Applied Economics and Policy Studies

Series Editors

Xuezheng Qin , *School of Economics, Peking University, Beijing, China*
Chunhui Yuan, *School of Economics and Management, Beijing University of Posts and Telecommunications, Beijing, China*
Xiaolong Li, *Department of Postal Management, Beijing University of Posts and Telecommunications, Beijing, China*

The Applied Economics and Policy Studies present latest theoretical and methodological discussions to bear on the scholarly works covering economic theories, econometric analyses, as well as multifaceted issues arising out of emerging concerns from different industries and debates surrounding latest policies. Situated at the forefront of the interdisciplinary fields of applied economics and policy studies, this book series seeks to bring together the scholarly insights centering on economic development, infrastructure development, macroeconomic policy, governance of welfare policy, policies and governance of emerging markets, and relevant subfields that trace to the discipline of applied economics, public policy, policy studies, and combined fields of the aforementioned. The book series of Applied Economics and Policy Studies is dedicated to the gathering of intellectual views by scholars and poli-cymakers. The publications included are relevant for scholars, policymakers, and students of economics, policy studies, and otherwise interdisciplinary programs.

Xiaolong Li · Chunhui Yuan · John Kent
Editors

Proceedings of the 7th International Conference on Economic Management and Green Development

Set 3

Editors
Xiaolong Li
Department of Postal Management
Beijing University of Posts
and Telecommunications
Beijing, China

Chunhui Yuan
School of Economics and Management
Beijing University of Posts
and Telecommunications
Beijing, China

John Kent
Supply Chain Management
University of Arkansas
Fayetteville, NC, USA

ISSN 2731-4006　　　　　　　　ISSN 2731-4014　(electronic)
Applied Economics and Policy Studies
ISBN 978-981-97-0522-1　　　　ISBN 978-981-97-0523-8　(eBook)
https://doi.org/10.1007/978-981-97-0523-8

© The Editor(s) (if applicable) and The Author(s), under exclusive license to Springer Nature Singapore Pte Ltd. 2024

This work is subject to copyright. All rights are solely and exclusively licensed by the Publisher, whether the whole or part of the material is concerned, specifically the rights of translation, reprinting, reuse of illustrations, recitation, broadcasting, reproduction on microfilms or in any other physical way, and transmission or information storage and retrieval, electronic adaptation, computer software, or by similar or dissimilar methodology now known or hereafter developed.
The use of general descriptive names, registered names, trademarks, service marks, etc. in this publication does not imply, even in the absence of a specific statement, that such names are exempt from the relevant protective laws and regulations and therefore free for general use.
The publisher, the authors, and the editors are safe to assume that the advice and information in this book are believed to be true and accurate at the date of publication. Neither the publisher nor the authors or the editors give a warranty, expressed or implied, with respect to the material contained herein or for any errors or omissions that may have been made. The publisher remains neutral with regard to jurisdictional claims in published maps and institutional affiliations.

This Springer imprint is published by the registered company Springer Nature Singapore Pte Ltd.
The registered company address is: 152 Beach Road, #21-01/04 Gateway East, Singapore 189721, Singapore

Paper in this product is recyclable.

Contents

International NGO Issues on Female Migrant Workers 1
   Yinwei Li

Time Lagged Effects of ESG Scores and Investor Attention on Stock
Returns 9
   Jiaqi Liu

Analyzing Reasons for the Selection of Investment Objects Based
on the Construction of Enterprise Ecological Value Network 18
   Caixiaoyang Ge

Analysis of the Motivation and Performance of Merger
and Reorganization of Companies Under Performance
Commitment--Based on the Dual Case Study of DF Company's
Acquisition of Pride and Fosber 27
   Liu Yu

Monetary Policy Regulation and Macroeconomic
Fluctuations—Empirical Research Based on VAR Model 41
   Xiaochen Liu

Recession Risk Prediction with Machine Learning and Big Panel Data 63
   Yunhao Yang

Investigate the Relationship Between Financial Risk and Financial
Performance: An Insight of China Life Insurance Company 88
   Shikang Wang

Model Innovation and Value Creation in E-commerce Platform
Ecosystems: A Case Study of Douyin 98
   Jiahang Hu and Yiming Zhong

An Investigation into the Relationship Between Transportation Network
and Economic Agglomeration 108
   Chenhao Zheng

A Study of the Dual Carbon Target and Green Finance Development
in Jiangxi Province 119
   Liwen Dai

Dynamic Correlation, Volatility Spillover Inside UK Capital Markets 129
  Mingze Yuan and Ziqi Guo

Challenges and Opportunities of Digital Construction of Chinese
Grassroots Government in the Information Age – Taking
the Construction of "Four Platforms" in Zhejiang Province as an Example 137
  Zhuofan Zong

Research on the Impact of Digitalization on Individual Investors'
Behavior from the Perspective of Behavioral Finance 146
  Zhihan Zhao

A Review of ESG Research in China: From the Perspective of Chinese
Enterprises 155
  Daoer Wang

PIC Planning Model and Geographic Information System Applied
on the Old District Renovation Using Intelligent Data Analysis 168
  Junyuan Li, Zihao Ma, and Xiyuan Zhang

Agriculture Trade Competitiveness, and Influencing Economic Factors:
A Study on China's Agricultural Trade 180
  Benjamin Kofi Tawiah Edjah

Financial Cloud Drives Digital Transformation of Enterprises:
——Taking Hisense's Application of Kingdee Financial Cloud
as an Example 188
  BoYong Chen and Zhuohao Zhang

Study on the Influence of Rural Revitalization on Regional Tourism
Development: An Empirical Analysis Based on the Data of 16
Prefectures in Yunnan Province 199
  Qing Wang

The Discussion of the Impact on the Stock Price After the Comments
or Recommendations from Stock Analysts–The Case Study on EV Stocks 214
  Jiaxi Zhang

The Effects of Transforming the CDMO Strategy on the Business
Performance of Porton Based on Financial Statement Analysis 224
  Lei Zhang

Economic Policy Uncertainty, ESG, and Corporate Performance 235
  Fumian Huang

Identification and Analysis of Risk Spillover Effect of Commercial Banks in China *Moran Wang*	247
Case Analysis of Kingfisher PLC's Operational Quality Based on the Perspective of Financial Report *Xinyi Song*	253
Comedic Violence Advertisement and Limiting Factors *Yuting Tong*	262
The Impacts of Goal Setting on Enterprises from a Corporate Social Responsibility Perspective *Yu Chen*	273
Behavioral Economics and Macroeconomics: Relationship Identification by Case of Economy Crisis in 2008 *Haocheng Yan*	280
The Impact of Endogenous Sentiment on US Stock Market Trading Volume *Lvqin Huang*	291
The Factors Affecting Electric Vehicle Adoption in the United States, 2016–2021 *Qing Hou, Shuai Zhou, and Guangqing Chi*	299
Assessing Endowment Effect in Different Cooperative Settings *Fengyi Zhang*	307
The Primary Performance Trait of Corporations with High Managerial Short-Termism *Yuping Wang*	314
Research on the Factors Affecting Inequality – Evidence from China *Gengqiang Xiao*	321
Accounting Measurement and Recognition of Digital Cryptocurrencies: Challenges, Practices, and Recommendations *Jiajun Ma*	328
Study on the Spillover Effect of Shanghai Crude Oil Futures Price Fluctuations on New Energy Stock Prices *Zhang Xinyu*	338

Exploring the Impact of Social Economic Status on Migrant Workers'
Sense of Social Equity from the Economic Sociology Perspective 350
   Hu Xinrui

Microeconomic Study of the Digital Economy's Importance
on Manufacturers' Management 365
   Yuyan Wang

Fintech Development and Corporate Innovation 373
   Chen Huan

Analysts' Characteristics and Forecast ability–An Empirical Study
from China's A-Share Market 382
   Mengyan Lei

Is There Salary Discrimination by Race and Nationality in the NBA?
A New Approach 391
   JiaYou Liang, ShuaiJie Zhao, and HaoYuan Zhu

Choice Overload Paradox in Online Shopping Environment 400
   Jiaxin Wang, Fang Han, Manting Ding, and Jia Zhang

The Influence of Endowment Effect on the Investment Decisions
in Hybrid Funds 414
   Huiqi Zhang

Research on Empowering Huawei's Financial Transformation
by Financial Shared Service Center 421
   Yiru Su

A Study on the Relevance of Corporate Solvency – A Case Study
of Procter & Gamble 431
   Huangzhiyi Zhang

ESG Performance Under Economic Policy Uncertainty: An Empirical
Study of Chinese Corporations 443
   Song Qiuge

Relationship Between Macroeconomy and Stock Market in the United
States 456
   Lixiang Zheng

Research on the Activated Utilization and Digital Innovation
Development of Cultural Heritage Under the Concept of Sustainable
Development 466
   Yuting Yu

Analysis of the Reasons for the Development of the New Energy
Vehicle Industry and Prospects —Taking BYD as an Example 478
   Boyu Liu

Challenges of Stock Prediction Based on LSTM Neural Network 490
   Rufeng Chen

Explore the Impact of Natural Factors on the Use of Shared Bicycles 500
   Liu Jiamei

Economic Dynamics Analysis of Higher Education Development 511
   Tian Mo

The Impact of Fintech on Enterprise Innovation: Take Companies
that Issue Fintech Concept Stocks as an Example 521
   Yuyao Sun

Resilience Assessment of the South-to-North Water Diversion Central
Route Project by Using Urban Futures Method 534
   Qiaozhi Zhang

Research on Factors Influencing the Rewarding Behavior of Virtual
Anchors' Fans 544
   Xinran Zhao

Analyzing the Reasons of BYD's Low-Profit Margin Through Financial
Data 555
   Tianqi Ma

Analysis and Forecast of USD/EUR Exchange Rate Based on ARIMA
and GARCH Models 566
   Jiatong Li, Jiawen Yin, and Rui Zhang

Forecasts on Euro-to-USD Exchange Rate Based on the ARIMA Model 576
   Qiaoyu Xie

Analysis and Forecasting of Exchange Rate Between Yuan and Dollar 588
   Sitian Yi

Forecast of China's Real Estate Industry Development Situation Based on ARIMA Model: Taking Vanke as an Example 598
Xiangyu Li

US Trade Balance Analysis on Imports and Exports Based on ETS and ARIMA Models 611
Shiqi Fan

Research on the Factors Affecting Mobility Rate Across States in the United States 626
Xinyu Shi

Exploring the Risks of Blockchain to the Financial Market and Its Countermeasures 633
Yujiang Duan, Fengfan Ge, and Zhixing Wen

To a Decentralized Future: Benefits that Blockchain Could Endow the Financing World 642
Yiping Li, Yuqing Liu, Ruixuan Sun, and Zihui Xu

Relevance Between ESG Scores and Annual Turnover: Evidence from 453 Industrial Hong Kong Stocks 652
Nanqi Liu, Changyou Qi, and Junjie Zhuge

How Does Years Since Immigration to the U.S.A. Affect Hourly Wage? 662
Shizhe Lyu

A Controversy in Sustainable Development: How Does Gender Diversity Affect the ESG Disclosure? 669
Bolin Fu, Keqing Wang, and Tianxin Zhou

Controlling Shareholders' Equity Pledges, Environmental Regulations and Corporate Green Performance—Based on Data from Listed Companies in Highly Polluting Industries 679
Mingfei Chen

ESG Performance's Effect on the Firm Performance the Evidence from Chinese A-share Market 690
Liqi Dong

The Factors Influence Purchase Intentions from the Consumer's Perspective and the Characteristics of Green Buyers 702
Ziyao Yang

A Study on the Motivation and Financial Performance of Haidilao's
Equity Crave-Out 716
  Tingxuan Dong

Study on the Reasons for the Failure of the Audit of Luckin Coffee
and Suggestions for Countermeasures 729
  Yufan Li

Baidu's Financial Competitiveness Research Based on DuPont Analysis
Method 738
  Yuqing Zhang

The Impact of COVID-19 on the Aviation Industry: Event Study on U.S.
Passenger Airline Stocks 752
  Yuxin Chen and Ziqing Gong

Predicting Customer Churn in a Telecommunications Company Using
Machine Learning 771
  Yinming Wu

Research on Real Estate Price Index Forecasting Based on ARIMA
Model: Taking Los Angeles as an Example 784
  Xiao Han

Research on the Reasons for Abnormal Changes in the Operation Status
of Domino's Pizza 796
  Yining Feng, Yunong Li, Jingyu Qin, and Yuankai Tao

Detect the Change Points in the Growth Rate of US Real Export Data
Based on Mean and Variance 804
  Yiwei Zhang

Forecasting the Stock Market Index with Dynamic ARIMA Model
and LSTM Model 815
  Siyuan Zhu

Public Goods Game Based on the Combination Model of Reputation
and Punishment 828
  Qing Liu

The Stylized Facts of Income Inequality in Mainland China, Korea
and Taiwan: Development and Comparison 836
  Yanshu Wang

Factors Influence Loan Default–A Credit Risk Analysis 849
   Xianya Qi

An Empirical Analysis of the Causal Relationship Between Equity
Incentives and Idiosyncratic Volatility in Chinese A-Share Listed
Companies 863
   Zhaoxuan Gan

An Empirical Analysis of the Relationship Between Chinese GDP
and Deposit Savings 873
   Yichuan Bai

FinTech Promotes the Development of Green Finance 885
   Heqing Huang and Qijie Yang

Comprehensive Analysis of China's Local Government Financing
Vehicle Debt 893
   Zihao Tang

The Relationship Between ESG Ratings and Financial Performance
of Coal Firms — the Case of China Shenhua and China Coal Energy 903
   Aimiao Zhang

Research on the Impact of Regulatory Inquiries Related to Information
Disclosure of Listed Companies – A Case Study of ANDON HEALTH 915
   Miaoxuan Ma

Research on Financial Competitiveness of a Listed Company Based
on DuPont Analysis Method 925
   Yile Kong and Xitong Zhu

Time Series Analysis in Pfizer Stock Prices in the Pre-
and Post-COVID-19 Scenarios 937
   Rixin Su

Stacking-Based Model for House Price Prediction 947
   Yiqian Zhou

A Dynamic Game Study on the "Big Data Discriminatory Pricing"
Behavior of E-commerce Platforms Under Government Regulation 959
   Zhuang Yao

Analysis on Marketing Strategy of Chinese Online Music Platform–QQ
Music 969
   Jiayi Hong

The Causality Between Executive Compensation, Equity Concentration, and Corporate Performance: A Multiple Regression Analysis 977
Xiao Rao

Exploring the Interplay Between Inflation, Energy Prices, and COVID-19 Amidst the Ukraine Conflict 986
Zeyao Li

An Empirical Analysis of Asset Pricing Models 998
Ziqi Chen, Zhenwu Sun, and Xiaoyu Wang

The Empirical Analysis of Asset Pricing Models in the Asia-Pacific Stock Market Under COVID-19 1008
Hui Wang

The Impact of Technological Change on Labour Market Outcomes and Income Inequality in China: An Empirical Analysis 1018
Xueyao Tong

The "Strong" Development of RMB 1025
Shengran Huang

Research on Business Value Assessment Model for New Generation Star 1035
Ziyi Xing

Fiduciary Duty Regime of Private Fund Managers: Insights from the US Regulatory Experience 1043
Jia Cheng

The Impact of Capital Globalization on Green Innovation: A Cross-Country Empirical Analysis 1054
Yuyang Yuan

Financing Constraints, Local Government Debt, and Corporate Stock Returns: An Empirical Analysis 1064
Yike Lu

Sustainable Supply Chains: A Comprehensive Analyse of Drivers and Practices 1075
Qichao Gong, Yuxi Wang, and Yuli Zhu

Innovating Online Operational Models for Independent Hotels: Assessing the Feasibility of a "Regional Independent Hotel Network Alliance" in Yunnan 1083
Qijing Li

Supply Chain Management in the Era of "Internet+": Case Analysis
of Agricultural Product Supply Chain 1094
   Huimin Liu, Yangmeng Liu, and Siyan Yi

An Empirical Study on the Causes of Default of US Dollar Debt
in the China's Property Based on Z-score Model 1102
   Yijing Wang

The Influence of Key Opinion Leaders on High-End Beauty Brands
in the Age of Self-media 1112
   Xilin Liu, Haonan Qian, and Haoyun Wen

Supply Chain Risk Management Process: Case Study of the Chinese
Aviation Industry in COVID-19 1120
   Jiangjia Xu

The Marketing Value of User-Generated Content in the Mobile Industry 1130
   Le Han, Zhuoer Wei, and Shuyan Zhang

Direct Carbon Emissions, Indirect Carbon Emissions, and International
Trade: An Analysis of OECD Member Countries 1143
   Yirong Xi

To What Extent Can We Use Google Trends to Predict Inflation
Statistically? 1156
   Minrui Huang and David Tai Li

A Literature Review on the Model of EGARCH-MIDAS, LMM, GBM
for Stock Market Prediction 1175
   Yingtong Wang

The Impact of Changes in Sales Prices of Non-durable Goods
on Consumers' Purchase Intentions When Using Online Shopping
Platforms 1185
   Zehao Xu

Analyzing Problems and Strategies of International Organizations
in Global Governance and Cooperation – Taking UNDP as an Example 1197
   Haosen Xu

Implementation of Monte-Carlo Simulations in Economy and Finance 1206
   Jintian Zhang

InstaCart Analysis: Use PCA with K-Means to Segment Grocery
Customers 1218
 Chenyu Lang

Research on the Influencing Factors of Housing Prices Based
on Multiple Regression: Taking Chongqing as an Example 1231
 Yijia Qi

Game Analysis of Cross-Border Entry of Enterprises into New Markets:
Case Study of Bytedance 1242
 Feiyue Lei and Lu Meng

Research on the Effectiveness of Clarifying Rumors by Listed
Companies in the Pharmaceutical Industry – Taking the Market
Reaction of Ling Pharmaceutical as an Example 1252
 Chuhan Wang, Beining Xu, and Qianwen Zhang

The Relationship Between ESG Performance and Financial Constraints
and Its Impact on Firm Value 1265
 Shengyang Qu

A Study on the Relationship Between ESG Performance and Stock
Returns – Take A-share Listed Company Stocks as the Example 1274
 Liqi Dong, Shifeng Deng, and Qian Gao

Digital Transformation in the New Energy Industry for Sustainable
Development: A Grounded Theory Analysis 1285
 Ming Liu

Causality Between Board Features and Corporate Innovation Level:
Empirical Evidence from Listed Companies in China 1295
 Zicheng Bu

Analysis of the Impact of Digital Inclusive Finance on Farmers' Income
Growth - An Empirical Analysis Based on 31 Provinces in China 1303
 Yuhan Sun

The Energy Consumption and Economic Growth 1315
 Yiguo Huang, Yizhen Zhang, and Heyu Cai

Research on the Merger and Acquisition Performance and Brand
Management of Cross-Border LBO—Take Qumei Home's Acquisition
of Norwegian Ekornes Company as an Example 1327
 Runbang Liu

The Impact of Investor Sentiment on Stock Returns 1361
  Xinran Fu

The Impact of Digitisation Degree on Agricultural Science
and Technology Innovation: Based on Panel Data of 31 Provinces
in China 1371
  Lanjie Huang

An Empirical Study on the Impact of Behavioural Bias on Investment
Decision-Making 1382
  Chutian Li

Matrix Factorization Model in Collaborative Filtering Algorithms
Based on Feedback Datasets 1405
  Yuqing Hu

Research on the Mall Customers Segmentation Based on K-means
and DBSCAN 1413
  Yifan Wang

Valuation and Analysis of the Canadian Banking Sector During
the COVID-19 Pandemic 1426
  Bo He

ChatGPT Concept Industry Valuation Analysis: Evidence from iFlytek
and Kunlun 1437
  Yajing Chen

Optimizing Trading Recommendations in Portfolio Trading: A Bilateral
Matching Theory Approach 1445
  Wenzheng Liu

The Impact of "Three Arrows" Policies on China's Real Estate Market:
An Event Study 1455
  Zixuan Wang, Yangjie Jin, and Jianuo Su

Corporate Social Responsibility Disclosure Quality and Stock Price
Crash Risk: Evidence from China 1474
  Minxing Zhu

An Analysis of the Effect of Social Medical Insurance on Family
Consumption 1491
  Siyun Yuan

The Influence of Impulsive Purchase on the Consumption Behaviour in Social Media 1503
Sirui Wang

Analysis of the Reasons of HNA Group's Bankruptcy and Future Prevention Measures for Enterprises 1513
Jiaheng Zhang

Cognitive Biases in Second-Hand and Pre-sale Real Estate Prices in Nanjing 1522
Bing Shen

How Targeted Poverty Alleviation Policy Program and Other Possible Factors Affect the Wellbeing of Chinese Seniors 1530
Xinru Fang

Investor Sentiment, Idiosyncratic Risk, and Stock Returns: Evidence from Australia 1548
Aiqi Li

Sovereign CDS Spreads and Covid-19 Pandemic 1559
Ying Xi

Portfolio Optimization for Major Industries in American Capital Market 1570
Xinyi Liu

The Impact of Investor Sentiment on Stock Returns Based on Machine Learning and Deep Learning Methods 1577
Xiangjun Chen

An Empirical Research on the Impact of ESG Performance on Chinese Stock Market 1597
Jiayun Yin

Research on the Application of Artificial Intelligence Technology in Risk Management of Commercial Banks 1606
Wensi Huang, Yiling Shi, and Wenjie Zhou

Exploring the Development Rule of GDP Based on Time-series Moran's Index 1616
Zhengjie Zang

An Empirical Study of U.S. Stock Market Forecasts and Trend Trading Strategies Based on ARIMA Model 1630
Siying Wang

Impact of 5G Commercial License Issuance on Stock Prices of Related
Listed Companies: Using Difference-in-Differences Model 1641
 Xi Zhou

Socio-Economic Determinants of National Saving in Pakistan 1649
 Munir Ahmad and Asghar Ali

Research on the Influence Mechanism of Experiential Interaction
on Consumers' Impulsive Buying 1664
 Liang Chen

A Qualitative Study on How the Covid-19 Pandemic Has Helped
in the Enablement of Entrepreneurial Ambitions Among Chinese
Entrepreneurs 1675
 Xiaodan Wang

The Application of Price-Earnings Ratio in Hong Kong Hang Seng
Index Futures Trading Strategy 1684
 Yishan Hou, Yifei Xu, and Shuye Zhou

The Effect of Governance Dimension of ESG on Corporate Performance 1694
 Huijia Zhang and Keyou Pang

Impact of Green Financing and Public Policies Towards Investment
Yield: Evidence from European and Asian Economies 1705
 Mirza Nasir Jahan Mehdi and Syed Ali Raza Hamid

The Long and Short Term Impact of COVID-19 on E-Commerce
and Retail Industries for US 1720
 Zixuan Li, Chenwen Song, and Tianrui Xiao

An Exploration of Bank Failure in Silicon Valley and the Interaction
of Failure Factors - Empirical Analysis Based on VAR Model 1746
 Tianqi Peng

Prediction of Lending Club Loan Defaulters 1765
 Xueyan Wang

Research on the CRE of China's Carbon Trading Pilot Policy 1778
 Jiayue Jiang, Meixin Wang, Mengzhen Xiao, Yuwei Yang, and Dan Wei

IEEE-CIS Fraud Detection Based on XGB 1785
 Zhijia Xiao

Unraveling the Link Between Federal Reserve Interest Rate Hikes
and the Chinese Stock Market 1797
   Jialin Li

Stock Market Volatility During and After the Covid-19 Pandemic:
Academic Perspectives 1809
   Yining Yang

Unveiling the Effects of the China-US Trade Conflict: A Comparative
Study of Stock Market Behaviors in the United States and China 1818
   Shuying Chen

Financial Analysis and Strategic Forecast of Tesla, Inc. 1831
   Xiaoke Wang

Mechanisms and Strategies of Smart Governance for Improving Urban
Resilience 1842
   Jianhang Du, Yongheng Hu, and Longzheng Du

The Impact of Low Carbon Economic Development on the Income
Gap Between Urban and Rural Residents - An Empirical Study Based
on Inter-provincial Panel Data in China 1848
   Yang Chengye

Addressing Credit Fraud Threat: Detected Through Supervised Machine
Learning Model 1863
   Yihan Yang

The Impact Caused by the COVID-19 Pandemic Re-opening on Catering
Industry in China: A Short-Term Perspective 1873
   Shiqi Pan

The Impact of the Russia-Ukraine War on Tesla: Evidence from ARIMA
Model 1882
   Jintian He

Research on the Link Between RMB Exchange Rate and Tesla's Stock
Price: A Long-Term Perspective 1893
   Jinhao Yu

Dynamic Impact of the Covid-19 on Cryptocurrency and Investment
Suggestion 1903
   Haozhe Hong

Research on the Relationship Between Chinese and American Stock Markets: Spillover Effects of Returns and Volatility 1914
Lin Liu

Research on the Impact of China's Industrial Structure Upgrading on the Balance of Payments Structure 1924
Yimeng Wang

The Impact of Digital Economy on Industrial Agglomeration 1933
Yuting Huang and Kaixvan Ma

Analysis of Influencing Factors of Housing Affordability Crisis in Vancouver 1949
Jiaxuan Chen

Analysis of the Impact of Female Executives on Corporate Financial Leverage 1960
XiangLin Cheng

Corporate Social Responsibility and Financial Performance: Evidence from Listed Firms in China 1971
Jiali Wang

The External Shock of the Epidemic on Employees' Turnover Intention in Central-Dominated China: The Mediating Effect of Automation and Teleworking 1987
Xinyu Chen

Research on the Mechanism of Farmers' Interest Linkage in Agricultural Technology Transformation 2001
Yuanyuan Chen

Analysis of Spatio-Temporal Evolution Patterns in the Green Development of Cluster-Type Cities: A Case Study of Zibo City in China 2010
Minne Liu

Correlation Between Chinese Outbound Tourism Numbers and Chinese Outward Foreign Direct Investment Study 2021
Peili Yu

Volatility Analysis Using High-Frequency Financial Data 2031
Junchi Wang

Can Environmental, Social and Governance Performance Alleviate
Financial Dilemma? 2043
   Junyi Wang

Reinforcement Learning for E-Commerce Dynamic Pricing 2051
   Hongxi Liu

Impact of ESG Performance on Firm Value and Its Transmission
Mechanism: Research Based on Industry Heterogeneity 2061
   Xingzhuo Liu

Author Index 2071

The Impact of Digitisation Degree on Agricultural Science and Technology Innovation: Based on Panel Data of 31 Provinces in China

Lanjie Huang(✉)

Faculty of Social Sciences, University of Southampton, Southampton SO17 1BJ, UK
lh3u21@soton.ac.uk

Abstract. Digitalisation can foster agricultural science and technology innovation in the age of the digital economy. A fixed effects model was employed to empirically assess the effects of digitisation on science, technology, and innovation in the agricultural industry using Chinese provincial panel data from 2011 to 2020. The results show that increased digitisation has contributed significantly to the development of science, technology, and innovation in the agricultural sector. After sorting out the impact paths of digitisation on agricultural science and technology innovation. This study argues that digitisation affects agricultural science and technology innovation through three main paths: rural education, digital inclusive finance, and digital transformation of agro-related enterprises. Education promotes agricultural innovation by improving the quality of the rural workforce, while digital inclusive finance promotes agricultural innovation by easing financing constraints. Agro-related enterprises accelerate the diffusion of innovation iterations mainly because they can achieve horizontal resource integration and value complementarity in digital innovation networks.

Keywords: Digitalisation · Agrotechnology · Innovation

1 Introduction

1.1 Background

China is a country with a large population, which will reach a total of approximately 1.4 billion by 2035, with 400 to 500 million people expected to still live in rural areas. The sound development of Chinese agriculture not only carries the food security of 1.4 billion people. It also carries the responsibility for the employment and livelihood of 400 to 500 million people in the countryside, as well as the protection and transmission of the ecological and cultural heritage of the countryside. Under the prerequisites of arable land resources and population size constraints, Chinese agriculture needs to find a new theoretical logic and practical path [1]. Some Chinese scholars believe that stimulating innovation in agricultural science and technology through increasing levels of digitisation, and thus improving the efficiency of agricultural production, is a sure way to move Chinese agriculture towards sound development. In theory, digital agriculture can indeed play a role in reducing production and transaction costs, increasing total factor productivity, and promoting quality and safety of agricultural products. In China, there is very limited scope for reducing costs through large-scale production. However, when the data element is introduced into the agricultural production function, the potential for cost reduction is huge. In the R&D segment, cross-innovations such as artificial intelligence with biotechnology and materials technology can change the technological path of breeding and improve R&D efficiency. Clarify the impact of digital development on agricultural science and technological innovation and make the right scientific recommendations. This will have a positive effect not only on Chinese agriculture, but also on other developing countries around the world.

1.2 Related Research

The effect of digitalization on innovation has been the subject of numerous empirical research. First, researchers have looked at how digitalisation affects corporate innovation. Based on data from Chinese A-share listed businesses from 2007 to 2020, Fu et al. investigated the effect of corporate digitalization on innovation. The results show that innovation output is significantly enhanced after firms undergo digital upgrading, and this result holds across various robustness tests. The empirical evidence supports the influence mechanism of external interaction. The impact of digital upgrading on innovation has a geographical spillover effect. Therefore, the authors argue that enterprises should be encouraged and supported to undertake digital upgrading and strengthen digital infrastructure [2]. Teng and Hao also believe that in the digital economy, digital transformation can facilitate the growth of high-quality businesses. Using a panel of Chinese A-share listed companies from 2007 to 2021, they conducted an empirical investigation to determine the mechanism of the digital cohort effect on firms' innovation investment. The results found that the digital cohort effect can significantly increase firms' innovation investment, which is achieved by intensifying industry competition [3]. In addition, Wang and Li used A-share listed enterprises as the research object and matched the macro data of digital financial inclusion with the micro data of enterprise innovation from 2011 to 2020. The theoretical logic and empirical analysis tested the following findings, digital inclusive finance can significantly promote corporate innovation, and this positive effect still holds after endogeneity test and robustness test [4].

The influence of digitalisation on regional creativity has been verified by other academics. Zhang et al. see the construction of integrated big data pilot zones as a quasi-natural experiment in regional digital transformation. They constructed a theoretical framework for the creation of integrated big data pilot zones to influence the level of urban innovation. They analysed panel data for 285 prefecture-level cities and listed companies in China from 2009 to 2019 using a two-difference approach, a three-difference approach, and a moderated mediating effects model. The impact effects and mechanisms of action of the establishment of big data comprehensive pilot zones on the innovation level of cities were empirically tested. According to the study, the integration of big data pilot zone construction considerably increased the level of urban innovation. The mechanism test showed that the creation of big data comprehensive pilot zones promoted urban innovation by optimising factor allocation efficiency, promoting industrial structure upgrading and enhancing entrepreneurial activity [5]. In addition, in her article, Cao illustrates that digitalisation and regional innovation are highly coupled. A new style of thinking, a new logical starting point, and a new cognitive schema that go beyond traditional innovation have been created as a result of the widespread use of digital technology. These changes have affected the observation scenario, elemental makeup, and process participation of regional innovation. In the innovation field, the digital "empathy" and "decentralised" synergy of intersubjectivity has been achieved. This breaks down the boundaries between the online and offline worlds of innovation and triggers an overall transformation of the regional innovation ecosystem. It has reconfigured the regional innovation framework, given rise to new regional innovation paradigms and combinations, and accelerated regional science and technology innovation into the path of paradigm revolution [6].

Extending to the national level, Yang et al. argue that digital transformation is driving profound changes across the economy and society, with a profound impact on the evolution of national innovation systems. They emphasize the effect of the digital transformation on the national innovation system in their article. The study concludes that, in terms of innovation agents, there is a greater diversity of types of agents and the formation of innovation networks that interact efficiently across geographies and organisations. In terms of innovation resources, data is both a core input factor for innovation activities and an important tool for improving the efficiency of resource allocation. In terms of innovation mechanism, digital technology breaks the traditional organisational mechanism based on the boundaries of disciplines and innovation chains, forming the development trend of integration and convergence [7].

Many academics have researched how digital financial inclusion affects agricultural innovation. Digital popular finance, as a type of digital product, combines digital technology and inclusive finance across borders, and has a good positive impact on agricultural technology innovation. Jiao and Liu experimentally investigated the effects of digital inclusive financing on the growth of rural industrial integration and the path of influence using provincial-level panel data collected in China from 2011 to 2019. Agricultural science and technology innovation was involved in the study as a mediating variable. The findings show that digital financial inclusion can indirectly foster the growth of rural industrial integration through advances in agricultural science and technology in addition to directly promoting it [8].

A number of scholars have also already conducted studies on the great contribution of digitalisation to quality agricultural development. Tang argues that digital technology has become a new tool for promoting quality development in agriculture and rural areas. Based on inspiration from the new structural economics, he constructs a theoretical framework for digital technology to empower high-quality agricultural and rural development, while verifying the practicality of the analytical framework with multiple cases. His research found that the digitisation of agricultural production, the digitisation of rural governance and the digitisation of people's lives are contributing to high-quality agricultural and rural development across the board [9]. Fan et al. then used a combination of entropy TOPSIS method and SDM model. They analysed the spatial and temporal characteristics of the green development level of agriculture in 30 Chinese provinces from 2010 to 2019 and the influence of the level of digitalisation on the green development of agriculture. The results show that the level of agricultural green development has steadily increased during the study period, showing obvious spatial clustering characteristics. An inverted U-shaped link exists between the level of digitization and the development of green agriculture and raising the level of digitization aids in the development of green agriculture. Further investigation revealed that digitisation had a spatial spillover effect on the growth of green agriculture, with digitisation in neighboring provinces playing a role in promoting and then inhibiting green agricultural development in the region. Based on the above findings, they put forward suggestions to increase investment in digital infrastructure, improve digital construction planning and ensure reasonable resource input [10]. Han also acknowledges the importance of digitalisation. They contend that the digital economy has emerged as a new engine of economic growth for national economies and is transforming the industrial landscape across a range of industries in the new wave of the information revolution. The digitisation of the entire agricultural chain has a catalytic and leading role in the transformation of rural industries, effectively promoting improvements in production efficiency, industrial structure, new markets for products, and synergistic division of labour among subjects across the chain. The transformation and upgrading of rural industries can be accomplished by fully utilizing the optimization and integration of digital technology in the allocation of agricultural production elements and its deep integration with agricultural production, operation, management, and services [11].

1.3 Objective

The relevant articles show the positive impact of digitisation on corporate innovation, regional innovation, and the national innovation system in China. At the same time, a number of articles also illustrate the significant contribution of digitisation to quality development in agriculture. It is therefore reasonable to assume in this paper that digitisation also has a significant impact on the intersection of the above two research directions. There is a research gap since no study has yet specifically examined how digitalization affects innovation in agricultural science and technology. As a result, this research empirically examines the relationship between the two using the degree of digitisation as the main explanatory variable and the level of innovation in agricultural science and technology as the predictor variable. By confirming the association between the two variables, the paper aims to offer more scientific recommendations on how to encourage agricultural science and technology innovation in the future.

2 Method

2.1 Model

Considering the possible lagged impact of digitisation development, this paper uses data with a one-period lag of the core explanatory variables. To empirically analyse the impact of digitisation development on agricultural science and technology innovation in China, the panel data regression model created in this study is as follows [12]:

$$AGP_{it} = \beta_0 + \beta_1 DIL_{t-1} + \sum_{k=1}^{n} \lambda_k X_{it} + \mu_i + \varepsilon_{i,t} \quad (1)$$

$$lnpat_{it} = \beta_0 + \beta_1 DIL_{t-1} + \sum_{k=1}^{n} \lambda_k X_{it} + \mu_i + \varepsilon_{i,t} \qquad (2)$$

i: Province
t: Year
DIL_{t-1}: Degree of digitisation in year t-1 in province i
AGP_{it}: Number of researchers engaged in agricultural science and technology innovation in year t in province i
$lnpat_{it}$: Number of patents in force in year t in province i
X_{it}: Control variables
μ_i: Fixed effects for provinces
$\varepsilon_{i,t}$: Model error term

As shown in Table 1, all the p-values for a robust Hausman test were less than 0.01, hence a fixed effects model should be used for the study in this paper.

Table 1. Hausmann test results.

	chi2(3)	Prob > chi2
lnpat	35.31	0.0000
AGP	50.21	0.0000

2.2 Variables

The primary explanatory factors for this study were selected from the Peking University Digital Finance Research Center's secondary indicator digitisation degree. The number of researchers in agricultural science and technology innovation as well as the quantity of active agricultural patents are the variables that are predicted. This is because the important determinants of the degree of innovation in a field of scientific research are its S&T inputs and outputs. The input of researchers is an important measure of S&T input, while the number of active agricultural patents is an important measurement of S&T output.However, there is no detailed data on the number of people engaged in science and technology activities in agriculture and effective patents in agriculture in the relevant statistics. In this paper, suitable alternative data was selected for estimation, and effective patents in agriculture were chosen as a proxy for effective domestic patents. The following formula was used to compute the number of researchers in agricultural science and technology innovation [13]:

$$AGP_{it} = \frac{AGDP_{it}}{GDP_{it}} \times RDP_{it} \qquad (3)$$

AGP_{it}: Number of researchers engaged in science, technology and innovation in the field of agriculture

$AGDP_{it}$: Regional agricultural GDP
GDP_{it}: Regional GDP
RDP_{it}: Number of R&D researchers

Control variables were selected based on articles that examined how to measure the level of science and technology innovation in the agricultural sector. The variables chosen were real human capital per capita in rural areas, the number of R&D institutions. A further variable is government financial expenditures on agriculture, forestry, and water [14, 15]. It is important to note that the indicator of agriculture, forestry, and water expenditure covers spending on agriculture, forestry, water conservation, poverty alleviation, and comprehensive agricultural development, according to the Chinese government's classification of revenue and expenditure.

2.3 Data

The panel data of 31 Chinese provinces from 2011 to 2020 were ultimately chosen for this article because data on digitisation indicators prior to 2011 and following 2020 were lacking. The *China Science and Technology Yearbook*, *China Statistical Yearbook*, and *China Rural Statistical Yearbook* were used to collect data on the predicted variables. Data for the primary explanation variables came from the Peking University Digital Finance Research Centre. The *China Financial Statistics Yearbook* and the *China Science and Technology Yearbook* were used to collect data on government expenditures on agriculture, forestry, and water as well as the number of R&D institutions. The Central University of Finance and Economics provided the information on real human capital per person in rural areas. Real human capital per capita in rural parts of each province was measured by this university's Human Capital and Labour Economics Research Centre. All yearbooks are published by the National Bureau of Statistics of China and have good credibility.

3 Results

The results of the AGP model show that the degree of digitisation is significantly and positively correlated with the number of researchers in agricultural science and technology innovation and passes the 1% significance level test. This means that the higher the level of digitisation, the greater the number of people involved in scientific and technological research in agriculture. For every unit increase in digitisation, there are 9 to 10 more researchers working on science, technology, and innovation in the agricultural sector.

The results of the lnpat model show that the degree of digitisation is significantly and positively correlated with the number of effective patents in agriculture and passes the 1% level of significance test. That is, the higher the degree of digitisation, the greater the number of effective patents in agriculture will be, as shown in Table 2 and Table 3.

Table 2. AGP model regression results.

variable	Coef.	t-value	p-value	R-sq	Prob > F
dil_lag	9.776637	3.75	0.001	0.3859	0.0000
aghc2	−20.73772	−1.77	0.086		
agpfe	.0005595	1.76	0.089		
ord	3.822371	2.65	0.013		

Table 3. Lnpat model regression results.

variable	Coef.	t-value	p-value	R-sq	Prob > F
dil_lag	.0015208	5.10	0.000	0.8169	0.0000
aghc2	.0057973	1.90	0.067		
agpfe	.0000000974	2.77	0.009		
ord	.0000287	0.86	0.396		

dil_lag: Digitisation degree with a one-year lag
aghc2: Real human capital per capita in rural areas
agpfe: Agriculture, forestry, and water expenditure
ord: The number of R&D institutions

4 Discussion

Countries all across the world are currently putting more focus on the development of innovation. Digital technology has become a significant contributor to the advancement of global innovation thanks to the ongoing development of big data and artificial intelligence. Digital productivity is driving the digital transformation of social production methods with unprecedented breadth and depth. By 2021, China's digital economy already accounted for 39.8% of GDP and reached RMB 45.5 trillion, making it one of the main engines of economic growth. The scale of information infrastructure construction is also growing. By June 2022, there were 1.051 billion Internet users in China, bringing the country's Internet penetration rate up to 74.4%. E-commerce is still doing well as digitalization's capability and level continue to grow. Online retail sales of physical goods in China have risen 12% year over year to RMB 10.8 trillion in 2021, making up 24.5% of all retail sales of social consumer goods. The scale of third-party payment transactions continued to expand. Business models in the service sector continue to innovate, with Internet healthcare, online education and telecommuting accelerating the digitisation of the service sector. In 2021, the scale of digitally deliverable services trade in China reached RMB 2.33 trillion, up 14.4% year-on-year. Agriculture's digital transformation has also been actively supported at the same time. Digital technologies like 5G, the Internet of Things, big data, and artificial intelligence are increasingly being applied to agricultural production and operations. Relevant key technology research and innovative application studies have been strengthened. China is committed to creating pilot demonstrations of the Internet of Things in agriculture, implementing intelligent water conservation projects, and promoting digital management and intelligent transformation of public infrastructure in water conservation. It has promoted the application of big data in agriculture and rural areas and established an information service system for the whole agricultural industry chain. It has also built the second largest species resource database and information system in the world and promoted digital management services for agricultural equipment [16].

The second National Conference on Big Data Strategy held in China emphasised the need to give full play to the role of data as a basic resource and an engine of innovation. Accelerate the formation of a digital economy with innovation as the main leader and support. The digitisation of the economy is seen as an important driver of innovation and development. Therefore, in the present and future stages of development, the role of science and technology innovation in the agricultural sector is even more prominent for China's agricultural development. Strengthen the innovation capacity of agro-related enterprises and reinforce their position as the main body of innovation. Playing their role as the core engine and key support of agricultural science and technology is a matter of high-quality agricultural development [17]. A new round of technological revolution and industrial change is taking place. Biotechnology, intelligent technology, new material technology and other advanced technologies are accelerating their penetration into the agricultural sector. In this context, China, as the world's largest producer and important trader of agricultural products, needs to improve its independent innovation capacity in key aspects and core areas such as seeds, plant protection, animal protection and agrochemicals. Some scholars believe that enhancing the construction of new digital infrastructure and improving technologies such as the Internet of Things, big data, and artificial intelligence. It will continue to catalyse the application and innovation of basic technologies in agriculture and rural areas and transform core key technologies. Following this, it will continue to expand high-quality, high-quality, and high-efficiency agriculture while encouraging the transformation and upgrading of the agricultural and rural structure [18].

Based on the above background, this paper argues that the role of digitalisation in promoting innovation in agricultural science and technology may be realised through the following pathways.

Firstly, digitalisation can promote the flow of urban quality educational resources to the countryside. Through distance education platforms, the information level of rural education can be effectively improved [9]. The good development of rural education can provide a larger pool of talents for agricultural science and technology innovation institutions and agro-related enterprises. Digital technology can also be used to achieve the interconnection and sharing of developmental public facilities such as digital libraries, digital television, and training courses in both urban and rural areas. Digital technology has effectively addressed the relative shortage of quality training resources in rural areas, thereby improving the quality of the rural workforce. When the literacy and skill quality of the rural workforce increases, they can more smoothly use various types of agricultural science and technology innovations and are more likely to achieve deeper applications of technology products. The higher the level of rural human capital, the more consumer demand there will be for agricultural science and technology innovation products [15].

Secondly, in the financial sector, the development of digitalisation is conducive to promoting a deeper digitalisation of inclusive finance, thus contributing to innovation in agricultural technology. The ease of digital technology allows the relevant counterparties to quickly access more useful information. Digital technology thus allows digital inclusive finance to quickly use the information obtained to reduce transaction costs and information costs. Bringing together and investing capital from scattered people in the agricultural technology innovation sector provides sufficient material security for technological advances in agriculture. Promoting innovation by alleviating financing constraints for agro-related enterprises and farmers [19].

Digitisation also affects agricultural science and technology innovation by influencing agro-related enterprises. Agribusiness is one of the main carriers of innovation in agricultural science and technology. Theoretically, digitisation drives the continuous optimisation of knowledge production methods, making open innovation the norm [20]. Agricultural enterprises are able to achieve horizontal resource integration and value complementation in digital innovation networks, accelerating the diffusion of innovation results and technological improvement [21]. In addition, some empirical studies have found that digital transformation by companies themselves can lead to increased investment in innovation [22].

5 Conclusion

This paper analyses the impact of digitalisation on the development of innovation in agricultural science and technology from a digital perspective. The relationship between the two is analysed quantitatively based on finding relevant proxy data. The results find that digitisation can facilitate the development of agricultural science and technology innovation. The impact pathways were analysed in three main ways. Firstly, digitisation can influence rural human resources through education and public facilities, thus influencing agricultural science and technology innovation. Secondly, it can alleviate the financing constraints of agriculture-related enterprises and farmers through digital inclusive finance. It thus promotes the advancement of science, technology, and innovation in the agricultural sector. Digitisation can also facilitate agriculture-related technological innovation by stimulating the digital transformation of agro-related enterprises. Based on the results of the empirical study, actively promoting investment and construction of national digital infrastructure and digital financial inclusion is conducive to the development of science and technology innovation in the agricultural sector. Providing more policy support, innovation incentives and intellectual property protection for agro-related enterprises also has a positive effect on science and technology innovation.

References

1. Wang, X.: Digitalization to help modernize agriculture. Stud. Labour Econ. **10**(6), 11–15 (2022)

2. Fu, W., Xi, X., Xu, B., Liu, X., Pan, Y.: How digital upgrading drives firm innovation: empirical evidence and mechanisms. Financ. Theory Pract. **44**(1), 92–99 (2023). https://doi.org/10.16339/j.cnki.hdxbcjb.2023.01.012
3. Teng, M., Shen, M.: How digital cohort effects affect firms' innovation inputs - A moderated mediation model. Sci. Technol. Prog. Response 1–9
4. Wang, M., Li, Z.: Digital inclusive finance and firm innovation: a theoretical logic and empirical test. J. Manag. **36**(1), 102–119 (2023). https://doi.org/10.19808/j.cnki.41-1408/F.2023.0008
5. Zhang, H., Yi, J., Xu, J.: How digital change affects urban innovation - empirical evidence based on the construction of a national integrated big data pilot zone. Sci. Stud. 1–21. https://doi.org/10.16192/j.cnki.1003-2053.20230406.005
6. Cao, Y.: The changing framework and paradigm reconstruction of regional science and technology innovation under digitalization drive. Acad. Forum **42**(1), 110–116 (2019). https://doi.org/10.16524/j.45-1002.2019.01.013
7. Yang, J., Li, Z., Kang, Q.: Study on the impact of digital transformation on national innovation system and countermeasures. Res. Develop. Manage. **32**(6), 26–38 (2020). https://doi.org/10.13581/j.cnki.rdm.20200193
8. Jiao, Q., Liu, Y.: Digital inclusive finance, agricultural technology innovation and integrated development of rural industries. Stat. Decis. Making **38**(18), 77–81 (2022). https://doi.org/10.13546/j.cnki.tjyjc.2022.18.015
9. Tang, W.: Digital technology-driven high-quality development of agriculture and rural areas: theoretical interpretation and practical path. J. Nanjing Agric. Univ. (Soc. Sci. Ed.) **22**(2), 1–9 (2022). https://doi.org/10.19714/j.cnki.1671-7465.2022.0018
10. Fan, S., Li, Y., Ma, X., Liu, H.: An empirical study on the impact of digitalization level on green development in agriculture - based on panel data from 30 Chinese provinces. World Agric. **12**, 4–16 (2021). https://doi.org/10.13856/j.cn11-1097/s.2021.12.001
11. Han, X., Liu, C., Liu, H.: Theoretical logic and practical path of digitalization of the whole agricultural chain to facilitate the transformation of rural industries. Reform **3**, 121–132 (2023)
12. Qi, Y., Liu, C., Ding, S.: Digital economy development, employment structure optimization and employment quality improvement. Econ. Dyn. **11**, 17–35 (2020)
13. Chen, Z., Zheng, R., Li, P.H., Huang, S.: Evaluation and analysis of the efficiency of agricultural science and technology innovation in Henan Province. J. Henan Agric. Univ. **52**(3), 464–469+484 (2018). https://doi.org/10.16445/j.cnki.1000-2340.2018.03.025
14. Wenzhong, D., Geng, P., Yanping, H.: Evaluation of Guangxi's agricultural science and technology innovation capacity from the perspective of innovation drive - based on entropy value and TOPSIS method material element evaluation model. Sci. Technol. Manage. Res. **39**(9), 82–89 (2019)
15. Wang, D., Ran, X.: Rural digitalization, human capital and integrated rural industrial development - empirical evidence based on provincial panel data in China. J. Chongqing Univ. (Soc. Sci. Ed.) **28**(02), 1–14 (2022)
16. Information Office of the State Council of the People's Republic of China, White Paper on "Building a Community of Destiny in Cyberspace Together" (full text). http://www.scio.gov.cn/zfbps/32832/Document/1732898/1732898.htm. Accessed 30 Apr 2023
17. Sun, L., Wang, X., Jin, Y., Mao, S.: Evolution of science and technology innovation capability of agricultural-related enterprises in China and the path to enhance it - Empirical evidence from listed agricultural-related enterprises. Issues Agric. Econ. **12**, 4–18 (2022). https://doi.org/10.13246/j.cnki.iae.20221017.001
18. Dong, X.: Innovative pathways for new digital infrastructure to drive high-quality development in rural agriculture. Learn. Pract. **01**, 33–42 (2023). https://doi.org/10.19624/j.cnki.cn42-1005/c.2023.01.010

19. Wan, J., Zhou, Q., Yi, X.: Digital finance, financing constraints and corporate innovation. Econ. Rev. **1**, 71–83 (2020). https://doi.org/10.19361/j.er.2020.01.05
20. Kang, J., Chen, K.: Digital innovation development economic system: framework, evolution and value-added effects. Sci. Res. Manage. **42**(4), 1 (2021). https://doi.org/10.19571/j.cnki.1000-2995.2021.04.001
21. Gaziz, S., Oteshova, A., Prodanova, N., Savina, N., Bokov, D.O.: Digital economy and its role in the process of economic development. J. Secur. Sustain. Issues **9**(4), 1225–1235 (2020). https://doi.org/10.9770/jssi.2020.9.4(9)
22. An, T., Wen, R.: Mechanisms and empirical evidence on the impact of digital transformation on innovation in Chinese enterprises. Modern Econ. Inquiry **5**, 1–14 (2022). https://doi.org/10.13891/j.cnki.mer.2022.05.003

An Empirical Study on the Impact of Behavioural Bias on Investment Decision-Making

Chutian Li(✉)

School of Finance, Dongbei University of Finance and Economics, Dalian 116025, China
1811521139@mail.sit.edu.cn

Abstract. Traditional finance theory assumes that investors are rational, but as socio-economic development continues, numerous real-life examples and anomalies have shaken the foundations of the "rational man" assumption. Behavioural finance believes that investors' perception and cognitive approach to the market and their own psychology deviate significantly from that of a rational person, and that securities investment behaviour is limited to logical rationality. In China's securities market, due to the time constraints of development, most investors are characterised by overconfidence and cognitive biases. Therefore, this paper takes Chinese individual investors as the research object, adopts the method of questionnaire research and empirical analysis, selects eight representative irrational investment behaviours according to the theory of behavioural finance, investigates the group characteristics of individual investors through descriptive statistics, variance analysis and the establishment of logistic regression models, and investigates in depth the influence of different irrational behaviours of different individual investors on their own investment decisions The final conclusions are drawn and recommendations are made for individual investors in China.

Keywords: Behavioural Finance · Irrational Investment Behaviour · Logistic Regression Models

1 Introduction

The "rational man assumption" is the cornerstone of traditional finance theory, whether it is Markowitz's Modern Portfolio Theory (MPT), the Capital Asset Pricing Model (CAPM) by Sharpe-Lintner-Mossin, or the Arbitrage Pricing Theory (ATP) by Ross based on the no-arbitrage principle are all based on this strong assumption [1]. However, with the gradual advancement of finance research, more and more anomalies began to appear in financial markets that could not be explained under the traditional rational man assumption, such as the "equity premium mystery", the "closed-end fund discount mystery" and the "small firm effect" have been discovered and proposed, opening the way for many scholars to challenge and revise the assumptions of traditional finance theory. In reality, people's actual decisions largely do not meet the "rational economic man" assumptions, in order to further research to explain the financial markets and investors' actual investment behaviour decisions, behavioural finance was born [2].

In the 19th century, Gustave le bon and Mackey initiated the theory of behavioural finance by studying the behaviour of groups of investors over time [3]. Richard Thaler introduced the concept of psychological accounts in 1980, and Shefrin and Statman analysed that investors have different risk preferences for different accounts [4]; In 1992, Grifin and Tversky (2002) created the theory of "overconfidence" and researchers Biljana N. Adebambo and Xuemin (Sterling) Yan found that companies with overconfident investors are relatively overvalued based on the market-to-book value ratio and valuation bias [5]. Daniel Kahneman and Amos Tversky, have systematically described "expectations theory", which better explains the "expected utility theory". Fischhoff, Slovie and Lichtenstein have argued that individuals can underestimate the likelihood of events that they cannot easily imagine happening [6]. Radu T. Pruna et al. introduced a well-known behavioural bias, loss aversion [7]. In the mid-1980s, Thaler and Shiller studied abnormal stock price fluctuations, investor psychology, and the "herding effect" in equity markets, and behavioural finance theory entered a new phase of development in this period [3].

The psychological characteristics of investors can be broadly summarised as being overconfident, relying on intuition or past experience to make judgements and decisions, and favouring harm over profit, but at the same time desiring to become rich. Under the influence of self-confidence, investors believe that their investment decisions are more scientific and logical than those of others [8]. Because investors' perceptions of market information can be influenced by their own mindset, emotions and other perceptions, they are prone to various biases: people seek simplistic strategies to solve problems and often end up making decisions that contain a large proportion of intuitive judgements, which called rules of thumb or heuristics. The main ones include representativeness bias, which focuses on representative characteristics at the expense of actual probabilities of occurrence, accessibility bias, which potentially overestimates the probability of easily associated events, and anchoring and adjustment bias, which adjusts the overall estimate of the probability of an event with reference to initial values; Framing effects affect people's attitudes to risk in the context of specific stakes choices, and individuals have an unstable choice of whether a gain or loss is certain for the same expected utility. The existence of mental accounts makes investors make different choices for different risky assets and show different risk preferences for different accounts: risk aversion in the face of losses and risk seeking in the face of gains, and this different psychological transition is well explained by mental accounts theory. The discussion of investors' irrational behaviour in this paper concludes eight representative behavioural finance theories: representativeness bias, anchoring effect, overconfidence, ambiguity aversion, framing effect, reflection effect, halo effect and mental accounts.

Compared to developed Western countries, China's securities market is still at an early stage of development, and investors are lacking in the mastery of investment knowledge and in the grasp of investment psychology and sensitivity, especially individual investors show a strong vulnerability and lagging reaction ability in the face of market investment risks. Individual investors in China's securities market trade very frequently and the turnover rate is as high as ten times or more than that of developed countries such as the United States, which not only shortens investors' stock holding time but also reduces investment returns; According to data, individual investors in China only hold 2.09 company shares, which is far below the standard of holding four company shares to enhance risk diversification; Most individual investors often have overconfidence in the investment process performance, which tends to cause excessive deviations in behaviour and effectiveness. Overall, China's securities market is characterised by high speculation, high turnover rates and frequent fluctuations in investments.

As more and more anomalies occur in the securities market, traditional finance theories are challenged and the study of behavioural finance is of great theoretical and practical importance in order to further improve investment theories. In practice, the factors that influence investors' investment decisions go far beyond the risk-return ratio proposed by traditional financial theory. Market sentiment, income levels and irrational psychology are also key factors that influence investors' investment decisions [9]. At the same time, the leapfrog development of China's securities market has made it impossible to cultivate a group of investors with a mature and rational investment psychology and philosophy. Therefore, this paper starts from eight representative irrational behaviours, elaborates on the content of behavioural finance theory and supplements it with a questionnaire survey to investigate the influence of irrational investment behaviours on the investment decisions of individual investors in China.

2 Methodology

2.1 Questionnaire

The purpose of this questionnaire is to collect the impact of various irrational investment behaviours on investors' investment decisions through the perspective of individual investors and to provide a database and support for subsequent statistical analysis in order to draw relevant conclusions and recommendations. The questionnaire is divided into three parts: basic information, irrational investment behaviours and investment decisions. The design of this questionnaire is mainly based on the more mature scales at home and abroad, with reference to the design of Li Jianxu's scale [10]. The questionnaire is personalized and described in relation to the topic of this research paper. In addition to the five basic background information of gender, age, occupation, annual household income and education level, the questionnaire also investigated four basic investment-related questions, namely the time of entry into the market, investment risk tolerance, investment capital as a proportion of total wealth and the degree of investment knowledge.

The eight types of irrational investment behaviours are: representativeness bias, anchoring effect, overconfidence, ambiguity aversion, framing effect, reflection effect, halo effect, and mental accounting. In the third part of the questionnaire, two scale questions were used to understand the investment decisions of individual investors in terms of their current investment frequency and future investment intentions. The average time taken to complete the questionnaire was 146.8 s. In order to make the survey more complete and comprehensive, this paper strictly controls the size and quality of the questionnaire, sets the invalid questionnaire below 90 s when conducting the survey online, and sets the question "Please select number 2" to screen and exclude the negative respondents to improve the efficiency of the questionnaire collection.

The reliability of the questionnaire will be measured by Cronbach's alpha, which is used to determine the stability and reliability of respondents' responses. In empirical analyses, Cronbach's reliability is usually tested using Cronbach's alpha. The closer the number is to 1, the greater the correlation between the answers to the individual questions, reflecting the better the reliability of the questionnaire answers. When the alpha value is greater than 0.8, it means that the questionnaire can meet the statistical needs, and when the alpha value is between 0.7 and 0.8, it means that the reliability is more reasonable. In this study, the main factors were measured in the form of scales, so testing the data quality of the measurement results is an important prerequisite to ensure that the subsequent analysis is meaningful. This paper uses SPSS software to analyze the reliability of the data for each of the two-scale questions in the questionnaire, and the results are shown in the Table 1.

Table 1. Results of confidence analysis.

Option	Item deleted scale mean	Item deleted scale variance	Corrected item total correlation	Cronbach's Alpha of the deleted item	Standardised α
B1	54.6	179.802	0.733	0.91	0.918
B2	54.63	179.922	0.701	0.911	
B3	54.62	180.293	0.717	0.911	
B4	54.6	180.025	0.718	0.911	
B5	54.62	179.161	0.735	0.91	
B6	54.62	179.806	0.722	0.91	
B7	54.61	180.686	0.687	0.911	
B8	54.63	180.402	0.724	0.91	
B9	54.59	179.98	0.711	0.911	
B10	55.63	232.432	−0.717	0.946	
B11	54.62	180.771	0.683	0.912	
B12	54.63	177.255	0.762	0.909	
B13	54.59	179.215	0.706	0.911	
B14	54.6	180.353	0.724	0.91	
B15	54.6	178.13	0.739	0.91	
B16	54.63	178.719	0.738	0.91	
C1	55.03	191.453	0.367	0.92	

According to the results of the reliability test, the overall reliability of the questionnaire reached 0.918, which exceeded 0.8, indicating that the reliability of the questionnaire was high and could be used for subsequent analysis and calculation.

Validity analysis is the analysis of the degree of accuracy of the measurement results. Content validity aims to detect the logic of the questionnaire design, to determine whether the questions set are relatively easy to understand, and whether the individual questions are reasonably set. The degree of correlation between the measured values and the measured results is the structural validity. The questionnaire was designed with reference to classical academic scales, and a pre-survey was conducted before the formal research to modify the content of the questionnaire to obtain better content validity. In terms of structural validity, the questionnaire was analyzed by SPSS software using the KMO and Bartlett's sphericity tests, with KMO values ranging from 0 to 1. The closer the value to 1, the better the structural validity. According to Table 2, the KMO value was 0.925 and Bartlett's sphericity test showed $P < 0.01$, indicating that the data had good structural validity.

Table 2. KMO and Bartlett's test.

KMO Sampling suitability number		0.925
Bartlett Sphericity Test	Approximate Cardinality	3147.481
	df	351
	Significance	0

2.2 Modelling

Table 3 below provides a clear explanation of the dependent and independent variables selected for this paper. Two questions were set under each item for irrational behaviour in the questionnaire, and in the process of econometric analysis, the scores of the two items were combined and the average of them was taken as the final score of each irrational behaviour.

Table 3. Assignment of independent and dependent variables.

Variable	Variable name	Symbol	Variable definition and assignment
Independent variable	Gender	Gender	Male = 1, Female = 1
	Age	Age	25-year-old and below = 1, 26–35 years old = 2, 36–45 years old = 3, 46–55 years old = 4, 56-year-old and above = 5

(*continued*)

Table 3. (*continued*)

Variable	Variable name	Symbol	Variable definition and assignment
	Occupation	Occ	Business units = 1, Financial related fields = 2, Medium and large enterprises = 3, Small Business = 4, Private, self-employed = 5, Other = 6
	Household income	Income	200,000 and below = 1, 200,000–400,000 = 2, 400,000–600,000 = 3, 600,000 and above = 4
	Education level	Edu	High School and below = 1, Associate = 2, Undergraduate = 3, Master and above = 4
	Market Entry Time	Entry	Within 1 year = 1, 1–3 years = 2, 3–5 years = 3, 5–10 years = 4, Over 10 years = 5
	Risk tolerance	Bear	Unacceptable loss = 1, Within 10% = 2, 10%-30% = 3, 30%-50% = 4, Above 50% = 5
	Investment ratio	Ratio	Below 10% = 1, 10%-30% = 2, 30% = 50% = 3, 50%-100% = 4, Above 100% (With borrowing) = 5
	Financial Knowledge	Know	Very knowledgeable = 1, General knowledgeable = 2, Less knowledgeable = 3
	Representativeness Bias	Rep	Strongly agree = 5, Agree = 4, General = 3, Disagree = 2, Strongly disagree = 1
	Anchoring Effect	Anc	Strongly agree = 5, Agree = 4, General = 3, Disagree = 2, Strongly disagree = 1
	Overconfidence	Over	Strongly agree = 5, Agree = 4, General = 3, Disagree = 2, Strongly disagree = 1
	Ambiguity Aversion	Amb	Strongly agree = 5, Agree = 4, General = 3, Disagree = 2, Strongly disagree = 1

(*continued*)

Table 3. (*continued*)

Variable	Variable name	Symbol	Variable definition and assignment
	Framing Effect	Frame	Strongly agree = 5, Agree = 4, General = 3, Disagree = 2, Strongly disagree = 1
	Reflection Effect	Ref	Strongly agree = 5, Agree = 4, General = 3, Disagree = 2, Strongly disagree = 1
	Halo Effect	Halo	Strongly agree = 5, Agree = 4, General = 3, Disagree = 2, Strongly disagree = 1
	Mental Accounting	Mental	Strongly agree = 5, Agree = 4, General = 3, Disagree = 2, Strongly disagree = 1
Dependent variable	Frequency of investment	Fre	Strongly agree = 5, Agree = 4, General = 3, Disagree = 2, Strongly disagree = 1
	Investment intentions	Int	NO = 0, YES = 1

The data survey of this paper adopts a questionnaire method and assigns values to individual investors' irrational investment behaviour and investment decisions on a five-level Richter classification scale. The Ordered Logistic regression model is used for the classed and ordered variable Y1. The analysis of the sample data from the above question shows that male and female investors tend to differ in their irrational behaviour, so this paper uses gender grouping to build an Ordered Logistic Regression model (formula (1)) for male and female investors respectively.

$$y^* = \alpha + \sum_{k=1}^{K} \beta_k x_k + \varepsilon \qquad (1)$$

y* is a latent variable that cannot be measured directly, and the intrinsic variability of the observed object is its main role, and ε is the error coefficient. Ordered Logistic is a non-linear model, so the stepwise iterative method of the great likelihood estimation method is chosen for the estimation of the parameters in this paper (formula (2)).

$$\frac{Inp(y \leq j)}{1 - p(y \leq j)} = \alpha_j + \sum_{i=1}^{n} b_i x_i \qquad (2)$$

The model has j = 1,2,3,4,5, denoting the 5 levels of investor investment frequency, y is the investment frequency of the respondent, x_i is the explanatory variable affecting investor investment frequency, the intercept term is α_j and the regression coefficient is b_i. For investors' investment decisions, the questionnaire also set "whether they will continue with their investment activities" in order to investigate investors' future investment intentions. Therefore, the second dependent variable "investment intention" is a binary categorical variable. For this variable Y2, a binary logistic regression model is used to analyze the effect of the respective variable X on investors' investment intention. For the dichotomous data Y, there are only two values, the number 1 represents YES and the number 0 represents NO.

$$In\left(\frac{P}{1-P}\right) = \beta_0 + \beta_1 X_1 + \beta_2 X_2 + \cdots + \beta_m X_m \quad (3)$$

In the model, Y = 1 represents the probability that the investor will choose to sustain investment activities is P, Y = 0 represents the probability that the investor will choose not to sustain investment activities is 1-P, X_m denotes the group m of independent variables, and β_m denotes the regression coefficient of the group m of independent variables, indicating the description of the influence of the respective variable factors on the respondents' future investment intention.

3 Empirical Results

3.1 Descriptive Statistics

According to Table 4, it can be seen that the gender of individual investors is evenly distributed, with the proportion of male investors slightly higher than that of female investors. In terms of age, the main group of individual investors is concentrated on the young and middle-aged group aged 26–45, with the number of individual investors aged 26–35 slightly higher than that of 36–45. In terms of their occupations, most of the survey respondents were working in large, medium, and small enterprises, with nearly half of the respondents working in small enterprises. In terms of income structure, most investors had a low-income level, with 85.7% earning less than $200,000 and less than 5% earning less than $200,000. In terms of income structure, the majority of investors have a low-income level, with 85.7% earning less than 200,000 yuan and less than 5% earning more than 400,000 yuan per year. In terms of education level, a large proportion of investors have a specialist or bachelor's degree, with 81.7% overall. From the personal characteristics of the sample, it can draw a general picture of the respondents. Most of the individual investors are working in small enterprises, with an annual income of 200,000 and are aged 35–45, with a concentration of college and bachelor's degrees, and belong to the middle class of society as a whole.

Table 4. Frequency analysis of demographic variables.

Variable	Option	N	Percentage	Mean	SD
Gender	Male	131	52.0%	1.48	0.50
	Female	121	48.0%		

(*continued*)

Table 4. (*continued*)

Variable	Option	N	Percentage	Mean	SD
Age	25-year-old and below	28	11.1%	2.63	1.01
	26–35 years old	96	38.1%		
	36–45 years old	81	32.1%		
	46–55 years old	35	13.9%		
	56-year-old and above	12	4.8%		
Occ	Business Units	18	7.1%	3.43	1.08
	Financial related Fields	24	9.5%		
	Medium and large Enterprises	71	28.2%		
	Small Enterprises	115	45.6%		
	Private, Self-employed	18	7.1%		
	Other	6	2.4%		
Income	200,000 and below	216	85.7%	1.19	0.52
	200,000–400,000	24	9.5%		
	400,000–600,000	11	4.4%		
	600,000 and above	1	0.4%		
Edu	High School and below	38	15.1%	2.39	0.78
	Associate	85	33.7%		
	Undergraduate	121	48.0%		
	Master and above	8	3.2%		

As Table 5 shown, in terms of the length of time investors have been in the market, 14.68% of investors have been in the market for less than one year and are at the introductory stage of investment. 69.1% of investors have been in the market for 1–5 years and have accumulated a certain amount of investment experience, with relatively rich investment philosophy and experience. In general, the time of entry into the market is evenly distributed, and the sample covers investors with different investment experience. In terms of risk tolerance, the proportion of investors who can bear risk losses of less than 10% is more than half, of which 11.51% cannot accept losses, indicating that most individual investors choose a more stable investment style. As seen from the proportion of investment assets to wealth, the number of investors with an investment weighting of less than 10% and between 10% and 30% is relatively small, both around 40%. From the investors' knowledge of investment, only 24.6% belong to the more professional investors, and most investors' risk tolerance and professional level are not enough.

Table 5. Statistical analysis of the investment background of the sample.

Variable	Option	N	Percentage
Entry	Within 1 year	37	14.7%
	1–3 years	103	40.9%
	3–5 years	71	28.2%
	5–10 years	35	13.9%
	Over 10 years	6	2.4%
Bear	Unacceptable loss	29	11.5%
	Within 10%	102	40.5%
	10%–30%	84	33.3%
	30%–50%	29	11.5%
	Above 50%	8	3.2%
Ratio	Below 10%	90	35.7%
	10%–30%	107	42.5%
	30%–50%	34	13.5%
	50%–100%	18	7.1%
	Above 100%(with borrowing)	3	1.2%
Know	Very knowledgeable	62	24.6%
	General knowledgeable	179	71%
	Less knowledgeable	11	4.4%

As can be seen from Fig. 1(a)(b), the proportion of respondents scoring 4 and above on representativeness bias was as high as 63.09%, with only 4.76% of investors not suffering from representativeness bias, indicating that most individuals are susceptible to representativeness bias as an irrational investment behaviour in the investment process. According to Fig. 1(c)(d), 63.49% of the overall sample scored 4–5 on the anchoring effect, with over 60% of individual investors reflecting the anchoring effect when making investment decisions. Figure 1(e)(f) shows that the proportion of investors scoring higher than 4 is as high as 63.5%, thus showing the prevalence of overconfidence manifestations in the investment market. Figure 1(g)(h) shows that over 60% of investors continue to be averse to ambiguity risk and stand out in the investment process. Figure 1(i)(j) shows that 69.44% of the investors surveyed scored 3, with a tendency towards a framing effect, while 26.19% scored 4 and above. When faced with the same question, people tend to avoid risk when asked in a profitable way, while they tend to take risks when asked in a losing way. Figure 1(k)(l) shows that 62.31% of all investors surveyed have a tendency to exhibit a reflexive effect. Figure 1(m)(n) shows that 65.08% of investors scored 4 and above, with a significant halo effect, indicating that many individual investors are influenced by authoritative information, brand culture and short-term benefits, thus increasing their desires to invest. Figure 1(o)(p) shows that up to a third of investors scored a perfect score on their mental accounting, indicating that investors are generally influenced by their mental accounting behaviour when making investment decisions.

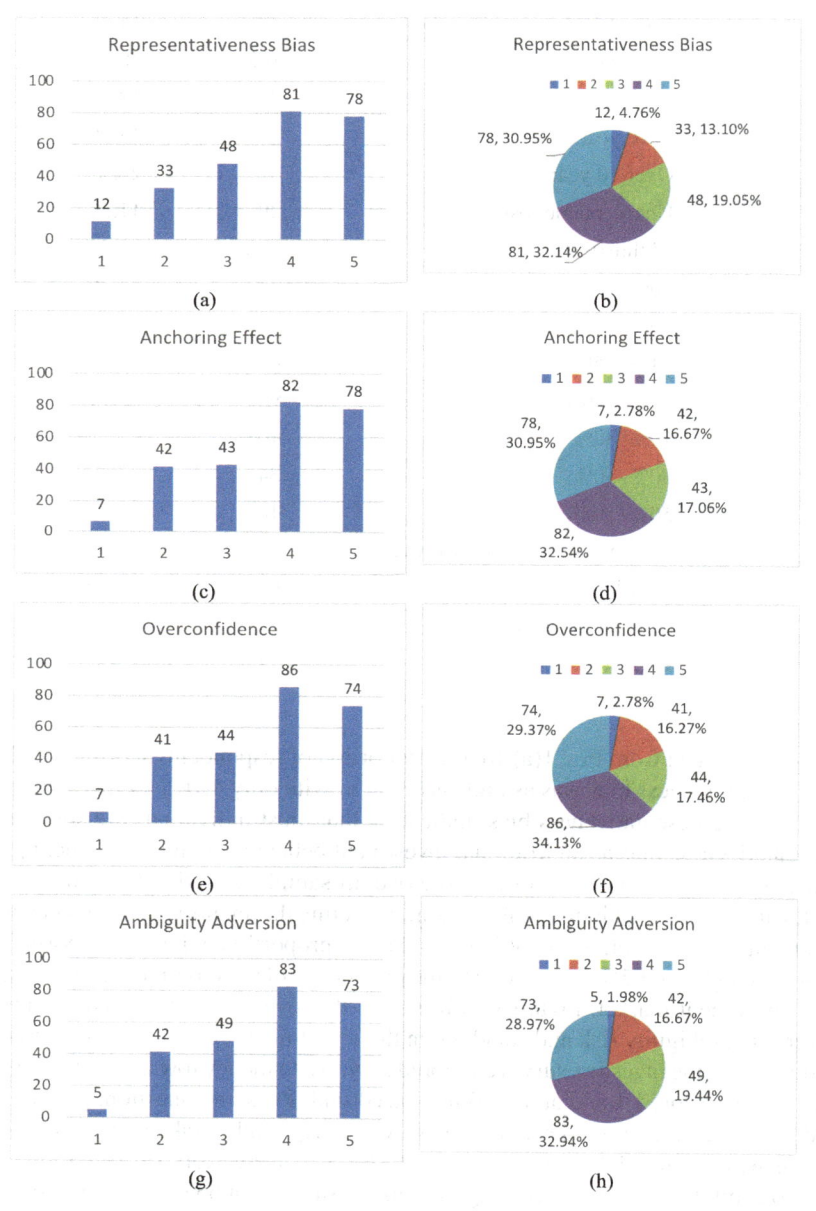

Fig. 1. Statistics of each irrational behaviour.

Framing Effect (i)

Category	Value
1	4
2	7
3	175
4	58
5	8

Framing Effect (j)

- 1: 4, 1.59%
- 2: 7, 2.78%
- 3: 175, 69.44%
- 4: 58, 23.02%
- 5: 8, 3.17%

Reflection Effect (k)

Category	Value
1	10
2	39
3	46
4	80
5	77

Reflection Effect (l)

- 1: 10, 3.97%
- 2: 39, 15.48%
- 3: 46, 18.25%
- 4: 80, 31.75%
- 5: 77, 30.56%

Halo Effect (m)

Category	Value
1	11
2	33
3	44
4	86
5	78

Halo Effect (n)

- 1: 11, 4.37%
- 2: 33, 13.10%
- 3: 44, 17.46%
- 4: 86, 34.13%
- 5: 78, 30.95%

Mental Accounting (o)

Category	Value
1	10
2	35
3	53
4	69
5	85

Mental Accounting (p)

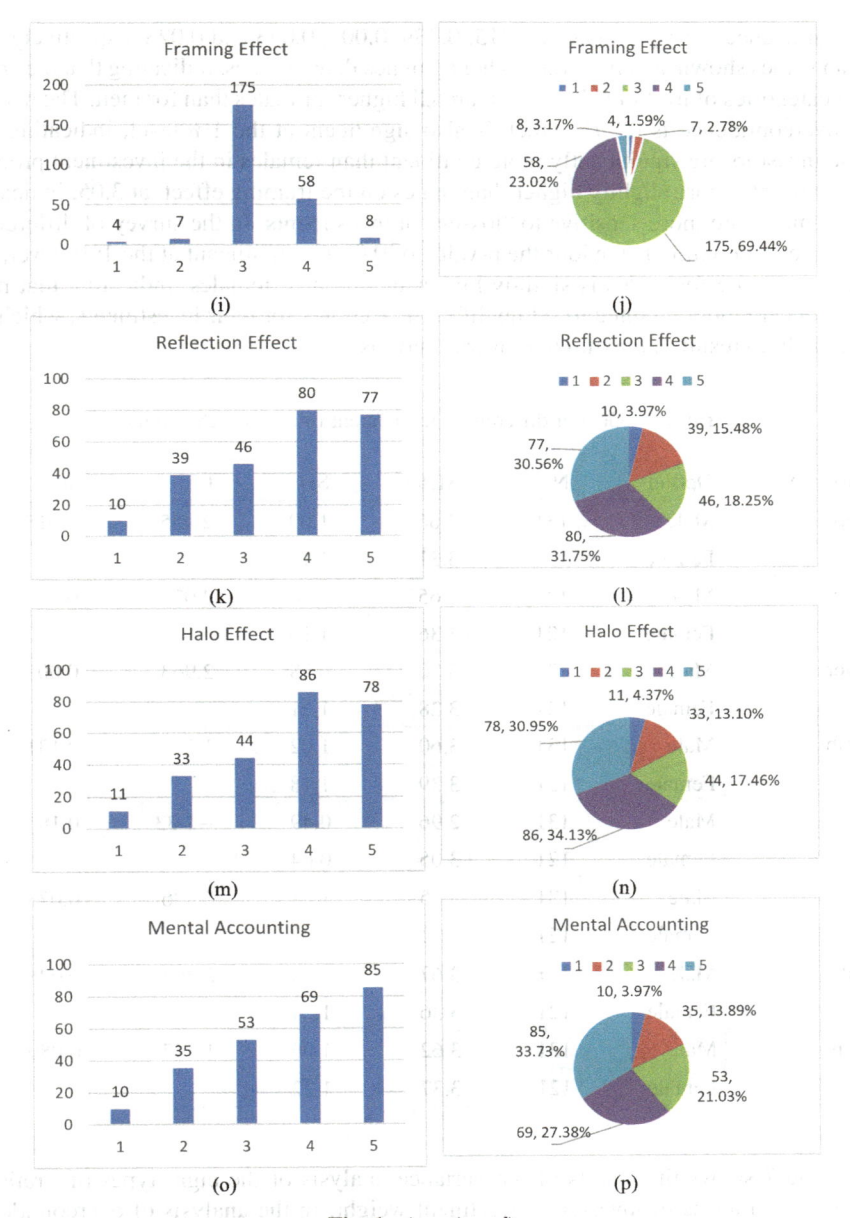

- 1: 10, 3.97%
- 2: 35, 13.89%
- 3: 53, 21.03%
- 4: 69, 27.38%
- 5: 85, 33.73%

Fig. 1. (*continued*)

3.2 Variance Analysis

The results of Table 6, which analyses the differences in the performance of irrational behaviours by gender, show that the representativeness bias, anchoring effect, overconfidence, reflection effect and halo effect are all significantly different at the 5% level of significance, with p-values of 0.015, 0.039, 0.003, 0.023 and 0.028 respectively. The mean values shown are all scored higher by males than females, indicating that the above four categories of irrational behaviour are all higher for males than for men. The p-value for overconfidence is 0.003, which is also significant at the 1% level, indicating that male investors are significantly more confident than females in the investment process. Females only score slightly higher than males on the framing effect, at 3.05, indicating that females are more sensitive to "losses" in investments. In the survey of differences in mental accounting behaviour the p-value of 0.089 is significant at the 10% level, and the mean score for males is slightly higher than that of females, indicating that male investors are more inclined to set up different accounts for their investments, which are less likely to result in maximizing overall returns.

Table 6. Gender differences in different irrational behaviours.

Variance	Option	N	Mean	SD	t	sig
Rep	Male	131	3.66	1.09	2.455	0.015
	Female	121	3.31	1.17		
Anc	Male	131	3.65	1.06	2.072	0.039
	Female	121	3.36	1.16		
Over	Male	131	3.70	0.98	2.963	0.003
	Female	121	3.28	1.21		
Amb	Male	131	3.60	1.02	1.516	0.131
	Female	121	3.39	1.18		
Frame	Male	131	2.96	0.49	−1.33	0.185
	Female	121	3.05	0.64		
Ref	Male	131	3.65	1.08	2.296	0.023
	Female	121	3.32	1.22		
Halo	Male	131	3.67	0.98	2.207	0.028
	Female	121	3.36	1.24		
Mental	Male	131	3.62	1.06	1.707	0.089
	Female	121	3.37	1.22		

Table 7 shows the results of the variance analysis of the eight types of irrational behaviour in terms of investors' investment weight. In the analysis of overconfidence behaviour, investors with less than 50% investment weight have a higher tendency to be overconfident than those with 50%–100% investment weight, and the overconfidence decreases with increasing investment weight to a certain extent. In the analysis of the variance of ambiguity aversion, investors with less than 10% investment weight score significantly higher than those with 30% investment weight and above, while investors with 10%–30% investment weight score significantly higher than those with 50% investment weight and above. This indicates that investors with lower investment weights have a higher tendency to be ambiguity averse, and that they prefer risks with known probabilities and are more likely to invest in areas they are familiar with and seek out familiar institutions and analysts. In the analysis of the reflection effect, investors with an investment weighting of less than 10% are more likely to have asymmetries in gain and loss preferences than those with an investment weighting of 50%–100%. In an investigation of the halo effect, investors with an investment weight of less than 10% are more likely to be directly influenced by authoritative judgments and some superficial factors than investors with an investment weight of 50% and above; The results of the psychological account variance analysis show that investors with less than 50% investment weighting have a significantly higher tendency to have a separate account than those with more than 50% investment weighting, indicating that investors with relatively low investment weighting are more likely to give their investment facilities a separate account and lose overall returns. Overall, investors with a lower investment weighting have a more pronounced tendency to behave in various irrational ways.

Table 7. Differences in investment funds as a % of total wealth by irrational behaviour.

Variance	Option	N	Mean	SD	F	sig	Multiple comparison
Rep	Below10%	90	3.57	1.02	0.926	0.450	/
	10%–30%	107	3.52	1.21			
	30%–50%	34	3.49	1.25			
	50%–100%	18	3.06	1.14			
	Above 100% (with borrowing)	3	3.00	1.00			
Anc	Below10%	90	3.60	1.09	1.873	0.116	/
	10%–30%	107	3.52	1.14			
	30%–50%	34	3.59	1.11			
	50%–100%	18	2.97	1.02			
	Above 100% (with borrowing)	3	2.50	1.00			
Over	Below10%	90	3.56	1.09	2.437	0.048	1 > 4,2 > 4,3 > 4
	10%–30%	107	3.53	1.11			
	30%–50%	34	3.63	1.14			
	50%–100%	18	2.89	1.09			
	Above 100% (with borrowing)	3	2.33	1.04			

(continued)

Table 7. (*continued*)

Variance	Option	N	Mean	SD	F	sig	Multiple comparison
Amb	Below 10%	90	3.69	0.99	4.407	0.002	1 > 3,1 > 4,1 > 5, 2 > 4,2 > 5,3 > 5
	10%–30%	107	3.55	1.17			
	30%–50%	34	3.25	1.02			
	50%–100%	18	3.00	0.99			
	Above 100% (with borrowing)	3	1.67	0.29			
Frame	Below10%	90	2.99	0.55	0.351	0.843	/
	10%–30%	107	3.03	0.61			
	30%–50%	34	3.04	0.62			
	50%–100%	18	2.89	0.32			
	Above 100% (with borrowing)	3	2.83	0.29			
Ref	Below10%	90	3.62	1.00	1.749	0.140	1 > 4
	10%–30%	107	3.44	1.27			
	30%–50%	34	3.65	1.14			
	50%–100%	18	3.03	1.25			
	Above 100% (with borrowing)	3	2.50	0.50			
Halo	Below 10%	90	3.63	1.05	2.003	0.095	1 > 4,1 > 5
	10%–30%	107	3.52	1.13			
	30%–50%	34	3.59	1.18			
	50%–100%	18	3.03	1.21			
	Above 100% (with borrowing)	3	2.33	0.76			
Mental	Below10%	90	3.64	1.04	4.243	0.002	1 > 4,1 > 5,2 > 4, 2 > 5,3 > 4,3 > 5
	10%–30%	107	3.52	1.13			
	30%–50%	34	3.62	1.09			
	50%–100%	18	2.64	1.42			
	Above 100% (with borrowing)	3	2.17	0.76			

3.3 Regressive Results

Based on the variance analysis in the previous section, it can be seen that individual investors of different genders have different biases towards irrational behaviour. Therefore, in this paper, Ordered Logistic regression models are built for male and female investors respectively, using gender as a subgroup to analyze the frequency of investors' investments. The regression results are shown in the table below, which passed the parallelism test and the model fit was good:

From Table 8, it can be seen that among the male investors surveyed, the coefficients of the four types of irrational investment behaviours, namely, representativeness bias, reflection effect, halo effect and psychological account, are significant, with the coefficient of representativeness bias being 0.677 and the p-value rejecting the original hypothesis at the 5% level (p = 0.038 < 0.05), indicating that male individual investors are easily influenced by positive publicity when making investments and will increase their investment frequency when dealing with normal returns on past investment products. The coefficient of the reflection effect is 0.512, with a p-value of 0.059 at the 10% level, indicating that male investors tend to be risk-averse when faced with the prospect of losses and risk-averse when faced with the prospect of gains, which positively influences their investment frequency; the coefficient of the halo effect is −0.619, which is significant (p = 0.036 < 0.05), indicating that male investors are susceptible to one-sided good data and authority figures when making investments; and finally the coefficient of the psychological account is significant at the 10% level (p = 0.095) at 0.538, indicating that most male investors are susceptible to psychological accounts of their investment sentiment and have high psychological fluctuations in their investments. The remaining four irrational behaviours had no significant effect on the investment frequency of male investors.

Table 8. Results of Ordered Logistic Model.

		Estimated value	SD	Wald	df	P	95% confidence interval Lowest	Highest
Threshold	[Fre = 1]	1.101	2.266	0.236	1	0.627	−3.339	5.541
	[Fre = 2]	2.392	2.278	1.103	1	0.294	−2.072	6.856
	[Fre = 3]	3.367	2.287	2.169	1	0.141	−1.114	7.849
	[Fre = 4]	5.391	2.302	5.484	1	0.019	0.879	9.903
Irrational behaviour	Rep	0.677	0.326	4.317	1	0.038**	0.038	1.316
	Anc	0.185	0.306	0.364	1	0.546	−0.416	0.785
	Over	0.257	0.323	0.634	1	0.426	−0.376	0.89
	Amb	−0.438	0.336	1.694	1	0.193	−1.097	0.222
	Frame	0.493	0.377	1.708	1	0.191	−0.246	1.232
	Ref	0.512	0.271	3.57	1	0.059*	−0.019	1.043
	Halo	−0.619	0.295	4.385	1	0.036**	−1.198	−0.04
	Mental	0.538	0.322	2.795	1	0.095*	−0.093	1.168

(*continued*)

Table 8. (continued)

		Estimated value	SD	Wald	df	P	95% confidence interval Lowest	Highest
Personal characteristics	Age	−0.195	0.186	1.104	1	0.293	−0.559	0.169
	Occ	−0.083	0.188	0.193	1	0.661	−0.451	0.286
	Income	0.476	0.483	0.973	1	0.324	−0.47	1.423
	Edu	−0.283	0.245	1.334	1	0.248	−0.762	0.197
	[Entry = 1]	−0.989	1.335	0.549	1	0.459	−3.607	1.628
	[Entry = 2]	−0.911	1.294	0.496	1	0.481	−3.447	1.624
	[Entry = 3]	−1.12	1.262	0.788	1	0.375	−3.593	1.352
	[Entry = 4]	0.15	1.365	0.012	1	0.913	−2.525	2.824
	[Entry = 5]	0a			0			
	[Bear = 1]	0.027	1.592	0	1	0.986	−3.093	3.148
	[Bear = 2]	−0.329	1.531	0.046	1	0.83	−3.33	2.673
	[Bear = 3]	−0.492	1.538	0.102	1	0.749	−3.505	2.522
	[Bear = 4]	−0.321	1.564	0.042	1	0.837	−3.386	2.744
	[Bear = 5]	0a			0			
	[Ratio = 1]	−1.232	0.834	2.184	1	0.139	−2.866	0.402
	[Ratio = 2]	−0.943	0.834	1.279	1	0.258	−2.578	0.692
	[Ratio = 3]	−1.329	0.889	2.236	1	0.135	−3.071	0.413
	[Ratio = 4]	0a			0			
	[Know = 1]	0.657	1.436	0.209	1	0.647	−2.157	3.472
	[Know = 2]	0.918	1.492	0.379	1	0.538	−2.006	3.843
	[Know = 3]	0a			0			

As can be seen from Table 9, the three irrational investment behaviours of anchoring effect, overconfidence and mental accounting have a significant impact on the investment frequency of female individual investors compared to male individual investors. The coefficient of the anchoring effect is −0.545, which is significant (p = 0.062 < 0.1), indicating that female investors are susceptible to the opinions of other market investors in the investment process, which leads to a decrease in investment frequency. The coefficient of overconfidence is 0.507, with a p-value of 0.074, which is significant at the 10% level, indicating that female individual investors are more significant overconfidence compared to male individual investors. Due to the safe pay-out and profitability of past investments, female investors tend to overestimate their ability to make personal decisions and increase their investment frequency. The psychological account coefficient of 0.789 was highly significant (p = 0.007 < 0.01), with female investors showing a more pronounced mental accounting than male investors, with the returns on some investments highly likely to affect female investors' positive investment sentiment and reflected through the channel of increased investment frequency. The remaining five irrational behaviours had no significant impact on female investors' investment frequency.

Table 9. Results of Ordered Logistic Model.

		Estimated value	SD	Wald	df	P	95% confidence interval Lowest Highest	
Threshold	[Fre = 1]	−1.172	3.151	0.138	1	0.71	−7.347	5.004
	[Fre = 2]	0.305	3.15	0.009	1	0.923	−5.869	6.479
	[Fre = 3]	1.24	3.15	0.155	1	0.694	−4.934	7.414
	[Fre = 4]	3.903	3.166	1.52	1	0.218	−2.302	10.109
Irrational behaviour	Rep	−0.116	0.243	0.229	1	0.632	−0.592	0.36
	Anc	−0.545	0.292	3.488	1	0.062*	−1.116	0.027
	Over	0.507	0.284	3.193	1	0.074*	−0.049	1.063
	Amb	0.115	0.287	0.161	1	0.688	−0.447	0.677
	Frame	−0.371	0.325	1.304	1	0.254	−1.007	0.266
	Ref	−0.012	0.301	0.002	1	0.967	−0.602	0.577
	Halo	−0.207	0.364	0.323	1	0.57	−0.919	0.506
	Mental	0.789	0.29	7.391	1	0.007***	0.22	1.357
Personal characteristics	Age	0.227	0.225	1.017	1	0.313	−0.214	0.668
	Income	0.463	0.362	1.635	1	0.201	−0.247	1.172
	Know	0.047	0.4	0.014	1	0.907	−0.738	0.832
	Bear	−0.223	0.202	1.224	1	0.268	−0.619	0.172
	Ratio	−0.183	0.203	0.818	1	0.366	−0.58	0.214
Personal characteristics	[Edu = 1]	1.272	1.062	1.434	1	0.231	−0.81	3.354
	[Edu = 2]	1.794	0.977	3.37	1	0.066	−0.121	3.71
	[Edu = 3]	0.464	0.951	0.238	1	0.626	−1.4	2.328
	[Edu = 4]	0a			0			
	[Entry = 1]	−2.057	2.288	0.809	1	0.369	−6.542	2.427
	[Entry = 2]	−1.425	2.198	0.42	1	0.517	−5.732	2.883
	[Entry = 3]	−2.4	2.224	1.166	1	0.28	−6.759	1.958

(continued)

Table 9. (continued)

		Estimated value	SD	Wald	df	P	95% confidence interval Lowest Highest	
	[Entry = 4]	−2.129	2.277	0.874	1	0.35	−6.592	2.335
	[Entry = 5]	0a			0			
	[Occ = 1]	1.491	1.479	1.017	1	0.313	−1.407	4.389
	[Occ = 2]	0.084	1.467	0.003	1	0.954	−2.792	2.959
	[Occ = 3]	1.115	1.339	0.694	1	0.405	−1.509	3.74
	[Occ = 4]	0.765	1.3	0.346	1	0.556	−1.784	3.313
	[Occ = 5]	−0.006	1.694	0	1	0.997	−3.326	3.313
	[Occ = 6]	0a			0			

For the investigation of investors' future investment intention, this questionnaire sets the question "Will you continue to invest?" The variable "investment intention" is therefore a binary categorical variable, therefore a binary logistic regression model was selected for the empirical analysis, aiming to investigate the impact of investors' personal characteristics and eight types of irrational investment behaviours on investors' future investment intentions. The regression results are shown in Table 10.

Table 10. Results of the binary logistic model analysis.

Variance	B	SD	Wald	df	P	Exp(B)	95% confidence interval for EXP(B) Lowest Highest	
Gender(1)	0.063	0.363	0.03	1	0.863	1.065	0.522	2.169
Age(1)	0.928	0.757	1.501	1	0.221	2.529	0.573	11.155
Age(2)	1.321	0.782	2.854	1	0.091*	3.746	0.809	17.339
Age(3)	0.827	0.853	0.939	1	0.333	2.286	0.429	12.173
Age(4)	1.167	1.269	0.845	1	0.358	3.212	0.267	38.656
Occ(1)	−0.709	0.896	0.626	1	0.429	0.492	0.085	2.849
Occ(2)	0.989	0.849	1.357	1	0.244	2.689	0.509	14.208
Occ(3)	0.998	0.84	1.412	1	0.235	2.713	0.523	14.07
Occ(4)	0.651	1.041	0.392	1	0.531	1.918	0.249	14.757
Occ(5)	1.101	1.422	0.599	1	0.439	3.008	0.185	48.855

(continued)

Table 10. (*continued*)

Variance	B	SD	Wald	df	P	Exp(B)	95% confidence interval for EXP(B) Lowest Highest	
Income(1)	0.744	0.723	1.059	1	0.303	2.104	0.51	8.672
Income(2)	1.676	1.264	1.757	1	0.185	5.343	0.448	63.653
Edu(1)	0.965	0.562	2.95	1	0.086*	2.625	0.873	7.897
Edu(2)	0.466	0.532	0.769	1	0.38	1.594	0.562	4.522
Edu(3)	−1.894	1.225	2.39	1	0.122	0.15	0.014	1.661
Entry(1)	1.76	0.55	10.229	1	0.001***	5.813	1.977	17.095
Entry(2)	0.678	0.575	1.389	1	0.239	1.97	0.638	6.083
Entry(3)	1.012	0.661	2.343	1	0.126	2.751	0.753	10.054
Entry(4)	0.065	1.407	0.002	1	0.963	1.068	0.068	16.818
Bear(1)	−0.911	0.731	1.552	1	0.213	0.402	0.096	1.686
Bear(2)	−0.583	0.73	0.638	1	0.424	0.558	0.134	2.334
Bear(3)	−1.784	0.844	4.475	1	0.034**	0.168	0.032	0.877
Bear(4)	−2.464	1.354	3.312	1	0.069*	0.085	0.006	1.209
Ratio(1)	−0.331	0.41	0.651	1	0.42	0.719	0.322	1.604
Ratio(2)	0.92	0.652	1.992	1	0.158	2.509	0.699	9
Ratio(3)	0.611	0.778	0.617	1	0.432	1.842	0.401	8.458
Ratio(4)	−1.398	2.609	0.287	1	0.592	0.247	0.001	41.026
Know(1)	0.04	0.47	0.007	1	0.932	1.041	0.414	2.613
Know(2)	3.666	2.338	2.459	1	0.117	39.111	0.4	3824.944
Rep	−0.094	0.278	0.114	1	0.736	0.91	0.527	1.571
Anc	−0.813	0.334	5.912	1	0.015**	0.443	0.23	0.854
Over	0.26	0.287	0.82	1	0.365	1.297	0.739	2.275
Amb	0.575	0.291	3.9	1	0.048**	1.778	1.004	3.147
Frame	−0.043	0.307	0.02	1	0.887	0.957	0.525	1.746
Ref	0.234	0.272	0.739	1	0.39	1.263	0.741	2.153
Halo	0.103	0.317	0.106	1	0.745	1.109	0.595	2.066
Mental	0.758	0.29	6.829	1	0.009***	2.134	1.209	3.768
c	−5.113	1.798	8.091	1	0.004***	0.006		

The gender of individual investors did not show significance ($p = 0.863 > 0.05$), with a regression coefficient of 0.063. Among investors of different ages, those aged 36–45 showed a p-value of 0.091, significant at the 10% level, with a regression coefficient of 1.321, indicating a greater intention to continue investing in the future as the age of the investor increases. Investors aged 36–45 are 3.746 times more likely to invest than investors aged 25 and under (OR = 3.746). The coefficients on investors' occupation and annual household income are also insignificant, with p-values greater than 0.05. The coefficient on investor's education level shows that investors with a specialist education level show a significant (p = 0.086 > 0.1), with an OR of 2.625, indicating that the investment intention of investors with a specialist education level is 2.625 times higher than that of investors with a high school education level or less. In the regression coefficient of investors' time in the market, the coefficient of time in the market between 1–3 years is significant at the 1% level (p = 0.001), and the OR value shows that the investment intention of investors with 1–3 years in the market is 5.813 times higher than that of investors within 1 year (OR = 5.813), the longer the time in the market, the stronger the future investment intention of investors. The regression coefficients for risk tolerance of 30%–50% and 50% or more were significant with p-values of 0.034 and 0.069 respectively, and the coefficients were negative, which combined with the OR values indicates that risk tolerance is negatively related to the investor's future investment intention. The p-values for the investor's investment weight and investment knowledge reserve did not reach the significance level.

From the regression results in the table above, it can be seen that the three irrational behaviours of anchoring effect, ambiguity aversion and mental accounting have a significant effect on investors' future investment intention. The coefficient of the mental accounting is 0.758, with a p-value of 0.009 at the 1% level and an OR of 2.134, indicating that for every 1 point increase in the investor's score on the psychological account, the investor's chance of winning future investment intentions increases by 113.4%, which has a significant positive effect on whether the investor will continue to invest. The coefficient of the anchoring effect is −0.813 (p = 0.015 < 0.05), indicating that the higher the score of the anchoring effect, the lower the investor's intention to invest in the future, and according to the OR (OR = 0.443), every 1 point increase in the score of the anchoring effect decreases the investor's odds of continuing to invest in the future by 55.7%. The regression coefficient of ambiguity aversion is 0.575 (p = 0.048 < 0.05) which is significant, corresponding to OR = 1.778. The regression coefficient of 0.575 (p0.048 < 0.05) is significant, corresponding to OR = 1.778. For every 1 point increasing in the score of ambiguity aversion, the probability of continued investment in the future increases by 77.8%, which shows that investors are cautious about their investment assets and most of them face greater psychological pressure when choosing new investment tracks and products.

4 Conclusion

This paper examines the irrational behavior of individual investors and its impact on investment decisions from the perspective of behavioral finance. The questionnaire data shows that most investors active in the investment market are concentrated in the young and middle-aged group aged 26–45, mostly working in small enterprises, with an annual income of around 200,000, and their education is concentrated in college and bachelor's degree. The analysis of the eight types of irrational investment behaviors shows that mental accounting is most evident when investors invest, followed by representativeness bias, anchoring effect, overconfidence, ambiguity aversion, reflection effect, and halo effect. Gender, age, education level, time in the market, and risk tolerance have significant effects on individual investors' future investment intentions, with risk tolerance having a negative effect on investors' investment intentions. The analysis of variance shows that different genders and investment weights exhibit different irrational behaviors, and different irrational investment behaviors also have a significant impact on individual investors' investment frequency and investment intention. Investors' investment knowledge is insufficient and lacks professionalism, and education level, time in the market, and risk tolerance all have a significant impact on individual investors' investment decisions. Therefore, investors need to improve their investment literacy and expertise to reduce the influence of irrational behavior and make more objective, comprehensive, and reasonable investment decisions in the investment process. Investors should analyze their own psychological tendencies and weaknesses, consciously pay attention to and correct their investment weaknesses, and improve their overall investment strategy skills and thinking skills.

The two regression models show that the four types of irrational investment behavior, namely representativeness bias, reflection effect, halo effect, and mental accounting, have a significant impact on the investment frequency of male individual investors, while the investment frequency of females is significantly affected by the anchoring effect, overconfidence, and mental accounting. Ambiguity aversion, anchoring effect, and mental accounting have significant effects on individual investors' future investment intentions, with ambiguity aversion being negatively related to investment intentions. However, the results obtained from the different sample sizes are often inconsistent. Future studies may include certain mediating variables, such as the inclusion of investors' investment sentiment as a mediating variable, to analyze in more depth the channels through which irrational behavior affects investors' investment decisions. Overall, the study highlights the importance of improving individual investors' investment literacy, understanding their own investment characteristics, and consciously correcting their investment weaknesses to make more rational investment decisions.

References

1. Yang, X., Wang, S.: Analysis of investor risk preferences in behavioral finance. J. Sichuan Univ. Philos. Soc. Sci. Ed. **1**, 24–29 (2006)
2. Duan, X.: Analysis and enlightenment of individual investors' investment behavior in China from the perspective of behavioral finance. Economist **3**, 113–115 (2020)
3. Chen, S.: Research on irrational behavior of A-client stock investment. Guangdong University of Finance and Economics (2021)
4. Shefrin, H., Statman, M.: Behavioral capital asset pricing theory. J. Financ. Quant. Anal. **29**, 323–349 (1994)
5. Adebambo, B.N., Yan, X.: Investor overconfidence, firm valuation, and corporate decisions. Manage. Sci. **64**, 5349–5369 (2017)
6. Lichtenstein, S., Fischhoff, B., Phillips, L.D.: Calibration of probabilities: the state of the art to 1980. In: Kahneman, D., Slovic, P., Tversky, A. (eds.), Judgment Under Uncertainty: Heuristics and Biases, pp. 306–334. Cambridge University Press, Cambridge (1982)
7. Pruna, R.T., Polukarov, M., Jennings, N.R.: Loss aversion in an agent-based asset pricing model. Quant. Financ. **2**, 275–290 (2020)

8. Chen, J., Zhang, K.: Research on securities investment behavior from the perspective of behavioral finance. China Manage. Informationization **25**(13), 155–157 (2022)
9. Gong, Y.: Research on the evolution and development trend of behavioral finance theory. Yunnan University of Finance and Economics (2022)
10. Li, J.: Analysis of the influence of irrational behavior on individual trust investment decision. China University of Political Science and Law (2021)

Matrix Factorization Model in Collaborative Filtering Algorithms Based on Feedback Datasets

Yuqing Hu(✉)

School of Finance, Capital University of Economics and Business, Beijing 100070, China
Huyuqing0525@outlook.com

Abstract. In recent years, with the advancement of internet technology, an increasing number of applications rely on recommendation systems to provide personalized recommendations to users in order to increase profits. The recommendation system has generated significant economic benefits and has become a popular research area. Collaborative Filtering (CF) is currently the most widely used method for building recommendation systems. CF techniques use user-item ratings in the form of user behavior as a source of information for prediction. The challenges in CF are being effectively addressed by Matrix Factorization (MF) algorithms. Implicit data, which has many advantages as a more accessible type of data, is increasingly being used in recommendation systems. This paper provides a detailed introduction to the knowledge framework of the collaborative filtering algorithm based on implicit feedback, describes the model for utilizing implicit data in this algorithm, and serves as a reference for future research. It is believed that this research has significant implications for promoting the development of personalized information services.

Keywords: Collaborative Filtering · Matrix Factorization · Recommendation System · Feedback Database

1 Introduction

In 1992, Goldberg created Tapestry, a personalized email system that used collaborative filtering and marked the beginning of recommendation systems. Over time, researchers and businesses began to recognize the value of these systems in both commercial and research fields. For instance, Netflix offered a $1 million prize in 2006 to improve their recommendation algorithm, which resulted in the rise of the field of recommendation algorithms and provided momentum for subsequent research.

Collaborative filtering is a technology that utilizes the preferences of similar users to automatically filter and select information for the target user. This is because users with similar preferences, social circles, and cultural backgrounds often share similar information needs. Collaborative filtering technology extracts user interests through browsing and search behavior, purchase history, or product ratings without interfering with the user's access, thereby enhancing the user's experience of the system. User-based and item-based methods are the most common types of collaborative filtering systems [1]. Matrix factorization, a technique used in collaborative filtering, has many advantages, such as powerful generalization ability, low space complexity, better scalability, and flexibility.

Implicit datasets are a type of dataset relative to explicit datasets, which are easier to obtain but do not reflect customer needs as clearly as the latter. The current direction of development for collaborative filtering algorithms is the combination of implicit datasets with matrix factorization technology [2].

The purpose of this article is to introduce the principles and classifications, datasets, and applicable algorithms of collaborative filtering and to indicate possible future research directions.

2 Collaborative Filtering Model

Collaborative filtering predicts the target user's interest in items they have not accessed yet by identifying similar users or items. Unlike content-based recommendation methods, collaborative filtering can capture complex concepts that are difficult to express using keywords and suggest new items based on similar users or items. Collaborative filtering algorithms can be classified into three categories: k-nearest neighbor-based models, matrix factorization-based models, and probabilistic graphical model-based models [3]. Within the matrix factorization category, there are three sub-categories: point-wise, pairwise, and column-wise matrix factorization models [4].

In addition, there are three popular algorithms in the matrix factorization category: the probabilistic matrix factorization model (PMF), the weighted matrix factorization model (WMF), and the pairwise interaction tensor factorization model (PITF), which are used for an item recommendation, rating prediction, and tag recommendation, respectively.

This section focuses on two commonly used collaborative filtering models: the k-nearest neighbor algorithm and the matrix factorization algorithm.

2.1 Collaborative Filtering Model Based on K-Nearest Neighbor

The K-Nearest Neighbor algorithm (KNN) is a widely used and adaptable machine learning model that can be divided into classification and regression models. The basic idea is to find the K most similar samples to the input sample in the training dataset and use the majority class or average attribute values of these K samples as the result.

The KNN algorithm has several applications in recommendation systems, including userKNN, itemKNN, SLIM, LOR-SLIM, and GL-SLIM [5].

For example, userKNN calculates the similarity between users in the training dataset to find K users with similar interests and predicts the preference of an input user for a certain item based on the preferences of those K similar users. Similarly, itemKNN calculates the similarity between items to find K similar items and recommends items based on a user's history of visiting items. The main challenges include how to calculate similarity between users or items, and how to use the obtained similarity to calculate the predicted result.

Similarity calculation in the basic KNN algorithm, such as ItemKNN, is based on the data vectors formed by the historical records of the items being visited. Similarity or distance measures are used to measure the degree of similarity, including Pearson correlation coefficient, cosine similarity, Jaccard similarity, and conditional probability similarity. For predicting preference values, simple average, weighted average, and weighted majority prediction methods are commonly used.

Both UserKNN and ItemKNN can be used for rating prediction and item recommendation. UserKNN is more suitable for personalized news recommendations, while ItemKNN is suitable for recommending products on e-commerce websites like Amazon. From a technical perspective, UserKNN is suitable for scenarios with fewer users, while ItemKNN is suitable for scenarios with fewer items. Compared with UserKNN, ItemKNN provides real-time personalized recommendations based on a user's history of visiting items, which satisfies the need for personalized recommendations and provides a reasonable recommendation explanation.

2.2 Collaborative Filtering Model Based on Matrix Factorization

Matrix factorization models are widely used and extended in the field of recommendation systems, applicable for rating prediction and product recommendation. It has good accuracy and scalability. Playing an important role in major recommendation system competitions. Such as the Netflix Prize, KDD Cup011 music recommendation Alibaba Big Data Competition, and so on. Specifically, matrix factorization is a typical dimensionality reduction technique that decomposes the original rating matrix (or count matrix) R into two hidden feature matrices: user hidden feature matrix P and product hidden feature matrix Q, where each user u (or product m) is represented by a real-valued vector much smaller than the valued vector P (or Qm), and the dimension of this vector is much small than the number of users or products. Therefore, the model can use two hidden feature matrices far smaller than the original data matrix to approximate the underlying meaning of the original feature matrix. Generally. The inner product of the user's hidden feature vector and the product's hidden feature vector represents the degree of the user's preference for the product Depending on the model's purpose, the matrix factorization model can be divided into two categories: (1) rating prediction matrix factorization model; (2) product recommendation matrix factorization model. Because of the different application purposes, the two types of models cannot generally be mixed, otherwise, the effect may be relatively poor. For example, PMF is generally used for rating prediction, and in many literatures, using PMF as a baseline method for product recommendation is obviously unreasonable [6].

2.3 Matrix Algorithm Based on Feedback Data Set

Feedback data, comprising a user's browsing, collection, and purchase behavior, may not always provide a definitive indication of their preferences for an item. This type of data is commonly referred to as implicit feedback, and it has two primary characteristics. Firstly, it lacks negative feedback. In explicit datasets, a low rating score typically suggests that the user does not like the item. However, in implicit datasets, the absence of any user action on an item does not necessarily mean the user dislikes it. Secondly, implicit feedback is vulnerable to noise. Behavioral data is utilized to infer user preferences, but it may not always be accurate. For instance, a user's purchase of a product on an e-commerce platform may not necessarily indicate that they like the product since it could have been bought for someone else. Similarly, a user's viewing of a video in a recommendation system may not necessarily indicate liking if the user simply fell asleep while watching it. These factors must be taken into consideration when working with implicit feedback data.

Explicit feedback datasets provide information about a user's preference for items, whereas implicit feedback datasets reflect the confidence level of observations. Explicit datasets indicate a user's liking for an item, while implicit datasets are based on the frequency of actions and provide confidence in the observed data. For example, if a user frequently views an item, they likely enjoy it. Appropriate evaluation metrics are necessary to evaluate the results of implicit feedback recommendations as they differ from explicit data. Mean square error can be used for evaluation in explicit datasets, whereas implicit datasets require specific evaluation metrics [7].

Due to the absence of explicit scoring information in implicit feedback scenarios, matrix decomposition is not an optimal approach. Some scholars have tackled this issue by implementing a 0–1 matrix decomposition method, which assigns a label of 1 to positive examples and 0 to negative ones. Nevertheless, including negative cases may introduce noise and compromise recommendation quality. An alternative is to reframe the recommendation task as a learning-to-rank problem, in which a sorter learns to rank the user's preferred items at the top. Various techniques have been proposed, including collaborative ranking and the Bayesian personalized ranking model. However, these techniques still require random negative examples when working with implicit feedback data, as they prioritize positive examples above negative ones [8].

3 Introduction to Suitable Algorithm

3.1 Alternative Least Squares

ALS is a popular machine learning model used in recommender systems. It is based on matrix factorization using SVD (Singular Value Decomposition) but with numerical approximations. ALS works by decomposing the interaction matrix between users and items into two smaller matrices, one for user embeddings and the other for item embeddings. These embeddings are designed in such a way that when a user's embedding is multiplied by an item's embedding, it gives an approximation of their interaction score. The resulting representation vectors for users and items exist in the same vector space, which allows recommendations to be made using cosine distances between the vectors. Essentially, the system recommends the 12 items with embedding vectors closest to the user embedding vector.

Alternating least squares (ALS) is a well-liked collaborative filtering recommendation technique that relies on models and is frequently employed in recommendation systems. It's based on a latent semantic model, also known as a latent factor model (LFM), which aims to uncover the interactions between users and items through a small number of factors [8]. This is achieved using matrix factorization (MF) to discover the relationships between users and latent factors and between latent factors and items. The algorithm completes the user-item matrix through dimensionality reduction and estimates the missing values. While similar to singular value decomposition (SVD), ALS is more suitable for matrices with missing values, since SVD is undefined for such matrices. For a user-item interaction matrix R ∈ RM × N, R represents the collection of matrices that contains user-item ratings, while M and N refer to the number of users and items, respectively. The latent factor model decomposes the original matrix R into two ma traces to multiply, as follows:

$$R \approx X^T Y = \sum_k x_{uk} y_{ki} \qquad (1)$$

Every user is symbolized by a vector Xu in k-dimensional space, and each item can be represented by a vector yi in the same space. These k characteristics are typically known as latent factors. The matrix factorization estimates entail computing the dot product of these two vectors. The aim is to decrease the squared difference between the forecasted ratings and the actual ratings in matrix R. This leads to a loss function that takes the form of Eq. (2).

$$L = \sum_{u, i \in R} (r_{ui} - x_u^T \cdot y_i)^2 + \lambda (\sum_{u \in X} \|x_u\|^2 + \sum_{i \in Y} \|y_i\|^2) \qquad (2)$$

In the previous equation, the symbol λ is a regularization factor, and the regularization terms are included to avoid overfitting the user and item vectors. The aim is to minimize this loss function, which is an optimization problem usually solved utilizing either stochastic gradient descent (SGD) or alternating least squares (ALS) optimization techniques. The ALS algorithm holds one of the vectors (such as yi) as a constant and computes the derivative of the loss function with respect to the other vector (such as xu), as shown in the following equation.

$$\frac{\partial L}{\partial x_u} = -2 \sum_i (r_{ui} - x_u^T \cdot y_i) y_i + 2\lambda x_u^T \qquad (3)$$

To minimize the squared difference, we can set the derivative to zero and solve for Xu using Eq. (4). Here, Y represents the matrix of all item vectors, and ru represents the ratings given by user u.

$$x_u^T = r_u Y \left(Y^T Y + \lambda I \right)^{-1} \qquad (4)$$

The same method can be used to calculate yi, the item vector for item i, using Eq. (5). Here, X represents the matrix of all user vectors, and ri represents the ratings given to item i. Note that in both equations, the regularization factor λ is included to prevent overfitting.

$$y_u^T = r_i Y X (X^T X + \lambda I)^{-1} \qquad (5)$$

The ALS algorithm can alternate between Eqs. (4) and (5) until the loss function converges or until a user-defined number of iterations is reached. The resulting X and Y matrices provide the optimal solution for the loss function L [9].

3.2 Stochastic Gradient Descent

Compared to the alternating least squares (ALS) technique, the stochastic gradient descent (SGD) algorithm is a more straightforward method. Each iteration estimates the gradient using a single randomly selected sample zt rather than computing the precise gradient of En(fw). Equation (6), which contains the weight vector, the learning rate at iteration t, and the gradient of the loss function with respect to the weight vector for the example zt at iteration t, is the update rule for SGD. The update rule for SGD with mini-batch is shown in Eq. (7) where n is the mini-batch's size [9].

$$\omega_{t+1} = \omega_t - \gamma_t \nabla_\omega Q(z_t, \omega_t) \quad (6)$$

$$\omega_{t+1} = \omega_t - \gamma \frac{1}{n} \sum_{i=1}^{n} \nabla_\omega Q(z_t, \omega_t) \quad (7)$$

4 The Analysis of Implicit Feedback Evaluation Methods

4.1 Classification Accuracy

Classification accuracy is widely used in implicit feedback recommendation algorithms to predict whether the algorithm can recommend items correctly and to measure the performance of the algorithm. Based on the user's preference for items, the actual recommendation situation is divided into four categories: True Positive (TP) when the user likes the recommended items and the algorithm recommends them; False Negative (FN) when the user likes the items but the algorithm does not recommend them; False Positive (FP) when the user does not like the items but the algorithm recommends them; and True Negative (TN) when the user does not like the items and the algorithm does not recommend them [10].

Precision. Precision refers to the proportion of items that are actually recommended to the target user by the implicit feedback algorithm, out of the total number of recommended items. Precision is commonly used to measure the performance of implicit feedback recommendation algorithms, with higher precision indicating better performance:

$$Precision = \frac{TP}{TP + FP} \quad (8)$$

F1 Metric. To evaluate an algorithm's performance, it is important to consider both precision and recall. The F1 metric is a measure that takes both into account and can be calculated using the formula:

$$F1 = \frac{2Recall \times Precision}{Recall + Precision} \quad (9)$$

It is desirable for an algorithm to have high values for both precision and recall. However, these metrics are often inversely related, meaning that when precision is increased, the recall may decrease and vice versa [2].

4.2 Ranking Accuracy

To measure the degree of consistency between the position order of items in the recommendation list and user preferences, average precision and mean percentage are commonly used to evaluate ranking-based implicit feedback.

Mean Average Precision. Mean Average Precision (MAP) is the average of precision scores for all target users, and it is mainly used for evaluating ranking-based implicit feedback recommendation systems. A higher MAP indicates that the items relevant to user preferences are ranked higher in the recommendation list, and thus, the ranking-based implicit feedback recommendation algorithm has higher precision:

$$MAP = \frac{\sum_{i \in U} AP_i}{|U|} \qquad (10)$$

AP_i refers to the average precision, i refers to target user.

Mean Percentage Ranking. Mean Percentage Ranking (MPR) is the average ranking position of all selected items by the target users and is commonly used as an evaluation method for ranking-based implicit feedback recommendations. MPR measures the satisfaction level of the target users with the recommendation list. A lower MPR value indicates better performance of the ranking-based implicit feedback recommendation algorithm in predicting the recall rate.

$$MPR = \frac{1}{|U|} \sum_i \frac{ind(i,j) \times rank_{i,j}}{\sum_i ind(i,j)} \qquad (11)$$

5 Conclusion

This article provides a detailed explanation of the principles and classifications of collaborative filtering systems, with a focus on the popular approach of using implicit datasets and matrix factorization for collaborative filtering. In the past few years, there has been a significant increase in the application of implicit feedback recommendations, particularly in industries such as video streaming, online music, social networks, and academia. For instance, online video platforms recommend suitable videos to users based on their historical viewing records and other contextual implicit feedback information, while personalized music websites analyze users' historical music records to recommend music that better fits their preferences. Social networks combine users' implicit feedback behavior with explicit preference-related behavior to more effectively recommend content that satisfies their needs.

To sum up, implicit feedback recommendation has made significant progress in various fields. Based on the analysis of existing research on implicit feedback recommendation in this study, future research can focus on the following areas:

1. Studying specific optimization of a certain evaluation criterion for three-dimensional egg collaborative sorting algorithms.

2. Studying the parallelization of various algorithms introduced in this paper, particularly the distributed/parallel implementation of these algorithms in large data sets using methods such as OpenMP, CUDA, MPI, and MapReduce.
3. Conducting practical application research of the various algorithms introduced in this paper in the field of information recommendation on the internet, particularly engineering implementation issues.

References

1. Xia, P.: Research on Collaborative Filtering Algorithm of Personalized Recommendation Technology (2012)
2. Kumar Bokde, D., Girase, S., Mukhopadhyay, D.: Role of matrix factorization model in collaborative filtering algorithm: a survey. Int. J. Adv. Found. Res. Comput. (IJAFRC). **1**(12) (2014). ISSN 2348–4853
3. Johnson, C.C.: Logistic matrix factorization for implicit feedback data. Adv. Neural Inf. Process. Syst. **27**(78), 1–9 (2014)
4. Wang, K.: Personalized recommender systems based on matrix factorization. East China Normal University, PhD dissertation (2017)
5. Christakopoulou, E., Karypis, G.: Local item-item models for top-n recommendation. In: Proceedings of the 10th ACM Conference on RecommendeSystems, pp. 67–74 (2016)
6. Wang, J., De Vries, A.P., Reinders, M.J.: Unifying user-based and item-based collaborative filtering approaches by similarity fusion. In: Proceedings of the 29th Annual International ACM SIGIR Conference on Research and Development in Information Retrieval, pp. 501–508 (2006)
7. Kumar Bokde, D., Girase, S., Mukhopadhyay, D.: Role of matrix factorization model in collaborative filtering algorithm: a survey. CoRR, abs/1503.07475 (2015)
8. Li, Z., Jin, D., Huang, X., Yuan, K.: A review of recommendation based on implicit feedback. J. Henan Univ. (Nat. Sci. Ed.) **03**, 305–319 (2022)
9. Chen, J., Fang, J., Liu, W., Tang, T., Chen, X., Yang, C.: Efficient and portable ALS matrix factorization for recommender systems. In: 2017 IEEE International Parallel and Distributed Processing Symposium Workshops (IPDPSW), pp. 409–418. IEEE (2017)
10. Bottou, L.: Stochastic gradient descent tricks. In: Montavon, G., Orr, G.B., Müller, K.-R. (eds.) Neural Networks: Tricks of the Trade. LNCS, vol. 7700, pp. 421–436. Springer, Heidelberg (2012). https://doi.org/10.1007/978-3-642-35289-8_25

Research on the Mall Customers Segmentation Based on K-means and DBSCAN

Yifan Wang[✉]

Tianjin University of Finance and Economics, Tianjin 300000, China
2020110527@stu.tjufe.edu.cn

Abstract. Studying customer classification of a shopping mall is important to understand the demographics, behavior, and preferences of customers, which can help in designing effective marketing strategies and improving customer experience to increase sales and revenue. It can also help in optimizing product placement and inventory management to cater to the needs of different customer segments. Based on the research background, the paper uses k-means and DBSCAN to classify mall customers, according to which the data is divided into 5 clusters and 6 clusters according to the elbow chart and K-mean, and the DBSCAN also divides the data into 6 clusters, but through the data ratio to the discovery, the cluster effect is not as good as the k-Mean effect. And in the final grouping based on k-means results, this article provides a business analysis of the 6 characteristic clusters, assumes 2 situations, and proposes solutions and optimization for these 2 situations that are conducive to the trader's improvement of the commodity and sales environment as a reference basis, thereby increasing trader's turnover, while also increasing consumer satisfaction and consumption effort.

Keywords: K-means · DBSCAN · clusters

1 Introduction

Customer classification in the shopping mall is of great significance for retailers and marketers. Retailers may improve their product offers and marketing tactics by monitoring consumer behavior and purchase patterns to better understand the requirements and preferences of their customers. Additionally, customer classification can help retailers identify their most valuable customers, allowing them to provide targeted promotions and personalized experiences to retain their loyalty. Furthermore, customer classification can assist retailers in improving store layout and product placement, leading to a better shopping experience for all customers. In summary, customer classification is a critical tool for retailers and marketers to enhance their understanding of customers, increase sales, and improve overall customer satisfaction.

Shopping malls are an essential part of modern society, serving as a central hub for commercial and social activities. As such, they offer a unique opportunity to understand consumer behavior and preferences. A considerable body of research has explored how consumers behave in shopping malls, with a particular focus on their motivations, needs, and decision-making processes.

© The Author(s), under exclusive license to Springer Nature Singapore Pte Ltd. 2024
X. Li et al. (Eds.): ICEMGD 2023, AEPS, pp. 1413–1425, 2024.
https://doi.org/10.1007/978-981-97-0523-8_129

Some studies have used psychographic profiling to classify consumers based on their personality traits, values, and lifestyles. This approach seeks to uncover the underlying psychological drivers that influence consumer behavior and preferences. Retailers may better satisfy the demands of their target customers by adjusting their marketing strategy and product offers by understanding these drivers [1–4].

Numerous studies have explored the classification of consumers in shopping malls, employing various approaches to better understand the factors that drive consumer behavior.

Demographic analysis has been a common method in studying consumer classification in shopping malls. According to research, demographic parameters including age, gender, income, and education level significantly affect buying preferences and habits [5–7]. For instance, studies have found that younger consumers tend to prefer fast-fashion retailers, while older consumers may prefer department stores or specialty shops.

Psychographic analysis has also been utilized to classify consumers in shopping malls. This approach involves identifying the psychological motivations that influence consumer behavior, such as personality traits, values, and lifestyles. Psychographic analysis has identified various groups of consumers based on their attitudes and shopping preferences, including brand loyalists, value seekers, and impulse shoppers [8, 9].

Behavioral analysis has also been used to classify consumers in shopping malls. Researchers have investigated different shopping behaviors such as browsing, impulse buying, and goal-directed shopping to identify different types of consumers. For example, some studies have identified recreational shoppers who enjoy browsing and window-shopping, while others have found goal-directed shoppers who are focused on finding specific products.

The literature on consumer classification in shopping malls highlights the importance of understanding consumer behavior for retailers and marketers. Retailers may better satisfy the demands of their target customers by customizing their marketing strategy and product offers by studying the numerous elements that influence consumer behavior. Ongoing research in this area can help to uncover new insights and trends in consumer behavior, allowing retailers to stay ahead of the curve in a competitive market [10, 11].

Despite the growing body of research on consumer behavior in shopping malls, there is still much to be learned about the complex dynamics at play. For instance, the rise of e-commerce and the COVID-19 pandemic have significantly impacted consumer behavior, highlighting the need for ongoing research and analysis. By continuing to explore and classify consumer behavior in shopping malls, retailers and marketers can gain valuable insights that can inform their business strategies and improve the shopping experience for consumers [12–15].

Therefore, this paper will focus on aggregate-level analyses, such as age, gender, income, consumption index and other factors, classifying customer groups, and trying to find shopping habits, attitudes and preferences across clusters. For instance, explore the concept of mall-shopping styles, which categorize consumers into different groups based on how they navigate the mall and their shopping motivations.

There are 2 main contributions in this paper. Firstly, enrich and expand existing literature on customer classification research. Secondly, this paper will give retailers some valuable insights to support their business strategies and improve consumer shopping experiences.

2 Data and Method

2.1 Data

This data set is some of the basic customer data output, through a supermarket shopping center membership card, such as customer ID, age, gender, annual income and consumption scores. Collected from Kaggle mall customer's data.

2.2 Method

This paper uses two clustering algorithms.

K-means. Unsupervised machine learning techniques like the k-means clustering algorithm are frequently used to classify related data points into groups. It is a common approach because it is easy to apply, efficient, and applicable to a variety of data formats and problem areas.

K-means clustering's objective is to divide a given dataset into k clusters; k is a user-defined parameter that denotes the number of desired clusters. Iteratively assigning data points to their closest centroid and updating the centroid until convergence is reached is how the method operates. The initial k centroids, which act as the focal points of each cluster, are chosen at random using the k-means algorithm. These initial centroids may be selected at random or according to a predetermined procedure. Each data point in the dataset is assigned to the closest centroids based on their Euclidean distance once the initial centroids have been selected. The square root of the sum of the squared coordinate difference between two points is used to calculate the Euclidean distance, which is a unit of distance between two locations in space [16–18].

The mean of each cluster is computed and is then used as the new centroid of that cluster once all the data points have been allocated to their closest centroid. Until the centroids stop shifting or a certain number of iterations has been achieved, this phase is repeated. The resulting clusters are then used for further analysis, such as identifying patterns and trends within the data. The clusters can also be used to make predictions about new data points based on their similarity to the existing clusters.

Scalability is one of the key benefits of k-means clustering. It can handle large datasets with a high number of dimensions and can be easily parallelized to speed up the clustering process. Additionally, k-means is a simple and efficient algorithm that can be easily implemented in most programming languages and software tools [19].

However, k-means clustering does have some limitations. The algorithm's need that the user identify the number of clusters—which could not always be known a priori—is one of its key drawbacks. It can be difficult to choose the ideal number of clusters, and choosing the wrong amount might provide less-than-ideal outcomes. K-means clustering also has the drawback of assuming spherical and equal-sized clusters, which may not necessarily be the case in real-world datasets. Despite these drawbacks, k-means clustering is a strong data analysis approach that has been extensively applied in a variety of fields, including customer segmentation, image processing, and data mining. K-means may offer important insights into the structure of the data and assist in identifying patterns and trends that might not be obvious from the raw data by clustering comparable data points.

Density-Based Spatial Clustering of Applications with Noise (DBSCAN). Density-Based Spatial Clustering of Applications with Noise (DBSCAN) is a well-liked unsupervised machine learning method for clustering related data points. It is particularly useful for datasets with complex shapes and varying densities.

DBSCAN does not need the user to specify the number of clusters, in contrast to other clustering techniques. Instead, it locates clusters depending on how densely the data points are distributed. The method groups together data points with a high density and close proximity to one another, while removing data points with a low density or isolation. The DBSCAN algorithm begins by randomly selecting an unvisited data point and checking its neighborhood to determine its density. All the data points that are located within a certain radius, known as the epsilon radius, of the selected data point are referred to as the data point's neighborhood. The chosen data point is designated as a core point if the neighborhood's total number of data points exceeds a predetermined minimum number, or minimum points. Once the core points have been identified, the algorithm proceeds to form clusters by expanding each core point's neighborhood to include all the neighboring data points that also satisfy the minimum points criterion. If a neighboring data point is also a core point, its neighborhood is added to the original neighborhood, and the process continues recursively until no new data points can be added to the cluster. Noisy data points are those that do not belong to any cluster. These data points are not near any core points and do not meet the minimum points requirement. DBSCAN's capability to handle datasets with complicated geometries and variable densities is one of its key features. DBSCAN is capable of handling datasets with different densities and can detect clusters of unusual forms and sizes, in contrast to other clustering algorithms like k-means. Additionally, DBSCAN is a more flexible and adaptable clustering technique since it does not need the user to define the number of clusters.

However, DBSCAN also has some limitations. One of the main limitations is that it requires the user to select appropriate values for the epsilon radius and minimum points parameters, which can be challenging for datasets with varying densities. Selecting inappropriate values can lead to the formation of suboptimal clusters or the exclusion of relevant data points. In summary, DBSCAN is a powerful clustering algorithm that can be used to identify clusters in datasets with complex shapes and varying densities. It is a flexible and versatile algorithm that does not require the user to specify the number of clusters, making it suitable for a wide range of applications. However, it also requires careful parameter selection to achieve optimal clustering results [20–22].

3 Results and Discussion

3.1 Description

Customers who are male have somewhat older average ages than those who are female (39.8 vs. 38.1). The age distribution of men is more even than that of women, and it is obvious that the 30- to 35-year-old age range is the largest. The K-S test, however, reveals that there are no statistically significant differences between the two groups. There are a few more female clients (112 vs. 87) than male consumers. 56% of all consumers are women. Males have a greater mean income than females (62.2 k$ vs. 59.2k$). Additionally, male customers' median income (62.5k$) is larger than female customers' (60k$). Both groups' standard deviations are comparable. One male member of the group stands out, earning roughly $145,000 per year. K-S test shows that these two groups are not statistically different. And the results shows in Fig. 1.

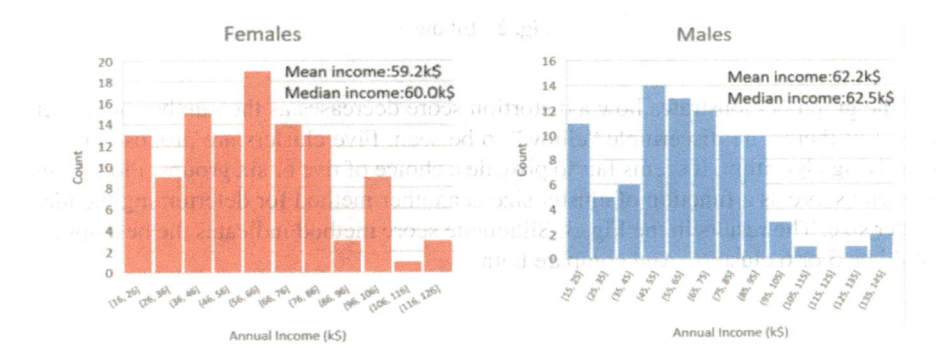

Fig. 1. Gender income

And a mean spending score for women (51.5) is higher than men (48.5). The K-S test p-value indicates that there is no evidence to reject the null-hypothesis, however the evidence is not so strong as in previous comparisons. Next the paper will calculate median income for all age groups. And the wealthy customers are in age of 25–45 years old. The biggest difference between women and men is visible in age groups 25–30 (male more rich) and 50–55 (female more rich).

3.2 Results of K-Means

Steps. The K-Means method consists of three key phases. 1. Use seed points to divide samples into beginning groups. Initial clusters will be formed by the samples that are closest to these seed points. 2. Determine the distances between the samples and the centroids of the groupings, then place the closest samples in each cluster. 3. Calculating freshly formed (updated) cluster centroids is the third stage. The elbow approach will be applied to locate a suitable number of clusters. The inertia for this approach will be estimated for a range of cluster sizes between 2 and 10. The rule is to choose the number of clusters on the graph where you notice a kink or "an elbow"2 in the Fig. 2.

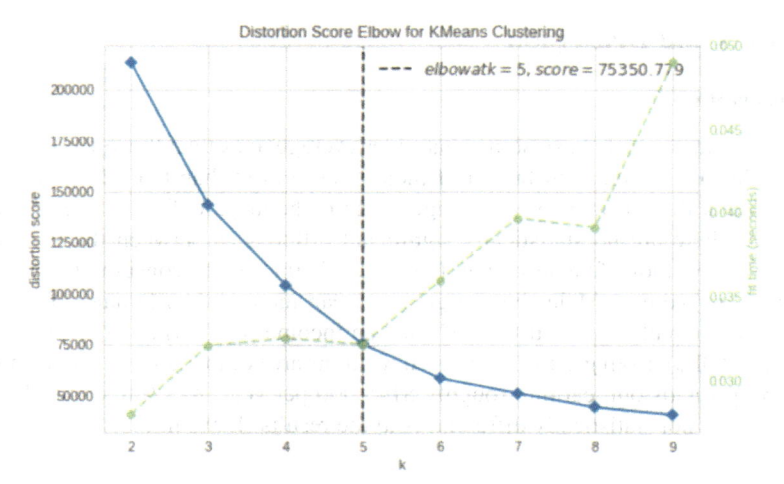

Fig. 2. Elbow

The graph demonstrates how a distortion score decreases as the number of clusters rises. But there's no discernible "elbow" to be seen. Five clusters are proposed by the underlying algorithm. It seems fair to provide a choice of five or six groups. Plotting the Silhouette score as a function of cluster size is another method for determining the ideal cluster size. The results in the Fig. 3. Silhouette score method indicates the best options would be 5 or 6 clusters. And compare both.

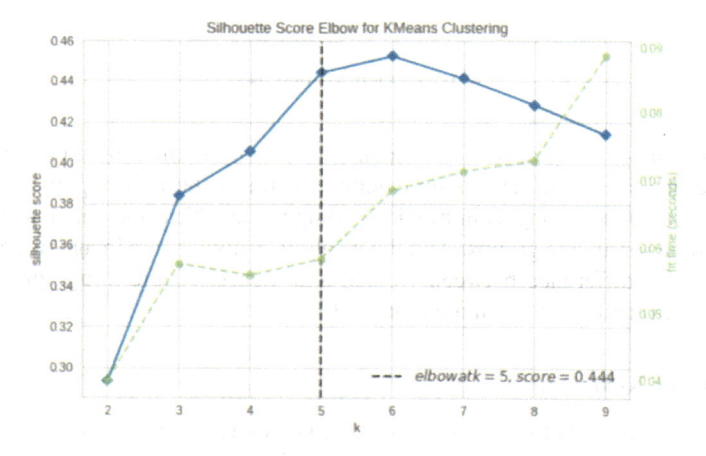

Fig. 3. Elbow2

Results of 5 Clusters. K-Means algorithm generated the following 5 clusters: And the results shows in Fig. 4.

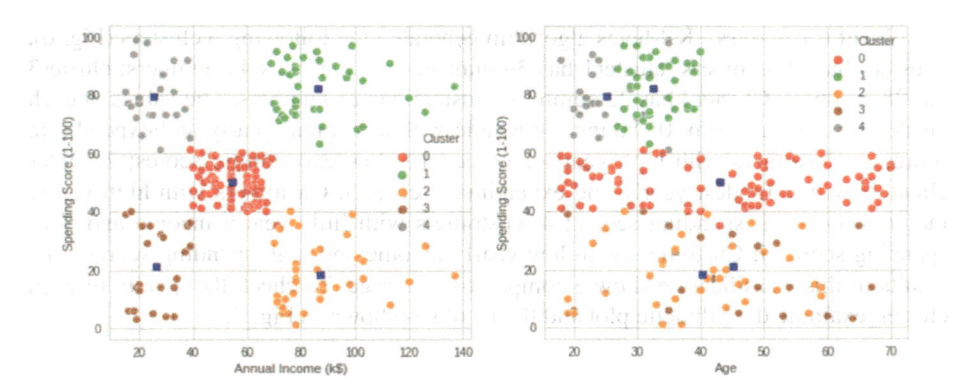

Fig. 4. Cluster result

K-means created 5 clusters. Cluster0 has 79 numbers; cluster1 has 39 numbers; cluster2 has 37 numbers; cluster3 has 23 numbers. Cluster4 has 22 numbers. Customers with low yearly incomes and high spending scores (n = 0); customers with medium annual incomes and high spending scores (n = 1); clients with high annual incomes and low spending scores (n = 3); and clients with low annual incomes and low spending scores (n = 4) are the other client groups.

There are no distinct groups is terms of customers age. The biggest cluster is a cluster number 1 with 79 observations ("medium-medium" clients). There are two the smallest ones each containing 23 observations (cluster 3 "high-high" and cluster 0 "low-high" clients). To check the quality of each cluster, examine the Silhuette plot and the results is shown in Fig. 5.

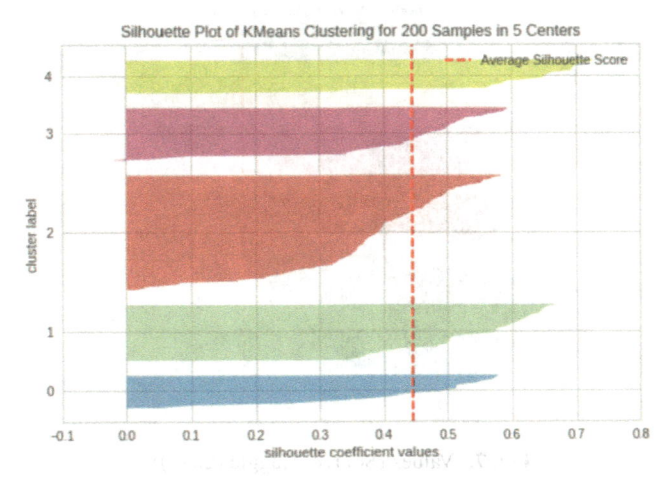

Fig. 5. Values of 5 clusters (Source: Kaggle (2023))

Results of 6 Clusters. K-Means algorithm generated the following 6 clusters (Fig. 6). Cluster0 has 35 numbers; cluster1 has 39 numbers; cluster2 has 45 numbers; cluster3 has 38 numbers. Cluster4 has 22 numbers; cluster5 has 21 numbers. The values of each cluster are very uniform. 0: Younger clientele with a medium yearly and expenditure score; 1: Customers with high yearly incomes and low expenditure scores; 2: Older clientele with a modest yearly and expenditure score; 3: Customers with high yearly incomes and high spending scores; 4: customers with little yearly income and poor spending score; 5: Customers with low yearly income and high spending scores; The results of this classification show a comparative average. To check the quality of each cluster, examine the Silhuette plot and the results is shown in Fig. 7.

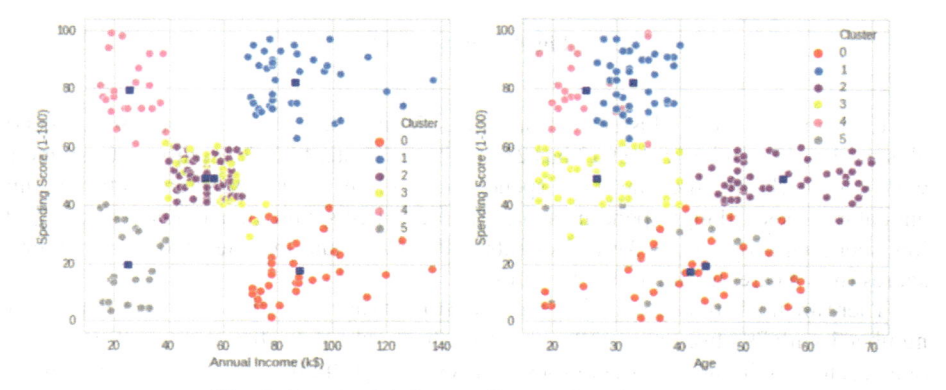

Fig. 6. Result of 6 clusters (Source: Kaggle (2023))

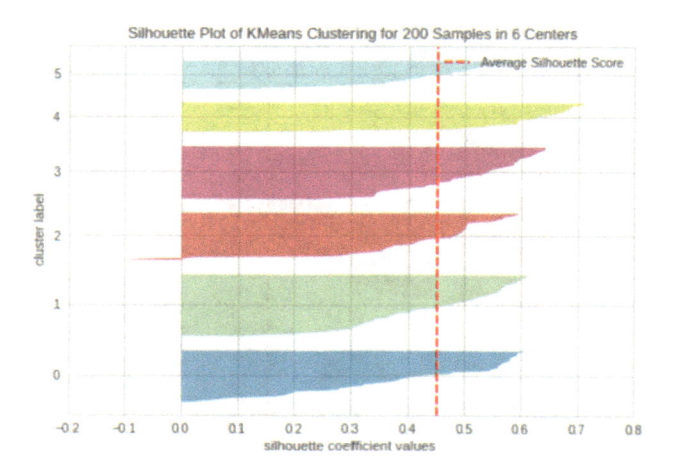

Fig. 7. Values (Source: Kaggle (2023))

3.3 Results by DBSCAN

In DBSCAN there are two major hyperparameters, first one Eps ε – distance, second is Min Pts – Minimum number of points within distance Eps. It is challenging to predict what values will be most effective at random. As a result, the paper first constructs a matrix of the combinations that are being looked at. Considering that DBSCAN bases its own cluster creation on those two factors. Check the number of generated clusters. Figure 8 shows how many clusters were generated by the DBSCAN algorithm for the respective parameters combinations.

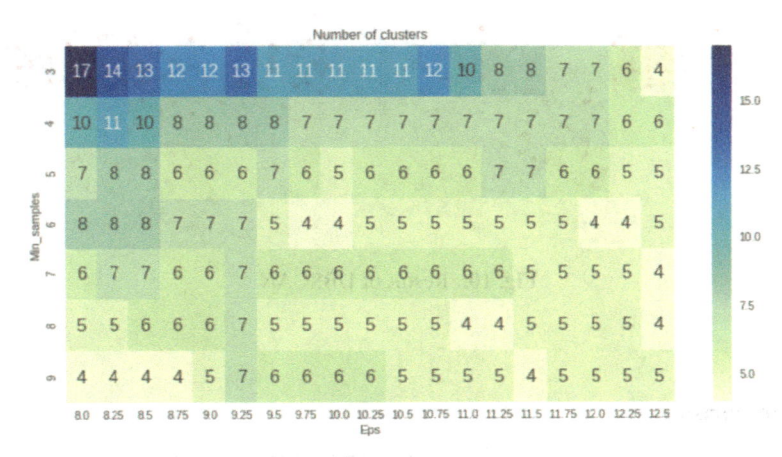

Fig. 8. Cluster result under DBSCAN

Figures depicts the findings, with the number of clusters ranging from 17 to 4. The majority of the combinations, however, result in 4–7 clusters. To decide which combination to choose the paper use a metric - a score and plot it as a heatmap (Fig. 9) again.

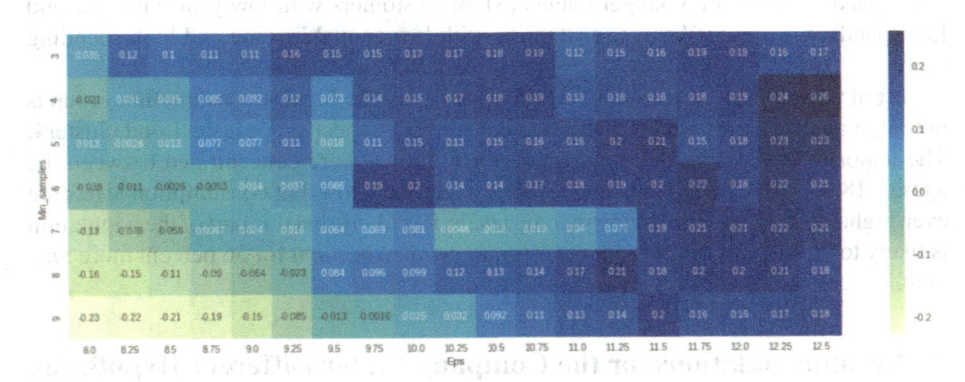

Fig. 9. Heatmap

DBSCAN created 5 clusters. Cluster1 has 112 numbers; cluster2 has 8 numbers; cluster3 has 34 numbers; cluster4 has 24 numbers. Sizes of clusters 1–5 vary significantly some have only 4 or 8 observations. And the results show in Fig. 10. There are some outliers; these points don't fit the criteria for distance and sample size needed to classify them as a cluster.

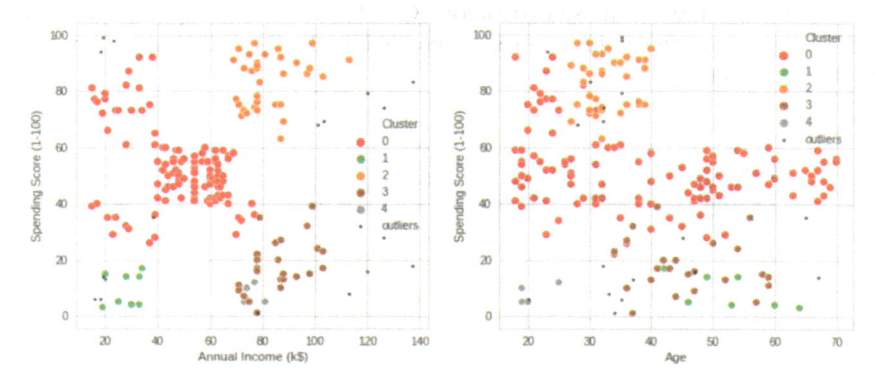

Fig. 10. Result of DBSCAN

3.4 Comparison

From the above comparisons. It is evident that DBSCAN was unable to produce accurate clusters. The most likely explanation is that DBCSAN attempts to locate clusters based on point density. DBSCAN will provide less-than-ideal results if one of our clusters is less dense than the others since it won't classify the least dense group as a cluster. K-Means algorithms then produced 6 logical groupings. Clients with low yearly income and high spending score are younger clients (0); those with medium annual income and medium spending score are older clients (2); and those with high annual income and high spending score are younger clients (3). 4: Customers with low yearly income and low spending score; 5: Younger customers with low annual income and high spending score.

From the 3D Fig. 11, it can be seen that the age of the highest consumption group is not large and is mainly divided into two categories, respectively cluster1 and cluster4. The majority of these higher-consumption age groups were concentrated between the ages of 18 and 30. Cluster 1 income levels are relatively low, but consumption levels are even higher than those with higher income levels, it is likely that this part of the population is likely to be students, In the consumer group, women account for 56 percent more than men.

4 Recommendations for the Company Under Different Hypothesis

There are the following hypothesis and recommendations.

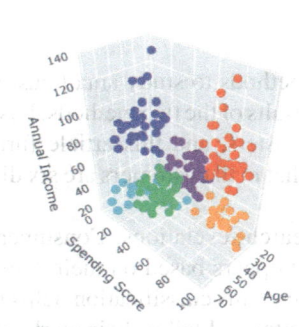

Fig. 11. Final result

4.1 Hypothesis1

The first hypothesis is that the company's products are for women, some women consume to buy for themselves, while some men consume for their sister or girlfriend to buy as a gift, and older people buy may be to give to their students or daughters.

4.2 Recommendations

Based on this hypothesis, there are three recommendations for the company:

First, because the product users are students, then the company can go to the university nearby to promote and promote their products. Secondly, company can empower your product, bind the product to love, for example, receiving the product is equal to receiving care, such as the role of roses. Finally, since the majority of users are women, I suggest that the company would prefer women around the age of 25 to work as salesmen, because women understand women better.

4.3 Hypothesis2

The second hypothesis is that the company's products are everyday goods, because the age of consumers affected is very broad, and the gender characteristics are not very obvious, so I guess it is possible for some toothpaste or other products.

4.4 Recommendations

Based on this hypothesis, there are two recommendations for the company. Firstly, divide products into different categories, because there are both women and men, so you can divide the products specifically into men's and women's use, such as the distinction of color and size, can be set in pink and blue two colors and pink a little bit small, blue is simple and a little bigger. Secondly, because the level of consumer's income is different, it is possible to divide products into different price ranges, so that no matter what kind of income group can consume.

5 Conclusion

This paper uses k-means and DBSCAN methods to study small customers, and the k-Means method is better by comparing the results of the two methods. It is more reasonable for k-means to divide the data into six clusters, and this article further suggests the company's strategy under the assumption that mall customers are six different consumer groups.

Through this study here are some research revelations. Consumer classification in shopping malls refers to the grouping of shoppers based on their demographic characteristics, shopping behavior, and preferences. This classification helps retailers and mall managers to understand their customers better and tailor their marketing strategies and offerings to meet their needs and preferences. For example, consumer classification can enhance the overall shopping experience by providing a sense of belonging and community. Shoppers who share similar characteristics and preferences can interact with each other and exchange recommendations and tips on where to find the best deals and products. Overall, consumer classification in shopping malls can be beneficial for both retailers and shoppers. It allows retailers to better understand their customers and tailor their offerings and marketing strategies, while shoppers can benefit from personalized recommendations and a more tailored shopping experience.

However, this paper also has some limitation. Firstly, customer behavior can change over time, making it difficult to maintain accurate classifications. A customer who was once a high-value customer may no longer be so due to changes in their buying habits or personal circumstances. Secondly, customer classification models may not be flexible enough to adapt to new data or changes in the market. This can limit their usefulness in identifying new customer segments or responding to changing customer needs.

References

1. Scammon, D.L., McMillan, S.F.: Consumer behavior segmentation: an investigation of the psychological motivations of self-expression and conformity. J. Mark. Commun. **13**(4), 267–283 (2007)
2. Chien, Y.-T., Wu, S.-I.: Consumer segmentation based on personality traits: exploring the differences in consumer behavior. J. Bus. Res. **68**(4), 814–820 (2015)
3. Antolin-Lopez, R., Munuera-Aleman, J.L., Galindo-Villardón, M.C.: A psychographic segmentation of the green consumer: evidence from a cluster analysis. J. Bus. Res. **68**(9), 2008–2019 (2015)
4. Craig, C.S., Douglas, S.P.: A psychographic approach to market segmentation: an application in the context of hedonic products. J. Consum. Res. **32**(4), 405–419 (2005)
5. Lee, Y.-E., Yang, H.: Consumer behavior segmentation based on online browsing behavior: empirical evidence from clickstream data. J. Bus. Res. **75**, 44–56 (2017)
6. Valor, C., Martín-Santana, J.D.: Market segmentation based on consumer attitudes towards corporate social responsibility: a cluster analysis. J. Bus. Res. **69**(9), 3433–3438 (2016)
7. Langarudi, S.P., Aguiar, J.M., Khodadad Hosseini, H.: Segmenting consumers based on their environmental values: a latent class analysis. J. Bus. Res. **104**, 111–124 (2019)
8. Gillespie, B., Hult, G.T.M., Griffith, D.J.: Consumer segmentation based on perceived risk and consumer innovativeness. J. Consum. Mark. **28**(3), 171–182 (2011)

9. Customers Clustering: K-Means, DBSCAN and AP (2022). https://www.kaggle.com/Code/Datark1/Customers-clustering-k-means-dbscan-and-ap/Notebook. www.kaggle.com. Accessed 24 Apr 2022
10. Jing, W., Zhao, C., Jiang, C.: An improvement method of DBSCAN algorithm on cloud computing. Procedia Comput. Sci. **147**, 596–604 (2019)
11. Ester, M., Kriegel, H.-P., Sander, J., Xu, X.: A density-based algorithm for discovering clusters in large spatial databases with noise. In: KDD-96 Proceedings, pp. 226–231 (1996)
12. Arthur, D., Vassilvitskii, S.: k-means++: the advantages of careful seeding. In: Proceedings of the eighteenth annual ACM-SIAM symposium on Discrete algorithms (2007)
13. Frey, B., Dueck, D.: Clustering by passing messages between data points. Science **315**(5814), 972–976 (2007)
14. Li, P., Ji, H., Wang, B., Huang, Z., Li, H.: Adjustable preference affinity propagation clustering. Pattern Recogn. Lett. **85**, 72–78 (2017)
15. Wenlong, H., Chung, F.-L., Wang, S.: Transfer affinity propagation-based clustering. Inf. Sci. **348**, 337–356 (2016)
16. Kanungo, T., Mount, D.M., Netanyahu, N.S., Piatko, C.D., Silverman, R., Wu, A.Y.: A k-means clustering algorithm. IEEE Trans. Pattern Anal. Mach. Intell. **24**(7), 881–892 (2002)
17. Arthur, D., Vassilvitskii, S.: k-Means++: the advantages of careful seeding. In: Proceedings of the Eighteenth Annual ACM-SIAM Symposium on Discrete Algorithms, pp. 1027–1035 (2007)
18. Cilibrasi, R., Vitányi, P.M.B.: Clustering by compression. IEEE Trans. Inf. Theory **51**(4), 1523–1545 (2005)
19. Delacruz, J.M., Benítez, J.M., Herrera, F.J.: A novel initialization method for the k-means algorithm using data transformation. Pattern Recogn. **48**(7), 2279–2289 (2015)
20. Wang, Y., Hu, Y., Li, J.: Improved DBSCAN algorithm. IEEE Trans. Knowl. Data Eng. **24**(3), 530–541 (2012)
21. Babenko, B., Tsai, M.-H., Belongie, S.J.: A survey of density-based clustering algorithms. In: Proceedings of the 14th International Conference on Computer Vision Workshops, pp. 40–48 (2013)
22. Sax, M.J., Schulte, F., Kottke, D.: DBSCAN revisited, revisited: why and how you should (still) use DBSCAN. ACM SIGKDD Explor. Newsl **22**(1), 33–41 (2021)

Valuation and Analysis of the Canadian Banking Sector During the COVID-19 Pandemic

Bo He[✉]

School of Finance and Management, Western University, Ontario N6A 3K7, Canada
bhe33@uwo.ca

Abstract. The 2019 coronavirus epidemic is an unprecedented disaster in human history. The economic crisis caused by the epidemic has caused many countries to face financial difficulties. The Bank of Canada has adopted an expansionary economic policy. As an industry that is relatively sensitive to changes in the overall economic market, the banking industry will undergo significant changes in the financial crisis and stimulating fiscal policies brought about by the COVID-19 epidemic. This research will use the price-earnings ratio method to evaluate and analyze all listed banks in Canada during the epidemic. By comparing the P/E ratios of various banks and the composite index of the Toronto Stock Exchange from 2019 to 2021, the study found that the stock prices of the Canadian banking industry are greatly undervalued, and have been undervalued after the implementation of macroeconomic policies. In the short term, Canadian banking industry profitability and stock prices will continue to rise, but will eventually fall. These results shed light on guiding further exploration of impact of COVID-19 on Canadian Banking Industry.

Keywords: COVID-19 · Canada · Banking

1 Introduction

As a global public health crisis, the 2019 coronavirus epidemic has spread to more than 200 countries and regions around the world. As of April 2020, the new coronavirus has caused a total of 504.4 million infections and 6.2 million deaths [1]. Under such an unprecedented public health crisis, everyone's life has been affected. In order to deal with the severe form of the epidemic, most countries have adopted a policy of closure and isolation to slow down the spread of the virus, and Canada is no exception [2]. The direct impact of the city closure policy is a new round of global economic crisis. Compared with the traditional economic depression, the impact of the city closure policy on the financial market is devastating [3]. The special financial crisis under the new crown epidemic has had a huge impact on various industries in Canada [4]. Data from the Toronto Stock Exchange shows that the Canadian stock market experienced a round of slump in early 2020. During this period, unlike other countries, both positive and negative news can hurt stock returns in the Canadian market [5]. It shows that Canadian investors prefer less risky and more stable industries in a crisis scenario, and the importance of expected returns becomes lower. Since then, the Bank of Canada has adopted a series of unconventional expansionary economic measures [6].

These policies have greatly increased the money supply in the Canadian money market, which is finally reflected in the stock price. The Canadian stock market rebounded rapidly in April and rose all the way. Compared with the overall market, Canada's banking industry has been less affected by the new crown epidemic, thanks to a relatively monopolistic and centralized system and strict supervision by an overall regulatory agency, which has been reflected in the 2008 financial crisis [7]. Some studies even show that in terms of performance alone, the new crown epidemic has no impact on the Canadian banking industry [8]. Howeverm the study only analyzed the three largest banks in Canada, and the conclusions may have limitations. The stability of the Canadian banking industry and stock prices under the background of the epidemic, as the industry most sensitive to national economic policies, the impact of stimulating economic policies on the banking industry, and the impact of crisis management during the epidemic on the banking industry after the epidemic is over the change. These arguments are very important for studying the valuation analysis of the Canadian banking industry under the new crown epidemic.

This article will first conduct valuation analysis on all listed banks in Canada, namely Royal Bank of Canada, Toronto-Dominion Bank, Bank of Montreal, Bank of Nova Scotia, and Canadian Imperial Bank of Commerce. Then compare the valuation results of different banks, and then compare the banking industry as a whole with the market, and finally draw the actual conclusion of the valuation results and point out the shortcomings of the research and the outlook for future research.

2 Method

The data for this research comes from the year-end financial reports of five Canadian listed banks and the related disclosures of Yahoo Finance and Investing.com. The research will conduct valuation analysis on all Canadian banks during the epidemic period (2019 to 2021) [9]. The mainstream banking valuation methods have been analyzed one by one, and the research found that the valuation methods have their own advantages and disadvantages, and there is no good one. Bad points, but for the banking industry, Deev recommends discounted cash flow models and option pricing models. The former involves market performance and risk factors to better predict the future, while the latter considers various factors of bank valuation to the greatest extent. In actual cases, the discounted cash flow model is not suitable for companies with negative net cash flow in certain periods, such as TD Bank. The original formulation of the option pricing model required many modifications before it could be used in practice [10].

Therefore, this article will use the relatively simple and commonly used relative valuation method price-earnings ratio model to value banks. By calculating the P/E ratios of different banks in different years during the COVID-19 pandemic, one compared and analyzed the specific performance of each bank during the COVID-19 pandemic. At the same time, the overall performance of the Canadian banking industry during the COVID-19 period is analyzed by comparing the composite index of the Toronto Stock Exchange, as well as investors' investment tendencies in the banking industry under special circumstances. This article will also use the Diluted Earning Per Share (DEPS) of each bank in the past 5 years to calculate the average growth rate to predict the future price-earnings ratio and finally get the forecasted valuation.

Table 1. 2019–2021 Royal bank of Canada P/E ratio.

	2019	2020	2021	2022
Diluted EPS	8.75	7.82	11.06	
Stock price (end of Dec.31)	102.75	104.59	134.25	
Price growth rate		1.791%	28.358%	
P/E ratio	11.74286	13.37468	12.13834	
P/E ratio growth rate		13.896%	−9.244%	
Average Diluted EPS growth rate 5Y	0.080098	0.051666	0.12648	
Diluted EPS Predict by Last Year	9.45086	8.224028	12.45887	
Stock price (Predict by Last Year)		110.9801	109.9937	151.2299
Stock price (Predict by Year 2019)		110.9801	119.2102	127.4403

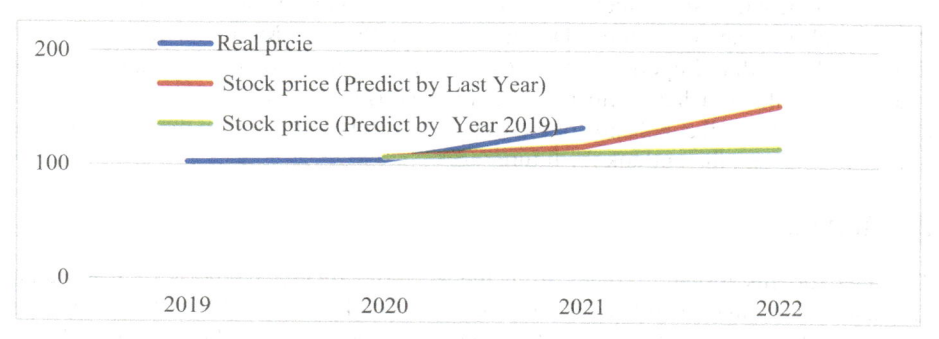

Fig. 1. Royal bank of Canada forecast stock price and comparison.

3 Results

3.1 Royal Bank of Canada

As shown in Table 1, the price-earnings ratio of Royal Bank of Canada is on the rise, which may mean that the bank's profitability has increased relatively. From the perspective of market stock prices, the stock price of Royal Bank of Canada has been less affected by the epidemic, but more affected by the stimulus fiscal policy of the Bank of Canada. After the implementation of expansionary economic policies such as quantitative easing, the share price and market value of Royal Bank of Canada will increase sharply in 2021, with a year-on-year increase of 28%. By comparing the price-earnings ratio and stock price of Royal Bank of Canada in 2020, the author found that the stock price of Royal Bank of Canada is relatively undervalued. From the perspective of forecasting, as shown in Fig. 1, the price-earnings ratio model cannot predict the impact of potential crises and opportunities, which is the reason for the large difference between the actual stock price and the predicted stock price. However, if there is no new crown epidemic and the overall market and enterprise value grow steadily, the valuation forecast of the price-earnings ratio method is relatively reliable.

3.2 Toronto-Dominion Bank

As shown in Table 2, the price-earnings ratio of TD Bank is on the rise. The profitability of TD Bank is relatively improved and the business may expand. Performance is less affected by the new crown, but it is stimulated by macroeconomic policies. From the stock price point of view, the stock price of TD Bank is relatively less affected by the epidemic, but the expansionary fiscal policy has a greater impact on it, with a year-on-year increase of 35%. It can be seen from Fig. 2 that the forecast value of the price-earnings ratio has certain significance for the market value of TD Bank, and the overall upward trend of the stock price is in line with the forecast.

Table 2. 2019–2021 TD bank P/E ratio.

	2019	2020	2021	2022
Diluted EPS	6.25	6.43	7.73	
Stock price(end of Dec.31)	72.83	71.92	96.98	
Price growth rate		−1.249%	34.844%	
P/E ratio	11.6528	11.18507	12.54592	
P/E ratio growth rate		−4.014%	12.167%	
Average Diluted EPS growth rate 5Y	0.084267	0.089689	0.108273	
Diluted EPS Predict by Last Year	6.776671	7.006703	8.566949	
Stock price (Predict by Last Year)		78.96719	78.37046	107.4803
Stock price (Predict by Year 2019)		78.96719	85.10439	91.24158

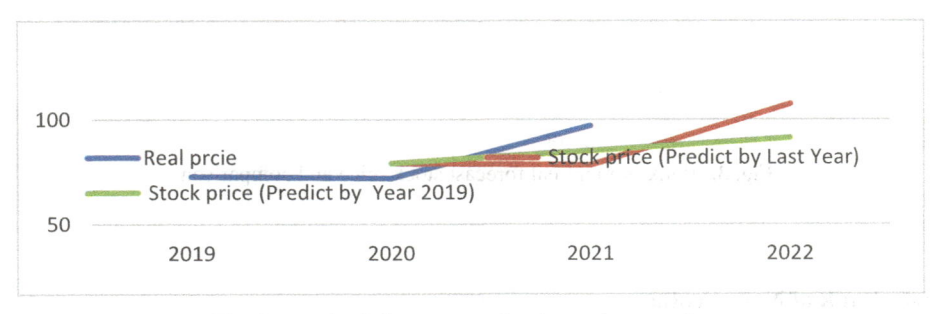

Fig. 2. TD bank forecast stock price and comparison.

3.3 Bank of Montreal

It can be seen from Table 3 that the price-earnings ratio of Bank of Montreal is on a downward trend, which shows that the profitability of Bank of Montreal has declined, and macroeconomic policies have had the opposite effect on its profitability. Bank stock prices show that the new crown epidemic has had a certain impact on the stock price of Bank of Montreal, but it is more affected by the fiscal policy of the Bank of Canada, which has increased by 40% year-on-year. However, combined with the growth rate of the price-earnings ratio, the stock price of Bank of Montreal in 2020 is relatively undervalued, but the stock price of Bank of Montreal in 21 years is seriously overvalued. Figure 3 shows this sharp rise concretely.

Table 3. 2019–2021 P/E ratio of bank of montreal.

	2019	2020	2021	2022
Diluted EPS	9.43	7.71	12.96	
Stock price (end of Dec.31)	100.64	96.78	136.19	
Price growth rate		−3.835%	40.721%	
P/E ratio	10.67232	12.55253	−10.50849	
P/E ratio growth rate		17.618%	−16.284%	
Average Diluted EPS growth rate 5Y	0.074448	0.025526	0.146855	
Diluted EPS (Predict by Last Year)	10.13204	7.906809	14.86324	
Stock price (Predict by Last Year)		108.1324	99.25045	156.1902
Stock price (Predict by Year 2019)		108.1324	115.6248	123.1173

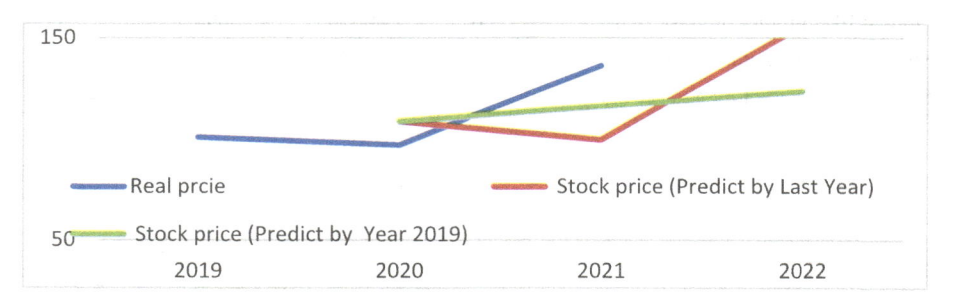

Fig. 3. Bank of montreal forecast stock price and comparison.

3.4 Bank of Nova Scotia

As shown in Table 4, the P/E ratio of Scotiabank has been on a steady upward trend within three years, which means that its profitability and business capabilities will further expand. The impact of the new crown epidemic on bank performance is small, and the stimulus fiscal policy has not improved its level of profitability. Judging from the stock price of Scotiabank, the stock price has dropped during the epidemic period. Through the comparison with the price-earnings ratio, it is found that the stock price of Scotiabank in

2020 is relatively undervalued, and the expansionary fiscal policy has greatly increased the stock price of Scotiabank. The growth rate reached 30%. Scotiabank shares are relatively overvalued in 2021. From Fig. 4, the price-earnings ratio model failed to predict the trend of Scotiabank stock.

Table 4. 2019–2021 Scotiabank P/E ratio.

	2019	2020	2021	2022
Diluted EPS	7.14	5.36	7.87	
Stock price (end of Dec.31)	73.35	68.8	89.55	
Price growth rate		−6.203%	30.160%	
P/E ratio	10.27311	12.83582	11.37865	
P/E ratio growth rate		24.946%	−11.352%	
Average Diluted EPS growth rate 5Y	0.046013	0.00385	0.078273	
Diluted EPS (Predict by Last Year)	7.468536	5.339382	8.486012	
Stock price (Predict by Last Year)		76.72508	68.53535	96.55938
Stock price (Predict by Year 2019)		76.72508	80.10017	83.47525

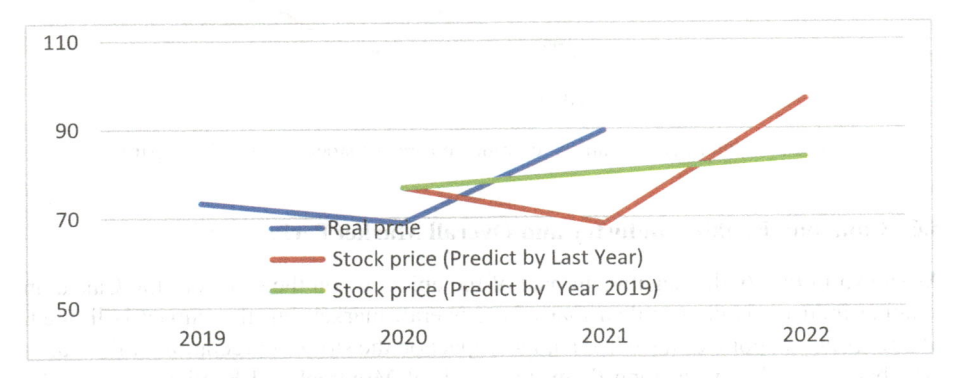

Fig. 4. Scotiabank forecast share price and comparison.

3.5 Canadian Imperial Bank of Commerce

As shown in Table 5, the price-to-earnings ratio of Canadian Imperial Bank of Commerce continues to rise, which means that the bank's profitability and business capabilities will further improve. From the stock price point of view, the new crown epidemic has not affected the Canadian Imperial Bank of Commerce, and the stock price is relatively undervalued in 2020, but Canada's macro-financial policy has greatly increased the bank's stock price, an increase of 35%. Figure 5 clearly shows the impact of macro-financial policies on the bank's stock price, and the forecast valuation of the price-earnings ratio has certain reference.

Table 5. 2019–2021 Canadian imperial bank of commerce P/E ratio.

	2019	2020	2021	2022
Diluted EPS	11.92	9.69	14.47	
Stock price(end of Dec.31)	54.03	54.36	73.72	
Price growth rate		0.611%	35.614%	
P/E ratio	4.532718	5.609907	5.094679	
P/E ratio growth rate		23.765%	−9.184%	
Average Diluted EPS growth rate 5Y	0.062	0.012	0.094	
Diluted EPS (Predict by Last Year)	12.65904	9.80628	15.83018	
Stock price (Predict by Last Year)		57.37986	55.01232	80.64968
Stock price (Predict by Year 2019)		57.37986	60.72972	64.07958

Fig. 5. Canadian imperial bank of commerce forecast stock price and comparison.

3.6 Canadian Banking Industry and Overall Market Performance

As shown in Fig. 6, the negative impact of the epidemic on the stocks of the Canadian banking industry is greater than that of the overall market, but the impact is limited. Macroeconomic policies have had a huge impact on the stock appreciation of the Canadian banking industry. Among them, the Bank of Montreal and Scotiabank have the largest fluctuations in the two years, while the smallest stock price fluctuations are the Royal Bank of Canada. The Royal Bank of Canada continues to have a higher stock price It proves that investors are more inclined to choose stocks with less price fluctuations and lower risk premiums when the market is facing risks. Relatively speaking, the stock price performance of Scotiabank is different from that of the banking industry as a whole. It has been most affected by the new crown epidemic and least affected by the central bank's stimulus fiscal policy. It can be seen from Table 6 that the overall impact of the epidemic on the Canadian stock market is not as large as predicted. Macroeconomic policies and post-epidemic economic recovery will greatly stimulate the Canadian stock market in 2021.

Figure 7 shows the P/E ratios of each bank in each year during the epidemic. It can be seen from Fig. 7 that the profitability of the top four banks in the Canadian

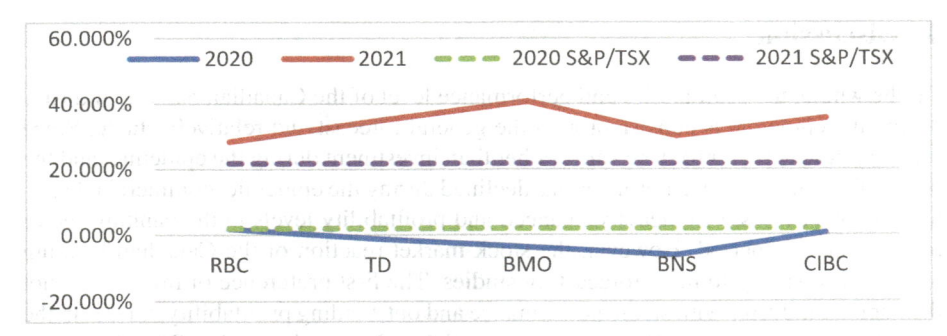

Fig. 6. Stock price growth rate.

Table 6. 2019–2021 Toronto stock exchange composite index.

	2019	2020	2021
S&P/TSX Composite (end of Dec.31)	17099.95	17433.36	21222.84
Growth rate		1.950%	21.737%

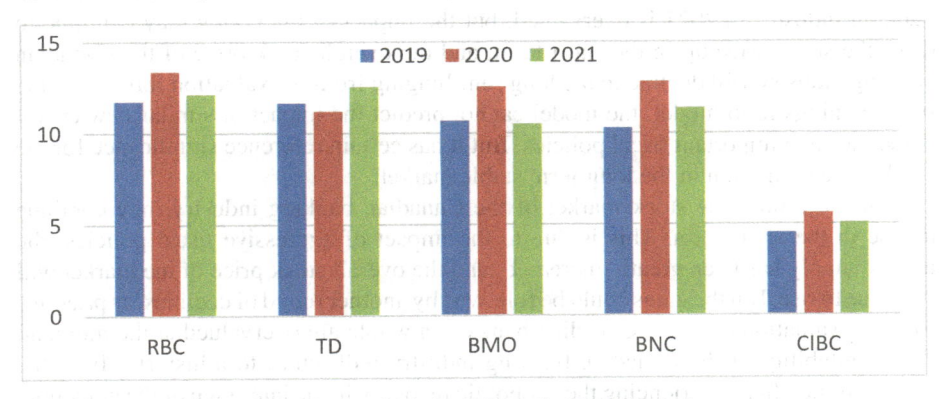

Fig. 7. Overall P/E ratio of Canadian banking industry

banking industry is similar, and the Canadian Imperial Bank of Commerce has relatively low profitability. The COVID-19 epidemic did not affect the overall profitability of the Canadian banking industry. On the contrary, the profitability of the Canadian banking industry increased during the COVID-19 epidemic and declined after the epidemic but was generally higher than the pre-epidemic level. Bank of Montreal and Scotiabank have seen the most fluctuations in profitability due to the impact of the epidemic, while TD Bank has the least volatility. TD Bank's profitability is affected by the epidemic and changes in macro-fiscal policy in contrast to the banking industry as a whole, which may be because the majority of TD Bank's business is related to retail banking.

4 Discussion

On the whole, the profitability and performance level of the Canadian banking industry during the epidemic is consistent with the general forecast and relatively stable. Since ordinary people prefer to store value rather than investment during the epidemic, and the profitability of ordinary enterprises has declined during the epidemic, commercial banks need to Businesses were heavily financed and profitability levels in the banking sector rose during this period. However, the stock market reaction of the Canadian banking industry is contrary to most forecasting studies. The first preference of investors is not the banking industry with stable performance and outstanding profitability. Shares in the Canadian banking sector fell amid a modest uptick in the broader market. This shows that the stock prices of the Canadian banking industry have been greatly undervalued during the epidemic. The expansionary fiscal policy of the Bank of Canada has had a small negative impact on the profitability of the Canadian banking industry. This may be because after the money supply has increased significantly, residents are no longer satisfied with depositing money in the bank but investing and consuming. However, bank stock prices are highly sensitive to stimulating economic policies. The stock prices of the Canadian banking industry will rise sharply in 2021 after the epidemic. Scotiabank, which has the smallest increase, also outperformed the market by nearly 10 percentage points, with an increase of close to 30%. Taken together, the overall stock price of the Canadian banking industry in 2021 is overvalued, but the impact of the policy may continue to drive the stock price up in the short term, and the overall stock price of the Canadian banking industry will decline in the long run. Judging from the valuation forecast of the price-earnings ratio model, the model cannot predict the impact of similar new crown epidemics and important fiscal policies. But it has certain reference significance for the stock price prediction in the long-term stable market.

For the future, the stock market of the Canadian banking industry may continue to rise in the short term. This is due to the impact of aggressive fiscal policies, the money supply has been greatly increased, and the overall stock price of the market will continue to rise. But the gains could be followed by another round of declines, as price-to-earnings valuations suggest Canadian banks as a whole are overvalued at the moment. The profitability of the Canadian banking industry will return to a historically stable upward trend after experiencing the economic recovery in the late stage of the epidemic, and the price-to-earnings ratio will rise steadily, but the specific situation depends on the changes and differences in the individual businesses of different banks. For a new round of economic crisis that may arise in the future, the Canadian banking industry once again proved its stable performance and profitability during the crisis of the new crown epidemic. The stability of the Canadian banking industry may be due to the relatively average market distribution of the Canadian banking industry. The price-earnings ratio shows that the profitability of the top four banks is equivalent, and there is no prominent monopoly. Investors should be more optimistic about the stock price performance of the Canadian banking industry during the crisis and believe in its ability to rise after the crisis.

It should be noted that due to the single valuation method used in this study, there are certain limitations. The valuation does not take into account factors such as the risk premium in crisis response, which makes the forecasted valuation part of the study likely to have a large error from the actual value. At the same time, the price-earnings ratio method does not take into account the differences in the business composition and profit ratio of different banks in the Canadian banking industry. For example, the price-earnings ratio of TD Bank and the overall market trend have the opposite trend during the epidemic. This may be due to the fact that most of its profitable business comes from retail central bank business rather than stored value and commercial banks. At the same time, this study did not analyze the price-earnings ratio and stock price changes in different quarters during the COVID-19 epidemic. In fact, the negative impact of the COVID-19 epidemic was concentrated in the first three months of 2020. It has been implemented in April and has had a huge impact on market share prices in April. The performance of the banking industry and the overall market in 2021 cannot fully represent the impact of macroeconomic policies. Changes in the bank's P/E growth rate and stock price growth rate may be more affected by the expansionary fiscal policy, and the increase in different quarters will reflect this change. There are also certain flaws in the data used in the research. The closing price at the end of the year cannot well reflect the differences in price changes of different stocks. Future research should consider year-to-year volatility in stock prices to determine whether stocks in the Canadian banking sector are more stable relative to the overall market. At the same time, future research should also consider other potential factors other than the epidemic and macroeconomic policies from 2019 to 2021, such as the impact of Russia-Ukraine conflicts and global economic changes.

5 Conclusion

In summary, this study found that the COVID-19 pandemic has led to a slight decline in the overall stock price of the Canadian banking industry, but the overall profitability has improved significantly. After the Bank of Canada implemented an unconventional expansionary fiscal policy, investors are generally optimistic about the impact of the policy on the banking industry, and the stock market prices of the Canadian banking industry have risen sharply. Compared with the profitability during the epidemic, the overall business profit of the banking industry has dropped significantly, but it has increased compared to before the epidemic. Due to the continued strong influence of unconventional expansionary economic policies, the overall market value of the Toronto Stock Exchange will continue to increase for quite a period of time, and the banking industry is no exception. The overall stock price of the industry will fall after the impact of the policy ends. By comparing the price-earnings ratio and stock price changes of Canadian banks in 2020, public investors did not invest in stocks in the banking industry as expected by the market. In fact, the business capability and profitability of the Canadian banking industry have once again proved its stability in the crisis. In a possible economic crisis in the future, Canadian banking stocks will be a relatively low-risk option with considerable returns. The research method of this paper is relatively simple. The company value and stock market fluctuations are affected by many factors. Further research should use more valuation and analysis indicators to improve the comprehensive analysis of the Canadian banking crisis response ability.

References

1. World health statistics 2022: monitoring health for the SDGs, sustainable development goals. Geneva: World Health Organization; 2022. Licence: CC BY-NC-SA 3.0 IGO
2. Cheng, C., Barceló, J., Hartnett, A.S., Kubinec, R., Messerschmidt, L.: COVID-19 government response event dataset (CoronaNet v. 1.0). Nat. Hum. Behav. **4**(7), 756–768 (2020)
3. Gopinath, G.: The great lockdown: Worst economic downturn since the great depression. IMF Blog **14**, 2020 (2020)
4. Lemieux, T., Milligan, K., Schirle, T., Skuterud, M.: Initial impacts of the COVID-19 pandemic on the Canadian labour market. Can. Public Policy **46**(S1), S55–S65 (2020)
5. Xu, L.: Stock return and the COVID-19 pandemic: evidence from Canada and the US. Financ. Res. Lett. **38**, 101872 (2021)
6. Talbot, D., Ordonez-Ponce, E.: Canadian banks' responses to COVID-19: a strategic positioning analysis. J. Sustain. Finan. Investment **12**(2), 423–430 (2022)
7. Bordo, M.D., Redish, A., Rockoff, H.: Why didn't Canada have a banking crisis in 2008 (or in 1930, or 1907, or…)? Econ. Hist. Rev. **68**(1), 218–243 (2015)
8. Salehi, A.: Assessing the impact of the Covid 19 pandemic on the banking system performance: evidence from the Canadian banking industry. Int. J. Finan. Bank. Stud. (2147-4486), 11(4), 01-16 (2022)
9. Deev, O.: Methods of bank valuation: a critical overview. Finan. Assets Investing **2**(3), 33–44 (2011)
10. Giammarino, R., Schwartz, E., Zechner, J.: Market valuation of bank assets and deposit insurance in Canada. Can. J. Econ. Revue Canadienne d'Economique **22**(1), 109–127 (1989)

ChatGPT Concept Industry Valuation Analysis: Evidence from iFlytek and Kunlun

Yajing Chen(✉)

Department of Finance, Hubei University of Economics, Wuhan 430000, China
1811581134@mail.sit.edu.cn

Abstract. At present, the explosion of GhatGPT has set off a new wave of technology in the world, and the value of related enterprises under the concept of ChatGPT has gradually become a hot topic for investors. However, there is not much research on the value of ChatGPT concept industry. In this paper, iFlytek and Kunlun, the leading companies of ChatGPT concept, are taken as the research objects, and the FCFF model based on two stages is used to evaluate them. Subsequently, the valuation range of the ChatGPT concept industry is calculated. It is concluded that iFlytek and Kunlun will usher in high growth in operating income and net profit, and the market value of iFlytek and Kunlun is still at a low level. ChatGPT concept industry value will be further improved, and provide relevant decisions for the improvement of enterprise value, to help investors clarify the industry status and market trend, and avoid blindly following the market.

Keywords: ChatGPT · Industry Valuation · FCFF Model

1 Introduction

Artificial intelligence is a strategic technology leading the future. China is vigorously promoting the development of artificial intelligence. The "Made in China 2025" issued by The State Council in May 2015 proposed that the production process be intelligent, and then AI related policies entered a period of intensive introduction. In October 2017, artificial intelligence was written into the report of the 19th National Congress, which will promote the deep integration of Internet, big data, artificial intelligence, and real economy. In July 2021, the Ministry of Industry and Information issued Construction Guidelines to promote the integration of AI with various fields, including transportation and finance.

At the end of 2020, ChatGPT was born, and then became popular all over the world. Many domestic enterprises are engaged in the research and development and production of ChatGPT products. Iflytek plans to combine ChatGPT with education products, and will release IFlytek AI learning machine on May 6. Kunlun released the first large and language model for benchmarking ChatGPT in China. The "Yanxi" artificial intelligence application platform backed by Jingdong + ChatGPT has identified four development directions. A shares added ChatGPT concept index, related concept stocks to achieve large fluctuations in the short term [1].

Domestic and foreign scholars have some research on the value of enterprises or industries. The capital value theory founded by Fisher first advocates that the discounted value of the cash flow that an enterprise can obtain in the future can be used to reflect the value of the enterprise [2]. The founders of MM theory believe that under certain assumptions, the market price of a firm is not related to its investment capital structure [3]. On this basis, Sharpe created the CAPM model, pointing out that the change of asset systematic risk will cause the necessary rate of return to change, and the increase of system risk will lead to the higher expected rate of return of asset realized in the future [4]. Black and Scholes subsequently proposed the option pricing model of duration interval (B-S model). Under the premise of long-term continuous operation, the value of the enterprise is obtained by adding the increasing value of various options [5]. Then, Song et al. used Real Options and Modern Capital Budgeting Theory to make a more in-depth study on the valuation of major investment opportunities in high-tech enterprises [6].

In China, enterprise value evaluation methods are often divided into income method, market method, cost method and option valuation method according to different theoretical bases, among which absolute valuation method and relative valuation method, mainly FCFF, are the two mainstream valuation methods at present [7]. Lin took Hengtong Optoelectronics as an example to conduct valuation research on high-tech companies, and the research results show that FCFF two-stage model can better reflect the value of high-tech companies [8]. Tang took Jiuyang Stock as an example to study the value evaluation of small home appliance enterprises, and the research conclusion pointed out that the use of FCFF two-stage model can more clearly show the actual operating conditions and future development potential of the company [9].

Jia concluded that the valuation of new consumer electronics enterprises producing a single category can be evaluated by using FCFF two-stage valuation model as the main valuation method, supplemented by relative valuation method [7]. In fact, there is not much literature on the asset value method and the market comparison method [10]. Liu used DDM combined with P/E and P/B methods to value the equity of Chinese commercial banks [10]. Combined with the specific development status of Suning Cloud service, Pan adopted free cash flow model, price-to-sales ratio method and so on to evaluate the value of Internet business companies such as Suning Cloud service [11]. Wang et al. used the relative valuation method to analyze the valuation of target companies in cross-border M&A [12].

At present, there are few researches on the industrial value of ChatGPT concept. In this paper, iFlytek and Kunlun, the leading enterprises of ChatGPT concept, are taken as the research objects. The traditional valuation method is used to evaluate the two companies based on the two-stage FCFF model, and then the valuation range of the ChatGPT concept industry is calculated. Explore the industry value of ChatGPT concept.

2 Method

This paper takes 2018–2022 as the sample period to carry out empirical research. The data in this paper come from the 2018–2022 annual report disclosed on the company's official website and related research reports of Radish Investment Research and make predictions accordingly. DCF is a valuation method commonly used by scholars who study enterprise value. DCF is divided into company discounted free cash flow model FCFF and equity discounted free cash flow model FCFE. Since the R&D and production of artificial intelligence have a large investment in the early stage, there may be two stages of explosive growth and stable growth in the later stage, and the FCFF model can be predicted by stages according to the development situation of the company. Therefore, this paper evaluates iFlytek and Kunlun through the two-stage FCFF model, and then calculates the industry valuation.

Based on the two-stage FCFF model, firstly, the profit forecast of iFlytek and the net profit forecast of Kunlun are predicted by the profit forecast of 5 research reports on iFlytek and 5 research reports on Kunlun. Secondly, based on the 2018–2022 financial statements of iFlytek and Kunlun, the free cash flow forecast is made. Finally, the discount rate is determined according to the weighted average cost of capital rate, and the valuation of the two companies is predicted to calculate the industry valuation.

The model formula of two-stage FCFF is shown as follows:

$$P = \sum_{t=1}^{n} \frac{FCFF_t}{(1+WACC)} + \frac{FCFF_{n+1}}{(WACC-g)(1+WACC)^n} \quad (1)$$

FCFF can be calculated as follows:

$$FCFF = NI + DD\&A - CEPEX - \Delta WC \quad (2)$$

where P refers to the enterprise valuation, n refers to the observation period, t refers to the rapid growth stage, n + 1 refers to the company entering the stage of stable growth, FCFFt refers to the free cash flow of the enterprise in the future year t, WACC refers to the weighted average cost of capital ratio, g refers to the sustainable growth rate after the enterprise enters the stage of stable growth, NI refers to the net profit. DD&A refers to depreciation and amortization, CEPEX refers to capital expenditure, and WC refers to working capital increase.

3 Empirical Analysis

3.1 Corporate Free Cash Flow Forecast

Based on the financial data of IFlytek and Kunlun in 2018–2022, this paper predicts the free cash flow of the two companies in 2023–2025. 1) Since the content of this paper is the expected cash flow of the two enterprises under the concept of ChatGPT, and ChatGPT belongs to the newly added sector, the financial data of previous years may be used to predict the company's net profit and operating income error may be large, so this paper uses the average of the net profit forecast and operating income forecast of the five securities companies. As the expected net profit and operating income of this valuation. As shown in Table 1 and Table 2, based on the financial data of iFlytek and Kunlun in 2018–2022, the ratio of depreciation and amortization, capital expenditure and working capital increase to total operating revenue is calculated, and the extreme value is deleted to take the average value. The average depreciation and amortization ratio of iFlytek and

Kunlun were 8.58% and 1.73% respectively. The increase of working capital accounted for 5.66% and −8.62% respectively. Kunlun's capital expenditure accounted for 0.96%. Since iFlytek's capex fluctuates widely, the average of the expected capex in the above research report is taken as the expected capex in this paper. Finally, the formula is used to forecast 2023–2025 free cash flow as given in Table 3 and Table 4.

3.2 Calculate WACC

WACC is calculated as follows:

$$WACC = \frac{E}{E+D} R_e + \frac{D}{E+D} R_d (1-T) \quad (3)$$

$$Re = R_f + \beta(R_m - R_f) \quad (4)$$

Here, R_f is the risk-free rate of return, which takes the average of the yield of China's 10-year Treasury bond in 2022; R_m the market rate of return, which takes the geometric mean of the 10-year SSE index; β is derived from the CSMAR database. The data of equity capital and debt capital is retrieved from the 2022 annual report. The results are presented in Table 5 and Table 6.

Table 1. 2018–2022 Main financial data of iFlytek Unit: RMB 100 million.

Item	2018	2019	2020	2021
Sale	79.17	100.79	130.25	183.14
DD&A	6.112	9.471	12.2947	14.2232
Capital Expenditure	18.23	18.87	12.49	20.82
ΔWorking Capital	−7.99	26.15	0.22	27.57

Table 2. 2018–2022 Main financial data of Kunlun Unit: RMB 100 million.

Item	2018	2019	2020	2021	2022
Sale	35.77	36.88	54.2	48.5	47.36
DD&A	0.43794	0.39706	1.2841	1.1309	0.78821
Capital Expenditure	0.1196	0.0381	0.866	0.5452	0.7783
ΔWorking Capital	−18.16	−9.54	25.22	−11.49	11.22

3.3 Value Estimation

Based on the two-stage FCFF valuation model, the period from 2023 to 2025 is set as the high number development stage, and the period after 2025 is set as the stable

Table 3. 2023–2025 Cash flow Statement forecast of iFlytek Unit: RMB 100 million.

Item	2023E	2024E	2025E
Sale	24883.34	32175.07	40569.16
NI	1744.474	2464.576	3375.754
DD&A	2134.033	2759.383	3479.273
Capital Expenditure	733	748.3333	727.3333
ΔWorking Capital	1408.981	1821.865	2297.167
Free Cash Flow	1736.526	2653.761	3830.527

Table 4. 2023–2025 Cash flow Statement forecast of Kunlun Unit: RMB 100 million.

Item	2023E	2024E	2025E
Sale	5315.6	5892	6464.6
NI	1382.338	1581.62	1774.752
DD&A	92.13194	102.1223	112.0468
Capital Expenditure	51.06108	56.59792	62.09825
ΔWorking Capital	−458.338	−508.038	−557.411
Free Cash Flow	1881.747	2135.183	2382.111

Table 5. WACC of IFlytek Deadline: December 31, 2022.

E		D	
E	168.47	Short-term borrowings	RMB 364million
		long-term loan	RMB 1714 million
		Total borrowings	RMB 2078 million
Rf	2.78%	Total interest on loans	RMB 65.36 million
Beta	116.07%	Rd	3.13%
Rm	4.93%	T	15.00%
Rm-Rf	2.15%	Rd(1-T)	2.66%
Re	5.27%	WACC	4.99%

development stage. The growth rate in the stable development stage is based on China's GDP growth rate of 3% in 2022. Iflytek's WACC was 4.9%; Kunlun's WACC is 5.69%. 2023–2025 free cash flow refer to the above. The two-stage FCFF valuation model was used to calculate the data, and the enterprise valuation of iFlytek was 155,660.5 million. The enterprise valuation of Kunlun is 71,288.64 million yuan. The results are summarized in Table 7 and Table 8.

Table 6. WACC of Kunlun Deadline: December 31, 2022.

E		D	
E	126.98	Short-term borrowings	RMB 618million
		long-term loan	RMB 0 million
		Total borrowings	RMB 618 million
Rf	2.78%	Total interest on loans	RMB 44.26 million
Beta	132.27%	Rd	7.16%
Rm	4.93%	T	15.00%
Rm-Rf	2.15%	Rd(1-T)	6.09%
Re	5.67%	WACC	5.69%

Table 7. IFlytek's valuation based on two-stage FCFF model Unit: RMB million.

Item	2023E	2024E	2025E	After 2025
Free Cash Flow	1736.526	2653.761	3830.527	
Discount	1654.04	2407.64	3310.191	148288.6274
WACC = 4.9%				
g = 3%				
Value = 155660.5 million				

Table 8. Kunlun's valuation based on two-stage FCFF model Unit: RMB million.

	2023E	2024E	2025E	After 2025
Free Cash Flow	1881.747	2135.183	2382.111	
Discount	1780.523	1911.647	2018	65578.47
WACC = 5.69%				
g = 3%				
Value = 71288.64 million				

3.4 Analysis

According to the floating market value ranking of ChatGPT concept components in the Royal Flow, IFlytek and Kunlun ranked the first and third, and the second three sixty zero was not considered in the sample scope due to the loss in 2022. In this paper, the industry value of ChatGPT is estimated by iFlytek and Kunlun. The industry value of ChatGPT concept is similar to the average valuation of iFlytek and Kunlun. The estimated industry value of ChatGPT concept is 1134.74 million yuan.

4 Conclusion

According to the market value ranking of the ChatGPT concept component stocks in Flushing, IFlytek and Kunlun Wanwei rank 1 and 3, and the second ranked 360 is not considered in the sample scope due to the loss in 2022. This paper expects the ChatGPT industry value to be estimated through the value estimates of IFlytek and Kunlun Wanwei. The ChatGPT concept industry value is approximated to the average valuation of IFlytek and Kunlun Wanwei. The ChatGPT concept industry value is estimated at RMB 113,474 million. Hence, ChatGPT industry has great development potential, and investors can choose to continue to follow the industry and excellent stocks in the medium and long term. Based on the analysis, ChatGPT industry has great development potential, and investors can choose to continue to follow the industry and excellent stocks in the medium and long term.

In the research process, due to the author's own limited understanding, the paper has the following shortcomings. Due to the limited ability of the author, the prediction of financial statements is not in-depth and comprehensive enough. As ChatGPT is a new business of the enterprise, it cannot use the previous financial statements to forecast net profit, and there is a certain deviation in using the average value of the forecast of the research report. This study uses traditional valuation methods for ChatGPT concept industry valuation. In the valuation stage, the valuation results are affected by the subjective judgment of personnel and there are certain deviations.

In the process of estimating enterprise value in the future, one needs to strengthen our own knowledge, further familiarize ourselves with the current situation and development of the industry and the enterprise, use a variety of methods for estimation and comparison, and accumulate experience, so as to make a more reasonable evaluation of the value of the industry or the enterprise. Taking Kunlun Wanwei and iFlytek as examples, this paper obtains the analysis result that ChatGPT industry valuation is low. Provide investors with relevant decision-making opinions, recommend investors to stick to the ChatGPT concept industry in the long term, and choose stocks with excellent performance to buy.

References

1. Zhao, L.: The ChatGPT index fluctuates sharply to warn against AI investment risks. Nat. Bus. Daily **4–13**, 001 (2023)
2. Irving, F.: The nature of capital and income. The Commercial Press **210**, 2 (2017)
3. Franco, M., Merton, H.M.: The cost of capital, corporation finance and the theory of investment. Am. Econ. Rev. **48**(3), 261–297 (1958)
4. Sharpe, W.F.: Capital asset prices: a theory of market equilibrium under conditions of risk. J. Finan. **19**(3), 425–442 (1964)
5. Scholes, M.S., Black, F.S.: The pricing of options and corporate liabilities. J. Polit. Econ. **81**(3), 637–654 (1973)
6. Yeon, S.J., Deok, J.L., Hyung, S.O.: Evaluation of new and renewable energy technologies in Korea using real options. Int. J. Energy Res. **37**(13), 1645–1656 (2013)
7. Jia, Y.: Research on the valuation of new consumer electronics enterprises. UESTC (2022)
8. Lin, L.: Research on the Valuation of high-tech listed companies. Shanghai Normal University (2010)

9. Tang, Y.: Value evaluation of small household appliance enterprises based on free cash flow: a case study of Joyoung stock. East China Jiaotong Univ. **1**, 59–60 (2020)
10. Liu, Y.: Analysis on the choice of bank equity valuation method. Finan. Forum **15**(07), 11–19 (2010)
11. Pan, Y.: Research on valuation of Suning Yunshang Group Co., LTD. HUST (2016)
12. Wang, H., Sun, C.: Valuation Analysis of transnational M&A target companies under different valuation methods. Commun. Finan. Account. **854**(18), 116–120 (2020)

Optimizing Trading Recommendations in Portfolio Trading: A Bilateral Matching Theory Approach

Wenzheng Liu(✉)

School of Ocean Engineering, Harbin Institute of Technology, Weihai 264209, China
wenzheng.liu.2021@uni.strath.ac.uk

Abstract. The development of information systems has greatly changed our way of life, and many group activities, including communication and trading, can be easily carried out online. Taking transactions as an example, including transactions of various items, online trading platforms provide a trading market, which can greatly improve trading efficiency and increase transaction volume. During trading, the market maker platform will assist customers in providing trading guidance services and facilitating a certain number of transactions when it is not possible to trade all. Examples of portfolio trading mainly include trading in the second-hand goods market, stock portfolio trading, and some small markets aimed at completing specific transactions. The transaction recommendation system is a user recommendation system based on a portfolio trading market matching mechanism algorithm. This trading recommendation system takes user information as input. This paper constructs a mathematical model of the market based on bilateral matching theory, and also visualizes it into a weighted bipartite graph. The parameters are obtained by solving the model based on the interior-point method and revised simplex method. The system feeds back the algorithm calculation results to users in the form of recommendation indices. The transaction recommendation system can be applied to software, web pages, and other trading platforms that can utilize backend computing power and have the ability to collect user information. The transaction recommendation system directly serves users.

Keywords: Portfolio Trading · Trading Recommendation System · Bilateral Matching Theory

1 Introduction

The rise of the Internet has brought revolutionary business transformation to many fields, and the digitization of traditional business is an inevitable trend. The financial industry has ushered in a wave of financial technology, and electronic banking has become popular in daily life. With the massive collection of information on the internet and the support of various social media, people have gradually formed unique community groups online, and the industries that serve these groups are mostly the products of traditional industries that have been digitized. The development of the Internet and the development of online communities have made trading activities more convenient and people's trading needs more vigorous. The rapid development and application of new concepts such as e-commerce have increased the demand for electronic market intermediaries, and the role of electronic intermediaries in commodity trading activities has become increasingly evident [1, 2]. Under the strong trading demand, the efficiency of individual free random matching is not enough to meet people's trading needs. People need more convenient and fast trading platforms and market services. The development of electronic market trading systems is precisely to meet people's trading needs.

The essence of an electronic trading market is an intermediary, which is a market operation behavior that applies modern electronic information technology to serve both trading parties, organizing transactions between them [3]. Portfolio trading refers to the process where buyers and sellers place the goods to be traded together and propose trading demands to market makers in the form of a combination, seeking buyers or sellers to trade. When each user holds a specific combination of transaction items and requests a transaction request from the platform, the platform collects this information as input. Electronic trading markets can achieve fast trading. It is worth mentioning that compared to traditional markets, backend platforms with high-performance computing capabilities can find the optimal solution based on customer data in matching models and objective functions. The solution set obtained from the backend is converted to the front end, providing potential buying or selling targets for each individual trading customer, and providing trading partner recommendation rating services. Obviously, compared to traditional trading markets, electronic trading markets as electronic intermediaries have obvious advantages in terms of efficiency and timeliness [4].

Based on the market matching theory and existing research, from the perspective of portfolio trading, this paper constructs a bilateral matching model, develops a solver, and continuously optimizes the optimal solution based on the interior point method and simplex method. The parameter solution set is fed back to users as an index to achieve a completely automated electronic trading service system. The solver development tool is the programming language Python. The profitability of electronic trading platforms generally relies on providing trading platforms and services for both buyers and sellers to collect service fees. Therefore, maximizing the number of commodity transactions is the most realistic demand of electronic trading platforms, and increasing the number of transactions will also improve user satisfaction, serving the common interests of both sides. This article aims to develop a solver with the goal of maximizing the number of commodity transactions. Under the objective function of maximizing the total number of commodity transactions in each round, reasonable constraints are constructed to meet the model assumptions and reality. Under multiple constraint conditions, the objective function is optimized and solved, and the obtained solution set is used in the front end for user trading guidance services.

2 Research Questions

The market matching theory was proposed by scholars Alvin E. Roth and Lloyd S. Shapley, who won the Nobel Prize in Economics in 2012 for their work on market matching theory. The bilateral matching theory is an important component of market matching theory. A typical example is the stable matching theory proposed by Gale and Shapley in the male and female mating market, known as the G-S algorithm [5]. Roth and his partners subsequently extended and applied the G-S algorithm, establishing a market design theory and practice of bilateral matching, Roth not only clearly defined the concepts of "bilateral" and "bilateral matching", but also analyzed practical cases of bilateral matching. Roth believes that bilateral refers to two sets of previously designated disjoint agents, while bilateral matching refers to the matching of bilateral agents in these markets [6]. The matching theory is derived from a systematic study of market matching function. The college admission and marital stability problems solved by the G-S algorithm when it was first proposed are the embodiment of market matching function [5]. In bilateral matching, the term "bilateral" refers to the fact that participants in the market always belong to one of two disjoint sets. "Matching" refers to the demand for bilateral transactions in the market, including the ranking of their preferences or the trading expectations [12]. The idea and modeling method of bilateral matching are very compatible with the demand for solving market matching problems. The holder of each portfolio is considered as an independent individual and belongs to only one party in a round of trading, and the two parties do not intersect with each other. The number of transactions represents the degree of preference of each individual, and the total number of transactions obtained by the algorithm represents the market's expectation of the number of transactions.

The research question of this article is based on bilateral matching, starting from a new perspective of portfolio trading. The potential trading partners are set as unknown, and the number of transactions is determined by the matching situation of individual goods held by both trading parties in the portfolio. Based on the above assumptions, establish a bilateral matching model for the market, with each transaction volume as the weight and corresponding to each pair of matchings. The unknown trading partners reflect the actual needs of traders, and the model's solution results will reflect the suggestion of pairing between buyers and sellers under the maximum number of commodity transactions, thus directly realizing the service role of electronic intermediaries, and solving some matching problems of portfolio transactions and the trading needs of customers.

3 Literature Review

The importance of electronic intermediaries in commodity transactions is already considerable. Nowadays, electronic intermediaries all over the world mostly serve customers in the form of software and web pages. Main projects such as COBRA, GAIA, AEBS, Meta broker, etc. [3]. Some job search apps, second-hand housing, and second-hand car trading apps are very common in China, with a large scale of advertising and promotion. NASDAQ, the earliest electronic stock trading system in the United States, was an electronic securities trading institution in the United States, early research mainly focused on single attribute matching of price attributes [7].

Currently, many scholars around the world are conducting research in various markets based on the rise of electronic intermediaries. Haiming Liang and others from the Northeast University of China designed an extended H-R algorithm based on matching satisfaction to establish a decision method for matching second-hand housing portfolio transactions. After considering the matching satisfaction of both buyers and sellers, the Pareto efficiency matching results were obtained. The proposed combination method supplements the original matching method for single second-hand house transactions. Meanwhile, this method still has the potential to solve other category-matching problems [8]. Zhongzhong Jiang and others, taking the actual B2C electronic intermediary as the background and considering the fuzzy demand information of both buyers and sellers, constructed an objective function based on modeling and optimization to maximize transaction matching degree and transaction quantity in the matching problem of second-hand housing transactions. Fully considering satisfaction makes the algorithm more reasonable and practical [9]. Hongbing Wang and others studied an electronic market with a core business of intermediary agents, constructed matching models and algorithms, and assisted users in finding suitable trading partners through communication between buyers and sellers. But this model and algorithm are more inclined to solve the one-to-many matching problem of a single user's perspective, which is more difficult to solve the problem of many-to-many perspectives for both buyers and sellers [10]. Tewari and others analyzed the functions of agent-based products and intermediary services, established models, and solved utility values to study the matching problem between buyers and sellers. By reading user input parameters, the user's attribute weights and utility functions were processed. The method can be applied to the catering industry to provide services for wireless internet users [11]. Jung and others considered the situation where multiple buyers correspond to multiple sellers, and from the perspective of mutual value domains between buyers and sellers, constructed constraints based on the degree of satisfaction of both parties' attributes, and constructed a constraint satisfaction problem model for solving. The developed solver was applied to real estate intermediary websites [12]. Based on the analysis of previous research, it can be seen that scholars have made progress in research not only on new methods but also on new perspectives [8–10]. In terms of application, the development of solvers for user platforms such as websites has also become a key concern for scholars [11, 12].

In summary, the design and application development innovation of the matching market based on computer technology mainly involves the introduction of new perspectives and mathematical models based on new perspectives, including objective functions and constraints based on model assumptions, developing solvers to optimize solutions then apply and serve the matching market under new perspectives.

4 Research Methods

The bilateral matching model can be visualized as a bipartite graph. After a certain number of buyers and sellers arrive, it can be approximated as the number of buyers equals the number of sellers. This paper demonstrates a simplified model of 5 to 5, as shown in Fig. 1. The left side of the bipartite graph represents the buyer, and the right side represents the seller. Each seller and seller will form a matching in the generalized model. Assuming the number of traders on one side is n, then all possible matching numbers are n*n. Each buyer and seller will submit a portfolio based on the transaction requirements. If the product combinations in the portfolio of a buyer and seller intersect, they are considered tradable. The corresponding matching weight is greater than 0. The weight is the maximum number of tradable products that can be traded between the two. But when the matching weight is 0, it can be considered that there is no transaction between the two, and the integration of this situation can be defined as no trading in this round. When conducting the simulation, the bipartite graph that reflects the real situation will remove the weight of 0 to better represent the potential trading partners of both buyers and sellers.

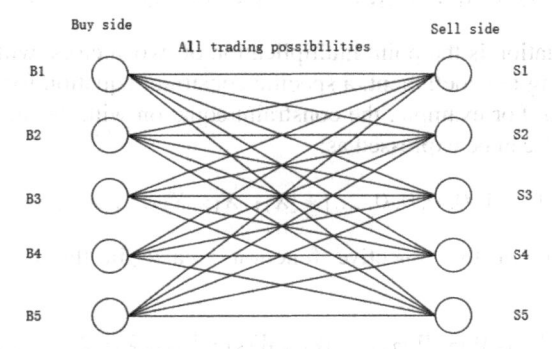

Fig. 1. A bilateral matching model including all trading possibilities.

The values to be solved in the model are defined as probabilities, which include the probability of trading with potential traders and the probability of not trading in this round. Each matching corresponds to a probability, denoted as X_{ij}, where each X_{ij} is a number between 0 and 1, $0 <= X_{ij} <= 1$, i represents the buyer, j represents the buyer. All traders also have a constraint on probability, and the sum of all potential trading partners' trading probabilities for each trader is 1, $\sum_i X_{ij} = 1$ and $\sum_j X_{ij} = 1$. The above equations constitute the constraint conditions for the optimization solution. The weight corresponding to each matching is denoted as W_{ij}, and the mathematical expectation of all matching weights is the mathematical expectation of the total number of market commodity transactions, denoted as $\sum_{ij} W_{ij} * X_{ij}$. The purpose of designing a matching market mechanism is to maximize the trading volume of goods, thus the objective function is $Max(\sum_{ij} W_{ij} * X_{ij})$, the value of expectation after solving the objective function is the maximum expected number of commodity transactions.

Taking the simplified model solution of 5 to 5 as an example, the probabilities corresponding to 5*5 matches are written in matrix form (matching possibilities matrix), as formula (1). In the matrix representation, the constraint can be defined as matrix elements are numbers between 0 and 1, and the sum of elements in any row and column of the matrix is 1.

$$X = \begin{bmatrix} X_{11} & X_{12} & X_{13} & X_{14} & X_{15} \\ X_{21} & X_{22} & X_{23} & X_{24} & X_{25} \\ X_{31} & X_{32} & X_{33} & X_{34} & X_{35} \\ X_{41} & X_{42} & X_{43} & X_{44} & X_{45} \\ X_{51} & X_{52} & X_{53} & X_{54} & X_{55} \end{bmatrix} \quad (1)$$

When calculating, for the convenience and speed of calculation, the matrix can be transformed into an array form:

$$X = [X_{11}, X_{12}, X_{13}, X_{14}, X_{15}, X_{21}, ..., X_{52}, X_{53}, X_{54}, X_{55}] \quad (2)$$

Constraints where the sum of elements in rows and columns is 1, can be expressed in the form of vector dot multiplication, as follows:

$$[C_{11}, C_{12}, C_{13}, ..., C_{54}, C_{55}] * [X_{11}, X_{12}, X_{13}, ..., X_{54}, X_{55}] = 1 \quad (3)$$

The above equation is the point multiplication of two vectors, with C_{ij} as the coefficient. By changing the coefficient, a specific constraint equation for a row or column can be constructed. For example, the constraint equation with the sum of the first row element values is 1 can be expressed as:

$$[1, 1, 1, 1, 1, 0, 0, 0, 0, ...] * [X_{11}, X_{12}, X_{13}, ..., X_{54}, X_{55}] = 1 \quad (4)$$

The expression of the objective function is also in the form of vector dot multiplication:

$$X_{max} = Max([W_{11}, W_{12}, W_{13}, ..., W_{54}, W_{55}] * [X_{11}, X_{12}, X_{13}, ..., X_{54}, X_{55}]) \quad (5)$$

The weight vector is determined by the actual situation and is a constant. The final optimization solution results include the objective function value and all probability values X_{ij} corresponding to matching.

5 Results

The calculation results of the model will be presented to users in the form of a recommended index of trading partners, which lists potential trading partners and the recommended index of potential trading partners, providing trading guidance services. The recommendation index includes the recommendation index of all potential trading partners and the recommendation index that is temporarily not traded. It is worth noting that the recommended trading partner for a single round of trading may not be optimal for a trader, but doing so will benefit the overall market in maximizing commodity trading volume, ensuring overall trading volume and satisfaction, and facilitating better subsequent trading.

The recommended index of trading partners received by each trader exists in the model in the form of 'probability', and the model optimizes and solves for the expected number of overall transactions. The trading partner recommendation rating system will try its best to increase trading volume for traders but will optimize the overall trading volume as the goal. For some individuals in special circumstances, not trading in this round will also be considered as a recommendation option, and a recommendation index will be set. Although platform recommendations may not necessarily be the optimal option, and customers also reserve the right to make their own choices, trading, when the platform does not recommend trading or blindly selecting the trader with the highest

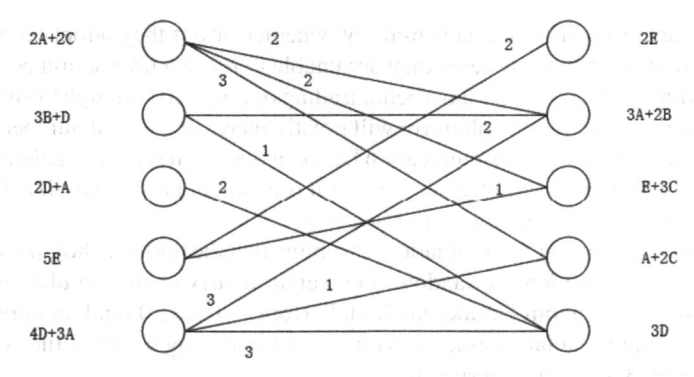

Fig. 2. The first simulation model.

transaction volume, is likely to not achieve the transaction, because the target trading object at this time is likely to have a better trading choice.

The simulation is demonstrated using a simplified 5*5 model to demonstrate the solver function. The visualization of the first simulation model is shown as Fig. 2.

There are five commodity categories in the market: A, B, C, D, and E, and each trader has different types and quantities of trading commodities. The portfolio of commodities held by the trader determines the weight of each matching, and the matchings with a weight of 0 have been removed in Fig. 3. The first set of model weight arrays is [0, 2, 2, 3, 0, 0, 2, 0, 0, 1, 0, 0, 0, 0, 2, 2, 0, 1, 0, 0, 0, 3, 0, 1, 3]. In this case, the potential trader information and recommendation index received by five buyers and five sellers can be simplified as formulas (6) and (7).

$$\begin{cases} B_1 = [0, 0, 0, 1, 0] \\ B_2 = [0, 0.5047, 0.4953, 0, 0] \\ B_3 = [0, 0, 0.5047, 0, 0.4953] \\ B_4 = [1, 0, 0, 0, 0] \\ B_5 = [0, 0.4953, 0, 0, 0.5047] \end{cases} \quad (6)$$

$$\begin{cases} S_1 = [0, 0, 0, 1, 0] \\ S_2 = [0, 0.5047, 0, 0, 0.4953] \\ S_3 = [0, 0.4953, 0.5047, 0, 0] \\ S_4 = [1, 0, 0, 0, 0] \\ S_5 = [0, 0, 0.4953, 0, 0.5047] \end{cases} \quad (7)$$

It can be seen that both parties from one matching receive the same recommendation index from the other party, for example, the S_5 recommendation index received by B_5 is the same as the B_5 recommendation index received by S_5. If the above traders fully follow the platform's guidance for trading, the final trading situation is [B_1(3/3), S_4(3/3)], [B_2(2/2), S_2(2/3)], [B_3(0/2)], [S_3(0/2)], [B_4(2/2), S_1(2/2)], [B_5(3/3), S_5(3/3)].

In the ten-person model of this group, 8 people reached a transaction and 7 people reached the maximum possible number of transactions. S3 and B3, which are unable to reach a transaction, may take the lead in trading in the absence of information. But after the platform achieves information symmetry, whether or not they adopt the platform's current round of no trading strategy, they are unable to reach a transaction because their potential trading partners always have better trading options. So although the information symmetry implemented by the platform will greatly increase the total number of market transactions and strengthen communication between traders, it is only beneficial for most traders. For a few types of traders, it may be more beneficial for individuals to make good use of information asymmetry to trade first.

Considering a more complex situation, assuming that the portfolio holdings of traders in the entire trading market are random, the weight matrix of the simulation model is generated using the random number method. Perform 10 and 20 random number simulations, and obtain the total transaction volume and matching curve of the commodity, as shown in Fig. 3 and Fig. 4, respectively.

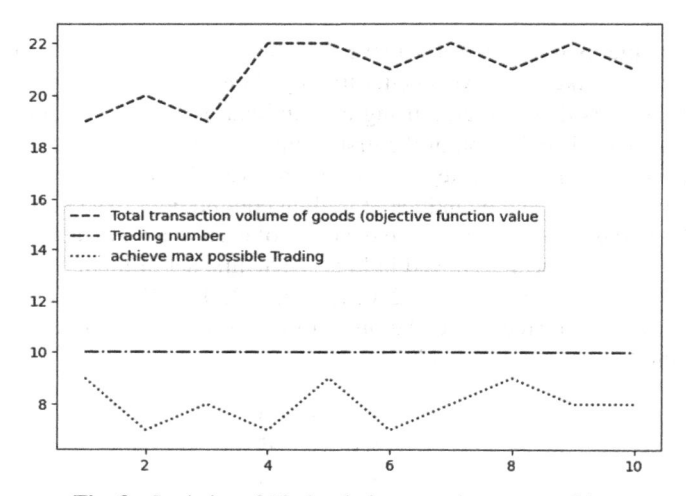

Fig. 3. Statistics of 10 simulation experiments matching.

From the above simulation results, it can be seen that the overall performance of the algorithm matching results is excellent. With a weight of 0–5 random numbers, a total trading volume of around 20 commodities can always be achieved in the random model. All traders in the first 10 groups of random experiments reached trades, and there were two sets of non-all trades between groups 11 and 20. The total trading volume in the non-all trades situation slightly decreased, but still maintained a certain level. The number of traders reaching the maximum possible trading volume fluctuates around 7.5 and is not affected by the trading volume.

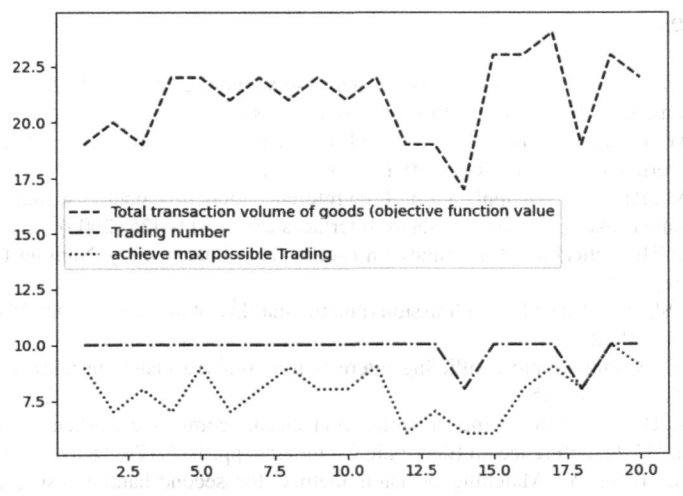

Fig. 4. Statistics of 20 simulation experiments matching.

6 Conclusion

The results obtained by the algorithm have a strong dependence on the model itself, and the number of transactions and matching situations are to some extent constrained by the specific holdings of the trader's portfolio. Secondly, there is no significant correlation between the number of transactions reached and two important reference parameters - the total trading volume of the commodity and the number of traders reaching the maximum possible trading volume. In non-extreme circumstances, both will remain to fluctuate within a certain range. Overall, the method proposed in this article can ensure the trading volume of goods and customer satisfaction under the assumption of a random market, causing both to fluctuate at a high level.

With the rise of e-commerce, people's shopping is becoming increasingly frequent, and secondary transactions will also become more common in the future. With the increasing variety of trading items, the application demand for portfolio trading is becoming increasingly apparent. The electronic combination trading platform not only provides convenience for everyone but also avoids waste and achieves full utilization of goods. The topic of this article is to made some research on the digitization, popularization, and efficiency of portfolio trading market, and proposed new insights in the design of portfolio trading mechanisms and solving methods. The method in this paper performs well in the portfolio trading market, plays a positive role in strengthening information symmetry, speeding up information circulation, and stabilizing the number of transactions. It proposes a new idea for the modeling and solving of portfolio transactions in the research of matching problems, and provides materials and references for future academic research.

References

1. Bhattacherjee, A.: Acceptance of e-commerce services: the case of electronic brokerages. IEEE Trans. Syst. Man Cybern. **30**(4), 411–420 (2000)
2. Sim, K.M., Chan, R.: A brokering protocol for agent-based e-commerce. IEEE Trans. Syst. Man, Cybern. Part C (Appl. Rev.), **30**(4), 474-484 (2000)
3. Blinov, M., Patel, A.: An application of the reference model for open distributed processing to electronic brokerage. Comput. Stand. Interfaces **25**(4), 411–425 (2003)
4. Jiang, X.: Theoretical and Case Study on E-commerce Intermediary. Nanjing University of Technology (2006)
5. Gale, D., Shapley, L.: College admissions and the stability of marriage. Amer. Math. Monthly **69**(1), 9–15 (1962)
6. Roth, A.E.: Common and conflicting interests in two-sided matching markets. Eur. Econ. Rev. **27**(1), 75–96 (1985)
7. Segev, A., Beam, C.: Brokering strategies in electronic commerce markets. In: Proceedings of the 1st ACM Conference on Electronic Commerce, pp. 167–176. Denver (1999)
8. Liang, H., Jiang, Y.: Matching decision method for second-hand housing combination transactions. Syst. Eng. Theory Pract. **35**(02), 358–367 (2015)
9. Jiang, Z., Fan, Z., Wang, D.: Multi-attribute commodity transaction matching problem with fuzzy information and unseparable demand in electronic intermediaries. Syst. Eng. Theory Pract. **31**(12), 2355–2366 (2011)
10. Wang, H., Wang, T., Xie, J.: Intelligent buying and selling interaction model. J. Comput. Sci. **26**(9), 1190–1195 (2003)
11. Tewari, G., Youll, J., Maes, P.: Personalized location-based brokering using an agent-based intermediary architecture. Decis. Support. Syst. **34**(2), 127–137 (2003)
12. Jung, J., Jo, G.: Brokerage between buyer and seller agents using constraint satisfaction problem models. Decis. Support. Syst. **28**(4), 293–304 (2000)

The Impact of "Three Arrows" Policies on China's Real Estate Market: An Event Study

Zixuan Wang[1], Yangjie Jin[2(✉)], and Jianuo Su[3]

[1] School of Economics and Management, Wuhan University, Wuhan 430072, China
[2] Faculty of Science and Technology, Beijing Normal University-Hong Kong Baptist University United International College, Zhuhai 519087, China
r130018025@mail.uic.edu.cn
[3] School of Business, Macau University of Science and Technology, Macau 999078, China

Abstract. China's economy has been sluggish in the wake of the COVID-19 pandemic, and consumer confidence has plummeted, leading to a gradual decline in the country's property sector. Plus, with the tightening of financing policies in previous years, numerous real estate enterprises have encountered financing difficulties and even risk bankruptcy. China must face up to the challenges of reviving its property sector. This study first summarizes China's real estate industry trends and policies in recent years. Then selects six real estate enterprises according to the "three arrows" policies (respectively published on November 21, November 23, and November 28, 2022) of real estate financing in the financial Article 16 issued by the government on November 11, 2022. Through event analysis, we find that the three-arrow policy issued by the government had a positive impact on the revival of the real estate industry.

Keywords: "Three Arrows" Policies · Real Estate Market · Financial Support · Event Study

1 Introduction

1.1 China's Real Estate Market

China's Real Estate Prices. Housing prices in China have risen yearly for the last ten years before decreasing slightly by around 3.21% in 2022. The housing price-to-capita disposable income ratio remains at a high level of 11 or more, and the housing leverage ratio remains high (Figs. 1 and 2).

Sales Status of Real Estate Enterprises. China's real estate demand market has been sluggish in the past two years. Figures 3 and 4 show a consistent trend of change in commercial housing sales volume and sales area: since July 2021, sales volume and sales area have declined compared to the same period of the previous year. 24.3% fewer sales areas and 26.7% fewer sales volume were recorded in 2022 than in the same period last year, bringing China's real estate market to a freezing point.

Fig. 1. Average price of commercial housing.

Fig. 2. Housing price-to-income ratio.

Fig. 3. Sales volume of commercial housing.

Inventory and Development Status of Real Estate Enterprises. Figure 5 shows that since July 2021, the area of commercial housing for sale in China has continued to rise year-on-year, and the growth rate reached the maximum of 14.9% in February 2023. The unsalable commercial housing has led to escalating inventory pressure on real estate enterprises, thus increasing cash flow pressure on real estate enterprises in the past two years. In addition, the construction starts also showed a decreasing trend affected by factors such as the slumping demand market and financial pressure.

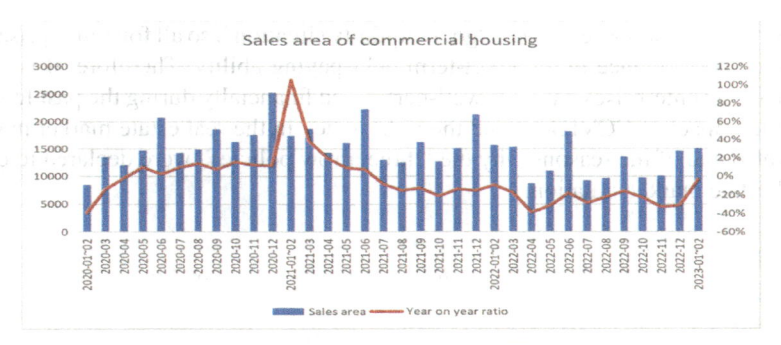

Fig. 4. Sales area of commercial housing.

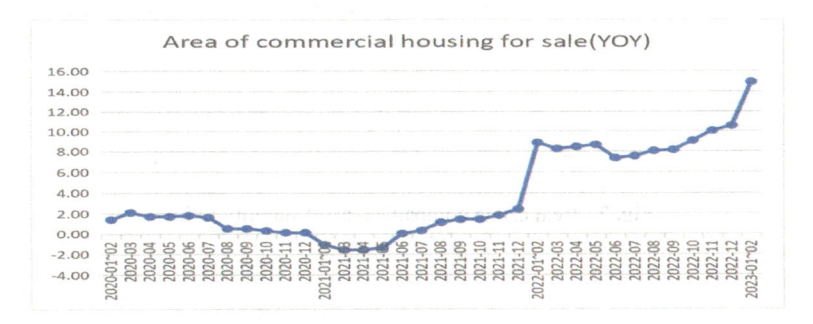

Fig. 5. Area of commercial housing for sale.

Fig. 6. Construction starts.

1.2 The Financial Condition of Real Estate Enterprises

The diagrams above are the companies' asset and liability ratio and the current ratio; these two financial indicators reflect the enterprises' ability to long-term and short-term debt paying. From Fig. 7, the data referring to all the companies' asset and liability ratios being much higher than 60%, which considers the "healthy financial condition line," so there may exist risks about companies' liquidity or problems related to cashflows. Also, Fig. 8 concludes that all those enterprises' current ratios are higher than one but lower than 2%, which is supposed to be a "good liquidity situation", so all four enterprises have an average performance in the short-term debt-paying ability. Therefore, it is evident that real estate enterprises have not well-performed financially during the past few years due to the impact of COVID-19 and the tight policy in the real estate market in China. That is also one of the reasons why the "three arrow policies" were declared to change the real estate market situation.

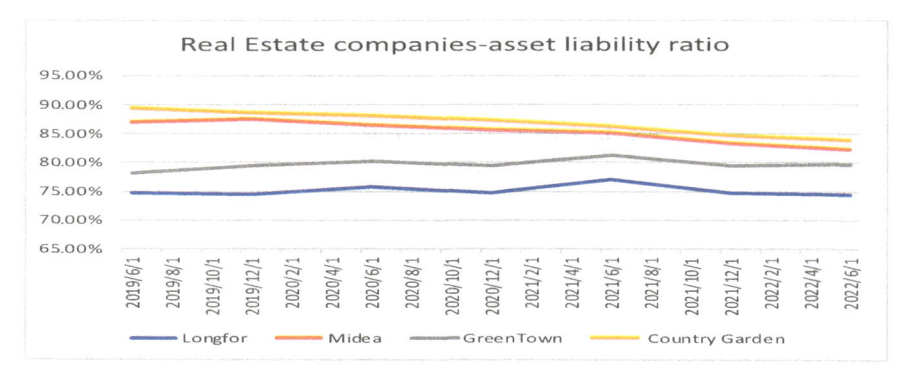

Fig. 7. Real estate companies' asset-liability ratio.

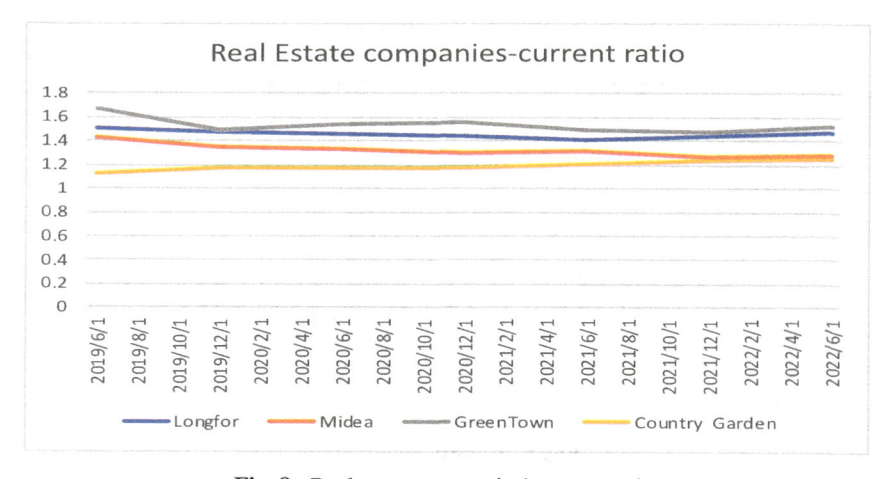

Fig. 8. Real estate companies' current ratio.

1.3 Policy Background

Overview of Real Estate Policies. Table 1 shows the major policies of China's real estate in the past five years. The leverage ratio of the household sector in some Chinese cities has risen rapidly, and the debt ratio of a large proportion of households has reached unsustainable levels. About half of the new savings resources were invested in the real estate sector recently. Accordingly, in 2016, the government set a tone that "houses are for living in, not for speculation.", which has guided the formulation of real estate policies since then. In addition, it points out that the excessive financing of the real estate industry squeezes the credit resources of other sectors and encourages real estate speculation, which makes the bubble problem more serious. After that, China's real estate financing has been tightened overall. In addition to bank loans and corporate bonds as the main financing channels, real estate enterprises' equity financing, ABS issuance, real estate funds, asset management financing, and so on have also been tightened (Table 2).

Table 1. Overview of significant real estate policies in China.

Date	Content of real estate policies
12/2016	The government proposed the tone of the real estate industry that ' the house is used for living, not for speculation.'
06/2019	China Banking and Insurance Regulatory Commission proposed real estate deleveraging
08/2020	The government issued a new real estate ' three red lines ' financing rules
12/2020	The Central Bank and the China Banking and Insurance Regulatory Commission issued a real estate loan concentration management approach
09/2021	The central bank's regular meeting set the tone of " two maintenance ": to maintain the healthy development of the real estate market, safeguard the legitimate rights and interests of housing consumers
11/2022	The central bank issued 16 financial support real estate rules. Support the real estate industry through the "three arrows" of real estate financing-credit financing, bond financing, and equity financing

Table 2. Overview of "three arrows" policies.

Date	"Three arrows" policies
11/11/2022	Notice on Doing a Good Job in the Current Financial Support for the Steady and Healthy Development of the Real Estate Market (referred to as the "Financial Article 16")
21/11/2022	"First arrow" -- credit financing support
23/11/2022	"Second arrow" -- bond financing support
28/11/2022	"Third arrow" -- equity financing support

Banks were eager to "close their umbrella" due to the "three red lines" policy of financing real estate enterprises, management of mortgage concentration, and recurrent outbreaks of the COVID-19 epidemic, banks were eager to "close their umbrella," leading to the real estate enterprise thunder explosion. Until the second half of 2021, credit policies were moderately corrected to maintain the real estate market's health, but the effect was limited. In 2022, China's real estate market experienced unprecedented challenges, including a sharp decline in commercial housing sales and frequent debt crises of real estate enterprises. To stabilize the property market, the central government has frequently released positive signals and strengthened policies from supporting the demand side to supporting the enterprise side. In November 2022, the central bank officially issued 16 measures of financial support for real estate. It continuously issued the "three arrows" policies on financing to improve the liquidity of real estate enterprises through credit, bonds, and equity, providing the most vital support for real estate enterprises' funding since the policy tightening and firing the first shot in the housing recovery.

In addition, regarding interest rate policy, China has implemented a more flexible and relatively loose monetary policy after the epidemic. Especially in 2022, to promote economic recovery, the central bank has adopted measures to reduce interest rates and reserve ratios to promote the steady growth of total monetary credit and maintain a steady decline in corporate synthetic financing costs. The one-year LPR was down five basis points in December 2021 and down ten basis points in January and August 2022, respectively. Five basis points reduced the 5-year loan prime rate in January and 15 basis points in May and August, respectively. However, since the reduction is not substantial, the residents ' purchasing power is out of line with the high housing price, and the financing threshold of housing enterprises has not been lowered, the central bank's reduction of LPR has not significantly boosted the real estate stock market.

Introduction of "Three arrows" policies. The "first arrow" mainly shows that financial institutions increase credit to real estate enterprises aimed at financial institutions to provide long-term, moderate credit funds of financial institutions to provide long-term cost.

The **"second arrow"** mainly supports housing enterprises to issue bonds before the end of November, which is aimed at helping private enterprises to issue bonds to support private enterprise bond issuance.

The **"third arrow"** mainly supports restoring the equity financing function of housing and housing-related enterprises. There are three main impacts of the "third arrow". Firstly, it helps resumption of mergers, acquisitions and reorganizations of listed companies involved in housing and supporting financing. Secondly, it actively plays the role of private equity investment funds. Lastly, it will resume the refinancing of listed housing enterprises and housing-related listed companies.

1.4 Research Purpose and Significance

This paper sorts of out relevant literature and summarizes the intervention rules of macro policy events on stock prices. Based on that, we study the impact of financing policies on the stock prices of real estate enterprises and banks.

For investors, in the face of major macro policy events, help them timely adjust the investment direction and strategy and find potential investment opportunities. By observing the effect of financing policies on real estate enterprises and banks' stock prices, this research can assess whether financing policies have played a positive role in the real estate and banking industry, then provide helpful advice for policymakers.

2 Literature Review

2.1 Event Study

Dolley is the introducer of the Event study [1]. She used an event study to explore the price effect of a stock split. Ball and Brown [2] studied the informativeness of earnings by event study used at present. Fama [3] studied the stock dividend effect. Brown and Warner [4] further perfected the event study and revised several statistical assumptions. Mackinlay A C and Campbell J Y [5] systematically combed the origin and development of event analysis and standardized it.

2.2 The Impact of Macro Policies on Stock Markets

Numerous studies have explored the impact of policy events on stock prices. For example, Baesel and Stein [6] argued that policy events are an important reason for the difference in stock returns. Pearce and Roley [7] concluded that there is a negative correlation between stock prices and unexpected changes in the money supply. Fleisher B [8] used the GARCH model to study and found that the government's intervention policy significantly affected China's stock market volatility. Sanjay, Marc, and Mukesh [9] used linear regression equations to analyze the impact of macroeconomic announcements regularly issued by the United States on the stock market and found that 17 reports significantly impact the stock market, but the other 6 have little impact. Suk-Joong, Michael, and Robert [10] found that predictable government policy information has little effect on the securities market, while unpredictable information would impact the securities market. Pincus [11] used the event study method to conclude that enacting the Sarbanes-Oxley Act significantly positively affects the stock market. Dooley and Hutchison [12] showed that the manufacturing and financial policies issued by the US government during the global financial crisis 2008 had a substantial impact on emerging nations' stock markets.

Lyu and Zhao [13] studied the effect of China's stock market price limits from the time and company size perspective. Wei [14] selected 12 policy events in China from 1992 to 2000 to analyze the efficiency of macro policies and concluded that China's stock market policies have strong anti-market trend characteristics, and the stock market's advance reaction to policies is evident, indicating that some investors have grasped the policy information in advance. Xu and Li [15] studied the impact of macro policies on the Chinese stock market through an event study. They found a positive correlation between the continuous policies and the Chinese stock market, but the degree of explanation is small. And the stock market operation is greatly affected by short-term policy events. Hu [16] conducted a comparative study on the abnormal fluctuations of stock indexes in the Shanghai and Shenzhen stock markets and found that the abnormal volatility of stock indexes is consistent with the time point of relevant policies, and policy events account for the first reason for stock index fluctuations. Wang et al. [17] An event-by-event study was conducted to examine the over-reaction of the Chinese stock market to policy information and provided evidence that the Chinese stock market has already over-reacted to policy information, and thus the market has not yet reached semi-robust efficiency; Compared with other research results on return information, the influence of policy on the market is more important, reflecting the apparent characteristics of "policy market". Yan and Xiao [18] used ARCH models to test the impact of policy events on the parts of stock market return changes. Wei and Zhang [19] used an event study to test the impact of macro-control policies on listed real estate companies and showed that the effect of various policies on real estate companies' stock price fluctuation is different; price is the most sensitive to monetary policies. The larger the asset scale, the less the real estate enterprises with state-owned backgrounds are affected by policies; on the contrary, the stock prices of listed real estate companies in coastal areas, mainly focusing on residential development and sales, are more sensitive to policies. Zhang and Ye [20] specifically divided policy events into nine categories and established an econometric model to detect the impact of policy events on China's stock market. They found that policy events affected stock market volatility differently, with more significant effects in bull and bear markets. Han and Hong [21] showed that industrial policies could bring high excess returns to investors in the short term after their announcement but have no effect on returns in the medium and long term. Liu [22] tested the impact of three red-line financing rules on the stock prices of different kinds of A-share real estate enterprises through an event study.

2.3 China's Real Estate Financing Methods

Li et al. [23] on the basis of sorting out the influence of China's real estate regulation policies on the financing of real estate enterprises and the current financing situation, and with the help of the DEA-BCC model, found that the efficiency of China's real estate financing is on the low side, and the insufficient scale efficiency severely restricts the improvement of the financing efficiency of China's real estate enterprises. Hu [24], through studying the characteristics, financing status, and current financing channels of the real estate industry and analyzing Vance's good diversified financing strategies, believes that the research on diversified financing channel strategies of real estate enterprises should not only control the financing structure according to their actual conditions but also balance internal and external financing to improve their level. Li [25] used the corporate growth model to explore the influence of financing variables. He finds that in the short term, financing preferences have a significant impact on corporate growth prospects. Given the financing problems of China's listed real estate companies, his research suggests expanding the diversification of real estate financing methods through reform and accelerating the development of the bond financing market.

Yang [26] explored real estate enterprises' financing structure and concluded that the current financing structure is consistent with China's national conditions. Liu [27] focused on the changes in the financing methods of China's real estate industry under the monetary tightening policies and concluded that diversification is the trend in financing. Zhang [28] analyzed the financing methods and problems of real estate enterprises and found financing strategies that aim to promote the development of the real estate industry. Guan [29] discussed the process for real estate companies and advised them to use multistage financing to expand the total financing amount. Ran [30] used case analysis and comparative analysis to conclude that the deleveraging policy will deduct financing scale in the short term but optimize the financing structure in a long time. Wang [31] further discussed the existing problems of real estate enterprises' financing and aimed to improve the financing channels under micro-control. Zhang [32] studied the three red-line policies during the epidemic and analyzed the problems existing in the financing of real estate enterprises. Cao and Li [33] learned the policies of "houses are for living in and not for speculative investment" with a dual difference model applied, showing that the guidelines help restrict obtaining loans from traditional institutions but increase commercial credit. Liu [34] analyzed how to have a good financing ability in the background of high-leverage expansion.

2.4 The Link Between Banking and Real Estate Industries

Most previous studies argued that banking is strongly related to real estate. Using the TVP-VAR model, Song et al. [35] analyzed the dynamic evolution path of housing price volatility and systemic risks of the real estate sector and banks in China. The research showed that the risk transmission of China's real estate sector is mainly conducted from liabilities through bank credit, and the impact of the risk of the real estate sector on the risk transmission intensity has apparent structural mutations. Liu [36] used the standard deviation method, Fama-French 3-factor model, and dynamic factor Copula model to compare the stock returns of China's real estate companies and banks and found that the risk trends of the two markets are the same. The joint default probability of the two is closely related to the risk trend. Jiang [37] adopted the dynamic stochastic general equilibrium (DSGE) model with financial intermediation to analyze the impact of real estate market fluctuations on the macro economy and the transmission mechanism and concluded that the rise in housing prices would increase bank leverage, expand credit and accumulate financial risks. Financial shocks within banks cause economic volatility by worsening bank balance sheets and tightening credit constraints.

2.5 The Impact of "Three Arrows" on the Real Estate Market

Ye [38] said in an interview with a "securities journal" reporter that as the supply-side financing support policies are introduced gradually, part of the estate enterprise financing problems is steadily alleviated. But while the current supply-side policy "to force", namely the thawing risk policy dynamics, is more significant, demand-side policy optimization is worth looking forward to more. Chen [39] pointed out in the report that on December 9, the real estate sector in the capital market continued to party A shares of Shenzhen Property A rose by the daily limit, while other stocks such as Joy City New Town Holding Vanke A Deep Room A rose. Hong Kong's stock real estate management and development sector has grown about 48%, A-share real estate ETF has increased more than 28%, and numerous stocks within the sector have doubled. Chang [40] mentioned in the report "The third arrow" is an essential measure to leverage our capital market's function actively. However, there is room for improvement in the normalization and compliance of listed housing enterprises, and it is expected that ensuring the delivery of buildings to improve the number of people's lives will be a crucial issue of business practice. At the same time, the audit requirements still need to be further evidence, and it is expected that the pressure of housing enterprises' equity financing issuance and sales end is also relatively large.

3 Methodology

The data analysis of this paper is based on an event study. Event study is a method of studying the impact of economic events on corporate value. The principle is to select a specific event, study the change in sample stock returns before and after the event, and then explain the impact of particular events on sample stock returns. The event study is based on the efficient market hypothesis that stock prices reflect all public information and investors are rational. Therefore, the Abnormal return can be calculated by eliminating the average return estimated by assuming that the event has not occurred in the actual return of the sample stock. The Abnormal return measures the degree of abnormal reaction of the stock price to the event and helps judge whether the stock price volatility is related to the event.

The abnormal return model in previous literature is mainly a market model. This paper uses the market model to examine abnormal returns by comparing whether a significant difference exists between returns in the estimation window and event window. The market model is presented as follows:

$$R_{i,t} = \alpha_i + \beta_i R_{mt} + \varepsilon_{i,t} \tag{1}$$

$$NR_{i,t} = \alpha_i + \beta_i R_{mt} \tag{2}$$

$$AR_{i,t} = R_{i,t} - (\alpha_{i,t} + \beta_{i,t} R_{mt}) \tag{3}$$

where $NR_{i,t}$ is the average return, $AR_{i,t}$ refers to the abnormal return, which is part of $R_{i,t}$ that excludes the average return and is usually represented by $\varepsilon_{i,t}$, $R_{i,t}$ is the actual return in the event window, α_i, β_i are estimated using the estimation window data.

The cumulated abnormal return of company i in the period of $[t_1, t_2]$ is calculated at the formula (4):

$$CAR_i(t_1, t_2) = \sum_{t=t_1}^{t_2} AR_{i,t} \tag{4}$$

The cumulative average abnormal return can be calculated by averaging CAR over all firms that are subject to the same event or type of event, as shown in formula (5):

$$CAAR_i(t_1, t_2) = \frac{1}{N} \sum_{i=1}^{N} CAR_i(t_1, t_2) \tag{5}$$

Further hypothesis testing is based on the results of CAR or CAAR. The null hypothesis is that "the event has no impact on the stock price"; that is, CAR in the event window should satisfy (Fig. 6):

$$CAR_i(t_1, t_2) \sim N(0, t\sigma_i^2) \tag{6}$$

This paper uses Z-test. If the test result is significantly different from 0, the null hypothesis will be rejected, indicating that the event significantly affects the stock price. Z-sore is calculated as:

$$Z_{CAR} = \frac{CAR_i(t_1, t_2)}{\sqrt{t\sigma_i^2}} \tag{7}$$

$$Z_{CAAR} = \frac{CAAR(t_1, t_2)}{\overline{\sigma}\sqrt{t}/\sqrt{N}} \quad (8)$$

when $\alpha = 0.05$, the standard error band is:

$$(-Z_{\alpha/2} \times \frac{1}{\sqrt{N}} \times \overline{\sigma} \times \sqrt{t}, Z_{\alpha/2} \times \frac{1}{\sqrt{N}} \times \overline{\sigma} \times \sqrt{t}) \quad (9)$$

where t is the number of days since the beginning of the event window, $\overline{\sigma} = \sqrt{\frac{1}{N}\sum_{j=1}^{N}\sigma_j^2}$, σ_j^2 is the variance of each firm in the estimation window. If CAR exceeds the range of confidence interval, it is considered that the null hypothesis can be rejected at the confidence level of α; that is, the study event impacts the stock price.

4 Data Analysis

4.1 Event Definition

The research chooses November 11, 2022, as an event at which the Central Bank and China Banking and Insurance Regulatory Commission jointly issued the Notice on Doing a Good Job in the Current Financial Support for the Steady and Healthy Development of the Real Estate Market ("Financial Article 16") (Table 3).

Table 3. Event definition.

Event	November 11,2022
Estimation Window	January 4,2021-October 20, 2022
Event Window	November 1,2022-December 23,2022 [−8, 30]

The event window is chosen from November 1,2022-December 23,2022, including the "Three Arrows" event.

4.2 Sample Selection

The research chooses Shanghai Composite Index as a reference value for studying A-shares and the Hang Seng Index as a reference value for studying Hong Kong stocks.

The data of the enterprises which have been selected for the research analysis involve six representative real estate companies in China. They are Vanke, Country Garden, Longfor, Green Town Group, China's top ten large-scale enterprises in the real estate market. Midea Real Estate represents innovative and technological companies that proliferated in the current years, and Radiance represents a minor enterprise in China's real estate industry.

Based on Table 4 which showed the rank of credit financial support provided by financial institutions, we selected the top 9 banks to study the impact of three arrows

Table 4. Bank credit ranking.

Bank	Line of credit	Bank	Line of credit
ICBC (Industrial and Commercial Bank)	655 billion	Bank of Communications	120 billion
Shanghai Pudong Development Bank	530 billion	Ping And Bank	50 billion
CIB	440 billion	Bank of Shanghai	40 billion
postal savings bank	280 billion	China Guangfa Bank (Not listed)	30 billion
Bank of China	220 billion	Shanghai Rural Commercial Bank	20 billion

on them, respectively ICBC, Shanghai Pudong Development Bank, CIB, Postal Savings Bank, Bank of China, Bank of Communications, Ping and Bank, Bank of Shanghai, Shanghai Rural Commercial Bank.

To better study the impact of the "Three Arrows" policies on the whole real estate enterprise, we choose the SSE Real Estate Index, which includes all the stocks listed on the Shanghai Stock Exchange in the industry, reflecting the boom of the whole real estate industry and the overall trend of stock prices.

All data is taken from Wind and iFinD. For each stock, however, we calculate the daily return using the everyday closing price and perform event analysis using the individual stock's return as the dependent variable and the market's return as the independent variable.

4.3 Empirical Results

The null hypothesis of this paper assumes that the real estate financing support policy does not affect the stock prices of real estate enterprises and commercial banks. The test results are as follows:

Figure 9 shows that in [-8,0] CAR has been on a downward trend; after the event, CAR has a brief rise, but not highly significant, indicating that Jinhui Holdings Co. Ltd has little affected in the whole period of "Three Arrows" probably because the second arrow's bond credit support is only 2 million, which is the least among all the real estate enterprises. But after [18, 30] Jinhui Holdings Co.Ltd had an upward trend after the release of the three arrows, it temporarily stimulated consumer confidence in the company.

Figure 10 shows that the property has had a significant positive impact since issuing Financial Article 16 on November 11. It has been rising steadily and out of the event window. On November 23, when the "Second Arrow" (bond financing support) was released, CAR significantly increased, indicating that bond financing support most obvious help the company. In short, it shows that the "Three Arrows" have considerably supported and positively impacted this property.

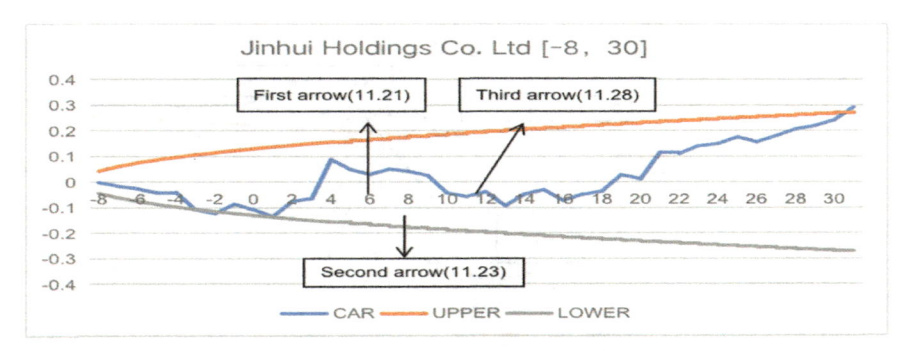

Fig. 9. CAR of Jinhui Holdings Co. Ltd.

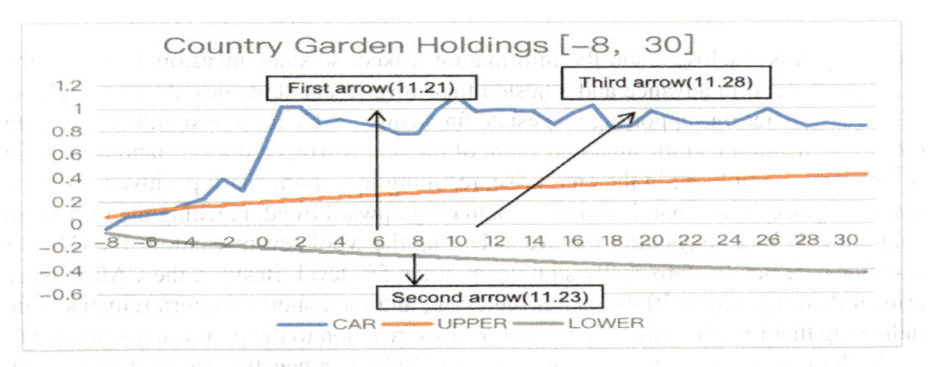

Fig. 10. CAR of Country Garden Holdings.

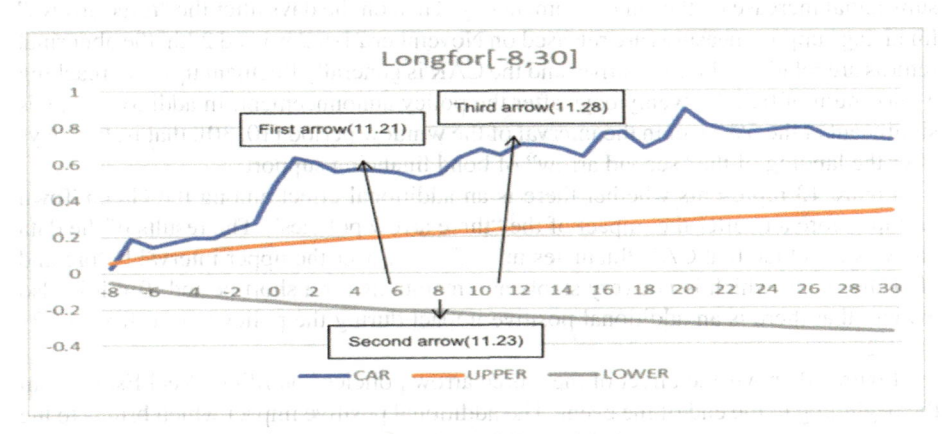

Fig. 11. CAR of Longfor.

According to the analysis results in Fig. 11–12, in the window of [−8, − 1], the CAR of Longfor has been positive. This may be because the National Association of Financial Market Institutional Investors held a meeting to discuss relevant matters before

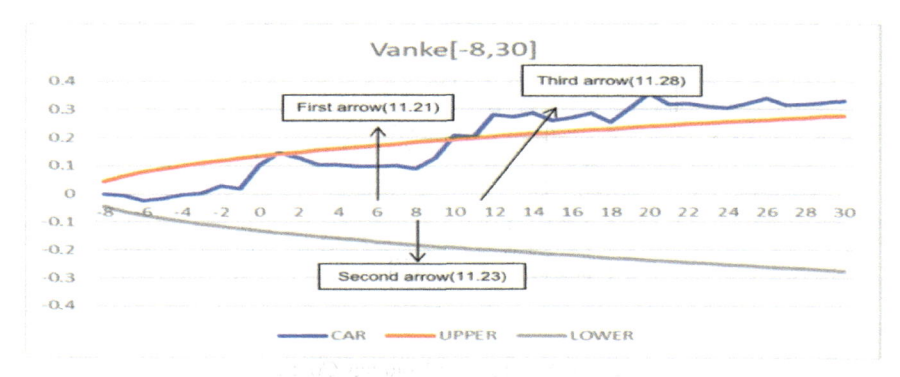

Fig. 12. CAR of Vanke.

the policy was disclosed, and the information leaked, so some investors predicted the stock price trend in advance and adjusted their investment strategies. After the release of the 16 policies on supporting real estate financing, the CAR has a significant jump to 0.6319, indicating that the announcement of the policy triggered a substantial increase in investors' confidence in the enterprise, resulting in a short, sharp positive impact on the stock price. After that, it shows a fluctuating upward trend, reaching the maximum value of 0.8939 20 days after the event. During the whole event window, the CAR of Longfor is basically statistically significant at the 5% level. Besides, the CAR is more critical than 0.5 within 30 days after the event, and the abnormal return remains high, indicating that Longfor has a significant positive reaction to the policy announcement.

In the window of $[-8, -3]$, the CAR of Vanke is a negative value close to zero. Three days before the policy is released, the CAR turns adverse to positive, and there is a substantial increase on the announcement day. Then on the days after the "three arrows" financing support measures are released on November 21st, 23rd and 28th, the abnormal returns are relatively large positive, and the CAR is generally fluctuant upward, reaching a maximum of 0.3579 twenty days after the policy announcement. In addition, CAR is significant at the 5% level in the interval of the window period [10, 30], that is, two days after the landing of the "second arrow" of bond financing support.

Figure 13 represents whether there is an additional effect among the Green Town Group before and after the impact of the "three arrow policies". The results of the data analysis conclude that CAR fluctuates up and down over the upper interval before and after the event, which is not very stable and maintains for a short period. But it is also evident that there is an additional positive impact during the policy period from 11.21 to 11.28.

Figure 14 shows the effect of the "three arrow policies" on Midea Real Estate from the beginning to the end of the event. The additional positive impact which brings to the enterprise exists for an extended period from the beginning of the event. The CAR is rising rapidly quickly and will retain a stable high level in the coming days. The CAR of Midea Real Estate maintains a sustained upward growth trend, and it is significant to conclude that Midea Real Estate has achieved great positive benefits due to the influence of the "three arrow policies."

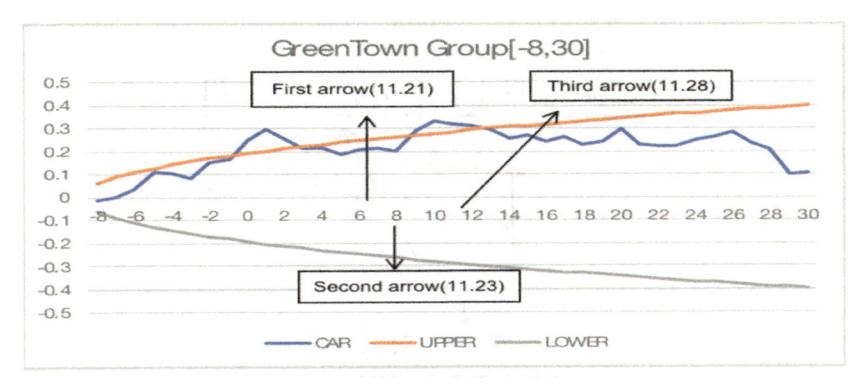

Fig. 13. CAR of Greentown Group.

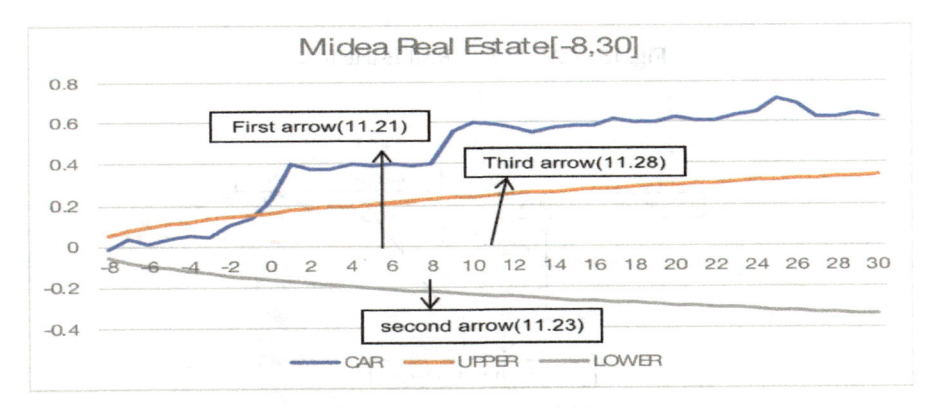

Fig. 14. CAR of Midea Real Estate.

In Fig. 15, the CAR of SSE Real Estate Index is a negative value approximately equal to zero in the window of $[-8, -1]$, and has been positive since the event date. It gradually increases in $[0,12]$, indicating that the positive impact of financing support policies on SSE Real Estate Index is rising. The CAR has remained stationary fluctuation after reaching a maximum of 0.1797 on the 12th. It's not significant at the 5% level during the event window. It shows that this round of financing support policies only has a weak positive effect on the stock price of the real estate industry in the short term. Further, compared with the above six real estate enterprises of large-scale and high-quality, the CAR of the SSE Real Estate Index in the event window is much smaller, indicating that the positive effect of this policy on the overall real estate industry in China is less than the impact on the top real estate enterprises.

According to the disclosed bank credit information, we select the stocks of the top 9 commercial banks in the credit amount to real estate enterprises and further calculate their cumulative average abnormal return in the event window. In Fig. 16, the CAAR generally shows an upward trend, and CAAR is positive within 30 days after the event, which is significant at the level of 5% for seven days after the event. Therefore, it can

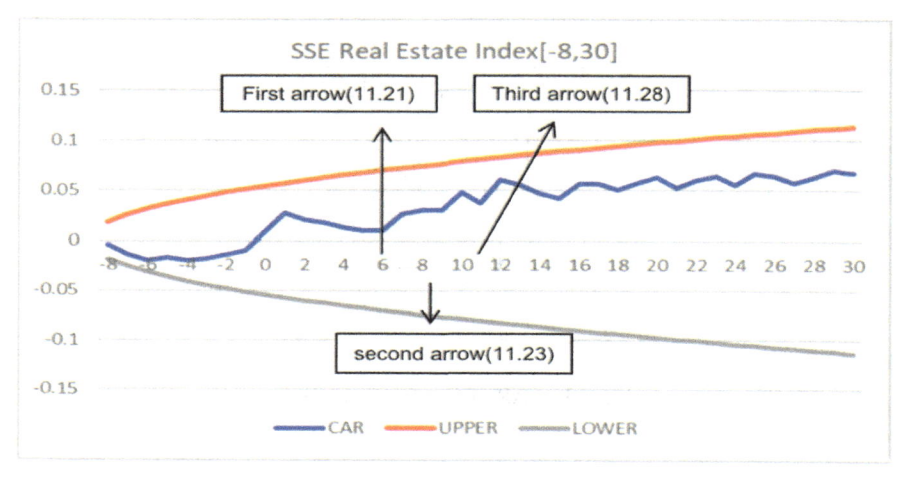

Fig. 15. CAR of SSE Real Estate Index.

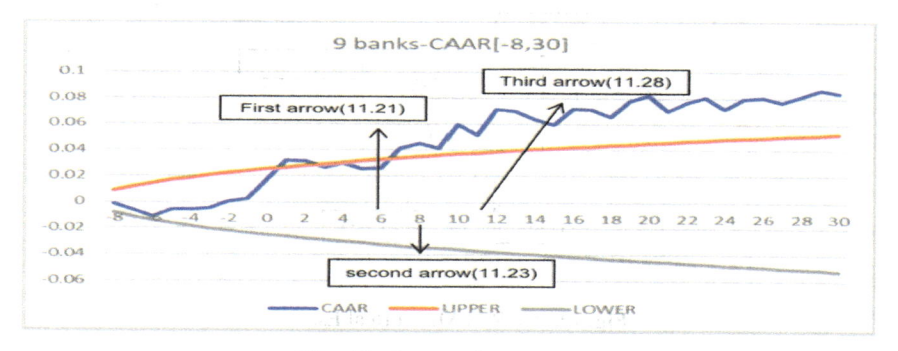

Fig. 16. CAAR of the 9 banks.

be concluded that the policy on financial support for real estate has indeed caused a continuous positive impact on the stock prices of commercial banks.

5 Conclusions

This study examines how real estate financial support policies affect the stock prices of real estate enterprises and commercial banks. The following conclusions can be drawn:

5.1 Influence of Real Estate Financial Support Policies on Real Estate Enterprises

The "three-arrow policies" have a generally positive impact on the whole real estate market due to the reason that the policy help promotes the financing progress and optimize the financing structure of real estate enterprises and of rare policy relaxation and incentive in the real estate market during the past ten years in China help to rebuild the lack of confidence in the whole market and lead to the goal of promoting the development of the real estate industry.

The real estate financing support policy impacted the Chinese real estate sector less than top-tier real estate enterprises. Large-sized real estate enterprises account for only 5% of all real estate enterprises nationwide, while small and medium-sized enterprises account for 95%. The policy prioritizes financing support for top-quality real estate enterprises, which has a more favorable impact on them than other small and medium-sized real estate enterprises.

5.2 Influence of Real Estate Financial Support Policies on Banks

Based on the historical data of the first five years, the correlation coefficient between the stock price of banking enterprises and the stock price of real estate enterprises is as high as 0.63, which shows that the trend of the two is strongly correlated. Based on empirical results and hypothesis testing, we conclude that real estate financial support policies also positively impact bank stock prices, which is consistent with the correlation between the two. Due to the strong correlation between banks and non-performing assets of real estate, the risks of China's real estate industry mainly affect bank risks through the debt transmission path and credit behavior [35]. During November 2022, with the warming of the real estate financing policy environment, the market's pessimism about the pressure on the asset quality of banks has weakened, the systemic risk of banks has been reduced, and the risk of house-related assets has been relieved, which are our main arguments of reasons for the stock market to repair the valuation of banks.

5.3 Suggestions and Improvement

Although the "Three Arrows" have helped the housing market recover, in the long run, there are still problems. For credit support and bond financing support, there is still considerable uncertainty about whether credit and bonds can be converted into financing. Because the housing enterprise financing support policy is mainly aimed at high-quality housing enterprises, the higher the quality of the housing enterprise to the intention of financing amount, thus in addition to a few of the risk exposure of enterprises, most housing enterprises are challenged to obtain financing. However, for equity financing support, investors' preferences match returns and risks and emphasize long-term investment principles.

To further promote the market recovery needs not only the financing support policy to resolve the risk but more essential is should also advance adjust even, encourage reasonable demand, release the related policy, promote the demand side, promote the enterprise's source of funds to improve, gradually form a virtuous cycle. For example, the government can additionally adjust and optimize restrictive measures such as "purchase limit and loan limit", and flexibly adjust the down payment ratio and stock mortgage interest rate is appropriate to reduce the pressure on home buyers to repay the loan.

References

1. Dolley, J.C.: Characteristics and procedure of common stock split-ups. Harv. Bus. Rev. **11**(3), 316–326 (1933)

2. Ball, R., Brown, P.: An empirical evaluation of accounting income numbers. J. Account. Res. **6**(2), 159–178 (1968)
3. Fama, E.F., Fisher, L., Jensen, M.C., Roll, R.: The adjustment of stock prices to new information. Int. Econ. Rev. **10**(1), 1–21 (1969). https://doi.org/10.2307/2525569
4. Brown, S.J., Warner, J.B.: Measuring security price performance. J. Finan. Econ. **8**(3), 205–258 (1980). https://doi.org/10.1016/0304-405X(80)90002-1
5. MacKinlay, A.C.: Event studies in economics and finance. J. Econ. Lit. **35**(1), 13–39 (1997)
6. Baesel, J.B., Stein, G.R.: The value of information: inferences from the profitability of insider trading. J. Finan. Quant. Anal. **14**(3), 553–571 (1979). https://doi.org/10.2307/2330188
7. Pearce, D.K., Roley, V.V.: The reaction of stock prices to unanticipated changes in money. J. Financ. **38**(4), 1323–1333 (1983)
8. Su, D., Fleisher, B.M.: Why does return volatility differ in Chinese stock markets? Pac. Basin Finan. J. **7**(5), 557–586 (1999)
9. Ramchander, S., Simpson, M.W., Chaudhry, M.K.: The influence of macroeconomic news on term and quality spreads. Q. Rev. Econ. Finan. **45**(1), 84–102 (2005). https://doi.org/10.1016/S1062-9769(03)00030-
10. Kim, S.J., McKenzie, M.D., Faff, R.W.: Macroeconomic news announcements and the role of expectations: evidence for US bond, stock and foreign exchange markets. J. Multinat. Financ. Manage. **14**(3), 217–232 (2004). https://doi.org/10.1016/j.mulfin.2003.02.001
11. Li, H., Pincus, M., Rego, S.O.: Market reaction to events surrounding the sarbanes-oxley act of 2002 and earnings management. Social Science Electronic Publishing
12. Dooley, M., Hutchison, M.: Transmission of the US subprime crisis to emerging markets: evidence on the decoupling–recoupling hypothesis. J. Int. Money Finan. **28**(8), 1331–1349 (2009)
13. Jihong, L., Zhenquan, Z.: The influence of fluctuation standstill on the rise and fall in stock market. Jilin Univ. J. Soc. Sci. **05**, 15–19 (2000). https://doi.org/10.15939/j.jujsse.2000.05.004
14. Yugen, W.: Statistical analysis on the policy effects on Shanghai's stock market. Stat. Res. **02**, 52–55 (2001). https://doi.org/10.19343/j.cnki.11-1302/c.2001.02.010
15. Xu, J., Li, Q.: An empirical analysis of the impact of macroeconomic policy on china's stock market. Econ. Res. J. (09), 12–21+95 (2001)
16. Jinyan, H.: Empirical analysis of policy effect, policy efficiency and policy market. Econ. Theory Bus. Manage. **08**, 49–53 (2002)
17. Chunfeng, W., Shuangcheng, L., Li, K.: Empirical study on the phenomenon of over-reaction and "policy market" in Chinese stock market. J. Northwest A&F Univ. (Soc. Sci. Ed.) **04**, 20–24 (2003)
18. Yan, W., Minzan, X.: Volatility of stock market yields and policy's impact. Contemp. Finan. Econ. **12**, 29–33 (2005)
19. Chenglong, W., Ding, Z.: Correlation between macroeconomic control on real estate market and fluctuations of real estate stocks——based on research of a share market. China Ind. Econ. **11**, 141–150 (2009). https://doi.org/10.19581/j.cnki.ciejournal.2009.11.014
20. Xinhong, Z., Chenglue, Y.: Empirical research on the policy effect of China ' s stock market. Macroeconomics **04**, 88–92 (2012). https://doi.org/10.16304/j.cnki.11-3952/f.2012.04.005
21. Qian, H., Yongmiao, H.: National industrial policy, asset price and investor behavior. Econ. Res. J. **12**, 143–158 (2014)
22. L, Mingya.: Research on the Impact of Three Red Line Financing Regulation on the Stock Price of Real Estate Enterprises (Master's Thesis, University of Electronic Science and Technology of China) (2022). https://kns.cnki.net/KCMS/detail/detail.aspx?dbname=CMFDTEMP&filename=1023413346.nh
23. Li, J., Liu, X., Zhao, Y. Based on the DEA analysis. China's real estate enterprises' financing efficiency in China's real estate, 539(18), 35–43 (2016). https://doi.org/10.13562/j.carolcarroll hina. Real estate 2016.18.004

24. Li, Z.: Financing methods and future financing trend forecast of chinese real estate companies. ranked, **495**(32), 29–31 (2018). 10.16266/j.carolcarrollnkicn11–4098/f2018.21.021
25. Hu, X.: Research on diversification strategy of China's real estate financing channels. China Small Medium-Sized Enterprises. **302**(01), 177–178 (2021)
26. Yang, H.: The innovative analysis of the financing structure of real estate enterprises. East China Econ. Manage. **22**(3), 66–70 (2008)
27. ZhiMin, L.: Analysis of real estate financing trends under monetary tightness policy. Finan. Econ. **12**, 36–38 (2011)
28. JianCheng, Z.: An analysis of the financing strategy of real estate enterprises in our country. Enterprise Reform Manage. **11**, 106–107 (2020)
29. Zhongzheng, G.: Research on the Choice of Financing Methods for Real Estate Companies Based on Regulatory Policies. Southeast University (2020)
30. Ting, R.: Research on the Financing Mode Innovation and Effect of Chinese Real Estate Enterprises Driven by the Deleveraging Policy——Taking Vanke as An Example (2021)
31. Xin, W.: Research on financing strategies of real estate enterprises under the background of macroeconomic regulation china's collective economy **17**, 71–73 (2021)
32. Xiang, Z.: Financing Strategies for Real Estate Enterprises under the "Three Red Lines Policy. Green Finan. Account. **09**, 30–32
33. Zhaowen, C.A.O., Qiuhong, L.I.: "The influence of "houses are for living in and not for speculative investment" policy on investment and financing of real estate enterprises. J. Chongqing Univ. Technol. (Soc. Sci.) **09**, 79–88 (2021)
34. Yuzu, L.: Research on the Influence of Macro-control Policies on the Financing Model of Real Estate Enterprises——Take Company A as an Example (2022)
35. Lingfeng, S., Hongyan, N., Zhilong, L.: Housing price fluctuation, implicit guarantee and banking systemic risk. Econ. Theory Bus. Manage. **03**, 16–26 (2018)
36. Juzhao, L.: Research on Trend and transmission characteristics between bank risk and real-estate risk: an empirical study based on China's stock market. Finan. Theory Pract. **01**, 28–38 (2022)
37. Zhenlong, J.: Real estate market fluctuations, effectiveness of macroprudential policy and two-pillar policy regulation. Stat. Res. **02**, 101–116 (2023). https://doi.org/10.19343/j.cnki.11-1302/c.2023.02.008
38. Ye, D.: Three Arrows" to help housing enterprises financing demand end policy "toolbox" still has space. Securities daily (A04) (2022). https://doi.org/10.28096/n.cnki.NCJRB2022.005255
39. Li, C.: Three arrows" power enterprise, dissolve the liquidity crisis. The securities times, 2022–12–10 (A03). DOI: 10.38329 / n.c. Nki NZJSB: 2022.005150
40. Chang, X.Y.: Housing enterprise financing to meet the "third arrow" investment bank to go all out at the same time frankly still have difficulties. Securities daily, 2022–12–08 (A04). DOI: 10.28096 / n.c nki. NCJRB. 2022.005254

Corporate Social Responsibility Disclosure Quality and Stock Price Crash Risk: Evidence from China

Minxing Zhu[✉]

Department of Finance, Zhongnan University of Economics and Law, Wuhan 430073, China
202021060074@stu.zuel.edu.cn

Abstract. In this paper we take China A-share listed companies from 2009 to 2019 as the sample and uses the fixed effects model to investigate the relevance between CSR disclosure quality and stock price crash risk. Specifically, the results show that: (1) There is a negative correlation between the disclosure quality and the stock price crash risk. (2) Under different financing constraints, there are important differences in the impact of disclosure quality on crash risk. In enterprises with higher financing constraints, the negative correlation between disclosure quality and future stock price crash risk will be weakened; (3) Compared to non-state firms, the inhibiting effect of CSR disclosure quality on crash risk is larger in state firms. Our work provides support for the positive impact of disclosure of CSR information on economic consequences, which is of great importance in stabilizing the stock market and promoting high quality economic development.

Keywords: Corporate Social Responsibility · Information Disclosure Quality · Stock Price Crash Risk · Financing Constraints

1 Introduction

1.1 Research Background

Recently, corporate social responsibility (CSR) has been widely concerned about. Surveys show that the number of companies disclosing non-financial information related to social issues is steadily increasing [1, 2]. China has implemented stricter disclosure requirements for social responsibility information for listed firms in recent years. Government explicitly state that listed companies should disclose their specific situations of undertaking and fulfilling social responsibility by the regulations and requirements of relevant departments. However, the current capital market is still imperfect, and information asymmetry hinders active interaction between enterprises and investors. Against this background, the public urgently hopes to enhance direct research on the CSR disclosure impact.

Stock price crash risk is an unexpected but rapid decline in stock price caused by cataclysmic crises in the financial market or public panic, which not only causes investors to suffer significant losses but also exacerbates market volatility and may even impact the real economy of the country. The information hiding hypothesis posits that the managers may conduct negative information management due to self-interest motives, resulting in a concentrated release of accumulated negative news that causes a negative impact on the stock price and ultimately crashes. CSR disclosure is a reflection of the interaction between enterprises and stakeholders, affecting external investors' perception and judgment of the company, and may strongly affect stock returns. Previous literature has shown that CSR disclosure directly reflects the company's fulfillment of social responsibility and can effectively alleviate information asymmetry between enterprises and stakeholders, increase mutual trust, and emphasize companies' competitive advantages [3–7].

However, there are still great differences in CSR disclosure quality among different enterprises, with overall low quality [8]. According to data from Rankins CSR Ratings, the average score for CSR disclosure of Chinese listed companies was between 40–45 points from 2015 to 2019. For example, in 2019, the highest score was 87 points, and the lowest score was only 15.72 points. Obviously, whether the quality of CSR information disclosed can reduce crash risk is worth studying.

In addition, financing constraints refer to the restrictions that companies face when financing from external investors. Financing constraints reflect different information disclosure environments and also reflect the difficulty of management manipulation of information disclosure. Companies with high financing constraints often have a higher extent of information asymmetry, and the agency problem is more severe. Therefore, the manipulation of social responsibility reports quality by management is more difficult to detect, thereby increasing their motivation [9]. At the same time, research has found that when companies face higher financing constraints, they prefer to cover up bad news through tone, which exacerbates the crash risk [10]. Based on this, introducing financing constraints and their influence on the relationship between the two will be conducive to better utilizing CSR disclosure and stabilizing the operation of the stock market.

1.2 Research Significance

The contribution of this article is threefold. First, by combining CSR disclosure quality, this paper adds to the literature on price crash risk. Prior research focused primarily on whether CSR or ESG would influence a firm's value or financial performance [11, 12]. Our study provides strong evidence that CSR disclosure is negatively correlated with crash risk, which in turn has a real impact on the financial market. Second, this work provides an in-depth analysis of moderating effects. Our results show that the ownership structure and funding constraints have a dampening effect on the negative correlation between the two. Third, the findings provide powerful evidence that is beneficial for the development of other emerging markets. Current research on CSR behavior and financial performance is primarily focused on developed economies. As developing countries become more involved in global social governance issues, however, quantifying the quality of information disclosure about social responsibility in emerging markets can provide new insights for research. In conclusion, our research is also practical for entrepreneurs and investors with an awareness of social responsibility. Governments are not only responsible for economic sustainability, but they should also be a moral obligation for all. The purpose of this work is to examine the positive role of CSR disclosure quality and to draw a positive feedback conclusion that corporate activities can bring stability to the financial market, providing a decision-making benchmark for corporate managers, investors, and regulators.

1.3 Research Methods and Findings

The CSR disclosure quality is derived from the scores of the "A-share Listed Company Social Responsibility Report Rating" issued by Rankins CSR Ratings. Consistent with prior research [13], the crash risk is calculated by the negative coefficient on the skewness of firm specific weekly returns and the asymmetric volatility of negative and positive stock returns. We use the fixed effect model, and robustness tests on alternative variables and the endogeneity of the sample, which supports the consistency of our study. We also analyzed the moderating mechanism of CSR disclosure, which shows that financing constraints will inhibit the negative correlation and differences in political resources caused by different ownership structures can lead to different relationships between CSR disclosure and the risk.

1.4 Structure of the Remaining Article

The remaining arrangement is organized as follows. Section 2 proposes literature review and hypotheses based on the explication of the construct. The methodology is described in Sect. 3, which includes the setting of econometric models, variable definitions, and data sources Sect. 4 presents the empirical analysis, including descriptive results, correlation analysis, regression analysis of benchmarks, and a series of moderation-effect analyses. Section 5 is the robustness test, which replaces the stock price crash risk measurement index and conducts tests for endogeneity via the Heckman two-stage approach. The research conclusion concludes with a summary and a further proposal of the theoretical significance and practical implications.

2 Literature Review and Hypothesis

2.1 Corporate Social Responsibility Information Disclosure Quality and Stock Price Crash Risk

Based on the framework of incomplete information rational expectations equilibrium and behavioral finance, relevant scholars constructed theoretical models at the market level to analyze the causes of crash risk. Caplin and Leahy proposed the "incomplete information hypothesis", showing that informed traders have more non-public information, while uninformed traders only know the original information of the stocks. The increased stock trading also brings information, and finally, the bad news is discovered, leading to a crash risk [14]. Hong and Stein proposed the "investor heterogeneous belief hypothesis", believing that in a market with short-selling constraints, investors have their information judgments about stock prices. Bullish investors hold more bad news, so they sell stocks hoping that bearish investors will buy them. Bearish investors continue to refuse to trade, while bullish investors keep lowering prices, causing a stock price crash [15]. Jin and

Myers began to shift their focus from the market level to the company level to study, pointing out that the crash risk at the company level is the probability of a significant negative deviation of individual stock returns from normal returns, and first proposed the "information hiding hypothesis", believing that the inherent root cause of the crash risk is the management's cover-up of negative information [16]. According to the "information asymmetry theory", there is a difference in the information that managers and investors have access to, especially since the diversification of information channels makes it impossible for investors to systematically grasp various information. Therefore, when the "scandal" that managers concealed erupts on a large scale in a very short time, it will cause dissatisfaction among external investors, who will sell a large number of stocks, causing the stock price to fall.

The CSR disclosure quality focuses on measuring the overall performance of enterprises and effectively alleviates information asymmetry. Zhang et al. found that enterprises with more readable CSR reports can better communicate with stakeholders about their legitimacy and adherence to social norms through easily understood language, which has significant value and relevance for investor decision making [17]. Kim et al. observing the potential effects of reputation and financial performance, also concluded that more readable corporate social responsibility reports can improve information transparency and establish trust with stakeholders [18]. Although Lee also pointed out that firms may use the CSR disclosure as a symbolic or greenwashing behavior, diverting stakeholder attention and scrutiny of their misconduct, thereby increasing the potential for corporate irresponsibility and subsequent risk of higher stock price crashes [19]. However, it is generally believed that the quality of CSR disclosure can measure various specific indicators in the categories of the company's environment, society, and corporate governance, reducing information asymmetry, alleviating investors' information disadvantage, enabling them to fully understand the company's development situation, and allowing the stock price to approach its intrinsic value, avoiding phenomena such as high stock prices and bubbles.

In addition, CSR disclosure quality is also beneficial in repairing the company's image for investors and demonstrating the company's sustainable development capabilities. Zhang et al. suggested that reputational damage from financial restatements can be partially repaired through higher quality CSR disclosures [17]. According to agency theory, managers of companies tend to hide negative news for their benefit. As negative news accumulates, however, it can result in a drastic decrease in the company's image, causing stock prices to fall sharply, and even triggering a stock market crash. High-quality CSR disclosure brings moral and reputation capital that can mitigate the impact of negative news on stock price and investments [20]. Additionally, Godfrey found that high-quality CSR disclosure represents good financial performance, and investors increase their tolerance and leniency towards the company in terms of both image and financial performance, attributing negative events to the managers' "unintentional" behavior, giving the company a buffer period to adjust their behavior and avoid a short-term stock price drop, reducing the risk [21]. In light of the above discussion, this article offers the hypothesis:

H1: CSR disclosure quality is significantly negatively correlated with stock price crash risk.

2.2 Financing Constraints

It is important to take into account the costs and financial state of the business before deciding to disclose. Darus et al. discovered that the more profitable a firm is, the more information it discloses about initiatives related to climate change [22]. Similarly, Lu and Abeysekera find that there is a positive effect of financial performance on the disclosure of CSR [23]. Al-Tuwaijri et al. investigated the interplay between information disclosure and economic performance, believing that firms with good economic condition tend to disclose some detailed environmental accidents and contingency plans [24].

At the same time, companies need financing to achieve smooth development and improve investment efficiency. Generally speaking, the more constrained financing is, the more challenging the firm is to obtain bank credit and, therefore, the stronger its willingness to obtain bank credit. Such companies have a stronger motivation to selectively disclose information and are more cautious in disclosing negative information because any increase in bank risk aversion caused by it is likely to affect their credit availability and may lead to a liquidity crisis, exacerbating financial risks and ultimately causing the company to fall into financial difficulties. In other words, companies with stronger financing constraints prefer to disclose negative information cautiously in order to obtain sustained and stable cash flows. If creditors do not discover the negative information that the firm has hidden and do not take corresponding actions, this will exacerbate the default risk caused by asymmetric information, and increase the crash risk. The literature on the level of funding constraints and corporate information disclosure has shown that greater funding constraints, which lowers the level of information disclosure, will increase the crash risk [22, 23]. In light of the above discussion, this paper proposes the second hypothesis:

H2: Holding other conditions constant, in firms with stronger financing constraints the negative correlation between CSR disclosure and the future crash risk will be weakened.

2.3 Ownership Structure

The direction of corporate disclosure is greatly influenced by its ownership and management structure [25]. Previous literature has produced inconsistent conclusions. Different types of ownership characteristics correspond to different production and operation objectives for enterprises. On the one hand, non-state-owned companies primarily aim to improve their business performance and maximize shareholder value, while state-owned holding companies shoulder certain political tasks in addition to improving business performance. Performance evaluation of state-owned enterprise executives is more diverse and not limited to corporate profits [26]. Their executives are more willing to undertake political responsibilities to achieve better promotion prospects. Therefore, state-owned holding companies often disclose more CSR information and reduce crash risk by improving the disclosure quality.

On the other hand, private enterprises lack close political connections and prefer to conduct substantive environmental improvement activities and actively disclose their environmental governance achievements to obtain political legitimacy and maintain good relations with the authorities. Bae found that non-state-owned enterprises are more willing to disclose CSR information to obtain legitimacy and economic benefits. As a result, firms with different ownership structures have different motivations for disclosure, which may lead to different relationships between CSR disclosure quality and crash risk [27]. In conclusion, findings from the existing literature are not unified. In this paper, we propose the competing hypotheses based on the above analysis:

H3a: The inhibitory effect of CSR disclosure quality on stock price crash risk is larger for state-owned holding companies compared to non-state-owned holding companies.

H3b: The inhibitory effect of CSR disclosure quality on share price crash risk is larger for non-state holding companies compared to state-owned holding companies.

3 Methodology

3.1 Data

This paper uses the scores of Rankins CSR Ratings (RKS) on companies' CSR reports from 2009 to 2019 as independent variables, and the crash risk data is selected as dependent variable. Other variable data corresponding to the same year were combined to form panel data for research. The reason for the end of the data in 2019 is that RKS mainly began to track and evaluate the ESG public information of CSI800 component stock companies from 2020. The data mainly comes from CSMAR and Wind. The following measures were taken for the collected sample: (1) excluding data with anomalies, and missing values were interpolated. (2) given that the financial industry has generally high debt characteristics, listed companies in the financial industry were removed. (3) considering companies with continuous losses may have an impact on the research, all ST, PT, *ST, and S*ST companies were removed. (4) to avoid the influence of IPO effects, samples of companies that went public in and after 2009 were excluded. (5) excluding samples where both earnings per share and net asset value per share are negative to obtain a sample of companies with normal operations. Finally, we obtain 433 sample companies and 4763 observations. In addition, to remove interference from extreme values, continuous variables less than 1% or greater than 99% are winsorized.

3.2 Variables

Dependent Variable. Drawing on related studies, we measure stock price crash risk (CRASHRISK) with NCSKEW and DUVOL [28, 29]. First, we regress the weekly returns of listed company stock, adjusted for market factors, to obtain the following equation:

$$r_{s,t} = \alpha + \beta_1 r_{m,t-2} + \beta_2 r_{m,t-1} + \beta_3 r_{m,t} + \beta_4 r_{m,t+1} + \beta_5 r_{m,t+2} + \varepsilon_{s,t} \quad (1)$$

In Eq. (1), $r_{s,t}$ is the weekly return of stock s in week t, adjusted for cash dividends; $r_{m,t}$ is the average weighted composite weekly market return, adjusted for cash dividends, in week t; and $\varepsilon_{s,t}$ is the residual, the portion of the stock's weekly return s that cannot be accounted for by the composite market return. The absolute value of $\varepsilon_{s,t}$ evaluates the risk.

Second, we take the logarithm of $\varepsilon_{s,t}$ in Eq. (1) to obtain the stock's weekly specific return:

$$W_{s,t} = ln(1 + \varepsilon_{s,t}) \qquad (2)$$

Finally, based on Eq. (2), we calculate NCSKEW and DUVOL.

$$NCSKEW_{s,t} = \frac{-n(n-1)^{3/2}\sum W_{s,t}^3}{(n-1)(n-2)(W_{s,t}^2)^{3/2}} \qquad (3)$$

In Eq. (3), $NCSKEW_{s,t}$ is a positive indicator, and the higher its value, the higher the stock price crash risk.

$$DUVOL_{s,t} = \ln\frac{(n_u - 1)\sum_{down} W_{s,t}^2}{(n_d - 2)\sum_{up} W_{s,t}^2} \qquad (4)$$

In Eq. (4), n_u and n_d are the numbers of weeks in which $W_{s,t}$ is greater or less than the average return in a year. The higher $DUVOL_{s,t}$ means the more $W_{s,t}$ tends to be negatively skewed.

Independent Variable. We calculate the CSR disclosure quality (denoted as CID) with the rating results of listed companies' social responsibility reports published by RKS, which adopts an original MCTI structured rating system to measure the content, technicality, and sector-specificity of social responsibility reports using an index method. Compared to other systems, the results of this system are more persuasive and applicable. A higher score in CSR means a better quality of corporate social responsibility disclosure.

Moderating Variables. The ownership structure (SOE) is divided according to the actual controlling shareholder. Assign a value of 1 if the sample enterprise is a state-owned enterprise, otherwise 0.

Financing constraints (KZ) are measured by the KZ index, which includes five aspects: operating cash flow (OCF), Tobin's Q ratio (TobinQ), leverage (LEV), dividend payout ratio (Dividends), and cash holdings (Cash) [30]. OCF/ASSET, Dividends/ASSET, and Cash/ASSET represent the ratios of operating cash flow, cash dividends, and cash balance to total assets, respectively. The larger KZ, the greater the financing constraints of the enterprise, and the calculation process is shown in Eq. (5).

$$KZ = -1.001909 \{*\} \text{ OCF/ASSET} + 3.139193 \{*\} \text{ LEV} - 39.3678 \{*\} \text{ Dividends/ASSET} \\ - 1.314759 \{*\} \text{ Cash/ASSET} + 0.2826389 \{*\} \text{ TobinqQ} \qquad (5)$$

Control Variables. We consider other factors that related to stock price crash risk, including the proportion of institutional investors' holdings (INS), leverage (LEV), return on equity (ROE), book to market ratio (BM), monthly turnover rate (TUR), average weekly return (RET) and the standard deviation of weekly returns (SIGMA).

3.3 Models

To verify H1, the following equation is constructed:

$$CRASHRISK_{s,t+1} = \alpha_0 + \alpha_1 CID_{s,t} + \alpha_2 INS_{s,t} + \alpha_3 LEV_{s,t} + \alpha_4 ROE_{s,t} + \alpha_5 BM_{s,t} + \alpha_6 TUR_{s,t} + \alpha_7 RET_{s,t} + \alpha_8 SIGMA_{s,t} + \Sigma YEAR_{s,t} + \Sigma IND_{s,t} + \varepsilon_{s,t} \quad (6)$$

where $CRASHRISK_{s,t+1}$ represents the crash risk of listed company s, measured by $NCSKEW_{s,t}$ and $DUVOL_{s,t}$. If α_1 is negative, then H1 is supported.

To test H2, the following equation is constructed:

$$CRASHRISK_{s,t+1} = \alpha_0 + \alpha_1 CID_{s,t} + \alpha_2 KZ_{s,t} + \alpha_3 CID_{s,t} \times KZ_{s,t} + \alpha_4 INS_{s,t} + \alpha_5 LEV_{s,t} + \alpha_6 ROE_{s,t} + \alpha_7 BM_{s,t} + \alpha_8 TUR_{s,t} + \alpha_9 RET_{s,t} + \alpha_{10} SIGMA_{s,t} + \Sigma YEAR_{s,t} + \Sigma IND_{s,t} + \varepsilon_{s,t} \quad (7)$$

To test the moderating effect of financing constraints, the interaction term $CID \times KZ$ are added to Eq. (7). If α_3 is positive, then its moderating role can be confirmed and H2 is supported.

To test research H3a and H3b, we divided the sample into two parts based on the structure of corporate ownership and Eq. (6) was regressed separately in different sample groups.

4 Empirical Analysis

4.1 Descriptive Results

Table 1 reports the mean and median values of NCSKEW are -0.369 and -0.319, and the mean and median of DUVOL are -0.253 and -0.255, indicating a relatively high risk of stock price crashes in the sample over the course of the study. With standard deviations of 0.87 and 0.465, we find significant differences across our samples. The average CID score is 39.631 compared to the maximum score of 78.498 and the minimum score of 13.071, suggesting that there are still differences between different firms and that the overall quality of CSR disclosure is low.

4.2 Correlation Analysis

As shown in Table 2, NCSKEW and DUVOL have a correlation coefficient of 0.868, which is significant at least at the 1% level, indicating that these two indicators are highly correlated and can be used simultaneously to measure risk. None of the correlation coefficients among the other variables are greater than 0.6, indicating that multicollinearity does not exist among the selected variables. At the 5% confidence level, the correlation coefficient between the CID and both NCSKEW and DUVOL is significant negative.

To further eliminate the possibility of multicollinearity, a VIF test was conducted and results show that the values were less than 5, indicating that the constructed model did not have a multicollinearity problem. In addition, considering that the panel data interval used in this study was only 11 years (2009–2019), which belongs to the type of "Large N small T" short panel data, the problem of "spurious regression" in this type of data is not significant and can often be ignored. Therefore, this study did not conduct a unit root test.

Table 1. Descriptive statistics [Owner-draw].

	Mean	Min	P25	Median	P75	Max	SD
NCSKEW	−0.369	−2.438	−0.743	−0.319	0.067	1.314	0.687
DUVOL	−0.253	−1.362	−0.559	−0.255	0.067	0.876	0.465
CID	39.631	9.749	30.825	37.131	46.350	78.498	13.071
SOE	0.713	0.000	0.000	1.000	1.000	1.000	0.453
KZ	1.364	−4.958	0.000	1.528	2.730	6.166	2.096
INS	0.522	0.018	0.386	0.545	0.672	0.921	0.210
LEV	0.494	0.078	0.357	0.506	0.636	0.890	0.189
ROE	0.084	−0.430	0.035	0.082	0.138	0.405	0.112
BM	1.370	0.114	0.514	0.919	1.772	7.016	1.304
TUR	−0.022	−0.853	−0.156	−0.013	0.108	0.792	0.283
RET	0.003	−0.014	−0.003	0.002	0.009	0.030	0.009
SIGMA	0.058	0.025	0.043	0.054	0.068	0.129	0.021

Table 2. Correlation matrix [Owner-draw].

	NCSKEW	DUVOL	CID	INS	LEV	ROE	BM	TUR	RET	SIGMA
NCSKEW	1									
DUVOL	0.868***	1								
CID	−0.033**	−0.034**	1							
INS	0.053***	0.047***	0.248***	1						
LEV	−0.084***	−0.079***	0.092***	0.087***	1					
ROE	0.083***	0.062***	0.0180	0.169***	−0.181***	1				
BM	−0.068***	−0.050***	0.252***	0.171***	0.550***	−0.193***	1			
TUR	−0.083***	−0.083***	0.00300	−0.075***	−0.00500	−0.056***	−0.045***	1		
RET	−0.166***	−0.203***	−0.081***	−0.033**	−0.0190	0.112***	−0.276***	0.475***	1	
SIGMA	−0.149***	−0.158***	−0.128***	−0.172***	0.0180	−0.119***	−0.295***	0.412***	0.518***	1

4.3 Baseline Analysis

Table 3 shows the basic regression results of CSR disclosure quality and crash risk. Compared with columns (1) and (2), when all control variables are taken into account, the regression coefficients for the CID are −0.002 and −0.001 in columns (3) and (4), which are significantly negatively correlated at the 5% confidence level, providing complete evidence that CSR disclosure can reduce the risk in the future. Hence, we prove H1.

4.4 Moderating Effect of Financing Constraints

Table 4 shows that the regression coefficient for CID remains negative and significant at the 5% level after the addition of the interaction term (CID × KZ) in columns (1) and

Table 3. Baseline results [Owner-draw].

	(1)	(2)	(3)	(4)
VARIABLES	NCSKEW	DUVOL	NCSKEW	DUVOL
CID	−0.001	−0.001	−0.002*	−0.001**
	(−1.31)	(−1.43)	(−1.92)	(−2.01)
INS			0.187***	0.128***
			(3.77)	(3.79)
LEV			0.023	0.003
			(0.32)	(0.06)
ROE			0.170	0.079
			(1.64)	(1.15)
BM			−0.066***	−0.038***
			(−5.72)	(−5.20)
TUR			0.015	0.036
			(0.30)	(1.08)
RET			−9.377***	−9.804***
			(−4.32)	(−7.17)
SIGMA			−7.249***	−4.129***
			(−7.60)	(−7.23)
Constant	−0.594***	−0.413***	0.059	0.033
	(−6.11)	(−6.48)	(0.52)	(0.46)
INDUSTRY& YEAR FE	YES	YES	YES	YES
Observations	4,762	4,762	4,762	4,762
R-squared	0.062	0.068	0.115	0.122

Robust t-statistics are reported in parentheses; *** $p < 0.01$, ** $p < 0.05$, * $p < 0.1$

(2), while the coefficient for CID × KZ is significantly positive. These results suggest that the efficiency of CSR disclosure is weakened and crash risk is increased in firms with strong financing constraints, which confirms H2.

4.5 Moderating Effect of Ownership Structure

To examine the moderating effect of ownership structure, we focus on the CID coefficient in the subgroup samples. As can be seen from the result in Table 5, CID has a negative relationship with both NCSKEW and DUVOL, but is significant only in state-owned enterprises, reflecting the motivation of state enterprises to reduce crash risk through more active use of environmental responsibility strategies than non-state enterprises.

Table 4. Moderating role of financing constraints [Owner-draw].

VARIABLES	(1) NCSKEW	(2) DUVOL
CID	−0.002**	−0.001**
	(−1.99)	(−2.09)
KZ	−0.008	−0.006
	(−1.19)	(−1.34)
CIDXKZ	0.001*	0.000**
	(1.92)	(2.00)
INS	0.183***	0.125***
	(3.68)	(3.70)
LEV	0.083	0.046
	(0.98)	(0.84)
ROE	0.120	0.043
	(1.06)	(0.57)
BM	−0.068***	−0.040***
	(−5.92)	(−5.42)
TUR	0.014	0.035
	(0.28)	(1.06)
RET	−9.283***	−9.737***
	(−4.28)	(−7.11)
SIGMA	−7.236***	−4.119***
	(−7.53)	(−7.15)
Constant	0.061	0.034
	(0.53)	(0.47)
INDUSTRY & YEAR FE	YES	YES
Observations	4,762	4,762
R − squared	0.116	0.123

Robust t-statistics are reported in parentheses; *** $p < 0.01$, ** $p < 0.05$, * $p < 0.1$

In order to reduce higher risk, state-owned enterprises pay more attention to the positive economic consequences of CSR disclosure and actively disclose quantitative or qualitative information. H3a is supported.

Table 5. Moderating role of corporate ownership [Owner-draw].

	(1)	(2)	(3)	(4)
VARIABLES	NCSKEW	DUVOL	NCSKEW	DUVOL
CID	−0.004**	−0.002*	−0.003	−0.002
	(−2.20)	(−1.81)	(−0.99)	(−0.90)
INS	0.119	0.125*	0.741***	0.374***
	(1.25)	(1.94)	(4.75)	(3.50)
LEV	−0.105	0.052	0.238	0.045
	(−0.75)	(0.55)	(1.05)	(0.29)
ROE	−0.174	−0.139	0.206	0.121
	(−1.28)	(−1.51)	(0.95)	(0.81)
BM	−0.042**	−0.010	−0.046	−0.042
	(−2.24)	(−0.79)	(−0.94)	(−1.24)
TUR	0.004	0.033	0.068	0.027
	(0.07)	(0.80)	(0.82)	(0.48)
RET	−10.779***	−11.125***	−10.738***	−8.042***
	(−4.64)	(−7.10)	(−3.31)	(−3.62)
SIGMA	−6.257***	−3.382***	−8.790***	−5.070***
	(−5.88)	(−4.71)	(−5.90)	(−4.96)
Constant	0.244	−0.025	−0.413	−0.157
	(0.73)	(−0.11)	(−1.48)	(−0.82)
INDUSTRY & YEAR FE	YES	YES	YES	YES
Observations	3,393	3,393	1,369	1,369
R-squared	0.102	0.114	0.138	0.139
	(0.07)	(0.80)	(0.82)	(0.48)
RET	−10.779***	−11.125***	−10.738***	−8.042***
	(−4.64)	(−7.10)	(−3.31)	(−3.62)
SIGMA	−6.257***	−3.382***	−8.790***	−5.070***

Robust t-statistics are reported in parentheses; *** $p < 0.01$, ** $p < 0.05$, * $p < 0.1$

5 Robustness Checks

5.1 Alternative Variables

Previous analyses only use continuous measures of NCSKEW and DUVOL. As a robustness check, we replace the results with the binary discrete measure of the probability of a stock price crash (CRASH). We define this variable as whether a stock experiences one or more weeks of crashes in one year. In this case, the firm is considered to be at risk of a stock price crash in that year and is recorded as 1, otherwise 0. We use Eq. (6)

to regress after substituting for the dependent variable, and report the result in Table 6. In columns (1) and (2), the correlation coefficients for the CID are both −0.001 and significant at the 1% level, indicating that the higher the quality of disclosure, the lower the risk of future stock price crashes, and H1 still holds.

Table 6. Alternative variables [Owner-draw].

VARIABLES	(1) CRASH	(2) CRASH
CID	−0.001***	−0.001***
	(−4.14)	(−4.04)
INS		0.040*
		(1.86)
LEV		0.014
		(0.47)
ROE		−0.033
		(−0.80)
BM		0.001
		(0.23)
TUR		−0.024
		(−1.13)
RET		−5.105***
		(−5.81)
SIGMA		1.054***
		(3.04)
Constant	0.124***	0.122**
	(2.67)	(2.31)
INDUSTRY & YEAR FE	YES	YES
Observations	4,692	4,692
R-squared	0.028	0.039

Robust t-statistics are reported in parentheses; *** $p < 0.01$, ** $p < 0.05$, * $p < 0.1$

5.2 Heckman Two-Stage Test

If the omitted variables that influence the CSR disclosure quality also affect the stock price crash risk, then the above regression results may represent spurious correlation. We uses the Heckman two-step test to overcome the endogeneity issue and the first step is to generate the dummy variable CSRD, which equals 1 only if CID is greater than the industry-year average. Using the regression results from the first stage, the ratio of inverse mills (IMR) is calculated, which is then incorporated into the second stage model for fitting. Despite the fact that the coefficient on IMR in the second stage regression of the Heckman model is significantly positive, the coefficient on CID is again significantly negative. This conclusion is still robust in Table 7.

Table 7. Heckman sample selection model [Owner-draw].

	(1)	(2)	
	1st Stage Probit Model	2nd Stage FE Model	
VARIABLES	CSRD	NCSKEW	DUVOL
LEV	0.153	0.782***	0.422***
	(1.19)	(3.94)	(3.11)
ROE	1.276***	5.307***	3.399***
	(7.10)	(3.86)	(3.61)
BM	0.152***	0.507***	0.335***
	(7.61)	(3.33)	(3.21)
CID		−0.003**	−0.002*
		(−2.54)	(−1.80)
INS		0.126*	0.123***
		(1.81)	(2.60)
TUR		0.058	0.045
		(0.83)	(0.95)
RET		−9.788***	−9.370***
		(−4.02)	(−5.62)
SIGMA		−9.653***	−4.764***
		(−9.49)	(−6.84)
IMR		6.325***	4.072***
		(3.75)	(3.53)
Constant	−0.158	−5.371***	−3.504***
	(−0.91)	(−3.54)	(−3.37)
INDUSTR & YEAR FE	YES	YES	YES
Observations	4762	2389	2389
R-squared	0.198	0.133	0.129

T-statistics are reported in parentheses; *** $p < 0.01$, ** $p < 0.05$, * $p < 0.1$

6 Conclusion

Responsible investing has received increasing attention from outside investors and inside managers in recent years. Enterprises need to maintain competitiveness in the fierce competition, actively engage in their social responsibilities while growing, combining their self-development with social advancement. Based on findings from the relevant literature and by summarizing and exploring emerging research perspectives, in this study, we examine the relationship between CSR disclosure quality and the stock price crash risk of publicly traded firms from 2009 to 2019, providing support for the mitigating effect between them. In particular, after controlling for other influential factors, we find that the higher the quality of CSR disclosure, the more positive governance signals can be transmitted to the outside world, generate a good reputational premium, and improve information transparency, which may counteract the harmful effects of "bad news". We also find that the financing constraint plays an important moderating role where strong financing constraints weaken the inhibiting effect of disclosure quality on crash risk. At the ownership level, this negative correlation of state holding companies is larger in magnitude. The above empirical results have passed robustness tests for key variable replacement and endogeneity problems.

From a policy perspective, the above verified evidence has the following implications: (1) For firms, if they can attach importance to improving the quality of CSR information disclosure, the financing environment, and relationships with investors, suppliers, and consumers, then high quality CSR disclosures may not only increase the transparency of corporate information but also constrain the risk of stock price crashes. (2) Investors should continually optimize their CSR investment strategy from an investor perspective and choose to invest in firms with higher social responsibility disclosure scores. It should scientifically and rationally assess the CSR disclosure quality to reduce the harm caused by stock price dips. (3) Relevant regulatory agencies should establish a robust mechanism for CSR disclosure and scientific implementation, to regulate its quality from the system level, and to effectively strengthen the scientific and perfect system of assessment, which is conducive to fostering stable development in China's stock market. We hope that this paper will eventually form a sound basis for further analysis.

References

1. Skouloudis, A., Evangelinos, K., Kourmousis, F.: Assessing non-financial reports according to the Global Reporting Initiative guidelines: evidence from Greece. J. Clean. Prod. **18**, 426–438 (2010)
2. Dhaliwal, D., Li, O.Z., Tsang, A., Yang, Y.G.: Corporate social responsibility disclosure and the cost of equity capital: the roles of stakeholder orientation and financial transparency. J. Account. Public Policy **33**, 328–355 (2014)
3. Gelb, D.S., Strawser, J.A.: Corporate social responsibility and financial disclosures: an alternative explanation for increased disclosure. J. Bus. Ethics **33**, 1–13 (2001)
4. Richardson, A.J., Welker, M.: Social disclosure, financial disclosure and the cost of equity capital. Acc. Organ. Soc. **26**, 597–616 (2001)
5. Shauki, E.: Perceptions on corporate social responsibility: a study in capturing public confidence. Corp. Soc. Responsib. Environ. Manag. **18**, 200–208 (2011)

6. El Ghoul, S., Guedhami, O., Kwok, C.C., Mishra, D.R.: Does corporate social responsibility affect the cost of capital? J. Bank. Finan. **35**, 2388–2406 (2011)
7. Taguchi, S., Kamijo, Y.: Disclosure Is a Gift That Encourages Trust and Reciprocity (2020). https://papers.ssrn.com/sol3/papers.cfm?abstract_id=3692382
8. Dahlsrud, A.: How corporate social responsibility is defined: an analysis of 37 definitions. Corp. Soc. Responsib. Environ. Manag. **15**, 1–13 (2008)
9. Winker, P.: Causes and effects of financing constraints at the firm level. Small Bus. Econ. **12**, 169–181 (1999)
10. He, G., Ren, H.M.: Are financially constrained firms susceptible to a stock price crash? Eur. J. Finan. **29**, 1–26 (2022)
11. Servaes, H., Tamayo, A.: The impact of corporate social responsibility on firm value: the role of customer awareness. Manage. Sci. **59**, 1045–1061 (2013)
12. Cho, S.J., Chung, C.Y., Young, J.: Study on the relationship between CSR and financial performance. Sustainability. **11**, 343 (2019)
13. Callen, J.L., Fang, X.: Institutional investor stability and crash risk: monitoring versus short-termism? J. Bank. Finan. **37**, 3047–3063 (2013)
14. Caplin, A., Leahy, J.: Business as usual, market crashes, and wisdom after the fact. Am. Econ. Rev. 548–565 (1994)
15. Hong, H., Stein, J.C.: Disagreement and the stock market. J. Econ. Perspect. **21**, 109–128 (2007)
16. Jin, L., Myers, S.C.: R2 around the world: new theory and new tests. J. Financ. Econ. **79**, 257–292 (2006)
17. Zhang, L., Shan, Y.G., Chang, M.: Can CSR disclosure protect firm reputation during financial restatements? J. Bus. Ethics **173**, 157–184 (2021)
18. Kim, Y., Park, M.S., Wier, B.: Is earnings quality associated with corporate social responsibility? Account. Rev. **87**, 761–796 (2012)
19. Lee, M.T.: Corporate social responsibility and stock price crash risk: evidence from an Asian emerging market. Manag. Financ. **42**, 963–979 (2016)
20. Godfrey, P.C., Merrill, C.B., Hansen, J.M.: The relationship between corporate social responsibility and shareholder value: an empirical test of the risk management hypothesis. Strateg. Manag. J. **30**, 425–445 (2009)
21. Godfrey, P.C.: The relationship between corporate philanthropy and shareholder wealth: a risk management perspective. Acad. Manag. Rev. **30**, 777–798 (2005)
22. Darus, F., Mohd Zuki, H.I., Yusoff, H.: The path to sustainability: understanding organisations' environmental initiatives and climate change in an emerging economy. Eur. J. Manag. Bus. Econ. **29**, 84–96 (2020)
23. Lu, Y., Abeysekera, I.: Stakeholders' power, corporate characteristics and social and environmental disclosure: evidence from China. J. Clean. Prod. **64**, 426–436 (2014)
24. Al-Tuwaijri, S.A., Christensen, T.E., Hughes Ii, K.E.: The relations among environmental disclosure, environmental performance, and economic performance: a simultaneous equations approach. Acc. Organ. Soc. **29**, 447–471 (2004)
25. Chau, G.K., Gray, S.J.: Ownership structure and corporate voluntary disclosure in Hong Kong and Singapore. Int. J. Account. **37**, 247–265 (2002)
26. Firth, M., Fung, P.M., Rui, O.M.: Corporate performance and CEO compensation in China. J. Corp. Finan. **12**, 693–714 (2006)
27. Bae, H.: Voluntary disclosure of environmental performance: do publicly and privately owned organizations face different incentives/disincentives? Am. Rev. Public Admin. **44**, 459–476 (2014)
28. Kim, J.B., Li, Y., Zhang, L.: Corporate tax avoidance and stock price crash risk: firm-level analysis. J. Financ. Econ. **100**, 639–662 (2011)

29. Hutton, A.P., Marcus, A.J., Tehranian, H.: Opaque financial reports, R2, and crash risk. J. Financ. Econ. **94**, 67–86 (2009)
30. Kaplan, S.N., Zingales, L.: Do investment-cash flow sensitivities provide useful measures of financing constraints? Q. J. Econ. **112**, 169–215 (1997)

An Analysis of the Effect of Social Medical Insurance on Family Consumption

Siyun Yuan(✉)

Department of Economics, University of Warwick, Coventry CV4 7FA, UK
u2126304@live.warwick.ac.uk

Abstract. Under the trend of the outbreak of the novel coronavirus in China, the social medical burden for people has become heavier. How to better solve the problem of medical treatment, increase family consumption and promote economic development has become a hot topic in the field of social economics. Therefore, the author aims to analyze the impact of social medical insurance on household consumption. Based on the data of the China Household Finance Survey (CHFS) of 2019, this paper empirically analyzes the influence mechanism of social medical insurance on household consumption by using the least square method and instrumental variable method from the microlevel. The results show that social medical insurance significantly affects family consumption, and the purchase of social medical insurance reduces family total consumption, family food consumption and family resident consumption. Heterogeneity tests indicate that families where the householder without employment enjoy a greater decline in consumption from purchasing social medical insurance compared to families where the householder has employment.

Keywords: Social Medical Insurance · Medical Insurance System · Medical Care · Family Consumption

1 Introduction

According to the 2021 China Statistical Yearbook released by the National Bureau of Statistics, the per capita expenditure on health care of Chinese residents increased from 1044.8 CNY in 2014 to 1902.3 CNY in 2019 [1]. This shows the significance of having social medical insurance in the society. Social medical insurance refers to a kind of social insurance in which insurance organizations provide material assistance for the loss of income and medical expenses caused by illness, injury, or disability. Family consumption refers to the daily living expenses of residents, including basic clothing, food, housing, transportation, education, and medical insurance expenses [2]. The purchase of medical insurance is targeted to provide a certain degree of protection in terms of medical expenses when facing certain risks in future life, thereby reducing the fluctuations caused by financial risks and reducing residents' capital consumption when dealing with risks [3]. Compared to foreign countries, the social medical insurance system in China was introduced relatively late. At present, the most widely covered social medical insurance systems in China are urban staff basic medical insurance, urban residents' basic medical insurance and new rural cooperative medical insurance [4]. China introduced basic medical insurance for urban workers in the late 20th century [3]. By the end of 2022, the number of people covered by basic medical insurance in China had reached 1.346 billion, with coverage stable at over 95% of the whole population [5].

It has become a question for the Chinese government and citizens whether the introduction of the social medical insurance system in China has matured until now and had the expected positive impact on reducing family overall expenditure. Zang Wenbin, Liu Guo-en, et al. empirically analyzed the impact of basic medical insurance for urban residents on urban household consumption by using panel data of household survey of China's urban residents' basic medical insurance in 2007 and 2008 in nine cities. They found out that the medical consumption expenditure of the insured family is about 13% higher than that of the uninsured family and insurance has the greatest impact on the medical consumption for low-income families [6]. Yuan Liyu used the data of the third period of Chinese Family Panel Studies (CFPS) from 2014 to 2018 and the Logit model to emphasize the promotion of the medical insurance system on residents' consumption level. The consumption level of residents in the central and eastern region has increased more from purchasing medical insurance than that in the western region [7]. This paper is going to explore the influence of having social medical insurance on family consumption in China up to 2019 and predict that social medical insurance will have an inverse effect on family consumption based on previous research. The results of this paper are conducive for people to make an evaluation of the current social medical insurance system in China and for the Chinese government to improve it more purposefully in the future.

2 Data, Model, and Variables Sources

This paper uses cross-sectional data from the 2019 China Household Finance Survey (CHFS). Samples of the 2019 China Household Finance Survey covered 29 provinces, 343 districts and counties, and 1,360 village committees across the country, collecting information from 34,643 households and 107,008 family members [8].

In terms of estimation methods, the OLS method is adopted in the benchmark model to test the influence of social medical insurance on family consumption behavior. The benchmark model is as follows:

$$C = \alpha + \beta \cdot I + \sum_{i=1}^{n} \gamma_i \cdot x_i + \mu \tag{1}$$

where C represents family consumption; I represents the purchase of social medical insurance; $\sum_{i=1}^{n} \gamma_i \cdot x_i$ represents other control variables affecting family consumption and μ is a random disturbance term.

This paper chose the explained variable, the explanatory variable, the control variable and the instrument variable, as shown in Table 1.

Table 1. Variable type, name, and description.

Variable Type	Variable Name	Variable Description
Explained variable	Family total consumption	The sum of the necessities and non-necessities consumption of all family members (in logarithm);
	Family food consumption	Total food consumption of the surveyed family (in logarithm);
	Family resident consumption	Total resident consumption of the surveyed family (in logarithm);
	Family education consumption	Total educational consumption of the surveyed family (in logarithm);
Explanatory variable	Social medical insurance	Dummy variable: whether the householder of the surveyed family has social medical insurance; 0 – No; 1 – Yes
Control variable	Family member	Number of family members in surveyed family;
	City level	Categorical variable: 1 - First-tier cities/New first-tier cities; 2 - Second-tier cities; 3 - Third-tier and below cities;
	Rural	Dummy variable: whether location of the surveyed family is rural; 0 – City/town; 1 – Rural
	Financial product	Dummy variable: whether the surveyed family has financial products; 0 – No; 1 – Yes
	Financial advisor	Dummy variable: whether the surveyed family has a financial adviser or investment adviser; 0 – No; 1 – Yes
	Work status	Dummy variable: whether the householder of the surveyed family has a job; 0 – No; 1 – Yes
	Credit card limit	Total credit card limit of the surveyed family (in logarithm)
	Family income	The sum of income of all family members (in logarithm);

(*continued*)

Table 1. (*continued*)

Variable Type	Variable Name	Variable Description
	Family assets	The sum of financial assets and non-financial assets of all family members (in logarithm);
Instrumental variable	Non-agricultural household registration	Dummy variable: 0 – The householder of the surveyed family has agricultural household registration/No registration; 1 – The householder of the surveyed family has non-agricultural household registration/Unified household registration;

3 Empirical Results

3.1 Model Construction

Based on the variables that are chosen from Table 1, the model is constructed following the equations:

$$\begin{aligned}ln(Familyconsumption) =\ &\alpha + \beta Socialmedicalinsurance \\&+ \gamma_1 Familymember + \gamma_2 Citylevel + \gamma_3 Rural + \gamma_4 Financialproduct \\&+ \gamma_5 Financialadvisor + \gamma_6 ln(creditcardlimit) \\&+ \gamma_7 ln(Familyincome) + \gamma_8 ln(Familyassets)\end{aligned} \quad (2)$$

3.2 OLS Estimation Result

This paper divides family consumption into five different forms to separate the influence of social medical insurance on various types of consumption: (1) total family consumption; (2) family food consumption; (3) family resident consumption; (4) family education consumption. Table 2 illustrates the OLS regression results of the four explained variables.

According to the OLS model analysis, as shown in Table 2, holding social medical insurance has significantly negative impacts on the family total consumption, family food consumption and family resident consumption. It has a positive impact on family education consumption, but the impact on educational consumption is not too significant.

The regression (1) result suggests that having social medical insurance has a negative impact on family total consumption at the 1% significance level, with an impact degree of -15.3%. This reflects that having social medical insurance does decrease family total consumption and families with social medical insurance spend 15.3% less than the family

Table 2. The impact of having social medical insurance on family consumption using OLS.

	(1) ln (Family total consumption)	(2) ln (Family food consumption)	(3) ln (Family resident consumption)	(4) ln (Family education consumption)
Social medical insurance	−0.153*** (−2.80)	−0.179*** (−3.29)	−0.272*** (−2.82)	0.0648 (0.49)
Family member	0.0936*** (9.13)	0.0707*** (6.91)	0.0301* (1.66)	0.196*** (7.95)
2. City level	−0.202*** (−5.26)	−0.136*** (-3.53)	−0.511*** (−7.50)	−0.230** (−2.50)
3. City level	−0.238*** (−7.73)	−0.140*** (−4.55)	−0.669*** (−12.31)	−0.306*** (−4.21)
Rural	−0.258*** (−2.97)	−0.238*** (−2.74)	−0.620*** (−4.03)	−0.342 (−1.51)
Financial product	−0.0519 (−1.48)	−0.0392 (−1.12)	−0.0446 (−0.72)	0.294*** (3.59)
Financial advisor	0.191** (2.20)	−0.0336 (−0.39)	0.0476 (0.31)	0.0126 (0.06)
Work status	0.0763** (2.29)	−0.0446 (−1.34)	0.121** (2.05)	0.478*** (6.00)
ln (Credit card limit)	0.119*** (10.09)	0.0767*** (6.49)	0.0928*** (4.43)	0.237*** (8.39)
ln (Family income)	0.0721*** (6.61)	0.0499*** (4.58)	0.0257 (1.33)	0.0787*** (3.06)
ln (Family assets)	0.123*** (11.15)	0.0805*** (7.34)	−0.0412** (−2.12)	0.179*** (6.78)
Constant	7.824*** (44.35)	7.914*** (44.96)	8.745*** (28.01)	2.408*** (5.70)
N	2380	2380	2380	2164

Notes: This table reports estimates from regression of family total consumption, family food consumption, family resident consumption and family education consumption on whether the householder of the surveyed family has social medical insurance. The P-values obtained are from the overall significance test with the null hypothesis that the effect of having social medical insurance equals zero. T statistics are reported in parentheses, *, ** and *** denote significance level of 10%, 5% and 1% respectively

without social medical insurance in terms of total consumption. This might be because a large proportion of a family's total consumption on medical expenses caused by illness, injury and disability is now saved. The results of control variables demonstrate that the large family generally spends more than the small family; the family in first-tier cities has higher total consumption than the family in second and lower tier cities; the family in rural areas has lower consumption than the family in cities and towns; the family that has financial product consume less; There is higher total consumption for the family with a financial advisor; family total consumption is higher when the householder of the family has a job; total consumption tends to increase with the credit card limit of the family; the greater the family income and assets, the higher the overall spending.

Regression (2), (3) and (4) prove whether social medical insurance has an impact on family consumption in the fields of food, housing and education separately. It is obvious that the coefficient of social medical insurance is -0.179 in regression (2), -0.272 in regression (3), remaining negative. These two estimates are significant under the 1% significant level, which means that purchasing social medical insurance also contributes to a decline in both family food consumption and family resident consumption. A possible reason for reducing food expenditure is because social medical insurance pays for hospital meals, reducing spending on specific healthy diets and nutritional interventions at home in the event of illness. Having social medical insurance leads to falling resident expenditure might because social medical insurance covers hospitalization expenses, which saves rent and other resident expenses for a period of time. The coefficient of social medical insurance in regression (4) is 0.0648, however, it is not significant.

Multicollinearity is the occurrence of high intercorrelations among two or more independent variables in a multiple regression model, which can lead to skewed or misleading results [9]. The multicollinearity test results of this model are shown in Table 3 below.

Table 3. Multicollinearity test.

Variable	VIF
Social medical insurance	1.03
Family member	1.09
City level 2 3	1.16 1.38
Rural	1.04
Financial product	1.18
Financial advisor	1.05
Work status	1.05
ln (credit card limit)	1.21
ln (Family income)	1.29
ln (Family assets)	1.51
Mean VIF	1.18

Table 3 illustrates that the mean VIF value of the model is 1.18, less than 2. The maximum value of VIF is 1.51, less than 10. As a result, it can be concluded that the correlation between explanatory variables is not high, which means that there is no multicollinearity problem in the model.

3.3 Instrumental Variable Method

In addition to OLS estimation, the instrumental variable method is also used to verify the causal relationship between social medical insurance and family total consumption. This model chose "non-agricultural household registration" as an instrument because it is predicted to have an effect on the likelihood of participation in social medical insurance but not a significant effect on family total consumption.

Table 4. First-stage equation of IV.

Social medical insurance	Coefficient	Std. Error	P > |t|
Non-agricultural household registration	0.0548***	4.71	0.000
Family member	0.00421	1.08	0.282
City level 2 3	−0.00646 0.0416***	−0.45 3.62	0.655 0.000
Rural	0.0390	1.18	0.238
Financial product	0.00329	0.25	0.803
Financial advisor	0.00135	0.04	0.967
Work status	0.0135	1.07	0.283
ln (credit card limit)	−0.00739*	−1.66	0.097
ln (Family income)	0.0119***	2.87	0.004
ln (Family assets)	0.0177***	4.23	0.000
Constant	0.552***	8.41	0.000

Notes: This table reports estimates from the regression of having social medical insurance on an indicator of having non-agricultural household registration. The P-values obtained are from the overall significance test with the null hypothesis that the effect of having non-agricultural household registration equals zero. T statistics are reported in parentheses, *, ** and *** denote significance level of 10%, 5% and 1% respectively

The first-stage equation is as follows:

$$Socialmedicalinsurance = \delta_0 \\ + \delta_1 Nonagriculturalhouseholdregistration + \delta_2 Familymember \\ + \delta_3 Citylevel + \delta_4 Rural + \delta_5 Financialproduct \\ + \delta_6 Financialadvisor + \delta_7 Workstatus + \delta_8 \ln(creditcardlimit) \\ + \delta_9 \ln(Familyincome) + \delta_{10} \ln(Familyassets) \quad (3)$$

Since non-agricultural household registration is predicted to be related to participation of social medical insurance, δ_1 should not equal to 0. The regression is run in Table 4 following the first-stage equation to test for the relevance of non-agricultural household registration as an instrument for social medical insurance.

Testing Instrument relevance condition

$$H_0 : \delta_1 = 0$$
$$F(1, 2361) = 22.23; Prob > F = 0.0000$$

The null hypothesis of the instrument relevance test is δ_1 equals to 0, and non-agricultural household registration unrelated with whether a person has social medical insurance. It is rejected for the reason that the Prob > F value is 0.0000, which means the coefficient 0.0548 is significant under the 1% significant level. This implies a notable positive correlation between social medical insurance and non-agricultural household registration, non-agricultural household registration satisfies the instrument relevance condition.

Table 5. The impact of having social medical insurance on family consumption using IV.

ln (Family total consumption)	Coefficient	Std. Error	P > |t|
Social medical insurance	−1.149*	−1.90	0.057
Family member	0.0953***	8.70	0.000
City level 2	−0.205***	−4.97	0.000
3	−0.190***	−4.54	0.000
Rural	−0.246***	−2.65	0.008
Financial product	−0.0453	−1.20	0.229
Financial advisor	0.175*	1.87	0.061
Work status	0.0838**	2.34	0.019
ln (credit card limit)	0.112***	8.44	0.000
ln (Family income)	0.0889***	6.21	0.000
ln (Family assets)	0.144***	8.19	0.000
Constant	8.316***	22.58	0.000

Notes: This table reports estimates from regression of family total consumption on whether the householder of the surveyed family has social medical insurance using an indicator of having non-agricultural household registration as instrument. The P-values obtained are from the overall significance test with the null hypothesis that the effect of having social medical insurance equals zero. T statistics are reported in parentheses, *, ** and *** denote significance level of 10%, 5% and 1% respectively.

Another necessary test for instrumental variable to be valid is the endogeneity test. In econometrics, endogeneity broadly refers to situations in which an explanatory variable is correlated with the error term [10]. The second-stage regression is run in Table 5 based on the equation:

$$\ln(\text{Family total consumption}) = \theta_0 + \theta_1 \overline{\text{Social medical insurance}}$$

$$+ \theta_2\text{Family member} + \theta_3\text{City level} + \theta_4\text{Rural} + \theta_5\text{Financial product}$$
$$+ \theta_6\text{Financial advisor} + \theta_7\text{Work status} + \theta_8\ln(\text{credit card limit})$$
$$+ \theta_9\ln(\text{Family income}) + \theta_{10}\ln(\text{Family assets}) \qquad (4)$$

Testing Instrument exogeneity condition.
Tests of endogeneity

$$H_0 : \text{Variables are exogenous}$$

Durbin (score) chi2(1) = 3.18887 (p = 0.0741)
Wu-Hausman F (1,2360) = 3.17567 (p = 0.0749)

The test results of instrument exogeneity condition are shown above. The endogeneity test obtained p values of 0.0741 and 0.0749, which is greater than 5% significant level. Hence the null hypothesis that variables in the second-stage equation are exogenous cannot be rejected; the non-agricultural household registration satisfies the instrument exogeneity condition.

Overall, non-agricultural household registration passed both the instrument relevance test and the instrument endogeneity test. It is, therefore, a valid instrument for social medical insurance. The model results in Table 5 again prove that having social medical insurance does have a negative impact on family total consumption at the 5% significant level.

4 Heterogeneity Test

Table 6 shows the heterogeneity analysis of the control variable 'work status'. It describes families where the householder has a job and families where the householder does not have a job and conducts the t-test for the differences between the two groups. The two regressions are constructed based on the two equations below:

$$\ln(\text{Family total consumption}) = \varphi_0 + \varphi_1 \text{ Social medical insurance}$$
$$+ \varphi_2\text{Family member} + \varphi_3\text{City level} + \varphi_4\text{Rural} + \varphi_5\text{Financial product}$$
$$+ \varphi_6\text{Financial advisor} + \varphi_7\ln(\text{credit card limit})$$
$$+ \varphi_8 \ln(\text{Family income}) + \varphi_9\ln(\text{Family assets}), \text{ if work status } = 1 \qquad (5)$$

$$\ln(\text{Family total consumption}) = \omega_0 + \omega_1 \text{ Social medical insurance}$$
$$+ \omega_2\text{Family member} + \omega_3\text{City level} + \omega_4\text{Rural} + \omega_5\text{Financial product}$$
$$+ \omega_6\text{Financial advisor} + \omega_7\ln(\text{credit card limit})$$
$$+ \omega_8 \ln(\text{Family income}) + \omega_9\ln(\text{Family assets}), \text{ if work status } = 0 \qquad (6)$$

By comparing regression (1) and regression (2) in Table 6, the coefficient of 'social medical insurance' in the householder who has a job group is −0.107, while it is −0.275 in the householder who does not have a job group. They are significant under 10% and 5% significant level, respectively. This can therefore be deduced that for families where

Table 6. Analysis of differences between the householder has job or does not have job.

	(5)	(6)
	ln (Family total consumption)	ln (Family total consumption)
Social medical insurance	−0.107*	−0.275**
	(−1.74)	(2.34)
Family member	0.0787***	0.150***
	(6.73)	(6.83)
2. City level	−0.216***	−0.157*
	(−4.94)	(−1.92)
3. City level	−0.242***	−0.218***
	(−7.19)	(−2.91)
Rural	−0.286***	0.546
	(−3.19)	(1.49)
Financial product	−0.0551	−0.00887
	(−1.38)	(−0.12)
Financial advisor	0.129	0.372**
	(1.28)	(2.16)
ln (credit card limit)	0.118***	0.103***
	(8.79)	(4.04)
ln (Family income)	0.0851***	0.0322
	(6.73)	(1.48)
ln (Family assets)	0.124***	0.118***
	(10.13)	(4.59)
Constant	7.752***	8.403***
	(39.39)	(20.66)
N	1925	455

Notes: This table reports estimates from regression of family total consumption on whether the householder of the surveyed family has social medical insurance for families where the householder has employment and families where the householder has no employment. Column 1 reports the effect for families where the householder has employment. Column 2 reports the effect for families where the householder is without employment. The P-values obtained are from the overall significance test with the null hypothesis that the effect of having social medical insurance equals zero. T statistics are reported in parentheses, *, ** and *** denote significance level of 10%, 5% and 1% respectively.

the householder has a job, holding social medical insurance results in a lower reduction in total consumption than for families where the householder does not have a job.

The coefficient of 'family member' in the householder having a job group is 0.0787, which significantly is less than 0.150 in the householder not having a job group. Since both of them are significant under 1% significant level, family total consumption increases with the number of family members. This also implies that increasing one family member in families where the householder has a job increases total consumption

7.13% less than in families where the householder does not have a job. The coefficients of '2. City level' in the two groups are -0.216 and -0.157 and they are significant under the 1% and 10% significant level respectively. This means that the gap in family total consumption between China's first and second-tier cities is wider for families where the householder has a job than for families where the householder does not have job. The coefficients of '3. City level' are -0.242 and -0.218 in the two groups respectively. This suggests that the gap in family total consumption between China's first and third-tier cities is also wider for families where the householder has a job than for families where the householder does not have a job. The coefficient of 'rural' is -0.286 in the householder who has a job group but 0.546 in the householder who does not have a job group. Because of the insignificance of 0.546, the result only indicates that for families where the householder has a job, living in rural areas costs 28.6% less than living in cities or towns. The coefficients of 'financial advisor' are 0.129 and 0.372 in the two groups respectively. Since the coefficient for the householder has a job group is not too significant, it shows that for families where the householder does not have a job, having a financial advisor increases total consumption by 37.2%. The coefficient of 'ln (credit card limit)' is 0.118 in the householder who has a job group, which is higher than 0.103 in the householder who does not have a job group. This can be explained as both groups' consumption is positively correlated with credit card limit. Families where the householder has a job increase more in total expenditure by having higher credit card limit compared to families where the householder does not have a job. The coefficients of 'ln (family income)' is only significant in the householder has a job group. This means that for families where the householder has a job, every 1% increase in total income leads to 8.51% increase in total consumption. The coefficients of 'ln (family asset)' are 0.124 and 0.118 in the two groups respectively. They are both significant under the 1% significant level, thus it shows that family total consumption increases with family assets and this positive correlation is greater for families where the householder has a job.

5 Conclusion

This paper uses microdata to study the influence of purchasing social medical insurance on family consumption and draws the following conclusions. After controlling for other variables, the purchase of social health insurance has a significant inverse effect on family total consumption, family food consumption and family resident consumption. OLS regression and instrumental variable regression illustrated that the purchase of social medical insurance significantly reduced family consumption at confidence levels of 1% and 5% respectively. Furthermore, the effect of social medical insurance on reducing family consumption differs between families where the householder has a job and families where the householder does not have a job. Families where the householder does not have a job enjoy a greater benefit in decreasing total expenditure from holding social medical insurance. China's social medical insurance has indeed contributed to reducing people's medical expenses, but the results show a decrease in overall family consumption and in non-medical expenses. Therefore, it is particularly crucial to improve the insurance system and promote an increase in overall family consumption, so that the increase in non-medical expenses exceeds the decrease in medical expenses. Finally, this paper only analyzed CHFS data up to 2019, meaning that changes in the data on COVID-19 outbreaks from 2020 till now are not accounted for, so this could be further improved by including the observations after 2019.

Acknowledgement. I have received valuable assistance from many people while completing this paper, in addition to my own efforts. Firstly, I would like to express my sincere gratitude to Prof. Xu Xin, who provided me with great support in finding an appropriate title and data for this paper. Secondly, I appreciate the enlightening guidance of all teachers and professors in the 'Econometrics for Data Science and Economic Application' project, which helped me a lot in organizing the framework of the paper and putting forward suggestions. Further, I am willing to thank all my friends and my parents for their persistent encouragement whenever I deny myself.

References

1. National Bureau of Statistics of China. China Statistical Yearbook 2021 (2021)
2. Du, Y.: The impact of basic medical insurance on promoting family consumption. Mod. Econ. Inf. (18), 364 (2018)
3. Li, H.: Analysis of the impact of basic medical insurance for urban residents on family consumption in China. J. Commer. Econ. (10), 33–35 (2018)
4. Xie, B., Han, J.: Impacts of basic medical insurance on household expenditure in urban and rural China. J. Bus. Econ. (05), 79–87 (2015)
5. China State Medical Insurance Administration. Medical Security Development Statistics Express (2022)
6. Zang, W., Liu, G., Xu, F., Xiong, X.: The impact of basic medical Insurance for urban residents on household consumption in China. Econ. Res. J. (07), 75–85 (2012)
7. Yuan, L.: Study on the influence of Chinese social basic medical Insurance on Household consumption (2021)
8. China Household Finance Survey and Research Center. Instructions for using data from 2019 China Household Finance Survey (CHFS) (2019)
9. Hayes, A.: Multicollinearity: meaning, examples, and FAQS, Investopedia. Investopedia (2023). https://www.investopedia.com/terms/m/multicollinearity.asp
10. Wooldridge, J.M.: Introductory Econometrics: A Modern Approach, p. 88, Fourth edn. South-Western, Australia (2009)

The Influence of Impulsive Purchase on the Consumption Behaviour in Social Media

Sirui Wang[✉]

Department of Science and Technology, Beijing Normal University-Hong Kong Baptist University United International College, Zhuhai 519080, Guangdong, China
q030016054@mail.uic.edu.cn

Abstract. As a life-sharing platform, social media has become one of the crucial channels to promote consumption, and shopping behaviour on the platform significantly impacts consumption decisions. The impact of impulse purchases on customers in the context of social media is examined in this article using the multiple linear regression method from the angles of stickiness and mental accounting. Using questionnaires, the study finds that impulse purchases positively affected stickiness and were positively correlated with mental accounting. In addition, stickiness acts as a mediating variable when impulsive consumption affects mental accounting. The study provides insight into how social media platforms and marketers use impulse buying behaviour to increase sales. By encouraging impulse purchases with more quality content, consumers can build a more engaged relationship with the platform and have more of a mental budget to prepare for their next impulse purchase. The study highlights the potential of impulse purchases as a powerful force that can influence consumer behaviour and decision-making processes on social media.

Keywords: Impulse Purchase · Stickiness · Mental Accounting

1 Introduction

As the trend of e-shopping has grown in recent years, more and more users share their shopping experiences on social media, driving the online community to join e-shopping. Therefore, it is crucial to research e-commerce's social media marketing activities (SMMAs) [1]. RED (XiaoHongShu), a new brand in China, operates on creating a cohesive social relationship among users through community building, marketing and publicity of products, and finally, increasing users' purchasing power [2]. Compared with other social commerce platforms (such as Taobao and TikTok), the operational focus of RED is not to promote user consumption but to create a community atmosphere, allowing users to explore their consumption needs. On the one hand, users actively share shopping experiences, beauty skills, travel experiences, and other content with the public out of their desire to share. On the other hand, the brand will invite users to share ordinary content while implanting brand product recommendations or experiences. This allows other users to unintentionally increase demand while relaxing with the content on the page.

Much literature on how social media affects impulse purchases, but very little research has explored the impact of impulse buying behaviour on consumers. Therefore, this study aims to explore the influence of impulsive purchases of social media on consumer attitudes, supplement the shortcomings of previous studies, and better understand the lasting influence on consumers after consumption to formulate more targeted marketing strategies for enterprises' long-term development.

Specifically, three types of impulse purchases (reminder, suggestion and planned) influence consumers' attitudes [3]. Therefore, the same three indicators were used in this study. Pure impulse purchases are not chosen because the reasons why consumers make pure impulse purchases are complex and mostly independent of platform operation. Referral propensity in social media increases user stickiness [4]. In addition, Impulsive consumption in group buying will increase users' mental accounting [5]. Therefore, this study uses stickiness and mental accounting indicators to examine the following two characteristics of consumer attitudes in the setting of social media. First, the impact of impulsive behaviour on social media platforms on consumer engagement and mental accounting. Then, it will be investigated how stickiness mediates when impulsive behaviour affects users' mental accounting. This study contributes to better marketing strategies and directions for social media platforms and promotes the development of the social media industry.

2 Methodology

This part introduces the design principle of the questionnaire, the hypothesis proposed, the data collection process, and the data analysis method.

2.1 Survey Design

This paper adopts a survey to explore the influence of impulse buying behaviour on consumers' attitudes. Referring to a questionnaire study on the influence of group buying behaviour on consumers [5]. This study modifies it into the usage background of social media and translates it into Chinese. The questionnaire is divided into three parts. The first part is primarily personal information collection, such as gender, age, economic level, etc. The second part is to understand the subjects' shopping habits and behavioural characteristics by asking questions such as purchase frequency and purchase amount. The third part is based on the subjects' experience of shopping on the RED platform or other shopping platforms according to the information recommended by the RED, which sets up five indicators: Impulse purchases from reminder (RIP).

from suggestions (SIP), planning (PIP), stickiness, and mental accounting. The specific problems of each indicator are shown in Table 1.

The third part used the Likert 5-point scale to evaluate the responses: "1" means totally disagree, and "5" means totally agree. Finally, this study also interviews subjects about their shopping experience with the RED. Using these indicators, this paper is going to verify the following hypotheses:

Hypothesis 1: impulse purchases from reminders, planning and suggestions all positively impact stickiness.

Hypothesis 2: impulse purchases from reminders, planning and suggestions all positively impact consumers' mental accounting.

Hypothesis 3: There is a mediating effect of stickiness on impulse purchases and consumers' mental accounting.

Table 1. Survey questions and the construction of indices.

Construct	Factors	Labelling
RIP	The RED blogger's tweets/videos remind me of items that suit my needs	I1
	Tweets/videos in the RED with explicit advertisement remind me of products that fit my needs	I2
	The detailed descriptions of products in the RED tweet/video remind me of products that fit my needs	I3
SIP	It is easy for me to buy products based on recommendations or suggestions from bloggers	S1
	When I see comments praising the product in a tweet/video, I tend to check it out and make a purchase	S2
	It is easy for me to be attracted to and buy products that showcase their functions on the platform	S3
PIP	When I browse RED in my spare time, I often place orders in RED or open other shopping APP for products that are not on the shopping list	P1
	I once went to RED to check out something I wanted to buy and ended up buying more than I had budgeted/needed	P2
	The increased pleasure I get from shopping at RED (including opening other shopping apps through RED) makes it worth my while to buy unexpected items	P3
Stickiness	After an impulse buy from a blogger, I pay attention to the information posted by the blogger again	ST1
	I recommend my favourite bloggers to people around me	ST2
	After an impulse purchase, I will increase the time and frequency of browsing the RED, even if it is not the blogger who planted grass before browsing	ST3
Mental accounting	I don't regret buying the products after seeing the information from RED	M1
	I believe it is wise to read the RED before making a purchase	M2
	When I see bloggers' recommendations or suggestions, I am willing to increase my original budget to buy bloggers' products	M3

2.2 Participants

There are 330 participants from all over China participated in the experiment. They answered the questions online via social media and were rewarded 5 yuan for participating. Participants signed an informed consent form before filling out the questionnaire.

2.3 Data Analysis Method

Part of the observations was dropped for no shopping experience in RED and calculated the frequency and percentage of different buying behaviour and characteristics of the remaining participants. Then, the reliability of the survey was calculated by Cronbach α and validity by the KMO test, Bartlett test, and factor analysis with varimax rotation. The questionnaire is eligible for factor analysis if the KMO test is higher than 0.8 and the Bartlett test is significant. Next, use the correlation matrix to study the correlation among RIP, SIP, PIP, mental accounting and stickiness. Also, the three types of impulse purchases were taken as independent variables and mental accounting and stickiness were taken as dependent variables for linear regression analysis, The two models built are as follows:

$$Stickiness = \beta_1\ Reminder + \beta_2\ Suggestion + \beta_3\ Planned + \varepsilon \quad (1)$$

$$Mental\ Accounting = \gamma_1\ Reminder + \gamma_2 Suggestion + \gamma_3 Planned + \delta \quad (2)$$

Using variance inflation factor (VIF) to test whether the independent variables have multicollinearity problems and it should be less than 10. Finally, a mediation model was established with stickiness as the mediating variable, impulse purchases as the independent variable, and mental accounting as the dependent variable. The flow of testing the mediation has three main steps [6]. The study follows these steps (see Fig. 1).

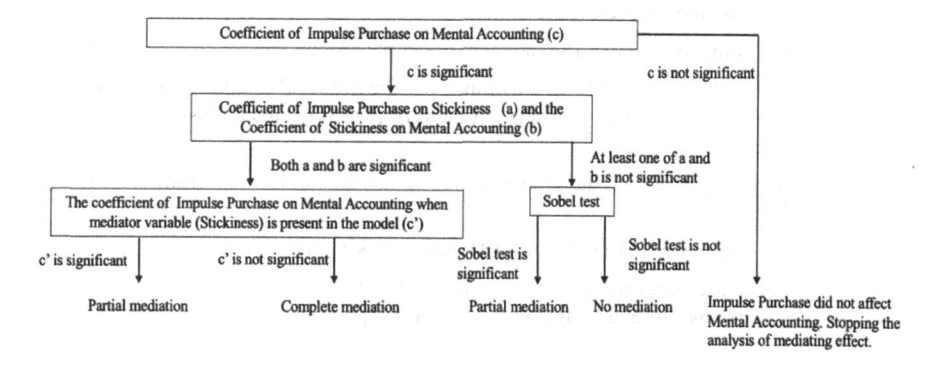

Fig. 1. Mediating Effect Test Procedure

3 Results

3.1 Descriptive Statistics

There are 330 questionnaires collected, and participants were aged between 19 and 25 (M = 57, SD = .379). Among them, 30 invalid questionnaires were screened out for those who had never used the RED or had zero shopping experience related to the RED, and 300 valid questionnaires remained, accounting for 90.9%. The fundamental data for the study's valid samples are presented in Table 2. In general, most of the respondents are aged 19–22 (91.2%), have consumption frequency related to the RED 1–5 times per month (67.3%), and spend 50–500 yuan (58.8%) on the RED. In addition, the skewness of age, monthly consumption level, and consumption amount of the RED range from -0.77 to 1.4, within the range of absolute value of 2, so the research data is normally distributed.

Table 2. Descriptive Statistics

Basic Information	Options and Classifications	Number of people	Proportion (%)
The average monthly consumption level	Less than ¥1,000	17	5.67
	Around¥ 1,001-¥2,000	189	63.00
	Around¥ 1,001-¥2,000	73	24.33
	Around¥ 1,001-¥2,000	11	3.67
	More than ¥4,001	10	3.33
Frequency related to shopping on RED	1-2 times	127	42.33
	3-5 times	95	31.67
	More than 5 times	78	26
Category of purchase (multiple choice)	Food/beverage	108	36
	Makeup/skin care	210	70
	Clothes/shoes/hats	212	70.67
	Household goods	87	29
	Others	12	4
The amount of monthly purchases related to RED	Less than ¥50	29	9.67
	Around¥ 51-¥100	86	28.67
	Around¥ 101-¥500	135	45
	Around¥ 501-¥1000	36	12
	More than ¥1001	14	4.66

3.2 Reliability and Validity Analysis

According to the reliability analysis, Cronbach's alpha for each construct was at least 0.7, indicating that the questionnaire had acceptable reliability. This study also examines the validity. KMO and Bartlett's tests were used to verify the validity, with the value of KMO being 0.90, which is significant (p < .001). The research data is very suitable for factor analysis. The validity of the finding is investigated using factor analysis with varimax rotation, and it is discovered that each factor is significant. Table 3 displays the findings of the reliability and validity measurements.

Table 3. Factor Analysis and Consistency Analysis

Construct	Factors	Factor loading	Eigenvalue	Cronbach's α
RIP	I1	0.789	2.329	0.849
	I2	0.809		
	I3	0.802		
SIP	S1	0.813	2.298	0.833
	S2	0.771		
	S3	0.814		
PIP	P1	0.797	2.307	0.865
	P2	0.786		
	P3	0.791		
Stickiness	ST1	0.793	2.319	0.844
	ST2	0.805		
	ST3	0.810		
Mental accounting	M1	0.815	2.385	0.873
	M2	0.832		
	M3	0.790		

Table 4. Correlation Matrix

	RIP	SIP	PIP	Stickiness	Mental Accounting
RIP	1				
SIP	0.456***	1			
PIP	0.562***	0.506***	1		
Stickiness	0.479***	0.470***	0.500***	1	
Mental accounting	0.493***	0.485***	0.538***	0.495***	1

Note: $^{*}p<0.1$ ** $p< 0.05$ *** $p < 0.01$

The association between mental accounting, stickiness, and three different types of impulse purchases is studied using correlation analysis, as shown in Table 4. The Pearson correlation coefficient is utilized to quantify the strength of the correlation. These results indicate that mental accounting and stickiness, RIP, SIP, and PIP all present significant values, and the correlation values are all greater than 0. It means positive correlations exist between mental accounting, stickiness, RIP, SIP, and PIP.

3.3 Regression Results

Using multiple linear regression to test the hypotheses. The results are summarized in Tables 5 and 6. The regression analysis findings on stickiness and impulsive purchasing are shown in Table 5 for Model 1. Reminder impulse purchases have a γ value of 0.240 (p < 0.001), which shows a strong positive relationship with stickiness. When the reminder impulse purchases increase by 1 time, the stickiness increases by 0.24 units. The other two types of impulse purchases have the same effect. Therefore, hypothesis 1 is supported. Among them, prompt impulse purchases have the most significant influence on stickiness. In addition, the variance inflation factor (VIF) in the entire study model is less than 2, indicating no dependence and that all dependent variables are free from multicollinearity problems.

Model 2 in Table 5 shows the regression analysis results between impulse purchases and mental accounting. With linear regression analysis taking RIP, SIP, and PIP as independent variables and mental accounting as the dependent variable, γ value of reminder impulse purchases is 0.250 (p < 0.001), demonstrating a significant positive association with mental accounting. When the reminder impulse purchases increase by 1 time, the mental accounting increases by 0.25 yuan. The other two types of impulse purchases have the same effect. In addition, VIF is larger than two, indicating that none of the independent variables exhibits the multicollinearity problem. Therefore, hypothesis 2 is supported.

Table 5. Regression Output of Impulse Purchases, Stickiness, and Mental Accounting.

	(1) Stickiness	(2) Mental Accounting
RIP	0.240*** (0.061)	0.250*** (0.065)
SIP	0.235*** (0.055)	0.253*** (0.058)
PIP	0.233*** (0.057)	0.301*** (0.060)
R^2	0.348	0.381
Adjusted R^2	0.341	0.375
F value	52.56	60.789

Note* p<0.1*** p< 0.05*** p < 0.01; standard errors are in parentheses

This study also investigated the mediating effect of stickiness on impulse buying behaviour and mental accounting. Model 5 in Table 6 investigates the r connection between impulse purchases, stickiness, and mental accounting. Following the flowchart in Fig. 1, the model satisfies the following conditions: the regression coefficient c equals 0.809 (p < 0.01), which means it is a significant correlation between Impulse purchases and Mental Accounting. The Regression coefficient b is equal to 0.219 (p < 0.01), and the coefficient a is equal to 0.708 (p < 0.01), which means both a and b are significant correlations. With mediating variables, the regression coefficient c' is 0.654 (p < 0.01), which means that under stickiness, there is also a significant correlation between Impulse purchases and Mental Accounting. The results show that this model is a partial mediation model. Therefore, the research hypothesis H3 is supported.

Table 6. Regression Output and Mediation Effect of Stickiness.

	(3) Mental Accounting	(4) Stickiness	(5) Mental Accounting
Impulse Purchases	0.809**	0.708**	0.654**
Stickiness			0.219**
R^2	0.381	0.348	0.407
Adjusted R^2	0.378	0.345	0.403
F value	183.090	158.723	101.855

Note: * $p<0.1$ ** $p< 0.05$ *** $p < 0.01$

3.4 Discussion

When studying the regression analysis of impulse purchases on mental accounting, this study predicts a difference from the literature [5]. This literature suggests that PIP have the most decisive influence on stickiness among the three types of impulse purchases. However, this paper noticed in Model 1 that suggested impulse buying behaviour has more influence on stickiness. In addition, this paper found that suggested impulse purchases had a significant impact on mental accounting, which was also inconsistent with the data in the literature [5]. However, recalling Model 2 in this paper, the regression coefficient of cue impulse purchases is smaller than that of the other two types of impulse purchases. The author further interviewed the subjects about their views on reminder impulse buying and found that the interviewees mentioned that when there was no solid goal-oriented purchase, they preferred to buy the products that appeared in tweets or videos without evident traces of advertisements on social media. The RED platform mainly serves female users, and women tend to be more goal-oriented toward their reward shopping when they buy impulsively [7]. However, except for women, as explained by the Self-Verification theory in literature, consumers are generally more inclined to believe the information they find rather than passively accept the information sold or persuaded [8].

A possible explanation for the mediation model is that users become more dependent on the platform when they have a satisfactory shopping experience associated with the platform. In addition, when they browse the RED, they will increase the mental accounting for the purchase of the product because of the good user experience, the use of the blogger or the recommendation of the public. The subjects interviewed after the study admitted that they used RED to look at the user experience when they wanted to shop but did not know exactly what to buy and ended up buying what they thought was a better product with more money than they had budgeted for. In addition, When users participate in social media as a social observation, the interactivity of social media, rather than the credibility of the content, affects their consumption behavior [9]. The interaction with the platform would positively affect impulse purchases tendency and further trigger impulsive buying behavior [10]. Therefore, the platform should attach importance to the interaction of users and cause them to consume impulsively to improve the stickiness of users to the platform and their mental accounting, to drive the consumption of higher limit next time.

4 Conclusion

This study takes the RED as an example to investigate the impact of Chinese users' impulsive social media consumption on user engagement and mental accounting. The findings demonstrate that impulsive purchases enhance user involvement and mental accounting. PIP have the most major influence on mental accounting, while reminder impulse buying has the most significant impact on stickiness. Therefore, social media platforms can adopt different strategies to increase users' impulse buying behaviour, stickiness to the platform, and mental accounting for shopping.

This study advances the field of research on impulsive purchases by describing how impulsive purchases affect consumers' later decision-making. The findings demonstrate that impulse purchases are not just random or irrational behaviour. In contrast, impulse purchases can broaden mental accounting and cultivate client engagement for further business interactions. Based on the results of this study, three practical implications are identified. First, social media platforms can stimulate consumers' shopping demand through discounts and other means to enhance their stickiness to the platform and their mental accounting for shopping. Secondly, compared with traditional shopping platforms, RED users prefer to relax and entertain themselves. Therefore, RED needs to develop more marketing strategies to make users happy while inadvertently showing them product information. Finally, social media can develop more marketing strategies by increasing customer engagement. Brands can increase user interaction through RED, developing and enhancing customers' mental accounting. At the same time, bloggers can also post more quality content to build good relationships with users. Our results suggest that expanding stickiness increases mental social media accounts. Once consumers become engaged with the platform, they will increase their spending on the products they want or are interested in.

Although this study contributes to understanding the impact of impulsive behaviour, a few limitations remain in this study. First, this study only focuses on RED, a social platform. Further research can be conducted on social media platforms such as TikTok and Bilibili, which have similar business models. Second, due to time constraints, this study adopted a cross-sectional study. In the future, longitudinal studies can be combined to forecast the influence of impulse buying behaviour on mental accounting and stickiness.

Thirdly, this experiment studied the mediating effect of stickiness on the impulse buying behaviour and mental accounting, and the results were partially mediating, indicating that there are more potential factors to be analyzed. The research may include social factors and network quality in the future.

References

1. Yadav, M., Rahman, Z.: The influence of social media marketing activities on customer loyalty. Benchmarking Int. J. **25**(9), 3882–3905 (2018)
2. Shao, M.: Research on UGC social e-commerce platform from the perspective of use and gratification theory – a case study of "Xiaohongshu." Home Drama **9**, 237–238 (2019)
3. Mohsin, D., Shamim, A., Yousaf, U., Ghazali, Z.: Customer relationship satisfaction and relationship improvement: key determinants of customer loyalty. Int. J. Mark. Princ. Pract. **3**, 6–12 (2013)
4. Köster, A., Matt, C., Hess, T.: Do all roads lead to rome? Exploring the relationship between social referrals, referral propensity and stickiness to video-on-demand websites. Bus. Inf. Syst. Eng. **63**(4), 349–366 (2021)
5. Wu, J., Chen, Y., Chien, S.: Impulse purchases and trust: the mediating effect of stickiness and the mental budgeting account. Cyberpsychol. Behav. Soc. Netw. **16**(10), 767–773 (2013)
6. Baron, R.M., Kenny, D.A.: The moderator–mediator variable distinction in social psychological research: conceptual, strategic, and statistical considerations. J. Pers. Soc. Psychol. **51**(6), 1173–1182 (1986)
7. Lucas, M., Koff, E.: The role of impulsivity and of self-perceived attractiveness in impulse buying in women. Personal. Individ. Differ. **56**, 111–115 (2014)
8. Szumowska, E., Wójcik, N.A., Szwed, P., Kruglanski, A.W.: Says who? Credibility effects in self-verification strivings. Psychol. Sci. **33**(5), 699–715 (2022)
9. Cao, D., Meadows, M., Wong, D., Xia, S.: Understanding consumers' social media engagement behaviour: an examination of the moderation effect of social media context. J. Bus. Res. **122**, 835–846 (2021)
10. Xiang, L., Zheng, X., Lee, M.K.O., Zhao, D.: Exploring consumers' impulse buying behavior on social commerce platform: the role of parasocial interaction. Int. J. Inf. Manag. **36**(3), 333–347 (2016)

Analysis of the Reasons of HNA Group's Bankruptcy and Future Prevention Measures for Enterprises

Jiaheng Zhang(✉)

Duke Kunshan University, No. 8 Duke Avenue, Kunshan 215316, Jiangsu Province, China
jz372@duke.edu

Abstract. This paper examines the reasons behind the bankruptcy of Hainan Airlines Group (HNA group), one of China's largest airlines. Through a comprehensive analysis of the airline's financial statements, industry trends, and regulatory environment, several factors have been identified that contributed to its downfall. These include Hainan Airlines' aggressive expansion strategy, excessive debt levels, fierce competition in the Chinese aviation market, and the impact of COVID-19 pandemic. Using a combination of quantitative and qualitative research methods, the paper provides insights into the underlying causes of the airline's financial distress and discusses the implications of its bankruptcy for the broader aviation industry in China. The findings suggest that Hainan Airlines' bankruptcy is a cautionary tale for other airlines seeking rapid growth and expansion and underscores the importance of sound financial management and risk mitigation strategies in the aviation sector.

Keywords: Hainan Airlines Group Bankruptcy · Financial Management · Financial Crisis

1 Introduction

Hainan Airlines Group was founded in January 1993 and listed on the Shanghai Stock Exchange on June 26, 1997. It was once one of the four major airlines in China [1]. The company's main business includes international and domestic air passenger and cargo transportation, as well as related services in the aviation transportation industry. In 2020, Hainan Airlines Group and its subsidiaries operated nearly 1,800 routes, covering Asia, North America, Europe, South America, and Oceania [2]. On October 31, 2021, the Higher People's Court of Hainan Province delivered a civil ruling to Hainan Airlines Group and related enterprises, declaring the bankruptcy reorganization of Hainan Airlines Group [2].

The purpose of this paper is to analyze the factors that contributed to Hainan Airlines' bankruptcy and provide insights into the underlying causes of the airline's financial distress. Using a combination of quantitative and qualitative research methods, the author examines the airline's financial statements, industry trends, and regulatory environment to identify the key drivers of its downfall. The author also discusses the implications of Hainan Airlines' bankruptcy for the broader aviation industry in China and the lessons that can be learned from this experience.

2 Analysis of the Reasons Behind the Financial Crisis of Hainan Airlines

2.1 Overexpansion

Hainan Airlines Group expanded too rapidly and aggressively, adding more routes, and increasing its fleet size without proper financial planning, leading to an increase in debt. Within a short period of time, HNA Group aggressively conducted cross-industry and interdisciplinarity in operations, acquiring numerous domestic and foreign companies through mergers and acquisitions. However, the quality of the acquisitions varied, and subsequent management and operations were poorly executed. Additionally, the synergy of diversified operations was weak, and segment integration proved challenging. The acquired subsidiaries repeatedly suffered losses, which in turn eroded the overall profitability of the group. Between 2017 and 2018, HNA Group successively acquired companies such as Shanxi Airlines and Lucky Air [3]. However, the acquired companies' operating income did not translate into net profits. Although operating income increased, net profit shifted from positive to negative.

2.2 Mismanagement

According to Figure 1, from 2016 to 2020, the turnover rate of accounts receivable of HNA Group decreased year by year, with a decrease of 81%, and the average cash collection period of the company became longer, External crises led to poor asset liquidity and declining debt-paying ability. It can be seen from Figure 2 that the sharp decrease in inventory turnover rate in 2017 was due to the merger of Tianjin Airlines Aviation Materials, which increased the total inventory by 1,114.83%. After the merger of HNA Technology in 2019, inventory increased significantly again, and the inventory turnover rate fell to 38.5 times in 2020. The total asset turnover rate showed a slow upward trend in the first four years, but dropped to 0.16 times in 2020, fully demonstrating the severe impact of the epidemic on the company's operations. Moreover, from Figure 3, the total asset turnover of Hainan Airlines Company is relatively low, indicating that the way the company uses its assets for operation is not efficient. This not only affects the company's profitability but also directly impacts the distribution of dividends for the publicly listed company.

Overall, HNA Group has gradually shown the consequences of poor management over the past five years. Although the development of its civil aviation main business is stable, its operational capability is only minimally ensured. External factors such as the epidemic have dealt a fatal blow to the company.

Accounts Receivable Turnover

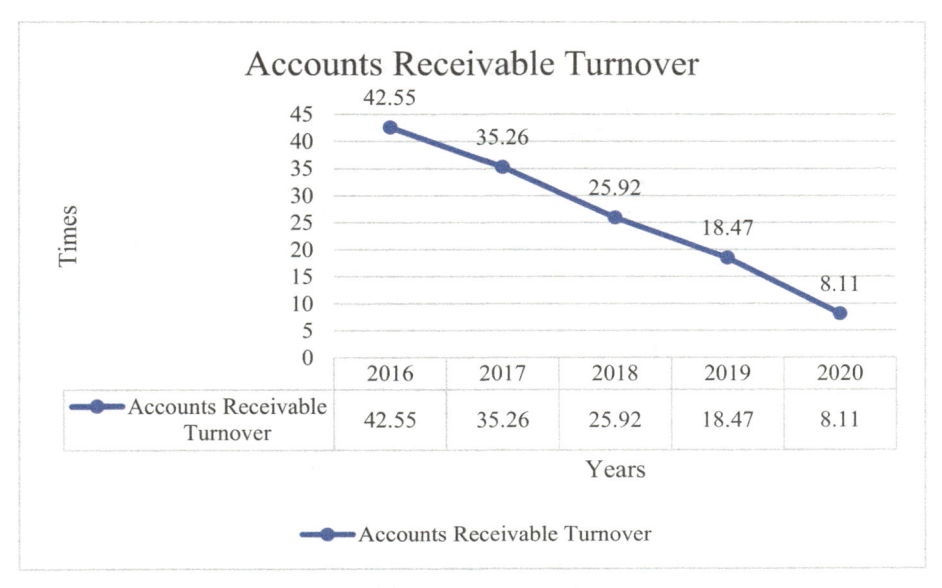

Years	2016	2017	2018	2019	2020
Accounts Receivable Turnover	42.55	35.26	25.92	18.47	8.11

Fig. 1. Accounts Receivable Turnover of HNA Group

Inventory Turnover

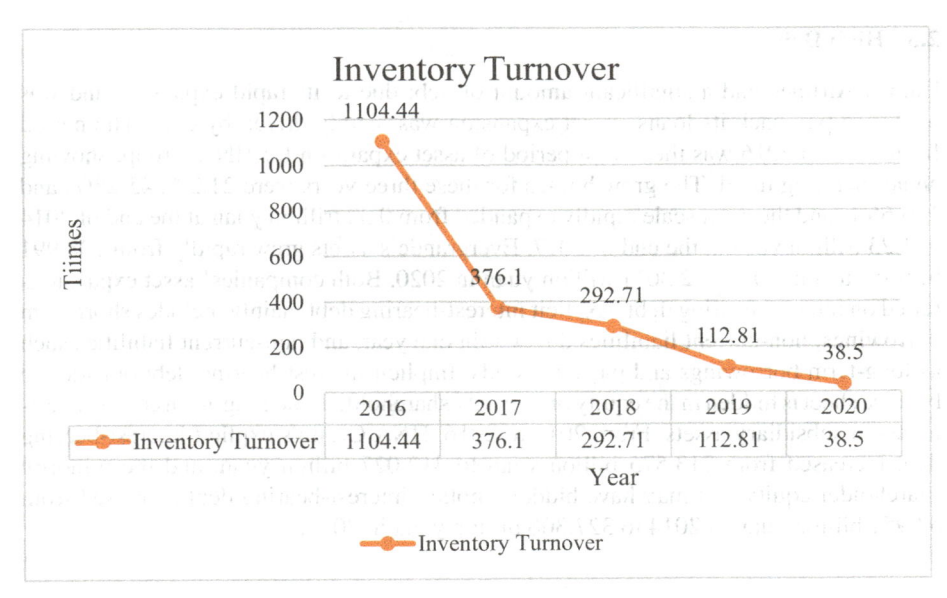

Year	2016	2017	2018	2019	2020
Inventory Turnover	1104.44	376.1	292.71	112.81	38.5

Fig. 2. Inventory Turnover of HNA Group

Total Assets Turnover

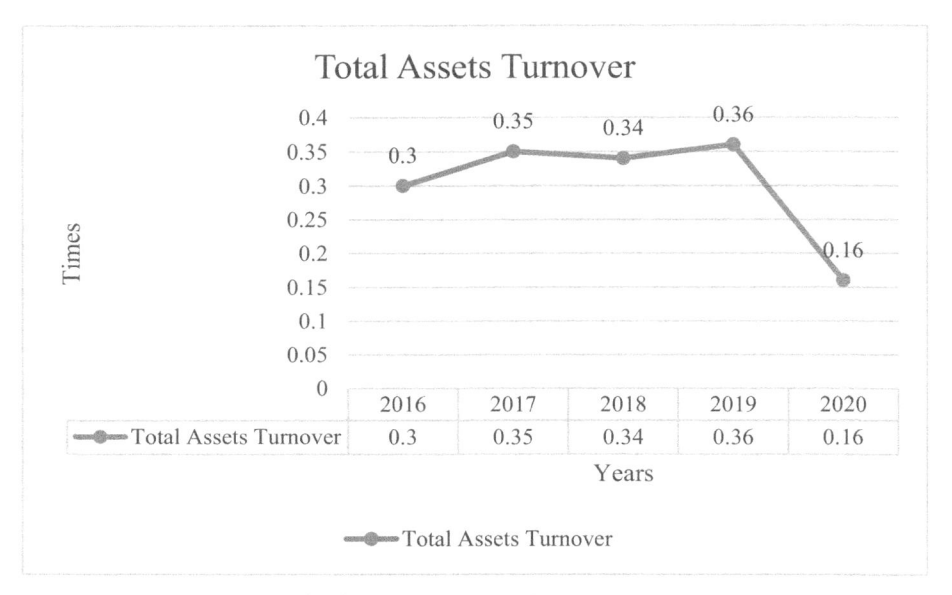

Years	2016	2017	2018	2019	2020
Total Assets Turnover	0.3	0.35	0.34	0.36	0.16

Fig. 3. Total Turnover of HNA Group

2.3 High Debt

Hainan Airlines had a significant amount of debt due to its rapid expansion and was unable to pay back its loans. Asset expansion was mainly driven by debt. The period from 2014 to 2016 was the fastest period of asset expansion for HNA Group, showing an accelerating trend. The growth rates for these three years were 21.2%, 45.28%, and 116.66%, and the asset scale rapidly expanded from 0.32 trillion yuan at the end of 2014 to 1.23 trillion yuan at the end of 2017. Evergrande's assets grew rapidly from 238.991 billion yuan in 2012 to 2.3011 trillion yuan in 2020. Both companies' asset expansions relied on interest-bearing debt. Explicit interest-bearing debt mainly includes short-term borrowings, non-current liabilities due within one year, and non-current liabilities such as long-term borrowings and payable bonds. Implicit interest-bearing debt outside the balance sheet is hidden in the equity of minority shareholders and long-term equity investments in subsidiary assets. From 2014 to 2016, HNA Group's explicit interest-bearing debt increased from 213.575 billion yuan to 412.027 billion yuan, and the minority shareholder equity that may have hidden implicit interest-bearing debt increased from 53.951 billion yuan in 2014 to 327.306 billion yuan in 2016.

Starting from the year 2000, under the background of large-scale mergers and acquisitions in major airlines, Hainan Airlines Group continuously carried out a large number of mergers and acquisitions in the aviation industry by leveraging financing and leverage methods beyond its own capital strength in order to gain a competitive advantage. Its huge debt constituted potential risks. Since 2018, Hainan Airlines Group has started to tighten its assets and dispose of acquired assets to save itself. The development of the aviation industry was further hit by the COVID-19 epidemic in 2020. Triggered by the epidemic, Hainan Airlines' outstanding debt of hundreds of billions of yuan made the company unable to sustain the burden, ultimately leading to bankruptcy and reorganization. As of the balance sheet date of 2020, the current liabilities of Hainan Airlines Group exceeded the current assets by approximately 112.6 billion yuan, with a net loss of 28.2 billion yuan attributable to shareholders' equity. Its huge debt set the stage for its subsequent bankruptcy.

2.4 Low Debt-Paying Ability

From Figure 4 and Table 1, it can be seen that, since 2017, the current ratio and quick ratio of HNA Group have decreased significantly, and the main reason for the change is the continuous increase in current liabilities. The upward trend of the debt-to-asset ratio in the past 5 years reflects an increasing long-term debt risk.

According to Figure 5, the interest coverage ratio was as low as 0.22 in 2018 and reached a new low of -10.64 in 2020. As the interest coverage rate of 1.5 is the minimum acceptable ratio for a cooperation and the tipping point refers to the threshold at which lenders are likely to deny the company any further loans. Therefore, it is even more difficult to maintain the aviation industry which was further hit by the COVID-19 epidemic

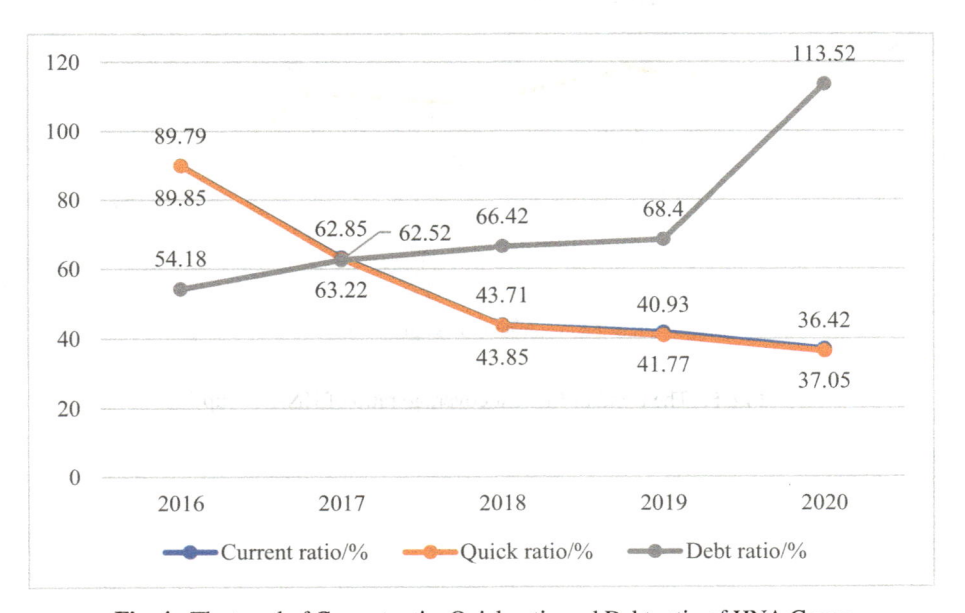

Fig. 4. The trend of Current ratio, Quick ratio and Debt ratio of HNA Group

in 2020. Triggered by the epidemic, Hainan Airlines' outstanding debt of hundreds of billions of yuan made the company unable to sustain the burden, ultimately leading to bankruptcy and reorganization. As of the balance sheet data of 2020, the current liabilities of Hainan Airlines Group exceeded the current assets by approximately 112.6 billion yuan, with a net loss of 28.2-billion-yuan attributable normal cash flow in 2020 [4]. In 2018, HNA Group suffered a loss of 3.591 billion yuan, a year-on-year decrease of 208.08%. The reason for the loss was that the company faced the risk of loss and decreased debt security due to the blood support provided to its parent company HNA Group. Through the analysis of debt-paying ability indicators, it was found that HNA Holdings' debt crisis was triggered by the loss in 2018, and the low interest coverage ratio raised questions about its sustainable operation. The impact of the COVID-19 pandemic in 2020 directly pushed HNA Holdings to the brink of bankruptcy.

Table 1. Debt-paying ability indicators of HNA Group from 2016 to 2020

	2016	2017	2018	2019	2020
Current ratio/%	89.85	63.22	43.85	41.77	37.05
Quick ratio/%	89.79	62.85	43.71	40.93	36.42
Debt ratio/%	54.18	62.52	66.42	68.4	113.52
Interest Coverage Ratio	1.9	3.29	0.22	1.19	−10.64

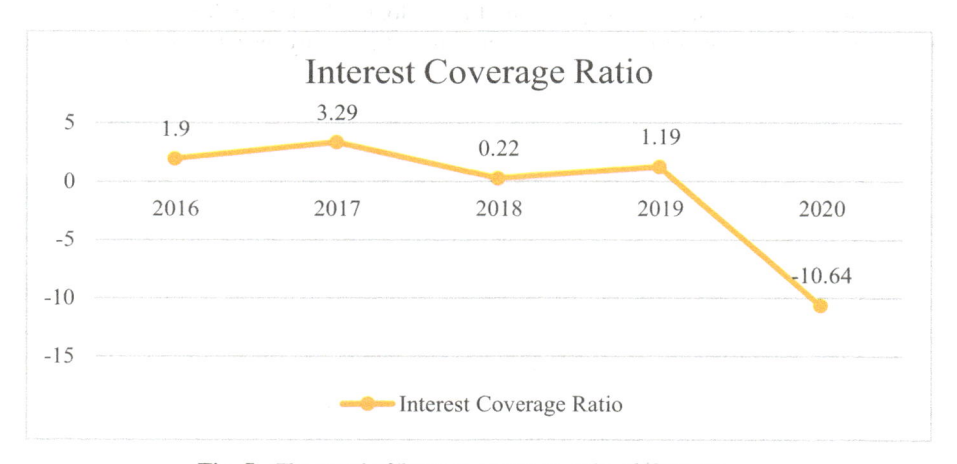

Fig. 5. The trend of Interest coverage ratio of HNA Group

2.5 Uncertainty in the External Environment

The development of the aviation industry is closely related to the macro economy. The aviation passenger and freight traffic are influenced to some extent by the macroeconomic cycle. When the macro economy is doing well, the demand for air transportation increases, while it decreases when the economy is performing poorly. After the outbreak of the "financial crisis" in 2008, the global macro economy entered a period of sustained depression. International economic theory holds that when the world economic growth rate is below 3%, the world economy enters a recessionary period [4]. The world economy's overall GDP growth rate has been in a sustained decline since 2010, with insufficient driving force for total market demand, which directly affects the volume of international flights. To mitigate the impact of the financial crisis on the economic environment, China adopted an active fiscal policy and loose monetary policy to stimulate economic growth, resulting in a loose financing environment in the market [5]. Against this backdrop, many enterprises adopted a high-leverage business model, relying on debt to maintain daily operations and aggressive expansion, laying hidden risks for debt defaults. At the same time, China's economic growth maintained a medium to high-speed growth rate of about 7% from 2010 to 2014, but after 2014, the country's economy entered a "new normal", with industrial upgrading and structural adjustment leading to a slowdown in economic growth, and the domestic economy maintaining a level below 7%, with significant downward pressure on economic development [6]. As a result, credit risks accumulated in the past through debt-fueled expansion continue to erupt, with the number and amount of bond defaults increasing year by year, leading to the continuous release of bond default risks, and default becoming "normalized".

As the macro economy enters a downward trend and global quantitative tightening, the decrease in total demand leads to a reduction in aviation transportation demand, directly affecting the company's main business income and reducing its profitability. The company's operating funds are reduced, making it easy to fall into financial difficulties. At the same time, when the economy is weak, it can lead to investors losing confidence in the market, resulting in a decrease in market capital liquidity, and companies facing refinancing difficulties. Therefore, in this economic environment, HNA Group's core business, Hainan Airlines, is easily prone to financial difficulties. In its high-debt situation, it is also difficult to obtain financing, causing HNA Group to suffer a great blow.

3 Financial Risk Prevention Measures

3.1 Priority to Developing Core Business, Plan Diversified Operations Reasonably

In order for companies to benefit from a diversification strategy, they must prioritize the development of their core business and plan their diversification strategy rationally. Firstly, companies must ensure the stable development of their core business, focus on their core business, and continuously enhance its core competitiveness. Only when the company's financial indicators such as debt-paying ability and profitability are relatively stable, can the company gradually try to diversify its operations. Secondly, companies must be cautious in implementing unrelated diversification, seek reasonable profit growth points, and carefully select industries to enter based on their own industry characteristics. This is because unrelated diversification will occupy more investment capital and cost expenses, and if there is not enough time to integrate and adjust the merged industry with the core business, the synergistic effect between the industries will not be fully realized. Instead, it will increase the conflict between the core business and non-core business, thereby increasing the company's financial risk.

3.2 Broaden Financing Channels and Establish a Reasonable Financing Structure

During its diversification process, HNA Group mainly used equity pledge and bond financing to raise funds, leading to a continuous decline in the company's liquidity. Therefore, the company should broaden its financing channels, formulate a reasonable financing structure, and establish and improve its financing system. On the one hand, the company can optimize and expand new financing methods by adjusting the proportion of equity and bond financing, thereby reducing the company's financing costs and effectively controlling its financial risks. On the other hand, the company should focus on its internal profitability, pay attention to changes in financial indicators and development trends, and promote its own development by enhancing internal retention. This will help the company maintain its surplus while formulating a reasonable financing structure.

3.3 Improve the Financial Risk Warning and Management System

As the diversification degree of an enterprise continues to increase, its scale will expand, and the risks it faces will also increase. Therefore, when an enterprise engages in diversified operations, it must control and manage its financial risks. Firstly, it is necessary to establish a financial risk warning system, relying on modern financial information integration systems to establish risk monitoring and transmission mechanisms, selecting reasonable warning indicators through qualitative and quantitative analysis methods, and establishing a comprehensive financial risk assessment mechanism to identify and alert on unreasonable data generated by various businesses. Secondly, attention should be paid to cultivating the awareness and ability of financial risk warning among the company's management and other managers. Regular training should be conducted to learn how to analyze and respond to financial risks, and a high-quality financial risk management system should be established. Finally, enterprises should improve their talent training and introduction mechanisms for diversified operations and introduce talents with strong financial risk awareness and rich experience to join the enterprise's management team to improve and optimize the corporate governance level and help diversified enterprises develop quickly and smoothly.

4 Conclusion

In conclusion, the bankruptcy of Hainan Airlines Group was the result of a combination of factors, including overexpansion, mismanagement, fierce competition in the aviation market, and the impact of the COVID-19 pandemic. Hainan Airlines expanded too rapidly and aggressively, leading to an increase in debt. The company's aggressive acquisition strategy was poorly executed, and the acquired subsidiaries repeatedly suffered losses, which eroded the overall profitability of the group. Hainan Airlines also faced mismanagement issues such as declining asset liquidity and declining debt-paying ability, as well as high debt levels.

This paper mainly focuses on the analysis of the reasons for the bankruptcy of Hainan Airlines Group but lacks a quantitative prediction of bankruptcy. Subsequent research will focus on the establishment of a financial crisis auditing early warning model, which can assess the bankruptcy risk of enterprises through data. This will help investment institutions, governments, and the companies themselves to make reasonable and timely decisions, thereby helping to reduce losses.

To prevent similar situations in the future, airlines should prioritize sound financial management and risk mitigation strategies in their operations. Companies should avoid excessive debt levels and aggressive expansion strategies without proper financial planning. Additionally, businesses should conduct thorough due diligence and post-acquisition integration to ensure the success of acquisitions. These measures will help ensure long-term financial stability for companies in the aviation industry. Hainan Airlines' bankruptcy serves as a cautionary tale for other airlines seeking rapid growth and expansion and highlights the importance of strategic planning and management in the aviation sector.

References

1. Nicholas, I.: Bigger is Better. Flightglobal, p. 43, 16–22 September 2003. Accessed 30 Oct 2012
2. Ouyang, Iris. HNA Group enters bankruptcy restructuring as China's largest asset buyer succumbs to debt after decade-long shopping spree. SCMP, 29 January 2021. Accessed 30 Jan 2021
3. Page, S., Li, J.: The formation of Hainan airlines: the inside story of how the pre-body of HNA group came to be. SSRN Electr. J. (2018).https://doi.org/10.2139/ssrn.3104281
4. These 5 charts reveal the Global Economic Outlook for 2022. World Economic Forum. (n.d.). https://www.weforum.org/agenda/2022/01/global-economic-outlook-5-charts-world-bank/. Accessed 29 Apr 2023
5. Kim, J., Wang, M., Park, D., Petalcorin, C.C.: Fiscal policy and economic growth: some evidence from China. Rev. World Econ. **157**(3), 555–582 (2021). https://doi.org/10.1007/s10290-021-00414-5
6. Ondris, P.: Analysis of the causes of the process of China'S GDP growth decline and perspective solutions. Part 1," Almanach (Actual Issues in World Economics and Politics), Ekonomická univerzita, Fakulta medzinárodných vzťahov, **14**(2), 22–36 (2019)

Cognitive Biases in Second-Hand and Pre-sale Real Estate Prices in Nanjing

Bing Shen(✉)

College of Economics and Management, Nanjing Forestry University, Nanjing 210037, China
shuyouruci968@njfu.edu.cn

Abstract. The real estate market has achieved rapid growth during the past few years due to urbanization, rising incomes, and some government policies aimed at promoting housing ownership. Therefore, the subject of the real estate market has long been studied as a core problem in the society, especially when it shapes the financial market. This article explores the effects of psychological biases such as loss aversion, endowment effect, herding effect, and animal spirits on the real estate market. These cognitive biases can lead to irrational behavior among buyers and sellers in the market, ultimately affecting the overall market's performance and efficiency. To illustrate the effects of cognitive biases, a comparison between the pre-sale and second-hand real estate markets has been examined. The objective of the article is to research the influence of behavioral economics on the real estate sector and offer methods for dealing with these problems. The study finds that cognitive effects can lead to rigid real estate prices and transactions, which can cause property bubbles in severe cases. The study also provides suggestions from both policymakers and property buyers, such as considering financial subsidies and sunk costs to constrain the effects of cognitive biases.

Keywords: Real Estate Market · Second-hand Market · Pre-sale Market · Cognitive Biases

1 Introduction

Cognitive biases in the real estate market have been a heated topic for researchers in recent years. It is important for people to realize that cognitive biases play significant roles in the real estate sector. Over the previous ten years, substantial growth has been seen in the property market. As the global economy recovered from the global financial crisis of 2008, the property market began to experience a rapid growth in demand and rising housing prices. However, a significant downturn with the restrictions imposed by the government had been seen in the real estate sector. In addition, the COVID-19 pandemic has had substantial effects on the real estate market, leading to several changes in house demand and supply. The Chinese real estate market plays a significant role of the economy of the country and a key source of investment for house investors.

It is vital for people to understand the real estate market through behavioral economics. Some researchers demonstrated that people who are loss averse tend to set higher reservation prices, which leads to higher prices in real estate. Additionally, higher prices can lead to longer negotiation times which can result in longer transaction times in the market. Apart from loss aversion, the endowment effect also plays an important role in real estate market. Endowment effect can lead house owners to overvalue their property. This overvaluation can lead to higher asking prices of real estates, contributing to higher market value. Additionally, herding has a great influence on the real estate market. Herding is a behavioral phenomenon that occurs when people tend to follow the actions of others. In the real estate market, the herding effect can cause a concentration of investors in a particular area, leading to an overheated market in that area. Moreover, animal spirits of investors can influence the real estate market. If investors are feeling optimistic about the overall market, they tend to be more likely to invest in properties, which can drive up overall prices. Conversely, if they are feeling pessimistic, they tend to be less likely to invest in properties, which leads to lower prices.

Consequently, the context of the article mainly concentrates on the phenomenon of the Nanjing real estate market over the past 10 years. Second-hand and pre-sale real estate market have been analyzed in order for property buyers and sellers to confirm the effects of cognitive bias in the real estate market. It reveals that several cognitive biases can have significant impacts on the real estate market through both investors and property sellers. What is more, multiple suggestions on these phenomena have been studied in this article in order to address cognitive bias in the real estate market. The contribution of the paper is to analyze the effects of cognitive biases and offer some solutions in addressing these problems in the real estate market.

2 Analysis on Nanjing's Real Estate Market

2.1 Background Description of Nanjing's Real Estate Market

Nanjing has gone through significant development in both the secondhand housing market and pre-sale housing market in the past 10 years. During the 10 years, there have been many changes in the main districts of Nanjing. The development of Nanjing's real estate market is attributed to ten major popular districts.

In terms of pre-sale real estate market, significant growth has been discovered in Nanjing's real estate market over the past 10 years. Pre-sale houses are new houses typically built during a specific pre-sale. From 2012 to 2014, the pre-sale real estate market was relatively stable. However, from 2015 to 2017, the real estate market experienced a rapid growth, with a surge in real estate construction projects. In 2017, the Nanjing government implemented strict regulations on pre-sale property prices. From 2018 to 2022, the overall market grew stably under the constraints of the government. Besides, the outbreak of the epidemic effectively reduced the number of new construction projects and stabilized the real estate market.

Properties that have been previously owned and lived in are referred to as second-hand real properties. The second-hand real estate market was relatively stable from 2012 to 2021. However, in 2022, the overall market began to cool down due to the epidemic, along with strict restrictions imposed by some authorities on the real estate market. These measures effectively lowered the price of second-hand real estate.

2.2 Cognitive Bias in Real Estate Prices

In the real estate market, cognitive bias can play a significant role in the real estate market, influencing both buying and selling behavior of homeowners. House owners are reluctant to sell their property for a price lower than what they initially paid for it because of loss aversion. Additionally, the endowment effect can lead house owners to overvalue their house property. As to the owners, they will develop a sentimental attachment to the property, which makes them to believe that their property is worth more than the market price. Also, the overall unstable prices can reflect the herding and animal spirits in the house owners' actions.

To analyze the effects of cognitive bias on real estate prices, comparisons between the prices of second-hand houses and pre-sale houses have been done. Nanjing house market exemplifies these two theories. The prices of second-hand and pre-sale houses has been studied in Nanjing over the past ten years.

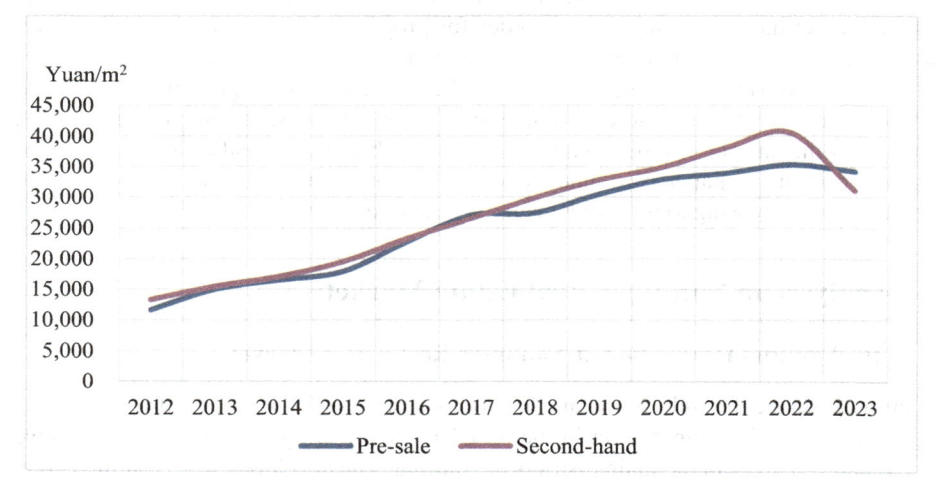

Fig. 1. Property price of the main districts of Nanjing (Source of data: https://www.cih-index.com/)

Figure 1 is divided into two main parts. Firstly, this diagram demonstrates the prices of second-hand and pre-sale houses between 2012 and 2023. As it is vividly shown in the diagram, the prices of second-hand houses have risen steadily between 2012 and 2022. In addition, the diagram also shows the prices of the pre-sale houses over the past ten years. Both the prices of second-hand houses and pre-sale houses have been rising over the past ten years. The overall prices in all the main districts have risen over the last decade, not just one single area. It is worth noting that property prices may be affected by government macro-regulation and the severe epidemic. Furthermore, it is evident from the diagram that second-hand houses are more expensive than the pre-sale houses due to the epidemic in general.

As to Figure 2, it shows the trend of second-hand house prices in Nanjing over the last ten years, and that prices have been rising every year. Some places in Nanjing

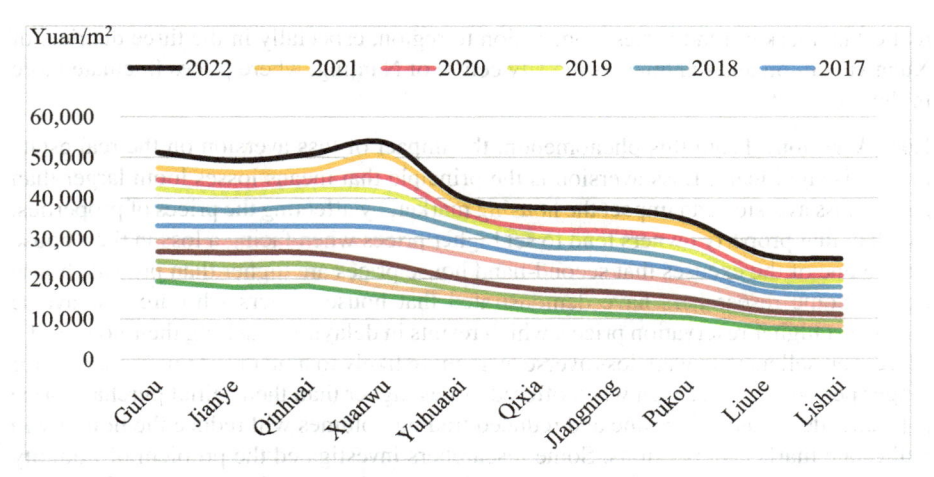

Fig. 2. Second-hand property prices trends in main districts of Nanjing (Source of data: https://www.cih-index.com/)

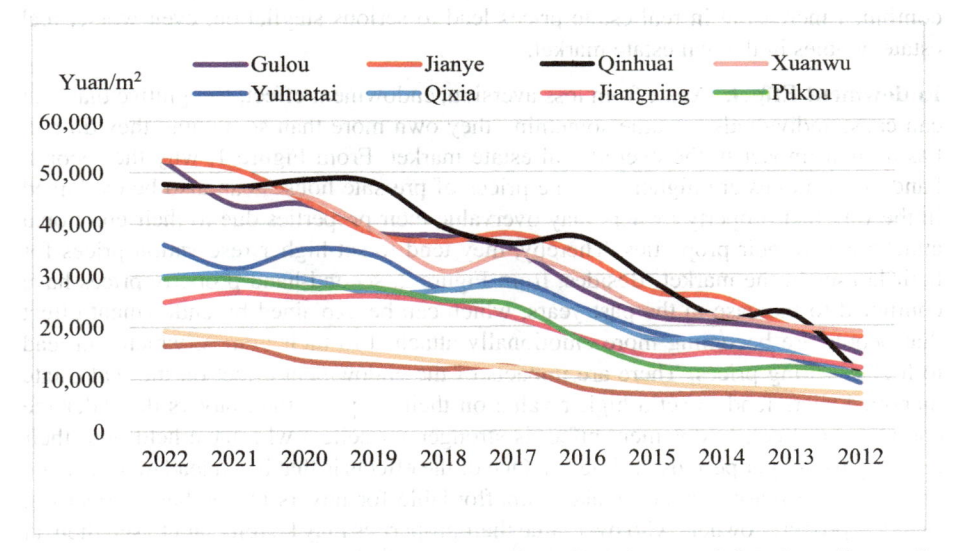

Fig. 3. Pre-sale property prices in main districts of Nanjing (Source of data: https://www.cih-index.com/)

have much higher second-hand property prices than others. Besides, places with higher second-hand property prices tend to be consistently high in areas with high prices, while prices are consistently low in capital areas. The difference in house prices between these two areas has been significant. Also, the difference in prices between these two areas has been large and has increased over time by about 2.5 times.

As to Figure 3, it reveals Nanjing's pre-sale real estate market during the previous 10 years. The overall house prices have increased by 2.5 times. Over the past 10 years, the real estate market trend varies from region to region, especially in the three districts of Xuanwu, Gulou and Qinhuai, as the city centre of Nanjing, where prices fluctuate more in these districts.

Loss Aversion. From this phenomenon, the impact of loss aversion on the real estate market is significant. Loss aversion is the principle that means losses loom larger than gains. Loss aversion can impact the housing market, by affecting the prices of properties. The fact that property owners tend to set higher prices when facing a loss in their house can be one of the excuses that second-hand house prices are higher than pre-sale house prices. Some researchers have demonstrated that house owners who are loss averse tend to set higher reservation prices, which results in delaying in selling their houses [1]. Moreover, sellers who were loss averse were more likely to hold onto their properties for longer periods of time, even when offered prices higher than their initial purchase price [2]. Extended transaction time and reduced trading volumes will reduce the liquidity in real estate market transactions. Some researchers investigated the problem of liquidity in the market and suggested that loss aversion contributes to the tendency of property markets to lose liquidity during down markets, as house owners resist lowering their demand down to pricing levels which maintain normal liquidity [3]. What's worse, continued increasing in real estate prices lead to serious stagflation, even worse, real estate bubbles in the real estate market.

Endowment Effect. Apart from loss aversion, endowment effect, a cognitive bias that can cause individuals to value something they own more than something they do not, has a great impact in the overall real estate market. From Figure 1, why the second-hand house prices are higher than the prices of pre-sale houses can also be explained in the way that property owners may overvalue their properties due to their emotional attachment to their properties. Thereby, they tend to set higher reservation prices for their houses in the market. Besides, from Figure 2, second-hand property prices have continued to increase in the past years, which can be explained by endowment effect that people are becoming more emotionally attached to their homes, which can lead to higher setting prices. There are impacts of the endowment effect on the real estate market. Sellers tend to set a higher value on their property than buyers do under the endowment effect. Endowment effect is stronger for sellers who have held onto their property for longer periods of time [4]. One of the effects is that it can lead to unrealistic pricing in the market, which make it unaffordable for buyers to purchase properties. Besides, property owners who overvalue their properties may be reluctant to sell them at market value, which can result in a shortage of available properties. When the demand is high, while there is a shortage of supply in properties, higher prices will occur in the market. Some researchers suggest that endowment effect may lead to the low turnover of housing stock in China's real estate market, which may have important implications for market efficiency and stability [5]. Furthermore, another effect of endowment effect is that it can lead to longer listing times in the market because house owners will set higher reservation prices and may be reluctant to negotiate and lower down their house prices, which will make the real estate market become rigid in transactions.

Herding. Herding also plays an important role in affecting the real estate market. Herding effect is a behavioral phenomenon that occurs when individuals follow the actions of others, rather than making independent decisions based on their own analysis. Some researchers demonstrated that investors are more likely to follow the behavior of their peers when the market is in a state of high uncertainty, which suggests that herding behavior may be a response to the perceived risk and uncertainty of the market [6]. According to the prices of pre-sale houses in Nanjing, it can be summarized that prices in some areas have been high in the past decade, while in other districts they have been low and there is a wide disparity in prices, which is related to the local environment but can still be explained by the herding effect. When sellers follow the actions of others, they may set higher reservation house prices. Investors perceive the market to be in a state of high uncertainty and react by following the behavior of others, rather than making independent decisions based on their analysis. Therefore, when investors follow the decisions made by others, they may invest in real estate assets that are overvalued, leading to continued increase in house prices in a particular district, which in severe cases would lead to market bubbles in the real estate market. In addition, herding behavior can also lead to a lack of liquidity in real estate prices between different places. This can lead to excessive house prices in a certain region, overheated property speculation, large disparities in house prices between different regions and, in serious cases, uneven regional development and unbalanced human resources.

Animal Spirit. Furthermore, there may have effects of animal spirits on the real estate market. Animal spirits are a term used to describe the psychological factors that drive human behavior, including decision-making in financial markets. One of the effects of animal spirits on the real estate market is that when animal spirits are high, people tend to be more optimistic and more likely to invest in real estate. Animal spirits can lead to excessive risk-taking and speculation, which can further exacerbate the formation of bubbles and credit crunches [7]. According to the prices of pre-sale houses in Nanjing, it can be summarized that prices in some areas have been high in the past decade, while in other districts they have been low, which is related to the animal spirits. People may be more willing to pay a premium for real estate assets under the high animal spirits. Conversely, when animal spirits are low, people tend to make conservative decisions and less likely to invest, which will lead to a crease in demand and a decline in prices. In addition, when animal spirits are high, investors tend to take on higher risk, leading to an increase in speculative investing. This phenomenon can lead to excessive property prices in a long period, which can explain the overall excessive price fluctuations in real estate.

3 Suggestions

There are growing appeals to address these situations in the past years. For some authorities, they should introduce relevant policies to prevent the property market from overheating. Property owners who are constrained by housing equity may benefit from financial assistance to help them make a transition to a new home [8]. For example, local government can provide some financial subsidies to property owners when they are facing a loss in their property. Policymakers may consider implementing measures to encourage long-term investment in property, rather than short-term speculation, in order to promote stability and sustainability in the market [9]. Besides, the government may need to consider the impact of loss aversion and reference points on the effectiveness of policies aimed at stimulating the housing market, such as tax incentives or subsidies. For some authorities such as the central bank can increase the deposit-reserve ratio to control real estate price by reducing the money circulating in the market through a monetary policy. Some researchers indicate that changes in monetary policy have a significant impact on real estate price growth in China. Specifically, an increase in the benchmark interest rate can cause real estate price growth to slow down, while an increase in the money supply leads to real estate price growth to speed up [10]. What is more, reducing transaction costs by reducing real estate commissions and taxes can help to make it easier for householders to sell their homes. In addition, limitations on down-payment costs and the amount of house property are of significant importance. Proper limitations in the market can boost the transactions in real estate market.

As for house buyers in the market, people are required to make prudent decisions under several cognitive bias. In addition, buyers need to consider the sunk costs in buying houses and avoid falling into the sales trap. At a certain total number of houses in the market, lower demand for the residential properties results in the lower house prices. In addition, for house sellers, they should conduct their own research to determine the value of their property and avoid herding effect. Besides, it is very significant to set a realistic reservation price for their property and avoid putting their houses on the market for too long.

4 Conclusion

The last years have seen a lot of discussion about the real estate market. Loss aversion, endowment effect, herding and animal spirits are four behavioral biases that can have significant impacts on real estate market. By comparing the prices of second-hand and pre-sale real estate market in Nanjing during the past 10 years, the study indicates that cognitive biases have great implications in the real estate market, including home prices, the length of transactions and real estate bubbles. Moreover, cognitive biases can also lead to less liquidity and stiff home prices. It is important for market participants to raise awareness of these psychological biases. As to the authorities, more regulations can be taken to mitigate the influence of these cogitative biases, which involves financial assistance and constraint in real estate prices. Besides, for house buyers and sellers, more caution is needed to face the overall complex real estate market such as considering sunk costs and making independent decisions. Understanding these cognitive biases and their effects on real estate prices is extremely important for both property sellers and buyers, as it can help them make more prudent decisions and contribute to a more stable and efficient real estate market.

The findings will be of interest to analyze the future behavior economic biases in real estate market. The insights gained from this study may be of assistance to make people deeply understand the overall real estate sector and avoid irrational decisions. Limitations are that the data analyzed in this article are not representative enough and that there are more real-life behavioral economics influencing the real estate industry. A further study could assess the long-term effects of cognitive biases in real estate market.

References

1. Genesove, D., Mayer, C.: Loss aversion and seller behavior: evidence from the housing market. Quart. J. Econ. **116**(4), 1233–1260 (2001)
2. Buisson, F.: Loss aversion and seller behavior: evidence from the housing market: comment. J. Bus. Econ. Stat. **30**(4), 564–567 (2012)
3. Bokhari, S., Geltner, D.: Loss aversion and anchoring in commercial real estate pricing: empirical evidence and price index implications. Real Estate Econ. **39**(4), 635–670 (2011)
4. Buisson, F.: Prospect theory and loss aversion in the housing market. J. Real Estate Res. **38**(2), 229–250 (2016)
5. Bao, H.X., Gong, C.M.: Endowment effect and housing decisions. Int. J. Strateg. Property Manag. **20**(4), 341–353 (2016)
6. Babalos, V., Balcilar, M., Gupta, R.: Herding behavior in real estate markets: novel evidence from a Markov-switching model. J. Behav. Exp. Finance **8**, 40–43 (2015)
7. Mondschean, T.S., Pecchenino, R.A.: Herd behavior or animal spirits: a possible explanation of credit crunches and bubbles. In: Allin, F.C., Michael, S.L., John H.W. (eds.) The Causes and Costs of Depository Institution Failures, pp. 233–245. Federal Reserve Bank of St. Louis: St. Louis, MO (1995)
8. Engelhardt, G.V.: Nominal loss aversion, housing equity constraints, and household mobility: evidence from the United States. J. Urban Econ. **53**(1), 171–195 (2003)
9. Li, H., Liang, L., Sun, C.: Does property return affect seller behavior? An empirical study of china's real estate market. Behav. Sci. **13**(1), 55 (2023)
10. Xu, X., Chen, T.: The effect of monetary policy on real estate price growth in China. Pacific-Basin Finance J. **20**(1), 62–77 (2012)

How Targeted Poverty Alleviation Policy Program and Other Possible Factors Affect the Wellbeing of Chinese Seniors
Based on the Alkire-Foster Methods

Xinru Fang(✉)

University California Santa Barbara, Goleta, CA 93117, USA
xinrufang@ucsb.edu

Abstract. This study conducted a linear regression analysis to investigate the correlational relationship between Chinese seniors' wellbeing and its possible determinants, in which a difference-in-difference model is adopted to analyze the monetary policy program in China. The study specifically examines several non-monetary possible determinants on seniors' wellbeing, including family characteristics, individual traits, etc. Meanwhile, it makes an attempt to define and conceptualize the notion wellbeing into a numerical, testable index based on Alkire-Foster methods. The results found that the monetary policy program imposes a positive impact on the wellbeing of seniors, but at the same time implies that the loss of young people in households leads to worse wellbeing status of seniors in families. Also, the results again put an emphasis on the significance of medical resources in determining seniors' wellbeing.

Keywords: Alkire-Foster Methods · Aging Problem · Wellbeing

1 Introduction

It is widely aware that China is now going through significant social change. Specifically, according to World Bank (2020), Chinese population falls for first time since 1961 along with declining birth rates over years. Meanwhile, the proportion of the senior population (those aged above 65 years) increased from 13.26% in 2010 to 14.9% in 2022. A continuously aging society with low birth rate is prompting changes in its demographic make-up and triggering the socio-economic challenges for statesmen. One of the heated topics in discussion is the challenges brought to the eldercare pattern in society, which is increasingly prominent in both academia and public domain.

There are currently three main types of eldercare models—family care, social care, and community care. Among the three types of eldercare model, family care is the most common interrelated elderly care model (Hongxin Li and Wei Li 2012). Seeing the family households as basic unit, the model naturally achieves the care function, which is described as the "feedback model" of family care proposed by Fei Xiaotong (1983).

However, the population aging in China is putting tremendous pressure on the family care eldercare model. Due to factors such as the family planning policy, population migration and separation of the elderly and young, the average size of Chinese households has continued to decrease since 1982, from an average of 4.41 people per household in 1982 to 2.27 people in 2021 (CEIC 2022). The United Nations estimated that the dependency ratio (ratio of non-labor force to labor force in households) will reach to 76.5% in 2055 from 37.7% in 2015 (2022). This means that there are fewer family members who can provide care for the elderly, and the overall caregiving burden of the family has increased. As the size of families has decreased, family structures have also become further simplified. The proportion of elderly people living with adult children has decreased, which means that many elderly people find it difficult to receive timely care from their families.

Expecting the backdrop of a significant weakening of the caregiving function of families, it then poses a significant question for the academia: how the family household characteristics in China affect the wellbeing of seniors in the context of family care in aging society? Substantial research has focused on the trend and mechanism of intergenerational support in affecting the seniors' wellbeing. Back in 1992, American scholar Krause has investigated the relationship between providing support to others and wellbeing in later life, focusing on the importance of social support networks in the well-being of seniors. Narrowing the discussion down in the Chinese context, some scholars showed that providing instrumental support to children as older parents and seniors' satisfaction about their descendants are positively correlated with the psychological well-being of elders (Chen 2016). Specifically, the impact of receiving support on seniors' well-being was fully mediated by their satisfaction with their descendants: parents who followed more traditional norms about family support have higher psychological well-being when provided functional support from their children.

Besides the discussion on intergenerational support affecting seniors' wellbeing, many scholars also argues that the pensions and other governmental policies play a mediating role in the relationship between family characteristics and wellbeing of seniors. Liu and Sun (2015) gave a comprehensive overview about China's pension system from a political-economic perspective. He concludes that while the Chinese pension system has established a universal non-contributory pension plan covering the previously ignored population, such as rural residents, it still lacks true universalism. An empirical study has justified the possible relationship by applying the ordered logit regression model based on a sample of 3815 retired urban residents aged over 60 (Abruquah et al. 2019). The results showed that while benefits from the public pension scheme generally enhanced life satisfaction, beneficiaries of certain pension schemes were more advantaged than others. Authors argued that life satisfaction was also affected by gender, residency, provincial level, the financial and emotional support from children as well as self-support abilities. However, the relative significance of each variable has not been articulated in previous research. Furthermore, since 2014 a policy program in China may impose a policy shock on seniors' life arguably, which is Targeted Poverty Alleviation (TPA) in China. Launched in late 2013, the program aims at raising roughly 70 million Chinese citizens out of poverty by the year 2020, through various economic approaches including microfinance, e-commerce, tourism, solar photovoltaic power generation, etc.

The impact of the policy program on the seniors' wellbeing has been remaining not identified and investigated in academia so far.

Besides lack of overall assessment on the weight of different variables affecting seniors' wellbeing during the 8-year period, there is also a more important concern, however. Previous research has not still defined the wellbeing of seniors in concrete, testable dimensions, but rather interchangeably apply life satisfaction of seniors to refer the wellbeing. In fact, there is actually an ongoing debate about the contested nature of well-being concepts in health and social science research and practice. Iglesias in 2016 compared three synthesizing approaches for measuring well-being in Switzerland. The three approaches are the subjective approach, which focuses on individuals' perceptions of their own well-being, the objective approach, which uses objective indicators such as income, and the capability approach, which considers the capabilities to lead fulfilling lives. The study finally concludes that each approach has its own advantages and limitations. Furthering the discussion, Vincent and Knight (2013) views well-being as a macro concept that encompasses both objective and subjective assessments, suggesting combining the three approaches for a comprehensive understanding of well-being. But still, the current academia has not reached a consensus about the general evaluation on wellbeing—a numerical testable standard for well-rounded assessment.

Given the lack of a general look at various variables as well as the unsettled debate on the notion "wellbeing", there is a need for empirical analysis to provide insight into them. And this study is an attempt to provide an empirical multidimensional evaluation on wellbeing and furthermore generally investigate the impact of family characteristics on seniors' wellbeing. Given the upheavals due to COVID-19 pandemic in 2020, which introduces uncertainty and disruption to seniors' wellbeing, all population researched thus only range from 2010 to 2018, and the situations during global pandemic are thus excluded from consideration. Narrowing the topic down, the research question is formulated as what are the characteristics of Chinese family households that determine the well-being index of senior citizens based on the evidence between 2010–2018?

2 Dataset

The data source is China Family Panel Studies (CFPS)—a nationally biennual and representative longitudinal survey of Chinese families. The sample size of CFPS is approximately 50,000 households and 150,000 individuals. The dataset uses a multi-stage, stratified, clustered sampling design to ensure that the sample is nationally representative of the Chinese population. For each sampled household in the study, scholars will interview respondents in person, and questions asked by interviewers will cover various aspects of household structure, income, education, health. Researchers track the same individuals and households twice a year, which provides valuable information on changes in individual and household characteristics and the factors that contribute to those changes.

3 Methods

Firstly, the dependent variable wellbeing of seniors is conceptualized into a numerical index, secondly, possible independent variables besides the "Targeted Poverty Alleviation" policy program are selected based on literature review, thirdly, linear regression analysis is conducted with the use of difference-in-difference model.

3.1 Construction of Multidimensional Wellbeing Index of Seniors (MWI)

Alkire-Foster Method

Formally, the wellbeing index for each senior, c_i, is calculated as a wellbeing matrix, $X = [x_{ij}]$, which is shown as below (Alkire and Foster, p. 477).

Firstly, let $X = [x_{ij}]$ denote the $n \times d$ wellbeing matrix

$$X = \begin{bmatrix} x_{ij} & \cdots & x_{nj} \\ \vdots & \ddots & \vdots \\ x_{id} & \cdots & x_{nd} \end{bmatrix}$$

Where

$$X_{ij} \geq 0 \quad (X_{ij} \in R_+)$$

x_i shows the individual $i = 1, 2, 3 \ldots, n$ wellbeing indicator in $j = 1, 2, 3 \ldots, d$ wellbeing domains. For each indicator j, a deprivation cutoff z_j is set. Let

$$z = (z_1, \ldots, z_j)$$

be the row vector that collects the deprivation cutoffs.

Given the condition $X_{ij} < z_j$, the i individual is identified as deprived in j. Given the X matrix and the z vector, a matrix of deprivation $\left[g_{ij}^0\right]$ is obtained such that

$$g_{ij}^0 = 1 \text{ if } X_{ij} < z_j$$

or

$$g_{ij}^0 = 0 \text{ if } X_{ij} > z_j$$

Let

$$W = (w_1, \ldots, w_d)$$

be the vector of weights that reveals the relative importance of each indicator. Then a deprivation score for each individual senior $i(c_i)$ is obtained by adding their weighted deprivations up:

$$c_i = \sum_{j=1}^{d} w_d g_{ij}^0$$

The c_i is the final wellbeing index of senior for induvial senior citizen.

The senior citizen will be further identified as either satisfying state or non-satisfying state through a cross-domain cut-off, k. That is:

$$\rho_k(x_i, z_j) = 1 \text{ if } c_i \geq k$$

or

$$\rho_k(x_i, z_j) = 0 \text{ if } c_i \geq k$$

Determination of Dimensions, Indicators, and Cross-Domain Cut-Off

See Table 1.

Table 1. Specific dimensions j and indicators x

Dimension	Indicator	z value derived	Weight
Physical health	Nutrition	BMI values >25 or <18.5	1/12
	Functional limits	If being disabled	1/12
	Self-report on health	Self-report on health is lower than 3	1/12
Mental health	Satisfaction on current life	Life satisfaction is lower than 3	1/16
	Satisfaction on the future	Future expectation is lower than 3	1/16
	Cognitive illness	The frequency of feeling nervous is over "sometimes"	1/16
	Social activities	If doing any social activity in 3 months	1/16
Living standards	Fuels	Not using natural gas when cooking	1/24
	Electricity	Power cut had happened in 3 months	1/24
	Water	Not using running water in life	1/24
	Housing conditions	Home cleanness rate is lower than 3	1/24
	Housing areas	House is no smaller than 25 square meters	1/24
	Necessities	Haven't had over 3 necessities listed in questionnaires	1/24

It's a common sense that the increase of poverty always leads to the decrease of wellbeing, thus poverty and wellbeing are often interwoven and seems dissecting the same problem from two sides. As a broad definition of poverty closely relates to a lack of wellbeing, "poverty" and "lack of wellbeing" are used almost interchangeably in academia. Therefore, the Multidimensional Wellbeing Index (MWI) in the report draws inspiration from Multidimension Poverty Index (MPI) as proposed by Alkire and Santos (2010), which become further contextualized in terms of seniors' life. Specifically, the dimension "health" in MPI is further dissected into two dimensions—physical health and mental health. As the dimension "education" in MPI plays a relatively little role in determining seniors' wellbeing, the dimension "education" is removed in the MWI. Also, as Vincent and Knight (2013) argue well-being shall also encompass objective assessments, material living conditions are considered based on a variety of research arguing their determining role in seniors' wellbeing (Pak 2020; Cheng et al. 2018; Galiani et al. 2019). As a result, there are totally three dimensions: physical health, mental health, and living standards.

For each indicator at certain dimension, there is a specific deprivation rule. Firstly, based on the BMI standards released by Center for Disease Control and Prevention, if one's BMI is 18.5 to 25, it falls within the Healthy Weight range. So, when BMI value is greater than 25 or smaller 18.5, the BMI indicator would be deprived. Secondly, if one report any type of disability, the indicator functional limit would be deprived to identify the disable people. Thirdly, on the range from 1 to 5, a greater value indicates a better situation people have, thus if one had chosen the value lower than middle value 3, it arguably indicates a relatively insufficient condition people might have. As indicators satisfaction on current life, expectation for future, frequency of feeling nervous (cognitive illness), and housing conditions adopt the 5-point range evaluation standard, these indicators would be deprived if the value reported is lower than 3. Fourthly, if one had not reported any social activity in the past three months, that would indicate arguably socially loneliness and the indicator social activity would be deprived. Fifthly, it's a common sense that the sample living conditions today include continuous use of electricity, running water and natural gas. Thus, if one had failed to achieve the sustaining use of electricity, water, or gas, the specific indicator would be deprived. Sixthly, as the official poverty standards in TAP program state that people whose housing areas are smaller than 25 square meter will be considered as citizens with poverty in terms of housing, indicator housing area would be deprived if one's housing area is smaller than 25 square meter.

Alkire and Foster (2011, pp. 482–483) suggest that the determination of the cross-domain cut-off, k, have normative implications. The value of the identification parameter, ρ_k, which is calculated based on the cross-domain thresholds is influenced by the attributes considered in the domain. In situations where deprivation in certain domains could lead to severe human rights violations, it may be appropriate to set the cross-dimension cut-off, k, to the minimum level. This would demonstrate that all human rights are of equal importance and are essential for human well-being. As the construction of multidimensional wellbeing index is largely based on the Alkire-Foster methodologies, I shall argue that any deficiency in each aspect of seniors' wellbeing may affect the wellbeing of seniors overall. So, the cross-domain cut-off is set at 33%.

3.2 Principle of Selecting Variables

The TPA policy targets at economic and financial development in low-income households, and therefore the regression analysis excludes all monetary factors and take more non-monetary factors related to family household characteristics into account. Previous studies have already provided sufficient variables relating to wealth inequality among households. The traditional literature includes level of education, ethnicity, gender, region, and other variables repeatedly mentioned by western academia (Kiefer 2008; Enkvist et al. 2012; Zhuang 2022). However, there are still several factors that differentiate the Chinese context with western context, which suggest some unique variables besides the traditional ones. For instance, the Chinese culture puts an emphasis on the filial piety, compared with the Western cultures. According to a 2014 survey, approximately "69.9% of older people wanted to age in their own home, while 41.3% expected their children to take care of themselves (Han et al. 2020)". Such huge demand for the intergenerational support is very likely to influence the well-being of different households by some degree.

3.3 Difference-in-Difference Model

To examine the causal impact of TPA program on seniors' wellbeing, a linear difference-in-difference model (DID) is applied based on observational data. Based on Kollamparambil and Etinzock (2019), the DID model is specified as following

$$c_{it} = \beta_0 + \beta_1 Post_{it} + \beta_2 Treat_{it} + \beta_3 (Post_{it} \times Treat_{it}) + \beta_4 X_{it} + \varepsilon_{it}$$

where the outcome variable multidimensional wellbeing index for an individual i at time t (c_{it}) is equal to the sum of a constant term (β_0), the treatment variable ($\beta_1 Post_{it}$), the post-intervention time period ($\beta_2 Treat_{it}$), the interaction between treatment and post-intervention ($\beta_3 (Post_{it} \times Treat_{it})$), and an error term ($\varepsilon_{it}$). The treatment in this case refers to the TPA policy program on seniors whose annual income level is below the 2300 yuan per year (Chen 2016), which was carried out by Chinese government at the beginning of 2015.

4 Results

The first part of the study is the descriptive analyses, including the statistics on indicators in the index as well as the summary of variables used in analysis, the second part is the results of the linear regression analyses, which include the situations based on extent of urbanization and regions.

4.1 Descriptive Analysis

Summary Statistics of Variables in Linear Regression Analysis
The chart below shows the summary statistics on the independent and dependent variables in the analysis, which reveals characteristics of the sampled population (Table 2).

Table 2. Overview of variables in linear regression analysis

Overview of variables	Mean	Std. Dev.	Min	Max
Multidimensional wellbeing index	.371	.099	.083	.722
Living in urban areas	.447	.497	0	1
Regions	2.261	1.069	1	4
Family size	4.169	1.965	1	19
Number of seniors in family	.373	.666	0	4
Number of middle-aged in family	2.63	1.336	0	10
Number of children in family	1.587	1.911	0	11
Ratio of elders over children	.081	.184	0	2
Dependency ratio	.685	.725	0	5
Percent of female in family	.523	.283	0	1
Percent of working people in family	.419	.381	0	1
Individual education level	6.793	4.763	0	22
Number of chronic diseases among elders	.431	.658	0	5
Distance to nearest medical center	.002	.012	0	1
If having functional limits	12	9.097	0	62
If doing any social activities	.088	.283	0	1
Number of pensions in households	.482	.95	0	7

The variable regions classify four regions of China into value 1 to 4, and its means 2.26 implies that people from eastern region and middle regions (more economically developed regions) are more sampled. And in terms of the extent of urban areas sampled, the mean 0.44 indicates relatively more people in rural areas are sampled.

Summary Statistics of Indicators in Multidimensional Wellbeing Index

The multidimensional wellbeing index (MWI) reflects the extent of seniors' both subjective and objective wellbeing, whose higher value indicates a worse wellbeing status of seniors. Specifically, the below shows the descriptive statistics on the MWI index and different indicators constituting the index (Table 3).

The mean of the combined result—MWI—is approximately 0.278, meaning a relatively high wellbeing status for seniors in sample generally. By contrast to the low value of MWI, three indicators higher than the mean of MWI are therefore worth of pondering, including housing conditions, future expectation, and cognitive illness.

Summary Statistics of Deprived Households Based on Cross-Domain Cutoff
See Table 4.

Based on the cross-domain cutoff on MWI, the percentage of households deprived in terms of their wellbeing display relatively considerable differences varying by urbanization, regions, and several household characteristics. Seniors living in urban areas are

Table 3. Overview of indicators in multidimensional wellbeing index

Indicators	Mean	Std. Dev.	Min	Max
Overall result (MWI)	.278	.074	.062	.542
Nutrition	.27	.444	0	1
Functional limits	0	.02	0	1
Self-report on health	.243	.429	0	1
Life Satisfaction	.185	.388	0	1
Future expectation	.89	.314	0	1
Cognitive illness	.991	.096	0	1
Social activities	.351	.215	0	1
Fuels	.392	.488	0	1
Electricity	.261	.439	0	1
Water	.052	.222	0	1
Housing cleanness	.347	.476	0	1
Housing areas	.008	.089	0	1
Necessities	.066	.248	0	1

Table 4. Summary on deprived households based on cross-domain cutoff

Types	Category	Percentage of deprived households
Gender	Male	.167
	Female	.168
Urbanization	Urban	.292
	Rural	.333
Regions	Eastern	.332
	Middle	.392
	Western	.465
	Northeastern	.41
Dependency ratio	Low dependency ratio	.394
	High dependency ratio	.46
Distance to Medical center	Short distance to medical center	.173
	Long distance to medical center	.397
Educational level	High educational level	.308
	Low educational level	.418

shown to have a relatively better wellbeing compared to those in rural settings. This is arguably due to better access to healthcare, social services, and economic opportunities in urban centers.

Summary Statistics of Wellbeing Status in Multidimensional Wellbeing Index
See Table 5.

Table 5. Summary on wellbeing status in multidimensional wellbeing index

Types	Variables	N	Mean of MWI	Percentage of Satisfying Status
Gender	Male	16560	.262	62.5%
	Female	15128	.263	62.5%
Urbanization	Rural	43580	.333	50.1%
	Urban	35166	.292	53.5%
Regions	Eastern	25458	.297	52.8%
	Western	19716	.313	51.2%
	Middle	21918	.332	50.1%
	North-eastern	12128	.319	50.8%

In terms of gender aspects, both male and female seniors have relatively same mean of MWI, which suggests that no significant difference in the general wellbeing of male and female Chinese seniors. While seniors living in rural areas have a higher mean value of MWI compared to those living in urban areas, indicating that rural seniors have worse wellbeing than their urban counterparts. It's again justified by the fact that the percentage of satisfying status for rural seniors is lower at 50.1% compared to 53.5% for urban seniors (Table 6).

Table 6. Summary on results of multidimensional wellbeing index with specific dimensions

Indicators	Mean		Std. Dev.	
	Before TPA	After TPA	Before TPA	After TPA
Overall result (MWI)	.281	.255	.075	.065
Nutrition	.164	.161	.37	.368
Functional limits	.312	.301	.455	.458
Self-report on health	.278	.334	.448	.471
Life Satisfaction	.197	.204	.398	.403
Future expectation	.869	.864	.337	.343
Cognitive illness	.991	.99	.096	.099

(*continued*)

Table 6. (*continued*)

Indicators	Mean		Std. Dev.	
	Before TPA	After TPA	Before TPA	After TPA
Social activities	.301	.21	.236	.125
Fuels	.391	.283	.488	.45
Electricity	.372	0	.483	0
Water	.035	0	.183	0
Housing cleanness	.347	.255	.476	.436
Housing areas	.005	.004	.071	.063
Necessities	.127	0	.333	0

Comparing the mean and standard deviation in every indicator between the period before Target Poverty Alleviation policy program carried out and after TPA, results show that most indicators show a decrease in both mean and standard deviation after TPA policy program. It shows that the wellbeing of seniors is improved and their wellbeing index are closer to the mean. Among the indicators, nutrition and functional limits show a small decrease in mean and standard deviation, indicating that the TPA policy program has improved the access to food and medical services for seniors, which has led to a reduction in functional limitations caused by poor nutrition and health conditions. It's justifiable as the TPA policy aims at directed the new rural cooperative medical system and major illness insurance towards the poor, while increasing support through medical assistance, temporary aid, and charitable relief.

4.2 Regression Analysis

Overall Results Based on Urban and Rural Areas

The chart below shows the results of linear regression analysis, including the coefficients of each variable with certain significance. The results are further classified into urban and rural areas (Table 7).

The results show that the TPA policy is significantly correlated with the wellbeing index across areas, and the negative correlation indicates its generally positive impact on seniors' wellbeing. Besides the monetary policy program, the variables related to medical conditions display great significance in correlation with the wellbeing index. Specifically, number of chronic disease of seniors is positively correlated with the wellbeing index whose coefficient is approximately 0.007. Comparatively, the distance to medical center has a far greater positive coefficient with the index, which is about 0.421. Other variables showing the great significance across rural and urban areas are educational level and percent of labor in the households. In addition, the two variables percent of female and number of pension in households have different extent of significance varying by regions, having a relatively smaller coefficient with the wellbeing index.

First, rural areas in China tend to have a weaker social welfare system and poorer access to medical services, which may make the financial and medical support provided

Table 7. Summary on regression results based on urban and rural areas

Variables	Overall	Urban areas	Rural areas
TPA policy effect	−0.0152***	−0.00138	−0.0193***
	(0.00494)	(0.00962)	(0.00574)
Time	0.0231***	0.0388***	0.0157***
	(0.00219)	(0.00343)	(0.00281)
Treated	0.0256***	0.00723	0.0255***
	(0.00394)	(0.00785)	(0.00450)
Dependency ratio	0.00124	−0.00389*	0.00565***
	(0.00137)	(0.00217)	(0.00174)
Number of senior chronic disease	0.00680***	0.00464**	0.00855***
	(0.00119)	(0.00189)	(0.00149)
Distance to medical center	0.421***	0.568***	0.367***
	(0.0867)	(0.197)	(0.0948)
Ratio of elders over young	0.00547	0.00332	0.00534
	(0.00570)	(0.00992)	(0.00683)
Percent of females in family	−0.00740**	−0.00152	−0.00555
	(0.00343)	(0.00586)	(0.00419)
Individual education level	−0.00314***	−0.00241***	−0.00275***
	(0.000202)	(0.000316)	(0.000269)
Percent of labor in households	0.0288***	0.0298***	0.0153***
	(0.00245)	(0.00411)	(0.00322)
Number of pension in household	0.00216**	−0.000648	0.00373***
	(0.000941)	(0.00148)	(0.00120)
Constant	0.285***	0.269***	0.292***
	(0.00407)	(0.00649)	(0.00514)
Observations	6,423	2,488	3,913
R-squared	0.105	0.121	0.068

Standard errors in parentheses, ***p < 0.01, **p < 0.05, *p < 0.1

by the TPA policy program more critical for seniors in these areas. By contrast, urban areas typically have better access to social welfare and medical services, which may make the impact of the TPA policy program less significant for seniors in these areas—justified by the greater significance of factors like the number of senior chronic disease and the number of pension in households.

Second, social and cultural factors, such as family structure and values, also differ between urban and rural areas in China. For instance, in rural areas, the prevalence of left-behind seniors who have been separated from their families due to work or migration may exacerbate social isolation and loneliness among seniors, negatively impacting their wellbeing. By contrast, in urban areas, seniors may have greater access to social activities and support networks, which may mitigate the impact of social isolation. The social and cultural factors may explain the different significance and effect of dependency ratio in rural areas. In rural areas, where seniors' physical and mental wellbeing heavily relies on the young, the greater dependency ratio implies the bigger problems faced with elders and thus decreases their wellbeing level. But in urban areas, where seniors' life less relies on the young people, the dependency ratio play a relatively smaller role in seniors' wellbeing.

Third, the differences in economic development and living standards between urban and rural areas may also affect seniors' wellbeing. While urban areas have seen rapid economic growth and increased access to modern amenities, many rural areas still struggle with poverty and limited access to basic needs, such as clean water and adequate housing. This may make the impact of the TPA policy program more critical for seniors in rural areas, who may face greater challenges in meeting their basic needs and accessing essential services.

What should also be noted is that the role of several variables concerning family characteristics reveals the dillemmas in current Chinese eldercare situations. Contrary to expectations, the percent of labor is shown to have a negative impact on seniors' wellbeing given its positive coefficient with the wellbeing index. It reveals the story of economic development from the perspective of seniors, however. As more young people keep busy bringing home bacon and neglect the family, seniors miss the young people to rely on and therefore lack their both physical support and mental accompany to sustain their wellbeing. It can be justified by the reversing effect of dependency ratio in affecting seniors' wellbeing varying by areas. In the rural areas, where the phenomena "empty-nest seniors and left-over children" are more prominent, the increasing dependency ratio implies the greater financial pressure on adults and increase their likeability of working outside the local communities, which triggers the loneliness of seniors in both physical and mental levels and therefore results in a loss of wellbeing as the positive correlation shows. By contrast, there is a positive correlation between dependency ratio and wellbeing index in the urban areas, where the income and capital play a more significant role in one's life. The greater financial pressures associated with increasing dependency ratio largely leads to worse material conditions and thus the wellbeing of seniors.

Besides that, the two variables distance to medical center and the number of chronic diseases are positively correlated with the wellbeing index, which is significant across both rural and urban areas. Based on common sense and empirical results, it's clear that more chronic diseases as well as longer distance to medical centers lead to worse physical health of seniors and possibly leads to more mental pressures. It can be argued that a more well-rounded medical environment has a mediating impact on the number of chronic diseases. Compared to eastern and middle regions, whose medical resources is relatively rich, variable number of chronic diseases has far greater coefficient with higher significance in western and north-eastern regions, where medical resources are in shortage. In eastern and middle regions, interestingly, variable distance to medical center imposes a greater impact on wellbeing index, while in other areas—poorer medical environment, the distance to medical center then lose its significance in determining seniors' wellbeing.In addition, the educational level proves to be negatively correlated with the wellbeing index and implies a positive role in affecting wellbeing. It's realized that one's better upbringing and knowledge will help pursue more physical and mental wellbeing—the educated are more likely to earn capital to improve their living environment and mentality.

Overall Results Based on Regions of China

The chart below shows the results that are classified based on different regions of China (Table 8).

Table 8. Summary on regression results based on regions of China

Variables	Eastern region	Middle region	Western region	North-eastern
TPA policy effect	−0.0217*	0.00623	−0.0318***	−0.0111
	(0.0120)	(0.00897)	(0.00733)	(0.0191)
Time	0.0238***	0.0334***	0.00650*	0.0454***
	(0.00409)	(0.00390)	(0.00371)	(0.00825)
Treated	0.0359***	−0.000535	0.0352***	0.0261
	(0.00969)	(0.00683)	(0.00594)	(0.0159)
Dependency ratio	−0.000773	0.00252	0.000181	−0.000638
	(0.00267)	(0.00242)	(0.00240)	(0.00432)
Number of senior chronic disease	0.00434*	0.00188	0.0131***	0.0104**
	(0.00237)	(0.00206)	(0.00194)	(0.00528)
Distance to medical center	0.451**	0.611***	0.0460	0.372
	(0.178)	(0.120)	(0.178)	(0.552)
Ratio of elders over young	0.0105	0.00140	0.00237	0.00758
	(0.0107)	(0.0114)	(0.00927)	(0.0178)
Percent of females in family	0.00606	−0.00906	−0.00873	−0.0335**
	(0.00690)	(0.00618)	(0.00534)	(0.0145)
Individual education level	−0.00101***	−0.00349***	−0.00400***	−0.00417***
	(0.000374)	(0.000377)	(0.000339)	(0.000824)
Percent of labor in households	0.0485***	0.0229***	0.0209***	0.0201**
	(0.00467)	(0.00452)	(0.00407)	(0.00990)
Number of pension in household	0.00447**	−0.00628***	0.00887***	0.00226
	(0.00179)	(0.00160)	(0.00179)	(0.00316)

(continued)

Table 8. (*continued*)

Variables	Eastern region	Middle region	Western region	North-eastern
Constant	0.249***	0.294***	0.306***	0.307***
	(0.00790)	(0.00747)	(0.00673)	(0.0157)
Observations	1,824	1,907	2,166	526
R-squared	0.112	0.112	0.132	0.165

Notes: Robust standard errors in parentheses. Significant at *10%, **5% and ***1%

China is a vast and diverse country, with significant regional economic, social, and demographic differences. The eastern region is considered more economically developed, with higher levels of urbanization, population density, per capita income, and access to education and medical resources. In contrast, the western region faces complex challenges, including a dispersed population, limited access to public services such as education and medical resources, and a challenging geographic environment. The middle region is a hub for manufacturing, home to a concentration of the population and industrial industries. Meanwhile, the northeastern region, a traditional heavy industrial base, is experiencing challenges due to national industrial policy shifts.

It's shown that the TPA policy had a more significant impact on seniors' wellbeing in the western region – the most impoverished area and the policy's primary targeted region. This is not surprising given that the western region's elderly population has a lower standard of living and less access to healthcare services. Interestingly, the number of seniors with chronic diseases had a higher coefficient and significance level in the western and northeastern regions. This may be due to the high aging population and relatively inadequate medical services in these regions. However, the variable distance to medical centers lost significance, suggesting that the TPA policy may have alleviated the issue of limited access to medical services.

The impact of the TPA policy on seniors' wellbeing varied depending on the economic and social environment, demographic characteristics, and healthcare system of each region. For instance, the western region's poverty and healthcare service shortages, coupled with its aging population, may have amplified the TPA policy's impact on seniors' wellbeing in this region. In contrast, the eastern region's higher per capita income and abundant healthcare resources may have reduced the TPA policy's impact on seniors' wellbeing.

5 Discussion

Firstly, the TPA policy program with different significance varying by areas and regions shall invite a closer inspection. The overall results justify the traditional view that the TPA policy program mainly targets at the low-income group in rural areas especially in the western regions. The coefficient of policy effect in rural area is −0.0193, greater than the overall coefficient of policy −0.0152. And the coefficient of policy—the influence of policy—become even greater when focusing on the western region, for which the coefficient further increases to −0.0318. The results cross-examine the comparative descriptive statistics on the wellbeing index between before-TPA period and after-TPA period at Sect. 4.1.4, where the overall wellbeing index and many indicators decrease – an improvement in seniors' wellbeing. Also, the empirical results clarify a lasting concern related to TPA policy. Some has been wondering that the TPA policy program mainly targets at the young population, and thus pay relatively few attentions to the wellbeing of seniors, which might not contribute to the wellbeing of seniors at all.

Secondly, percentage of labor and dependency ratio point to key issues in the household eldercare pattern in Chinese aging society. The findings regarding the impact of family characteristics on seniors' wellbeing in the context of Chinese eldercare situations highlight several important implications. Firstly, the negative relationship between the percent of labor and seniors' wellbeing challenges the prevailing expectations. This suggests that as more young people become preoccupied with work and neglect their familial duties, seniors experience a lack of physical support and emotional companionship, which adversely affects their wellbeing. In rural areas characterized by the prevalence of "empty-nest seniors and left-over children", the increasing dependency ratio exacerbates the financial pressure on adults, leading to their likeliness to seek employment outside their local communities. Consequently, this triggers a sense of loneliness and negatively impacts seniors' wellbeing, as the positive correlation suggests. On the other hand, in urban areas where income and capital hold greater significance, the positive correlation between dependency ratio and wellbeing index implies that the financial pressures associated with an increasing dependency ratio result in worse material conditions, thereby affecting seniors' overall wellbeing.

On societal level, results again put an emphasis on the medical environment provided to senior citizens. It is evident, both intuitively and empirically, that a greater number of chronic diseases and longer distances to medical centers contribute to poorer physical health among seniors and potentially result in increased mental pressures. Notably, the coefficient and significance of the number of chronic diseases display greater magnitude in western and north-eastern regions, where medical resources are relatively scarce, compared to the eastern and middle regions that enjoy richer medical resources. In these eastern and middle regions, however, it is intriguing to observe that the distance to medical centers exerts a stronger influence on the wellbeing index. Conversely, in regions characterized by a poorer medical environment, the distance to medical centers loses its significance in determining the wellbeing of seniors.

What remains unclear in the study, however, is the impact and significance of variable pension in affecting seniors' wellbeing. Displaying great significance across areas and regions, the welfare policy is positively correlated with the wellbeing index, which indicates a negative impact on seniors' wellbeing. It could be the case that each province in China has different pension policy and promote the welfare to different extent, which leads to the confusion and unambiguity in the effect of pension. It can be by part justified by that variable pension loses its significance in affecting wellbeing index in north-eastern region as shown in the Sect. 4.2.2. As the region which has some of the lowest birth rates and average pension incomes, the reliance of younger generations on pensions leads to an ineffective pension system contributing to seniors' wellbeing. But still, the unexplainable result requires future research to examine its effect on seniors' wellbeing especially based on different social context and geographical locations. Besides research on pension, it's also suggested that the future research shall take a closer look at how disparity between urban and rural areas leads to the different impact of policies and variables.

6 Conclusion

The study attempts to conceptualize seniors' wellbeing into a multidimensional numerical index based on Alkire-Foster methods, and incorporate a difference-in-difference model in the linear regression to evaluate the effect of TPA on seniors' wellbeing. Results show that TPA does have a positive impact on seniors' wellbeing especially in rural area and western region. The study further depicts a dilemma of rural seniors relying on household, who might lose support from the young as their kids become migrant workers in cities. Also, the study again puts an emphasis on the importance of medical resources in improving seniors' wellbeing. Future research shall continue to look at the specific relationship between the seniors' wellbeing and certain variable in more specific social content and geographical condition, such as pension.

References

Abruquah, L.A., Yin, X., Ding, Y.: Old age support in urban China: the role of pension schemes, self-support ability and intergenerational assistance. Int. J. Environ. Res. Public Health **16**(11), 1918 (2019). https://doi.org/10.3390/ijerph16111918

Alkire, S., Foster, J.: Counting and multidimensional poverty measurement. J. Public Econ. **95**(7–8), 476–487 (2011). https://doi.org/10.1016/j.jpubeco.2010.11.006

CEICdata.com: China population: no of person per household (2023). https://www.ceicdata.com/en/china/population-no-of-person-per-household

Chen, X., Silverstein, M.: Intergenerational social support and the psychological well-being of older parents in China. Res. Aging **22**(1), 43–65 (2000). https://doi.org/10.1177/0164027500221003

Chen, X.: We will resolutely win the battle against poverty and achieve the goal of a moderately prosperous society in all respects on schedule. CCP official news (2016). Npc.gov.cn. http://www.npc.gov.cn/npc/c541/201601/87a6480eb1e3442398c46f37f7f2aded.shtml

Cheng, L., Liu, H., Zhang, Y., Zhao, Z.: The health implications of social pensions: evidence from China's new rural pension scheme. J. Compar. Econ. **46**(1), 53–77 (2018). https://doi.org/10.1016/j.jce.2016.12.002

Enkvist, Å., Ekström, H., Elmståhl, S.: What factors affect life satisfaction. (LS) among the oldest-old? Arch. Gerontol. Geriatr. **54**(1), 140–145 (2012). https://doi.org/10.1016/j.archger.2011.03.013

Fei, X.: Elderly support in changing family structures: revisiting the changes in family structures in China. J. Peking Univ. (Philos. Soc. Sci. Ed.) (03), (1983). CNKI:SUN:BDZK.0.1983-03-001

Galiani, S., Gertler, P., Bando, R.: The effects of non-contributory pensions on material and subjective well being. Econ. Dev. Cult. Change (2019). https://doi.org/10.1086/702859

Han, Y., He, Y., Lyu, J., Yu, C., Bian, M., Lee, L.: Aging in China: perspectives on public health. Global Health J. **4**(1), 11–17 (2020). https://doi.org/10.1016/j.glohj.2020.01.002

Iglesias, K., Suter, C., Beycan, T., Vani, B.P.: Exploring multidimensional well-being in Switzerland: comparing three synthesizing approaches. Soc. Indic. Res. **134**(3), 847–875 (2016). https://doi.org/10.1007/s11205-016-1452-9

Imbens, G.W., Angrist, J.D.: Identification and estimation of local average treatment effects. Econometrica **62**(2), 467–475 (1994). https://doi.org/10.2307/2951620

Krause, N.: Anticipated support, received support, and economic stress among older adults. J. Gerontol. B Psychol. Sci. Soc. Sci. **52B**(6), P284–P293 (1997). https://doi.org/10.1093/geronb/52b.6.p284

Krause, N., Herzog, A.R., Baker, E.: Providing support to others and well-being in later life. J. Gerontol. **47**(5), P300–P311 (1992). https://doi.org/10.1093/geronj/47.5.p300

Kiefer, R.A.: An integrative review of the concept of well-being. Holist. Nurs. Pract. **22**(5), 244–252 (2008). https://doi.org/10.1097/01.hnp.0000334915.16186.b2

Kollamparambil, U., Etinzock, M.N.: Subjective well-being impact of old age pension in South Africa: a difference in difference analysis across the gender divide. South Afr. J. Econ. Manag. Sci. **22**(1), (2019). https://doi.org/10.4102/sajems.v22i1.2996

Liu, T., Sun, L.: Pension reform in China. J. Aging Soc. Policy **28**(1), 15–28 (2015). https://doi.org/10.1080/08959420.2016.1111725

Pak, T.-Y.: Social protection for happiness? The impact of social pension reform on subjective well-being of the Korean elderly. J. Policy Model. **42**(2), 349–366 (2020). https://doi.org/10.1016/j.jpolmod.2019.12.001. www.sciencedirect.com/science/article/pii/S0161893820300016#bib0015. Accessed 6 Mar 2023

Population, total - China | Data (2022). Worldbank org. https://data.worldbank.org/indicator/SP.POP.TOTL?locations=CN

La Placa, V., McNaught, A., Knight, A.: Discourse on wellbeing in research and practice. Int. J. Wellbeing **3**(1), (2013). https://www.internationaljournalofwellbeing.org/index.php/ijow/article/view/177

Xinhong, L., Wei, L.: Research on domestic and international models of elderly care. Econ. Manag. (12), 18–22 (2012).CNKI:SUN:JJGL.0.2012-12-003

Zhigang, Y., Lin, C.: The trend and mechanism of intergenerational income mobility in China: an analysis from the perspective of human capital, social capital and wealth. World Econ. **36**(7), 880–898 (2013). https://doi.org/10.1111/twec.12043

Zhuang, J.: Income and wealth inequality in Asia and the Pacific: trends, causes, and policy remedies. Asian Econ. Policy Rev. **18**(1), 15–41 (2022)

Investor Sentiment, Idiosyncratic Risk, and Stock Returns: Evidence from Australia

Aiqi Li(✉)

SKEMA Business School, 2/9 Avocet Street, Holden Hill, SA 5088, Australia
inclinedsky@hotmail.com

Abstract. In the study, the link between idiosyncratic risk and excess return is discussed using a sample of common stocks in the Australian technology sector from January 2017 to December 2022. Furthermore, the investor sentiment variable is introduced to investigate the connection between idiosyncratic risk and excess return in both high and low investor sentiment volatility. The measurement of idiosyncratic risk follows previous studies using the fama-french three-factor model, and the correlation between idiosyncratic risk and excess return is measured using the firm-level Fama-Macbeth regressions model. The results show that the correlation is not statistically significant before the introduction of the investor sentiment variable. However, there is a significant positive correlation after the introduction of the investor sentiment variable.

Keywords: Idiosyncratic Risk · Excess Return · Investor Sentiment · Fama-french Model · Cross-sectional Regression

1 Introduction

Academic debate on the subject of idiosyncratic risk and stock returns has long been a hot topic. Because it believes that all investors in a perfectly competitive market have the same investment expectations and risk preferences, classical economic theory views market risk as the only factor influencing security prices. But in the real market, this is not the case. Due to arbitrage policy limitations and inherent arbitrage costs, arbitrageurs are unable to fully offset the market's knowledge asymmetry problem, which undermines the fundamental tenet of classical economic theory. Thus, idiosyncratic risk has been included in numerous empirical investigations, but the academic community is still divided regarding how the two are related. A part of researchers believe that there is a positive relationship between idiosyncratic risk and return [1], and a part of scholars believe that there is a negative relationship [2], while some scholars question the correlation between the two [3]. In my paper, I continue to discuss the relationship between idiosyncratic risk and stock returns. Unlike most research publications in the past that include samples from the U.S. and China, few empirical studies have opted to employ Australia as a sample. I am original in choosing a sample of listed stocks in the Australian technology sector. The smaller size of the Australian market compared to the U.S. stock market means that it is more susceptible to changes in the Asian market compared to the European stock market. It also has a relatively more stable regulatory environment compared to the Asian stock market, with continuity and transparency of policies, because of which it does not fully apply to other sample findings.

In this essay, I also look at the impact of investor emotion on the correlation between stock returns and idiosyncratic risk. Investor sentiment, which refers to investors' aggregate attitudes and views about the market and specific equities, is a crucial element impacting stock returns and financial market risk. Mood swings can cause "noise" trading—unsophisticated trading—on financial markets, which can impact stock returns [4].

The impact of investor sentiment on stock returns has been widely studied, and many empirical studies have shown that investor sentiment can have a significant impact on stock returns [5, 6], but there are few articles examining the relationship between investor sentiment, idiosyncratic risk, and stock returns. In the two relevant articles I found, the authors both chose stocks of multinational corporations as the subject of their study, and there is no relevant literature with a single market as a sample. So that I can fill the gap in this area, I decide to investigate the Australian stock market as a sample. In addition, I focus on the technological sector in Australian common stock market in this paper, because technology stocks are often considered high-growth stocks. Therefore investors are more sensitive to their future earnings prospects. In addition, the value of companies in the technology sector may be difficult to capture by traditional valuation factors due to their growth stage. It is crucial to consider the impact of idiosyncratic risk on stock values.

The remainder of this article is structured as follows. Section 2 presents the sources of sample data and the relevant variables and models. Section 3 presents the empirical results, including heterogeneous risk and stock return regression results, and investor sentiment regression results. Section 4 is a model reliability test, and Sect. 5 concludes the study and makes suggestions for future research.

2 Literature Review

2.1 Idiosyncratic Risk and Return

A fundamental financial model called the Capital Asset Pricing Model (CAPM), created by Sharpe in 1964 [7], tries to quantify the correlation between stock return and beta coefficient, which is strongly related to the risk premium. The model suggests that only market risk should be valued in equilibrium since investor diversification may completely eliminate idiosyncratic risk. However, empirical studies have produced results that challenge this assumption. For example, Douglas [8] and Lintner [9] observed that the variance of residuals derived from a market model has a substantial impact on the cross-sectional variation of average stock returns. These studies were taken as early evidence that the standard CAPM was inadequate. Barberis and Huang [10] found a link between expected returns and idiosyncratic risk, while Malkiel and Xu [11] provided compelling empirical support for the relevance of idiosyncratic risk in illuminating the expected stock returns, even after controlling for the factor of size. One possible reason for the influence of idiosyncratic risk on stock return is that real-world portfolios cannot be fully hedged.

In a study by Goetzmann and Kumar [12], it was discovered that more than 25% of investor portfolios featured just one stock, more than half had no more than three stocks, and less than 10% of portfolios contained more than ten stocks.

Conversely, some research questioned the relation between idiosyncratic risk and risk. Ang et al. [2] examined a negative relation between idiosyncratic risk and returns in 23 developed countries. Then this result was partly supported by Rachwalski, M. and Wen, Q [13], who identified a temporary negative relation between idiosyncratic risk levels and returns and a persistent positive relation between idiosyncratic risk and returns. Meanwhile, Liu, Z. et al. [3] believed that there is no meaningful association between returns and idiosyncratic volatility. I continue to explore idiosyncratic volatility effect in Australia, which add new evidence for the debate.

2.2 Sentiment Index and Return

Furthermore, this study introduces a sentiment index to explore the relationship between idiosyncratic risk and return in optimistic and pessimistic market conditions. Investor sentiment, defined as excessively positive or negative affect, has been extensively studied in relation to stock returns. Some literature directly studied the impact of investor sentiment on financial returns, attempting to predict stock prices from investor sentiment, such as Bollen, J et al. [5], Bozhkov, S. et al. [6] who utilized machine learning models to forecast stock prices based on tweet sentiment. Other studies have explored the indirect effect of investor sentiment on stock returns. According to research by Nartea, G. V. et al. [14], the economic policy uncertainty premium is greater during times of weak market sentiment, suggesting that risk-averse investors are ready to pay more for stocks during these times. Amromin G and Sharpe S [15] argued that investors' trading behaviors in optimistic and pessimistic periods are asymmetric, with investors expecting higher returns and trading more actively in prosperous times. Similarly, Antoniou, C. et al. [16] observed that noise trading is prominent during optimistic periods, while conventional beta pricing dominates during pessimistic periods. In addition, Wang W [17] examined the role of institutional investor sentiment in determining the beta-return relation.

However, previous research rarely focused on the role of investor sentiment in the relationship of idiosyncratic risk and returns. Although some literature has combined sentiment index and idiosyncratic risk on stock mispricing [11, 18], their sample was from Chinese cross-listed companies and American Depository Receipt. In this paper, I expand the sample of research to stocks of listed companies in Australian technology sector. Besides, I choose recent data from January 2017 to December 2022, which also expand the time range of relevant research. Besides, I choose recent data from 2017 January to 2022 December, which also expand the time range of relevant research.

3 Methodology

3.1 Data Description

The study data were obtained from Thomson Reuters and Bloomberg. From January 2017 to December 2022, this sample included 21 technology sector common stocks in January 2017, which increased to 72 stocks in December 2022. All relevant daily and monthly stock return indices and company characteristics data, including closing prices, capitalization, and book-to-market ratios. To reduce noise in the idiosyncratic risk calculations, I removed numbers with negative BM (book-to-market ratio), daily returns below −1, and monthly returns above 2. To prevent outliers from substantially affecting the data, I winsorize capitalisation and BM between 5% and 95%.

I follow Ang et al. [2] and Liu, Z et al. [3]to calculate idiosyncratic risk, choosing the return of the past 22 trading days at the beginning of the month, and to regress stock excess return and idiosyncratic risk, choosing the monthly return in t + 1 month. In addition, I use the Australian one-year treasury rate as the risk-free rate and the ASX200 index as the market return indicator.

3.2 Investor Sentiment

I measure investor sentiment using Confidence Indicators in OECD Indicator for Australia (CCI) and the National Australia Bank Business Confidence (NBCI). The OECD Indicator for Australia is a composite indicator based on a variety of economic indicators, including the Consumer Confidence Index. Compared to other investor sentiment indicators, it has the advantage of including a variety of economic indicators to reflect not only consumer sentiment, but also the overall economic situation in a comprehensive manner. In addition, the OECD Indicator for Australia has a reliable data source and covers a wide time frame, so it can be used as an important reference indicator when studying a sample of Australian technology stocks. The National Australia Bank Business Confidence Index (NBCI) provides a unique perspective on the overall business environment and potential economic growth in Australia, as it captures the views and expectations of Australian business owners and managers, compared to other broad-based indicators of investor sentiment, with a particular focus on businesses operating in Australia.

3.3 Idiosyncratic Risk

Selecting a mean equation is necessary for estimating predicted idiosyncratic risk, and various factor models result in various estimations of residual volatility, which eventually influences the definition of idiosyncratic risk. Since the idiosyncratic variance is a second moment, the number of components in the mean equation does not appear to have a major effect on the results in practise. In recent studies, many researchers have adopted the three-factor Fama-French model to measure idiosyncratic risk, building on the findings of Fama and French [19, 20]. This model includes the market excess return as well as two additional factors, SMB and HML. Liu, Z et al. [3] innovated FF3 and Partially referenced the formula proposed by Ang et al. [2], this new IVOL (individual stock volatility) formula, I choose the model to calculate idiosyncratic risk in Australia stock market. Meanwhile, I also follow their way to estimate each company's idiosyncratic risk at the previous 22 trading days:

$$R_{i,t} = \alpha + \beta_{MKT,i,m} MKT_t + \beta_{SMB,i,m} SMB_t + \beta_{HML,i,m} HML_t + \epsilon_{i,t} \quad (1)$$

where the 22 trading days that ended on the last trading day of month m − 1 are referred to as day t in this instance. R_i,t and MKT_t, respectively, stand for the excess returns of the firm i and the market over the risk-free rate. SMB and HML stand for small-to-big firm excess returns and high book-to-market (HML) firm excess returns over low book-to-market (LBL) firm, respectively. As opposed to HML, which is calculated as the difference between the returns of the bottom third and top third of all firms ranked by book-to-market ratio, SMB is the difference between the returns of the upper half and lower half of all firms ranked by market capitalisation.

3.4 Control Variables

To control for the effect of other factors on the relationship between idiosyncratic risk and expected return, referring to Antoniou, C. et al. [16], Long, H. et al. [21], Liu, Z et al. [3], I consider the following commonly used control variables:

Market capitalization (SIZE): the logarithm of the market capitalization at the end of month t as the market capitalization in month t.
Value: Value is the book-to-market ratio at the end of $t - 6$.
Momentum (MOM): MOM at time t is the stock's return for the past 11 months, lagged by one month, i.e. from $t - 12$ months to $t - 1$ months.
Short-term reversal (REV): stock return for $t - 1$ month (i.e., last month).

3.5 Diosyncratic Risk and Returns

I employ univariate portfolio-level analysis to group all stocks based on individual stock volatility. I divide all stocks into three groups at the beginning of the month, then calculate equal-weighted and value-weighted raw returns for each portfolio. Through this method, the volatility levels of individual stocks can be divided into three groups: high, medium and low. This helps to better capture the relationship between volatility and expected returns, and also allows for a more accurate calculation of expected returns for each group.

Then, I follow firm-level Fama-Macbeth [22] regressions with monthly data:

$$R_{i,t+1} = \beta_{0,t} + \beta_{1,t}IV_{i,t} + \beta_{2,t}SIZE_{i,t} + \beta_{3,t}VALUE_{i,t} + +\beta_{k,t}Control_{k,t} + \epsilon_{i,t} \quad (2)$$

where R_i,t + 1is realized stock return in month t + 1. IV(IVOL) is realized idiosyncratic volatility as defined previously.

4 Empirical Results

4.1 Idiosyncratic Risk

Table 1 presents the mean idiosyncratic volatility for equal-weighted (EWIV) and value-weighted (VWIV). EWIV is computed as the standard deviation of residuals obtained from Eq. (1), while VWIV is calculated as the market capitalization-weighted individual stock volatility from the previous 22 trading days. The results show that the mean value of EWIV is 0.056, while the mean value of VWIV is 0.047. The latter value is higher than that reported for the Chinese market [23] and the French market [3]. I think the reason is that I just research technological industry, but other empirical results focus on all industry, and growth stocks are more susceptible to idiosyncratic risk.

Moreover, the lower mean value of VWIV compared to EWIV suggests that the idiosyncratic volatility of small firms is higher than that of large firms, consistent with results observed in the French and US markets.

Shown as Panel B, the correlation of two variables is 0.7676, which means that EWIV and VWIV are highly correlated with each other.

Table 1. Descriptive statistics for EWIV, VWIV.

Panel A: Summary statistics

	mean	sd	min	max
EWIV	0.056	0.014	0.037	0.123
VWIV	0.047	0.023	0.000	0.172

Panel B: Correlation Table

	EWIV	VWIV
EWIV	1.0000	
VWIV	0.7676	1.0000

4.2 Univariate Portfolio-Level Analysis

I construct three portfolios sorted by equal-weighted volatility (EWIV) and value-weighted volatility (VWIV) respectively, as shown in Table 2, and I examine the average monthly raw return and FF-3 alpha of equal-weighted and value-weighted portfolios for each of the three portfolios, according to the innovative function of the fama-french three-factor model proposed by Liu, Z et al. [3]. From this table, the results show that there are a significantly negative relationship between idiosyncratic volatility and the raw returns, but volatility spreads (high-low) are −2.4851 are 4.8961 respectively, which are not statistically significant. The same pattern is also can be seen in FF-3 alpha. The conclusion is in line with Liu, Z et al. [3] and Ang et al. [2]. Furthermore, the mean absolute values of raw return and FF-3α are greater in the groups of high EWIV and high VWIV compared to the low groups.

4.3 Firm-Level Cross-Sectional Regressions

I examine how individual stock volatility affects stock pricing in this part using cross-sectional regressions based on Fama and MacBeth [22]. The model includes the variables IV, size, value, momentum, and reversal. Table 3 shows the regression results by dividing EWIV into three portfolios from large to small in order of ranking. The results show that there is a slight positive relationship between EWIV and one-month ahead stock excess return in low EWIV portfolio and is significant at the 10% level. However, the correlations is statistically insignificant in high EWIV. Meanwhile, the effects of momentum, reversal and value are not be found in all portfolios, size effect is just been found in low EWIV portfolio at 5% level (Table 4).

Table 2. Raw returns and FF-3 alpha of portfolios sorted by idiosyncratic volatility.

	Raw Return		FF-3 Alpha	
	Mean	Std. Dev	Mean	Std. Error
Equal-weighted				
high EWIV	−1.0656 (−38.8571)	0.0274	−0.0048 (−3.0288)	0.5646
medium EWIV	−1.4339 (−52.9861)	0.2699	0.0042 (3.3991)	0.0012
low EWIV	−0.9702 (−36.24)	0.2675	0.0011 (1.2426)	0.0009
high-low	−0.0964 (−2.4851)		−0.0059 (−3.2252)	
Value-weighted				
high VWIV	−1.2182 (−45.0271)	0.0270	0.0013 (8.9964)	0.0001
medium VWIV	−1.2136 (−39.2968)	0.0309	0.0008 (23.9170)	0.0000
low VWIV	−1.0419 (−44.5493)	0.2338	0.0009 (23.8108)	0.0000
high-low	−0.1763 (4.8961)		0.0004 (−2.4097)	

Table 3. Characteristics of portfolios sorted by idiosyncratic volatility.

	EWIV	SIZE	Value	Momentum	REV
high EWIV	0.091 (1.60)	−0.000 (−1.26)	0.000 (1.56)	−0.003 (−0.29)	−0.002 (−1.13)
medium EWIV	0.112 (0.47)	−0.000 (−0.56)	0.000 (1.21)	0.002 (0.39)	−0.002 (−0.29)
low EWIV	0.2562* (−1.95)	−0.000** (−2.21)	0.000 (0.79)	0.058 (−0.79)	−0.079 (−0.99)

t-statistics in parentheses *** $p < 0.01$, ** $p < 0.05$, * $p < 0.1$.

4.4 EPU Premium Conditioned on Investor Sentiment

In order to examine the impact of idiosyncratic risk on stock price under two scenarios of high and low sentiment volatility, we then incorporate investor sentiment as a precondition. Defining diff_CCI according to the formula (CCI_t/CCI_t-1)-1, dividing the sample into two parts, low diff_CCI and high diff_CCI, and conducting one cross-sectional regression in each group. The results are shown in Table 5, the correlations of equal-weighted and value-weighted idiosyncratic volatility in low or high diff_CCI are

Table 4. Correlation table for cross-sectional regressions.

	R_t + 1	EWIV	SIZE	Value	Momentum	REV
R_t + 1	1.0000					
EWIV	0.1025	1.0000				
SIZE	−0.0067	−0.0640	1.0000			
Value	0.0524	0.0071	0.2409	1.0000		
Momentum	0.0060	−0.0340	0.2002	0.2449	1.0000	
REV	0.8276	0.0836	0.0178	0.0502	−0.0041	1.0000

Note: From the correlation coefficient matrix in the above table, the correlation between most of the variables is low and there is no clear indication of multicollinearity. After cross-sectional regression, I perform a VIF test and the VIF values of all variables were around 1, so I can exclude multicollinearity.

positive significantly, and the correlation is higher when mood swings are high, 0.234 and 0.221 in the EWIV and VWIV groups, respectively.

The results also show that SIZE and $t + 1$ month return are negatively correlated in low mood swing period, but it is not significant in high diff_CCI period. REV and return are positively correlated and statistically significant in the case of high volatility of sentiment. Similarly, VALUE, Momentum (MOM) and short-term reversal(REV) also all correlate with raw return during low diff_CCI period, and their correlations are not significant during the high diff_CCI period.

As indicated in Table 6, I substitute the investor sentiment variable with the National Australia Bank Business Confidence (NBCI), define (NBCI_t/NBCI_t-1)-1 as diff_NBCI, and divide the sample into low diff_NBCI and high diff_NBCI for the regression in order to assess the robustness of the results. Like the previous experiment, the correlations between IV during the low and high diff_NBCI periods are both positively significant. However, the correlation during the high diff_NBCI period is lower than during the low period. From these two experiments, it can be concluded that idiosyncratic volatility and excess return are correlated both in periods of low and high volatility in sentiment, but there is no robust evidence that the correlation is stronger when sentiment volatility is high.

Table 5. Relation of return and volatility sorted by Consumer Confidence Index (CCI).

	Equal-weighted		Value-weighted	
	low diff_CCI	high diff_CCI	low diff_CCI	high diff_CCI
IV	0.157***	0.234***	0.158***	0.221***
	(9.570)	(0.0649)	(9.640)	(3.486)
SIZE	−0.001**	−0.000770	−0.001**	−0.001
	(−2.356)	(0.000532)	(−2.373)	(−1.461)
VALUE	−0.000*	0.000273***	−0.000*	0.000***
	(−1.916)	(0.000105)	(−1.882)	(2.638)
MOM	0.011**	−0.00659	0.011**	−0.007
	(2.446)	(0.00936)	(2.460)	(−0.707)
REV	−0.002***	−0.00417	−0.002***	−0.004
	(−2.715)	(0.00953)	(−2.725)	(−0.425)
Constant	−0.006***	−0.00943**	−0.006***	−0.008**
	(−4.718)	(0.00409)	(−4.730)	(−2.140)

t-statistics in parentheses *** $p < 0.01$, ** $p < 0.05$, * $p < 0.1$.

Table 6. Relation of return and volatility sorted by National Australia Bank Business Confidence (NBCI).

	Equal-weighted		Value-weighted	
	low diff_NBCI	high diff_NBCI	low diff_NBCI	high diff_NBCI
IV	0.196***	0.159***	0.194***	0.148***
	(4.121)	(6.191)	(4.111)	(5.893)
SIZE	−0.001	−0.001**	−0.001	−0.001**
	(−1.359)	(−2.491)	(−1.371)	(−2.552)
VALUE	0.000**	0.000	0.000**	0.000
	(2.182)	(0.572)	(2.223)	(0.601)
MOM	−0.003	0.010*	−0.003	0.010*
	(−0.266)	(1.903)	(−0.255)	(1.874)
REV	−0.003	0.008*	−0.003	0.009*
	(−1.626)	(1.657)	(−1.626)	(1.690)
Constant	−0.007*	−0.007***	−0.007*	−0.006***
	(−1.937)	(−3.596)	(−1.881)	(−3.258)

t-statistics in parentheses *** $p < 0.01$, ** $p < 0.05$, * $p < 0.1$.

5 Conclusion

In the above empirical study, I examine the relationship between idiosyncratic risk and excess return using a sample of common shares of 72 companies in the Australian technology sector. According to the results of the study, before the inclusion of the investor sentiment variable, there was no statistically substantial association between idiosyncratic risk and excess returns in either cross-sectional regression or portfolio analysis. After the inclusion of investor sentiment, there is a substantial positive correlation between idiosyncratic risk and excess returns. However, the correlation does not follow a certain pattern during low and high sentiment periods, probably due to the significant differences in the measures of investor sentiment indicators used. This paper provides new evidential support for Ang's study [2] before the introduction of the investor sentiment variable, but questions Ang's findings [2] after the introduction of the investor sentiment variable. Further research is still needed on whether there is a correlation between idiosyncratic risk, excess return and investor sentiment amount.

References

1. Lee, B.S., Li, L.: The idiosyncratic risk-return relation: a quantile regression approach based on the prospect theory. J. Behav. Financ. **17**(2), 124–143 (2016)
2. Ang, A., Hodrick, R.J., Xing, Y., Zhang, X.: The cross-section of volatility and expected returns. J. Financ. **61**, 259–299 (2006)
3. Liu, Z., Nartea, G., Wu, J.: Patterns and pricing of idiosyncratic volatility in the French stock market. Theor. Econ. Lett. **8**, 79–97 (2018)
4. Black, F.: Noise. J. Financ. **41**(3), 529–543 (1986)
5. Bollen, J., Mao, H., Zeng, X.: Twitter mood predicts the stock market. J. Comput. Sci. **2**(1), 1–8 (2011)
6. Bozhkov, S., Lee, H., Sivarajah, U., et al.: Idiosyncratic risk and the cross-section of stock returns: the role of mean-reverting idiosyncratic volatility. Ann. Oper. Res. **294**, 419–452 (2020)
7. Sharpe, W.F.: Capital asset prices: a theory of market equilibrium under conditions of risk. J. Financ. **19**(3), 425–442 (1964)
8. Douglas, G.W.: Risk in the equity markets: An empirical appraisal of market efficiency. Yale Econ. Essays **9**, 3–45 (1969)
9. Lintner, J.: Security prices, risk, and maximal gains from diversification. J. Financ. **20**(4), 587–615 (1965)
10. Barberis, N., Huang, M.: Mental accounting, loss aversion, and individual stock returns. J. Financ. **56**(4), 1247–1292 (2001)
11. Malkiel, B.G., Xu, Y.: Risk and return revisited. J. Portf. Manag. **23**(3), 9–14 (1997)
12. Goetzmann, W., Kumar, A.: Equity portfolio diversification. Rev. Financ. **12**(3), 433–463 (2008)
13. Rachwalski, M., Wen, Q.: Idiosyncratic risk innovations and the idiosyncratic risk-return relation. Rev. Asset. Pric. Stud. **6**(2), 303–328 (2016)
14. Nartea, G.V., Bai, H., Wu, J.: Investor sentiment and the economic policy uncertainty premium. Pac.-Basin Financ. J. 101438 (2020)
15. Amromin, G., Sharpe, S.: Expectations of risk and return among household investors: are their Sharpe ratios countercyclical? Working Paper 17 (2009)

16. Antoniou, C., Doukas, J.A., Subrahmanyam, A.: Investor sentiment, beta, and the cost of equity capital. Manag. Sci. **62**(2), 347–367 (2016)
17. Wang, W.: Institutional investor sentiment, beta, and stock returns. Financ. Res. Lett. 101374 (2019)
18. Li, Y., Zhang, Y.: Investor sentiment, idiosyncratic risk, and stock price premium: evidence from Chinese cross-listed companies. SAGE Open **11**(2) (2021)
19. Fama, E., French, K.R.: The cross-section of expected. J. Financ. **47**(2), 427–465 (1992)
20. Fama, E., French, K.R.: Common risk factors in the returns on stocks and bonds. J. Financ. Econ. **33**(1), 3–56 (1993)
21. Long, H., Jiang, Y., Zhu, Y.: Idiosyncratic tail risk and expected stock returns: evidence from the Chinese stock markets. Financ. Res. Lett. **24**, 129–136 (2018)
22. Fama, E.F., MacBeth, J.D.: Risk, return, and equilibrium: empirical tests. J. Polit. Econ. **81**(3), 607–636 (1973)
23. Kong, G.W., Kong, D.M.: Institutional investors' trading in speculation: evidence from China. South Afr. J. Econ. **83**(4), 617–631 (2015)

Sovereign CDS Spreads and Covid-19 Pandemic

Ying Xi(✉)

School of Economics and Management, BJTU, Weihai 264200, China
21711113@bjtu.edu.cn

Abstract. Shaken by the global economic impact of COVID-19, sovereign CDS spread change across countries. The article explores the drivers affecting U.S. sovereign CDS spreads before and during the pandemic by analyzing data from two periods, January 2, 2017, to December 31, 2019, and January 1, 2020, to April 27, 2021, to forecast U.S. sovereign CDS spreads using a support vector regression machine and the forecast results of U.S. sovereign CDS spreads are partially analyzed by the average impact value algorithm. It is found that U.S. sovereign CDS spreads mainly showed a downward trend before the COVID-19 pandemic, a significant increase in U.S. sovereign CDS spreads during the initial period of the epidemic, and an overall downward trend despite a transient increase in the subsequent period. Before the COVID-19 pandemic, domestic factors are more essential for U.S. sovereign CDS spreads, but during the pandemic, domestic factors become less important, and global factors become more important for U.S. sovereign CDS spreads. This paper concludes that global drivers are more important for U.S. sovereign CDS spreads than domestic drivers during a widespread global epidemic.

Keywords: Sovereign CDS Spreads · MIV · SVR · K-CV · Covid-19

1 Introduction

Macro-level financial deterioration caused by the pandemic can increase the country's risk. As the core of country risk, sovereign risk is a macro risk to global financial transactions and can directly affect the behavioral decisions of participating financial traders [1, 2]. After the COVID-19 pandemic, studies that characterized sovereign CDS spreads as a sovereign risk emerged. Up to now, many studies have focused on analyzing the impact of the COVID-19 pandemic on sovereign CDS spreads, while most scholars focus on the correlation between corporate CDS spreads and pandemics within countries, a shock of pandemics on sovereign risk, etc. [3–6]. There are fewer studies on the factors influencing sovereign risk before and after the pandemic, so this paper investigates the drivers of sovereign risk before and after the pandemic through machine learning.

This paper uses a support vector regression machine neural network to do regression prediction analysis to filter out the important drivers of sovereign CDS spreads based on a combination of mean impact values and the importance of the respective variables on sovereign CDS spreads, followed by an analysis of the changes in indicators of factors driving U.S. sovereign CDS spreads before and during the COVID-19 pandemic [7]. Firstly, a neural network algorithm is used to efficiently predict the U.S. sovereign CDS spreads across time using a regression. Then the importance of each influencing factor on the regression forecasts of U.S. sovereign CDS spreads is analyzed based on the average impact value algorithm. Finally, the variability of the drivers before and during the COVID-19 pandemic is analyzed, and thus the scientific and effective prediction of U.S. sovereign risk during the special period (the COVID-19 pandemic) is important for maintaining global economic stability and asset safety of investors in financial transactions.

2 Models and Data

2.1 Introduction of the Model

Support vector regression machine is based on the fundamental idea of first mapping the initial data to a high-dimensional eigenspace, and the optimal separating hyperplane is found by a nonlinear mapping function followed by linear regression with minimum mean square error in the high-dimensional feature space [7]. Recently, SVR got extensively applied in various regression problems and showed good predictive performance [8]. In this paper, the SVR model is chosen for regression prediction, a radial basis kernel function is selected, and cross-validation (CV, Cross Validation) is used to find the parameters c of the penalty, and g of the kernel function are chosen optimally for classification.

Given the set of data samples as $(x_1, y_1), (x_2, y_2), \cdots, (x_k, y_k)$, $i = 1, 2, 3 \cdots, k$, which $x_i \in R^n$, $y_i \in R$. The regression function is expressed as follows [9].

$$L_g(f(x), y) = \begin{cases} |f(x) - y| - g, & if : |f(x) - y| > g \\ 0, & else \end{cases} \quad (1)$$

The following maximization function approach is solved through the use of kernel functions $K(x, y)$ for solving and constructing decision hyperplanes in higher dimensional spaces:

$$W(\alpha, \alpha^*) = -\frac{1}{2} \sum_{i,j=1}^{k} (\alpha_i - \alpha_i^*)(\alpha_j - \alpha_j^*) K(x_i \cdot x_j) - g \sum_{i=1}^{k} (\alpha_i + \alpha_i^*) + \sum_{i=1}^{k} y_i(\alpha_i - \alpha_i^*) \quad (2)$$

Restrictions:

$$s.t. \begin{cases} \sum_{i=1}^{k}(\alpha_i - \alpha_i^*) = 0 \\ \alpha_i, \alpha_i^* \in [0, C], i = 1, 2, \cdots, k \end{cases} \quad (3)$$

The corresponding functional regression is:

$$f(x) = \sum_{i=1}^{k}(\alpha_i - \alpha_i^*) K(x_i \cdot x_j) \quad (4)$$

Dombi et al. presented MIV to reflect weight matrix variations in neural networks, and MIV serves as an indicator for evaluating one of the best correlations between variables in a neural network, with its absolute magnitude signifying the relative influence of importance [10].

2.2 Model Prediction Performance Evaluation Metrics

This paper uses three evaluation criteria to assess the accuracy of the regression prediction model:

Mean Absolute Error (MAE)

$$MAE = \frac{1}{n}\sum_{i=1}^{n}|\hat{y_i} - y_i| \qquad (5)$$

Mean Square Error (MSE)

$$MSE = \frac{1}{n}\sum_{i=1}^{n}(\hat{y_i} - y_i)^2 \qquad (6)$$

Root Mean Square Error (RMSE)

$$RMSE = \sqrt{\frac{1}{n}\sum_{i=1}^{n}(y_i - \hat{y_i})^2} \qquad (7)$$

Coefficient of determination (R squared)

$$R^2 = 1 - \frac{\frac{1}{n}\sum_{i=1}^{n}(y_i - \hat{y_i})^2}{\frac{1}{n}\sum_{i=1}^{n}(y_i - \overline{y_i})^2} \qquad (8)$$

2.3 Data

The U.S. 5-year sovereign CDS spread as a forecaster for this paper, and the data is obtained from DataStream [10]. All explanatory variables are obtained from Investing, and the sample period before the epidemic is January 3, 2017, to December 31, 2019, and the sample period during the epidemic is January 2, 2020, to April 27, 2021 [11]. The paper finally obtained 1086 daily observations for each variable series by temporal matching for the dependent and independent variables and removing missing values, including 754 daily observations for each variable series before the epidemic and 332 daily observations for each variable series during the epidemic. Through the study of Li and other scholars, this paper identified 7 global factors and 3 national factors, for a total of 10 daily explanatory variables, as shown in Table 1 [7].

Table 1. Influence factors of US sovereign CDS spreads [7]

Index	Symbol
A. Global Factors	
U.S. 10-Year Treasury Yield	UTR10
Panic Index	VIX
Crude Oil ETF Volatility Index	CVX
Gold ETF Volatility Index	OVX

(*continued*)

Table 1. (*continued*)

Index	Symbol
Gold Price Futures	GFP
WTI Crude Oil Futures Price	WTIFP
Brent Crude Oil Spot Price	BrentFP
B. National Factors	
US Dollar Index	DI
S&P 500 Index	SP500
U.S. 5-Year Treasury Yield	UTR5

The overall U.S. sovereign CDS spreads showed a downward trend prior to the pandemic outbreak, indicating a downward trend in U.S. sovereign risk. Experiencing sharp fluctuations in U.S. sovereign CDS spreads following a pandemic outbreak in its initial stages indicates elevated U.S. sovereign risk. It is worth noting that after a pandemic outbreak in its initial stages, U.S. sovereign CDS spreads slowed down the upward trend and gradually showed a downward trend within a shorter period, indicating that U.S. sovereign risk has been on a significant downward trend since then.

2.4 Correlation Coefficient

Pearson correlation coefficients were chosen to calculate the correlation coefficient values of U.S. sovereign CDS spreads and their influencing factors for two time periods before and during the pandemic, as shown in Figs. 1 and 2, respectively.

For pre-pandemic U.S. sovereign CDS spreads, it can be found that all six global factors are negatively correlated and all two domestic factors are negatively correlated with U.S. sovereign CDS spreads except for the U.S. Treasury 10-year yield, while all two domestic factors are negatively correlated with U.S. sovereign CDS spreads except for the U.S. Treasury 5-year yield. The absolute value of the correlation coefficient between the S&P 500 Index and the U.S. sovereign CDS spread is equal to 0.848 among all the influencing factors, and there is a very strong correlation between the two. The correlation coefficient in absolute value is 0.6629 between the price of gold futures and the spread of U.S. sovereign CDS, with a strong correlation between the two. With absolute values ranging between 0.3 and 0.5, the correlation coefficients between the five global factors other than the gold volatility index moderately correlate with U.S. sovereign CDS spreads. Coefficients of correlation between the dollar index, the five-year U.S. Treasury yield, and the U.S. sovereign CDS spread have absolute values ranging from 0.1 to 0.3, and these two domestic influences exhibit a weak correlation with the U.S. sovereign CDS spread. The lowest absolute value of the coefficient of correlation between the gold volatility index as well as the U.S. sovereign CDS spread lies at 0.03657.

Then, being affected by the pandemic, sovereign CDS in the United States seems to be a different situation as a result of its spread in the epidemic. It is found that the correlation between the three global factors and the US sovereign CDS spreads is positive except for the two crude oil futures prices and gold futures prices and 10-year U.S. treasury yields, while the correlation between the two domestic factors and the US sovereign DS spreads is negative except for the US dollar index. Analyzing the strength of the correlations specifically, with the exception of gold futures prices and five-year U.S. Treasury yields, the absolute values of the correlation coefficients between all eight influencing variables and Sovereign CDS spread in the U.S. are above 0.6, which have strong correlations. Unlike before the pandemic, the two crude oil futures prices and the gold volatility and panic index have stronger correlations with sovereign CDS spreads, while a weaker correlation between gold futures prices and U.S. sovereign CDS spreads.

As a result of these analyses, for the U.S. before the COVID-19 pandemic outbreak, domestic factors have a stronger correlation with their sovereign CDS spreads, while for the U.S. during the pandemic, in addition to the increased correlation between domestic factors and U.S. sovereign CDS spreads, global factors show a stronger correlation with U.S. sovereign CDS spreads.

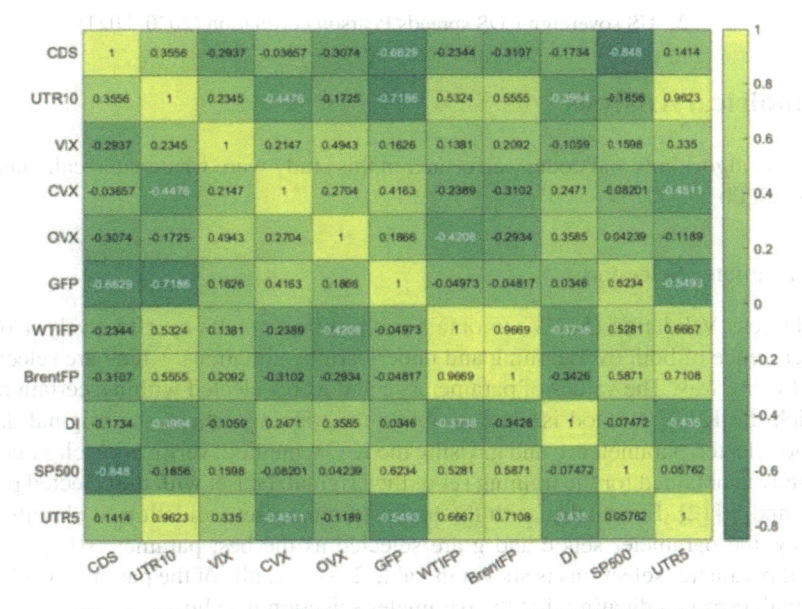

Fig. 1. US sovereign CDS spreads Pearson correlation (2017–2019)

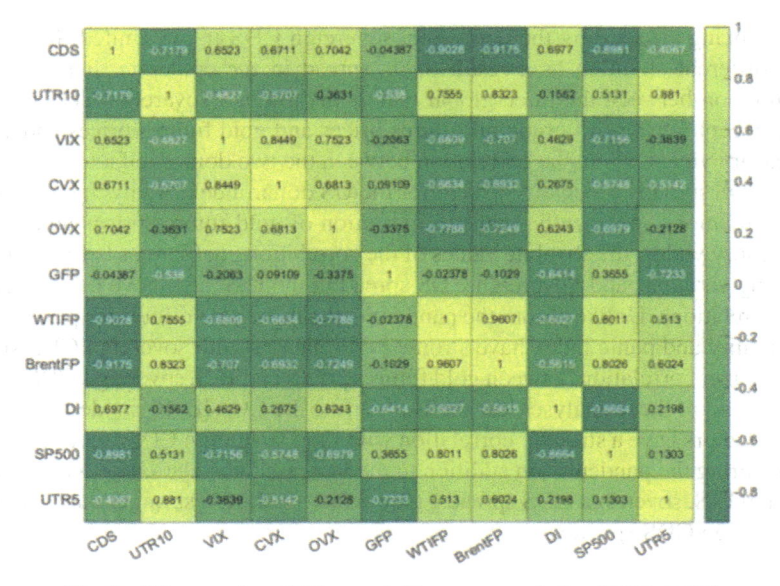

Fig. 2. US sovereign CDS spreads Pearson correlation (2020–2021)

3 Empirical Analysis

The model algorithms and codes performed in this study were written and calculated on Matlab 2020b.

3.1 Parameter Selection

K-fold Cross Validation (K-CV) to obtain more robust results by effectively avoiding the occurrence of both overlearning and underlearning situations, which are selected in the following way. The values of parameters c and g are selected within a certain range, in which the K-CV method is used to obtain the training data of the original dataset with the selected parameters c and g. Using the K-CV method, verification classification accurately is obtained for the training set of the original dataset with the selected parameters c and g [12]. Eventually, with the highest training set validation of classification accuracy, the parameter sets c and g are selected as the best parameters(Fig. 3). The result of parameter selections is shown in Table 2. The results of the parameter selection have small errors, indicating that the parameter selection is valid.

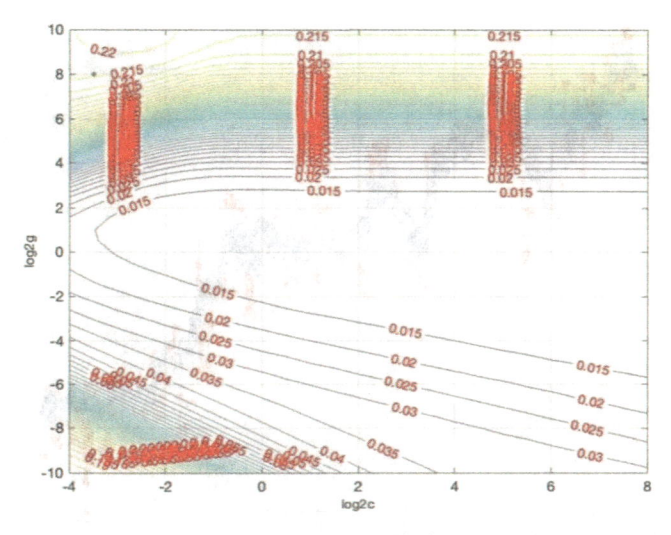

Fig. 3. Select the best parameters by cross-validation c&g (2017.1.3–2019.12.31)

Table 2. Results of K-fold Cross Validation parameter selection

Best Cross Validation	2017.1.3–2019.12.31	2020.1.2–2021.4.27
MSE	0.22%	0.22%
c	0.176777	0.0625
g	1024	1024

3.2 Regression Prediction

It uses the best parameters c&g achieved under the K-CV method to train the SVM, followed by regression prediction on the original data. The final regression prediction result plots are shown in Figs. 4 and 5. The prediction performance is shown in Table 3, which shows that the regression prediction model predicts better results.

Before the pandemic, the coefficient of determination was used in the regression prediction of U.S. sovereign CDS spreads is 0.96257. The variance in the dependent variable is explained by the regression relationship, indicating a percentage of 96.257%. Indicating a better fit and a more realistic fit function. During the pandemic, there is a regression prediction being conducted for U.S. sovereign CDS spread is 0.98141, it showed that the regression relationship explained 98.141% of the variation of the dependent variable, indicating that the fit was better and the fitting function more realistic.

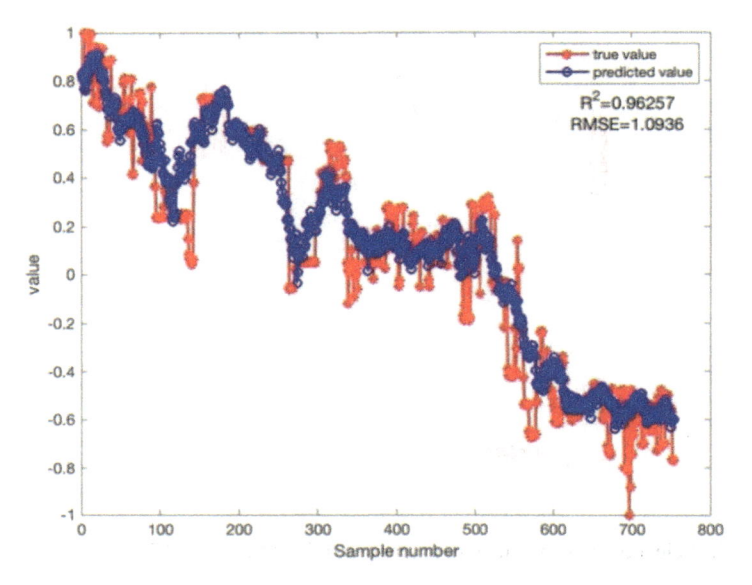

Fig. 4. Regression prediction results graph (2017.1.3–2019.12.31)

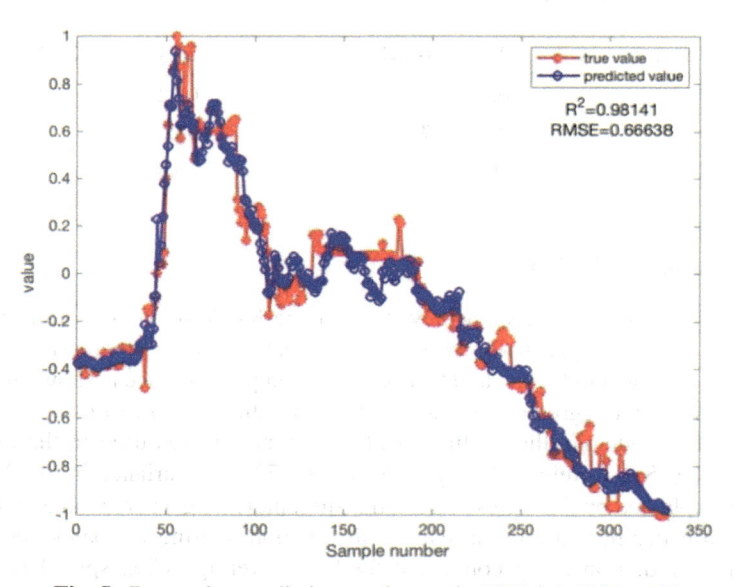

Fig. 5. Regression prediction results graph (2020.1.2–2021.4.27)

Table 3. Support vector regression error calculation

	2017.1.3–2019.12.31	2020.1.2–2021.4.27
mean absolute error MAE	0.040244	0.029396
mean square error MSE	1.1961	0.44407
root mean square error RMSE	1.0936	0.66638
coefficient of determination R^2	0.96257	0.98141

4 Importance of Identifying Influencing Factors

Before and during the pandemic, to identify the drivers of U.S. sovereign CDS spreads, the MIV values of each influencing factor of sovereign CDS spreads on U.S. sovereign CDS spreads are derived based on the SVR forecast results combined with MIV, respectively (Table 4 and Table 5.) For the U.S. before the pandemic outbreak, the top four important influencing factors on U.S. sovereign CDS spreads are the Panic Index, S&P 500 Index, Oil Volatility Index, and Gold Futures Price, which together contribute more than 66% of the degree of influence, with the Panic Index having 24.87% of the influence, indicating its influence on the sovereign CDS spreads of the U.S. with strong predictability. Meanwhile, U.S. five-year Treasuries, crude oil futures, In terms of the degree of influence on the U.S. sovereign CDS spread, the U.S. dollar index ranks in the last three positions, with a total influence value of less than 11%, showing a lower influence status. The analysis found that global factors show strong predictability on U.S. sovereign CDS spreads, while the degree of influence of the domestic factor S&P 500 Index on U.S. sovereign CDS spreads is 18.39%, indicating its comparative importance in predicting U.S. sovereign CDS spreads.

Table 4. SVR-MIV Forecast Results Prior to Pandemic Outbreak

Variable	MIV-percent
VIX	24.97%
SP500	18.39%
OVX	11.93%
GFP	11.20%
CVX	7.94%
UTR10	7.41%
BrentFP	7.17%
UTR5	4.88%
WTIFP	3.77%
DI	2.33%

For the U.S. during the pandemic, the Panic Index, crude oil futures prices, crude oil volatility, gold volatility, and the S&P 500 are in the top five significant influencers of U.S. sovereign CDS spreads, with a joint influence on U.S. sovereign CDS spreads of more than 83%, demonstrating the significant predictability of these five factors on U.S. sovereign CDS spreads. At the same time, the dollar index and gold futures price levels are at low impact levels. Domestic factors have had less impact on U.S. sovereign CDS spreads during the pandemic than global factors.

Table 5. SVR-MIV Forecast Results for U.S. Sovereign CDS Spreads Prior to the Pandemic Period

Variable	MIV-percent
VIX	24.81%
WTIFP	22.87%
OVX	14.83%
CVX	13.15%
SP500	10.05%
UTR5	4.46%
BrentFP	3.07%
UTR10	3.03%
DI	2.37%
GFP	1.36%

In summary, the panic index, crude oil, and oil volatility indexes are more predictive of U.S. sovereign CDS spread forecasts before and during the pandemic. The pandemic period saw a decrease in the influence of the S&P 500 Index and U.S. 10-year Treasury yield on U.S. sovereign CDS spreads compared to the pre-pandemic period. Conversely, crude oil futures prices had a more significant impact on U.S. sovereign CDS spreads during the pandemic period. These findings suggest that global factors had a greater influence on U.S. sovereign CDS spreads during the pandemic than before. Overall, the pandemic period brought about changes in the factors that influence U.S. sovereign CDS spreads.

5 Conclusion

The global economy has been greatly affected by the COVID-19 crisis, which could result in a national economic crisis and increase sovereign risk for global investors. Thus, scientific and effective forecasting of U.S. sovereign risk in special periods is important to maintain global economic stability and the asset security of investors in financial transactions. The study discovered that the U.S. sovereign CDS spreads initially fluctuated strongly during the pandemic outbreak but eventually followed a decreasing trend. Overall, there was a decline in the U.S. sovereign CDS spreads. The degree of influence of global factors on U.S. sovereign CDS spreads increased during the pandemic compared with before the outbreak. Therefore, global investors and international financial regulators can pay more attention to international economic and financial factors to predict U.S. sovereign risk in the face of a global emergency like COVID-19. This paper does not consider daily or monthly indicators of the severity of COVID-19 in the forecasting model, and the algorithms and models used in this paper are more classical and can be further improved in terms of parameter selection algorithms for regression forecasting.

References

1. Annaert, J., Ceuster, M.D., Roy, P.V., Vespro, C.: What determines Euro area bank CDS spreads? J. Int. Money Financ. **32**, 444–461 (2013)
2. Badaoui, S., Cathcart, L., Jahel, L.E.: Do sovereign credit default swaps represent a clean measure of sovereign default risk? A factor model approach. J. Bank. Finance **37**, 2392–2407 (2013)
3. Daehler, T.B., Aizenman, J., Jinjarak, Y.: Emerging markets sovereign CDS spreads during COVID-19: economics versus epidemiology news. Econ. Model. **100** (2021)
4. Augustin, P., Sokolovski, V., Subrahmanyam, M.G., Tomio, D.: In sickness and in debt: The COVID-19 impact on sovereign credit risk. J. Financ. Econ. **143**, 1251–1274 (2021)
5. Andrieș, A.M., Ongena, S., Sprincean, N.: The COVID-19 pandemic and sovereign bond risk. North Am. J. Econ. Financ. **58** (2021)
6. Bizuneh, M., Geremew, M.: Assessing the impact of Covid-19 pandemic on emerging market economies' (EMEs) sovereign bond risk premium and fiscal solvency. East. Econ. J. **47**, 519–545 (2021)
7. Li, J.P., Wang, J., Feng, Q.Q., Sun, X.L.: Forecasting sovereign CDS spreads based on multiple determinants. China J. Econometrics (02), 362–376 (2021)
8. Dalal, A., Bagherimehrab, M., Sanders, B.C.: Quantum-assisted support vector regression for detecting facial landmarks, pp. 1–20 (2021)
9. Cai, G.C.: Research on stock price prediction based on support vector regression machine (Master's thesis, Hangzhou University of Electronic Science and Technology) (2009)
10. Data, Datastream. https://www.refinitiv.cn/zh/products/datastream-macroeconomic-ana lysis?utm_campaign=748972_BAUBaiduBrandProductPaidSearch2023&elqCampaignId= 20637&utm_source=Baidu&utm_medium=CPC&utm_content=Product%20Name%20-% 20Exact&utm_term=Datastream
11. Data, investing. cn. https://cn.investing.com/
12. MATLAB Chinese Forum. MATLAB neural networks 30 case studies. Beijing University of Aeronautics and Astronautics Press (2010)

Portfolio Optimization for Major Industries in American Capital Market

Xinyi Liu[✉]

Cornell University, Ithaca, USA
xl936@cornell.edu

Abstract. This study focuses on portfolio optimization of five companies in the American capital market using the mean variance model. The importance of portfolio construction is emphasized, considering its significance in mitigating risk and maximizing returns for investors. Historical financial data and market information of five selected companies from 2013 to 2023 are analyzed. In this work, 10,000 investment portfolios are simulated using Monte Carlo simulation. The portfolio with the highest Sharpe ratio and the portfolio with the lowest volatility are then determined using the mean variance model. The performance of these two portfolios is assessed by comparing them to real income data covering nearly two months after the asset weights for these two portfolios have been determined. The result of this study shows that Apple processes the largest proportion of the maximum Sharpe ratio portfolio, while Google for the minimum volatility portfolio. By comparing the cumulative return of the two portfolios with the NASDAQ 100 Index, it is discovered that both portfolios outperformed the benchmark index. The insights gained from this research offer valuable guidance to investors, enabling them to make informed decisions in constructing optimal portfolios that align with their risk and return preferences.

Keywords: Ortfolio Optimization · Mean-Variance

1 Introduction

The 20th and 21st centuries have seen the emergence of several large corporations that have become household names, such as Apple and Amazon. These companies are leaders in their respective industries, ranging from technology to retail to finance and energy. Given their size and influence, these companies are often included in investment portfolios. However, constructing an optimal portfolio that includes these companies presents a challenge due to the vast number of available assets and the complex interrelationships between them. In this situation, portfolio optimization approaches offer big companies a useful tool for managing their portfolios effectively.

Previous studies have shown that the mean-variance model is an effective tool for portfolio optimization [1–3]. Since Harry Markowitz first put forward the concept in 1952, it has grown to be an essential component of contemporary portfolio theory. In order to manage the portfolios of large American companies, experts have recently applied the mean-variance model to different sectors. Using financial and non-financial aspects, such as regulatory and compliance risks, liquidity concerns, and consumer behavior, Yang and Chan [4] suggested a mean-variance optimization methodology for companies. The study discovered that the mean-variance framework performed better than conventional methods for optimizing a portfolio. Similarly, a study by Yao et al. [5] proposed a dynamic mean-variance optimization model for portfolio management of companies. The model takes into account the dynamic nature of the different industries and considers multiple risk factors, including market risk, operational risk, and regulatory risk. The study found that the dynamic mean-variance model can effectively manage portfolio risk and outperform traditional portfolio optimization methods.

Overall, the mean-variance model is an effective tool for optimizing portfolios, and its use in different sectors has the potential to enhance portfolio management for different businesses and investors. In recent years, the application of mean-variance model in portfolio optimization has been extended to various asset classes including stocks, bonds, and commodities [6–8]. However, few studies have focused on optimizing the portfolio of American capital companies using this model.

The detailed investigation process can be summarized as follow: First, the daily stock prices data from January 2013 to January 2023 for each of the 5 companies are collected. The expected returns and covariance matrix of the stock returns are calculated based on historical data. Utilizing these calculations, an optimization algorithm is employed to determine the optimal portfolio weights for each company. The results demonstrate that the optimized portfolios yield higher expected returns and lower risks compared to equally weighted portfolios. The mean variance model enables the identification of optimal portfolio weights for each company, facilitating the construction of a diversified investment portfolio. Lastly, through the evaluation of the obtained results, the study identifies limitations such as limited historical data and potential variations in future market conditions.

2 Data

The paper selects five representative stocks of U.S. capital market. The ticker of these 5 assets are AMZN, AAPL, NFLX, GOOG, and META.

Daily stock price data of the aforementioned companies was gathered from January 1, 1989, to December 31, 2018, for the purpose of optimizing the portfolio of American capital corporations. An optimization technique was then employed to identify the best portfolio that maximizes return for a specific level of risk. The data for this study was sourced from Yahoo Finance (Tables 1, 2, and Fig. 1).

3 Method

The concept of mean-variance optimization, initially introduced by Harry Markowitz in his seminal 1952 study, has revolutionized the field of portfolio management, transforming it into a scientific discipline. Markowitz's pioneering work established that an optimal allocation can be achieved by strategically combining assets with diverse expected returns and volatilities.

Table 1. Selected Stocks.

	Company
AMZN	Amazon.com, Inc.
AAPL	Apple Inc.
NFLX	Netflix, Inc.
GOOG	Alphabet Inc.
META	Meta Platforms, Inc.

Table 2. Descriptive statistics of the selected assets.

	Min	Max	Mean	Std Dev	Cumulative Return
AAPL	12.03	180.43	60.46	49.11	7.71%
AMZN	12.41	186.57	73.78	53.29	6.53%
GOOG	17.51	150.71	59.32	35.17	4.93%
META	22.90	382.18	155.58	83.90	4.30%
NFLX	13.14	691.69	239.05	174.23	22.43%

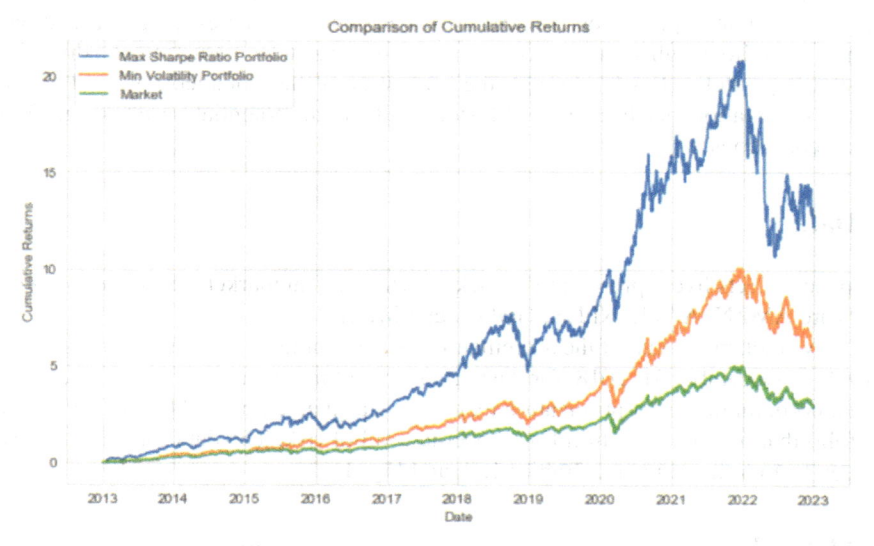

Fig. 1. Cumulative returns of the stocks.

The expected return of a portfolio is calculated using the formula:

$$E_{(r_p)} = \sum_i w_i E(r_i)$$

The variance (risk) of the portfolio return is calculated by the following equation:

$$\sigma_p^2 = \sum_i \sum_j w_j w_i \, Cov(r_i, r_j)$$

The sharpe ratio of one portfolio is calculated as follows:

$$SR = \frac{E_{(r_p)} - R_f}{\sigma_p}$$

In summary, mean-variance optimization, as conceptualized by Markowitz, has significantly influenced portfolio management by enabling the identification of optimal asset allocations. Understanding the minimum variance frontier, efficient frontier, and the calculation of expected returns, variances, and the Sharpe Ratio empowers researchers and practitioners to make informed decisions in constructing portfolios that strike a balance between risk and return.

4 Result

To begin with, the paper employs the Monte Carlo Method to generate 100,000 portfolio outcomes with various weights. Figure 2 illustrates the scatter plot, where the efficient frontier is highlighted by the blue edge.

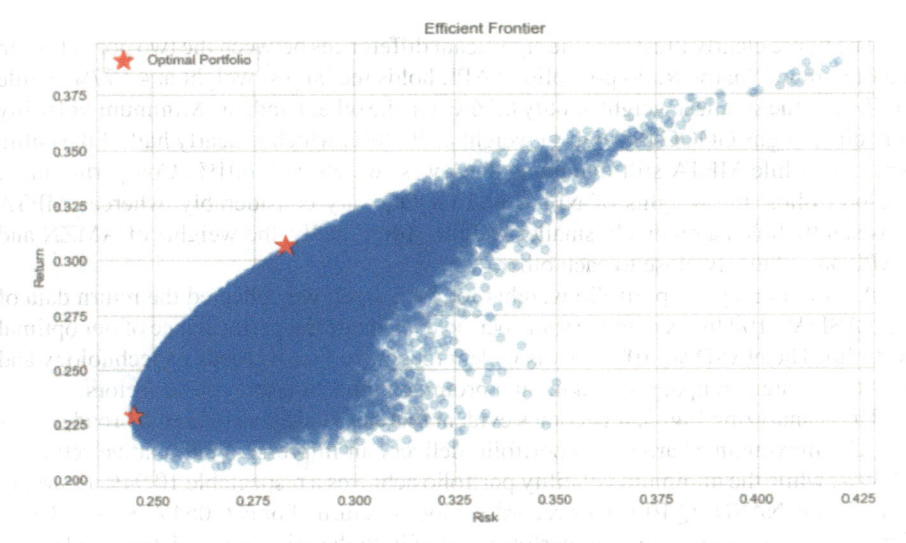

Fig. 2. Efficient frontier retrieved by Monte Carlo Method.

By analyzing this chart and utilizing the mean variance model, we can determine the optimal portfolio, which is calculated and labeled in Fig. 2. Obtaining the two asset allocations allows the next step: the calculation of the portfolio return. Using the test set from January 2013 to January 2023 together with the stock weights, the daily portfolio returns can be gained, and furthermore, the cumulative returns. Specifically, the Maximum Sharpe Ratio portfolio and the Minimum Volatility portfolio stand out as key candidates. The former offers the highest excess return per unit of risk, while the latter boasts the lowest risk within the effective set mentioned earlier. The following tables present the calculated portfolio weights, along with the corresponding Sharpe Ratio and Volatility (Tables 3 and 4).

Table 3. Asset weights under two criterions.

	AMZN	AAPL	NFLX	META	GOOG
Maximum Sharpe Ratio portfolio	8.06%	47.77%	34.20%	0.063%	9.91%
Minimum Volatility portfolio	10.68%	36.87%	2.44%	0.801%	49.20%

Table 4. Portfolio characteristics of the two portfolios.

	Sharp Ratio	Volatility	Returns
Maximum Sharpe Ratio portfolio	107.82%	28.03%	30.22%
Minimum Volatility portfolio	91.94%	24.52%	22.54%

The figure clearly illustrates the significant differences between the two portfolios. In the Maximum Sharpe Ratio portfolio, AAPL holds the largest weight at 47.77%, while META has the smallest weight of only 0.26%. On the other hand, the Minimum Volatility portfolio assigns GOOG the highest weight at 49.20%, which is nearly half of the entire portfolio, while META still maintains the lowest weight at 0.801%. Comparing these two portfolios, the weights of NFLX and GOOG vary considerably, whereas META consistently holds a relatively smaller weight. Additionally, the weights of AMZN and AAPL are relatively close to each other.

After obtaining the portfolio weights for each asset, we collected the return data of the NASDAQ 100 Index over the same period to evaluate the performance of our optimal portfolio. The NASDAQ 100 index is widely recognized for its focus on technology and growth-oriented companies, making it a prominent benchmark in these sectors.

Upon analyzing Fig. 3, it becomes evident that our study surpasses the broader market. The maximum Sharpe ratio portfolio delivers an impressive cumulative return of 22.39%, while the minimum volatility portfolio achieves a respectable 10.94% return. In contrast, the NASDAQ 100 index records a modest return of only 0.064%. Figure 3 consistently showcases the superior performance of both the minimum volatility and maximum Sharpe ratio portfolios compared to the NASDAQ 100 index throughout the entire observed period. Remarkably, the cumulative returns of the maximum Sharpe ratio and minimum volatility portfolios experienced a significant surge over the last three years, contrasting with the stable performance of the NASDAQ 100 index. Consequently, we can confidently assert that not only does the maximum Sharpe ratio portfolio outperform the market as a whole, but it also outperforms the minimum volatility portfolio in terms of return performance.

Fig. 3. Comparison of Maximum Sharpe Ratio, Minimum variance portfolio and the market level.

5 Conclusion and Discussion

In conclusion, this research focuses on optimizing portfolios of five representative companies in the American capital market through the mean variance model. The significance of portfolio construction is underscored as it helps investors mitigate risk and maximize returns. Historical financial data and market information are carefully examined, and Monte Carlo simulation is employed to simulate 10,000 random investment portfolios. By applying the mean variance model, the portfolios with the highest Sharpe ratio and lowest volatility are identified. These portfolios are then evaluated using real income data spanning ten months. The findings reveal that Apple dominates the portfolio with the highest Sharpe ratio for 47.77%, while Google dominates the portfolio with the lowest volatility for 49.20%, almost 1/2 of the total portfolio. Notably, both portfolios outperform the NASDAQ 100 Index. This research provides valuable guidance to investors, assisting them in constructing optimal portfolios that align with their risk and return preferences.

One limitation of this study is its sole reliance on the standard mean-variance model for portfolio optimization. Although the mean-variance model is widely used and provides valuable insights, it assumes static correlation coefficients between assets. In reality, correlations among assets can change over time, especially during periods of market turbulence. By incorporating dynamic correlation coefficients, the study could have captured a more realistic representation of the portfolio's risk characteristics. Furthermore, other risk measures beyond volatility, such as downside risk or tail risk, could have been explored as potential avenues for future research. Incorporating these factors would enhance the robustness and comprehensiveness of the study's findings.

References

1. Markowitz, H.M.: Portfolio selection. J. Financ. **7**(1), 77–91 (1952)
2. Sharpe, W.F.: Capital asset prices: a theory of market equilibrium under conditions of risk. J. Financ. **19**(3), 425–442 (1964)
3. Lintner, J.: The valuation of risk assets and the selection of risky investments in stock portfolios and capital budgets. Rev. Econ. Stat. **47**(1), 13–37 (1965)
4. Yang, J., Chan, W.H.: The mean-variance portfolio optimization model: a systematic review and future research areas. Int. J. Financ. Stud. **7**(1), 8 (2019)
5. Yao, C., Liu, X., Zhou, Z., Xiong, X.: A mean-variance model with fuzzy random variables for portfolio selection problem. Mathematics **8**(2), 201 (2020)
6. Zhang, Y., Zhang, H., Huang, L.: Mean-variance portfolio selection with a randomized rule for portfolio selection problem. J. Intell. Fuzzy Syst. **31**(4), 2273–2283 (2016)
7. Rachev, S.T., Stoyanov, S.V., Fabozzi, F.J., Focardi, S.M.: Mean-variance portfolio optimization when means and covariances are fuzzy. J. Portf. Manag. **44**(1), 55–66 (2018)
8. Song, X., Ma, Z., Li, Y., Li, X., Li, J.: Portfolio selection based on a mean-variance model with interval probability. Complexity **2019**, 1–14 (2019)

The Impact of Investor Sentiment on Stock Returns Based on Machine Learning and Deep Learning Methods

Xiangjun Chen(✉)

Shandong University, Jinan 264209, Shandong, China
`chenxiangjunn@outlook.com`

Abstract. The popularity of artificial intelligence, as demonstrated by ChatGPT, continues to drive the remarkable growth of AI-related concept stocks in the market and has a significant influence on the overall performance of technology stocks. However, multiple factors affect the stock prices of technology companies. This study seeks to examine how investor sentiment impacts the stock returns of technology companies using the Fama-French three-factor model. We employ principal component analysis to conduct factor analysis, create an investor sentiment factor, and propose the utilization of a TiDE time series model based on a multilayer perceptron (MLP) to forecast stock returns. We progressively introduce four indicators, namely book-to-market ratio, market return, total market value, and the investor sentiment factor, and observe a substantial improvement in the accuracy of stock return predictions. Additionally, when investors feel more positive about a particular stock or the market as a whole, there tends to be an increase in stock returns. Conversely, when investor sentiment is negative, there tends to be a decrease in stock returns. Comparing the TiDE model with machine learning methods like Random Forest and Gradient Boosting, as well as deep learning methods such as LSTM and Transformer, we find that the TiDE model enhances prediction accuracy and reduces the disparity between predicted and actual values in time series forecasting tasks. On the one hand, this study helps investors better understand the impact of investor sentiment on the stock prices of technology companies in China's financial markets. On the other hand, it provides empirical research evidence for applying artificial intelligence in the financial field. In the future, this research result can be useful in applying to a wider range of stock markets and other financial fields.

Keywords: Investor Sentiment · Stock Return · Deep Learning · Machine Learning

1 Introduction

Following the cessation of the COVID-19, stock markets across the globe have gradually experienced a financial recovery. In light of the pandemic's global spread, an increasing number of companies have shifted towards online operations, presenting opportunities for the analysis and forecasting of technology company stock markets. Because of the typically high valuations and price-to-earnings ratios of technology stocks, which are closely linked to expected returns, conducting market research on technology stocks holds significant academic merit. Starting from the Fama-French three-factor model (FF3) [1], researchers have been exploring the optimal combination of various indicators to explain expected returns. Kumar and Lee [2] conducted a study based on the trading activities of investors and found that retail investors tend to concentrate their trading activities on companies with smaller sizes, lower prices, higher book-to-market ratios, and lower institutional ownership. In Schmeling's study [3] on the international expected stock returns of 18 industrialized countries, it was shown that the level of consumer confidence plays a crucial role in determining the overall returns of a country's stock market. According to Liu, Stambaugh, and Yuan's research [4] on the Chinese stock market, both the size and value factors have a considerable influence on predicting stock returns. These results align with prior studies conducted in various markets, suggesting that size and value play crucial roles in determining stock returns across different regions and economies.

Investor sentiment has been an important factor influencing stock returns in financial markets. According to a study by Fisher and Statman [5], there appears to be a direct relationship between investor sentiment and stock returns, with positive sentiment correlating with higher returns. Baker and Wurgler [6] further explored the concept of emotional trading behavior, where investors trade based on their emotions rather than rational judgment. On the other hand, Barber et al. [7] analyzed individual investors' trading behavior to investigate whether retail trading has an impact on the market. Gao, Gu, and Koedijk [8] found that when institutional investors are more optimistic about the market, stock prices tend to rise in the short term. Conversely, when institutional investors are more pessimistic, stock prices may decline. Studying investor sentiment has become increasingly meaningful because of the continuous development of financial markets and the constantly developing behavior of investors.

Factor models in the field of asset pricing are one of the most crucial methods for explaining stock market volatility. Over the past few decades, many scholars have studied factor models and proposed different theories and models. Among them, the Capital Asset Pricing Model (CAPM) and the three-factor model proposed by Sharpe [9], Lintner [10], Fama, and French [1] have been widely applied in asset pricing and portfolio construction. CAPM considers that the risk of an asset is positively related to its expected return. Lintner [10] extended the concept of risk factors on the basis of CAPM and proposed three factors, namely, market risk, individual stock risk, and market size, to explain variations in stock returns. Fama and French [1] further introduced two additional factors, namely, book-to-market ratio and market liquidity, and constructed the three-factor model. This model has performed well in empirical research and has become one of the classic models in asset pricing. Furthermore, Carhart [11] proposed a four-factor model and found that the "momentum" factor can significantly impact investment portfolio returns. On the other hand, Fama and French [12] decomposed market size as well as the book-to-market ratio into more detailed factors such as high value, high momentum, and high quality. They constructed the five-factor model. These factor models provide essential references for constructing investment portfolios and risk control and have become classic theories in the field of asset pricing. In conclusion, factor models are one of the important concepts in capital asset pricing and have significant implications for effectively explaining stock market volatility and constructing investment portfolios.

In recent years, increasing numbers of researchers have applied machine learning (ML) and useful deep learning (DL) techniques to finance, aiming to improve the accuracy of stock indicator predictions. This trend is mainly due to the difficulty of traditional methods in capturing the complexity and non-linear features of financial data. Therefore, many scholars have proposed various models and algorithms for stock prediction. Hochreiter and Schmidhuber [13] proposed the use of LSTM recurrent neural networks to predict changes in stock prices; Bao, Yue, and Rao [14] proposed a method to predict time series data on financial markets. Their framework utilizes both stacked AE(AutoEncoders) and LSTM; while Gu, Kelly, and Xiu [15] applied machine learning techniques to empirical asset pricing by reinforcement learning to predict the returns of different stocks and applied it to portfolio construction. Overall, these studies have made significant contributions to applying deep learning and machine learning in the field of finance, helping us understand the advantages and limitations of different algorithms and models for predicting stock prices.

In this article, we focus on the relationship between investor sentiment and stock returns in the A-share market's technology companies and further explore the potential of deep learning methods in large-scale time series prediction. Our contribution is to use principal component analysis to select stock features related to investor sentiment and combine them into the SENT composite index to represent the level of investor sentiment. Then, we innovatively used the TiDE time series model to predict stock returns, gradually incorporating market factors, size factors, book-to-market ratio factors, and investor sentiment factors to explore the significance of sentiment. We also compared various methods, including Random Forest, Gradient Boosting, Xgboost, SVM, LSTM, and Transformer. The experimental results showed that TiDE had the strongest predictive ability. Finally, we draw the conclusion based on empirical analysis that incorporating investor sentiment factors is helpful in explaining stock returns. Investor sentiment and stock returns are positively correlated relationship. The results of this research emphasize the importance of investor sentiment in driving the behavior of the stock market and provide new ideas for investor decision-making. In addition, our research has theoretical value and practical significance, which can promote investors' better understanding of market changes and provide assistance in formulating more scientific investment strategies.

The paper is structured as follows: Sect. 2 provides a description of the data, variance analysis, and data preprocessing; Sect. 3 introduces the factor analysis, along with the factor regression model that considers FF3 and investor sentiment. The prediction models LSTM, SVM, and Xgboost are also performed. The results of factor analysis, factor regression, and model prediction are presented in Sect. 4. The last section provides our conclusions based on the findings.

2 Data

2.1 Data Source

This study focuses on the stock data of technology-listed companies in the A-share market. It excludes stocks flagged with risk warnings (ST, *ST), newly listed stocks, and stocks with significant data gaps in the research sample. As a result, it retains 36 technology-listed companies' stocks for analysis. With a daily data frequency, the sample period for this study covers from January 2012 to December 2022, resulting in a total of 52,802 observations. The dataset includes variables such as stock turnover rate (TR), trading volume growth rate (AGR), price-earnings ratio (PE), trading volume (VOL), return rate, total market value (MV), one-year deposit interest rate, Shanghai Composite Index, and book-to-market ratio (BM). We use these variables to construct investor sentiment factors, market factors, size factors, and book-to-market ratio factors. The primary data for these variables are sourced from the CSMAR database, while the industry classification follows the China Securities Regulatory Commission's 2012 version of industry classification standards.

This study's primary objective is to analyze investor sentiment's impact on stock returns and accurately predict future stock returns by using ML and DL models. Therefore, the selected independent variables in this study should effectively reflect stock returns to a certain extent or exhibit a certain level of correlation with stock returns. Building upon the FF3, this study incorporates investor sentiment factors, market factors, size factors, and BM factors as independent variables to analyze the key factors influencing stock returns. Additionally, ML and DL models are developed to forecast stock returns.

Furthermore, in order to conduct a comprehensive analysis of time series at a horizontal level, Table 1 presents the definitions and measurements of the selected variables in this study for each sample data.

The Shanghai Composite Index helps us understand the overall trends, market conditions, and current operating status of the Chinese stock market, as well as its impact on various sectors and individual stocks. It facilitates the analysis of the market's cyclic fluctuations and enables the inference of future trends based on these patterns, thereby enhancing the accuracy of predicting stock returns. Figure 1 illustrates the changes in the closing values of the Shanghai Composite Index from 2012 to 2022. Furthermore, Fig. 2 displays the stock price variations of two technology-listed companies, Huakong Seg and Nanfu Bio, over time. It shows that stock prices tend to rise accordingly with an upward trend in the market. Conversely, in a downward market trend, stock prices decline. Therefore, incorporating the Shanghai Composite Index as a market factor enhances the ability to forecast stock returns.

2.2 Variable Analysis

Descriptive Statistical Analysis. In this article, we conduct a descriptive statistical analysis of the sample data. We use measures, including the number of samples(N), the mean, standard deviation(sd), median(p50), maximum value(max), and minimum(min) value, to describe the overall characteristics of the data. Table 2 shows the result.

Table 1. Definition and measurement of each variable.

Variables	Measurement
TR	The number of shares traded on a given day relative to the total number of shares in circulation on that same day
AGR	The ratio of the difference between the transaction amount and the previous day's transaction amount
PE	The ratio of stock price to annual earnings per share
VOL	–
Return rate	–
Risk-free return rate	The one-year deposit rate announced by the central bank is converted into the daily interest rate
Market return	Use the Shanghai Composite Index instead
MV	–
BM	Use the Shanghai Composite Index instead of the ratio of book value to total market value at the end of the last quarter

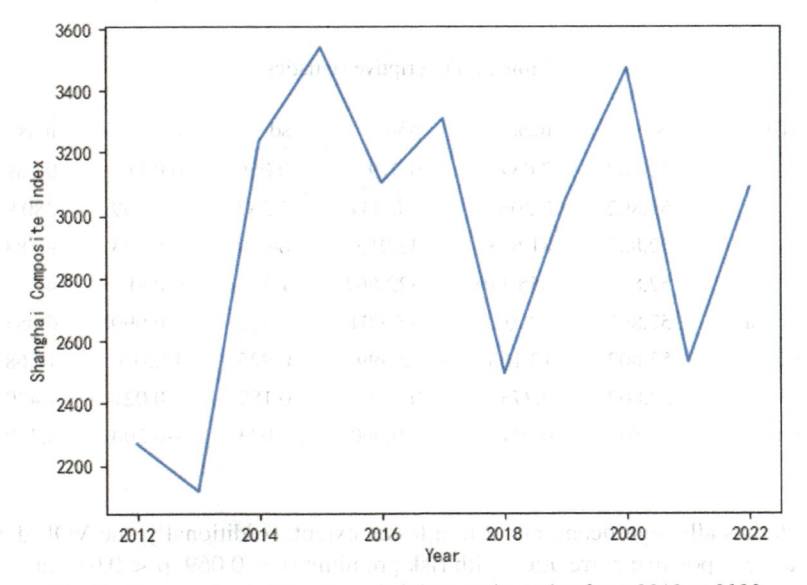

Fig. 1. Change chart of the Shanghai Composite Index from 2012 to 2020.

Correlation Analysis. Table 3 presents the correlation coefficients. The TR of individual stocks shows a weak positive correlation with risk premium ($r = 0.090$, $p < 0.01$), demonstrating a strong significance level. Similarly, the AGR exhibits a weak positive correlation with risk premium ($r = 0.092$, $p < 0.01$), indicating a strong significance level. The PE demonstrates a weak positive correlation with risk premium ($r = 0.05$, $p < 0.01$)

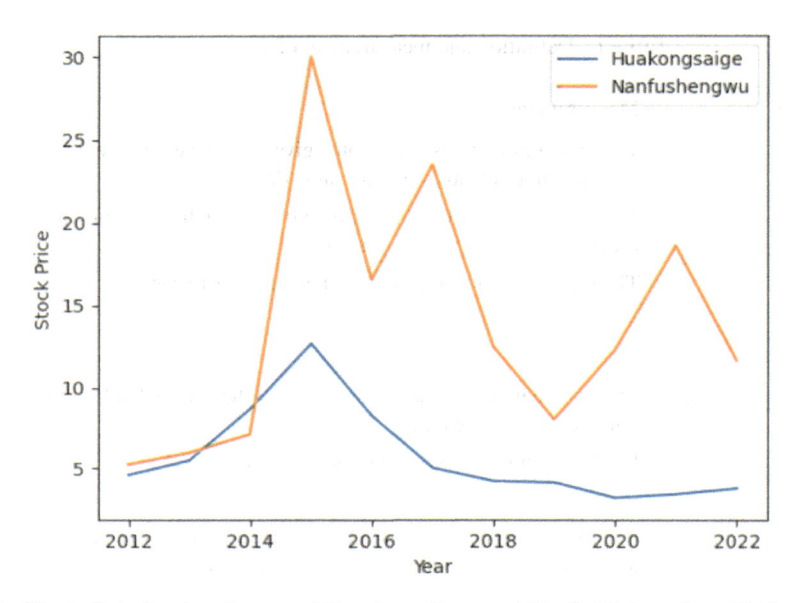

Fig. 2. Chart of stock price changes of Huacheng Sager and Nanfu Biology from 2012 to 2022

Table 2. Descriptive statistics.

VARIABLES	N	mean	p50	sd	min	max
TR	52,802	0.037	0.019	0.056	0.000	0.789
AGR	52,802	0.206	−0.044	3.337	−0.999	280.9
PE	52,802	81.673	42.016	669.8	−6,963	9,583
VOL	52,802	655.170	322.667	1,326	0.030	44,397
Market return	52,802	−0.005	−0.004	0.012	−0.090	0.053
$\log(MV)$	52,802	13.163	12.999	0.925	11.313	16.68
BM	52,802	0.273	0.239	0.189	−0.021	1.430
Risk premium	52,802	0.001	−0.000	0.033	−0.200	0.200

that is statistically significant, albeit to a lesser extent. Additionally, the VOL demonstrates a weak positive correlation with risk premium ($r = 0.069$, $p < 0.01$) and shows a strong significance level. Market return exhibits a strong positive correlation with risk premium ($r = 0.413$, $p < 0.01$), demonstrating a high significance level. The logarithm of total market capitalization shows a weak positive correlation with risk premium ($r = 0.018$, $p < 0.01$), which is statistically significant. Furthermore, the BM exhibits a weak negative correlation with risk premium ($r = -0.034$, $p < 0.01$), demonstrating a strong significance level. Overall, the correlations between each variable and risk premium are weak but statistically significant. These findings establish a solid statistical foundation for further research.

Table 3. Correlation coefficients.

	TR	AGR	PE	VOL	Market return	log(MV)	BM	Risk premium
TR	1							
AGR	0.136***	1						
PE	0.019***	−0.00500	1					
VOL	0.365***	0.053***	0.00500	1				
Market return	0.021***	0.00200	0.00600	0.016***	1			
log(MV)	−0.042***	−0.00100	0.00600	0.188***	0.041***	1		
BM	−0.101***	−0.018***	−0.066***	−0.038***	−0.00300	−0.297***	1	
Risk premium	0.090***	0.092***	0.00500	0.069***	0.413***	0.018***	−0.034***	1

Tips: ***: $p < 0.01$; **: $p < 0.05$; *: $p < 0.1$

2.3 Data Preprocessing

Missing Value Handling. In addressing the issue of missing values, this study employs a wide range of factor indicators with varying quality. Some factors exhibit a higher frequency of missing values, while others have fewer missing values. For factors with relatively few missing values, we utilize K-means clustering. Specifically, we select the K nearest observed sequence values to the missing value and estimate the missing data for the sample by calculating the weighted average based on the distances. We directly exclude the corresponding samples from the analysis for factors with a significant number of missing values.

Outlier Handling. An outlier refers to an exceptionally high or low value within a sample. After removing missing samples, this study replaces data points outside the 0.1% and 99.9% quantiles with the corresponding data from the 0.1% and 99% quantiles, respectively.

Standardization Processing. It is common to encounter inconsistent data scales during data processing. Larger numerical values may dominate the overall distribution. Therefore, Data standardization is necessary to address these issues. In this study, we employ the Z-score method for standardization, as illustrated by the following formula:

$$x' = \frac{x - \bar{x}}{\sigma} \quad (1)$$

3 Method

In this study, the principal component analysis (PCA) technique is predominantly employed to construct a composite indicator called SENT. This composite indicator incorporates four different investor sentiment indicators with the aim of elucidating investor sentiment. Furthermore, it investigates the impact of market factors, size factors, book-to-market ratio factors, and investor sentiment factors on returns. To be more specific, this study utilizes the FF3 as a framework for regression analysis and incorporates the investor sentiment factor. To forecast stock returns, we use the TiDE time series model. The effectiveness of this model is validated by comparing it with various benchmark models.

3.1 Factor Analysis

At present, Baker and Wurgler [16] introduced the widely adopted approach for constructing an emotion index. They used the principal component analysis method to eliminate trait components that are not associated with emotions. As a result, they obtained a more refined dataset that specifically captures emotional aspects. In particular, they chose proxy variables that can effectively represent investor sentiment, including measures such as turnover rate, number of new accounts, and other relevant data. Then, they used these variables to carry out multiple linear regression with macroeconomic variables such as CPI and obtained the residuals. This procedure allows for the removal of the impact that basic factors have on investor sentiment. However, due to the selection of distinct proxy variables, it is essential to conduct separate principal component analyses on the residual sequences associated with these variables. It is useful to eliminate trait factors linked to the proxy variables and extract shared information. Hui-qin et al. used this methodology. Hui-qin et al. [17] utilized four indirect indicators, namely TR, AGR, PE, and VOL, to explain investor sentiment. They used principal component analysis to combine these indicators into a composite measure that represents investor sentiment. Experimental results confirmed that this composite indicator exhibited stronger explanatory power for stock returns compared to individual indicators. Furthermore, the study demonstrated that investor sentiment has a more significant short-term impact than long-term impact.

Factor analysis is a frequently used method for data dimensionality reduction. Its primary purpose is to explain the correlation between observed variables by identifying latent variables to achieve dimensionality reduction of the original data. The fundamental idea behind factor analysis is to represent the observed data as a combination of several underlying factors and an error term. Direct measurement cannot get factors that are unobservable variables that influence the observed data, but the covariance matrix of the observed variables can achieve it. To be more specific, the algorithmic procedure of factor analysis typically involves the following steps:

(1) Assuming that the observed data is composed of a linear model consisting of k factors and an error term:

$$x_i = \lambda_{1i}f_1 + \lambda_{2i}f_2 + \ldots + \lambda_{ki}f_k + \epsilon_i \tag{2}$$

x_i is the i-th observation, λ_{ji} is the contribution of the j-th factor to the i-th observation data, f_j is the j-th factor, ϵ_i is the error term of this data.

(2) Suppose that the mean value of factor f is 0, the variance is 1, and is not correlated.

$$E(f_j) = 0, Var(f_j) = 1, Cov(f_i, f_j) = 0 (i \neq j) \tag{3}$$

(3) The factor loading matrix Λ and the covariance matrix Ψ of the error term are solved by the maximum likelihood estimation method.
(4) The factor load matrix Λ is rotated through the factor rotation method to better interpret the data.

The formula of factor analysis is as follows:

(1) The covariance matrix of observed data

$$S = \frac{1}{n-1} \sum_{i=1}^{n} (x_i - \bar{x})(x_i - \bar{x})^T \tag{4}$$

n is the number of observations, and x_i is the i-th observation, $\bar{x}$ is the mean of all observations.

(2) Component matrix

$$\Lambda = [\lambda_{ji}]_{k \times p} \tag{5}$$

k is the number of factors and p is the dimension of the observed data. λ_{ji} represents the contribution of the j-th factor to the i-th observed data.

(3) The covariance matrix of the error term

$$\Psi = diag(\psi_1, \psi_2, \ldots, \psi_p) \tag{6}$$

ψ_i is the variance of the error term of the i-th observed data.

(4) Standardized component matrix

$$\varphi_{ji} = \frac{\lambda_{ji}}{\sqrt{\psi_i}} \tag{7}$$

$\sqrt{\psi_i}$ is the standard deviation of the error term of the observation i

(5) Factor score

$$f_j = \sum_{i=1}^{p} \varphi_{ji} z_i \tag{8}$$

z_i is the standardized score of the i-th observation data, which can be expressed as:

$$z_i = \frac{x_i - \bar{x_i}}{s_i} \tag{9}$$

$\bar{x_i}$ is the mean of observation i and s_i is the standard deviation of this data.

(6) Observation data reconstruction

$$x_{ij} = \mu_i + \sum_{j=1}^{k} \lambda_{ji} f_j + \epsilon_{ij} \tag{10}$$

μ_i is the mean of the i-th observation.

It is vital to note that the results of factor analysis may be affected by issues such as data missingness and multicollinearity. Additionally, careful consideration should be given to selecting the number of factors and the rotation method based on the specific circumstances.

3.2 Factor Regression Model

In 1992, Fama and French [1] conducted a study to identify factors that contribute to differences in stock return rates. Their findings suggested that MV, BM, and PE of listed companies are key determinants of variations in stock returns. By examining the relationship between investment returns and various factors, it is possible to assess the influence of investor sentiment on stock returns. This method introduces the investor sentiment factor to evaluate its impact on the stock returns of technology companies based on FF3. The primary equation for this study is as follows:

$$R_{i,t} - R_{f,t} = \alpha_{i,t} + \beta_1(R_{m,t} - R_{f,t}) - \beta_2 ln(MV_{i,t}) + \beta_3 BM_{i,t} + \beta_4 SENT_{i,t} + \varepsilon_{i,t} \tag{11}$$

The variables are described in Table 4.

Table 4. Formula variable definition.

Variable	Note	computing method
$R_{i,t}$	The yield of stock i in period t	–
$R_{f,t}$	Risk-free rate	It is calculated by converting the one-year deposit rate announced by the central bank into the daily interest rate (one-year deposit rate /360)
$R_{m,t}$	Market Return	Use the Shanghai Composite Index instead
$ln(MV_{i,t})$	The size of stock i in period t	The total market value of period t is expressed as the natural log
$BM_{i,t}$	The size of stock i in time t the Book-to-Market ratio of stock i in time t	The ratio of the book value at the end of the last quarter to the total market value of the T-period
$SENT_{i,t}$	Investor sentiment in stock i at phase t	The data can be obtained by PCA
$\alpha_{i,t}$	Intercept term	–
$\beta_1 \sim \beta_4$	The coefficient of each variable	–
$\varepsilon_{i,t}$	Random error term	–

3.3 Prediction Model

We aim to predict the returns for the T + 1 trading day with data from the previous T trading days by employing a time-series model to gradually introduce market factors, size factors, book-to-market ratio factors, and investor sentiment factors. To achieve this goal, we introduce the TiDE model to explore the influence of incorporating investor sentiment indicators on predicting stock returns. We also compare the TiDE model with multiple benchmark models to validate its superiority in time-series prediction problems.

TiDE: Time-Series Dense Encoder. Das et al. [18] proposed that MLP (Multilayer Perceptron) has limitations in fitting the nonlinearity between time series and other temporal variables when dealing with complex time series problems. Therefore, they upgraded the MLP time-series prediction model and introduced a novel TiDE model, which achieved the highest known performance on multiple datasets. The TiDE model is composed of MLPs, focusing on addressing issues, which include previous linear models being unable to capture the nonlinear relationship between the prediction window and historical window, as well as the inability to model external variables effectively.

The Residual Block, which is the critical foundational unit of the TiDE model, consists of a Dense+ReLU layer, a Dense linear layer, and an Add&Layernorm layer. This foundational block also builds all other components of the TiDE model. The model includes four main parts: Feature Projection, Dense Encoder, Dense Decoder, and Temporal Decoder.

The Feature Projection component maps external variables to a lower-dimensional vector using the Residual Block, primarily aiming to reduce the dimensionality of the external variables. The Dense Encoder part concatenates the historical sequence, attribute information, and the lower-dimensional vector mapped from external variables. It uses multiple layers of Residual Blocks to map this concatenated input, eventually obtaining an encoded result denoted as "e". The Dense Decoder part takes the encoded result "e", maps it into "g" using multiple layers of Residual Blocks, and reshapes "g" into a matrix of dimensions [p, H]. "H" corresponds to the length of the prediction window, and "p" represents the output dimension of the decoder. It means that the prediction window generates a vector at each time point. The Temporal Decoder combines the previous "g" with the external variables "x" by concatenating them along the temporal dimension. A Residual Block is then employed to map the output results for each time. After that, incorporating the direct mapping results from the historical sequence establishes a residual connection. Finally, This process generates the final prediction results. Figure 3 shows the architecture of the TiDE model is illustrated.

In each prediction, we use the market factors, size factors, BM factors, and investor sentiment factors from the preceding 36 days to forecast the next trading day's return. To create features and labels from the time series data, we employ a moving window approach, dividing the entire dataset into 80% training set and 20% test set.

Benchmark Models - RF, GBDT, XGBoost, SVR, LSTM, Transformer. We select robust and high-performance machine learning and deep learning methods, including RF, GBDT, XGBoost, SVR, LSTM, and Transformer, for benchmarking TiDE. We will briefly introduce these methods in the following paragraphs.

Random Forest. As a method of ensemble learning, RF consists of multiple decision trees. Each decision tree trains on a randomly selected sample and a set of randomly chosen features. Afterward, voting determines the final prediction. Many researchers, such as Khaidem et al. [19], have previously applied Random Forest to predict financial data. It enables to handle a large number of input variables and nonlinear relationships. Therefore, Random Forest is an excellent choice for time series forecasting problems that involve a significant number of features.

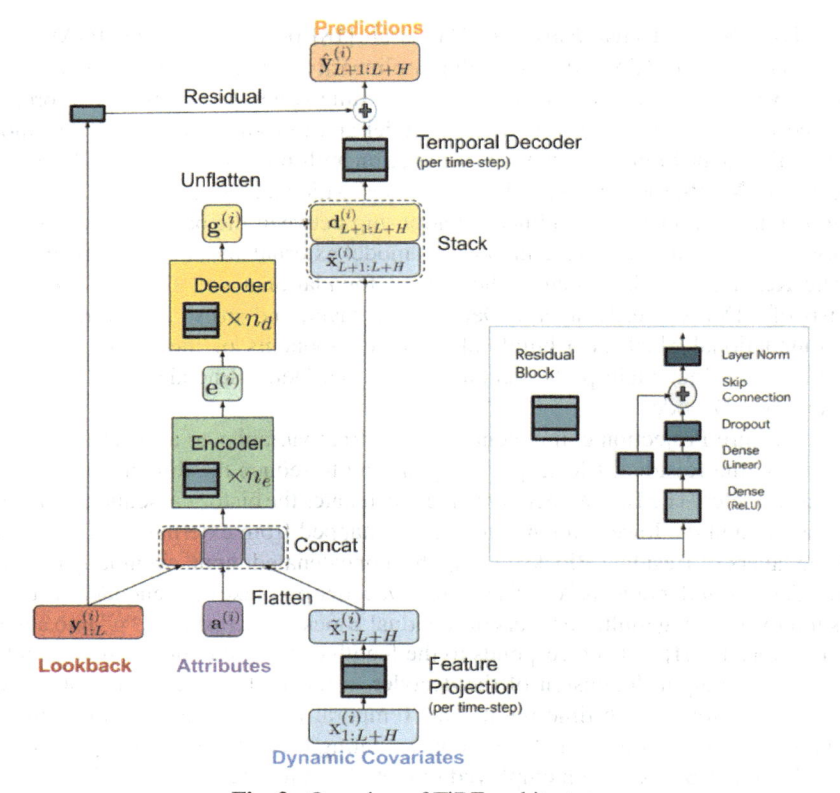

Fig. 3. Overview of TiDE architecture.

Gradient Boosting. GBDT is a machine learning algorithm based on ensemble learning that predicts the target variable by iteratively training multiple decision trees. Its main idea is to use the difference between the previous model's predictions and true values as a new target variable for training in each iteration, continuously improving the model's predictive capability. Compared to using a single decision tree for prediction, GBDT can more accurately predict the target variable because it gradually optimizes the model's predictive performance and has strong noise resistance. When applied to time series forecasting, it can generate a prediction model using historical data and utilize that model to forecast future values. As a direct result of its ability to capture trends and periodic changes in time series data, GBDT is often more effective in handling time series data than traditional moving average models or exponential smoothing models.

Extreme Gradient Boosting. As an ensemble learning algorithm, XGBoost is based on decision trees that combine multiple weak classifiers to construct a more powerful classifier, which is useful for classification and regression tasks. It is an enhanced version of GBDT that utilizes the Taylor expansion in optimizing the objective function and incorporates regularization terms in the loss function to control model complexity. Moreover, it can adaptively learn complex nonlinear interactions between features and handle high-dimensional sparse data, enabling it to capture intricate structures and trends present in time series.

Support Vector Regression. SVR is a type of algorithm that is used to predict numerical outputs. Its main objective is to find an optimal function that can map training samples onto a hyperplane in a high-dimensional space while minimizing prediction errors and maintaining model simplicity. In time series forecasting, SVR can establish models by using time as an input variable and previous observations as features. When dealing with nonlinear relationships, SVR can utilize kernel functions to transform the input data into a higher-dimensional feature space, thereby capturing the relationships between the data more effectively. In this experiment, we employ the linear kernel function.

Long Short-Term Memory. LSTM is primarily designed to tackle the concerns of vanishing and exploding gradients that arise during the training of long sequences. It is a deep-learning model with promising performance in time series forecasting. Fischer and Krauss [20] utilized LSTM networks for predicting financial time series and showcased their efficacy in extracting valuable insights from intricate financial time series data. In this study, based on a moving window approach in the time series data, we built a deep learning LSTM framework to predict the stock return features.

In this study, the construction of the deep learning LSTM framework based on the moving window approach was accomplished using neural network components, including LSTM layers, Dropout layers, and Dense layers. The implementation of this framework was conducted using the PyTorch deep learning framework. The activation function used in the framework was ReLU, and the optimization algorithm utilized was Adam. Figure 4 analyzed the structure of the LSTM model.

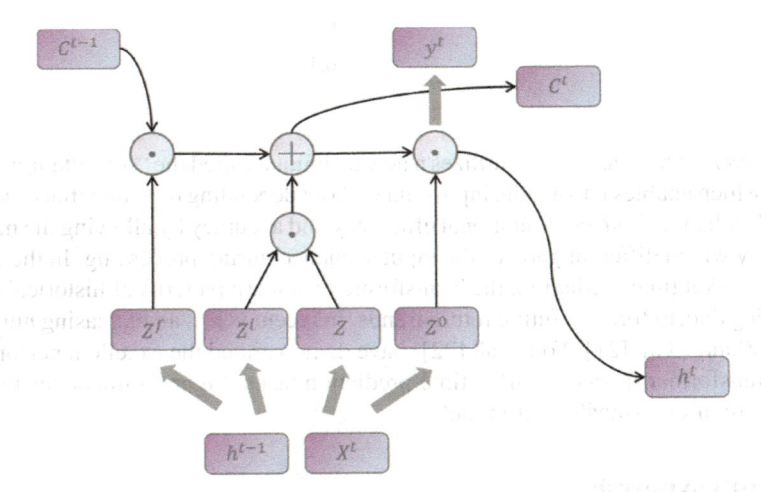

Fig. 4. LSTM model structure.

The main formula is as follows:

$$C^t = z^f \cdot C^{t-1} + z^i \cdot z \tag{12}$$

$$y^t = \sigma\left(W'h^t\right) \tag{13}$$

$$h^t = z^O \cdot \tanh\left(C^t\right) \tag{14}$$

C^t represents the state at time t; z^f represents the forget gate state, which plays a crucial role in determining which information from the previous state $C^{(t-1)}$ should be excluded; x^t represents the input at time t; z^i represents the signal for the select gate, which controls selective memorization of the input x^t; h^t represents the passed state at time t. The symbol "·" denotes matrix multiplication, and "+" denotes matrix addition. In the LSTM model, there are three stages: forget stage, the select memory stage, and the output stage. In the forgotten stage, the forget gate state z^f calculated at time t is used to determine which information from the previous state C^{t-1} needs to be forgotten. In the select memory stage, the input value x^t at time t is selectively memorized. Lastly, the output stage determines the information to be output as the current state and applies the tanh activation function to modify the state from the previous stage. Table 5 presents the specific parameter configurations for LSTM.

Table 5. Parameter settings.

Parameter	Settings
epochs	100
layers	2
learning rate	5
sequence_length	32
batch_size	64
dropout	0.1

Transformer. The Transformer utilizes a new technique called the "self-attention mechanism," which enables it to handle input data without depending on sequential order. This approach enhances both computational efficiency and accuracy by allowing the model to selectively weigh different parts of the input sequence during processing. In the context of stock market time prediction, the Transformer can learn patterns of historical returns and trading data to forecast future return trends. In recent years, an increasing number of studies (Zhang et al. [21], Yoo et al. [22]) have demonstrated the excellent performance of the Transformer in stock market time prediction tasks. Figure 5 illustrates the main architecture of our Transformer model.

4 Results Analysis

4.1 Factor Analysis Results

Factor Analysis Based on Principal Component Analysis. In this study, the selected indirect indicators of investor sentiment are stock turnover rate (TR), growth rate of

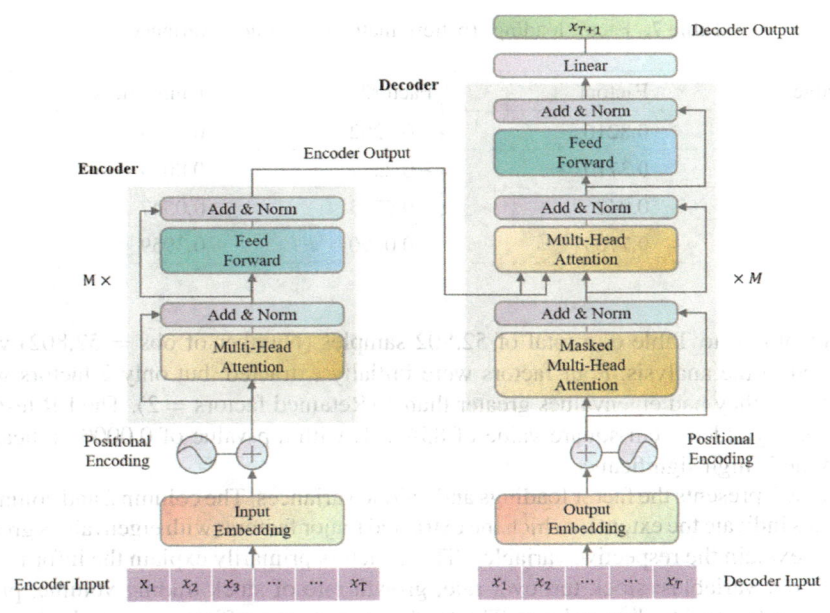

Fig. 5. The architecture of Transformer. In this architecture, the historical stock data $x_1, x_2, \cdots, x_T$ is provided as input data to the Transformer model. The model processes the input data through multiple self-attention layers and feedforward neural networks, allowing it to learn complex patterns in the historical data. Finally, the model produces a predicted stock price x_{T+1} as its output, which represents the estimated value of the stock at time $T+1$ based on the historical data.

stock trading volume (AGR), price-earnings ratio (PE), and trading volume (VOL). The data sources are presented in Table 4. The four variables were standardized to eliminate the influence of measurement units, and the results were listed in Table 6 after factor analysis.

Table 6. Factor analysis/correlation.

Number of obs = 52,802 Retained factors = 2 Number of params = 6				
Factor	Eigenvalue	Difference	Proportion	Cumulative
Factor1	1.40927	0.40734	0.3523	0.3523
Factor2	1.00193	0.03832	0.2505	0.6028
Factor3	0.96361	0.33844	0.2409	0.8437
Factor4	0.62518		0.1563	1.0000

LR test: independent vs. saturated: chi2(6) = 8541.71 Prob > chi2 = 0.0000

Table 7. Factor loadings (pattern matrix) and unique variances.

Variable	Factor1	Factor2	Uniqueness
TR	0.8216	0.0202	0.3324
AGR	0.3710	−0.2377	0.8059
PE	0.0426	0.9713	0.0547
VOL	0.7763	0.0390	0.3959

According to Table 6, a total of 52,802 samples (Number of obs = 52,802) were involved in the analysis. Four factors were initially extracted, but only 2 factors were retained as they had eigenvalues greater than 1 (Retained factors = 2). The LR test for the model yielded a chi-square value of 8541.71, with a p-value of 0.0000, indicating the model's high significance.

Table 7 presents the factor loadings and unique variances. The column 2 and column 3 columns indicate the extent to which the extracted major factors (with eigenvalues greater than 1) explain the respective variables. These factors primarily explain the information of the four variables: stock turnover rate, growth rate of stock trading volume, price-earnings ratio, and trading volume. The final factor score coefficient matrix is shown in Table 8.

Table 8. Scoring coefficients.

Variable	Factor1	Factor2
TR	0.57962	0.02018
AGR	0.26324	−0.23723
PE	0.03026	0.96947
VOL	0.55084	0.03889

Calculation of Investor Sentiment (SENT). The scores for each principal component are as follows:

$$F_1 = 0.57962 \times TR + 0.26324 \times AGR + 0.03026 \times PE + 0.55084 \times VOL \quad (15)$$

$$F_2 = 0.02018 \times TR - 0.23723 \times AGR + 0.96947 \times PE - 0.03889 \times VOL \quad (16)$$

$$SENT = \frac{35.23\% \times F_1 + 25.05\% \times F_2}{60.28} \% \quad (17)$$

Therefore, the expression for investor sentiment is as follows:

$$SENT = 0.211 \times TR + 0.128 \times AGR + 0.243 \times PE - 0.166 \times VOL \quad (18)$$

where SENT represents the investor sentiment indicator, TR represents the turnover rate indicator, VOL represents the current trading volume indicator, and AGR represents the growth rate of the trading volume indicator.

4.2 Regression Analysis Results

After quantifying the investor sentiment indicator (SENT) through factor analysis, a regression analysis was conducted using the FF3. The independent variables included Rm-Rf, ln(MV), and BM, while the dependent variable was R-Rf. Table 9 presents the results of regression analysis.

Table 9. The regression analysis results.

$R_i - R_f$	Coefficient	std. err.	t	P > |t|	[95% conf. Interval]	
$R_m - R_f$	1.116	0.011	104.08	0.000	1.095	1.137
marketValue	−0.001	0.000	−3.01	0.003	−0.001	−0.000
BM	−0.005	0.001	−6.75	0.000	−0.006	−0.003
SENT	0.003	0.000	18.96	0.000	0.003	0.004
_cons	0.013	0.002	6.59	0.000	0.009	0.017

From Table 10, it can be observed that the p-values for all indicators are less than 0.05, indicating the high significance of the model. The regression equation can be derived as follows:

$$R_i - R_f = 1.116 \times (R_m - R_f) - 0.001 \times marketValue \\ - 0.005 \times BM + 0.003 \times SENT + 0.01 \quad (19)$$

According to Eq. (19), the conclusion shows that there exists a direct relationship between investor sentiment and stock returns, with positive sentiment correlating with higher returns.

4.3 Prediction Model Results

Based on the factor model, the prediction was performed using RF, GBDT, XGBoost, SVR, LSTM, Transformer, and TiDE models by gradually adding variables. Table 10 presents the performance of the models evaluated by four metrics: MAE, MSE, RMSE, and R-squared.

The results of stepwise regression show that as ln (MV), BM, SENT is introduced, the MAE, MSE, and RMSE of these models gradually decrease, while the R-squared value increases. This indicates that the model's explanatory power regarding the sample's stock returns is enhanced by the incorporation of the investor sentiment factor. The observable shift in patterns implies that fluctuations in investor sentiment hold considerable sway over stock returns.

Table 10. Each factor and stock return.

	Variable	MAE	MSE	RMSE
RF	ln(MV)	0.596	0.512	0.715
	ln(MV), BM	0.578	0.484	0.696
	ln(MV), BM, SENT	0.353	0.319	0.353
GBDT	ln(MV)	2.347	11.113	3.337
	ln(MV), BM	2.343	11.064	3.326
	ln(MV), BM, SENT	2.336	11.308	3.363
XGBoost	ln(MV)	0.051	0.005	0.068
	ln(MV), BM	0.051	0.005	0.068
	ln(MV), BM, SENT	0.050	0.005	0.067
SVR	ln(MV)	2.347	11.113	3.337
	ln(MV), BM	2.343	11.064	3.326
	ln(MV), BM, SENT	2.336	11.308	3.363
LSTM	ln(MV)	3.314	12.067	4.467
	ln(MV), BM	3.310	12.008	4.321
	ln(MV), BM, SENT	3.308	11.093	4.102
Transformer	ln(MV)	2.376	11.089	3.364
	ln(MV), BM	2.310	11.012	3.312
	ln(MV), BM, SENT	2.308	10.093	3.100
TiDE	ln(MV)	0.103	0.546	0.856
	ln(MV), BM	0.100	0.512	0.841
	ln(MV), BM, SENT	0.098	0.478	0.819

5 Conclusion

In this study, we primarily investigate the impact of investor sentiment on stock returns using data from 36 technology-listed companies. Based on the principal component analysis, we filter out the idiosyncratic components unrelated to sentiment from four indicators: individual stock returns, the growth rate of trading volume, price-to-earnings ratio, and trading volume. We synthesize these components to create the composite indicator SENT, representing investor sentiment. Regression analysis is conducted by gradually introducing market factors, size factors, book-to-market ratio factors, and investor sentiment factors, using the TiDE model to forecast stock returns.

The research findings indicate that individual stock returns, the growth rate of trading volume, price-to-earnings ratio, and trading volume effectively explain investor sentiment and the inclusion of the investor sentiment factor contributes to the explanation of stock returns. The TiDE model significantly improves predictive accuracy.

Although a substantial dataset is used in the experiment, many data points with missing values are excluded during the data preprocessing stage. However, in cases of data gaps, it may be challenging to accurately analyze and model the entire dataset, leading to potential errors. Furthermore, the research focuses solely on technology-listed companies, and the use of the Shanghai Composite Index returns as a measure of market risk portfolio introduces some errors, which may affect the accuracy and generalizability of the conclusions. Therefore, future research should involve reasonable approaches to handle missing values in the dataset. Additionally, different types of companies can be included as research subjects or more refined market risk indicators can be utilized for analysis, specifically tailored to technology stocks. Furthermore, exploring the influence of other factors such as the macroeconomic environment and industry characteristics on stock returns can provide a more comprehensive understanding of the topic.

References

1. Fama, E.F., French, K.R.: The cross-section of expected stock returns. J. Financ. **47**(2), 427–465 (1992)
2. Kumar, A., Lee, C.M.: Retail investor sentiment and return comovements. J. Financ. **61**(5), 2451–2486 (2006)
3. Schmeling, M.: Investor sentiment and stock returns: some international evidence. J. Empir. Financ. **16**(3), 394–408 (2009)
4. Liu, J., Stambaugh, R.F., Yuan, Y.: Size and value in China. J. Financ. Econ. **134**(1), 48–69 (2019)
5. Fisher, K.L., Statman, M.: Investor sentiment and stock returns. Financ. Anal. J. **56**(2) (2000)
6. Baker, M., Wurgler, J.: Investor sentiment in the stock market. J. Econ. Perspect. **21**(2), 129–151 (2007)
7. Barber, B.M., Odean, T., Zhu, N.: Do retail trades move markets? Rev. Financ. Stud. **22**(1), 151–186 (2008)
8. Gao, X., Gu, C., Koedijk, K.: Institutional investor sentiment and aggregate stock returns. Eur. Financ. Manag. **27**(5), 899–924 (2021)
9. Sharpe, W.F.: Capital asset prices: a theory of market equilibrium under conditions of risk. J. Financ. **19**(3), 425–442 (1964)
10. Lintner, J.: The valuation of risk assets and the selection of risky investments in stock portfolios and capital budgets. In: Stochastic Optimization Models in Finance, pp. 131–155. Academic Press (1975)
11. Carhart, M.M.: On persistence in mutual fund performance. J. Financ. **52**(1), 57–82 (1997)
12. Fama, E.F., French, K.R.: A five-factor asset pricing model. J. Financ. Econ. **116**(1), 1–22 (2015)
13. Hochreiter, S., Schmidhuber, J.: Long short-term memory. Neural Comput. **9**(8), 1735–1780 (1997)
14. Bao, W., Yue, J., Rao, Y.: A deep learning framework for financial time series using stacked autoencoders and long-short term memory. PLoS ONE **12**(7), e0180944 (2017)
15. Gu, S., Kelly, B., Xiu, D.: Empirical asset pricing via machine learning. Rev. Financ. Stud. **33**(5), 2223–2273 (2020)
16. Baker, M., Wurgler, J.: Investor sentiment and the cross-section of stock returns. J. Financ. **61**(4), 1645–1680 (2006)
17. Zhou, H., Tu, Y., Li, P., Chen, J.: # br# Impact of black swan events on stock price based on perspective of investor sentiment. J. Beijing Univ. Posts Telecommun. (Soc. Sci. Ed.) **21**(3), 43 (2019)

18. Das, A., Kong, W., Leach, A., Sen, R., Yu, R.: Long-term Forecasting with TiDE: Time-series Dense Encoder. arXiv preprint arXiv:2304.08424 (2023)
19. Khaidem, L., Saha, S., Dey, S.R.: Predicting the direction of stock market prices using random forest. arXiv preprint arXiv:1605.00003 (2016)
20. Fischer, T., Krauss, C.: Deep learning with long short-term memory networks for financial market predictions. Eur. J. Oper. Res. **270**(2), 654–669 (2018)
21. Zhang, Q., Qin, C., Zhang, Y., Bao, F., Zhang, C., Liu, P.: Transformer-based attention network for stock movement prediction. Expert Syst. Appl. **202**, 117239 (2022)
22. Yoo, J., Soun, Y., Park, Y.C., Kang, U.: Accurate multivariate stock movement prediction via data-axis transformer with multi-level contexts. In: Proceedings of the 27th ACM SIGKDD Conference on Knowledge Discovery & Data Mining, pp. 2037–2045 (2021)

An Empirical Research on the Impact of ESG Performance on Chinese Stock Market

Jiayun Yin[✉]

School of Economics and Management, Tsinghua University, Beijing 100084, China
yinjy20@mails.tsinghua.edu.cn

Abstract. With the rapid growth and spread of ESG-related investment, governments have introduced various policies related to environmental protection and sustainable development, and the attention to ESG-related investment concepts in China has significantly increased. Against this background, this study uses data from listed companies in the Chinese A-share market as a sample to empirically test the relationship between the ESG performance of companies and excess returns and volatility of stocks. The results show that: the ESG performance of a company is not significantly correlated with its stock excess returns, but negatively correlated with its stock price volatility. This means that good ESG performance can reduce stock price volatility, but has no definite impact on excess returns. The innovation of this study lies in applying ESG investment concepts to the Chinese market and attempting to analyze the rationality of Chinese ESG rating agencies using ESG ratings from Chinese institutions. This provides a new perspective for investors' and enterprises' ESG practice, which is conducive to future expansion and research, as well as the further development of ESG-related investment concepts in China.

Keywords: Environmental, Social and Governance · Excess Return · Stock Volatility

1 Introduction

With the rapid development of the economy, global-ranged environmental issues such as resource scarcity and climate change are constantly emerging, widening the wealth gap and highlighting social inequality. In this context, the ESG concept proposed by United Nations Environment Program (2004) received widespread attention. It assesses enterprises through three dimensions: E (Environmental), S (Social), and G (Governance), with a special focus on enterprises that contribute to social value and have sustainable growth potential. This weakens the importance of returns in investment decisions, prioritizing the positive impact of enterprises on the environment and society.

ESG ratings can reflect many issues that cannot be reflected in traditional corporate financial data analysis, and these issues are likely to be of concern to investors. From bonds' perspective, the score of G in ESG is mainly about factors such as corporate governance which plays an important role in analyzing corporations' debt default risk.

According to Liu et al.'s paper, there is a significant negative correlation between ESG performance and corporate default risk. Therefore, adding ESG indicators can improve the accuracy of early warning models to a certain extent [1]. From an enterprise's perspective, an ESG score also helps the asset management process. On the one hand, the construction of an ESG score helps investors understand the business strategy and management level, therefore it can reduce financing costs. The research done by Zhang demonstrated the idea that ESG performance has an impact on the dynamic adjustment of capital structure by alleviating corporate financing constraints and reducing the cost of equity capital [2]. On the other hand, Hu et al. found that ESG rating significantly promotes the green transformation of enterprises through market incentive mechanisms and external supervision mechanisms [3].

Although the ESG investment concept has developed significantly in places such as the United States and the United States, it was not until recent years that it began to receive attention due to the relatively imperfect development of the Chinese market. Whether ESG investment also works well in the Chinese market becomes a main concern for investors. Wu believes that ESG performance can enhance the stock value of the company [4]. Similarly, Liu et al. also think that the ESG performance of a company can transmit good corporate trait information to the stock price, thereby promoting an increase in stock returns [5]. However, the study of Li suggests that ESG only has a certain and limited positive correlation with excess returns in medium to long-term investments, and the impact of ESG ratings on short-term investments is not significant [6]. Furthermore, Wang found ESG rating only has a significant positive correlation with the excess return on investment of limited industries [7].

Based on previous studies listed above, this study considers a wider range of Chinese listed companies' stocks. This study aims to draw on relevant research ideas and use existing data to determine whether the ESG level of a company is correlated with excess returns and volatility of stocks.

2 Methodology

2.1 Data Selection

This study's sample and data are acquired from the Wind database. The research sample was from A-share listed companies before 2023 May. In order to better reflect the impact of ESG ratings on excess returns and stock price volatility of general enterprises, this study conducted the following sample screening process: (1) excluded samples of listed companies in the financial and related industries; (2) excluded samples of listed companies processed by ST and ST* (delisting risk warnings); (3) excluded samples of listed companies which have no ESG rating score. After this sample screening process, the final sample consists of 4,586 observations.

2.2 Variables Construction

Explained Variables. The explained variables in this study are the excess returns of stocks and the volatilities of stock prices, and both can be directly acquired from the Wind database.

Explanatory Variable. The explanatory variable in this study is the ESG performance scored by Wind, which is also directly acquired from the Wind database. The reason why the Wind ESG rating was chosen instead of the FTSE ESG rating is that Wind has a higher level of understanding of China's macroeconomic situation and listed companies. More importantly, after sample screening, the number of Chinese listed companies that obtained Wind scores was 4,586, while the number of Chinese listed companies with FTSE ESG scores was only 795. Choosing Wind ESG scores can better obtain universal conclusions applicable to Chinese A-share listed companies. The following Table 1 shows the explained and explanatory variables set by this study.

Control Variables. In addition to ESG, there are other factors that can affect the stock value of a company, so it is necessary to set control variables. The following Table 2 shows the control variables set by this study.

Table 1. Definition of explained and explanatory variables.

Variables	Definition
Alpha	The excess return of a stock, directly acquired from Wind database, which is one of the explained variables in this study
Var	The volatility of a stock price, directly acquired from Wind database, which is one of the explained variables in this study
ESG	The Wind ESG score of a A-share listed corporation, directly acquired from Wind database, which is the explanatory variable in this study

Table 2. Definition of control variables.

Variables	Definition
MV	The market value of a stock which is used to measure a company's scale, directly acquired from Wind database
Tobin_Q	Tobin Q value is the ratio of a company's stock market value to the asset replacement cost represented by the stock, used to measure the company's performance, indirectly used the data acquired from Wind database and the formula to calculate
Industry	Dummy Variables based on the Wind II industry standard According to the previous research from Wei, a value of 1 is assigned to relatively heavy asset industries such as transportation, materials, and energy, while a value of 2 is assigned to relatively light asset industries such as retail, media, consumption, telecommunications, and healthcare [8]
EPS	The earnings per share of a stock is used to measure a company's profitability, directly acquired from Wind database

2.3 Model Construction

To study the impact of ESG ratings on excess returns and stock price volatilities, this study constructs the following linear regression model. Formula (1) is to get the correlation between excess returns and ESG scores; and Formula (2) Formula (2) is to get the correlation between stock price volatilities and ESG scores.

$$Alpha = \alpha + \beta_1 ESG + \beta_2 MV + \beta_3 Tobin\_Q + \beta_4 Industry + \beta_5 EPS + \varepsilon \quad (1)$$

$$Var = \alpha + \beta_1 ESG + \beta_2 MV + \beta_3 Tobin\_Q + \beta_4 Industry + \beta_5 EPS + \varepsilon \quad (2)$$

Among these variables, MV, Tobin_Q, Industry, and EPS are several control variables that have been introduced above. Alpha and Var are the excess return and stock price volatility of a stock, respectively, corresponding to the explained variable mentioned above. ESG refers to the ESG score of a company, corresponding to the explanatory variable mentioned above.

2.4 Research Method

This study is based on a linear model and adopts methods such as OLS for research. This study conducts a robustness test by replacing the ESG scoring mechanism with FTSE scoring instead of Wind scoring. Furthermore, it tests the rationality of Wind ESG scores by conducting a regression model between the Wind ESG rating and the FTSE ESG rating.

3 Results

3.1 Descriptive Statistics

Table 3 below reports the descriptive statistic for the main variables. It can be seen from the table: (1) The mean value of Alpha is 0.348, of Var, is 6.022, of ESG is 6.161, of MV, is 1.506e+10, of Tobin_Q, is 1.804, of Industry is 1.504, and of EPS is 0.536. These indicate that there are significant excess returns in investing in A-share Chinese listed companies, so the adaptation of the CAPM model in the Chinese market is limited. (2) There are significant fluctuations in stock returns in the Chinese market, and there are also significant differences in ESG ratings among different companies, according to the standard deviation of corresponding variables. (3) There are also significant differences between companies' Tobin_Q values and EPS, which means different companies' profitability are significantly different.

In Table 4 below, correlations among the main variables are shown in the correlation matrix. Overall, Alpha with Var, and MV with EPS are significantly correlated with each other, while other factors are found to be correlated with one another to a moderate and even slight degree. Moreover, according to the VIF analysis showed in Panel B, since the VIFs between different variables are significantly smaller than 5, it can be considered that there is no obvious collinearity between the respective variables.

Table 3. Descriptive statistics.

Variables	N	mean	sd	min	max
Alpha	4,586	0.348	1.092	−11.60	34.23
Var	4,586	6.022	2.557	1.450	57.29
ESG	4,586	6.161	0.776	3.380	9.390
MV	4,586	1.506e+10	5.472e+10	2.729e+08	2.149e+12
Tobin_Q	4,586	1.804	1.362	0.127	22.74
Industry	4,586	1.504	0.500	1	2
EPS	4,586	0.536	1.430	−9.729	52.75

Table 4. Correlation among main variables.

Variables	Alpha	Var	ESG	MV	Tobin_Q	Industry	EPS
Panel A. Correlation matrix							
Alpha	1.000						
Var	0.568	1.000					
ESG	0.027	−0.023	1.000				
MV	0.001	−0.046	0.210	1.000			
Tobin_Q	0.262	0.219	0.039	0.109	1.000		
Industry	0.173	0.129	0.097	0.016	0.174	1.000	
EPS	−0.038	0.012	0.125	0.491	0.118	0.023	1.000
Panel B. VIF analysis							
Variable	MV	EPS	ESG	Tobin_Q	Industry	Mean	Variable
VIF	1.36	1.33	1.06	1.05	1.04	1.17	VIF
1/VIF	0.734489	0.754570	0.946757	0.953367	0.961128		1/VIF

3.2 Regression Results

Since there is no obvious collinearity between main variables, OLS can be used to conduct the linear regression model. Table 5 and Table 6 shows the regression results according to the model (1) and (2), respectively.

According to the regression results of model (1) reported in Table 5, the p-values of explanatory variable ESG score is not significant under significance level $\alpha = 0.1$, while the p-values of control variables Tobin_Q, Industry, EPS are significant. The coefficient value of ESG score is 0.012, indicating that there's no significant correlation between the excess return and ESG. This phenomenon can be explained by the following reasons according to the research of Ba et al.: (1) ESG related investments have not received high attention in the Chinese market, and most investors still focus on economic returns, so they tend to invest in companies with good financial performance and strong

Table 5. Regression results of model (1).

Alpha	Coef.	St.Err.	t-value	p-value	[95% Conf	Interval]	Sig
ESG	.012	.014	0.87	.383	−.015	.038	
MV	0	0	0.36	.72	0	0	
Tobin_Q	.13	.008	17.13	0	.115	.145	***
Industry	.189	.021	9.05	0	.148	.229	***
EPS	−.037	.008	−4.58	0	−.053	−.021	***
Constant	−.215	.087	−2.48	.013	−.385	−.045	**
Mean dependent var	0.364			SD dependent var		0.725	
R-squared	0.090			Number of obs		4586	
F-test	91.057			Prob > F		0.000	
Akaike crit. (AIC)	9634.903			Bayesian crit. (BIC)		9667.056	

Note: *** $p < .01$, ** $p < .05$, * $p < .1$.

profitability; (2) ESG related ratings may have a certain degree of subjectivity and cannot reflect the medium to long-term growth potential of the enterprise; (3) At present, ESG ratings in Chinese market mainly rely on public data from enterprises, and the quality of information disclosure varies, largely depending on the enterprise itself [9].

Table 6. Regression results of model (2).

Var	Coef.	St.Err.	t-value	p-value	[95% Conf	Interval]	Sig
ESG	−.085	.045	−1.90	.058	−.173	.003	*
MV	0	0	−4.65	0	0	0	***
Tobin_Q	.358	.025	14.23	0	.309	.407	***
Industry	.454	.069	6.57	0	.318	.589	***
EPS	.043	.027	1.60	.109	−.01	.096	
Constant	−.085	.045	−1.90	.058	−.173	.003	*
Mean dependent var	5.917			SD dependent var		2.367	
R-squared	0.063			Number of obs		4585	
F-test	61.067			Prob > F		0.000	
Akaike crit. (AIC)	20626.696			Bayesian crit. (BIC)		20658.848	

Note: *** $p < .01$, ** $p < .05$, * $p < .1$.

According to the regression results of model (2) reported in Table 6, the p-value of the explanatory variable ESG score is negatively correlated with the volatility of stock price under significance level $\alpha = 0.1$, while the p-values of control variables MV, Tobin_Q, and Industry. The coefficient value of the ESG score is −0.085, indicating that there's a significant negative correlation between the stock price volatility and ESG. This finding is consistent with the research made by Liu & Zhang, and Feng. According to this research, the mechanism can be explained by the following statements: (1) ESG ratings can alleviate information asymmetry and provide stakeholders with a more comprehensive understanding of a company's operations; (2) Companies with higher ESG scores perform better in environmental, social, and corporate governance, and have a higher ability to withstand risks, resulting in less volatility in stock prices; (3) Companies with higher ESG scores have stronger sustainability, better reputation, are more favored by investors, and are more likely to receive market support compared to companies with lower ESG ratings, thereby reducing the volatility of enterprise stock prices [10, 11].

3.3 Robustness Check

Based on the above regression results, it was found that the high or low Wind ESG score did not have a significant impact on the excess returns of stocks. However, considering the subjectivity of Wind's ESG score, it may not be accurate enough for some companies. In the first part of the robustness test, this study uses the FTSE ESG score to conduct regression analysis on the stock excess return. Table 7 reports the new regression results on FTSE ESG score data.

Table 7. Robustness Check for Regression Model (1).

Alpha	Coef.	St.Err.	t-value	p-value	[95% Conf	Interval]	Sig
ESG	−.043	.036	−1.22	.222	−.113	.026	
MV	0	0	2.87	.004	0	0	***
Tobin_Q	.047	.015	3.08	.002	.017	.076	***
Industry	.207	.044	4.68	0	.12	.293	***
EPS	−.041	.01	−4.16	0	−.061	−.022	***
Constant	−.097	.083	−1.17	.241	−.259	.065	
Mean dependent var	0.232			SD dependent var		0.601	
R-squared	0.069			Number of obs		795	
F-test	11.711			Prob > F		0.000	
Akaike crit. (AIC)	1398.493			Bayesian crit. (BIC)		1421.884	

Note: *** $p < .01$, ** $p < .05$, * $p < .1$.

According to the robustness check regression model, the correlation between Alpha and FTSE ESG score is still not significant under significance level $\alpha = 0.1$, which is consistent with the previous regression model based on Wind ESG data. Based on the above regression results, it was found that the higher Wind ESG scores have a significant negative impact on the volatility of stocks. Similarly, this study uses the FTSE ESG score to conduct regression analysis on the stock volatility in case of the inaccuracy of the Wind ESG score. Table 8 reports the new regression results on FTSE ESG score data.

Table 8. Robustness Check for Regression Model (2).

Var	Coef.	St.Err.	t-value	p-value	[95% Conf	Interval]	Sig
ESG	−.066	.097	−0.68	.487	−.254	.127	*
MV	0	0	−3.69	0	0	0	***
Tobin_Q	.292	.041	7.09	0	.211	.373	***
Industry	.415	.12	3.45	.001	.179	.651	***
EPS	.049	.027	1.81	.07	−.004	.102	*
Constant	4.232	.225	18.79	0	3.79	4.674	***
Mean dependent var	5.288			SD dependent var		1.691	
R-squared	0.126			Number of obs		795	
F-test	22.780			Prob > F		0.000	
Akaike crit. (AIC)	2992.819			Bayesian crit. (BIC)		3016.210	

Note: *** $p < .01$, ** $p < .05$, * $p < .1$.

According to the robustness check regression model, the correlation between Var and FTSE ESG score is still significant negative under significance level $\alpha = 0.1$, which is consistent with the previous regression model based on Wind ESG data.

4 Conclusion

This study is based on Wind ESG rating data and related financial data of listed companies in the Chinese A-share market, combined with relevant theories and research results, to construct a regression model, and explore the relationship between ESG performance of companies, excess returns on stock investments, and return volatility. The results indicate that: firstly, the ESG performance of a company does not have a significant impact on its excess return on investment; Secondly, there is a negative correlation between the ESG performance of enterprises and the volatility of their stock prices. Enterprises with higher ESG scores have lower volatility in their stock prices. These results have passed the robustness check, which may indicate that Wind ESG scores have rationality and accuracy to some extent.

On the one hand, ESG-related investments have not received enough attention in the Chinese market, ESG-related ratings may have a certain degree of subjectivity and cannot reflect the actual performance of companies, especially when the quality of information disclosure varies, the accuracy of ESG scores are mainly depending on the enterprise itself. ESG ratings can mitigate information asymmetry and bring a better report to companies, making it easier for these companies to win the favor of investors and have stronger risk resistance, thereby reducing stock price volatility.

This study has explored the main topics considering the relationship between ESG scores and investment excess return or stock price volatility in the Chinese market. However, much remains uncertain because there are still several limitations. For example, there is still no unified and internationally recognized standard for ESG rating, so there is a certain degree of difference in the ratings given by multiple institutions, especially the limited number of Chinese-listed companies that have received internationally recognized ESG ratings, while domestic ESG rating agencies in China do not have widespread recognition. This may cause bias in this study. Moreover, how the ESG standard fit in the Chinese market and the investors' preference for ESG rating is still continuously changing.

References

1. Liu, X., Chang, R., Zhang, J., Di, H.: Research on enterprise default risk warning considering ESG performance. Financ. Theory Pract. (04), 45–57 (2023)
2. Zhang, L.: The mechanism and data testing of the impact of ESG performance on the dynamic adjustment of capital structure. Chin. Bus. Theory (07), 111–116 (2023)
3. Hu, J., Yu, X., Han, Y.: Can ESG rating promote green transformation of enterprises-verification based on multi-time point double difference method. Res. Quant. Econ. Tech. Econ. **40**, 90–111 (2023)
4. Wu, H.: The impact of corporate ESG performance on stock value. Bus. Exhib. Econ. (09), 97–100 (2023)
5. Liu, X., Wu, X., Kong, X.: ESG performance and stock returns of listed companies: based on the information content of enterprise traits in stock prices. Friends Account. (10), 85–93 (2023)
6. Li, Y.: Analysis of the Impact of ESG Ratings on Excess Returns of A-share Stocks. Hebei University of Finance (2022)
7. Wang, R.: Research on the Impact of ESG Scoring on the Excess Return of Companies. School of Foreign Affairs (2022)
8. Wei, B.: The impact of ESG performance on domestic corporate bond financing. Financ. Market Res. (07), 26–35 (2021)
9. Ba, S., Wang, B., Wang, Z.: The domestic and international practices and future trends of ESG investment development. Fujian Financ. (02), 36–46 (2023)
10. Liu, H., Zhang, Z.: Research on the impact of ESG performance, innovation efficiency, and stock price volatility - based on A-share listed companies. Wuhan Financ. (02), 37–43+64 (2023)
11. Feng, W.: Research on the Impact of ESG Ratings of Listed Companies on Stock Price Volatility. University of Electronic Science and Technology (2022)

Research on the Application of Artificial Intelligence Technology in Risk Management of Commercial Banks

Wensi Huang[1(✉)], Yiling Shi[2], and Wenjie Zhou[3]

[1] School of Economics, Guangdong University of Technology, Guangzhou 510520, China
1811571124@mail.sit.edu.cn
[2] Economic Management, Shanxi Institute of Energy, Jinzhong 030604, China
[3] School of Economics and Management, Guangdong Technology of College, Zhaoqing 526100, China

Abstract. With the continuous progress and application of artificial intelligence (AI) technology, the use of AI technology in the management of commercial banks has received more and more attention. In this paper, we take commercial bank risk management as the research topic, combine the mainstream technology and examine the specific application. First, it is addressed how commercial banks assess credit risk by using data mining, natural language processing, machine learning (ML), and deep learning (DL) in commercial banks' credit risk assessment is discussed. Then, the risk control of commercial banks is discussed from three aspects: data mining and analysis, risk control model building, and risk control decision-making. After that, the advantages of AI in commercial banks, such as dealing with nonlinear problems, excellent data acquisition, and real-time monitoring of transactions, are discussed. And the limitations of AI in commercial banks, such as data discrimination and interpretability are discussed. It turns out that risk management involves, AI technology can effectively improve credit risk assessment results and can effectively prevent fraud risks. The value of this dissertation is to afford a reference for the research and practice of AI in areas related to risk management applications.

Keywords: Artificial Intelligence Technology · Commercial Banks · Risk Management · Applications

1 Introduction

In 2023, the bankruptcy of the Silicon Valley Bank of the United States and the bankruptcy of Signature Bank will cause turmoil in the global financial market. The restructuring of Credit Suisse will further increase the global attention to the risk management of commercial banks. In the realm of traditional commercial banking, numerous deficiencies exist within the field of risk management.

In the field of credit risk assessment, traditional evaluation methods face two primary challenges. Firstly, traditional evaluation methods struggle to address non-linear problems. In the credit scoring of traditional commercial banks, techniques such as logistic regression and discriminant analysis are employed to determine the likelihood of default [1]. Secondly, there are limitations in the data sources used, as they are often single-sourced and of questionable quality. This data hampers the accurate reflection of the true creditworthiness of individuals, particularly for those who have not previously engaged in borrowing or lending activities with banks, making it more challenging to assess their credit risk [2]. In the field of credit card fraud, traditional commercial banks exhibit a lag in their response time. It is often the case that certain banks only advise cardholders to change their passwords and related information after a fraud incident has already occurred [3]. In the field of anti-money laundering, commercial banks face a lag in monitoring money laundering activities perpetrated by illicit entities. However, intelligent anti-money laundering systems can effectively detect these illicit financial transactions more efficiently [4].

Numerous scholars have employed AI technologies in areas such as credit risk and anti-fraud risk in commercial banks to enhance risk management practices in traditional commercial banking. Credit risk assessment can incorporate methods such as ML, DL, Bayesian networks, artificial neural networks, and recurrent neural networks [5–7]. Credit card risk can be addressed using gradient-boosting decision trees [8]. AI techniques and ML algorithms can be employed in addressing anti-fraud risks [9, 10].

This paper intends to investigate the use of AI in commercial banks' risk management. Firstly, this paper discusses the application of data mining, natural language processing, ML, DL, and risk model construction in credit risk assessment. Lastly, this paper summarizes the previous discussions and provides recommendations for future development directions. This paper provides an in-depth analysis of the application of AI technology in risk management within the commercial banking sector. It begins by discussing the current utilization of AI technology in commercial banks' risk management practices. Subsequently, the paper discusses the advantages and limitations associated with the implementation of AI in this context. Furthermore, it explores the potential future development directions and highlights the emerging application prospects of AI technology in commercial banks' risk management. The comprehensive insights presented in this study contribute to the existing academic literature and offer valuable guidance for researchers and practitioners in the field of commercial banking risk management.

2 Application of Artificial Intelligence Technology in Risk Management of Commercial Banks

2.1 Credit Risk Assessment Based on Artificial Intelligence Technology

Data Mining. Data mining is the first step of AI in commercial banking credit risk assessment. Jin [11] argued that credit risk assessment in banks utilizes data mining and analytical techniques in extracting valuable information from vast amounts of data, aiming to enhance the accuracy of risk evaluation. Commercial banks accumulate a large amount of data in their day-to-day operations, including customer information, transaction records, market data, economic indicators, etc. These data contain a wealth of helpful information, but without analysis, it is difficult to derive meaningful conclusions.

During the process of data mining, commercial banks need to perform operations such as data cleansing, preprocessing, and feature extraction to enhance data quality and accuracy. Moreover, commercial banks must employ appropriate algorithms and models for data mining and analysis, such as cluster analysis, association rule mining, classifiers, regression analysis, and more. Through these algorithms and models, commercial banks can delve into the inherent patterns and features within the data, uncover hidden risk signals behind the data, and enhance the accuracy of risk identification and prediction.

Natural Language Processing. Natural language processing is the second step of AI in credit risk assessment. In risk assessment, a significant amount of information is expressed in natural language form, such as news reports, financial statement analysis, social media information, etc. By utilizing natural language processing techniques, it is possible to transform this textual information into structured data and analyze and model them, enabling a better understanding of the nature of risk events and timely detection of their occurrences. Sheng [12] argued that utilizing natural language processing techniques can lead to better evaluation of risk issues within contracts. Natural language processing techniques primarily encompass text classification, sentiment analysis, and entity recognition. Among these, text classification is a technique that categorizes text based on its topic or category, enabling automatic classification and organization of a large volume of textual information. Sentiment analysis, on the other hand, involves identifying and categorizing the emotions expressed in text. It allows for a quick understanding of people's emotional inclination toward specific events, thus enabling the prediction of future development trends. Zheng [13] argued that incorporating natural language processing techniques into intelligent customer service chatbots can enhance the user experience. Entity recognition, on the other hand, involves using natural language processing techniques to identify entities within the text, such as names of people, locations, organizations, etc., and standardize them for subsequent analysis.

Applying natural language processing techniques enables commercial banks to gain a more comprehensive and accurate understanding of risk events, providing them with additional information support for decision-making. For instance, commercial banks can utilize natural language processing techniques to analyze and categorize massive amounts of information from sources like news reports and social media. This enables them to promptly identify various risks and issue early warnings for events that may impact their banking operations. Specifically, natural language processing techniques are also a crucial application of DL in the field of risk assessment. They can assist banking institutions in analyzing customers' textual information, such as loan applications and collateral documents, to extract features and establish models for risk assessment.

Machine Learning and Deep Learning. ML and DL are the third steps of AI in credit risk assessment. In the area of risk assessment, ML and DL techniques are widely applied. This is because these two technologies can extract patterns from the data obtained after data mining and natural language processing and establish models for risk prediction and risk management. In the evolution of AI, ML is an important technique, and DL is a variant of ML that operates on neural networks. It is a novel learning approach that enables more accurate risk prediction and improves the effectiveness of risk assessment.

Machine is an automated learning technique based on data. By learning and analyzing the data, it discovers patterns and constructs predictive models. Gu [14] argued that using

ML techniques to analyze customer risk factors and build a logistic model to calculate their probability of default. In the field of risk assessment, ML algorithms can be used to construct classification models, clustering models, regression models, and more to facilitate risk identification and evaluation. In the risk management of commercial banks, the application of ML and DL methods in risk assessment covers various aspects, such as credit scoring, fraud detection, default prediction, and more. To perform credit scoring, one can employ classifiers that utilize algorithms such as logistic regression, support vector machines, and random forests. These classifiers learn the credit characteristics and behavior of customers from historical data to score and classify them. For fraud detection, algorithms based on both supervised and unsupervised learning can be used. Techniques such as decision trees, neural networks, and clustering analysis can be applied to monitor and identify fraudulent transaction behaviors, thereby mitigating fraud risks. For default prediction, models based on regression analysis, decision trees, and neural networks, among other algorithms, can be used. These models consider the features and behaviors of customers from multiple angles to predict the probability of default.

Indeed, DL is a specialized form of ML that simulates the workings of the human neural system. It involves learning through multi-layered neural networks. In the field of risk assessment, there are various DL algorithms, such as Multi-Layer Perceptron (MLP), Autoencoders (AE), Recurrent Neural Networks (RNN), and Long Short-Term Memory Networks (LSTM). Zhou and Shang [15] argued that utilizing LSTM models and the R-theory can reduce the error in predicting stock volatility. Yang [6] argued that using a DL framework, a stacked denoising autoencoder neural network algorithm can be employed to reduce the factors that affect the evaluation performance of the model. In the field of risk assessment, DL can be applied to handle large amounts of unstructured data, such as images, speech, text, and more, thereby improving the accuracy of risk prediction. ML and DL are utilized in risk assessment to process and comprehend vast amounts of data, extract relevant characteristics, and construct predictive models that aid in identifying and assessing potential risks.

Risk Model Construction. The construction of risk assessment models based on AI technology typically involves three critical steps. Firstly, through data mining and natural language processing techniques, the various structured and unstructured data of the customers are processed and transformed to extract useful information and patterns. This includes operations such as data cleaning, preprocessing, and feature extraction, which transform textual data into a structured form, allowing the extraction of key features and indicators related to the customers. Secondly, the processed data is analyzed and modeled using ML and DL algorithms. These algorithms can learn patterns and relationships from large amounts of data and establish predictive models related to risks. By training and evaluating the models, potential risks of customers can be identified, providing a basis for risk assessment. Lastly, the risk assessment model is constructed. Customer data is inputted into the model, and time series analysis and calculations are performed to derive the risk coefficients for the customers. Xia [16] argued that using multiple models to construct a risk assessment indicator system, followed by data analysis, enables the construction of a risk assessment model. These risk coefficients can serve as references to assist banking institutions in assessing and managing risks and making corresponding decisions and measures. This AI-based risk assessment method can improve efficiency, accuracy, and predictive capabilities, providing crucial support for risk management in commercial banks. Figure 1 shows the flowchart for constructing a risk model based on AI technology.

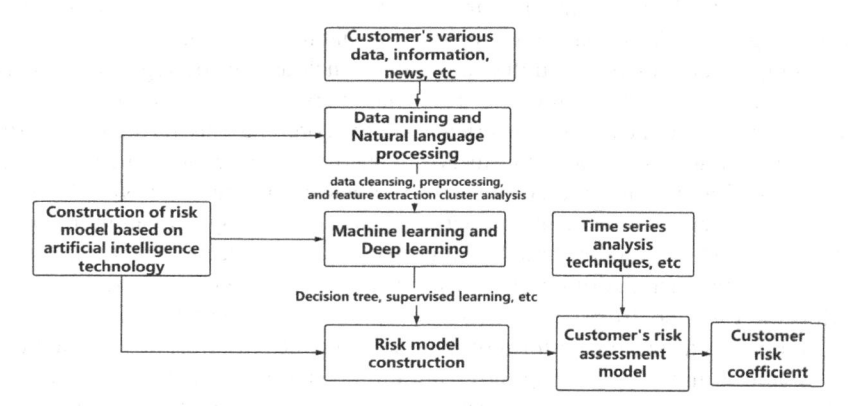

Fig. 1. Flow Chart for Building a Risk Model Based on AI Technology.

2.2 Risk Control of Commercial Banks Based on Artificial Intelligence Technology

Data Mining and Analysis. Data mining is the first step to controlling the possible risks of commercial banks under AI technology. In the context of continuous improvement of commercial banks' credit business and continuous innovation of risk control evaluation systems, digital transformation has become the main trend and general direction, which will put forward higher requirements for digital risk control relying on big data and financial technologies such as AI. On the issue of how to obtain data and what kind of data to obtain, Yang [17] mentioned in his article that the key to laying a good foundation for the database is to clarify the core of financial risk and how to use cutting-edge technologies to obtain data for mastery. First, commercial banks need to use these technologies to analyze the current environment they are in and also to anticipate the changes they may encounter in the future. In doing this, it is necessary to focus on mining and processing data and information related to commercial banks, collecting and classifying them, and storing them after finishing them. Secondly, with the development of the combination of AI and commercial banks, the database is constantly supplemented and modified to establish an intelligent information platform as a way to promote the real-time sharing of data. Zhao [18] proposes that through big data analysis, technology mining, and AI, we can integrate data information through multiple channels and cite more customer-related data to solve the problem of "information asymmetry" and establish a more accurate and comprehensive risk control system. The main purpose is to realize intelligent risk identification and establish an intelligent anti-fraud platform before lending, establish a credit factory business model during lending, realize the separation of key positions and reduce operational risks to a certain sense, improve the exploitation process of intelligence and automation after lending, and realize differentiated post-lending management by improving the post-lending early warning model and classifying customers into risk levels.

Commercial banks can strengthen their internal database construction through data mining combined with network data platforms and cloud computing technologies and establish a corresponding visualization platform while optimizing the management model. At the same time, commercial banks can also use this to pay attention to customers' asset information promptly when promoting and handling customers' business, effectively combining risk management and network information technology, which can greatly improve the scientific nature of the business operation, management, and decision-making as well as reduce the riskiness of customers' investment and create better conditions for risk control.

Risk Control Model Establishment. Establishing a risk control model is the second step to controlling the possible risks of commercial banks under AI technology. At present, most commercial banks in China have established corresponding risk control models and carried out supply chain financial services in conjunction with their situations. In their article, He and Cui [19] delineate several supply chain models of commercial banks in detail, combining their situation with commercial banks' credit risks and other issues for research, specifically, prepayment financing, inventory financing, and accounts receivable finance models. The finance models for accounts receivable, inventories, and prepayment financing models are studied. According to the accounts receivable finance concept, some small and medium-sized businesses lend to commercial banks, commercial banks can establish a set of credit review processes to determine whether there is a real trade contract before deciding whether to issue funds and reduce the risk of funding through the balance sheet and other data information; the inventory financing model refers to the fact that when commercial banks lend to small and medium-sized enterprises with insufficient operating capital, they select qualified third-party logistics. If the financier is unable to repay the loan on maturity, the commercial bank can request the third party to sell the pledged goods to obtain funds; the advance financing model means that the commercial bank acts as an intermediary to advance the payment for the SME and then recovers the payment on maturity, relying on the creditworthiness of the SME. These three emerging models combined with AI and technologies such as big data can capture the credit risk assessment of financing enterprises to reduce the risk of financial business.

At the same time, building digital risk control models can achieve full process monitoring of each business, and the system will freeze accounts and quickly warn when risks are detected, which can significantly reduce potential losses, such as establishing relevant anti-fraud models and default models, which can help commercial banks prevent credit risks.

Risk Control Decision. Making risk control decisions is the third step of risk control. After getting the relevant data and modeling, how to use this information to make decisions is a very important step, and He [20] believes that currently there are some limitations due to AI technology in commercial banks' risk management, and AI mainly relies on big data, ML and intelligent algorithms and other technologies for data storage and memory learning, so it cannot risk at all.

Based on the consideration of this problem, Zhao et al. [21] elaborate on risk control decision-making based on the establishment of Internet financial risk models, pointing out that commercial banks and other financial enterprises must pay attention to anti-fraud and establish and improve a practical risk control decision system from the business level, the level of supervision mechanism, and the level of national development strategy. First of all, for the design of financial product models, different financial products should be designed for different consumers and investors to truly demonstrate the benefits and risks of this product, for commercial banks and other financial enterprises should have a sufficient grasp and familiarity with the financial product industry they invest in, to analyze and set the corresponding risk control mechanism, to choose the best leverage level and strengthen leverage risk control. For example, according to the progress history of China's P2P and the current lack of industry norms and regulatory mechanisms, many financial enterprises and platforms will carry out some illegal fundraising and money laundering crimes. Although the government has strengthened supervision and management, the use of AI technology and big data technology for anti-fraud risk management still needs to be continuously strengthened; finally, it is about the national development strategy level of decision-making, because, first of all, commercial banks and other financial enterprises are the existence of the multi-dimensional and complex business model, in combination with ML, data analysis, and other technologies, it is more likely to appear in the regulatory gap, after escaping the monitoring of the financial industry, there will be more risk hidden dangers, once the outbreak, the impact on the whole national economy is huge. Therefore, the state also needs to establish a corresponding regulatory body for this purpose and intervene in the financial direction. Figure 2 shows the logical framework for the risk control section.

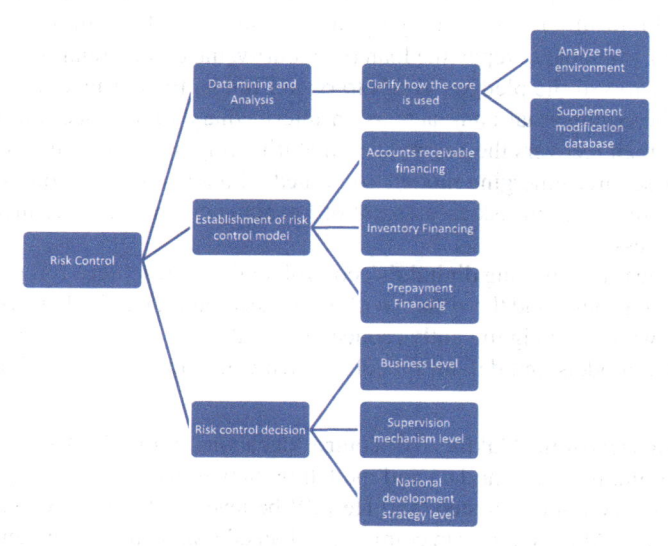

Fig. 2. Risk control framework diagram.

3 The Application Advantages and Limitations of Artificial Intelligence in Risk Management within Commercial Banks

3.1 The Advantages of Artificial Intelligence in Credit Risk Assessment within Commercial Banks

The Capability to Address Nonlinear Relationships in Traditional Models. In traditional credit risk assessment within commercial banks, linear regression models are commonly employed. However, by integrating AI technologies such as ML and neural networks with these traditional models, it becomes possible to address the prevalent issue of nonlinearity in risk relationships. This integration has the potential to significantly enhance the accuracy of credit rating models used by commercial banks when evaluating the creditworthiness of borrowers [22].

Excellent Data Acquisition Capabilities. In the era of big data, traditional commercial banks face challenges such as limited access to information and difficulties in efficiently processing vast amounts of data. However, AI technology can overcome these challenges by leveraging large-scale data from multiple sources and across various dimensions. This capability helps to address the limitations faced by traditional banks in terms of data acquisition. With AI technology, once a sufficient amount of information is obtained, it can rapidly process vast quantities of data and uncover the behavioral patterns of customers. This enables efficient evaluation of credit risk for clients, enhancing the overall risk management capabilities of commercial banks. By harnessing the power of AI, banks can gain valuable insights from extensive data sources, resulting in more accurate and efficient credit risk assessments for their customers [23].

3.2 The Advantages of Artificial Intelligence in Risk Control in Commercial Banks

Enhanced Effectiveness in the Prevention and Detection of Fraudulent Transactions. Traditional anti-fraud models commonly rely on supervised algorithms, which exhibit limited capabilities in addressing diverse variations of fraud and identifying emerging fraud patterns. By leveraging appropriate ML algorithms, the prevention and detection of fraudulent transactions can be significantly enhanced [4]. ML techniques demonstrate the ability to provide early warning signals for fraud risks, including credit card fraud and other forms of fraudulent activities.

Real-Time Transaction Monitoring. Building an anti-fraud system for commercial banks with neural network models as the core enables real-time supervision of online financial services across various channels. When customers engage in various online financial transactions, information such as customer identity and the transaction amount is obtained to assess the fraud risk associated with the transaction. Based on the evaluation results, measures such as approval or blocking are taken [24].

3.3 Limitations of Artificial Intelligence in Risk Management in Commercial Banks

Data Discrimination. AI algorithms have the potential to exhibit bias towards gender, race, and other data attributes. Zhou [25] argued that AI algorithms' biases and discrimination primarily stem from data bias and model bias. The issue of the digital divide arises in the context of AI-based credit risk assessment, as it heavily relies on big data. However, obtaining data for the elderly population can be challenging [26]. This poses a disadvantage in assessing the credit risk of older individuals.

Interpretability. In credit risk assessment, it is generally believed that more complex models tend to achieve better results. However, there is a trade-off between the complexity of AI algorithm models and their interpretability. Therefore, model interpretability becomes a major concern in the application of AI algorithms. There is some debate regarding interpretability, with some scholars leaning towards adding certain methods to the model for interpretation [27]. On the other hand, some scholars argue that explanations in ML are unable to accurately capture their true meaning [28].

4 Conclusions

This article focuses on the application of AI technology in the risk management of commercial banks. The primary research approach is to explore ML, natural language processing, and other AI technologies in identifying and mitigating potential risks, improving decision-making processes, and enhancing overall operational efficiency. The main conclusion is that applying AI technology in risk management can help commercial banks better manage risks, achieve sustainable growth and profitability, and navigate future challenges. However, the study lacks empirical research on the effectiveness and sustainability of AI technology in practical operations. To address the lack of empirical research, more case studies and experiments should be conducted to test the feasibility and scalability of AI-based risk management solutions, and researchers can collaborate with commercial banks to collect more data and feedback for the refinement and improvement of existing models and algorithms.

Authors Contribution. All the authors contributed equally and their names were listed in alphabetical order.

References

1. Leo, M., Sharma, S., Maddulety, K.: Machine learning in banking risk management: a literature review. Risks 7(1), 29 (2019)
2. Jiang, Z., Chen, J., Zhang, C.: Financial technology empowers risk management transformation of commercial banks. Contemp. Econ. Manag. 41(01), 85–90 (2019)
3. Priya, G., Saradha, S.: Fraud detection and prevention using machine learning algorithms: a review. In: International Conference on Electrical Energy Systems (ICEES), pp. 564–568. IEEE (2021)

4. Kannan, S., Somasundaram, K.: Autoregressive-based outlier algorithm to detect money laundering activities. J. Money Laundering Control **20**(2), 190–202 (2017)
5. Jagtiani, J., Lemieux, C.: The roles of alternative data and machine learning in fintech lending: evidence from the Lending Club consumer platform. Financ. Manag. **48**(4), 1009–1029 (2019)
6. Yang, D.: Research on personal credit risk assessment based on deep learning. Central University of Finance and Economics (2019)
7. Teles, G., Rodrigues, J.J.P.C., et al.: Artificial neural network and Bayesian network models for credit risk prediction. J. Artif. Intell. Syst. **2**(1), 118–132 (2020)
8. Si, M., Guo, W., Chen, C.: Artificial intelligence-based Lasso-GBDT credit card risk rating method. Rural Financ. Re. (05), 28–38 (2022)
9. Wang, W.: Application of artificial intelligence in the field of financial anti-fraud. China Sci. Technol. Inf. **592**(20), 72–74 (2018)
10. Cao, H., Zhang, X., Zhu, R., Huang, X.: The application and practice of machine learning models in real-time anti-fraud in the digital financial era. J. Intell. Sci. Technol. **1**(04), 342–351 (2019)
11. Jin, K.: Research on credit risk assessment method for bank users based on data mining. Shenyang University of Technology (2022)
12. Sheng, Y.: Research on Contract Risk Assessment Based on Natural Language Processing. Harbin Engineering University (2017)
13. Zheng, Y.: Research on the Application of Artificial Intelligence in Commercial Bank Management. Chongqing University of Technology and Industry (2021)
14. Gu, Z., Hu, L.: Research on customer credit risk assessment of commercial banks from the perspective of machine learning. Financ. Dev. Res. **481**(01), 79–84 (2022)
15. Zhou, Z., Shang, R.: Prediction and application of high frequency volatility of CSI 300–a deep learning based approach. J. Shanghai Lixin Coll. Account. Financ. (4), 60–74 (2019)
16. Xia, M.: Study on the construction of credit decision model of commercial banks for small and micro enterprises under big data. Chongqing University of Technology and Business (2022)
17. Yang, C.: Research on financial risk control strategy of small and medium-sized enterprises under the background of big data. Natl. Circul. Econ. (29), 38–41 (2022)
18. Zhao, D.: Research on the digital transformation of inclusive finance of commercial banks in China. Southwest Financ. (12), 35–43 (2020)
19. He, S., Cui, D.: Financial risk control of supply chain of commercial banks under the background of financial technology. J. Shenyang Normal Univ. (Soc. Sci. Ed.) **47**(01), 103–109 (2023)
20. He, R.: Research on risk control and management of commercial banks. Economic management Abstracts
21. Zhao, R., Zhao, J., Liu, Y.: Model evaluation and control decision-making of Internet financial risk. Enterp. Reform Manag. (15), 3–7 (2021)
22. Sadok, H., Sakka, F., Maknouzi, M.: Artificial intelligence and bank credit analysis. A review. Cogent Econ. Financ. **10**(1), 2023262 (2022)
23. Addo, P.M., Guegan, D., Hassani, B.: Credit risk analysis using machine and deep learning models. Risks **6**(2), 38 (2018)
24. Xing, G.: Relying on big data technology to build an intelligent risk control system for commercial banks. China Financ. Comput. (08), 19–22 (2018)
25. Zhou, N., Zhang, Z., Nair, V.N., Singhal, H., Chen, J.: Bias, fairness and accountability with artificial intelligence and machine learning algorithms. Int. Stat. Rev. **90**(3), 468–480 (2022)
26. Rosales, A., Fernández-Ardèvol, M.: Ageism in the era of digital platforms. Convergence **26**(5–6), 1074–1087 (2020)
27. Bussmann, N., Giudici, P., Marinelli, D., et al.: Explainable machine learning in credit risk management. Comput. Econ. **57**, 203–216 (2021)
28. Rudin, C.: Stop explaining black box machine learning models for high stakes decisions and use interpretable models instead. Nat. Mach. Intell. **1**(5), 206–215 (2019)

Exploring the Development Rule of GDP Based on Time-series Moran's Index

Zhengjie Zang(✉)

Department of business and management, Monash University, Melbourn 3168, Australia
zzan0003@student.monash.edu

Abstract. To study the development rule of GDP, this paper extends the application of Moran's index from static analysis to dynamic perspectives. The time-series Moran's indices of GDP is calculated to explore the aggregation characteristics of GDP in China. Then, population size, employed population factor, and legal entity factor, are considered to calculate the Moran's indices of unit indices GDP. From these Moran's indices, several pieces of hidden information are mined. From the time-series Moran's indices of unit population GDP, the migration trend from undeveloped regions to developed regions can be found. From the time-series Moran's indices of unit employed population GDP, the phenomenon of income distribution imbalance can be evaluated. From the time-series Moran's indices of unit legal entity GDP, the self-organization property of enterprises is discovered. All these results are meaningful for analyzing the role of GDP to social economy and for determining the increasing law of GDP.

Keywords: Eeconomy · Moran's index · Time-series · GDP

1 Introduction

China's rapid growth for decades have contributed to the global economy, Many researchers pay increasing attention to Chinese reform, and attempt to explore trends of economic development [1, 2]. Gross domestic product(GDP) is the most remarkable index to reflect the development of economy, and several methods are used to build the relationship between economic factors and GDP and to dig the variation rule of GDP [3–5].

Analyzing the trend of GDP is necessary while assessing a country's economic situation. However, China covers large areas and has a considerable population. The total GDP of China can express the macro development trends but ignore the imbalance in different provinces [6]. The development levels of economy in different regions of China vary given the excessive amounts of influence factors. Many regions makes excellent progress, but many regions are slow in advancing their economy. To explore the rule of economic development, many studies have been made from variouse perspectives, such as the arrangement of financial factors, the advantage of resources, and the policies among others. Several studies also probe what factors will influence the economicy development and the role mechanism of these factors.

Researchers present the integrated effect apparent in economic progress for different regions, and the developed region may be connected together [7]; they also analyze the reasons why these phenomena occur and think the developed regions possess strong and attractivecapital, talents, and resources. To explore the rule of economic development, the gross domestic product(GDP) is regarded as dependent, and many other factors are regarded as independents; then, the relationship between the dependent and independents can be determined on the basis of mathematical model [8]; additionally, the predicting results of dependent can be calculated when the values of independents are input. These methods are efficient at macro level, and can be accepted easily. Then many undeveloped regions wished to keep up with the developed regions by referring to the model of developed regions in developing relevant policies.

Actually, in GDP as an absolute index, mere emphasis on the absolute value of GDP is insufficient because many factors will be ignored. For example, the GDP is very high in a region, but the population size of this region is very large; only a few areas contribute to the GDP. Therefore, only GDP can be solely used tot assess the economic development of this region. Emanuele Felice [9] found this problem, and attempted to use relative indices, GDP per worker (productivity), and employment, to discuss the regional inequality and the differences in the development paths of different regions. In addition, the spatial relationship of these relative indices requires consideration. Therefore, studying the development rule of GDP based on relative indices and spatial analysis method is very meaningful. This paper will further explore this topic by using GDP in different regions of China.

The rest of this paper is organized as follows: The "Literature Review" section discusses the relavent methods used in analyzing economic development, especially GDP. The "Data and Methodology" section describes the method of assessing the spatial characteristics of relative indices set up in this paper. The "Discussion" section explains the development laws of GDP hidden in time-series Moran's indices. The "Conclusion" section concludes this research.

2 Literature Review

While assessing a country's economic situation, GDP must be the core parameter of concern. The trends and nature of the GDP changes are given extra attention [10]. China has been the world's second largest economy [2] and the research on the the enonomy of China is very extensive. X. Wang, Y. Wang, Zheng et al examined the impact of human capital on the green economy, and think that the development of China's green economy relied more on improving the human capital stock than the human capital structure [11]. Yan, Zhou, Diao et al considered the air pollution causes spatial coupling with population and economy [12]. Chang, Pang, He et al explored the spatial relationship between nightlight and tourism economy; they found that the spatial agglomeration coupling index is higher in North China, South-Central China, and the coastal regions of East China and relatively lower in Southwest and Northwest China [13]. These studies show the regional inequality on the economic development; as the research moves along, regional inequality is a subject capturing the growing attention of economic historians and economists [9]. Cheng, Y. Wang, Z. Wang et al discovered that rural development inequality is an important practical issue during the course of full establishment of a moderately well-off society in modern China based on the data of Jinlin Province, and found the strategy of relieving such inequality [14]. The development inequality even exists in a small region. Preference [15] analyzed the spatial economic pattern at county level on the basis of the data of per capita GDP and three industries (i.e. primary, secondary and tertiary industries) in Chang-Zhu-Tan urban agglomeration; they proved the remarkable difference in economic development between the northern and southern county units. Guan, Lei, and Han found that aging level was also unequal by regional differences, urban-rural differences, and minority differences [16].

From the researches above, we can sum up the several methods used in analyzing the development of GDP, such as the mathematical approach [17], statistics method [3, 6], machine learning method [8], and the spatial-temporal analysis method [18]. Among these methods, the theory of spatial autocorrelation analysis is a key element in geographical analysis, it can reveal the spatial–temporal pattern of an economic index, reflect the spatial clustering characteristics, and analyze the mechanism between the development of economy and spatial attribution [19]. In a number of measurements of spatial correlation, two are commonly used. One is Moran's index, and the other is Geary's coefficient. The former is a generalization of Pearson's correlation coefficient, and the latter is analogous to the Durbin-Watson statistic of regression analysis. Nonetheless, in practice, Moran's index is more significant to spatial analysis [20, 21].

Existing research has shown that many scholars pay their attention to the GDP, and a variety of methods are used in analyzing the rule of GDP. However, the research based on the unit indices GDP is lacking. Actually, the unit indices GDP can better reflect the principle of economic development. Meanwhile, the research on the Moran's index of the unit indices GDP is insufficient. The most important property of Moran's index, the time-series characteristics, is not mined. Indeed, a rigorous study may yield other valuable findings. Therefore, analyzing the rule of economy based on the Moran's indices of unit indices GDP must be more effective.

3 Data and Methodology

3.1 Original Data and Preliminary Processing

Many factors influence the economic development of a region, the main factors include the population factor [16], policy factor [20], nature factor [6, 22], education factor [11], and technological factor [7]. These factors are qualitative indices. To quantify and analyze the relationship between them and the development of economy, this paper uses gross population of a region to express population factor, policy factor, and natrue factor because nature conditions and national policies decide the trend of population development and the migration trend. The employed population is used to espress the education factor because the higher the education level, the higher the chances people are employed. Meanwhile, the number of legal entity is used to express the techonlogical factor because enterprises are the carrier of technology.

Therefore, this paper uses the original data of GDPs as shown in Table 1, gross population, gross employed population, and numbers of legal entity of every region (including every province, autonomous region, and municipality) from the National

Bureau of Statistics of China. To build the relationships between GDPs to the gross population, the employed population and the number of legal entity, the ratios of GDP are calculated to the gross population, the gross urban employed population, and the counts of legal entity. Then, the indices of unit population GDP (UPG), unit employed population GDP (UEPG) and unit legal entity GDP (ULEG) are obtained. Tables 2, 3, and 4 show the results.

Table 1. GDPs of different regions (Unit: 100 million yuan).

Region	2022	2021	2020	2019	2018	2017	2016	2015	2014	2013
Beijing city	41611	41045.6	35943.3	35445.1	33106	29883	27041.2	24779.1	22926	21134.6
Tianjin city	16311.3	15685.1	14008	14055.5	13362.9	12450.6	11477.2	10879.5	10640.6	9945.4
Hebei province	42370.4	40397.1	36013.8	34978.6	32494.6	30640.8	28474.1	26398.4	25208.9	24259.6
Shanxi province	25642.6	22870.4	17835.6	16961.6	15958.1	14484.3	11946.4	11836.4	12094.7	11987.2
Inner mongolia autonomous region	23158.7	21166	17258	17212.5	16140.8	14898.1	13789.3	12949	12158.2	11392.4
Liaoning province	28975.1	27569.5	25011.4	24855.3	23510.5	21693	20392.5	20210.3	20025.7	19208.8
Jilin province	13070.2	13163.8	12256	11726.8	11253.8	10922	10427	10018	9966.5	9427.9
Heilongjiang province	15901	14858.2	13633.4	13544.4	12846.5	12313	11895	11690	12170.8	11849.1
Shanghai city	44652.8	43653.2	38963.8	37987.6	36011.8	32925	29887	26887	25269.8	23204.1
Jiangsu province	122875.6	117392.4	102807.7	98656.8	93207.6	85869.8	77350.9	71255.9	64830.5	59349.4
Zhejiang province	77715.4	74040.8	64689.1	62462	58002.8	52403.1	47254	43507.7	40023.5	37334.6
Anhui province	45045	42565.2	38061.5	36845.5	34010.9	29676.2	26307.7	23831.2	22519.7	20584
Fujian province	53109.9	49566.1	43608.6	42326.6	38687.8	33842.4	29609.4	26819.5	24942.1	22503.8
Jiangxi province	32074.7	29827.8	25782	24667.3	22716.5	20210.8	18388.6	16780.9	15667.8	14300.2
Shandong province	87435.1	82875.2	72798.2	70540.5	66648.9	63012.1	58762.5	55288.8	50774.8	47344.3
Henan province	61345.1	58071.4	54259.4	53717.8	49935.9	44824.9	40249.3	37084.1	34574.8	31632.5
Hubei province	53734.9	50091.2	43004.5	45429	42022	37235	33353	30344	28242.1	25378
Hunan province	48670.4	45713.5	41542.6	39894.1	36329.7	33828.1	30853.5	28538.6	25881.3	23545.2
Guangdong province	129118.6	124719.5	111151.6	107986.9	99945.2	91648.7	82163.2	74732.4	68173	62503.4

(continued)

Table 1. (continued)

Region	2022	2021	2020	2019	2018	2017	2016	2015	2014	2013
Guangxi zhuang Autonomous Region	26300.9	25209.1	22120.9	21237.1	19627.8	17790.7	16116.6	14797.8	13587.8	12448.4
Hainan province	6818.2	6504.1	5566.2	5330.8	4910.7	4497.5	4090.2	3734.2	3449	3115.9
Chongqing city	29129	28077.3	25041.4	23605.8	21588.8	20066.3	18023	16040.5	14623.8	13027.6
Sichuan province	56749.8	54088	48501.6	46363.8	42902.1	37905.1	33138.5	30342	28891.3	26518
Guizhou province	20164.6	19458.6	17860.4	16769.3	15353.2	13605.4	11792.4	10541	9173.1	7973.1
Yunnan province	28954.2	27161.6	24555.7	23223.8	20880.6	18486	16369	14960	14041.7	12825.5
Tibet Autonomous Region	2132.6	2080.2	1902.7	1697.8	1548.4	1349	1173	1043	939.7	828.2
Shaanxi province	32772.7	30121.7	26014.1	25793.2	23941.9	21473.5	19045.8	17898.8	17402.5	15905.4
Gansu province	11201.6	10225.5	8979.7	8718.3	8104.1	7336.7	6907.9	6556.6	6518.4	6014.5
Qinghai province	3610.1	3385.1	3009.8	2941.1	2748	2465.1	2258.2	2011	1847.7	1713.3
Ningxia Hui Autonomous Region	5069.6	4588.2	3956.3	3748.5	3510.2	3200.3	2781.4	2579.4	2473.9	2327.7
Xinjiang Uygur Autonomous Region	17741.3	16311.6	13800.7	13597.1	12809.4	11159.9	9630.8	9306.9	9264.5	8392.6

Table 2. Value of UPG (Unit: 10 thousand yuan).

Region	2021	2020	2019	2018	2017	2016	2015	2014	2013
Beijing city	18.75085	16.41996	16.18498	15.10310	13.62033	12.31945	11.32500	10.56011	9.94569
Tianjin city	11.42396	10.09950	10.14838	9.66226	8.83021	7.95371	7.56046	7.44619	7.05348
Hebei province	5.42389	4.82500	4.69701	4.37579	4.13562	3.86089	3.59406	3.44243	3.32870
Shanxi province	6.57195	5.11049	4.85033	4.55685	4.12658	3.39966	3.36357	3.42820	3.39100
Inner mongolia autonomous region	8.81917	7.18186	7.12733	6.66424	6.12335	5.66063	5.30697	4.96456	4.64049

(continued)

Table 2. (*continued*)

Region	2021	2020	2019	2018	2017	2016	2015	2014	2013
Liaoning province	6.51915	5.87812	5.81139	5.47903	5.03084	4.71285	4.65890	4.59516	4.40064
Jilin province	5.54265	5.10880	4.79036	4.53052	4.32383	4.06194	3.83391	3.77233	3.53370
Heilongjiang province	4.75462	4.29940	4.16111	3.86129	3.62254	3.43488	3.31255	3.37328	3.23216
Shanghai city	17.53845	15.66049	15.31141	14.55022	13.35158	12.11471	10.93857	10.24313	9.47880
Jiangsu province	13.80275	12.12784	11.64917	11.03571	10.19468	9.22932	8.56956	7.82883	7.24480
Zhejiang province	11.32122	10.00141	9.79796	9.24642	8.49321	7.78228	7.26946	6.79516	6.45481
Anhui province	6.96306	6.23448	6.04818	5.59758	4.89949	4.36063	3.96460	3.75516	3.43754
Fujian province	11.83809	10.48032	10.23123	9.42685	8.32531	7.37286	6.73180	6.32246	5.79248
Jiangxi province	6.60345	5.70524	5.46220	5.03357	4.48034	4.08999	3.74156	3.49728	3.19486
Shandong province	8.14899	7.16165	6.98006	6.61396	6.28048	5.89216	5.60397	5.17688	4.85782
Henan province	5.87589	5.45814	5.42549	5.06244	4.56047	4.11631	3.82271	3.58474	3.30435
Hubei province	8.59197	7.48555	7.66475	7.10191	6.30674	5.66746	5.18701	4.85593	4.37703
Hunan province	6.90328	6.25171	6.00815	5.47546	5.09997	4.65713	4.31423	3.91488	3.56745
Guangdong province	9.83282	8.80478	8.64656	8.09404	7.54869	6.89983	6.39942	5.93376	5.54600
Guangxi zhuang Autonomous Region	5.00478	4.40743	4.26277	3.96762	3.62558	3.31822	3.07583	2.84860	2.63124
Hainan province	6.37657	5.50020	5.35759	5.00071	4.62706	4.27398	3.95153	3.68483	3.38685
Chongqing city	8.74138	7.80349	7.40458	6.82542	6.38241	5.79518	5.22492	4.80572	4.32667
Sichuan province	6.46058	5.79400	5.55189	5.15588	4.57294	4.01630	3.70205	3.54974	3.27019
Guizhou province	5.05156	4.62945	4.35793	4.01706	3.57754	3.13795	2.84277	2.49472	2.19524
Yunnan province	5.79139	5.20028	4.92656	4.43985	3.93906	3.49989	3.20824	3.01777	2.76352
Tibet Autonomous Region	5.68361	5.19863	4.70305	4.37401	3.86533	3.45000	3.16061	2.89138	2.61262
Shaanxi province	7.61803	6.57752	6.53986	6.09054	5.50038	4.91631	4.65387	4.54730	4.18123
Gansu province	4.10663	3.59044	3.47481	3.22231	2.90908	2.74123	2.59873	2.57542	2.37071
Qinghai provice	5.69882	5.07555	4.98492	4.68143	4.20666	3.88007	3.48527	3.20781	3.00053
Ningxia Hui Autonomous Region	6.32855	5.48724	5.22803	4.94394	4.53943	4.00201	3.77105	3.64882	3.49505
Xinjiang Uygur Autonomous Region	6.30035	5.32846	5.31344	5.08310	4.49996	3.96656	3.90226	3.98473	3.67291

Table 3. Value of UEPG (Unit: 10 thousand yuan).

Region	2021	2020	2019	2018	2017	2016	2015	2014	2013
Beijing city	54.04292	48.57859	44.79350	40.40767	36.76098	34.16450	31.87843	30.32941	28.47178
Tianjin city	61.17434	54.86878	52.17335	51.39577	46.19889	40.13007	36.90468	36.00880	32.88823
Hebei province	71.37297	64.17284	60.72674	59.04888	57.24043	44.51861	41.01678	38.41649	37.12825
Shanxi province	51.63784	40.29733	38.45296	37.47792	33.78656	27.74361	26.88258	26.75227	25.83448
Inner mongolia autonomous region	79.06612	63.77679	61.27625	59.25404	53.09373	47.03035	43.40932	40.32570	37.49967
Liaoning province	60.19541	52.45680	49.72054	46.87101	41.75746	36.38919	32.68160	30.10478	27.87520
Jilin province	51.68355	47.54073	42.28922	40.29288	35.56496	32.37193	30.81513	29.80413	27.86022
Heilongjiang province	47.74486	43.08913	38.74256	32.71327	29.81356	27.99482	26.96655	26.99224	25.32941
Shanghai city	63.90455	60.35208	53.04790	56.20696	52.07180	47.60593	42.19554	38.94252	37.49855
Jiangsu province	89.33973	76.57929	74.04999	63.29458	57.84036	51.66026	45.90935	40.45837	39.47941
Zhejiang province	71.56466	63.06210	63.26547	57.23019	49.69474	44.54143	40.15848	36.29591	34.84005
Anhui province	75.57741	67.29402	63.41738	57.42175	57.48973	50.87546	46.38225	43.16600	39.60747
Fujian province	85.60639	71.97326	66.17667	54.84519	50.32327	44.27243	40.44563	38.10281	34.94379
Jiangxi province	66.57991	57.10299	54.60992	52.13794	43.60475	39.00021	34.92383	33.67247	32.13528
Shandong province	74.77687	66.28262	65.80271	59.03357	52.82262	48.34430	44.70672	40.09698	36.68395
Henan province	63.43828	56.23318	55.49360	51.62400	39.69264	35.15223	32.93729	31.17937	29.39823
Hubei province	77.82971	68.13134	69.48455	64.32267	53.57554	46.36869	42.60003	39.95770	36.43647
Hunan province	75.43482	68.67681	66.85789	66.50137	59.79866	54.28132	49.28095	43.28700	39.17671
Guangdong province	59.08357	53.30245	52.30403	50.12046	46.68570	41.97139	38.36366	34.54771	31.77600
Guangxi zhuang Autonomous Region	61.44065	53.90083	52.55407	50.74405	44.70025	40.15097	36.50173	33.84259	30.88933
Hainan province	57.20405	51.30138	52.16047	49.30422	44.57384	40.41700	37.19323	33.98030	31.53745
Chongqing city	78.40631	67.53344	63.04968	55.18609	49.37574	43.64979	38.59601	35.28058	32.40697
Sichuan province	62.06311	56.27942	58.77019	54.96042	47.84789	42.08063	38.14205	35.72561	31.33775
Guizhou province	57.79210	53.26693	52.22454	49.76726	43.16434	37.97874	34.27967	30.10535	26.87260
Yunnan province	75.84920	68.55304	63.19401	48.90070	43.76420	39.06683	36.07427	33.46449	29.95912
Tibet Autonomous Region	46.74607	45.62830	37.89732	41.96206	40.51051	37.23810	31.22754	28.91385	26.71613

(*continued*)

Table 3. (*continued*)

Region	2021	2020	2019	2018	2017	2016	2015	2014	2013
Shaanxi province	63.28088	53.13337	51.45262	48.54400	42.07190	37.24247	34.97225	33.69313	31.47714
Gansu province	39.13318	34.24752	34.45968	32.85002	28.30517	26.46705	25.04431	24.62561	23.43920
Qinghai province	50.44858	45.32831	43.89701	43.82775	38.94313	35.78764	32.07337	29.23576	26.68692
Ningxia Hui Autonomous Region	64.89675	57.25470	53.55000	51.62059	45.01125	39.34088	35.28591	33.79645	32.23961
Xinjiang Uygur Autonomous Region	50.31339	42.72663	42.65088	41.97051	33.31313	30.04930	29.34079	29.26248	27.11664

3.2 Analysis of Global Moran's Indices of GDPs

To mine the spatial structure and correlations of GDP, the global Moran's index of GDP is calculated according to Eq. (1). Table 5 shows the results.

$$I = \frac{n}{S_0} \times \frac{\sum_{i=1}^{n} \sum_{j=1}^{n} w_{ij}(y_i - \bar{y})(y_j - \bar{y})}{\sum_{i=1}^{n} (y_i - \bar{y})^2} \quad (1)$$

where $S_0 = \sum_{i=1}^{n} \sum_{j=1}^{n} w_{ij}$, n is the count of space; y_i and y_j are the attributes of space i and j; $\bar{y}$ is the mean of attributes in all space; and w_{ij} is the weight be tween spaces i and j. In this paper, $w_{ij} = 1$ as space i and j is adjacent, or $w_{ij} = 0$.

Moran's index ranges from -1 to 1. A positive I indicates a positive spatial correlation between the indices of regions and represents the characteristics of spatial agglomeration. A negative and significant I indicates that the indices between regions have negative spatial correlation, representing discrete spatial characteristics. If the value of I is 0, the observed values are randomly distributed between regions [11].

In Table 5, the global Moran's indices reflect the aggregation degree of GDP in different regions. The larger the Moran's index, the higher the aggregation degree. Table 4 shows that GDPs have strong aggregation effect in China. Z-score and p value show the testing results of Moran's index, and the values demonstrate that the Moran's indices are credible.

Table 4. Value of ULEG (Unit: 100 million yuan).

Region	2021	2020	2019	2018	2017	2016	2015	2014	2013
Beijing city	0.03155	0.03059	0.03881	0.03323	0.04153	0.03802	0.03517	0.03470	0.03354
Tianjin city	0.03866	0.03774	0.04369	0.04411	0.02801	0.02933	0.03398	0.04028	0.04641
Hebei province	0.02574	0.02472	0.02653	0.02586	0.02670	0.03626	0.04189	0.04748	0.05369
Shanxi province	0.02569	0.02308	0.02676	0.02864	0.02411	0.02395	0.03097	0.03967	0.05001

(*continued*)

Table 4. (continued)

Region	2021	2020	2019	2018	2017	2016	2015	2014	2013
Inner mongolia autonomous region	0.04215	0.03927	0.04510	0.04586	0.04530	0.05065	0.05584	0.05827	0.06854
Liaoning province	0.03543	0.03340	0.04001	0.03649	0.03310	0.03419	0.03658	0.04003	0.04478
Jilin province	0.04378	0.05155	0.05530	0.05294	0.05225	0.05390	0.05524	0.05790	0.06939
Heilongjiang province	0.04124	0.03959	0.04577	0.04194	0.03672	0.04725	0.05188	0.05822	0.06625
Shanghai city	0.08084	0.07313	0.07875	0.08074	0.06796	0.06441	0.05994	0.05821	0.05618
Jiangsu province	0.03808	0.04048	0.04239	0.04437	0.03645	0.04055	0.04593	0.04821	0.05537
Zhejiang province	0.02970	0.02841	0.03278	0.03640	0.02924	0.03156	0.03232	0.03239	0.03730
Anhui province	0.03239	0.03279	0.03893	0.03753	0.03400	0.04040	0.04218	0.04814	0.05652
Fujian province	0.03577	0.03769	0.04497	0.05189	0.03890	0.03939	0.04037	0.04406	0.05719
Jiangxi province	0.03390	0.03367	0.04326	0.04387	0.03527	0.03957	0.04353	0.04798	0.05584
Shandong province	0.02541	0.02561	0.03055	0.03495	0.03127	0.03557	0.04354	0.04869	0.05558
Henan province	0.02972	0.03284	0.03786	0.03556	0.04645	0.04928	0.04859	0.05543	0.06018
Hubei province	0.03714	0.03634	0.04512	0.04627	0.03946	0.04258	0.04473	0.04974	0.05784
Hunan province	0.04885	0.04998	0.05934	0.05331	0.04938	0.05583	0.06099	0.06091	0.05644
Guangdong province	0.03432	0.03152	0.03224	0.03162	0.04688	0.05400	0.05349	0.05263	0.05762
Guangxi zhuang Autonomous Region	0.02977	0.02931	0.03311	0.03476	0.03299	0.03397	0.03676	0.04061	0.04771
Hainan province	0.03441	0.03966	0.04246	0.04366	0.04480	0.04816	0.04907	0.05421	0.06387
Chongqing city	0.03854	0.03896	0.03992	0.03641	0.03352	0.03381	0.03526	0.03869	0.04441
Sichuan province	0.05570	0.05190	0.05345	0.05052	0.06017	0.06104	0.06192	0.06252	0.06759
Guizhou province	0.03067	0.03286	0.03559	0.03376	0.03039	0.03473	0.03972	0.04371	0.05056
Yunnan province	0.03471	0.03311	0.04064	0.03896	0.03193	0.03622	0.04013	0.05033	0.06095
Tibet Autonomous Region	0.03787	0.03814	0.03451	0.03112	0.05071	0.04400	0.03934	0.03594	0.03907
Shaanxi province	0.04111	0.03775	0.04394	0.04109	0.04641	0.04817	0.04999	0.05611	0.06296
Gansu province	0.02978	0.02968	0.03270	0.02721	0.03299	0.03278	0.03342	0.03749	0.04391
Qinghai provice	0.02726	0.02684	0.02985	0.03004	0.02266	0.03455	0.03429	0.03548	0.04660
Ningxia Hui Autonomous Region	0.02901	0.02957	0.03310	0.04135	0.03534	0.03436	0.03927	0.04530	0.05118
Xinjiang Uygur Autonomous Region	0.04469	0.04194	0.05051	0.04849	0.04468	0.04337	0.04737	0.05232	0.06068

Table 5. Moran's indices of GDP in different years.

Parameters	2013	2014	2015	2016	2017	2018	2019	2020	2021	2022
Moran's Indices	0.168	0.170	0.170	0.175	0.176	0.184	0.186	0.184	0.187	0.191
z-score	2.352	2.377	2.382	2.439	2.457	2.545	2.569	2.551	2.583	2.626
p	0.0186	0.0174	0.0171	0.0147	0.0140	0.0109	0.0102	0.0107	0.0098	0.0086

We now compare Tables 1 and 2. In Table 1, the GDPs of every region increase from one year to another. In Table 4, we can also see that Moran's index increases roughly from one year to another too. This finding illustrates that the GDPs in developed regions grow faster despite the steady increase in the economy of every province, and the economic development is even more unbalanced. Then, whether the unit indices GDPs accord with this rule will be discussed in the next subsection.

3.3 Analysis of Global Moran's Indices of Unit Indices GDP

To further detail the influence of the population and employed population to the GDP, the Moran's indices of UPG and UEPG are calculated on the basis of Eq. (1), and Table 5 shows the results. Given that the Z-scores are all over 2.4, and p values are all less than 0.02, their values are not shown in Table 6.

Table 6. Moran's indices of UPG and UEPG in different years.

Parameters	2013	2014	2015	2016	2017	2018	2019	2020	2021
Moran's Indices of UPG	0.217	0.203	0.197	0.189	0.184	0.177	0.173	0.167	0.172
Moran's Indices of UEPG	0.307	0.262	0.259	0.229	0.217	0.267	0.328	0.295	0.298

In Table 6, the Moran's indices of UPG nearly decrease with the increase in year, this trend goes against the GDP. That is, the aggregation effect is relieved once the population factor is considered. The reason is the people in underdeveloped regions tend to move to developed regions, and the population in developed regions increases constantly. The GDPs in developed regions are high, but the population size is also large. Consequently, the advantage of the unit population GDP is insufficient. Then, the aggregation effect of the unit population GDP decreases correspondingly.

Table 6 also shows the Moran's indices of UEPG decreasing from 2013 to 2017; then, they increase from 2018 to 2021. The Moran's index reaches the lowest value in 2017. This result shows that the aggregation effect of UEPG is very large in 2013. Then, the aggregation effect eases up gradually from 2013 to 2017, which means the differences in UEPG between different regions decrease as well. Nonetheless, the aggregation effect of UEPG improves from 2018 to 2021. Contrasting Table 3 with Table 1, we can find an interesting result: the UEPGs in the developed regions, such as Guangdong Province, Shanghai City, and Zhejiang Province, are rather low. The high value regions lie in Jiangsu Province, Inner Mongolia Autonomous Region, Fujian Province, Hubei Province, Chongqing City, Yunnan Province, Hunan Province, and Anhui Province; some of them are undeveloped regions. Then, comparing the Moran's indices of UPG and UEPG in Table 5, we can find the rule of people's income. Hypothesizing the income in proportion to UEPG, when the Moran's index of UEPG is very large, the UEPG is very high in some regions; then, the income will concentrate in a small portion of people, and the distribution of wealth will be unbalanced. When the Moran's index of UEPG is small, then, the gap of UEPG in different regions is narrow. Certainly, the distribution of wealth will tend to be balanced.

Moreover, the employed population size commonly depends on the number of legal entity. To explore whether ULEG has the aggregation attribution, this paper calculates the Moran's indices of ULEG, and Table 7 shows the results.

Table 7. Moran's indices of ULEG in different years.

Parameters	2013	2014	2015	2016	2017	2018	2019	2020	2021
Moran's Indices of ULEG	−0.063	−0.038	−0.058	−0.072	−0.132	−0.013	−0.039	−0.049	−0.065
z−score	−0.335	−0.049	−0.270	−0.437	−1.122	0.257	−0.067	−0.189	−0.424
p	0.7378	0.9605	0.787	0.662	0.262	0.797	0.946	0.851	0.671

In Table 6, the z-score and p value show that ULEG lacks an aggregation effect. The most of Moran's indices of ULEG are nearing zero. Accordingly, the ULEG of different regions tends toward the random distribution.

In Table 4, we can also see intuitively that the ULEG of Shanghai is the highest, but the ULEG of the surrounding regions, such as Jiangsu Province, Zhejiang Province, and Anhui Province, are rather modest. This finding illustrates that the production value of the legal entity does not rely on the regions; whatever the region, whether in developed region or undeveloped region, the internal factors of the enterprises are the key factors.

4 Discussion

Calculating Moran's index is a method to analyze the spatial autocorrelation of an observation value. Most of the studies calculate the Moran's index, judge the aggregation effect, and then discuss which region is surrounded by high value or low value of one parameter. The same is done in the analysis of GDP of a region. Few studies explore the transformation law of Moran's index of GDP. Actually, Moran's index is variable in different periods; the Moran's index will change when the values of a parameter in a region and adjacent regions have changed. The Moran's index will increase when the values of a parameter in the region and adjacent regions have similar increasing trend, or the Moran's index will decrease.

Based on this theory, the changing rule of GDP can be analyzed. In this paper, GDP is an absolute index, and their Moran's indices change from small to large with the addition of years. This process can show that the new economic pattern of multicenter is forming, the economic centers have stronger appeal to talents, technologies, and capital. Then, migration of population is inevitable. We all know Guangdong Province, Jiangsu Province, and Zhejiang Province are developed provinces, given their extremely high GDPs. In Table 1, we can see their populations have a net increase. The population in Guangdong Province have increased to 14.14 million people from 2013 to 2021, Zhejiang Province to 7.56 million, and Jiangsu Province to 3.13 million. By contrast, the population size has decreased to 5.41 million in undeveloped Heilongjiang Province.

Only through this phenomenon, the migration of population relieves the gap of the unit population GDP in different regions, which can be seen from the Moran's index of UPG in Table 2. Therefore, comparing the Moran's indices of GDP and UPG, the moving trend of population can be detected.

Upon seeing the UEPG, some of higher values are in developed region, such as in Jiangsu Province and Shandong Province. Some of them are in undeveloped regions, such as the Inner Mongolia Autonomous Region and Yunnan Province. In some developed regions, such as Guangdong Province and Shanghai City, the UEPGs are rather low. Moreover, the Moran's indices of UEPG decrease gradually and then increase again, which actually involves income distribution. Whether distribution of income is balanced is very important, as it reflects the redistribution of social wealth. Certainly, several methods can be used to evaluate the wealth gap. This paper discovers a new method, that is, if combining the Moran's index of UPG, the Moran's index of UEPG can reflect the change in income from a rather micro perspective. Once the Moran's index of UPG is not very high, and the Moran's indices decrease gradually from one year to another, then, high Moran's index of UEPG, especially the Moran's indices that increase continuously with the addition of years, is a disadvantage. This scenario will make a small portion of people obtain a lot of income while worsening income inequality.

In Table 7, the Moran's indices of ULEG show that the self-organization ability of the legal entity is very strong. Enterprises will organize production according their characteristics. The output value and benefit should be the concerns of enterprises themselves. Supplying the good social environment is enough for government, as it will promote enterprises to work hard and to produce higher GDP.

5 Conclusion

This paper extends the application of Moran's index, which is a useful index to express the spatial autocorrelation of a parameter. However, its information is not used efficiently from a static view. The author analyzes the development rule of GDP of China based on time-series Moran's indices. The results show that the time-series Moran's indices can mine the deep law of GDP, and the more information hidden in the Moran's index can be used adequately.

The time-series Moran's indices of GDP shows that the new economic pattern is becoming increasingly apparent, the development levels of several economic centers are progressively increasing, and the leading role of developed region is stronger. However, when considering the population size, the Moran's indices of UPG show a decreasing trend, and the aggregation effect of UPG somewhat slows down in developed regions. That is, the population resource advantage is not used well, and the demographic dividend needs to be exploited further. Once UEPG and the Moran's index of UEPG are compared, we can judge the trend of income distribution: excessively high Moran's index reflects the inequality of income distribution. The Moran's index of ULEG shows that legal entities have self-organization characteristics. Government supplying a good social environment is very important. As for the production value, enterprises should be concerned of it.

The author also recognizes that this study produces preliminary results for the development rule of GDP based on time-series Moran's index and unit indices GDP. Some rules of GDP can be concluded, but the quantitative relations are not very clear. For example, what degree the Moran's index of UEPG reaches is the threshold, and what degree the index of UPG reaches is reasonable. Therefore, further studying these questions is necessary to improve the precision of the research on GDP.

Furthermore, GDP may be affected by many chance factors. For example, owing to the change in policy and the epidemic, this paper only analyzes GDP from the official data without considering the inner factors. For relevant policy making, the studies must comprehensively focus on the inner factors driving the development of GDP.

6 Declaration of Interest Statement

The author states no conflict of interest.

References

1. Overholt, W.: China and the evolution of the world economy. China Econ. Rev. **40**, 267–271 (2016)
2. Zhang, H., Li, M., Zéman, Z.: Study on chinese technical economy and global social responsibility. J. Phys. Conf. Series **1187**, 052092 (2019)
3. Ferrari, G.: Comparisons of GDP over time and across space: the state of the art. E STUDIOS DE E CONOMÍA A PLICADA **36**(1), 149–166 (2018)
4. Afonso, O., Neves, P.C., Pinto, T.: The non-observed economy and economic growth: a eta-analysis. Econ. Syst. **44**, 100746 (2020)
5. Ball, C., French, J.: Exploring what stock markets tell us about GDP in theory and practice. Res. Econ. **75**, 330–344 (2021)
6. Hu, S., Yang, C., Zhu, X., Zheng, Z., Cao, Y.: Distributions of region size and GDP and their relation. Physica A **430**, 46–56 (2015)
7. Li, Y., Zhang, J.: Moran index analysis of the impact of financial elements on macroeconomic efficiency. J. Southwest Univ. (Nat. Sci. Ed.) **42**(3), 124–129 (2020)
8. Xu, X., Rogers, R.A., Estrada, M.A.R.: A novel prediction model: ELM-ABC for annual GDP in the case of SCO countries. Comput. Econ. (2022). https://doi.org/10.1007/s10614-022-10311-0
9. Felice, E.: The roots of a dual equilibrium: GDP, productivity and structural change in the Italian regions in the long-run (1871-2011). In: Economic History Working Papers, Banca d'Italia, no. 40 (2017). ISSN 2281-6089 (print), ISSN 2281-6097
10. Yu, Y., et al.: National green GDP assessment and prediction for China Based on a CA-markov land use simulation model. Sustainability **11**, 576 (2019)
11. Wang, X., Wang, Y., Zheng, R., Wang, J., Cheng, Y.: Impact of human capital on the green economy: empirical evidence from 30 Chinese provinces. Environ. Sci. Pollut. Res. **30**, 12785–12797 (2023)
12. Yan, D., Zhou, M., Diao, Y., Yang, M.: Air pollution in China: Spatial patterns and spatial coupling with population and economy. Front. Environ. Sci. (2022). https://doi.org/10.3389/fenvs.2022.1040131
13. Chang, P., Pang, X., He, X., Zhu, Y., Zhou, C.: Exploring the spatial relationship between nighttime light and tourism economy: evidence from 31 provinces in China. Sustainability **14**, 7350 (2022)
14. Cheng, Y., Wang, Y., Wang, Z., Luo, X.: Changing rural development inequality in Jilin Province, Northeast China. Chin. Geogr. Sci. **23**(5), 620–633 (2013)

15. Dong, M., Zou, B., Pu, Q., Wan, N., Yang, L., Luo, Y.: Spatial pattern evolution and casual analysis of county level economy in Changsha-Zhuzhou-Xiangtan Urban agglomeration, China. Chin. Geogr. Sci. **24**(5), 620–630 (2014)
16. Guan, D., Lei, L., Han, Z.: Spatial-temporal variation of population aging: a case study of China's Liaoning Province. Complexity, 1–13 (2020)
17. Juan, G., Eyckmans, J., Rousseau, S.: Defining and measuring the circular economy: a mathematical approach. Ecol. Econ. **157**, 369–372 (2019)
18. Ji, J., Tang, Z., Zhang, W., Liu, W., Jin, B., et al.: Spatiotemporal and multiscale analysis of the coupling coordination degree between economic development equality and co-environmental quality in China from 2001 to 2020. Remote Sens. **14**, 737 (2022)
19. Zhang, R., Lu, J.: Spatial-temporal pattern and convergence characteristics of provincial urban land use effificiency under environmental constraints in China. Int. J. Environ. Res. Public Health **19**, 10729 (2022)
20. Chen, Y.: New approaches for calculating moran's index of spatial autocorrelation. Plos One **8**(7), e68336 (2013)
21. Chen, Y.: An analytical process of spatial autocorrelation functions based on Moran's index. Plos One (2021). https://doi.org/10.1371/journal.pone.0249589
22. Newell, R.G., Prest, B.C., Sexton, S.E.: The GDP-temperature relationship: implications for climate change damages. J. Environ. Econ. Manag. **108**, 102445 (2021)

An Empirical Study of U.S. Stock Market Forecasts and Trend Trading Strategies Based on ARIMA Model

Siying Wang[✉]

Mathematical Sciences, Anhui University, Hefei 230000, AH, China
c12214011@stu.ahu.edu.cn

Abstract. Financial forecasting is an important practical guidance for discovering objective trends in financial development and guiding financial investments. According to domestic and foreign research, many scholars have made forecasts for the stock market with various methods. This paper applies the ARIMA model to forecast the future U.S. stock market returns by studying the S&P S&P500 index. It also explores the feasibility of trend-based trading strategies that are commonly used. The original data is collected from the wind database, and the data is the closing price of the S&P 500 index, ranging from 2000-1-3 to 2023-4-27. The data is divided into two parts: modeling data and testing data. The results show that the prediction model is in the form of ARIMA (3, 1, 4), and the average accuracy of the model is 1.8%, which indicates that the model is real and effective. At the same time, this paper verifies that the trading strategy of chasing up and killing down is feasible. The research results can provide theoretical empirical reference for financial investment. However, it is also found that the ARIMA model used in this paper should be combined with other models for more refinement in the prediction effect.

Keywords: S&P 500 · ARIMA Model · Forecast

1 Introduction

The United States is the largest developed country in the world and the largest economy in the world today. And the world's largest volume of stock market today is also located in the United States, which means that the impact of the U.S. stock market on the global economy is also very huge. With the development of economic globalization, economic activities among countries influence each other, financial capital among financial markets penetrate each other, and the trend of linkage among international stock markets becomes more and more obvious. As a representative of the stock market, the study of the U.S. stock market is of great interest.

The stock market is a barometer of the economy and an important reference when analyzing the economic situation. On the one hand, the stock market affects the real economy; on the other hand, the stock market reflects and predicts economic trends and economic cycles. Therefore, stock market quotes are of great significance for financial decisions, economic analysis and policy implementation. Both for stock market investors and company managers, they urgently need to know the future trends of the stock market and future changes in earnings, so that they can make more accurate investment decisions or avoid possible financial risks. The state of the stock market can be simply divided into a bull market and a bear market. A bull market is currently considered to have started when the stock index increases 20% from its low point, and a bear market is considered to have started when the stock index decreases 20% from its high point [1]. However, the current state of the market is unknown. Therefore, it is important to accurately identify and predict the state of the stock market.

Along with the Dow Jones Industrial Average, Nasdaq Composite, and Standard & Poor's 500 Index (S&P 500), collectively known as the "Big Three", the S&P 500 is one of the most well-known indices on the American stock market [2]. The S&P 500 is a list of the 500 most powerful publicly traded companies selected by the S&P index committee from a number of important industries. Therefore, the S&P 500 is a better reflection of the current U.S. economy and the actual situation of the entire market. In this paper, we use the historical data of S&P500 index to determine and predict the future trend of stock market changes and prepare for what may happen next.

This paper theoretically reviews the literature on stock market forecasting and research by domestic and foreign scholars and summarizes various methods of stock market forecasting. There are three main approaches to stock market forecasting, one is the stochastic process forecasting model, represented by Ling and Feng, who used Markov's method to forecast the transition of bull and bear markets [3]. Second, stock price volatility forecasting models based on statistical theory, such as GARCH model [4], Logit model [5], support vector machine [6], Multi-Factor model [7], etc. Third, Stock market prediction by neural network prediction model, represented as artificial intelligence prediction model [8]. Historical information is fed into the machine to predict future trends by fitting a non-linear relationship between stock prices and historical information. Bull and bear market forecasts are based on price volatility forecasts, and the two research methods are similar [9, 10].

This paper intends to take the S&P 500 index as the research object to predict the future stock market trend by identifying the bull and bear market states of the stock market. It can also empirically demonstrate the trend trading strategy of chasing the bull and the bear by means of a statistical approach.

2 Method

2.1 Data Source

S&P 500 was put forward in 1957 in Standard & Poor's, which is consistent with the reality of the American stock market. Since July 1, 1976, it has been composed of 400 industrial stocks, 20 transportation stocks, 40 public utility stocks and 40 financial stocks. The characteristics of S&P 500 are large sampling range, strong representativeness, strong accuracy and strong continuity. Since the S&P 500 Index always has 500 constituents, it is not affected by new stock issues and can be used to describe investors' returns. The base period of the plan is from 1941 to 1942, and the basic target is set at 10.

By weighting the number of new shares issued, and according to different time points. Use the following equation to calculate the index.

$$S\&P500 = \frac{\text{Adjusted market capitalization of constituents in the reporting period}}{\text{Base period market capitalization}} * 10 \tag{1}$$

In this case, the market value of the base period is a constant. It is clear that the S&P 500 index's data information serves as a crucial benchmark for research on the American stock market. Therefore, the S&P 500 index is selected as a proxy variable to reflect the return and volatility of the U.S. stock market in this paper.

In this paper, the daily trading data of S&P 500 index from January 3, 2000 to April 27, 2023 were obtained from WANDER Data Online as a sample. Finally, a total of 5867 sets of daily data for the S&P 500 were obtained. The data were divided into two parts, where the data for the period 2000-1-3 to 2022-12-30 were used for model building and the data for the period 2023-1-3 to 2023-4-27 were used for testing. The following Fig. 1 shows original data.

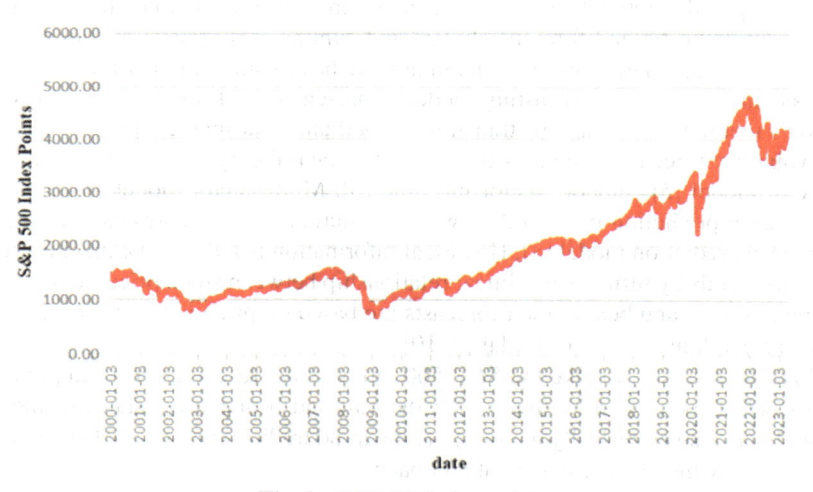

Fig. 1. S&P 500 index points.

2.2 Variable Description

The simple and logarithmic rates of return are the two most commonly used measures of return calculation. Although simple rates of return are usually used in the stock market, log rates of return and simple rates of return yield approximately equal results when price variability is minimal. Logarithmically processed return data are smoother and additive in time, which facilitates the calculation of continuous compound interest. Therefore, logarithmic returns are mostly chosen as the object of study when studying the pattern of changes in stock prices or stock price indices. The formula for calculating the logarithmic rate of return is shown as follows.

$$R_t = ln\frac{Price_t}{Price_{t-1}} \quad (2)$$

where R_t is the return on day t, $Price_t$ indicates the closing price on day t, and $Price_{t-1}$ indicates the closing price on day t-1.

2.3 Mathematical Statistics Method

Box and Jenkins created the differential autoregressive moving average model, sometimes known as the ARIMA (p, d, q) model, in 1976. A moving average model is MR(q), and an autoregressive model is AR(p), where p is the number of moving average terms and q is the number of regression terms. In ARIMA, d stands for the quantity of different orders. The standard ARMA (p, q) expression (where θ is a constant term).

$$Y_t = \theta + a_1 Y_{t-1} + a_2 Y_{t-2} + \cdots + a_p Y_{t-p} + \beta_0 \mu_t + \beta_1 \mu_{t-1} + \cdots + \beta_q \mu_{t-q} \quad (3)$$

where ARMA (p, d, q) is the d-order model of ARMA (p, q).

3 Results and Discussion

3.1 Parameter Determination

First, parameters p, d, and q need to be determined and the corresponding ARIMA (p, d, q) model needs to be established. When the data were not put through the process, the ADF test showed a statistic of 1.381, which was greater than the 10% threshold of −2.568, and raw data had unit roots and were unstable. Raw data were converted to log returns after first-order differencing. The stability of the data series was then tested by ADF test, and the ADF test statistic was that the original data had a unit root and was unstable. After the first-order difference test, the ADF test statistic is −57.556, which is less than the 1% critical value of −3.436, and the original data series becomes a smooth series, so the data series is a first-order difference smooth series, so the parameter d = 1. Figure 2 shows first-order difference plot of the data series.

3.2 Estimated Values

In ARMA (p, d, q) model, the parameters p and q are determined with the help of the correlation and partial correlation plots. The model results can be seen in Table 1. Since the data are first-order differential smooth series, the values of p and q can be determined from the autocorrelation coefficient (ACF) in Fig. 3 and the partial correlation coefficient (PACF) plots in Fig. 4 to be 3 and 4, respectively, thus forming the ARIMA (3,1,4) model.

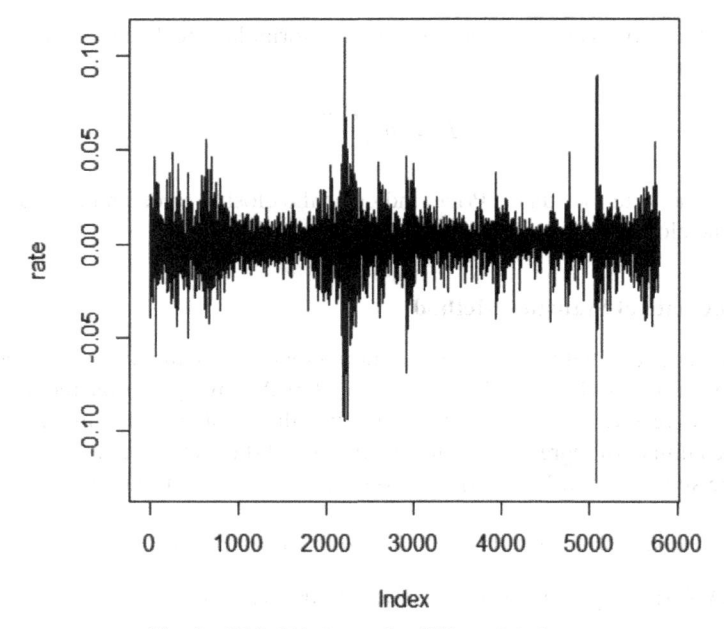

Fig. 2. S&P 500 first order differential chart.

Table 1. ARIMA (3,1,4) parameter estimation.

Variable	Coefficient	Std. Error
C	0.0002	0.0001
AR (1)	0.4644	0.1910
AR (2)	0.3535	0.1481
AR (3)	−0.4968	0.1770
MA (1)	−0.5716	0.1909
MA (2)	−0.3106	0.1550
MA (3)	0.5507	0.1760
MA (4)	−0.0938	0.0218

3.3 Test Model

To test the fit and reliability of the ARMA (3,1,4) model, the residuals of the model estimation results were judged for the presence of white noise to correct the relevant parameters. By determining the maximum lag order of 15 for the residual series generated by the ARMA (3,1,4) model, the residual correlation plots in Fig. 5 and the Q statistics in Fig. 6 were calculated.

It was found that the sample autocorrelation function of the residual series was within the set region and the corresponding probability error was less than 5%, so it could be

Series x1

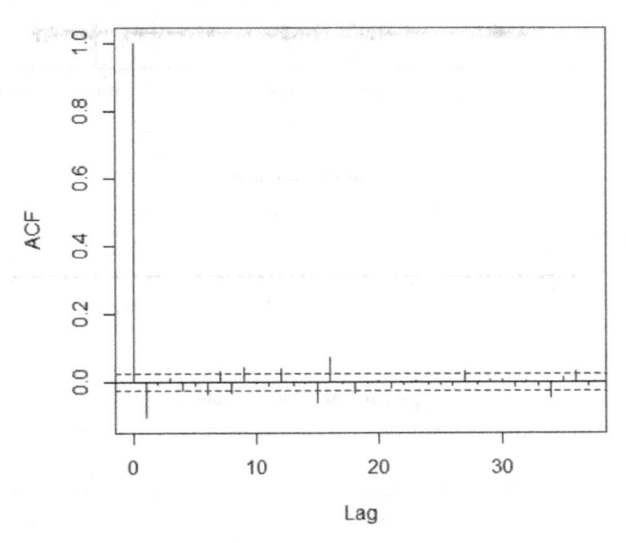

Fig. 3. ACF chart.

Series x1

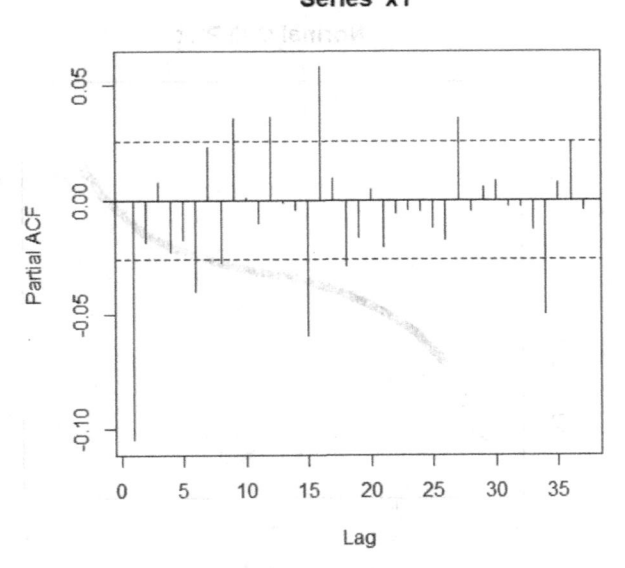

Fig. 4. PACF chart.

judged that there was no autocorrelation in the residual series, and therefore the model could be considered to have passed the test.

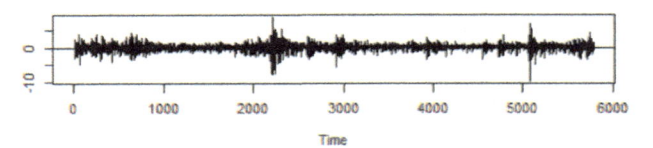

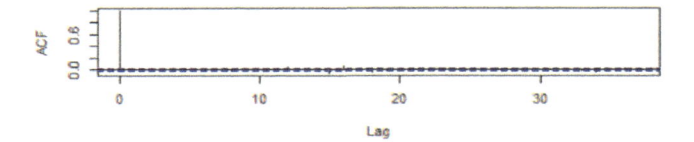

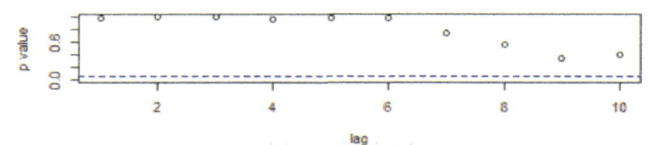

Fig. 5. Residual Correlation Chart.

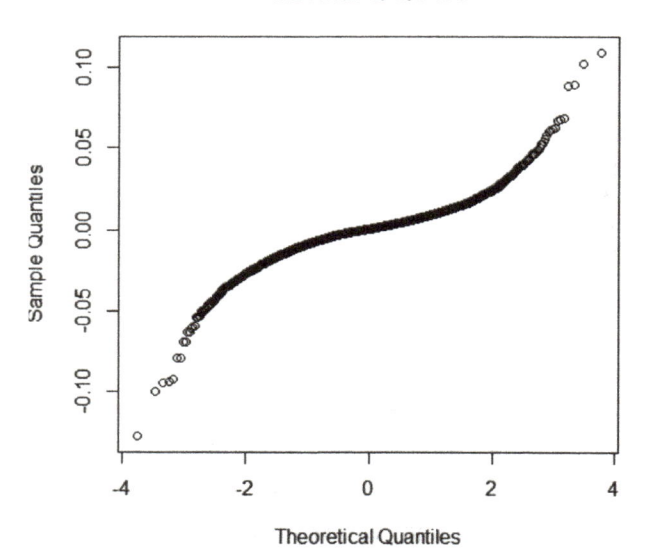

Fig. 6. QQ chart.

3.4 Prediction Results

In order to test the accuracy of the model, the S&P 500 index data for 80 days from 2023–1-3 to 2023–4-27 are used as the test data. Figure 7 shows the fit of the forecast results. Figure 8 shows the actual S&P 500 trend.

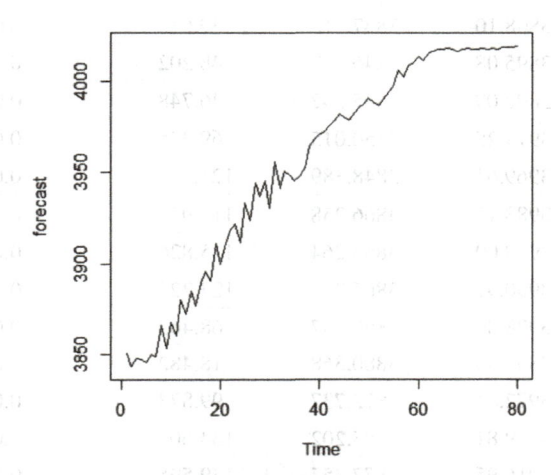

Fig. 7. Fitted graph of prediction results.

Fig. 8. Fitted graph of prediction results.

Table 2 shows the estimates of S indicators for the period from January 3, 2000 to December 30, 2020 (too much data to show only part of it). From Table 2, it can be seen that the maximum relative error is 4.8%, but not more than 5%. The average relative error is 2.8%, so the proposed model can be considered valid.

Table 2. ARIMA (2,1,9) parameter estimation.

Date	Predict	Actual	Absolute error	Relative error
2023-01-03	3824.14	3850.074	25.934	0.007
2023-01-04	3852.97	3842.785	10.185	0.003
2023-01-05	3808.10	3847.716	39.616	0.010
2023-01-06	3895.08	3846.878	48.202	0.012
2023-01-09	3892.09	3845.342	46.748	0.012
2023-01-10	3919.25	3850.015	69.235	0.018
2023-01-11	3969.61	3848.389	121.221	0.031
2023-01-12	3983.17	3866.258	116.912	0.029
2023-01-13	3999.09	3853.264	145.826	0.036
2023-01-17	3990.97	3867.743	123.227	0.031
2023-01-18	3928.86	3860.397	68.463	0.017
2023-01-19	3898.85	3880.368	18.482	0.005
2023-01-20	3972.61	3872.737	99.873	0.025
2023-01-23	4019.81	3885.202	134.608	0.033
2023-01-24	4016.95	3877.355	139.595	0.035
2023-01-25	4016.22	3889.946	126.274	0.031
2023-01-26	4060.43	3895.858	164.572	0.041
2023-01-27	4070.56	3899.693	170.867	0.042
2023-01-30	4017.77	3911.444	106.326	0.026
2023-01-31	4076.60	3923.028	153.572	0.038
2023-02-01	4119.21	3977.412	141.798	0.034
2023-02-02	4179.76	3989.058	190.702	0.046
2023-02-03	4136.48	3945.467	191.013	0.046
2023-02-06	4111.08	3938.220	172.86	0.042
2023-02-07	4164.00	3963.539	200.461	0.048
2023-02-08	4117.86	3924.157	193.703	0.047
2023-02-09	4081.50	3944.663	136.837	0.034
2023-02-10	4090.46	3937.133	153.327	0.037

3.5 Trading Strategies

Trend trading strategy of chasing up and down is a common trading strategy that people use when trading stocks, by catching the change point of the trend and operating quickly in a short period of time so as to gain profit.

As seen in Fig. 9, there is already an upward trend by the end of 2022 and it is possible to make a trade to buy the stock and thus make some profit in 2023.

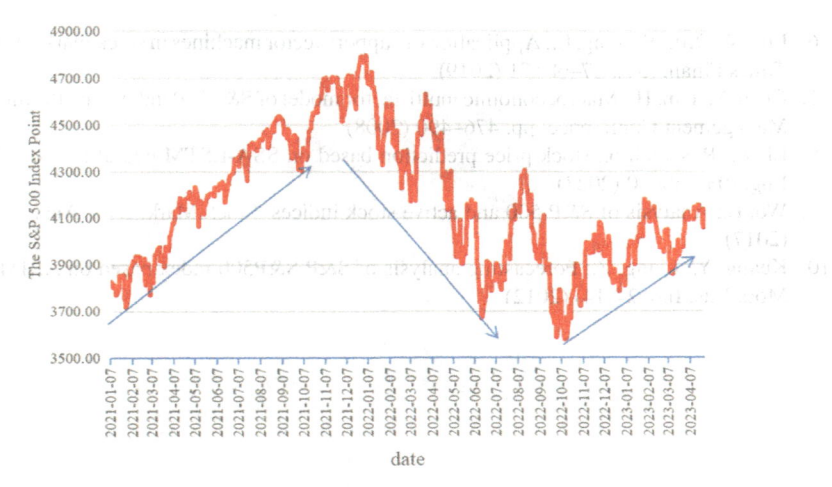

Fig. 9. S&P500 trend chart.

4 Conclusion

In this paper, a time series forecasting method of financial market based on difference moving mean is proposed. The data are divided into two parts, where the data from 2000-1-3 to 2020-12-30 are used for modeling, and the second stage is to use the data from 2023-1-3 to 2023-4-27 for verification. The prediction model is ARIMA (3,1,4), and the prediction accuracy error is less than 5%, so the model is valid and can be used for practical applications. During the research of this paper, the following problems were found. The S&P500 index data is also random like other financial data, which brings uncertainty to the data prediction and increases the difficulty of prediction. This paper needs to combine other data analysis models to improve the accuracy of data prediction. Second, using the S&P 500 index to represent the return volatility in the U.S. stock market will ignore the small and medium-sized enterprises and the GEM situation. Also, the data selection is daily, which is high frequency data and somewhat complicated to analyze. Finally, the yield data of each stage has its own characteristics and should be analyzed separately according to the stage, not generalized.

References

1. Chen, K., Chen, W.: An empirical study on the characteristics of A-share bull and bear markets and trading strategies to catch up and kill down. Spec. Econ. Zone (2), 46–52 (2017)
2. Li, P.: Study on S&P500 index. Secur. Mark. Herald (2), 44–46 (2000)
3. Lin, F.: Forecasts of the "bull-bear" market transition in China's stock market. China Collect. Econ. (25), 90–92 (2019)
4. Lin, W., Chen, H., Zhou, L., Meng, X.: Analysis of risk predictive ability of Chinese stock market based on VaR-GARCH model family. Stat. Decis. Mak. **35**(21), 151–155 (2019)
5. Zheng, M., Miao, J.: Application of logit model in Shanghai stock market forecasting. Stat. Decis. Mak. (06), 102–104 (2007)

6. Luo, W., Xu, W., Tang, L.: Application of support vector machines in stock market forecasting. Times Finan. (31), 67–68+71 (2019)
7. Chen, Y., Pan, H.: Macroeconomic multi-factor model of S&P500 index. In: 3th Annual China Management Conference, pp. 476–490 (2008)
8. Li, X.: Research on stock price prediction based on SSA-LSTM neural network. Inf. Syst. Eng. (03), 48–50 (2023)
9. Wo, L.: Analysis of S&P 500 and active stock indices. Stock Mark. Dyn. Anal. (11), 11–12 (2017)
10. Kuang, Y., Liang, Z.: Forecasting analysis of S&P S&P500 index based on ARIMA model. Mod. Bus. Ind. **24**(14) (2012)

Impact of 5G Commercial License Issuance on Stock Prices of Related Listed Companies: Using Difference-in-Differences Model

Xi Zhou(✉)

School of Business, Macau University of Science and Technology, Macau 999078, China
`2009853ub011008@student.must.mo.edu`

Abstract. As the rapid expansion of 5G commercialization in China recently, people are paying attention to how policy events impact the performance of the stock market. This paper will use difference-in-differences model to analyze the impact of 5G commercial license issuance on stock prices of related listed companies. The researcher selects 105 eligible listed companies in this industry as the research sample and divides them into a treatment group and a control group according to the degree of correlation of the concept of 5G. After analyzing by difference-in-differences model, the issuance of 5G commercial licenses has a significant positive impact on the stock prices of the relevant companies. The positive impact of this policy on companies effectively promotes the commercialization of 5G in China and facilitates China's adaptation to the accelerated development of 5G globally. Finally, this article suggests investors actively focus on policy trends and strengthen their analysis ability of data-level information in the investment process. At the same time, the government needs to make sure the accuracy, immediacy, and continuity of policy promulgation.

Keywords: 5G Commercial License Issuance · Stock Prices · Difference-in-differences Model

1 Introduction

5G, as the leading direction of the latest generation of communication technology advancement, has been developed very well in a range of worldwide in the past decade. Facing the fiercely competitive environment, China is also actively promoting the deployment and commercialization of 5G networks [1]. On June 6, 2019, there are four operators recieved the 5G commercial licenses from the Ministry of Industry and Information Technology of the People's Republic of China (MIIT): China Telecom, China Mobile, China Unicom, and China Broadcasting and Television. In October of the same year, MIIT officially approved the opening gate for 5G base stations to enter the network and the related licenses, and the disclosure of this news brought great volatility to 5G-related stocks -- China officially entered the first year of 5G commercialization [2]. As we all know, policy events are closely related to the stock market performance. At the same time, major policy events directly affect investors' confidence, judgment, and investment behavior, which in turn affects the share prices of related listed companies and their yields [3].

Due to the increasing attention from the market on 5G commercialization, the influence of the issuance of 5G commercial licenses on the stock prices of related companies has also started to cause concern of some scholars. In recent years, not many studies directly explored the impact of 5G-related policies on the stock prices of Chinese listed companies. Regarding the impact of policies on share prices, studies focused on two main topics: the first one focuses on the impact of investors' attention on the market performance of 5G concept stock companies [2]; another one focuses on the mechanism of policy events affecting stock returns [3]. Existing studies have been devoted to exploring the variables that affect stock prices and exploring the ways in which these variables affect stock prices [4, 5], but lack a comparison of stock price changes before and after the policy shock, and do not set a control group to highlight the intensity of changes in affected companies.

Hence, this paper takes the listed companies in communications industry classified by Shenyin Wanguo Research & Consulting and listed companies that have high correlation to 5G introduced by Communication Industry Daily (online) as the research object and selects 105 eligible listed companies in this industry as the research sample. This paper applies difference-in-differences model and covers 22 domestic listed companies as the treatment group. These companies can be classified into seven groups: base stations, chip modules, antenna feed systems, optical fiber and cable segment, optical module segment, RF device segment, and communication construction segment. After that, the researcher uses the data from the treatment group to compare with the data from a control group consisting of 83 stocks of listed companies in the communication industry. It can help us to study the impact of the policy event of 5G license issuance on the share prices of the above-mentioned companies. Finally, the research results show that the issuance of 5G commercial licenses brings a significant positive market reaction to the listed companies with a high 5G correlation. Compared to other communication industry's listed companies, companies directly affected by the 5G conception show a sustained increase in share prices.

Therefore, this paper contributes to the related research field in two aspects: Firstly, by using of difference-in-differences model, such analysis can sufficiently eliminate the bias between the treatment and control groups [6], and to some extent, it can also reduce the effects caused by selection bias and external factors [7]. In this way, it can obtain a more accurate and reliable estimated result. Secondly, the operation of comparing the stock price changes before and after the policy shock has strong theoretical and practical meaning, which can guide investors to properly understand the intensity of changes in 5G-related policies on the company's stock price.

2 Methodology

2.1 Event Definition and Sample Selection

The event in this article refers to the issuance of 5G commercial licenses by the Ministry of Industry and Information Technology of the People's Republic of China (MIIT) to four telecoms operators on 6 June 2019. Since this event occurred in a relatively recent year, constructing event dummy variables in terms of "year" will result in too little time data to fit the regression equation well. Therefore, this article chooses to construct the dummy variables by using "week" as the time unit. As Lu said in 2021, DID model estimates require at least one year of data before and after the year of policy implementation [8]. So this article choose week 20 of 2018 as the first week and week 23 of 2020 as the last week (week 106). Week 23 of 2019 as the 54th week when the policy event occurred, which means at the 54th week the policy started to affect the stock price. To better demonstrate the effect of the policy on share prices, 23 listed companies with high correlation to 5G which are introduced by Communication Industry Daily (online) were selected as the treatment group. At the same time, 87 stocks in the communications industry under the Shenyin Wanguo Research & Consulting's Standard were used as the control group (excluding Hong Kong stocks, those already included in the treatment group, and those listed after the occurrence of the policy event).

The summary statistics of variables about the regression model are shown in Table 1. All sample data in this paper was obtained from the CSMAR database.

Table 1. Descriptive statistics.

VARIABLES	(1) N	(2) mean	(3) S.D.	(4) min	(5) max
Number	11,025	5,513	3,183	1	11,025
Week (t)	11,025	53.94	30.40	1	106
Weekly closing price	11,025	17.58	13.69	1.120	144.8
Weekly stock market value	11,025	7.018e + 06	1.196e + 07	398,650	1.766e + 08
Momentum	11,025	−0.256	5.586	−84.45	51.94

2.2 Model Construction and Variable Description

This article uses a difference-in-differences model to test the impact of the policy event of "5G commercial license issuance" on the stock prices of relevant listed companies, and constructs the following multiple regression model:

$$Weeklyclosingprice_{it} = \beta_0 + \beta_1 \times did_{it} + \beta_2 \times Time_t + \beta_3 \times Treatment_i + \beta_4 \times Momentum + \beta_5 \times Weeklystockmarketvalue + \varepsilon_{it} \quad (1)$$

Weeklyclosingprice$_{it}$ use the closing price on the last trading day of week i to represent the stock price of stock i in week t; *Time*$_t$ denotes the start time of the policy event and the subscript t represents the number of weeks. If Week <= 54, then *Time*$_t$ = 0; if Week > 54, then *Time*$_t$ = 1; *Treatment*$_i$ denotes whether stock i is directly affected by the policy; if yes, *Treatment*$_i$ = 1, representing the stock is contained in the treatment group; if no, *Treatment*$_i$ = 0, representing the stock is contained in the control group; The interaction *did*$_{it}$ is the core explanatory variable, indicating the effects arising from the implementation of the policy. If stock i is directly affected by the policy in week t, *did*$_{it}$ = 1; otherwise, *did*$_{it}$ = 0; *Momentum* represents stock momentum, which refers to the speed or rate of change in the price of a stock. Calculated by subtracting the closing price of the current period from the closing price 10 days earlier [9]; *Weeklystockmarketvalue* represents the market value of an individual stock, which is calculated as the market price per share multiply total number of shares issued ε_{it} is a stochastic disturbance term.

The explanatory summary of the variables selected for study in this paper is shown in Table 2:

Table 2. Summary table of variables.

Variable	Explanation
Weeklyclosingprice	The weekly closing price of a single stock
did$_{it}$	The interaction term, which represents the effect after the policy is implemented
Time$_t$	Dummy variable, which that represents when the policy event began
Treatment$_i$	Dummy variable, whether is the stock directly affected by the policy
Momentum	The control variable, momentum
Weeklystockmarketvalue	Control variable, market value of individual stocks

3 Empirical Analysis

3.1 Parallel Trend Test

The parallel trend hypothesis is based on the principle of testing whether the stock prices of the treatment and control groups had a parallel growth trend before the policy occurred. In this article, the average share price of the treatment and control groups was calculated from week 1 to week 106. With week 54 being the occurrence time of the policy, plotting the trend changes before and after the policy.

The plotted results are shown in Fig. 1:

As the line can be seen in Fig. 1, the weekly average share prices of the treatment group and the control group are basically in parallel from week 1 to week 53. After the policy event of "5G commercial license issuance" in week 54, the gap between the

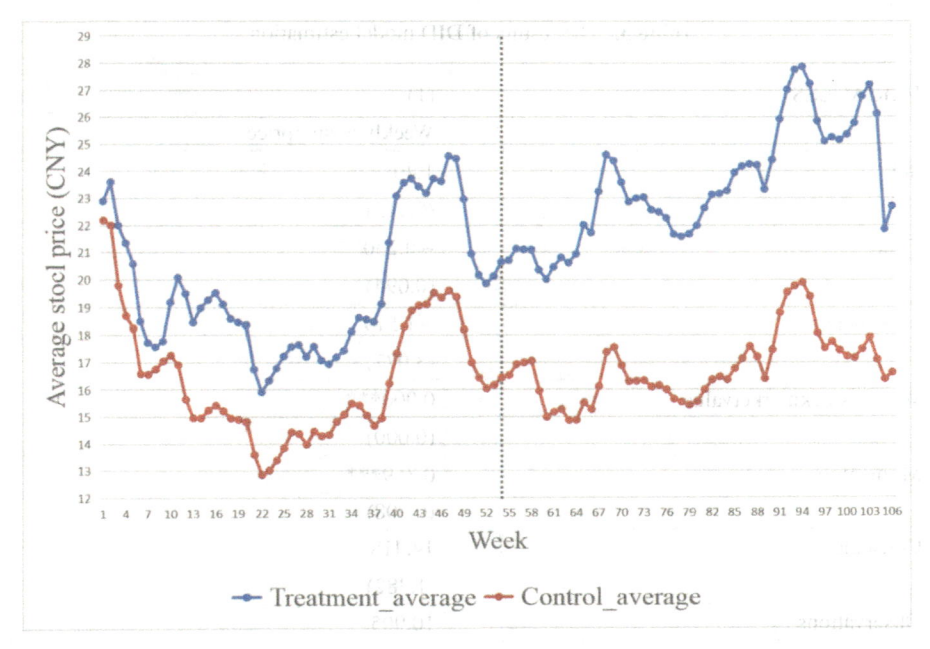

Fig. 1. Parallel trend test diagram.

treatment group and the control group widened. This result can be judged to satisfy the assumption of a double-difference parallel trend.

3.2 Analysis of Results

This paper assess the weekly average share price of the sample companies by using difference-in-differences model, and Table 3 presents the regression results. The regression result shows that, at the 1% level of significance, the coefficient of the core explanatory variable *did* is significantly positive, with a coefficient of 1.408. The coefficient indicates that the event has a certain positive effect on the company's share price to a certain extent. The reason for this situation is: after the issuance of licenses, the relevant companies will accelerate the pace of construction of 5G networks, driving the common development of the entire industry [10]. Investors will be keenly aware of this market change and hold optimistic expectations for 5G-related stocks, so they will buy shares and raise the stock price.

3.3 Placebo Test

The results in Sects. 2.1 and 2.2 present that the enforcement of the policy did produce a policy effect. At the same time, it can say that there was no obvious difference between the experimental and control groups before the implementation of the policy. However, it is unknown whether the policy effect shown by the difference-in-differences model was also influenced by other factors, and therefore a placebo test is required.

Table 3. The results of DID model estimation.

VARIABLES	(1)
	Weeklyclosingprice
did	1.408***
	(0.213)
Time	−0.230**
	(0.094)
Treatment	−1.519
	(3.077)
Weeklystockmarketvalue	0.000***
	(0.000)
Momentum	0.359***
	(0.008)
Constant	14.418***
	(1.382)
Observations	10,905
Number of Code	104

Notes: *** $p < 0.01$, ** $p < 0.05$, * $p < 0.1$

Many people narrow the sample to the the time period before the policy was occurred and randomize another policy implementation time to have placebo testing. The sample for this article is week 1 to week 106 and the policy implementation time is week 54. Hence, this placebo assumes that the policy happpened before week 54. Similar to Yue's [11] and Wang's [12] placebo test in 2019, this research sets the placebo test sample between week 1 and week 54 and sets the policy implementation time at week 25. As the results in Table 4, the coefficient on *did_new* is insignificant and even negative. Such results allow for the exclusion of other potentially unobservable factors, which means the policy effects estimated in this article are robust.

Table 4. Placebo test result.

VARIABLES	(1)
	Weeklyclosingprice
did_new	
	−0.195
	(0.241)
Time	−1.021***
	(0.111)
Treatment	−2.021
	(2.671)
Weeklystockmarketvalue	0.000***
	(0.000)
Momentum	0.283***
	(0.008)
Constant	14.629***
	(1.199)
Observations	5,512
Number of Code	104

Notes: Standard errors in parentheses. *** $p < 0.01$, ** $p < 0.05$, * $p < 0.1$

4 Conclusion

This article has tested the implementation effect of the 5G commercial licensing policy using a difference-in-differences model based on panel data on the weekly average share prices of companies with a strong association with the 5G concept and selected companies in the telecommunications industry for the period 2018–2020. Here are the main findings:

First, the issuance of 5G commercial licenses has a extremely positive relationship with the stock prices of the relevant companies. Second, the positive impact of this policy on companies effectively promotes the commercialization of 5G in China and facilitates China's adaptation to the accelerated development of 5G globally. Third, the rapid development of 5G networks will meet the demand for better network services from users in multiple industries in China and help economic development.

In summary, small and medium-sized investors should actively pay attention to policy trends in the investment process, in order to gain excess returns from them. In the future, investors can also actively pay attention to 5G-related policies released by relevant authorities to explore investment opportunities. At the same time, small and medium-sized investors should also strengthen their analysis ability of data-level information to enhance their investment judgment. There is no doubt that the issuance of 5G commercial licenses has brought positive excess returns to the communications industry as a whole, but through analysis, researchers can see that the issuance of 5G commercial licenses has only had a significant positive impact on companies with a high correlation to the 5G concept. Therefore, after deciding to invest in a certain industry, investors should understand and analyze more at the data level to understand the nature, size, operation, profitability, and future development prospects of different companies.

In addition, government, as the policy maker and promulgator, any decree issued by the government can have a significant impact on the whole market. In this way, it is important for the government to ensure that its policies are precise and clear such as when policies will take effect and whom policies will be directed. So that, policies can be accurately understood by all parties in the market. At the same time, the government has an obligation to ensure that policies are issued in a timely manner. The government should make its policies public on official paths in time to reduce market anxiety and panic due to uncertainty. Finally, the government should also ensure continuity of policy. The government should ensure that the implementation of its policies is in place to demonstrate its determination to achieve them. For example, in this case, the issuance of 5G commercial licenses was preceded by a number of policies related to 5G development by MIIT and other relevant departments, so that the issuance of 5G commercial licenses did not appear abrupt. Only by ensuring continuity of policy, investors and related businesses will be more likely to agree with the government's policy objectives, and market forces will continue to move towards a common goal.

References

1. Li, J.: A study on the current status of 5G technology development. Wirel. Connect. Technol. **17**(1), 12–13 (2020)
2. Zhu, H.: The Impact of Investors' Attention on the Market Performance of 5G Concept Stocks. Harbin Institute of Technology, Harbin (2021)
3. Shi, Q.: Research on the Impact of 5G Commercial License Issuance on the Stock Returns of 5G Communication Industry. Southwest University of Science and Technology, Mianyang (2021)
4. Lei, T., Yu, S.: The impact of unexpected events on stock prices. China Bus. J, **2021**(1), 88–89 (2021)
5. Fan, Q., Wang, T.: The impact of Shanghai-Hong Kong Stock Connect policy on A-H share price premium. Finan. Res. Lett. **21**, 222–227 (2017)
6. Lechner, M.: The estimation of causal effects by difference-in-difference methods. Found. Trends Econ. **4**, 165–224 (2011)
7. Wang, D., Li, M.: Carbon reduction effects based on a double difference model. J. Hebei Univ. Geosci. **45**(4), 104–109 (2022)
8. Lu, J., Yan, Y., Wang, T.: A study on the micro effects of green credit policy: a perspective of technological innovation and resource reallocation. China Ind. Econ. **1**, 174–192 (2021)
9. Murphy, J. J.: Technical analysis of the financial markets: a comprehensive guide to trading methods and applications (1999)
10. China builds world's largest 5G network three years after issuance of 5G commercial li-cences. SyndiGate Media Inc. 11. (2022)
11. Lu, Y., Lu, Y., Wu, S., et al.: The outbound investment promotion effect of the "Belt and Road" initiative: a double-difference test based on Chinese firms' greenfield investment from 2005 to 2016. Econ. Res. **54**(624(09)), 189–204 (2019)
12. Wang, Y., Wu, H.: How innovative monetary policy works in China: the collateral channel. Econ. Stud. **54**(12), 86–101 (2019)

Socio-Economic Determinants of National Saving in Pakistan

Munir Ahmad[1(✉)] and Asghar Ali[2]

[1] School Education Department Punjab, Jhang, Pakistan
munirahmad5489@gmail.com
[2] University of Agriculture Faisalabad, Faisalabad, Pakistan
asghar.ali@uaf.edu.pk

Abstract. Savings have energetic role in growth of an economy. A vigorous saving rate is very significant component, which is part of all major economies of the world. The socio-economic determinants of saving in Pakistan were determined in present study. It used time span of 1973–2018 in case of Pakistan. We applied Autoregressive Distributive Lag Approach (ARDL) for long run co-integration and Error Correction Model (ECM) for short run empirical estimation. Two models were used to estimate economic and social impact on National Saving in Pakistan. The empirical results indicated that the Gross Domestic Product, Government's Current Expenditure, Fiscal Deficit, Worker's Remittances, Unemployment rate and Inflation rate determined the saving rate in Pakistan. Whereas Demographic variable Age Dependency Ratio, Government Size, Urban Population, Rural Population found responsible social variable which determined saving in Pakistan. As per empirical results, it is found that the GDP,, government current expenditure, interest rate, workers remittance, fiscal deficit, inflation rate, and unemployment rate have both short and long run effect on national savings. It is suggested that fiscal and monetary tools should be used efficiently to handle the economic factors positively as improvement in GDP, reduction in inflation rate and unemployment rate that heavily influenced national saving rate in Pakistan.

Keywords: National saving · ARDL · Determinants · Social factors · fiscal deficit · remittances

1 Introduction

The most important and good thing in any economy of a nation is its saving that can play a vital rate its financial welfare. A healthy saving rate is very important element which all major economies of the world have. Investment is like a fuel for any growing economy. Savings play very important role for the betterments of any economy and it is essential for it. Keynesian is also of the view that whatever a nation saves is invested later on. The national savings are indirectly basis of the new capital. All the major economies of the world are top saver like USA, China and Japan. The most important element in the development of any economy is savings of any nation. Macroeconomics instability is

© The Author(s), under exclusive license to Springer Nature Singapore Pte Ltd. 2024
X. Li et al. (Eds.): ICEMGD 2023, AEPS, pp. 1649–1663, 2024.
https://doi.org/10.1007/978-981-97-0523-8_149

major issue of Pakistan economy now basic reason of slow economic growth in Pakistan is the insufficient saving rate. High level of consumption is the main reason behind the low savings in Pakistan Agarwal [1], Antonino and Yallwe [2].

The Harrod-Domar theory emphasizes the importance of saving levels and capital out ratios in economic growth. Capital stock saving is crucial for capital accumulation and social relations. Savings impact productivity, consumption, and income distribution. It is crucial to identify factors affecting national savings. Pakistan's culture is redirected, leading to arrogance, squandering, and imbalanced expenditures Ahmad and Asghar [3].

Pakistan's low saver rate, at 21.4% of GDP, negatively impacts the country's economy and development. The country's financial institutions struggle to change saving patterns, and Pakistan seeks to raise domestic saving rates to influence foreign savings and invest in human and physical capital. Attansio et al. [4].

During 2003–07, foreign inflows boosted Pakistan's economy, but failed to increase domestic investment, despite high income rates and domestic savings. Antonino and Yallwe [2], Ahmad and Asghar [3], Attansio et al. [4].

Pakistan should take steps to boost domestic savings and attract FDI to address low trends. National savings are essential for an economy's growth, but low saving rates have led to a shortage of capital. Despite reaching 7.3% in real GDP, this acceleration has turned into deceleration. Salma et al. [5].

In long term low level of saving rate has been possibility economy move in to vicious circle of low investment, low growth rate, low productivity and ultimately low per capita income. On other hand, high saving rate can boost up by high capital, high investment, high productivity and high growth rate. Savings lead to economic growth as it has noticeable effect on the economic growth rate, also higher savings had to capital growth. Savings are considered by the government savings in public sector and savings produced by public sector enterpriser in the form of internal resources. Personal savings is defined when the people consume less than their income then financial market can channelized from lender saver to borrower-spender or these savings can be used by the saver for social purposes Attanasio et al. [4], Khalid and Mahmood [6].

Pakistan's economy almost has regular budget deficit throughout its history. It has an average saving rate; saving rate during 70s and 80's was pertly rash. In the decade of 1970s average savings was counted 9.44% to GDP Ahmad and Asghar [3].

Pakistan's average saving rate was 8.74% in the 1980s, leading to the launch of Structural Adjustment Programs (SAP) to address budget imbalances. The government modernized the National Savings Scheme, fixed interest rates, and introduced tax breaks to encourage savers. The saving rate increased significantly in the early 1990s, reaching 17.5% in 1991. The average saving rate from 2000 to 2020 was 9.3%, with the highest rate in 2004 and the lowest in 2019.Agarwal [1], Ahmad and Asghar [3], Khalid and Mahmood [6].

1.1 Theoretic Framework of National Savings

National Savings can be divided into private and public sectors, including household and corporate savings. Public sector savings are collected by government and enterprises. Personal saving occurs when spending is under income, and funds can be used for social causes through the financial market.

The amount of undistributed corporate profits is called Business savings. It can be measured Such as follows.

$$\text{Income Identity} = Y = C + I + G + NX \quad (1)$$

The amount of money that is left over after a nation has consumed or expended all of its resources is known as national saving. Anything that is not spent in a free market is presumed to be saved and subsequently invested:

$$NS = Y - C - G - NX = I \quad (2)$$

$$Y - C - G = N.S = I + NX \quad (3)$$

As national savings are consisted on private and public savings, we can divide it into its components, by inducing Taxes (t) into the above equation.

We get:

$$[(Y - T) - C] + [T - G] = I + NX \quad (4)$$

(Y − T) In Eq. (4) is disposable income without consumption expenditure (C) is private savings such as [(Y − T) − C]. Public saving comprises on government revenue minus government expenditure (T-G). Taxes (T) are the amount which is paid by the people to Government. If in an economy the revenue of government income are more its expenditures, this particular situation is called Budget Surplus. On other hand the situation in which expenditures are greater than income is called Budget deficit. In case of surplus budget, savings of any economy are positive and on other situation of deficit budget, saving is negative. It also called dis-saving condition.

Pakistan's budget deficit has led to low public sector savings, causing significant variation in the economy. The 1990s structural Adjustment Program improved financial sector rehabilitation, but private savings never became negative. Husain [7].

2 Review of Literature

A lot of studies comprise on national and international economies had been reviewed in current paper. Some previous studies were reviewed on private savings and others were on public savings.

Jilani et al. [8], Shaheen et al. [9], Matur et al. [10], Nasir and Khalid [11], Narayan and Siyabi [12], Khan et al. [13], Gleizer [14] highlighted the association between Gross Domestic Production and Savings. They found positive relationship between GDP and Savings.

According to Khan et al. [13] Per capita income and Age dependency ratio had indirect influence over saving. Real interest rate has positive correlation with national saving. In Jilani et al. [8] it is also found inverse relation between Fiscal deficit, inflation rate and interest rate with national saving. In Dipietro [15] it is estimated the negative impact of Government Size over national saving. Narayan and Siyabi [12] also presented positive correlation between national income and national saving.

In Nasir and Mahmood [11] it is also revealed direct Government Current Expenditure and interest relationship with national saving. Vicelette [16] argued that if Pakistan wanted to sustain its growth and increase its investment, it has to increase its national saving. It may ultimate increase its gross domestic production. Gleizer [14] estimated two different models by using explanatory variable real GDP, real foreign saving per capita and real interest rate. Carbone [17] used panel data and found negative effect of dependency ration over national saving. Habbel and Luis [18] presented that world saving rate is getting decrease gradually due to increase in consumption.

In Sajid and Sarfraz [19] there was found that long run causality occurs from GDP to private saving. Farhan and Akram [20] presented negative relationship between inflation, age dependency ratio and saving and positive correlation between income and saving. Ahmad and Asghar [3] showed negative association between exchange rate and national saving. Matur et al. [10] also found inverse relation with saving. Teshome et al. [21] designated that 79.2% of his respondent had household saving. Shaheen et al. [9] showed negative correlation between trade openness and national saving.

3 Materials and Methods

3.1 Data Source

For the empirical study, the data set from 1973 to 2018 was employed. The information obtained from a number of sources, including the World Development Indicators (WDI), the International Financial Statistics (IFS), the State Bank of Pakistan, the 2015 Handbook of Statistics Review, and several issues of the Pakistani Economic Surveys. WDI [22].

3.2 Descriptions of the Data and Variables

The dependent variable in this study, National Saving (NS) is used in both of the models. GDP is summation of Market value of all goods and services produced in a country.

Data is in percent of GDP. The difference of payments made to domestic individuals from foreigner and foreign individuals to domestic citizen are termed as net foreign factor income in the economy.

The total government revenues minus total expenditures are defined as Budget Deficits (BD). If expedite are more than incomes this has negative value and called Budget deficit whereas If it has positive value then there is a budget surplus Hutchison [23]. Government Current Expenditures (GCE) represented by variable "The general government final consumption expenditures: It is taken as a proxy of GCE because the general govt. Final consumption (GGFC) expenditures are more reliable and near to the definition of government current expenditure that can be used as proxy variable in place of Government Current Expenditure (GCE). These (GGFC) expenditures are the summation of all current expenditures of government for purchases of goods and services. These expenditures are also included compensation of employees, national defense and security. But it did not include the government military expenditures. The interest rate imposed by the banks on their loans is called Interest Rate (IR) Desroches and Francis

[24]. The cost of living is termed as Inflation Rate (INF). Inflation is represented by Consumer Price Index (CPI).

All transfers made to persons who have moved to other economies and who have jobs or plan to keep them for more than a year. Some developing nations classify worker remittances as factor income receipts, making them a part of gross national income (GNI). The World Bank observed a worldwide definitional framework for GNI. Therefore, it is possible that the association of employees' remittances would vary from national customs.

The second model consisting on social factors affecting national saving are Age Dependency Ratio, Government size, Urban and Rural population. Age dependency ratio is demographic variable. It is ratio of number of dependence have age interval below than 15 year to older than 64 to working age people Bossworth and Chodrow-Reich [25]. For instance, if the value of ADR is 0.8, its means that 8 people are dependent out of 10 working people. The second variable in social model is Government Size (GS). It is tough to measure in numerical form. So we use a proxy to calculate the government size is 'the ratio of government spending and GDP' Dipietro [15]. These spending are consumptions and investment of a government. Rural population is the population living in rural areas of Pakistan and is calculated difference between total population and urban population. The part of population living in small or big cities in Pakistan is called urban population Bossworth and Chodrow-Reich [25].

3.3 Empirical Model

The Review of Literature postulated that there should be a healthy econometric model. All major social and economic determinants of national savings in Pakistan are broadly included in the econometric model. This is reason of creating two separated models comprising on social and economic model. The social model highlighted the relationship between social variables and national savings and on the other second model showing the relationships of economic variables and national savings in Pakistan. The reason behind the two separate models is to estimate social and economic determinant separately. This act will provide saving behavior in Pakistan separately.

This regression will give a comprehensive understanding of saving structure in Pakistan.

3.4 Model of Economic Savings in the Nation

Every significant variable that has an impact on national savings is addressed in the economic model. It comprised the following metrics: Gross Domestic Product (GDP), Budget Deficit (BD), Interest Rate (IR), Government Current Expenditure (GCE), Inflation Rate (INF), and Worker's Remittances (WR).

$$NS_t = \beta_0 + \beta_1 GDP_t + \beta_2 GCE_t + \beta_3 FD_t + \beta_4 WR_t + \beta_5 INF_t + IR_t + \epsilon_t \quad (5)$$

3.5 Social Model of National Saving

Through previous literature it was come to know that it is very important to discuss the impact social factors on national savings in Pakistan. We analyzed some social factors such as Government Size (GS), Demographic variable Age Dependency Ratio (ADR), Urban and Rural population

$$NS_t = \beta_0 + \beta_1 GS_t + \beta_2 ADR_t + \beta_3 RPOP_t + \beta_4 UPOP_t + \epsilon_t \qquad (6)$$

where $\beta_1 < 0, \beta_2 < 0, \beta_3 < 0$ and $\beta_4 < 0 / \beta_3 > 0$.

3.6 Empirical Estimation Techniques

In this study, we aimed to draw attention to the economic and social aspects that influence national saving. Co-integration may be done using a variety of methods, including Engle and Granger [26], Pesaran et al. [27], Pesaran and Pesaran [28] and the Auto Regressive Distributive Lagged Model (ARDL). Ordinary Least Squares is the test used in ARDL. Based on the findings of the Augmented Dickey Fuller Test, we used the Auto Regressive Distributive Lag Model in this article. The findings of the ADF test revealed that the stationarity level varies to some extent. Some variables remain constant at their current level, while others remain constant at the initial difference level. This stationarity property recommended that we use the ARDL approach to verify co-integration. Another benefit of the Auto Regressive Distributive Lag Model is that it might take a few lags to fully represent the data generation process in the general-to-specific level modeling framework Laurencesen and Chai [29].

Firstly, we applied Augmented Dickey Fuller Test Dickey and Fuller [30], Dickey and Fuller [31] for unit root. The assumption of Bound Test is that the variable included in the model must be integrated at Level and or First difference I(0), I(1) respectively. If any variable that is integrated at 2nd difference in the model then the F-Statistics provide spurious results Pesaran et al. [28], Ouattara [32].

Table 1. Unit Root

Variable	T-Value	Prob	Level
National Saving	−2.6213	[0.0962]	I(0)
GDP	−4.6102	[0.0005]	I(0)
GCE	−8.3126	[0.0000]	I(1)
Inflation	−3.4326	[0.0148]	I(0)
Fiscal Deficit	−3.0504	[0.0378]	I(0)
Interest Rate	−8.3016	[0.0000]	I(1)
Worker's Remittances	−8.0372	[0.0000]	I(1)
Government Size	−5.4495	[0.0000]	I(0)
Urban Population	−4.0001	[0.0034]	I(1)
Rural Population	−5.3745	[0.0001]	I(1)
Age Dependency Ratio	−4.4849	[0.0000]	I(1)

(*), (**) and (***) shows significance @ 1%, 5% and 10% respectively.

Table 2. Statistics for Lag Length t Test Selection

Model 1	Akaike Information Criteria	Schwarz Criteria	Log Likelihood
Lag 1	27.42*	29.60*	−560.91*
Lag 2	28.00	32.26	−511.12
Model 2			
Lag 1	9.2122*	10.4167*	−177.2823*
Lag 2	9.6436	11.8739	−157.1590
Lag 3	9.4765	12.7533	−123.7467

(*) shows the maximum lag to be selected.

4 Empirical Outcome

The Augmented Dickey Fuller Test was used to determine the stationarity of the variables, and the results are shown in Table 1. The findings demonstrated that certain variables are discovered at first difference level I(1) and some are stationary at level I(0).

The dependent variable, national saving, is stationary at level with a t-statistic at a 10% level of significance, as indicated in the table above. As a result, the GDP, inflation, fiscal deficit, and government size are all stable at the same level, with t-values of − 4.6102, −3.4326, −3.0504, and −5.4495 at 1%, 5%, and 10%, respectively.

Government Current Expenditure (GCE), Interest rate, Worker's Remittances, Urban and Rural Population and Age Dependency Ratio are stationary at first level of significance I(1) having t-values of −8.3126, −8.0372, −4.001, −5.3745, and −4.4849 respectively at 1%, 5% and 10%.

Later on, we applied Pesaran and Pesaran [28] presented Autoregressive Distributed Lag Model. We also applied Akaike Information Criterion (AIC), Schwarz Bayesian Criterion (SBC) and Hannan-Quinn Criterion (HQC) for the selection of number of lags.

The most significant lag duration for the economic model and social model in Table 2 above was shown to be 1. Three separate tests, including the Schwarz Criterion, the Akaike Information criterion, and the Log Likelihood, were used to corroborate the lag length basis. The models of economic and social forces have the same optimum lags that minimize the Schwarz Criteria. In order to estimate the model of economic and social aspects, the Auto Regressive Distributive Lag technique to co-integration was used once the best lag length had been determined.

Table 3. Autoregressive Distributed Lag (ARDL) Estimates

Repressors	Coefficient	Standard Error	T-Ratio	[Prob]
NS(−1)	0.385*	0.113	3.397	[0.002]
GDP	0.229***	0.174	1.316	[0.096]
GDP(−1)	0.316***	0.175	1.812	[0.078]
GCE	0.085**	0.161	0.529	[0.060]
FD	−0.269	0.194	−1.391	[0.173]
WR	0.373**	0.163	2.291	[0.028]
Inflation	−0.179*	0.064	2.808	[0.008]
IR	−0.338*	0.121	−2.794	[0.008]
C	16.059*	2.889	5.558	[0.000]
R Square	0.86	Adjusted R Square		0.77
Akaike Info. Criterion	−95.51	Schwarz Bayesian Criterion		−103.64
DW-statistic	2.08	Equation Log-likelihood		−86.51

(*), (**) and (***) shows significance @ 1%, 5% and 10% respectively.

Table 4. Wald Test

Test Statistic	Value	Df	Probability
F-statistic	109.533	(6, 40)	0.000
Chi-square	657.20	6	0.000

In Table 3, results of Auto Regressive Distributed Lag Model are presented. GDP, Government Current Expenditure, Worker's Remittances, Inflation and Interest rate have significant impact on National Savings in Pakistan. The R^2 of current estimation is 86% which is indication of goodness fit of the model and adjusted R2 value found 0.77, it means that 77% of the determinants of national saving in Pakistan captured in

Table 5. Diagnostic Tests

	Test Applicable	CHISQ (1)	Prob.
Serial correlation	Lagrange multiplier	0.3352	[0.611]
Functional form	Ramsey's reset test	2.5693	[0.154]
Normality	Test of skewness and kurtosis	0.6119	[.000]
Hetroscedasticity	White test	0.4708	[0504]

current model. The value of lag of national saving has positive and significant impact on dependent variable. GDP, lag value of GDP, GCE, WR have direct relationship with dependent variable national saving with coefficient values of 0.229, 0.316, 0.085 and 0.373 respectively. These values are significant at 1%, 5% and 10% level of significant.

One percent change in GDP will bring 0.229% increase in National savings in Pakistan. Government Current Expenditure also has direct correlation with dependent variable. One percent change in GCE will increase 0.085% in national savings. Because of private savings in Pakistan are high throughout the history, that's why the Government current expenditures are positively impact on saving. Worker's Remittances has also positive and significant effect on national savings. It means one percent increase in worker's remittances will bring 0.373% increase in national savings in Pakistan. When the magnitude of Worker's Remittances go high, it increase the Money Supply of an economy and ultimately the saving rate getting on up gradually due to MPC that is always less than 1. People consume less and save more.

The results of the studies like Modigilani [33]. In Jilani et al. [8], Salma et al. [5], Athurkorela and Sen [34], Paiva and Jahan [35], and Nurudeen [36] results were showed similar correlations as showed in this study. Interest Rate, Inflation rate, and Fiscal Deficit have negative and significant influence on national saving. The coefficient values are −0.338, −0.179, −0.269 respectively at 1%, 5% and 10% level of significant.

Rate of interest have both effect on saving, positive or negative. In this it shows negative impact, it means when rate of interest go on it will reduce saving and vice versa. Inflation rate increase the level of prices and due to this consumption level increase and magnitude of MPC increase and MPS decrease. In Gleizer [14], Paiva and Jahan [35], Nurudeen [36] and Gale and Orszag [37] same results found that there is insignificant impact of interest rate on national savings. Jilani et al. [8], Engle and Granger [26] have also same results as in the present research.

In Table 4 "Wald test" results are presented. The calculated F-Statistics is 109.533and is significant at 1% level of significant. These results are showing that there is cointegration relationship among the variables. F−statistics is also highly significant which indicated overall goodness of fit.

Table 5 is showing Diagnostic tests that there is no econometric problem such as autocorrelation, conflict to normal distribution existed in current model. There is not Hetroscedasticity in the model. Similarly, no model specification bias existed with reference to functional form as well.

In Table 6 the results of Long run coefficient under ARDL approach are presented. GDP, IR, Inflation, and Worker's Remittances are statistically significant having 0.886, −0.549, −0.293 and 0.608 respectively. Fiscal deficits and Government Current Expenditure are not statistically significant.

Table 6. Estimated Long Run Coefficients, using the ARDL Approach

Regressor	Coefficient	Standard Error	T Ratio	Prob.
GDP	0.886	0.3378	2.624	0.013
GCE	0.139	0.255	0.544	0.590
IR	−0.549	0.162	−3.384	0.002
FD	−0.438	0.300	−1.460	0.153
INF	−0.293	0.111	−2.627	0.013
WR	0.608	0.244	2.485	0.018
C	26,112	3.134	8.329	0.000

(*), (**) and (***) shows significance @ 1%, 5% and 10% respectively

Table 7. Error Correction Mechanisms for the Selected ARDL Model

Regressor	Coefficient	Standard Error	T-Ratios	Prob.
dGDP	0.229***	0.174	2.316	[[0.096]
dGCE	0.085**	0.161	0.529	[0.060]
dFD	−0.269	0.94	−1.391	[0.173]
dWR	0.374**	0.164	2.291	[0.028]
dINF	−0.179*	0.064	−2.808	[0.008]
dIR	−0.338*	0.121	−2.793	[0.008]
Ecm (−1)	−0.615*	0.113	−5.426	[0.000]

(*), (**) and (***) shows significance @ 1%, 5% and 10% respectively.

$$ECM = NS + 0.8866 * GDP + 0.1388 * GCE + 0.4382 * FD - 0.6075 * WR + 0.0.2926 * INF - 0.5490 * IR - 26.112 * C.1.3$$

(7)

In Table 7 it shows the short term relationship of workers' remittances, Fiscal deficit, interest rate, inflation rate GDP and Government Current Expenditure are significant relationship with national saving, with coefficient 0.374, −0.338, −0.179, 0.229 and 0.085 significant at 1%, 5% and 10% level of significant respectively. Agarwal [1], Attanasio et al. [4], and Sajid and Sarfraz [19] also showed same relationships. The rate

Table 8. Autoregressive Distributed Lag Estimates

Regressor	Coefficient	Standard Error	T-Ratio	[Prob.]
NS(−1)	0.459	0.138	3.3264	[0.002]
RPOP	−0.060	0.123	−0.493	[0.623]
UPOP	−0.374	0.132	−2.843	[0.007]
ADR	−0.006	0.069	−1.093	[0.027]
GS	0.835	0.877	0.953	[0.046]
R^2	0.75		Adjusted R^2	0.72
DW-Stats	1.87		F-Stat (4, 40)	[0.000]

(*), (**) and (***) shows significance @ 1%, 5% and 10% respectively.

Table 9. Wald Test

Test Statistic	Value	Df	Probability
F-statistic	620.1494	(4, 42)	[0.0000]
Chi-square	2458.59	4	[0.0000]

Table 10. Diagnostic Tests

	Test Applicable	CHSQ	Probabilities
Serial correlation	Lagrange multiplier	0.0062	[0.937]
Functional form	Ramsey's reset test	2.271	[0.132]
Normality	Test of skewness and kurtosis	1.256	[0.534]
Hetroscedasticity	White test	3.051	[0.810]

Table 11. Estimated Long Run Coefficients, using the ARDL Approach

Regressor	Coefficient	Standard Error	T Ratio	Prob.
RPOP	−0.1123	0.2273	−0.494	[0.624]
UPOP	0.6925	0.1687	4.105	[0.000]
ADR	−0.0118	0.1282	−0.092	[0.027]
GS	1.5456	1.6992	0.909	[0.368]

(*), (**) and (***) shows significance @ 1%, 5% and 10% respectively.

of interest found insignificant in both short and long run. Many previous studies are also supportive to this result.

Table 12. Error Correction Representations for the Selected ARDL Model

Regressor	Coefficient	Standard Error	T-Ratios	Prob.
dRPOP	−0.0607	0.1232	−0.4928	[0.625]
dUPOP	0.3744	0.1317	2.8432	[0.007]
dADR	−0.0064	0.0692	0.0623	[0.927*]
dGS	0.8356	0.8770	1.9528	[0.046]
Ecm(−1)	−0.5406	0.1381	−0.3.91	[0.000]*

(*), (**) and (***) shows significance @ 1%, 5% and 10% respectively.

Engle and Granger [26] presented the Error Correction Mechanism (ECM) meant that the integration the behavior of economic in short-run variables with its long-run behavior. It is one period lag value of error terms. ECM is gotten from the long-run correlation. Whereas the ECM (−1) value captures the adjustment from short to long run period.

In short run, ECM determined the speed of adjustments from long run equilibrium. The constant value of ECM (−1) pointed out the adjustment process of disequilibrium towards equilibrium in long run. In current study, the value of ECM (−1) −0.61 is negative and statistically significant. This coefficient value showed that the adjustment process is quit fast. It means 61% will readjust this as compare to last year Engle and Granger [26].

4.1 Empirical Analysis for Social Model

In this section the analysis of social model are presented. The results are generated by applying Auto Regressive Distributive lag approach. According to Schwarz Criterion the lag length is lag one to be appropriate lag length.

In Table 8, results of Auto Regressive Distributed Lag Model are presented. GDP, Government Current Expenditure, Worker's Remittances, Inflation and Interest rate have significant impact on National Savings in Pakistan. The R^2 of current estimation is 75% which is indication of goodness fit of the model and adjusted R^2 value found 0.72, it means that 72% of the determinants of national saving in Pakistan captured in current model.

The value of lag of national saving has positive and significant impact on dependent variable. Rural population, Urban Population, and Age Dependency Ratio have indirect relationship with dependent variable national saving with coefficient values of 0.0.0607, 0.374, and 0.0.0064 respectively. These values are significant at 1%, 5% and 10% level of significant.

One percent change in Rural Population will bring 0.0.60% decrease in National savings in Pakistan. Urban Population also has indirect correlation with dependent variable. One percent change in urban population will decrease 0.0.374% in national savings. Age Dependency Ratio has also negative and significant effect on national savings. It means one percent increase in Age Dependency Ratio will bring 0.0.006% decrease in national savings in Pakistan.

Government Size has positive relationship because government size consists on government consumption divided by gross domestic product. Due to high consumption trend in urban areas and high migration trend from rural to urban areas it is insignificant. And government size positive and significant relationship with national saving in Pakistan Dipietro [15].

In Table 9 "Wald test" of Social Model results are presented. The calculated F-Statistics is 620.149 and is significant at 1% level of significant. These results are showing that there is co-integration relationship among the variables. The overall goodness of fit is showed by F –statistics which is also highly significant and indication of good ft.

Table 10 is showing Diagnostic tests of social factors that there is no econometric problem such as autocorrelation, conflict to normal distribution existed in current model. There is not Hetroscedasticity in the model. Similarly, no model specification bias existed with reference to functional form as well.

In Table 11 the results of Social Model's Long run coefficient under ARDL approach are presented. RPOP, UPOP, ADR, and Government Size are statistically significant having -0.1123, 0.6925, -0.0118 and 1.5456 respectively. Rural Population and Government Size are not statistically significant (Table 12).

$$ECM = NS - 0.1123 * RPOP - 0.6925 * UPOP + 0.011854 * ADR - 1.5456 * GS \quad (8)$$

In Table 7 it shows the short term relationship of Urban Population and Government Size are significant relationship with national saving, with coefficient 0.374, and 0.8356 significant at 1%, and 5% level of significant respectively. It is also observed that Rural Population and Age Dependency Ratio are insignificant in long run as well as in short run.

Engle and Grangle presented the Error Correction Mechanism (ECM) meant that the integration the behavior of economic in short-run variables with its long-run behavior. It is one period lag value of error terms. ECM is gotten from the long-run correlation. Whereas the ECM (-1) value captures the adjustment from short to long run period.

In short run, ECM determined the speed of adjustments from long run equilibrium. The constant value of ECM (-1) pointed out the adjustment process of disequilibrium towards equilibrium in long run. In current study, the value of ECM (-1) -0.54 is negative and statistically significant. This coefficient value showed that the adjustment process is quit fast. It means 54% will readjust this as compare to last year Engle and Granger [26].

The coefficient of ECM term showed that 54% of the disequilibrium of last year in national saving will adjust this year.

5 Conclusion and Policy Recommendation

In this study, we determined the social and economic factors of national savings in Pakistan. As indicated earlier, Pakistan is low level of saving country because it has consumption loving population/nation Gale and Orszag [37], Financial Stability Review [38]. We applied Autoregressive Distributive Lag Model (ARDL) for long run and Error Correction Mechanism (ECM) for short run dynamics and speed of adjustment respectively.

According to our results Gross Domestic Product, Worker's Remittances, Government Size and Government Current Expenditure have positive impact on national saving, the dependent variable. Fiscal deficit, Inflation, Urban and Rural Population and interest rate have negative impact on national saving International Financial Statistics [39]. On the basis of our findings it is suggested that GDP should increase, due to foreign inflows it can be boosted up in the economy. Worker's Remittances can play an important role in this regard. Budget Deficit, Government Current Expenditure are negatively impact on national savings, so government should cut down their non-productive expenditure. New Jobs opportunities must bet created because of this urbanization could be controlled.

The trend of dependence must be minimized. The technical education should be given importance. People should be convinced to get technical education for productive activities while continuing their basic routine to bear their own daily basis expanses. For this concerned authorities must held workshops, highlighting the issue.

References

1. Agarwal, P.: The relation between saving and growth: co-integration and causality evidence from Asia. Appl. Econ. **33**, 499–513 (2001)
2. Antonino, B., Yallwe, A.H.: Fiscal deficit, national saving and Sustainability of economics growth in emerging economies: a dynamic GMM panel data approach. Int. J. Econ. Financ. Issues **2**, 126–140 (2012)
3. Ahmad, M., Asghar, T.: Estimation of saving behavior in Pakistan using micro data. Lahore J. Econ. **9**, 1–40 (2004)
4. Attanasio, O., Picci, L., Scorcu, A.: Saving, growth and investment. Rev. Econ. Stat. **82**, 182–211 (2000)
5. Salma, S., Ali, M.M., Maryam, F., Javed, F.: Impact of foreign capital inflows on domestic saving of Pakistan. Interdepend. J. Contemp. Res. Bus. **4**, 443–457 (2013)
6. Khalid, A., Mahmood, H.: Macroeconomics determinants of national savings revisited. a small open Pakistan economy. World Appl. Sci. J. **21**, 49–57 (2013)
7. Husain, A.M.: Private saving and its determinants: the case of Pakistan. Pak. Dev. Rev. **35**, 49–70 (1996)
8. Jilani, S., Salam, A.S., Azam, F.C., Ahsan, S.: Determinants of national saving in Pakistan: an explanatory study. Asian Soc. Sci. **9**, 254–262 (2013)
9. Shaheen, S., Ali, M.M.: Impact of foreign capital inflows on domestic saving of Pakistan. Interdisc. J. Contemp. Res. Bus. **4**(10), 443 (2013)
10. Matur, P.E., Ali, S., Seema, B.: Determinants of private savings and interaction between public and private savings in Turkey. Topics Middle East. Afr. Econ. **14**, 102–125 (2012)
11. Nasir, S., Khalid, M.: Saving-investment behavior in Pakistan: an empirical investigation. Pak. Dev. Rev. **43**, 665–680 (2004)
12. Narayan, P., Siyabi, S.A.L.: An empirical investigation of the determinants of Oman's national savings. Econ. Bull. **51**, 1–7 (2005)
13. Khan, H.A., Hasan, L., Afia, M.: Dependency ratio, foreign capital inflows and the rate of savings in Pakistan. Pak. Dev. Rev. **31**, 843–856 (1992)
14. Gleizer, L.D.: Saving and real interest rates in Brazil. In: International Monetary Fund, Econometrica. Handbook of Statistics 2010, vol. 9, pp. 63–92. State Bank of Pakistan (1991)
15. Dipietro, W.R.: Government size, government effectiveness, and national savings rates. J. Econ. Literat. **79**, 1–12 (2009)

16. Vicelette, G.A.: Determinants of savings in Pakistan, A World Bank Document: Working Paper Series Report, No.10, SASPR-10 (2006)
17. Carbone, E.: The effect of unemployment on saving. An experimental analysis with panel data, pp. 1–57. University of New York (2003)
18. Hebbel, S.K., Luis, S.: World saving: trends and Theories. Estodios De Economia **25**, 192–215 (1998)
19. Sajid, G.M., Sarfaraz, M.: Savings and economic growth in Pakistan: an issue of Causality. Pak. Dev. Rev. **46**, 17–36 (2008)
20. Farhan, M., Akram, M.: Does income level affect saving behavior in Pakistan: an ARDL approach to co-integration for empirical assessment. East J. Phycol. Bus. **3**, 62–72 (2011)
21. Teshome, G., Kassa, B., Emana, B., Haji, J.: Determinants of real household savings in Ethopia: the case of East Hararghe zone, Oromia regional state. J. Econ. Sustain. Dev. **4**, 66–77 (2013)
22. World Development Indicators (CD-ROM 2012, online). World Bank (2012)
23. Hutchison, M.M.: Budget policy and the decline of national saving revisited. Bank Int. Settle. **33**, 1–65 (1992)
24. Desroches, B., Francis, M.: World real interest rates: A global saving and investment perspective. International Department, Bank of Canada (2007)
25. Bossworth, B., Chodorow-Reich, G.: Saving and demographic change: the global dimension. In: 8th Annual Joint Conference on the Brookings Institution (2006)
26. Engle, R., Granger, C.: Co-integration and error correction: representation estimation and testing. Econometrica **55**, 251–276 (1987)
27. Pesaran, H.M., Shin, Y., Smith, J.R.: Bound testing approaches to the analysis of level relationships. J. Appl. Economet. **16**, 289–326 (2001)
28. Pesaran, M.H., Pesaran, B.: Micro.t 4.0: Interactive Econometric Analysis. Oxford University Press, Oxford (1997)
29. Laurenceson, J., Chai, J.C.H.: Financial Reform and Economic Development in China. Edward Elgar, Cheltenham (2003)
30. Dickey, D., Fuller, W.A.: Distribution of the estimates for autoregressive time series with Unit Root. J. Am. Stat. Assoc. **74**, 427–431 (1979)
31. Dickey, D., Fuller, W.: Likelihood ratio statistics for autoregressive time series with a unit root. Econometrica **49**, 1057–1072 (1981)
32. Ouattara, B.: Modeling the long run determinants of private investment in senigal", Centre for Research in Economic Development and International Trade (CREDIT), No. 04/05, University of Nottingham (2004)
33. Modigliani, F.: Life cycle, individual thrift and the wealth of Nations. Am. Econ. Rev. **76**, 297–313 (1986)
34. Athukorala, P.C., Sen, K.: The determinants of private savings in India. World Dev. **32**, 491–503 (2003)
35. Paiva, C., Jahan, S.: An empirical study of Private saving in Brazil. Braz. J. Polit. Econ. **23**, 121–132 (2003)
36. Nurudeen, A.: Saving-Economic growth nexus in Nigeria 1970–2007: Granger Causality and Co-integration analysis. Rev. Econ. Bus. Stud. **3**, 93–104 (2010)
37. Gale, W.G., Orszag, P.R.: Budget deficits, national saving, and interest rates. Brook. Pap. Econ. Act. **2**, 101–187 (2004)
38. Financial Stability Review. Trends in Financial Savings. State Bank of Pakistan, pp. 1–61 (2012)
39. International Financial Statistics. International Monetary Fund (2008)

Research on the Influence Mechanism of Experiential Interaction on Consumers' Impulsive Buying

Liang Chen(✉)

School of Business, Anhui University, Hefei 230039, Anhui, China
`liangc0301@163.com`

Abstract. The experiential interaction between consumers and merchants is an important method for increasing consumers' propensity to purchase in the context of consumption upgrades, and it is also an important factor that traditional offline supermarkets cannot disregard when attempting to reverse the situation. Experiential interaction is divided into four dimensions based on the S-O-R model, experiential marketing theory, and interactive marketing theory: sensory experiential interaction, emotional experiential interaction, entertainment experiential interaction, and behavioral experiential interaction. Price sensitivity plays a moderating and mediating function between interaction and consumer impulse purchases. The questionnaires were distributed to offline supermarkets in main cities of Anhui Province, and SPSS and AMOS were utilized for statistical analysis and hypothesis testing. The results indicate that flow experience partially mediates the relationship between experiential interaction and impulsive purchasing, while price sensitivity moderates the relationship between flow experience and impulsive purchasing.

Keywords: Experiential Interaction · Impulse Buying · SOR Theory · Flow Experience · Price Sensitivity

1 Introduction

Online shopping's convenience and speed have put offline supermarkets under more operational pressure. Community group purchasing at low prices, repeated epidemics, and cost rises have made offline supermarket development more difficult in recent years. According to the "2021 Supermarket Format Survey Bulletin" published by the China Chain Store and Franchise Association, 67.1% of supermarket companies' sales will decrease year-over-year in 2021, and 72.2% of companies' net profits will decrease in 2020 [1]. Traditional offline supermarkets must change to survive the fierce market competition. In the e-commerce era, Meng Chenyang studied traditional offline supermarkets' digital transformation tactics [2]. Traditional offline supermarkets' consumer-level transition has not been studied. Consumption is mostly by consumers. Numerous studies have shown that internet shoppers are influenced by external variables and impulsive.

Thus, would the external environment cause customers to make impulsive offline purchases? This article investigates how this phenomenon affects consumers' impulsive purchases through experiential interaction with merchants.

Environmental psychology's S-O-R model examines how environmental stimuli affect consumers' psychology and behavior [3]. This research proposes that consumers' flow experience and impulse purchasing behavior might be stimulated by merchants' experiential contact. Based on a literature analysis and classification, this research examines how flow experience and the S-O-R model affect customers' impulsive purchases. The Guotai Junan Securities special report on the consumer industry found that the younger generation not only owns strong consumption ability, dare to spend money, and price sensitivity is "the lowest in history" [4]. The offline supermarket survey also found that the younger generation is more likely to act on impulse purchase. This paper investigates the regulating effect of price sensitivity on consumers' impulsive purchases, enriches the relevant theories, and offers traditional offline supermarkets some guidance when seeking solutions.

2 Research Hypothesis

2.1 The Impact of Experiential Interaction on Impulsive Purchase

Sensory, emotional, entertaining, and behavioral experience involvement affects customers' buy intent [5]. Offline supermarkets buyers' sensory experience engagement leaves a lasting impression of the merchant's products and services. Offline shopping is emotional. Supermarket customers encounter emotional resonance, entertainment experiential engagement, and product-entertainment pairings. The extent to which consumers' offline shopping experiences change their purchase behavior and lifestyle [5]. Customers like brick-and-mortar supermarkets with distinctive designs. Consumer-merchant connections are engaged. Study hypothesizes:

H1: Experiential interaction has a significant positive impact on impulsive buying.

H1a: Sensory experiential interaction has a significant positive impact on impulsive buying.

H1b: Emotional experiential interaction has a significant positive impact on impulsive buying Significant positive effect.

H1c: Entertainment experiential interaction has a significant positive effect on impulsive buying.

H1d: Behavioral experiential interaction has a significant positive effect on impulsive buying.

2.2 The Mediating Role of Flow Experience

Hausman et al. found that the exterior environment motivates consumers and improves flow, boosting their buy propensity [6]. Another study found that offline marketing plus an intelligent purchasing experience provide a "immersive" shopping experience that influences consumer behavior [7]. Consumers' perception of products and purchasing behavior will be influenced by offline supermarket merchants' contentment and pleasure. Thus, experiential engagement between consumers and merchants can help generate consumers' flow experience, which might encourage impulsive buying. This study hypothesizes:

H2: Flow experience plays a mediating role in the impact of experiential interaction on impulsive buying.

H2a: Flow experience plays a mediating role in the impact of sensory experiential interaction on impulsive buying.

H2b: Heart Flow experience plays a mediating role in the impact of emotional experiential interaction on impulsive buying.

H2c: Flow experience plays a mediating role in the impact of entertainment experiential interaction on impulsive buying.

H2d: Flow experience mediates the effect of behavioral experiential interaction on impulsive buying Mediating effect of purchase.

2.3 Moderating Effect of Price Sensitivity

Consumer price sensitivity is how much they notice price changes [8]. Xiong Ying found that consumers with high price sensitivity had a reduced effect of consuming experience on consumer reconstruction behavior [9], while consumers with low price sensitivity have a considerable effect. This paper believes that after consumers have experiential interactions with merchants in offline supermarkets and have a flow experience, consumers with high price sensitivity will restrain their impulsive consumption behavior, while consumers with low price sensitivity will make more impulsive purchases. Thus, this paper hypothesizes:

H3: Price sensitivity plays a moderating role in the process of flow experience on impulsive buying (Fig. 1).

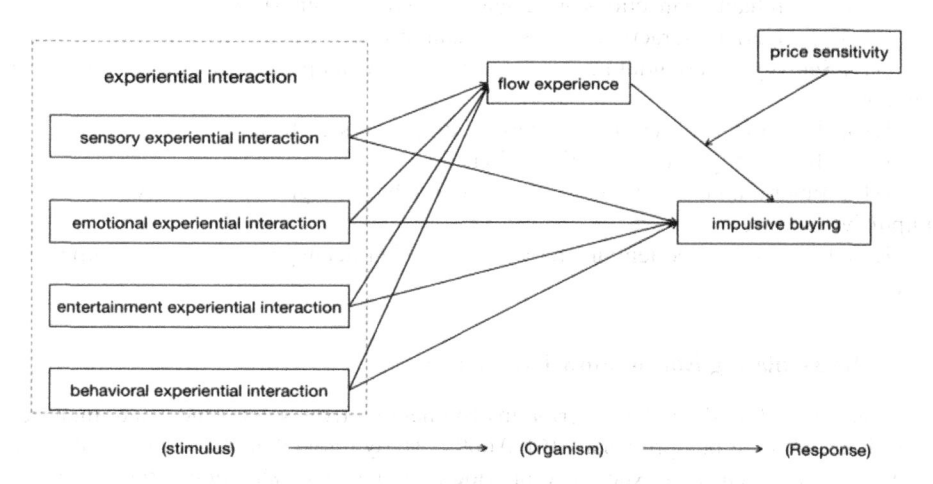

Fig. 1. The theoretical framework of this study (original)

3 Study Design

3.1 Variable Measurement and Sample Data Collection

Variable Measurement and Scale Design. This work examines interpersonal interaction, flow experience, impulsive buying, and price sensitivity. Sensory and emotional experiential contact are subdivided. Interactive, entertaining, and behavioral experiential interaction are the four dimensions, whereas the remaining variables are measured in one dimension. To build the final scale, this study uses the 5-level Likert scale, draws insights from mature scales in the US and elsewhere, and talks with experts. Using the "1 strongly disagree" to "5 strongly agree" scale, examinees must objectively evaluate each item depending on their individual situation [10]. The experiential interaction scale is based on Brakus JJ et al. and Dong Jingjing et al. [11], the impulsive purchasing scale is based on Qin Xiao and Rook [12, 13], and the price sensitivity scale is based on Wang Qian and modified [14].

Sample Data Collection. This report studies offline supermarket and merchant customers. The official survey questionnaire will be circulated January–May 2022. Sample data are mostly collected in the province's major cities. The traditional supermarkets bought cheap trinkets to give out as incentives for customers to fill out the surveys. 97.5% of 485 questionnaires were legitimate after 12 invalid ones were removed. Table 2 shows that 53.1% of the samples were female, 38.7% were between 18 and 25, 69.7% had a bachelor's degree, 35.8% were private enterprise workers, and 33.8% had a monthly wage between 4,000 and 6,000 yuan (Table 1).

3.2 Common Method Bias Test

This research controls the common method bias scale's reliability and validity using anonymous assessment and partial item reversal [15]. Harman's single-factor test assessed the data's method deviation. In this investigation, unrotated exploratory component analysis produced seven factors with characteristic roots greater than 1, the first of which explained a considerable amount of the variance. This study had no substantial common technique bias because the variation was 37.061%, less than 40% [16].

3.3 Reliability and Validity Test

Cronbach's coefficients assess reliability tests. Table 3 shows sensory, emotional, entertainment, behavioral, flow, and pricing sensitivity. The questionnaire's impulsive purchasing Cronbach's coefficients are all over 0.8, indicating strong reliability.

In this paper, exploratory and confirmatory factor analyses are utilized to assess the questionnaire's validity. Table 3 displays exploratory factor analysis results. The KMO values of all research variables exceed 0.6, and the p-values of Bartlett coefficients are all significant, indicating that the sample data are appropriate for factor analysis. The results of the confirmatory factor analysis indicate that all of the model's fitting indicators have reached the standard (χ^2/df=0.988, RMSEA = 0.000, GFI = 0.967, AGFI = 0.955, NFI = 0.968, RFI = 0.960), indicating that the model fits well, as shown in Table 4. The

Table 1. Sample distribution

kind	Category	Frequency	Percentage
Gender	Man	222	46.9
	Woman	251	53.1
Age	Under 18	51	10.8
	18–25	183	38.7
	25–35	130	27.5
	35–45	80	16.9
	Over 45	29	6.1
Highest Academic Qualification	High school or below	122	25.8
	University (undergraduate, junior college or equivalent)	329	69.6
	Postgraduate (Master, Ph.D.)	22	4.7
Occupation	student	54	11.4
	Office worker	64	13.5
	Employees of state-owned enterprise	120	25.4
	Private enterprise employees	182	38.5
	Self employed/Freelancer	41	8.7
	the emeritus and retired	12	2.5
Monthly income	2000 yuan and below	58	12.3
	2001–4000 yuan	124	26.2
	4001–6000 yuan	160	33.8
	6001–8000 yuan	84	17.8
	More than 8000 yuan	47	9.9
total		473	100.0

average extraction variance of sensory experiential interaction, emotional experiential interaction, entertainment experiential interaction, behavioral experiential interaction, flow experience, price sensitivity, and impulse purchasing is greater than 0.5. The reliability (CR) is greater than 0.80, which indicates that the convergent validity is optimal. In addition, Table 5 reveals significant correlations between sensory experiential interaction, emotional experiential interaction, entertainment experiential interaction, behavioral experiential interaction, flow experience, price sensitivity, and impulse purchasing ($p < 0.01$), the correlation coefficients are all less than 0.70, the multicollinearity problem between the variables is not evident, and the correlation coefficients are all less than 0.70.

Table 2. Reliability test and Exploratory Factor Analysis (original)

Dimension	N	Cronbach's α coefficient	KMO	Bartlett test p-value
Sensory experiential interaction	3	0.806	0.713	0.000
Emotional experiential interaction	3	0.808	0.712	0.000
Entertainment experiential interaction	3	0.832	0.722	0.000
Behavioral experiential interaction	3	0.892	0.691	0.000
Flow experience	3	0.804	0.711	0.000
Price sensitivity	3	0.889	0.677	0.000
Impulsive buying	4	0.863	0.831	0.000

Table 3. Convergence validity (original)

Path			Effect value	AVE	CR
GG3	<—	Sensory experiential interaction	0.76	0.5814	0.8064
GG2	<—	Sensory experiential interaction	0.781		
GG1	<—	Sensory experiential interaction	0.746		
QG3	<—	Emotional experiential interaction	0.774	0.5849	0.8084
QG2	<—	Emotional experiential interaction	0.717		
QG1	<—	Emotional experiential interaction	0.801		
YL3	<—	Entertainment experiential interaction	0.759	0.623	0.832
YL2	<—	Entertainment experiential interaction	0.805		
YL1	<—	Entertainment experiential interaction	0.803		
XW3	<—	Behavioral experiential interaction	0.786	0.7477	0.8977
XW2	<—	Behavioral experiential interaction	0.797		
XW1	<—	Behavioral experiential interaction	0.995		
XL3	<—	Flow experience	0.765	0.5777	0.804

(*continued*)

Table 3. (continued)

Path			Effect value	AVE	CR
XL2	<—	Flow experience	0.768		
XL1	<—	Flow experience	0.747		
JG3	<—	Price sensitivity	0.778	0.7475	0.8976
JG2	<—	Price sensitivity	0.802		
JG1	<—	Price sensitivity	0.997		
CD4	<—	Impulsive buying	0.78	0.6125	0.8634
CD3	<—	Impulsive buying	0.799		
CD2	<—	Impulsive buying	0.763		
CD1	<—	Impulsive buying	0.788		

Table 4. Discrimination validity (original)

	Sensory experiential interaction	Emotional experiential interaction	Entertainment experiential interaction	Behavioral experiential interaction	Flow experience	Price sensitivity	Impulsive buying
Sensory experiential interaction	0.5814						
Emotional experiential interaction	0.409***	0.5849					
Entertainment experiential interaction	0.456***	0.344***	0.623				
Behavioral experiential interaction	0.319***	0.3***	0.333***	0.7477			
Flow experience	0.426***	0.393***	0.4***	0.346***	0.5777		
Price sensitivity	0.289***	0.287***	0.4***	0.274***	0.348***	0.7475	
Impulsive buying	0.535***	0.446***	0.538***	0.409***	0.484***	0.41***	0.6125
AVE square root	0.762	0.765	0.789	0.865	0.760	0.865	0.783

Note:*** Indicates that the P value is less than 0.001, the diagonal line is the AVE average variance variation extraction amount

4 Empirical Analysis

4.1 Mediating Effect Test

This paper tests the mediating effect of flow experience using Amos Graphics 24.0 software. In this paper, Bootstrap analysis will be applied to the data, 2000 samples will be drawn, and the PC and BC confidence interval will be 95%. Table 6 demonstrates the results.

As shown in Table 6, in the path of sensory experiential interaction → flow experience → impulsive purchase, at the 95% confidence level, the confidence intervals of PC and BC are [0.007, 0.085], [0.009, 0.089] respectively, all intervals do not contain 0, indicating that indirect effects exist, and the indirect effect value is 0.020, indicating that flow experience has a significant mediating effect between sensory experiential interaction and impulsive purchase, the total effect value of sensory experiential interaction → impulsive purchase is 0.071, and the mediation effect accounts for 28.17% of the total effect, indicating that flow experience plays a partial mediating role in the path from sensory experiential interaction to impulse purchase, that is, H1a and H2a are established. In the path of emotional experiential interaction → flow experience → impulsive purchase, at the 95% confidence level, the confidence intervals of PC and BC are [0.008,0.079] and [0.009,0.082] respectively, and the confidence intervals do not contain 0, indicating the existence of an indirect effect, the indirect effect value is 0.019, indicating that flow experience significantly mediates the relationship between emotional experiential interaction and impulsive purchase, the total effect of it accounts for 30.16 percent of the total effect, indicating that flow experience partially mediates the path of emotional experiential interaction → impulsive purchase, i.e., H1b and H2a are supported.

In the path of entertainment experiential interaction → flow experience → impulsive purchase, at the 95% confidence level, the confidence intervals of PC and BC are [0.005, 0.066] and [0.006, 0.071] respectively, and the intervals do not contain 0, indicating that the indirect effect exists, and the indirect effect value is 0.016, indicating that flow experience has a significant mediating effect between entertainment experiential interaction and impulsive purchase, the total effect value of entertainment experiential interaction → impulsive purchase is 0.064, and the mediating effect of it accounts for 25% of the total effect, indicating that flow experience plays a partial mediating role in the path from entertainment experiential interaction to impulse purchase, i.e., H1c and H2c are established. In the path of behavioral experiential interaction → flow experience → impulsive purchase, at the 95% confidence level, the confidence intervals of PC and BC are [0.006, 0.060] and [0.007, 0.064] respectively, and the intervals do not contain 0, indicating the existence of an indirect effect, the indirect effect value is 0.014, indicating that flow experience has a significant mediating effect between behavioral experiential interaction and impulsive purchase, It accounts for 27.45% of the total effect, indicating that flow experience plays a partial mediating role in the path of behavioral experiential interaction → impulsive purchase, i.e., H1d and H2d are established.

Table 5. Mediating effect test result (original)

Path	Effect value	SE	Bias-corrected 95%CI			Percentile 95%CI		
			lower	upper	P	lower	upper	P
GG → XL → CD	0.039	0.020	0.009	0.089	0.007	0.007	0.085	0.011
QG → XL → CD	0.037	0.019	0.009	0.082	0.006	0.008	0.079	0.008
YL → XL → CD	0.030	0.016	0.006	0.071	0.008	0.005	0.066	0.014
XW → XL → CD	0.029	0.014	0.007	0.064	0.006	0.006	0.060	0.008

4.2 Moderated Mediation Effect Test

Price sensitivity moderates the mediation effect connection in this paper using Amos Graphics24.0. This study follows Edwards and Lambert's advice and uses the Bootstrap method to investigate if the mediation effect varies with moderator variable values [17], 2000 sample extractions, and a 95% confidence range for PC and BC. Table 7 shows results. In the path of sensory experiential interaction-flow experience-impulsive purchase, at the 95% confidence level, the confidence intervals of BC and PC under high grouping are [−0.016, 0.063], [−0.021, 0.053], respectively, The interval does not contain 0, indicating that the mediation effect under high grouping is not significant, the confidence intervals of BC and PC under low grouping are [0.007,0.101], [0.006,0.098], and the interval contains 0, indicating that under low grouping the mediating effect is significant. Under high grouping, the 95% confidence intervals of BC and PC under emotional experiential interaction-flow experience-impulsive purchase are [−0.018, 0.056] and [−0.021, 0.054]. Under high grouping, the interval does not contain 0, indicating that the mediation effect is not significant, under low grouping, the confidence intervals of BC and PC are [0.009,0.1], [0.008,0.097], and the interval contains 0, indicating that the mediation effect is significant.

At the 95% confidence level, the confidence intervals for BC and PC under high grouping for the entertainment experiential interaction-flow experience-impulsive purchase path are [−0.014, 0.055], [−0.019, 0.05], respectively. The interval does not contain 0, indicating that the mediation effect is not significant under high grouping, the confidence intervals for BC and PC under low grouping are [0.007,0.089], [0.005,0.084], and the interval contains 0, indicating that the mediation effect is significant under low grouping. In the path of behavioral experiential interaction-flow experience-impulsive purchase, the confidence intervals of BC and PC under high grouping are [−0.013, 0.043], [−0.016, 0.038], respectively, at the 95% confidence level. The interval does not contain 0, indicating that the mediation effect is not significant under high grouping, the confidence intervals for BC and PC under low grouping are [0.006,0.071], [0.005,0.07], and the interval contains 0, indicating that the mediation effect is significant under low grouping.

In conclusion, hypothesis H3 is supported.

Table 6. Moderated mediation effect test result (original)

Path	Parameter	Effect value	Bias-corrected 95%CI			Percentile 95%CI		
			lower	upper	P	lower	upper	P
GG → XL → CD	int_high	0.015	−0.016	0.063	0.265	−0.021	0.053	0.395
	int_mean	0.028	0.002	0.075	0.03	0.001	0.07	0.045
	int_low	0.041	0.007	0.101	0.012	0.006	0.098	0.016
QG → XL → CD	int_high	0.015	−0.018	0.056	0.327	−0.021	0.054	0.39
	int_mean	0.029	0.002	0.072	0.032	0.001	0.069	0.041
	int_low	0.042	0.009	0.1	0.009	0.008	0.097	0.012
YL → XL → CD	int_high	0.013	−0.014	0.055	0.288	−0.019	0.05	0.394
	int_mean	0.025	0.003	0.066	0.024	0	0.06	0.045
	int_low	0.036	0.007	0.089	0.01	0.005	0.084	0.016
XW → XL → CD	int_high	0.011	−0.013	0.043	0.279	−0.016	0.038	0.39
	int_mean	0.021	0.002	0.051	0.027	0.001	0.049	0.041
	int_low	0.03	0.006	0.071	0.01	0.005	0.07	0.012

Note: int_high, int_mean, and int_low represent the high, medium, and low groups of the mediation effect, respectively

5 Conclusion

This paper uses the S-O-R model to study offline supermarket customers' impulse purchases, stressing the role of experiential contact between consumers and merchants on spontaneous purchases. Empirical examination of 473 customers' antecedent traits and willingness trajectories revealed the following: First, the more experiential interaction between consumers and merchants, the easier it is to produce impulsive buying behavior, second, consumers in offline supermarkets are more likely to have a flow experience when they interact with merchants based on motivations like enjoyment and accomplishment, which positively promotes impulsive buying behavior, and third, offline supermarket shoppers are more likely to be impulsive. After the supermarket-merchant contact and flow experience, high-price-sensitive consumers will restrain their impulsive consumption, while low-price sensitive consumers would not. Less price sensitive, consumers buy more impulsively. The questionnaire sample is limited, thus future research should increase it to get more accurate and generalizable results. Second, consumer-retailer experiential contact affects impulsive buying in complex ways. Other mediating and moderating variables will join price sensitivity and flow experience. Influence impulse purchases through sensory encounters. Divide the variable factor of experiential contact between offline supermarket consumers and merchants in future study.

References

1. Yilan Business. Closing 23 stores in two months, physical retail is still difficult (2022). https://view.inews.qq.com/a/20220318A0312X00. Accessed 29July 2022

2. Meng, C.: Research on transformation strategies of traditional supermarkets under the e-commerce era. China Int. Finan. Econ. Chin. Engl. (24), 127–131 (2016)
3. Zhao, B., Wang, Y.: The influence of e-commerce anchor characteristics on consumers' purchase intention. Bus. Res. (1), 1–6 (2021)
4. Yu, M., Miao, Q.: Change and Innovation: The New Consumption Era. Guotai Junan Securities Research Institute, Shanghai (2021)
5. Dong, J., Xu, Z., Fang, Q., et al.: Model construction of the impact of online experiential interaction between consumers and merchants on their purchase intention. J. Manag. (11), 1722–1730 (2018)
6. Hausman, A.V., Siekpe, J.S.: The effect of web interface features on consumer online purchase intentions. J. Bus. Res. (1), 5–13 (2009)
7. Wang, X., Xu, X., Wang, X.: Research on the impact of smart shopping experience on consumers' purchase intention. Cons. Econ. **38**(03), 87–96 (2022)
8. Pu, Y.: User paid marketing strategy of paid knowledge products——take the "Trial Experience" of Zhihu platform as an example. Modern Bus. (33), 11–15 (2020)
9. Ying, X.: Analysis of the relationship between consumer experience and repurchase behavior under the background of new retail—based on the perspective of price sensitivity heterogeneity. Bus. Econ. Res. (4), 61–64 (2022)
10. Liu, X., Wu, J.: Shopping community value co-creation behavior and purchase intention - the mediating role of perceived value. J. Chongqing Technol. Bus. Univ. Soc. Sci. Ed.
11. Brakus, J.J., Schmitt, B.H., Zarantonello, L.: Brand experience: what is it? how is it measured? does it affect loyalty?. J. Mark. (5), 52–68 (2009)
12. Xiao, Q.: Research on the Influence of Social Interaction on Consumers' Impulsive Purchase Intention in Online Group Buying, p. 5. Shandong University, Jinan (2019)
13. Rook, D.W.: Normative influences on impulse buying behavior. J. Cons. Res. (22), 305–313 (1995)
14. Qian, W.: Research on the Effect of Promotional Discount Level on Purchase Intention under Time Limit and Price Sensitivity Adjustment, p. 3. Nanjing University of Finance and Economics, Nanjing (2019)
15. Zhou, H., Long, L.: Statistical testing and control methods for common method bias. Adv. Psychol. Sci. (6), 942–950 (2004)
16. Wei, H., Feng, R.: Research on the influence mechanism of organizational support on employee creativity——based on job insecurity. Leadership Sci. (10), 64–67 (2021)
17. Edwards, J.R., Lambert, L.S.: Methods for integrating moderation and mediation: a general analytical framework using moderated path analysis. Psychol. Methods **12**(1), 1–22 (2007)

A Qualitative Study on How the Covid-19 Pandemic Has Helped in the Enablement of Entrepreneurial Ambitions Among Chinese Entrepreneurs

Xiaodan Wang[✉]

Innovation Management and Entrepreneurship FT, The University of Manchester, Manchester M13 9PL, UK
mgk19xw@gmail.com

Abstract. The impact of any crisis on entrepreneurial motivation has been widely studied in the extant literature. However, most studies have assumed a negative relationship between problems and entrepreneurial causes. Through this study, the researcher aimed to explore the positive impact of a crisis on entrepreneurial ambitions. To achieve this, the researcher conducted semi-structured interviews with nine Chinese entrepreneurs who started their ventures in China between 2020 and 2022. The study revealed a positive relationship between crises and entrepreneurial ambition. Changing market conditions and personal factors were found to have enabled the development of entrepreneurial dreams among Chinese entrepreneurs. Additionally, the study revealed that the Chinese government played a significant role in sustaining their entrepreneurial aspirations during the Covid-19 pandemic. From this study, it can be concluded that a crisis can present various entrepreneurial opportunities, and individuals must focus on leveraging the benefits that a problem might give.

Keywords: Entrepreneurial Motivation · Chinese Entrepreneurs · Covid-19 Pandemic · Entrepreneurial Opportunities

1 Introduction

The impact of a crisis on entrepreneurial motivation has been extensively explored in the literature, with most studies assuming a negative association between concerns and entrepreneurial ambitions. For example, Arrighetti [1] found that a crisis can be a significant obstacle that impacts an entrepreneur's potential to start a new venture. Nonetheless, it is also essential to recognize the positive impact of a crisis on entrepreneurial ambitions. A problem can disrupt existing industries and markets at a macro level, creating new market demand [2]. At a micro-level, people who lose their jobs during a crisis may be motivated to search for novel opportunities to generate income [3]. This research aims to investigate the influence of the Coronavirus crisis on entrepreneurial ambition, mainly focusing on the circumstances that may lead to a positive relationship between the two. Entrepreneurialism has been emphasized by the Chinese government since 2015, as it plays a unique role in China's economic strategy [4]. According to a report, approximately 23.7 million new business ventures were created in China in 2019 [5].

Nevertheless, that same year, the city of Wuhan became the initial epicenter of the Covid-19 outbreak, marking the beginning of a global pandemic that had profound consequences. Due to prolonged lockdowns imposed by governments worldwide, the unemployment rate increased globally, with organizations laying off many employees [6]. Despite these challenges, recent reports suggest that the Covid-19 pandemic in China has triggered a flood of entrepreneurialism in the nation [7]. Even with the population suffering from the coronavirus, there has been a 5% increase, accounting for almost 25 million new ventures created in the country [5]. However, the underlying factors that drove these entrepreneurs to undertake the risk of initiating new ventures during a crisis remain unclear. Therefore, investigating the impact of the Coronavirus pandemic in facilitating the rise of multiple entrepreneurial ventures in China and comprehending how entrepreneurs sustained their ambition amid uncertain circumstances offers an engaging avenue for research.

2 Literature Review

2.1 Entrepreneurial Motives

The motivation to start an entrepreneurial venture varies among individuals, whether they are potential entrepreneurs or new entrepreneurs. The most common categorization of entrepreneurial motives splits them into two major types: necessity motives and opportunity motives [8]. Necessity-based entrepreneurship refers to the creation of small-scale ventures to fulfill an individual's survival needs [9], while opportunity-based entrepreneurship refers to the creation of ventures in response to entrepreneurial opportunities presented by the external environment [10]. Therefore, motives play a significant role in enabling entrepreneurial ambition among people. The difference between entrepreneurs holding necessity motives and those with opportunity motives is a matter of debate [11]. Some studies show that there is no significant difference. For example, a survey of entrepreneurs from Czechia, Hungary, and Serbia found that the personality trait of an individual rather than their motive helps to shape entrepreneurial ambition [12].

In contrast, other studies suggest that investigating this difference is worthwhile. For instance, the tendency of Chinese females to engage in necessity-based entrepreneurship activities for creating small-scale, low-revenue businesses is more than that of Chinese males [9]. This study highlights a positive association between the gender of an entrepreneur and their entrepreneurial motive. However, there is a gap in the literature on whether the necessity motive, opportunity motive, or personality traits prompt Chinese entrepreneurs to start entrepreneurial ventures during the Covid-19 pandemic. Given the labor market's potential challenges, such crises might amplify the need for necessary entrepreneurship. Alternatively, these crises may introduce new market opportunities by disrupting established industries, creating space for new ventures to emerge within this environment. The following two subsections will consider Covid-19's role in prompting entrepreneurial action by shifting market demand and supply-side support structures.

2.2 The Influence of the Corona Virus Pandemic on Consumer Behaviour

During the Covid-19 period, there was a significant shift in consumer behavior toward products and services. The only change is stockpiling behavior. Due to the fear of lockdown, people started accumulating [13]. Consequently, the supply chain of prominent FMCG brands was adversely impacted, revealing its inefficiency in effectively responding to the unforeseen and volatile consumer demand. For instance, a study by Wang [14] found that during panic buying situations, Chinese consumers were willing to pay a premium of 60.47% for fresh food reserves. The second change is an overreliance on online food delivery applications. Due to the strict lockdown of 100 days in the spring season 2020 in China, restaurants, bakeries, and other eateries were closed [15]. As a result, the Chinese depended on food delivery applications that burdened China's existing online food delivery system [15]. The third change is the increased demand for disinfectant products. In China, the need for disinfectants increased tremendously as their consumption increased in the commercial and residential sectors [16]. These examples clearly show a change in demand, and the existing supply could not cope with this variable demand. However, it is unclear how this change has been perceived as an opportunity to start novel ventures in China. This research effectively addresses the apparent gap in the existing literature.

2.3 Role of Government in Supporting Entrepreneurial Ventures

The Chinese government has constantly supported entrepreneurial ventures in the pre-pandemic era [17]. During the pandemic era as well, novel experiences in China benefitted from a range of various measures taken by the Chinese government, such as tax exemptions and financial assistance [18, 19]. However, the support received by the novel Chinese entrepreneurs in actuality from the Chinese government has not yet been studied directly from the entrepreneurs' perspective in the extant literature. This study fills this evident gap in the literature.

3 Research Methodology

3.1 Research Design

The rationale behind employing a qualitative research design for this study is grounded in investigating the research questions from the participant's standpoint rather than relying solely on the researcher's viewpoint [20]. The primary focus of this research is to capture the first-hand experiences of Chinese entrepreneurs who embarked on their entrepreneurial ventures during the Covid-19 pandemic. Therefore, it was imperative to gather insights and obtain responses to the three research questions directly from the perspective of these entrepreneurs. By opting for a qualitative research design, the study successfully delved into the lived experiences and viewpoints of the participants, thus substantiating the choice of this methodology.

3.2 Research Participants and Sampling Procedure

The initial instance of the Covid-19 virus was documented in late 2019 in Wuhan, a city in China [21]. Therefore, entrepreneurs who started their ventures in China during 2020–2022 were the population of interest for this research work. The researcher selected nine such entrepreneurs using a snowball sampling method. This sampling technique has been cited as the one in which the researcher takes assistance from one or more research participants to reach other potential participants [22]. It has also been cited that such a sampling method is helpful in those cases where the members of the target population share certain specific traits, and it seems complicated for the researcher to reach these members [23]. This research aimed to identify Chinese entrepreneurs who started entrepreneurial ventures between 2020–2022. This shows that these Chinese entrepreneurs share a specific trait of risk-taking during the uncertain times of the pandemic. Also, the recency of the research period made it difficult for the researcher to identify these entrepreneurs due to the lack of available data about their novel entrepreneurial ventures.

3.3 Data Collection and Transcription Mechanism

To gather data, the researcher utilized semi-structured interviews, which consisted of questions not arranged in a specific order but designed in line with the three research questions. The interview guide was prepared before data collection to ensure a focused interview direction [24]. Considering the geographical limitations, the interviews were conducted via telephone. The discussions took place in the Chinese language and involved the participation of 9 Chinese entrepreneurs. Subsequently, the data gathered from the interviews were translated into English for analysis.

3.4 Data Analysis

After transcribing the data, the researcher employed thematic analysis as the chosen method to analyze the collected information. The thematic analysis involves the coding of data to identify different themes, as described by Clarke, Braun, and Hayfield. This approach enables researchers to explore and uncover broader patterns within the data, as emphasized by Terry [25]. A notable strength of the thematic analysis is its ability to reveal both surface-level (semantic) and underlying (latent) patterns present in the data, as highlighted by Clarke, Braun, and Hayfield [26]. Given the advantageous features of thematic analysis, it was deemed suitable for the specific objectives of this study.

4 Findings

From the application of thematic analysis, various themes were discovered. These themes have been used to develop Fig. 1, which shows multiple pieces' relationships. In the finding section, the researcher indicated the supporting quotes as useful in discovering themes and relationships among them.

4.1 Theme 1: Crisis

The foremost theme that emerged from applying thematic analysis is the crisis. Most respondents referred to the Covid-19 pandemic as a crisis that disturbed the normal functioning of the lives of individuals. Some of the supporting quotes are:

"The international borders closed due to the pandemic" (Interviewee 1).

"No one has ever imagined such a scenario where everything will be closed down, and people will be confined to their homes only" (Interviewee 2).

"During the pandemic, most of the business activities came to a halt" (Interviewee 3).

Thus, from the analysis of these statements, it is clear that the Covid-19 pandemic was essentially perceived as a crisis by entrepreneurs in China.

4.2 Theme 2: Market Conditions

According to the prevailing consensus among respondents, the Covid-19 pandemic has brought about substantial changes in market conditions. In particular, they noted a significant alteration in the market landscape for existing products, alongside a noticeable surge in demand for new developments arising from the effects of the pandemic.

Increased Demand for Existing Products and Entrepreneurial Ambition. According to most respondents, the Coronavirus pandemic led to a mismanagement of the supply chain due to a surge in demand that exceeded the capacity of the existing supply in China. This undoubtedly led to the enablement of entrepreneurial ambition. Some of the supporting quotes are:

"Bakeries closed, and most of the people are inefficient in baking. So, I got an idea of supplying rice cooker cake and take advantage of this rising demand for sweet products among Chinese." (Interviewee 3).

"Demand for home-cooked food increased as the families were ill due to Covid-19. Then, I realized why not start a small business delivering Liangpi to homes. Since these noodles are cold, these could be delivered to even far-off places" (Interviewee 5).

"Personal hygiene mattered most during the pandemic. Demand was rising, and stocks were getting over. I thought my homemade soaps could greatly help people" (Interviewee 6).

New Product Demands and Entrepreneurial Ambition. According to the prevailing consensus among most respondents, the Covid-19 pandemic significantly disrupted individuals' daily routines and activities. This disruption prompted a noticeable increase in consumer demand for various new products as a means of managing and adapting to the pandemic's impact. This undoubtedly led to the enablement of entrepreneurial ambition. Some of the supporting quotes are:

"So, I would say Covid-19 triggered the demand for my digital learning kits for toddlers." (Interviewee 2).

"The socialization was practically zero during the pandemic. My gaming app allowed families to come together to play Xiangqi with each other using mobile phones" (Interviewee 4).

"The pandemic presented various challenges, and parents could not cope with demanding toddlers who had nothing to do during the lockdown." (Interviewee 7).

4.3 Theme 3: Personal Factors

According to the majority of respondents, the outbreak of the Coronavirus pandemic resulted in a significant disruption to the regular functioning of daily life. Furthermore, three prominent factors were identified as contributors to the facilitation of entrepreneurial ambition among Chinese entrepreneurs, driven by personal motivations.

Availability of Time and Entrepreneurial Ambition. Most entrepreneurs reported that due to the prolonged lockdown during the pandemic, there was enough idle time available which motivated them to do something productive. Some of the supporting quotes are:

"Initially, I thought that it was a great time to create a bond with my family and kids, but then I realized that I can certainly use this time for creating something of my own." (Interviewee 3).

"Ah, you see, I was all free at that time, which pushed me to do something new, which I was never able to do before as an executive manager of an IT firm" (Interviewee 5).

"The lockdown proved to be a boom for my venture. I got ample time to set an ambition that is still a driving force for me" (Interviewee 6).

"I was isolated due to illness and got enough me-time which helped me frame my entrepreneurial ambition" (Interviewee 7).

Survival and Entrepreneurial Ambition. Most of the entrepreneurs reported that the motivation behind their entrepreneurial ambition was to support themselves and their families financially during the pandemic. Some of the supporting quotes are:

"The tuition centers got closed, so I started this online tutoring venture to support my livelihood during these unpredictable times" (Interviewee 2).

"But then when I was jobless…that's when I got motivated to start a home-cooked food business of my own" (Interviewee 3).

Personal Fulfilment and Entrepreneurial Ambition. Some entrepreneurs reported that their desire for personal fulfillment motivated them to start an entrepreneurial venture. Some of the supporting quotes are:

"My wife and I felt that it would be very fulfilling to have something we can call all ours" (Interviewee 9).

"For me, having a gaming app of my own was always a dream, and the Covid-19 pandemic helped me live my dream. I still feel that I am dreaming…" (Interviewee 4).

"The pandemic helped me achieve my goal in life…" (Interviewee 7).

4.4 Theme 4: Government Support and Entrepreneurial Ambition

The majority of the entrepreneurs reported that the support from the Chinese government has helped in the sustainment of their entrepreneurial ambition during the Covid-19 pandemic. Some of the supporting quotes are:

The strict zero covid policy has helped small home-based businesses grow. Due to this policy, I am now a proud owner of a home-based bakery..." (Interviewee 3).

"Of course, the Chinese government has supported my entrepreneurial venture. The rent waivers helped me survive..." (Interviewee 5).

"There was always a feeling of support from the Chinese government. Even little help in terms of a tax refund can help a small startup sustain during such unpredictable times..." (Interviewee 7).

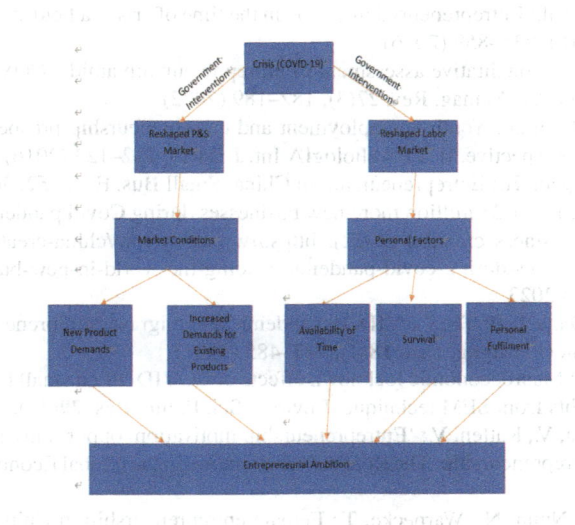

Fig. 1. Findings of the study.

5 Discussion and Conclusion

This research explored the impact of significant global crises, particularly the Covid-19 crisis, on entrepreneurial ambition and the conditions under which that relationship might be optimistic. From this study, it has been found that changing market conditions, i.e., increased demand for existing products and new product demands, and personal factors, i.e., availability of time, survival, and personal fulfillment, were the major factors that positively impacted entrepreneurial ambition. The Chinese government also played a significant role through strict zero-covid policy, rent waivers, and tax refunds helped the entrepreneurs sustain their entrepreneurial dream during the Covid-19 pandemic. From this study, even a crisis can boost entrepreneurial aspirations. During uncertain times, instead of being demotivated, people must concentrate on leveraging the benefits that a problem might present.

It is important to note that the current report acknowledges a limitation regarding the sample size, which may impact the quality and reliability of the research findings. The small sample size can limit the ability to derive meaningful conclusions and accurately predict the broader population being studied. To address this limitation, future research endeavors could expand the sample size to include a more extensive and diverse participant base. Researchers can obtain more robust conclusions about the relationship between crises, such as the Covid-19 pandemic, and entrepreneurship. This will enhance the validity and generalizability of the findings.

References

1. Arrighetti, A., et al.: Entrepreneurial intention in the time of crisis: a field study. Int. J. Entrep. Behav. Res. **22**(6), 835–859 (2016)
2. Nasar, A., et al.: A qualitative assessment of entrepreneurship amidst COVID-19 pandemic in Pakistan. Asia Pac. Manag. Rev. **27**(3), 182–189 (2022)
3. Abimbola, O.H., et al.: Youth unemployment and entrepreneurship prospects in Nigeria: a developmental perspective. IFE PsychologIA Int. J. **24**(2), 112–123 (2016)
4. He, C., Lu, J., Qian, H.: Entrepreneurship in China. Small Bus. Econ. **52**, 563–572 (2019)
5. UHY. China created 1.25 million more new businesses during Covid pandemic – leading the world in new business creation (2022). https://www.uhy.com/china-created-1-25-million-more-new-businesses-during-covid-pandemic-leading-the-world-in-new-business-creation/. Accessed 31 Jan 2023
6. Vorobeva, E., Dana, L.P.: The COVID-19 pandemic and migrant entrepreneurship: responses to the market shock. Migrat. Lett. **18**(4), 477–485 (2021)
7. Xiao, D., Su, J.: Macroeconomic lockdown effects of COVID-19 on small business in China: empirical insights from SEM technique. Environ. Sci. Pollut. Res. **29**(42), 44–56 (2022)
8. Mota, A., Braga, V., Ratten, V.: 'Entrepreneurship motivation: opportunity and necessity. In: Sustainable Entrepreneurship: The Role of Collaboration in the Global Economy, pp. 139–165 (2019)
9. Hernandez, L., Nunn, N., Warnecke, T.: Female entrepreneurship in China: opportunity-or necessity-based? Int. J. Entrep. Small Bus. **15**(4), 411–434 (2012)
10. Ma, R., Huang, Y.C.: Opportunity-based strategic orientation, knowledge acquisition, and entrepreneurial alertness: the perspective of the global sourcing suppliers in China. J. Small Bus. Manag. **54**(3), 953–972 (2016)
11. Jafari-Sadeghi, V.: The motivational factors of business venturing: Opportunity versus necessity? a gendered perspective on European countries. J. Bus. Res. **113**(1), 279–289 (2020)
12. Zarnadze, G., et al.: Personality traits and business environment for entrepreneurial motivation. Administ. Sci. **12**(4), 1–18 (2022)
13. Amaral, N.B., Chang, B., Burns, R.: Understanding consumer stockpiling: insights provided during the COVID-19 pandemic. J. Consum. Aff. **56**(1), 211–236 (2022)
14. Wang, E., et al.: Consumer food stockpiling behavior and willingness to pay for food reserves in COVID-19. Food Secur. **12**(1), 739–747 (2020)
15. Lin, Y., et al.: Supply chain sustainability during COVID-19: last mile food delivery in China. Sustainability **14**(3), 148–165 (2022)
16. Wei, W., et al.: Radiotherapy workflow and protection procedures during the Coronavirus Disease 2019 (COVID-19) outbreak: experience of the hubei Cancer Hospital in Wuhan, China. Radiother. Oncol. **148**, 203–210 (2020)
17. Su, Z., Xie, E., Wang, D.: Entrepreneurial orientation, managerial networking, and new venture performance in China. J. Small Bus. Manag. **53**(1), 228–248 (2015)
18. Chen, J., et al.: Riding out the covid-19 storm: how government policies affect SMEs in China. China Econ. Rev. **75**(1) (2022)
19. Meyer, K.E., Prashantham, S., Xu, S.: Entrepreneurship and the post-COVID-19 recovery in emerging economies. Manag. Organ. Rev. **17**(5), 1101–1118 (2021)

20. Merriam, S.B., Grenier, R.S.: Qualitative Research in Practice: Examples for Discussion and Analysis. John Wiley & Sons Inc., Hoboken (2019)
21. Abebe, E.C., et al.: The newly emerged COVID-19 disease: a systemic review. Virol. J. **17**(1), 1–8 (2020)
22. Naderifar, M., Goli, H., Ghaljaie, F.: Snowball sampling: a purposeful method of sampling in qualitative research. Strides Dev. Med. Educ. **14**(3), 1–4 (2017)
23. Goodman, L.A.: Comment: On respondent-driven sampling and snowball sampling in hard-to-reach populations and snowball sampling not in hard-to-reach populations. Sociol. Methodol. **41**(1), 347–353 (2011)
24. Kallio, H., et al.: Systematic methodological review: developing a framework for a qualitative semi-structured interview guide. J. Adv. Nurs. **72**(12), 2954–2965 (2016)
25. Terry, G., et al.: Thematic analysis. SAGE Handb. Qual. Res. Psychol. **2**, 17–37 (2017)
26. Clarke, V., Braun, V., Hayfield, N.: Thematic analysis. Qual. Psychol. Pract. Guide Res. Methods **3**, 222–248 (2015)

The Application of Price-Earnings Ratio in Hong Kong Hang Seng Index Futures Trading Strategy

Yishan Hou[1], Yifei Xu[2(✉)], and Shuye Zhou[3]

[1] College of Finance and Statistics, Hunan University, Changsha 410082, China
[2] BNU Business School, Beijing Normal University, Beijing 100875, China
202011030069@mail.bnu.edu.cn
[3] School of Economics, Dongbei University of Finance and Economics, Dalian 11600, China

Abstract. Recent years, affected by the international situation, the volatility of Hong Kong stock market has increased, and investors face higher risks while having more opportunities. Whether the Price-Earnings ratio (P/E ratio) can not only be able to predict changes in stock market, but also formulate speculative strategies has been one of the research hotspots in recent years. But there is still a research gap in the use of the P/E ratio on the feasibility of HK stock market. Therefore, this paper constructs an investment strategy based on the P/E ratio indicator and uses R language to simulate the historical data collected by the Hong Kong Hang Seng Index and its P/E ratio in the last 5 years. According to results, the average success rate of this strategy reached more than 60%, of which the nearest quarter reached the highest success rate of 67.07%, indicating that the strategy is feasible. This means that this strategy can provide investors with a basis for investment decisions to obtain higher returns by mining the predictive role of the P/E ratio in the investment field.

Keywords: Hang Seng Index · P/E Ratio · Trading Strategy · Hang Seng Index Futures

1 Introduction

Hong Kong is a non-sovereign offshore financial market with free capital flows. The Hang Seng Index is highly vulnerable to various political and economic factors, both domestic and foreign. These factors have been identified as one of the leading causes of the increased volatility observed in the index in recent years. In 2022, the Hang Seng Index experienced a significant downturn, falling by 25.72% in a brief 18-day trading period between February 18th and March 15th. This abrupt decrease in value was attributed to several factors, including inflationary risks that had emerged from the Russia-Ukraine situation, the delisting of technology companies, and the decision to increase interest rates by the Federal Reserve. The Hang Seng Index (HIS) is an essential price index in the Hong Kong capital market. Because it reflects the price trend of the Hong Kong capital market. The HIS takes 33 representative stocks of Hong Kong stock market as sample. Hang Seng Index futures are stock index futures based on the HSI. Unlike the CSI 300 index and other indices in mainland China, HSI futures have longer trading hours and different limits on the amount of increase or decrease. HSI futures have a minimum volatility of 1 index point and an unlimited maximum volatility.

The Hong Kong stock market's increased volatility has on the one hand increased the potential returns for investors, but on the other hand increased the risks associated with investing. The P/E ratio, which is the ratio of stock price to earnings per share, is a measure of the risk to investors, has long been used by investors to evaluate IPOs, large cap stocks or individual stocks as an important investment evaluation indicator, it is also used to determine whether a security is overvalued or undervalued.

Over the course of 70 years, researchers have extensively studied the price-earnings ratio, with initial research stemming from Benjamin's concept of value investing. In recent years, scholars have conducted in-depth studies using Vector autoregressive model (VAR) and Autoregressive Integrated Moving (ARIMA) models to confirm the usefulness of P/E indicators in the investment field. Ikoku et al. used the Nigerian Stock Exchange as an object, explored whether the stock P/E ratio indicator has the ability to predict stock prices. They found that the information contain in P/E ratio can be used to predict stock price trends and determine whether there is a stock market bubble [1]. Gupta argued that price-to-earnings (P/E) ratios have a great significance on predicting overall stock prices in selected markets. He suggested that investors can use P/E ratios and price margins as a guide to assess stock prices and the investment potential of securities [2]. Similarly, Mayur found that for blue-chip or large-cap companies, the higher the current value of the stock P/E ratio is, the higher the future price of the stock and the lower the return [3]. Specifically, Truong found that investing in low P/E stocks consistently yields high returns by examining the performance of low P/E stocks on the New Zealand Stock Exchange [4]. Based on a study of the performance of portfolios constructed with P/E ratios, Bodhanwala demonstrated that portfolios with low P/E ratios in the Indian stock market earnings ratio portfolios outperformed the benchmark market returns [5]. Sharma found that there was a significant positive correlation between the PE index and the S&P 500 index returns in the US. When the PE index was lower, it resulted in lower S&P 500 returns, and when the PE index was higher, it led to higher S&P 500 returns [6].

These years, a large number of other scholars had also conducted research in this regard. When studying the relationship between the P/E ratio of the domestic ChiNext board and the company's growth, profitability and risk, Ye found that the P/E ratio indicator does not correctly reflect the company's true financial position or company fundamentals [7]. However, most scholars believe that there is a significant correlation between the P/E ratio and the following year's stock earnings, and the P/E ratio indicator can guide investment to some extent. Chen et al. found that the price-earnings ratio of Shanghai and Shenzhen listed companies showed a positive correlation with the growth indicators composed of net profit growth rate, operating income growth rate and total asset growth rate [8]. In addition, many scholars have found that there was a significant correlation between the P/E ratio and the following year's stock earnings, and the P/E ratio indicator could guide investment to a certain extent. For example, Zhang found that there was a strong negative correlation between the price-to-earnings ratio (P/E) of stocks listed on the Shanghai Stock Exchange from 1991 to 2004 and the average daily returned in the following year [9]. Yu and Hu found that the deviation rate of the previous P/E ratio had a good guiding effect on the trend of the Shanghai Composite Index in the later stage [10].

Therefore, it is necessary to conduct an in-depth study on the feasibility of using the P/E ratio as an investment strategy and exploring the use of this ratio of the HSI to formulate investment strategies. Utilizing it in the investment field can provide investors with a basis for making investment decisions that lead to greater returns.

From the existing research on the price-earnings ratio, it is not difficult to find that the price-earnings ratio can be used to judge whether there is a bubble in the price of securities and help investors predict the future price trend of securities to a certain extent. Besides, there are relevant empirical studies that also show a significant correlation between this ratio and the return of the stock index. Therefore, studying a feasible investment strategy on the P/E ratio is necessary. It can help investors analysis the market, so that they can make more informed investment decisions and obtain higher returns.

2 Methods

The trading strategy adopted in this study is a speculative strategy. The speculative strategy is divided into two main strategies: long and short speculation, depending on the part of the position to be opened. Long speculation is when a speculator expects the price of a stock index futures market to rise and buys the contract in order to profit from the hedge after the price rises; short speculation is when a speculator expects the price of a stock index futures market to fall and sells the contract in order to profit from the hedge after the price falls.

In this study, the Hang Seng Index P/E ratio is used as a reference for trading Hang Seng Index futures. In general, the ratio of the Hang Seng Index is less than a specific value A, indicating that the market as a whole is undervalued and suitable for buying. While the P/E ratio is super than a particular value B, indicating that the market as a whole is overvalued and needs to be liquidated. However, since the P/E ratio fluctuates between 9x and 15x in the last 5 years, the lower bound is set to 10x and the upper bound is set to 14x.

$$P/E\ ratio = \frac{Price\ per\ Share}{Earnings\ per\ Share} \quad (1)$$

$$Contract\ Expiry\ Points - Agreed\ Trading\ Points = Bid/Ask\ Spread \quad (2)$$

For the long strategy, when the P/E ratio is less than 10x on a trading day, market player can buy the contract at the current contract price and close the position on the contract delivery date. And the strategy is successful if the value of futures contract is larger than the buying value when the position is closed.

For short strategies, when the P/E ratio for a trading day is greater than 14x, market player can sell the contract short at the current price and close it on the contract delivery date. If the value of the futures contract at the time of closing is less than the value of the short sale, the strategy is successful, as Fig. 1 shows.

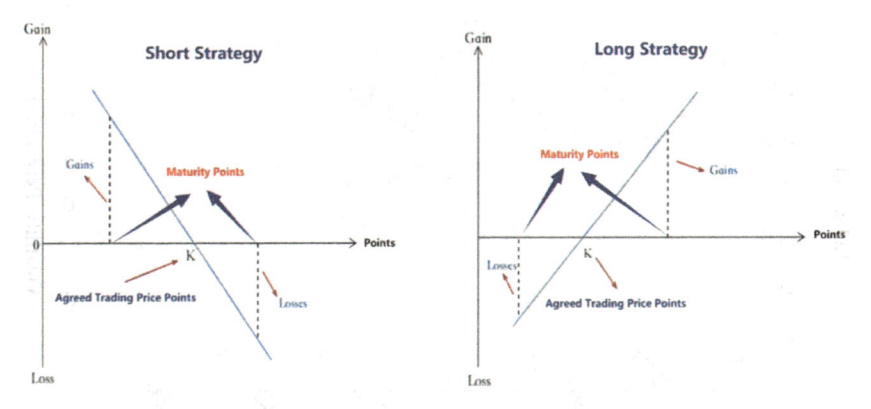

Fig. 1. The profit and loss chart of strategic.

3 Results and Discussion

3.1 Descriptive Statistics

The data used below comes from iFind. This study selects the Hang Seng Futures Index and Hang Seng Index P/E ratio from 2018/5/2 to 2023/4/27. The size of the ratio is used as a reference data and the closing price of the Hang Seng Futures Index is used as the transaction data to study the trading strategy of futures; a total of 1183 data are deducted for non-trading days.

Figure 2 shows the data for the Hang Seng Index for the last five years from 2018/4/30 to 2023/4/27. The overall trend of the HSI is oscillating downward during this period. The HSI bottomed out in 2022/11, and then showed a V-shaped reversal to usher in a 3-month general upward trend, supported by global liquidity expectations on valuation and the optimization of the national anti-epidemic policy and the economic recovery window.

Figure 3 shows the trend of the Hang Seng Futures Index over the past five years. Its overall trend is similar to the trend of the HSI, with overall fluctuations to the downside. The overall range of increase and decrease is between −7% and 10%.

Figure 4 shows the P/E ratio of the HSI over this period. The ratio fluctuates within the range of 9x to 15x in the past five years from 2018/4 to 2023/4, with a median of 10.38x and an average of 10.83x. The current P/E ratio is in the 22.29% quartile of the historical 5-year range. The P/E ratio of less than 10x in the last five years accounts for 30.76% of the overall statistics, and the ratio of more than 14x accounts for 4.20% of the overall statistics. Therefore, when the P/E ratio is lower than 10, HSI futures can be considered undervalued, and when the P/E ratio is greater than 14, HSI futures can be considered overvalued. Based on it, this paper takes A value of 10 and B value of 14.

Figure 5 illustrates the historical volatility of the Index of Hang Seng Futures. The volatility changes in the last 20 days are large, and the volatility range in the last 120 days is basically between 15% and 30%, indicating that there is some risk in the Hang Seng Index futures market.

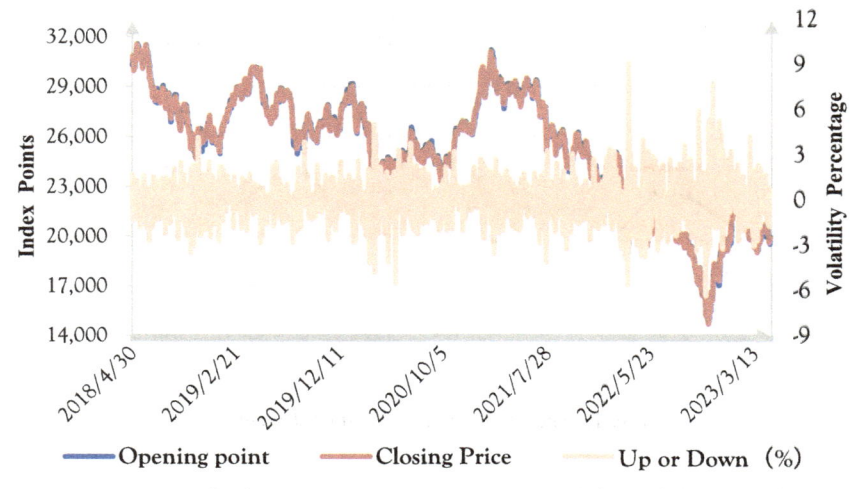

Fig. 2. Hang seng index (2018/4/30~2023/4/27).

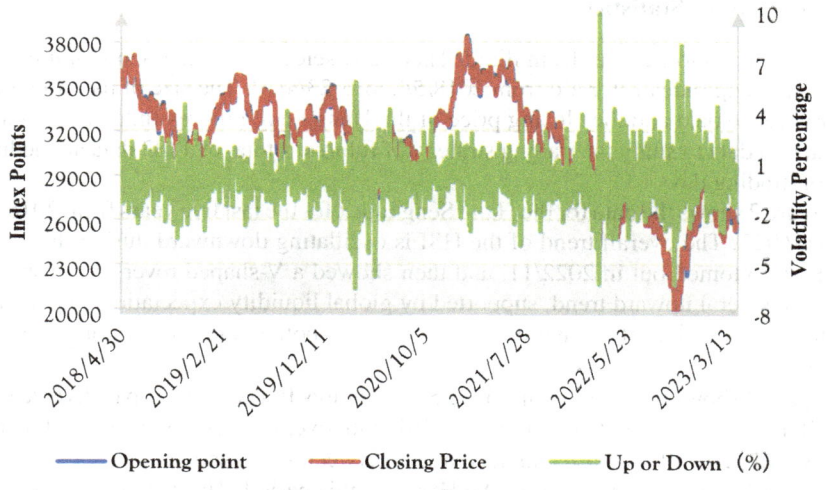

Fig. 3. Hang seng futures index (2018/4/30~2023/4/28).

Figure 6 shows the statistics of the last five years' returns. The returns show a normal distribution overall, with an average return of −0.0285% and an Alpha of −0.0598.

3.2 Assumption

To simplify the study, the first assumption is that the delivery dates of the contracts are all the second last business day of the delivery month specified in the contract; and then it is assumed that the last assumption is that futures are traded in volumes of 1 unit; it is also assumed that the futures contracts traded are the four contracts of current month contract, following month contract and two nearest calendar quarter month contracts.

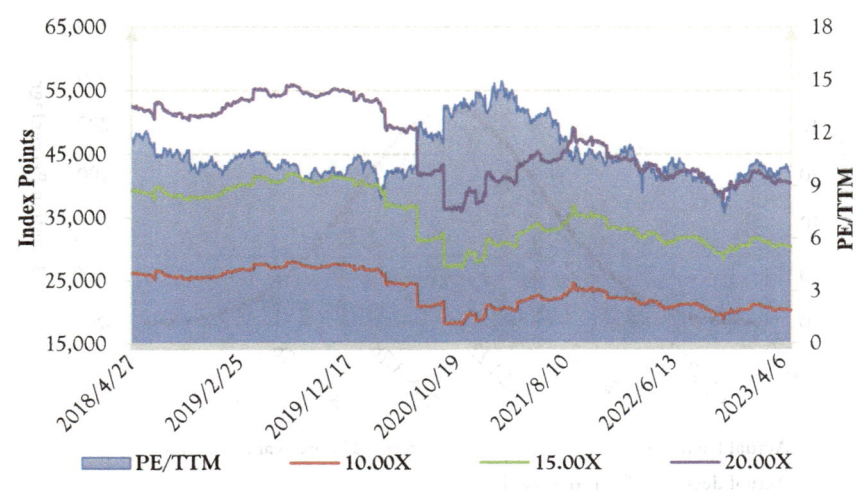

Fig. 4. Hang seng index P/E ratio (2018/4/27~2023/4/27).

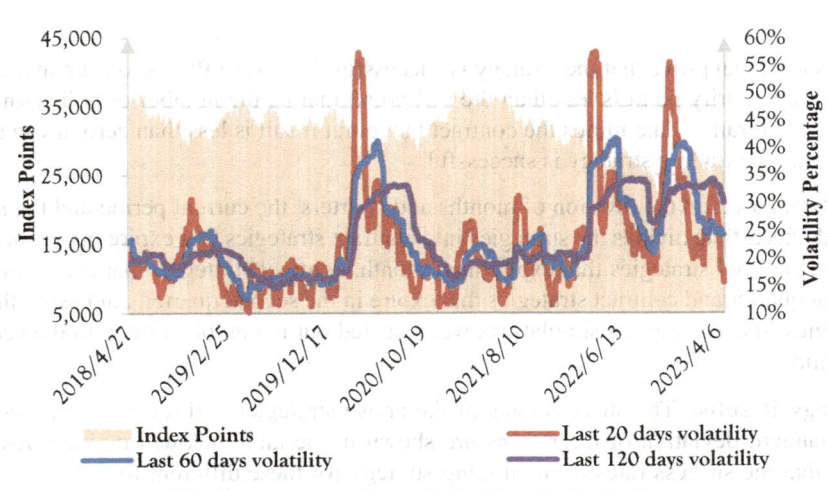

Fig. 5. Hang seng futures index historical volatility.

3.3 Empirical Analysis

Strategy Implementation. This study selects the Hang Seng Futures Index and the HSI P/E ratio from 2018/5/2 to 2023/4/27 as the research indicators firstly. And then this study screens out the data with a P/E ratio of below 10 or a P/E ratio higher than 14. With R language as the main data analysis tool, we have designed the following verification scheme. First of all, the plus or negative of the result of the contract expiration date minus the number of contracting buying points from the data screened out earlier is used as a reference value for the success of the trading strategy. Specifically, when the P/E ratio is less than 10, if the maturity point is greater than the buy point, that is, the number of points on the contract expiration date minus the contract buy point result is greater

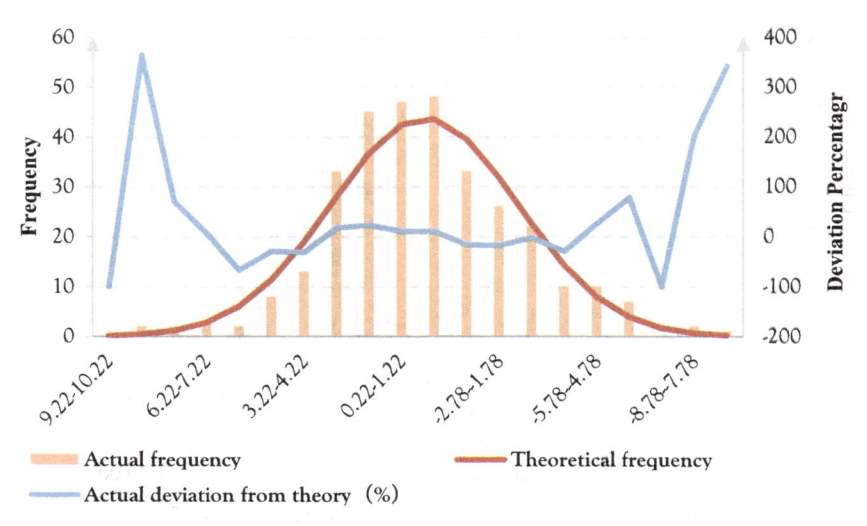

Fig. 6. Return statistics.

than zero, it can prove that the strategy is successful; When the P/E ratio is greater than 14, if the maturity point is less than the sell point, that is, the number of points on the contract expiration date minus the contract buy point result is less than zero, it can also prove that the trading strategy is successful.

Then, based on the division of months and quarters, the current period and the next period, this article divides the strategies into contract strategies that expire in the current month, contract strategies that expire next month, contract strategies that expire in the nearest quarter and contract strategies that expire in the second quarter. And using these strategies, specific trading simulations were carried out in combination with the actual P/E ratio.

Strategy Results. The success rates of the above strategies and the average, median and standard deviation of the returns are shown in the table below. Empirical results show that the success rates of the trading strategy for these different futures contracts are all above 50% except current month contract. Specifically, the success rate of the current month contract is 49.41%, the next month contract is 60.82%, the nearest quarter contract is 67.07%, and the second quarter contract is 64.03%, as Table 1 shows.

Table 1. Strategy results.

Contract Type	Success Rate	Mean	Median	Std
Current month	49.41%	27.56	0.00	1244.74
Next month	60.82%	471.73	569.96	2267.36
Nearest quarter	67.07%	394.39	396.71	2283.54
The 2nd quarter	64.03%	312.87	753.45	3238.95

3.4 Statistical Analysis

The quartiles of returns for the various strategies are shown in the Table 2 below:

Table 2. The quartiles of returns.

Quantile	0%	25%	50%	75%	100%
Current month	−4436.90	−531.02	0.00	581.94	4982.33
Next month	−6082.96	−670.50	569.96	2105.03	5703.43
Nearest quarter	−5046.97	−686.00	396.71	1908.50	6605.39
The 2nd quarter	−7492.80	−2827.71	753.45	2934.30	7106.87

The histogram of the distribution of returns is as Fig. 7. As can be seen from the four charts below, for all four contracts, the strategy's returns are mostly spread between −4000 and 4000 pips, with the returns of the second quarter contract strategy more concentrated at both ends of the spectrum, and the peak frequency of returns for the remaining three expiry time contracts all between −2000 and 2000.

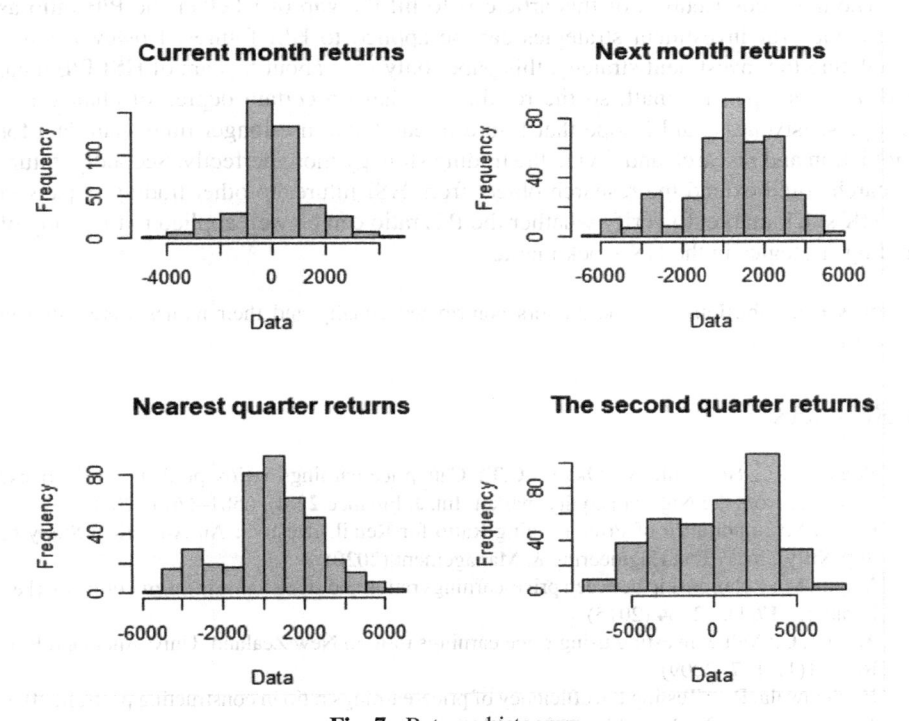

Fig. 7. Returns histogram.

4 Conclusion

This article designs a trading strategy for the Hang Seng Index futures market with the P/E ratio as a reference indicator, which has certain investment significance and reference value. By selecting the P/E ratio as the basic indicator of the trading strategy, this article proposes a new trading strategy. The empirical results show that the investment strategy based on the P/E ratio proposed in this article can help investors achieve objective returns in the HSI futures market and is feasible. The P/E ratio is an effective basic metrics of trading strategies that can increase investor returns and lower risks. Applying trading strategies based on it can effectively improve the success rate of trading and reduce risk, helping investors increase their investment profits, and providing a reference for index futures speculative trading strategies and new ideas for investment decisions in emerging markets.

Among the four trading strategies proposed, the contract strategy with the most recent quarter expiration has the highest average success rate. This article speculates that the main reason is that the strategy has a longer time span and more real-time time, and the investment strategy with the P/E ratio as a reference is also more suitable for investments with a long-term horizon. Therefore, this article suggests that when investing in indices with a long-term span, investors can use "buy when the price-earnings ratio is less than 10, sell when it is greater than 14" as a reference for investment.

The main contribution of this article is to fill the gap of whether the P/E ratio as a reference for investment strategies can be applied to HSI futures. However, when simulating the investment strategy, this paper only uses about 5 years of HSI P/E data, and the time span is small, so the results may have a certain degree of chance and less persuasiveness, and I hope that future research can use longer time span data for simulation and research and divide the trading strategy more perfectly. Secondly, future research could extend the research object from HSI futures to other trading objects in the HK stock market to verify whether the P/E ratio can be well applied to the study of trading strategies in the HK stock market.

Authors Contribution. All the authors contributed equally and their names were listed in alphabetical order.

References

1. Ikoku, A.E., Hosseini, A., Okany, C.T.: Can price-earnings ratios predict stock prices? Evidence from the Nigerian equity market. Int. J. Finance **22**(4), 6581–6611 (2010)
2. Gupta, S.: Importance of Price Earning Ratio for Retail Investors: An Analytical Study of Top Nifty Stock. Test Engineering & Management (2020)
3. Mayur, M.: Relationship between price-earnings ratios and stock value in an emerging market. Paradigm **19**(1), 52–64 (2015)
4. Truong, C.: Value investing using price earnings ratio in New Zealand. Univ. Auckland Bus. Rev. **11**(1), 1–7 (2009)
5. Bodhanwala, R.J.: Testing the efficiency of price-earnings ratio in constructing portfolio. IUP J. Appl. Finance **20**(3), 1111–1118 (2014)
6. Sharma, M., et al.: Volatility and returns analysis of U.S. PE index. J. Private Equity **14**, 38–41 (2011)

7. Hui, Y.: Is P/E ratio a valid indicator of investment decision analysis: based on an empirical analysis of the financial status quality of gem companies. Account. Econ. Res. **26**(3), 41–51 (2012)
8. Chen, G.R., Liu, R.: Can P/E ratio be an effective indicator for investment decision analysis: empirical data from china a-shares. J. Account. Res. **9**, 9–16 (2011)
9. Zhang, W.P.: Analysis of P/E ratio and stock return in shanghai stock market: a test of the effectiveness of shanghai stock market. East China Econ. Manag. **19**(9), 45–149 (2005)
10. Yu, Y., Hu, X.K.: An empirical analysis of the theoretical price-to-earnings ratio of china's stock market. Econ. Perspect. **6**, 89–91 (2011)

The Effect of Governance Dimension of ESG on Corporate Performance

Huijia Zhang(✉) and Keyou Pang

School of Tourism Management, Macao Institute for Tourism Studies, Avenida Padre Tomás Pereira, S.N., Taipa, Macao SAR, China
z1999614@yahoo.com

Abstract. Since the Chinese government put forward the "dual carbon target", China's ESG has entered a stage of rapid development, and people from all walks of life pay increased attention to the ESG governance concept of listed companies. Most of the current research on ESG and economic consequences focuses on the environmental (E) and social (E) dimensions, with a need for more research on the governance (G) dimension. Using the governance dimension score and Tobin's Q as measurement indicators, this paper proves that the governance dimension of ESG significantly promotes corporate performance by studying the operational mechanism between the governance dimension and corporate performance. The research conclusions enrich the research literature on the factors influencing the economic consequences of ESG, and provide practical implications for various stakeholders.

Keywords: ESG · Governance · Corporate Performance

1 Introduction

With the advancement of global Sustainable Development Goals, the capital market is paying increasing attention to the concept of ESG (environmental, social, and governance). ESG refers to non-economic factors that evaluate companies implementing sustainable development models, fulfilling social responsibilities, and utilizing modern management methods. Among them, the quality of governance dimension directly affects the long-term development of enterprises, investors' trust and society's stability. Good governance practices can also help firms reduce risks and costs and improve efficiency and innovation. All these factors can directly or indirectly affect enterprises' profitability and market competitiveness [1, 2]. In this research, Tobin's Q is selected as an indicator to measure corporate performance, and the data of 14420 listed companies in the A-share market from 2012 to 2021 are used as samples for empirical analysis. The study proves that the governance dimension of ESG will positively promote corporate performance.

Economic impacts are essential indicators for investment. Recently, the economic impacts related to ESG have been focused on by scholars and investors. Admittedly, the economic impact of ESG has much mutual research, but there still needs to be more effort on the Governance dimension. Matsumura et al. analyzed information about corporate environmental performance and discovered that companies with strong environmental and social performance tended to have better overall performance [3]. According to Kaul and Luo's study in 2018, companies can benefit from practicing corporate social responsibility. They discovered that if a company's social responsibility is tied to its core business or does not interfere with non-profit activities, it can lead to economic advantages [4]. Theoretically, this study provides a reference for the influencing mechanism between governance dimensions and corporate performance. Examining the connection between governance dimensions and corporate performance can benefit companies seeking to implement ESG practices. Utilizing relevant theories can offer practical recommendations for companies.

The remainder of the paper can be organized as follows: The first part is the introduction, which introduces the relevant research background and explains this paper's theoretical significance and practical significance. The second part is the literature review. This section combs the research results on the relationship between ESG, governance dimension, and corporate performance to provide theoretical guidance for subsequent empirical research. The third part is the hypothesis development, analyzing the specific mechanism of the influence of governance dimension on corporate performance and putting forward the research hypothesis of this paper. The fourth part is the research design, which expounds on the scope of sample selection, data source, model, and the definition of the main variables involved in constructing the model. The fifth part is the empirical analysis. After the empirical analysis of the samples, the conclusion is drawn, the empirical results are analyzed, and the research hypothesis proposed above is tested to analyze whether the hypothesis is valid. The last part is the conclusion, which summarizes this paper's research content and achievements and summarizes and points out the shortcomings of the research.

2 Literature Review

2.1 ESG

The ESG principle considers a company's environmental (E), social (S), and governance (G) factors in a comprehensive framework. Based on the theory of CSR, ESG is surpassing CSR and becoming an essential indicator for measuring the overall health of a company due to its institutional advantages in measurability, enforceability, and profitability [5]. ESG is a method of investing that aims to achieve long-term growth in value. Governments and organizations worldwide highly appreciate the development of ESG [6].

ESG research primarily concentrates on various aspects, including shareholder value, organizational performance, corporate charity, transparency, and institutional theory. Scholars are delving into the intricacies of environment, society, and governance. The correlation between ESG and its economic impact is a highly discussed topic. In 2020, Awaysheh and colleagues utilized the KLD database to assess the ESG status of various companies. Their findings indicated that the top-performing companies exhibited higher operational performance and market valuation than their peers. These results persisted even when the governance (G) dimension was excluded from the analysis [7]. Mackey et al. hypothesized a favorable relationship between ESG practices and corporate values by utilizing the KLD database [8]. In recent years, listed companies worldwide have been transforming their business objectives, and the goal of maximizing profits is gradually fading into history. ESG goals that contribute to sustainable development are becoming mainstream. The concept of ESG is in its early stages in China, and both the market acceptance and the completeness of supporting systems need to be improved. Environment, society, and corporate governance are crucial to the development of companies, and poor ESG performance is likely to bring risks to enterprises, leading to a decrease in profitability and damage to corporate interests. Research on the consequences of ESG and the economy can help companies realize the importance of ESG development.

2.2 Governance Dimension of ESG

ESG rating agencies mainly evaluate corporate governance from the perspectives of governance objectives, governance structure, incentive mechanism, business ethics, and controversial events [9]. As companies separate ownership and management roles, an issue called the agency problem can arise over time [10]. Jesen and Mecking believed that corporate governance should focus on the inconsistency between the ultimate goals of shareholders and senior corporate managers, and good corporate governance should form common interests between owners and actual managers [11]. Corporate governance aims to transfer management control while protecting shareholder interests. It focuses on the company's longevity, growth, principles, and financial success.

Most studies that explore how environmental, social, and governance (ESG) factors impact corporate performance or value tend to ignore the importance of overall governance. These studies focus on the relationship between specific aspects of corporate governance and overall corporate value. Regarding ownership structure, Doan et al. pointed out that increasing ownership concentration and enhancing shareholders' rights are conducive to improving corporate value [12]. Regarding board governance, Tan et al. emphasized the importance of board size on business performance [13]. Manita et al. found that diverse gender representation on the board of directors positively impacts accounting and market performance [14]. As stated by Zhu et al., an increased presence of independent directors can effectively mitigate agency conflicts and incentivize the board of directors to prioritize long-term growth when deliberating on decisions [15].

Regarding corporate governance supervision, Bai et al. believe that internal supervision methods, such as strengthening the accountability of the board of supervisors, can improve the quality of internal control and financial performance [16]. The economic consequences of a company are influenced by various factors, including governance which is crucial to its performance. This study uses the corporate governance score in ESG rating to examine the connection between governance and performance.

In order to promote sustainability development, governance (G) is essential in light of the advancements made in both the economy and society [17]. Studies indicate that implementing effective corporate governance mechanisms to support ESG initiatives can enhance the long-term value of organizations. [18–20]. Corporate governance is a crucial method for overseeing and balancing the operations of enterprises, ensuring their healthy functioning. It plays a vital role in promoting stable development in the social economy. It is advantageous for companies to investigate the correlation between governance dimensions and economic outcomes in ESG, as this can help enhance their internal environment, resulting in higher returns and sustainable growth.

2.3 Cooperate Performance

Scholars use different research methods and indicators when conducting academic research on cooperate performance. The main methods include the stock valuation method based on financial data, the stock valuation method based on market data, and the valuation method based on the future cash flow of enterprises. The leading research indicators can be summarized as return on total assets, return on equity, stock return, earnings per share, asset-liability ratio, profit margin, growth rate, operating income, and Tobin's Q value. The existing literature on corporate performance shows that the method based on financial data does not consider the differences in systemic risk, temporary imbalance effect, tax law, and accounting practices related to R&D, inventory valuation, and advertising, resulting in measurement bias [21]. Tobin's Q is a valuation method based on market data, which can measure the relationship between the market value of an enterprise and the actual asset value. Tobin's Q is a valuation technique that uses market data to determine the relationship between a company's market value and tangible asset value. It calculates the ratio of market value to real asset value and is commonly used as an indicator to assess corporate performance. The higher Tobin's Q is, the higher the market value of the cooperate is relative to the actual asset value, which means that the market holds a higher expectation for the future profit prospect of the cooperate. Tobin's Q can be used to study the investment efficiency and market competitiveness of enterprises in different industries and countries, which has a specific reference value for comparing the value of different enterprises and industries [22–24]. In summary, this study chooses Tobin's Q as the measure indicator of cooperate performance.

3 Hypothesis Development

Internally, fraud, misappropriation of public funds, and corruption are serious issues that damage an enterprise's value and share price. Corporate governance includes compliance and internal control systems that reduce the risk of adverse events and protect the corporate value and financial performance [25]. Liu & Zhu believe that improving corporate governance will enhance the company's financial security in the future, thus promoting the improvement of the company's profitability [26]. The principal-agent problem can hurt a company's financial performance. Management is accountable to external groups, which can conflict with maximizing profits for shareholders [10, 11]. If the management does not prioritize the interests of shareholders, it can lead to the principal-agent problem. However, implementing good corporate governance can effectively address this issue by minimizing agency costs, information asymmetry, and communication costs. For example, ESG corporate governance dimension can reduce agency risk by introducing external supervision to ease the information asymmetry between shareholders and management. This approach can ultimately maximize the benefits for corporate shareholders and enhance the company's profitability [17].

From the perspective of the external environment of the company, systemic risk is the risk that may cause some or all of the financial system to be damaged, thus causing a wide range of financial services disorders and causing a severe impact on the real economy. Companies with good governance can better withstand systemic financial risks and are less vulnerable to shocks [27]. Suitable shareholder governance mechanisms can help companies attract potential investors [28]. Reducing the cost of capital through lower systemic risk and higher valuations can enhance the financial performance of a company.

H1: *The governance (G) dimension of ESG positively correlates with the cooperate performance.*

4 Research Design

4.1 Sample and Data

This study uses firms listed in Shanghai and Shenzhen stock exchanges between 2012 and 2021 as samples, and focuses on the impact of the governance (G) dimension of ESG scores on the financial performance of firms. ESG rating data is sourced from the WIND database, while other relevant data is sourced from the CSMAR database. The specific sample selection process is as follows: firstly, financial and insurance firms are excluded. These firms have significant differences in their main business, size, and information disclosure compared to other listed firms. Secondly, (*) ST-listed firms are excluded. These firms have significant differences in their financial indicators and information disclosure compared to other firms. Thirdly, firms listed in the same year are excluded, as they have a shorter period for information disclosure, creating significant differences compared to other firms. Fourthly, samples with missing variables (such as audit fees and control variables) are excluded. Finally, a total of 14420 firm-year sample observations are obtained.

4.2 Model Design and Variable Definition

In order to verify the relationship between governance (G) dimension score in ESG and corporate performance (H1), models (1) (2) (3) are intended to be used for the empirical test:

$$TobinQA_{i,t+1} = \alpha_0 + \beta_1 G_{i,t} + \beta_2 CONTRS_{i,t} + \beta_3 YEARFE_{i,t} + \beta_4 FIRM_{i,t} \quad (1)$$

$$TobinQB_{i,t+1} = \alpha_0 + \beta_1 G_{i,t} + \beta_2 CONTRS_{i,t} + \beta_3 YEARFE_{i,t} + \beta_4 FIRM_{i,t} \quad (2)$$

$$TobinQC_{i,t+1} = \alpha_0 + \beta_1 G_{i,t} + \beta_2 CONTRS_{i,t} + \beta_3 YEARFE_{i,t} + \beta_4 FIRM_{i,t} \quad (3)$$

Tobin's Q is the dependent variable in this article, representing the cooperate performance of company i in period t + 1. In order to ensure the reliability of the study, the researcher chooses Tobin's Q values of three different measurement methods as the dependent variable. The article intends to use the ratio of net profit and total assets of listed companies to measure financial performance. G (governance) is the independent variable in this article, which represents the score of the G dimension in ESG for the company i in period t. CONTR represents all control variables in this article. Based on existing research literature, this paper intends to control company size (SIZE), asset-liability ratio (LEV), fixed assets (PPE), cash flow from operating activities (CFO), the proportion of independent directors (INDEP), and Board size (BSIZE). YEAR and FIRM are fixed effects controlled in this article. The variable definitions and value-taking methods are shown in Table 1.

Table 1. Variable definitions.

Variable	Description
Market value A	A shares * Current closing price of A shares + Current closing price of domestically listed foreign capital shares B shares * Current closing price of domestically listed foreign capital shares B shares + (Total number of shares - RMB ordinary shares - domestically listed foreign capital shares B shares) * (ending value of total owners' equity/ending value of paid-in capital) + ending value of total liabilities
Market value B	(Total capital stock -- domestically listed foreign capital shares B shares) * Current closing price of A shares + domestically listed foreign capital shares B shares * current closing price of B shares + current ending value of total liabilities
TobinQA	Market value A/total assets
TobinQB	Market value A/(Total assets - net intangible assets - net goodwill)
TobinQC	Market value B/total assets
G	Governance, take the score of G dimension in ESG
SIZE	The size of the company is equal to the natural log of the total assets
LEV	Asset-liability ratio, total liabilities divided by total assets
PPE	Original cost of Property, Plant, and Equipment less accumulated depreciation
CFO	Cash flows from operating activities, the cash flow generated by an enterprise in the normal course of operation
INDEP	Proportion of independent directors, the number of independent directors divided by the total number of directors on the board
BSIZE	Board size, the natural logarithm of the total number of board members
YEAR	Year fix effects
FIRM	Firm fix effects

5 Empirical Results

5.1 Descriptive Statistics

Table 2 presents the descriptive statistics of the dependent, independent, and control variables. The average values of TobinQA, TobinQB, and TobinQC are 1.886, 2.087, and 2.338, respectively. The standard deviation of TobinQ is greater than 1, indicating a significant difference in the cooperate performance of the companies in the sample. The average score of governance dimension (G) is 6.381, and the standard deviation is 1.231, indicating that each company's score of governance dimension (G) varies greatly. Among the control variables, the average value of company size is 22.357, and the standard deviation is 1.446, indicating significant differences in company size in the samples. The average proportion of independent directors is 0.381, which exceeds the regulation that at least 1/3 of the board members of listed companies should be independent directors. The descriptive statistical values of other control variables are reasonably distributed.

Table 2. Descriptive statistics result.

Variable	N	Mean	SD	p25	p50	p75
TobinQA	14420	1.886	1.261	1.170	1.499	2.071
TobinQB	14420	2.087	1.413	1.271	1.655	2.315
TobinQC	14420	2.338	1.762	1.233	1.773	2.727
G	14420	6.381	1.231	6.000	6.000	7.000
SIZE	14420	22.357	1.446	21.343	22.128	23.096
PPE	14420	0.191	0.154	0.070	0.159	0.276
CFO	14420	0.048	0.069	0.010	0.048	0.088
LEV	14420	0.430	0.213	0.260	0.417	0.580
INDEP	14420	0.381	0.073	0.333	0.364	0.429
BSIZE	14420	2.280	0.265	2.197	2.303	2.485

5.2 Regression Analysis

Table 3 presents the baseline regression results. Equations (1), (2), and (3) test the impact of governance dimension scores on cooperate performance, respectively. The regression coefficients of the governance dimension score (G) are 0.048, 0.047, and 0.041, respectively, and are all significant at the level of 1%, suggesting that the higher the governance dimension score of the company in ESG rating is, the better the corporate performance is, and H1 is verified. The analysis of the governance dimension in ESG alone proves the importance of corporate governance for firm performance. Previous practice and research on ESG have paid more attention to environmental and social dimensions. According to the results of this study, companies need to pay attention to this previously neglected dimension in practicing ESG.

Among the control variables, firm size and cash flow from operating activities are significantly related to the dependent variable. Large listed companies have high information transparency and low operational risk, and it is relatively easy to obtain financing, increasing corporate value to a certain extent. The result shows that corporate governance significantly impacts firms' value. Interestingly, there is a negative correlation between firm size and Tobin's Q, which means that larger firms may have lower value if their governance is not improved over time. There is a positive relationship between cash flow from operating activities, which refers to the cash flow generated by the company from normal operating activities, which is usually the primary source of the company's operations, and company performance. While there is a negative correlation between the asset-liability ratio and corporate performance, it is not significant. This suggests that having too much debt can negatively impact a company's performance. Therefore, enterprises need to use financial leverage reasonably to avoid any adverse effects on their performance.

Ownership structure and board characteristics are essential to corporate governance, and many scholars have studied their relationship with economic consequences. Based on the samples of top companies in India, Jackling and Johl pointed out that larger board sizes positively affect performance [29]. Alqatan et al. took financial companies in the United Kingdom as samples to study and pointed out a correlation between board independence and corporate performance [30]. The findings of this study indicate that the size of the board and the number of independent directors do not significantly impact the outcome variables. The researchers suggest that the influence of ownership structure and board characteristics on economic consequences may be limited by regional factors or a nonlinear relationship, based on analysis of previous literature.

Table 3. Baseline regression results.

	(1) TobinQA	(2) TobinQB	(3) TobinQC
G	0.048***	0.047***	0.041***
	(4.72)	(4.15)	(3.51)
Size	−0.362***	−0.229***	−0.638***
	(−12.68)	(−7.17)	(−19.16)
PPE	0.005	−0.153	−0.623***
	(0.03)	(−0.96)	(−3.76)
CFO	0.472***	0.601***	0.754***
	(3.76)	(4.27)	(5.15)
LEV	−0.162*	−0.328***	−0.759***
	(−1.70)	(−3.08)	(−6.84)
INDEP	0.082	0.051	0.276*
	(0.67)	(0.37)	(1.94)
BSIZE	−0.039	−0.058	0.041
	(−1.03)	(−1.35)	(0.92)
Constant	9.790***	7.180***	16.508***
	(15.52)	(10.15)	(22.44)
Firm	YES	YES	YES
Year	YES	YES	YES
N	14037	14037	14037
r2_a	0.708	0.708	0.779

Note: ***, **, * represent the significance levels of 1%, 5%, and 10%, respectively

6 Conclusion

In recent years, more and more investors have taken ESG as a systematic indicator to judge its impact on enterprise value. At the same time, ESG has been vigorously advocated in helping enterprises build sustainable development models, and fulfill social responsibilities and modern management methods. Relevant systematic studies still need to be improved. This paper reviews relevant literature and theories and hypothesizes the influencing mechanism between governance dimensions and corporate performance. The researchers used Stata.17 software to conduct regression analysis on the data of 14420 Chinese listed companies. The empirical results show that the relationship between corporate governance dimensions and firm performance is positive and significant. The e results also point out that the control variables, firm size and cash flow from operating activities significantly affect the model. When the company pays more attention to its governance mode and rectifies the problems such as excessive management compensation and internal corruption, it will undoubtedly reduce the management cost of the company and express positive signals to the social investors, which is conducive to establishing a good image of the company and attracting more investment, thus improving the corporate value. In actively practicing the ESG development concept, enterprises need to pay attention to the governance dimension and achieve high-quality development of enterprises more comprehensively. Enterprises should further improve the transparency of corporate governance, regularly publish business data to the public, carry out accurate information disclosure procedures, accept social supervision, and reverse promote the improvement of the internal management ability of enterprises. In addition, enterprises should carry out system updates, revision and training, and formulate detailed and practical rules of corporate governance system based on the actual situation of enterprises to ensure that each system not only meets the management needs but also gives full play to the actual effectiveness.

The implementation of the ESG concept not only needs the cooperation of industries and enterprises but also needs the support of the external environment, especially supporting incentive and restraint mechanisms. As an essential participant in the capital market, the behavior of investors has a certain feedback and correction effect on some problems existing in the capital market. Investors should also be aware of the positive effect of governance dimensions on corporate performance, so they can refer to the performance of corporate governance dimensions when selecting investment objects to make investment decisions to improve investment reliability.

This study still has limitations. Because the development of ESG in China is just in its infancy, ESG scores and other data for Chinese companies only cover a decade, making longer-term trends insufficiently observable. This paper does not introduce moderating and mediating variables, so exploring the influence mechanism may not be comprehensive enough. This paper focuses on Chinese-listed companies, and the findings may not be persuasive in a cross-cultural context. Future studies can consider adding samples from different countries and regions, which can further increase the universality of research results.

References

1. Gurol, B., Lagasio, V.: Corporate governance and market performance of European banks: analysing differences and similarities between one-tier and two-tier models. Int. J. Bus. Gov. Ethics **15**(1), 21–37 (2021)
2. Adeloye, G.: Effect of corporate governance on the performance of financial institutions in Nigeria. Sci. J. Bus. Manag. **9**(2), 119 (2021)

3. Matsumura, E.M., Prakash, R., Vera-Munoz, S.C.: Firm-value effects of carbon emissions and carbon disclosures. Account. Rev. **89**(2), 695–724 (2014)
4. Kaul, A., Luo, J.: An economic case for CSR: the comparative efficiency of for-profit firms in meeting consumer demand for social goods. Strateg. Manag. J. **39**(6), 1650–1677 (2018)
5. The evolution of ESG from CSR (2022). https://www.lexology.com/library/detail.aspx?g=80bbe258-a1df-4d4c-88f0-6b7a2d2cbd6a
6. Li, T.T., Wang, K., Sueyoshi, T., Wang, D.D.: ESG: Research progress and future prospects. Sustainability **13**(21), 11663 (2021)
7. Awaysheh, A., Heron, R.A., Perry, T., Wilson, J.I.: On the relation between corporate social responsibility and financial performance. Strateg. Manag. J. **41**(6), 965–987 (2020)
8. Mackey, A., Mackey, T.B., Barney, J.B.: Corporate social responsibility and firm performance: investor preferences and corporate strategies. Acad. Manag. Rev. **32**(3), 817–835 (2007)
9. Wong, W.C., Batten, J.A., Mohamed-Arshad, S.B., Nordin, S., Adzis, A.A.: Does ESG certification add firm value? Financ. Res. Lett. **39**, 101593 (2021)
10. Berle, A.A., Means, G.G.C.: The modern corporation and private property. Transaction Publishers (1991)
11. Jensen, M.C., Meckling, W.H.: Theory of the firm: Managerial behavior, agency costs and ownership structure. J. Financ. Econ. **3**(4), 305–360 (1976)
12. Doan, A.T., Le, A.T., Tran, Q.: Economic uncertainty, ownership structure and small and medium enterprises performance. Aust. Econ. Pap. **59**(2), 102–137 (2020)
13. Tan, X., Song, Z., Yang, T.: Empirical analysis of equity structure and operating performance of listed banks in China. Financial Research **11**, 144–154 (2010)
14. Manita, R., Bruna, M.G., Dang, R., Houanti, L.H.: Board gender diversity and ESG disclosure: evidence from the USA. J. Appl. Account. Res. (2018)
15. Zhu, J., Rao, P., Bao, M.: Equity structure, credit behavior and bank performance: an empirical study based on data from urban commercial banks in China. Financial Res. **7**, 31–47 (2012)
16. Bai, H., Han, R., Sun, Y.: The impact of internal control of listed companies in the securities industry on financial performance. China Prices **4**, 95–98 (2021)
17. Li, J., Yang, Z., Chen, J., Cui, W.: Mechanism research of ESG promoting corporate performance: Based on the perspective of corporate innovation. Sci. Sci. Manag. S&T **42**(9), 71–89 (2021)
18. Brammer, S., Millington, A.: Does it pay to be different? An analysis of the relationship between corporate social and financial performance. Strateg. Manag. J. **29**(12), 1325–1343 (2008)
19. Eccles, R.G., Ioannou, I., Serafeim, G.: The impact of corporate sustainability on organizational processes and performance. Manage. Sci. **60**(11), 2835–2857 (2014)
20. Esteban-Sanchez, P., de la Cuesta-Gonzalez, M., Paredes-Gazquez, J.D.: Corporate social performance and its relation with corporate financial performance: International evidence in the banking industry. J. Clean. Prod. **162**, 1102–1110 (2017)
21. Benston, G.J.: The validity of profits−structure studies with particular reference to the FTC's line of business data. Am. Econ. Rev. **75**, 37–67 (1985)
22. Tobin, J.: A general equilibrium approach to monetary theory. J. Money Credit Bank. **1**(1), 15–29 (1969)
23. Tobin, J.: On the efficiency of the financial system. Lloyds Bank Rev. **153**, 1–15 (1984)
24. Hayashi, F.: Tobin's marginal Q and average Q: a neoclassical interpretation. Econometrica **50**(1), 213–224 (1982)
25. Hong, H., Kacperczyk, M.: The price of sin: the effects of social norms on markets. J. Financ. Econ. **93**(1), 15–36 (2009)
26. Liu, Y., Zhu, L.: An empirical study on corporate governance and enterprise value. Manage. Rev. **23**(2), 45–52 (2011)

27. Gregory, A., Tharyan, R., Whittaker, J.: Corporate social responsibility and firm value: disaggregating the effects on cash flow, risk and growth. J. Bus. Ethics **124**, 633–657 (2014)
28. El Ghoul, S., Guedhami, O., Kwok, C., Mishra, R.: Does corporate social responsibility affect the cost of capital? J. Bank. Finance **35**(9), 2388–2406 (2011)
29. Jackling, B., Johl, S.: Board structure and firm performance: evidence from India's top companies. Corp. Gov. Int. Rev. **17**(4), 492–509 (2009)
30. Alqatan, D.A., Chbib, I., Hussainey, K.: How does board structure impact on firm performance in the UK? Corp. Board Role Duties Compos. **15**(2) (2019)

Impact of Green Financing and Public Policies Towards Investment Yield: Evidence from European and Asian Economies

Mirza Nasir Jahan Mehdi[1(✉)] and Syed Ali Raza Hamid[2]

[1] Management Sciences, Uswa Institute of Higher Education (Punjab University), Islamabad 45750, Pakistan
`dr.mirza.hod_bba@uihe.edu.pk`
[2] HIMS, Hamdard University Islamabad, Islamabad 45600, Pakistan
`ali.raza@hamdard.edu.pk`

Abstract. The green investment & financing are the key concerned areas of the prevalent green management which are inspected by most of the green investors to ascertain the viability for the appropriate investment opportunities in the green investment regions. This study is oriented to examine the expected relationship between green financing, public policies and investment yield, which ultimately affect the green investors of the targeted Asian and European economies. The cross section data for the period of 2011–2022 related to green, public policy and controlling variables; have been congregated from the websites and reports of Bloom Berg NEF, WBI, IFS, Federal Banks of Asia & Europe, Global Financial Development Database, and ADBI. After checking the different diagnostics tests, and calculating the descriptive statistics, the long term effect of green financing and public policies towards investment yield through Pooled OLS, DOLS, and FMOLS are analyzed in the E-Views. The empirically calculated findings declare that Green Mutual Funds, Green Wage Rate, and Local Weather Forecast affect insignificantly on the investment yield, while rest of the factors affect significantly on the investment yield (ROI), which lead to meet the maximum objectives of this study. The significant results proclaim the empirical allegiance of all the study factors in the Asian & European green markets. The insignificant findings instigate the policy makers to reappraise the green considerations and flaws in promoting the green innovations must be controlled by some concrete green policies and green investment awareness programs. By and large, the lenient low green financing cost can boost the green projects in the long run.

Keywords: Green Financing · Investment Yield · Renewability · Sustainability · Cross Section · Public Policy · Financial Development Database · Diagnostic Tests · Policy Makers

1 Introduction

The phenomenon of green financial economy is capturing the due attention of the investors, household consumers, business suppliers, and government agencies, rapidly since the last two decades in this global village [4]. Undoubtedly, the concept of the green financing and investment, was in vogue in the developed economy including USA, China, France, Germany, Russia and many more others, even though during the last five decades, on the theoretical and practical grounds [10]. Green financing these days, contrary to the conventional financing, emphasizes on the needs of the green management for the renewable energy and sustainable development projects, which are compatible to keep this planet from the mass destruction that can be expected due to the lavish utilization of the existent resources [2]. Until recently, during the past era since 2012–2022, many of the sustainable and energy related projects are funded by the green investment financing programs for the promotion of the wind energy, solar energy, biogas fuels, and hydropower (Amran et al., 2020). In the report published by International Energy Agency (IEA), the global final energy source from the renewable projects amounted to 19.20% which will reach to almost > 50% by 2030 from the current renewable energy panels in the European and Asian states, while the electricity generation from the energy sustainable financing projects was only 18.43% during the 2020 [23] owing to less attention towards green sustainable activities.

Public Policies are oriented towards financial economic stability, prices stability in the states, encouraging the investment opportunities, to retain the optimum level of resources, to pursue the employment level, accelerating the rate of economic growth, and the capital formation, to retain the balance between political & administrative structures, to collect the taxes revenues, And to operate the public spending [26]. Public Policies are settled down by the experts and policy makers at institutional and federal levels. These policy makers are directed to structure the policies keeping in view the state economic conditions, interests groups, different NGSs, political parties' agendas, innovative scientific and technological adoptions, finding the public opinions through surveys, and by taking the concerns of the business community [63]. The policy related decisions are affected by many factors including the political upheavals, law & order uncertainty, and financial distractions. Ideological differences at individuals & state level, pragmatic applications of the policy contents also constitute the policy making effective. For the green investment growth, the policy makers of the state & financial institutions are joined in hands [51].

In the Asian and European economies, the policy makers at state level are spending huge funds on R&D green projects to follow the green renewable energy and sustainable funding projects. The green firms, ultimately, are also inclined either towards the green financing institutions for the funds to meet the infrastructure requisites, or by offering its green funds' schemes to collect the funds from the investors at domestic and institutional level (Adedoyin et al., 2020). Public spending, R&D, employment level and, labor rates, interest rate, infrastructural planning are considered the eminent notions for the green financing and economic growth, that resultantly leads to the investment yield, the investor is expected for. One of the critical indicators of the investment yield, is also the political stability that controls the green financing schemes in the Asian and European Arenas [3]. The Human Capital Index (HCI) and Foreign Exchange Rates (FXR) are the other controlling drivers of the green management economy, to promote the yields to the green investors. On the other hand, the failure of the economies to meet Public Expenditure deficits and Taxation deficits, is due to state inability to establish the balance between these two indicators, leading to crises of green funds, which lowers the investment returns affixed with the green projects [34].

The Asian and European Economies are keenly directed towards the green management schemes. To realize the green projects, the green firms are oriented for the green funds, a sufficient portion of these funds, is borrowed from the green investors at domestic and at institutional level. These investors are risk-tolerant and risk-aversion simultaneously [53]. The Asian investors are especially, ambitious towards their parts of earnings as early as these can be recovered. The investors delegate their compact responsibility towards the stockholders and borrowers (firm owners) for the dividend policy, retained earnings and the growth of variant profitability ratios like ROI, ROE, ROCE and the size of many more financial ratios towards parallel market industry indicators [43]. On the other hands, the European investors of the developed states are more attentive towards the growth of the green firms rather it is slow, being observed the key value of the renewable energy generations and disasters [16]. Evidently, the financial health (investment yield) of the green industry's firms, to some ways are also the product of the profound public policies towards fiscal and monetary grounds simultaneously [13].

2 A Critical Review of Literature

Jin et al. (2021) indicated that green financing can promote the green energy and renewable projects, including the wind energy, biogas energy, and fossil fuels as China is the sole biggest consumer of the total energy, that is comprised almost the 27% of the total world energy (Energy Outlook, 2018). Besides, the green environmental technologies, infrastructures and advance equipment can be produced easily and affordability to purchase the green products by the smaller firms becomes possible though the green financing like green bonds [46], green mutual funds and green investment funds [24, 33, 58]. Through the green funded power plants, the researchers investigated the emissions of CO_2 and identified the green effects of CO_2 on green firms' financial growth [11, 27]. The core inclusion behind the green financing is concerned with the environment friendly energy & sustainable schemes to facilitate the economic growth and ultimately evade the risk embedded with the growth of these sustainable products [49, 56]. Recently, He et al. (2019) presented an innovative description for the green financing and its productive applications. To him (2019), green financing makes possible the human capital resources for the green funded renewable energy production and the protection for sustainable environment dilemma [45, 64]. Mengumi et al. (2022) indicate that green credit schemes, green insurance funds, green mutual funds, green investment securities, and green carbon finance; can produce the renewable investment efficiency for low energy consumption projects, high efficient green firms, and for the low polluted sustainable environment (Zhang et al., 2016; He et al., 2018; [9]). For the successful planning and implementation by the green financing firms [42, 52], the Asian Development Bank (ADB, 2017) has determined the three key impediments for the green firms. First, they should identify the right kind of renewable & sustainable green project. Secondly, the green firms' evaluators and investors [38] should identify the complex planning that can be implemented for the both public and private green financing programs and finally, the green analyst must structure the green financing products (i.e. green investment funds, green investment bonds, and green climatic & environmental funds etc.) towards green renewable and sustainable projects (Zhongming et al., 2017). Furthermore, the ASEAN countries (Azhgaliyeva et al., 2020; Banga, 2019) are also busy in attempt to get closed the pool of financial markets' investors to realize them degradation of energy & sustainability issues, and ultimately to advise for investing in the green financial products to settle their contributions towards mankind safety and get their due financial benefits through these green projects as well (North, 2016; Volz, 2018; 48).

Public Policies are settled down all over the world to meet the energy and sustainable needs of water, air, oxygen, CO_2 and fresh environment, for the settlers of this globe. Similarly, efforts are being made to restore the energy and sustainable deficiency in the European and Asian regions [6; Ghasemi et al., 2019). The chief interest of the political and public institutions is to provide a guidelines and policy structure to the green financing firms and green products' investors (Iram et al., 2020). Policy institutions debate that GDP/capita is increased for the countries, where the green renewable energy & sustainable projects are initiated to foresee the deficiency of the oxygen, water and air (Zhang and Zhang, 2018). On the other hand, Wu et al. (2021) identify that private expenditures for R&D to explore the green needs and green Problems, are not sufficient to meet the green financing needs satisfactory. In the light of this deficiency, the public sector involvement becomes crucial to meet the capital funds needs for the planning and implementation of the green activities (Anser, 2019; Facchini and Seghezza, 2018; Yang, 2017). Likewise, restructuring the fiscal and monetary policies are compatible to channel the funds from the public sector, investors and other green stakeholders towards green R&D activities; ultimately out of these capital funds, an adequate portion can be spent on labor & infrastructure expenses [53, 54]. Strategically, Lepitzki and Axsen (2018) and Iqbal et al. (2020) assert that R&D is the significant driver that can foster the green renewable and sustainable energy projects in the remote sustainable regions [6, 34].

Alonso-Conde et al. (2020) depicted the need for green bond financing for renewable and sustainable projects to observe the effects of green financing on the profitability (ROI) of the green listed firms. They (2020) identified that the global energy consumption through coal can be reduced to 3.5% per annum if the renewable energy projects are financed through the green financing bonds [30, 44]. According to Bhutta et al. (2022) the cashflows after taxes, interests and all other expenses, overall can mitigate or reduce the risk of the green firms. This risk-aversion and capital flows makes it possible the financial earning indicators (ROI) of the green firms to be accepted by the green investors [15, 18]. Conversely, the green firms are less attentive to increase the Retained Earnings, Dividend Payout Ratio, Return on Equity, Return on Investment, and Return on Capital Employed [19, 65]. On the other side, Brunnschweiler (2010) determined that cost of capital affects the profitability (ROI) of green firms badly owing to that higher cost of capital of the loan institutions the green financing firms which are tilted to borrow the green loans, or collect the capital funds through green bonds, green mutual funds, green investment securities, or other types of green financial Instruments [21, 25, 60].

The main objective of this study is aimed to generate the significant short term and long term relationship among the green financing indicators, public policy related factors, controlling determinants and measurement of investment yield return. This relationship covers the main paradigm of the core problem statement area of this green financing renewable sustainable study. The conceptual pretext of all the determinants and investment yield, has already been elaborated through the following diagram (Fig. 1):

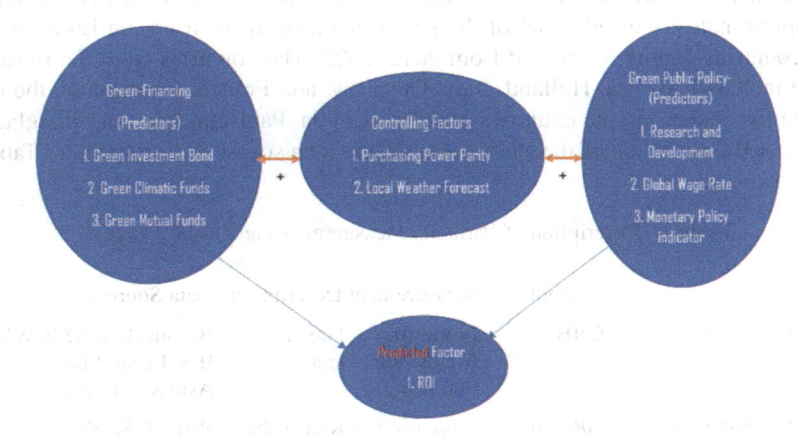

Fig. 1. .

To test the linkage for all the dimensions of green financing and public policies along with the controlling effect, with the dimensions of investment yield; the following propositions are established after observing the theoretical and empirical grounds of all the dimensions.

Proposition First: Green financing dimensions (1. Green Investment Bond- H1; Green Climatic Funds-H2; Green Mutual Funds-H-3: influence the investment yield parameters (ROI) positively.

Proposition Second: Public Policy factors (Research and Development- H4; Global Wage Rate- H5; Monetary Policy indicator-H6), affect significantly on investment yield.

Proposition Third: The Controlling indicators (Purchasing Power Parity-H7; Local Weather Forecast-H8) in combined with green financing indicators and Public policy dimensions, have significant interaction with the investment yield.

3 Variables, Data and Methods of the Study

This section is oriented to elaborate in details the data collection tools, data variables & specifications, and finally the econometric methods of the study to retrieve the hypothesized study's target issues on the grounds of empirical justification.

3.1 Variables and Data Description

This study is segmented to apply the Slack Based Method (SBM), a data envelopment analysis approach that weighs the multidimensional indicators according to their proportion. According to [38], this data driven approach has the capacity to reduce the number of factors, because it indicates the performance improvement directions in addition to the performance evaluation criteria. It was decided to cut short our sample to 200 firms of ten countries of merely Asian and European Blocks. All this was obviously conducted keeping in view the Slack Based Method, a practical data envelope approach to evade the aftermath's hindrances during data compilation. Subsequently, we applied the proportionate balanced panel of the green financing firms from ten European and Asian countries coping the period from 2012–2022. The countries from the European belt are included Austria, Holland, Italy, Germany, and France; whereas, on the other hand the five Asian sample countries are China, India, Pakistan, Iran, and Bangladesh. A condensed description of the study variable and data sources, is provided in Table 1.

Table 1. Description of Variable, Measurements and Data Sources.

Variables	Symbol	Measurement Description	Data Sources
Green Investment Bonds	GItB	Proportion of Green Bonds/Total Debt Financing	Bloom Berg NEF, WBI, IFS, Federal Banks of Asia & Europe,
Green Renew-Climatic Funds	GRnClF	Proportion of Renewable Funds/TDF	WBI, IFS, WER, IEA-World Energy Outlook, EPA
Green Mutual Funds	GMutF	Proportion of Green Mutual Funds /TDF	Bloom Berg NEF,ADBI, WBI, GFDDB
Research and Development	RDT	Cost of Patents + Cost of copy rights	WBI, IFS, Financial Times, Annual NNDP Reports
Global Wage Rate	GWgRt	Total Labor/GDP	WBI, Annual UNDP Reports, HDI, Ministry of Labor
Monetary Policy indicator	MonPolI	% share of capital to green firms/Total GDP	WBI, IFS, ADBI, ECB
Purchasing Power Parity	PrPwPt	FXR = local currency value. Value/$ value	Federal Banks of Asia & Europe, GFDDB
Local Weather Forecast	LWtrFt	Actual volume of Air Pressure – Expected Volume of Air Pressure	MWF, UNEP, WMO, IPCC
Return on Investment	RInvt	Net Gain/Initial Cost * 100	Global Financial Development Database

Note: All the variables are constructed from the empirical studies & theoretical backgrounds

3.2 Econometric Methods and Models

To test the effect of green financing factors on the investment yield (ROI), we at the first stage structured a very basic econometric models that are given below;

$$Yit = f(GItB; GRnClF; GMutF; RDT; GWgRt; MonPoll; PrPwPt; LWtrFt)$$

Firstly, we conducted the Pearson Pairwise Correlation Test: Cross Section Dependence Test (CD). Aftermath, Panel Unit Root Test was undertaken to check the stationarity of data series at order or at first level. The general econometric equation for the to examine the unit root into the data is depicted as the following;

$$D(Y_t) = \alpha_0 + \beta_t + YY_{t-1} + D(Y_t(-1)) + \mu_t \quad (1)$$

Keeping in view the time series segment of Panel data series, the Ordinary Least Squared (OLS) & Dynamic Ordinary Least Squared (DOLS) methods, are also projected to estimate the combined long term produced results. Besides, to generate the long term findings for all the study variables from all the sample countries are also produced through Fully Modified Ordinary Least Squared (FMOLS) estimation econometrical technique.

$$\ln(RInvt)it = \beta 1i \ln(GItB)it + \beta 2i \ln(GRnClF)it + \beta 3i \ln(GMutF)it \\ + \beta 4i \ln(RDt) + \beta 5i \ln(GWgRt)it + \beta 6i \ln(MonPoll) \\ + \beta 7i \ln(PwPt)it + \beta 8i \ln(LWtrFt)it + \Psi it$$

4 Empirical Results Through Estimated Steps

This part of the study forges the estimated results through different Parametric & non-Parametric tests. These kinds of step-wise estimation methods through different tests are compiled by Bhattacharya et al. (2016), Mehrara et al. (2012) and, Apergis & Payne (2010). To combat the statically differences, we calculated the descriptive statistics (Table 2) first of all like others studies of this are. The results are shown below.

To make ensure the heterogeneity across different countries of Asian & European regions (Table 3), we estimated the average annual growth/annum of the concerned modified determinants. Following the heterogeneous panel models (separate regression for each sample country), we notice a limited homogeneity among the countries.

The results of the Table 4 demonstrate the significance of most of the famous Cointegration tests as maximum p-statistics are significant.

For the long term Panel Analysis, the three regression models entail: Pooled ordinary least squared (OLS), dynamic ordinary least squared (DOLS), and fully modified ordinary least squared (FMOLS) are estimated in the E-VIEWS as presented in Table 5 given below.

Table 2. Summary Statistics.

Variables	Mean	St. Dev	Minimum	Maximum	Skewness	Kurtosis	N
GItB	1127.7984	1543.6735	254.9845	3487.8453	2.9854	11.8736	
GRnClF	9864.3765	7893.9825	284.8734	15432.9846	4.6754	20.7453	
GMutF	432.9845	367.9654	238.4539	4532.7636	−1.5482	−5.5429	
RDT	894.4679	798.5843	298.3864	4539.7639	2.8320	10.5639	
GWgRt	675.9870	765.9387	50.4527	2398.5937	6.3921	−46.3920	
MonPolI	.9876	0.7538	.2876	3.6754	5.2973	37.9847	
PrPwPt	0.6758	0.8745	0.1745	5.9374	2.6730	−8.7648	
LWtrFt	37.8654	43.6728	25.9376	874.390	−1.7562	6.5420	
RInvt	0.8736	1.0828	0.3461	2.8730	−2.8927	9.4835	

Source: The Step-based Statistical Empirical Analysis

Table 3. Average Annual Growth (%) of the Variables Corresponding to European Region.

	Austria	Holland	Italy	Germany	France	China	India	Pakistan	Iran	Ban-Desh
GItB	7.45	6.45	4.23	9.89	5.67	4.82	2.85	3.76	3.45	−2.86
GRnClF	−1.34	4.45	7.49	8.87	5.46	3.30	2.57	3.87	4.37	3.93
GMutF	2.67	8.67	−3.56	4.56	1.17	1.39	3.26	−1.48	2.38	2.87
RDT	4.82	2.85	3.76	3.45	−2.86	1.18	2.18	1.92	3.30	3.76
GWgRt	1.39	3.26	−1.48	2.38	2.87	.74	1.12	.65	2.38	2.29
MonPolI	1.85	4.62	3.78	3.95	4.47	2.67	8.67	−3.56	4.56	1.17
PrPwPt	2.38	3.83	2.86	3.90	4.28	−3.48	3.26	−5.78	−1.18	3.27
LWtrFt	2.63	3.76	2.25	4.28	3.97	1.85	4.62	3.78	3.95	4.47
RInvt	3.30	2.57	3.87	4.37	3.93	−2.56	4.92	2.37	8.84	6.38

Note: the growth statistics are derived by the authors' self-econometric analysis

Table 4. Panel Cointegration Results.

Tests' Types	Panel Tests' Names	Statistics	p-value
Pedroni	Augmented Dickey Fuller Test	−8.4672	0.0000***
	Phillips-Perron (PP-Test)	−7.7638	0.0000***
	Modified Phillips-Perron Test	2.7847	0.0004***
Kao	Dickey Fuller Test	−2.5762	0.0070***
	Augmented Dickey Fuller Test	−2.2674	0.0145**

(*continued*)

Table 4. (*continued*)

Tests' Types	Panel Tests' Names	Statistics	p-value
	Modified Dickey Fuller Test	−0.3246	0.5673
	Unadjusted Dickey Fuller Test	−1.5763	0.0646***
	Unadjusted Modified Dickey Fuller Test	1.3247	0.1257
Westerlund	Variance Ratio Statistics	−1.4763	0.0783***

Note: p-values are significant at 0.01 (***), 0.05 (**) & 0.1 (*)

Table 5. Panel Analysis of the Variables.

Variables	Polled OLS-Statistics			DOLS-Statistics			FMOLS-Statistics		
	Coefficient	t-stats	p-value	Coefficients	t-stats	p-value	Coefficient	t-stats	p-value
Intercept									
GItB	0.4309 (0.0225)	19.15**	0.0043	0.4215 (0.02341)	17.98**	0.0042	0.4056 (0.0223)	18.18**	0.0044
GRnClF	−69.5708 (32.56)	−2.10**	0.0442	−67.5608 (34.25)	−1.973**	0.0431	−72.4385 (35.92)	−2.016**	0.0431
GMutF	15.876 (75.53)	0.210	0.0738	12.874 (87.23)	0.147	0.0734	13.758 (78.47)	0.1754	0.0628
RDT	−18.76 (0.5648)	−33.22**	0.0015	−16.47 (0.3762)	−43.77**	0.0041	−14.52 (0.4541)	−31.97**	0.0025
GWgRt	−7.58 (45.98)	−0.165	0.548	−6.90 (57.87)	−0.119	0.645	−8.95 (42.73)	−0.209	0.443
MonPolI	−2562.467 (1407.226)	−1.821	0.067	−2348.672 (1522.487)	−1.54	0.058	−2638.487 (1397.337)	−1.890	0.062
PrPwPt	−3.6745 (1.4387)	−2.55**	0.0437	−3.8722 (1.3585)	−2.85**	0.0492	−3.3756 (1.5582)	−2.170**	0.0339
LWtrFt	11.597 (75.6487)	0.153	0.5527	10.487 (78.472)	0.133	0.5481	9.7528 (80.487)	0.1211	0.4527
R^2-value	0.7462			0.7212			0.7384		
F-Stats	114.508			127.634			122.582		

Note: S.E are in parenthesis; (DV: Return on Investment and P/E Ratio, (**) stands that results are significant at 0.05 level.

5 Findings and Discussions of Green Investment Based Study

This section of the study interprets the findings of multiple estimated steps as well as exposes the empirical discussion of the findings with the support of theoretical and empirical grounds. The Table 2 displays the summary statistics of all the study variables. We can conclude that all the predictors are fitted to illustrate the predictors and controlling factors. The mean values for both the factors are satisfactory (if MV > 3). It can be marked by the Table 2, that most of the mean values are acceptable. On the other hand, the dispersion values (S.D) are low around the mean values for all the factors, except than only few factors. The similar kind of mean and S.D findings are observed in the research projects of Bhattacharya et al. (2016) and Apergis and Payne (2010). The pervasive findings (Table 3) highlight the average annual growth of the ten European and Asian Countries. The statistics justify the reasonable and admitted growth factor across each individual sample country. The growths in factors, are realistic (if Growth Rate $< 5\%$) and trumpet the increasing trends of green investment modes by the global investors to save this planet from the mass destruction of energy crises in the future. By and large, the findings (Table 3) as regards Asian & European countries intricate the adoption of green financing and sustainability projects ultimately to increase the yields for the green investors. The findings [17, 40, 65] also empirically justify the similar heterogeneity among the panel countries of Asia and Europe. There is slightly difference of values in the findings of OLS, DOLS and FMOLS which can be observed by the statistics of the Table 5. This can be complied with the findings that green investment (GItB) affect significantly on the investment yields (t-value $= 19.15 > 1.96$; p-value $= 0.0043$) through OLS model. These significant values describe the benefits for the green investors through green bonds purchasing in the green capital markets. These significant statistics are consistent with the findings of Zhang et al. (2021), and Barua & Chiesa (2019). For the green renewable climatic funds (GRnClF), the findings of Table 5 (t-value $= -1.973 > 1.96$; p-value $= 0.0431$) through DOLS model, demolish that 'GRnClF' significantly impacts the investment yield (ROI) yielding the significant attractions for the investors who are looking to invest their idle funds in the green renewable climatic securities in the open capital markets [9, 32, 42]. The second hypothesis is empirically targeted to meet the concerned objective positively. On the other hand, in case of green mutual funds (GMutF), the insignificant findings (t-value $= 0.1754 < 1.96$; p-value $= 0.0628$) are noticed in the Table 5 through FMOLS model. The insignificant effect of GMutF to predict the ROI, does not meet the third green financing objective, all which also tends to reject the third hypothesis of the study. This insignificance reveals the little awareness of the green investors for mutual funds or owing to its risky nature in the capital markets. The similar findings are observed by Abolhosseini & Heshmati (2014), Wang & Zhi (2016) and Lyeonov et al. (2019). As regards the Public Policy Factors affecting the investment yield, it has been confirmed through the findings of Table 5 that policy factor namely green research and development (RDT), has significant effect (t-value $= 43.77$ for RDT from FMOLS) on the investment yield, and this significant finding is inclined to accept the 4th hypothesis of this green financing study. This significant finding disseminate the high consideration research & development funds. These findings support the results of studies [28, 48, 51]. On the converse side, the findings of Table 5 disclose that two policy factors green wage rate (GWgRt) and monitory policy (MonPolI) have insignificant effects towards investment yield (ROI). These insignificant findings declare that green projects are not affected owing to increase or decrease in the wage rates of the workers who are involved into the green financing projects. These insignificant findings validate the rejection of 5th and 6th hypotheses respectively, and resultantly don't fulfill the correspondent objectives. Criscuolo and Menon (2015), Taghizadeh and Yoshino (2020), and Lamperti et al. (2021), also identified the similar insignificant effects of wage rates and monitory policy factors towards the financial growth. According to FMOLS model, the findings expose that PrPwPt significantly influences the green investment yield owing to the t-value (2.17) and ultimately significant p-values (0.0339). This all is the indication for the espousal of incremental management incentives to target the green financing strategies, which can eventually cause the higher investment yield in return. Sun et al. (2020), and Raberto et al. (2019), determined the similar significant in their observations in their divergent studies. Therefore, we are destined to accept the 7th hypothesis of the study to meet our concerned objective. Finally, the findings (t-value = 0.133 & p-stats = 0.5481) of local weather forecast (LWtrFt) in the Table 5 through the MOLS model, presage that LWtrFt has the insignificant impact on the investment yields, and in return final hypothesis (8th) is rejected. This empirically denotes that water, energy, biogases, and weather can insignificantly cause the decrease in green financing and investment yield which is controversial on the real grounds w.r.t green renewable strategies. This insignificant result is coherent with the studies [36, 55, 59]. Not but not the least, the R2 statistical values (Table 5) of Pooled OLS, DOLS, and FMOLS (074, 0.72, and 0.73) are also empirically justified that show the maxim effect of the green financing, policy factors, and controlling factors on the investment yields. Similarly, the fitness (F-stats) of all the three regression models is also effective leading to the strengths of the three OLS models (114.51, 127.634, and 122.58) to measure the investment yield.

6 Conclusion and Policy Implications

The green management and green sustainable projects are being occupied by the motivational researchers and practitioners. This is why, this study is a stab to curve the green financing issues prevailing in the far-flung areas of the European and Asian states. The study illuminates the impacts of the green financing factors to yield the consummate rewards for the green investors. To conclude, the effects of green financing factors (Green Investment Bond; Green Renew-Climatic Funds; and Green Mutual Funds), policy related factors (Research and Development; Global Wage Rate; and Monetary Policy indicator), and controlling factors (Purchasing Power Parity; and Local Weather Forecast) are acceded to achieve the forecasted investment yields for the period 2011–2022 by the empirical designation of models namely Pooled OLS, DOLS, and FMOLS. It is concluded from the Panel OLS, DOLS, and FMOLS Analysis that only the Green Mutual Funds, Green Wage Rate, and Local Weather Forecast affect insignificantly on the investment yields, while all the rest of the factors impact significantly leading to meet the uttermost objectives of this green financing study. The results of the study are the indications for a lot of conclusions which are drawn on the grounds of strong empirical rationales and these are mostly described in the previous debate. On the grounds of the results, a few of the policy related implications are structured. Firstly, the awareness for the green financing modes and green banking must be differentiated by the policy makers. Secondly, policy as regards the green mutual funds must be structured and floated among the green investors through different platforms, like social media, seminars, webinars, conferences & workshops for the promotion of green schemes. Third, the policy institutions must be dictated by the governance of the countries to ascertain the green financing policies while the implementation of any green renewable and sustainable project. Fourth, the green firms must be briefed and polished about the awareness of R&D projects relevant to green renewability. Fifth, the green firms must be tilted and forced by the policy implementations to serve the labor of the green projects with due and market wages. Finally, the local weather authorities must be equipped with the appropriable instrument to measure the weather forecast for the operations of green projects. The weather authorities must be ascertained the literacy and training of the field workers of the weather departments.

References

1. Abolhosseini, S., Heshmati, A.: The main support mechanisms to finance renewable energy development. Renew. Sustain. Energy Rev. **40**, 876–885 (2014)
2. Adedoyin, F.F., Alola, A.A., Bekun, F.V.: An assessment of environmental sustainability corridor: the role of economic expansion and research and development in EU countries. Sci. Total. Environ. **713**, 136726 (2020)
3. Afonso, A., Furceri, D.: Government size, composition, volatility and economic growth. Eur. J. Polit. Econ. **26**(4), 517–532 (2010)
4. Agliardi, E., Agliardi, R.: Financing environmentally-sustainable projects with green bonds. Environ. Dev. Econ. **24**(6), 608–623 (2019)
5. Alonso-Conde, A.B., Rojo-Suárez, J.: On the effect of green bonds on the profitability and credit quality of project financing. Sustainability **12**(16), 6695 (2020)
6. Aly, A., Jensen, S.S., Pedersen, A.B.: Solar power potential of Tanzania: identifying CSP and PV hot spots through a GIS multicriteria decision making analysis. Renewable Energy **113**, 159–175 (2017)
7. Amran, A., Nejati, M., Ooi, S.K., Darus, F.: Exploring issues and challenges of green financing in Malaysia: perspectives of financial institutions. Sustain. Soc. Responsib. Account. Report. Syst. 255–266 (2018)
8. Anser, M.K.: Impact of energy consumption and human activities on carbon emissions in Pakistan: application of STIRPAT model. Environ. Sci. Pollut. Res. **26**(13), 13453–13463 (2019). https://doi.org/10.1007/s11356-019-04859-y
9. Apergis, N.: Renewable energy and its finance as a solution to the environmental degradation. Environ. Kuznets Curve (EKC) 55–63 (2019)
10. Apergis, N., Payne, J.E.: Renewable energy consumption and economic growth: evidence from a panel of OECD countries. Energy Policy **38**(1), 656–660 (2010)
11. Arabi, B., Munisamy, S., Emrouznejad, A., Shadman, F.: Power industry restructuring and eco-efficiency changes: a new slacks-based model in Malmquist-Luenberger Index measurement. Energy Pol. **68**, 132–145 (2014)
12. Azhgaliyeva, D., Kapoor, A., Liu, Y.: Green bonds for financing renewable energy and energy efficiency in South-East Asia: a review of policies. J. Sustain. Finance Invest. **10**(2), 113–140 (2020)
13. Azhgaliyeva, D., Kapsalyamova, Z., Low, L.: Implications of fiscal and financial policies on unlocking green finance and green investment. In: Sachs, J., Woo, W., Yoshino, N., Taghizadeh-Hesary, F. (eds.) Handbook of Green Finance, pp. 427–457. Springer, Singapore (2019). https://doi.org/10.1007/978-981-13-0227-5_32
14. Banga, J.: The green bond market: a potential source of climate finance for developing countries. J. Sustain. Finance Invest. **9**(1), 17–32 (2019)
15. Barua, S., Chiesa, M.: Sustainable financing practices through green bonds: what affects the funding size? Bus. Strateg. Environ. **28**(6), 1131–1147 (2019)
16. Bhattacharya, M., Paramati, S.R., Ozturk, I., Bhattacharya, S.: The effect of renewable energy consumption on economic growth: evidence from top 38 countries. Appl. Energy **162**, 733–741 (2016)

17. Bhutta, U.S., Tariq, A., Farrukh, M., Raza, A., Iqbal, M.K.: Green bonds for sustainable development: Review of literature on development and impact of green bonds. Technol. Forecast. Soc. Chang. **175**, 121378 (2022)
18. Bieliński, T., Mosionek-Schweda, M.: Green bonds as a financial instrument for environmental projects funding. Unia Europejska. pl **248**(1), 13–21 (2018)
19. Bobinaite, V., Tarvydas, D.: Financing instruments and channels for the increasing production and consumption of renewable energy: Lithuanian case. Renew. Sustain. Energy Rev. **38**, 259–276 (2014)
20. Brunnschweiler, C.N.: Finance for renewable energy: an empirical analysis of developing and transition economies. Environ. Dev. Econ. **15**(3), 241–274 (2010)
21. Carlos, R.M., Khang, D.B.: Characterization of biomass energy projects in Southeast Asia. Biomass Bioenerg. **32**(6), 525–532 (2008)
22. Criscuolo, C., Menon, C.: Environmental policies and risk finance in the green sector: cross-country evidence. Energy Pol. **83**, 38–56 (2015)
23. D'Orazio, P., Dirks, M.W.: Exploring the effects of climate-related financial policies on carbon emissions in G20 countries: a panel quantile regression approach. Environ. Sci. Pollut. Res. Res. **29**(5), 7678–7702 (2022)
24. Esso, L.J., Keho, Y.: Energy consumption, economic growth and carbon emissions: cointegration and causality evidence from selected African countries. Energy **114**, 492–497 (2016)
25. Eyraud, L., Wane, M.A., Zhang, M.C., Clements, M.B.J.: Who's going green and why? Trends and determinants of green investment. International Monetary Fund (2011)
26. Facchini, F., Seghezza, E.: Public spending structure, minimal state and economic growth in France (1870–2010). Econ. Model. **72**, 151–164 (2018)
27. Fan, M., Shao, S., Yang, L.: Combining global Malmquist-Luenberger index a generalized method of moments to investigate industrial total factor CO2 emission performance: a case of Shanghai (China). Energy Pol. **79**, 189–201 (2015)
28. Geddes, A., Schmidt, T.S., Steffen, B.: The multiple roles of state investment banks in low-carbon energy finance: an analysis of Australia, the UK and Germany. Energy Policy **115**, 158–170 (2018)
29. Ghasemi, G., Noorollahi, Y., Alavi, H., Marzband, M., Shahbazi, M.: Theoretical and technical potential evaluation of solar power generation in Iran. Renewable Energy **138**, 1250–1261 (2019)
30. Glomsrød, S., Wei, T.: Business as unusual: the implications of fossil divestment and green bonds for financial flows, economic growth and energy market. Energy Sustain. Dev. **44**, 1–10 (2018)
31. He, L., Liu, R., Zhong, Z., Wang, D., Xia, Y.: Can green financial development promote renewable energy investment efficiency? A consideration of bank credit. Renewable Energy **143**, 974–984 (2019)
32. Hossain, M.: Green finance in Bangladesh: Policies, institutions, and challenges (No. 892). ADBI Working Paper (2018)
33. Huang, J., Du, D., Tao, Q.: An analysis of technological factors and energy intensity in China. Energy Pol. **109**, 1–9 (2017)
34. Huntington, H.G.: Crude oil trade and current account deficits. Energy Econ. **50**, 70–79 (2015)
35. Iram, R., Anser, M.K., Awan, R.U., Ali, A., Abbas, Q., Chaudhry, I.S.: Prioritization of renewable solar energy to prevent energy insecurity: an integrated role. Singapore Econ. Rev. **66**(02), 391–412 (2021)
36. Irfan, M., Razzaq, A., Sharif, A., Yang, X.: Influence mechanism between green finance and green innovation: exploring regional policy intervention effects in China. Technol. Forecast. Soc. Chang. **182**, 121882 (2022)

37. Jin, Y., Gao, X., Wang, M.: The financing efficiency of listed energy conservation and environmental protection firms: evidence and implications for green finance in China. Energy Policy **153**, 112254 (2021)
38. Lamperti, F., Bosetti, V., Roventini, A., Tavoni, M., Treibich, T.: Three green financial policies to address climate risks. J. Financ. Stab. **54**, 100875 (2021)
39. Lepitzki, J., Axsen, J.: The role of a low carbon fuel standard in achieving long-term GHG reduction targets. Energy Policy **119**, 423–440 (2018)
40. Lin, B., Zhu, J.: Fiscal spending and green economic growth: evidence from China. Energy Econ. **83**, 264–271 (2019)
41. Lyeonov, S., Pimonenko, T., Bilan, Y., Štreimikienė, D., Mentel, G.: Assessment of green investments' impact on sustainable development: Linking gross domestic product per capita, greenhouse gas emissions and renewable energy. Energies **12**(20), 3891 (2019)
42. Mehta, A., Sandhu, S.C., Kinkead, B.: Catalyzing Green Finance: A Concept for Leveraging Blended Finance for Green Development. Asian Development Bank (2017)
43. Mngumi, F., Shaorong, S., Shair, F., Waqas, M.: Does green finance mitigate the effects of climate variability: role of renewable energy investment and infrastructure? Environ. Sci. Pollut. Res. 1–13 (2022)
44. Müllner, J.: International project finance: review and implications for international finance and international business. Manag. Rev. Q. **67**(2), 97–133 (2017)
45. Ng, A.W.: From sustainability accounting to a green financing system: Institutional legitimacy and market heterogeneity in a global financial centre. J. Clean. Prod. **195**, 585–592 (2018)
46. Ng, T.H., Tao, J.Y.: Bond financing for renewable energy in Asia. Energy Pol. **95**, 509–517 (2016)
47. North, D.C.: Institutions and economic theory. Am. Econ. **61**(1), 72–76 (2016)
48. Peimani, H.: Financial barriers for development of renewable and green energy projects in Asia. In: Sachs, J., Woo, W., Yoshino, N., Taghizadeh-Hesary, F. (eds.) Handbook of Green Finance, pp. 15–34. Springer, Singapore (2019). https://doi.org/10.1007/978-981-13-0227-5_14
49. Pham, L.: Is it risky to go green? A volatility analysis of the green bond market. J. Sustain. Finance Invest. **6**(4), 263–291 (2016)
50. Raberto, M., Ozel, B., Ponta, L., Teglio, A., Cincotti, S.: From financial instability to green finance: the role of banking and credit market regulation in the Eurace model. J. Evol. Econ. **29**(1), 429–465 (2019)
51. Sachs, J.D., Woo, W.T., Yoshino, N., Taghizadeh-Hesary, F.: Why is green finance important? (2019)
52. Sachs, J., Woo, W.T., Yoshino, N., Taghizadeh-Hesary, F. (eds.): Handbook of Green Finance: Energy Security and Sustainable Development. Springer, Singapore (2019). https://doi.org/10.1007/978-981-13-0227-5
53. Shah, S.A.A., Zhou, P., Walasai, G.D., Mohsin, M.: Energy security and environmental sustainability index of South Asian countries: a composite index approach. Ecol. Ind. **106**, 105507 (2019)
54. Sun, H., Pofoura, A.K., Mensah, I.A., Li, L., Mohsin, M.: The role of environmental entrepreneurship for sustainable development: evidence from 35 countries in Sub-Saharan Africa. Sci. Total. Environ. **741**, 140132 (2020)
55. Taghizadeh-Hesary, F., Yoshino, N.: Sustainable solutions for green financing and investment in renewable energy projects. Energies **13**(4), 788 (2020)
56. Taghizadeh-Hesary, F., Yoshino, N., Phoumin, H.: Analyzing the characteristics of green bond markets to facilitate green finance in the post-COVID-19 world. Sustainability **13**(10), 5719 (2021)
57. Volz, U.: Fostering green finance for sustainable development in Asia. In: Routledge Handbook of Banking and Finance in Asia, pp. 488–504. Routledge (2018)

58. Wang, C., Liao, H., Pan, S.-Y., Zhao, L.-T., Wei, Y.-M.: The fluctuations of China's energy intensity: biased technical change. Appl. Energy **135**, 407–414 (2014)
59. Wang, Y., Zhi, Q.: The role of green finance in environmental protection: two aspects of market mechanism and policies. Energy Procedia **104**, 311–316 (2016)
60. Wiser, R.H., Pickle, S.J.: Financing investments in renewable energy: the impacts of policy design. Renew. Sustain. Energy Rev. **2**(4), 361–386 (1998)
61. Wu, M., Wu, J., Zang, C.: A comprehensive evaluation of the eco-carrying capacity and green economy in the Guangdong-Hong Kong-Macao Greater Bay Area, China. J. Clean. Prod. **281**, 124945 (2021)
62. Yang, J.S.: The governance environment and innovative SMEs. Small Bus. Econ. **48**(3), 525–541 (2016). https://doi.org/10.1007/s11187-016-9802-1
63. Yoshino, N., Taghizadeh-Hesary, F., Nakahigashi, M.: Modelling the social funding and spillover tax for addressing the green energy financing gap. Econ. Model. **77**, 34–41 (2019)
64. Zeng, X.W., Liu, Y.Q., Man, M.J., Shen, Q.L.: Measurement analysis of China's green finance development. China Yanan Cadre Coll **6**, 112–121 (2014)
65. Zhang, R., Li, Y., Liu, Y.: Green bond issuance and corporate cost of capital. Pac. Basin Financ. J. **69**, 101626 (2021)
66. Zhang, Y.J., Zhang, K.B.: The linkage of CO_2 emissions for China, EU, and USA: evidence from the regional and sectoral analyses. Environ. Sci. Pollut. Res. **25**(20), 20179–20192 (2018)

The Long and Short Term Impact of COVID-19 on E-Commerce and Retail Industries for US

Zixuan Li[1(✉)], Chenwen Song[2], and Tianrui Xiao[3]

[1] Faculty of Social Science and Art, The University of Sydney, Sydney 2006, Australia
Li-zixuan2001@126.com
[2] Faculty of Commerce, The University of Melbourne, Melbourne 3010, Australia
[3] Economics and Management School, Wuhan University, Wuhan 430072, China

Abstract. COVID-19 limits people's travel and social distance, causing online retail sales to explode. The Internet as a shopping method can overcome the limitations of physical shops, such as space limitations and time constraints. At the same time, online shopping makes it easier for consumers to compare prices, quality, and styles and pursue a personalized experience between items. However, the literature does not provide a clear answer to whether consumers have changed their habits and prefer to shop online or whether this is simply a choice forced upon them during the pandemic. This research aims to use event study and forecasting models to analyze the impact of COVID-19 on the e-Commerce and retail sectors. Evidence showed in this paper suggests that after gaining a temporary advantage during the pandemic, the e-commerce sector will slow its growth in the post-epidemic era and even reach new all-time lows.

Keywords: Covid-19 · E-Commerce · Retail Industries · Case Study

1 Introduction

The global pandemic outbreak of 2020 has brought about a dramatic change in consumer Channels. Established in the 1960s, e-Commerce flourished with the advent of many advanced technologies. Additionally, the emergence of the online platforms eBay and Amazon in the 1990s saw the e-Commerce industry grow by leaps and bounds [1]. Although e-commerce became popular a decade ago, the pandemic has accelerated the process of fast digitalization. Related figures show that e-commerce sales grew by US$244.2 billion in 2020, the first year of the pandemic, up 43% compared to US$571.2 billion in 2019 [2]. Forbes data suggests that 81% of US consumers have never purchased groceries online in 2019, and the outbreak of Covid-19 has changed how they buy, with 79% of US consumers already ordering groceries online by 2020 [3]. Over a year, more buyers flocked to the online shopping market. In Southeast Asia, 34% of those buying clothing online indicated that this was their first attempt to buy online, and 94% of users of the new digital service intend to continue using it after the pandemic [4]. Moreover,

---

Z. Li, C. Song and T. Xiao—These authors contributed equally to this work and should be considered co-first authors.

the Amazon Business Report for 2021 states that 56% of SMEs are mainly motivated to accelerate their digital transformation efforts because they have been forced to move to remote work with limited face-to-face operations; however, ultimately, both buyers and sellers have been facilitated and benefited by unlocking new technologies and features adopted for online shopping [5].

The risk of possible infection has made the shopping experience stressful for consumers, and the social alienation and limited opening hours of public places due to the blockade imposed by the government have made people reconsider new modes of shopping. Consumers seem to have been forced to change their habits and prioritise online shopping when shopping [1]. Many academics believe that the online shopping boom will not dissipate even after the end of COVID-19, as the pandemic has accelerated consumer adaptation to online shopping [6], and this change in consumer habits during the pandemic will continue for decades in the e-commerce industry [7]. However, McKinsey's data show that only about 13–16% of consumers in Italy, Germany, and France are satisfied with their online grocery service. Further, e-commerce giant Amazon's growth has slowed in the post-epidemic era, and last year Amazon announced job cuts because it had hired too many workers during the coronavirus pandemic and overextended its logistics operations [8, 9]. The last reported quarter 2022 Q4 Amazon's net income was $278.00 million, down by -98% year-over-year from $14,323.00 million [10]. This article will explore whether COVID-19 had an impact on the e-commerce and retail industries and whether this effect could continue in the post-pandemic era.

2 Methodology

This article uses mainly the CAPM model and the event study approach to detect abnormal returns in e-commerce and retail indices during the pandemic.

2.1 CAPM Model

The capital asset pricing model (CAPM) is used as a regression model to estimate the return on investment. CAPM is an idealised financial mathematics method for determining the expected returns on capital investment, such as the stock in this research. This model identifies, quantifies, and translates risk into an estimated variable of expected return on equity. The basic assumption for CAPM is that all investors are risk-averse and can invest or borrow unlimited capital at a risk-free rate.

A general expression of CAPM is as follows:

$$E(R_i) = R_f + \beta_i * (E(R_m) - R_f) \ldots \tag{1}$$

In this research, the expression will be transformed as follow:

$$E(R_i) - R_f = \beta_i * (E(R_m) - R_f) \ldots \tag{2}$$

To construct a general regression estimation model for stock:

$$E(R_i) - R_f = \alpha_i + \beta_i * (E(R_m) - R_f) \ldots \tag{3}$$

where:

E (R_i) - R_f: stock return premium, (IBUY, Amazon, XRT, Walmart, and Target in this research)

(R_m) - R_f: market return premium, (S&P 500 in this research)

3 Event Study

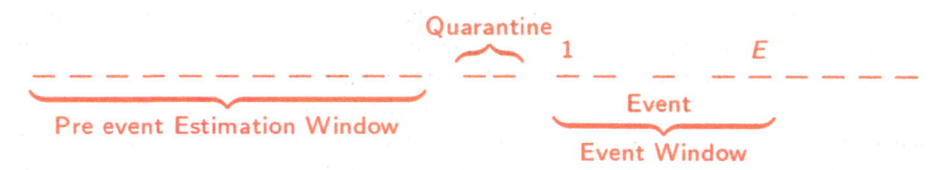

Fig. 1. Event study timeline.

The returns that should occur during the event window are predicted using the CAPM model, i.e.,

$$NR_t - r_f = \alpha + \beta_i * (R_m - r_f), t = 1, ..., E \ldots \quad (4)$$

Then, Formula 5 define the so-called Abnormal Returns inside the event window.

$$AR_t = \overbrace{R_t}^{Treated} - \overbrace{(\alpha + r_f + \beta * (R_m - r_f))}^{Control}, t = 1, ..., E \ldots \quad (5)$$

In practise, the parameters α, β are estimated using the estimation window data (from 2018/01/14 to 2020/01/13). Additionally, AR t tests conducted by R were used to test the impact of COVID-19 on objective indices.

The abnormal return should satisfy

$$AR_t = \varepsilon_t \sim N(0, \sigma^2), t = 1, ..., E \ldots \quad (6)$$

$$t_{statistics} = (\sum AR/N)/(\sigma/\sqrt{N}) \ldots \quad (7)$$

This study uses the P-value of the t-test to observe whether there is an obvious abnormal return during the pandemic. If the P-value is small, usually less than 0.05, the null hypothesis (there is no abnormal return) is typically rejected because it means that the observed result is unlikely to be caused by random error but may be caused by true differences. In addition, this article also shows the results of t-tests on cumulative abnormal return in graphs by comparing CAR(t) with $\pm Z_{\partial/2}\ \sigma\ \sqrt{t}/\sqrt{N}$ for two sided α-level tests.

The cumulated abnormal return for each t in the event window.

$$CAR(t) = \sum_{s=1}^{t} AR_s = \sum_{s=1}^{t} \varepsilon_t \sim N(0, t\sigma^2), t = 1, ..., E \ldots \quad (8)$$

In this article, the estimation window and four different event windows were selected according to the start and end dates from the pandemic period that are most likely to affect COVID-19 restrictions in the US (Fig. 1 and Table 1).

January 23, 2020: lockdown of Wuhan due to COVID-19
March 11, 2020: COVID-19 is declared a global pandemic
May 28, 2020: US COVID-19 Deaths Pass the 100,000 Mark
July 1, 2020: Mask restrictions and home quarantine orders in the US due to the outbreak have been largely lifted.
September 14: US Airports Stop Screening International Travelers

Table 1. Event windows time [owner-draw].

Event Windows	Date
Event Window 1	2020/3/11–2020/7/01
Event Window 2	2020/3/11–2020/9/14
Event Window 3	2020/1/23–2020/5/28
Event Window 4	2020/1/23–2022/12/31

4 E-Commerce

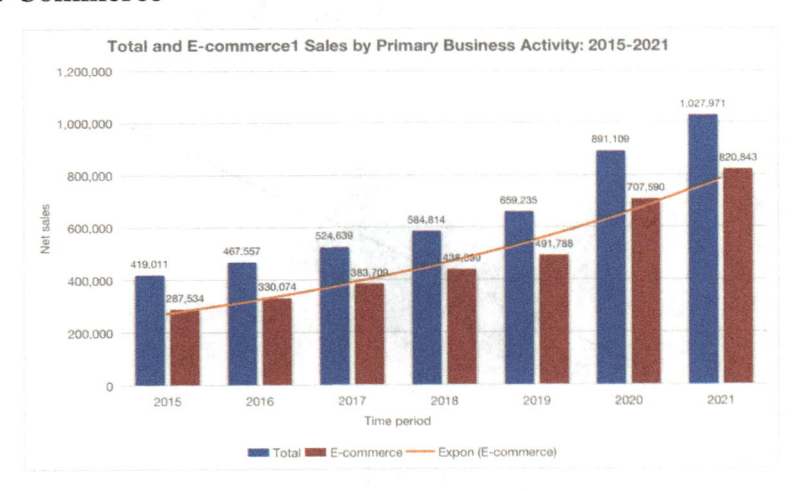

Fig. 2. Total and e-commerce sales [owner-draw].

According to Mayumi Brewster's reports, using data from the United States Census Bureau's Annual Retail Trade Survey (ARTS), the Fig. 2 implys that e-commerce sales by primary business activity have a general increasing trend from 2015 to 2021, but the increase became especially considerable during the pandemic. There is a dramatic surge of e-commerce sales by $215.8 billion or 43.9% in 2020, the first year of the pandemic, rising from $491.8 billion in 2019 to $707.6 billion in 2020. Therefore, it is valuable to estimate the data generated in the US e-commerce industry to discover the influence of COVID.

4.1 Amazon

Amazon, founded in 1994 is currently one of the most influential and biggest companies in the E-Commerce industry. It offers a wide range of products and services to consumers around the world with net sales reaching over $386 billion in 2020. Also, this retail giant's overall revenue continued to grow significantly due to Covid-19 and its net sales of second quarter of 2020 alone tripled from the previous year.

4.2 CAPM for Amazon

For OLS estimation of equation to provide consistent estimate of α and β with minimum variance within the class of unbiased linear estimator, the linear regression model in Fig. 3 shows there is a strong relationship between S&P500 return and Amazon return (beta = 1.5) and the required return for Amazon is much higher than the return expected from the market due to premium risk. However, this beta may be overestimated, as people may have learnt from the pandemic and adjusted the beta on Amazon downward according to CAPM.

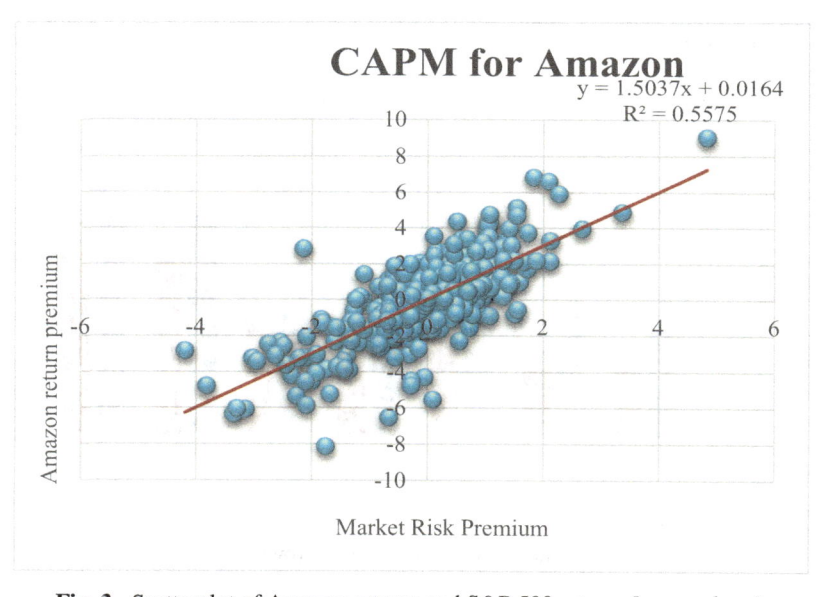

Fig. 3. Scatterplot of Amazon returns and S&P 500 returns [owner-draw].

Beta in the CAPM model plays a pivotal role in portfolio construction, as it measures the volatility or systematic risk of an individual security or portfolio compared to the whole market. Generally, a beta greater than 1 means that the stock is riskier than the market, and the stock usually has a higher return than the market as risk premium. Before the pandemic, stocks in the e-Commerce and technology sectors typically amplified the direction of the market. For example, Amazon's volatility or risk premium was greater

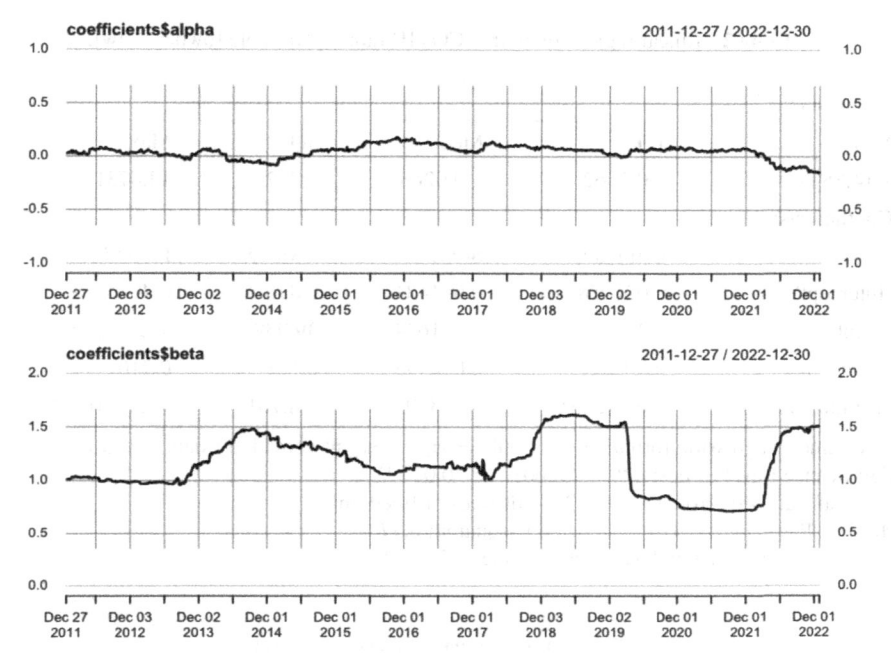

Fig. 4. The Covid-19 Beta effect [owner-draw].

than the market risk premium, as shown in Fig. 4. However, the beta of Amazon showed a sharp decline during the coronavirus pandemic, leaving it with a beta much less than 1. This shift not only changed the relationship between market risk and return but also have a profound impact on how investors construct and minimize the risk of their portfolios. Therefore, Amazon is a good hedging stock for investors during the pandemic period.

$$r_{it} = \hat{\alpha} + \alpha_1 Covid + \beta r_{mt} + \beta_1 r_{mt}*Covid \ldots \quad (9)$$

Similarly, the result of linear regression with a COVID Dummy Variable indicates that market return has a significant positive relationship (the coefficient $\beta = 1.2629$) with the return of Amazon, and the interaction between market return and Covid-19 has a significant negative effect (the coefficient $\beta_1 = -0.472231$). However, the covid-19 variable alone does not have a statistically significant impact on the dependent variable. The overall pandemic beta is 0.79 for Amazon, which is also lower than 1 (see Table 2).

According to the result of the t test for different events for four different event windows. As shown in Figs. 5, 6, 7 and 8, there is strong evidence to reject null hypotheses (H0: no abnormal return), which means that Amazon presented an abnormal return during the pandemic. Also, what is interesting about the result in Fig. 7 is that the cumulative abnormal return of Amazon showed an obviously positive abnormal return in the short term, crossing the upper boundary of the confidence interval; nevertheless, the cumulative abnormal return became negative in the post-pandemic era and showed statistical significance in the long run. Moreover, as can be seen in Fig. 9 Amazon's abnormal returns show very large volatility from March to November 2020, and it begins to return to relatively flat volatility in 2021 (see Fig. 10).

Table 2. Linear regression with a COVID dummy variable [owner-draw].

Residuals:				
Min	1Q	Median	3Q	Max
−14.8837	−0.7562	−0.0263	0.7426	14.4731

Coefficients:				
	Estimate	Std.Error	T value	Pr(>/t/)
(Intercept)	0.026058	0.031481	0.828	0.408
xr_mt	1.262987	0.031624	39.938	< 2e−16***
covid_dv	0.008858	0.078483	0.113	0.910
xr_mt:covid_dv	−0.472231	0.053899	−8.761	< 2e−16***

Note. Linear regression formula lm(formula = xr_it ~ xr_mt* covid_dv, data = data)
Significance Level Codes: 0 "***" 0.001 "**" 0.01 "*"
Residual standard error: 1.648 on 3267 degrees of freedom
Multiple R-squared: 0.3706, Adjusted R-squared: 0.37
F-statistic: 641.1 on 3 and 3267 DF, p-value < 2.2e−16

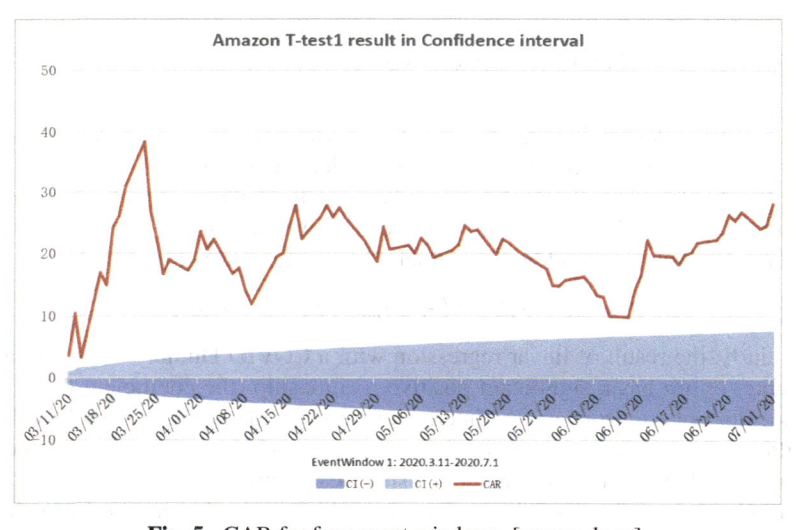

Fig. 5. CAR for four event windows. [owner-draw].

The positive abnormal return of Amazon can be explained by following channels:

1) Restrictions on movement change consumption bundles towards the kinds of goods that Amazon specializes in favoring Amazon and other retailers over providers of travel and other unavailable services.
2) Widespread lockdowns and social distancing measures implemented during the pandemic change shop access, favoring online shopping options over street-front stores. As people sought to purchase essential items, groceries, and other products from

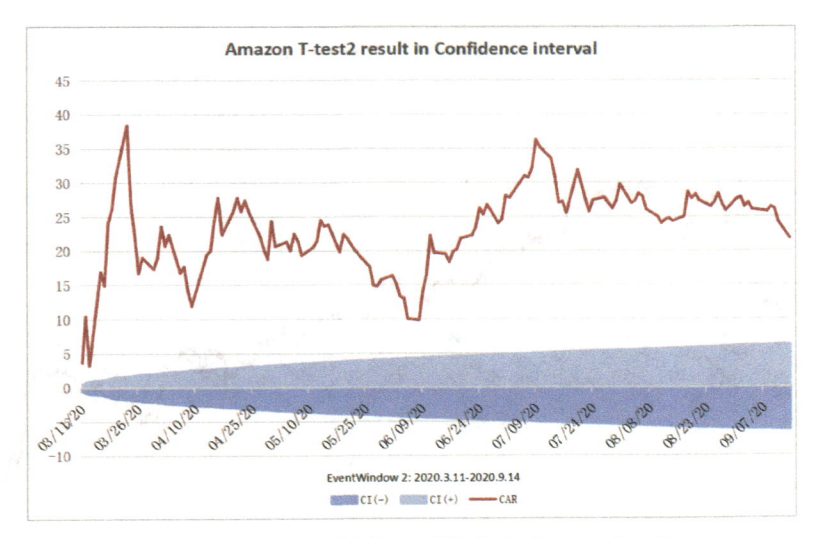

Fig. 6. CAR for Four Event Windows. [owner-draw].

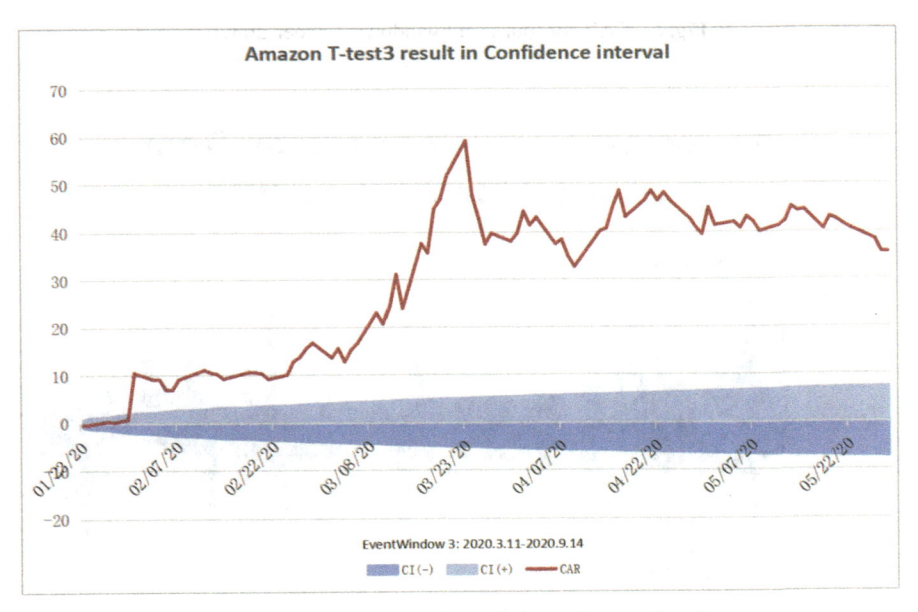

Fig. 7. CAR for four event windows. [owner-draw].

the safety of their homes, Amazon experienced a significant increase in sales and revenue. Amazon experienced a significant increase in sales and revenue.

3) Investor Confidence: The pandemic highlighted the resilience and adaptability of Amazon's business model, which contributed to increased investor confidence. Many investors saw Amazon as a safe investment during uncertain times, leading to a higher

Fig. 8. CAR for four event windows. [owner-draw].

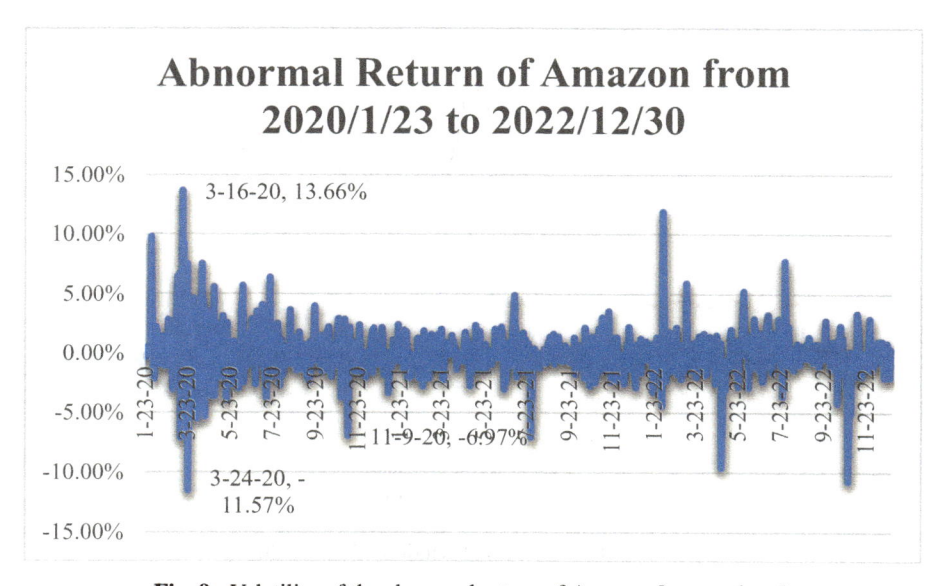

Fig. 9. Volatility of the abnormal return of Amazon [owner-draw].

demand for the company's stock. The combination of strong financial performance and positive market sentiment drove up the stock price, resulting in abnormal returns.

However, Professor Konan claims Amazon may have reached maturity, as for the first time in decade Amazon sales are not in double digits, with year-on-year sales growth in the past between 20–40% and a slowdown of just 9.4% in 2022 [11]. Similarly, the Fig. 11 demonstrates that Amazon net sales have been on a continuous growth trend, but its growth rate plummets by showing the trajectory of Amazon net sales after taking log. After removing the cyclical fluctuations brought about by Christmas, the linear regression model for log Amazon net sales shows Amazon's growth slows severely in the latter half of 2021 and 2022 and has an unprecedented residual of more than -0.3, compared with previous growth rate (see Fig. 12).

Fig. 10. The Trajectory of Amazon Net Sales.

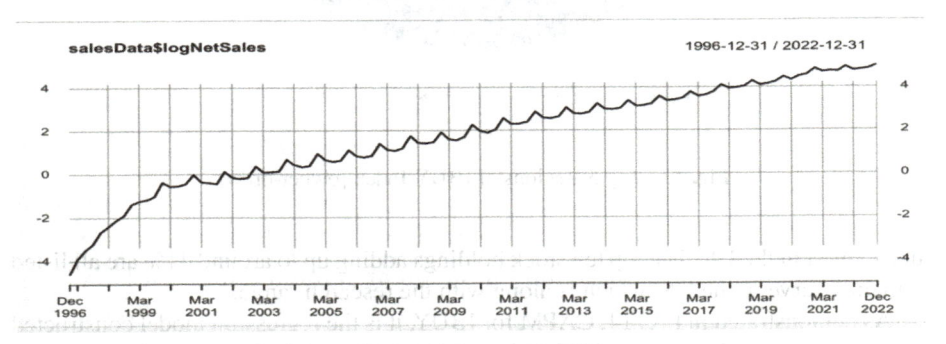

Fig. 11. The Trajectory of Log Amazon Net Sales [owner-draw].

4.3 IBUY

The Amplify Online Retail ETF (IBUY) index is chosen to analyse the e-commerce industry for mainly three reasons. Firstly, it is one of the oldest ETFs launched on 19th April 2016. Secondly, it tracks the EQM Online Retail Index, which is a globally diverse basket of publicly traded companies that obtain 70% or more revenue from online sales. This suggests that it generally includes the main subjects of the sample to investigate. Thirdly, as shown in Fig. 13. Top 5 Regions of IBUY Index, approximately 75% of the

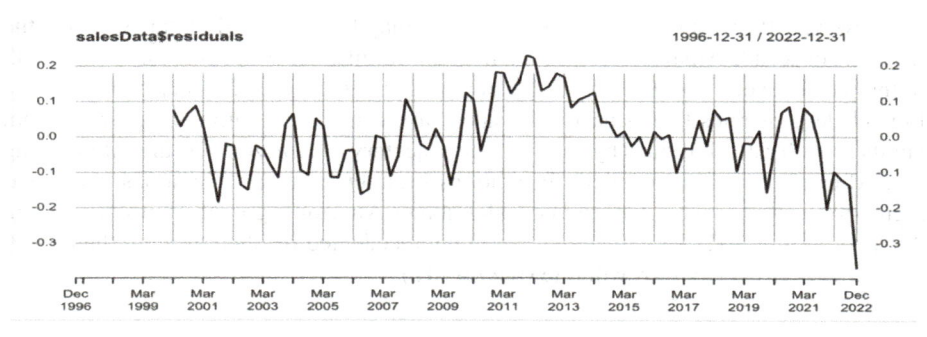

Fig. 12. Residual of Linear Regression Model of Amazon Net Sales [owner-draw].

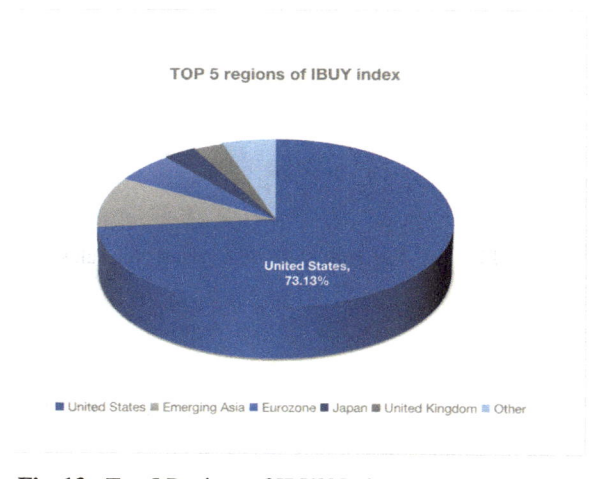

Fig. 13. Top 5 Regions of IBUY Index [owner-draw].

funds invest in the US. The top ten stock holdings adding up to around 41% are all listed or mainly serve in the US, which is along with the research range.

As demonstrated in Fig. 14. CAPM for IBUY, it is the regression model constructed by the adjusted market return of IBUY from 2018.1.12 to 2020.1.13. This demonstrated an extremely high positive-correlated relationship between the S&P 500 and the IBUY index. This means there is a strong strength between the S&P 500 and the IBUY index. The major reason for this high correlation is both S&P 500 and IBUY include a wide range of goods and services sustaining daily activities. In addition, there is a relatively high R square, 0.628, which means that IBUY funds as a typical e-Commerce ETF could explain the 62.8% variance of S&P 5000. Thus, it is reasonable to have a high connection between indexes.

As shown in the Fig. 15. General Trend of IBUY, there is a small drop at the beginning of the COVID period from 55.844 to 36.99, but a considerable increasing trend throughout the COVID period and peaked at 137.75, which is inconsistent with the general opinion of economic stagnation and consumption reduction caused by COVID.

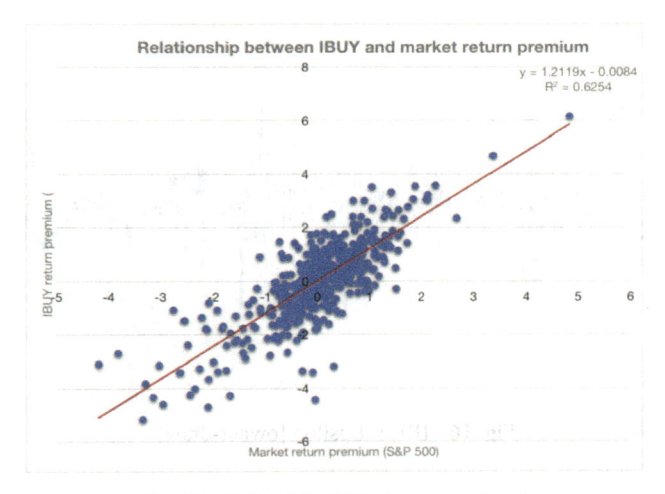

Fig. 14. CAPM for IBUY [owner-draw].

Fig. 15. General trend of IBUY [owner-draw].

Figure 16 IBUY Epsilon demonstrates the fluctuation of the adjusted IBUY market return during the COVID period. It clearly shows that the pandemic has a very large influence on the e-commerce industry in the beginning period of COVID (2020.1.13–2020.4.13), leading to extreme up and down. However, it is more accurate to use econometric methods to analyse the impact of COVID on the USA e-commerce industry through hypothesis testing. Setting the null hypothesis that there is no difference between the actual IBUY point and the estimated IBUY point constructed by the regression model plotted as previously during the COVID time.

After running the hypothesis test for four event windows, all four hypotheses that demonstrate a meaningful result shown in Fig. 17. P-Value Results of IBUY. According to the P-value generated by the event study, the null hypothesis that there is no difference

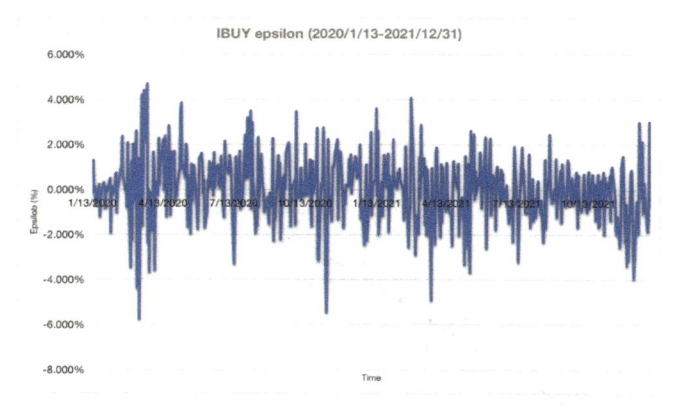

Fig. 16. IBUY Epsilon [owner-draw].

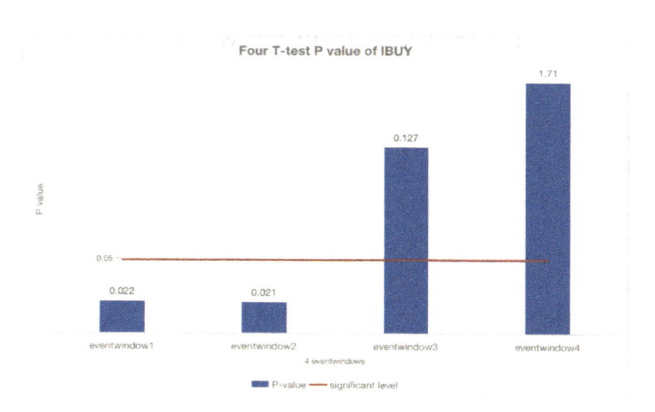

Fig. 17. P-Value results of IBUY [owner-draw].

between the estimated IBUY point and the actual IBUY point could be rejected. This suggests that COVID influenced the e-Commerce industry through the IBUY index.

As demonstrated in the Figs. 18, 19, 20 and 21. Event windows for IBUY, there is significant evidence to show that the pandemic has had a positive impact on the e-Commerce industry in the beginning period of COVID from 2020.3.11 to 2020.7.1 from (the event window 1). The fourth event window p-value also suggests a long-term impact, which suggests the pandemic has a significant positive impact on the e-commerce industry by increasing the total purchase through online platforms. This is because of the lockdown policy issued on March 17th people have to purchase some part of their goods and services online. As a result, the positive impact for the short and long term on the e-commerce industry could be demonstrated through the IBUY index during the COVID.

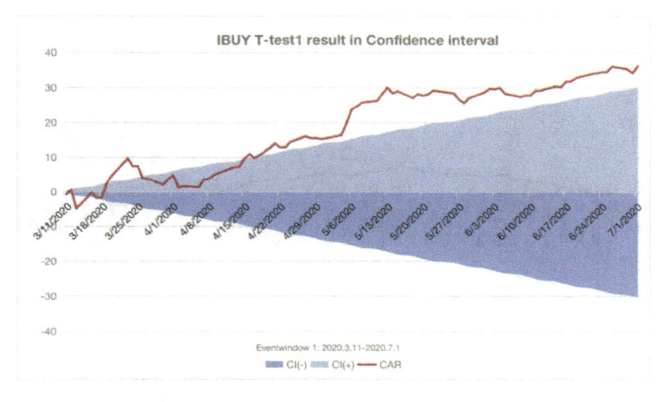

Fig. 18. Event windows for IBUY [owner-draw].

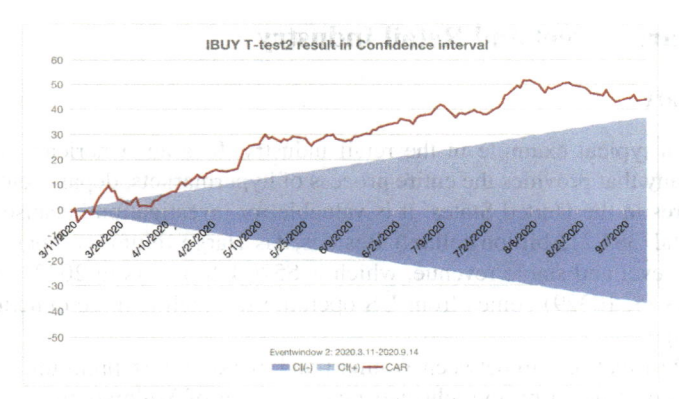

Fig. 19. Event windows for IBUY [owner-draw].

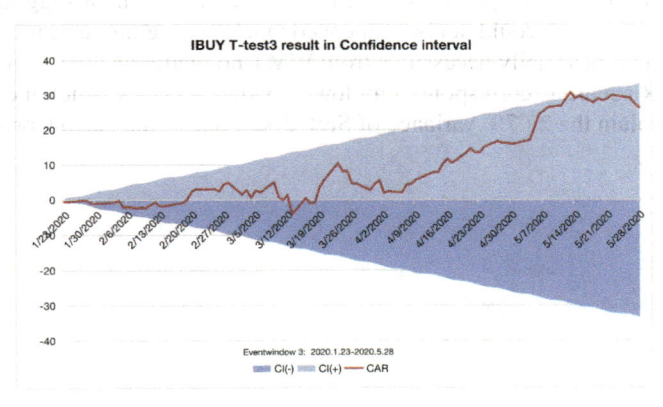

Fig. 20. Event windows for IBUY [owner-draw].

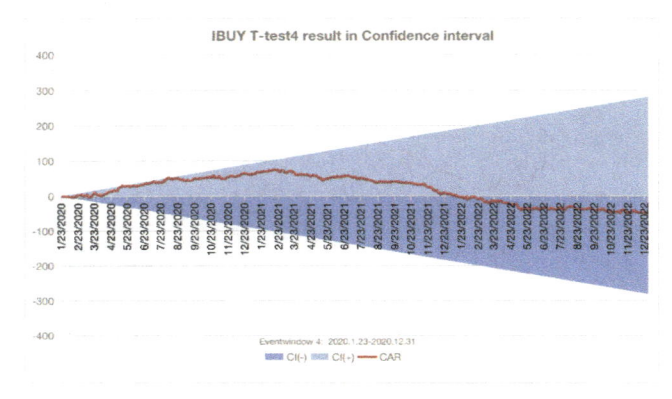

Fig. 21. Event windows for IBUY [Owner-draw]

5 Walmart, Target and Retail Industry

5.1 Walmart

Walmart is a typical example in the retail industry. It is an American multinational retail company that provides the entire process of hypermarkets, department stores, and grocery stores in the United States. It is valuable for investigation because of its large market capital (384.213 billion dollars). Besides, it is a large volume company worldwide with a high level and stable revenue, which is $570 US dollars in 2022. Additionally, 65% of sales ($510329) comes from US operations, which is in conjunction with the research range.

Figure 22 Relationship between Walmart and market return premium is the regression model constructed by the adjusted market return of Walmart from 2018.1.12 to 2020.1.13. The correlation between WMT and SP500 is less strong than that of Amazon (0.628) because WMT provides more daily necessities, which suggests that it has narrow sales scales and would not be influenced much by external reasons. After all, citizens have to purchase daily necessities from WMT no matter whether there is COVID. Besides, the R square is correspondingly lower, which suggests which means Walmart could only explain the 22.7% variance of S&P 5000, due to the narrow product range.

Fig. 22. Relationship between Walmart and market return premium [owner-draw].

Fig. 23. Walmart returns [owner-draw].

Figure 23 Walmart returns and Fig. 24 Walmart epsilon demonstrate the adjusted market returns and epsilon trends for Walmart from 2020.1.13–2021.12.31. Both graphs show that there is a surge in 2020.3.17 because President Trump issued new guidelines urging people to avoid social gatherings of more than ten people and to restrict discretionary travel. Citizens in the US have to purchase and stock up on daily necessities from

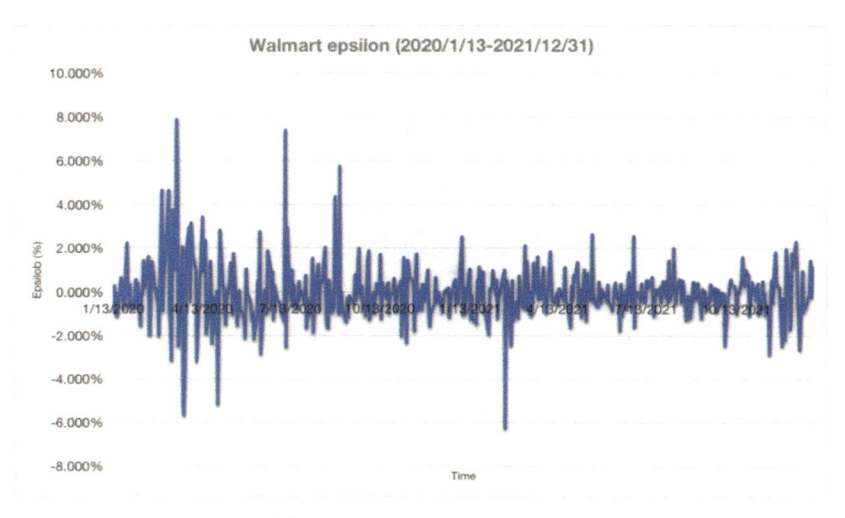

Fig. 24. Walmart epsilon [owner-draw].

supermarkets, such as Walmart. There are some other considerable fluctuates that need to ignore due to the internal event in Walmart. For example, in 2020.4.29 Walmart has to pay a 14 million dollar fine for a judgement settlement which leads to a significant drop in epsilon. Generally, the pandemic has dramatic influence at the beginning period, but less effect or almost no influence in the consequence time and post-pandemic period.

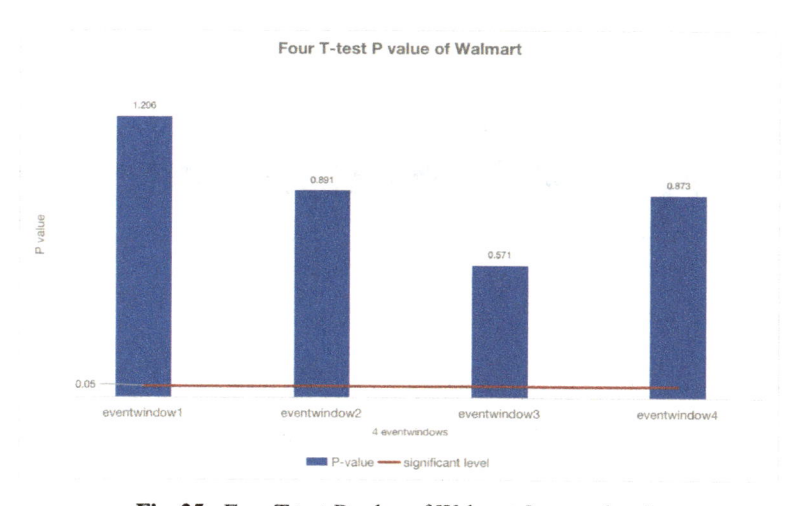

Fig. 25. Four T-test P value of Walmart [owner-draw].

After constructing the hypothesis test and relative event, graphs show that there is no influence on WMT, P-value of which are all above the significant level, presented in Fig. 25. Four T-test P value of Walmart. This suggests that there is no influence in both

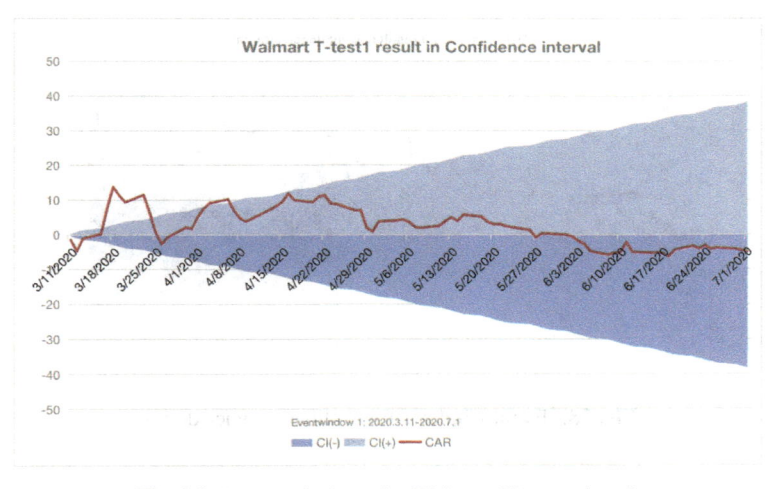

Fig. 26. Event windows for Walmart [Owner-draw].

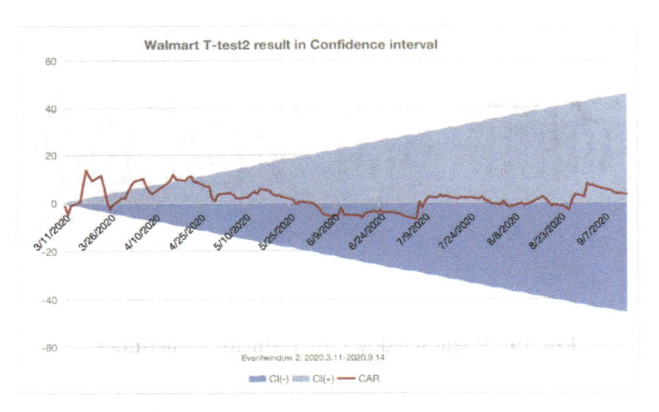

Fig. 27. Event windows for Walmart [owner-draw].

short run and long run even in the middle and later periods of the pandemic. To be more specifically, Fig. 26, 27, 28 and 29. Event windows for Walmart discuss the influence on four eventwindow of Walmart by presented as the confidence interval, which all have the same result as the P value that the COVID would not infuence the Walmart.

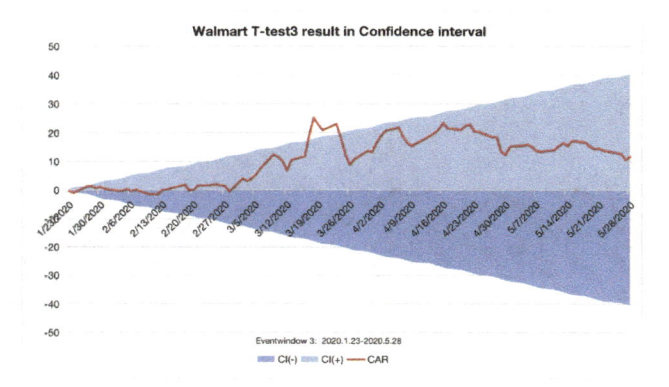

Fig. 28. Event windows for Walmart [owner-draw].

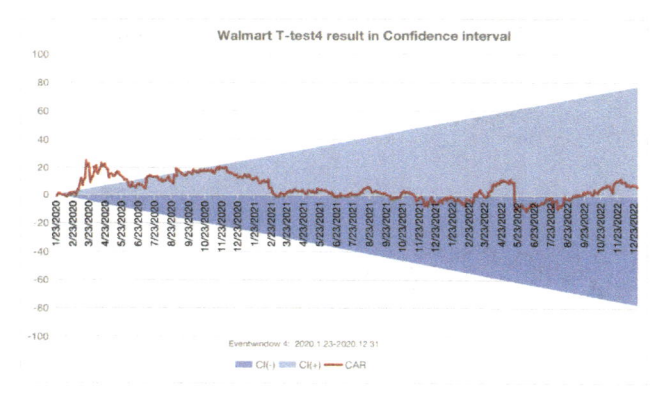

Fig. 29. Event windows for Walmart [owner-draw].

5.2 TGT and XRT

The retail industry has experienced a drastic transformation in recent decades. The technological revolution has further revolutionized the face of the retail industry. As a result, each industry aims to obtain a better understanding of its customers to formulate business strategies. The next part is for the target and XRT stock trading returns affected by the COVID-19 event. Target, the second-largest retail leader in the United States, noted in its 2021 earnings report that it had grown steadily in recent years, seemingly unaffected by COVID-19. At the same time, XRT, as an index fund of the retail sector of the US stock market, can better reflect the sales status of the entire retail industry and people's attention.

The correlation between TGT and XRT is also tested to find out whether one of them could be used to predict the return of the other. As shown in Fig. 30, the results turn out to be a low level of correlation with less than 0.5 and an undesirable r square, which suggests a low level of model fit. That is to say, although the target belongs to a large

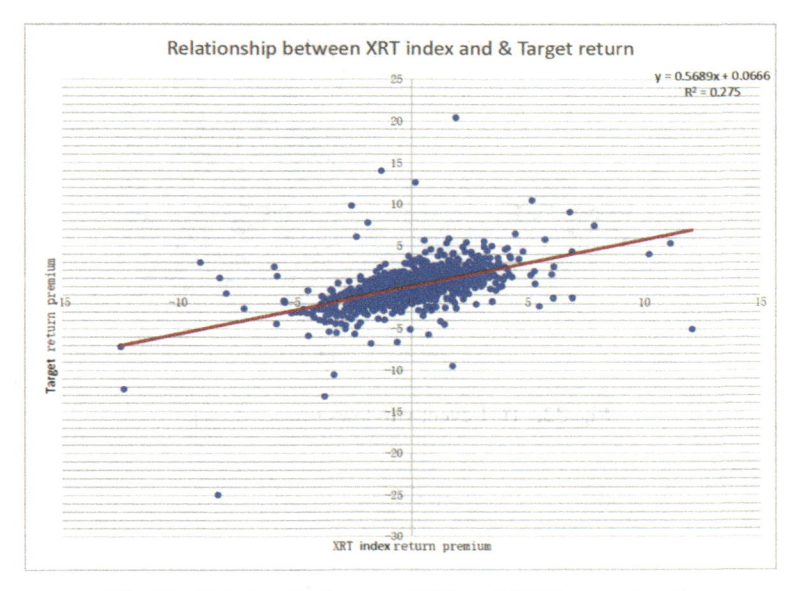

Fig. 30. Relationship between TGT and XRT [owner-draw].

part of the retail industry, due to its leading position and flexible sales model, it will not be affected by the same impact as other retail enterprises.

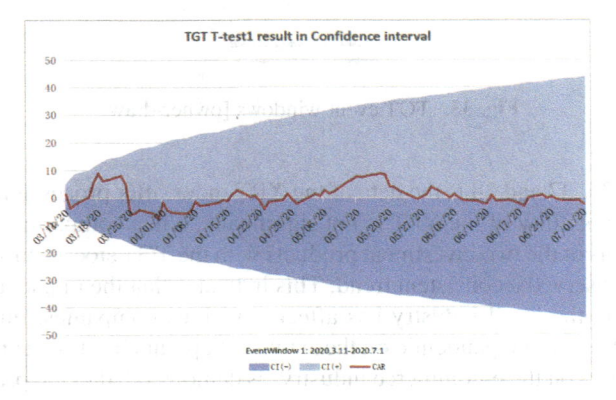

Fig. 31. TGT event windows [owner-draw].

After processing the regression model and time series model of Target, Fig. 31, 32, 33 and 34 shows that Target's return didn't suffer great fluctuations in all the time windows, This also means that TGT, as a leading company, is well-prepared and adjusted to face the COVID-19 pandemic. Furthermore, we can observe that TGT has accumulated consistent abnormal returns over the past two years, indicating that the impact of the COVID-19 pandemic on TGT stock returns is not significant in t-tests.

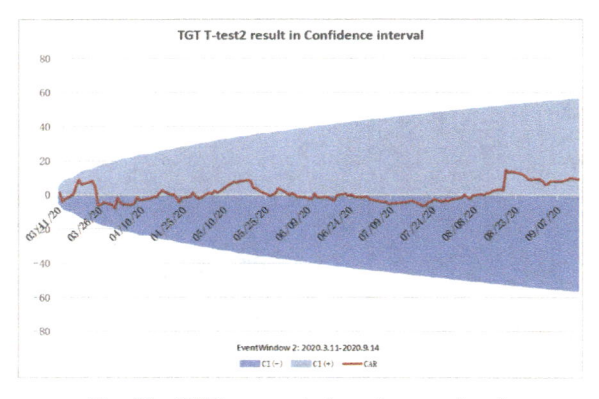

Fig. 32. TGT event windows [owner-draw].

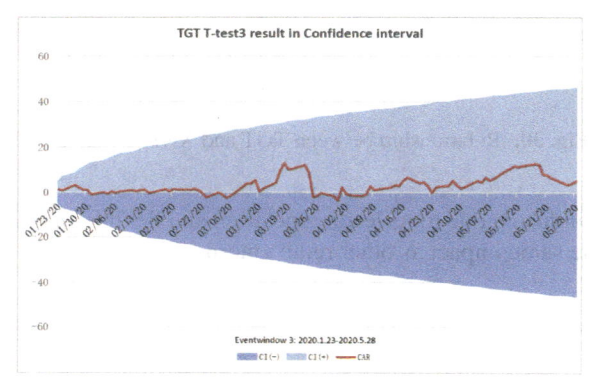

Fig. 33. TGT event windows [owner-draw].

Figure 35, 36, 37 and 38 is the data of the XRT index after procession, it can also be found that the volatility of the XRT is not significant. When comparing the cumulative abnormal returns of the two investment products with the TGT stock returns in four event windows, we observed a consistent trend. This indicates that the impact of the COVID-19 pandemic on the retail industry has affected various companies. Furthermore, the insignificant effect of the pandemic on these two data points in t-tests contrasts with the significant impact on the e-commerce industry, as demonstrated in the previous analysis of the e-commerce industry.

5.3 ARIMA Prediction Model

ARIMA model is a time series forecasting model that combines autoregression, differencing, and moving average components. The high-order version of the ARIMA model can improve the accuracy of the prediction by increasing the order of the model. These higher-order models often include seasonal and long-term dependencies modeling, which requires more complex differencing and modeling methods for the data.

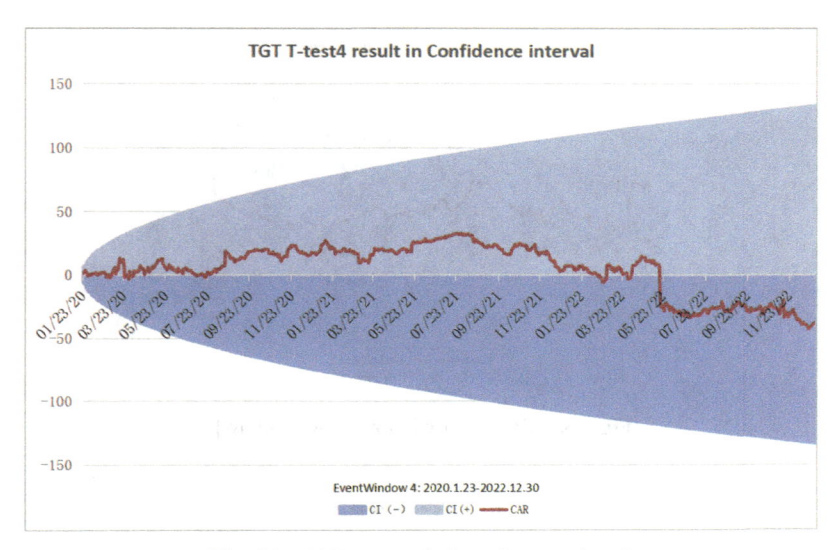

Fig. 34. TGT event windows [owner-draw].

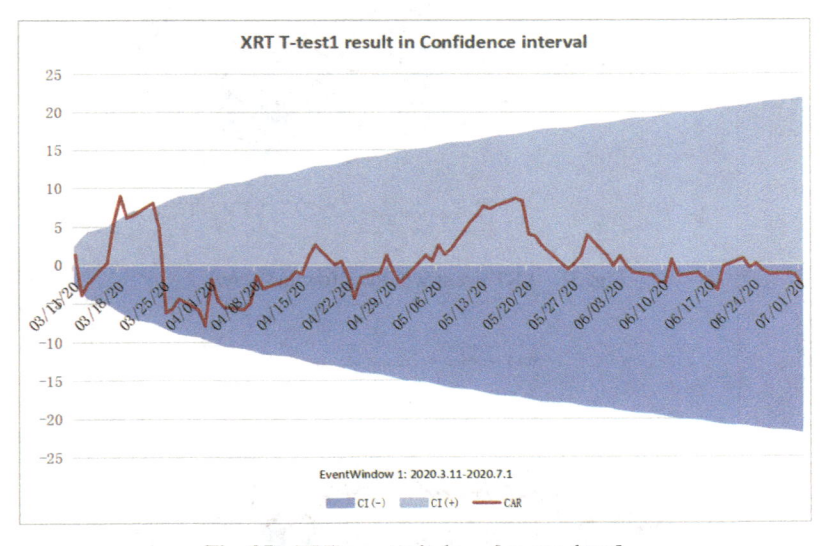

Fig. 35. XRT event windows [owner-draw].

The high-order version of the ARIMA model can also incorporate exogenous variables, which can affect the model prediction results.

After analyzing the XRT index using the high-order ARIMA model in R language, it can be observed that the forecast of returns is not optimistic (Fig. 39), as it has remained at a relatively low level, and its volatility is also high. As the supply chain crisis gripped the world last year, large retailers spent a lot on purchases for fear of running out of

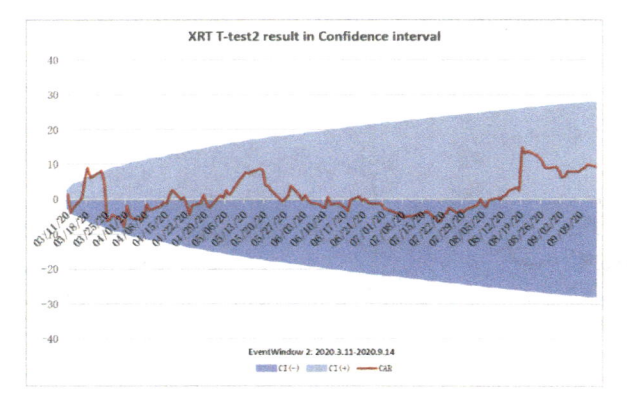

Fig. 36. XRT event windows [owner-draw].

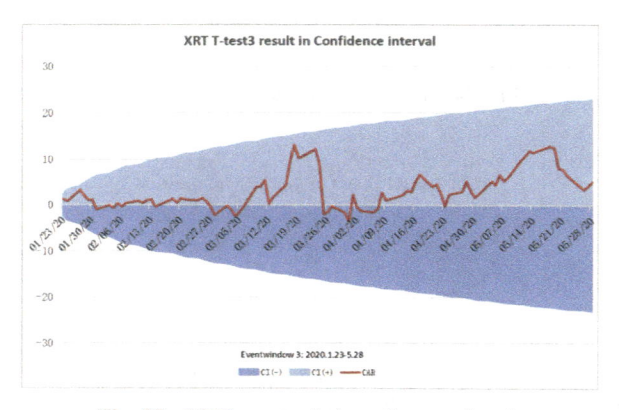

Fig. 37. XRT event windows [owner-draw].

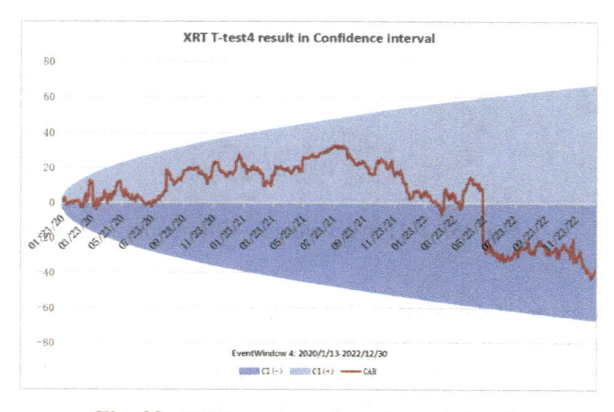

Fig. 38. XRT event windows [owner-draw].

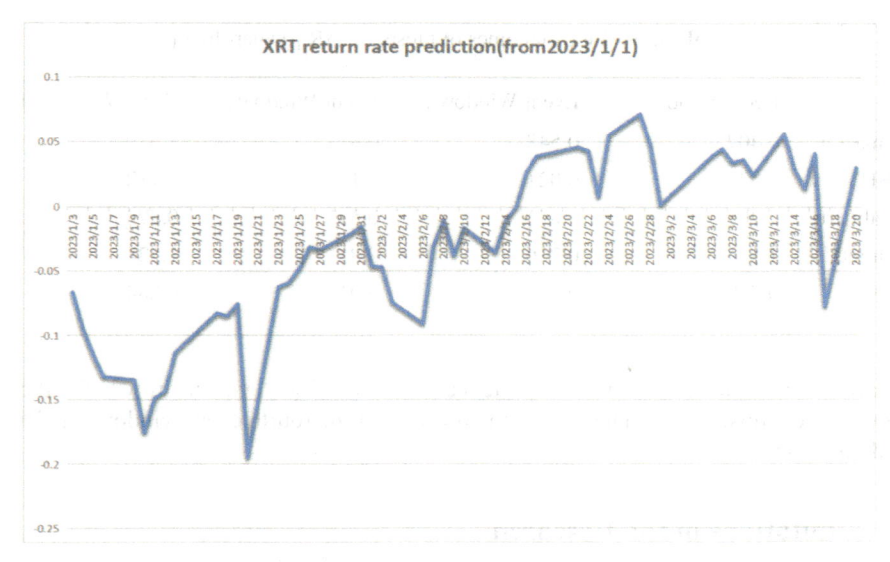

Fig. 39. Prediction of XRT return [owner-draw].

goods to sell. Retailers such as Walmart, Costco, and Target chartered their own ships to ensure shipping, which this year has turned out to be the cause of high inventory.

5.4 Results Analysis

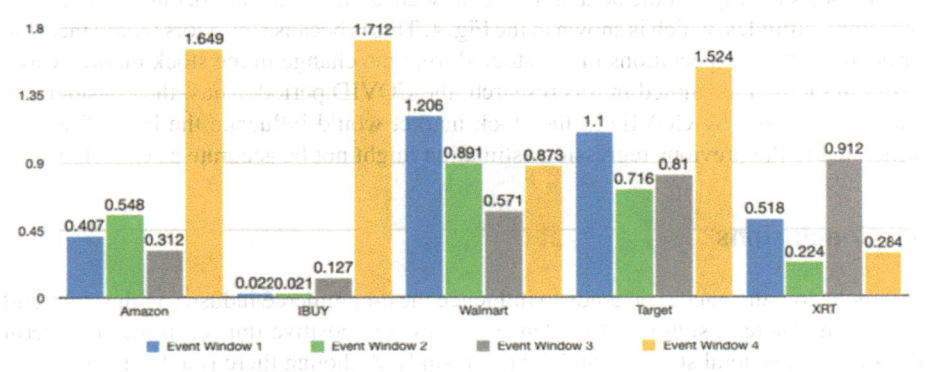

Fig. 40. P Value outcomes of t tests for AR [owner-draw].

The Fig. 40 and Table 3 show that there was significant difference in IBUY abnormal return and relatively low p-value for Amazon compared with others. Overall, these results indicate that the e-commerce sector grew rapidly during the early stage of the pandemic and with statistically significant abnormal returns, and the retail sector was not significantly affected by the economic downturn. More importantly, in the post-pandemic era, the advantages accumulated in the early stages of the pandemic will be

Table 3. P Value outcomes of t tests for AR [Owner-draw].

	Event Window 1	Event Window 2	Event Window 3	Event Window 4
Amazon	0.407	0.548	0.312	1.649
IBUY	0.022	0.021	0.127	1.712
Walmart	1.206	0.891	0.571	0.873
Target	1.1	0.716	0.81	1.524
XRT	0.518	0.224	0.912	0.284

significantly weakened or even experience a serious slowdown in growth for the e-Commerce industry, as can be seen in the p values of the fourth event window for IBUY and Amazon.

6 Limitations of the Research

Generally, the limitations of this research are caused by the difference between the settings of the models and the real-life situation. First, the CAPM model is used to construct the regressions for estimation, which leads to several discrepancies. For example, there might be more than one factor influencing the stock return premiums, such as the stock capital, which suggests that the coefficients generated from the regression model might not be highly simulated in real-life situations. In addition, the CAPM model could only generate fixed coefficients, which would not be changed by time series. However, there is evidence showing that the beta of the stock, such as Amazon, varied, due to changes in investors' attitudes, which is shown in the Fig. 4. This is because investors would increase or decrease their expectations of the stock during the change in the stock market, especially in the period studied in this research, the COVID period. Thus, the considerable variations caused by COVID in the stock market would influence the beta of stocks, which led to the previous regression estimation might not be accurate as expected.

7 Conclusions

In conclusion, the pandemic tends to influence the e-commerce industry in the short and long term. There is significant evidence to show the positive impact in the short term through both general statistics and the event study. Although there is a downward trend of the e-commerce industry in statistical analysis, the actual influence of the pandemic in the long run is ambiguous. Since the e-commerce industry has reached maturity after the pandemic, it is suggested that the increasing magnitude would gradually decrease. For example, Amazon's net sales increased dramatically during pandemic, and reached maintenance after the pandemic. Compared to retail industries and typical companies such as Walmart and Target, there is no evidence showing a statistically significant impact in the short run and no significant evidence to prove the long-term impact on returns in the retail industry. This is probably because the retail industries are more focused on daily necessities, so the sales volume could not fluctuate much due to external factors. Although there might be some limitations of this research, the result is still convincing that COVID had a positive impact on the e-commerce industry in short term through the IBUY index and typical example Amazon compare its counterparts, in the retail industry.

References

1. Taher, G.: E-commerce: advantages and limitations. Int. J. Acad. Res. Account. Finance Manag. Sci. **11**(1), 153–165 (2021)
2. Mayumi, B.: Annual retail trade survey shows impact of online shopping on retail sales during COVID-19 pandemic. United States census bureau (2022). https://www.census.gov/library/stories/2022/04/ecommerce-sales-surged-during-pandemic.html
3. Tyrväinen, O., Karjaluoto, H.: Online grocery shopping before and during the COVID-19 pandemic: a meta-analytical review. Telematics Inform. **71**, 101839 (2022). https://doi.org/10.1016/j.tele.2022.101839
4. Stegglals, P.: Post-pandemic consumer behavior and habits - think with google apac. Google (2021). https://www.thinkwithgoogle.com/intl/en-apac/consumer-insights/consumertrends/consumer-behavior-psychology-post-pandemic/. Accessed 4 Mar 2023
5. Press Center. 2021 Amazon Business B2B E-commerce in evolution Report highlights gaps, opportunities in E-procurement process. Press Center (2021). https://press.aboutamazon.com/2021/6/2021-amazon-business-b2b-e-commerce-in-evolution-report-highlights-gaps-opportunities-in-e-procurement-process
6. Kim, R.Y.: The impact of COVID-19 on consumers: preparing for digital sales. IEEE Eng. Manage. Rev. **48**(3), 212–218 (2020)
7. Chaudhary, H.: Analyzing the paradigm shift of consumer behavior towards E-Commerce during pandemic lockdown. Available at SSRN 3664668 (2020)
8. How European shoppers will buy groceries in the next normal. McKinsey & Company (2020). https://www.mckinsey.com/industries/retail/our-insights/how-european-shoppers-will-buy-groceries-in-the-next-normal
9. O'Donovan, C.: Amazon grew relentlessly. Now it's getting lean. The Washington Post (2023). https://www.washingtonpost.com/technology/2023/03/27/amazon-layoffs-job-cuts/
10. Amazon net income 2004–2022. Marketplace Pulse (2023). https://www.marketplacepulse.com/stats/amazon-net-income
11. Kohan, S.E.: Walmart, Amazon, and the Home Depot agree, consumer spending will slow in 2023. Forbes (2023). https://www.forbes.com/sites/shelleykohan/2023/02/25/walmart-amazon-and-the-home-depot-agree-consumer-spending-will-slow-in-2023/?sh=71c6e1244ca5

An Exploration of Bank Failure in Silicon Valley and the Interaction of Failure Factors - Empirical Analysis Based on VAR Model

Tianqi Peng(✉)

Beijing University of Technology, Beijing 100124, China
`tianqi.peng@ucdconnect.ie`

Abstract. The bankruptcy of Silicon Valley Bank (hereinafter referred to as SVB), as a topical issue, was a bank liquidity crisis event mainly triggered by the rising interest rates of the Federal Reserve. In order to further reveal the risks in the business structure of Silicon Valley Bank and to provide theoretical support for SVB's cash outflow and maturity mismatch phenomenon, this paper uses the Fed interest rate, SVB's Treasury asset ratio, bond-weighted duration and cash balance to total assets ratio as the research objects. It analyses the impact of the Fed interest rate on SVB's financial indicators and the interaction between the indicators through unit root test and co-integration test using Var model. The interaction between the indicators is analysed by impulse response and variance decomposition to examine the magnitude, peak and persistence of the impact of shocks. Finally, with the lagged forecast responses, the omissions of Basel III are presented, and some suggestions are made for future precautionary measures in the banking sector.

Keywords: Silicon Valley Bank · Credit Risk · Maturity Mismatch · Var model · Impulse Response · Basel III

1 Introduction

On March 8, 2023, Silicon Valley Bank (SVB), a prominent financial institution in the United States, shocked the market by announcing plans to sell its securities portfolio and issue stocks to raise emergency funds. This announcement triggered a wave of panic among depositors and investors, leading to a run on deposits and a rapid sell-off of SVB's stocks. Within 48 h of the turmoil, on March 10, the California Department of Financial Protection and Innovation (DFPI) declared the closure of SVB due to its insufficient liquidity and insolvency, appointing the Federal Deposit Insurance Corporation (FDIC) as the bankruptcy trustee [1].

In addition, He, J. [2] highlights the ineffectiveness of Basel III, the prominent standard for banking regulation, in regulating HTM securities, despite its utilization of the capital adequacy ratio as a regulatory indicator. Xiong, Q. [3] also pointed out that it is the one of the immediate trigger of the bankruptcy. Besides, the lack of quantitative indicators of bank customer concentration, and the risk of bank runs could not be directly measured by the Accord. Furthermore, Basel III does not limit the proportion of commercial banks' HTM holdings to portfolio assets, which allows for radical asset allocation by all types of commercial banks and making it an easy tool for the manipulation of commercial banks' financial statement data and regulatory measures.

On the one hand, Silicon Valley Bank's bankruptcy was also largely due to its aggressive asset allocation. With the Federal Reserve's interest rate hike leading to huge losses on its asset side and heavy unrealised gains and losse (Fang, Y., & Yuan, Y. [4]). On the other hand, against the backdrop of the interest rate hike, SVB's single client group had difficulty raising funds and offering deposits leading to pressure on SVB's liability side, exacerbating its unrealised losses and triggering investor panic and a run (Huang, G. [5]).

In order to investigate the problem of SVB's asset structure allocation in the context of the Fed's interest rate changes and the limitations of Basel III, as well as to explain at a theoretical level its maturity mismatch leading to large cash outflows, a VAR model was selected to study the bankruptcy of Silicon Valley Bank.

2 Limitations of the Basel III Regulation of SVB Insolvency

Currently, the regulatory framework for Systemically Important Financial Institutions (SIFIs), represented by the Basel Accord, primarily focuses on traditional licensed financial institutions such as banks and insurance companies. Ba, Y., & Shang, H. [6] states it establishes standardized methods and rules for identifying, assessing, and regulating risks, Su, Y. [7]. Also states that it integrates risk management with the capital establishment, thereby promoting the concept of capital resilience against risks.

Basel III builds on the previous Basel II and Basel I and introduces the concept of macro-prudential regulation to effectively guard against systemic risk (Li, T. [8]). Li, Q. [9] figures out it raises minimum capital requirements, increases leverage ratios, liquidity ratios and requires increased information disclosure, and Dai, X. [10] also illustrates that it has important guidance for banking supervision in the areas of capital regulation, and liquidity risk control, systemically important bank supervision and leverage ratio regulation.

With the Fed's aggressive rate hikes, SVBs suffered huge losses on the asset side. Liu, Z., Xiao, J., et al. [11] have pointed out that if we calculate SVB's HTM asset float, its US $17.5 billion unrealised loss at end-2022 has This exceeds its capital equity of US$15.39 billion and is on the verge of technical insolvency.

However, SVB's core Tier 1, Tier 1 and capital adequacy ratios of 12.05% (15.26%), 15.40 (15.26%) and 16.18% (16.05%) respectively in 2022 are well above the regulatory capital requirements in Basel III. Han, H. [12] suggests that this is due to distortions in the regulatory measures, as unrealised losses on HTM bonds are not reflected in the Basel III regulatory measures.

Besides, it is important to note that the Basel Accord fails to provide specific quantitative indicators to assess bank customer concentration and measure the risk of bank runs directly (Liu, X., & Ju, Z. [13]). This limitation poses a challenge in effectively monitoring and addressing these critical risks within the banking industry. Moreover, Basel III does not impose any restrictions on the proportion of commercial banks' holdings of assets classified as "held-to-maturity" (HTM) in relation to their overall portfolio assets. This regulatory gap enables all types of commercial banks to engage in radical asset allocation strategies, which, in turn, can facilitate the manipulation of financial statement data and undermine the effectiveness of regulatory measures.

3 Model Design and Indicator Selection

In order to investigate the problem of SVB's asset structure allocation in the context of the Fed's interest rate changes and the limitations of Basel III, this study selects quarterly data from Q1 2000 to Q4 2022, comprising a total of 92 samples. The shadow interest rate proposed by Wu and Xia [14] is used to measure the monetary policy effects under the zero lower bound constraint, denoted as FRRS (Shadow). The ratio of total U.S. government securities to total assets of Silicon Valley Bank is obtained from the official website of myfin.us financial institution and the quarterly reports of Silicon Valley Bank, denoted as TAR (Treasury-asset ratio). The weighted average duration of held-to-maturity (HTM) fixed-income products of Silicon Valley Bank is obtained from quarterly reports since Q4 2002 [15]. For the quarterly data of HTM in 2000 and 2001, which Silicon Valley Bank no longer publicly discloses, the annual data from the annual reports of the bank in the corresponding years are adjusted and used instead, denoted as HTM. To ensure consistency among variable data, the cash balance-total deposit ratio (CTR) is used to quantify the cash outflow of Silicon Valley Bank, which is the ratio of cash balance to total deposit, collected and organized from the bank's quarterly reports.

FFRS: represents the monetary policy of the Federal Reserve System (Fed) in the United States and reflects the macroeconomic environment.

TAR: reflects SVB's bond investment strategy and measures the bank's asset allocation status.

$$TAR = \frac{Total\ U.S.\ Government\ securities}{Total\ Assets}$$

HTM: reflects the weighted average duration of bonds in the bank's investment portfolio, which measures the impact of interest rate changes on bond prices. Here, w_t represents the weight of the bond at time t.

$$HTM = \sum_{t=1}^{T} t \times w_t$$

CTR: reflects the proportion of SVB's cash reserves to its total deposits, quantifying the bank's liquidity status.

$$CTR = \frac{Cash\ balance}{Total\ Deposit}$$

Considering the potential interdependence among the indicators, this study employs a non-structural approach to fit the relationship model between variables, namely the Vector Autoregression (VAR) model. The VAR model extends the single-variable autoregression to the "vector" autoregression composed of multivariate time series variables. In this model, each endogenous variable in the system is treated as a function of lagged values of other variables, thus constructing a multiple-equation system, and estimating the dynamic relationship of all endogenous variables through regression.

$$Y_t = \alpha + \pi_1 \cdot Y_{t-1} + \pi_2 \cdot Y_{t-2} + \cdots + \pi_p \cdot Y_{t-p} + \mu_i$$

According to the VAR model, Y_t is a 4-dimensional vector that includes the values of the four variables mentioned above at time t. Y_t represents a column vector that includes *FFRS*, *TAR*, *HTM*, and *CTR*, where t represents the period, p represents the lag order of all endogenous variables, π represents the matrix of coefficients, and μ_i represents the random disturbance term.

In accordance with the requirements of the VAR model, we do not take the logarithm of variables that are "ratios" in order to reduce the potential influence of eliminating the relationship between variables before normalization.

3.1 Unit Root Test

The ADF test was employed to examine the stationarity of variables, with the AIC criterion being used for unit root testing. The results of the tests are shown in Table 1. It can be observed that the Federal Funds Rate Shadow Rate (FFRS), Treasury Asset Ratio (TAR), Duration of Held-to-Maturity Securities (HTM), and Cash-to-Total-Deposit Ratio (CTR) are all first-order integrated at the 1% significance level, indicating that they are stationary series at the 1% significance level.

3.2 Johansen Co-integration Test

Based on the VAR model, the Johansen system cointegration test was selected. According to the stationary test results, all four variables have no time trend term T, while two variables have intercept term C. Therefore, cointegration tests were conducted with and without intercept term C, as well as without time trend term T.

From Table 2, it can be seen that the T statistic or Max-Eigen value is greater than the 0.05 critical value, and the p-value is less than 0.05. Rejecting the null hypothesis of "no cointegration relationship", it indicates that the four variables have a long-term stable cointegration relationship and the regression results are significant. In addition, the data of the model variables are mostly ratios. In order to preserve the potential influence between the variable data, our model does not choose to take logarithms or perform first-order difference operations on the sample data.

Table 1. Unit root test results.

Variables	ADF test values	(C, T)	Critical values (1%, 5%, 10%)	Stability conclusion
FFRS	−3.119882	(C,0)	−2.590910, −1.944445, −1.614392	Steady
DFFRS	−3.595233	(0,0)	−2.590910, −1.944445, −1.614392	Steady
TAR	0.393663	(0,0)	−2.590910, −1.944445, −1.614392	Unstable
DTAR	−6.857351	(0,0)	−2.590910, −1.944445, −1.614392	Steady
HTM	1.816265	(0,0)	−2.590622, −1.944404, −1.614417	Unstable
DHTM	−8.331930	(0,0)	−2.590910, −1.944445, −1.614392	Steady
CTR	−1.379106	(C,0)	−2.590622, −1.944404, −1.614417	Unstable
DCTR	−8.547803	(0,0)	−2.590910, −1.944445, −1.614392	Steady

Source: obtained by the authors using Eviews 12.0 software
Note: (C, T) indicates whether the ADF test equation includes the constant and time-trend terms

Table 2. Co-integration test results.

Type	Trace Statistic/(Max-Eigen) Value	0.05Critical	Prob,
C Not available	54.51999	28.85353	0.0010
	40.17493	24.15921	0.0107
C is available	66.32054	54.07904	0.0028
	35.66246	28.58808	0.0053

Source: obtained by the authors using Eviews 12.0 software

3.3 Determine the Optimal Lag Order

The optimal lag length for the two stages of the VAR model were determined using Eviews 12.0 software, and the results are shown in Tables 3. Based on the principle of selecting the lag length with the fewest degrees of freedom and comprehensive consideration of the model, the lag length for both stages of this model was selected as 2.

Table 3. Lag orders under each criterion.

Lag	LogL	LR	FPE	AIC	SC	HQ
0	272.3159	NA	1.98e−08	−6.388473	−6.272720	−6.341941
1	699.6765	803.8449	1.10e−12	−16.18277	−15.60401*	−15.95011
2	725.0143	45.24609	8.85e−13*	−16.40510*	−15.36332	−15.98632*
3	736.2015	18.91167	9.99e−13	−16.29051	−14.78572	−15.68560
4	750.8355	23.34484	1.05e−12	−16.25799	−14.29018	−15.46695
5	762.4492	17.42056	1.18e−12	−16.15355	−13.72274	−15.17639
6	783.7190	29.87893*	1.08e−12	−16.27902	−13.38519	−15.11573

Source: obtained by the authors using Eviews 12.0 software

4 Var Model Determination for SVB

$$Y_t = \alpha + \pi_1 \cdot Y_{t-1} + \pi_2 \cdot Y_{t-2} + \mu i$$

$$\text{of which, } Y_t = \begin{bmatrix} FFRS \\ TAR \\ HTM \\ CTR \end{bmatrix}$$

$$Y_t = \begin{bmatrix} 0.046505 \\ 0.005530 \\ 0.000222 \\ 0.098503 \end{bmatrix} + \begin{bmatrix} 0.804090 & 0.206903 & -0.007556 & -1.208644 \\ -0.309830 & 0.996205 & 0.032618 & -0.903942 \\ -0.422888 & -0.172156 & 1.591255 & 5.287761 \\ -0.005731 & 0.004844 & -4.96E-05 & 1.067008 \end{bmatrix} Y_{t-1}$$
$$+ \begin{bmatrix} 0.022380 & -0.035401 & -0.006761 & 1.150202 \\ 0.165647 & -0.049695 & -0.035408 & 0.875993 \\ 0.053275 & -0.355257 & -0.640891 & -6.147177 \\ 0.016654 & -0.003163 & 0.001050 & -0.073253 \end{bmatrix} Y_{t-2}$$

To analyze the dynamic relationship between the federal funds shadow rate, SVB bond-to-asset ratio, changes in cash balance, and the duration of maturing bonds, it is necessary to ensure the stability of the VAR model. The main criterion for judging the stability of the VAR model is whether the eigenvalues are within the unit circle. When the eigenvalues are within the unit circle, the VAR model is considered stable; if the eigenvalues are outside the unit circle, the VAR model is unstable. As shown in Fig. 1, all eigenvalues are within the unit circle and their corresponding moduli are less than 1, indicating that the VAR model is stable. This lays the foundation for subsequent impulse response and variance decomposition analyses.

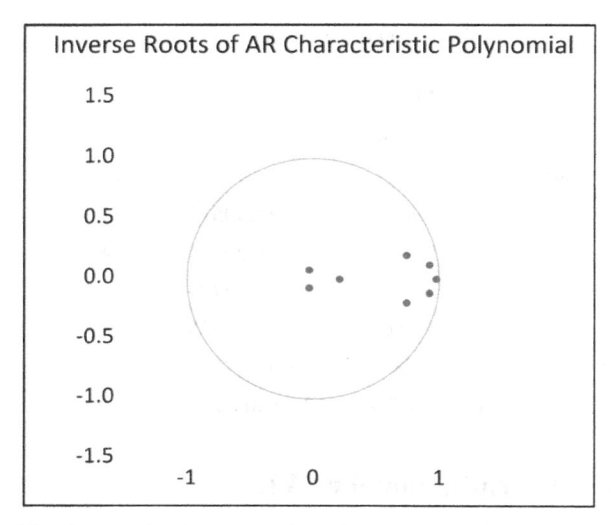

Fig. 1. SVB bankruptcy variable model stability test results.

4.1 Predictive Analysis of Granger Causality Test

Based on the qualitative analysis of Silicon Valley Bank, in the model which mainly investigate the predictive effects of FFRS on CTR, HTM, and TAR, as well as the predictive effects of TAR and HTM on CTR. Since HTM and FFR variables are obtained by averaging monthly data to obtain quarterly data, and it can't be found the monthly data for HTM, the accuracy of the model's sample data may be affected to some extent. In this case, in order to increase the model's fault-tolerance and mitigate potential issues due to inaccurate data, we have chosen a relatively loose significance level of α, which is 10%. The degree of predictive performance is shown in Table 4.

Table 4. Degree of Granger causal prediction between variables.

Dependent Variable	Independent Variable	Prob.	Predicted Significance
CTR	TAR	0.0270	Significance
CTR	HTM	0.0600	Significance
CTR	FFRS	0.5046	Insignificance
TAR	FFRS	0.0075	Significance
HTM	FFRS	0.9192	Insignificance

Source: obtained by the authors using Eviews 12.0 software

In the Granger causality tests, we found that the qualitative analysis results related to the Silicon Valley Bank bankruptcy were largely validated. Specifically, the SVB's government bond asset allocation and the duration of the maturing bonds had a significant predictive effect on changes in the bank's cash balance, while the federal shadow interest rate had a significant predictive effect on the proportion of SVB's government bond assets. However, there were two Granger test results that did not fully match our previous qualitative analysis, namely, the federal interest rate's predictive effect on changes in cash balance and the weighted duration of HTM bonds. Despite this, we believe that such deviations from our expectations are reasonable in some extent.

Analysis of the Reasons for the Insignificant Prediction of CTR by FFRS. Although it is believed that the federal funds rate typically has an impact on bank cash balances in qualitative analysis, observations from the Fig. 4 indicate that SVB may have responded differently to interest rate changes during the 2008 financial crisis compared to other banks. At this time, the bank's cash management strategy may have focused more on risk management rather than profit-seeking, and SVB may have increased its cash reserves to ensure sufficient liquidity to cope with market volatility and credit risk. This unique situation may have resulted in a less significant predictive effect of the federal funds rate on SVB's cash balance changes.

Furthermore, since 2019, Silicon Valley Bank has been in a period of aggressive investment in long-term assets. Qualitative analysis shows that during this period, the predictive effect of the federal funds rate on changes in SVB's cash balances, maturity duration of bonds, and allocation of government bonds has weakened. This reflects the bank's unstable operational status and problems with its asset structure, where bank rates should have a certain predictive effect on these three variables in a normally operating commercial bank. Nevertheless, over time, the weight of government bond allocation (TAR) and the bond-weighted duration (HTM) still show significant predictive power on SVB's cash balance changes (CTR), which is consistent with the Granger causality test results.

Analysis of the Reasons for the Insignificant Prediction of HTM by FFRS. From Fig. 8, it can be seen that SVB, as a commercial bank that should primarily focus on lending, did not consider HTM maturing bonds as its core business prior to setting an aggressive allocation in US government bonds in 2019. This business has been in a developmental state. This means that the bank's business structure did not prioritize long-term bond business as its core, which may have reduced the sensitivity of the still-to-be-scaled maturing bond business to changes in interest rates, and made the federal benchmark shadow interest rate less significant for SVB's duration forecast. Therefore, this deviation also serves as a reasonable possibility.

Since 2019, SVB's aggressive allocation of long-term assets has better explained the bank's significant cash outflows in the later period. This objectively reflects structural issues in SVB's banking business and is also one of the important reasons for its bankruptcy in the later period.

5 Empirical Analysis of SVB Bankruptcy Factors Based on Var (2) Model - Impulse Response Function Analysis

Using impulse response functions can help examine the short-term dynamic impact relationship between the Federal Reserve shadow interest rate and the Silicon Valley Bank's asset allocation to government bonds, the duration of maturing bonds, and changes in cash balance. It can also help further explain the objective phenomenon of how the asset allocation to government bonds and duration of maturing bonds cause liquidity outflows and bankruptcy. Impulse response functions mainly to observe the theoretical explanation of the objective factors leading to the bankruptcy of Silicon Valley Bank by giving a standard deviation shock to the Federal Reserve shadow interest rate, the asset allocation to government bonds, and the duration of maturing bonds. Additionally, exploring some predictions regarding the bank's structural adjustment if it had not gone bankrupt in the later period.

Moreover, the model can use non-stationary time series data to conduct impulse response under the premise of having a cointegration relationship, which may result in non-convergence. However, it can still provide useful information on the short- and medium-term interaction between variables.

5.1 Dynamic Impact of Shocks to FFRS on TAR

As shown in Figs. 2 and 3, a positive shock of one standard deviation in the federal shadow interest rate, i.e., a tightening monetary policy by the Federal Reserve, leads to a short-term decline (TAR < 0) in Silicon Valley Bank's proportion of government bonds. The negative response reaches its minimum value of −0.035 in the 11th quarter and gradually converges to the long-term equilibrium level in the 22nd quarter.

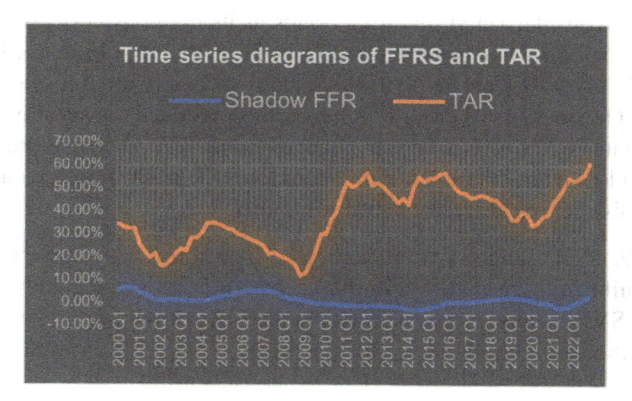

Fig. 2. Time series diagrams of FFRS and TAR.

Based on the response function in Fig. 3 the further predictions can be made on SVB's future asset allocation based on the federal funds rate. If SVB had not gone bankrupt, within eleven quarters (three years) of implementing this allocation strategy

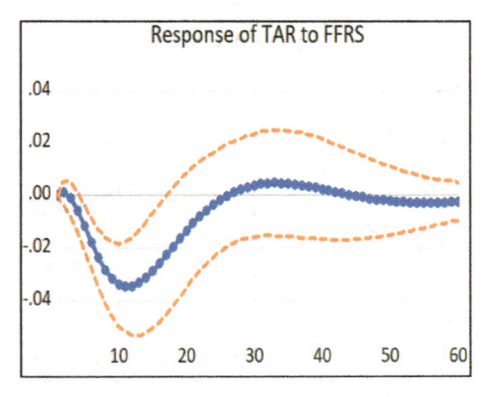

Fig. 3. Impulse response of TAR to FFRS. Source: obtained by the authors using Eviews12.0

in 2021, SVB's proportion of government bonds would have shown a downward trend. Within 22 quarters (five years) of lag, SVB may adopt a series of strategies to optimize asset allocation and mitigate interest rate risk, and therefore the proportion of government bonds will gradually converge to a stable level in the long term.

5.2 Dynamic Impact of Shocks to FFRS on CTR

According to Fig. 4 & Fig. 5, given a one standard deviation positive shock to the shadow interest rate, i.e. the background of the Federal Reserve raising interest rates, Silicon Valley Bank's cash balance changes decrease in the short term (i.e. cash outflow), with a negative response (CTR < 0), reaching a maximum value of -0.016 after about four quarters (one year), and in the long term the cash balance changes increase (i.e. cash inflow), with a positive response (CTR > 0), reaching a maximum value of 0.012 after about fifteen quarters and gradually returning to the long-term equilibrium level.

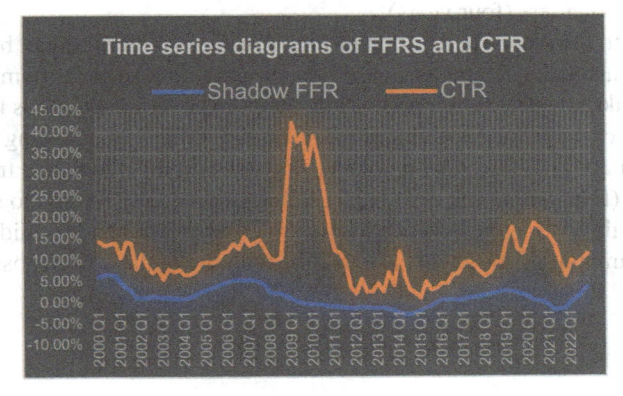

Fig. 4. Time series diagrams of FFRS and CTR.

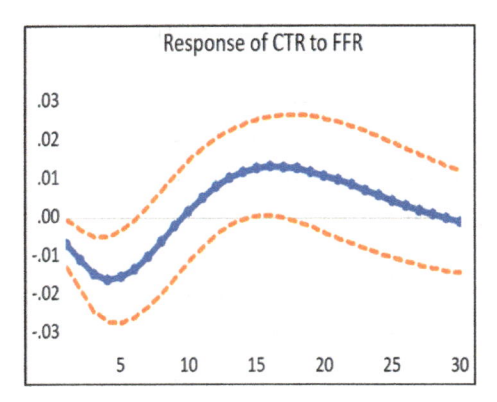

Fig. 5. Impulse response of CTR to FFRS. Source: obtained by the authors using Eviews12.0

Based on the response function in Fig. 5, further predictions can be made about the future cash balance changes of SVB in response to fluctuations in the federal shadow interest rate. Assuming that SVB does not go bankrupt, in the four quarters (approximately one year) following the implementation of the asset allocation strategy in 2021, SVB may experience a certain degree of cash outflow, followed by a slowdown in the outflow trend. However, in approximately 16 quarters (four years) from now, in 2025, SVB will receive cash inflows from five-year bonds reaching maturity. This prediction is consistent with objective facts.

5.3 Dynamic Impact of Shocks to TAR on CTR

According to Fig. 6 and Fig. 7, a positive shock of one standard deviation in SVB's bond assets will immediately lead to a negative response in SVB's cash balance (i.e., cash outflow, CTR < 0). The negative impact will reach its minimum value of -0.023 after a lag of two quarters, and then gradually return to long-term equilibrium and converge after a lag of 17 quarters (four years).

According to the response function in Fig. 7 further predictions can be made about SVB's future cash balance changes based on its asset allocation. Assuming that SVB does not go bankrupt, after its aggressive allocation to government bonds from Q2 2020 to Q4 2021, its cash balance will initially decrease significantly, reaching its maximum cash outflow in 2022, followed by a gradual slowdown in the downward trend. After 17 quarters of lag (four years), the cash balance change gradually returns to stability. This reflects that while SVB aggressively allocated to government bonds, it did not reserve a proportionate amount of sufficient cash to cope with the outflow of deposits.

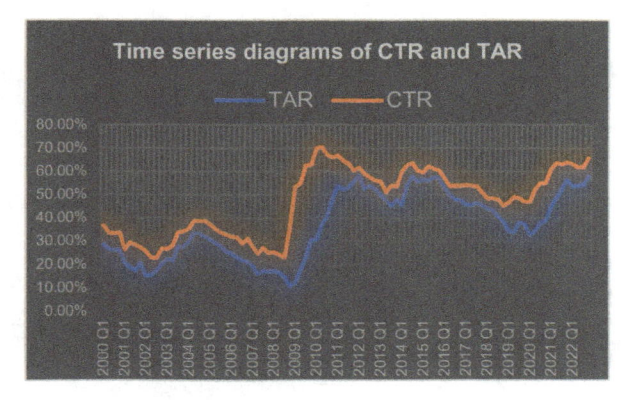

Fig. 6. Time series diagrams of CTR and TAR.

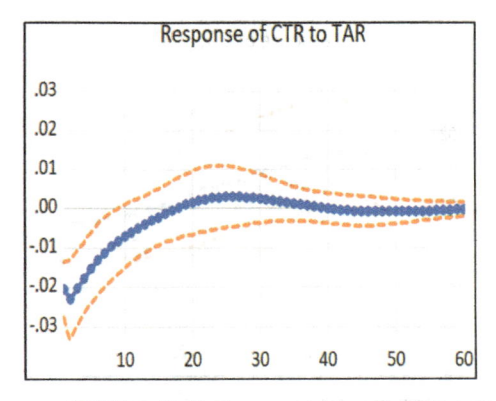

Fig. 7. Impulse response of CTR to TAR. Source: obtained by the authors using Eviews12.0

5.4 Dynamic Impact of Shocks to HTM on CTR

Given a positive shock of one standard deviation in SVB's bond maturity, as shown in Fig. 8 & Fig. 9, i.e., an increase in bond maturity, it will lead to an immediate positive response in Silicon Valley Bank's cash balance (i.e., cash inflow), with a positive CTR. The maximum positive impact will be reached after a lag of seven quarters (two years), with a value of 0.016, and then gradually return to the long-term equilibrium level after a lag of twenty quarters (five years).

Based on the response function in Fig. 9, we can further predict the future cash balance changes of SVB based on the changes in bond duration. If SVB does not go bankrupt, after purchasing a large amount of long-term government bonds in 2020, its cash balance will show a positive response (i.e., cash inflow) starting from the second lagged quarter. After twenty lagged quarters (five years), i.e., in 2025, the cash inflow reaches its maximum response value. At this time, a large amount of five-year government bonds purchased by SVB will mature, and the principal and interest of the bonds will be returned to the

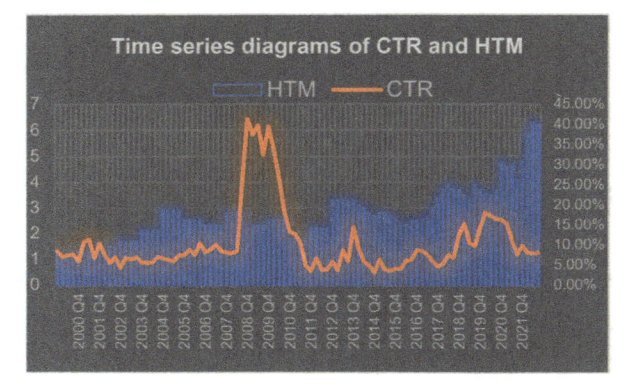

Fig. 8. Time series diagrams of CTR and HTM.

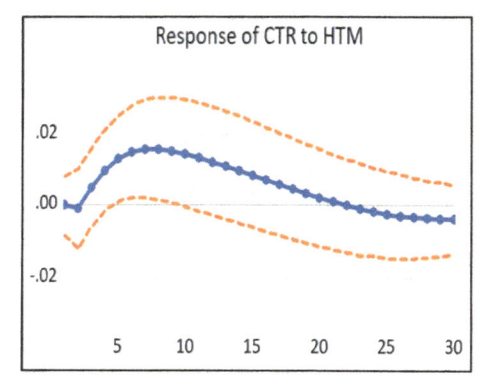

Fig. 9. Impulse response of CTR to HTM. Source: obtained by the authors using Eviews12.0

bank, resulting in cash income for the bank. This theoretically explains the phenomenon of increased cash inflows for SVB after the maturity of its five-year Treasury bonds.

5.5 A Brief Theoretical Analysis of the Causes of SVB Bankruptcy Instances Based on Impulse Response

Starting from the first quarter of 2020 and based on four impulse response graphs, this part analyzes the bankruptcy process of Silicon Valley Bank (SVB). Over the eight quarters from 2020 to 2021, the Federal Reserve implemented a large-scale interest rate cut policy in response to the economic downturn caused by the COVID-19 pandemic, reducing the interest rate to zero to stimulate the economy (FFRS experienced negative shocks). The Federal Reserve's benchmark interest rate plays an important guiding role in commercial banks' loan interest rates. As the interest rate remains at zero, commercial banks' loan interest rates also correspondingly decrease to near-zero. With the rise of the global technology company financing boom, technology startups, as SVB's main customers, have deposited large sums of money into SVB (CTR exhibits a positive response, with maximum response in the first quarter of 2021 after four quarters).

In this context, SVB's lending yield was lower than the yield of long-term government bonds. Influenced by the Federal Reserve's monetary policy foresight, SVB did not engage in a large amount of traditional lending business but chose to buy a large number of long-term government bonds (TAR exhibited a positive response, with a maximum response in the fourth quarter of 2022 after the eleventh quarter), causing the proportion of government bonds in SVB's portfolio to increase.

In the fourth quarter of 2021, as the Federal Reserve gradually implemented a normalised monetary policy and raised the federal funds rate for the ninth consecutive time (FFRS suffered a positive shock), the price of long-term Treasuries fell significantly. To contain losses and address potential liquidity risk, SVB sold a large number of bonds with longer maturities (TAR responded negatively, with the response reaching a minimum in Q3 2024 after the eleventh quarter). Due to SVB's own public disclosure of its exposure to liquidity risk, no one would have been willing to invest at a discount without an emergency, as they would not even be able to recover their principal. Under this forward-looking influence, SVB's customers began to waver in their confidence in the stability of its asset structure and withdrew their deposits, leading to a massive outflow of deposits, which in turn further exacerbated SVB's liquidity crisis and eventually led to a run (exogenous, with a significant drop in CTR). Ultimately, this chain of events led to the bankruptcy of SVB. Had this exogenous factor not arisen, it is likely that SVB would have used this cash for lending, as predicted by the impulse response function, leading to a cash outflow in 2023 (negative CTR response, with a minimum in the first quarter of 2023).

SVB's unrealized losses were severe, and it was unable to realize the cash inflow from purchasing a large number of long-term government bonds that was predicted in the impulse response function 16 quarters later (CTR exhibits maximum positive response in 2025), leading to a mismatch between government bond yields (SVB's assets) and deposit outflows (SVB's liabilities), and ultimately resulting in bankruptcy. This phenomenon indicates that the bankruptcy risk of SVB is extremely serious and also reveals problems in SVB's business structure. The above predicted analysis explains the phenomenon of cash outflows and mismatch of maturities that led to the bankruptcy of Silicon Valley Bank from a theoretical perspective.

6 Empirical Analysis of SVB Bankruptcy Factors Based on Var (2) Model - Variance Decomposition Analysis

Variance decomposition analyzes the contribution of each structural shock to endogenous variable changes, which can reflect the relative importance of various stochastic disturbances in the system that affect endogenous variables (Fig. 10 & Table 5).

Based on the results of the variance decomposition, FFRS shows that the majority of standard deviation fluctuations are self-contained and not significantly affected by other variables, with a decrease from 100% in the first period to 87% in the seventeenth period, while other variables contributions start at 0% and increase to 13% in the tenth period. TAR initially has full self-containment (100%), but later decreases to 20%, while

FFRS and CTR both show increasing contributions from 0% in the initial period to 45% and 29%, respectively, in the tenth period. HTM's standard deviation is relatively stable and mainly self-contained, remaining at 94% from the first period (97%) to the tenth period. CTR's standard deviation is mostly influenced by other variables, while TAR and HTM show an increase in their contributions from 33% and 0% in the first period to 43% and 18%, respectively, in the tenth period, with CTR carrying over 60% of the standard deviation in later periods.

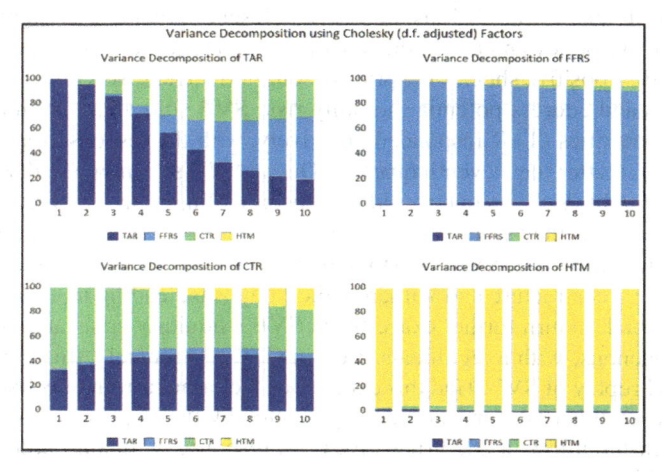

Fig. 10. SVB variance decomposition. Source: obtained by the authors using Eviews12.0

Table 5. Values of variance decomposition of SVB variables.

Variances	Period	S.E	TAR	FFRS	CTR	HTM
TAR	1	0.023507	100.0000	0.000000	0.000000	0.000000
	2	0.030104	95.66223	0.102218	4.036799	0.198751
	3	0.034810	86.14506	1.607598	11.21290	1.034438
	4	0.039416	72.20601	6.353046	19.36043	2.080519
	5	0.044822	56.86564	14.41826	25.84460	2.871505
	6	0.051294	43.43546	23.92603	29.44193	3.196579
	7	0.058632	33.47429	32.83670	30.55682	3.132185
	8	0.066420	26.82726	40.13160	30.18908	2.852053

(continued)

Table 5. (*continued*)

Variances	Period	S.E	TAR	FFRS	CTR	HTM
	9	0.074225	22.67012	45.67536	29.15842	2.496105
	10	0.081690	20.19163	49.72100	27.94075	2.146616
FFRS	1	0.003680	0.215029	99.78497	0.000000	0.000000
	2	0.006816	0.594358	98.54500	0.025838	0.834805
	3	0.009641	1.077936	96.94799	0.176033	1.798039
	4	0.012032	1.530679	95.29243	0.488628	2.688263
	5	0.013980	1.966775	93.62863	0.954809	3.449787
	6	0.015530	2.406365	91.99866	1.542756	4.052217
	7	0.016741	2.860136	90.45029	2.206255	4.483324
	8	0.017676	3.330398	89.02717	2.893649	4.748782
	9	0.018390	3.813062	87.76049	3.556190	4.870262
	10	0.018930	4.299364	86.66526	4.154493	4.880879
CTR	1	0.038261	33.22150	1.660504	65.11800	0.000000
	2	0.051481	37.89351	2.495659	59.51790	0.092927
	3	0.059621	41.48396	3.585934	54.59186	0.338251
	4	0.065277	44.32815	4.491098	49.66660	1.514148
	5	0.069459	46.14218	5.016249	45.25484	3.586731
	6	0.072685	46.95979	5.132471	41.62033	6.287411
	7	0.075271	46.91904	4.956538	38.81402	9.310402
	8	0.077446	46.18952	4.686581	36.75074	12.37315
	9	0.079388	44.95020	4.530153	35.28268	15.23697
	10	0.081221	43.38307	4.644509	34.25010	17.72232
HTM	1	0.234609	1.691524	0.178338	0.809558	97.32058
	2	0.337121	1.536418	0.091368	2.571922	95.80029
	3	0.405390	1.193490	0.063438	3.565677	95.17740
	4	0.452803	0.965434	0.053707	4.212068	94.76879
	5	0.486454	0.843083	0.049264	4.642977	94.46468
	6	0.510489	0.802211	0.045157	4.916546	94.23609
	7	0.527598	0.815830	0.043581	5.069744	94.07085
	8	0.539673	0.859009	0.054334	5.132463	93.95419

(*continued*)

Table 5. (*continued*)

Variances	Period	S.E	TAR	FFRS	CTR	HTM
	9	0.548126	0.911283	0.094111	5.131625	93.86298
	10	0.554047	0.957961	0.184207	5.091812	93.76602

Source: obtained by the authors using Eviews12.0

7 Conclusions and Suggestions

7.1 On Bank Asset Structure and Liquidity Risk

While refining the Basel III regulatory measures, according to Fig. 3, SVB's TAR only reached the minimum value of response in the twelfth quarter (three years) after the Fed's interest rate hike, and banks do not react to interest rate changes in a timely manner, so they should appropriately improve their own interest rate sensitivity to reduce liquidity risk arising from the maturity mismatch phenomenon. In addition, according to Fig. 9, a positive movement in HTM leads to a lagged inflow of cash. In other words, whether it is SVB's own aggressive allocation to Treasuries or rising interest rates, an increase in HTM will further lead to a lag in unrealised returns, which is a direct cause of the maturity mismatch phenomenon. Commercial banks should therefore pay more attention to the relationship between HTM and unrealised gains and losses, and reduce the proportion of treasury assets (especially long-maturity bonds) to total assets during the interest rate climbing phase to reduce investor panic caused by the surfacing of unrealised losses.

7.2 On Bank Supervision and Regulatory Measurement

Commercial Banks are Required to Disclose Additional Capital Adequacy Ratios for HTM Securities. Basel III regulatory indicators can calculate the difference between the fair value and amortised cost of HTM bonds, estimate their unrealised gains and losses, and include them in the calculation of the capital adequacy ratio so that the capital adequacy ratio can better reflect the interest rate risk of banks.

Limit the Proportion of HTM Bonds to the Total Portfolio Assets of Commercial Banks. The lack of restrictions on the proportion of HTM (held-to-maturity) securities and the possible reclassification of available-for-sale (AFS) securities as HTM securities can create opportunities for commercial banks to manipulate financial statement data and regulatory metrics. To address this issue, supervisory authorities should develop rules and regulations to limit the proportion of HTM securities held by commercial banks and set limits on the number of AFS securities that can be reclassified as HTM securities. By implementing these measures, supervisory authorities can reduce the potential for abuse and ensure the integrity and reliability of financial reporting and regulatory indicators in the banking sector.

Optimising the Structure of the Customer Base. Customer concentration also manifests itself in a certain type of customer segment, where the economic behaviour of the same type of customer segment is characterised by "concerted action", which is transmitted to commercial banks when the external environment has an adverse impact on a certain type of customer segment. As existing regulatory agreements cannot quantify the concentration of banks' customers and the risk of runs, commercial banks should appropriately expand their business audience and reduce customer concentration in order to reduce the risk of runs on banks from the same customer base under the influence of exogenous factors.

Conduct Regular Stress Tests. Commercial banks should take proactive measures to conduct comprehensive and systematic stress tests on a regular basis. Through scientifically sound stress tests, the risks faced by commercial banks in various businesses and under extreme conditions can be detected and identified in a timely manner. Particularly in the areas of liquidity and capital, commercial banks should attach great importance to the results of stress tests as an important basis for decision-making and risk management practices, and take appropriate risk control and response measures to maintain their ability to operate soundly and sustain their growth.

References

1. Ma, M.: Regulatory vigilance needed for small and medium-sized financial institutions, macro policies should emphasize synergy. Financial Times 001 (2023)
2. He, J.: Reflections on the bankruptcy of Silicon Valley Bank and asset-liability management. Banker (04), 40–43 (2023)
3. Xiong, Q., Lv, H., Chu, X., Huang, X.: The impact and implications of the collapse of Silicon Valley Bank in the United States. Int. Finance (04), 57–66 (2023)
4. Fang, Y., Yuan, Y.: Causes and countermeasures of the run on Silicon Valley Bank and North Rock Bank. Financ. Account. Mon. (09), 14–18 (2023)
5. Huang, G.: Lessons from the systemic financial risks of Silicon Valley Bank's bankruptcy. Banker (04), 35–36 (2023)
6. Ba, Y., Shang, H.: Exploring the systemic importance regulation of financial technology companies from the perspective of Basel accord. North China Finance **03**, 14–28 (2023)
7. Su, Y.: Insights into the risk management of Chinese commercial banks from Basel III. Invest. Entrepreneurship (23), 10–12 (2022)
8. Li, T.: Evolution and new requirements of the final version of Basel III. Shanghai Finance (07), 40–46 (2018)
9. Li, Q.: The impact of Basel agreements on risk regulation of commercial banks. Coop. Econ. Technol. (05), 79–80 (2017)
10. Dai, X.: The process of implementing the Basel agreement system in China and its impact on the commercial banking industry. In Shanghai Law Society (Eds.) Collected Papers of Shanghai Law Research, Volume 23, 2022 - Research on the Rule of Law in Social Governance, pp. 56–69 (2023)
11. Liu, Z., Xiao, J., et al.: "CICC Macro I The Impact of Silicon Valley Bank's Collapse Should Not Be Underestimated" (2023). https://www.cicc.com/
12. Han, H., Peng, Y., Liu, Q., Chen, H.: Research on silicon valley bank's bankruptcy under the background of Basel III: a dual perspective based on business model and regulatory measurement. Finance Account. Mon. (09), 3–13 (2023)

13. Liu, X., Ju, Z.: How to be a resilient commercial bank: Insights from Silicon Valley banks. Banker (04), 37–39 (2023)
14. Wu, J.C., Xia, F.D.: Shadow rate. J. Money Credit Bank. (2016). https://sites.google.com/view/jingcynthiawu/shadow-rates
15. Silicon Valley Bank: Quarterly Reports from Q1 2000 to Q4 2022

Prediction of Lending Club Loan Defaulters

Xueyan Wang(✉)

UCL Information Management of Business, University College of London, London WC1E 6AE, UK
zceiaaa@ucl.ac.uk

Abstract. This article analyzes the loan defaulter's prediction of Lending Club. Since the emergence of more and more repayment problems brings risks and capital losses to the company, it is crucial for managers to research the relevant factors of loan failure. The data is collected from Kaggle website, and it contains the data from the United States during the period of 2007–2015. In this paper, comparative analysis, group analysis and index analysis are used to analyze the dataset. What's more, there are three methods to predict the model building, which are Artificial Neural Networks, XG-Boost Classifier and Random Forest Classifier. Additionally, it can be found that the main factors affecting loan defaulters are installment, terms, grades, interest rate and so on. And when establishing the model, it is found that, Artificial Neural Networks (ANNs) algorithm is more suitable for the analysis and prediction of these data. Lending Club's analysis of failed loans can help managers develop strategies to reduce business risks and maximize profits.

Keywords: Loan · Artificial Neural Network · XGBoost · Random Forest

1 Introduction

Nowadays, many borrowers can easily borrow from the Lending Club company at low interest rates, this brings a lot of potential risks and financial losses to Lending Club [1]. The purpose of this paper is to use Machine Learning (ML) and some logical analysis to classify customers into different types of lenders and credit levels by analyzing their loan profiles. Additionally, in order to explore the main factors behind loan default, this paper analyzes the degree to which different factors influence the failure. In short, the main business purpose is to cut down the amount of credit loss and utilize this for its portfolio and risk assessment.

In recent years, the loan problem has been a crucial issue for various banks and the entire financial industry to explore. For example, Zhang, Wang and Liu have modeled profit as an indicator and explained the relationship between inputs and forecast values and the key factors affecting the forecast values [2]. Meanwhile, Kim and Shin also used Machine Learning to predict the bank loan defaulters, and he found that the Support Vector Machine (SVC) was the best algorithm to predict the data [3]. In addition, Ming-Chun Tsai et al. studied the loan default model and used four prediction methods of

DA, LR, NN and DEA-DA to compare the applicability of prediction. Eventually, they found that DEA-DA and NN were more suitable for predicting this model [4]. Stein explored the relationship between default predictions and loan profits in the paper, using power curves to infer that more powerful models are more profitable than weaker ones and providing a simulation example [5]. Moreover, Walsemann et al. used the Linear Regression model and Neural Network prediction model to improve the accuracy of data prediction in the report and finally found that the Neural Network model had quite obvious advantages in the prediction of results [6]. Over the past few years, the studies of loan defaults have not stopped. Many people have studied the relationship between loan defaults and different influencing factors. On the one hand, the issuance of loans brings great income to the company, and on the other hand, it also brings potential risks. In order to find a balance between loan revenue and risk, lenders need to control the risk of loans. Therefore, the risk assessment prediction of each loan has become an inevitable work. Based on the above research and reasons, this paper analyzes the relationship between different factors and loan status and compares the accuracy of the three analysis methods when building the model.

This paper analyzes Lending Club notebooks in the basic order of Machine Learning. Firstly, in the data processing stage, the original data is sorted and cleaned to determine the total number of valid data for subsequent analysis. Then in the data analysis part, the relationship between the key factors that may have an impact and the loan status is analyzed in turn, and the specific analysis methods such as frequency histogram, box plot and cross-analysis table are used here. After the data analysis, the appropriate prediction model is established according to the conclusions obtained. Here, the three algorithms, Artificial Neural Networks (ANNs), XG Boost Classifier and Random Forest Classifier, are used to evaluate the results of the model. What's more, the performance of the three models is compared in the end, and the most suitable prediction model is selected. Based on the above research, this paper puts forward recommendations and strategies for the future development of the Lending Club.

2 Introduce and Explore Data

From the collected dataset, there are 28 basic descriptions of particular data set (columns), such as loan amount, interest rate and installment, which are basic definitions of loan defaulters. For more relevant information about the data, ask the author or see the original notebook on the Kaggle website. What's more, there are a total of 396,030 records, and the number of non-empty columns is 28, which paves the way for subsequent data cleaning.

There are several columns here, so the investigation of valid and invalid values for each data is important. It can be found that there are no missing values (396030 non-null values) in most of the factors, except that there are many null values in the 6 data of employment-title, employment-length, title, revolving utilization, public record bankruptcies and mortgage-accounts. (See Table 1) Then, these factors will be deleted or filled in vacant data in the subsequent data cleaning process.

Table 1. The non-null values of 6 factors.

Dataset	Non-null values
employment title	373103 non-nul
employment length	377729 non-null
title	394275 non-null
revolving utilization	395754 non-null
mortgage account	358235 non-null
public record bankruptcies	395495 non-null

3 Data Cleaning

After reading these data, it's the Data Cleaning part. First, the missing data and repetitive functions are crucial to be deleted or completed. As mentioned before, the total amount of data is 396,030, and there are 28 influencing factors. In order to further verify the conclusion of missing data, the percentage of 5 factors with missing data is calculated here. (See Table 2) It can be clearly found that employment-title (5.789%), employment-length (4.621%) and mortgage-account (9.543%) have high missing rates. Therefore, next this paper did a more comprehensive exploration of each factor to determine how to deal with these columns.

Table 2. The missing percentage of 5 factors.

Factors	Number of missing values	Percentage
employment title	22927	5.789%
employment length	18301	4.621%
title	1755	0.443%
revolving utilization	276	0.070%
mortgage account	37795	9.543%
public record bankruptcies	535	0.135%

First, there are too many employment titles in real life, and it is impossible for us to include every one of them. So, it is impossible to count the number of unique employment titles across all the data and found that there are 173,105 unique titles, which is a huge number. In addition, there are many missing data for this factor. Therefore, employment title will not be considered in this paper. Moreover, moving on to the analysis of the employment length. There are 12 types of employment length, which are 10+ years, 4 years, <1 year, 6 years, 9 years, 2 years, 3 years, 8 years, 7 years, 5 years and 1 year and NaN years. This study then considered the relationship between loan status and different employment lengths, as shown in Table 3. Obviously, no matter how long of the length, the ratio of loan status is roughly 8:2, which indicates that there is no direct connection between the repayment status of borrowers and their employment length. In addition, the data missing rate of this factor is 4.621%, which is a high rate. To sum up, this paper dropped the employment length column.

Table 3. Relationship between loan status and different employment lengths.

employment length	the percentage of Fully Paid	the percentage of Charged Off	Ratio
10+years	0.82	0.18	Fully paid: Charged Off = 8: 2
4 years	0.81	0.19	
<1 year	0.81	0.21	
6 years	0.79	0.19	
9 years	0.80	0.20	
2 years	0.81	0.19	
3 years	0.80	0.20	
8 years	0.80	0.20	
7 years	0.81	0.19	
5 years	0.81	0.19	
1 year	0.81	0.20	

In addition, this study listed the top five titles and purposes with the largest number and found that these rankings were basically the same: debt consolidation, credit card, home improvement and other. In other words, the analysis of the purpose column can replace the title column, and there are no missing values in the purpose column, which is more conducive to the subsequent data analysis. Therefore, this paper kept the purpose column and removed the title.

What's more, through comparison, it can be found that under the factor of mortgage account, the ratio of loan status is about 1.5:1 (218458:139777), which is helpful for subsequent research. So here were proposed three methods to fill the missing data to retain this column: the first one is to fill the missing data by building a model, such as a linear model. But this approach can be relatively complicated. Secondly, filling this column based on the average of the other columns, which is relatively simple. Finally, classifying the column and making NaN a separate category is another option. Each method is not 100% correct. The second approach was chosen here. First reviewed the other columns to see which are highly correlated with mortgage accounts. The results are shown in Fig. 1. The highest correlation is between the total account and the mortgage account. Therefore, Here choose the data in the total account column to calculate the missing data. Start by grouping the data frame according to the total account and calculating each entry's average mortgage account. Therefore, the mortgage account column was kept.

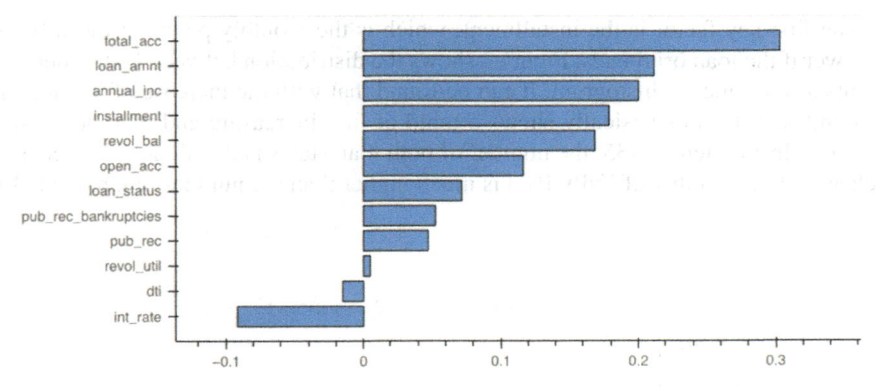

Fig. 1. The correlation between the mortgage account and other columns.

Finally, revolving utilization and public record bankruptcies, these two characteristics have missing data points, but make up less than 0.5% of the total data. So, this paper deleted the rows missing those values in those columns with the formula. All in all, this paper removed three columns (employment title, employment length and title), and finally, there are 39529 data and 24 columns.

4 Data Analysis

After getting familiar with the data and working with it, this paper started to analyze the data. In order to understand the impact of different factors on the status of loans, it's crucial to visualize the data and analyze it using summary statistics.

First, the paper determined the ratio of current loan status. As shown in Fig. 2, the number of Fully Paid (318,357) far exceeds the number of Charged Off (77673), and their ratio is about 4:1. Then this paper analyzed the relationship between different factors and the account of loans and compared the number of two loan states under the same factor.

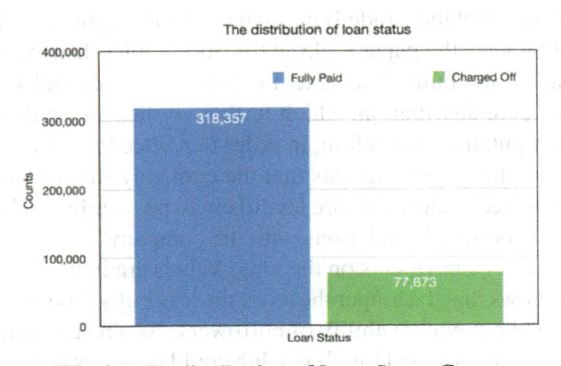

Fig. 2. The distribution of Loan Status Counts

The first key factor is the installment, which is the monthly payment owed by the borrower if the loan originates. Figure 3 shows the distribution between Installment and Counts as a frequency histogram. It can be found that with the increase of Installment, the number of Counts basically shows a trend of first increasing and then decreasing, and when Installment is 335, the number of both loan states is the highest. Moreover, it is clear that the number of Fully Paid is much higher than the number of Charged Off.

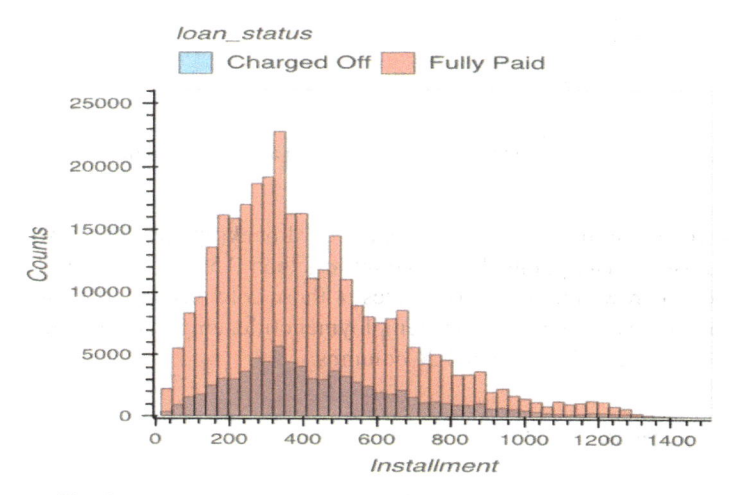

Fig. 3. Distribution between Installment and Loan Status Counts.

Then, about the Grades, Lending club assigned loan grades, and the unique grades are B, A, C, E, D, F, G, and then separate these 7 grades into Sub-Grades.

Figure 4 is the distribution diagram of Grades, from which it can see that the total Count number of the two loan states is Grade B with the most and Grade G with the least. Secondly, in the Fully Paid loan state, the number of Grade B is also the largest. However, for the state Charged Off, the number of Grade C is the largest. From this, the paper roughly deduces that the Grade B group has a better reputation. To further explore the distribution of Grades, the paper looks at the Sub-Grades distribution (Fig. 5). It can be easily found that in the Fully Paid state, the region of grades B1 to B5 is the highest point of the entire curve distribution, which further verifies the conjecture that Grade B group has a better reputation. Therefore, in order to reduce the business risk and capital loss of the company, this paper suggests that the company should focus on developing customers with high credit rates, who are less likely to be overdue on loans and can form long-term and great cooperative relations with the company.

Term is the number of payments on the loan. Values are in months and can be either 36 or 60. Figure 6 shows that the longer the term, the less Fully Paid. From this, long-term lending will affect the repayment ability of borrowers. As a result, long-term loans have a higher risk of losing money, and Lending Club could consider adding more 36 months loan term.

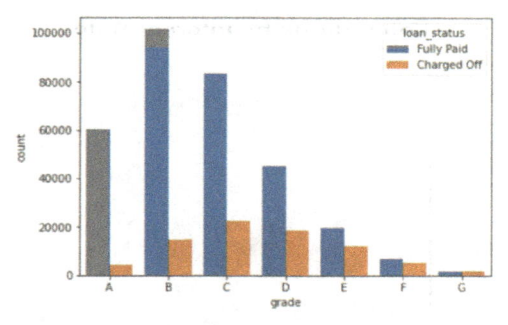

Fig. 4. Distribution between Grades and Loan Status Counts.

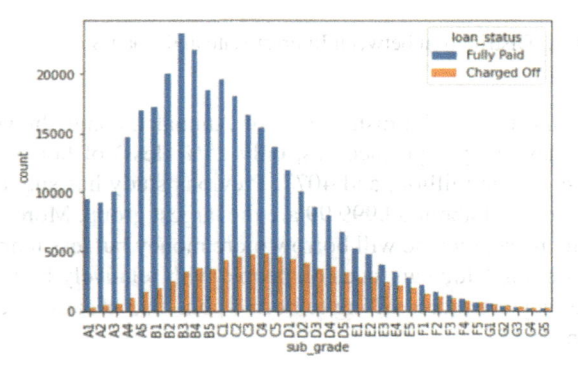

Fig. 5. Distribution between Sub-Grades and Loan Status Counts.

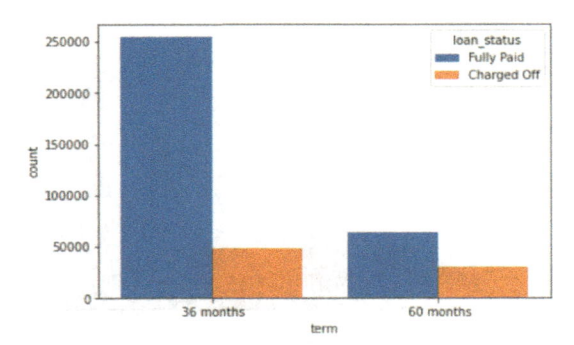

Fig. 6. Distribution between Terms and Loan Status Counts.

The Fig. 7 is the distribution between Interest Rate and Loans Status Counts. With the increasing of Interest Rate, the Loans Counts are roughly increasing and decreasing. It seems that loans with high interest rate are more likely to be unpaid. In addition, if the Interest Rate increases, people tend to borrow less. Therefore, Lending club company chooses the 12 or 13 Interest Rate is the best choice.

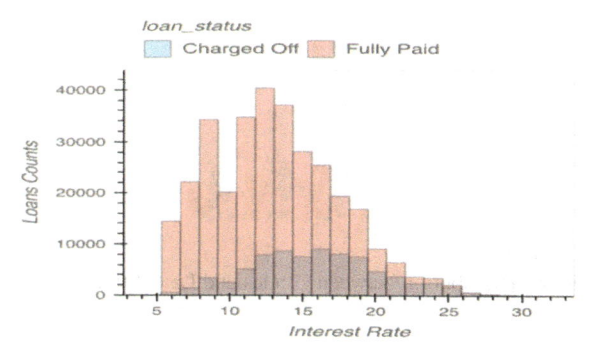

Fig. 7. Distribution between Interest Rate and Loan Status Counts.

According to the Fig. 8, the distribution of Annual Income shows that borrowers generally do not have very high incomes, only 25% (less) of borrowers have annual incomes in excess of one million, and 4077. Previous study has suggested that people with an annual income of about 99,999.99 are the largest group. Moreover, if a person's Annual Income increase, then he will borrow more money but less than proportionately [7]. Therefore, Lending Club can focus on people with relatively high Annual Income, not only because they are more willing to borrow, but also because they are capable of repaying the loan.

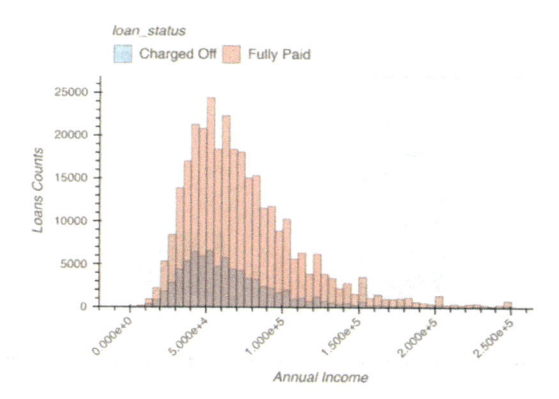

Fig. 8. Distribution between Annual Income and Loan Status.

The last crucial factor is the Mortgage Account. Figure 9 shows the distribution relationship between Mortgage Account and Loan Status Count. "0" and "1" in Fig. 9 represented the number of mortgage accounts, and the number of mortgages with a small number is replaced with "0", on the contrary, "1" represented a high number. It can be seen that the state of Charged Off has little effect under different quantities. However, the Fully Paid status increases as the number of mortgages increases.

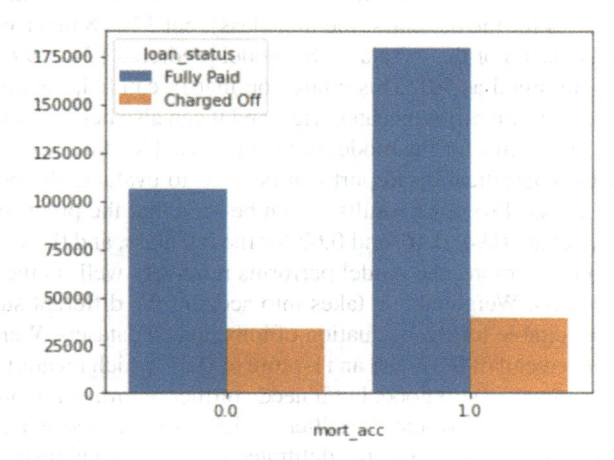

Fig. 9. Distribution between Mortgage Account and Loan Status.

After analyzing these essential factors, this paper can indicate that Instalments, Grades, Terms, and Interest rates impact the loan defaulters of the Lending Club. The company can take specific measures mentioned before to minimize the risk while optimizing the profit.

5 Models Building

This paper uses 3 methods to build the models: Artificial Neural Networks (ANNs), XGBoost Classifier, Random Forest Classifier.

The first method is Artificial Neural Networks (ANNs) is a kind of intelligent neural system which simulates biological neural network by computer network system. It not only has the computing ability to deal with numerical data, but also has the learning, association and memory ability to deal with knowledge [8]. It uses AUC prediction plots to have separate training and testing results. From the train results, precision is the accuracy of the model on positive samples, recall is the accuracy of the model on all positive samples, f1-score is the weighted harmonic mean of precision and recall, and accuracy is the accuracy of the model as a whole. Macro avg and weighted avg are the average metrics for all classes respectively, where weighted avg takes into account the different support of each class, so it is more suitable for the evaluation of imbalanced data sets. As we can know from the results, the overall model has an accuracy of 88.84%. The recall rate of the model for negative samples is low, only 0.46. The recall rate for positive samples is very high, reaching 0.99. This means that the model may have some misjudgment when predicting negative samples but perform better when predicting positive samples. At the same time, the overall accuracy is 0.89, which can be considered as the overall performance of the model is still good.

The Accuracy Score in the test results show that the overall accuracy of the model is 88.87%, which means that the model correctly classified 88.87% of the total samples on the test set. The Confusion Matrix shows the confusion matrix. The model predicted 11,682 correct classes for the 0.0 class (the first class), but 13,798 incorrectly classified as 1.0 (the second class). For the 1.0 class, the model predicted 104,219 correct classes, but 724 were misclassified as 0.0. This confusion matrix can help us understand how well the model performs on different categories, and it can also help us determine which categories are more difficult for the model to distinguish. The precision, recall, and f1-score metrics in the Classification Report can be used to evaluate the performance of the classification model. From the results, it can be seen that the precision, recall, and f1-score of the model are 0.94, 0.46, and 0.62 for the 0.0 class, and 0.88, 0.99, and 0.93 for the 1.0 class. Furthermore, the model performs relatively well on the 1.0 class, but poorly on the 0.0 class. Weighted avg takes into account the different support of each class, so it is more suitable for the evaluation of imbalanced datasets. Weighted avg has a precision of 0.89, a recall of 0.89, and an f1-score of 0.87, which means that the overall performance of the model is still good, but it needs further optimization on the 0.0 class.

The second method is XGBoost Classifier, which also uses the Area Under Curve (AUC) (Fig. 10) [9]. The AUC is the area delimited by the axis and takes a value of 0.5 to 1. The closer the AUC is to 1.0, the more realistic it is. Figure 10 shows that the AUC value is 0.91, which is a high value, indicating that the authenticity of this method is relatively reliable.

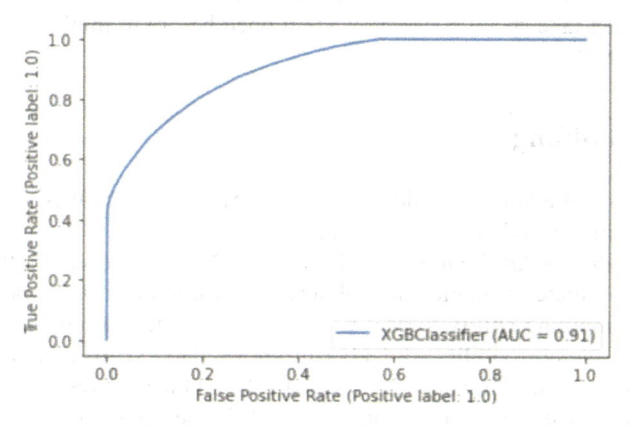

Fig. 10. AUC of XGBoost Classifier.

First, from the train results, the accuracy is 89.60%. What's more, a Classification Report is given showing the precision, recall and f1-score of classifying each class (0 and 1) respectively. Class 0 has a recall of 0.50, which is low, but a precision of 0.95. Class 1 has a precision of 0.89 and a recall of 0.99, both of which perform very well. The last two columns are weighted avg and macro avg, which count the average of all categories. Additionally, the Confusion Matrix shows how well the true labels are classified from the predicted labels. The elements on the diagonal are the number of correctly classified samples, the other elements are incorrect. In this confusion matrix, there are 25828 correct classifications and 25837 incorrect classifications for class 0; Class 1 has 1423 misclassifications and 209055 correct classifications.

From the test results, it can be seen that the correct classification rate of this model for all sample classifications is 88.94%. Precision is the fraction of examples that were actually positive when the model predicted positive examples. The precision values are 0.91 and 0.89, respectively. Recall is the proportion of positive examples that the model was able to predict correctly when the sample was positive, with a recall of 0.48 and 0.99. The F1-score is the harmonic mean of precision and recall, with an F1-score of 0.63 and 0.94, respectively. Macro avg is the average of precision, recall, F1-score of all classes with equal weights. Weighted avg means that the weighted average is calculated based on the number of samples in each class. The weighted avg precision, recall and F1-score of this model are 0.89, 0.89 and 0.88, respectively. Additionally, the Confusion Matrix predicted results compare to the actual results. The results of the model in the confusion matrix are unbalanced, and the recall rates of class 1.0 and 0.0 are very different. It can be seen that the model has a good prediction effect for the 1.0 class, but the prediction effect for the 0.0 class is poor.

There is the third method, Random Forest Classifier, which is always used in relevant investigations [10]. The train results are perfect and pretty matched. The Accuracy Score is 100.00%, and all classifications are 1.00. Additionally, the Confusion Matrix predicted results compare to the actual results. The results of the model in the confusion matrix are very balanced. Therefore, the model has a much perfect prediction effect for both the 0.0 class and 1.0 class.

From the test results, the overall model has an accuracy of 88.94%. The recall rate of the model for negative samples is low, only 0.46. The recall rate for positive samples is very high, reaching 0.99. This means that the model may have some misjudgment when predicting negative samples but perform better when predicting positive samples. At the same time, the overall accuracy is 0.89, which can be considered as the overall performance of the model is still good.

Figure 11 shows the results of test and train of the three algorithms. It can be found that ANNs algorithm has better prediction degree in both test and train. The roc-auc-score metric for each algorithm is the metric used to measure the predictive performance of the classification model. This metric has a value between 0.5 and 1.0, where closer to 1.0 means that the model has better predictive performance.

According to the results in the table (Table 4), the roc-auc-score of ANNS algorithm is 0.905, which is much higher than the scores of the other two algorithms, indicating that ANNS algorithm may be more suitable for solving the problem than RANDOM FOREST and XGBOOST algorithms on this dataset.

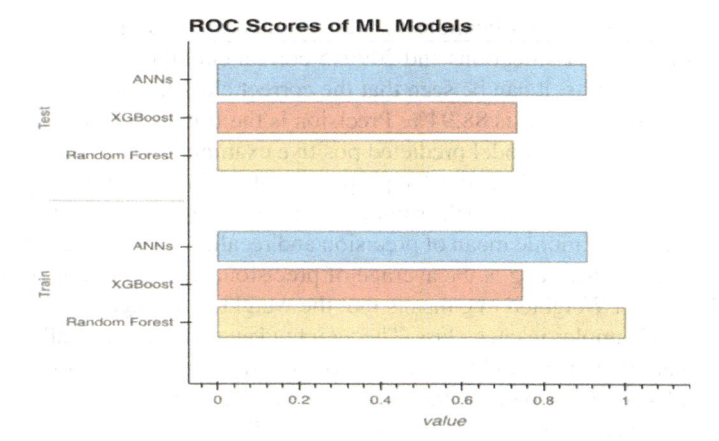

Fig. 11. Comparison of results of the three algorithms.

Table 4. ROC of three algorithms.

	roc-auc-score
ANNs	0.905
XGBoost classifier	0.734
Random Forest Classifier	0.725

6 Conclusion

In order to reduce the operating risk and credit loss of Lending Club company, managers should select target customers more carefully according to different influencing factors. For example, among the company's customers, the average repayment ability of Grade B group is better, so we can focus on developing this group of customers and reduce the loan to Grade E group customers. What's more, in the repayment term, the repayment rate of the short-term repayment project of 36-month is significantly higher than that of the 60-month project. Therefore, the company can increase the short-term loan maturity to reduce the risk of capital loss.

In addition to this optimization of currently existing policies, managers should also reduce risks through other multifaceted measures. Firstly, the risk management model is applied to estimate the risk level of the customer. The implementation of this measure will effectively judge the reputation and ability of the customer, and fundamentally judge the potential risk of the customer. Additionally, the relevant departments should improve the guaranteed policy of borrowers to ensure that someone is responsible for the loan, which is an important way to reduce the loss of funds of the company. Finally, as a mature Lending company, Lending Club should always be sensitive to changes in the economic market.

References

1. Chang, S., Kim, S.D., Kondo, G.: Predicting default risk of lending club loans. Mach. Learn. 1–5 (2015)
2. Zhang, L., Wang, J., Liu, Z.: What should lenders be more concerned about? Developing a profit-driven loan default prediction model. Expert Syst. Appl. **213**, 118938 (2023)
3. Kim, D.S., Shin, S.: The economic explainability of machine learning and standard econometric models-an application to the US mortgage default risk. Int. J. Strateg. Prop. Manag. **25**(5), 396–412 (2021)
4. Tsai, M.C., Lin, S.P., Cheng, C.C., Lin, Y.P.: The consumer loan default predicting model–an application of DEA–DA and neural network. Expert Syst. Appl. **36**(9), 11682–11690 (2009)
5. Stein, R.M.: The relationship between default prediction and lending profits: integrating ROC analysis and loan pricing. J. Bank. Finance **29**(5), 1213–1236 (2005)
6. Walsemann, K.M., Gee, G.C., Gentile, D.: Sick of our loans: Student borrowing and the mental health of young adults in the United States. Soc Sci Med **124**, 85–93 (2015)
7. Kruk, M.E., Goldmann, E., Galea, S.: Borrowing and selling to pay for health care in low-and middle-income countries. Health Aff. **28**(4), 1056–1066 (2009)
8. Jain, A.K., Mao, J., Mohiuddin, K.M.: Artificial neural networks: a tutorial. Computer **29**(3), 31–44 (1996)
9. Saigo, H., Nowozin, S., Kadowaki, T., Kudo, T., Tsuda, K.: GBoost: a mathematical programming approach to graph classification and regression. Mach. Learn. **75**, 69–89 (2009)
10. IBM. www.https://www.ibm.com/topics/random-forest. Accessed 21 June 2023

Research on the CRE of China's Carbon Trading Pilot Policy

Jiayue Jiang[1(✉)], Meixin Wang[2], Mengzhen Xiao[3], Yuwei Yang[4], and Dan Wei[5]

[1] The University of Auckland, City Campus, Auckland 1012, New Zealand
jephoneymoons@163.com
[2] Air China, Huadu District, 163 Yingbin Avenue, Guangzhou, China
[3] State Grid Guang'an Power Supply Company, No. 199 Jin'an Avenue, Guang'an, Sichuan, China
[4] State Administration of Taxation Chongzhou Tax Bureau, No. 16 East Section Xihe Avenue, Chongzhou, Chengdu, Sichuan, China
[5] Jianyang City URCDGSC, No. 6 Renmin Road, Shehongba Street, Jianyang, Chengdu, Sichuan, China

Abstract. In this paper, the empirical analysis was carried out by DID model based on the panel data of 294 cities from 2006 to 2019, exploring the carbon reduction effects (CRE) under the policy of China's trading pilot. The results are yielded as follows: The overall CRE of China's carbon trading pilot policy is significant and it includes both "policy effect" (triggered by corresponding actions taken by those enterprises due to the market mechanism) and "subject effect" (triggered by local governments' administrative interference due to the Hawthorne Effect). Also, the results show a fact that the CRE may not meet the emission expectation to the degree of pilot period when the policy is promoted to a comprehensive level. In fact, carbon trading policy has formed a relatively stable emission-cost expectation for the emission enterprises, and the enterprises can achieve carbon emission reduction by improving green technology innovation and reducing energy consumption intensity.

Keywords: CRE · China's Carbon Trading · Policy Shock

1 Introduction

The development of science always comes with more human activities which often have a substantial impact on climate change, making global climate warming a worldwide issue. In some developing country like China, carbon trading pilot policy is approved and implemented to cope with carbon dioxide emissions and its economic development. With a carbon market being established in 2021 nationally, the operation of carbon market in China now changes from "partial pilot" to "national promotion" after setting up trading pilot areas in 7 provinces and cities. As a policy-innovation mechanism with Chinese characteristics, this so-called "pilot first and then popularize" pattern can conduct an

---

J. Jiang, M. Wang, M. Xiao, Y. Yang, and D. Wei—These authors contributed equally.

© The Author(s), under exclusive license to Springer Nature Singapore Pte Ltd. 2024
X. Li et al. (Eds.): ICEMGD 2023, AEPS, pp. 1778–1784, 2024.
https://doi.org/10.1007/978-981-97-0523-8_158

accurate assessment of policy effects under the premise of effectively controlling the risks that may result from the implementation of new policies, but there is an obvious problem arising: the selection of pilot areas. In the actual practice, this selection is inevitably affected by some political bias and Hawthorne Effect. As a result, some policies that have achieved remarkable results in the pilot stage may not achieve the desired effect in the overall promotion [1]. Hence, based on the institutional background of the Chinese-style policy experiment scenario, the CRE of the carbon trading pilot will be divided into two components: "policy effect" and "subject effect", and this paper will be exploring the existence of these two, and putting forward targeted suggestions.

2 Literature Reviews and Research Hypotheses

2.1 The CRE in Carbon Market

Since the implementation of China's carbon trading policy, researchers have conducted researches from different angles. Some works measure the effectiveness and actual effects of the carbon market as a whole [3, 4]. Others conduct separate studies or sub-regional surveys for each pilot project to analyze its heterogeneity [2, 5]. Scholars have reached a consensus on the effectiveness of China's CRE in carbon market, they mainly carried out research from three aspects: technological progress [6], energy consumption [7], and industrial structure [8].

2.2 Policy Effect

The analytical objects of the policy effect are the enterprises that emit emissions. Due to the implementation of carbon trading policies, these enterprises will face stricter carbon-emission constraints. Compared with command-based regulations, market-based environmental regulations allow enterprises to have a greater right to choose independently, effectively avoiding the uncertain risks brought about by "moblizing carbon reduction". As pointed out in the relevant literature [4–8], enterprises can reduce carbon emissions from two ways: Technological innovation (long-term decision, the fundamental way to achieve emission reduction) and energy consumption (short-term decision, the direct way to achieve emission reduction). Based on the above analysis, we put forward the following hypotheses:

H1–1: Carbon trading policies can motivate enterprises to innovate green technologies, and the generation of such incentives takes a certain amount of time to accumulate.

H1–2: The implementation of carbon trading policies directly affects the energy consumption behaviours of enterprises, thereby reduces the energy consumption intensity of pilot areas.

2.3 Subject Effect

As for the subject effect, local governments are the analytical target. Under the institutional background of Chinese-style policy experimentation, local governments are always under the incentive of promotion, and all the policy preferences of the central government may become the direction of local governments' performance efforts. Therefore, when a certain area becomes a "pilot", the main political officials will generate a strong motivation to redouble the mobilization of administrative resources to ensure the success of carbon trading policy pilots [3]. Based on this idea, we propose the following two hypotheses:

H2–1: The implementation of the pilot policy will strengthen the emphasis on environmental protection issues such as carbon emissions in the work arrangements of the pilot areas.

H2–2: In a Chinese-style policy experiment scenario, realizing that the redistribution of administrative resources caused by one's "pilot" status will reduce the performance of local governments in terms of economic growth.

3 Data and Method

3.1 Data

The sample is arranged from 2006 to 2019 of 294 cities, and we collected data from various databases: (1) Carbon emission data comes from China Carbon Emissions Accounting Database (CEADs). (2) Economic growth target and environmental-word frequency data from city government work reports. (3) Green patent technology applications come from the national intellectual property database. (4) Other relevant data sources come from *China Urban Statistical Yearbook, China Regional Economic Statistical Yearbook and statistical yearbooks of various provinces and cities*.

In the empirical regression, the natural logarithm is taken for indicators such as per capita carbon emissions, per capita GDP, population density, and the number of industrial enterprises above designated size. The descriptive statistics of related variables are shown in Table 1.

3.2 Variables

Explained Variables. We draw upon the idea of Wu Yinyin et al. [4], and based on the county-level carbon emission data fitted by Chen et al. $lnPerCO2_{it}$ denotes the per capita carbon emissions simulated based on nighttime light data, and $lnPerCO2E_{it}$ denotes the per capita carbon emissions calculated based on energy consumption.

Core Explanatory Variables. The core explanatory variable is policy-shock ($DIDset_{it}$). The experimental group included the seven official pilots approved by the NDRC in 2011, and other provinces which voluntarily established carbon markets at the end of 2016. The policy-impact time is considered to be 2011, as it is the start year of the official pilot scheme. While the start time in Fujian and Sichuan is set in 2016. The Corporate behaviour is represented by per capita green patent applications ($GreenTch_{it}$) and energy consumption intensity ($lnEnerInt_{it}$). Government behaviour is expressed by both the frequency of environmental protection words (EvrWord$_{it}$) in the government work reports, and the fluctuation of economic growth and performance caused by the tilt of administrative resources to "pilot" tasks under the Hawthorne Effect. "Unplanned

Table 1. Descriptive statistics results.

	Treatment group					Control group				
VarName	Obs	Mean	SD	Min	Max	Obs	Mean	SD	Min	Max
lnPerCO2	441	6.173	0.388	4.905	7.579	3535	6.393	0.626	4.019	8.671
lnPerCO2E	441	5.140	1.037	1.731	6.876	3535	4.858	1.091	1.083	9.260
EcoPerf	441	−0.818	1.673	−9.700	4.400	3535	−0.193	2.809	−22.000	15.100
GreenTch	441	1.863	2.946	0.029	19.528	3535	0.717	1.407	0	18.719
lnEnerInt	441	6.508	0.654	3.78	8.308	3535	6.557	0.766	4.302	10.973
GreenTch	441	1.863	2.946	0.029	19.528	3535	0.717	1.407	0	18.719
EvrWord	432	0.649	0.240	0.197	1.603	3530	0.502	0.228	−0.097	2.287
HIS	441	6.576	0.374	5.857	7.652	3535	6.429	0.348	5.517	7.516
RICE	441	0.901	0.048	0.728	0.997	3535	0.873	0.069	0.557	0.997
IS	441	2,773	2,777	0.165	17.44	3535	1.87	2,812	0.056	54,179
lnPerGDP	441	10,648	0.549	9,425	11,913	3535	10,218	0.697	7.921	12.359
y2rate	441	0.462	0.086	0.162	0.693	3535	0.48	0.112	0.117	0.91
y3rate	441	0.430	0.104	0.271	0.835	3535	0.387	0.096	0.086	0.792
FisSlf	441	0.488	0.220	0.135	0.995	3535	0.463	0.221	0.027	0.999
lngsqy_gy	441	7.114	0.903	5.468	9.207	3535	6.472	1.127	2.944	10.631
lnpopDen	441	6.271	0.933	4.617	8.814	3535	5.665	0.933	1.623	8.577
market	441	11.779	2.219	6.076	18.049	3535	10.187	2.687	3.037	19.163
FdiRate	441	1.769	1.859	0	11.448	3535	1.873	2.478	0	90.507

growth" ($EcoPerf_{it}$) is represented by the actual GDP growth rate of the year from the local government work reports.

Control Variables. In the regression, referring to the ideas of Wu Yinyin et al. [4], control variables are selected as follows: (1) The level of economic development $lnPerGDP$, , expressed by per capita GDP. (2) Industrial structure, expressed by the proportion of the secondary industry y2rat e and the proportion of the tertiary industry $y3rate$. . (3) Financial self-sufficiency rate $FisSlf$ is the ratio of the general budgetary revenue of the local government to the general budgetary expenditure. (4) The number of industrial enterprises above designated size $lngsqy\_gy$. . (5) Population density $lnpopDen$. . (6) The marketization level *market* is replaced by the provincial marketization level. (7) The proportion of foreign investment $FdiRate$, expressed as the ratio of foreign direct investment to GDP.

3.3 Models

The DID model is commonly used in economics to assess the impact of policy shocks. In order to evaluate and test the CRE of China's carbon market, we set the following benchmark model:

$$Y_{it} = \alpha_0 + \alpha DID_{it} + \beta X_{it} + u_i + \lambda_t + \varepsilon_{it}$$

Among them, the subscript i and t represent the city and year, Y_{it} denotes the per capita carbon emission level, which is the explained variable. The core explanatory variable DID_{it} = $treat_i$ × $post_{it}$ indicates whether it is affected by the policy, $treat_i$ indicates whether it is the experimental group, and $post_{it}$ indicates the time of the policy shock. X_{it} represents a series of control variables that have an impact on carbon emissions, such as per capita GDP, u_i, λ_t respectively represent the individual and year fixed effects, and ϵ_{it} are error terms.

4 Emperical Tests and Result Analysis

4.1 Fundamental Regression

We use two-way fixed-effects regression to estimate the baseline model, and the results are shown in Table 2. From columns (1) to (4), no matter which carbon emission measurement is used and whether control variables are introduced, the CRE of carbon trading policies is very significant. From the absolute value of the coefficient, the carbon trading policy has a greater CRE on carbon emissions measured on the basis of energy consumption. The reason may be that the target of carbon trading policy is enterprises rather than residents. The carbon emissions measured based on energy consumption mainly represent the production carbon emissions from enterprises, while the carbon emissions measured based on night-light simulation also include both production and living carbon emissions. This is also confirmed by the fact that the mean value of lnPerCO2 is larger than that of lnPerCO2E in the descriptive statistics.

Table 2. Regression results of carbon trading pilot CRE test.

	(1)	(2)	(3)	(4)
	lnPerCO2	lnPerCO2	lnPerCO2E	lnPerCO2E
DIDset	−0.0494***	−0.0607***	−0.0513**	−0.0790***
	(−4.22)	(−6.46)	(−2.26)	(−3.45)
lnPerGDP		0.6187***		0.6789***
		(13.93)		(8.38)
_cons	6.3744***	1.0295*	4.8951***	−1.7037
	(2883.06)	(1.69)	(855.81)	(−1.42)
control variables	No	Yes	No	Yes
ID/Year	Yes/Yes	Yes/Yes	Yes/Yes	Yes/Yes
N	3976	3976	3976	3976
r2	0.9619	0.9718	0.9180	0.9230

The t values are in parentheses. ***p < 0.01, **p < 0.05, *p < 0.1. Due to space limitations, the control variable coefficients are not shown, the same below.

4.2 Function Channel Test

Table 3 shows the channel test regression results of the carbon trading pilot: the policy effect and the subject effect. Column (1) shows that carbon trading pilots have promoted green technology innovation at a 5% significance level, and the H1–1 part is certified. Column (2) shows that the carbon trading policy has suppressed the energy consumption intensity of the pilot area at a significant level of 1%, and H1–2 is proved. It can be seen that the carbon trading policy promotes enterprises to innovate green technologies and reduce energy consumption, thereby reducing the level of carbon emissions. This conclusion is consistent with the existing literature. Column (3) shows that the implementation of the policy has significantly increased the frequency of environmental protection-related words in the local government work report, which directly indicates the existence of the subject effect, and H2–1 is proved. Column (4) shows that the implementation of the policy has significantly suppressed the economic growth performance of the pilot areas, which indirectly indicates that the subject effect exists and is quite obvious, and H2–2 is proved.

Table 3. The function channel test of the carbon trading pilot.

	(1)	(2)	(3)	(4)
	Policy effect		Subject effect	
	GreenTch	lnEnerInt	EvrWord	EcoPerf
DIDset	0.1987**	−0.0846***	0.0372***	−0.4068***
	(2.38)	(−3.37)	(2.75)	(−2.80)
_cons	5.9056	11.6622***	−0.1118	−3.2081***
	(1.64)	(9.83)	(−0.46)	(−2.64)
control variables	Yes	Yes	Yes	Yes
ID/Year	Yes/Yes	Yes/Yes	Yes/Yes	Yes/Yes
N	3976	3976	3679	3593
r2	0.7012	0.8453	0.5003	0.406 3

Robust t-statistics in parentheses. *** $p < 0.01$, ** $p < 0.05$, * $p < 0.1$.

4.3 Placebo Test

We use two strategies to conduct a placebo test to exclude the influence of unknown factors other than policy shocks on the estimated results. The first one draws only the "pseudo-treatment group" at random, and the second draws both the "pseudo-treatment group" and the "pseudo-shock time". Specifically, we randomly select 64 cities among the 294 sample cities as the "pseudo-treatment group". Considering the difference between the official pilot and the voluntary pilot, we randomly select two years as the "pseudo-shock time". The above sampling was repeated 500 times, and the parameters were estimated according to the benchmark regression model. The results show that the estimated coefficients of actual policy shocks and virtual policy shocks are significantly different, indicating that the results are robust.

5 Conclusions

China's carbon trading pilot has a significant CRE. Besides, the CRE of China's carbon market includes not only the policy effect caused by enterprises responding to market-based environmental regulations, but also the subject effect caused by the efforts of local governments knowing their "pilot" status. This finding explains the phenomenon that some past literatures pointed out that the CRE had already appeared in the year when the pilot list was announced (when carbon trading market was not yet in its operation), and indicates that the existing literatures may have overestimated the CRE of carbon trading pilots as well. This means that when the carbon trading policy is transformed from a partial pilot to a comprehensive promotion, its CRE may not reach the same level as in the pilot period.

Although the subject effect in the Chinese-style policy experiment scenario has led to an overestimation of the CRE, this does not mean that the carbon trading policy itself has no CRE at all. In fact, only from the impact of carbon trading policies on enterprises, the implementation of carbon trading policies has formed relatively stable emission cost expectations for emission companies, which in turn prompts companies to achieve carbon emission reductions by enhancing green technology innovation and reducing energy consumption intensity.

References

1. Li, Z.: Multiple logics of policy pilot promotion——based on the analysis of smart city pilots in China. J. Publ. Adm. **16**(03), 145–156+175 (2019)
2. Lu, C.: The "Policy Experiment" mechanism of administrative reconsideration reform and its reflection. J. China Univ. Polit. Sci. Law (06), 153-163 (2013)
3. Wang, W., et al.: Emission-reduction effectiveness evaluation and impact factor analysis of China's carbon emission trading pilot mechanism. China Popul. Resour. Environ. **28**(04), 26–34 (2018)
4. Wu, Y., et al.: Research on the carbon emission-reduction effect of China's carbon market: Based on the synergy of market mechanism and administrative intervention. China Ind. Econ. **08**, 114–132 (2021)
5. Dong, Z., Wang, H.: Effectiveness test of market-based environmental regulation policy: empirical evidence from the perspective of carbon emissions trading policy. Stat. Res. **38**(10), 48–61 (2021)
6. Li, G., Zhang, W.: Research on industrial carbon emissions and emission reduction mechanisms under China's carbon trading. China Popul. Resour. Environ. **27**(10), 141–148 (2017)
7. Huang, X., Zhang, X., Liu, Y.: Has China's carbon trading policy achieved environmental dividends?. Econ. Rev. (06), 86–99 (2018)
8. Qi, S., Cheng, S., Cui, J.: Environmental and economic effects of China's carbon market pilots: empirical evidence based on a DID model. J. Clean. Prod. **279**, 123720 (2017)

IEEE-CIS Fraud Detection Based on XGB

Zhijia Xiao(✉)

School of Data Science, Chinese University of Hongkong (Shenzhen), Shenzhen 518172, China
zhijiaxiao@link.cuhk.edu.cn

Abstract. As a result of the world switching to using credit cards in place of cash due to the quick advancement of technology, fraud incidents have increased. Fraud deals with circumstances in which there is criminal intent, yet it is usually difficult to discern. Much research indicate that global losses based on credit card fraud will exceed $35 billion by 2020. The credit card's providers or those financial banks should protect users from any fraud risk they might confront. As a result, this work provides a machine learning-based strategy to identify fraudulent transactions using data from the Kaggle-obtained IEEE-CIS Fraud Detection dataset. The model combines three most efficient ensemble models including Categorical Boost (CatBoost), Extreme Boost (XGBoost) and LightGBM (LGBM). Instead of training the model directly, this paper provides detailed data preprocessing and feature engineering methods in order to choose all the key variables and remove features having low correlation with the label. The results indicate that the final model introduced in this paper achieved best among all other models as getting 96.77% score. The result in this paper benefits the related corporations in financial activities.

Keywords: Fraud Transaction Detection · Machine Learning · XGBoost · CatBoost · LighGBM

1 Introduction

As technological advances promote communication and commerce, they also lead to an increase in fraud. According to investigation from Chaudhary and his team, fraud refers to obtaining goods/services and money by illegal way [1]. Because attackers can directly take the information from victims, credit cards are among the frauds that are most likely to be the target. Banking services industry researcher Weatherford estimates that credit card theft cost banking institutions more than $1 billion in US dollars [2].

Many insurance companies have invested millions of dollars in fraud detection algorithms to protect high-risk transactions and clients. Many related works explored various models and pipelines to improve the detection methodology. For instance, Zareapoor, and Shamsolmoali trained a bagging classifier for fraud transaction detection [3]. His model performed great on real-world problems and was quite straightforward for implementation. Additionally, they used cross validation techniques to assess their models using a comprehensive dataset from the UCSD-FICO competition that included labels for legal and fraudulent data. However, their bagging classifier is unable to directly address time series issues. For the purpose of detecting credit card fraud, Tran et al. employed the best anomaly detection techniques [4]. The effectiveness of this strategy was demonstrated by his team using actual data from European credit card users. The results of the studies demonstrated that their methods produced a high level of detection accuracy and a low proportion of false alarms. Their real time data-driven approach did well on that certain dataset but the parameters in the ensemble model are very likely to be overfitting. Awoyemi et al. employed 10-fold cross-validation techniques to assess their experiments using the dataset from the ULB Machine Learning Group [5]. 100,000 credit card transaction records with classifications for genuine and fraudulent transactions were included in the collection. Zhang's research chose XGBoost-based model. Compared to SVM, Random Forest, and Logistic Regression, it performed better [6]. They established a comprehensive model. But similarly, they did not put more emphasis on those low correlation variables.

Thus, an XGB model with new UID features is built to identify whether each transaction is fraudulent or not. To solve problems in the previous projects, this model first preprocesses the dataset, focus more on the time-series problem and transfer the time delta into the concrete transaction time. Among the datasets, the training set samples are about 590,000 (fraud accounts for 3.5%), and the test set samples are about 500,000. This paper applies several methods to combine and reduce features, including some encoding functions to aggregate features, remove Nan variables, analyze those outliers, combine variables with high correlation and apply PCA to reduce dimension and select feature. Furthermore, the final model applies time consistency on feature selection and post process to improve performance. Then the final model combines three efficient ensemble classifiers and get great performance with 96.77% score.

This paper constructed as follows. Section 2 is the data description and related analysis. Section 3 refers to feature engineering, Sect. 4 presents the feature selection. Section 5 describes the methods and results. Section 6 concludes the paper.

2 Data Description and Analysis

2.1 Data Description

The IEEE-CIS Fraud Dataset, which includes a variety of features from device type to product features, was developed from Vesta's actual e-commerce transactions. This data set includes two tables, including the transaction table and identity table. The key, Transaction ID, can be used to connect these two different types of tables.

The Transaction Table contains 394 features including 22 categorical features and 372 numeric features. Instead of a true timestamp, the TransactionDT is a time delta from a specified reference date and time. The D1-D15 represent time deltas, such as the number of days since the last transaction. C1 through C14 are keeping track of things like how many addresses are discovered to be linked to the payment card. D1 to D15 represent timedelta, such as the number of days since the last transaction. M1 through M9 are identical, including the card names, addresses, etc. Rich features created by Vesta engineers are included in V columns, such as ranking, counting, and other entity relations. This paper will show how to get the exact transaction date time from these two features in Data Preprocessing section. These variables are summarized in Table 1.

Table 1. Transaction Table.

Variables	Variable Description	Type
TransactionID	Transaction ID	Categorical
isFraud	Binary Label	Categorical
TransactionDT	Transaction Delta	Numerical
TransactionAmt	Transaction Amount	Numerical
card1-card6	Payment Card Information	Categorical
addr1-addr2	Address	Categorical
C1-C14	Counting	Numerical
D1-D15	Timedelta	Numerical
M1-M9	Match	Categorical
V1-V339	Vesta engineered rich features	Numerical
R_email domain	Recipient Email Domain	Categorical
P_email domain	Purchaser Email Domain	Categorical
dist1-dist2	Country Distance	Numerical

According to Table 2, there are 41 features total in the identity table, including ID, category, and numerical features. DeviceType can be a desktop, mobile, or unidentified device type. DeviceInfo is a representation of device data. They are gathered by the partners in digital security and Vesta's fraud prevention system. For the sake of contract compliance and privacy protection, all identity information is masking and won't be disclosed.

Table 2. Identification Table.

Variables	Variable Description	Type
TransactionID	ID of transaction	Categorical
DeviceType	Device Type	Categorical
DeviceInfo	Device Information	Categorical
id01-id11	Identification Data	Numerical
id12-id38	Identification Data	Categorical

These two tables have the common key called TransactionID. However, Nan values exist in this table and will be solved in the feature engineering section. For instance, they will be replaced by -999 to show that they are missing values.

The sample size and feature dimensions are Train transactions shape (590,540, 394), identity (144,233, 41), Test transactions shape (506,691, 393) and identity (141,907, 41).

2.2 Labeling Logic

The reasoning behind the labeling is to classify transactions immediately after those with a user account, email address linked to isFraud. If none of them are discovered within 120 days, the transaction is deemed to be legitimate (isFraud = 0). Therefore, rather than predicting fraudulent transactions, this model seeks to predict fraudulent clients (credit cards).

After 120 days, a card becomes isFraud = 0. It is rarely seen in the training data. The training dataset has 73838 clients (credit cards) with 2 or more transactions. The pie chart below shows that 71575 (96.9%) of those are always isFraud = 0 and 2134 (2.9%) are always isFraud = 1. Only 129 (0.2%) have a mixture of isFraud = 0 and isFraud = 1 (See Fig. 1).

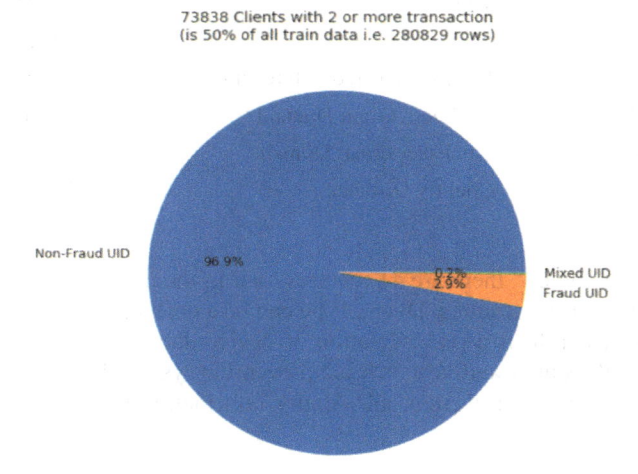

Fig. 1. Amount of Fraud / Non-Fraud UID.

The cardholder may not have known about the fraudulent activity or may have forgotten to report it in time and after the claim period has passed in the real world. In certain situations, alleged fraud may be presented as legitimate, but it is impossible to identify them. Vesta believes that they are a small percentage and rare cases.

2.3 Data Preprocessing

The D Columns will be transformed into their original transaction date time by the following formula.

D15n = Transaction_Day - D15,

Transaction_Day = TransactionDT / (24*60*60).

Then this variable is multiplied by Fig. 2 and 3 show how the Transaction delta change into Transaction date time.

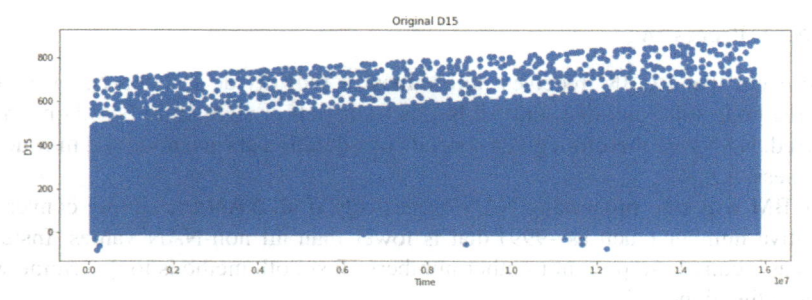

Fig. 2. TransactionDT.

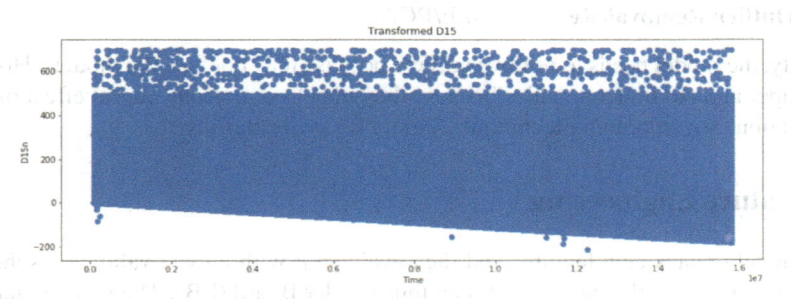

Fig. 3. Transaction Date Time.

2.4 Encoding Functions

Frequency encoding (encode_FE) performs frequency encoding by combining the test and train data before encoding.

A potent method that enables LGBM to determine whether column values are common or uncommon is frequency encoding. To illustrate, LGBM can benefit from knowing which credit cards are used infrequently.

The Group Statistics / Aggregations (encode_AG) function creates aggregated characteristics including aggregated mean and standard deviation.

When given group statistics, LGBM may decide if a number is frequent or rare for a specific group. You provide pandas three variables to work with in order to calculate group statistics. You specify the group, the relevant variable, and the kind of statistic. To exploit the new UID, the model needed to create numerous aggregated group features, and 47 new features were created in the feature engineering phase.

Label Encoding (encode_LE) transforms categorical features into encoded labels.Combination Encoding (encode_CB) combines two columns This helps LGBM because by themselves, for example, card1 and card2 may not correlate with target and therefore LGBM won't split them at a tree node. But the interaction uid = card1_card2 may correlate with target and now LGBM will split it. Numeric columns can combine with adding, subtracting, multiplying, etc.

2.5 NAN Processing

In the event that LGBM receives null values, it will divide the non-NAN values at each tree node split and then send all NANs to the left or right child based on which is preferred. NANs are therefore given special consideration at each node and may develop overfitness.

LGBM will stop processing NAN excessively if all NAN are simply converted to a negative number (such as -999) that is lower than all non-NAN values. Instead, it will treat it equally important to other numbers. Test both methods to determine which produces the highest CV.

2.6 Outlier Removal/Relax/Smooth/PCA

Usually, the model needs to remove outliers because they confuse the models. However, this paper aims to find anomalies because they may have a strong causal effect on fraud transaction. So, smoothing techniques should be used carefully.

3 Feature Engineering

The model creates new features and then evaluate it with a local validation scheme to see if they improve the model's CV and thus Leader Board (LB). Then the model keeps beneficial features and discard the others.

3.1 Creating Magic Feature

To prevent overfitting on the train and public test dataset, this model cannot directly use the client UIDs and those columns that help identify clients including the D, V, and ID columns. Also, it cannot add UID as a new column because 68.2% of clients in the private test dataset are not in the training dataset. The magic feature is the key.

Two things make up the magic. The UID feature is used to check customers. Second, aggregated group characteristics are produced by the encode functions. The column UID is then removed, and the client/card description is merely comprised of aggregate data.

The training and test data have different sets of clients so the model can find which columns help differentiate clients by performing adversarial validation. According to the Fig. 4, the most important columns to identify users are D10n, D1n, TransactionAmt, etc. These are the columns this paper must use to find the clients.

The model first creates a UID using card/D/C/V columns and almost all 600 000 unique cards and respective clients. The model combines card1, addr and D1 to indicate the card issue date. And card1 + addr + D10 or D15 affiliated account creation or first activity date. The model can also take all the C, M columns and do Python code: new_features = df.groupby ('uid') [CM_columns].agg (['mean']).

The model will find customers (credit cards) thanks to this. This UID is not flawless. Numerous UID values include two or more customers. The model will recognize this, separate UIDs, and identify the single clients by adding further splits to its trees.

Now the model has the ability to classify clients that it has never seen before. This new feature helps post process predictions and validate how models perform on seen

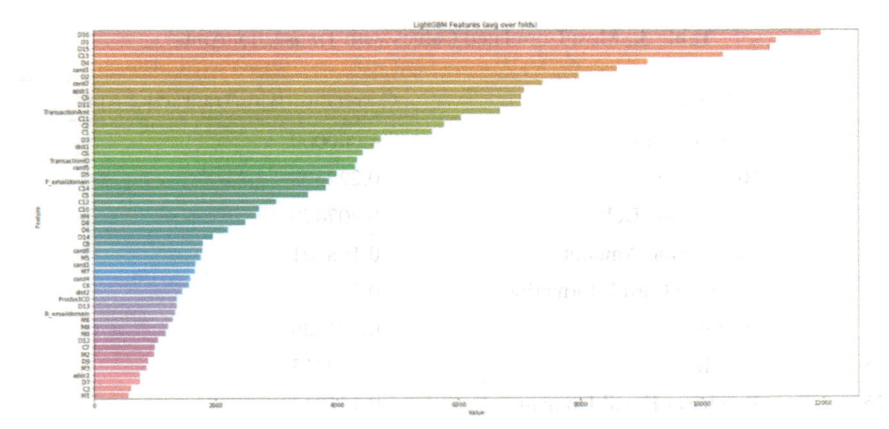

Fig. 4. Importance of Features.

versus unseen clients. Producing new UIDs by a script also helps following EDA, special validation tests, and post process.

3.2 Exploratory Data Analysis (EDA)

The first 95 V columns and original 53 columns are operated by Liukis 's great EDA. This part includes features such as TransactionID, isFraud, card, addr, etc. Each variable is separated to three labels: fraud, no-fraud and test set. They are visualized by scatter plot to show their distribution and changes over time. Take TranctionAmt as an example in Fig. 5 and Table 3, they show the time series results and correlated features in a descending order.

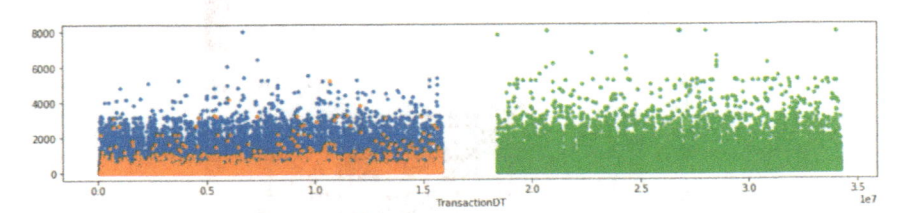

Fig. 5. TransactionAmt Values Over Time (blue = no-fraud, orange = fraud, green = test).

Deotte's EDA was used for processing the remaining 300 columns for V and ID columns. This paper first employs three techniques to decrease the number of V columns. The V columns seem to be connected and redundant. Consequently, subgroups inside each block of V columns that are correlated ($r > 0.75$). Then, one column from each subset, namely permutation importance, can be used to replace the entire block. The subsets [1–11] exist in the block V1-V11, for instance, and the model can choose the sets including [1, 3, 4, 6, 8] to represent the corresponding block without sacrificing a lot of information. The model then use one of three techniques: apply PCA to each group

Table 3. Most Correlated Calues with TransactionAmt.

	Column	Correlation with TransactionAmt
0	TransactionAmt	1.000000
1	Binary Label	0.222308
2	Transaction Delta	0.207470
3	Transaction Amount	0.198601
4	Payment Card Information	0.197351
5	Address	0.191320
375	Match	−0.139413
376	Purchaser Email Domain	−0.141014
377	Recipient Email Domain	−0.142297
378	Country Distance	−0.144958
379	Timedelta	−0.149459

separately, choose the largest possible subset of uncorrelated columns from each group, or replace each group with the average of all columns.

Afterward, these reduced groups were further evaluated using feature selection techniques below. For example, the block V322-V339 failed "time consistency" and was removed from the models. The smaller set for V columns still exhibits significant internal correlation, as shown in Fig. 6 below. These V columns have a lot of overlap.

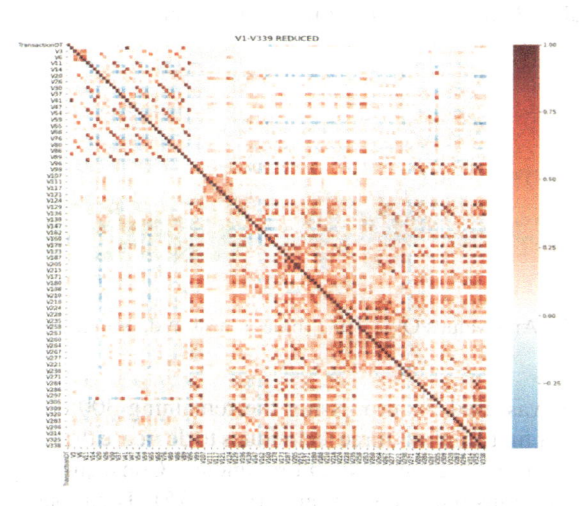

Fig. 6. Internal correlation between V1 ~ V339.

4 Feature Selection

Feature selection is important because the origin data set have many columns and preferred to keep the models efficient. The XGB had 250 features and would train 6 folds in 10 min. Since this paper created lots of new features in the last section, the model can use forward feature selection based on single or groups of features, recursive feature elimination, LGBM importance, or permutation importance to determine which are useful. Also, this paper has finished the following process in other sections: permutation importance, train/test distribution analysis.

"Time consistency" is the ability to predict isFraud for the last month of the train dataset using a single model that was trained by a small group of features from the first month of the train dataset. This assesses consistency of a feature over time on its own. Although 95% were, 5% of the columns damaged the models. They had a validation AUC of 0.40 and a training AUC of about 0.60. Alternatively put, some features discovered patterns in the present that weren't there in the future. This document double-checks each test with other tests to avoid any complications that could arise from potential interactions.

Each model uses only one feature and is trained using the training data from the first month. The model then forecasts isFraud in the training data's most recent month. Both the training accuracy score and the validation accuracy score should be higher than AUC = 0.5 for this study. 19 features are being eliminated since they turn out to have failed this test. Seven D columns that are primarily NAN are also deleted. For instance, the model block V322-V339 was eliminated because it failed the "time consistency" test.

5 Models and Results

5.1 Model Selection

This section mainly focuses on the XGBoost model. According to previous investigations, by including regularization to handle sparse data and weighted quantile drawings for tree learning, XGBoost optimizes the loss function [7–10]. Additionally, they aid in the development of quick and scalable tree boosting systems. Some of these studies include cache access patterns and data compression. These techniques and insights enable XGBoost to surpass the bulk of other machine learning algorithms in terms of speed and precision. The XGBoost technology can be used to GPU computers or distributed systems, which is practical for engineers or data scientists.

The decision trees in LightGBM (LGBM), according to Essam Al Daoud, are grown leaf-by-leaf rather than examining all of the preceding leaves for each new leaf [11].

Target-based statistics and permutation approaches are used in Categorical Boosting (CatBoost), which focuses on categorical columns. At each fresh split of the existing tree, CatBoost uses the greedy strategy to address the exponential increase of the feature combination (Al Daoud, 2019).

In total, all the models introduced above are proved to be helpful for the fraud detection. Thus, the final model contains 3 typical GBDT pipelines main models with single scores in Table 4.

Table 4. Leader Board Scores for Three Main Models.

Model	Public LB	Private LB
CatBoost	0.964	0.940
LGBM	0.962	0.938
XGBoost	0.960	0.932
Simple Blend (equal weights)	0.967	0.945

During these experiments, each model was predicting well a different group of UIDs in test set: CatBoost did well on all groups, XGB - best for known, LGBM - best for unknown.

5.2 Validation Strategy

This paper first split the dataset into proportion of training 75% and predicting 25%. Then apply various validation strategies such as training on first 4 months of train, skip a month, predict last month. This paper also does train 2, skip 2, and predict 2 and train 1 skip 4 predict 1 and reviews Leader Board scores (which is just train 6, skip 1, predict 1 and no less valid than other holdouts).

The paper also analyzes models by how well they classified known versus unknown clients using the script's UIDs. When training on the first 5 months and predicting the last month, the Table 5 shows that 3 models have their own advantages.

Table 5. Performance of Three Main Models.

Models	Advantages	AUC Scores
XGBoost	Predicting known UIDs	0.9972
LGBM	Predicting unknown UIDs	0.9212
CatBoost	Predicting questionable UIDs	0.9883

When doing ensemble and/or stack on these models, the resultant model excelled in all three categories. It could predict known, unknown, and questionable UIDs, which are transactions that the script could not confidently link to other transactions, forward in time with great accuracy.

The model performed a GroupKFold using the month as groups for the prediction. The training data includes from December 2017 to May 2018. The article uses the terms 12, 13, 14, 15, 16, and 17 to identify these months. Group K Fold's Fold 1 will simulate utilizing the months 13 through 17 and the projected month 12. The model trained on months 13 through 17 will also be able to predict the test.csv file, which moves forward in time.

5.3 Post Process

Analysis reveals that a single client's transactions are either all isFraud = 0 or all isFraud = 1, respectively. As a result, each of their predictions is identical. With the exception of the isFraud values from the train dataset, the post process replaces all predictions from one client with their average prediction. There are two slightly different variations of the model. They are applied sequentially. Note the models do not use the script's UIDs. The models found clients by themselves as described above. As seen in Table 6 above, the XGB model's Public LB increases from LB 0.960 to 0.962 after performing post processing. And raises its Private LB from LB 0.932 to 0.934. This represents an increase of LB 0.0016.

Table 6. Performance of Post Process based on XGB.

Models	Public LB	Private LB
XGB	0.960	0.932
XGB + Post Process	0.962	0.934

5.4 Results

The final model was a combination of 3 high scoring single models. CatBoost, LGBM, and XGB. And the model engineered features independently.

One final submission was a stack where LGBM was trained on top of the predictions of CAT and XGB. The concrete scores are shown in Table 7. Other final submission was an ensemble with equal weights. Both submissions were post processed by taking all predictions from a single client (credit card) and replacing them with that client's average prediction. This post processing increases LB by 0.001.

Table 7. Final Models.

Models	Public LB	Private LB
LGBM + CAT + XGB (Stack)	0.9677	0.9459
LGBM + CAT + XGB (Stack + Post Processing)	0.9687	0.9469

6 Conclusion

In summary, this study suggests a machine learning-based methodology. For detecting fraud transactions in the context of the increasing use of credit cards and the subsequent rise in fraudulent activities. The model combines three powerful ensemble algorithms, namely CatBoost, XGBoost, and LGBM, to improve the detection accuracy. The study utilizes the certain fraud transaction dataset from Kaggle and emphasizes the importance of data preprocessing and feature engineering techniques in selecting relevant variables and eliminating irrelevant features. The results demonstrate that the proposed model outperforms other models, achieving an impressive accuracy score of 96.77%. This model can be beneficial for credit card providers and financial institutions in protecting users from potential fraud risks.

In real life, with similar inputs, those financial companies and credit card providers can directly apply the final model and it will detect the fraud accounts and transactions. This fraud detection and prevention technology will enhance customer satisfaction while also saving millions of dollars annually. Customers can use their chips hassle-free with improved accuracy fraud detection.

References

1. Chaudhary, K., Yadav, J., Mallick, B.: A review of fraud detection techniques: credit card. Int. J. Comput. Appl. **45**(1), 39–44 (2012)
2. Weatherford, M.: Mining for fraud. IEEE Intell. Syst. **17**(4), 4–6 (2002)
3. Zareapoor, M., Shamsolmoali, P.: Application of credit card fraud detection: based on bagging ensemble classifier. Procedia Comput. Sci. **48**, 679–685 (2015)
4. Tran, P.H., Tran, K.P., Huong, T.T., Heuchenne, C., HienTran, P., Le, T.M.H.: Real time data-driven approaches for credit card fraud detection. In: Proceedings of the 2018 International Conference on e-business and Applications, pp. 6–9 (2018)
5. Awoyemi, J.O., Adetunmbi, A.O., Oluwadare, S.A.: Credit card fraud detection using machine learning techniques: a comparative analysis. In: 2017 International Conference on Computing Networking and Informatics, pp. 1–9 (2017)
6. Zhang, Y., Tong, J., Wang, Z., Gao, F.: Customer transaction fraud detection using XGBoost model. In: 2020 International Conference on Computer Engineering and Application, pp. 554–558 (2020)
7. Song, K., Yan, F., Ding, T., Gao, L., Lu, S.: A steel property optimization model based on the XGBoost algorithm and improved PSO. Comput. Mater. Sci. **174**, 109472 (2020)
8. Shi, R., Xu, X., Li, J., Li, Y.: Prediction and analysis of train arrival delay based on XGBoost and Bayesian optimization. Appl. Soft Comput. **109**, 107538 (2021)
9. Pan, S., Zheng, Z., Guo, Z., Luo, H.: An optimized XGBoost method for predicting reservoir porosity using petrophysical logs. J. Petrol. Sci. Eng. **208**, 109520 (2022)
10. Chen, T., Guestrin, C.: XGBoost: a scalable tree boosting system. In: Proceedings of the 22nd ACM SIGKDD International Conference on Knowledge Discovery and Data Mining, pp. 785–794 (2016)
11. Daoud, A.E.: Comparison between XGBoost, LightGBM and CatBoost using a home credit dataset. Int. J. Comput. Inf. Eng. **13**(1), 6–10 (2019)

Unraveling the Link Between Federal Reserve Interest Rate Hikes and the Chinese Stock Market

Jialin Li

School of Economics, Xiamen University, Xiamen 361005, China
1720080105@xy.dlpu.edu.cn

Abstract. In response to the severe inflation following the COVID-19 pandemic, the Federal Reserve initiated a round of interest rate hikes starting from March 2022. In order to explore the impact of this action by the Federal Reserve on the Chinese stock market, this paper selects data from January 4, 2022, to June 9, 2023, including the US dollar index, Shanghai Composite Index, Shenzhen stock index, and Growth Enterprise Index. A VAR model is utilized to investigate the interrelationships and dynamics among these four variables, and impulse response graphs of the three Chinese stock indices under this shock are plotted. Additionally, an ARMA-GARCH model is established to analyze the heterogeneity of the influence of the sudden fluctuation of the US dollar on the instability of the Chinese stock market. The research indicates that the Federal Reserve's interest rate adjustments have a negative impact on the Chinese stock market and suggests that policymakers should focus on how to quickly respond to short-term negative effects caused by shocks in order to stabilize the economy, while investors can benefit from stock market volatility and exchange rate fluctuations through reasonable expectations.

Keywords: Federal Reserve Interest Rate Hikes · Chinese stock market · VAR · ARMA-GARCH-X

1 Introduction

In 2019, the outbreak of COVID-19 caused a severe recession in the world economy. In order to stimulate the domestic economy, the Federal Reserve adopted aggressive monetary and fiscal policies. On the one hand, the Federal Reserve injected liquidity into the market on a large scale, creating a loose financing environment to vigorously stimulate investment and consumption, in order to boost economic development. In 2020, the Federal Reserve's total assets increased by 77% year-on-year [1]. On the other hand, by heavily increasing its holdings of US Treasury bonds, the Fed stimulated the economy and significantly increased the income of US residents, thus stimulating total social demand. In June 2020, the percentage of public debt to GDP increased by 20.59%, reaching 25.15% in December of the same year [1]. The supply shock caused by this series of measures led to unexpected inflation in the US dollar.

Against this backdrop, the Federal Reserve has implemented tight policy measures since March 2020 in order to revert the inflation rate to its long-term target of 2% [1]. To date, the Fed has conducted 10 interest rate hikes, with a cumulative increase of 500 basis points.

The monetary policy of the Federal Reserve has a certain spillover effect on foreign economies. Since March 2022, the Federal Funds Rate in the United States has been continuously increasing. From 0.08% in February 2020 to 5.08% in May 2023 [1], the interest rate differential between China and the US has narrowed, with an even inverted yield curve. As the Fed continues its interest rate hike process, China is facing pressure and risks such as short-term capital outflows, external market contraction, and exchange rate fluctuations.

Studying the relationship between the Federal Reserve interest rate hike and the Chinese stock market is important to gain insights into the global economic dynamics, inform policy decisions, ensure financial stability, and guide investment strategies. This paper investigates the effect of the Federal Reserve's decision to raise interest rates on the performance of the Chinese stock market. The following sections outline the structure of this paper. Firstly, a review of existing research is provided to give context, followed by a description of the research design in the second section. The third part presents empirical results and corresponding analyses, while the fourth section discusses the research findings in light of existing studies and provides recommendations for policymakers and investors. The final part is a summary of the paper's conclusions.

2 Literature Review

There have been studies and discussions conducted among scholars on the spillover effects of the Fed's interest rate hike on foreign countries.

Firstly, the impact of the Fed's monetary policy will affect foreign stock markets. Luc Laeven & Hui Tong has found that global stock prices are strongly affected by US interest rate changes, where the US's contractionary monetary policy leads to a global decline in stock prices [2]. Similarly, Irfan Akbar Kazi,Hakimzadi Wagan & Farhan Akbar has found that due to a contractionary monetary policy, the OECD member countries' stock prices were significantly lowered [3]. Additionally, Zhuo Huang,Chen Tong,Han Qiu & Yan Shen has also discovered that US policy uncertainty has a negative impact on China's stock market [4].

Furthermore, the Fed's interest rate hike would influence foreign stock markets through various means. The monetary policy shock has a rapidly strong impact on typical emerging market interest rates and exchange rates [5]. Asset prices, interest rates, and trade channels play a primary role in the transmission of the US's monetary policy effects to foreign markets [3].

The Fed's interest rate hike affects exchange rates in several ways. Valentina Bruno & Hyun Song Shin believes that this measure may cause a tightening of the US dollar, reducing international capital flows and causing the US dollar to appreciate [6]. Moreover, the uncertainty of US economic policies is also a crucial factor affecting the exchange rate decline [7]. The impact of exchange rate fluctuations on foreign stock markets is transmitted through several channels. Silvia Miranda Agrippino & Hélène Rey argues that the tightening of the US dollar leads to a global decline in asset prices, and floating exchange rate countries will be affected by spillover effects [8]. Jérôme Héricourt & Sandra Poncet states that exchange rate fluctuations hinder trade and amplify the financial fragility of enterprises [9], affecting stock prices. Exchange rate fluctuations to a certain extent led to stock market volatility, and the degree of its effects is correlated with the strength of interaction and speculative demand [10].

Apart from the effects caused by exchange rates, the Fed's monetary policy affects stock prices in foreign countries by influencing their interest rates [2]. Meanwhile, Peter Tillmann believes that changes in different countries' interest rates lead to capital flows, which also have a significant impact on stock prices [11].

Overall, scholars have conducted a certain degree of research on the topic of Federal Reserve interest rate adjustments. Firstly, there are papers discussing the influence of United States' monetary policy on global stock markets. in different regions and countries of various types. Additionally, scholars have focused on the channels of influence, exploring the effects of Federal Reserve rate hikes on exchange rates, interest rates, and foreign trade, thereby further impacting stock markets in other countries. In this paper, based on existing viewpoints, this paper select a representative stock index in China to more targetedly investigate the repercussions of the Federal Reserve's decision to increase interest rates on the Chinese stock market, thus providing a certain degree of supplementary research to the relevant field.

3 Research Design

3.1 Data Source

This paper selects the US dollar index and the Shanghai Composite Index, Shenzhen stock index, and Growth Enterprise Index from January 4, 2022, to June 9, 2023, for analysis, exploring the consequences of the Federal Reserve's decision to raise interest rates on the Chinese stock market. The data used in this paper are all from the CEIC database [1]. In addition, the data is preliminarily processed by calculating the daily returns of each index using the daily index data. Specifically, the difference between the index on the current day and the previous day is divided by the index on the previous day, and the result obtained is the return on that day. Furthermore, the index data and return data are transformed using a formula and analyzed further on a logarithmic scale using Stata.

3.2 Augmented Dickey–Fuller (ADF) Unit Root Test

Given that the data utilized in this study comprises time series data, it is crucial to assess the data's stationarity prior to constructing a model for subsequent analysis. In this paper, unit root tests are used, with the null hypothesis set as the existence of a unit root. If the test result rejects the null hypothesis, the sequence is considered stationary.

From the results in Table 1, it can be observed that the index data is not significant and unable to reject the null hypothesis, indicating that the sequence is non-stationary. On the other hand, the return data can reject the null hypothesis at a probability level of 99%, indicating that the sequence is stationary. Therefore, this study uses index return data for subsequent research.

Table 1. Weak Stationarity Test: ADF test.

	t	p
Price		
US Dollar	−1.519	0.8224
SSEC	−2.840	0.1827
SZSE	−2.709	0.2324
GEM	−2.646	0.2591
Return		
US Dollar	−14.449	0.0000***
SSEC	−13.181	0.0000***
SZSE	−13.089	0.0000***
GEM	−12.965	0.0000***

3.3 Vector Autoregression (VAR) Model

As this study involves the mutual influence and dynamic relationship of multiple variable time series, this paper adopt the VAR model proposed by Sims [12, 13]. This model regresses several lagged variables of all variables on all current variables. Four independent time series variables are used in this paper. Equations (1)-(4) represent the equations for the US dollar index, Shanghai Composite Index, Shenzhen stock index, and Growth Enterprise Index, respectively. Taking Eq. (1) as an example, it includes the return rates of lagged items for each index, and the final term is the error term. Equation (5) represents the matrix form of the equation.

$$dollar_t = \alpha_1 + \phi_{11} dollar_{t-1} + \cdots + \phi_{1p} dollar_{t-p} + \beta_{11} ssec_{t-1} + \cdots + \beta_{1p} ssec_{t-p}$$
$$+ \delta_{11} szse_{t-1} + \cdots + \delta_{1p} szse_{t-p} + \gamma_{11} gem_{t-1} + \cdots + \gamma_{1p} gem_{t-p} + \varepsilon_{1t} \quad (1)$$

$$ssec_t = \alpha_2 + \phi_{21} dollar_{t-1} + \cdots + \phi_{2p} dollar_{t-p} + \beta_{21} ssec_{t-1} + \cdots + \beta_{2p} ssec_{t-p}$$
$$+ \delta_{21} szse_{t-1} + \cdots + \delta_{2p} szse_{t-p} + \gamma_{12} gem_{t-1} + \cdots + \gamma_{2p} gem_{t-p} + \varepsilon_{2t} \quad (2)$$

$$szse_t = \alpha_3 + \phi_{31} dollar_{t-1} + \cdots + \phi_{3p} dollar_{t-p} + \beta_{31} ssec_{t-1} + \cdots + \beta_{3p} ssec_{t-p}$$
$$+ \delta_{31} szse_{t-1} + \cdots + \delta_{3p} szse_{t-p} + \gamma_{13} gem_{t-1} + \cdots + \gamma_{3p} gem_{t-p} + \varepsilon_{3t} \quad (3)$$

$$gem_t = \alpha_4 + \phi_{41} dollar_{t-1} + \cdots + \phi_{4p} dollar_{t-p} + \beta_{41} ssec_{t-1} + \cdots + \beta_{4p} ssec_{t-p}$$
$$+ \delta_{41} szse_{t-1} + \cdots + \delta_{4p} szse_{t-p} + \gamma_{14} gem_{t-1} + \cdots + \gamma_{4p} gem_{t-p} + \varepsilon_{4t} \quad (4)$$

$$\begin{bmatrix} dollar_t \\ ssec_t \\ szse_t \\ gem_t \end{bmatrix} = \begin{bmatrix} \alpha_1 \\ \alpha_2 \\ \alpha_3 \\ \alpha_4 \end{bmatrix} + \begin{bmatrix} \phi_{11} \cdots \phi_{1p} \\ \phi_{21} \cdots \phi_{2p} \\ \phi_{31} \cdots \phi_{3p} \\ \phi_{41} \cdots \phi_{4p} \end{bmatrix} \begin{bmatrix} dollar_{t-1} \\ \vdots \\ dollar_{t-p} \end{bmatrix} + \begin{bmatrix} \beta_{11} \cdots \beta_{1p} \\ \beta_{21} \cdots \beta_{2p} \\ \beta_{31} \cdots \beta_{3p} \\ \beta_{41} \cdots \beta_{4p} \end{bmatrix} \begin{bmatrix} ssec_{t-1} \\ \vdots \\ ssec_{t-p} \end{bmatrix}$$
$$+ \begin{bmatrix} \delta_{11} \cdots \delta_{1p} \\ \delta_{21} \cdots \delta_{2p} \\ \delta_{31} \cdots \delta_{3p} \\ \delta_{41} \cdots \delta_{4p} \end{bmatrix} \begin{bmatrix} szse_{t-1} \\ \vdots \\ szse_{t-p} \end{bmatrix} + \begin{bmatrix} \gamma_{11} \cdots \gamma_{1p} \\ \gamma_{21} \cdots \gamma_{2p} \\ \gamma_{31} \cdots \gamma_{3p} \\ \gamma_{41} \cdots \gamma_{4p} \end{bmatrix} \begin{bmatrix} gem_{t-1} \\ \vdots \\ gem_{t-p} \end{bmatrix} + \begin{bmatrix} \varepsilon_{1t} \\ \varepsilon_{2t} \\ \varepsilon_{3t} \\ \varepsilon_{4t} \end{bmatrix} \quad (5)$$

3.4 ARMA-GARCH Model

Firstly, as shown in Eq. 6, this paper establishes the ARMA model. The AR(p) model $\varnothing_0 + \sum_{i=1}^{p} \varnothing_i x_{t-1}$ is used to predict the selected Chinese stock indexes based on the historical data from January 4, 2022, while the MA(q) model $\alpha_i - \sum_{i=1}^{q} \varnothing_i \alpha_{t-1}$ uses past volatility to predict the future.

$$x_t = \phi_0 + \sum_{i=1}^{p} \phi_i x_{t-1} + \alpha_i - \sum_{i=1}^{q} \phi_i \alpha_{t-1} \quad (6)$$

In this study, the GARCH model is used for analysis. This paper construct ARMA-GARCH models of the return and volatility of three Chinese stock indexes to investigate the correlation between the increase in interest rates by the Federal Reserve and the fluctuations observed in the Chinese stock market. Compared with the ARCH model, this model has fewer parameters to estimate, and thus provides more accurate predictions for future conditional variance. By introducing an explanatory variable σ_{t-1}^2, , higher-order ARCH(p) models can be simplified into GARCH(1,1) models. The specific GARCH (1,1) model setting is shown in Eq. 7, where the second term represents the ARCH part, and the third term represents the GARCH part.

$$\alpha_t^2 = \alpha_0 + \alpha_1 \varepsilon_{t-1^2} + \beta_t dollar_t + \gamma_1 \sigma_{t-1^2} \quad (7)$$

4 Empirical Results and Analysis

4.1 Order of VAR Model

This paper conducts research on the interrelationships between several variables based on the VAR model. Firstly, the order is determined to identify the lag period to be used. The maximum lag period is set to 12. And after calculating information criterion, the appropriate lag order is determined based on the number of *. Table 2 shows that the optimal lag order is 1.

Next, a test for the stationarity of the model is conducted. If the VAR model does not exhibit stationarity, the impulse response function will not converge to zero, and the

Table 2. Likelihood ratio test and information criterion

Lag	LL	LR	p	FPE	AIC	HQIC	SBIC
0	4886.03			2.0e-18	−29.4098	−29.3915*	−29.364*
1	4903.65	35.243*	0.004	2.0e-18*	−29.4196*	−29.3282	−29.1904
2	4914.57	21.838	0.148	2.0e-18	−29.389	−29.2244	−28.9764
3	4923.23	17.311	0.366	2.1e-18	−29.3447	−29.1071	−28.7488
4	4935.15	23.855	0.093	2.2e-18	−29.3202	−29.0094	−28.5408
5	4945.57	20.84	0.185	2.2e-18	−29.2866	−28.9026	−28.3238
6	4950.94	10.738	0.825	2.4e-18	−29.2225	−28.7655	−28.0764
7	4959.61	17.338	0.364	2.5e-18	−29.1784	−28.6482	−27.8489
8	4967.35	15.481	0.490	2.6e-18	−29.1286	−28.5253	−27.6157
9	4974.72	14.734	0.544	2.8e-18	−29.0766	−28.4002	−27.3804
10	4980.41	11.379	0.785	3.0e-18	−29.0145	−28.2649	−27.1349
11	4990.97	21.119	0.174	3.1e-18	−28.9817	−28.159	−26.9187
12	4997.18	12.419	0.715	3.3e-18	−28.9228	−28.0269	−26.6764

Fed's interest rate adjustment will have a long-term impact on the Chinese stock market. If all points are within the circle, the model can be considered stable. As depicted in Fig. 1, it is evident that all eigenvalues of the coefficient matrices are within the unit circle. Therefore, the VAR (1) system is stable, and there is no need to re-estimate the lagged terms, allowing for further analysis to be conducted.

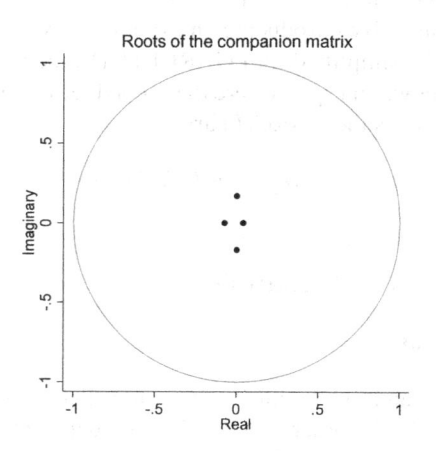

Fig. 1. Unit root test. Photo credit: Original

4.2 Impulse Response

This study explores the dynamic influence of three additional variables (GEM, SZSE, and SSEC) in the VAR model, regarding their response to fluctuations in the US dollar index, particularly during periods of increased interest rates set by the Federal Reserve. In this paper, a 30-period impulse response function is calculated and the pulse response diagrams for the four variables after the impact are plotted.

Figure 2 reflects the impact of the US dollar index on the other three variables in the VAR system. The horizontal axis represents unit time, with one day being used as the unit. The vertical axis indicates the percentage change of each relevant Chinese stock market index after being impacted.

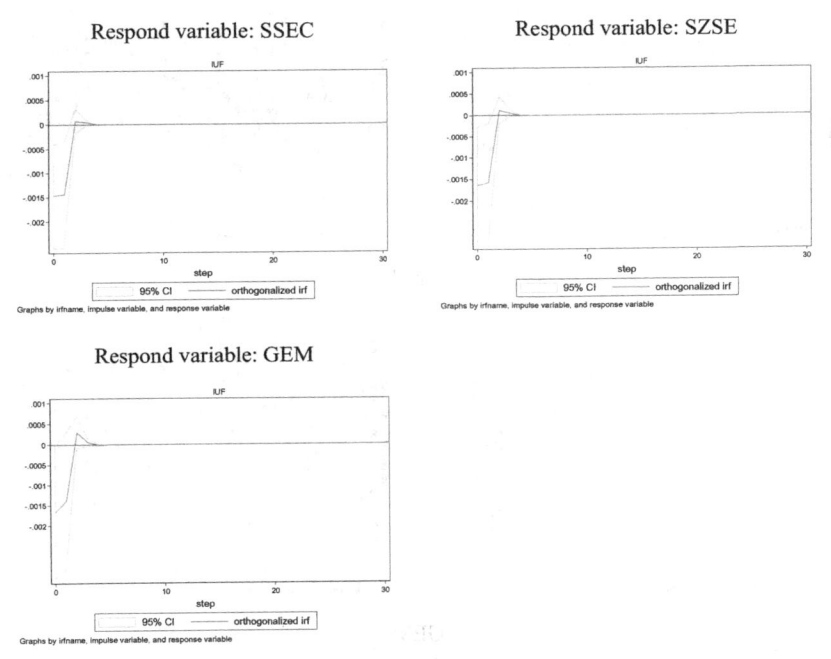

Fig. 2. Impulse and response (Impulse variable: US Dollar). Photo credit: Original

Figure 2 reveals that the three Chinese stock indices were all impacted by the fluctuations in the US dollar index. The impacts lasted for approximately five days and all indices experienced an initial decline but gradually became immune to the impacts towards the end of the period.

More specifically, after being negatively affected by the US Federal Reserve's interest rate hike, all three indices experienced a gradual reduction in the impacts over time and saw an increase in the second to third day. Among them, SZSE and GEM were more severely impacted with a decline of around 0.16%, while SSEC experienced a decline of approximately 0.14%. GEM responded more quickly to the impacts, with a reduction of negative effects by around 0.04% on the first day after the crisis, compared to only 0.01%

for the other two indices. Moreover, GEM also had the most significant overreaction among the three indices, reaching 0.03%, compared to 0.01% for SZSE and less than 0.01% for SSEC.

4.3 ARMA Specification

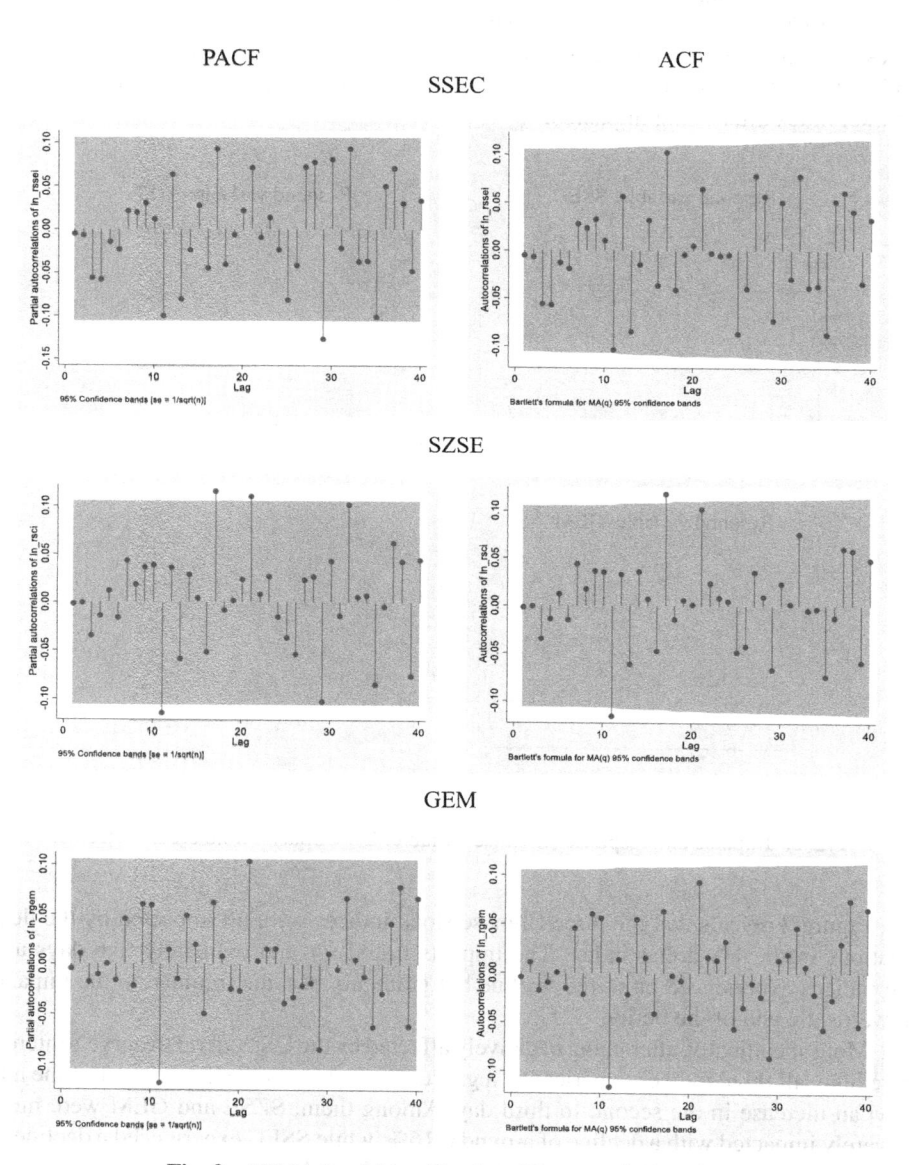

Fig. 3. ARMA (p, q) identification. Photo credit: Original

For the ARMA model, this study employed PACF and ACF to determine the orders of the AR and MA models, respectively, choosing the values outside the range as the orders used. As shown in the Fig. 3, the AR orders for SSEC, SZSE, and GEM were 29, 11, and 11, respectively, while the MA orders were all 11.

4.4 ARMA-GARCH Estimation Results and Variance Equation

This study plots the logarithmic values of the stock index returns. As shown in Fig. 4, it is obvious that the volatility of the earlier values is significantly greater than that of the later values, or in other words, the fluctuations are concentrated in the earlier and middle periods of the selected time period. Therefore, it can be preliminarily confirmed that the index exhibits conditional heteroscedasticity.

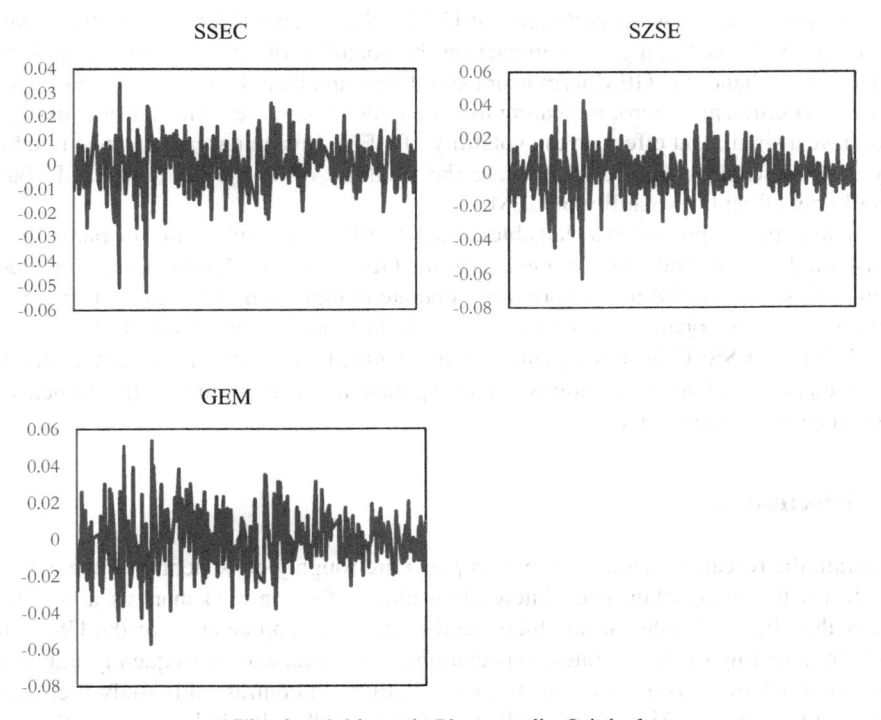

Fig. 4. Yield trend. Photo credit: Original

Furthermore, this study conducts further research based on the ARMA-GARCH model to verify the heteroskedasticity conditions and examine the impact of the US dollar index on the Chinese stock index. The results are presented in Table 3.

As shown in the table, both the ARCH and GARCH terms of the three Chinese stock indices are significant, further confirming the presence of conditional heteroskedasticity in all three indices. Regarding the influence of US dollar fluctuations on the volatility of Chinese stock indices, both the SSE Composite Index (SSEC) and the Shenzhen

Table 3. ARMA-GARCHX regression: variance equation

	(1) SSEC		(2) SZSE		(3) GEM	
	Coef.	p	Coef.	p	Coef.	p
US dollar	155.5678	0.056*	226.0923	0.076*	193.0961	0.515
ARCH	0.0698	0.002***	0.0547	0.008***	0.0496	0.008***
GARCH	0.8559	0.000***	0.9224	0.000***	0.9396	0.000***
Constant	0.0000	0.950	−0.0006	0.230	−0.0010	0.130

Component Index (SZSE) are affected by changes in the US dollar index at a 90% confidence level, moving in the same direction as the US dollar. The impact on both indices is significant, with coefficients of 155.5678 and 226.0923, respectively, meaning that the US dollar has a greater impact on the volatility of SZSE compared to SSEC. On the other hand, the GEM term is not significant and there is insufficient evidence to reject a coefficient of zero, indicating that the Federal Reserve's interest rate hike does not have a significant effect on the volatility of GEM. In summary, an interest rate hike by the Fed would significantly increase the volatility of both SSEC and SZSE, but it would not affect the volatility of GEM.

This paper proposes that a plausible explanation lies in the substantial disparity in size between the SZSE and SSEC compared to the GEM market. Moreover, the constituent companies of the GEM market primarily operate in high-tech sectors, characterized by relatively shorter operational histories and smaller market capitalization. Conversely, the SZSE and SSEC host companies of larger magnitude, with a substantial fraction engaged in cross-border operations, rendering them more susceptible to the influence of external environmental factors.

5 Discussion

Overall, the research conclusions of this paper are roughly consistent with the existing studies on the impact of the Fed's interest rate hikes on foreign stock markets, all of which show that the Fed's interest rate hikes tend to cause an appreciation of the US dollar, thereby affecting exchange rates, expectations, and trade, and consequently impacting foreign stock markets and increasing their volatility. In contrast, this study focuses on three representative Chinese stock indices and uses the US dollar index to reflect the Fed's interest rate hikes, which more comprehensively reflects their impact on the Chinese stock market. This study provides a theoretical reference for policymakers to formulate policies to deal with the impact and for investors to profit from the changes.

This study finds that the effect of the Federal Reserve's increase in interest rates on the performance of the Chinese stock market is relatively short-lived, but it does exacerbate market volatility. Therefore, policymakers can accelerate the market-oriented interest rate and exchange rate reforms, diversify financial instruments, reduce the flow of hot money under shocks, rapidly respond to short-term shocks, and stabilize the domestic economic environment to mitigate the negative impact on economic development [14].

In addition, accelerating the internationalization of the RMB and flexibly applying monetary policy tools can also help alleviate the negative impact of the Fed's interest rate hikes.

Investors can also profit by capitalizing on the characteristic changes in the stock market during a downturn. On the one hand, they can profit by utilizing currency conversion at the point when the policy is issued, and the US dollar appreciates by reasonably anticipating US policies. On the other hand, firstly, considering the impact of the US Federal Reserve's monetary policies on the volatility of the Chinese stock market, investors can likewise profit through short-term investments by taking advantage of the fluctuations in the stock market. Additionally, when taking all factors into account, investors can also utilize this characteristic to profit as the US Federal Reserve's interest rate hikes immediately negatively impact the Chinese stock market.

6 Conclusion

This study examines the impact of the US Federal Reserve's interest rate hike since 2022 on the Chinese stock market, which can be of significant theoretical and practical significance for policy makers and investors. Previous research has shown that changes in the US monetary policy, including interest rate hikes, have important implications for the global financial market. Given China's status as a prominent developing economy, it is crucial to analyze the consequences of the US interest rate increase on China's stock market, considering its heightened susceptibility to such fluctuations.

The study adopts the US dollar index as a proxy for the impact of the US Federal Reserve's interest rate hike and uses SSEC, SZSE, and GEM to represent China's stock market. SSEC and SZSE, being established exchanges, are seen as a barometer for the overall state of the economy, while GEM represents a high-tech, emerging innovative sector that is potentially more sensitive to external shocks. As such, these indices provide a comprehensive basis for investigating the impact of the US interest rate hike on China's stock market.

Based on a regression analysis of index returns, the study finds that the US Federal Reserve's interest rate hike immediately produces negative impacts on all three indices of China's stock market, with GEM responding the fastest to mitigate the negative effects. Interestingly, the impact on SSEC is the smallest, perhaps owing to its relative stability as compared to the other two indices. Moreover, three days after the impact, all three indices exhibit a slight rebound, indicating a quick recovery from the initial shock. Notably, the impact subsequently disappears completely after three days. It is also indicated that the interest rate hike by the US Federal Reserve is likely to increase the volatility of SSEC and SZSE, while having no significant effect on GEM's volatility.

References

1. CEIC Database Homepage. https://insights-ceicdata-com-s.libproxy.xmu.edu.cn/Untitled-insight/views
2. Laeven, L., Tong, H.: US monetary shocks and global stock prices. J. Finan. Intermed. **21**(3), 530–47 (2012)

3. Kazi, I.A., Wagan, H., Akbar, F.: The changing international transmission of U.S. monetary policy shocks: is there evidence of contagion effect on OECD countries. Econ. Model. **30**, 90–116 (2013)
4. Huang, Z., Tong, C., Qiu, H., Shen, Y.: The spillover of macroeconomic uncertainty between the U.S. and China. Econ. Lett. **171**, 123–127 (2018)
5. Bartosz, M.: External shocks, U.S. monetary policy and macroeconomic fluctuations in emerging markets. J. Monetary Econ. **54**(8), 2512–2520 (2007)
6. Valentina, B., Hyun, S.S.: Capital flows and the risk-taking channel of monetary policy. Working paper series: Monetary economics (TN.18942) (2013)
7. Han, L., Qi, M., Yin, L.: Macroeconomic policy uncertainty shocks on the Chinese economy: a GVAR analysis. Appl. Econ. **48**(51), 4907–4921 (2016)
8. Miranda-Agrippino, S., Rey, H.: US monetary policy and the global financial cycle. Rev. Econ. Stud. **87**(6), 2754–2776 (2020)
9. Héricourt, J., Poncet, S.: Exchange rate volatility, financial constraints, and trade: empirical evidence from Chinese firms. World Bank Econ. Rev. **29**(3), 550–578 (2015)
10. Dieci, R., Westerhoff, F.: Heterogeneous speculators, endogenous fluctuations and interacting markets: a model of stock prices and exchange rates. J. Econ. Dynam. Control **34**(4), 743–764 (2009)
11. Peter, T.: Capital inflows and asset prices: Evidence from emerging Asia. J. Bank. Finan. **37**(3), 717–729 (2013)
12. Sims, C.A.: Macroeconomics and reality. Econometrica **48**(1), 1 (1980)
13. Sims, C.A.: The role of approximate prior restrictions in distributed lag estimation. J. Am. Stat. Assoc. **67**(337), 169–175 (1972)
14. Neanidis, K.C.: Volatile capital flows and economic growth: the role of banking supervision. J. Finan. Stab. **40**, 77–93 (2018)

Stock Market Volatility During and After the Covid-19 Pandemic: Academic Perspectives

Yining Yang(✉)

SILC Business School, Shanghai University, Shanghai 201800, China
yangyn1218@shu.edu.cn

Abstract. The Covid-19 aroused severe fluctuations in global stock markets widely and rapidly, while there lacks sufficient studies concerning shock caused by the Covid-19 to stock markets systematically. Through systematic review, this research summarizes features of stock market volatility during and after the pandemic by covering general characteristics and spillovers effect of the volatility. Specifically, the coronavirus would lead to significant volatility of the stock market through various and complex approaches, including economic losses, investor sentiment and policies, and this volatility would change with the stage of the coronavirus. Inside the stock market, as centres of volatility contagion, industrial, consumption and energy sectors, would transmit risks due to high correlations between sectors with mechanism varying from stage to stage, but industries isolating risks still exist in the long term. Although research on volatility spillovers between financial submarkets particularly during the epidemic are limited, previous empirical studies reveal that stock, foreign exchange and bond markets would transmit risks to each other. Furthermore, the Covid-19 has promoted cross-border stock market risk contagion significantly. These arguments present a systematic view of shock aroused by the Covid-19 to risks of stock markets, providing directions for further research and assisting investors of capital markets in identifying and managing portfolio risks, especially under the background of severe public health crises. In particular, investors are suggested to realize dynamic changes of stock market volatility and its transmission inside and between various markets, increase proportion of stocks isolating risk, and diversify investment portfolio with safe-haven assets, such as gold.

Keywords: Stock market volatility · Volatility spillovers · Risk contagion · Covid-19 · Systematic review

1 Introduction

In December 2019, the Covid-19 outbreak has resulted in stagnation in business activities and spread of panic, inflicting serious damage on the global economy which was experiencing a weak recovery. A significant symbol of this economic damage is a high fluctuation in the global capital markets [1], posing a threat to stability of the financial system. As a key segment of financial markets, the stock market has experienced significant volatility with a wide scope and a rapid speed. As the following Fig. 1 shown, the main global stock markets presented a steady growth with slight volatility before the first quarter of 2020, while there has been a sharp decline in global stock indexes since the eruption of the Covid-19 pandemic. For instance, NASDAQ Composite Index and Shanghai Composite Index approximately decreased by 15.31% and 10.86% respectively from January to the end of March in 2020.

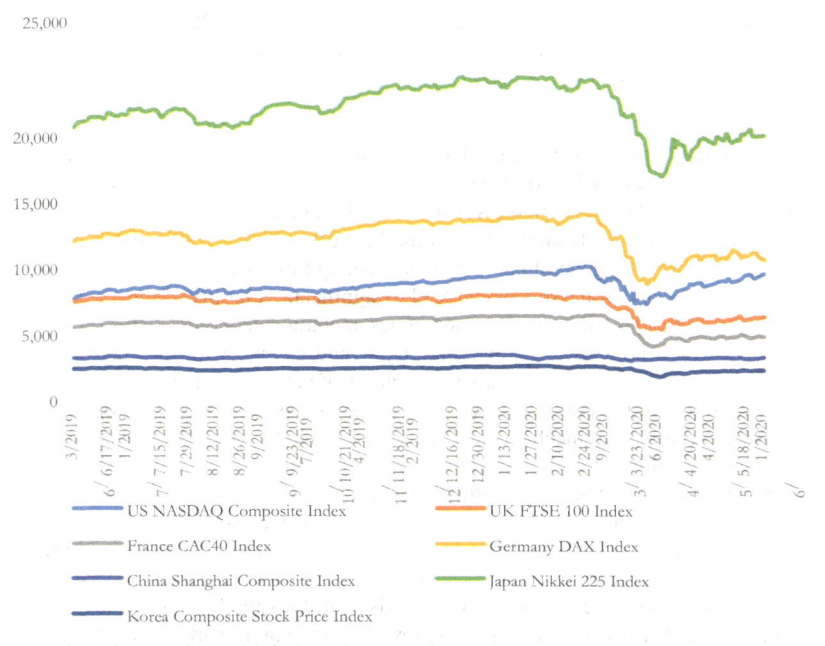

Fig. 1. Stock Indexes of the Global Main Stock Markets from June 2019 to June 2020. Data source: NASDAQ, FTSE Russell, Paris Bourse, Deutsche Börse AG, Shanghai Stock Exchange, Nihon Keizai Shimbun and Korea Exchange. Photo credit: Original

However, current researches concerning the negative influence of the Covid-19 mainly focus on perspectives of public governance, monetary policy, industrial structure and the financial market as a whole, while specific studies emphasize on stock market volatility aroused by the coronavirus are relatively limited. In addition, these limited researches merely highlight volatility of stock market in particular countries or in single aspect, especially volatility spillovers between specific countries, lacking comprehensiveness.

Therefore, based on the existing literature, this systematic review aims to analyse stock market volatility intensified by the Covid-19 pandemic regarding its features and volatility spillovers. This review contributes to assisting investors in identifying characteristics of stock market volatility caused by external shocks during and after the severe public health crises, with the Covid-19 epidemic serving as a typical example, so that they will be able to allocate assets and manage risks more rationally with awareness of cross-market and cross-border stock market risk contagion.

This research will firstly identify general features of the stock market volatility intensified by outbreak of the coronavirus disease, and then reveal the risk transmission among different industry sectors inside the stock market in Sect. 2. Apart from the volatility of stock markets itself, Sect. 3 will further discuss volatility spillovers between stock market and other financial submarkets, including foreign exchange and bond markets, and Sect. 4 will present risk contagion of stock markets across different countries during and after the public health crisis. Furthermore, Sect. 5 will conclude this research, provide relevant suggestions concerning portfolio allocation for investors of capital markets, and point out potential direction for further research.

2 Stock Market Volatility

2.1 Overall Features

Volatility of the stock market aroused by the coronavirus pandemic is significant and complex, and this impact has varied with different stages of the pandemic.

For wild fluctuation of the stock market, considering limited data samples at the beginning of the coronavirus period, major researches compared this global pandemic with other similar public health emergencies, such as Spanish Flu pandemic in 1918 with the peak of global fatality rate in the contemporary world, and implemented regression analysis with data of 48 countries to predict that the Covid-19 would lead to a decrease in real GDP by approximately 6% on average in these 48 typical countries [2]. In fact, according to open data disclosed by the World Bank, there is a 3.31% decline in the global GDP of 2020 compared with the previous year, which is not as passive as prediction of the research mentioned above but still reflects the negative influence on macro economy imposed by the pandemic. Under this serious harm to macro economy, the global health emergency has evoked a tremendous shock to the market of stock. With event-study analysis on the basis of daily data from 2009 to 2020, the coronavirus disease has affected the financial markets significantly, among which stock markets and foreign exchange markets have suffered the most serious shock [3]. Specifically, the empirical results reveal that outbreak of the coronavirus has imposed a significantly positive and substantial influence on the stock market volatility temporarily, implementing exponential GARCH models, and from the long-term perspective, using an extended GARCH-MIDAS model [4, 5].

Complexity of stock market risk mainly derives from the transmission mechanisms of stock market volatility brought by the Covid-19 outbreak. Firstly, the rapid spread of coronavirus directly caused economic losses through stagnant production and disruptions of supply chains, resulting in a significant decline in stock market returns [6, 7]. Furthermore, uncertainty of this public health emergency, accompanied with information asymmetry, has intensified investor pessimism and panic, which would reflect in their herding and regret aversion [8, 9], implying that investors would mimic investment behaviour of each other and reduce their holding shares to avoid losses without rationality. As a result, investors in the stock market tend to sell their holdings blindly, promoting stock price synchronicity and leading to further abnormal volatility in the stock market [10]. Instead, they prefer to transfer funds to invest in safe haven assets, such as gold, as demonstrated by a general significant increase in international spot price of gold since the beginning of 2020 shown in Fig. 2 below. Besides, to curb economic recession and boost development of the financial markets during and after the coronavirus outbreak, the governments tend to implement proactive fiscal policy and expansionary monetary policy by various policy instruments, such as increasing government expenditure and decreasing interest rate. Both policies would affect stock prices directly and indirectly, and then arouse volatility of the stock market, based on empirical results of event-study methodology [11].

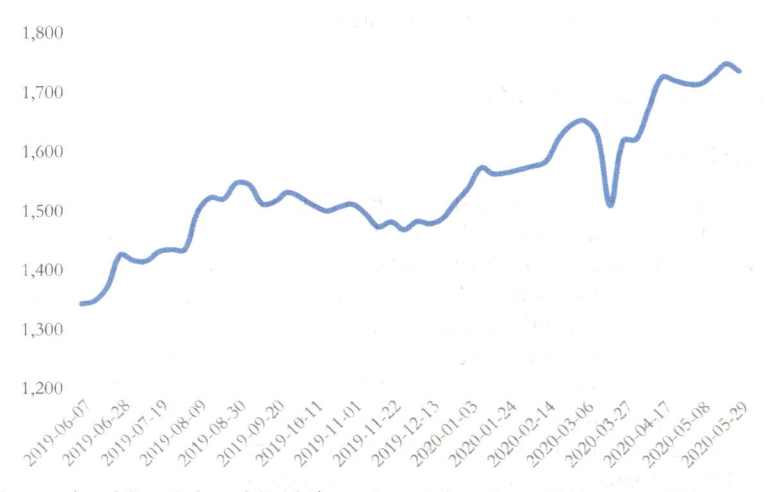

Fig. 2. International Spot Price of Gold ($ per Ounce) from June 2019 to June 2020. Data source: National Bureau of Statistics of China. Photo credit: Original

Moreover, stock market risk changes with the stage of the Covid-19 epidemic. Considering different stages of infectious diseases, including the coronavirus, with different characteristics, current research infers and verifies that stock market volatility also depended on the stages of the Covid-19 pandemic [12]. Specifically, according to trend analysis of the research, at the outbreak and control stages of the epidemic from January to March in 2020, index of stock price fluctuated drastically in the shape of 'M', while this index rose gently at the recovery phase after March [12].

Therefore, wild fluctuations demonstrated in the stock market have resulted from the outbreak of the global health emergency through various and complex approaches, such as economic losses, investor sentiment and policies, and characteristics of these fluctuations depend on the stages of the epidemic.

2.2 Risk Transmission Inside the Stock Market

Inside the stock market, high correlation and interdependence between industry sectors aggravate risk transmission among industry chains, leading to an overall increasing volatility of the stock market.

Centres of risk transmission mainly include industrial, consumption and energy sectors, based on Regular Vine Copula models [13]. As the core driver of the economic development which connects closely with abundant industry sectors with a wide range, industrial sectors might face limitation of production, especially in the early stage of the coronavirus [13]. For the consumption sector, temporary close of physical stores, limited commodity production and express delivery services have dented consumer confidence as reflected by declining Consumer Confidence Index (CCI) in China in Fig. 3. This index, the comprehensive measure of Chinese consumers' subjective feeling of the current economic condition, living standard, consumption expenditure and employment status, is compiled by China Economic Monitoring & Analysis Center, and it is positively related to consumer confidence with a neutral stance denoted by CCI of 100 [14]. Therefore, as shown in Fig. 3, during the Covid-19 outbreak, although consumers were still confident to consume as CCI exceeded 100, there has been a sharp decline in CCI since the beginning of 2020, implying that consumer confidence of China have been weaken significantly aroused by the pandemic.

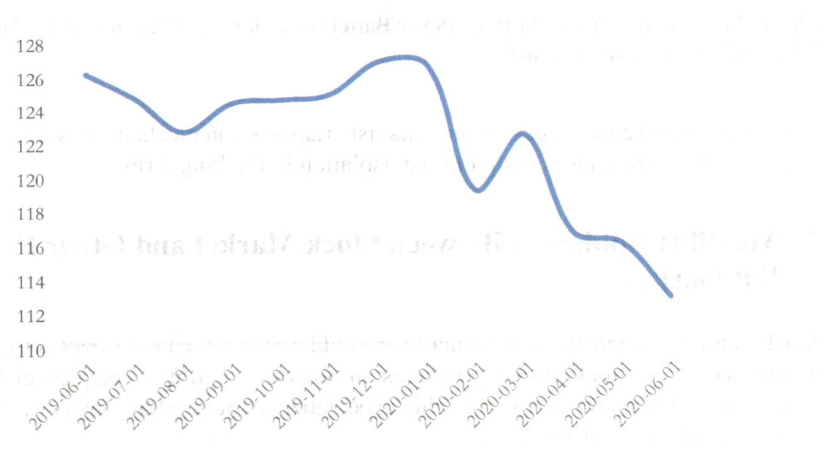

Fig. 3. Consumer Confidence Index (CCI) in China from June 2019 to June 2020. Data source: China Economic Monitoring & Analysis Center. Photo credit: Original

In addition, significant volatility derived from energy sectors might result from severe fluctuation of international crude oil price due to both the Covid-19 epidemic in December 2019 and the Russia-Ukraine war in February 2022 illustrated by Fig. 4.

For risk transmission mechanism during the Covid-19 pandemic, the correlations between industry sectors generally increased temporarily, while in the long term, they would increase or remain flat, apart from the declining correlation coefficient between consumption and information technology sectors [13]. It implies that affected by the Covid-19 outbreak, risk transmission and contagion existed between general industry sectors in the short run. However, in the longer term, there exists industry sectors that realize risk isolation in the stock market, such as information technology sector, with consideration of popular telecommuting and online education during the period of the coronavirus.

To sum up, volatility inside the stock market that has been intensified by the coronavirus would be transmitted from several key industry sectors, including industrial,

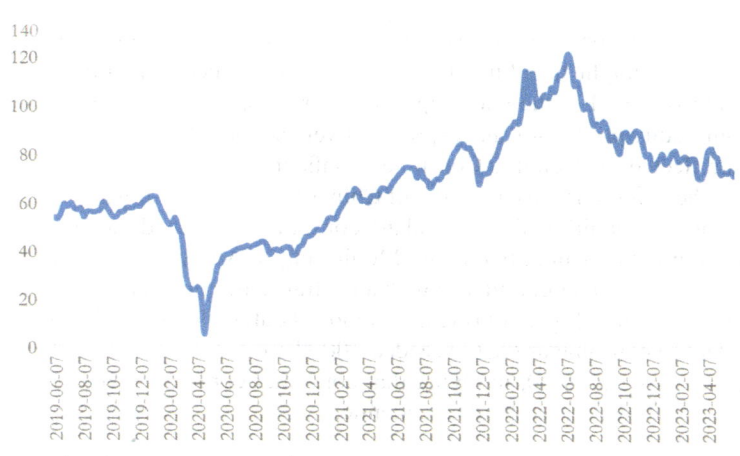

Fig. 4. International Crude Oil Price ($ per Barrel) from June 2019 to June 2023. Data source: NASDAQ. Photo credit: Original

consumption and energy sectors, and this risk transmission mechanism would vary from stage to stage with sectors realizing risk isolation in the long term.

3 Volatility Spillovers Between Stock Market and Other Financial Submarkets

Stock, foreign exchange and bond markets would transmit their risks between each other, among which the stock market possesses an obvious volatility contagion effect on the bond market, but relevant research which specialize in these effects under the context of the Covid-19 are relatively limited.

Various research verify that by means of GARCH models, risk contagion between the stock and foreign exchange markets is bidirectional [15, 16]. These bidirectional volatility spillovers effects are not symmetrical [17]. However, this research is unable to conclude a stronger risk spillover effect between these two markets, since different empirical studies apply different models with different data and draw contrary conclusions [18, 19].

Between the markets of stock and bond, there also exists bidirectional volatility spillovers effects based on empirical results of GARCH models [20, 21]. Furthermore, the stock market possesses a stronger risk contagion effect, compared with the bond market, as concluded by most research [22, 23].

Hence, it is reasonable to infer that wild and complex fluctuations in the stock market, aroused by the epidemic, would be transmitted to other financial submarkets, taking the foreign exchange and bond markets as typical examples, because of the volatility spillovers effects. However, this conclusion should be verified by further empirical research with consideration of additional specific fluctuations aroused by the coronavirus outbreak.

4 Volatility Spillovers of Stock Markets Across Different Countries

With the rapid advance of globalization, stock market volatility has been transmitted between different countries during the epidemic period, resulting in systematic risk spillovers of the stock markets.

Using daily return data of stock markets worldwide, empirical results of nonparametric Mann-Whitney tests reveal that the outbreak of the coronavirus worldwide has caused significant detriment to international stock markets, and spillover effects between major countries have been intensified [24], which are more significant than the risk contagion in 2008, when the global financial crisis unfolded [25]. Specifically, volatility contagion effect of a single stock market on the global stock markets displays positive correlation with severity of the Covid-19 epidemic in the country that this market belongs to [26]. In particular, the outbreak of the pandemic has tightened the connections between European, American and Chinese stock markets [27], among which European stock markets with severe pandemic have become the volatility spillovers centre of international stock markets [25]. Apart from European stock markets, the direction of risk contagion between American and Chinese stock markets has been altered by the coronavirus. Through a copula-based Conditional Value-at-Risk model, empirical results imply that before the pandemic outbreak, the stock market of America would impose a stronger risk spillovers effect on that of China than the opposite direction, while the comparison result has become exactly contrary during the Covid-19 [28].

Therefore, the Covid-19 would tighten risk correlations among stock markets worldwide, intensifying stock market volatility spillovers across different countries.

5 Conclusion

Since December 2019, the Covid-19 pandemic has impeded development and stability of the global macro economy significantly. As the barometer of the macroeconomy and financial markets, stock markets worldwide have experienced wild fluctuations during the pandemic period. However, there lacks systematic research in relation to the influence of the coronavirus on stock market risks from various and comprehensive perspectives. Therefore, propose of this systematic review is to analyse volatility of the stock market during and after the coronavirus period systematically, including its own features and its cross-market and cross-border spillovers effects, so that investors in financial markets are able to conduct portfolio allocation and risk management reasonably when they face exogenous shock, such as the Covid-19.

Affected by complex factors which include economic losses, investor panic and policies, stock markets have experienced significant volatility, whose features would vary from stage to stage of the Covid-19. Specifically, volatility of stock markets mainly originates from industrial, consumption and energy sectors inside the market, and these sectors would transmit their risks to other sectors in both short and long term. However, there still exists industry sectors that succeed in isolating risks in the long term during this epidemic period, such as the information technology sector. In terms of cross-market stock market risk contagion, even though research that specialize in the spillovers effect during and after the Covid-19 period are relatively limited, previous empirical results have shown that risks would be transmitted between stock, foreign exchange and bond markets. For cross-border stock market volatility spillovers effect, the Covid-19 has strengthened volatility spillovers effect of stock markets between different countries and altered risk contagion direction, with the risk spillovers centre of European stock markets.

Considering these characteristics during the period of a public health emergency, for investment of stock, investors are recommended to pay attention to dynamic changes of both stock market volatility and its transmission between industry sectors, and emphasize on industries which can isolate risks, such as the information technology sector and relevant markets. In terms of the whole portfolio allocation, due to the volatility contagion effect of a stock market on other financial submarkets in various countries, investors are suggested to diversify their investment portfolio, such as considering gold with its hedging potential and ability of safe haven, in order to spread their risk during this era of a public health emergency.

Among the existing literature, major research concerning the stock market during the pandemic attach importance to the cross-border volatility spillovers effect. By comparison, studies with respect to shock evoked by the Covid-19 to specific risk transmission mechanism inside the stock market and cross-market volatility spillovers effect of the market are limited and highlighted for further research.

References

1. Shen, Y., Li, C., Zhao, X., Wang, X.: Research on the risk contagion effect of global stock market under major risk events. Int. Econ. Trade Res. **39**, 82–99 (2023)
2. Barro, R.J., Ursua, J.F., Weng, J.: The coronavirus and the great influenza pandemic: lessons from the "Spanish Flu" for the coronavirus's potential effects on mortality and economic activity (2020). https://www.nber.org/system/files/working_papers/w26866/w26866.pdf
3. Fang, Y., Shao, Z., Huang, C.: Capital market opening and cross-border risk contagion prevention and control—evidence from Shanghai-Hong Kong stock connect program. Stud. Int. Finan. **413**, 65–75 (2021)
4. Haroon, S.A.R.R.: COVID-19: media coverage and financial markets behavior— a sectoral inquiry. J. Behav. Exp. Financ. **27**, 100343 (2020)
5. Bai, L., Wei, Y., Wei, G., Li, X., Zhang, S.: Infectious disease pandemic and permanent volatility of international stock markets: a long-term perspective. Financ. Res. Lett. **40**, 101709 (2021)
6. Zhang, Z., Zhu, S., Lv, F.: Research on the impact of the COVID-19 pandemic on capital markets. Friends Account. **642**, 131–137 (2020)
7. Yang, Z., Chen, Y., Zhang, P.: Macroeconomic shock, financial risk transmission and governance response to major public emergencies. J. Manag. World **36**, 13–35+7 (2020)
8. Chen, Y., Shen, Y., Wang, J.: Financial market reaction to dramatic public health shocks. J. Financ. Res. **6**, 20–39 (2020)
9. Ahmed, B.: Understanding the impact of investor sentiment on the price formation process: a review of the conduct of American stock markets. J. Econ. Asymmetr. **22**, e00172 (2020)
10. Cheng, C., Liu, K.: Research on the impact of capital markets under COVID-19— based on stock price synchronization. J. Industr. Technol. Econ. **40**, 125–135 (2021)
11. Tian, J., Wang, W.: Does macro-policy implementation shock stock market after the financial crisis? —based on high frequency data analysis. Rev. Econ. Manag. **34**, 130–137 (2018)

12. Lan, B., Zhuang, L.: Research on the impact of COVID-19 epidemic on financial market shocks. Stat. Decis. **37**, 129–133 (2021)
13. Yu, J., Jin, X., Liu, Y.: Multiscale inter-sectoral dependence structure and dynamic evolution of Chinese stock market under sudden crisis—a study of COVID-19 epidemic. J. Ind. Technol. Econ. **42**, 70–79 (2023)
14. Ma, W., Jiang, X.: The influence of consumer confidence on real economy under the background of "double cycle": analysis based on VAR model. Econ. Manag. **36**, 10–18 (2022)
15. Zhao, H.: Dynamic relationship between exchange rate and stock price: evidence from China. Res. Int. Bus. Financ. **24**, 103–112 (2010)
16. Morales-Zumaquero, S.-R.: Volatility spillovers between foreign exchange and stock markets in industrialized countries. Q. Rev. Econ. Finance **70**, 121–136 (2018)
17. Reboredo, J.C., Rivera-Castro, M.A., Ugolini, A.: Downside and upside risk spillovers between exchange rates and stock prices. J. Bank. Finance **62**, 76–96 (2016)
18. Kumar, M.: Returns and volatility spillover between stock prices and exchange rates: empirical evidence from IBSA countries. Int. J. Emerg. Mark. **8**, 108–128 (2013)
19. Zhou, B., Zhang, H., Cao, Q.: Industry heterogeneity of volatility spillover effects between RMB exchange rate and stock market. Taxation Econ. **5**, 55–61 (2021)
20. Dean, W.G., Faff, R.W., Loudon, G.F.: Asymmetry in return and volatility spillover between equity and bond markets in Australia. Pac. Basin Financ. J. **18**, 272–289 (2010)
21. Yue, Z., Zhang, Y.: Empirical research on the spillover effect of money market and bond market on Shanghai and Shenzhen 300 Index. Macroeconomics **3**, 100–108+135 (2014)
22. Liu, L., Lv, Y., Wang, Y.: Give or receive spillovers across Chinese financial markets. Modern Finan. Econ.-J. Tianjin Univ. Finan. Econ. **35**, 81–90 (2015)
23. Mcmillan, D.G.: Interrelation and spillover effects between stocks and bonds: crossmarket and cross-asset evidence. Stud. Econ. Financ. **37**, 561–582 (2020)
24. He, Q., Liu, J., Wang, S.: The impact of COVID-19 on stock markets. Econ. Polit. Stud. **8**, 275–288 (2020)
25. Yuan, M., Hu, D.: Study of risk spillover effect of global stock market against background of COVID-19 impact. Finan. Forum **26**, 36–48 (2021)
26. Yang, Z., Wang, S.: Systemic financial risk contagion of global stock market under public health emergency: empirical evidence from COVID19 epidemic. Econ. Res. J. **56**, 22–38 (2021)
27. Ye, W., Zhao, J., Miao, B.: Study on the interrelationship and risk spillover effects of liquidity risks in European, American and domestic stock markets: against the background of epidemic outbreaks. J. Appl. Stat. Manag. **40**, 292–309 (2021)
28. Hanif, W., Mensi, W., Vo, X.V.: Impacts of COVID-19 outbreak on the spillovers between US and Chinese stock sectors. Financ. Res. Lett. **40**, 101922 (2021)

Unveiling the Effects of the China-US Trade Conflict: A Comparative Study of Stock Market Behaviors in the United States and China

Shuying Chen[✉]

School of Business, Wake Forest University, Winston-Salem, North Caroline 27109, USA
Chens419@wfu.edu

Abstract. The world's economic environment has been significantly impacted by the United States and China's developing trade conflict. This paper investigates the impact of this trade conflict on the stock markets of both countries, utilizing a decade-long data (2010–2019) of the S&P 500 and Shanghai Composite Index (SSEC), including the period of the trade conflict. The research uses the Augmented Dickey-Fuller (ADF) test to evaluate data stationarity, and an ARIMA model (Autoregressive Integrated Moving Average) to forecast stock market actions. Significant findings of this study indicate differing effects of the conflict on the two nations' stock markets. The U.S. market, represented by the Nasdaq index, showed short-term fluctuations during the conflict, aligning closely with long-term predictions, which denotes its capacity to adjust and maintain robustness in the face of such economic upheavals. Conversely, China's market, as per the SSEC, reflected a substantial divergence between actual and predicted values during the trade conflict, suggesting potential long-term economic repercussions. The research is significant as it underscores the divergent impacts of geopolitical events on various national economies. It provides valuable insights for policymakers and investors alike, emphasizing the importance of strategic management and careful evaluation of geopolitical risks and events. The paper suggests that while markets may show resilience in the face of conflicts, the potential for long-term impacts should not be overlooked.

Keywords: Trade Conflict · Stock Market Analysis · Geopolitical Risks · US-China Relations · Investment Strategies

1 Introduction

The growing trade conflict between the United States and China has dramatically altered the global economic stage, affecting both the economies involved directly and the worldwide economy at large. This research endeavors to elucidate the ramifications of this enduring trade conflict on the stock markets of both nations. The S&P 500 and the Shanghai Composite Index (SSEC) have been selected as indicative indices of these markets. This study scrutinizes data over ten years (2010–2019), encompassing the ongoing China-US trade conflict, to evaluate how much this economic dispute has influenced stock market behavior.

The backbone of this research design is a comprehensive time-series analysis utilizing robust techniques like the Augmented Dickey-Fuller (ADF) test and the Autoregressive Integrated Moving Average (ARIMA) model. The ADF test helps identify the presence of unit roots and stochastic trends in the stock prices, contributing to the reliability and consistency of the dataset. Meanwhile, the ARIMA model, known for its predictive and modeling capabilities for time-dependent variables, is harnessed to scrutinize the market indices' past values and correlated variables.

For fine-tuning the model, tools like the Partial Autocorrelation Function (PACF) and Autocorrelation Function (ACF) are employed to ascertain the order of the ARIMA model. These combined processes ensure the construction of a model optimally suited to capture the subtleties of the market indices during the observed period.

Preliminary findings suggest a pronounced disparity in the trade conflict's impacts on the US and Chinese markets. The US stock market shows resilience, with the market's inherent capacity absorbing short-term fluctuations in the long term. In contrast, China's market consistently diverges between anticipated and actual outcomes, implying a more severe, enduring impact.

This research aims to provide a sophisticated picture of how global trade disputes arise, like the US-China standoff, can reverberate through financial markets, influencing their behaviors. The anticipated research findings should contribute to policy debates, guide investor decisions, and stimulate further academic inquiries into economic conflicts and their broader implications. As this exploration continues, the complexities and interconnectedness of global financial markets during intense geopolitical strife become increasingly apparent, highlighting the enduring effects of these economic tremors.

The remainder of the paper is structured as follows: Sect. 2 dives deep into a thorough analysis of the literature, highlighting previous research works pertinent to trade conflicts, stock market dynamics, and the influence of geopolitical tensions on global economic activities. The research design is presented in Sect. 3, which goes into detail on the data sources, the Augmented Dickey-Fuller (ADF) test for stationarity, and the use of the AutoRegressive Integrated Moving Average (ARIMA) model to study and forecast stock market behavior. Section 4 is dedicated to the empirical results and analysis. It provides the ARIMA model's order and discusses the observed impact of the China-US trade conflict on the Nasdaq and SSEC indices. The penultimate section, Sect. 5, gives a detailed discussion of the findings, drawing parallels with the existing literature and highlighting the research implications. The paper is concluded in Sect. 6, which summarizes the major findings and offers useful suggestions for investors and policymakers based on the learnings from the study.

2 Literature Review

2.1 The Trade Conflict

The post-World War II era has seen the United States hold sway as the dominant power, sustaining a liberal international order. However, the landscape of global power is shifting as China's rapid ascendancy challenges the established US hegemony, instigating power competition and potential conflict [1]. China's contestation of US dominance can be underscored by three strategic endeavors in recent years: the Belt and Road Initiative

(BRI), the Asian Infrastructure Investment Bank (AIIB), and the "Made in China 2025" industrial development plan [1].

The BRI, which pays homage to the historic Silk Road, is a bold endeavor to promote global peace, infrastructure growth, and regional economic cooperation. Currently involving around 70 countries, the initiative has found favor with many nations across the globe. Across a direct challenge to the traditional financial institutions dominated by the US and its allies, the AIIB, a multilateral development bank led by China, provides financial backing for infrastructure projects across Asia. The "Made in China 2025" policy, which focuses on industries including robotics, advanced information technology, aviation, and new energy vehicles, also acts as a ten-year blueprint for transforming China into a leader in the high-tech industry. This strategy aims to lessen China's reliance on foreign technology and increase domestic competitiveness [1].

From 2018 onwards, the US and China have engaged in a tit-for-tat imposition of trade restrictions, causing a considerable escalation in tariffs. As a result, the tariffs on Chinese imports into the US have surged from 2.6% to 17.5%, while tariffs on US imports into China have risen from 6.2% to 16.4% [2]. These escalations were felt most acutely in 2019, leading to a dramatic import reduction of up to 40%. The sectors most impacted included petroleum, metals, and agriculture, although imports of Computer, Electronic, and Optic Equipment saw an increase, potentially driven by apprehensions of future export restrictions [2].

This escalating trade conflict between the US and China is fueled by the US's grievances with perceived unfair trade practices by China and deep-seated differences in their political and economic systems. The US perceives China's economic model as antithetical to the principles of free trade and views China's meteoric rise as a direct challenge to its hegemonic status, prompting efforts to counterbalance China's growth and reaffirm its dominance [3]. Such economic confrontation adversely affects both nations, likely reducing foreign direct investment and diminishing market shares. The conflict stems from opposing perspectives, with the US accusing China of unfair trade practices, while China disputes the US's characterization of its rise as a threat [3].

In its retaliatory measures, China strategically targeted industries in regions with high Republican voter concentration, especially in swing districts where even minor shifts in voting patterns could significantly influence election outcomes. For instance, the decision to impose retaliatory tariffs on nuts adversely affected Republican-leaning counties in California's twenty-first district, which anticipated a tight race in the 2018 election. Thus, the unfolding US-China trade conflict has far-reaching implications, reverberating across global power dynamics, economic systems, and electoral politics [4].

2.2 Semiconductor Industry

The USA-China trade conflict, described by some as a nascent tech war, has provoked a discernible shift in global economic dynamics. The conflict has resulted in the USA implementing tighter regulations on foreign investments and restrictive measures on domestic firms engaging with Chinese tech companies [3]. Consequently, the semiconductor industry has emerged as a focal point in this tussle, with significant implications for global value chains and national security [5].

In particular, the semiconductor industry has experienced a radical transformation. Reduced trade barriers and the inclusion of China in the international economy resulted in many American semiconductors manufactured in third countries. The focus has pivoted from physical production to an emphasis on intellectual property rights. This shift has challenged US policymakers seeking to regulate foreign firms, forcing them to grapple with complex legal implications [5].

Export controls on semiconductors introduced in response to national security concerns proved to be a convoluted legal process and had unintended consequences. Initially, the controls had limited reach but high potential costs for US firms. Policymakers eventually had to extend these controls to include inputs from semiconductor manufacturers in Taiwan and South Korea. However, US semiconductor companies, traditionally requesting trade restrictions, opposed these tariff measures [5].

The US and China's Phase One deal, announced in February 2020, was a temporary ceasefire. It included China's promise to buy an additional $200 billion worth of US goods and services in 2020 and 2021, even if it did not remove the recently imposed tariffs. Semiconductors were among the products included in the deal, reflecting their central role in this ongoing conflict [5].

Initial export controls on semiconductors were criticized for their expansive scope and inefficacy in achieving their intended purpose. These controls potentially restricted sales of US semiconductors to companies like Huawei that were not directly involved in national security-sensitive activities, raising economic concerns [5]. Further export controls were enacted in 2020 to mitigate these shortcomings, targeting semiconductor manufacturing equipment and introducing the Foreign Direct Product Rule (FDPR). This rule aimed to limit foreign chipmakers' access to US-made equipment unless they agreed to cease sales to Huawei, hoping to induce reliance on US manufacturing equipment and persuade foreign companies to comply with US restrictions on Huawei [5].

Investment restrictions were also implemented to address national security concerns in the semiconductor industry. The Committee on Foreign Investment in the United States (CFIUS) reviewed, and potentially blocked, foreign acquisitions of American companies deemed a security risk. This led to scrutiny of Chinese attempts to acquire semiconductor companies, deterring potential mergers and acquisitions [5].

The saga of the semiconductor industry during the US-China trade disputes showcases the evolving political economy of trade policy within global value chains. As tensions escalate and the global supply chain and distribution of semiconductor manufacturing capabilities transform, the ramifications remain uncertain. Given semiconductors' significant role in various sectors, these issues demand careful consideration from policymakers, industry stakeholders, and researchers [5].

2.3 Global Economy

The US-China trade tensions have significantly affected global markets and altered global value chains (GVCs). As a direct consequence of these tensions, trade diversion has been manifested in the increased trade interactions between the US and third countries, including Mexico, the EU, Taiwan, and Vietnam. Sectors like motor vehicles, manufacturing, transport equipment, and electrical equipment have notably benefited from this diversion. [2]. China's trade diversion, on the other hand, showed a different pattern, with import reductions not only from the US but also from third countries, reflecting a reorganization of value chains. East Asian economies have adjusted their value chains, reducing exports to China while increasing those to the US [2].

Despite the ongoing conflict, the global impact is expected to be relatively marginal, with global GDP projected to decrease by 0.08% to 0.25%, suggesting a limited direct impact on the world economy. However, certain countries and sectors might bear the brunt of this conflict more significantly [6]. East Asian countries, notably those heavily involved in global supply chains and exporting intermediate goods to China, might experience the conflict's negative impacts [6].

Trade policy plays a pivotal role in shaping the structure and dynamics of GVCs. Trade restrictions like tariffs and quotas can directly impact the flow of goods and services across borders, affecting the competitiveness of firms operating within these GVCs. On the flip side, trade agreements aim to facilitate the integration of countries into GVCs by promoting market access, harmonizing regulations, and establishing standard rules.

In response to trade restrictions, firms within GVCs employ strategies to mitigate the adverse effects and maintain competitiveness. These tactics include modifying value chain operations and changing production locations, end markets, and suppliers [7]. Consequently, these actions can prompt a restructuring of GVCs in several ways. Firms might shift their production networks to countries with more favorable trade policies, leading to new production locations and value chain activities. This geographical dispersion of production and reconfiguration of GVCs aids firms in adapting to trade restrictions.

Furthermore, switching suppliers to bypass trade restrictions can redefine lead firm-supplier relationships, potentially leading to changes in the distribution of tasks and responsibilities within GVCs. Firms investing in upgrading their value chain activities may also introduce new technologies, processes, and products, driving technological upgrading and innovation within GVCs [7].

The restructuring of GVCs in response to trade restrictions can have mixed implications. It can enhance the resilience and competitiveness of firms by diversifying their production and sourcing networks and promoting technological upgrading. However, it can also disrupt existing GVC relationships, increase transaction costs, and introduce new uncertainties [7]. Thus, the strategies of switching and upgrading remain crucial for firms navigating trade restrictions within GVCs. These strategies demand strategic choices regarding production locations, end markets, suppliers, and investments in economic upgrading [7].

2.4 Review

Global markets and global value chains (GVCs) have been significantly impacted by the US-China trade conflict. China, through its initiatives like the Belt and Road, Asian Infrastructure Investment Bank, and "Made in China 2025" policy, has challenged US dominance. The trade conflict has resulted in shifts in production locations, suppliers, and end markets, with the semiconductor industry becoming a focal point of contention. The conflict has led to a reconfiguration of GVCs, leading to both resilience and disruption.

This article explores the intersection of geopolitics, economics, and technology, offering a nuanced understanding of the US-China trade conflict's impact on the global semiconductor industry and GVCs. It discusses firms' adaptive strategies within GVCs and highlights the implications of policy decisions on these global networks.

3 Research Design

3.1 Data Source

The data used in this paper originated from investing.com [8], a well-established and widely recognized financial platform. Investing.com offers diverse data on various financial instruments covering global and regional markets. This paper extracts S&P 500 and Shanghai Composite Index (SSEC)'s past ten years of the stock price on a weekly and monthly basis. The time spent covers the stock price from 2010 to 2019, which includes the stock price during the China-US trade conflict period.

3.2 Weak Stationarity Test

In this study, the unit root, stochastic trend, and stability of the statical features of the time series are examined using the Augmented Dickey-Fuller (ADF) test. The series is stationary as opposed to having a root unit, which is the alternative hypothesis for the ADF test. The p-value of the raw data for the data in Table 1 is most certainly higher than the significance level of 0.05, indicating that there isn't enough data to rule out the null hypothesis. Regarding the first and second-order difference, the variables have a very small p-value that is close to 0, indicating strong evidence to reject the null hypothesis, and variables are likely to be stationary. For the modeling and analysis process in the data, it is better to contain stationary variables because the relationship and pattern in the data remain constant over the time series, which allows for more straightforward and reliable statistical modeling. By having trend invariance and removing trend components, the analysis would get an improved regression and a more explicit long-term relationship between the stock and its prices.

3.3 Autoregressive Integrated Moving Average (ARIMA) Model

In time series analysis, the ARIMA (AutoRegressive Integrated Moving Average) model is used to forecast and model a dependent variable's behavior based on its historical values and the values of other correlated variables. The model incorporates three critical components. The first component is autoregressive (AR). This component correlates the current value of the dependent variable with its previous values, predicated on the assumption that the current value is linearly affected by its antecedents, which suggests that future events are influenced by their historical occurrences. The integrated (I) component deals with non-stationary data, where the statistical properties, such as mean and variance, change over time. The ARIMA model applies differencing to the data to achieve a state of stationarity. The moving average (MA) component is leveraged to analyze past error terms' impact on the dependent variable's current value. The ARIMA model is made up of these three elements, and it is often written as ARIMA (p, d, q). The letters 'p' and 'q' in this notation stand for the order of the autoregressive component, 'd' stands for the quantity of differences required for stationarity, and 'p' stands for the order of the moving average component.

Table 1. Weak stationarity test.

	t	p
Raw		
Nasdaq - monthly	−3.021	0.1263
Nasdaq - weekly	−3.579	0.0317
SSEC – monthly	−2.544	0.3064
SSEC - weekly	−2.332	0.4161
1st order difference		
Nasdaq - monthly	−8.331	0.0000
Nasdaq - weekly	−16.093	0.0000
SSEC – monthly	−7.198	0.0000
SSEC - weekly	−12.870	0.0000
2nd order difference		
Nasdaq - monthly	−12.888	0.0000
Nasdaq - weekly	−26.172	0.0000
SSEC – monthly	−11.303	0.0000
SSEC - weekly	−23.443	0.0000

4 Empirical Results and Analysis

4.1 Order of ARIMA Model

The order of an ARIMA model determined by analyzing two essential tools, the Partial Autocorrelation Function (PACF) and Autocorrelation Function (ACF) plots. The autoregressive (AR) component's order (p) can be found using the PACF plot. PACF displays the relationship between the time series' most recent value and its prior values while also accounting for the impact of intermediate lags. An optimal approach to determining the order (p) is to observe when significant PACF values begin to become statistically insignificant beyond a certain lag. For Nasdaq on monthly basis, the order of AR is 5. For Nasdaq on weekly basis, the order of AR is 8. For SSEC on monthly basis, the order of AR is 4, and the order of SSEC on weekly basis is 5. The differencing operation is applied to the time series data in the Integrated (I) component of the ARIMA model. All model has an order of differencing of 2, which means the original time series has been differenced twice. The moving average (MA) component's order (q) can be found using the ACF plot. The last significant lag in the ACF plot can be used as a predictor of the order (q) for the MA component of the ARIMA model. The ACF indicates the correlation between the current value of the time series and its lagged values. For the four groups of time series data, the orders are all 1, indicating that the model incorporates one lagged error term (Fig. 1).

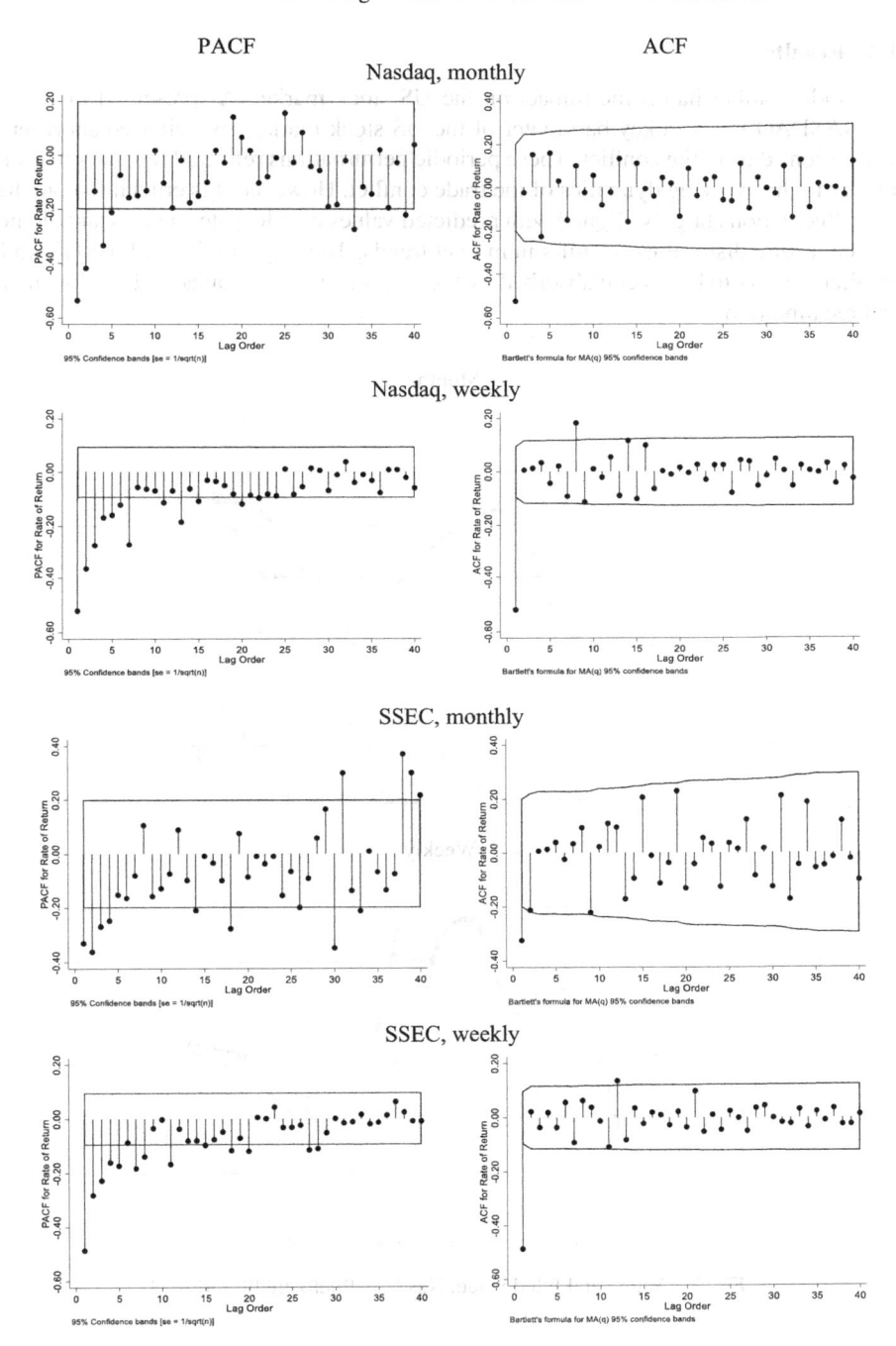

Fig. 1. PACF and ACF. Photo credit: Original

4.2 Results

The trade conflict had some impact on the US stock market. As presented in Fig. 2, the NASDAQ index, a key barometer of the US stock market, experienced short-term fluctuations during the conflict. These periodic perturbations reflected the market's sensitivity to the evolving dynamics of the trade conflict. However, it is crucial to note that these fluctuations largely aligned with predicted values on a long-term basis and did not induce lasting distortions or shifts in market trends. The impact of the China-US trade conflict appears to have been absorbed by the market's inherent capacity for adjustment and recalibration.

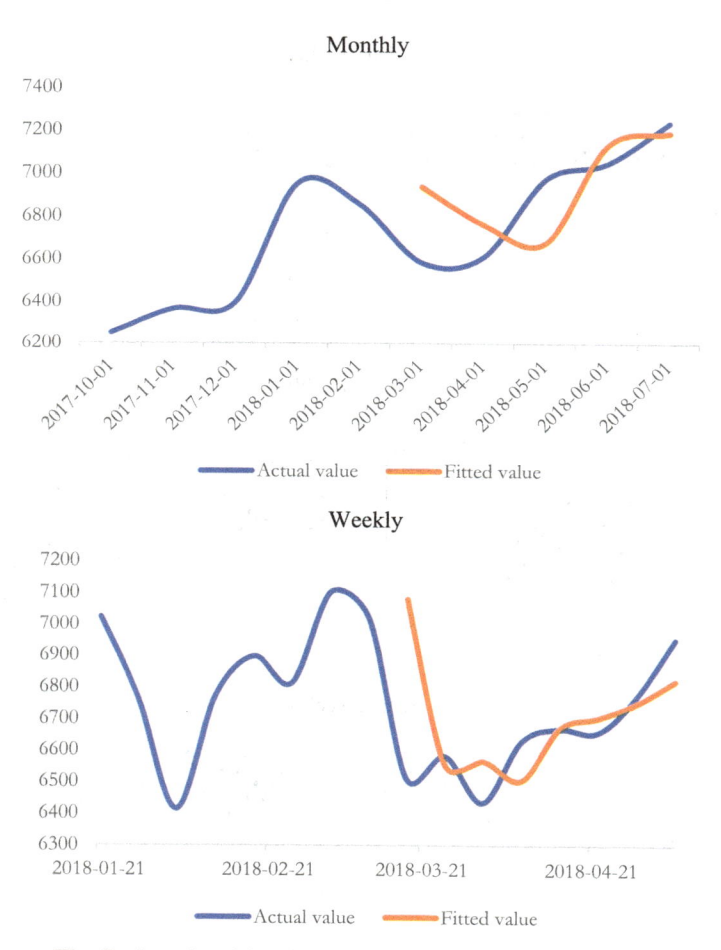

Fig. 2. Actual and fitted value, Nasdaq. Photo credit: Original

On the other hand, the China-US trade conflict has exhibited more significant effects on China's economic indicators. As evidenced in Fig. 3, a distinct divergence can be observed between the actual line, which represents the observed data, and the fitted line, which signifies the predicted values. This divergence suggests that the actual economic outcomes deviated substantially from what was anticipated, indicating a noteworthy impact of the trade conflict. More importantly, this difference doesn't appear to be a short-term anomaly, but rather an ongoing trend. This sustained divergence signals the possibility of long-term economic repercussions for China as a result of the trade conflict, a stark contrast to the more transient effects observed in the US stock market.

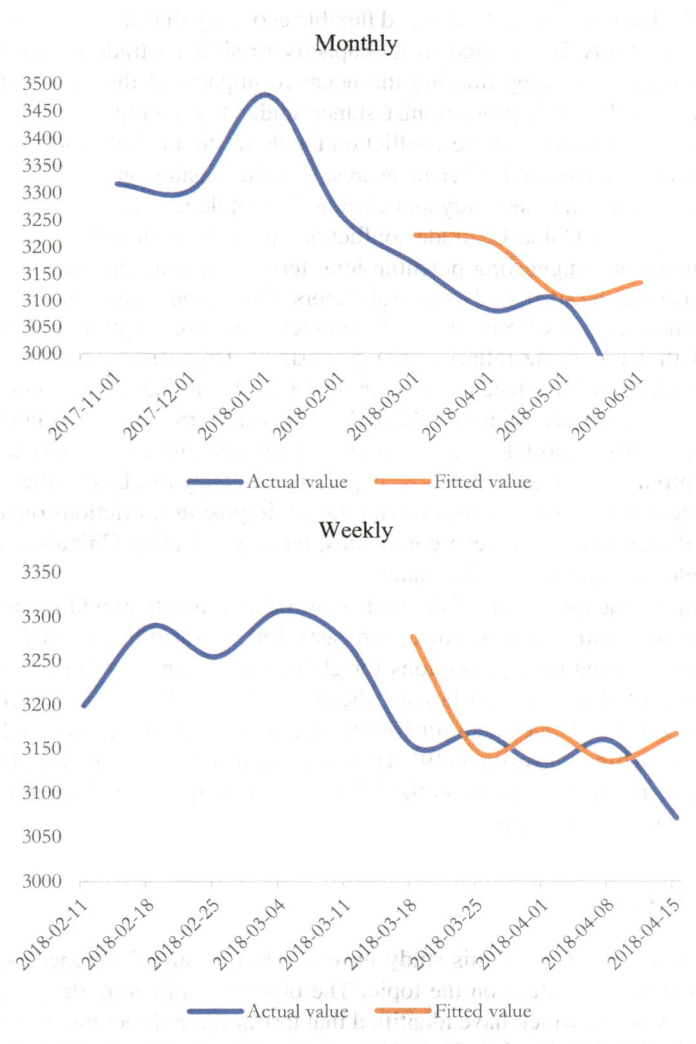

Fig. 3. Actual and fitted value, SSEC. Photo credit: Original

4.3 Analysis

The observed fluctuations in the NASDAQ index amidst the US-China trade conflict suggest the US stock market's inherent resilience and adaptability. Although the market showed short-term sensitivities to the unfolding dynamics of the trade conflict, these fluctuations largely aligned with long-term predictions, implying no significant long-term market distortions [3]. This resilience can be attributed to a few factors.

Firstly, the US has a more diverse and flexible economy that can absorb such shocks better. This flexibility is reflected in its capacity to shift its trade relations to other countries or regions, thereby diluting the negative impacts of the trade conflict with China. Secondly, the US's protectionist stance under the Trump administration may have mitigated some effects of the conflict on the domestic market, shielding domestic industries through tariffs and other measures, despite debates on the impacts of such protectionism on income inequality and chronic budget deficits [3].

Contrastingly, the China-US trade conflict had more pronounced effects on China's economic indicators, suggesting potential long-term economic repercussions [3]. This stark difference can be attributed to several factors. Firstly, the trade conflict has exposed China's dependence on the US market and its vulnerability to disruptions in bilateral trade relations. With a significant reliance on exports and foreign direct investment, China's economic model may have faced significant setbacks due to the ongoing conflict.

Secondly, the US's accusations of China's unfair trade practices, especially related to intellectual property rights (IPR), technology transfer, and innovation, have led to tariffs on Chinese products, impacting Chinese exporters adversely [5]. Lastly, the conflict has extended to technology-related issues, with the US imposing restrictions on technology transfers and certain Chinese tech companies, thereby affecting China's ambitions to ascend the global technology value chain.

Furthermore, the escalation of the trade conflict and threats of additional measures have resulted in negative global growth forecasts. International bodies such as the IMF and ADB have revised their projections for global and Asian growth downward, indicating the impact of the conflict beyond the two nations. This global uncertainty has led to weak export and sales data for China, increased investor caution, and restricted high-tech foreign direct investment [9]. Therefore, while the trade conflict's impact may be relatively minor and transient on the US market, it may pose substantial long-term challenges for China's economy.

5 Discussion

The conclusions presented in this study have similarities and differences when compared with existing literature on the topic. The observed shift in trade patterns aligns with previous studies, which have identified that tariffs can redirect trade from efficient producers, like China, to slightly less efficient ones, such as Vietnam and Mexico [10]. However, the present study extends this understanding by illustrating the US-China trade conflict's broader economic and sectoral impacts.

The findings suggest that this trade conflict does not merely disrupt the global supply chain, dampens economic growth and creates uncertainties that affect investor confidence and business decisions [3, 6]. These insights provide a comprehensive analysis of the multidimensional impacts of the trade conflict, extending beyond the traditional focus on trade imbalances.

For policymakers, the research underscores the potential for long-term damage to domestic and global economies from protracted trade conflicts. Policymakers should consider the direct effects of tariffs on the targeted sectors and the indirect consequences on investor confidence, global supply chains, and economic growth. They may need to consider collaborative and multilateral solutions to address the root causes of trade disputes rather than escalating tit-for-tat tariff impositions.

From an investor's perspective, this study offers valuable insights into the potential risks and uncertainties brought about by the trade conflict. It suggests that investors must be cautious and strategic in their decision-making, considering the likelihood of ongoing volatility and the possibility of firms changing their production, supplier, or market focus [10]. Moreover, the findings highlight the need for investors to consider a sector-level understanding of the effects due to the varied impacts across different industries [11].

This research provides an in-depth understanding of the multifaceted implications of trade conflicts, shedding light on the dynamic adjustments in global trade patterns and the broader socioeconomic consequences. It highlights the need for further research into the strategies firms adopt to navigate the changing trade environment and the impacts of these strategies on global supply chains and economic growth.

6 Conclusion

In conclusion, this research reveals that the trade conflict between the United States and China has far-reaching impacts on the financial landscape of both countries and the global economy. The significant findings indicate that the conflict influences the stock markets differently in these two nations.

Short-term fluctuations were observed during the trade conflict for the U.S. stock market, represented by the Nasdaq index. However, these oscillations aligned closely with long-term predicted values, implying the market's inherent resilience and capacity to adjust and recalibrate in response to external shocks. This demonstrates the robustness of the U.S. stock market and its ability to absorb and recover from the impacts of the trade conflict in the long term.

On the contrary, China's stock market, represented by the SSEC, displayed a considerable deviation between actual and predicted values during the conflict period. This discrepancy indicates the significant impacts of the trade conflict on China's economy. Notably, these effects are not short-lived but indicative of a persistent trend, suggesting potential long-term economic repercussions for China.

Therefore, this analysis underlines the complex dynamics and diverse impacts of the China-U.S. trade conflict on different national markets. It reinforces the importance of geopolitical events in shaping economic and financial landscapes and offers insights for policymakers, investors, and businesses navigating these changes. The results serve as a reminder of the interconnectedness of global financial markets and the need for careful consideration and strategic management of geopolitical risks and events.

References

1. Kim, M.-H.: A real driver of US–China trade conflict: the Sino–US competition for global hegemony and its implications for the future. Int. Trade Polit. Dev. **3**(1), 30–40 (2019)
2. Bekkers, E., Schroeter, S.: An economic analysis of the US China trade conflict, WTO Staff Working Paper, No. ERSD-2020-04, World Trade Organization (WTO), Geneva (2020)
3. Kwan, C.H.: The China–US trade war: deep-rooted causes, shifting focus and uncertain prospects. Asian Econ. Policy Rev. **15**, 55–72 (2020)
4. Kim, S., Margalit, Y.: Tariffs as electoral weapons: the political geography of the US–China trade war. Int. Organ. **75**(1), 1–38 (2021)
5. Bown, C.P.: How the United States marched the semiconductor industry into its trade war with China. SSRN (2021)
6. Pasrk, S.: Trade conflict between the U.S. and China: what are the impacts on the Chinese economy? Int. Organ. Res. J. **15**(2), 153–168 (2020). (in English). https://doi.org/10.17323/19967845-2020-02-10
7. Gereffi, G., Lim, H.-C., Lee, J.: Trade policies, firm strategies, and adaptive reconfigurations of Global value chains. J. Int. Bus. Policy (2021). https://doi.org/10.1057/s42214-021-00102-z
8. Investing Homepage. Investing.com
9. Carvalho, M., Azevedo, A., Massuquetti, A.: Emerging countries and the effects of the trade war between Us and China. MDPI (2019, May 13). https://www.mdpi.com/2227-7099/7/2/45
10. The Economist Newspaper. (n.d.-a). New research counts the costs of the Sino-american trade war. The Economist. https://www.economist.com/finance-and-economics/2022/01/01/new-research-counts-the-costs-of-the-sino-american-trade-war
11. The impact of trade conflict on developing Asia (EWP 566). (n.d.). https://www.adb.org/sites/default/files/publication/471496/ewp-566-impact-trade-conflict-asia.pdf

Financial Analysis and Strategic Forecast of Tesla, Inc.

Xiaoke Wang[✉]

College of Arts and Science, New York University, New York, NY 10003, USA
xw2212@nyu.edu

Abstract. This report provides a comprehensive analysis of Tesla, one of the leading companies in the electric vehicle industry. The report begins with an introduction, providing a company description, an industry overview, and recent events related to Tesla. The accounting analysis section focuses on key aspects such as revenue recognition, inventory valuation, operating lease vehicles, digital assets, and solar energy. It examines Tesla's financial statements and accounting practices to evaluate their accuracy and transparency. The performance evaluation section assesses Tesla's liquidity, solvency, efficiency, and profitability. Financial ratios are computed and compared with selected competitors to provide insights into Tesla's financial health and performance. Based on the findings, a forecast is presented for Tesla's future performance, considering the company's growth strategies, such as increasing manufacturing capacity and expanding into new markets. The report also discusses potential impacts on Tesla from industry trends, including recent policies related to electric vehicles. Overall, the report concludes that Tesla has demonstrated strong financial performance and market dominance in its industry. It focuses on innovation, expanding production capacity, and global expansion positions it for continued success. However, investors are advised to closely monitor industry developments, competitive pressures, and changing policies to make informed investment decisions. At the same time, this report provides valuable insights for investors, industry analysts, and stakeholders interested in understanding Tesla's fundamental analysis and its potential trajectory in the coming years.

Keywords: Accounting Analysis · Performance Evaluation · Strategic Forecast

1 Introduction

Tesla Inc. Was established in 2003 and has since become a leader in the electric vehicle (EV) sector, revolutionizing the automobile industry around the world with its cutting-edge technology and environmentally friendly energy sources. By delving into Tesla's annual report and employing a comprehensive fundamental analysis to evaluate various aspects of Tesla's financial performance, this report will predict the company's prospects for the future. Considering factors such as revenue recognition, inventory valuation, and performance evaluation metrics related to liquidity, solvency, efficiency, and profitability, we will assess Tesla's financial health and provide insights into its future outlook.

Moreover, we will compare Tesla with its main competitors on key performance ratios and predict how Tesla will be affected in the future. Through this analysis, investors and stakeholders can gain a better understanding of Tesla's position in the electric vehicle industry and make informed decisions regarding their investments. As a result, investors are recommended to hold onto Tesla stocks given the company's strong financial performance, growth prospects, and position as a market leader in the electric vehicle industry. Also, diversification of investment portfolios, monitoring industry trends and policies, and conducting ongoing analysis is essential to make informed investment decisions.

Located in Palo Alto, California, Tesla, Inc. is a well-known American manufacturer of electric vehicles and clean energy. The business creates, develops, produces, and markets solar energy systems, electric vehicles, and devices for energy storage. The Model S, Model 3, Model X, and Model Y are some of Tesla's most well-known vehicle models, and each has seen substantial growth in popularity and market acceptance. Tesla's strategic objective goes beyond just making cars; the corporation wants to hasten the global switch to renewable energy. In addition to making electric automobiles, Tesla also provides energy storage systems with its Powerwall and Powerpack products as well as solar energy solutions through its SolarCity subsidiary. This diversification allows Tesla to establish a comprehensive ecosystem of sustainable energy products and services [1].

The automotive industry is undergoing a transformative shift towards electrification and sustainable mobility. With the increasing global concerns over climate change and the need for reducing greenhouse gas emissions, governments and consumers alike are pushing for cleaner and more efficient transportation solutions. In this transformation, Tesla has been at the fore, leading the EV sector and upending conventional automakers [2]. An increase in consumer demand for environmentally friendly transportation options, government incentives, and technology improvements have all contributed to the tremendous expansion of the worldwide electric vehicle market in recent years. According to Britannica, electric vehicle sales accounted for 4.2% of total global car sales in 2020, and this figure is projected to rise to 14% by 2025 [3]. Tesla has positioned itself as a market leader in this growing industry, capturing a substantial market share and expanding its presence globally [4].

Tesla's recent annual report provides insights into the company's performance and key events that have shaped its operations. It is essential to consider notable developments that may have influenced Tesla's financial position and outlook. One significant recent event is Tesla's expansion into new markets. The company has been actively increasing its production capacity and establishing Gigafactories worldwide to meet the growing demand for its electric vehicles. Notably, Tesla established its Gigafactory in Shanghai, China, which significantly increased the company's footprint in the largest automobile market in the world [1]. A notable achievement for the corporation was also made when Tesla was included in the S&P 500 index in December 2020. This recognition further enhanced Tesla's reputation and credibility in the financial markets and attracted a broader investor base. To promote innovation and keep a competitive edge, Tesla has also been making significant investments in research and development (R&D) [5]. The company's ongoing advancements in battery technology and autonomous driving capabilities have garnered attention and positioned Tesla as an industry leader in terms of technological innovation.

2 Accounting Analysis

2.1 Revenue Recognition

Revenue recognition is a critical aspect of Tesla's financial analysis as it provides insights into how the company records its revenue from different sources. Tesla's revenue recognition policies are disclosed in its financial statements and footnotes, shedding light on the timing and method used to recognize revenue. Tesla's 10-K report for the fiscal year ended December 31, 2022 states that the company primarily records revenue when there is convincing evidence of an agreement, the goods have been delivered or the services have been rendered, the price is fixed or determinable, and the likelihood of collection is reassuringly high [1].

For automotive sales, Tesla recognizes revenue upon the delivery or transfer of control to the customer, which generally occurs at the time of vehicle delivery. Revenue from energy generation and storage products, including solar energy systems and energy storage products, is recognized when control transfers to the customer, typically upon system energization or completion of installation. Services revenue, such as maintenance and software updates, is recognized over the period when the services are performed. Tesla also recognizes revenue related to Full Self-Driving (FSD) features and upgrades. Revenue from FSD features is recognized when the features are made available to customers, as long as all other revenue recognition criteria are met. If features are delivered on a standalone basis, the revenue is allocated between the vehicle and the FSD features. The portion attributable to the FSD features is recognized over the estimated period during which the features are expected to be provided.

Understanding Tesla's revenue recognition policies allows stakeholders to assess the company's revenue growth, the timing of revenue recognition, and the impact of potential changes in those policies on financial performance. It also provides insights into the reliability and sustainability of Tesla's revenue streams.

2.2 Inventory Valuation

Calculating Tesla's cost of goods sold (COGS) and carrying value of its inventory on the company's balance sheet and income statement both depend on accurate inventory valuation. According to Tesla's financial filings, the weighted-average cost technique is used to evaluate its inventories. Based on the average price of all comparable items in stock, the cost of inventory is determined using this method. The majority of the raw materials, works-in-progress, and finished commodities in Tesla's inventory are connected to the manufacture of its electric automobiles. The carrying value of inventory includes direct material costs, direct labor costs, and allocated overhead. Based on projections of future demand and market conditions, inventory is considered to be impaired if its carrying value exceeds its net realizable value.

In recent years, Tesla's inventory levels have increased substantially, reflecting the company's efforts to meet the growing demand for its electric vehicles. However, managing inventory levels is crucial to avoid excessive carrying costs and obsolescence risks. Stakeholders should keep a careful eye on Tesla's inventory turnover ratio, which evaluates the effectiveness of inventory management by determining how rapidly inventory is sold or used in production. Additionally, fluctuations in the value of inventory may impact Tesla's financial statements. Changes in raw material costs, currency exchange rates, or unexpected disruptions in the supply chain can affect the valuation of inventory and consequently impact COGS and gross margins. Analyzing Tesla's inventory valuation practices and understanding the factors influencing inventory levels and costs provides valuable insights into the company's operational efficiency and profitability.

2.3 Operating Lease Vehicles

In addition to vehicle sales, Tesla offers customers the option to lease vehicles through operating lease arrangements. Operating lease vehicles are recorded as assets on Tesla's balance sheet and generate lease revenue over the lease term. These lease arrangements allow customers to use Tesla vehicles for a specified period, usually ranging from two to four years, while Tesla retains ownership of the vehicles. In order to reflect the manner in which the lessee receives the benefit of the lease, Tesla records lease income on a straight-line basis for the course of the lease. The revenue recognized for operating lease vehicles is presented as lease revenue in Tesla's financial statements. This revenue contributes to Tesla's overall revenue and should be considered when evaluating the company's financial performance.

Analyzing Tesla's operating lease vehicles can provide insights into the company's customer demand, leasing strategies, and revenue stability. It is important to assess the growth and profitability of the operating lease business segment, as well as any potential risks associated with lessee defaults, residual value uncertainties, or changes in lease accounting standards.

2.4 Digital Assets

Tesla's involvement in digital assets is an area that requires attention in the accounting analysis. Tesla has made large investments in digital assets like cryptocurrencies even though the firm is best known for its electric cars and other sustainable energy goods. In Tesla's annual report, it is essential to examine any disclosures related to digital assets, including the recognition, measurement, and valuation of these assets. Tesla's accounting treatment of digital assets may depend on the specific nature of the assets held, such as Bitcoin, and the purpose of holding these assets, whether for investment or operational reasons.

Understanding how Tesla accounts for digital assets is crucial as it may impact the company's financial statements and overall financial performance. Changes in the valuation of digital assets can have significant implications for Tesla's balance sheet, particularly in terms of asset values and potential impairments. It is important to analyze Tesla's disclosures and assess the risks and opportunities associated with digital asset investments.

2.5 Solar Energy

Tesla's involvement in the solar energy sector is another aspect to consider in the accounting analysis. Through its subsidiary SolarCity, Tesla offers solar energy solutions, including solar panels and related energy storage products. Analyzing Tesla's accounting practices in the solar energy segment provides insights into the company's revenue recognition, cost allocation, and profitability in this business line. Similar to the revenue recognition policies discussed earlier, revenue from solar energy products is recognized when control transfers to the customer, typically upon system energization or completion of installation. Understanding the revenue recognition criteria specific to solar energy products helps evaluate the revenue growth and sustainability of Tesla's solar energy business.

Additionally, assessing the cost structure and profitability of Tesla's solar energy segment is essential. This includes analyzing the cost of solar panels, installation costs, and associated expenses. Evaluating the profitability of solar energy products allows stakeholders to assess the long-term viability of Tesla's diversification into the clean energy market.

3 Performance Evaluation

This section will calculate some key ratios and evaluate Tesla's financial performance. At the same time, we will assess the performance of Tesla's main competitors with similar market capitalization, including Ford Motor Company, General Motors, and NIO Inc. [6]. With the comparison results, we can analyze how Tesla performed in its market.

3.1 Liquidity

As shown in Table 1, Tesla exhibits a strong liquidity position with a current ratio of 2.26. This shows that the business has enough liquid assets to pay its short-term obligations. Additionally, Tesla's fast ratio of 1.90, which separates current assets from inventory, demonstrates a good capacity to satisfy short-term obligations without primarily relying on inventory conversion. Ford Motor Company, in contrast, displays a fast ratio of 1.03 and a current ratio that is noticeably lower at 1.20. These numbers show that Tesla has a slightly worse liquidity position. The fast ratio of Ford Motor Company indicates a moderate ability to satisfy short-term obligations without largely relying on inventory, even though it keeps enough current assets to cover current liabilities.

Similar to Ford Motor Company, General Motors has a 1.10 current ratio and a 0.90 quick ratio. These numbers suggest a slightly poorer liquidity position in comparison to Ford Motor Company and Tesla. Although General Motors has enough current assets to satisfy its liabilities for the present period, its quick ratio points to a reduced capacity for meeting obligations for the immediate future without resorting extensively to inventory conversion. The current ratio for NIO Inc. is 1.29, and the quick ratio is 0.85. According to these measures, Tesla and Ford Motor Company are in a slightly worse situation than General Motors when it comes to liquidity, while Tesla and Ford are in a somewhat better position. Although NIO Inc. Shows that it has enough current assets to cover its

Table 1. Liquidity ratios of Tesla and its competitors [7].

Company name	Current ratio	Quick Ratio
Tesla	2.26	1.90
Ford Motor Company	1.20	1.03
General Motors (GuruFocus, 2023)	1.10	0.90
NIO Inc	1.29	0.85

current liabilities, its quick ratio indicates that it may not be able to satisfy its short-term obligations without resorting extensively to inventory.

Considering these liquidity ratios, Tesla holds advantages compared with its competitors, exhibiting a robust liquidity position with a higher current ratio and quick ratio. This shows that Tesla has a higher ability to efficiently manage liquidity risks and meet short-term financial obligations. It is important to keep in mind, nevertheless, that in order to provide a complete picture of a company's overall financial performance and health, liquidity analysis should be carried out in conjunction with a thorough assessment of other financial and non-financial elements.

3.2 Solvency

The debt-to-equity ratio calculates how much money a company receives from creditors as opposed to shareholders for funding. A lower debt-to-equity ratio shows that more of the company's assets are financed by shareholders' equity, which lowers the risk of financial instability. The interest coverage ratio, which evaluates the company's capability to make interest payments on outstanding debt, is another measure of solvency.

Table 2. Solvency ratios of Tesla and its competitors.

Company name	Debt-to-Equity Ratio	Interest Coverage Ratio
Tesla	0.07	71.45
Ford Motor Company	3.22	21.1
General Motors	2.61	33.8
NIO Inc	0.97	−28.3

In Table 2, Tesla has a substantially lower level of debt relative to its equity, with a debt-to-equity ratio of 0.07. This suggests a cautious capital structure and decreased likelihood of financial distress. Moreover, Tesla exhibits a robust interest coverage ratio of 71.45, implying a substantial ability to cover interest expenses with its EBIT. The high interest coverage ratio reinforces Tesla's capacity to service its interest payments comfortably and indicates a strong solvency position.

On the other hand, Ford Motor Company presents a higher debt-to-equity ratio of 3.22, indicating a larger proportion of financing provided by creditors compared to shareholders. This suggests a higher financial risk and potential vulnerability to changes in the economic environment. Although Ford Motor Company's debt-to-equity ratio is higher than Tesla's, it remains within a range that is commonly observed in the automotive industry. The interest coverage ratio of 21.1 indicates that Ford Motor Company generates sufficient earnings to cover its interest expenses, albeit at a relatively lower level compared to Tesla. Similarly, General Motors exhibits a debt-to-equity ratio of 2.61, reflecting a higher reliance on debt financing in comparison to equity. This poses a greater financial risk and may increase the company's vulnerability to economic downturns or changes in interest rates. However, General Motors maintains a relatively higher interest coverage ratio of 33.8, suggesting a solid ability to meet its interest obligations.

NIO Inc., in contrast, exhibits a debt-to-equity ratio that is 0.97, which indicates a moderate degree of debt in comparison to equity. This reflects a conservative capital structure and suggests a lower risk of financial instability. However, NIO Inc. Reports a negative interest coverage ratio of -28.3, suggesting challenges in generating sufficient earnings to cover interest expenses. The company's capacity to pay interest is put in doubt by this negative ratio. While a lower interest coverage ratio generally indicates a weak solvency position, a comprehensive evaluation requires considering other factors, including debt maturity schedules, profitability, and cash flow generation.

With a substantially lower debt-to-equity ratio and a greater interest coverage ratio than its rivals, Tesla stands out among its peers overall and demonstrates a strong solvency position. Ford Motor Company and General Motors report higher debt-to-equity ratios, implying relatively higher financial risks, but maintain acceptable interest coverage ratios. NIO Inc., while maintaining a conservative debt-to-equity ratio, faces challenges with its negative interest coverage ratio, suggesting a need for improved profitability and cash flow generation to meet interest obligations.

3.3 Efficiency

Tesla, with an asset turnover ratio of 0.99, demonstrates a moderate efficiency in generating sales from its total assets. This ratio suggests that Tesla generates approximately $0.99 in revenue for every dollar of assets employed. Although the asset turnover ratio is not particularly high, it is important to consider that the automotive industry typically requires significant capital investment in assets, which can impact this ratio. Moreover, Tesla exhibits a relatively high inventory turnover ratio of 4.72, indicating efficient management of its inventory and a faster rate of inventory conversion into sales. Ford Motor Company, General Motors, and NIO Inc. All show lower asset turnover ratios compared to Tesla. Ford Motor Company has an asset turnover ratio of 0.62, indicating a lower efficiency in generating sales from its total assets compared to Tesla. Similarly, General Motors and NIO Inc. Report asset turnover ratios of 0.59 and 0.61, respectively, suggesting a relatively lower revenue generation from their asset base.

Regarding the inventory turnover ratio in Table 3, all competitors demonstrate higher ratios compared to Tesla. Ford Motor Company, General Motors, and NIO Inc. Exhibit inventory turnover ratios of 9.55, 9.58, and 2.08, respectively. These figures imply that these companies have more frequent inventory turnover and a faster rate of converting inventory into sales compared to Tesla. However, it is essential to consider that efficiency ratios can vary across industries, business models, and product offerings. The automotive

Table 3. Efficiency ratios of Tesla and its competitors.

Company name	Asset Turnover Ratio	Inventory Turnover Ratio
Tesla	0.99	4.72
Ford Motor Company	0.62	9.55
General Motors	0.59	9.58
NIO Inc	0.61	2.08

industry, in particular, may have variations in asset turnover and inventory turnover ratios due to different production and sales strategies.

In conclusion, Tesla's efficiency ratios indicate a moderate efficiency in asset utilization and a relatively higher efficiency in managing inventory compared to its competitors. While Tesla's asset turnover ratio is not particularly high, its inventory turnover ratio demonstrates effective inventory management practices. However, Ford Motor Company and General Motors exhibit higher inventory turnover ratios, indicating a more efficient management of their inventories.

3.4 Profitability

As Table 4 shown, Tesla with a gross profit margin of $20.853 billion, showcases a robust ability to generate profits after accounting for COGS. This indicates effective management of production costs and pricing strategies. Furthermore, Tesla's operating profit margin of 15.33% demonstrates the company's ability to generate operating profits from each dollar of revenue after considering both COGS and operating expenses. Moreover, Tesla's return on assets (ROA) of 15.18% signifies its efficiency in utilizing its assets to generate profits.

Ford Motor Company, on the other hand, reports a gross profit margin of $25.025 billion, which is higher than Tesla's. However, its operating profit margin of 4.25% and ROA of 1.15% indicate relatively lower profitability and efficiency in asset utilization compared to Tesla. These figures suggest that Ford Motor Company faces challenges in generating operating profits and maximizing profitability from its asset base. General Motors presents a gross profit margin of $20.981 billion, which is comparable to Tesla. However, General Motors reports an operating profit margin of 7.21% and ROA of 3.61%, indicating a moderate profitability level and relatively better efficiency in utilizing its assets compared to Ford Motor Company. NIO Inc. Demonstrates a lower gross profit margin of $7.135 billion, indicating a comparatively lower ability to generate profits from its revenue after considering COGS. Additionally, NIO Inc.'s operating profit margin of 4.1% and negative ROA of -20.0% suggest challenges in generating operating profits and a lack of efficiency in utilizing its assets effectively.

In conclusion, Tesla emerges as the leader among its competitors in terms of profitability ratios, showcasing a strong gross profit margin, operating profit margin, and positive return on assets. While Ford Motor Company and General Motors exhibit comparable gross profit margins, they lag behind Tesla in terms of operating profit margin

Table 4. Profitability ratios of Tesla and its competitors.

Company name	Gross Profit Margin (for the twelve months ending March 31, 2023)	Operating Profit Margin	Return on assets (ROA)
Tesla	$20.853B	15.33%	15.18%
Ford Motor Company	$25.025B	4.25%	1.15%
General Motors	$20.981B	7.21%	3.61%
NIO Inc	$7.135B	4.1%	−20.0%

and ROA. NIO Inc. Faces challenges with its lower profitability ratios and negative ROA, suggesting a need for improvement in generating profits and optimizing asset utilization.

4 Strategic Forecast

The last section has learned a great deal about the financial health and operational effectiveness of Tesla by examining the company's performance in the areas of liquidity, solvency, profitability, and efficiency. Based on the assessment of these key factors, we can now provide a strategic forecast for Tesla.

4.1 Overview of Tesla's Performance in 2022

In the last year, Tesla has performed well across a number of important financial metrics. The company has a strong ability to meet short-term obligations and efficiently manage liquidity risks, as shown by its liquidity position, which is demonstrated by its current ratio of 2.26 and a quick ratio of 1.90. Tesla's solvency ratios also show a strong financial position and the capacity to pay off long-term debt, with a high interest coverage ratio of 71.45 and a low debt-to-equity ratio of 0.07. Tesla has a gross profit margin of $20.853 billion, an operating profit margin of 15.33%, and a return on assets (ROA) of 15.18%, all of which are highly profitable metrics that demonstrate the company's capacity to turn a profit from operations and make efficient use of its assets. Moreover, Tesla's efficiency ratios demonstrate a moderate level of asset utilization and efficient management of inventory, with an asset turnover ratio of 0.99 and an inventory turnover ratio of 4.72.

4.2 Forecast for the Next 2–3 Years

Tesla's development strategies and growth plans are expected to play a significant role in shaping its future performance. One key driver for Tesla's future success is its focus on increasing manufacturing capacity. By expanding production facilities and optimizing production processes, Tesla aims to achieve economies of scale and long-term cost savings. The increased manufacturing capacity will enable Tesla to meet the growing demand for its electric vehicles and other energy products, ultimately boosting its revenue and profitability. In addition to expanding manufacturing capacity, Tesla has been actively investing in R&D to enhance its product offerings and technology. The company's focus on innovations such as autonomous driving, battery technology, and renewable energy solutions positions it well for future growth and market leadership. These investments in R&D are expected to further differentiate Tesla from its competitors and strengthen its competitive advantage.

Furthermore, Tesla's foray into new markets, including China and Europe, presents significant growth opportunities. By expanding its presence globally, Tesla can tap into a larger customer base and gain market share in regions with favorable policies and incentives for electric vehicles [8]. This expansion strategy aligns with the increasing global focus on sustainability and the transition towards cleaner energy alternatives, creating a favorable market environment for Tesla's products.

4.3 Impact of Industry Trends

Tesla's performance and future prospects are also influenced by broader industry trends and policies. Recent policies and regulations promoting clean energy and electric mobility, such as stricter emission standards and government incentives, have contributed to the increasing adoption of electric vehicles [3]. As governments worldwide push for greener transportation solutions, Tesla stands to benefit from the growing demand for its electric vehicles and clean energy solutions. However, changes in government policies, such as shifts in subsidies or the imposition of tariffs, could impact Tesla's competitive position and profitability in certain markets. Another industry trend worth noting is the increasing competition in the electric vehicle market. Despite the fact that Tesla now has a sizable market share, both seasoned automakers and recent entrants are stepping up their attempts to challenge Tesla's hegemony [9]. As competition intensifies, Tesla will need to continually innovate, optimize costs, and maintain its reputation for technological excellence to retain its market leadership.

Furthermore, the availability and cost of key raw materials for electric vehicle production, such as lithium, nickel, and cobalt, can significantly impact Tesla's manufacturing operations and profitability. Any disruptions or price fluctuations in the supply chain for these critical materials could pose challenges to Tesla's production and potentially increase costs. In addition to industry trends, geopolitical factors and trade policies can also have an impact on Tesla's operations. Changes in trade agreements, tariffs, or restrictions on international trade could affect Tesla's global supply chain and increase costs. It is crucial for the company to closely monitor geopolitical developments and adapt its strategies accordingly to mitigate potential risks.

5 Conclusion

In conclusion, Tesla has showcased strong liquidity with a comfortable current ratio and quick ratio, indicating its ability to meet short-term obligations. The company's solvency ratios highlight a conservative capital structure and a robust ability to service long-term debt obligations. Furthermore, Tesla has demonstrated favorable profitability ratios, including a healthy gross profit margin, operating profit margin, and return on assets. The efficiency ratios indicate a moderate level of asset utilization and effective inventory management. Looking ahead, Tesla's growth strategies, including increasing manufacturing capacity, investing in R&D, and expanding into new markets, position the company for future success. These initiatives, coupled with the industry's growing focus on sustainability and government policies supporting electric vehicles, create a favorable environment for Tesla's growth.

This analysis provides the following recommendations for investors: First, considering Tesla's strong financial performance, growth prospects, and the company's position as a market leader in the electric vehicle industry, holding onto Tesla stocks could be a viable option. The company's consistent innovation, expanding production capacity, and global presence provide a foundation for future growth. Also, while Tesla has exhibited strong performance, it is wise for investors to maintain a diversified portfolio. Investing in a range of industries and companies can help mitigate risks associated with individual stock performance. Moreover, as the electric vehicle industry evolves, investors should stay updated on industry trends, changes in government policies, and emerging competition. This will enable them to assess potential risks and opportunities and make informed investment decisions. Additionally, investors should regularly monitor Tesla's financial reports, industry developments, and market conditions to make informed investment decisions. This will help them stay abreast of any changes that may impact Tesla's performance and adjust their investment strategies accordingly.

References

1. Tesla Official Website. https://www.tesla.com/. Accessed 27 May 2023
2. Statista. Automotive Industry. https://www.statista.com/topics/1487/automotive-industry/. Accessed 27 May 2023
3. Liu, J.-H., Meng, Z.: Innovation model analysis of new energy vehicles: taking toyota, tesla and BYD as an example. Procedia Eng. **174**, 965–972 (2017)
4. Tesla, Inc. (TSLA) - Financials. Yahoo Finance. https://finance.yahoo.com/quote/TSLA/financials/. Accessed 27 May 2023
5. Tesla, Inc. (2022) Form 10-K. U.S. Securities and Exchange Commission. https://www.sec.gov/Archives/edgar/data/1318605/000095017023001409/tsla-20221231.htm. Accessed 27 May 2023
6. Who Are Tesla's (TSLA) Main Competitors? Investopedia. https://www.investopedia.com/ask/answers/120314/who-are-teslas-tsla-main-competitors.asp#toc-teslas-competitors. Accessed 27 May 2023
7. Lalithchandraa, B.N., Rajendhiran, N.: Liquidity ratio: an important financial metrics. Turk. J. Comput. Math. Educ. **12**(2), 1113–1114 (2021)
8. Yan, J.: BYD and Tesla's competitive advantages and future development prospects. BCP Bus. Manag. **18**, 442–450 (2022). https://doi.org/10.54691/bcpbm.v18i.583
9. IEA (2023), Global EV Outlook 2023, IEA, Paris. https://www.iea.org/reports/global-ev-outlook-2023. License: CC BY 4.0

Mechanisms and Strategies of Smart Governance for Improving Urban Resilience

Jianhang Du[1(✉)], Yongheng Hu[2], and Longzheng Du[2]

[1] University of Finance and Economics Mongolia, Ulaanbaatar 13381, Mongolia
dlz4305@163.com

[2] Zhejiang International Studies University, Hangzhou 310023, China

Abstract. This study employs panel models to analyze the regression outcomes derived from panel data of 29 key cities spanning 2014 to 2020. Meanwhile, it investigates the impact paths of smart governance to enhance urban resilience. The findings in the study include: (1) Smart governance has improved the social, economic, and infrastructure resilience of cities through the application of information technology. Additionally, it has enhanced the social and economic resilience of cities through e-governance. (2) Information technology has a negative impact on environmental resilience. (3) E-government has a significantly adverse effect on infrastructure resilience, while almost no impact on environmental resilience.

Keywords: Smart governance · Urban resilience · Sustainability

1 Introduction

Urbanization is developing rapidly worldwide [1]. Its acceleration is accompanied by ecological damage, environmental pollution, traffic jams, and other problems, which impact the complex and open system repeatedly. So cities are revealed to be more vulnerable [2], and they urgently need to improve their resilience to respond to various uncertain shocks and achieve sustainable development effectively [3]. The stagnation of the sustainable development goals (SDGs) stems from the tension and challenges from economic growth, social equality, and environmental performance [4–6]. Traditional production factors such as labor, land, and capital are positively correlated with the economic dimension, but not strongly associated with the social and environmental dimensions; while smart governance is positively correlated with all dimensions of urban sustainability [2].

The concept of smart governance is consistent with that of smart city, which makes extensive use of ICT to optimize resource utilization and promote sustainable development of economy, environmental protection and society [7, 8]. Kitchin [9] revealed two main ideas for smart cities: (1) Smart cities should use new thinking paradigm to do everything related to governance and economy. (2) Smart cities are based on big data and ICT.

Smart governance can be divided into two categories according to whether it is based on digital technology. One is regarded as wise or smart governance, which mainly contains the meaning of open and democratic governance, and has nothing to do with big data and ICT [7]; the other on smart governance is based on ICT application and digital technology innovation [8]. At present, we still know little about the environmental, social and economic impacts of ICT-enabled governance [10], especially in China where digital technology is developing rapidly. So this is taken as the research topic of this paper.

The significance of this study on the mechanisms by which smart governance enhances urban resilience are as follows: Scholars at home and abroad have been studying the relationship between smart cities and urban resilience. However, research specifically focusing on the paths through which smart governance influences urban resilience has not been explored. Therefore, analyzing the mechanisms through which smart governance enhances urban resilience is of great significance for Chinese cities in the digital economy era to achieve urban resilience.

2 Empirical Analysis of the Mechanisms

2.1 Model Setting

This study employs a panel model to test the proposed framework. The sample consists of 29 key cities selected from the 2014–2020 survey report on the development of e-government services by provincial governments and key cities in China. The collected panel data are analyzed using the following model:

$$Ur_{it} = \beta_0 + \beta_1 smartGov + \beta_2 X_{it} + \mu_i + v_t + u_{it} \tag{1}$$

where i stands for the city; t for the time; Ur_{it} for the urban resilience index with four dimensions expressed by four indices. $SmartGov_{it}$ defining smart governance, is a comprehensive expression of two explanatory variables. X_{it} represents a set of control variables; μ_i the individual factor; v_t the time factor; u_{it} the error term. In this study, separate regressions are conducted for the two independent variables and the four dependent variables. If the regression coefficients are significantly positive, then the independent variables have a promoting effect on the dependent variables, meaning smart governance enhances a specific aspect of urban resilience. Conversely, if the coefficients are not significant, then the desired effect is not achieved.

2.2 Description of the Variables

Explained Variable. The explained variable in this study is the level of urban resilience, which is measured using the urban resilience index, encompassing four dimensions: ecological resilience, economic resilience, social resilience, and infrastructure resilience. This study adopts a set of indices referenced from relevant studies [2]. The dimensions of economy, society, environment, and infrastructure constitute the indicator system for measuring urban resilience. Using relevant data from the National Bureau of Statistics of China, these four indices are expressed by the rate of harmless treatment of household garbage, regional GDP, total retail sales of social consumer goods, and the number of hospitals and healthcare clinics.

Core Explanatory Variable. This study proposes an evaluation indicator system for smart governance, emphasizing the role of smartness and collaboration in achieving social objectives in urban governance. It highlights the importance of achieving a balance between urban economy, environment, and society to achieve sustainable development. The core explanatory variable is smart governance, divided into two dimensions: EGDI and information and communication technology (ICT). Data are sourced from the National Bureau of Statistics of China and China E-Government Network. For the e-government development index, relevant data are from the research report on the development of e-government service levels in Chinese provincial governments and key cities. Three indices, namely fixed telephone users, international internet users, and employment in information transmission, computer services, and software industries, are selected for the ICT index, synthesized by using the entropy weighting method (Table 1).

Table 1. Evaluation index system of smart governance.

	Primary indices	Secondary indices	Interpretation of secondary indices
Smart governance	EGDI	Index of online service effectiveness	They are reflective of the level of administrative services provided by the local government department in terms of open collaboration and efficient interaction
		Index of online transaction popularity	
		Index of service completeness	
		Index of service coverage	
		Index of service guidelines accuracy	
	ICT	Number of fixed-line telephone users	They are reflective of the level of urban information technology
		Number of international Internet users	
		Number of employees in information transmission, computer services, and software industry	

Control Variables. Due to potential interference from variables describing city characteristics on urban resilience, this study incorporates control variables from some research [2], including (1) trade openness measured by the proportion of total imports and exports to GDP; (2) urbanization rate by the proportion of urban permanent population to the total permanent population of prefecture-level cities; (3) technological investment by the logarithm of government expenditure on science and technology.

3 Data Sources and Processing

This study selects 29 key cities from the research report on the development of e-government service at the provincial level in China, covering the period from 2014 to 2020, as the experimental subjects. The dependent variable is the urban resilience level (Ur) with the data sourced from the National Bureau of Statistics of China. The explanatory variable includes EGDI and ICT, sourced from the National Bureau of Statistics of China and China E-Government Network, respectively. The control variables are obtained from the National Bureau of Statistics of China.

4 Empirical Testing

4.1 Analysis of Benchmark Regression Results

The benchmark regression is conducted separately for the different measures of the independent and dependent variables. Table 2 presents the results of the benchmark regression for the panel model.

Table 2. Benchmark regression results.

	Environmental resilience		Infrastructure resilience	
EGDI	0.0668		−0.3823***	
	(0.0408)		(−0.0968)	
ICT		−2.7134**		55.0421***
		(−1.2399)		(10.1814)
control variables	controlled	controlled	controlled	controlled
R-sq	0.0834	0.0607	0.5598	0.5493
N	169	197	174	203
	Economic resilience		Social resilience	
EGDI	0.1167*		0.1933**	
	(0.0673)		(0.0937)	
ICT		34.1376***		49.0039***
		(7.0012)		(8.8783)
control variables	controlled	controlled	controlled	controlled
R-sq	0.8706	0.8802	0.7668	0.7783
N	174	198	172	201

The determinate coefficient (R-squared) for environmental resilience is 0.08 and 0.06, indicating that the model has a moderate fit and can only explain 8% and 6% of the variation in the dependent variables, respectively. On the other hand, the models for infrastructure resilience, economic resilience, and social resilience exhibit a better fit, as they are able to explain more than half of the variation in the dependent variables.

Generally, it can be observed from the above that the coefficient of ICT impacting on environmental resilience is significantly negative; e-governance has a significant negative impact on infrastructure resilience. Meanwhile, the coefficient of information technology on infrastructure resilience is significantly positive; both e-governance and information technology have significantly positive coefficients on urban economic resilience; the coefficients of e-governance and information technology on social resilience are also significantly positive.

4.2 Robustness Test

To further examine the regression results, the independent variables are simultaneously included in Model (2) based on Model (1). In the following model, $EGDI_{it}$ represents the level of e-governance, and ICT_{it} defines information technology:

$$Ur_{it} = \beta_0 + \beta_1 EGDI_{it} + \beta_2 ICT_{it} + \beta_3 X_{it} + \mu_i + v_t + u_{it} \quad (2)$$

Table 3. Regression results.

	Social resilience	Environmental resilience	Economic resilience	Infrastructure resilience
EGDI	0.230**	0.077	0.142*	−0.348**
	(2.929)	(1.76)	(2.446)	(−4.139)
ICT	48.645**	−1.026	33.564**	45.714**
	(4.895)	(−0.138)	(4.557)	(4.272)
Control variable	control	control	control	control
R-sq	0.796	0.078	0.885	0.603
N	172	169	174	174

Table 3 validates the benchmark regression results.

5 Conclusions and Strategies

This study is based on panel data from 29 key cities in China from 2014 to 2020. Using panel regression models, it explores the impact mechanisms of smart governance on improving urban resilience. The research findings suggest that smart governance enhances the social, economic, and infrastructure resilience of cities through the application of information technology. Additionally, through e-government, the social and economic resilience of cities is further improved. However, the impact of information technology on environmental resilience is negative, displaying that the government's support for enhancing urban resilience through information technology is not strong enough. E-government has a significant negative impact on infrastructure resilience and little impact on environmental resilience.

Based on the above analysis, we propose the following strategies: First, e-government service platforms and operational models should be optimized. Second, the smartification of diverse stakeholders should be promoted. Third, the development and utilization of digital technologies should be advanced. Fourth, relevant policies and regulations should be improved to regulate market order.

References

1. Du, L., Lin, W.: Does the application of industrial robots overcome the Solow paradox? Evid. China Technol. Soc. **68**, 101932 (2022)
2. Giuliodori, A., Berrone, P., Ricart, J.E.: Where smart meets sustainability: the role of smart governance in achieving the sustainable development goals in cities. BRQ Bus. Res. Q. **26**(1), 27–44 (2023)
3. Moyer, J.D., Hedden, S.: Are we on the right path to achieve the sustainable development goals? World Dev. **127**, 104749 (2020)
4. Ribeiro, P.J.G., Gonçalves, L.A.P.J.: Urban resilience: a conceptual framework. Sustain. Cities Soc. **50**, 101625 (2019)
5. Haffar, M., Searcy, C.: Classification of trade-offs encountered in the practice of corporate sustainability. J. Bus. Ethics **140**, 495–522 (2017)
6. Xiong, N., Du, L.: Can Confucian culture promote enterprise total factor productivity? Evidence from China. Int. J. Emerg. Mark. ahead-of-print No. ahead-of-print (2023)
7. Odendaal, N.: Information and communication technology and local governance: understanding the difference between cities in developed and emerging economies. Comput. Environ. Urban Syst. **27**, 585–607 (2003)
8. Caragliu, A., Del Bo, C., Nijkamp, P.: Smart cities in Europe. J. Urban Technol. **18**(2), 65–82 (2011)
9. Kitchin, R.: Making sense of smart cities: addressing present shortcomings. Camb. J. Reg. Econ. Soc. **8**, 131–136 (2014)
10. Tomor, Z., Meijer, A., Michels, A., Geertman, S.: Smart governance for sustainable cities: findings from a systematic literature review. J. Urban Technol. **26**(4), 3–27 (2019)

The Impact of Low Carbon Economic Development on the Income Gap Between Urban and Rural Residents - An Empirical Study Based on Inter-provincial Panel Data in China

Yang Chengye(✉)

Shanghai Lixin University of Accounting and Finance, Shanghai, China
Eden030922@gmail.com

Abstract. The aim of this paper is to explore the impact of low-carbon economic development on the income gap between urban and rural residents in China. By analyzing the current situation of the wide income gap between urban and rural residents and the challenges posed by global climate change to urbanization, this paper argues that developing a low-carbon economy is an effective way to address the income gap and to cope with climate change. The low-carbon economy accomplishes synergistic growth of the economy, society, and natural environment and has a significant influence on the income gap between urban and rural populations. This is done through technological innovation and efficient energy usage. Therefore, promoting the transformative development of a low-carbon economy and the synergistic development of the urban and rural economies is a sure way to achieve sustainable development and a concrete manifestation of the implementation of Xi Jinping's thought on socialism with Chinese characteristics for a new era.

Keywords: Low Carbon Economy · Theil Index · Urban-Rural Income Gap · Urbanization

1 Introduction

The large income disparity between urban and rural people has been a significant issue for China during the expansion of the economy as it is a key indicator of urban-rural inequality [1, 2]. Following the reform and opening, China's national economy used to concentrate its resources on urban areas with less support for rural growth, which caused the disparity in income between urban and rural residents in China to widen even further and now stands at a considerably larger level than the average for the rest of the world [3, 4]. The biggest issue is the sharp increase in the total demand for energy in cities, as well as the enormous demand for urban infrastructure, housing, and other necessities due to the world's fast urbanization. An efficient strategy to reconcile the contradiction between urbanization and climate change is through a low-carbon economy. Humanity has made a strategic decision in response to climate change to move toward a low-carbon economy. In order to realize the objective of the harmonious growth of the economy, society, and the environment, it is driven by sustainable development concept and employs a variety of techniques, including technical innovation.

This paper, which is based on China's low-carbon economy theory and practice, aims to analyze the impact of China's low-carbon economic development of the gap in the absence of climate change.

2 Review of the Literature

2.1 Low-Carbon Economy

The idea of low-carbon economy and the low-carbon economy model have arisen in response to the worsening effects of global climate change. The idea of low-carbon economy was developed as the result of the Kyoto Protocol [5]. Low-carbon economy is an economic development model based on low energy consumption, low pollution and low emissions, which is mainly manifested in the improvement of energy efficiency, optimization of energy structure and rationalization of consumption behavior [6]. There are still numerous disagreements on what a low-carbon economy means both domestically and internationally, despite the fact that more and more governments are acknowledging the concept and are gradually putting the low-carbon economy development model into effect. While developing countries are more development-oriented and focus on how can a win-win situation be achieved between the reduction of emissions and the development of the economy, developed countries are more compliance-oriented and define their governance objectives in terms of compliance with their international greenhouse gas emission control commitments [7].

2.2 The Income Gap Between Urban and Rural Dwellers

Existing research suggests that urbanization [8], transport infrastructure [9], financial development [10], and demographic structure [11] can affect the income gap. The expansion of the digital economy, the digital divide, and the income discrepancy between population in urban and rural areas all make significant contributions to this concept. However, the financial and industrial structures are the only two viewpoints from which the development of the digital economy is taken into account, and this only accounts for one side of the story. On the other side, the study on the growth of the low-carbon economy explores its effects on the difference in income between people living in urban and rural areas from two angles: the success of environmental regulation and the growth of green industries.

2.3 Transformative Development of Low-Carbon Economy and Synergistic Development of Urban and Rural Economy

A new global trend that is influencing the economic and social evolution of many nations is the growth of low-carbon economy in transition. The income gap in China is still very wide, and coordinating development between urban and rural areas through the optimization of the structure of the industry is a key strategy for closing this income gap [12]. Rural areas will not be able to benefit from such development due to a lack of human resources, research, and technology, which will have an impact on farmers' income levels. Second, the growth of low-carbon economy necessitates the presence of numerous energy-efficient and environmentally benign industries, which are absent from rural areas.

This modifies how industries are organized in both urban and rural locations, which will have an impact on both populations' income levels. Additionally, the transition to low-carbon economy may result in some changes to the environment and social security, which will have a different degree of impact on urban and rural people. The size and evolution of the income gap will be affected by these changes.

2.4 Review of the Literature

It is clear from reading the aforementioned literature evaluation that the literature described above has flaws.

Although the existing literature on the topic of the impact of low-carbon economy on the income gap mentions the need to boost investment in science and technology and foster the demand for highly skilled workers and employment growth, it is only briefly touched upon how to achieve a synergistic development of the urban and rural economies. To understand more about the following relationship between the development of a low-carbon economic transition and the co-development of urban and rural economies, this paper further investigates the impact of low-carbon economic transition on urban-rural economic structure, regional openness, and population ageing through an empirical study using a panel data set of Chinese provinces.

3 Formulation of the Research Hypothesis

This study makes the following two claims about how the growth of a low-carbon economy can impact the wealth gap.

First, through influencing the pace of urbanization, a low-carbon economy can reduce the economic gap [13]. A change in the organization of the industry, demographic occupation, and urban territorial space all take place in tandem with the process of urbanization [14]. Technology- and knowledge-intensive sectors are low-carbon industries, such as the information technology sector, with very low energy and material consumption and minimal environmental impact. In terms of hardware and software, the information technology sector has the benefits of low energy consumption and low emissions, and there is significant room for growth in low-carbon economy. It is challenging for the surplus of rural labor to meet the cities' demand for new talent in the low-carbon economy, though, because rural residents typically have lower levels of education than their urban counterparts. They also have a smaller pool of human capital and find it more challenging to comprehend and use the smart technological products and services of the low-carbon economy. The "digital divide" that migrant workers must overcome makes it difficult for them to fully benefit from the "reverse urbanization" phenomenon brought about by the new round of tertiary development. The growth of low-carbon economy in China has facilitated industry reorganization and modernization, expanding the wage gap between urban and rural dwellers. The digital divide brought on by further promoting the low-carbon economy has a negative impact on the surplus labor force that moves from rural areas to the cities in search of work, which in turn widens the income gap. As a result, although low-carbon economic development can encourage urbanization. In conclusion, this paper puts out a first hypothesis:

H_1: The income gap and low-carbon economic development are inversely correlated.

Second, through environmental control rules, a low-carbon economy can affect income gap [15]. So, can China's environmental control policies combine economic development with environmental and ecological protection? What effect does environmental regulation have on the income gap? Few studies have focused on the conflict between environmental protection and economic inequality, which is how environmental quality and income disparities interact. As a result, this paper examines the relationship between environmental regulation and the income gap based on research on low-carbon economic development. It also examines the effect of environmental regulation on the income gap between urban and rural residents using a theoretical research model, proposing second hypothesis:

H_2: The income gap between urban and rural residents can be impacted by environmental regulatory policies in the development of low carbon economy.

Overall, there is a positive correlation between the income gap between people living in urban and rural areas and the level of low-carbon economy development. To this end, this paper aims to argue for the validity of this hypothesis through econometric modelling analysis.

4 Study Design

4.1 Measurement of Low Carbon Economic Development

To measure how far the low-carbon economy has advanced, there is no accurate statistic. In this study, carbon intensity is used as an indicator to gauge how far a low-carbon economy has come. The amount of carbon dioxide emitted per dollar of GDP or per unit of energy use is referred to as carbon intensity. The following are the justifications for selecting carbon intensity as a measure of the low-carbon economy development stage:

The relationship between economic growth and carbon emissions can be readily seen in the intensity of carbon emissions. If carbon intensity decreases, it shows a slowing in economic growth relative to carbon emissions, showing advancement in the creation of a low-carbon economy.

Carbon intensity is easy to measure and compare: Carbon intensity can be derived from relatively simple calculations and is easily comparable, so it can be used as a significant indicator of low-carbon economy development.

4.2 Measuring the Income Gap Between People Living in Urban and Rural Areas

In China, the Thiel index and the ratio of disposable income between urban and rural inhabitants are frequently used to gauge the disparity in income between the two populations. Relative to the ratio of disposable income of urban and rural residents, the Thiel index takes into account the factor of population changes and decomposes the urban-rural residents' income gap into inter-group and intra-group gaps, which is more reflective of the income gap [16]. Theil is used in this work to measure the income gap between urban and rural residents in the main regression and the ratio of disposable income between urban and rural residents in the robustness test. Theil index is a reliable predictor, and a higher value corresponds to a wider income gap, which is calculated as shown in the following equation:

$$Theil_{it} = \sum_{i=2}^{2} \left(\frac{y_{i,t}}{y_t}\right) \times ln\left[\frac{y_{i,t}}{y_t} \bigg/ \frac{x_{i,t}}{x_t}\right] \quad (1)$$

where i = 1 and i = 2 denote urban and rural areas respectively, t denotes year, y denotes disposable income and x denotes population.

4.3 Construction of the Model

Given the possible non-linear effects of low carbon economic development on the income gap between urban and rural areas, the following econometric model is constructed:

$$Theil_{i/t} = \beta_0 + \beta_1 \ln STR_{i/t} + \beta_2 \ln AGDP_{i/t} + \beta_3 Primary_{i/t} + \beta_4 Intensity_{i/t} + \beta_5 Open_{it} + \beta_6 \ln Old_{i/t} + \mu_i + v_i + \varepsilon_{i/t} \quad (2)$$

where 't' denotes the year and 'I' denotes the province, municipality or autonomous region.

This paper measures the extent of ageing in terms of the old-age dependency ratio in urban areas (Table 1).

Table 1. Definition of variables.

Variable	Calculation method
Theil	The calculation is shown in Eq. (1)
Primary	Primary sector output
STR	Share of secondary and tertiary sectors in GDP
Intensity	Carbon emission/GDP
AGDP	Gross regional product per capita
Open	Total imports and exports/GDP
Old	Elderly dependency ratio in urban areas
Gap	Urban income/rural income

4.4 Data Sources

This study examines the effects of low-carbon economic development on 2006–2018 income gap using data from 31 provinces, municipalities directly under the Central

Government, and autonomous regions. The historical China Rural Statistical Yearbook, the historical Regional Statistical Yearbooks of each province, municipality, and autonomous region, and the Wind database serve as the primary sources of data. Any pertinent gaps in the data are filled by manually compiling the annual statistical bulletins of each region, and additional information is gleaned from the Internet. The paper finally obtained 403 observations, which constitute the balanced panel data. All the continuous variables are scaled down at the 1% and 99% levels to eliminate the effect of extreme values on the study (Table 2).

Table 2. Covariance diagnosis.

Variable	VIF	1/VIF
AGDP	2.550	0.393
STR	2.480	0.403
Open	2.360	0.424
Intensity	1.930	0.517
Primary	1.600	0.624
Old	1.100	0.906
Mean	VIF	2

Table 3. Relevance analysis.

Theil	Intens ~ y	Primary	STR	AGDP	Open	Old	
Theil	1						
Intensity	0.476***	1					
Primary	−0.096*	−0.262***	1				
STR	−0.502***	−0.262***	−0.266***	1			
AGDP	−0.808***	−0.550***	0.0570	0.664***	1		
Open	−0.568***	−0.425***	−0.346***	0.618***	0.551***	1	
Old	−0.117**	−0.0440	0.0180	0.097*	0.0290	−0.0790	1

Notes: *** $p < 0.01$, ** $p < 0.05$, * $p < 0.10$; Standard errors with strong heteroskedasticity are in parenthesis. Positive coefficients show how the urban-rural income gap is affected by a low-carbon economy; negative coefficients show how the urban-rural income gap is affected by a low-carbon economy.

4.5 Descriptive Statistics of Variables

The VIF values for each variable were less than 10 through the cointegration diagnostics, and there was no significant multicollinearity between the variables to allow for regression analysis (see Table 4).

Table 4. Descriptive statistics.

Variable	Sum	Mean	P50	SD	Min	Max
Theil	403	0.108	0.101	0.0490	0.0190	0.261
Intensity	390	0.0230	0.0190	0.0150	0.00300	0.0860
Primary	403	6.842	7.164	1.149	3.863	8.507
STR	403	0.892	0.894	0.0560	0.698	0.997
AGDP	403	10.42	10.45	0.600	8.717	12.01
Open	390	0.303	0.139	0.366	0.0170	1.721
Old	403	2.447	2.485	0.263	1.560	3.001

Table 3 reports the results of descriptive statistics for all variables used in the regressions in this paper. As relevant data were missing for some areas, linear interpolation was applied in this paper to estimate the values of these missing data points. The mean value of the Thiel index is 0.110, while the minimum and maximum values are 0.019 and 0.276 respectively, which indicates that there are significant differences in the income gap in various Chinese regions. Nevertheless, there are also notable regional variations in the degree of low-carbon economy development. The eastern region is where the development of low-carbon economy is at its maximum level, whereas the western region is where it is at a relatively low level. This pattern is consistent with the current circumstances in China.

The eastern regions, such as Zhejiang, Guangdong and Beijing, are at the forefront of China's economic development. These regions are represented by the digital economy, which is leading the way nationwide. Prominent digital economy companies, such as Alibaba, Tencent, Jingdong, Today's Headlines and Baidu, have risen to prominence in these regions. These companies are leading the way in the digital economy and driving the rapid development of related industries. Their achievements in the low-carbon economy reflect their advancement in sustainable development and environmental protection.

In contrast, the development level of the low-carbon economy in the western region is relatively low. The information and communication infrastructure in some western provinces is still being gradually improved, and there is a gap compared to the eastern regions. This may be due to a number of factors such as the relatively low starting point, weaker development base and smaller market size in the western region. However, with the support of national policies and the efforts of the western region itself, the potential for low-carbon economy development in the western region is still huge.

5 Empirical Analysis

Table 5 reports and compares the results of the least squares, fixed effects and random effects regressions in this paper. In this paper, Theil, Intensity, STR, and AGDP are regressed. The p-value of the results is less than 0.05 by Hausman's test. The fixed effects model is picked in place of the initial theory. The regression results for Intensity are not significant and the preliminary hypothesis is that there is an inverted U-shaped relationship between this variable and the explanatory variables. In this study, the squared terms of Theil, Intensity, and intensity were regressed. The results are displayed in Table 6, which demonstrates that Theil and Intensity variables have an inverted U-shaped connection. In addition, the proportion of primary and secondary industries is controlled for in this study, and neither the sign nor the significance of the regression coefficient of intensity are altered. This suggests that at the initial stages of development, the digital economy can significantly and favorably affect the gap in income. However, as the low carbon economy develops, its impact on this gap will be inhibited, and the overall inverted U-shaped relationship between the two is shown, which supports the hypothesis H_1 of this paper.

After further controlling for other control variables, the sign of the regression coefficient of Intensity remained unchanged. This suggests that environmental regulations, represented by carbon emissions intensity, can positively enhance the efficiency of green economic growth in the national sample, which supports hypothesis H_2 of this paper.

Table 5. Empirical results of low-carbon economic research on the income gap.

	Ols	Fe	Re
Intensity	−0.206	0.179	0.214*
	(0.128)	(0.120)	(0.126)
Primary	−0.003*	−0.044***	−0.020***
	(0.002)	(0.004)	(0.003)
STR	0.151***	−0.096***	0.006
	(0.038)	(0.037)	(0.036)
AGDP	−0.064***	−0.007*	−0.029***
	(0.004)	(0.004)	(0.004)
Open	−0.039***	−0.012***	−0.014***
	(0.006)	(0.004)	(0.004)
Old	−0.021***	−0.002	−0.000
	(0.006)	(0.002)	(0.003)
_cons	0.728***	0.576***	0.537***
_cons	(0.039)	(0.030)	(0.031)
N	390	390	390
R^2	0.697	0.889	
Hausman	Prob > chibar2 = 0.0000		

Notes: *** p < 0.01, ** p < 0.05, * p < 0.10; Standard errors with strong heteroskedasticity are in parenthesis. Positive coefficients show how the urban-rural income gap is affected by a low-carbon economy; negative coefficients show how the urban-rural income gap is affected by a low-carbon economy.

Table 6. Income disparities between urban and rural residents and low-carbon economic development.

	Theil
Intensity	4.507***
	(0.456)
$Intensity^2$	−44.210***
	(6.510)
_cons	0.035***
	(0.006)
N	390.000
R^2	0.309

Notes: *** $p < 0.01$, ** $p < 0.05$, * $p < 0.10$; Standard errors with strong heteroskedasticity are in parenthesis. Positive coefficients show how the urban-rural income gap is affected by a low-carbon economy; negative coefficients show how the urban-rural income gap is affected by a low-carbon economy.

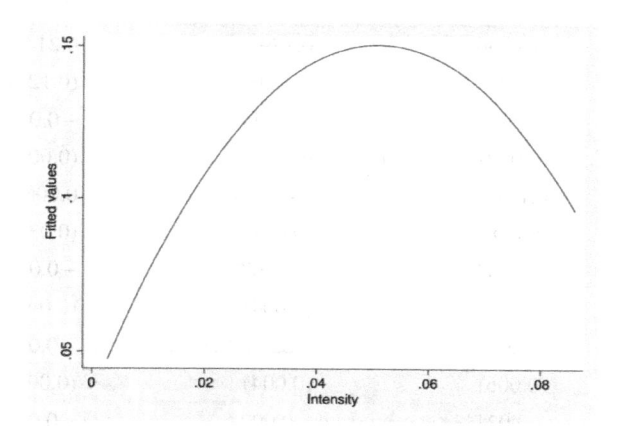

Fig. 1. Inverted U-shaped relationship between Theil and Intensity.

6 Mechanism Testing and Analysis

6.1 Substitution of Explanatory Variables

First, this study measures the income gap. It does so by comparing urban to rural income ratios. The related regression results, which are shown in column (1) of Table 7, show that the study's conclusions are still valid (see Fig. 1).

Table 7. Robustness tests.

	(1)	(2)	(3)
	Ols	Fe	Re
Intensity	−0.927	1.110	1.208
	(1.570)	(1.430)	(1.394)
Primary	−0.086***	−0.240***	−0.151***
	(0.020)	(0.053)	(0.040)
STR	1.649***	0.532	0.904**
	(0.465)	(0.438)	(0.404)
AGDP	−0.547***	−0.245***	−0.325***
	(0.045)	(0.052)	(0.041)
Open	−0.202***	−0.141***	−0.150***
	(0.070)	(0.042)	(0.041)
Old	−0.186***	0.036	0.040
	(0.070)	(0.028)	(0.028)
_cons	8.121***	6.422***	6.296***
	(0.478)	(0.353)	(0.346)
N	390	390	390
R^2	0.489	0.828	

Notes: *** $p < 0.01$, ** $p < 0.05$, * $p < 0.10$; Standard errors with strong heteroskedasticity are in parenthesis. Positive coefficients show how the urban-rural income gap is affected by a low-carbon economy; negative coefficients show how the urban-rural income gap is affected by a low-carbon economy.

6.2 Test for Lagged Effects

Considering that the effect of GDP on the income gap does not necessarily occur in the current period, and there may be a certain lag effect, regressions were conducted by adding data with one and two lags. The results of regression that took into account explanatory variables with one and two delays are shown in Table 8. This leads us to the conclusion that the income gap is still significantly impacted by the lag effect of GDP, which is a genuine phenomenon.

Table 8. Hysteresis effect.

	(1)	(2)	(3)
	Theil	Lag 1 stage	Lag 2 stage
Intensity	0.179	0.381***	0.468***
	(0.120)	(0.122)	(0.125)
Primary	−0.044***	−0.048***	−0.046***
	(0.004)	(0.004)	(0.004)
STR	−0.096***	−0.141***	−0.143***
	(0.037)	(0.034)	(0.034)
AGDP	−0.007*	−0.015*	0.003
	(0.004)	(0.009)	(0.006)
Open	−0.012***	−0.007**	−0.002
	(0.004)	(0.003)	(0.003)
Old	−0.002	−0.002	0.000
	(0.002)	(0.002)	(0.002)
L.AGDP		0.010	
		(0.008)	
L2.AGDP			−0.008*
			(0.005)
_cons	0.576***	0.615***	0.590***
	(0.030)	(0.029)	(0.030)
N	390	360	330
R^2	0.889	0.915	0.922

Notes: *** $p < 0.01$, ** $p < 0.05$, * $p < 0.10$; Standard errors with strong heteroskedasticity are in parenthesis. Positive coefficients show how the urban-rural income gap is affected by a low-carbon economy; negative coefficients show how the urban-rural income gap is affected by a low-carbon economy.

6.3 Moderating Effects

In order to evaluate how the low carbon economy affects income gap, this study uses AGDP multiplied by Open as a moderating variable. The findings show that even after considering the effect of GDP multiplied by Open, the moderating variable still shows a significant association with the variable Theil's index of income gap (see Table 9).

This conclusion shows that the open AGDP component alters the growth of the income gap. This moderating factor, in particular, may have a moderating effect on the income gap throughout the transition to a low-carbon economy. Increased GDP multiplied by Open denotes greater economic activity and openness to the outside world. In this case, economic growth that is low in carbon is likely to happen faster and more thoroughly. Low-carbon economic development is probably going to contribute positively

Table 9. Moderating effects.

	(1)	(2)
	Theil	Theil
Intensity	0.179	−0.060
	(0.120)	(0.114)
Primary	−0.044***	−0.021***
	(0.004)	(0.005)
STR	−0.096***	0.068*
	(0.037)	(0.039)
AGDP	−0.007*	−0.039***
	(0.004)	(0.006)
Open	−0.012***	−0.293***
	(0.004)	(0.035)
Old	−0.002	0.001
	(0.002)	(0.002)
TJ		0.026***
		(0.003)
_cons	0.576***	0.596***
	(0.030)	(0.027)
N	390	390
R^2	0.889	0.906

Notes: *** $p < 0.01$, ** $p < 0.05$, * $p < 0.10$; Standard errors with strong heteroskedasticity are in parenthesis. Positive coefficients show how the urban-rural income gap is affected by a low-carbon economy; negative coefficients show how the urban-rural income gap is affected by a low-carbon economy.

to closing the wealth gap between urban and rural populations because of its emphasis on environmental preservation and sustainability. This is because the environmental and new industries arising from low-carbon economic development usually have higher value-added and employment potential, thus providing more employment opportunities and sources of income, and helping to narrow the income gap.

6.4 Heterogeneity Analysis

The data were divided into four groups for heterogeneity analysis using AGDP as the criterion, the first group from 8.71654 to 10.0028, the second group from 10.0094 to 10.4628, the third group from 10.834 to 12.0086 and the fourth group from 10.8072 to 12.1226. Through the study, it was found that as the AGDP increases, the correlation between carbon emission intensity and the Thiel index the correlation between carbon emission intensity and the Thiel index also becomes more and more significant, and the contribution of carbon emission intensity to the Thiel index is also increasing (Table 10).

Table 10. Heterogeneity analysis.

	(1)	(2)	(3)	(4)
	Theil	Theil	Theil	Theil
Intensity	0.017	0.411	0.405***	0.397
	(0.284)	(0.273)	(0.137)	(0.351)
Primary	0.110***	−0.072***	−0.019*	−0.026***
	(0.041)	(0.023)	(0.010)	(0.003)
STR	0.783**	−0.214*	0.092	−0.463***
	(0.306)	(0.127)	(0.105)	(0.090)
AGDP	−0.153***	0.016	−0.038***	0.007**
	(0.044)	(0.023)	(0.012)	(0.003)
Open	0.009	−0.070***	−0.026***	0.004**
	(0.038)	(0.018)	(0.005)	(0.002)
Old	0.011	−0.002	−0.000	−0.007***
	(0.007)	(0.004)	(0.002)	(0.002)
_cons	0.211*	0.667***	0.555***	0.605***
	(0.117)	(0.071)	(0.054)	(0.075)
N	98	99	100	93
R^2	0.727	0.818	0.889	0.848

Notes: *** $p < 0.01$, ** $p < 0.05$, * $p < 0.10$; Standard errors with strong heteroskedasticity are in parenthesis. Positive coefficients show how the urban-rural income gap is affected by a low-carbon economy; negative coefficients show how the urban-rural income gap is affected by a low-carbon economy.

In the second half of analysis, this paper argues that low-carbon economic growth will have an effect on the income gap between urban and rural residents from the viewpoints of environmental regulation and urbanization. In the early stages of low-carbon economic development, the low-carbon economy will exacerbate the income gap between urban and rural populations by accelerating the urbanization process and growing the tertiary sector. The urban-rural digital divide is becoming more significant as the low-carbon economy develops further, the urbanization process is hampered, and rural residents' skill levels are lower than those urban areas, which causes the low-carbon economy's growth to widen the income gap. Due to the development of low-carbon economy, the income gap has widened.

7 Conclusion

Low-carbon economy and large differences in income between rural and urban residents are two hot issues in China nowadays, and they are also important influencing factors for sustainable social development. Therefore, this paper builds an econometric model based on sample data from 2006–2018 in China to re-investigate the relationship between the two from the perspective of environmental regulation and urbanization, and the results of the theoretical and empirical evidence are as follows:

This article examines the effect of a low-carbon economy on the income gap between urban and rural residents. The gap is significantly correlated with the level of development of the low carbon economy, according to studies utilizing econometric models. As the low-carbon economy continues to develop, this income gap will widen, leading to issues like the urban-rural digital divide. Through mechanism testing, it was found that low carbon economic development would affect the income gap between people living in urban and rural areas by influencing environmental regulations and the urbanization process. Further research found that:

First, the results demonstrate that both urban and rural economies are significantly impacted by the shift to low-carbon economy. With the advancement of low-carbon economy, green and high-tech industries in urban areas show rapid growth, while traditional industries in rural areas are restricted to a certain extent. This alteration in the industrial structure has caused the income gap to increase.

Second, the study shows that the expansion of low-carbon economy has strengthened the ties between urban and rural areas economically and increased the region degree of openness. With the transition to low-carbon economy, the advantages of urban areas in terms of technology, capital and talent have been further exploited, attracting more resources to cities, thereby increasing the gap. Specifically, the innovation and technological advances brought about by the low-carbon economic transition have made urban areas a hotspot for investment and entrepreneurship, thus accelerating the development of the urban economy. However, rural areas are relatively weaker in attracting resources and investment, and therefore have fewer opportunities for income growth than urban areas, which leads to widen gap.

Thirdly, the study found that the low-carbon economic transition has had a significant impact on the extent of population ageing. With the development of low-carbon economy, employment opportunities in rural areas are reduced, leading to a stronger tendency for the younger population to concentrate in urban areas. By contrast, metropolitan areas have a relatively young population structure because of the attraction of a younger population, which further exacerbates the ageing of the population in rural areas. In summary, the low-carbon economic transition has had a significant impact on the extent of population ageing and an indirect effect on the income gap.

References

1. Lagakos, D.: Urban-rural gaps in the developing world: does internal migration offer opportunities? J. Econ. Perspect. **34** (2020)
2. Sicular, T., Yue, X., Gustafsson, B., Li, S.: The Urban–Rural Income Gap and Inequality in China. Rev. Income Wealth **53**(1), 93–126 (2010)

3. Lei, G., Xiaoma, T., Hong, W.: Empirical evidence on local fiscal finance, urbanization and urban-rural income gap. China Popul.-Resour. Environ. **25**(09), 93–99 (2015). https://kns.cnki.net/kcms/detail/37.1196.n.20150824.1614.012.html
4. Yuan, Y., Wang, M., Zhu, Y., Huang, X., Xiong, X.: Urbanization's effects on the urban-rural income gap in China: a meta-regression analysis. Land Use Policy **99**, 104995 (2023)
5. Bao, J., Miao, Y., Chen, F.: Low-carbon economy: a new change in the way of human economic development. China Ind. Econ. (04), 153–160 (2008). https://doi.org/10.19581/j.cnki.ciejournal.2008.04.018
6. Li, Y., Zhu, S., Luo, L., Yang, D.: Theoretical exploration of low carbon development as a macroeconomic goal - based on the Chinese scenario. Manag. World (06), 1–8 (2017). https://doi.org/10.19744/j.cnki.11-1235/f.2017.06.002
7. Poon, K.W.: Strategic cognition, development paradigm and strategic initiatives of ecological civilization construction in the new era. Dongyue Discuss. Ser. **39**(03), 14–20+191 (2018). https://doi.org/10.15981/j.cnki.dongyueluncong.2018.03.002
8. Lu, M., Chen, Z.: Urbanization, urban tendency economic policies and the rural-urban income gap. Econ. Res. (6), 9 (2004)
9. Yang, X., Shi, D.: Transportation infrastructure, factor mobility and urban-rural income gap. South. Econ. (09), 35–50 (2019). https://doi.org/10.19592/j.cnki.scje.361764
10. Wang, Y.C., Wen, T.: Study on the economic growth effect and heterogeneity of digital finance. Mod. Econ. Discuss. (11), 14 (2020)
11. Jiaxu, W., Bo, F., Shujuan, W.: Does population aging exacerbate urban-rural income inequality - an empirical analysis based on inter-provincial panel data in China. Contemp. Econ. Sci. **39**(4), 10 (2017)
12. Chen, B., Lin, Y.: Development strategies, urbanization, and the rural-urban income gap in China. Soc. Sci. China (04), 81–102+206 (2013)
13. Liu, S., Xia, Y.: The development path of low carbon economy in the context of new urbanization. J. Soc. Sci., Hunan Normal Univ. **41**(03), 84–87 (2012)
14. Chen, W., Wu, W.: Digital economy development, digital divide and income gap between urban and rural residents. South. Econ. (11), 1–17 (2021). https://doi.org/10.19592/j.cnki.scje.390621
15. Bao, T.: Do environmental regulations widen or narrow the rural-urban income gap? --based on the dual perspectives of economic efficiency and economic structure. J. Yunnan Univ. Finan. Econ. **38**(03), 1–20 (2022). https://doi.org/10.16537/j.cnki.jynufe.000767
16. Liang, S., Liu, P.: Digital inclusive finance and rural-urban income gap. J. Capital Univ. Econ. Bus. **21**(01), 33–41 (2019). https://doi.org/10.13504/j.cnki.issn1008-2700.2019.01.004

Addressing Credit Fraud Threat: Detected Through Supervised Machine Learning Model

Yihan Yang[✉]

Ivey Business School, Western University, London, ON N6G 0N1, Canada
Ryang.hba2024@ivey.ca

Abstract. In the modern digital age, the rising risk of credit fraud has posed a great challenge to financial institutions and credit card users. This paper follows the analysis of credit card fraud detection notebooks on Kaggle, aiming to improve the accuracy of the automated monitoring system model and the efficiency of institutional operations. Based on realistic credit card transaction records of European cardholders in 2013, a data-driven fraud detection model is trained in the form of a confusion matrix using multiple algorithms as well as various oversampling techniques. The algorithmic models using Random Forest classifier and SMOTE techniques show the best performance based on the assessment criteria of accuracy, specificity and fraud detection rate. From a business application standpoint, in addition to ongoing system maintenance and improvement, credit institutions can work on offering personalized risk monitoring services, negotiating for multi-platform data-sharing cooperation and promoting user education to prevent future fraudulent activities.

Keywords: Credit Fraud · Random Forest · SMOTE

1 Introduction

In an era of rapid digitalization with a growing desire for convenience, card payments have replaced the use of cash as the most common way of purchasing payments. As of 2022, 82% of U.S. adults have had a credit card [1]. According to a February 2023 Forbes Advisor survey, 36% of U.S. customers typically use a physical or virtual credit card to pay for their purchases [2]. While credit cards bring benefits to consumers, they also present potential security risks, where credit card fraud has emerged as a major threat. According to the Nilson Report, a leading authority in the payments industry, the forecasted credit card fraud losses are expected to reach a staggering $408.5 billion worldwide over the next decade, emphasizing the urgency and imperative of addressing this problem [3].

Credit card fraud can cause great negative impacts on financial institutions, making it necessary to deploy a Fraud Detection System (FDS). From the customer's perspective, people may opt to switch to a more secure credit provider, when they experience credit card fraud or believe their financial information is at risk. Implementing an FDS signifies a bank's dedication to safeguarding its clients against fraud, boosting customer patronage and trust. Additionally, manual investigation of fraudulent transactions can be extremely time-consuming and resource intensive for the bank's day-to-day operation, as investigators can only review a handful of alerts per day. Due to the tiny probability of fraudulent transactions occurring, manual detection is inefficient, or even infeasible, costing huge financial losses. Implementing an FDS automates the fraud detection process, enabling banks to efficiently identify any disputed transactions in real time while reducing operational costs.

In recent years, considerable scholars and researchers have devoted themselves to technological innovation in the field of credit card fraud. In the past literature. In the past literature, fraud detection strategies and machine learning algorithms have been extensively studied and compared. Among them, several studies have proposed and proved that a random forest algorithm is an effective approach. A team conducted a comparative study of several common machine learning algorithms to evaluate their performance in fraudulent transaction detection, including logistic regression, random forest, Naive Bayes, and multilayer perceptron. The results of the tested algorithms suggest that the random forest methodology performed the best [4]. Another analysis compared the Random Forest and AdaBoost algorithms. Although both algorithms had similar accuracy rates, the Random Forest algorithm outperformed in terms of precision, recall, and F1 scores [5].

In addition, there are several other methods and algorithms that have been found to be effective in the field of fraud detection. Altab Althar Taha and Sareef Jameel Malbery proposed the OLightGBM method, which combines an optimized optical gradient boosting machine with a Bayesian-based hyperparametric optimization algorithm. Their research demonstrates that OLightGBM performs exceptionally well in fraud detection, exhibiting an ideal shape of the ROC curve with an AUC of 92.88% and achieving an impressive 98.4% accuracy [6]. Another study introduces a new approach for detection that integrates the use of neural network ensemble classifiers and hybrid data resampling techniques. The experimental results demonstrate that the proposed long short-term memory (LSTM) ensemble classifier, trained with resampled data, achieves a 99.6% sensitivity and 99.8% specificity [7].

Furthermore, a study focused on combining unsupervised outlier detection techniques with a supervised credit card fraud detection classifier, finding that the clustered approach performs well by using k-means clustering to obtain outlier scores [8]. However, excessive use of outliers raises concerns about overfitting and variance problems.

Some other authors investigated the effectiveness of using the isolated forest algorithm in detection. Although the experimental implementation achieved an accuracy of over 99.6% on the entire dataset, the accuracy dropped to 28% in tests on a randomly selected tenth of the dataset [9]. This drop in accuracy can be attributed to the apparently imbalanced dataset, demonstrating the significant impact and making a balanced dataset critical. Finally, another study evaluated the application and performance of eight methodologies, with special consideration on dealing with imbalanced datasets. The study points out that the traditional imbalanced data processing methods may generate many false positives, resulting in some important fraud cases going undetected [10].

2 Data Description

2.1 Dataset Information

To build the detection model, the cleaned data, imported for analysis, consists of the transaction records made by European credit cards users in September 2013. The dataset contains 284,807 rows and 31 columns, with each row representing a credit card transaction. These columns relate to information about the transaction, such as the date, the different features (V1 to V28), the amount, and the class, broken down as follows in Table 1.

Table 1. Detailed explanation of column variables in the dataset.

Column variables	Explanation
Time	Time represents the duration in seconds between the first and the current transaction
V1-V28	V1-V28 are the principal components. Due to privacy concerns, the database does not define the customer and background information. The raw data was reduced in dimension using a PCA technique, resulting in the final 28 anonymized features seen in the columns
Amount	The amount column indicates the corresponding transaction amount
Class	The class column is the dependent variable using one hot encoding technique to denote whether or not the credit card transaction is fraudulent, assigning a "1" as the fraudulent transaction and a "0" otherwise

2.2 Exploratory Data Analysis

With the 284,807 transactions recorded in the dataset, the largest transaction amount is 25,691 USD, while the average value of all transactions is only 88.35 USD (Table 2). The distribution graph of transaction value indicates that the entire dataset is heavily right skewed with most of the transactions being rather small in the transaction amount (Fig. 1). Therefore, it can be concluded that a record with extremely large values is likely to have anomalies or exceptional circumstances that require additional attention. They can be excluded from the original data as outliers, but a trade-off needs to be determined between the amount of data used for training and the impact of extreme values on the model.

Table 2. Selected example of the descriptive statistics analysis.

	Count	Mean	Std	Min	25%	50%	75%	Max
Amount	284,807	88.34	250.12	0.00	5.60	22.00	77.17	25,691.16
Class	284,807	0.00173	0.0415	0	0	0	0	1

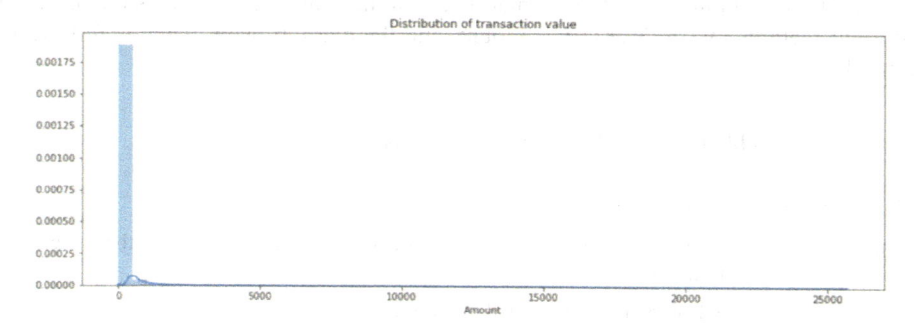

Fig. 1. Distribution of transaction value.

In terms of the class label column, the numerical average of this column reflects the truthful fraud rate, revealing that only 0.173% of all transactions in the data are fraudulent. Based on the rarely occurring nature of fraud, as demonstrated by both ratios and graphs, there are non-negligible differences between the quantity of normal and fraudulent transactions (Fig. 2). Thus, it is critical to deal with unbalanced data sets and ensure that sufficient data can be used to represent the minor data types to build the model.

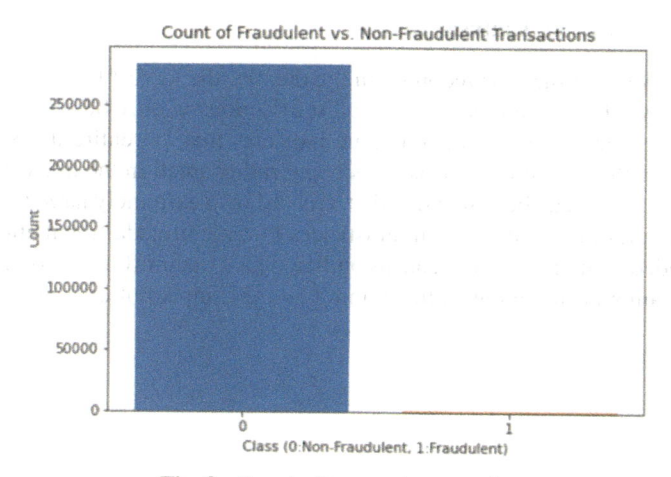

Fig. 2. Count of transaction records.

3 Data Processing

Since standard machine learning algorithms tend to disregard the minority and follow a procedure that focuses on the dominant class [11]. With only 0.17% of transactions being fraudulent while 99.83% being normal, the existing data imbalance places a considerable effect on model performance as well as reliability. The following 4 methods can be implemented to oversample the minority to achieve the balance (See Table 3):

Table 3. Oversampling techniques.

Oversampling Technique	Methodology
Synthetic Minority Over-sampling Technique (SMOTE)	SMOTE generates synthetic samples for minority categories in unbalanced datasets by interpolating along a line, that connects the randomly selected minority samples and their nearest neighbours
Borderline-SMOTE	BSMOTE focuses on samples near the boundary between the minority and the majority. Unlike SMOTE, BSMOTE first identifies boundary samples and generates synthetic samples only for those samples that are more likely to be misclassified
Borderline-SMOTE SVM	As the name implies, this algorithm combines Boundary-SMOTE with a Support Vector Machine (SVM) classifier to generate synthetic samples for samples near the decision boundary identified using the SVM classifier to improve the performance of the classifier
Adaptive Synthetic Sampling (ADASYN)	This method adaptively generates a different number of synthetic samples for all the minor samples depending on the distribution of the different classes around the sample, paying more attention to those samples that are more difficult to classify

To summarize, the main difference between these algorithms is the way they identify and generate synthetic samples. After dividing the data into 50% training group and 50% test group, the next step was to process the raw data using different oversampling methods to achieve a similar or equal count of fraudulent or non-fraudulent records (Table 4). A total of 284,315 fraudulent records (containing both original and synthetic records) will eventually be obtained, matching the original number of non-fraudulent data.

Table 4. Oversampling result.

		Algorithms			
		SMOTE	BSMOTE	SMOTESVM	ADASYN
Counter	0 (Non-fraud)	284,315	284,315	284,315	284,315
	1(fraud)	284,315	284,315	284,315	284,298

4 Fraud Detection Model

A confusion matrix is built to analyze the dummy classifier, displaying the actual (in a row) and predicted (in a column) class labels of the dataset, and provides valuable insight into the model performance (Table 5). The matrix contains 4 components: True Positive (TP) represents a correct determination of normal records; False Positive (FP) shows the type I error, where some normal transactions are misclassified as fraudulent, leading to unnecessary investigation and human intervention; False Negative (FN) represents the type II error, where the model fails to identify fraudulent transactions. It is the most essential threat, as it will lead to enormous potential business loss; True Negative (TN) is the most important element, denoting fraudulent transactions that are correctly predicted.

Table 5. Confusion Matrix.

Confusion Matrix		Predicted Status	
		Non-Fraud	Fraud
Actual Status	Non-Fraud	TP	FP (Type I error)
	Fraud	FN (Type II error)	TN

4.1 Valuable Performance Evaluation Metrics

The model can be assessed using several performance metrics, including accuracy, specificity, and fraud detection rate.

Accuracy comes in first, which provides an overall assessment, and demonstrates how many transactions can be accurately predicted. Nevertheless, this metric has no value in any unbalanced dataset because it assesses the accuracy of TP and TN as a whole, whereas NP, the subject of our study, is only a small fraction. Therefore, accuracy, in this case, cannot be used to determine whether the model is effective in identifying fraud.

Specificity measures the proportion of actual fraudulent cases that the model correctly identifies out of all predicted fraud. A higher specificity score indicates that fewer manual interventions are needed to repeatedly check the disputed transactions. In addition, the fraud detection rate can be used to measure whether all fraudulent transactions are accurately identified and not missed. A valuable model will have high specificity and high fraud detection rate, so that all fraudulent transactions can be effectively detected, and potential losses can be minimized.

4.2 Machine Learning Algorithm

In this study, a total of nine algorithms, as well as four oversampling methods, were applied to develop a robust and accurate fraud detection model. These models are designed to effectively differentiate between fraudulent or legitimate credit card transactions. To measure the effectiveness of these models, three key performance metrics were used to thoroughly evaluate and analyze their capabilities and performance.

As can be seen from the Tables 6 and 7, most of the fraud detection models exhibit high accuracy when applied to both training and testing datasets, but their performance in terms of specificity and detection rate is unsatisfactory. While the overall accuracy of the models is high, indicating a large number of correct predictions, the low specificity implies that many legitimate transactions are incorrectly identified as fraudulent. This may potentially lead to unnecessary investigations and inconvenience to customers. In addition, the low fraud detection rate suggests that the model may not be able to effectively identify true fraud situations, which would potentially lead to undetected fraudulent activity, and result in ongoing losses to customers and credit institutions. Therefore, although the model has high overall accuracy, due to its poor specificity and low detection rate, there is a need for the model to be improved in order to increase its effectiveness in accurately identifying fraudulent transactions.

Table 6. Train and test result summary (1).

Algorithms	Accuracy for training set	Accuracy for testing set	Specificity for total set	Detection rate for total set
LogisticRegression/SMOTE	97.21%	97.18%	7.13%	89.23%
LogisticRegression/BSMOTE	99.05%	99.06%	15.80%	86.79%
LogisticRegression/SMOTESVM	99.23%	99.22%	14.25%	85.16%
LogisticRegression/ADASYN	97.00%	97.04%	6.78%	89.43%
GaussianNB/SMOTE	86.73%	86.79%	15.34%	75.61%
GaussianNB/BSMOTE	94.39%	94.42%	21.54%	63.01%
GaussianNB/SMOTESVM	96.64%	96.71%	29.09%	58.94%
GaussianNB/ADASYN	87.00%	86.93%	15.12%	78.46%
KNeighborsClassifier/SMOTE	100.00%	97.35%	8.26%	100.00%
KNeighborsClassifier/BSMOTE	100.00%	99.85%	57.23%	73.98%
KNeighborsClassifier/SMOTESVM	100.00%	99.86%	57.94%	74.19%
KNeighborsClassifier/ADASYN	100.00%	97.32%	8.09%	100.00%
DecisionTreeClassifier/SMOTE	99.80%	99.61%	29.12%	97.36%

Table 7. Train and test result summary (2).

Algorithms	Accuracy for training set	Accuracy for testing set	Specificity for total set	Detection rate for total set
DecisionTreeClassifier/ADASYN	99.87%	99.71%	34.75%	98.17%
RandomForestClassifier/SMOTE	100.00%	99.99%	93.89%	100.00%
RandomForestClassifier/BSMOTE	99.99%	99.98%	96.61%	92.68%
RandomForestClassifier/ADASYN	100.00%	99.99%	93.89%	100.00%
GradientBoostingClassifier/SMOTE	99.91%	99.82%	48.30%	98.37%
GradientBoostingClassifier/SMOTESVM	95.87%	95.93%	27.67%	59.55%
GradientBoostingClassifier/ADASYN	99.99%	99.94%	74.70%	99.59%
XGClassifier/SMOTE	100.00%	99.98%	91.26%	99.80%
XGClassifier/BSMOTE	100.00%	99.98%	95.62%	93.09%
XGClassifier/SMOTESVM	100.00%	99.98%	95.61%	92.89%
XGClassifier/ADASYN	100.00%	99.98%	88.79%	99.80%
LGBMClassifier/SMOTE	99.98%	99.95%	70.11%	99.19%
LGBMClassifier/BSMOTE	100.00%	99.98%	93.69%	93.50%
LinearDiscriminantAnalysis/SMOTE	93.26%	93.22%	11.20%	83.13%
LinearDiscriminantAnalysis/BSMOTE	98.08%	98.14%	31.23%	68.29%
LinearDiscriminantAnalysis/SMOTESVM	98.35%	98.32%	62.20%	62.20%

4.3 Best Model

The algorithmic model, using the random forest classifier and SMOTE technique performs exceptionally well on the important measures (Fig. 3). The ROC curve of the model for the training dataset shows a perfect AUC of 1, indicating that the trained model can accurately classify fraudulent and legitimate transactions, making it an ideal classifier (Fig. 4).

An accuracy of 99.9% was shown in the test results, enabling the model exhibits an impressive and accurate prediction capability. In addition, the model achieved a perfect fraud detection rate of 100%, which means that all fraudulent transactions are successfully identified by the model. Furthermore, the model has a high specificity of about 93.9%, indicating that only a very small percentage of normal records are misclassified as fraudulent. This could be attributed to the fact that a few normal records may have some anomalies that pose a higher risk. However, only a small number of additional resources are required for re-detection, which is consistent with the goal of minimizing costs.

Overall, the superior accuracy, perfect fraud detection rate and high specificity make the model an effective tool for identifying fraudulent transactions, that can help credit institution optimize their resource allocation and reduce unnecessary expenses and losses.

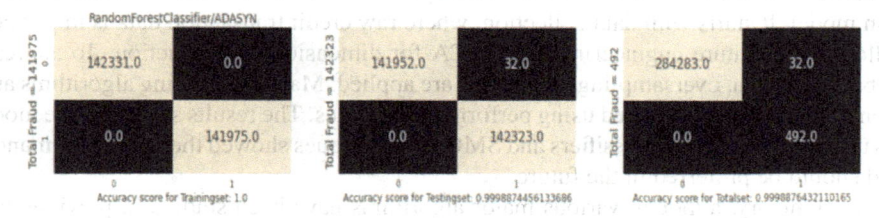

Fig. 3. Train and test result of Random Forest Classifier /SMOTE.

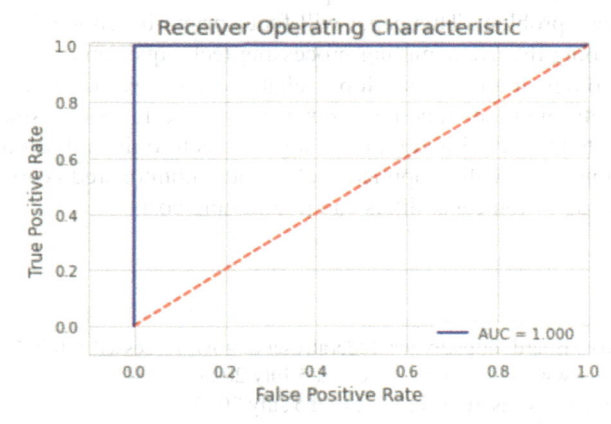

Fig. 4. ROC Curve of trainset using Random Forest Classifier /SMOTE.

5 Business Application and Future Development

First, continuous system maintenance and optimization of the model guarantee the long-term effectiveness of the application. In addition, credit institutions can improve their monitoring systems based on users' purchase history and behavioural habits. This system can combine supervised and unsupervised machine learning techniques. Supervised techniques rely on historical transaction data to identify fraud, while unsupervised outlier detection techniques use outliers in the transaction distribution to identify potential types of fraudulent activity, even previously unseen types. As a result, they can develop personalized risk assessments for different customers and provide proactive alerts. In the future, cross-platform data sharing and cooperation between multiple credit institutions can be established to integrate data information and improve the overall quality of fraud detection. At the same time, there is a need to improve network security and enhance privacy protection measures for user's information on data-sharing platforms. In addition to internal operations management, institutions should provide education to users to raise their security awareness when using credit cards and empower them with effective precautions to reduce the risk of fraud.

6 Conclusion

In conclusion, the paper follows a structured procedure to build an effective fraud detection model. It starts with data collection, where raw credit transaction data is imported, followed by feature engineering using PCA for dimensionality reduction. To address imbalanced data, oversampling techniques are applied. Machine learning algorithms are then employed and evaluated using performance metrics. The results show that the models using random forest classifiers and SMOTE techniques showed the best performance and should be preferred in the future.

In summary, although various major algorithms have been studied in previous literature, there is still room for improving the accuracy of credit card fraud detection. Rare research has been conducted on the application of methods and algorithms to solve the data imbalance problem. This paper will focus primarily on the data-driven detection model, combing the oversampling processing techniques and supervised machine learning methodology. It aims to develop a reliable data-based fraud detection program that can accurately pinpoint fraudulent transactions. The following study utilized the dataset from September 2013 and multiple algorithms to train and test the model. The resulting detection model will be applied to efficiently monitor credit card security while optimizing fraud detection capabilities and minimizing costs.

References

1. Federal Reserve Board. https://www.federalreserve.gov/. Accessed 5 July 2023
2. Forbes. https://www.forbes.com/. Accessed 5 July 2023
3. Inscribe. https://www.inscribe.ai/. Accessed 5 July 2023
4. Varmedja, D., Karanovic, M., Sladojevic, S., Arsenovic, M., Anderla, A.: Credit card fraud detection - machine learning methods. In: International Symposium INFOTEH-JAHORINA (INFOTEH) (2019)
5. Sailusha, R., Gnaneswar, V., Ramesh, R., Rao, G.R.: Credit card fraud detection using machine learning. In: International Conference on Intelligent Computing and Control Systems (2020)
6. Taha, A.A., Malebary, S.J.: An intelligent approach to credit card fraud detection using an optimized light gradient boosting machine. IEEE Access **8**, 25579–25587 (2020)
7. Esenogho, E., Mienye, I.D., Swart, T.G., Aruleba, K., Obaido, G.: A neural network ensemble with feature engineering for improved credit card fraud detection. IEEE Access **10**, 16400–16407 (2022)
8. Carcillo, F., Le Borgne, Y.-A., Caelen, O., Kessaci, Y., Oblé, F., Bontempi, G.: Combining unsupervised and supervised learning in credit card fraud detection. Inf. Sci. **557**, 317–331 (2021)
9. Maniraj, S.P., Saini, A., Ahmed, S., Sarkar, S.D.: Credit card fraud detection using machine learning and data science. Int. J. Eng. Res. **08**(09), 110–115 (2019)
10. Makki, S., Assaghir, Z., Taher, Y., Haque, R., Hacid, M.-S., Zeineddine, H.: An experimental study with imbalanced classification approaches for credit card fraud detection. IEEE Access **7**, 93010–93022 (2019)
11. Towards Data Science. https://towardsdatascience.com/. Accessed 5 July 2023

The Impact Caused by the COVID-19 Pandemic Re-opening on Catering Industry in China: A Short-Term Perspective

Shiqi Pan[✉]

College of Computer Science and Technology, Jilin University, Changchun 130012, Jilin, China

pansq1020@mails.jlu.edu.cn

Abstract. As the development of rational epidemic prevention policies, catering industry was under a period of recovery after the downturn caused by Covid-19. Depending on some studies, Covid-19 pandemic have great impacts on consumer behavior including eating less in public restaurants and having high requirements on restaurant environment; as a result, many restaurants suffer heavy losses. The implementation of full deblocking policy is double-edged for the rebound of catering industry market. In this article, we focused on catering factory market in China and daily stock data from February 2020 to June 2023 is extracted. The study used the ARIMA model to assess the relationship between variables. Based on the result, the deblocking policy have an obvious positive simulation on catering industry in short term but already have the tendency to get into a bull market. The study analysis the degree of the impact caused by the Covid-19 on catering industry in China and offers its stakeholders to avoid investors pile into a stock and other follow.

Keywords: Covid-19 Pandemic · Catering Industry · Stock Returns · Over-reaction

1 Introduction

Statistics show that among the top industries most impacted by the outbreak, the catering sector came in at number two [1]. In China, the coronavirus pandemic has had a significant impact on catering industry. In 2020, total catering sales in China was less than 4 trillion yuan affected by the new coronavirus epidemic [2]. Then in December 2020, the catering sector in China is on the mend. However, the domestic epidemic occurred frequently at the beginning of 2022 and the catering business was severely impacted in several locations. Total catering industry revenue in China was 20040 billion yuan in the first half of 2022, a 7.7% year-over-year decline. Later in 2023, after the implementation of lockdown policy, the economic recovery accelerated month by month, and catering became a reliable means to drive economic growth [3].

The impacts of Covid-19 on catering industry fall into two major categories, the first being the changes in consumer behavior, and the second being the actual impacts on individuals and employees in retail and food service. To be more exact, consumer behavior can be divided into social behavior and psychological behavior. In terms of social behavior, people were eating less in public restaurants because of restriction from social distancing affected by the epidemic, which makes many restaurants suffer heavy losses [4].

Chenyu Zhang et al. had found close association between consumer's psychological behavior and Covid-19 in China. Based on LDA (Latent Dirichlet Allocation) topic analysis results, prior to the epidemic, consumers were more inclined to frequent celebrity restaurants and place a higher value on food quality, while after the outbreak, consumers are more concerned with modifications to meals, the eating experience and the prevention of epidemics [5]. Meanwhile, the number of parcels and takeaways is also increasing. In terms of sentiment analysis, consumer confidence in the rehabilitation and growth of the catering business is evident from the emotional state of consumers after the outbreak, which is more optimistic than it was before the pandemic.

Additionally, individuals and employees in retail and food service were under great pressure. During the pandemic, workers in the food service industry face a wide variety of unknown risks to their daily work, mainly including infection and infecting others, isolation and various customer demands. Therefore, they are experiencing heightened mental distress due to where they work and the daily discrimination they experience there [6].

These previous studies highlighted how Covid-19 altered people's behaviors and habits from consumer side and employee side. With the open of the epidemic, study on changed consumer preference and catering industry might help enterprises to recovery faster from the epidemic. In that way, stock price might rise and it may stimulate stock return volatility. However, only a few studies discussed how exactly the stock price of the catering factory reacts to changes in the Covid-19 pandemic. To fill the void, this study will take catering industry in China as an example to study the impact caused by the Covid-19 pandemic on catering industry stock price in China form a short-term perspective. The study will find out the impacts through the compare between the predicted data and the actual data using the time series model and history information.

The rest of this paper is structured as follows: information about the data source, data stability, and the models in this paper is covered in Sect. 2. Section 3 follows, with a full discussion of the results from the ARIMA model, as well as additional analysis on the compare between predicted data and the actual data. Following that, there is a discussion on the study's focus, objective, and importance. Finally, Sect. 5 reiterates the final conclusion briefly.

2 Research Design

2.1 Data Source

Data on catering industry market in China is available in many financial terminals, and the study extracted daily and weekly closing stock prices respectively from February 3,2020 to June 6,2023, from the Wind financial terminal (https://www.wind.com.cn/portal/zh/WFT/index.html). Meanwhile this paper takes December 12,2022 as the opening time node, because the new epidemic prevention policy enacted by the China State

Council on this day ended the three-year long strict control measures including social distancing rules, lockdown measures and self-quarantines [7]. Data from February 3,2020 to December 12,2022 therefore is regarded as historical information used to predicted what would the stock prices go on if the open policy of Covid-19 did not carry out. Then the study compares the predicted data and the actual data from December 12,2022 to June 6,2023 to find out the impacts on catering industry causing by the Covid-19 both in short term and long term.

2.2 Weak Stationarity Test: ADF Test

Testing whether or not the data are stationary is the essential to prediction. Based on the ADF test in Stata in Table 1, the p-value for daily and weekly catering industry closing stock prices in China are both not equal to 0, which is considered not statistically significant.

To solve the problem, catering industry stock returns are obtained by dividing the difference between two days' closing stock prices by the one on the previous day, and data is calculated by the formula $\ln(1 + x)$. The second order difference are given by dividing the difference between two days' stock returns by the one on the previous day, the transform formula is as same as the first difference. Processing the daily and weekly raw data following the formula above respectively, and continuing analysis in the logarithmic scale.

The p-value for daily catering industry stock return and weekly catering industry stock return in China are all equal to 0, consequently, the data-driven model is now feasible.

Table 1. Weak stationarity test.

	t	p
Daily		
Raw	−2.034	0.5830
1st order difference	−16.979	0.0000
2nd order difference	−30.063	0.0000
Weekly		
Raw	−2.165	0.5096
1st order difference	−8.913	0.0000
2nd order difference	−13.065	0.0000

2.3 Auto Regressive Integrated Moving Average (ARIMA) Model

ARIMA model is a combination of Auto Regressive model, Moving Average model and difference method, and it has been applied in many prediction problems [8]. The model is used to express in the form of ARIMA (p, d, q), where the parameter p and q are the lag orders of AR Model and MA model respectively and parameter d is the order of the difference.

AR Part. The study's choice of model was the AR model, and the separate time serious variables was denoted by x_t, , resulting in an AR (p) model.

$$x_t = \Phi_0 + \Phi_1 x_{t-1} + \cdots + \Phi_p x_{t-p} + \alpha_t + e_{,t} \qquad (1)$$

The Eq. (1) above is for catering industry stock return. To clarify, in Eq. (1) $\Phi_0 + \Phi_1 x_{t-1} + \cdots + \Phi_p x_{t-p} + \alpha_t$ represents a linear function of past lags of catering factory stock return in China, while e_t is the error term.

MA Part. Based on the AR model, MA model constrain that the order of the model is limited. Moreover, MA model is a linear function of white noise hence the model is naturally stationary.

$$x_t = c_0 + a_t - \theta_1 a_{a-t} - \cdots - \theta_1 a_{t-1} + e_t \qquad (2)$$

Similar to AR model, in Eq. (2) $c_0 + a_t - \theta_1 a_{t-1} - \cdots - \theta_1 a_{t-1}$ represents a linear function of past lags of catering industry stock return in China, while e_t is the error term.

ARMA (p, q). Equation (5) displays the ARMA model's general formulation. The AR(p) is represented by the abbreviated component $\Phi_0 + \sum_{i=1}^{p} \Phi_i y_{t-i}$, , whereas MA(q) completes the equation. Future value is predicted by AR(p) model by applying historical catering stock returns from February 3,2020 to December 12,2020, while MA(q) forecasts using an error term.

$$y_t = \Phi_0 + \sum_{i=1}^{p} \Phi_i y_{t-1} + \alpha_t - \sum_{i=1}^{p} \theta_i a_{t-1} \qquad (3)$$

3 Empirical Results and Analysis

3.1 Order of ARIMA Model

To determine the lag orders for AR(p) and MA(q) in relation to the order of the stock return in logarithm, PACF and ACF can be useful. The study built ARIMA model for both daily stock return and weekly stock weekly because all of the four figures present the trailing.

The daily stock return of catering industry in China is transformed by the formula of first order difference, while the weekly stock return of it is operated in the second order difference.

For both PACF and ACF plots in the Fig. 1, the first portion beyond the critical values is 8; this shows that AR(p) and MA(q) both have orders of 8, and that the values of p and q are equal to 8.

In the Fig. 2, the first portion for PACF plots beyond the crucial value is 7, showing that AR(p) have order 7. As for ACF plots, all value after lag order 1 are within two standard deviations, illustrating that MA(q) have order 1.

PACF   ACF

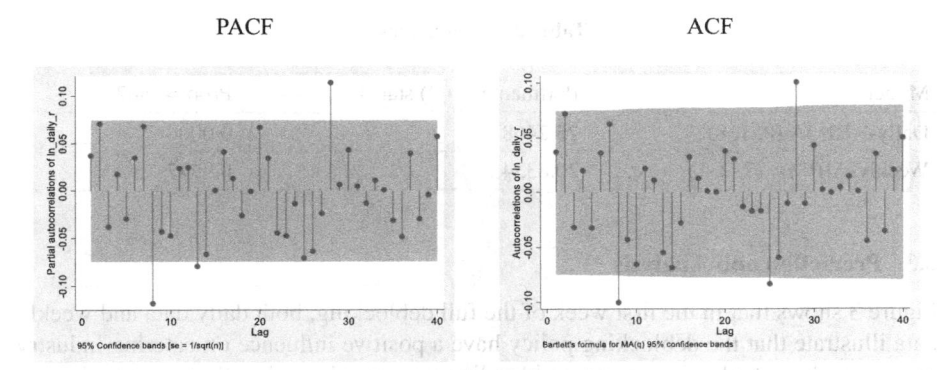

Fig. 1. PACF and ACF of daily stock return. Photo credit: Original

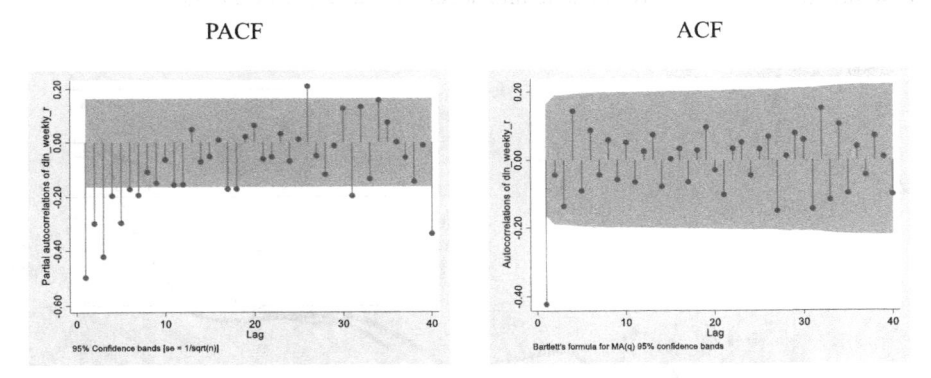

PACF   ACF

Fig. 2. PACF and ACF of weekly stock return. Photo credit: Original

3.2 ARIMA Estimation Results

After the discussion of lag orders for modeling, Daily-ARIMA (8,1,8) and Weekly-ARIMA (7,2,1) was built for daily and weekly time series respectively.

Table 2 contains the residual test for two ARIMA models had been built. P-value for the Weekly-ARIMA model is greatly larger than 0.1. However, P-value for the Daily-ARIMA model is less than 0.1 and approximately equal to 0, which is considered as rejecting the null hypothesis and. In other words, the residual sequence of Daily-ARIMA model is not white noise sequence. Although the Daily model fails the residual test, the main purpose of this study is not giving accurate predictions, therefore the model still has application value.

Table 2. Residual test.

Model	Portmanteau (Q) statistic	Prob > chi2
Daily-ARIMA (8, 1, 8)	75.2468	0.0006
Weekly-ARIMA (7, 2, 1)	20.8334	0.9947

3.3 Prediction and Analysis

Figure 3 shows that in the first week of the full deblocking, both daily data and weekly data illustrate that the deblocking policy have a positive influence on catering industry market as the actual value shown in blue line was mainly higher than the fitted value shown in orange line. Although the stock price seems to have no response to the opening in the first three days, it is reasonable and acceptable as a period of "lag".

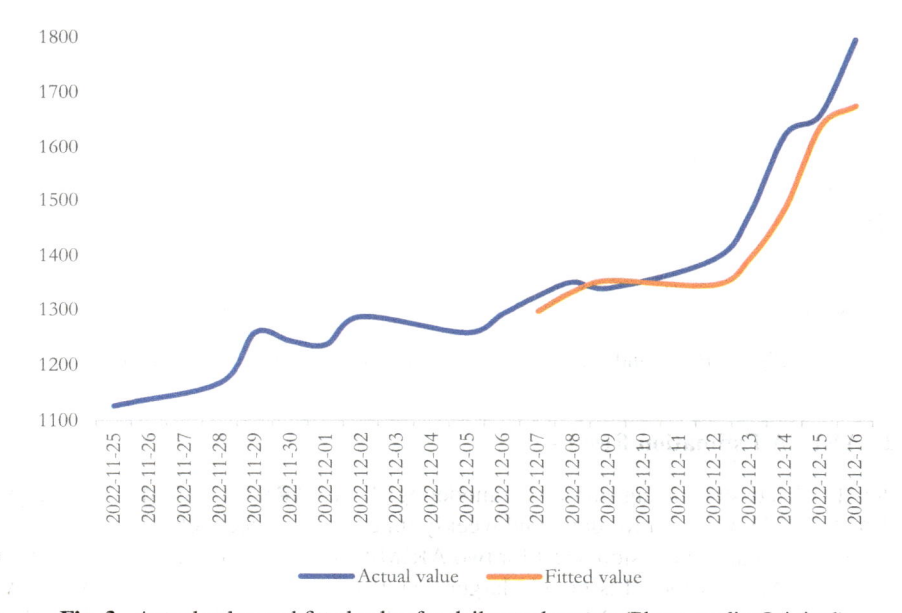

Fig. 3. Actual value and fitted value for daily stock return (Photo credit: Original).

Combining two figures, the stimulation effect of the opening policy did not last for long time. Actual value of catering industry stock price kept higher than fitted value of that until the fifth week. Meanwhile the stimulation degree rase in the first week but started to fall down in the second week, mainly keeping up a stable level in the next two weeks.

The sharply decline of the stock prices shown in the Fig. 4 can be explained as the phenomenon of over-reaction in behavioral economics. The book Irrational Exuberance, written by Robert Shiller, the expert of behavioral economics, published in March 2000 and called the then-rising stock market as "an irrational, self-driven and self-inflating bubble" [9]. Historical research has found out that investors will become more pessimistic about stocks that suffer losses but become more optimistic about lucrative stocks [10]. In fact, the rise in stock prices of catering industry is inevitable and predictable hence the passenger flow volume for restaurants would surge after the lockdown. Then tons of investors would buy the stocks and that would keep the stock prices going up. In this way, the implement of opening policy caused the catering industry rase rapidly in a short term and eventually lead to a bull market.

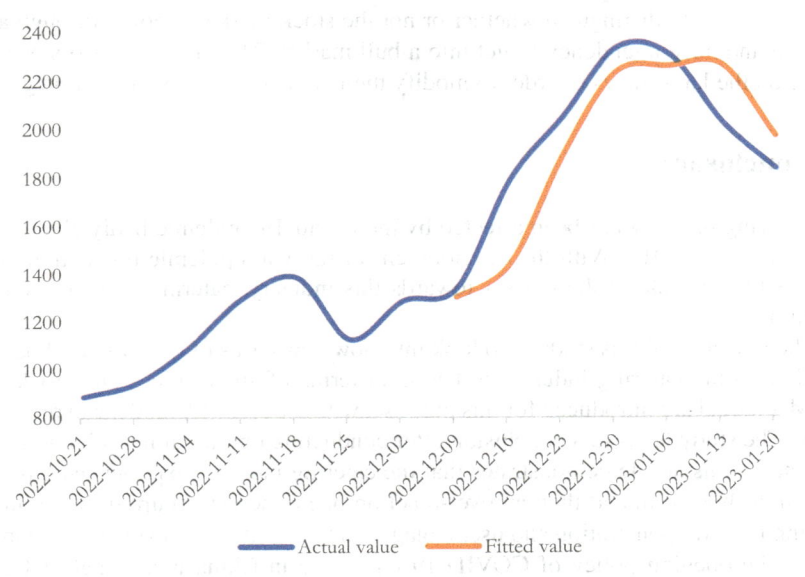

Fig. 4. Actual value and fitted value for weekly stock return (Photo credit: Original).

4 Discussion

In comparison to historical studies, this paper focuses on how COVID-19 pandemic affects the stock return of catering industry in China, whereas existing articles discuss the COVID-19 pandemic impact on mental health, living habits, interactive behaviors, information dissemination or infodemic on social media. Although some articles investigate stock market performance during the pandemic, their conclusions and topics are more related to other industries such as healthcare, education, social media and energy, and so on. However, one similarity between us in analyzing stock market volatility is that many authors adopted methodology or related transformations such as AR model, MR model, ARIMA model, VAR model, or others in their research to determine stock market movements.

Through this study, managers of catering companies could pay more attention to designing contingency strategies for the emergence of potential black swan events in order to avoid the creation of a bad atmosphere so that the whole industry supply chain on catering industry is relatively stable and can optimize the company's profit model. Further, supervise stakeholders and market participants with catering industry accounts, such as policymakers or organizations, taking responsibility to regulate and assure the direction of the discussion is vital, especially in the case of an accident.

The strict epidemic control had inflicted heavy losses on the physical catering stores, but the Covid-19 is only a temporary setback for this industry, and it serves as a reminder for catering industry to widen the industrial chain and build brand effect. According to the findings of this study, it is important for investors who are concerned about catering industry stocks to distinguish whether or not the stock market is going through a overreaction and have a tendency to get into a bull market. Therefore, investors need keep an eye on the latest news in order to modify their short-term investment strategies.

5 Conclusion

The catering industry has been affected by the Covid-19 epidemic badly all around the world started at 2019. With the development of rational epidemic prevention policies and positive attitude of the masses towards this industry, catering industry is under a period of recovery.

The objective of this study is to look into how new cases of the Covid-19 pandemic correlate to the catering industry in China in terms of stock prices and stock return. ARIMA model are introduced for this purpose, with the ARIMA model can predict time series. The study leads to a conclusion after conducting empirical investigation.

Finally, this article demonstrates that the catering industry experienced a period of surge in a short term and then an over-reaction phenomenon occurred. It is a fact that catering industry penetration and user engagement were at a low level among pandemic period, the opening policy of COVID-19 pandemic in China is a signal of Business recovery. The pandemic impact on the long-term future of the catering industry stock return and its volatility will eventually diminish and return to normal, following the general trend of the stock market.

One weakness of this paper is that it only focuses on the impact of the epidemic on stock prices and does not discuss other factors such as stock volatility. At the same time, this study focuses on the short-term impact only, and further research is needed on the long-term impact caused by epidemic on the catering industry.

References

1. Data of CDA Data Science Research Institute (2020). https://baijiahao.baidu.com/s?id=1657787884046607639
2. Data of Food China website. A comprehensive interpretation of dining! The White Paper on the ecology of China's Catering Industry in 2022 was officially released (2022). http://food.china.com.cn/2022-08/12/content_78369879.htm
3. Data of 21jingji website. "China's Catering Consumption Trend in 2023" released: China's catering consumption K-shaped differentiation is obvious (2023). https://www.21jingji.com/article/20230522/herald/c77090f5ad53899c56eab784166cad99.html

4. Data of China Cuisine Association. Novel Coronavirus Pneumonia Epidemic Situation and Development Trend Analysis Report 2020 China (2020). http://www.ccas.com.cn/site/content/204393.html
5. Zhang, C., Jiang, J., Jin, H., Chen, T.: The impact of COVID-19 on consumers' psychological behavior based on data mining for online user comments in the catering industry in China. Int. J. Environ. Res. Public Health **18**(8), 4178 (2021)
6. Rosemberg, M.-A., Adams, M., Polick, C., Li, W.V., Dang, J., Hsin-Chun Tsai, J.: COVID-19 and mental health of food retail, food service, and hospitality workers. J. Occup. Environ. Hyg. **18**(4–5), 169–179 (2021)
7. Lee, S., Liu, B., Jung, S., Kim, B.: The effect of vaccination during the COVID-19 for the restaurant industry. Int. J. Hospit. Manag. **110**, 103451 (2023)
8. Chang, Q.: Study on the impact of epidemic situation on catering industry and its countermeasures——from the perspective of takeout business. Int. J. Front. Sociol. 4(12) (2022)
9. Li, F., Liu, J., Zhang, M., Liao, S., Hu, W.: Assessment of economic recovery in Hebei Province, China, under the COVID-19 pandemic using nighttime light data. Remote Sens. **15**(1), 22 (2023)
10. Sullistiawan, D., Rudiawarni, F.A., Feliana, Y.K., Grigorescu, A.: Do investors overreact to COVID-19 outbreak? An experimental study using sequential disclosures. Contemp. Econ. **17**(1), 43–57 (2023)

The Impact of the Russia-Ukraine War on Tesla: Evidence from ARIMA Model

Jintian He(✉)

College of Art and Science, State University of New York at Stony Brook, New York 11794, USA
Jintian.he@stonybrook.edu

Abstract. This paper examines the impact of geopolitical events, specifically the Russia-Ukraine war, on Tesla's stock price. This study utilizes an autoregressive integrated moving average (ARIMA) model to analyze weekly and monthly stock closing prices from February 2022 to June 2023. The core objective of the study is to examine what impact an increase in oil prices due to the Russia-Ukraine war would have on the electric vehicle industry, specifically Tesla Inc. The main findings showed that escalating tensions led to an initial spike in Tesla's stock price, driven by higher oil prices and the urgency for alternative energy sources. However, while eventually stabilizing at the end of the forecast period, supply chain disruptions caused by the war led to a significant drop in inventory values. This study contributes to the financial literature by integrating geopolitical risk assessment into stock price forecasting models, demonstrating how ARIMA can be used in the context of unforeseen international crises. The study highlights the need for resilience in global supply chains and highlights potential areas for policy intervention. It also demonstrates that investors view geopolitical risk as an integral part of their investment strategy, further emphasizing the need for tools such as ARIMA in financial forecasting and decision making.

Keywords: Russia · Russo-Ukrainian War · Tesla · ARIMA Model

1 Introduction

On 24 February 2022, Russia invaded and occupied parts of Ukraine in a major escalation of the Russia-Ukrain War [1]. At the same time, since Russia was a major oil exporter, the dramatic decrease in oil production during the war and the fact that the Biden administration banned Russian oil exports to the United States to impose sanctions on Russia, led to a 42% increase in oil prices during the first year of the war [2]. As shown in Fig. 1 below, the dotted line shows the start of the Russo-Ukrainian war on February 24, 2022, when the price of oil was $90+, and within the next ten days, by March 2, 2022, the price of oil had soared to $115+. The significant increase in energy prices led to an increase in the cost of almost all goods and services, further increasing inflationary expectations. At the same time, oil being the blood of industry, American industry was naturally affected significantly [3].

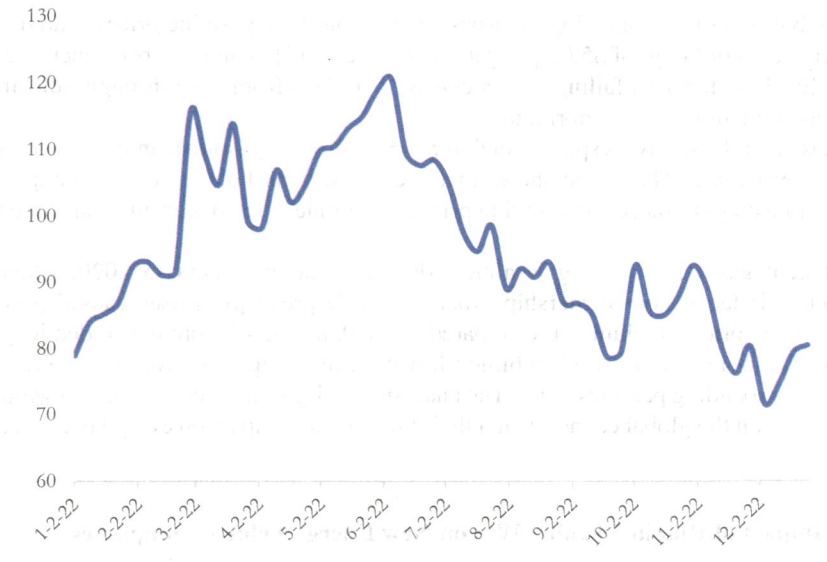

Fig. 1. Changes in oil prices in 2022. Data source: Crude oil price data from 2022.1.2 to 2022.12.2 were downloaded from investing.com and plotted in a line chart table on excel. (Photo credit: Original) [4]

In this article, Tesla, a well-known American company, was selected as an example, and all stock data of Tesla since its IPO were used, and ARIMA was used for modeling as well as analysis to study how Tesla's stock price was influenced by the price of oil. It also predicts the future direction of Tesla's stock price.

This paper has the remaining five parts, the second part 2. Literature review introduces the relationship between war and oil prices, and the impact of war on the new energy vehicle industry. The third part, Research Design, explains the data sources and the analysis of the closing price of Tesla shares using ADF and ARMA. The fourth section, Empirical Results and Analysis, summarizes and analyzes the results obtained in the third section, and then makes a forecast for the market. The fifth section, Discussion, explains how this paper differs from the existing literature and how it can be understood and used by policy makers and regulators. The sixth section concludes the paper.

2 Literature Review

2.1 The Direction of U.S. Oil Prices Due to the Russian-Ukrainian War

President Biden announced that the United States will not support Putin's war, calling the new sanctions against Russia a "powerful blow" to its ability to finance ongoing conflicts. Although the United States imports about 100,000 barrels of oil per day from Russia, this represents only 5% of Russia's total crude oil exports and 8% of U.S. oil and petroleum product imports [5].

However, these restrictions have inadvertently led to an increase in already rising oil and gasoline prices, putting further financial pressure on consumers, businesses, and the global economy. Following the Russian invasion, U.S. gasoline prices soared 42%, reaching a record high of $5.02 per gallon on June 14 [2]. While the price increase was short-lived, with prices falling for 98 consecutive days from June through September, the economic impact was enormous.

Last year, U.S. drivers spent a total of $528 bilslion on gasoline, an increase of $120 billion over 2021. This surge shows that each U.S. household is still spending about $900 more on gasoline, despite falling prices since June when prices hit an all-time high [2].

Recent gasoline spending is almost double what was spent in 2020, when the pandemic-induced homeownership order and widespread job losses caused gasoline demand and prices to plummet. Compared to 2019, the year before the epidemic, gasoline spending increased by $156 billion last year, resulting in an average of $1,200 in additional spending per household. The analysis highlights the ripple effects of geopolitical events on the global economy and their far-reaching impact on everyday consumers [2].

2.2 Impact of Russia-Ukraine War on New Energy Vehicle Companies

The Russian-Ukrainian conflict has had a profound impact on the global supply of key raw materials for electric vehicles (EVs). With the EU targeting zero emissions by 2050, demand for copper, aluminum and silicon is expected to increase, but the war threatens these supply chains, delaying the timeline. Russia supplies a significant portion of the EU's palladium, aluminum, nickel, platinum, copper, cobalt, and lithium [5]. The war has also affected the production of Ukrainian neon gas, an important component of electric vehicle batteries [6].

In addition, a large portion of the uranium used in European nuclear reactors comes from Russia. The conflict has prevented the price of clean technologies such as lithium-ion batteries from falling, driving lithium prices up two and a half times this year. Cobalt prices are at record levels, while increases in nickel and neon costs are expected to add $3,000 to the price of each electric vehicle.

Meanwhile, U.S. electric vehicle prices continue to rise, averaging about $63,000 in January, about 35% higher than the industry average for all vehicles. In the case of Tesla, the subject of our analysis, Tesla has raised the price of its Model 3 sedan by 18%, largely due to supply chain disruptions. This situation presents significant challenges as mainstream consumers are unwilling to pay a significant premium for technology they have not yet fully adopted [7].

However, rising oil prices will increase consumers' daily car costs, then will prompt consumers to reduce demand for oil cars, while various governments are now supporting electrified transportation, so more people will transform to use new energy transportation. According to the sample survey, close to 40% of U.S. citizens decided to purchase an electric vehicle in the next five years. Also, after the increase in gas prices, Tesla's order revenue increased by 80% compared to before the increase in gas prices, which is good news for Tesla [8].

3 Research Design

3.1 Data Source

This paper critically examines the impact of the Russia-Ukraine war on Tesla's stock market performance. Using data from investing.com, this paper analyzes Tesla's weekly and monthly closing stock prices since its initial public offering (IPO) [9]. Given that the conflict erupted on February 24, 2022, this paper strategically extracted stock price data from February 2022 to June 2023. The stock price data for this period provides a comprehensive understanding of Tesla's financial dynamics in the midst of the geopolitical crisis. To improve the accuracy of the study, weekly and monthly data were scrutinized. Through this methodical approach, this paper endeavored to provide a detailed and accurate analysis of how the Russia-Ukraine war affected Tesla's stock market performance over a defined period of time.

3.2 Log Returns

This study combines an analysis of Tesla's closing stock price from February 2022 to June 2023 using data processed by Stata. To capture the nuances of Tesla's stock performance, the investigation uses a logarithmic transformation, a method that helps stabilize volatility and present proportional changes more clearly.

The procedure begins with the calculation of the log price. This part uses the mathematical formula:

$$Return_t = \ln(1 + price_t) \tag{1}$$

where "$price_t$" represents the closing price of each trading day. In Stata, this is done using the command gen ln_index1 = ln(1 + index1), which generates a new variable "ln_index1", indicating the log price.

This paper then calculate the log returns to gain insight into the exponential growth rate of stock prices. This is done in Stata using the command gen ln_index1r = d.ln_index1. Here, d.ln_index1' indicates the first difference of 'ln_index1', resulting in the log returning the variable 'ln_index1r'.

3.3 Weak Stationarity Test: ADF Test

In this paper, the Augmented Dickey-Fuller (ADF) test was employed to test for the stationarity of the weekly and monthly closing stock prices of Tesla. Stationarity, a prerequisite for the accurate application of many time series models, including the ARIMA model deployed in this study, signifies that the statistical properties of a series are constant over time.

In both the weekly and monthly data, the raw series have high p-values, indicating failing to reject the null hypothesis of the ADF test – that the series has a unit root and is therefore not stationary. However, after taking the first and second order differences, the p-values drop to zero. This suggests that the differenced series are stationary as it is workable to reject the null hypothesis at any conventional level of significance.

These results offer crucial insights into the 'I' component of the ARIMA model. It suggests that, to ensure stationarity, the first (in the case of the monthly data) or second (in the case of the weekly data) differences of the series should be taken prior to the application of the ARIMA model. The enhanced model accuracy resulting from this stationarity ensures more reliable predictions and interpretations of Tesla's stock price behavior amid the Russia-Ukraine conflict (Table 1).

Table 1. Weak stationarity test.

	t	p
Weekly data		
Raw	−1.832	0.6894
1st order difference	−16.549	0
2ne order difference	−31.609	0
Monthly data		
Raw	−1.476	0.8370
1st order difference	−8.188	0

3.4 ARIMA Model

Autoregressive (AR(p)): In the context of Tesla's stock prices, an autoregressive component would mean that today's stock price can be forecasted from the stock prices of the previous 'p' days. For example, if continuing work with an AR (1) model, today's stock price would be dependent on yesterday's stock price, plus some error.

For instance, the AR (1) model:

$$X_t = c + \varphi_1 * X_{t-1} + \varepsilon_t \qquad (2)$$

This could be interpreted as today's (time t) Tesla's stock price (X_t) being equal to a constant term (c), plus a factor of yesterday's (time t − 1) stock price ($\varphi_1 * X_{t-1}$), plus some random error (ε_t).

Integrated (I(d)): The integrated part in the model refers to the differencing of the observations. This helps in making the time series data stationary. For instance, if this paper have a series of Tesla's stock prices that exhibits a trend (thereby making it non-stationary), this paper could apply differencing to remove this trend and make the series stationary.

For example, a first-order differenced series I (1) is calculated as:

$$X_t = \mu + \varepsilon_t + \theta_1 * \varepsilon_{t-1} \qquad (3)$$

$$\Delta X_t = X_t - X_{t-1} \qquad (4)$$

where ΔX_t represents the change in stock price from one day (t-1) to the next (t).

Moving Average (MA(q)): The moving average part involves modeling the error term ε_t as a linear combination of the past 'q' error terms. For instance, if this paper has an MA (1) model, it suggests that the error today (ε_t) is a function of the error in the previous day (ε_{t-1}).

For instance, the MA (1) model:

$$X_t = \mu + \varepsilon_t + \theta_1 * \varepsilon_{t-1} \tag{5}$$

It could be interpreted as today's Tesla's stock price (X_t) being equal to a constant term (μ), plus today's error term (ε_t), plus a factor of yesterday's error term ($\theta_1 * \varepsilon_{t-1}$).

This mix of AR and MA processes helps model a wide array of time series data. The coefficients on the lagged values and errors (the θ's) in the ARMA model represent the effect those values have on the current point in the series.

In the context of Tesla stock price analysis, the ARMA model would use both past stock prices and past forecast errors to predict the future stock price. It gives an equation that, when given the past 'p' observed prices and 'q' observed errors, can be used to estimate the next stock price.

$$X_t = \theta_1 + \sum_{i=1}^{p} \theta_i * X_{t-1} + a_t - \sum_{i=1}^{q} \theta_i * a_{t-1} \tag{6}$$

4 Empirical Results and Analysis

4.1 Order Identification

In both graphs, the horizontal lines typically seen above and below zero on the y-axis represent the confidence intervals (usually at 95%). If a spike extends beyond these intervals, it's considered statistically significant. According to the weekly PACF and ACF graphs in Fig. 2, the Y-axis (the horizontal lines) is the dependent variable, PACF, and ACF of the log of Logarithmic return of TSLA, and the X-axis is the time lag order. The area bounded in y-axix which means by y = ±2 standard error refers to the 95% confidence interval for AR(p) and MA(q).

According to Table 2, the p-values are 0.3881 and 0.7081. The p-values are quite high for both models, which fail to reject the null hypothesis. In simpler terms, this indicates that the residuals in the models are independently distributed, and there is no autocorrelation present, and implies that the models have captured the underlying correlation structure in the data.

4.2 Forecasting and Analysis

In the model, the weekly and monthly stock closing prices of Tesla after the outbreak of the Russian-Ukrainian war show some interesting trends. For the weekly data from Fig. 3, an initial spike followed by a sharp decline after the fifth week is observed; for the monthly data from Fig. 4, a similar pattern of rising and then a significant decline after the second month is observed.

PACF   ACF
Weekly data

Monthly data

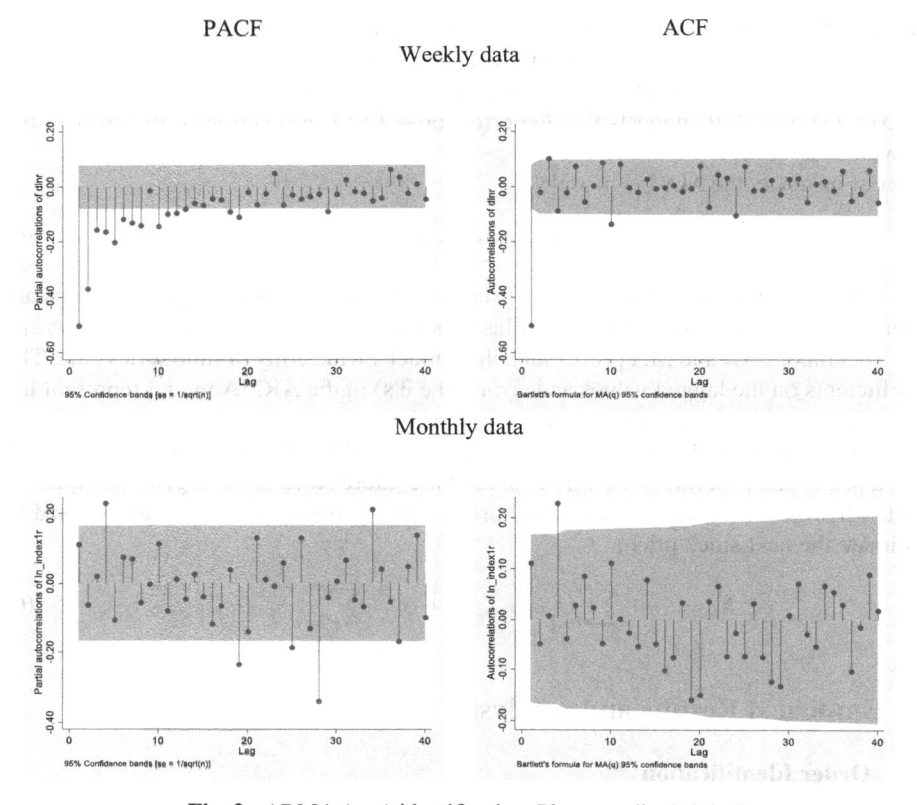

Fig. 2. ARMA (p, q) identification. Photo credit: Original

Table 2. Residual test.

Model	Portmanteau (Q) statistic	Prob > chi2
Weekly-ARIMA (8, 2, 1)	41.9074	0.3881
Monthly-ARIMA (4, 1, 4)	34.6807	0.7081

The rise in Tesla stock price in the early weeks and first month of the war could be attributed to the market's perception of electric vehicles (EVs) as a viable alternative to rising oil prices due to the war. Investors could have seen Tesla, a leader in the EV industry, as a safe haven that would have pushed its stock price higher. This initial spike could also have been driven by market speculation, which is not uncommon during periods of heightened geopolitical tensions.

However, the subsequent decline may be related to several factors. The escalating war could disrupt the supply chain for key electric vehicle components. As mentioned earlier, Russia and Ukraine are major suppliers of raw materials critical to EV batteries (e.g., nickel, palladium, and semiconductor-grade neon gas). These supply disruptions

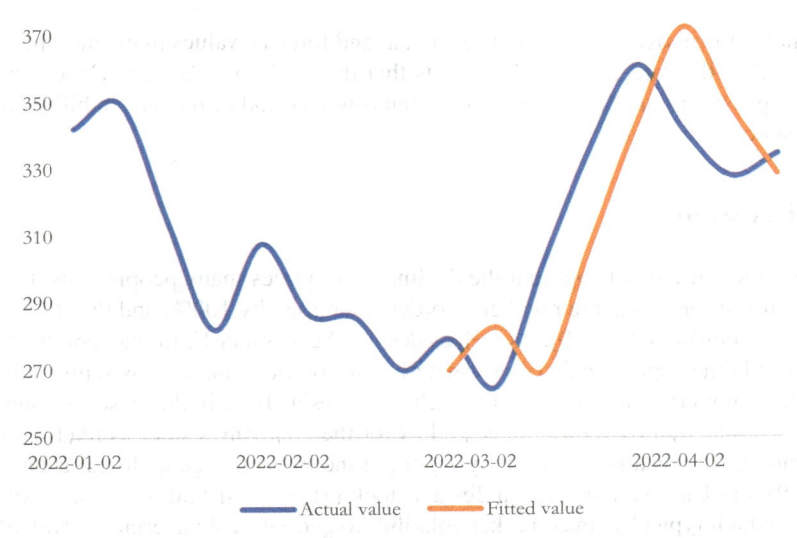

Fig. 3. Actual value and fitted value, Weekly data (Photo credit: Original).

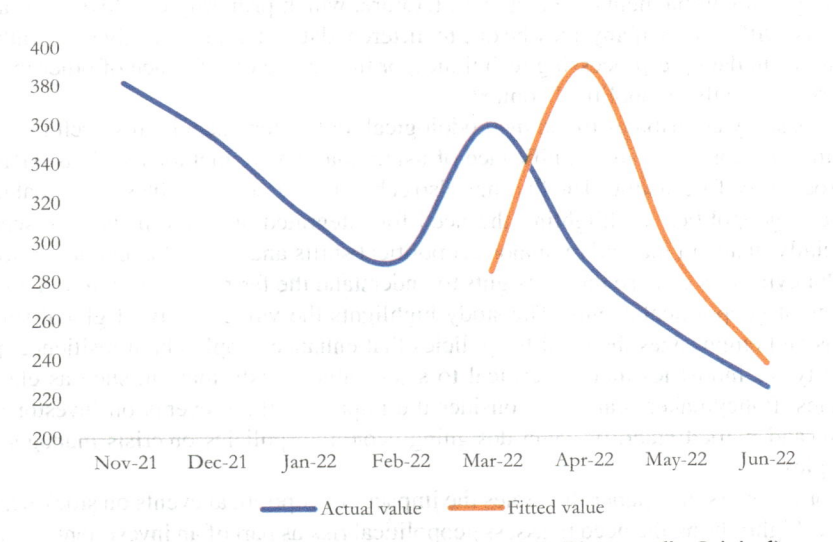

Fig. 4. Actual value and fitted value, Monthly data (Photo credit: Original).

would inevitably affect Tesla's production capacity and could lead to a decline in investor confidence, which could cause the stock price to fall.

In addition, the steady decline in oil prices from all-time highs could erode investor enthusiasm for electric vehicle stocks such as Tesla. As oil prices become cheaper, the urgency to move to electric vehicles may lessen, which could affect Tesla's market perception.

Finally, the narrowing gap between actual and forecast values in the monthly model at the end of the forecast period suggests that the model is adapting to the new price trend, suggesting that the market may be entering a period of relative stability after the initial shock of the war.

5 Discussion

Existing literature points out that the decline in oil prices many people consider a permanent transition Tesla, the number of orders increased by 100%, and the stock is on a continuous upward trend [10]. As well as despite the Russian-Ukrainian conflict has led to a break in the supply chain of raw materials for production, such as semiconductors, but still cannot affect the strong trading chain of Tesla, Tesla in this case still intends to increase production by 2 million as well as for the company's stock is ready to rise in preparation. The results of this study highlight the impact of geopolitical events, such as the Russia-Ukraine conflict, on Tesla's stock price, consistent with the existing literature, which typically links market volatility to geopolitical uncertainty. Notably, the use of the ARIMA model in this study provides a quantitative dimension to this understanding and complements the existing literature, which primarily employs qualitative analysis. Differences, if any, may be due to different data intervals (weekly vs. monthly), variations in data pre-processing techniques, or the degree of influence of other market factors outside the geopolitical context.

This study contributes to the methodological toolkit for financial research by highlighting the feasibility and significance of using quantitative methods such as ARIMA for stock price forecasting. The findings also echo the interconnectedness of global markets and geopolitics, highlighting the need for integrated analysis in future research, especially in an era marked by major geopolitical shifts and technological disruptions.

Policymakers can use these insights to understand the far-reaching economic implications of geopolitical events. The study highlights the vulnerability of global supply chains and emphasizes the need for policies that enhance supply chain resilience, particularly for industries that are critical to sustainable transformation, such as electric vehicles. Policymakers can also consider the impact of these events on investor sentiment and market stability when designing economic policies or crisis management strategies.

For investors, this paper illustrates the impact of geopolitical events on stock performance, highlighting the need to assess geopolitical risk as part of an investment strategy. Tesla investors in particular can appreciate the company's exposure to the global supply chain and the impact of raw material prices on the value of its stock. In addition, the predictive power of the ARIMA model shown here could potentially be adopted or adapted to forecast other stock prices to inform investment decisions. However, investors should view these forecasts as part of a broader analytical framework, combining them with other market indicators and risk assessment tools to gain comprehensive investment insights.

6 Conclusion

This paper provides a comprehensive analysis of the impact of the Russia-Ukraine conflict on Tesla's stock price using an ARIMA model, demonstrating the intricate relationship between geopolitical events, global commodity markets, and stock prices. The study uses weekly and monthly data for the period from February 2022 to June 2023, a period of high geopolitical tensions and subsequent disruptions in global supply chains.

The findings show that Tesla shares rose sharply in the initial weeks and first month after the outbreak of war, likely due to higher oil prices during this period. As a leader in the electric vehicle (EV) industry, Tesla was seen as the safer choice, which pushed up its share price. However, the initial spike may have been driven by market speculation and urgency for energy alternatives, rather than Tesla's inherent market dominance.

The study also found that Tesla's stock price declined significantly in both weekly and monthly numbers after the initial spike. This decline has been linked to disruptions in the supply of key raw materials for electric vehicle batteries, such as nickel, palladium and semiconductor-grade neon gas, due to the escalation of the war. The steady decline in oil prices from historic highs may also have dampened investor enthusiasm for electric vehicle stocks such as Tesla, causing its stock price to fall.

At the end of the forecast period, the model shows that the gap between actual and forecast stock values is narrowing, suggesting that the market may be stabilizing after the initial shock triggered by the war. These findings underscore the utility of forecasting models such as ARIMA in dealing with stock market volatility and informing policy decisions and investment strategies in the face of geopolitical uncertainty.

References

1. Askew, J.: Ukraine War: A month-by-month timeline of the conflict so far. Euronews (2023). https://www.euronews.com/2023/01/30/ukraine-war-a-month-by-month-timeline-of-the-conflict-in-2022
2. Chapman, M.: As war in Ukraine intensifies, US gasoline hits record $4.17. AP News (2022). https://apnews.com/article/russia-ukraine-business-europe-05ba4a25cbee9b5281804d3a5b60f058
3. Isidore, C.: One year into Ukraine War, US gas prices are lower. here's what to expect ahead. CNN (2023). http://www.cnn.com/2023/02/25/energy/us-gas-prices-one-year-after-invasion/index.html
4. Sangita, S.: Opinion: Impact of the Russia-Ukraine War on the Global EV Industry. Emobilityplus (2022). https://emobilityplus.com/2022/05/27/opinion-impact-of-the-russia-ukraine-war-on-the-global-ev-industry/
5. Hockenos, P., Schwägerl, C., Conniff, R., Struzik, E.: How Russia's war is putting Green Tech progress in jeopardy. Yale E360 (2022). https://e360.yale.edu/features/russiaukraine-war-metals-electric-vehicles-renewables
6. Reuters. How Russia's invasion of Ukraine means more expensive EVS. Euronews (2022). https://www.euronews.com/next/2022/03/08/first-covid-now-war-russia-s-invasion-of-ukraine-is-dashing-hopes-of-more-affordable-elect
7. Bustos, C.: Tesla orders surge 100% as people turn to electric cars amid high gas prices. Entrepreneur (2022). https://www.entrepreneur.com/business-news/tesla-orders-surge-100-as-people-turn-to-electric-cars/421969

8. Evannex. Will soaring oil & gas prices cause Tesla's stock to rise? InsideEVs (2022). https://insideevs.com/news/575074/tesla-stock-market-rising-gas-prices/
9. Investing.com, crude oil price. https://cn.investing.com/commodities/crude-oil
10. Popli, N.: High gas prices drive up interest in electric vehicles. Time (2022). https://time.com/6173178/high-gas-prices-electric-vehicles/

Research on the Link Between RMB Exchange Rate and Tesla's Stock Price: A Long-Term Perspective

Jinhao Yu(✉)

International College, Xiamen University, Xiamen 361005, China
u7722325@anu.edu.au

Abstract. After China's exchange rate reform, the exchange rate has changed more frequently. The foreign exchange market has an increasing impact on the securities market. This paper analyzes the link between Tesla's stock price and exchange rate of the renminbi against US dollar by establishing VAR model and ARMA-GARCHX model. In the empirical analysis, this paper uses Tesla's daily stock price from June 29, 2010, to June 9, 2023 and the daily exchange rate in the same period as the research data. And the unit root test, impulse response analysis and ARMA GARCHX estimation are used to test the data. Through empirical analysis, this paper concludes that the exchange rate will indeed have an impact on Tesla's stock price, and this impact is mainly negative. Compared with other studies in the same field, the research object selected in this paper is more detailed and specific. This study helps to predict the change of Tesla's share price and preserve the stability of financial markets in the event of exchange rate changes, and investors, policy makers and Tesla itself can also adjust their strategies and plans according to this law. Policy makers can apply the conclusions of this paper to affect the stock market by manipulating exchange rate changes.

Keywords: Exchange Rate · Stock Price · VAR Model · ARMA-GARCHX Model

1 Introduction

Tesla has developed rapidly since its listing on the Nasdaq Stock Exchange on June 29, 2010, and now has become the world's largest new energy vehicle company. Tesla's share price has been rising all the way, with a record 13 consecutive days of rising in June 2023 raising Tesla's share price by more than 40% and a market value increase of nearly $240 billion [1]. Tesla's rapid development is closely related to Tesla's super factory in Shanghai, China. Since Tesla's Shanghai Super factory was put into operation in 2020, Tesla's global delivery in 2021 has increased by more than 80%, and Tesla's Shanghai Super factory's delivery in 2023 is expected to exceed the total delivery of Tesla's factories in other countries, At the same time, the Chinese market contributes more than 30% of Tesla's sales, which shows that the Chinese market is very important to Tesla. Moreover, with the gradual opening of China's financial market after the reform and opening-up, the flow of international capital is becoming more and more frequent, so the impact of exchange rate is becoming more and more significant. Especially after China's exchange rate reform, the RMB exchange rate has changed from unilateral appreciation to two-way volatility. And the volatility and uncertainty have increased significantly, which may lead to changes in Tesla's stock price. The study of the link between Tesla's stock price and exchange rate helps to explore and analyze the link between exchange rate market and stock market, which is important to preserve the good operation of financial markets.

The first part of this paper is introduction. This part will introduce the research background, significance, and research purposes. The second part is literature review. In this part, there is a collation and analysis of the relevant literature. The third part is the experiment design. This part will introduce the data sources and model settings of this paper. The fourth part is the empirical analysis part, which will use VAR model and ARMA-GARCHX model to carry out the empirical test and summarize the results of the empirical test. The fifth part is the discussion part, which analyzes the research conclusion of this paper. The last part is a summary of the main research results of this paper.

2 Literature Review

In the field of Finance, there are two mainstream assumptions to explain the link between exchange rates and the prices of stocks. First, DOM Busch R and Fischer S. put forward the flow-oriented hypothesis. He believes that the exchange rates can lead to changes in the stock prices of companies by affecting trade in goods [2]; Second, Branson put forward the stock-oriented hypothesis. He considers that the change of capital account is an important way for exchange rate to affect the stock price of enterprises [3]. Kim and Yang found that capital inflows will increase asset prices and affect stock prices by studying Asian financial markets [4]. Kumar built the nonlinear Granger causality test and NARDL test to analyze India's exchange rate, petroleum price and stock price. His results show that there is an unidirectional and non-linear causal link between exchange rate and stock price [5]. Shahrestani and Rafei studied the impact of petroleum price and exchange rate on stock price of Tehran stock exchange under different state transitions through MS-VAR model. The results show that there are different state probability transitions between the prices of stock and exchange rates [6]. Wong used the MGARCH model to analyze the relation between the prices of stocks and exchange rates in seven countries, including Japan, the Philippines, and the United Kingdom [7]. The results proved that there was a negative correlation between exchange rates and the prices of stock. Aloui and Aïssa used the Vine-Copula model to explore the multivariate dependency link between U.S. crude, exchange rate, and stock returns. They pointed out that there was a negative Kendall dependency link between stock returns and dollar exchange rate, but also a positive tail dependency relationship [8]. Zhu et al. constructed the financial index under the same framework of exchange rate, interest rate and stock price, and found that there was a statistical causal relationship between the three [9]. However, not all studies show a significant connection between the prices of stocks and exchange rates. Adeniyi and kumeka studied the connection between exchange rates and the prices of stocks of 54 listed companies in Nigeria and found that for most listed companies, the link between stock prices and exchange rates is not prominent [10]. Liang from the two countries relative sensitivity factors of common stock of the stock prices point explains the connection between the prices of stocks and exchange rates, finding that rising exchange rates may have a negative influence on the prices of stocks in a long period time [11].

From the above literature, we can see that most of the literature believes that exchange rate will affect stock prices. Several papers have also pointed out that rising exchange rates will have a negative influence on the prices of stocks. However, the research object of the above literature is the whole stock market, and there is no research on the stock of a specific listed company. In this paper, I collect data, establish models, empirical analysis. And I summarize the results of empirical analysis, pointing out how to use the research results of this paper.

3 Research Design

3.1 Data Source

This paper uses Tesla's daily stock price from June 29, 2010, to June 9, 2023, and the daily exchange rate in the same period as the research data. Tesla's daily share price comes from stock price data released on the NASDAQ Exchange, and the daily exchange rate comes from data released by the Bank of China on the Renminbi to US Dollar Exchange Rate. Besides, the time series data cannot be directly analyzed quantitatively, so it is necessary to take logarithms to eliminate the influence of Heteroscedasticity in time series data. Among them, lNTESLA is Tesla's log stock price, LNER is the log exchange rate, LNTESLAR is Tesla's log stock price yield, and LNERR is the log exchange rate yield.

3.2 Weak Stationarity Test

Because many economic data are not stable in real life, it is requisite to first conduct ADF unit root test on the data first in order to ensure that the data used in the empirical study is stable and prevent false regression of time variable data (Table 1).

Table 1. Weak Stationarity Test: ADF test.

	t	p
Price		
Tesla	−1.772	0.7183
USD to RMB	−2.053	0.5722
Return		
Tesla	−39.767	0.0000***
USD to RMB	−39.665	0.0000***

From the unit root test, it's clear to see that Tesla's log and exchange rate data accept the original assumption that there is a unit root, indicating that this series is a nonstationary time series, which means Tesla's log stock price data and log exchange rate data are unstable. After the first order difference, Tesla's log stock price yield data and log exchange rate yield data are obtained. It can be seen that Tesla's log stock price yield and log exchange rate yield data reject the original hypothesis at the significant level of 1%, which proves that the data after the first order difference is stable. Therefore, this paper selects these two sets of stable data for empirical analysis.

3.3 VAR Model Setting

This paper selects vector auto-regressive model to empirically test the link between Tesla's stock price and exchange rate. Vector auto-regressive model or VAR model for short, is a very commonly used econometric model, which can be used to analyze the dynamic relationship between variables in multiple time series. There are two variables in the data selected in this paper, so the binary VAR model is selected, and the model formula is shown in the table below:

$$Y_t = C_1 + \sum\nolimits_1^n \alpha_i Y_{t-i} + \sum\nolimits_1^n \beta_i X_{t-i} + \varepsilon_1, t = 1.2\ldots, n \qquad (1)$$

$$X_t = C_2 + \sum\nolimits_1^n \alpha_i X_{t-i} + \sum\nolimits_1^n \beta_i Y_{t-i} + \varepsilon_2, t = 1.2\ldots, n \qquad (2)$$

3.4 ARMA-GARCHX Model Setting

ARMA-GARCHX model needs to model the mean and variance respectively, because the residuals in ARMA model are white noise and have no research significance, so the residuals should meet the GARCH process; In the GARCH model, the mean equation is a constant, which also has no research significance, so the mean should meet ARMA. The APMA model is shown in the table below:

$$x_t = \emptyset_0 + \sum_{i=1}^{p} \emptyset_i x_{t-i} + \alpha_i - \sum_{i=1}^{q} \emptyset_i \alpha_{t-i} \qquad (3)$$

$\emptyset_0 + \sum_{i=1}^{p} \emptyset_i x_{t-i}$ represents the AR model, which is used to describe the impact of historical values on current values. And $\alpha_i - \sum_{i=1}^{q} \emptyset_i \alpha_{t-i}$ represents the MA model, which uses past volatility to estimate the future and the last part of the model.

The GARCH model is as follows:

$$\sigma_t^2 = \alpha_0 + a_1 \alpha_{t-1}^2 + \beta_1 \sigma_{t-1}^2 \qquad (4)$$

In the Eq. (4), term $a_1 \alpha_{t-1}^2$ is ARCH part and $\beta_1 \sigma_{t-1}^2$ represents GARCH part.

4 Empirical Results and Analysis

4.1 Order of VAR Model

Then, this part will determine the optimal number of lag periods. The test results of the number of lag periods of truss's stock price yield and exchange rate yield are as follows. From the test results, it can determine that the optimal number of lag periods is 12 (Table 2).

Table 2. Likelihood ratio test and information criterion.

Lag	LL	LR	p	FPE	AIC	HQIC	SBIC
0	22211.9			3.9e−09	−13.6845	−13.6831*	−13.6807*
1	22218.2	12.653	0.013	3.9e−09	−13.6859	−13.6819	−13.6746
2	22222.9	9.3683	0.053	3.9e−09*	−13.6863*	−13.6796	−13.6676
3	22225.8	5.7764	0.216	3.9e−09	−13.6856	−13.6762	−13.6594
4	22227.5	3.5351	0.473	3.9e−09	−13.6842	−13.6722	−13.6505
5	22229.6	4.2207	0.377	3.9e−09	−13.6831	−13.6683	−13.6418
6	22231.3	3.311	0.507	3.9e−09	−13.6816	−13.6642	−13.6329
7	22235.3	7.9197	0.095	3.9e−09	−13.6816	−13.6615	−13.6254
8	22240.6	10.673	0.030	3.9e−09	−13.6824	−13.6596	−13.6187
9	22243.1	5.0496	0.282	3.9e−09	−13.6815	−13.656	−13.6103
10	22245.6	4.9334	0.294	3.9e−09	−13.6806	−13.6524	−13.6018
11	22245.8	0.3511	0.986	3.9e−09	−13.6782	−13.6473	−13.592
12	22251.7	11.924*	0.018	3.9e−09	−13.6794	−13.6459	−13.5857

4.2 Impulse Response

Before impulse response, we need to test the stability of the model. The test results are as Fig. 1:

From the test results, it's clear to see that all points are distributed in the unit circle, which means that the model established by the time series data used in this paper is stable. So it can be used for impulse response analysis. The impulse response results are as Fig. 2:

From the results of impulse response (Fig. 2), it can be concluded that LNERR has a negative correlation with LNTESLAR in this period. The negative impact of phase 12 is the largest, reaching the lowest point of −0.014. While the positive impact of phase 2 is the largest, reaching the highest point of 0.0005, showing a complete convergence after phase 25. Impulse response results can show that increasing LNERR by one unit in the current period will mainly have a negative impact on the future period of LNTESLAR.

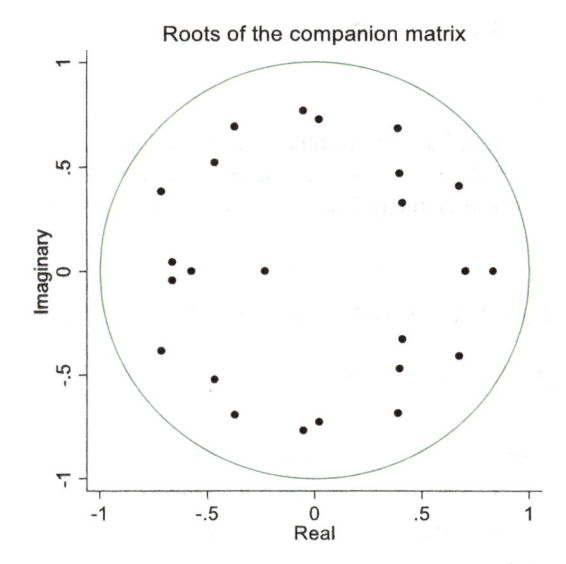

Fig. 1. Unit root test(Photo credit: Original).

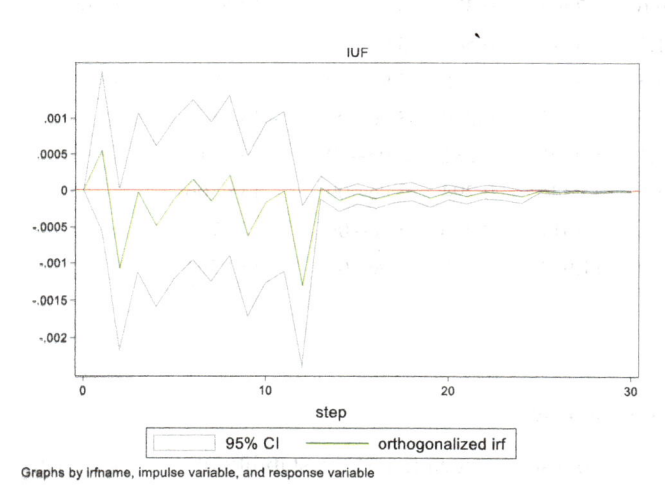

Fig. 2. Impulse and response (Impulse variable: USD to RMB) (Photo credit: Original).

Figure 3 shows Tesla's stock price changes in 2022. From the chart, it's easy to find that Tesla's stock price has a significant downward trend after the Federal Reserve began raising interest rates for the first time in March 2022. This is the same as the conclusion reached above, the Fed's interest rate hike will lead to the depreciation of the RMB, which will raise the RMB exchange rate and Tesla's stock price will fall.

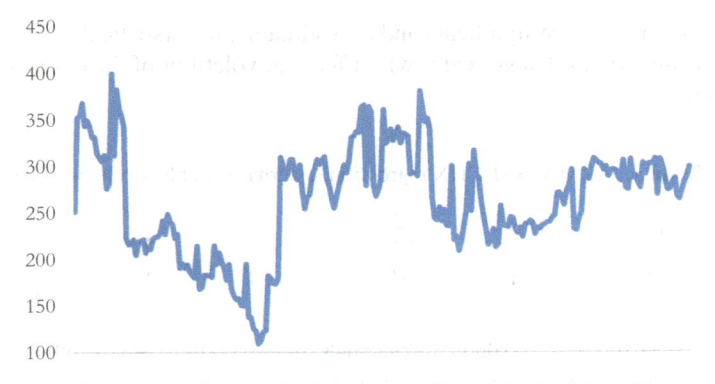

Fig. 3. Changes in Tesla Stock Price (Photo credit: Original).

4.3 ARMA Specification

Before using the ARMA GARCHX model to predict, we need to find the best the lag orders for AR(p) and MA(q). PACF and ACF can be used to derive the lag orders of AR (P) and MA (q), as shown in Fig. 4:

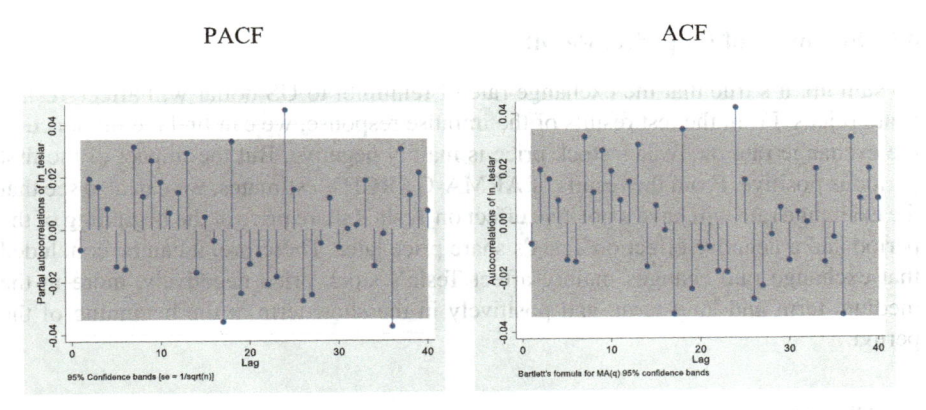

Fig. 4. ARMA (p, q) identification. Photo credit: Original

As can be seen from the above figure, the first part exceeding the critical value in PACF and ACF diagrams is 24, so the optimal order of AR (P) and MA (q) is 24 and the values of P and Q are 24.

4.4 ARMA-GARCH Estimation Results and Variance Equation

Tables 3 shows the ARMA-GARCHX model estimation results and the variance equation. From the table, it's easy to find that all the GARCH and ARCH terms both have p-values less than 0.05 in the variance equation. The results mean the GARCH and ARCH terms are significant. Furthermore, all the Logs but L1 in column (3) have p-values less than 0.05, proving they are significant and the estimating has statistical significance. The results show that the exchange really will affect the volatility of Tesla stock price to a certain degree.

Table 3. ARMA-GARCHX regression, external variable: exchange rate.

	(1)		(2)		(3)	
	Coef.	p	Coef.	p	Coef.	p
Exchange rate						
L0	284.1006	0.000	293.5648	0.000	−319.2692	0.000
L1	−11.74465	0.000	−233.2797	0.000	−85.0995	0.445
L2			−11.75571	0.000	362.2137	0.000
ARCH	0.0440537	0.000	0.0413848	0.000	0.0409543	0.000
GARCH	0.9504988	0.000	0.9513231	0.000	0.9500162	0.000
Constant	−11.74465	0.000	−11.75571	0.000	−11.79292	0.000

4.5 Summary of Empirical Results

To sum up, it's true that the exchange rate of renminbi to US dollar will affect Tesla's share prices. From the test results of the impulse response, we can find the influence of the exchange rate on Tesla's stock price is mainly negative. But the impact of the first period is positive. From the results of ARMA-GARCHX estimates, we can also see that the exchange rate will have a positive effect on Tesla's share price at the beginning of the period and a negative effect on Tesla's share price later. Therefore, it can be concluded that exchange rate changes mainly affect Tesla's stock price negatively, more in the medium term and long term, and positively in the short term at the beginning of the period.

5 Discussion

Compared with other studies, this paper selects a specific company stock as the research object, while most of the existing literature takes the financial market of the whole country as the research object, and the research object of this paper is more detailed. The conclusion of this paper is roughly the same as that of the existing literature. This paper also finds that the rising exchange rate does influence Tesla's stock price, and the impact is mainly negative. However, this paper finds that Tesla's stock prices are affected positively by the rising exchange at the beginning of the period in the process of empirical research, which can fill the gap of some related research in a certain way.

Because the exchange rate will affect the stock price, company director and investors need to pay more attention to the change of exchange rate so that they can eliminate the influence of exchange rate fluctuations on the company's operation so that they may avoid losses to the company or themselves. For policy makers, the conclusions of this paper can help them better regulate financial markets. Policy guidance can affect the stock price of listed companies by regulating the exchange rate, to regulate the market. When policy makers need to raise the share prices of Listed Companies in the short term, they can raise the exchange rate; When policy makers need to raise the share prices of Listed Companies in the medium and long term, they can lower the exchange rate. The conclusions of this paper can help investors make profits in the stock market. According to the conclusion of this paper, when the exchange rate rises, stock prices may ascend in the short term and decline in the medium and long term. Therefore, investors can make their own investment choices according to this law.

6 Conclusion

The objection of the study is to find the link between Tesla's stock prices and exchange rates. Besides, the paper also wants to analysis what kinds of impact will the change of exchange rate have on Tesla's share price. VAR and ARMA-GARCH models are introduced for the purpose, this study uses VAR models to explore the impulse response and the ARMA-GARCH model is used to assess the stock returns and conditional variances. After the empirical analysis, this paper has led to some conclusions.

Firstly, this paper demonstrates that the exchange rate does influence Tesla's stock price. The influence of exchange rate on the prices of stocks is mostly negative. Secondly, in the short run at the beginning of the period, the rising exchange rate will affect stock prices of Tesla negatively; in the medium term, the exchange rate will have a negative influence on stock prices of Tesla. And the impact is diminishing over time. Changes in exchange rates will influence stock prices, and thus financial markets. The research results of this paper can help to explain the impact of exchange rate on financial markets, so the use of the conclusions of this paper can help to preserve the regular operation of the financial market and promote the rapid development of financial markets.

References

1. Investing. Cn.investing.com. Accessed 9 June 2023
2. Dom Busch, R., Fischer, S.: Exchange rates and the current account. Am. Econ. Rev. **5**, 960–971 (1980)
3. Branson, W.H.: Macroeconomic Determinants of Real Exchange Rate. National Bureau of Economic Research Working Paper (1981)
4. Kim, S., Yang, D.Y.: The impact of capital inflows on asset prices in emerging Asian economies: is too much money chasing too little good. Open Econ. Rev. **22**(2), 293–315 (2011)
5. Kumar, S.: Asymmetric impact of oil prices on exchange rate and stock prices. Q. Rev. Econ. Financ. **72**, 41–51 (2019)
6. Shahrestani, P., Rafei, M.: The impact of oil price shocks on Tehran Stock Exchange returns: application of the Markov switching vector autoregressive models. Resour. Policy **65**, 101579 (2020)
7. Wong, T.H.: Real exchange rate returns and real stock price returns. Int. Rev. Econ. Financ. **49**, 340–352 (2017)

8. Aloui, R., Aïssa, M.S.B.: Relationship between oil, stock prices and exchange rates: a vine copula based GARCH method. North Am. J. Econ. Financ. **37**, 458–471 (2016)
9. Zhu, S., Kavanagh, E., O'Sullivan, N.: Inflation targeting and financial conditions: UK monetary policy during the great moderation and financial crisis. J. Financ. Stab. **53**, 100834 (2021)
10. Adeniyi, O., Kumeka, T.: Exchange rate and stock prices in Nigeria: firm level evidence. J. Afr. Bus. **21**(2), 235–263 (2020)
11. Liang, D.: Conditional correlation between exchange rates and stock prices. Q. Rev. Econ. Financ. **80**, 452–463 (2021)

Dynamic Impact of the Covid-19 on Cryptocurrency and Investment Suggestion

Haozhe Hong[✉]

International College, Jinan University, Guangzhou 511486, China
`hong2001@stu2020.jnu.edu.cn`

Abstract. Under the external impact of the COVID-19 epidemic, traditional financial markets have been negatively affected. In order to further explore the impact of COVID-19 on the cryptocurrency market price and investment, this paper adopts the comparative experiment method and use the ARIMA model to build the price trend of cryptocurrency before the outbreak point as a control group without COVID-19, and compares it with the real price trend of cryptocurrency affected by COVID-19 as an experimental group. Studies have found that external shocks such as the COVID-19 pandemic can cause cryptocurrency prices to rise significantly in the short term and lead to overreactions. Within a month after the shock occurs, the price converges to an equilibrium price that is higher than the initial price. This shows that when external shocks such as the COVID-19 pandemic occur, investors can increase their positions in cryptocurrencies to increase their safe-haven assets, and policymakers need to adopt opposite market policies for traditional financial markets and cryptocurrency markets in order to prevent large cash flows from traditional financial markets to cryptocurrency markets, which may result in increased instability in both. This paper has constructive significance for investors' rational investment behavior and policymakers' efficient market policy methods when external shocks such as COVID-19 occur.

Keywords: Contrast Experiment Method · Experimental Group · Control Group · Cryptocurrency Prices · Investment

1 Introduction

The COVID-19 pandemic has had a certain external impact on global financial markets. Xu Changling's paper, a study of the impact of the COVID-19 epidemic on major international financial markets [1], found that the Dow Jones Index and the Standard & Poor's index, which are "barometers" of the financial market, plunged, falling by as much as 30%, and the US stock market suffered multiple circuit breakers. At the same time, commodity markets were also highly volatile, with the price of West Texas Intermediate Crude Oil (WTI) falling from $17.50 to −$37.63. While investors are looking for safe havens, policy makers are also looking for ways to keep financial markets stable.

This paper uses the ARIMA model to construct the price trend of various cryptocurrencies in the absence of COVID-19 as the control group, and compares the data with the real price trend of cryptocurrencies as the experimental group, so as to quantitatively determine the impact of COVID-19 pandemic on the price of cryptocurrencies. This paper also predicts changes in the cryptocurrency market and reasonable investor responses to external shocks like the COVID-19 pandemic.

Firstly, on the impact of COVID-19 on financial markets. The paper examining the impact of the novel coronavirus on financial markets found that the impact of the novel coronavirus on the stock market was wavy [2], while the impact on the cryptocurrency market was relatively smooth. On this basis, this paper further elaborates the specific impact of the COVID-19 epidemic on the cryptocurrency market price, and uses ARIMA model and quantitative methods to judge the trend of cryptocurrency changes in different market sizes.

Moreover, there is the macroeconomic impact of the coronavirus pandemic. Feng Yifan and Wang Di pointed out in their paper on the impact of the novel coronavirus epidemic on the global economy and China's response [3], that the global novel coronavirus epidemic has impacted the normal operation of the global economy as a non-economic factor, and countries are forced to adjust their monetary policies, fiscal policies and trade policies to ease the downward pressure on the economy. On this basis, this paper explores that when external shocks such as the novel coronavirus outbreak occur, policy makers should adopt opposite market policies for the traditional financial market and the cryptocurrency market at the same time to prevent the aggravation of national economic fluctuations more effectively.

Further, in terms of the impact of the COVID-19 pandemic on cryptocurrencies. In a paper on the study of the New coronavirus epidemic, digital currency volatility and risk contagion [4], it is pointed out that although the digital currency market has certain local risk resistance, digital currency does not have systematic risk aversion ability and investment attributes dominate. On this basis, this paper further explores that investors should build a safe haven asset by adding positions in cryptocurrencies at near-equilibrium prices within a month after the outbreak of the COVID-19 pandemic, so as to avoid speculation caused by large purchases of digital currencies in the short term.

In addition, in the feasibility of the research method. This paper, the occurrence of the new coronavirus epidemic is controlled as a single variable, and then the ARIMA model is used to predict the price of cryptocurrency, and the comparison experiment is conducted with the real data. According to the proof made by Ahmer sabah in Bitcoin Price Prediction using ARIMA Model [5], the ARIMA model has practicability in the collection of historical data of bitcoin price and the prediction of future trend. The proof shows that it is legitimately to extend the ARIMA model to the category of cryptocurrencies that Bitcoin belongs to.

Besides, the innovation of this study is to quantify the increase of non-systemic risk from external shocks such as the COVID-19 pandemic and examine its impact on cryptocurrency prices. The literature related to this paper can be found in the paper of Bitcoin a better safe-haven investment than gold and commodities [6], which published by Shahzad and other scholars in 2019.The paper demonstrated in: Bitcoin in the case of internal shocks in the market to show the investment hedging properties and price trends.

However, this paper expands on the general price performance of cryptocurrencies under the event of external shocks to the market, which has not studied before.

2 Methodology

In this part, the paper will introduce the research methods in detail, including: data sources for modeling, unit root test and ARIMA model setting and other research settings and concepts.

The research design is mainly as follows: Firstly, the author chooses three cryptocurrencies with relatively large, medium, and small market sizes, namely Bitcoin, Ethereum and Tron. Moreover, the research collected all their price data and set the date of the COVID-19 outbreak as January 24, 2020. A logarithmic series of closing prices for the three currencies is then generated, as well as a logarithmic yield series. After that, the stationarity of the logarithmic series and the logarithmic return series of the three currencies is tested. The order of AR and MA are determined by drawing PACF and ACF graphs for three logarithmic return sequences. Finally, the ARIMA (p, d, q) model is constructed to predict the price of cryptocurrency after the outbreak of COVID-19.

In the summary part, comparative experiment method is adopted, and "whether the new coronavirus epidemic occurs" is controlled as a single variable. Moreover, the modeling data is used as the control group, and the actual price trend of each currency is compared as the experimental group. Compare two groups to obtain the impact of the new coronavirus epidemic on the price and investment of cryptocurrency.

2.1 Data Sources

The authors first downloaded weekly and monthly closing price data for Bitcoin, Ethereum and Tron from Investing [7] since their launch. After importing all the data into STATA, the time of the outbreak of COVID-19 was set as January 24, 2020, in order to use only the data before that time point for modeling.

Finally, the author will generate the logarithmic series and the logarithmic return series from the closing price data of the three currencies collected mainly for the following two reasons: 1. Ensure that the data after the difference is stationary data, which is convenient for time series model modeling and prediction. In the cryptocurrency market, there is usually a volatility in cryptocurrency closing prices over time, while logarithmic sequences have better stationarity. 2. Adjust the approximate normal distribution of the data to conform to the modeling assumptions of the time series model. Cryptocurrency closing prices typically show a right-skewed distribution with increased extreme values and large fluctuations, however, adjusting the closing prices to a logarithmic series will reduce the impact of outliers and make the data more consistent with a normal distribution.

2.2 Weak Stationarity Test

In this section, the author conducts a unit root test on the logarithmic price series of the three currencies constructed before, in order to judge whether the time series has

Table 1. Stationarity test.

	t	p
Bitcoin, Weekly data		
Raw	−2.037	0.5813
1st order difference	−14.991	0
2ne order difference	−27.372	0
Bitcoin, Monthly data		
Raw	−2.590	0.2847
1st order difference	−7.391	0.0000
2ne order difference	−12.899	0.0000
Ethereum, Weekly data		
Raw	−2.362	0.3999
1st order difference	−10.969	0
2ne order difference	−19.343	0
Tron, Weekly data		
Raw	−3.267	0.0719
1st order difference	−13.727	0
2ne order difference	−24.748	0

stationarity. Only when there is no unit root in the test result, that is, when the sequence is stable, can the subsequent ARIMA model modeling and prediction be carried out.

As shown in Table 1, this paper not only tests the stability of the weekly price series of the three currencies, but also tests the stability of the monthly price series of Bitcoin, laying the groundwork for the subsequent modeling to predict the long-term impact of the novel coronavirus epidemic. Simultaneously, the stationarity of time series under first and second difference is also tested.

In general, the T-values of the original sequences of the four sequences are not less than the critical value in the test results, and their P-values are also in a high position (Although the P-value of the original sequence of Tron is equal to 0.0719, it still has higher instability than the sequence after difference). Indicating that the null hypothesis cannot be rejected, that is, they all have unit roots and the sequences are not stable. On the other hand, The T-values of the four series differences are all greater than the critical value, and the p-values are all smaller than the significance level. It shows that the null hypothesis can be rejected, that is, the four kinds of time series after difference are considered stationary.

To sum up, the stationarity of the sequence after second-order difference is the best. Subsequent ARIMA models will be modeled using the data after second-order difference.

2.3 Order Determination and ARIMA Model Settings

In order to construct the ARIMA model, the authors not only determining the sequences using second-order difference, but also calculating the partial autocorrelation coefficients and autocorrelation coefficients of the four sequences respectively, as shown in the figure below.

Firstly, from the PACF chart of Bitcoin week data, it can be determined that the order of the AR model is 5. When the PACF value exceeds the confidence interval, the first point in the confidence interval is truncation, and the fifth order corresponding to it is the order of the AR model. Similarly, according to the monthly data of Bitcoin, the weekly data of Ethereum, and the weekly data of Tron, the PACF chart is obtained respectively. When the PACF value exceeds the confidence interval, the corresponding order of the points first falling at confidence interval are the seventh, sixth and fifth order respectively, which means the order of their AR models are 7, 6 and 5 respectively.

In addition, in the ACF chart, when the ACF value exceeds the confidence interval, the first point falling into the confidence interval is truncation. The order corresponding to this point is the order of the MA model. The ACF chart obtained from the weekly data of Bitcoin, monthly data of Bitcoin, weekly data of Ethereum and weekly data of Tron can be seen in Fig. 1. The corresponding order of all their truncation is 1. It shows that, the order of MA models of these four sequences is 1.

In summary, combined with the previously obtained modeling data from second-order difference sequences, the ARIMA models established for the four sequences are as follows: Bitcoin Weekly-ARIMA (5, 2, 1); Bitcoin Monthly-ARIMA (7, 2, 1); Ethereum Weekly-ARIMA (6, 2, 1); Tron Weekly-ARIMA (5, 2, 1).

2.4 Residual Test of ARIMA Model

After the ARIMA model is used for fitting, the author conducts residual test to check whether the residual after modeling conforms to the white noise sequence, and then judges the quality of model fitting. The residual test results after ARIMA model fitting for the four sequences are shown in the Table 2.

It can be seen from the Table 2 that: (1) The Q statistic of Bitcoin Weekly-ARIMA (5, 2, 1) is low, and the corresponding Prob > chi2 is 0.9929. This means that in the weekly data of Bitcoin, the residual sequence of this ARIMA model is not relevant, and the autocorrelation is not significant; (2) Similarly, in Bitcoin Monthly-ARIMA (7, 2, 1), the value of Q statistic is low and Prob > chi2 value is greater than the critical value, that is, the null hypothesis cannot be rejected, indicating that the data fitted by the model is not significantly different from the theoretical expectation; (3) On the other hand, the Q statistics of Ethereum Weekly-ARIMA (6, 2, 1) and Tron Weekly ARIMA (5, 2, 1) are both in the high level, indicating that their residual sequences have strong autocorrelation. Although the Prob > chi2 value of Ethereum Weekly-ARIMA (6, 2, 1) is 0.6386, their residual sequence still has some noise; (4) To sum up, in the extent that can be adjusted, Bitcoin Weekly-ARIMA (5, 2, 1) and Bitcoin Monthly-ARIMA (7, 2, 1) has a higher goodness of fit, but the fitting effects of Ethereum Weekly-ARIMA (6, 2, 1) and Tron Weekly-ARIMA (5, 2, 1) were relatively poor.

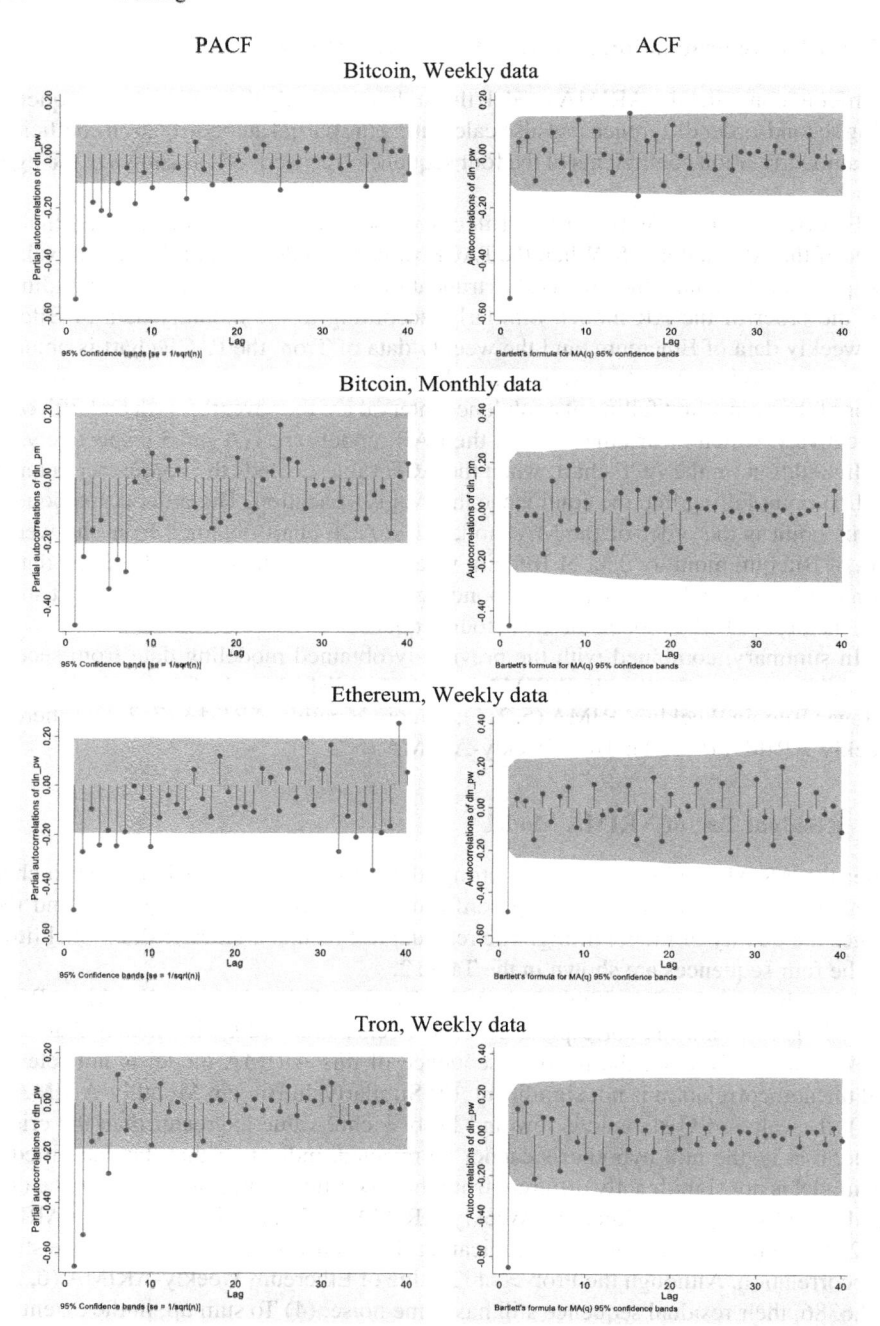

Fig. 1. ARMA (p, q) identification. Photo credit: Original

Table 2. Residual test.

Model	Portmanteau (Q) statistic	Prob > chi2
Bitcoin Weekly-ARIMA (5, 2, 1)	21.4122	0.9929
Bitcoin Monthly-ARIMA (7, 2, 1)	17.4160	0.9993
Ethereum Weekly-ARIMA (6, 2, 1)	99.1662	0.6386
Tron Weekly-ARIMA (5, 2, 1)	86.8570	0

3 Empirical Results and Predictive Analysis

The experiment selected the weekly prices of three cryptocurrencies with large, medium, and small market size to explore the short-term impact of the novel coronavirus epidemic on the prices of different cryptocurrencies.

And the author chose the monthly price of Bitcoin, which is the most representative cryptocurrency, to explore the long-term impact of the COVID-19 pandemic on cryptocurrency prices. The prediction results obtained after fitting the ARIMA model are shown in the figures below. For the prediction and comparison results of each chart, the author's summary analyses are as follow:

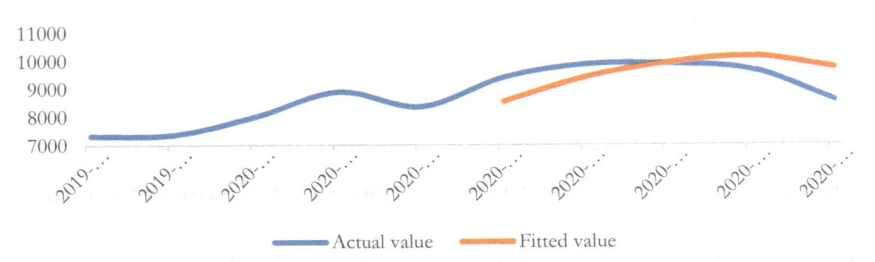

Fig. 2. Actual value and fitted value, Bitcoin-Weekly data (Photo credit: Original).

First of all, the result of Fig. 2 shows that: At the place of horizontal coordinate 2020-1-24, where the author set as the point that the COVID-19 outbreak occurred. It can be found that there is a large difference between the price curve of bitcoin in the control group that controls the non-occurrence of COVID-19 and the real price curve in the experimental group. This shows that in the very short term, the price of bitcoin has reacted very quickly to the COVID-19 outbreak. That is to say, the price of bitcoin was highly sensitive to the COVID-19 and greatly affected in the short term. And the difference between the orange and blue lines on the vertical axis represents how much bitcoin's price has been affected by the COVID-19 pandemic.

Simultaneously, the Actual value line in blue is above the Fitted value line in orange. This shows that in the ultra-short term on a weekly basis, the COVID-19 epidemic will have a large degree of positive impact on the price of bitcoin. The author considers that when the global financial market suffers from external shocks, investors will tend to buy cryptocurrencies as safe-haven assets, which leads to bitcoin price rise when the epidemic occurs.

Besides, Fig. 2 shows that in February 2020, the Actual value line crossed the Fitted value line from the top to down, indicating that there was an overreaction in the cryptocurrency market under the influence of the novel coronavirus epidemic. As pointed out in a paper on Investor behavior of Stock index Futures based on behavioral finance [8], immature financial markets are more susceptible to the following behaviors of irrational investors. The author analyzes that this may be due to investors overreacting to the negative news in the financial market and overbuying cryptocurrencies as safe-haven assets, which results in a bubble in the price of cryptocurrencies.In the paper Nvestor Sent and Momentum Strategies published by Jiang Dan and other scholars in 2021 [9], it can be seen that overreaction does exist in financial markets. Further, in 2017, Li Xiaoming and other scholars published Investor sentiment, momentum, and post-earnings announcement drift [10]. It showed that Investor sentiment affects investment behavior and thus price movements in financial markets.

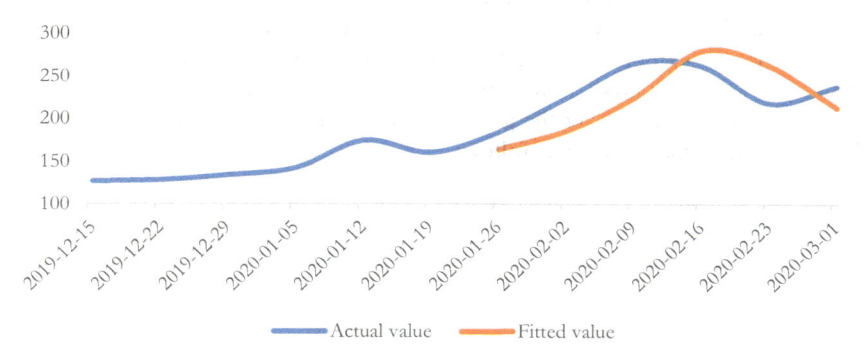

Fig. 3. Actual value and fitted value, Ethereum-Weekly data (Photo credit: Original).

Comparing the price trends of Ethereum and Tron in Fig. 3 and Fig. 4 with Bitcon price trend in Fig. 2, it can be found that: Fig. 3 shows that in March 2020, Ethereum's Actual value line re-crosses the Fitted value line from below to up. This shows that the actual cryptocurrency price after the bubble caused by the overreaction disappears, and its equilibrium price after astringe is still higher than the price in the absence of the COVID-19 pandemic. In other words, the COVID-19 pandemic actually has a real positive impact on the market price of cryptocurrencies.

In the ultra-short period from 2020-1-24 to 2020-2-23, the author compares the difference between Actual value line and fitted value line in the figures of three market size cryptocurrencies and find that: Cryptocurrencies with a larger market size have a smaller difference between the actual value of the price and the fitted value, such as Bitcoin here. However, the smaller the market size of the cryptocurrency, the greater the difference between the actual value and the fitted value of the price, such as Ethereum and Tron here. In other words, the larger the market size of the cryptocurrency, the less

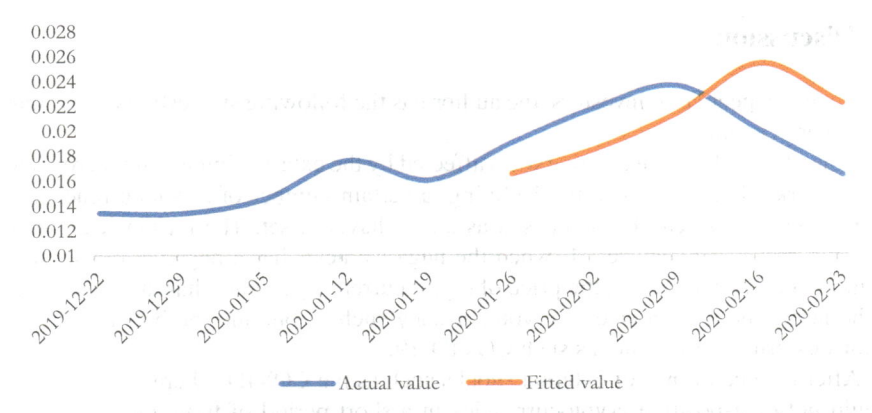

Fig. 4. Actual value and fitted value, Tron-Weekly data (Photo credit: Original).

affected by the COVID-19, the better its stability against external shocks. The smaller the market size of the cryptocurrency, the less stable it is under external shocks.

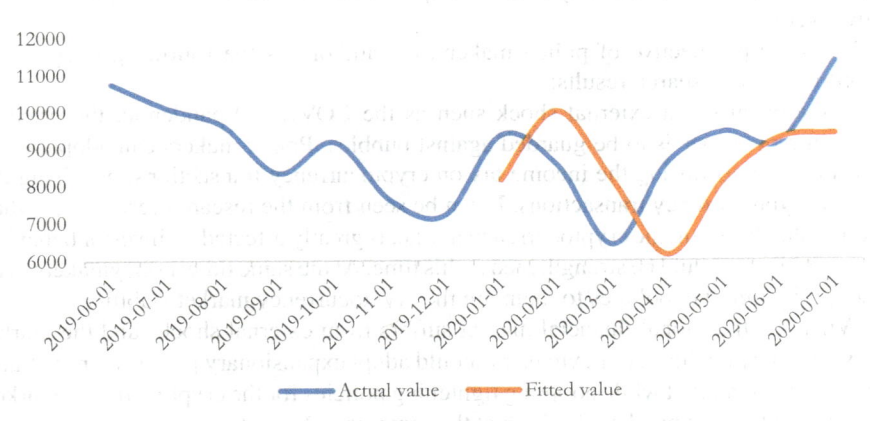

Fig. 5. Actual value and fitted value, Bitcoin-Monthly data (Photo credit: Original).

As can be seen from Fig. 5 that after the COVID-19 outbreak occurred on 2020-1-24, the price of bitcoin rose continuously in April and May after falling in March. Its Actual value even accelerated in June and July compared to the Fitted value. The author analyzes that it may be due to the global spread of the COVID-19 in March, and the US stock market fell sharply which even caused several circuit breakers occurred, resulting in a small decline in the price of bitcoin. However, when most of the world's stock markets officially entered a bear market, the price of bitcoin rose instead of falling, reflecting the safe-haven asset attributes of cryptocurrencies when the market is subjected to external shocks. To sum up, the author predicts that if the financial market is subjected to greater external shocks or the traditional stock index declines more sharply, the price of cryptocurrencies will increase. And there is a lag of one to two months for such changes in cryptocurrency prices.

4 Discussion

From the perspective of investors, the author has the following suggestions according to the research results:

When the global financial market is affected by the external impact of macro factors, or the market index is generally declining, a certain number of cryptocurrencies with a large market size can be purchased as a safe haven asset. The reasons can be seen from the predictive analyses: 1, when the negative news has a negative impact on the traditional financial market, the price of cryptocurrency generally has an upward trend; 2, the larger the market size of cryptocurrency such as bitcoin, the better its stability against external market shocks such COVID-19.

After the occurrence of external shocks such as the COVID-19 epidemic, investors should not over-position cryptocurrencies in a short period of time, otherwise it will change from investment behavior into speculation. From the previous analysis, there is an overreaction in the market price of the cryptocurrency, and the price will fall back to the equilibrium price within a month after the acceleration of the price. At the same time, this also shows that if investors want to speculate, they should increase their positions in cryptocurrencies immediately after the impact, and end in a super-short period of one to two weeks.

From the perspective of policy makers, the author has the following suggestions according to the research results:

In the event of an external shock such as the COVID-19 pandemic, the price of cryptocurrencies needs to be guarded against bubbles. Policy makers can adopt policy measures such as raising the income tax on cryptocurrency transactions, or raising the fees for cryptocurrency transactions. It can be seen from the research results that when external shocks occur, the cryptocurrency market is greatly affected by investor behavior, and supervision should be strengthened at this time. At the same time, policymakers need to adopt tight market policies to maintain the cryptocurrency market stability.

When the traditional financial market suffers from external shocks and the market index generally declines, policymakers should adopt expansionary policies for the traditional financial market while adopting tightening policies for the cryptocurrency market, or even adopt circuit breakers for both at the same time. It can be seen from the research results that when the traditional financial market is frustrated, investors tend to withdraw a large amount of money from the traditional financial market and put it into the cryptocurrency market, which will increase the instability of both markets and increase the systemic risk of both. Policy makers need to adopt opposite market policies for both markets at the same time to effectively maintain two kinds of markets' stability.

5 Conclusion

In this paper, a comparative experiment method is adopted, with the price of the cryptocurrency with the COVID-19 outbreak as the experimental group, and the price of the cryptocurrency without the COVID-19 outbreak in the model as the control group. The ARIMA model was built in the control group and compared with the experimental group. The main conclusions from the study are as follows:

In terms of the impact of COVID-19 on cryptocurrency prices:

External shocks such as the COVID-19 pandemic will have a larger positive impact on cryptocurrency prices. (1) After external shocks such as the COVID-19 pandemic, cryptocurrency prices are heavily influenced by investor behavior, leading to overreaction and a certain bubble, and will converge to an equilibrium price within a month; (2) The larger the market size, the better the stability of cryptocurrencies against external shocks; (3) Cryptocurrencies can act as safe-haven assets in the event of external shocks such as the COVID-19 pandemic; (4) In terms of the impact of COVID-19 on investment; (5) Investors can increase their positions in cryptocurrencies when external shocks such as the COVID-19 pandemic occur, but should avoid their own overreaction that leads to speculation; (6) When external shocks such as the COVID-19 pandemic occur, policymakers should simultaneously adopt opposite policies towards both traditional financial markets and cryptocurrency markets to maintain the stability of both markets.

To sum up, the outbreak of COVID-19 has different aspects of the impact on cryptocurrency prices and investment. As investors, we should be rational and not blindly follow the trend, and as policy makers, we should consider the situation of the two markets comprehensively to make policies.

References

1. Xu, C.: Study on the impact of COVID-19 on major international financial markets. Spec. Zone Econ. (11), 81–84 (2022)
2. Bo, L., Lei, Z.: Study on the impact of COVID-19 on financial market. Stat. Decis. (05), 129–133 (2021)
3. Yifan, F., Di, W.: The impact of COVID-19 on the global economy and China's response. Low Carbon World (09), 255–256 (2021)
4. Bo, L., Lei, Z.: Study on the COVID-19 epidemic, digital currency fluctuations and risk infection. J. Yunnan Univ. Financ. Econ. (05), 1–13 (2021)
5. Sabah, A.: Bitcoin Price Prediction using ARIMA Model (2019)
6. Shahzad, J.S.J.H.: Bitcoin: a better safe-haven investment gold and commodities. Econ. Lett. **147**, 81–84 (2016)
7. Investing. https://cn.investing.com/
8. Shen, J.: The stock index futures investors behavior based on behavioral finance research. Ph.D. dissertation, Southwestern University of Finance and Economics (2013)
9. Jiang, D., Tian, G., Yu, L.: Investor sent and momentum strategies. J. Behav. Financ. **22**(1), 18–35 (2021)
10. Li, X., Zhang, X., Zhao, X.: Investor sentiment, momentum, and post-earnings announcement drift. J. Bus. Financ. Acc. **44**(1–2), 156–183 (2017)

Research on the Relationship Between Chinese and American Stock Markets: Spillover Effects of Returns and Volatility

Lin Liu[✉]

School of Business and Management, Jilin University, Changchun 130012, China
liulin3419@jlu.edu.com

Abstract. In the context of economic globalization and financial sector liberalization, the economies of countries are increasingly vulnerable to international capital flows. This article selects the Shanghai Composite Index and Nasdaq Index from January 1, 2010 to December 31, 2019. Using VAR and ARMA-GACH models, the average side effects and volatility side effects of China's A-share market and the US stock market were studied, the existence of side effects was examined, the causes of side effects were analyzed on the basis of empirical results, and appropriate policy recommendations were put forward to regulators to avoid the external risks of Chinese stock market as much as possible to seek long-term stable development. This paper proves that both the ARCH volatility side factors and the GARCH volatility spillover factors in the NASDAQ SSE yield series have passed the importance level test, indicating that SSE reflects the indirect impact of ARCH and GARCH volatility on the NASDAQ index.

Keywords: ARMA-GARCH model · NASDAQ index · Shanghai composite Index · Spillover effect

1 Introduction

Under the background of economic globalization and financial liberalization, the economy and finance of various countries are more and more susceptible to the influence of international capital flow. With China's accession to the WTO, China's economic reform has been promoted, which has made China's economy more market-oriented and more open, and the connection with foreign stock markets has become increasingly large. China's A-share market and the US stock market are the world's first and second largest stock markets. In 2018, the US imposed tariffs on Chinese trade, which triggered Sino-US friction and further affected the global financial turmoil. In the analysis of spillover effects of stock market volatility in China and the US. Wang Shuo et al. [1] can see from the comparative analysis of the monetary environment in the Chinese and US markets that the long-term low interest rate and quantitative easing policies in the United States reduce the effect of value investment, while China's prudent monetary policy is conducive to value discovery in the stock market, which in turn fully reflects the effectiveness of hybrid strategies. Li Yuanguang and Wang Jing [2] argue that the US stock market has a one-way short-term volatility spillover effect on China's Shanghai stock market. Based on the data of six price indices, Zou Jiajun and Yao Jinhai [3] created a multi-resolution wavelet analysis model, analyzed the dynamic characteristics of the fluctuation components of stock indexes of different scales. They found significant differences in the long-term stability of Chinese and U.S. stock markets. The short-term volatility of the Chinese and US stock markets is slightly different, and the short-term volatility of China's three largest stock indices is much smaller than the three largest US stock indices.

Maghyereh et al. [4] concluded that the results show that relations between the United States and the Middle East and between the United States and North Africa before 2008 were relatively little. However, relations between the US and North Africa and between the US and the Middle East since 2008 have significantly strengthened. And all this was done by Gamba-Santamaria et al. [5] using the DCC-GARCH method, this paper makes an empirical analysis on the securities markets of several major part of economies such as the United States and Latin America. The results show that in most of the period, Brazil is the issuer of spillover, Colombia and Mexico are the issuers of spillover, while the spillover effect of American securities market on Latin American securities market is obviously enhanced after the economic crisis. Golosnoy et al. [6] through the analysis of the correlation coefficients of the United States stock market, Japanese stock market and Germany stock market, the results show that before the economic crisis, the correlation coefficient between the Japanese market and the market of the United States and between the Germany market and the US market are relatively small. However, the inflow and outflow of foreign capital have the greatest impact on China's stock market, among which the spillover effect of foreign capital is the greatest. Volatility spillovers from US equities to Japanese and German equities increased significantly.

Using the VAR and GACH model, the Granger test and the momentum function to analyze the dynamics of the NASDAQ index on the Chinese Shanghai Composite Index and the Shenzhen Component Index, Shuanni Zhang and Shuanglan Zhang [7] found that the US stock market had a vital impact on the Chinese stock market. These tensions have lasting consequences, but are weakening. According to Li Changzhi and Fang Fang [8], American investor sentiment generally has a positive impact on the return rate of the Chinese stock market. However, there is a reversal phenomenon, which means that American investor sentiment will initially have a negative impact on the return rate of the Chinese stock market before turning positive. Less time is required for US investor sentiment to spread; the "securities investment liabilities" project's magnitude has a stronger influence on the returns of the Chinese stock market. Yang Zhongming [9] selected stock indices in China, a major country in China and Hong Kong using a forward-delay correlation model, a data exchange model and an EGARCH model in a three-part study of daily stock index data in major China, Hong Kong and the EGARCH model, and found that stock indices in the future weak model are not used in the future correlation model. The link between the Chinese and American stock markets is long-term balance. The three stock markets' degree of contribution to the equilibrium price and the strength of their guiding relationship are both meticulously measured in the information sharing model. Finally, it is discovered using the EGARCH model that there is clear volatility aggregation and "leverage effect" in the three locations. Additionally, when dealing with the effects of fresh information, the stock markets in the three locations are more vulnerable to bad news. Before and after the beginning of the new crown pneumonia pandemic, Pan Qunxing et al.[10] chose intraday and overnight return data of the Shanghai Composite Index and the S&P 500 Index as samples. They discovered that both before and after the pandemic, the Chinese and American stock markets had spiking components. Chinese stock markets are more likely and more likely to cause a spike spillover in US stocks. The likelihood and severity of jump spillover in the Chinese and US stock markets are delayed by one day. There is a jump leverage effect in the US stock market, and the impact of the leap on the future volatility of the Chinese stock market is even more significant.

In this paper, the US and Chinese mainland stocks are selected as the research objects. The VAR model and ARMA-GARCH-X model are used respectively. Shanghai Composite Index was officially released on July 15, 1991. It has a long history and great influence in China's stock market. It includes heavy stocks and small and medium-sized stocks, with a wide coverage, which can basically reflect the overall development of China's overall economy. For so many years, it is also the "broad market index" that investors often talk about. Nasdaq Index (IXIC), founded in 1981. Nasdaq's basic index is 100, including all new technology industries.

The rest of this paper is structured as follows:information about the data source, data stability, and the models in this paper is covered in Sect. 2. Section 3 follows, with a full discussion of the results from the VAR model and the ARMA-GARCH model, as well as additional analysis on the stock return, stock volatility, and market participants' behavior. Following that, there is a discussion on the study's focus, objective, and importance. Finally, Sect. 5 reiterates conclusion briefly.

2 Research Design

2.1 Data Source

In this paper, the US and Chinese mainland stocks are selected as the research objects. The VAR model and ARMA-GARCH-X model are used respectively, and the returns of Shanghai Stock Exchange Index and NASDAQ Index are selected as the research objects. This article uses data from January 2010 to December 2019 to avoid the impact of the US economic crisis and the global pandemic. Data are from Yingwei Financial situation and daily data are selected.

2.2 Weak Stationarity Test: ADF

Checking that the data is stable is the first step before proceeding. According to the ADF test conducted by Stata, the p value of Nasdaq index in Table 1 is 0, and the p value of the logarithmic return rate of Shanghai Composite Index and Nasdaq Index is 0, which is considered to be statistically significant. Because of these findings, the evidence is sufficient to reject that the variable has a unit root. In other words, the model built on the data works, and the data is smooth.

Table 1. Weak Stationarity Test: ADF test

Index	t	p
SSEC	−2.436	0.3605
Nasdaq	−4.106	0.0062***
Return		
SSEC	−35.403	0.0000***
Nasdaq	−35.648	0.0000***

2.3 Vector Autoregression (VAR) Model

The use of the VAR model can be traced back to a study on linear stochastic difference equations and research on the autoregressive nature used for Tinbergen's model before reaching Sim's [11] well-known contribution to VAR model application. The VAR model can be employed to capture the relationship between multiple variables while avoiding the challenge of model construction based on rigorous economic theory.

About using VAR model to test the mean spillover effect of time series. Let the return on the Shanghai Composite Index (RSSEC) and the return on the Nasdaq Composite Index (RIXIC), R_t is a two-dimensional column vector. Where $R_t = (R_t SSEC, R_t IXIC)$.

$$R_t = \mu_t + \sum_{i=1}^{p} \tau_i R_{t-1} + \varepsilon_t \tag{1}$$

In Eq. (1), E is a two-dimensional disturbance vector; U is a two-dimensional column vector, representing the random error column vector; F are all second-order parameter matrices, which can be obtained:

$$\begin{cases} R_t SSEC = \mu_{1,t} + \sum_{i=1}^{p} \gamma_{11,t} R_{t-1} SSEC + \sum_{i=1}^{p} \gamma_{12,t} R_{t-1} IXIC + \varepsilon_{1,t} \\ R_t IXIC = \mu_{2,t} + \sum_{i=1}^{p} \gamma_{21,t} R_{t-1} SSEC + \sum_{i=1}^{p} \gamma_{21,t} R_{t-1} IXIC + \varepsilon_{2,t} \end{cases} \tag{2}$$

In formula (2), where is the variance of the mean value. For the mean spillover effect of the return rate, explain its meaning. If r is 0 or not significant, there is no mean spillover effect between the return rate of Shanghai Stock Exchange Index and the return rate of Nasdaq index; If r is 0 or not significant, then there is no mean spillover effect between Nasdaq index return and SSE index return.

2.4 ARMA-GARCH Model

The ARMA-GARCH model can evaluate both the return and volatility of the Shanghai composite Index and Nasdaq index. This model is broken down into two sections in this paper: ARMA and GARCH.

$$y_t = \varphi_0 + \sum_{i=1}^{p} \varphi_i y_{t-i} + \alpha_i - \sum_{i=1}^{q} \varphi_i \alpha_{t-i} \tag{3}$$

The general expression of the ARMA model is shown in Eq. (3). AR(p) is represented by the $\varphi_0 + \sum_{i=1}^{p} \varphi_i y_{t-i}$ component, and the rest is MA(q). AR(p) estimates the future value based on past returns of the Shanghai and Nasdaq indices between January 2010 and December 2019, while MA(q) uses an error term to make predictions.

And then another GARCH. In this paper, we will discuss GARCH (1,1), where the former denotes the autoregressive range and the latter denotes the moving average range. GARCH(1,1) was chosen because it has fewer parameters than ARCH(p). This is ideal for multiple time series to identify data spikes, and it requires only one lag to perform the analysis. Therefore, this paper chooses the GARCH (1,1) model.

$$\sigma_t^2 = \alpha_{0,1} + \alpha_1 \varepsilon_{t-1}^2 + \beta_t index_t + \gamma_t \sigma_{t-1}^2 \qquad (4)$$

In formula (4), the $\alpha_1 \varepsilon_{t-1}^2$ term is the ARCH part, the $\gamma_1 \sigma_{t-1}^2$ term is the GARCH part, and the additional term $\beta_t index_t$ outside the generalized formula as an additional explanatory variable in the model.

3 Empirical Results and Analysis

3.1 Order of VAR Model

To determine the optimal delay sequence for a VAR model, statistical criteria and other LR information for each delay must be evaluated. The data is followed by an asterisk (*) to indicate the desired order of delay.

Table 2. Likelihood ratio test and information criterion

Lag	LL	LR	p	FPE	AIC	HQIC	SBIC
0	14517			2.1e–08	−12.0008	−11.9991*	−11.996*
1	14519.5	5.0237	0.285	2.1e–08	−11.9996	−11.9943	−11.9852
2	14523	6.9804	0.137	2.1e–08	−11.9991	−11.9904	−11.9752
3	14525.8	5.6528	0.227	2.1e–08	−11.9982	−11.986	−11.9647
4	14525.8	6.0341	0.197	2.1e–08	−11.9974	−11.9817	−11.9543
5	14542	26.386	0.000	2.1e–08	−12.005	−11.9858	−11.9523
6	14547	9.9942	0.041	2.1e–08	−12.0058	−11.9831	−11.9435
7	14553	11.966*	0.018	2.1e–08	−12.0074	−11.9813	−11.9356
8	14557.4	8.7651	0.067	2.1e–08*	−12.0077*	−11.9781	−11.9263
9	14559.9	5.1466	0.273	2.1e–08	−12.0066	−11.9735	−11.9156
10	14563.3	6.6553	0.155	2,1e–08	−12.006	−11.9694	−11.9055
11	14567.4	8.2257	0.084*	2.1e–08	−12.0061	−11.9661	−11.896
12	14568.4	2.015	0.733	2.1e–08	−12.0036	−11.9601	−11.8839

Table 2 reveals that lags 7, 8, and 11 all have that sign. A comparison of AIC differences is necessary to determine the optimal lag order.

Once you have determined the order of the VAR models, it is important to check if the VAR models are static. Next, determine the performance of the model by performing a device root test and drawing a circle of devices with a root. In Fig. 1, the entire trajectory is clearly within the circle, which means that there is no need to recalculate the gender, and the 3D VAR (7) is a stable model.

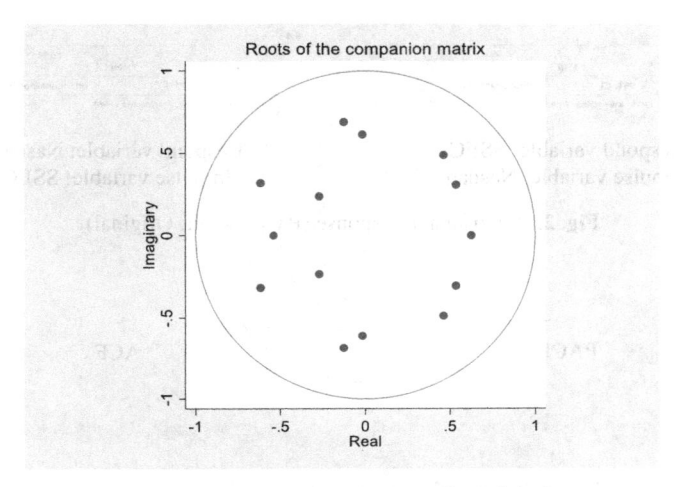

Fig. 1. Unit root test (Photo credit: Original)

3.2 Impulse Response

When one of the stock indexes has a shock of the standard deviation unit size, the dynamic change of the overall model, which pulses the corresponding analysis. Figure 2 shows that the impact of the SSE index return on the Nasdaq index return is small (the maximum impact is less than 0.1%). Similarly, the impact of the Nasdaq index yield shock on the Shanghai Index yield is very small (the maximum is around 0.025%). Due to the continuous escalation of the Sino-US trade war, the global economy, including the US financial market, has exposed more and more risks, which makes the US stock market, which already has the need to adjust, once the volatility increases, there will be unimaginable consequences. China's stock market is in the adjustment of structure, reduce leverage in the pain period of operation, the overall at a historic low, and the support of the national macroeconomic policy makes the stable operation of China's stock market more solid foundation. As a result, the future volatility of China's stock market will be gradually controlled, and the decline will be effectively contained. At the same time, the Sino-US trade war has prompted China's trade business with the US to gradually shift to other countries, making the extent of China's economy affected by the US economy gradually reduced. Therefore, even if the US stock market has huge fluctuations in the future, the impact on China's stock market will be weakened a lot, which confirms the aforementioned conclusion that the influence of the US stock market on China's stock market is gradually weakening.

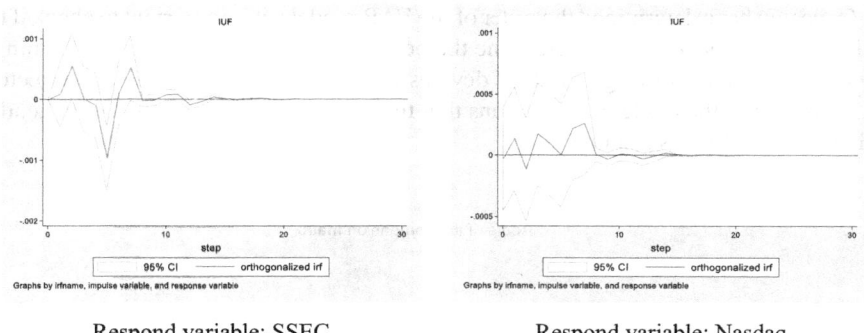

Respond variable: SSEC
Impulse variable: Nasdaq

Respond variable: Nasdaq
Impulse variable: SSEC

Fig. 2. Impulse and response (Photo credit: Original)

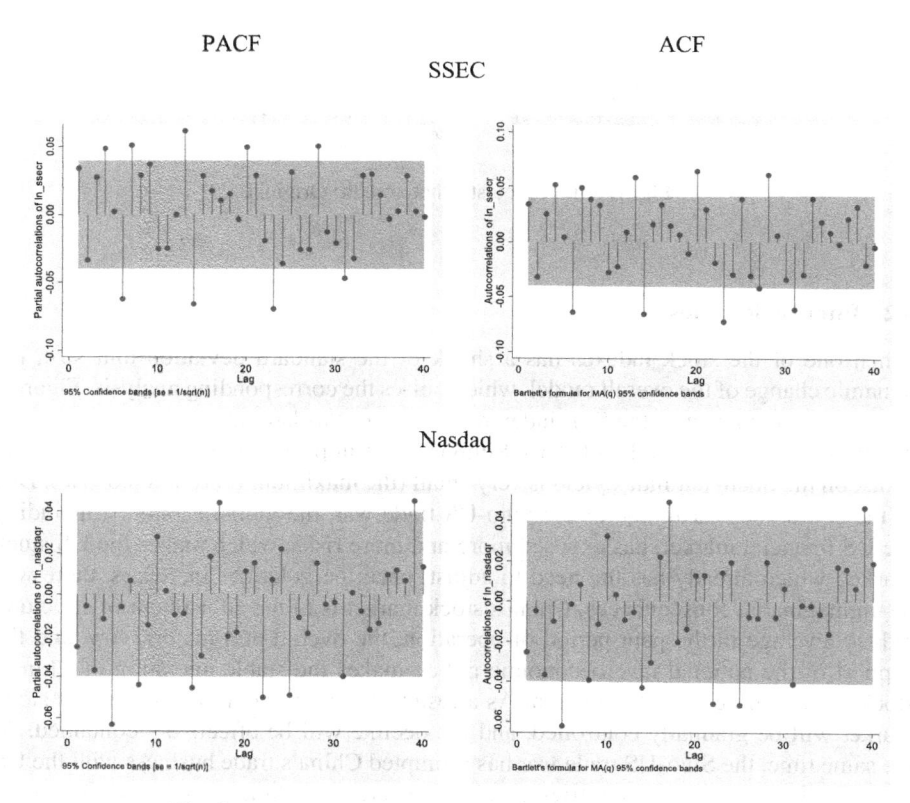

PACF   ACF

SSEC

Nasdaq

Fig. 3. ARMA (p, q) identification (Photo credit: Original)

3.3 ARMA Specification

For the logarithmic sequence of SSEC returns, both PACF and ACF are useful for deriving the lag sequences AR(p) and MA(q). In addition to the target values in Fig. 3, the first part of the PACF and ACF charts is 4, indicating that the order of AR(p) and MA(q) is equal to 4, and both p and q have values of 4. For the NASDAQ, in addition to the target value, the first part of the PACF and ACF charts is 6, which means that both AR(p) and MA(q) have 6 orders, and both p and q values are 6.

3.4 ARMA-GARCH Estimation Results and Variance Equation

Table 3 contains the model estimates and the variance equation. The p values of ARCH and GARCH terms in the variance equation are both less than 0.01, indicating that they are significant. The existence of conditional heteroscedasticity meets the main requirements of GARCH model construction, which means that SSE index and Nasdaq index returns have significant conditional heteroscedasticity. The coefficient p value of AR model and MA model is less than 0.01, which means they are significant. The SSE yield has a material impact on the volatility of the Nasdaq, and vice versa.

Table 3. ARMA-GARCHX regression: variance equation

	(1) SSEC			(2) Nasdaq		
	Coef.	Std. Err.	P	Coef.	Std. Err.	P
SSEC-sigma				.8174072	.2681639	0.000***
Nasdaq-sigma	2.275585	0.7884554	0.004***			
ARCH	0.0408145	0.0041022	0.000***	.1339849	.012597	0.000***
GARCH	0.9396152	0.0038913	0.000***	.8118115	.0166082	0.000***
Constant	−14.78988	0.2371109	0.000***	−12.19926	.1266047	0.000***

4 Discussion

As for the test of the transmission mechanism of the Chinese and US stock markets, whether it is at the period of Sino-US trade war or the outbreak of the epidemic, compared with the normalization of the Chinese and US stock markets, the volatility spillover effect during the two crises is significantly enhanced. This empirical result verifies the theory of market contagion hypothesis, in which the volatility of stocks of various countries is particularly correlated during crises, and verifies the stock market spillover mechanism of China and the United States based on crisis period. As for the other two transmission mechanisms, based on economic fundamentals and investor behavior, it is particularly difficult to collect economic fundamentals and the data of investor behavior cannot be quantified, and it is difficult to fully convince the spillover effect analysis, so it cannot be verified in the empirical part of this paper. According to the above research conclusions, compared with the American stock market, China's A-share market has A slightly weaker ability to resist risks and most investors show irrational behaviors. As a result, when volatility in the U.S. market affect the class A stock market, volatility in the U.S. stock market easily cause strong confusion on the Chinese stock exchange due to the poor preventive capability of the A-stock exchange.

5 Conclusion

China is not only one of the fastest-growing developing countries in the world, but also the largest developing country in the world. It has close economic, trade and financial ties with the United States, which has greatly promoted the mutual ties between the two countries. This paper tests the relevance between Chinese and American stock market from 2010 to 2019, and selects Shanghai Composite Index, NASDAQ, and other stock markets as samples. The fluctuations of stock market are analyzed by VAR method, the fluctuations of stock market are analyzed by ARMA-GARCH method, and the rate of return and variance of stock market are estimated by ARMA-GARCH method. This paper makes an empirical analysis of this.

This paper confirms that the volatility spillover of ARCH and GARCH of Shanghai Composite Stock Market on American stock market does not reach a significant level, indicating that Shanghai Stock Exchange has arch and Garch spillover effects on American stock market and NASDAQ stock market. These two kinds of spillover effects did not reach a significant level. The results show that the volatility spillover factors of ARCH and GARCH in the stock market of Shanghai Stock Exchange are verified in the significance test of 1%. From this, we can draw the conclusion that American stock has A volatility spillover effect on Chinese stock market.

Therefore, Chinese equity investors shouldn't ignore the influence of the US stock market on the Chinese stock market, and still need to pay attention to the fluctuations of the US Dow Jones Industrial Index and Nasdaq index to make appropriate investment decisions. Due to the time difference between the two countries, it provides investors with a reference to the US stock market to predict the possibility of China's stock market, pay attention to the US stock market in the evening, to find reference information for the next day in China's stock market investment. When the US stock market plummets, investors can consider shorting stocks, and when the US stock market skyrockets, investors can consider going long stocks.

Regulators should learn the operating system and operating conditions of mature markets, optimize the structure of China's stock market to some extent, and reduce the losses caused by risks in the face of sudden crises and risks. In addition, improving the supervision of the information disclosure system of listed companies is also conducive to stabilizing investor sentiment and avoiding overconfidence or herd effect among investors. At present, most investors in China tend to speculate, and it is difficult to make a reasonable judgment on the arrival of risks. The improvement of information disclosure will enable investors to face the stock trading more rationally. The volatility of the stock market also decreases accordingly. The more reasonable the supervision of listed companies, the better the guidance of the market, and the more stable development of the stock market.

References

1. Wang, S., Zhu, Y.Z., Xu, B.: Research on hybrid strategy of momentum and value effect based on Chinese and American stock markets. J. Zhejiang Univ. Sci. Technol. **34**(04), 338–346 (2022)
2. Li, Y., Wang, J.: Non-linear short-term volatility spillover effect between Shanghai Stock Exchange, Hong Kong Stock Exchange and US Stock Exchange after the Shanghai-Hong Kong Stock Connect: Based on the time-varying perspective of exchange rate fluctuation inhibiting stock market volatility. Finan. Account. Monthly **18**, 163–170 (2018)
3. Zou, J., Yao, J.H.: Comparative study on price volatility of Chinese and American stock markets based on wavelet multi-resolution. Price Monthly **02**, 9–15 (2023)
4. Maghyerch, A.I., Awartani, B., Hilu, K.A.: Dynamic transmissions between the U.S. and equity marketsin the MENA countries: new evidence from pre-global financial crisis. Q. Rev. Econ. Finan. **56**, 123–138 (2015)
5. Gamba-Santamaria, S., Gomez-Gonzalez, J.E., Hurtado-Guarin, J.L., Melo-Velandia, L.F.: Stock market volatility spillovers: evidence for latin America. Finan. Res. Lett. **20**(1), 207–216 (2016)
6. Golosnoy, V., Gribisch, B., Liesenfeld, R.: Intre-daily volatility spillovers in international stockmaikets. Rev. Finan. Stud. **3**(2), 281–307 (2015)
7. Zhang, S.N., Zhang, S.L.: Research on the volatility spillover effect of American Stock market to Chinese stock market: based on VAR model and GARCH (1,1) model. China Collect. Econ. **22**, 166–168 (2019)
8. Li, C.Z., Fang, F.: Research on the correlation between returns and investor sentiment in Chinese and American stock markets. New Finan. **04**, 12–18 (2020)
9. Yang, Z.M.: Research on the correlation of Chinese and American stock markets during the economic crisis: based on the comparative analysis of A-share, Hong Kong Stock and American stock markets. Natl. Circ. Econ. **31**, 154–156 (2021)
10. Pan, Q.X., Sun, Y.J., Gao, T.Q., Du, X.L.: Research on the spillover effect of jumps and the impact of jumps on future volatility in Chinese and American stock markets. Finan. Theory Pract. **01**, 12–24 (2023)
11. Sims, C.A.: The role of approximate prior restrictions in distributed lag estimation. Am. Stat. Assoc. **67**(337), 169–175 (1972)

Research on the Impact of China's Industrial Structure Upgrading on the Balance of Payments Structure

Yimeng Wang(✉)

University of Sussex, Brighton BN19BJ, UK
3048177637@qq.com

Abstract. China's primary industry has experienced slow growth in labor productivity, while the secondary industry, despite having a complete industrial chain, faces challenges such as low value-added products, high energy consumption, and ecological impacts. Although the tertiary industry has witnessed rapid development, there remains a significant gap in terms of standards and quality in the modern service sector. Since China's accession to the WTO, the country's import and export volumes have increased substantially, maintaining a trade surplus in the current account. This study aims to collect continuous data from 1982 to 2021 and utilize comparative analysis and QCA analysis methods to examine the characteristics of China's industrial structure and balance of payments structure. The findings suggest that upgrading the industrial structure can help balance and optimize the structure of the balance of payments.

Keywords: Industrial Structure Upgrading · Labor Productivity · Balance of Payments Structure · Current Account · Financial Capital Account

1 Introduction

The acceleration of China's industrial structure transformation and upgrading is expected to significantly impact the country's balance of payments structure. And its goal is to evolve from a stage of high-speed growth to a stage of high-quality development, from a resource-based and labor-intensive type to a technology-driven, innovative, green and sustainable development type. This topic has garnered attention from both domestic and foreign business and academic communities, leading to various perspectives and interpretations. This paper adopts the Balassa-Samuelson Hypothesis [1] (BSH) perspective to assess the upgrading of China's industrial structure based on labor productivity. The net balance of import and export trade and the net financial capital account are utilized as measurement indicators for the balance of payments structure. Labor productivity is further divided into labor force and industrial output value categories. The study employs the Qualitative Comparative Analysis (QCA) method to analyze the adequacy relationship between labor productivity and the upgrading of the industrial structure. By employing these analytical approaches, this research aims to shed light on the complex dynamics between labor productivity and industrial structure upgrading.

2 Overview of China's Industrial Structure Upgrading and Balance of Payments

2.1 Evolution and Characteristics of China's Industrial Structure

Going back in history, agriculture and the labor force engaged in agriculture used to play a dominant role in China's social and economic structure for more than 4,000 years according to Lyu [2]. After 1950, to expedite the establishment of a comprehensive industrial system, the Chinese government made a strategic decision to prioritize the development of heavy industry in its path towards industrialization. At the end of 2001, China joined the World Trade Organization (WTO).

Table 1. Changes in China's industrial structure from 1982 to 2021. Unit: %

	Proportion of Primary Industry in GDP (%)	Proportion of secondary industry in GDP (%)	Proportion of Tertiary industry in GDP (%)
1982	32.8	44.6	22.6
1990	27.05	41.61	31.34
2000	16.35	50.23	33.42
2010	9.33	46.50	44.17
2020	7.65	37.82	54.53
2021	7.3	39.4	53.3

Note: The data in the table comes from the National Bureau of Statistics of China [3]

Table 2. Changes in the Population Structure of China's Industrial Labor Force from 1982 to 2021. Unit: %

	Proportion of labor force in the primary industry in the total labor force (%)	Proportion of secondary industry labor force in total labor force (%)	Proportion of tertiary industry labor force in total labor force (%)	Total labor force (ten thousand)
1982	68.13	18.43	13.44	45295
1990	60.10	21.40	18.50	64749
2000	50.00	22.50	27.50	72085
2010	36.70	28.70	34.60	76105
2020	23.60	28.70	47.70	75064
2021	22.87	29.08	48.05	74652

Note: The data in the table are from the National Bureau of Statistics of China

As can be seen from Tables 1 and 2, as China's industrial structure changes, the distribution of the labor force population in the three industries also changes, and labor productivity steadily increases.

2.2 Analysis of Structural Changes and Development Trends of China's Balance of Payments

China's balance of payments data has shown notable trends since its compilation and publication began in 1982. Starting from the mid-1980s, China's current account has generally maintained a surplus. This indicates that the value of China's exports of goods and services has exceeded the value of its imports during this period.

Similarly, China's capital and financial account (excluding reserve assets) has mostly shown a surplus in each year, demonstrating a net inflow of capital and financial transactions into the country. However, it is important to note that there have been exceptions to this trend. Specifically, in the years 2014, 2015, and 2016, China's capital and financial account experienced deficits. These deficits were influenced by factors such as the tightening of monetary policy by the United States and the implementation of trade protectionism measures [4] (Table 3).

Table 3. Structure of China's balance of payments. Unit: $100 million

	1982	1990	2000	2010	2019	2020
Current account (Goods and services)	48	107	288	2230	1318	3697
Financial items (financial accounts not of reserve nature)	−17	−28	20	2822	73	−778

Note: Data are from the State Administration of Foreign Exchange of China

China's long-term export-oriented economic orientation has become one of the important reasons for the weakening of domestic effective supply and insufficient effective demand, resulting in a long-term imbalance in the structure of the balance of payments that Lin in 2018 [5].

3 Methodology

In this paper, the necessary and sufficient causality is examined through the application of fuzzy set qualitative comparative analysis (fsQCA), a method suitable for studying asymmetric and configurational parameters, as demonstrated by Ragin [6]. This analytical approach allows for exploring multiple possibilities. Firstly, fsQCA can determine whether a single condition is necessary for achieving the desired outcome.

In presenting our results, we adopt the conventional notations: core conditions indicated by ● (present) or ⊗ (absent), peripheral conditions represented by ● (present) or ⊗ (absent), and a blank space to signify instances where the presence or absence of conditions does not significantly impact the outcome, as shown by Fiss in 2011 [7].

According to the previous domestic and foreign theoretical literature, this paper will study the impact of labor productivity of three industries in China on the balance of payments structure. This paper uses the latest relevant time series data from 1982 to 2021 (data from the National Bureau of Statistics of China and the State Administration of Foreign Exchange of China) as the sample data for empirical research.

4 Result and Analysis

4.1 Research Process

Utilizing the fsQCA method, we performed two types of causality analyses: necessary causality ("No Y without X") and sufficient causality ("If X, then Y"). This two-step analytical approach enables us to ascertain whether certain strategies are essential and/or adequate for achieving high performance within intricate operational contexts.

Consistent with established QCA practices, our study initially carried out a fuzzy-set analysis of necessary conditions, as depicted in the table, employing a consistency benchmark of 0.90.

Table 4. Analysis of necessary conditions in fsQCA.

	Net balance of current account		Net difference between capital and financial account	
	Consistency	Coverage	Consistency	Coverage
proportion of primary industry	0.899	0.874	0.624	0.663
proportion of primary industry	0.349	0.339	0.617	0.654
employees in the primary industry	0.426	0.378	0.721	0.700
~employees in the primary industry	0.708	0.759	0.522	0.611
proportion of secondary industry	0.883	0.896	0.592	0.657
~proportion of secondary industry	0.353	0.328	0.622	0.632
employees in the secondary industry	0.936	0.843	0.686	0.675
~employees in the secondary industry	0.313	0.330	0.585	0.674
proportion of tertiary industry	0.845	0.910	0.551	0.648
~proportion of tertiary industry	0.387	0.343	0.646	0.625
employees in the tertiary industry	0.899	0.877	0.632	0.674
~employees in the tertiary industry	0.352	0.340	0.614	0.649

In Table 4, among all the values, only the consistency of the number of laborers in the secondary industry in the net current account stands at 0.936, exceeding the standard 0.9. This high consistency arises from the stable proportion of the population engaged in the secondary industry, which remains between 20% and 30% throughout the year.

This stability indicates a constant labor force contributing to the production and export of goods, thereby helping to maintain trade balance. Moreover, a stable proportion of the population in the secondary industry signifies a continuous supply of highly skilled labor, technological progress, and increased productive capacity, enhancing the competitiveness of the industrial sector and boosting exports. These factors create favorable terms of trade and have the potential to increase the net value of the current account.

In the analysis of configuration adequacy, this paper adopts a case frequency threshold of 1, an original consistency threshold of 0.8, and a PRI (Proportional Reduction in Inconsistency) consistency threshold of 0.70 [8]. As depicted in the figure, the findings show that one configuration (s1) can impact the net value of the current account, while two configurations (s2, s3) can influence the net value of the financial capital account (Table 5).

Table 5. Configurations (fsQCA).

	Net balance of current account	Net difference between capital and financial account	
	s1	s2	s3
Proportion of primary industry	●	●	⊗
Employees in the primary industry		●	●
Proportion of secondary industry	●	●	⊗
Employees in the secondary industry	●		●
Proportion of tertiary industry	●	●	⊗
Employees in the tertiary industry	●	●	⊗
Raw coverage	0.826	0.343	0.373
unique coverage	0.826	0.070	0.100
Consistency	0.918	0.959	0.950
solution coverage	0.826	0.443	
Solution consistency	0.918	0.945	

Configuration s1 is the only solution of each labor productivity factor to the net value of current account. Because the proportion of labor in the primary industry dropped from 68% in 1982 to 22% in 2021, the primary industry often involves the production and export of raw materials and agricultural products. A decline in the number of workers in this sector may lead to a reduction in the production and export of primary goods, the terms of trade being the ratio of export prices to import prices. The reduction of labor force in the primary industry may affect the terms of trade if it leads to changes in the relative price of primary products, which also indicates that labor force shifts to other industries. While the labor force population of the primary industry might not be a necessary condition for these effects, it does demonstrate that the industrial structure's upgrading can have a positive impact on current items, such as trade balances and terms of trade.

Configuration s2 is one of the solutions of each labor productivity factor to the net value of current financial capital account. Due to the fierce competition in the global market, the industry needs to constantly innovate and adapt to maintain its competitiveness. Configuration s3 is another solution of each labor productivity factor to the net value of the current financial capital account. S3 and s2 show completely different results, so it can be concluded that the impact of industrial structure upgrading on the long-term effect of import and export trade is significant but unpredictable.

4.2 Robustness Test

This paper includes robustness tests to examine the configuration of the business environment that leads to high Total Factor Productivity (TFP). The employed method is Qualitative Comparative Analysis (QCA), which is based on set theory. When slight modifications are made to the analysis, if there is a sub-set relationship between the results, the substantive interpretation of the research findings remains unchanged, indicating robustness [9].

In the first robustness test, the threshold of case frequency is increased from 1 to 2. This adjustment results in two configurations that align closely with the existing configurations, demonstrating consistent findings.

In the second robustness test, the PRI (Parsimonious Consistency Index) consistency level is reduced from 0.7 to 0.65. Despite this adjustment, the configurations obtained still encompass the existing configurations, indicating the robustness of the research findings.

4.3 Analysis of Various Configurations

The researcher highlights the various configurations (s1, s2, s3) that emerge when considering the influence of labor productivity factors on the net value of the current account and the current financial capital account. It underscores the importance of industrial structure upgrading and its implications for trade.

The study states that configuration s1 emerges as the sole solution indicating the influence of labor productivity factors on the net value of the current account. It emphasizes the declining proportion of labor in the primary industry over time, which can result in a decrease in the production and export of primary goods. This reduction in the labor force of the primary industry can affect the terms of trade, which is the ratio of export prices to import prices. This study suggests that the shift of labor force to other industries due to the upgrading of the industrial structure has a positive impact on the current account.

In contrast, this study describes configurations s2 and s3 are presented as solutions for labor productivity factors affecting the net value of the current financial capital account. It is mentioned that due to global market competition, industries need to constantly innovate and adapt to maintain competitiveness. The paper concludes that s2 and s3 show completely different results, indicating that the impact of industrial structure upgrading on the long-term effects of import and export trade is significant but unpredictable. But now China is facing the problem that the working-age labor force continues to decrease [10].

5 Discussion

According to data released by China's National Bureau of Statistics, "China's working-age population between the ages of 15 and 59 has been declining year by year since 2012." The decline is due to the decades-long downturn in the fertility rate. According to China's seventh National Census, "from 2010 to 2020, China's total fertility rate was only 1.3." According to demographic theory, the total fertility rate needs to reach 2.1 to achieve an equilibrium between births and deaths. The downward trend of the labor force population has a direct negative impact on GDP growth and the structure of the balance of payments. To leverage its population advantage, the Chinese government must prioritize and consistently increase investment in education, including vocational skills training and lifelong learning. By doing so, China can effectively transform its large population base (with a total population of 1.412 billion in 2022) into a highly skilled labor force. Presently, the percentage of individuals holding a bachelor's degree or higher in China's total population is less than 4%, with doctors accounting for approximately 0.06%. Nevertheless, the sheer scale of the population has generated the world's largest pool of tech talent, with 10.76 million graduates in 2021 alone.

Education plays a vital role in harnessing the potential of the population base and fostering talent advantage. It enables the promotion of independent scientific and technological innovation, guiding the trajectory of scientific and technological development. Through the integration of emerging technologies across various industries, education facilitates the transformation of resource-based and labor-intensive sectors into technology-driven, innovative, environmentally friendly, and sustainable industries. This process drives the upgrade of the industrial structure and enhances labor productivity.

By reversing the decline in output caused by the diminishing working-age population and maintaining a competitive edge in the international market, China can effectively balance its balance of payments structure. This will contribute to solving the challenges associated with "getting old before getting rich" and the "Lewis turning point" in China's economic development.

The Balassa-Samuelson effect hypothesis mentions that the increase in labor productivity will lead to the increase in wages and remuneration, which will lead to the increase in prices, and the nominal exchange rate and the real exchange rate will also follow the rise according to Bela Balassa in 1961 [1]. The expectation of RMB appreciation will attract international capital flows and have a positive impact on the financial account of China's balance of payments.

6 Conclusion

In conclusion, this analysis examines the structure and progress of the primary, secondary, and tertiary industries, highlighting the potential consequences of a decline in the proportion of workers in the primary sector within the total current account workforce. Such a decline typically indicates a shift in the economy towards sectors like manufacturing or services. Reducing the primary industry labor force can lead to decreased production and export of raw materials and agricultural products, negatively impacting the trade balance and potentially resulting in a more significant trade deficit, thereby affecting the net current account.

The influence of stabilizing the labor force in the secondary industry on the net current account is more nuanced than the overall labor force. A stable proportion of the secondary industry contributes to enhanced export competitiveness and a steady manufacturing foundation, potentially resulting in increased exports and an improved net current account. However, concerning the current net financial capital account, the secondary industry's labor share stability may not directly impact it. The net capital account primarily focuses on capital flows like foreign direct investment and portfolio investment. While a stable secondary sector workforce size can foster a favorable investment climate, the effect on the net capital account depends on various factors, including investment policy, economic stability, and investor sentiment.

The employed population in the tertiary industry is steadily growing, with population and output value being vital prerequisites for its development. Enhancing the tertiary sector and population necessitates creating an appealing business environment, investing in infrastructure, promoting innovation and digitization, strengthening education and training, fostering collaboration, supporting work-life balance, and implementing effective marketing strategies.

Technological advancements, heightened labor productivity, and the integrity and diversity of the industrial chain are crucial for long-term sustainable development. Consequently, the government should prioritize improving the quality and skills of the labor force, fostering innovation and competition, enhancing the industrial chain, and propelling the industry towards environmentally friendly and zero-carbon practices.

However, it is essential to note that while the stability of the secondary industry can promote economic predictability, a lack of adaptability may stifle innovation. Insufficient education and training can result in labor shortages in the tertiary industry. Therefore, managing these labor shifts effectively requires prudent economic planning and policy implementation to mitigate potential challenges while maximizing the benefits for long-term sustainable growth. Also, this paper provides an in-depth analysis of China's industry, and these recommendations have certain regional limitations, so future research will focus on more countries and perspectives.

Acknowledgement. First of all, they have increased my understanding of professional expertise as well as my academic writing abilities. I was impressed by their strict academic requirements, extensive professional knowledge and patient teaching attitude.

References

1. Balassa, B.: The theory of economic integration (1961)
2. Simian, L.: General History of China. Qunyan Press, Beijing (2015)
3. National Bureau of Statistics of China. http://www.stats.gov.cn/sj/
4. Yin, W.: Characteristics and trend outlook of China's industrial structure changes during the 14th five-year plan period. China Prices (9) (2021)
5. Lin, Y.: Interpreting China's Economy. Peking University Press, Beijing (2018)
6. Ragin, C.C.: Redesigning social inquiry: fuzzy sets and beyond. Wiley Online Library (2008)
7. Fiss, P.C.: Building better causal theories: a fuzzy set approach to typologies in organization research. Acad. Manag. J. **54**(2), 393–420 (2011)
8. Du, Y., Liu, Q., Cheng, J.: Management World, (9): What Kind of business environment leads to high entrepreneurial activity in cities
9. Zhang, M., Du, Y.: Application of QCA method in organization and management research: positioning, strategy and direction. J. Manag. **16**(9), 1312–1323 (2019)
10. Jian, Q.: China's labor market outlook in 2023. China Social Science Network (2023)

The Impact of Digital Economy on Industrial Agglomeration

Yuting Huang and Kaixvan Ma[✉]

Beijing Wuzi University, Beijing 101149, China
1666561634@qq.com

Abstract. In an era characterized by swift digital economy development, strengthening traditional industries and aiding industrial agglomeration with digital economy. This paper examines the effects and process of the digital economy on industrial agglomeration using by developing an indicator system, employing the entropy weight approach to assess the digital economy, and industrial agglomeration is measured using the location entropy approach. According to research, the digital economy can stimulate the establishment of industrial agglomeration, and this boosting influence is particularly visible in locations located in the eastern region, where marketization, population density and technological innovation is significant. The development of the circulation industry plays a significant promoting role in the process of promoting industrial agglomeration through the digital economy. Therefore, we should actively develop the digital economy and boost infrastructure building; Promote the combination of online and offline industrial clusters, actively build online clusters, shorten the geographical distance between enterprises, and accelerate industrial integration; Develop the circulation industry, reduce production and transportation costs, enhance urbanization level, and attract capital to assist in industrial agglomeration.

Keywords: Digital Economy · Circulation Industry · Industrial Agglomeration · Regulation Effect

1 Introduction

With the emergence of a new technological revolution and industrial change around the world, a novel mode of production with Big data as the focus and digital technology as the engine has emerged. Human society has quickly moved towards the era of digital economy, and has become a horse drawn carriage promote the rapid recovery of the world economy. With its high technology, high penetration, high integration, and high growth features, the digital economy profoundly integrates with the actual economy and accelerates the changes and modernizing of traditional industrial structures. The "2035 Vision Plan Outline" feature a chapter on "accelerating the growth of technology and building a digital China," highlighting the "building of new benefits in the digital economy", and becoming a lighthouse for China's digital economy. Writing a new chapter for the expansion of the digital economy has shown the way forward. It was discovered that China's digital economy has maintained a consistent growing trend by measuring the percentage of the scale of the digital economy to GDP. From 2011 to 2020, the digital economy's share of GDP climbed from 19.47% to 38.6%, showing a clear upward trend (Fig. 1). The digital economy is a fresh impetus for increasing China's economic growth in both quantity and effectiveness, as well as an exciting opportunity for industrial agglomeration [1]. In the 2022 Central Government Work Report, it was proposed to "speed up the development of modern manufacturing agglomerations, implement the national advantageous emerging industry clustering project, provide strong support in the areas of funding, talent, as well as additional aspects, and encourage the industry's transition to the mid to high end". The digital economy will affect the economic geography pattern. On the one hand, the uneven economic geography pattern is caused by incomplete infrastructure and the "digital divide" [2], which leads to uneven information distribution, significant spatial and regional disparities, and imbalanced industrial development; The convergence of the digital and physical economies shortens geographical distance, enables various enterprises to cooperate and develop online, reduces development costs, and is conducive to industrial development.

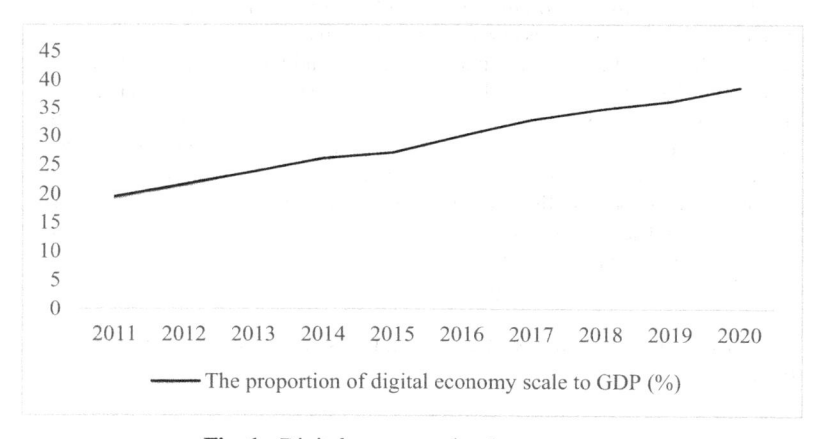

Fig. 1. Digital economy development map.

Circulation industry can indirectly guide the optimization of labor force [3], Promote the conversion of foreign trade to domestic sales, generating greater consumption and production capacity [4]. The circulation industry also has a strong ability to absorb employment, accelerate the optimization of land, labor and other factors [5]. At the same time, it has constructed supply chain activities, reduced trade costs, and enabled different industries, different formats, and different enterprises to combine and develop within a certain geographical range [6], further promoting the formation of industrial agglomeration. For example, the rapid growth of Alibaba's digital industry belt has expanded from less than 100 and 52 cities in 2013 to 3000 and 163 cities in 2021. Various provinces have formed digital industry belts with industry attributes. The digital industry belt is a new form of industrial organization that has emerged under the growth of digital economy, it is a "new industrial cluster" development model that integrates the offline industrial chain and online industrial ecology, playing a bridging role in the development of digital industrial clusters and advanced manufacturing industrial clusters, and increasingly becoming an important support for enhancing industrial resilience and vitality. The digital industrial belts developed in various areas varies due to the diverse growth of the circulatory industry in different locations. The digital transformation of Shantou enterprises drives the transformation of traditional wholesale markets to develop the underwear industry; Dongguan is building an "O2O New Wholesale" model in the field of industrial internet to develop the clothing industry, and so on. Therefore, it is critical to clarify the influence of the development circulation industry on the industrial agglomeration of digital economy.

Nowadays industrial agglomeration faces challenges such as technology shortage, high costs, financing difficulties, and low innovation. Existing scholars can reduce coordination costs, promote cooperation and division of labor [7], attract technical talents, capital and other production factors, and help in the transformation of conventional sectors to boost industrial agglomeration formation [8]; Some scholars feel that the digital economy has altered the innovation process within businesses as well as the collaborative innovation mechanism between various industrial organizations. The connection, repercussions, and dissemination effects between the information and communications sector and other industries are pushing industrial structure upgrades. However, there is no literature directly studying the impact of the development of the communication industry on the digital economy, as well as the link between production and consumption in circulation, Compared with existing literature, this article plays an indispensable role in industrial agglomeration, and its marginal contribution is as follows: (1) as the hub of production and consumption, circulation industry development is used as a moderating variable to study the impact of circulation industry as an intermediate link between production and consumption; (2) further subdivided the impact of marketization level, population density, and technological innovation level on industrial agglomeration.

2 Literature Reviews

2.1 Digital Economy and Industrial Agglomeration

The internet based economy is a new motor for industrial agglomeration as well as an exciting opportunity for enhancing the effectiveness of economic development [1]. Digital economy encourages structure upgrading, and growth of the market economy makes the digital economy to play a greater part in industrial structure upgrade [9]. But most scholars on the influence of the digital economy, using the method of empirical analysis of heterogeneity, believe that technology innovation improves the digital economy, that it can promote worker productivity and promote electronic devices transference to promote industrial structure upgrading, that it can also accelerate the evolution and improvement of industrial structure, and that the influence of the industrial structure upgrade has nonlinear characteristics and regional heterogeneity [10]. In the domestic literature research, the relationship between the two believes that the digital economy propels China's manufacturing structure to the medium and high-end [11]. The emerging information technology not only improves the effectiveness of the market but also promotes the scale of production and the refinement of the industrial chain [12]. The complete integration of the digital and real economies has become an innovative catalyst for promoting industrial change and upgrade [13], enterprises can use the internet to accomplish the upgrading and optimization of a single structure, improve resource allocation and utilization efficiency [14], some scholars introduced empirical studies of metrological models and discovered that digital economy showed a significant beneficial correlation with industrial structure [15], it is found that it can indirectly affect structure upgrading by affecting human capital as well as technological and scientific advances [16]; The industrial integration impact may all be used to adapt, change, and upgrade the industrial structure [17]. From the research on the adjustment of industrial structure of different industries in digital economy, digital supports industry structure upgrading by cracking the congestion in the creativity chain, enhancing manufacturing chain quality, maximizing supply chain efficiency, and extending the area of service chain [18]. Moreover, there are geographical variances in the digital economy's modification of industrial structure [19], and nonlinear characteristics and spatial spillover characteristics [20]. Digital economy can greatly reduce the coordination costs of enterprises by attracting a large amount of labor, utilizing its permeability, and promoting division of labor and cooperation between enterprises [7]. By lowering the cost of transactions, expanding the market, and fostering knowledge spillovers can effectively promote the degree of specialization and diversification in various regions, which is also influenced by the size of enterprises and the level of urbanization. It has the potential to impact industrial structure modification under the control of digitalization [21], and the growth of the digital economy has fully unlocked and liberated the high-quality development of industrial agglomeration [22]. From the standpoint of real economy and digital economy integration, the development of digital economy enables regions to enhance their industrial agglomeration level by leveraging their respective endowment advantages, utilizing existing industrial foundations, cultivating and attracting high-tech talents, and establishing high-tech industrial parks [23]. From the perspective of digital technology innovation, cities with higher levels of digital technology innovation have more innovation capital. The aggregation of factors such as human capital and information technology will promote industrial specialization and division of labor [8]. From the perspective of product demand, it is believed that in areas with developed digital economies, the growth of the digital industry will inevitably increase the demand for intermediate goods, leading to the phenomenon of industrial agglomeration [24]. From a macro, meso, and micro perspective, it is believed that the emergence of the Internet is capable of enhancing the overall efficiency of cities along with manufacturing industries [25], and that increasing the intensity of digital technology diffusion between regions will also improve the rectifying impact that industrial agglomeration on resource mismatch, providing better development space for industrial agglomeration [26]. The following is hypothesis in this paper:

Hypothesis 1: The growth of the digital economy promotes the growth of a local industrial agglomeration.

2.2 Digital Economy and the Development of Circulation Industry

In the field of circulation industry, the digital economy promotes the expansion of the circulation industry and improves circulation efficiency by shortening circulation time and reducing circulation costs [27]. The extensive use of technology in the circulation industry has gradually infiltrated and integrated from the transaction link to the innovative research and development, research and design, application sales and other links, as well as the modernization and optimization of the circulation industry chain [28], improving the circulation industry's informatization level, and maximizing resource allocation. First, improve the digital transformation of the circulation industry, shorten the circulation transaction time through intelligent development, and apply digital technology to enable rapid and accurate feedback of goods or service information [27]. And the time for the circulation industry chain to obtain effective information is shortened, improving the supply and demand matching ability of the circulation industry, enabling goods or services to flow quickly from the production end to the consumer end, and meeting the needs of consumer groups efficiently and accurately, The informatization, digitization, and visualization of the supply chain shortening the time required for the circulation industry and opening up a broader consumer market. Secondly, efficient and precise consumption accelerates circulation and transactions, while also reducing the cost of capital turnover and transaction costs. Nowadays, e-commerce platforms are widely emerging, the information of goods or services is gradually open and transparent, and consumers have more and diversified demands. The application of big data can provide consumers with more appropriate and accurate consumer products [29], which greatly reduces the costs caused by product price differences, information asymmetry, and supply and demand mismatch, and eliminates many barriers in the transaction process, the following is hypothesis in this paper:

Hypothesis 2: The development of the digital economy has promoted the development of the regional circulation industry.

2.3 Digital Economy, Development of Circulation Industry, and Industrial Agglomeration

Circulation, as a key link connecting production and consumption, the manufacturing industry's development is greatly influenced by the circulation industry's quick development. Digitalization of circulation promotes industrial agglomeration by providing a better platform for production, circulation, distribution, and consumption to be more efficient [30], and by reducing labor intensity, labor productivity, transportation costs, and land rent costs in the industry, as well as increasing urbanization levels [31]. The circulation industry and the level of urbanization develop together. Areas with a high level of urbanization will attract a large amount of capital, labor and other factor resources, create more jobs [32], develop various infrastructure, expand trade markets, and guide industries to gather in the region [33]. The expansion of the size of cities and towns also increases the capacity for the expansion of industrial clusters [34], the growth of the circulation industry may reduce the industry's production costs by lowering transportation expenses, as well as indirectly improve factor productivity of the manufacturing industry [35], thereby guiding labor optimization [3] and promoting the formation of industrial clusters. However, the traditional circulation industry has many problems in the transaction link, cost, time, and supply and demand matching. It needs to use the penetration of digital technology to complete its own Digital Revolution, apply the high penetration of digital economy, integrate with the traditional circulation industry, drive its upstream and downstream industries' innovative technology, digitization, and informatization [28], and give full play to the regulatory effect of the development of the circulation industry in industrial agglomeration. The development of the circulation industry provides a better production platform and agglomeration environment for industrial agglomeration, making industrial production, product circulation, allocation and sales of factor resources more efficient. In addition, data elements are another important element of modern industry, closely integrated with industrial production,, forming emerging formats, and supporting the growth of the local economy, the following is hypothesis in this paper:

Hypothesis 3: In the digital economy, the development of the circulation industry is crucial for fostering the development of industrial clusters.

A survey of current literature reveals that there are few pertinent mechanism tests and empirical testing, and that the research on the influence of the digital economy on industries begins from the perspective of industrial structure. There hasn't been any research done in tandem with the growth of the circulation sector to examine how the digital economy's impact on industrial agglomeration relates to that growth. The digital economy is rapidly integrating with the circulation industry, and information network technology has developed rapidly in the circulation industry. The development of the circulation industry has reduced industrial production costs and promoted trade exchanges with upstream and downstream industries. This article uses a model to examine relationships and mechanisms between them. Based on differences in spatial regions and different indicators in different regions, a more in-depth analysis of the heterogeneity characteristics of the digital economy on industrial agglomeration is conducted, and relevant recommendations are proposed to improve the formation of industrial agglomeration.

3 Empirical Design

3.1 Basic Model

The following model is developed to study the impact of digital economy development on manufacturing industry agglomeration:

$$aggl_{it} = \alpha_0 + \alpha_1 dige_{it} + \alpha_2 X_{it} + \mu_i + \theta_t + \varepsilon_{it} \qquad (1)$$

Among them, $aggl_{it}$ representative provinces i t years manufacturing agglomeration level; $dige_{it}$ representative provinces i t years of digital level of economic development; X_{it} representative control variable; μ_i and θ_t represents individual and time fixed effects; ε_{it} represents the random perturbation terms.

To studying the effect of digital level of economic development of circulation industry development, build bidirectional fixed effects model as follows:

$$docl_{it} = m_0 + m_1 dige_{it} + m_2 X_{it} + \mu_i + \theta_t + \varepsilon_{it} \qquad (2)$$

The transfer items of digital economy and circulation industry development are added to the model (1) to verify the regulatory role of the development of circulation industry in the influence of digital economy on industrial agglomeration.

$$aggl_{it} = \beta_0 + \beta_1 dige_{it} + \beta_2 doc_{it} + \beta_3 X_{it} + \mu_i + \theta_t + \varepsilon_{it} \qquad (3)$$

$$aggl_{it} = \gamma_0 + \gamma_1 dige_{it} + \gamma_2 doc_{it} + \gamma_3 dige_{it} * doc_{it} + \gamma_4 X_{it} + \mu_i + \theta_t + \varepsilon_{it} \quad (4)$$

Among these, the $doc1_{it}$ represents provinces i t years of the development level of circulation industry; doc_{it} show will $doc1_{it}$ The median is the standard, taking 1 greater than the median, and taking 0 otherwise, $dige_{it}*doc_{it}$ is the digital economy and the circulation the interaction term of industry development.

3.2 Variable Design and Data

Explained variables: industrial agglomeration ($aggl_{it}$). The methods for measuring industrial agglomeration include location entropy method, Hufendal index method, cluster analysis method, location gini coefficient method and industry cluster index method. This paper using the location entropy method [36] to measure manufacturing industrial agglomeration, the formula is provided as formula (5):

$$aggl = \frac{q_{ij}/q_i}{q_j/Q} \quad (5)$$

where, i indicates the province, j indicates the manufacturing industry, and q_{ij} represents the number of employment in manufacturing industries in i province, and Q indicates the total number of employment nationwide.

Interpretive variables: digital economy ($dige_{it}$). Most scholars for the provincial level of the digital economy measure using entropy weight, entropy method and principal component analysis, this study draws on ZhaoTao [37, 38], measuring the digital economy by using the entropy method (Table 1).

Table 1. Indicator system.

Level 1 indicators	Secondary indicators	unit	Indicator attributes
Digital economy development scale	Total postal business	kilometres	+
	Express business revenue	Wan Yuan	+
	Total telecom business	100 million	+
Digital economy infrastructure	Mobile phone penetration rate	Department / 100 people	+
	Internet broadband access to the users	Ten thousand households	+
	Talent support (the number of ordinary colleges and universities)	individual	+

Adjustment variables: the development of the circulation industry (doc_{it}). Measured by the specialization level of circulation industry, according to the definition of industrial specialization in Glaeser and Dekle [39], in the regulation effect model, the median is the standard, the province with the circulation development level higher than the median is 1, otherwise, 0.

$$docl_{it} = \frac{n_{it}}{N_{it}} \qquad (6)$$

Among these, the $docl_{it}$ refers to the professional level of the circulation industry, used to measure the growth level of the circulation industry, n_{it} is i province t year circulation industry urban unit employment number, N_{it} it is the final number of urban units in t.

Control variables: financial level (Fin): this paper refers to the study of Zhao Tao [37], measured by the ratio of the sum of the balance of regional institutional deposits and loans to gross regional product; degree of government intervention (gov): the percentage of fiscal expenditure to GDP measures the degree of intervention by governments; urbanization level (urban): to measure the level of urbanization by using the proportion of the urban population, at the same time, it is log-treated; level of transportation infrastructure (tra): transportation infrastructure is the basic condition of the industry, in this paper, we refer to the methods of Gong Xinshu [40], etc., using the following formula:

$$Trade = \frac{total\ mileage\ of\ regional\ highways}{area} * 100\% \qquad (7)$$

For study and analysis in this work, the panel data of 31 Chinese provinces from 2011 to 2020 were chosen. The China City Statistical Yearbook and EPS database provided the first data. The interpolation method was used for the individual data with missing values. Table 2 displays the descriptive statistical findings for the research variables.

Table 2. Descriptive statistics (sample size = 310).

Variables	Mean	Std.Dev	Min	Max
Industrial agglomeration (aggl)	0.810	0.353	0.0830	1.782
Development level of digital economy (dige)	0.230	0.133	0.0190	0.892
Circulation industry development level (doc)	0.050	0.501	0.000	1.000
Financial Level (Fin)	0.284	0.210	0.110	1.379
Degree of government intervention (gov)	2.664	1.094	0.882	6.761
Urbanization level (urban)	4.035	0.234	3.127	4.495
Transport infrastructure level (tra)	0.432	0.391	0.0130	2.087

4 Empirical Analysis

4.1 Benchmark Regression

The regression is performed on formula (1) to examine the influence of digital economic growth on industrial agglomeration, and the findings are displayed in Table 3. Table 3 (1) shows results without controlling variables. The results of the digital economy on industrial agglomeration is shown in Table 3 columns (2) through columns (5) when the four control variables are introduced one at a time. The digital economy coefficient is determined to be significantly positive, proving that hypothesis 1 is correct. Using the regression of formula (2), the digital economy component is found to be substantially positive in Table 3 column 6, indicating that the digital economy can significantly contribute in its growth of the circulation industry. Hypothesis 2 is correct.

Table 3. Benchmark regression.

variables	aggl					doc1
	(1)	(2)	(3)	(4)	(5)	(6)
dige	0.551**	0.549**	0.554**	0.564**	0.599**	0.075*
	(0.253)	(0.260)	(0.256)	(0.258)	(0.282)	(0.044)
gov		−0.029	−0.055	−0.075	0.119	0.248***
		(0.258)	(0.248)	(0.255)	(0.276)	(0.088)
tra			0.086	0.087*	0.116*	−0.010
			(0.051)	(0.048)	(0.060)	(0.010)
fin				0.003	−0.005	−0.021**
				(0.024)	(0.020)	(0.010)
urban					0.505*	0.003
					(0.276)	(0.024)
_cons	0.765***	0.773***	0.743***	0.740***	−1.291	0.016
	(0.048)	(0.089)	(0.092)	(0.093)	(1.094)	(0.013)
Fixed effects	Yes	Yes	Yes	Yes	Yes	Yes
R^2	0.105	0.105	0.113	0.113	0.145	0.208
N	310	310	310	310	310	310

4.2 The Regulating Effect of the Development of the Circulation Industry

The findings are displayed in Table 4. Table 4 (2), the regression coefficient of interaction between digital economy and circulation industry development is 0.266, and R^2 changes is 0.015, indicating that the regulation effect is significant. The growth of the circulation industry is crucial for advancing the progress of the digital economy promotes agglomeration and hypothesis 3 is verified. May be due to the circulation industry developed areas, driving the construction of infrastructure, the urbanization level is higher, attracts a lot of capital and labor, and the production materials of transportation cost is lower, produce greater consumption and production capacity, provide more jobs, promote the local industrial agglomeration.

Table 4. Results of moderating effect.

variables	aggl	
	(1)	(2)
dige	0.582*	0.385*
	(0.288)	(0.216)
doc	0.051	−0.007
	(0.033)	(0.037)
dige*doc		0.266*
		(0.138)
gov	0.123	0.275
	(0.252)	(0.256)
tra	0.121**	0.123*
	(0.057)	(0.061)
fin	0.002	−0.004
	(0.020)	(0.017)
urban	0.572**	0.610**
	(0.271)	(0.278)
_cons	−1.591	−1.730
	(1.088)	(1.127)
Fixed effects	Yes	Yes
R^2	0.170	0.185
N	310	310

4.3 Heterogeneity Analysis

Group the samples by region and perform benchmark regression was conducted in each to examine the heterogeneity of the influence of the digital economy on industrial agglomeration in the area. The outcomes are displayed in Table 5. The digital economy strongly promotes industrial agglomeration in the eastern region. The cause of this difference may be that the eastern economy and circulation industry development level overall higher, is advantageous to the production of raw materials to reduce production costs and information transmission. Beneficial to forming industrial agglomeration. And digital economy infrastructure of the cental and west region is relatively backward, relatively poor industry development environment, circulation industry is underdeveloped, all kinds of costs and information congestion, cause the role of the digital economy is limited.

A group regression was then performed according to different degrees of various indicators in different regions, as shown in Table 6. First, this article uses the marketization index constructed by Fan Gang [41] to measure the level of marketization, in the provinces of the median, the median sample for high marketization level group, below the median sample for marketization level group [42], and regression analysis, can be

Table 5. Heterogeneity analysis based on location

variables	In the area		
	east	central	west
	(1)	(2)	(3)
dige	0.997**	0.852	−0.324
	(0.415)	(0.842)	(0.315)
gov	0.565	0.308	−0.050
	(0.986)	(0.741)	(0.220)
tra	−0.208	−0.423	0.064
	(0.999)	(0.305)	(0.043)
fin	0.007	−0.117	−0.010
	(0.031)	(0.081)	(0.015)
urban	0.463	−0.457	0.117
	(0.645)	(1.372)	(0.457)
_cons	−1.080	2.705	0.252
	(2.500)	(5.355)	(1.726)
Fixed effects	Yes	Yes	Yes
R^2	0.418	0.295	0.413
N	100	100	110

found that in the low marketization level of digital economy of industrial agglomeration is not significant and negative, this shows that the regional market foundation is not perfect, hindered the development of digital economy and industry, is not conducive to the formation of industrial agglomeration. Second, this paper to the median of the standard, the whole sample is divided into low density, high density and regression analysis respectively, the results can be found in the population density is high, the digital economy in promoting industrial agglomeration, the higher the population density, provides the resources of industrial development must labor, promote the formation of industrial agglomeration. Third, this research project measures the level of technical innovation using the number of patent applications [43]. It can be seen that in cities with low level of technological innovation, the impact of digital economy on industrial agglomeration is not significant and negative, which shows that regions with low level of technological innovation lack independent introduction, and the industry is underdeveloped.

4.4 Robustness Test

The explanatory variable lags for one period. This article will re estimate industrial agglomeration with explanatory variables lagging for one period to test the robustness of the model. As demonstrated in column (1) of Table 7, the coefficient of the digital economy's development level with a one-period lag is still favorably significant.

Table 6. Analysis of the heterogeneity.

variables	Marketization level		density of population		Technology innovation level	
	High marketization level	Low marketization level	high density	low density	High innovation group	Low innovation group
	(1)	(2)	(3)	(4)	(5)	(6)
dige	0.794*	−0.205	1.037***	−0.087	0.792*	−0.411
	(0.449)	(0.471)	(0.232)	(0.115)	(0.458)	(0.568)
gov	0.330	−0.015	0.929***	−0.058	0.177	−0.045
	(0.908)	(0.259)	(0.289)	(0.250)	(1.231)	(0.258)
tra	0.352	0.106**	0.083	0.065**	0.719	0.108**
	(0.673)	(0.042)	(0.159)	(0.031)	(0.476)	(0.048)
fin	0.004	0.003	−0.070***	−0.016	0.014	−0.004
	(0.059)	(0.014)	(0.025)	(0.012)	(0.082)	(0.013)
urban	0.746	−0.098	0.886*	0.384*	1.065**	−0.089
	(0.513)	(0.324)	(0.431)	(0.192)	(0.481)	(0.297)
_cons	−2.225	0.954	−2.872	−0.650	−3.643*	0.982
	(2.162)	(1.253)	(1.766)	(0.757)	(1.957)	(1.168)
Fixed effects	Yes	Yes	Yes	Yes	Yes	Yes
R^2	0.207	0.306	0.360	0.123	0.190	0.270
N	155	155	155	155	155	155

Replace the explained variable. For the purpose of trying to get more reliable regression results, the calculation formula in this paper is as Eq. (5), which is based on the research of Sun Zhichao [44], using the industrial agglomeration of GDP and population proportion to replace the measure of employment to conduct the robustness test. The calculation formula is as Eq. (5). The results are displayed in Table 7 (2), and it can be seen that even when the explained factors are replaced, the coefficient of digital economy development level remains substantial and positive, demonstrating that the prior results are resilient.

$$Aggl1 = \frac{(\frac{GDP \text{ of the secondary industry}}{resident\ population})}{(\frac{national\ secondary\ industry\ GDP}{national\ resident\ population})} \tag{8}$$

Table 7. Robustness test.

variables	The explanatory variables lag behind the one phase (1)	Replacement by the explanatory variable (2)
L.dige	0.691**	
	(0.280)	
dige		36.421**
		(16.001)
gov	0.046	−15.732
	(0.239)	(15.924)
tra	0.184**	1.854
	(0.087)	(2.520)
fin	0.004	0.743
	(0.018)	(1.423)
urban	0.653*	16.357
	(0.323)	(10.333)
_cons	−1.938	−38.016
	(1.304)	(40.601)
Fixed effects	Yes	Yes
R^2	0.145	0.420
N	279	310

5 Conclusion

This paper employs the models to examine how the expansion of the digital economy has affected industrial agglomeration and the regulatory impact of the development of the circulation industry. According to research, the growth of the digital economy significantly promotes the formation of industrial agglomeration, and the growth of the circulation industry significantly promotes the formation of industrial agglomeration in the digital economy. Moreover, with a more actively improving effect in the eastern region. In addition, in the high level of marketization areas with dense populations and high levels of technological innovation also have more significant promoting effects.

The following enlightenments are drawn by this article from the earlier analysis: Develop the digital economy first, then upgrade the infrastructure. This study comes to the conclusion that the growth of the digital economy can aid in the creation of industrial agglomerations. The foundation for developing a digital economy is to build an infrastructure that is flawless, vigorously push for the development of digital infrastructure, particularly by fully utilizing the permeability, efficiency, lowering trade costs, advancing the level of growth of the circulation industry. Simultaneously, emphasis should be placed on encouraging the digital transformation of old industrial infrastructure, fully utilizing the information dividend that the digital economy has brought to the sector and developing the regional economy. Secondly, the combination of online and offline industrial clusters. Online agglomeration can help promote industrial integration and development, and improve competitiveness. With the digital economy, industrial agglomeration can no longer rely closely on offline agglomeration. The degree of industrial integration will rapidly decline. As a result of the digital economy's impact, online agglomeration can enable enterprises to have no distance and use digital technology to quickly connect and exchange products and services online, enhancing the quality of goods and services provided by upstream and downstream businesses. And online clustering can provide more information and job opportunities. Thirdly, develop the circulation industry and enhance the level of urbanization. Regions with developed circulation laws have lower trade costs, easier access for enterprises to low-cost raw materials, and densely populated areas with more employment opportunities and higher levels of urbanization. These are all factors conducive to the formation of industrial clusters.

References

1. Qiao, S.: Analysis of the impact of digital economy on industrial structure upgrading based on stata. In: 2021 2nd International Conference on Big Data Economy and Information Management (BDEIM), Sanya, China, pp. 31–35 (2021)
2. An, T., Yang, C.: Internet reshaping the geographical pattern of China's economy: micro mechanisms and macro effects. Econ. Res. **55**(02), 4–19 (2020)
3. Zhang, J., Zhao, Q.: Research on the transformation and upgrading of business model of circulation supply chain driven by new retail. Bus. Econ. Manag. **11**, 5–15 (2018)
4. Cong, Y.: Circulation industry development and urbanization——empirical research based on the panel data model. China's Circ. Econ. **28**(07), 31–38 (2014)
5. Wang, S., Si, Z.: Analysis of the mechanism and factors of the influence of the circulation industry on the new urbanization based on the dynamic panel data——take Jiangsu Province as an example. Circ. Econ. China **31**(06), 8–16 (2017)
6. Zhan, H.: The mechanism of trade circulation industry agglomeration on the transformation and upgrading of manufacturing industry——Based on the perspective of competition and cooperation of cluster supply chain network. China's Circ. Econ. **28**(09), 59–65 (2014)
7. Liu, W., et al.: Does the digital economy reduce air pollution in China? a perspective from industrial agglomeration. Energy Rep. **9**, 3625–3641 (2023). ISSN 2352-4847
8. Lu, Y., Fang, X., Zhang, S.: Digital economy, space spillover and high-quality development of urban economy. Econ. Longitude **38**(06), 21–31 (2021)
9. Meng, Y., Wang, C., Zhang, W.: Nonlinear impacts of information and communications technology investment on industrial structure upgrading: the role of marketization. Appl. Econ. Lett. **30**(3), 336–342 (2023)
10. Guan, H., Guo, B., Zhang, J.: Study on the impact of the digital economy on the upgrading of industrial structures—empirical analysis based on cities in China. Sustainability **14**(18), 11378 (2022)
11. Zhang, Y.: The development ideas and main tasks of digital economy driving the industrial structure to the middle and high-end. Econ. Hor. **394**(09), 85–91 (2018)
12. Yao, Z.: The Regional marketization level and the competition of the digital economy——based on the analysis of the inter-provincial spatial distribution characteristics of the digital economy index. Jianghan Forum (12), 23–33 (2020)

13. Li, C., Li, D., Zhou, C.: The mechanism of digital economy driving the transformation and upgrading of manufacturing industry——analysis based on the perspective of industrial chain. Bus. Res. **514**(02), 73–82 (2020)
14. Chen, B., Wang, W.: Internet development, industrial agglomeration structure and green innovation efficiency. Econ. Manag. East China **35**(04), 42–56 (2021)
15. Chen, X., Yang, X.: The influence of digital economy development on the upgrading of industrial structure——based on the theory of grey correlation entropy and dissipation structure. Reform **325**(03), 26–39 (2021)
16. Liu, Y., Chen, X.: The impact of China's Digital economy development on the upgrading of industrial structure. Econ. Manag. Res. **42**(08), 15–29 (2021)
17. Ding, Z.: Research on the mechanism of digital economy driving high-quality economic development: a theoretical analysis framework. Disc. Mod. Econ. **457**(01), 85–92 (2020)
18. Zhao, X.: Research on the transformation and upgrading of china's manufacturing driven by digital economy. Zhongzhou Acad. J. **252**(12), 36–41 (2017)
19. Chang, Z., Qian, M.: Analysis of the intermediary effect of information technology affecting industrial structure optimization and upgrading———empirical evidence from the provincial level in China. Econ. Theory Econ. Manag. (6), 39–42 (2018)
20. Chen, Y., Zhang, X.: Mechanism of digital economy development on regional industrial structure optimization——based on empirical analysis of provincial panel data from 2011 to 2019. Finan. Theory Series **297**(04), 14–23 (2023)
21. Hui, P., Lu, Y., Wang, Q.: How does heterogeneous industrial agglomeration affect the total factor energy efficiency of China's digital economy. Energy **268**, 126654 (2023). ISSN 0360-5442
22. Tian, G., Chen, F.: Digital economy, industrial agglomeration and high-quality development of manufacturing industry in the Yellow River Basin. Stat. Decis.-Mak. **38**(21), 10–14 (2022)
23. Zhang, L., Liang, Y., Gong, R.: Study on the dynamic impact of digital economy on urban-rural income gap——evidence from 31 provinces (autonomous regions and municipalities) in China. Econ. Issues Explor. **488**(03), 18–40 (2023)
24. Ye, T., Wang, X.: The influence of digital economy on coordinated and balanced development——on the realization path of common prosperity. Econ. Dyn. **743**(01), 73–88 (2023)
25. Huang, Q., Yu, Y., Zhang, S.: Internet development and manufacturing productivity improvement: internal mechanisms and Chinese experience. China Ind. Econ. **377**(08), 5–23 (2019)
26. Wu, Y., Tao, K., Peng, J.: Industrial collaborative agglomeration, digital technology support and resource misallocation. Sci. Res. Manag. **44**(01), 125–135 (2023)
27. Xie, L., Li, S., Wang, X.: Analysis of self-operation and joint operation in China's retail industry. Bus. Econ. Manag. **331**(05), 5–14 (2019)
28. Tang, H., Chen, X., Zhang, J.: Digital economy, circulation efficiency and upgrading of industrial structure. Bus. Econ. Manag. **361**(11), 5–20 (2021)
29. Bai, Y., Song, L.: A political and economic analysis of the impact of the digital economy on economic activities. J. Lanzhou Univ. (Soc. Sci. Ed.) **49**(04), 78–85 (2021)
30. Zhou, J., Wang, P.: The pressure and countermeasures of China's industrial structure upgrading under the new development pattern. Econ. Hor. (6), 94–99 (2021)
31. Fan, X., Kang, X.: Empirical analysis of manufacturing industry agglomeration degree measurement and influencing factors in Shaanxi Province. Econ. Geogr. **33**(09), 115–119 + 160 (2013)
32. Cong, Y.: Circulation industry development and urbanization - empirical research based on Panel data model. China Circ. Econ. **28**(07), 31–38 (2014)
33. Yan, W., Han, Y, Yang, Y.: Research on the relationship between urbanization and commodity circulation: theory and Empirical Evidence. Econ. Res. (02), 75–83 (2004)

34. Ma, G., Cai, L.: Research on the mechanism of interaction between urbanization and industrial agglomeration. J. Harbin Inst. Technol. (Soc. Sci. Ed.) **21**(05), 127–134 (2019)
35. Song, Z., Chang, D., Ding, N.: Influence of circulation industry and structural adjustment of manufacturing industry. Ind. Econ. China (8), 5–14 (2010)
36. Meng, F., Yan, Z.: Industrial intelligence, industrial agglomeration and carbon productivity. Sci. Res.: 1–18 (2023)
37. Zhao, T., Zhang, Z., Liang, S.: Digital economy, entrepreneurial activity and high-quality development——empirical evidence from Chinese cities. Manage World **36**(10), 65–76 (2020)
38. Yang, R., Xu, X.: The influence of digital economy on the high-quality development of commercial circulation industry. China's Circ. Econ. **37**(05), 28–40 (2023)
39. Glaesere, L., Kallal, H.D., Scheinkman, J.A., et al.: Growth in cities. J. Polit. Econ. **100**(6), 1126–1152 (1992)
40. Wang, Z., Zhang, H., Gong, X., et al.: Logistics industry agglomeration, market segmentation and regional green economic efficiency. Econ. Longitude **35**(05), 87–93 (2018)
41. Fan, G., Wang, X., Ma, G.: The contribution of China's marketization process to economic growth. Econ. Res. **46**(09), 4–16 (2011)
42. Li, L., Wang, T.: Export, innovation and enterprise domestic sales——based on upstream and downstream perspective. Int. Trade Issues **472**(04), 142–157 (2022)
43. Sun, Z., Wang, T., Guo, H., et al.: Technological innovation, industrial agglomeration, and economic development. Econ. Issues **527**(07), 77–86 (2023)
44. Huang, Y., Wen, W.: The development of circulation industry, spatial interaction, and urban economic growth. Ind. Econ. Res. (04), 75–87 (2019)

Analysis of Influencing Factors of Housing Affordability Crisis in Vancouver

Jiaxuan Chen(✉)

Vancouver College, 5401 Hudson St, Vancouver, BC V6M 0C5, Canada
`jchen@vancouvercollege.ca, jason1112chen@gmail.com`

Abstract. Vancouver, renowned for its natural beauty and livability, is experiencing an ongoing and severe housing affordability crisis. This paper delves into the factors behind skyrocketing housing prices and seeks to understand the unique aspects of this market that contribute to the affordability crisis. Drawing upon data from 2005 to 2022, the study explores various determinants, including labor market, interest rates, social housing, economic growth, foreign money, and zoning regulations. The analysis reveals that the unaffordability of housing in Vancouver is not solely attributed to a specific reason, but a combination of issues behind the market and nonmarket forces in the housing market that ultimately created the imbalance between the income level and housing prices. The Housing Affordability Index is used to measure housing affordability, which considers the median income of a typical household in Vancouver as a parameter. Besides, this study highlights the critical role of foreign money inflow and zoning regulations through which the demand composition and the supply shock create a market failure.

Keywords: Vancouver · Housing Affordability Crisis · Capital Inflow · Zoning Regulations

1 Introduction

Over the past few decades, Vancouver has gained a reputation for having one of the world's most expensive real estate markets. Since the federal government stopped funding public housing in the late 1980s, accompanied by increasing numbers of immigrants, housing affordability has been a hot topic for a long time. Among all the Canadian Cities, Vancouver's housing prices have been significantly higher than other Census Metropolitan Areas (CMA) according to the Canadian Real Estate Association (CREA), as illustrated in Fig. 1. As a beautiful city with no extreme summer and winter climates and decent amenities, Vancouver is often marked as one of the world's most livable cities [1]. However, the increasing unaffordability of housing creates a high barrier to entry for people to enjoy the good living conditions in Vancouver, even some of the original residents in the city are unable to afford to live there anymore [2].

Previous studies had analyzed the potential culprit of Vancouver's housing affordability crisis, specifically, focusing on the effect of foreign buyers [3]. Other potential causes

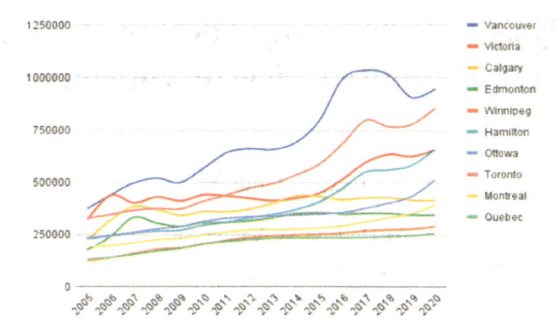

Fig. 1. Housing Benchmark Price Comparison in 10 Canadian Cities; Data Source: CREA.

of unaffordable housing prices around the world have been identified as well, including the effect of zoning laws [4], income inequality [5, 6], and non-market housing [6, 7].

Addressing the housing affordability crisis needs a collaborative effort from policy-makers, private developers, and residents to create a more balanced and equitable housing market. But before that, it is crucial to identify the root causes of such an issue. This paper identifies the likely factors behind the rapid growth in home prices in Vancouver and analyzes what unique factors have contributed to Vancouver's particular problems. This paper discusses the specific demand composition of Vancouver, and how different supply-side influencing factors are playing their roles in the issue. The following section of this essay will respectively discuss the definition of housing affordability, data sources, the roles of housing and the labor market, low-interest rates, social housing, economic growth, foreign buyers, and zoning regulations.

2 Housing Affordability

Housing affordability refers to the ability of the median citizen to buy a house given her or his income. Firstly, it is important to acknowledge that one would expect prices to increase with economic growth. However, as shown below in Fig. 2, changes in median income are not kept in pace with the faster price change in the Vancouver Housing Market. Housing affordability is a combined problem that shows an imbalance between the labor market's and the housing market's equilibrium prices. Therefore, this paper not only examines the housing prices in Vancouver or contrasts them to other cities; it also focuses on understanding housing unaffordability in a way that is relative to the median income of a typical household in Vancouver. At least one market failure should exist whether in the housing or labor markets, reflecting a significant producer surplus in the market.

In this paper, following the National Association of Realtors, housing affordability can be measured by Housing Affordability Index (HAI):

$$HAI = \left(\frac{median\ income}{qualifying\ income}\right) * 100\% \tag{1}$$

where

$$qualifying\ income = monthly\ payment * 12 * 4 \tag{2}$$

$$monthly\,payment = P\left(\frac{i(1+i)^n}{(1+i)^{n-1}}\right) \qquad (3)$$

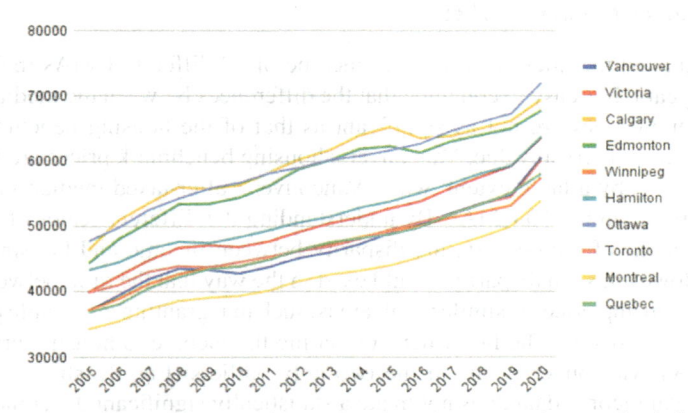

Fig. 2. Median Income Comparison in 10 Canadian Cities; Data Source: Statistics Canada.

In formula 3, i is the annual interest rate, n is the time interval, and P represents the loan value. It is not economically sustainable if a person is spending more than 25 percent of their income on housing, therefore, when calculating the qualifying income, it equals to monthly payment times 12, which gives the annual correspondent, and times it by 4 to calculate a person's lowest income if they want to economically sustainably to buy a house.

In the following part of the paper, HAI will be used to examine different trends in the housing market.

3 Analysis of Influencing Factors

This section focuses on explaining the potential influencing factors of the Vancouver Housing Affordability Crisis. The analysis uses data which are typically annual observations from 2005 to 2022, which can more accurately reflect the current economic development of Vancouver.

The primary data sources are shown below:

(1) Statistics Canada, the data source of the after-taxed median income
(2) Canadian Real Estate Association (CREA), the data source of the seasonally adjusted benchmark prices of houses.
(3) Real Estate Board of Greater Vancouver (REBGV)'s monthly market watch, the data source of housing sales.

Secondary sources are shown below:

(1) National Bank of Canada (NBC), which gains data on interest rates from the charter banks in the country. It serves as the data source of the mortgage interest rate.

(2) Metro Vancouver Housing Data Book 2022, which gains and analyzes data from the Canada Housing and Mortgage Corporation (CHMC). It serves as the data source of housing starts.

3.1 Housing or Labour Market

Figure 2 depicted the after-taxed median income of 10 different CMAs in Canada for the past 15 years. It is easy to conclude that the differences between the median incomes among different cities are not as significant as that of the housing benchmark prices (Fig. 1) in their numerical value. Vancouver's housing benchmark prices are the highest among all cities, by a large extent, while Vancouver's after-taxed median income is in the middle between the 10 CMAs. By understanding the different scales of economies in different areas of the country, the disparity between income and housing prices is expected. However, such disparity should exist in the way that the ratio between median income and housing prices is similar in all areas, such that granting affordable purchasing power to those citizens. The fact when comparing the income to housing price ratio in the 10 CMAs, Vancouver is one of the two only outliers (Fig. 3), showing that even though median income data does not make a statistically significant difference between the different CMAs, the housing prices data do indicate such a difference.

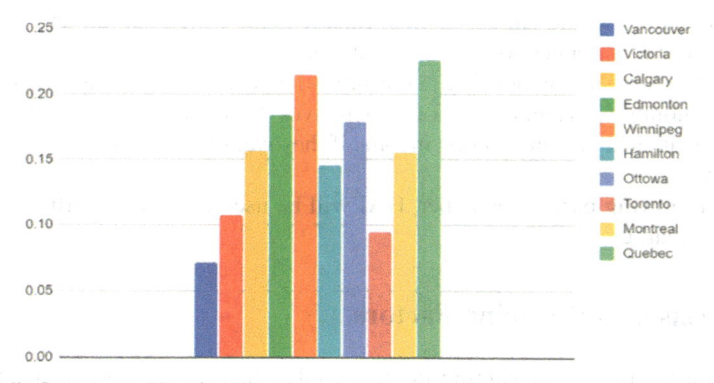

Fig. 3. Media Income to Housing Benchmark Price Ratio; Data Sources: Statistics Canada & CREA.

Therefore, it is clear that the housing market is experiencing a market failure, with prices being set way beyond the socially optimal market equilibrium. In other words, Vancouver is not experiencing a poverty issue, and the unaffordable housing prices are contributed mainly by the inefficient housing market, which is yet to become socially optimal. The reason why houses are unaffordable in Vancouver is not that people are earning too little, but that houses are too expensive for people who earn around the median income to afford.

3.2 Interest Rates

Although lower interest rates would allow people with lower incomes to afford a more expensive house to increase the housing demand, it does not explain the fact that Vancouver's housing prices are uniquely higher than other Canadian cities [3]. Additionally, in Fig. 4, a regression represents the correlation between the change in 5-year mortgage interest rates and the change in home prices in Vancouver. The R-squared ends up being around 0.08, which is not statistically significant. As interest rates are the same in all Canadian cities, while there is no statistically significant correlation between interest rates and housing prices, it leads to the conclusion that low-interest rate is not the specific reason why Vancouver's housing prices are too high, while it may be a factor influencing the overall trend in Canadian housing.

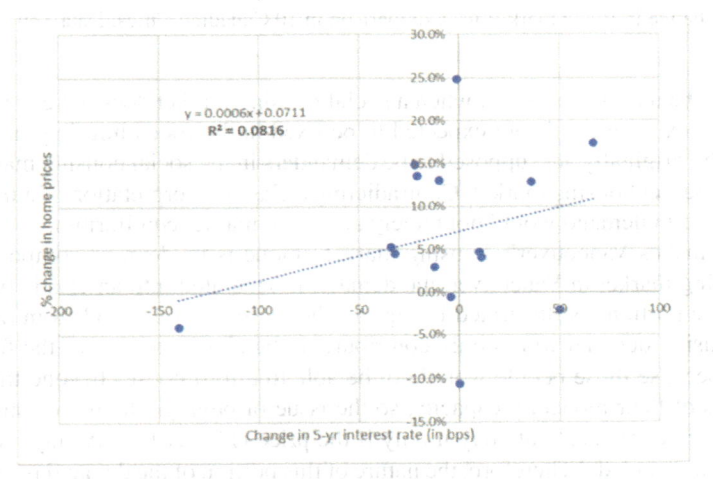

Fig. 4. Correlation Between Changes in 5-yr interest rate and Change in home prices; Data Sources: CREA & National Bank of Canada retrieved from Charter Banks.

3.3 Social Housing

Another point where the government is commonly attacked is Vancouver's lack of social housing. Social housing was defunded by the federal government as far as back in the 1980s. In Fig. 5, looking at the change in benchmark price in the 10 CMAs in the period between 2005 and 2021, when social housing is already no longer a thing, Vancouver's fluctuation still turns out to be big and is the biggest one among the ten cities, which empirically supports that social housing is not the root behind the high housing price in Vancouver.

Market housing and social housing are meant to be two separate markets. Social housing targets a specific portion of home buyers whose income is lower than a certain social standard and who cannot afford market housing. The suppliers of such houses would not be motivated by profitability, at least not from the demand side. Considering

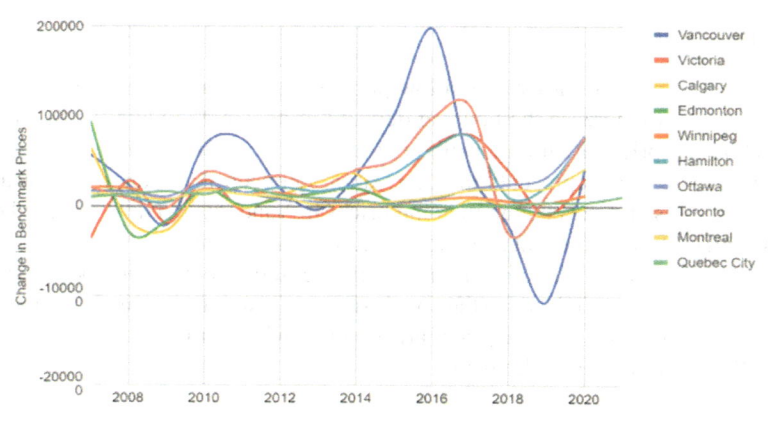

Fig. 5. Change in Benchmark Price Comparison in 10 Canadian Cities. Data Source: CREA.

housing to be a basic necessity, when a social housing market does not exist, or a huge shortage is existing and is not expected to be fixed in the social housing market, those people who originally are supposed to be demanders in the social housing market would enter the market housing market. Contradicting a classic interpretation of a free market, this increase in demand would not hugely affect the market equilibrium.

What makes Vancouver's housing market unique is its demand composition. In a free housing market in Vancouver, the demand is separated into an elastic portion and an inelastic portion, as illustrated in Fig. 6. The increase in demand from the original social housing demand would only contribute to the elastic portion of the free-market demand because those people would not be able to afford houses beyond that specific price A as of their monetary capacity, so the issue of buying a home for this group of low-income people is about "buy it only if the price is lower than A, anything beyond that is not demanded." Therefore, the nature of this portion of the demand is very elastic. When only this portion of demand is increased, while the equilibrium price is already set beyond A, which precisely describes the situation when social housing is defunded, then this increase in demand would do very little to the change in the equilibrium price. Therefore, even though the lack of social housing would be a huge topic to be discussed in the homelessness issue in Vancouver, it is not the reason why the housing price is so high.

3.4 Economic Growth

When an economy is doing well, an increase in aggregate demand would cause an increase in the average price level, which also comes with increased wages. Therefore, if Vancouver's housing price is increasing at a faster rate than the median income, it is not conclusive to say that this increase in housing price is caused by economic growth, or at least, not all of it. As mentioned above in Sect. 3.2, the disparity between the housing prices in cities is way higher than that of the income. Economic growth is a sign that represents a better standard of living, and an unreasonable decrease in housing affordability is not expected. HAI for Vancouver for 2006 to 2020 shows a trend of

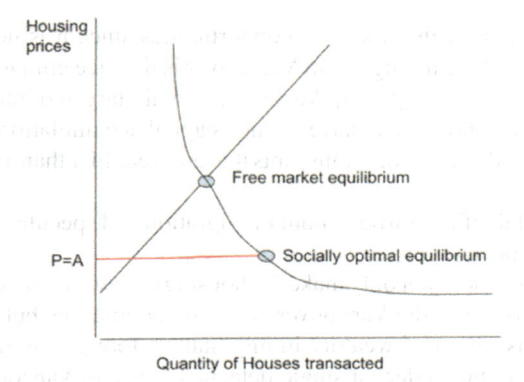

Fig. 6. Vancouver Housing Market Demand-Supply Curve without Supply Shock.

decreasing for the most part as Fig. 7 shows, representing the housing prices increasing in a way that includes an "extra-inflation" beyond the numerical price increase brought by economic growth. The increase in wages is set to be the standard for price increases here. Otherwise, economic growth cannot represent a growth in living standards for the average citizen. Considering that, the disparity of economic growth between different Canadian cities does not explain the unique unaffordable housing prices in Vancouver.

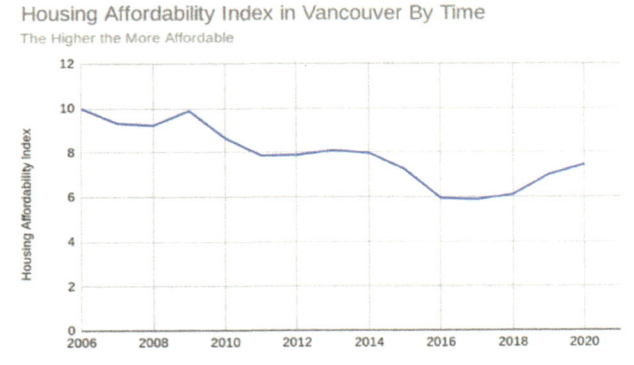

Fig. 7. Housing Affordability Index in Vancouver by Time; Data Sources: Statistics Canada, CREA, National Bank of Canada Retrieved from Charter Bank.

3.5 Foreign Money and Demand Composition

The effect of foreign money in Vancouver is enormous, where foreign money is usually buying up the high-priced portion of the Vancouver housing market. About 88% of houses that are priced beyond 5 million dollars in the University Endowment Land are purchased by non-Anglican named Chinese [8], and 66% of 172 sampled single-detached houses in Vancouver are purchased by the same group [7]. Different from other west coast cities where people may arrive to search for better opportunities, Vancouver does not provide immigrants with a lot of job opportunities since it is not home to any big industries—the main drive to migrate to Vancouver is the nice climate, stable amenities, and comfortable environment [9, 10]. Vancouver's main targeted immigrant population is the wealthy people who already have enough capital accumulation from abroad—the city is receiving a good amount of immigrants that are wealthier than a typical native-born Vancouverite.

Therefore, capital inflow, through both immigration and speculation, becomes a very crucial fact in Vancouver.

This capital inflow does not only make the housing demand in Vancouver accountable for the money that is not in the Vancouver economy circulation, but it also changes the demand shape. This group of wealthy immigrants or foreign investors are willing to spend more money to buy a decent single detached house in Vancouver for them to be able to enjoy the nice climate and friendly environment in Vancouver (or better speculate for a larger return), granting the inelastic price portion of this part of the demand, as shown in Fig. 6. Since this portion of demand is specifically focusing on high-priced houses, therefore, single detached houses would be the main focus for analysis. Figure 8 depicts the comparison of changes in benchmark prices in single detached houses and the housing sales, which shows a minute amount of changes in houses transacted in the market have been explained by changes in housing prices. This observed fact aligns with the theory's prerequisite, which, therefore, supports the theory in wealthy immigrants and foreign buyers reshape the demand of the Vancouver Housing Market to create an inelastic portion at the low quantity level.

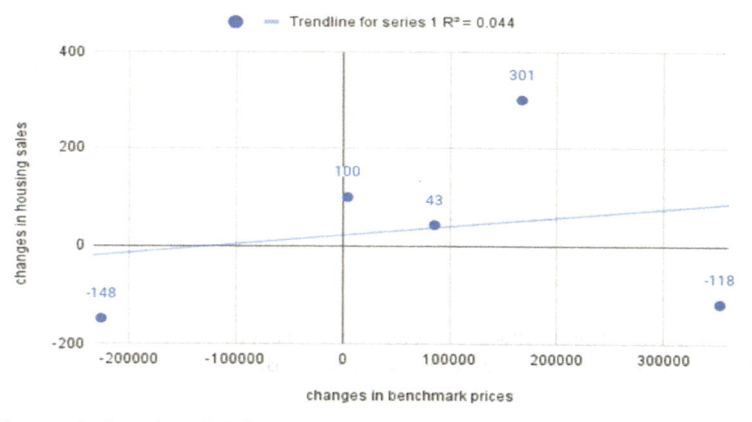

Fig. 8. Changes in Benchmark Prices vs. Changes in Housing Sales; Data Source: CREA and REBGV.

One fact that supports the counterargument is that less than 10% of the residential units in Vancouver are foreign-owned for investment purposes. However, the market influence of such investments is not determined by the quantity they buy up in the market. Despite not being very huge in number, they act as outliers that hugely change the trend of demand in the Vancouver housing market. As illustrated in Fig. 6, in a housing market that is purely determined by free demand and supply (all else unchanged), wealthy immigrants and foreign investors make up the inelastic portion of the demand, despite the quantity demanded at this portion being very low, because of the high corresponding prices, it brings the equilibrium price way higher than the socially optimal one, where homes are priced at a price that a typical Vancouverite can afford. The market is already experiencing a huge market failure since housing is a necessity; a free-market equilibrium that makes housing unaffordable for a typical Vancouver resident reflects huge negative externalities.

Unlike the determinants mentioned in Sects. 3.1 to 3.4 of this paper, foreign money inflow is unique to Vancouver. Therefore, this point is not rebuttable by looking at Fig. 1. Similar to the low-income portion of the population, the holders of foreign money are hugely affecting the demand composition of market housing, the one significant difference between these two groups of people is that the holders of foreign money can influence the equilibrium prices while the elastic portion cannot. Through that, it is obvious to see how foreign money is one of the root causes of the skyrocketing housing prices in Vancouver.

3.6 The Effect of Zoning Regulations

Zoning is considered to be one of the main culprits of housing unaffordability [4], and it applies specifically to Vancouver as well. Figure 9.a depicts the zoning map of today's city of Vancouver, where most area in the city is zoned to be a single detached house or duplex district. Single-detached house districts allow nothing to be built around a house except for its backyard and garage. Duplex districts allow two units of houses to be built on a single lot. These land use laws would be considered very inefficient regarding Vancouver's large population and limited land. Contrasting with another huge metropolis in Canada, Montreal's zoning map depicts the complete opposite, where it does not specify what type of houses can be built in a residential zone (Fig. 9.b). The zoning laws in Vancouver hugely limit the supply of houses in the housing market. Given the demand being so inelastic at the low quantity, this limitation in supply would cause a massive increase in equilibrium price as illustrated in Fig. 10. It is easily seen that resources in the market are not close to allocative efficiency.

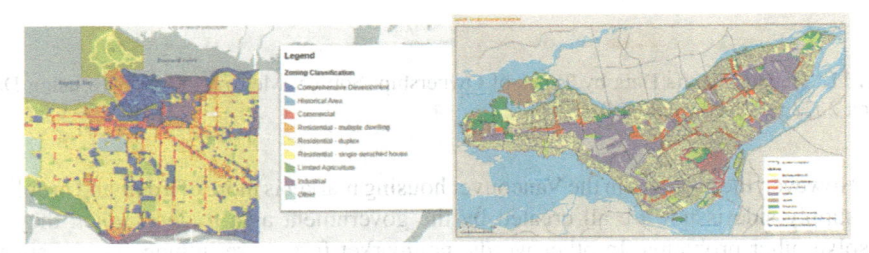

Fig. 9. a. Vancouver Zoning Map; Source: City of Vancouver (left). **b.** Montreal Zoning Map; Source: l'affctation du sol et la densite d'occupation (right).

Besides that, banning building rental apartments further solidifies the problem. In 1974, the City of Vancouver stopped funding the construction of rental apartments in the

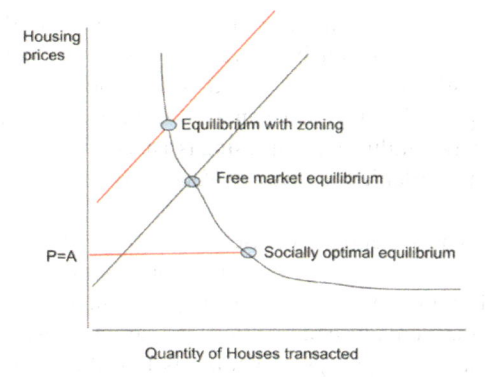

Fig. 10. Vancouver Housing Market Demand-Supply Curve with Supply Shock.

city, and since then, the rental housing starts have been very low, as illustrated in Fig. 11. The Strata Act of 2000 prohibits the owners of Condominiums to rent their properties out, creating a vast market shortage for rental housing. These legislations further limit the supply of housing in Vancouver, contributing to the huge unaffordability of the Vancouver housing market and further distorting the situation. Therefore, the role that the legislative body can play here is very crucial.

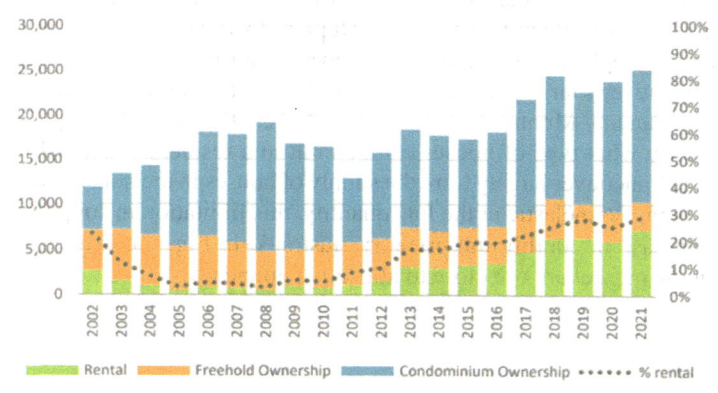

Fig. 11. Housing Starts Data by Types of Ownership; Source: Metro Vancouver Housing Data Book 2022 retrieved from CMHC.

However, the problem in the Vancouver housing market is more of a demand problem; the supply-side issues are all created by the government as a tradeoff when they try to solve other problems. In other words, nonmarket forces are influencing the supply exacerbating the problem created by the unique demand composition in Vancouver Housing Market. Therefore, when it comes to de-escalating the problem, terminating or reforming the supply is relatively plausible and easier to achieve while having a brand-new demand composition has a long way to go.

4 Conclusion

Vancouver Housing Crisis is a prolonged issue that has affected everybody in Vancouver to a certain extent. This paper focuses on explaining the housing affordability crisis in Vancouver with affordability being defined by HAI, thus classifying Vancouver as the most unaffordable city in Canada which has a qualifying income that is around 10 times larger than the median income of a typical Vancouver resident.

By considering household incomes, it was concluded that the housing affordability crisis in Vancouver is a housing market issue, not a poverty issue. Low-interest rates are not the reason the housing market is failing. Besides that, economic growth is not the root cause either. In Sect. 3, this paper concludes that the root causes of the housing unaffordability issues are the foreign money influence on the demand composition and the limitation on supply due to the zoning regulations.

This paper explores the root causes of Vancouver's housing price increase without proposing solutions. It acknowledges wealthy immigration, speculation, and zoning laws as contributors to the issue but does not examine their potential benefits for the economy and society. The paper provides a theory of the demand composition of the Vancouver Housing Market, which aligns with real-time statistics but lacks empirical analysis. The essay relies on median income, potentially misleading regarding economic inequality's impact on the housing crisis. Future research should consider different quantiles and examine the role of inequality more comprehensively.

References

1. Cox, W.: Housing Affordability and the Standard of Living in Vancouver. Policycommons.net, Canadian Electronic Library (2023). Accessed 2 Apr 2023
2. Brunet-Jailly, E.: Vancouver: the sustainable city. J. Urban Affairs **30**(4), 375–88 (2008). Accessed 24 Apr 2021
3. Gordon, J.: Vancouver's Housing Affordability Crisis: Causes, Consequences, and Solutions. Simon Fraser University, 2016, pp. 3–24. Accessed 26 Apr. 2023
4. Glaeser, E.L., Gyourko, J.: The impact of zoning on housing affordability. National Bureau of Economic Research (2002). Accessed 31 Mar 2023
5. Matlack, J.L., Vigdor, J.L.: Do rising tides lift all prices? income inequality and housing affordability. National Bureau of Economic Research (2006). Accessed 2 Apr 2023
6. Favilukis, J., et al.: Affordable housing and city welfare. Rev. Econ. Stud. **90**, 293–330 (2022). Accessed 22 May 2022
7. Sieg, H., Yoon, C.: Waiting for affordable housing in New York City. National Bureau of Economic Research (2019). Accessed 9 May 2023
8. Yan, A.: Ownership patterns of single family homes sales on the west side neighborhoods of the city of Vancouver: a case study (2015). https://www.slideshare.net/. Accessed 9 May 2023
9. Helliwell, J.F., et al.: How happy are your neighbours? variation in life satisfaction among 1200 Canadian neighbourhoods and communities. PLOS ONE **14**(1), e0210091 (2019). Accessed 22 May 2023
10. Yu, L.: An empirical study of recent mainland Chinese migration to Vancouver. J. Can. Hist. Assoc. **19**(2), 180–196 (2009). Accessed 22 May 2022

Analysis of the Impact of Female Executives on Corporate Financial Leverage

XiangLin Cheng[✉]

Changsha Tianxin District, Changsha 410035, China
cxianglin08@gmail.com

Abstract. This study examines the role of female executives in corporate financial leverage using data from all domestic companies in China from 2010 to 2021. The sample is carefully screened, and the fixed-effects model is employed for regression analysis. The results indicate that the proportion of female executives is negatively correlated with financial leverage, supporting the hypothesis that female executives have an inhibitory effect on corporate leverage. Further endogeneity tests and robustness checks confirm the robustness of the findings. Additionally, we conduct heterogeneity tests considering state-owned versus non-state-owned enterprises and small versus large enterprises. The results reveal that the negative correlation between the proportion of female executives and financial leverage is more pronounced in non-state-owned and large enterprises, while it is not significant in state-owned and small enterprises. These differences could be attributed to variations in corporate governance structures and decision-making processes. The findings of this research provide valuable policy implications for companies aiming to enhance their financial management and risk management practices. Recognizing the importance of female executives in shaping financial decisions, companies are encouraged to promote gender diversity in leadership positions and create an inclusive environment for talent selection and advancement. By understanding the impact of female executives on financial leverage, companies can make informed decisions and mitigate potential risks associated with aggressive financing behaviors.

Keywords: Female Executives · Financial Leverage · Gender Diversity

1 Introduction

Funds are the lifeblood of enterprises, and the more abundant the funds, the greater the potential for business development. However, relying solely on internal funds is often insufficient to meet the needs of a growing enterprise. From the perspective of financial management, debt financing becomes an indispensable source of funds for modern businesses. The financial leverage effect mainly arises from debt financing, which is a double-edged sword. While it can satisfy the funding requirements and provide financial leverage benefits to the company, it also exposes the company to financial risks, leading to potential losses. For instance, as financial leverage increases, the cost of financing for the company may rise. With the refinement of the division of labor and the development of market economies, female executives have emerged and taken on increasingly important roles in the capital markets. The gender of top executives may influence management style, risk preferences, and value orientation, leading to certain heterogeneity in company decision-making and outcomes. As a result, the role of female executives has become a recent research focus, with numerous scholars investigating their positive impact on earnings management, corporate performance, investment efficiency, and corporate social responsibility fulfillment. The question remains whether female executives can play a role in corporate financing decisions and, if so, whether this role is promotive or inhibitory.

Therefore, this paper selects all domestic companies from 2010 to 2021 as empirical samples and uses a fixed-effect model to investigate the impact of female executives on corporate financial leverage. The regression results show that female executives have an inhibitory effect on financial leverage. This paper aims to make the following contributions: Firstly, it explores a new channel, the gender of executive team members, to investigate the influencing factors of corporate financial leverage, thereby expanding the literature on the determinants of financial leverage. Secondly, it incorporates female executives and corporate financial leverage into the same research framework, revealing the inhibitory effect of female executives on financial leverage, providing empirical evidence to better understand the influence of female behavioral characteristics on their financing decisions. Thirdly, this study offers insights into the composition of executive teams, emphasizing the indispensable role of female executives in corporate governance.

2 Literature Review

There are many factors that influence corporate financial leverage. From an internal perspective, we can start with the formula of the financial leverage ratio (EBIT/(EBIT - I)), and the factors affecting the role of financial leverage can be deduced as follows: Earnings Before Interest and Taxes (EBIT), Interest Rate on Debt (I), and Capital Structure (Debt/Asset). Under other fixed conditions, EBIT is negatively correlated with the financial leverage ratio. Similarly, with the EBIT margin and capital structure unchanged, the higher the interest rate on debt, the higher the financial leverage ratio. Under constant EBIT and debt interest rate, the higher the debt-to-equity ratio, the higher the financial leverage ratio [1].

From an external perspective, industry characteristics, national policies, and economic cycles can also influence corporate financing decisions. From an industry perspective, high-growth industries with ample future investment opportunities tend to choose equity financing, resulting in lower debt levels. On the other hand, industries with relatively smaller investment opportunities and slower growth are inclined to rely on significant debt financing [2]. At the national policy level, expansionary fiscal policies by the government can provide more investment opportunities for companies, leading them to increase their debt-to-equity ratios to expand investments. Similarly, when the central bank adopts an expansionary monetary policy and lowers interest rates, the financing costs for companies decrease, stimulating them to increase their debt financing ratios. Economic cycles also play a role, as companies tend to increase their financial leverage in favorable economic conditions to exploit the positive effect of financial leverage [3].

Additionally, managerial traits have a certain influence on corporate financing decisions. Based on the rational assumption and information asymmetry theory, the pecking order theory of financing suggests that when companies have sufficient internal funds, managers are more inclined to use internal funds first, then consider low-information-cost debt financing, and finally turn to equity financing. However, studies by Li Huidong et al. found that Chinese listed companies prioritize equity financing over debt financing in terms of innovation investment [4]. Therefore, whether the financing sequence of domestic companies conforms to the pecking order theory of financing remains to be examined. With the rise of behavioral finance, more research focuses on managerial irrational factors, and from an overconfidence perspective, explains financing sequences. Many studies abroad indicate that overconfident managers tend to overestimate their own abilities and underestimate external risks, leading to aggressive financing strategies, increased financial leverage, and a preference for debt financing over equity financing [5, 6]. Many domestic studies also show that managers' levels of overconfidence affect the extent of internal cash flow utilization in companies, and companies often prioritize long-term debt financing over internal financing [7, 8]. Wu Guotong and Li Yanxi found that overconfident management leads to larger-scale and longer-term debt financing for companies [9].

Most of the above studies assume that managers are homogeneous, but it is essential to note that there is heterogeneity among company managers. The moral development of men and women, influenced by their values towards work, can affect their future ethical behavior [10]. Studies have found that female employees tend to be more "moral" [21]. According to gender socialization theory, female executive characteristics can influence corporate strategic decision-making. In recent years, gender diversity has been increasingly valued, and the role of women in modern society and the economy is becoming more prominent. Foreign studies by Faccio et al. found that companies with female CEOs have higher survival rates and stability compared to those with male CEOs [11]. In domestic research, many scholars have shown that female executives play a positive role in corporate earnings management [12], company performance [13], investment efficiency [14], and corporate social responsibility [15]. Xu Zongyu and Yang Yuanyuan further found that female executives play an important role in reducing company litigation risk and audit fees [16].

Regarding the influence of female executives on corporate financing decisions, scholars have analyzed the relationship between female gender traits and risk aversion from the perspectives of physiology, social psychology, and behavior. Compared to male executives, female executives are more cautious and risk-averse during the decision-making process [17]. Generally, female executives are less likely to make relatively aggressive financing decisions, and their rational traits can regulate aggressive financing and other irrational behaviors caused by overconfidence, leading to a preference for lower-cost internal financing and further optimizing the capital structure of external financing. Data show that female-led companies have financing levels approximately 90% lower than male-led companies [18]. Zhang Ailian, Pan Mengmeng, and Liu Bai suggest that when the proportion of female executives exceeds 25%, their impact on the company's debt financing cost changes from positive correlation to significantly negative correlation

[19]. In other words, when the threshold of 25% is exceeded, the increase in the proportion of female executives helps to reduce the company's debt financing cost, thereby having a positive impact on the further development of the company. Zhang Changzheng and Zhang Xinyue also found that debt financing has a "stepwise" negative impact on R&D investment, and the participation of female executives in corporate governance enhances this inhibitory effect [20].

Gender, as one of the important manifestations of managerial heterogeneity, has a certain influence on corporate decision-making and risk preferences. Currently, most research focuses on the impact on company litigation risk, audit fees, investment efficiency, and corporate performance, with limited literature exploring its role in financing decisions. Therefore, this study will investigate the influence of female executives on corporate financing strategies and consequently on the company's financial leverage. By identifying the role of female executives in corporate financing decisions, it will be possible to regulate aggressive financing behavior and prevent debt risks caused by excessive financing.

3 Research Design

3.1 Sample Selection and Data Source

This study uses all domestic companies from 2010 to 2021 as the initial sample and applies the following screening criteria: (1) Exclude "ST" listed companies; (2) Exclude companies in the financial and real estate industries; (3) Exclude companies with fewer than 50 employees; (4) Exclude companies with negative equity. Data on the proportion of female executives and other variables are obtained from the CSMAR database.

3.2 Measurement of Key Variables

Financial leverage is measured by (Net Profit + Income Tax Expense + Financial Expenses)/(Net Profit + Income Tax Expense). The proportion of female executives is calculated as the ratio of the number of female executives to the total number of executives (Table 1).

3.3 Regression Model

To test the proposed hypotheses, a fixed-effects model is constructed. The study controls for other variables that may influence corporate financial leverage while also accounting for time fixed effects, individual fixed effects, and industry and city interaction fixed effects. The regression equation is as follows:

$$FL_{it} = \alpha + \beta_1 \text{Female}_{it} + X'_{it}\varphi + \eta_i + \gamma_t + \mu_{ind \times t} + \varepsilon_{ct}$$

where FL represents the financial leverage of company i in year t, Female represents the proportion of female executives in company i in year t, X is the vector of control variables, η_i represents individual fixed effects, γ_t represents time fixed effects, $\mu_{ind \times t}$ represents industry and city interaction fixed effects, and ε_{ct} represents the error term.

Table 1. Measurement of variables.

Variable Type	Variable Name	Variable Symbol	Variable Measurement
Dependent Variable	Financial Leverage	FL	(Net Profit + Income Tax Expense + Financial Expenses)/(Net Profit + Income Tax Expense))
Independent Variable	Proportion of Female Executives	Female	Proportion of female executives in relation to the total number of executives
Control Variables	Company Age	Age	Difference between the establishment year and the current year of the company
	Company Size	Size	Natural logarithm of total assets of the company
	Capital Structure	D/A	Total liabilities divided by total assets
	ROA	ROA	Ratio of net profit to total assets
	Proportion of shares held by the largest shareholder	Top1	Proportion of shares held by the largest shareholder
	Current Ratio	CR	Ratio of current assets to current liabilities

4 Empirical Analysis

4.1 Descriptive Statistics

The mean (median) of the corporate financial leverage variable (FL) is 1.47 (1.16), indicating that the financial leverage ratio of Chinese listed companies is around 1.2 times (see Table 2).

However, there is significant individual variation, with the maximum value reaching 8.3 times, while some companies have high financial interest expenses, approximately double their earnings before interest and taxes. The mean (median) of the female executive proportion variable (Female) is 0.16 (0.14), indicating that the proportion of female executives in Chinese listed companies is only around 14%. The maximum shareholder ownership variable has a maximum value (minimum value) of 75% (8.92%), showing significant variation in the concentration of equity ownership among individual companies. The same applies to the current ratio variable, indicating significant variation in companies' liquidity.

Table 2. Descriptive statistics.

Variable	Mean	Median	SD	Max	Min
FL	1.4684	1.1564	1.0496	8.2995	0.5018
Female	0.1613	0.1429	0.1650	0.6667	0.0000
Age	16.9966	17.0000	5.8690	32.0000	4.0000
Size	22.0001	21.8272	1.2901	25.9847	19.4304
D/A	0.4114	0.4027	0.2040	0.8845	0.0497
ROA	0.0426	0.0415	0.0617	0.2112	−0.2346
Top1	35.0611	33.0000	15.0130	75.0000	8.9200
TobinQ	2.0493	1.6302	1.2968	8.5446	0.8683
CR	2.6281	1.6784	2.8531	18.0746	0.3152

4.2 Multiple Regression Results Analysis

Assuming that female executives have an inhibitory effect on corporate financial leverage, Table 3 presents the results of the OLS regression. From the table, it can be observed that both the coefficient of the explanatory variable (Female) and the control variables (D/A, ROA, Top1, CR) are significantly different from zero at the 10% level. As the time fixed effects, individual fixed effects, and industry and city fixed effects are successively added, the explanatory power of the model gradually increases, with R-square increasing from 39.54% to 42.16%.

As shown in column (5) of Table 3, the coefficient of the female executive proportion variable (Female) is significantly negative at the 1% level (−0.1492), supporting the hypothesis that there is a negative correlation between female executives and financial leverage.

4.3 Endogeneity Test

Considering the potential endogeneity between female executives and financial leverage, we find that the proportion of female executives in other companies in the same region in the same year is exogenous to the financial leverage of that company and is correlated with our variable Female. Therefore, we use the proportion of female executives in other companies in the same region in the same year as an instrumental variable. As shown in column (3) of Table 4, the coefficient of Female is significantly negative at the 5% level (−0.1353), consistent with the results of the hypothesis test in the previous sections. Even after controlling for endogeneity issues, the evidence remains supportive.

4.4 Robustness Test

Winsorization. To test the influence of outliers, we conducted 1.5%, 2.5%, and 5% winsorization of the data. The regression results show that the coefficient of Female remains significantly negative at the 1% level (−0.1367, −0.1108, −0.0736), consistent with the previous test results (Table 5).

Table 3. Baseline regression.

	(1) FL	(2) FL	(3) FL	(4) FL	(5) FL
Female	−0.4380***	−0.1570***	−0.0945*	−0.0945*	−0.1492***
	(0.0356)	(0.0342)	(0.0552)	(0.0551)	(0.0571)
Age		−0.0018*	−0.0148***	−0.0035	0.0171
		(0.0010)	(0.0023)	(0.0194)	(0.0200)
Size		−0.0234***	−0.0145	−0.0081	−0.0131
		(0.0054)	(0.0138)	(0.0140)	(0.0152)
D/A		1.9203***	1.9604***	1.9723***	1.8659***
		(0.0421)	(0.0651)	(0.0656)	(0.0705)
ROA		−6.4368***	−7.8715***	−7.7648***	−7.3380***
		(0.1537)	(0.1919)	(0.1943)	(0.2085)
Top1		−0.0017***	−0.0039***	−0.0043***	−0.0046***
		(0.0004)	(0.0009)	(0.0009)	(0.0010)
TobinQ		0.0082*	−0.0050	0.0004	0.0034
		(0.0048)	(0.0058)	(0.0065)	(0.0068)
CR		0.0195***	0.0124***	0.0147***	0.0146***
		(0.0025)	(0.0033)	(0.0033)	(0.0035)
_cons	1.5389***	1.6178***	1.8101***	1.4665***	1.2484***
	(0.0082)	(0.1153)	(0.2788)	(0.4478)	(0.4722)
Year	No	No	Yes	Yes	Yes
SPE	No	No	No	Yes	Yes
IND × City	No	No	No	No	Yes
N	31994	29282	28811	28811	27171
Adj. R^2	0.0047	0.2238	0.3954	0.3981	0.4216

Sample Period. Special periods (e.g., 2012: the 18th Party Congress; 2019–2021: COVID-19 pandemic) may have an impact on the regression results. For example, the 18th Party Congress proposed the goal of building a moderately prosperous society in all respects. To achieve sustainable economic development and significant progress in the balance, coordination, and sustainability of development, GDP and per capita income for urban and rural residents should double compared to 2010. Companies may increase investment and production in response to the national call. During the COVID-19 pandemic, the Chinese economy slowed down, and companies may have a less optimistic outlook on the overall environment, leading to a lower debt ratio. Therefore, we divided the data into different periods, namely, 2012–2021, 2010–2019, and 2012–2019. The coefficient of Female remains significantly negative at the 1%, 10%, and 5% levels,

Table 4. Endogeneity test.

	(1) FL	(2) FL	(3) FL
Female	−0.1199**	−0.1484**	−0.1353**
	(0.0588)	(0.0581)	(0.0599)
Control Variables	Yes	Yes	Yes
SPE	Yes	Yes	Yes
Year	No	Yes	Yes
IND × City	No	No	Yes
N	27171	27094	26949
Adj. R^2	−0.1139	0.4399	0.4631

Table 5. Winsorization.

	(1) 1.5% FL	(2) 2.5% FL	(3) 5% FL
Female	−0.1367***	−0.1108***	−0.0736***
	(0.0484)	(0.0382)	(0.0244)
Control Variables	Yes	Yes	Yes
SPE	Yes	Yes	Yes
Year	Yes	Yes	Yes
IND × City	Yes	Yes	Yes
N	27171	27171	27171
Adj. R^2	0.4648	0.5251	0.6245

respectively (−0.1707, −0.1227, −0.1571), consistent with the previous test results (Table 6).

4.5 Heterogeneity Test

Considering the Difference Between State-Owned and Non-State-Owned Enterprises. We further examine whether our research findings differ between state-owned and non-state-owned enterprises. The results show that in the sample of state-owned enterprises, the coefficient of the proportion of female executives is not significant. However, in the sample of non-state-owned enterprises, the coefficient of the proportion of female executives is significantly negative at the 10% level (−0.1096). The reason for this difference may be that state-owned enterprises have stricter borrowing ratios and loan approval processes, limiting the impact of female executives.

Table 6. Sample period.

	(1) 2012–2021	(2) 2010–2019	(3) 2012–2019
	FL	FL	FL
Female	−0.1707***	−0.1227*	−0.1571**
	(0.0639)	(0.0655)	(0.0755)
Control Variables	Yes	Yes	Yes
SPE	Yes	Yes	Yes
Year	Yes	Yes	Yes
IND × City	Yes	Yes	Yes
N	22004	22611	17443
Adj. R^2	0.4582	0.4454	0.4986

Considering the Difference Between Small and Large Enterprises. To further investigate whether our research findings differ between small and large enterprises, we divide the sample into small and large enterprises based on the median of enterprise size. The results indicate that in the sample of small enterprises, the coefficient of the proportion of female executives is not significant. However, in the sample of large enterprises, the coefficient of the proportion of female executives is significantly negative at the 5% level (−0.2224). The reason for this difference may be that in small enterprises, executive power is relatively concentrated, and female executives have lower say, making it difficult for them to exert their influence effectively (Table 7).

Table 7. Heterogeneity test.

	(1) State-owned Enterprises	(2) Non-state-owned Enterprises	(3) Large Enterprises	(4) Small Enterprises
	FL	FL	FL	FL
Female	−0.0915	−0.1096*	−0.2224**	−0.1189
	(0.1212)	(0.0611)	(0.1011)	(0.0955)
Control Variables	Yes	Yes	Yes	Yes
SPE	Yes	Yes	Yes	Yes
Year	Yes	Yes	Yes	Yes
IND × City	Yes	Yes	Yes	Yes
N	9552	16435	13511	12052
Adj. R2	0.5040	0.3493	0.4595	0.4282

5 Conclusion

With the increasing importance of female executives, this study investigates the role of female executives in corporate financial leverage. The empirical sample includes all domestic companies from 2010 to 2021, which were carefully selected. The fixed-effects model was used for regression analysis, and the results indicate that companies with a higher proportion of female executives tend to have lower financial leverage. After conducting a series of robustness and endogeneity tests, the research findings remain robust. However, this study has certain limitations: first, the research data only extend until 2021; second, the generalizability of the research conclusions to the global context during China's transition phase requires further examination.

Based on the findings of this study, several policy implications can be drawn. The risk aversion tendencies and other traits of female executives play a crucial role in corporate financing decisions. Companies should recognize the significance of selecting and appointing female executives and establish a scientific and rational talent selection and promotion system. Regarding external recruitment, gender discrimination should be avoided, and equal opportunities for men and women should be encouraged. Internally, regular inspections, guidance, and support for female employees are essential to break the "glass ceiling" and remove barriers for women to enter executive positions.

References

1. Liu, L.: The dual effects of financial leverage on enterprises under corporate debt financing. China Manag. Informationization **15**(06), 25–26 (2012)
2. Chen, A.: Exploring the relationship between industry competition characteristics and corporate financing decision-making. Contemp. Econ. **219**(10), 48–49 (2009)
3. Wang, B.: Current situation and influencing factors analysis of financial leverage application in domestic enterprises. Mod. Bus. (30), 139–140 (2018). https://doi.org/10.14097/j.cnki.5392/2018.30.070
4. Li, H., Tang, Y., Zuo, J.: Using own money or others' money for innovation? a study based on the financing structure and corporate innovation of chinese listed companies. Finan. Res. **392**(02), 170–183 (2013)
5. Malmendier, U., Tate, G.: CEO overconfidence and corporate investment. J. Financ. **60**(6), 2661–2700 (2005)
6. Graham, J.R., Harvey, C.R., Puri, M.: Managerial attitudes and corporate actions. J. Finan. Econ. **109**(1), 103–121 (2013)
7. Ye, B., Yuan, J.: Managerial confidence, corporate investment, and corporate value: empirical evidence from Chinese listed companies. China Soft Sci. (02), 97–108 (2008)
8. Liu, Y., Guo, J.: The impact of managerial overconfidence on corporate financing order. Sci. Res. Manag. **33**(11), 84–88 (2012)
9. Wu, G., Li, Y.: Managerial over-optimism and corporate debt financing decision-making. Ind. Technol. Econ. **38**(11), 130–144 (2019)
10. England, G.W., Lee, R.: The relationship between managerial values and managerial success in the United States, Japan, India, and Australia. J. Appl. Psychol. **59**(4), 411 (1974)
11. Faccio, M., Marchica, M.T., Mura, R.: CEO gender, corporate risk-taking, and the efficiency of capital allocation. J. Corp. Finan. **39**, 193–209 (2016)

12. Zhou, Z., Xiu, Z.: Can female executives reduce earnings management? empirical evidence from China's capital market. J. Central South Univ. Econ. Law **206**(05), 95–102+132+159–160 (2014)
13. Wang, J., Wang, L.: Research on the impact of female executives on the performance of listed companies, Econ. Trade Pract. (12), 137 (2017)
14. Su, L.: Female executives, internal control quality, and non-efficient investment. Finan. Account. Commun. **836**(36), 39–42 (2019). https://doi.org/10.16144/j.cnki.issn1002-8072.2019.36.008
15. Zhu, W., Deng, L.: Can female executives promote corporate social responsibility? empirical evidence from Chinese A-share listed companies. China Econ. Issues (04), 119–135 (2017). https://doi.org/10.19365/j.issn1000-4181.2017.04.11
16. Xu, Z., Yang, Y.: Female executives, litigation risk, and audit fees. J. Finan. Econ. Res. **35**(05), 132–146 (2020)
17. Palvia, A., Vähämaa, E., Vähämaa, S.: Are female CEOs and chairwomen more conservative and risk averse? evidence from the banking industry during the financial crisis. J. Bus. Ethics **131**, 577–594 (2015)
18. Yan, J.: An empirical study on the gender of private small and medium-sized enterprise owners and financing constraints. Bus. Econ. Manag. (05), 50–57 (2011). https://doi.org/10.14134/j.cnki.cn33-1336/f.2011.05.007
19. Zhang, A., Pan, M., Liu, B.: The influence of overconfidence on corporate financing preference: a correction based on the gender of top managers. Theor. Pract. Res. Finan. **40**(04), 53–59 (2019). https://doi.org/10.16339/j.cnki.hdxbcjb.2019.04.031
20. Zhang, C., Zhang, X.: The, "Stair-Step" negative impact of debt financing on R&D investment: the moderating role of female executives. Soft Sci. **37**(02), 35–43 (2023). https://doi.org/10.13956/j.ss.1001-8409.2023.02.05
21. Franke, G.R., Crown, D.F., Spake, D.F.: Gender differences in ethical perceptions of business practices: a social role theory perspective. J. Appl. Psychol. **82**(6), 920 (1997)

Corporate Social Responsibility and Financial Performance: Evidence from Listed Firms in China

Jiali Wang[✉]

Skylark Investment, No. 258 Dongfang Road, Suzhou, Jiangsu, China
carriewang103@hotmail.com

Abstract. Research on the relationship between corporate social responsibility (CSR) and firm performance has grown exponentially over the past few decades, especially in developed economies. As one of the largest economies, the level of CSR development in China is relatively low and CSR-related topics have not been deeply studied until recent years. A few researchers examined a significant and positive link between CSR and financial performance among Chinese firms. However, the data source and methodology employed in prior studies had many limitations. This paper introduces a methodology to explore the relationship between CSR and financial performance with CSR Development Index issued by Chinese Academy of Social Sciences (CASS) since 2009, which is a more systematic CSR measure comparing to existing literature. With a sample consisting of 110 listed firms in China over the period of 2011–2014, fixed effects panel data analysis is adopted and tested to be the most appropriate methodology. Results using pooled OLS and random effects panel analysis are also included for better comparisons. The econometrics results show that there is no significant relationship between the two variables in the same year and in following years when incorporating lagged variables. In other words, CSR could not affect financial performance of Chinese listed firms. This conclusion indicates that the development and awareness of CSR in China still have much room for improvement.

Keywords: Corporate Social Responsibility (CSR) · Financial Performance · CSR Development Index · State-Owned Enterprises

1 Introduction

Corporate social responsibility (CSR), as well as environmental, social and governance (ESG) have become two of the key topics in the field of business management and academic studies. China government has issued relevant standards, regulations and laws to improve the CSR performance of Chinese companies in recent years. However, the *CSR Blue Book* published by Chinese Academy of Social Science (CASS) suggested that with a scale from 0 to 100, the average CSR score of the top 300 companies in China was only 36.1 points and more than 40% of them were marked below 20 points in 2021 [1]. And the average score of 2014 was 34.22, which indicated a fact that the level of CSR implementation in China was not only in a relatively low level, but also improved in a slow progress. The most important reason for Chinese companies not actively engaging in CSR might be the uncertainties to the costs and benefits of CSR activities, as many Chinese firms are still struggling for survival in the highly competitive market. This phenomenon requires deep research on the relationship between CSR and financial performance in China.

Many researchers have done empirical research on CSR-CFP relationship in China [2–4]. However, there are some limitations and gaps because of lacking of reliable and consistent data. This research will focus on listed firms in China during the period of 2011–2014, including state-owned and non state-owned firms. The empirical contribution is to improve the methodology by adopting fixed effects panel data analysis instead of simple OLS or cross-sectional regression analysis. Moreover, the CSR Development Index will be employed as the CSR measure in this study, which has been issued by CASS since 2009. It was only available in hard copies and in Chinese language before 2017, so it has not been widely used by prior researchers. With the improved methodology and CSR measure, this study will provide some deep insights on the relationship between CSR and financial performance among Chinese firms.

2 Data and Methodology

2.1 Variable Selection

Since 2009, CASS have started to conduct annual research on the CSR activities in China and evaluate social performance of China's top 100 state-owned enterprises (SOEs), top 100 non state-owned enterprises (non-SOEs) and top 100 foreign-financed enterprises in each year. The research and evaluation process were guided by the existing methodologies of many international CSR rating systems and standards [2]. This index is constructed to rate each firm with the overall CSR and four CSR-related indicators on responsibility management (RM), market responsibility (MR), social responsibility (SR) and environmental responsibility (ER) separately. There is no online resource for this index before 2017, so paper copies of Chinese CSR Blue Book published in the year 2011, 2012, 2013 and 2014 were obtained from the CASS official website and then manually inputted for further research.

For financial performance, three of the most widely used accounting-based measures have been employed: ROA (return on assets), ROE (return on equity) and EPS (earnings per share). The choice of accounting-based measures depends on the characteristics of Chinese market and it does not mean this type of measure is superior to market-based measure. As Chinese stock markets are still in the developing stage and are highly volatile than other developed markets, as the majority investors are individuals who lack of professions and experiences [5]. Their buying/selling decisions have been examined to have weak relationship with CSR performance unless serious scandals happened, which are quite different from institutional investors who care more about social responsibility. Therefore, CSR activities and performance might have stronger impacts on other stakeholders such as customers, employees and communities. Accounting-based measures are more suitable in the investigation on CSR-CFP relationship in China.

This study also includes a series of control variables that have been examined or predicted to be influential to the CSR-CFP relationship in previous literature. These control variables include *Size* measured by the logarithm of total assets, *Risk* measured by debt to assets ratio and firm age. A dummy variable *SOE* (equals to 1 if SOE and 0 otherwise) is used to control the different characteristics between SOEs and non-SOEs. Finally, a dummy variable *Industry* is included since financial performance and social performance varying across different industries. The data for financial performance and control variables were collected from CSMAR Database.

2.2 Hypothesis

To estimate the relationship between CSR and CFP, two hypotheses are proposed for regression analysis. Hypothesis 1 of this study expects a negative impact of CSR on current year's CFP for Chinese listed firms. Although CSR activities could create huge costs with no benefits for the same year, some benefits could be realised in following period(s). Hypothesis 2 predicts the relationship between CSR and CFP with time-lagged effects. A positive relationship is expected between CSR and financial performance in the following year.

Hypothesis 1. *The overall CSR performance has a negative impact on the corporate financial performance in the same year for listed firms in China.*

Hypothesis 2. *The overall CSR performance has a positive impact on the corporate financial performance in the following year(s) for listed firms in China.*

2.3 Econometrics Models

Considering the possible variances across firms, modelling using panel data is expected to be more appropriate for this study. The double dimensionality of a panel data set could improve the quality of the evidence by controlling for factors that vary across firms that are not included in the model and avoiding bias due to these omitted variables [6]. Also, the panel data analysis consists of two approaches: fixed effects and random effects. Several post-estimation tests will be conducted on all models in order to decide the most appropriate approach in next section.

The following three econometric models are developed to examine the previous two hypotheses empirically. The dummy variables *SOE* and *Industry* will be omitted in fixed-effect panel data analysis, as time-invariant differences between firms are already controlled. While in POLS and random effects analysis, these time-invariant variables will be included. Model I is developed to estimate Hypothesis 1 and Model II with one-year lagged variables is developed to estimate Hypothesis 2. In order to further estimate the CSR-CFP relationship, Model III is an additional model incorporating two-year lagged variable, as the impact of CSR activities might be delayed for more than one year. Detailed descriptions or definitions for each variable are presented in Table A1.

Model I

$$CFP_{it} = \alpha_i + \beta_1 CSR_{it} + \beta_2 Size_{it} + \beta_3 Risk_{it} + \beta_4 Age_{it} + \beta_5 SOE + \beta_6 Industry + u_{it}$$

Model II

$$CFP_{it} = \alpha_i + \beta_1 CSR_{it-1} + \beta_2 Size_{it-1} + \beta_3 Risk_{it-1} + \beta_4 Age_{it-1} + \beta_5 SOE + \beta_6 Industry + u_{it}$$

Model III

$$CFP_{it} = \alpha_i + \beta_1 CSR_{it-2} + \beta_2 Size_{it-2} + \beta_3 Risk_{it-2} + \beta_4 Age_{it-2} + \beta_5 SOE + \beta_6 Industry + u_{it}$$

In each equation, $\alpha_i (i = 1, 2, 3 \ldots n)$ represents the unknown intercept that varies across each firm and u_{it} is the error term. The term i and t refer to the firm and year of each observation. The term *t-1* and *t-2* refer to the one-year lag and two-year lag, respectively. The term β_n is the coefficient of each independent and control variable. The dependent variable CFP_{it} measures corporate financial performance with three indicators: ROA, ROE and EPS. Each indicator will be tested and analysed separately in the next section. The main independent variable CSR_{it} represents the scores from the CSR Development Index, which measures the overall CSR performance of each firm in each year. $Size_{it}$, $Risk_{it}$, Age_{it}, SOE_{it} and $Industry_{it}$ are included as control variables.

2.4 Sample

The sample of this study consists of 110 Chinese firms listed on Shanghai Stock Exchange (72 firms), Shenzhen Stock Exchange (19 firms) and Stock Exchange of Hong Kong (19 firms). The research period is from 2011 to 2014, while the performance data for 2010 and 2015 are also included as lagged variables. The data set is organized using Microsoft Excel 2011 and the regression analysis is conducted with Stata. There are 110 Chinese listed firms left in the sample with 67 SOEs and 43 non-SOEs.

3 Empirical Results

The descriptive statistics and the Pearson's correlation matrix for all variables are conducted and presented in Appendix. Many existing studies on CSP-CFP relationship have adopted cross-sectional or simple OLS (ordinary least squares) regression analysis, while panel data analysis could provide more evidence in depth [3]. In the first step of this study, pooled OLS (POLS), random effects (RE) and fixed effects (FE) panel data analysis are performed for each model separately in order to examine whether the significant CSR-CFP relationship mentioned in previous studies exists in this study. Next, three important post-estimation tests are conducted to decide the most appropriate approach among POLS, FE and RE. Results for the LM test and Hausman test are shown in Table A7 in Appendix, which suggest that FE panel analysis is the most appropriate approach for most models. RE approach is more appropriate when using EPS as the CFP measure in Model I and Model II. Further tests using least squares dummy variable model (LSDV) confirm that only firm effects are needed and no time effects are required.

3.1 Model I: CSR Impacts on Financial Performance for the Same Year

Table 1 presents the results the regression results of Model I, which estimates the impact of CSR on financial performance (three measures) for the same year. As shown in Panel A, the POLS results show that the relationship between CSR and CFP is negative and significant at the $p \leq 0.01$ level, when ROA and ROE are dependent variables. This result is not consistent with some of previous studies, as many of them found positive relationship between CSR and CFP [3, 4, 7]. It is in line with Rutledge et al., who tested the CSR-CFP relationship with POLS method using the same CSR measure as this study on large SOEs firms in China [2]. Thus, Hypothesis 1 holds when using POLS approach, while this is not the most appropriate estimation.

Panel B of Table 1 presents the results using FE panel analysis with firm fixed effects, which is the most appropriate estimation when CFP measure is ROA and ROE according to Hausman test. Consistent with the finding of some previous studies, CSR is no longer a significant determinant of CFP [8]. This finding suggests that CSR might not influence the current year's financial performance anymore, so Hypothesis 1 does not hold after controlling for the firm fixed effects. The signs of coefficients for other variables are generally as expected. Size is positive and significant in each model ($p \leq 0.01$ for ROA and $p \leq 0.001$ for ROE), as larger firms have better financial performance. Risk is negative and highly significant ($p \leq 0.001$), which suggests that lower risk could lead to better performance. Age is a negative and highly significant ($p \leq 0.001$) determinant of financial performance, indicating that younger firms might have better financial performance. The R-squared values have been largely improved with FE approach, which indicates controlling for firm-fixed effects estimation could explain more variance of the CFP.

Panel C of Table 1 shows the results using random effects, which is the most appropriate approach when CFP is measured by EPS. Again, there is no statistically significant relationship between CSR and EPS. Both size and risk are highly significant ($p \leq 0.001$) determinants of CFP (measured by EPS). The coefficient for SOE is negative and significant at the $p \leq 0.1$ level, indicating that non-SOEs have better financial performance measured by EPS than non-SOEs.

Table 1. Pooled OLS, fixed effects and random effects regression results of Model I.

Panel A: Pooled OLS regression analysis			
Dependent variable:	ROA	ROE	EPS
CSR	-0.081^{**}	-0.071^{**}	-0.001
Size	0.655^{***}	2.776^{***}	0.276^{***}
Risk	-0.120^{***}	-0.049	-0.014^{***}
Age	0.006	0.047	0.003
SOE	-1.158^{**}	-4.778^{**}	-0.611^{***}
Industry	-1.009	-0.233	-0.011
Constant	5.820^{***}	-11.294^{**}	-1.116^{***}

(*continued*)

Table 1. (*continued*)

Panel A: Pooled OLS regression analysis			
Dependent variable:	ROA	ROE	EPS
R2	0.205	0.126	0.203
Panel B: Fixed effects panel analysis (with firm fixed effects)			
Dependent variable:	**ROA**	**ROE**	EPS
CSR	0.007	0.049	−0.001
Size	2.171**	11.902***	0.318**
Risk	−0.283***	−0.940***	−0.032***
Age	−0.619***	−2.078***	0.003
SOE	Omitted	Omitted	Omitted
Industry	Omitted	Omitted	Omitted
Constant	8.099	−27.786	−0.804
R^2	0.710	0.627	0.900
Panel C: Random effects panel analysis			
Dependent variable:	ROA	ROE	**EPS**
CSR	−0.026+	−0.001	−0.045
Size	0.688***	0.318**	3.000***
Risk	−0.146***	−0.032***	−0.252***
Age	−0.006	0.003	0.026
SOE	−0.016	Omitted	−5.180
Industry	−0.070	Omitted	−0.134
Constant	7.030***	−0.804	−8.267
R^2	0.202	0.900	0.113

+ $p \leq 0.1$; * $p \leq 0.05$; ** $p \leq 0.01$; *** $p \leq 0.001$. The R-squared values reported for RE models are overall R-squared values.

3.2 Model II: CSR Impacts on Financial Performance After One Year

Model II tests the relationship between CSR and financial performance with one-year lagged variables. Again, the Hausman test shows that FE approach with firm fixed effects is the most appropriate approach when CFP is measured by ROA and ROE, while RE approach is more appropriate when CFP is measured by EPS. Table 2 presents the results for this model using three approaches with three CFP measures. Unfortunately, results of POLS, FE and RE approaches consistently show that there is no significant relationship between CSR and CFP of next year with all three measures. Better CSR performance in the first year could not affect financial performance in the second year, so Hypothesis 2 does not hold. The signs of the insignificant coefficients are still negative, which might indicate that the direction of the impacts of CSR is the same as in Model I. The expected benefits of CSR on financial performance have not released.

For other variables, results with FE approach presented in Panel B suggest little statistically significant relationship between the dependent and all independent variables. The coefficients of size turn to be negative and significant at the $p \leq 0.01$ level when ROA is dependent variable and at the $p \leq 0.05$ level when ROE is dependent variable. These results suggest that the larger listed Chinese firms might experience poorer financial performance next year after controlling for firm fixed effects. Also, risk becomes a significant positive coefficient at the $p \leq 0.01$ level when CFP is measured by ROE. These results might require further investigations in future research. The results using RE approach are presented in the Panel C. The coefficients of size are positive and are significant at the $p \leq 0.01$ level when EPS is dependent variable.

Table 2. Pooled OLS, fixed effects and random effects regression results of Model II.

Panel A: Pooled OLS regression analysis			
Dependent variable:	ROA	ROE	EPS
CSR_{t-1}	−0.011	−0.038	−0.009
$Size_{t-1}$	0.410**	1.898***	0.268***
$Risk_{t-1}$	−0.084***	0.022	−0.011***
Age_{t-1}	0.010	0.042	0.002
SOE	−0.846*	−3.737**	−0.660***
Industry	−0.022	0.076	−0.003
Constant	4.491***	−11.728***	−1.315***
R2	0.113	0.112	0.203
Panel B: Fixed effects panel analysis (firm fixed effects)			
Dependent variable:	ROA	ROE	EPS
CSR_{t-1}	−0.016	−0.050	−0.007
$Size_{t-1}$	−1.836**	−5.299*	−0.056
$Risk_{t-1}$	0.054	0.288**	0.007
Age_{t-1}	0.164	0.331	0.015
SOE	Omitted	Omitted	Omitted
Industry	Omitted	Omitted	Omitted
Constant	17.759**	46.30*	1.028**
R^2	0.687	0.627	0.901
Panel C: Random effects panel analysis			
Dependent variable:	ROA	ROE	EPS
CSR_{t-1}	−0.012	−0.044	−0.007

(*continued*)

Table 2. (*continued*)

Panel A: Pooled OLS regression analysis			
Dependent variable:	ROA	ROE	EPS
Size$_{t-1}$	0.258	1.614**	0.195**
Risk$_{t-1}$	−0.059***	0.053	−0.006
Age$_{t-1}$	0.009	0.035	0.001
SOE	−0.624	−3.195+	−0.551+
Industry	−0.025	0.098	0.012
Constant	4.555**	−10.636*	−0.924*
R^2	0.110	0.109	0.190

$^+ p \leq 0.1$; $^* p \leq 0.05$; $^{**} p \leq 0.01$; $^{***} p \leq 0.001$. The R-squared values reported for RE models are overall R-squared values.

3.3 Model III: CSR Impacts on Financial Performance After Two years

In order to further verify the possible relationship between CSR and CFP among listed firms in China, Model III incorporates two-year lagged variables. The econometrics results are presented in Table 3. Again, there is no significant relationship between CSR and financial performance with any of three CFP measures using any of three approaches. The Hausman test suggests that FE model is more appropriate for all three CFP measures than RE and POLS approaches. However, as shown in Panel B of Table 3, there are few significant results using FE approach excepting for the control variable age, which is negatively related to CFP at the $p \leq 0.05$ level. Therefore, there is no significant relationship between CSR and financial performance after two years.

Table 3. Pooled OLS, fixed effects and random effects regression results of Model III.

Panel A: Pooled OLS regression analysis			
Dependent variable:	ROA	ROE	EPS
CSR	−0.010	−0.042	0.003
Size	0.291*	1.678***	0.253***
Risk	−0.073***	0.036	−0.009+
Age	0.008	0031	0.003
SOE	−0.962*	−3.703**	−0.684***
Industry	−1.009	−0.233	0.009
Constant	1.134	−33.030***	−4.800***
R2	0.120	0.116	0.193

(*continued*)

Table 3. (*continued*)

Panel A: Pooled OLS regression analysis			
Dependent variable:	ROA	ROE	EPS
Panel B: Fixed effects panel analysis (with firm fixed effects)			
Dependent variable:	**ROA**	**ROE**	**EPS**
CSR	0.002	−0.037	−0.002
Size	−0.517	−6.08	−0.044
Risk	0.012	0.126	0.005
Age	−0.355*	−0.888*	−0.048*
SOE	Omitted	Omitted	Omitted
Industry	Omitted	Omitted	Omitted
Constant	21.066	52.647	2.206
R^2	0.772	0.654	0.922
Panel C: Random effects panel analysis			
Dependent variable:	ROA	ROE	EPS
CSR	−0.048	−0.007	−0.007
Size	1.594**	0.204***	0.204***
Risk	0.040	−0.003	−0.003
Age	0.019	−0.002	−0.002
SOE	−3.452+	−0.595**	−0.595**
Industry	0.134	0.015	0.015
Constant	−31.056	−3.903***	−3.903***
R^2	0.115	0.184	0.184

+ $p \leq 0.1$; * $p \leq 0.05$; ** $p \leq 0.01$; *** $p \leq 0.001$. The R−squared values reported for RE models are overall R-squared values.

A robustness check is conducted by replacing the overall CSR score with the four specific indicators and regressing them one by one as the main independent variable. As shown in Table A9 in Appendix, the results are generally identical to the previous results, which means the insignificant results are stable and reliable.

4 Conclusion

The econometrics results of this study prove that CSR performance has no significant impact on financial performance in the same year (Model I), after one year (Model II) and after two years (Model III). The only significant relationship between CSR and CFP is evidenced in Model I using the POLS regression method, while it is not the most appropriate estimation according to the Hausman test. Therefore, this study concludes that there is little relationship between CSR and financial performance among listed firms in China during the period of 2011–2014.

The stakeholder perspective suggests that good CSR performance of a firm could gain legitimacy and reliability from stakeholders, which could further lead to increase in economic benefits in theory [5]. There should be some reasons behind the non-significant relationship between CSR and CFP examined in this study. One possible reason could be the benefits of good CSR performance of Chinese firms are not realised through financial performance. For example, it is difficult to trace the outcomes of CSR efforts related to employees with financial performance, especially with accounting figures. The costs of improving working conditions or other welfares would lead to huge costs, while benefits such as improvement in morale and overall satisfaction are difficult to measure. Another important reason is related to the reactions from Chinese stakeholders, including consumers, employees, suppliers and communities. For example, providing high quality and eco-friendly products should allow the firm to charge higher prices and gain market share [9]. Unlike consumers in developed economies who fully understand the concept of sustainability [10], many Chinese people are not as well informed or well educated about the concepts of social responsibilities and sustainability. In other words, attempts done by Chinese firms related to CSR might not affect the behaviours of stakeholders.

With improved methodology and better CSR measure, the finding of this study is different from the significant and positive results examined in some prior studies on CSR-CFP relationship in China. The new evidence successfully reflects the actual situation of poor CSR development, especially for the high costs of CSR activities and low awareness among Chinese consumers. Therefore, related government authorities could encourage firms to conduct more CSR activities with reasonable rewards to reduce any concerns about high costs. At the same time, public awareness about CSR and sustainability should be further improved through education and media. For firm managers who are planning for CSR activities, there should be fewer worries about CSR might hurt financial performance, as this study examined that there is no significant relationship between the CSR and CFP in the current and following years.

Appendix

CSR scores were collected from CSR Development Index by CASS 2011–2014. Data for financial performance and control variables were collected from CSMAR Database (Table A2).

Table A1. Variable Definitions.

Variable	Description or Definition
Dependent Variable	
CFP	(Corporate Financial Performance)
-ROA	Return on assets (in percentage)
-ROE	Return on equity (in percentage)
-EPS	Earnings per share (RMB)
Independent Variable	
CSR	Overall score for corporate social responsibility
Control Variables	
Size	Natural logarithm of total assets (RMB in millions)
Risk	Debt ratio, equals to total liabilities divided by total assets (in percentage)
Age	Age from the registration date of the firm
SOE	SOE dummy, equals to 1 if the firm is SOE, 0 otherwise
Industry	Type of industry of the firm coded from 1 to 11 (details see Sect. 4.3)

Table A2. Industry segmentation (Panel A) and descriptive statistics for CSR scores (Panel B).

		RM	MR	SR	ER	Overall CSR
Panel A	Obs					
Mean	440	35.21	42.39	39.01	33.40	39.32
Median	440	31.85	45.00	41.35	33.30	40.25
Maximum	440	100	95.80	96.30	100	89.50
Minimum	440	0	0	0	0	0
Standard Deviation	440	29.47	25.52	26.40	26.72	26.15
Panel B	N					
Mining & Petroleum	12	56.79	57.46	60.69	46.59	56.70
Construction & Real Estate	10	28.86	34.83	36.31	23.82	32.77
Food & Textiles	8	12.21	27.05	16.08	15.47	18.78
Chemicals & Pharmaceuticals	9	18.54	25.82	20.54	17.51	21.11
Refining, Rubber & Plastic	2	40.64	50.61	44.88	43.53	45.41

(*continued*)

Table A2. (*continued*)

		RM	MR	SR	ER	Overall CSR
Steel & Heavy Manufacturing	15	28.40	41.32	34.66	30.01	34.60
Computers, Electronics & Autos	13	31.81	40.00	33.82	28.81	35.00
Transportation	9	45.63	43.13	51.23	42.67	48.25
Telephone & Electricity Utilities	11	55.30	54.23	52.57	54.29	57.36
Wholesale & Retail	6	11.51	22.94	17.99	9.79	18.01
Banking & Financial Services	15	41.98	54.20	45.95	42.89	49.27

RM, MR, SR and ER are responsibility management, market responsibility, social responsibility and environmental reasonability. CSR scores are collected from CSR Development Index developed by CASS (2011–2014) (Table A3).

Table A3. Descriptive statistics over the period of 2011–2014.

Variable	Mean	Median	Minimum	Maximum	Standard Deviation
CSR score	39.32	40.25	0	89.50	26.15
Return on assets (%)	3.27	2.48	−27.71	22.65	3.27
Return on equity (%)	10.44	11.08	−96.45	68.25	13.06
Earnings per share (RMB)	0.69	0.40	−1.41	7.31	0.69
Total assets (RMB in millions)	923776	81600	1520.19	20609953	2916932
Debt ratio (%)	66.44	67.76	9.14	95.18	17.99
Age	17.87	16	3	142	14.18

Each variable contains 440 observations (Tables A4, A5 and A6).

Table A4. Correlation matrices for Model I.

	CSR	ROA	ROE	EPS	Size	Risk	Age	SOE	Industry
CSR	1.000								

(*continued*)

Table A4. (*continued*)

	CSR	ROA	ROE	EPS	Size	Risk	Age	SOE	Industry
ROA	−0.074	1.000							
ROE	0.004	0.749***	1.000						
EPS	0.106*	0.484***	0.510***	1.000					
Size	0.494***	−0.052	0.266***	0.317**	1.000				
Risk	0.119*	−0.386***	−0.091 +	−0.005	0.482***	1.000			
Age	0.0052	0.018	0.067	0.073	0.067	0.007	1.000		
SOE	0.446***	−0.099*	−0.098 +	−0.11*	0.344***	0.055	−0.004	1.000	
Industry	0.094*	−0.132**	0.070	−0.091 +	0.376***	0.301***	0.214**	0.050	1.000

+$p \leq 0.1$; *$p \leq 0.05$; **$p \leq 0.01$; ***$p \leq 0.001$. ROA, ROE and EPS are three measures of corporate financial performance (CFP) and they will be regressed separately in regression analysis.

Table A5. Correlation matrices for Model II.

	CSR_{t-1}	ROA	ROE	EPS	$Size_{t-1}$	$Risk_{t-1}$	Age_{t-1}
CSRt-1	1.000						
ROA	−0.055	1.000					
ROE	0.021	0.791***	1.000				
EPS	0.104*	0.512***	0.571***	1.000			
Sizet-1	0.486***	−0.022	0.293***	0.342***	1.000		
Riskt-1	0.129**	−0.337***	0.119	−0.034	0.510***	1.000	
Aget-1	0.0052	0.041	0.077	0.066	0.070	−0.008	1.000

+$p \leq 0.1$; *$p \leq 0.05$; **$p \leq 0.01$; ***$p \leq 0.001$.

Table A6. Correlation matrices for Model III.

	CSR_{t-2}	ROA	ROE	EPS	$Size_{t-2}$	$Risk_{t-2}$	Age_{t-2}
CSRt-2	1.000						
ROA	−0.055	1.000					
ROE	0.021	0.791***	1.000				
EPS	0.104*	0.512***	0.571***	1.000			
Sizet-2	0.486***	−0.022	0.293***	0.342***	1.000		
Riskt-2	0.129**	−0.337***	0.119	−0.034	0.510***	1.000	
Aget-2	0.0052	0.041	0.077	0.066	0.070	−0.008	1.000

+$p \leq 0.1$; *$p \leq 0.05$; **$p \leq 0.01$; ***$p \leq 0.001$.

Table A7. Results for Breusch-Pagan Lagrange Multiplier (LM) test and Hausman test.

	LM test		Hausman test		Most appropriate approach
	Chibar2	P-value	Chi2	P-value	
Model I					
ROA	140.89	0.0000	31.92	0.0000	Fixed effects
ROE	66.71	0.0000	60.35	0.0000	Fixed effects
EPS	439.68	0.0000	6.88	0.1424	Random effects
Model II					
ROA	167.05	0.0000	16.43	0.0025	Fixed effects
ROE	108.41	0.0000	11.24	0.0240	Fixed effects
EPS	454.98	0.0000	6.92	0.1402	Random effects
Model III					
ROA	114.85	0.0000	11.56	0.0210	Fixed effects
ROE	48.17	0.0000	11.33	0.0231	Fixed effects
EPS	237.50	0.0000	10.32	0.0354	Fixed effects

The results for Hausman test are determined at the $p \leq 0.05$ significant level (Tables A8).

Table A8. Robustness check: correlation matrices.

	RM	MR	SR	ER
RM	1.000			
MR	0.801***	1.000		
SR	0.888***	0.848***	1.000	
ER	0.851***	0.802***	0.870***	1.000
ROA	−0.081+	−0.059	−0.083+	−0.053
ROE	−0.019	0.0103	−0.023	0.021
EPS	0.126**	0.066	0.062	0.108*
Size	0.429***	0.484***	0.472***	0.454***
Risk	0.080+	0.086+	0.111*	0.097*
Age	−0.001	−0.018	−0.019	0.017

+$p \leq 0.1$; *$p \leq 0.05$; **$p \leq 0.01$; ***$p \leq 0.001$. RM, MR, SR and ER refer to responsibility management, market responsibility, social responsibility and environmental responsibility. The rest part of the correlation matrices is identical to Table 2 in the main text Sect. 5.

(1) $ROA_{it} = \alpha_i + \beta_1 RM_{it} + \beta_2 Size_{it} + \beta_3 Risk_{it} + \beta_4 Age_{it} + \beta_5 SOE + \beta_6 Industry + u_{it}$

(2) $ROA_{it} = \alpha_i + \beta_1 MR_{it} + \beta_2 Size_{it} + \beta_3 Risk_{it} + \beta_4 Age_{it} + \beta_5 SOE + \beta_6 Industry + u_{it}$
(3) $ROA_{it} = \alpha_i + \beta_1 SR_{it} + \beta_2 Size_{it} + \beta_3 Risk_{it} + \beta_4 Age_{it} + \beta_5 SOE + \beta_6 Industry + u_{it}$
(4) $ROA_{it} = \alpha_i + \beta_1 ER_{it} + \beta_2 Size_{it} + \beta_3 Risk_{it} + \beta_4 Age_{it} + \beta_5 SOE + \beta_6 Industry + u_{it}$

Table A9. Robustness check: pooled OLS, fixed effects and random effects regression results for Model I using ROA as dependent variable.

	(1)	(2)	(3)	(4)
Panel A: Pooled OLS regression analysis				
RM	−0.018*			
MR		−0.018*		
SR			−0.020*	
ER				−0.013
Size	0.659***	0.658***	0.663***	0.621***
Risk	−0.121***	−0.121***	−0.120***	−0.120***
Age	0.006	0.005	0.006	0.006
SOE	−1.131**	−1.175***	−1.074**	−1.268**
Industry	−0.115*	−0.109+	−0.120*	−0.102*
Constant	5.781***	5.948***	5.820***	5.921***
R2	0.208	0.205	0.118	0.202
Panel B: Fixed effects panel analysis				
RM	−0.004			
MR		0.002		
SR			0.001	
ER				0.012
Size	2.147**	2.172**	2.163**	2.152**
Risk	−0.283***	−0.283***	−0.283***	−0.282***
Age	−0.620***	−0.599***	−0.592***	−0.640***
SOE	Omitted	Omitted	Omitted	Omitted
Industry	Omitted	Omitted	Omitted	Omitted
Constant	8.365	7.914	7.968	8.510
R2	0.710	0.710	0.710	0.711
Panel C: Random effects panel analysis				
RM	−0.010*			
MR		−0.015		

(*continued*)

Table A9. (*continued*)

Panel A: Pooled OLS regression analysis

	(1)	(2)	(3)	(4)
SR			−0.017⁺	
ER				−0.007
Size	0.706***	0.676***	0.693***	0.631***
Risk	−0.146***	−0.146***	−0.145***	−0.145***
Age	−0.004	−0.007	−0.006	−0.006
SOE	−1.144*	−1.200⁺	−1.106	−1.330*
Industry	−0.079	−0.068	−0.093	−0.062
Constant	6.871***	7.206***	7.029***	7.269***
R^2	0.206	0.202	0.204	0.198

+p ≤ 0.1; *p ≤ 0.05; **p ≤ 0.01; ***p ≤ 0.001.

References

1. Chinese Academy of Social Science (CASS). CSR Blue Book. Beijing: Social Science Academic Press (2021)
2. Rutledge, R.W., et al.: An examination of the relationship between corporate social responsibility and financial performance: the case of Chinese state-owned enterprises. Adv. Environ. Account. Manag. **5**, 81–113 (2014)
3. Fang, X., Zhu, W.: Empirical research of the relationship between corporate social responsibility and add value: based on China's listed company panel data of 2005–2011. J. Appl. Sci. **13**(19), 3952–3960 (2013)
4. Chen, H., Wang, X.: Corporate social responsibility and corporate financial performance in China: an empirical research from Chinese firms. Corp. Gover. Int. J. Bus. Soc. **11**(4), 361–370 (2011)
5. Cheng, S., Lin, K.Z., Wong, W.: Corporate social responsibility reporting and firm performance: evidence from China. J. Manag. Gov. **20**(3), 503–523 (2015)
6. Baltagi, B.H.: Econometric Analysis of Panel Data, 5th edn. John Wiley & Sons, Hoboken (2013)
7. Margolis, J.D., Elfenbein, H.A., Walsh, J.P.: Does it pay to be good? a meta-analysis and redirection of research on the relationship between corporate social and financial performance. Working paper, Harvard Business School, Cambridge (2007)
8. Nelling, E., Webb, E.: Corporate social responsibility and financial performance: the "virtuous circle" revisited. Rev. Quant. Finan. Acc. **32**(2), 197–209 (2009)
9. Sprinkle, G.B., Maines, L.A.: The benefits and costs of corporate social responsibility. Bus. Horiz. **53**(5), 445–453 (2010)
10. Van Beurden, P., Gössling, T.: The worth of values–a literature review on the relation between corporate social and financial performance. J. Bus. Ethics **82**(2), 407–424 (2008)

The External Shock of the Epidemic on Employees' Turnover Intention in Central-Dominated China: The Mediating Effect of Automation and Teleworking

Xinyu Chen(✉)

The University of Melbourne, Melbourne 3010, Australia
xinychen1116@gmail.com

Abstract. Taking the special time window of COVID-19, the research identifies the influence of the epidemic crisis and the related policies on the key indicator of the active employment policy - the turnover intention of low-wage employees in the context of the 'employment promotion strategy' in central-authorized China. The research aims to justify the mechanism behind the effect through the mediators of automation and teleworking, which, on the other hand, is related to the upper-level design of the "Made in China 2025" strategy. The empirical research is based on a sample size of 9,917 in Guangdong Province, China, and the survey is conducted at the mid-point of the pandemic trajectory. Probit models and path analysis were used in exploring the effects between constructs. Based on the results, the authors found that the COVID-19 pandemic has a strong positive effect on the turnover intention of employees in Guangdong Province, subject to an unequal influence on the rural-hukou labour force. Also, built on the path analysis, the author identified that the adoption of automation and teleworking negatively correlated with the effect of the pandemic while positively related to the leave intention of employees, and the adoption of automation and teleworking can mitigate the total effect of COVID-19 on the turnover intention.

Keywords: COVID-19 · Turnover Intention · Teleworking · Automation

1 Introduction

COVID-related policies in China were strict before the end of 2022 [1]. However, an abrupt reversal of policy was made later. The pandemic crisis in either stage reveals the top-down nature of the Chinese Communist Party (CCP) and Xi's highly centralized leadership style [2]. For example, at a heavy cost to maintain the dynamic zero-COVID policy, Shenzhen required a 24h COVID-negative passport for citizens [3], responding to the remarks of the Political Bureau of the Communist Party of China Central Committee [4]. In this case, the strict restriction policies were fully enforced and implemented by local governments and street-level bureaucracy [5], contributing to a distinctive trajectory across waves of the pandemic and the inaccessibility and reduction of labour-intensive jobs.

In addition to the temporary COVID-related policies, the nature of the labor market and employment relations in China is a dividend from other countries under the "top-level" design of the central government [6]. First, inherited from the transaction towards a market-orientated labor market coupled with the Hukou (household registration) system, a labor force dualism – formal and informal (temporary) sectors – attributes to the gaps across the urban-rural-migrant social welfare systems, making the migrants suffer unevenly high unemployment and little social assistance [7, 8]. Second, the employment relationship is regulated mainly through legalization and policies from the central government, with limited support from the government-supporting union [9] and weak labor nongovernmental organizations [10]. To this extent, workers prioritize quitting the job and treat it as an approach under workplace threats [11], thus leading to a high turnover rate in a common place [12]. Third, the employment promotion strategy is stressed as a major strategic policy goal under "top-level design", promoting flexible employment opportunities [6] and encouraging a fiscal stimulus package rewarding small and medium enterprises [13] and relaxed taxes and social insurance contributions [14].

Furthermore, China experienced a boom in the adoption of robotics and machine tools in 2021 [15], leading to the expedient and exaggerated reactions of migrants towards the long-term shock of replacement. Teleworking was introduced as the short-term solution and the long-term design, albeit the rural-urban digital gap [16] and the manual nature of low-skilled work.

Therefore, based on the Guangdong Employer-Employee Survey in 2021, this article conducts a quantitative analysis of the leave intentions of the workers in China under the shock of the COVID-19 pandemic. Section 2 provides a summary of the literature review and hypotheses. Section 3 includes an identification of variables and a description of the method. The obtained results of empirical research are analyzed in Sect. 4 and a discussion of the results is introduced in Sect. 5. The COVID-19 pandemic dramatically changed how people live and work. This paper documents the development of new working modes and employee management during and after the COVID-19 pandemic.

2 Literature Review and Hypothesis

2.1 The COVID-19 Pandemic and Turnover Intention

Research in the Western background recorded an increased turnover in low-paid, high-turnover industries [17], which is associated with the uptrend of job openings made available due to the recovery from COVID-19 [18]. In this circumstance, the turnover decision of workers – especially the inner migrants - in China during the pandemic needs to be discussed in the dual labor market and the government-led policies.

First, the problem of an insufficient coverage of social insurance [19], unemployment policy benefits, and social assistance [20] among the migrant was made more significant due to the epidemic. Moreover, limited unemployment subsidies were introduced in response to the employment promotion led by upper-level policymakers [13]. Both suggest a high risk of turnover. Second, the outbreak of COVID-19 suggested a tight labor market. The economic growth dropped from 6% to −6.8% and the urban unemployment rate raised from 5.3% to 6.2% [21]. As a consequence, incumbent employees are more reluctant to quit. In combination with the former-mentioned discussion, the following hypothesis is proposed:

H1a: The pandemic would decrease voluntary turnover intention, especially the rural-hukou workers.

On the other hand, the mobility restriction led to the coexistence of a high turnover rate of migrants [22] and a labor shortage in the manufacturing sector [23]. The local governments implement assistance accordingly: first, under the employment promotion policy [6], more training and shuttle buses were provided to encourage labor mobility, thereby further relieving the pressure of the job vacancies in the labor-intensive industry and new jobs in small and middle enterprises; second, more job opportunities were provided to rural laborers nearby and the possibility of flexible employment was promoted. For example, online shop owners, express couriers, and takeout deliverymen are popular among recent migrants [24]. Given the indication of increased labor demand, the hypothesis is subject to:

H1b: The pandemic would increase the voluntary turnover intention of employees, especially the rural-hukou workers.

2.2 Automation and Turnover Intention

The unstoppable and irreversible trend of adoption of robotic and autonomous systems can have a latent effect on employee turnover [25] and an unequal negative impact on low-skilled groups [26]. Across the pre- and post-pandemic era, the transaction towards automation is processed under the upper-level "Made in China 2025" strategy [27] and the proposed action plan by local governments [28]. Notwithstanding that the training scheme and education subsidy could relieve the skilled-unskilled wage gap [29], the use of robots would inevitably widen wage inequality even if people switch over to the service sector where there is an increasing number of new jobs emerging [30]. Following the accelerated automation during the pandemic, low-wage and low-skilled workers might lower their turnover intention in the face of fewer employment opportunities in the manufacturing sectors and lower income in other informal sectors. Hence, the hypothesis is given:

H2a: The influence of the pandemic is positively mediated via the development of automation on the leave intention of employees.

However, given that the automation technology application in the manufacturing industry is still in a relatively early stage in China [31], the introduction of automation indicates a productivity effect rather than a displacement effect, as the mechanical equipment aims to improve the efficiency of the low-skilled workers [32]. In combination with automation and the pandemic, Zhang et al. suggest that investment in robotic technology can mitigate the unemployment associated with the public crisis, serving as a positive signal [28]. Therefore, the boosted robotic installation might encourage the leave intention of the workers in a positive labor market with increasing demand. The hypothesis yields:

H2b: The influence of the pandemic is negatively mediated via the development of automation on the leave intention of employees.

2.3 Telework and Turnover Intention

Although the pandemic developed telecommuting and other more flexible working practices [33] – a solution to decrease turnover intention [34] and maintain productivity during the lockdown [35] – most low-wage employees doing physical work can hardly access to such working mode. In this regard, their working time and wages were reduced due to the the pandemic-related constriction [36]. In China, because enough rural migrants are the laborers in the manufacturing sector, their inaccessibility to work would not cause a wage reduction but high turnover [22]. Thus, the accessibility to telework might be a strong motivator for retention during the epidemic:

H3a: The influence of the pandemic is negatively mediated via the availability of teleworking on the leave intention of employees.

H3b: The pandemic would be positively mediated via teleworking regarding the rural-hukou workers.

The conceptual model presented in Fig. 1 was proposed according to the above hypotheses.

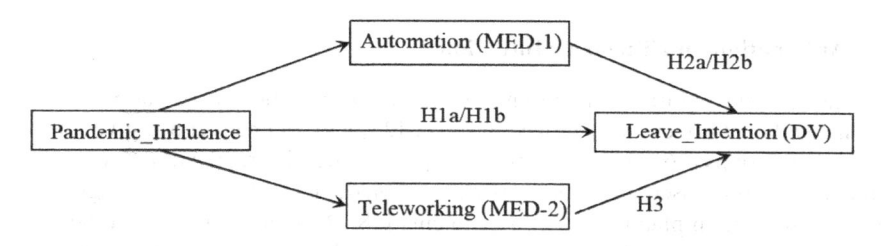

Fig. 1. Conceptual model and hypotheses.

3 Methodology

3.1 Data and Sample

The data under research is sourced from the Guangdong Employer-Employee Survey (GDEES) carried out in Guangdong province from January to July 2021 - the year after the outbreak of the pandemic - with a sample size of 9,917 across 2,053 enterprises. The GDEES is designed and conducted by the Labour and Social Security Research Centre of South China Normal University and supported by the Human Resources and Social Security across Guangdong Province. In the GDEES database, data are collected via the method of quota sampling. The GDEES survey covers 21 cities in Guangdong province, including the two most economically significant cities, Guangzhou and Shenzhen, each with a sample size of 200 firms and 1,000 employees, seven Tier-2 cities, each with a sample size of 100 companies and 500 employees, and the other twelve cities of 80 companies and 400 employees. The dataset applied in the analysis accounts for 7,505 samples from 1,668 companies. Among these 7,505 samples, 4,157 are from Tier-1 and Tier-2 cities, taking 55.39%; the other 3,348 come from less-developed cities, taking 44.61% of the dataset.

3.2 Variables and Descriptive Statistics

Turnover intention, defined as the extent to which someone is planning to quit his or her current job, is the dependent variable measured by the question: "Have you considered voluntary leave after the outbreak of the pandemic?". It was recorded as a dummy variable. The respondents with the answer "not considered" were tagged as "0" while the ones who answered with "considered - do small business", "considered - engage in flexible employment", and "considered - transfer to another company" were tagged as "1".

Pandemic influence, the variable of interest, is based on the question "By the end of December 2021, to what extent has your firm's production capacity recovered?". The firms that achieved their maximum output were labeled as "unaffected" while the rest that failed to reach their production capacity were labeled as "affected". Overall, a small proportion of firms are fully recovered from COVID-19, accounting for 32.57%. Unsurprisingly, the employees in the firm without the pain of the pandemic reported a lower percentage of 8.05 in contrast to their counterparts under the impact of the pandemic, at a significant level of 99%.

Automation is recorded by the question "Have you introduced automation, robots, computer numerical control (CNC) machinery tools, etc. during the pandemic?". The answers are "Never", "Plan-to", "Small volume", and "Large volume". Similarly, the variable is transferred to a dummy variable: the former two categories of "Never" and "Plan-to" are recorded as "0", and the other two of "Small volume" and "Large volume" are recorded as "1", tagged as adopted the automation. Although 29.69% of the enterprises introduced robotic technologies, only 5.48% of those applied automation heavily. For enterprises that recovered from the pandemic and those that remain unrecovered, there is no significant gap between the groups with and without leave intentions identified.

Teleworking is measured by the question "Have you experienced working from home during the pandemic?", with an answer of rather positive (1 = have teleworking experience) or negative (0 = no teleworking experience). The majority (67.24%) of the subjects reported no experience with homeworking. Furthermore, while there is no significant gap within the firms under no impact, there is a gap (2.30%) between the percentage of the employees with and without leave intention in the firms that do not recover from the pandemic.

Control variables include tenure, wage, working hours (both variables are transferred to natural logarithms), and demographic characteristics. As shown in Table 1, regardless of the influence of the COVID-19 pandemic, the younger (Gap = 2.15; 1.97), unmarried (Gap = 9.58%; 5.75%), and rural-hukou employees (Gap = 4.22%; 9.61%) with shorter tenure (Gap = 1.04; 1.58), less wage (Gap = 0.04; 0.03) and longer working time (Gap = −0.02; −0.02) would take a higher proportion in the group in consideration of another job, consistent with the conclusion of other research [37, 38].

Table 1. The summary statistics.

Variables	Influenced by the Pandemic			Uninfluenced by the Pandemic		
	With Leave Intention	Without Leave Intention	Gap	With Leave Intention	Without Leave Intention	Gap
Automation	26.60%	25.81%	−0.79%	38.92%	35.71%	−3.20%
Teleworking	33.52%	31.22%	−2.30%*	36.97%	35.13%	−1.83%
Age	32.92	35.07	2.15***	32.08	34.06	1.97***
Gender (Male = 1)	38.64%	39.97%	1.33%	46.04%	40.11%	−5.94%**
Education	12.96	12.86	−0.11*	13.19	13.26	0.065
Marital status (Married = 1)	65.08%	74.66%	9.58%***	66.06%	71.81%	5.75%***
Hukou (Rural = 1)	62.28%	58.05%	4.22%***	68.42%	58.81%	9.61%***
Tenure	5.41	6.45	1.04***	4.66	6.25	1.58***
Ln wage	8.23	8.26	0.04***	8.32	8.35	0.03**
Ln hours	2.14	2.10	−0.02***	2.14	2.12	−0.02***
Manufacturing Industry	51.16%	47.56%	−3.6%**	61.38%	57.44%	−3.93%**

Notes: * $p < 0.05$, ** $p < 0.01$, *** $p < 0.001$

4 Results

4.1 Baseline Estimates

First, a baseline model is introduced to fit a Probit Model, the variable of interest – the influence of the pandemic - is positively correlated with the leave intention at a coefficient of 0.2102. In the case of the results of the marginal effects, compared to the employees in the companies that recovered from the pandemic, the leaving intention of the workers in the firms unable to restore their full productivity would have increased by 0.0582. Furthermore, the indicator of the pandemic influence holds across two Probit models at a significant level of 99%. Therefore, employees would be more likely to consider leaving their positions under the circumstance of the COVID-19 pandemic. Thus, hypothesis 1b is supported partially.

Second, according to Table 2, the tenure and wage are negatively related to the dependent variable of the quit intention – a 1% increase of each variable accounts for a decrease of the voluntary turnover possibility by 0.19 and 0.03 [$0.0728 * \ln(1.01)$] percentage points respectively. Furthermore, a 1% increase in working hours would increase the dependent variable by [$0.1753 * \ln(1.01)$], accounting for 0.08 percentage points. The results of the demographic variables suggest that the males (dx/dy = 0.0420), unmarried (dx/dy = −0.0253), and older (dx/dy = −0.0055) individuals are more likely

Table 2. Probit Models for the turnover intention & marginal effects of the coefficients - dy/dx.

	Coef.	dy/dx	Coef.	dy/dx
Pandemic (influenced = 1)	0.2102*** (0.0425)	0.0582*** (0.0119)	0.2253*** (0.0434)	0.0598*** (0.0115)
Age	−0.0209*** (0.0034)	−0.0055*** (0.0009)	−0.0205*** (0.0034)	−0.0054*** (0.0009)
Gender (Male = 1)	0.1587*** (0.0415)	0.0420*** (0.0110)	0.1498*** (0.0425)	0.0397*** (0.0112)
Education	0.0108 (0.0155)	0.0029 (0.0041)	0.0003 (0.0163)	0.0001 (0.0043)
Marital status (Married = 1)	−0.0955* (0.0501)	−0.0253* (0.0133)	−0.1110** (0.0510)	−0.0295** (0.0135)
Hukou (Rural = 1)	0.0838** (0.0416)	0.0222** (0.0110)	0.0944** (0.0427)	0.0250** (0.0113)
Tenure	−0.00728* (0.0041)	−0.0019* (0.0011)	−0.0066 (0.0042)	−0.0018 (0.0011)
Ln wage	−0.2752*** (0.0551)	−0.0728*** (0.0145)	−0.2786*** (0.0575)	−0.0739*** (0.0152)
Ln hours	0.6626*** (0.1569)	0.1753*** (0.0414)	0.6890*** (0.1613)	0.1828*** (0.0427)
Industry (manufacturing = 1)	0.0937** (0.0405)	0.0248** (0.0107)	0.0780* (0.0441)	0.0207* (0.0117)
Automation			0.0428 (0.0461)	0.0114 (0.0122)
Teleworking			0.1064** (0.0454)	0.0283** (0.0120)
Cons	0.4781 (0.5223)		0.4435 (0.5395)	
N	5,846		5,600	
Pseudo R^2	0.0343		0.0356	

Notes: * $p < 0.05$, ** $p < 0.01$, *** $p < 0.001$

to consider leaving their current employers, leaving education a negligible effect on the quit intentions. Referring to the indicator of hukou, the result suggests that the possibility of the employees with rural hukou considering leaving their current jobs would be 2.22 percentage points lower than those of the workers with urban hukou. In addition, the potential hazard rate among the workers in the manufactory industry would be 2.48 percentage points higher, significant at a 95% level. Besides, the result of Pseudo R^2 also indicates that the inclusion of the demographic variables would uplift the total variance explained.

Third, Probit model 2 implies that the inclusion of the variables of automation and teleworking contributes to limited raise in the Pseudo R^2, in which case, those variables lead to a minor variation. On the one hand, there is no significant correlation between the indicator of automation and the dependent variable of pandemic impact, which, to some extent, rejects both H2a and H2b. For the variable of teleworking, an increase of 1% teleworking leads to an increase of the voluntary turnover possibility by 0.0283, at a significant level of 95%, which rejects H3a.

In consideration of the Chinese-specific circumstance with a hukou system, the difference between the labor force with rural and urban hukou is analyzed to investigate the underlying inequality effect. The result (Table 3) indicts the cluster of employees with rural hukou. The 1% increase in the percentage of enterprises under the influence of the pandemic is correlated with an increase of 8.80% in the turnover intention, which is larger than an increase of 3.98% in leaving intention among the cluster with urban hukou. The pandemic would account for a heavier influence on those rural-hukou laborers referring to their turnover intention, further verifying H1b. Additionally, the variable of teleworking records a significant positive coefficient of 0.1583 within the urban-hukou cluster solely, denoting that the positive effect of remote working on the turnover intention mostly results from the flexibility shared by urban-hukou holders. H3b is potently supported.

Overall, a positive effect of the pandemic and teleworking method on the leave intention of employees is observed, in favor of H1b and H3b. In the next section, path analysis would be employed to uncover the mechanism of how the influence of the pandemic is decoded in the decision-making of the employees and to examine the reliability of the results of the baseline models.

4.2 Path Analysis

Given H2 and H3, the assumption is held that the indicator of interest - pandemic influence - might affect the dependent variable through the mediators of automation and teleworking to affect the turnover intentions. Considering Probit Model (1) in the previous section, the decomposition of the Probit coefficient would be conducted into its direct and indirect parts and simple magnitude measures would be provided [39].

The results in Table 4 and Fig. 2 display that the influence of the pandemic has significant effects on both the identified mediators of Automation and Teleworking, in which case, both the medicating variables identified indicate no endogeneity and therefore can be further analysed. In detail, the results imply a negative correlation between the pandemic influence and automation (PI $\rightarrow$ AT $= -0.3266$), in which respect, the firms under server pain of COVID-19 would be less likely to have adopted the shift towards automation. Also, the impact of COVID-19 is negatively associated with teleworking (PI $\rightarrow$ TW $= -0.1055$): the employees in enterprises unrecovered from the economic shock of the pandemic made less available of the remote working choice. Again, both Automation and Teleworking attribute a positive effect on the leave intention of employees, with path coefficients of 0.0764 and 0.0654 respectively.

Table 5 reports the results of decomposition with the 'product of coefficients' method of the influence of the pandemic on the turnover intention with the mediators. Both the indirect and direct effects are statistically significant, albeit the direct effect has a positive coefficient of 0.2266, and the indirect effect accounts for a negative magnitude of 0.0978,

Table 3. Probit Models for the turnover intention & the marginal effects by Cluster of Hukou.

	Hukou = Rural		Hukou = Urban	
	Coef.	dy/dx	Coef.	dy/dx
Pandemic (influenced = 1)	0.3648***	0.0880***	0.1412***	0.0398***
	(0.0716)	(0.0171)	(0.0550)	(0.0155)
Age	−0.0209***	−0.0053***	−0.0196***	−0.0055***
	(0.0034)	(0.0013)	(0.0044)	(0.0012)
Gender (Male = 1)	0.0267*	0.0267*	0.1726***	0.0487***
	(0.0415)	(0.0112)	(0.0559)	(0.0157)
Education	0.0019	0.0018	−0.0057	−0.0016
	(0.0155)	(0.0066)	(0.0204)	(0.0058)
Marital status (Married = 1)	−0.0176*	−0.0176	−0.1386**	−0.0391**
	(0.0193)	(0.0013)	(0.0665)	(0.0187)
Tenure	−0.0016*	−0.0017	−0.0062*	−0.0017*
	(0.0015)	(0.0015)	(0.0015)	(0.0016)
Ln wage	−0.0629***	−0.0629***	−0.2931***	−0.0827***
	(0.0206)	(0.0206)	(0.0782)	(0.0220)
Ln hours	0.2028***	0.2028***	0.6197***	0.1748 ***
	(0.0711)	(0.0711)	(0.1946)	(0.0547)
Industry (manufacturing = 1)	0.0138	0.0138	0.0876	0.0247**
	(0.0170)	(0.0170)	(0.0569)	(0.0160)
Automation	0.0126	0 .0126	0.0320	0.0090
	(0.0187)	(0.0187)	(00573)	(0.0162)
Teleworking	0.0369	0.0089**	0.1581***	0.0446***
	(0.0169)	(0.0169)	(0.0598)	(0.0168)
Cons	−0.0735		0.8504	
	(0.8548)		(0.7157)	
chi2(1) =	6.05			
Prob > chi2	0.0139			

Note(s): * $p < 0.05$, ** $p < 0.01$, *** $p < 0.001$

attributing to a positive total effect on the dependent variable of the pandemic influence. In other words, whereas the pandemic influence proved to have a dominant direct effect on leave intention, its negative indirect effect offsets the positive total effect on the dependent variable of hazard rate via the mediators of automation and teleworking. Simply put, the introduction of combined automation and teleworking can weaken the negative influence of the pandemic on leave intention; nevertheless, the employees in firms unrecovered from the pandemic crisis would be more possible to consider leaving, regardless of the introduction of automation and remote working.

In terms of the relative measures of the indirect effect, the positive effect of the influence of the pandemic is mediated by automation, whose magnitude overtakes which

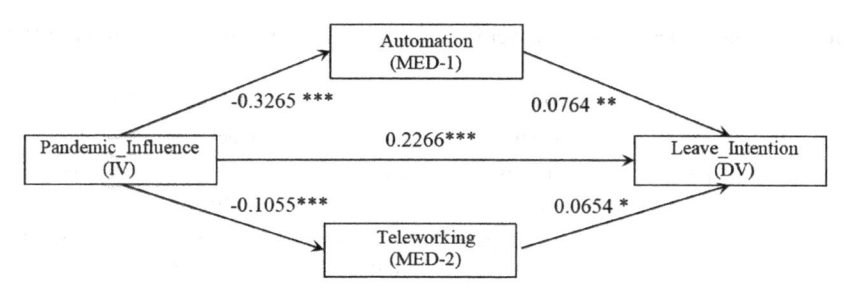

```
                    Automation
                    (MED-1)
          -0.3265***        0.0764**
Pandemic_Influence   0.2266***      Leave_Intention
      (IV)                              (DV)
          -0.1055***        0.0654*
                   Teleworking
                    (MED-2)
```

Fig. 2. The conceptual model with the values of path coefficients.

Table 4. Standardized path coefficients for the proposed model.

Hypothesized path	Link Direction	Path Coefficient	Z-Value	N
PI → AT	Negative	−0.3266*** (0.0564)	−9.82	6,943
PI → TW	Negative	−0.1055*** (0.0330)	−3.20	6,986
AT → LI	Positive	0.0764** (0.0384)	1.99	6,943
TW → LI	Positive	0.0654* (0.0386)	1.75	6,986
PI → LI	Positive	0.2266*** (0.0386)	5.87	6,764

Notes: * $p < 0.05$, ** $p < 0.01$, *** $p < 0.001$

Table 5. Effects of MEDs on IV.

	Coefficients	z
Total effect	0.1287*** (0.0386)	5.87
Direct effect	0.2266*** (0.0386)	5.83
Indirect effect	−0.0978*** (0.0198)	−4.95
via Automation	−0.0740*** (0.0147)	−5.04
via Teleworking	−0.0239*** (0.0085)	−2.81

Notes: * $p < 0.05$, ** $p < 0.01$, *** $p < 0.001$

of teleworking, subject to a negative magnitude of −0.0740, accounting for 75.66% of the indirect effect. In this way, the introduction of automation would be more likely to have an impact on softening employee turnover decision-making in the context of the COVID-19 pandemic, supporting H2b. Also, despite the relatively smaller magnitude (−0.0239), taking 24.44% of the indirect effect, the availability of teleworking would mitigate the positive relation between the pandemic and the turnover intention, indicating the approval of H3a.

5 Discussion

The research investigates how turnover intention developed during the epidemic crisis in China, where the upper-level design - dualism in social insurance - takes the dominant position in coordinating the labor market and industrial relations. Furthermore, as a dividend from the Western countries, the accelerated transaction of teleworking and automation in China has diverse influences under the industry-upgrading and employment promotion strategy.

First, a significant positive influence of the pandemic on leave intention in Guangdong Province is documented, which might be resulting from the pandemic-related public health policies constricting mobility and consistent employment promotion strategy. Under the dualism in China, the employees with rural hukou have a higher turnover intention, congruent with the historical records [22] and their prolonged working time thrived from the closed-loop production systems during pandemic outbreaks [40].

Furthermore, the analysis implies that the mechanism of the pathways of robotic adoption and teleworking would dilute the negative influence of the pandemic on turnover intention to some extent. Without a significant influence on turnover intention, automation softens the epidemic-related leave indirectly via the dying-down investment in the machines and the replacement-triggered turnover. Moreover, the accessibility of homeworking contributes to an increased turnover, especially among the labor with urban hukou – more likely the high-skilled workers – suggesting the shifts in working methods and potential effect of government promotion to encourage flexibility. The result denotes that the enterprises that failed to recover are less available for teleworking, which might indicate the manual work nature or limited digitalization.

Notably, a considerable positive association between the pandemic and the turnover intention resulting from the direct effect. It is possible that the leave intention might be incited by the restriction of traveling across provinces – which attributes to both the inaccessibility to the positions and the labor shortage in the areas abundant with labor-intensive companies (i.e., Guangdong) - and the central employment promotion policy after the outbreak of COVID-19 rather than the organizational change.

6 Conclusion

Generally, this study underscores labor retention under the influence of the COVID-19 pandemic in China. In this paper, it is found that, in China, the pandemic has a strong positive effect on the intention of employees to leave their positions, and the pandemic attack accounts for a dual mechanism: the adoption of automation and teleworking could weaken the effect of COVID-19 on the enterprises while both solutions would be positively correlated with the turnover intention of their employees. In another word, the relaxation of both solutions on the positive effect of the pandemic on turnover intention results from the negative influence of the epidemic on the progress to invest in automation and make available for teleworking which encourage voluntary leave. Apart from the disadvantages in terms of social security, there is a severe impact of the pandemic on the turnover intention of the group with rural hukou.

References

1. World Bank Group. World Bank East Asia and Pacific Economic Update, October 2022: Reforms for Recovery. WORLD BANK GROUP (2020). https://doi.org/10.1596/978-1-4648-1921-6
2. Gill, B.: China in the COVID world: continued challenges for a rising power. NATO Defense College (2020). http://www.jstor.org/stable/resrep27744
3. Wu, S., Huang, Z., Grant-Muller, S., Gu, D., Yang, L.: Modelling the reopen strategy from dynamic zero-COVID in China considering the sequela and reinfection. Sci. Rep. **13**, 7343 (2023). https://doi.org/10.1038/s41598-023-34207-7
4. Xinhua. Vice-premier reiterates dynamic zero-COVID policy (2022). http://english.www.gov.cn/statecouncil/sunchunlan/202205/10/content_WS62799c37c6d02e533532a753.html
5. Qin, X., Owen, C.: The CCP, campaign governance and COVID-19: evidence from Shanghai. J. Chin. Polit. Sci. 1–26 (2022)
6. Qian, J.: The Political Economy of Making and Implementing Social Policy in China. Palgrave Macmillan, Singapore (2021)
7. He, A.J., Zhang, C., Qian, J.: COVID-19 and social inequality in China: the local–migrant divide and the limits of social protections in a pandemic. Policy Soc. **41**(2), 275–290 (2022)
8. Li, T., Barwick, P.J., Deng, Y., Huang, X., Li, S.: The COVID-19 pandemic and unemployment: evidence from mobile phone data from China. J. Urban Econ. **135**, 103543 (2023)
9. Leung, P.P.: Labor Activists and the New Working Class in China Strike Leaders' Struggles. Palgrave Macmillan, New York (2015)
10. Franceschini, I., Nesossi, E.: State repression of Chinese Labor NGOs: a chilling effect? China J. **80**, 111–129 (2018)
11. Chan, K.C.: The Challenge of Labour in China: Strikes and the Changing Labour Regime in Global Factories. Routledge, London (2010)
12. Chen, Y., Kim, Y.K., Liu, Z., Wang, G., Zhao, G.:. Can HPWS and unions work together to reduce employee turnover intention in foreign MNCs in China? In: Advances in Industrial and Labor Relations, 2017: Shifts in Workplace Voice, Justice, Negotiation and Conflict Resolution in Contemporary Workplaces. Emerald Publishing Limited (2018)
13. Lu, Q., Cai, Z., Chen, B., Liu, T.: Social policy responses to the COVID-19 crisis in China in 2020. Int. J. Environ. Res. Public Health **17**(16), 5796 (2020)
14. Wong, C., Qian, J.: COVID-19 highlights need to strengthen China's social safety net (I): the unemployment insurance scheme. East Asian Institute Background Brief, No.1572, National University of Singapore (2020)
15. IFR. China: Robot installations grew by 44 percent. IFR (2022). https://ifr.org/ifr-press-releases/news/china-robot-installations-grew-by-44-percent
16. Song, Z., Wang, C., Bergmann, L.: China's prefectural digital divide: spatial analysis and multivariate determinants of ICT diffusion. Int. J. Inf. Manag. **52**, 102072 (2020). https://doi.org/10.1016/j.ijinfomgt.2020.102072

17. Weissmann, J.: Everyone Is Quitting Their Job. Slate (2021). https://slate.com/business/2021/06/workers-quitting-jobs-woohoo.html
18. Fontinelle, A.: The Great Resignation. Investopedia (2022). https://www.investopedia.com/the-great-resignation-5199074
19. Qian, J., Wen, Z.: Extension of social insurance coverage to informal economy workers in China: an administrative and institutional perspective. Int. Soc. Secur. Rev. **74**(1), 79–102 (2021)
20. Chen, S., et al.: Barriers of effective health insurance coverage for rural-to-urban migrant workers in China: a systematic review and policy gap analysis. BMC Public Health **20**(408), 1–16 (2020)
21. Moscarini, G., Postel-Vinay, F.: Did the job ladder fail after the great recession? J. Labor Econ. **34**(S1), S55–S93 (2016). https://www.jstor.org/stable/26588431
22. Che, L., Du, H., Chan, K.W.: Unequal pain: a sketch of the impact of the Covid-19 pandemic on migrants' employment in China. Eurasian Geogr. Econ. **61**(4–5), 448–463 (2020). https://doi.org/10.1080/15387216.2020.1791726
23. International Finance. Decoding China's blue-collar labour shortage (2022). https://internationalfinance.com/decoding-chinas-blue-collar-labour-shortage/
24. Bing, K.: Innovation-led growth can help resolve labor shortage issue. China Daily (2023). https://www.chinadaily.com.cn/a/202302/21/WS63f3fe0ba31057c47ebafd1e.html
25. Domini, G., Grazzi, M., Moschella, D., Treibich, T.: For whom the bell tolls: the firm-level effects of automation on wage and gender inequality. Res. Policy **51**(7), 104533 (2022). https://doi.org/10.1016/j.respol.2022.104533
26. Nazareno, L., Schiff, D.S.: The impact of automation and artificial intelligence on worker well-being. Technol. Soc. **67**, 101679 (2021). https://doi.org/10.1016/j.techsoc.2021.101679
27. Xinhua. China to invest big in "Made in China 2025" strategy (2017). http://english.www.gov.cn/state_council/ministries/2017/10/12/content_281475904600274.html
28. Zhang, P., Qin, Y., Liang, H., Zhou, L.: Robotization and labour demand in post-pandemic era: Microeconomic evidence from China. Technol. Forecast. Soc. Chang. **192**, 122523 (2023). https://doi.org/10.1016/j.techfore.2023.122523
29. Zhang, P.: Can public subsidy on education reduce wage inequality in the presence of automation? Econ. Res. **35**(1), 6850–6866 (2022). https://doi.org/10.1080/1331677x.2022.2053783
30. Zhang, P.: Automation, wage inequality and implications of a robot tax. Int. Rev. Econ. Financ. **59**, 500–509 (2019). https://doi.org/10.1016/j.iref.2018.10.013
31. Cheng, H., Jia, R., Li, D., Li, H.: The rise of robots in China. Journal of Economic Perspectives **33**(2), 71–88 (2019)
32. Qin, X., Xu, W., Chen, H., Zhong, J., Sun, Y., Li, X.: Automation, firm employment and skill upgrading: firm-level evidence from China. Ind. Innov. **29**(9), 1075–1107 (2022). https://doi.org/10.1080/13662716.2022.2122411
33. Ancillo, A., Núñez, M., Gavrila, S.: Workplace change within the COVID-19 context: a grounded theory approach. Econ. Res.-Ekonomska Istraživanja **34**(1), 2297–2316 (2021). https://doi.org/10.1080/1331677X.2020.1862689
34. Delanoeije, J., Verbruggen, M.: Between-person and within-person effects of telework: a quasi-field experiment. Eur. J. Work Organ. Psy. **29**(6), 795–808 (2020). https://doi.org/10.1080/1359432X.2020.1774557
35. Sharma, S., Singh, G., Sharma, R., Jones, P., Kraus, S., Dwivedi, Y.K.: Digital health innovation: exploring adoption of COVID-19 digital contact tracing apps. IEEE Trans. Eng. Manag. 1–17 (2020). https://doi.org/10.1109/TEM.2020.3019033
36. Yasenov, V.: Who can work from home? In: Social Science Research Network (2020). https://doi.org/10.2139/ssrn.3590895

37. Aliaga, M.B.: Gender inequality during the pandemic: perspectives of women workers in Latin America and the Caribbean. Int. J. Labour Res. **10**(1), 91–107 (2021)
38. Grugel, J., Barlow, M., Lines, T., Gigaudo, M.E., Omukuti, J.: The gendered face of COVID-19 in the Global South: the development, gender and health nexus, 1st edn.. Bristol University Press (2022). https://doi.org/10.2307/j.ctv2jn91v9
39. Karlson, K. B., Holm, A., Breen, R.: Comparing regression coefficients between same-sample nested models using logit and probit: a new method. Sociol. Methodol. **42**, 286–313 (2012). http://www.jstor.org/stable/23409353
40. CLB. October 2022 labour news roundup: Average weekly working hours increased under pandemic. China Labour Bulletin (2022). https://clb.org.hk/en/content/october-2022-labour-news-roundup-average-weekly-working-hours-increased-under-pandemic

Research on the Mechanism of Farmers' Interest Linkage in Agricultural Technology Transformation
A Case Study of 22 National Agricultural Science and Technology Parks in Shandong Province

Yuanyuan Chen(✉)

School of Economics, Shandong University of Finance and Economics, Jinan, China
yuan_erchen@163.com

Abstract. By categorizing the mechanisms of interest linkage in 22 national agricultural science and technology parks in Shandong Province and combining scholarly research, this study reveals that the overall operational efficiency of agricultural science and technology parks in Shandong Province is relatively high. The main cooperation models are "company + farmers" and "base + farmers," which may be closely related to enterprise operations. By establishing an intelligent pig game model, three cooperation models are identified between agricultural science and technology parks and farmers: government-oriented, industry-driven, and government-participatory models. The selection of these models is influenced by financial environment, intermediary institutions, and government finances. The study suggests the need for further optimization of the agricultural financial environment, the establishment of a robust agricultural information platform, and strengthened government support for agricultural science and technology parks. These findings provide valuable insights for the transformation of agricultural technology achievements.

Keywords: Agricultural Technology Transformation · Interest Linkage mechanism · Agricultural Science and Technology Park

1 Introduction

The transformation of agricultural technology achievements is a crucial factor in promoting modern agricultural development and facilitating the rational allocation of technological and agricultural resources. Zhao Ying and Bu Fengxian proposed, from a systemic perspective, to comprehensively consider the interest demands of various subjects involved in technology transformation, emphasizing the holistic nature of the agricultural technology achievement transformation system [1]. Many scholars have highlighted the three main elements in the process of agricultural technology achievement transformation: the supply and demand entities of technology transformation, and intermediary entities. They emphasize the need for coordinated efforts among these entities to achieve the transformation of technological achievements [2]. Currently, domestic research on technology transformation has mostly focused on systems for connecting and disseminating technological achievements and their utilization, with limited exploration from the perspective of interest mechanisms. In China's agricultural technology achievement transformation, the imbalance between supply and demand for agricultural technology innovation and inadequate technology dissemination pose challenges. The lack of effective mechanisms linking interests stands as a significant factor contributing to the imbalance in the supply and demand for agricultural technology achievements [3]. Scholars both domestically and internationally have underscored the importance of farmers as key stakeholders in the process of technology achievement transformation. Thus, promoting the successful transformation of agricultural technology requires a keen consideration of farmers' interest demands and the establishment of robust interest linkage mechanisms. This holds crucial significance for advancing the transformation of agricultural technology achievements.

2 Theoretical Analysis of Farmers' Interest Linkage Mechanism in Promoting Agricultural Technology Transformation

Agricultural technology extension categorizes the transformation of technological achievements into three main components: transformation subjects, transformation targets, and transformation recipients. According to the theory of farmer behavior change, three major factors influence changes in farmer behavior. First, the need for economic development and increased income serves as the most fundamental and initial driving force. Second, the impetus of market development, as a market economy requires technological innovation to expedite progress. Third, the guiding role of the government, which formulates policies to guide farmer behavior in support of agricultural production.

To achieve efficient transformation of technological achievements, it is necessary to establish a stable connection between various stages of agricultural production and the pre- and post-production phases. This involves constructing an interest linkage mechanism that promotes shared benefits and shared risks between farmers and agricultural science and technology parks. Dominated by agricultural science and technology parks, the mode of technological transformation utilizes technology, market, and information interfaces between the park and farmers. This approach facilitates the integration of modern agricultural technology into the various stages of pre-production, production, and post-production. Agricultural science and technology parks, owing to their relatively comprehensive and expansive extension systems, offer technological services to small-scale farmers. Leveraging technology demonstrations and socialized services, these parks mobilize a significant portion of farmers within their surrounding regions, thus fostering collective development among local farmers. Simultaneously, this approach aids in gathering technology demand information from dispersed farmers, providing feedback to technology providers, and offering a basis for refining technological achievements and research topics. The technological transformation model led by agricultural science and technology parks can stimulate the fundamental drive of farmers. Under governmental guidance and through the alignment of agricultural science and technology parks with the market, farmers are encouraged to engage in production development using advanced technologies. This effectively facilitates the transformation of technological achievements.

3 Efficiency of Agricultural Science and Technology Parks in Shandong Province and Classification of Interest Linkage Mechanisms

Agricultural technological innovation, the transfer of agricultural technological achievements, and the development of high-tech agriculture require agricultural science and technology parks to serve as intermediaries and carriers. The construction of agricultural science and technology parks in Shandong is at the forefront nationally, representing a significant breakthrough in China's agricultural technological innovation. As of December 2021, Shandong Province has a total of 22 national-level agricultural science and technology parks, ranking first in terms of quantity nationwide.

3.1 Efficiency of Agricultural Science and Technology Parks in Shandong Province

Based on the comprehensive operational efficiency and scale benefit assessment of agricultural science and technology parks in various cities in Shandong Province in 2017 conducted by Yu Kun and other scholars (see Table 1), it can be concluded that, apart from cities such as Zibo, Linyi, Liaocheng, Binzhou, and Heze, the comprehensive efficiency of the agricultural science and technology parks in the remaining 12 cities in Shandong Province is all 1. This indicates that, overall, the agricultural science and technology parks in Shandong Province operate at a relatively high level. Twelve prefecture-level cities have both pure technical efficiency and scale efficiency reaching 1, indicating that over two-thirds of the elements of production and utilization in agricultural science and technology parks in Shandong Province have reached the highest level, resulting in high technology input-output ratios and rational resource allocation [4].

3.2 Classification of Interest Linkage Mechanisms in Shandong Province's Agricultural Science and Technology Parks

Based on the classification of various scholars in existing literature regarding interest linkage mechanisms and in consideration of the situation of Shandong Province's national agricultural science and technology parks and small-scale farmers, this study classifies the interest linkage mechanisms in Shandong Province's agricultural science and technology parks into four types: "Cooperative + Farmers," "Base + Farmers," "Enterprise + Farmers," and "Cooperative Dual Equity Participation." Table 2 presents the classification results for the 22 national agricultural science and technology parks in Shandong Province.

From the results in the table, it can be observed that the main interest linkage models between Shandong Province's national agricultural science and technology parks and farmers are the "Enterprise + Farmers" and "Base + Farmers" models. Among them, the "Company + Base + Farmers" model exists in three parks. The high-level construction

Table 1. Operational efficiency of agricultural science and technology parks in various cities in Shandong province in 2017.

Region	Comprehensive Efficiency	Pure Technical Efficiency	Scale Efficiency
Jinan City	1.00	1.00	1.00
Qingdao City	1.00	1.00	1.00
Zibo City	0.52	0.88	0.59
Zaozhuang City	1.00	1.00	1.00
Dongying City	1.00	1.00	1.00
Yantai City	1.00	1.00	1.00
Weifang City	1.00	1.00	1.00
Jining City	1.00	1.00	1.00
Tai'an City	1.00	1.00	1.00
Weihai City	1.00	1.00	1.00
Rizhao City	1.00	1.00	1.00
Laiwu City	1.00	1.00	1.00
Linyi City	0.60	1.00	0.60
Dezhou City	1.00	1.00	1.00
Liaocheng City	0.57	0.69	0.83
Binzhou City	0.25	0.50	0.50
Heze City	0.41	0.43	0.95

Source: Calculated and organized by the author based on available data

Table 2. Classification of interest linkage models between Shandong province's national agricultural science and technology parks and farmers.

Type	Specific Model	Parks
Cooperative + Farmers		Zoucheng, Binxian, Zaozhuang
	R&D + Company + Cooperative + Farmers	Zibo
Base + Farmers		Jining, Linyi, Jinan, Weifang, Zaozhuang, Tai'an
	Company + Base + Farmers	Laiwu, Shouguang, Linyi
Enterprise + Farmers		Binxian, Weihai, Qixia, Yantai, Rizhao, Dongying, Heze, Binzhou

(*continued*)

Table 2. (*continued*)

Type	Specific Model	Parks
	Contract Farming	Jimo, Qingdao
	Industrial Park + Farmers	Liaocheng, Dezhou
Dual Equity Participation	Agricultural Leading Agricultural Science and Technology Park + Cooperative + Family Farm + Farmers	Laiwu
	Base Farmers, Farmers' Cooperative "Minimum Guarantee + Dividend"	Zibo

Source: Compiled by the author based on relevant documents

of agricultural science and technology parks in Shandong Province might be closely related to enterprise operations.

4 Game Theory Analysis of Interests Between Agricultural Science and Technology Parks and Farmers

The sustainable and stable operation and development of agricultural science and technology parks require a rational basis for interest linkage mechanisms. Drawing on the research model of Bai Li and Zhao Banghong regarding the development model and interest linkage mechanism of edible mushroom industry in Yixian County, this study constructs an intelligent pig game model for the fund investment of agricultural science and technology parks and farmers. The model is used to analyze the four cooperation modes and interest linkage mechanisms between agricultural science and technology parks and farmers [5].

4.1 Hypothesis Analysis and Model Construction

The cost input before the production process mainly includes seedling costs and greenhouse construction expenses. This paper takes the decision of who builds the greenhouse first as the starting point for the game, with both agricultural science and technology parks and small-scale farmers having the options to build or not build.

Before establishing the model, the following assumptions are made:

In the production process, the cost of purchasing advanced seedlings is B, and the cost of building a greenhouse is P. Under the condition that farmers adopt advanced seedlings, receive production technology guidance from agricultural science and technology parks, and have their products uniformly sold by the parks, the unit greenhouse output value is R. In the absence of technology guidance and with independent dispersed operations, the unit greenhouse output value obtained by farmers is S. Agricultural science and technology parks use their capital, technology, and information technology advantages.

Under the condition of using advanced seeds, the sales income of a single greenhouse is M. Under the scale economy condition, agricultural science and technology parks introduce advanced seeds and receive government support, achieving unit area sales income N. The cost of employing farmers to manage greenhouses and pick fruits in agricultural science and technology parks is denoted as L, and in this case, farmers' wages are the main consideration. Farmers need to incur high self-built greenhouse construction costs and loans, resulting in borrowing costs D. Agricultural science and technology parks autonomously purchase new seedlings and construct greenhouses, providing them free of charge to farmers and enjoying government subsidies denoted as G. Because farmers bear certain technological risks in independent dispersed operations without technical guidance, $R > S$. Under government subsidies and achieving economies of scale, the income $N > M$.

Under the aforementioned assumptions, there are four main cooperation modes and interest linkage mechanisms between agricultural science and technology parks and farmers:

1. "Enterprise + Farmers" Industry-Driven Model: In this mode, companies invest in developing and establishing production bases and greenhouses, sign contracts with farmers, hire them, and guide them in standardized production management. Farmers, however, need to pay for seed purchases and build their own greenhouses. In this scenario, farmers require loans to meet upfront investments, with their production costs comprising seed costs B, greenhouse construction costs P, and loan costs D. Their income is denoted as R. The costs for agricultural science and technology parks include greenhouse construction costs P and farmer wages L. Their income mainly consists of the production and sales income M and the difference in purchase and sales (M-R).

2. "Market + Farmers" Market Order Model: In this mode, leading agricultural science and technology parks are responsible for purchasing products grown by farmers. Farmers bear higher costs in this case, requiring loans for upfront investment, with their production costs including seed costs B, greenhouse construction costs P, and loan costs D. Their income is denoted as S. Because farmers bear certain technological risks in independent dispersed operations without technical guidance, $R > S$. At this point, the profit for agricultural science and technology parks is the difference between purchases and sales (M-S).

3. Government Participation Model: In this hypothetical scenario, government-supported agricultural science and technology parks provide farmers with free production bases, technical guidance, and unified sales. Farmers themselves purchase advanced seeds and engage in production operations. Under this condition, farmers' production costs are mainly seed costs B, and their profit is the unit greenhouse output value R. The construction costs of agricultural science and technology parks are represented by building costs P, with their income coming from the difference between purchases and sales N-R, along with government subsidies G.

4. Neither party purchases advanced seeds, assuming a profit of 0 (Table 3).

Table 3. Profit matrix between agricultural science and technology parks and small-scale farmers.

		Agricultural Science and Technology Park	
		Build Greenhouse	Don't Build Greenhouse
Farmer	Build Greenhouse	(M-L-P + (M-R),R-B-P-D)	(M-S,S-B-D-P)
	Don't Build Greenhouse	(G + N-R-P,R-B)	(0,0)

4.2 Intelligent Pig Game Model Analysis

Through the intelligent pig game analysis between agricultural science and technology parks and small-scale farmers, when farmers choose to build greenhouses, the difference in profits between the agricultural science and technology park building greenhouses and not building greenhouses is represented as (M-L-P-R-S). The unit greenhouse output value S for farmers in the absence of technical guidance and their unit greenhouse output value under technical guidance are both greater than zero and only increase, so in order to achieve (M-L-P-R-S) > 0, the only option is to increase M. This implies that agricultural science and technology parks, leveraging their financial, technological, and informational advantages, choose the option of single greenhouse sales income through advanced seed adoption. In this scenario, the industry-driven cooperation mode can be selected; otherwise, the agricultural science and technology park opts not to build greenhouses.

In the situation where farmers do not build greenhouses, whether the agricultural science and technology park builds greenhouses depends on whether the condition (G + N-R-P) > 0 can be satisfied. Here, the main consideration is the sales income N from single greenhouses under economies of scale conditions in the agricultural science and technology park and the intensity of government subsidies. Given the policies in China that strongly promote technological development and advance agricultural science and technology park construction, it is highly likely that this inequality will be satisfied. At this point, the development model falls under the government participation category.

4.3 Conclusion

Based on the analysis of the interests of both agricultural science and technology parks and farmers, the following conclusions can be drawn: when farmers choose to build greenhouses in agricultural science and technology parks, their optimal choice is not to build greenhouses. In situations where agricultural science and technology parks do not build greenhouses, farmers' behavior choices are primarily influenced by loan costs. In regions with relatively well-developed agricultural financial systems, the option of building greenhouses and adopting a market-oriented cooperation mode can be considered. If the management costs of forming a cooperative society for farmers are minimal, they can further opt for the agricultural cooperative society and market integration model. In cases where farmers choose to build greenhouses, if the single greenhouse income in agricultural science and technology parks is relatively high, the optimal choice for both parties is to build greenhouses, indicating an industry-driven cooperation mode. Otherwise, the agricultural science and technology park chooses not to build greenhouses.

In scenarios where farmers do not build greenhouses, given China's vigorous efforts to promote technological development and advance agricultural science and technology park construction, the choice for agricultural science and technology parks to build greenhouses may yield higher returns. In this context, the development model aligns with government participation.

5 Conclusion

Agricultural science and technology parks, as mediums for the conversion of scientific achievements, have been vigorously promoted by the nation. The notable achievements of Shandong Province's agricultural science and technology parks serve as a model and leading example for the construction of similar parks nationwide. Based on the evaluation results of the operational efficiency of Shandong's agricultural science and technology parks, it can be concluded that the overall operational level of these parks is relatively high. Over two-thirds of the regions in the province have achieved the highest level of element production utilization in agricultural science and technology parks, with high input-output ratios of technology and reasonable resource allocation. Through further analysis of the cooperation models and interest connection mechanisms between the 22 national agricultural science and technology parks in Shandong Province and farmers, the final findings reveal that the current predominant interest connection mechanisms are the "enterprise + farmers" and "base + farmers" models. The high-level construction of agricultural science and technology parks in Shandong Province may be closely linked to business operations. This aspect could be explored and analyzed further in future research.

By establishing the intelligent pig game model analysis, this paper concludes that the cooperation models and interest connection mechanisms between agricultural science and technology parks and farmers primarily fall into three categories: government-driven, industry-driven, and government participation. The selection of these modes is significantly influenced by factors such as farmers' financial environment for loans, the efficiency of information transmission by intermediary organizations, and the intensity of government support. Within the market-oriented cooperation model and interest connection mechanism, the government needs to enhance the rural financial system and provide a more diverse range of rural credit methods to alleviate farmers' loan pressure. In the industry-driven cooperation model, efforts should focus on strengthening the information transmission mechanism and platform for the conversion of agricultural technology achievements, facilitating successful agricultural outcomes. In the government participation development model, the government should increase support for various types of business entities and invest in scientific and technological funds to foster the conversion of agricultural technology achievements. The establishment of a solid relationship between agricultural science and technology parks and farmers' interests should prioritize the well-being of farmers and construct a more rational interest connection mechanism. Effective management of the distribution of interests with farmers is crucial in this regard.

References

1. Zhao, Y., Bu, F.: A systemic observation on agricultural technology achievement transformation. Guangdong Agric. Sci. **2009**(12), 340–342 (2009). https://doi.org/10.16768/j.issn.1004-874x.2009.12.103
2. Wang, S.L., Teng, Y.: Research on the coupling and interaction mechanism of subjects in agricultural technology achievement transformation. Sci. Technol. Manag. Res. **35**(11), 197–200 (2015)
3. Guo, L.S.: Analysis of the problems in agricultural technology achievement transformation (Part I). Chin. Agric. Sci. Bull. **2004**(04), 304–306 (2004)
4. Yu, K., Wu, S., Zhang, C.Y., Wu, Y.C., Chen, X.Y.: Development process, distribution characteristics, and inspirations of agricultural science and technology parks in Shandong Province. Sci. Technol. Manag. Res. **41**(01), 62–69 (2021)
5. Bai, L., Zhao, B.H.: Research on the selection of industrial poverty alleviation models and benefit connection mechanisms: a case study of edible mushroom industry development in Yixian County, Hebei Province. Hebei Acad. J. **35**(04), 158–162 (2015)

Analysis of Spatio-Temporal Evolution Patterns in the Green Development of Cluster-Type Cities: A Case Study of Zibo City in China

Minne Liu(✉)

Nanjing Normal University, Nanjing 210023, China
211302195@njnu.edu.cn

Abstract. The cluster-type city, characterized by a unique spatial configuration of relatively independent urban regions, grapples with substantial obstacles in its quest for high-quality urban development, a context in which the importance of green urban development has increased markedly. This research, taking Zibo City in China as an illustrative case, employs the Entropy Value Method-Technique for Order Preference by Similarity to Ideal Solution (TOPSIS) model to comprehensively gauge the degrees and spatio-temporal traits of urban green development across disparate districts and dissect influential determinants. The investigation's outcomes suggest that the levels of urban green development in all districts of Zibo City exhibit an overall undulating but ascending trajectory, with regions of high value chiefly centralized and areas of low value dispersed in the northern and southern zones. The weighted examination of indicators at each tier unveils that high-quality economic development and the extent of environmental construction serve as substantial catalysts in bolstering resource utilization efficiency, thereby playing a pivotal part in the city's green development. Zibo, as both an industrial city in transition as well as a regenerative city, confronts disparities and challenges in its urbanization progress.

Keywords: Urban Green Development · Entropy Approach-TOPSIS Modeling · Cluster-Type Cities · Urban Sustainable Development

1 Introduction

In the span of the last three decades, China's urbanization process has undergone swift growth, elevating the urbanization rate from 26.42% in 1990 to 63.89% in 2020 [1]. However, the crude development strategy has engendered problems such as resource squandering [2], environmental contamination [3], and excessive exploitation and irrational configuration of land use [4]. Considering that green sustainable development refines the structure of land use and alleviates the discord between urban progression and ecological conservation, promoting green urban sustainability has grown paramount in China's current urbanization stage. During the 19th National Congress, the state unveiled the paradigm of transitioning China's economic development from high-speed to high-quality, prioritizing high-quality urbanization as the fundamental transformational goal and the prospective course of urban evolution to achieve sustainable city development of a high caliber [5]. Simultaneously, the report from the 19th National Congress emphatically called for the execution of green development principles and the advancement of ecological civilization construction to address the clash between urban progression and environmental preservation [6].

The principal aims of this research are two-fold: (1) to scrutinize the spatio-temporal evolution patterns of green development levels in small and medium-sized cities from a micro-perspective, and (2) to investigate the characteristics of Zibo's green development as well as the key factors impacting its progression. This study serves as a foundational reference, facilitating balanced and sustainable development across economic, social, and ecological spheres within the city. The implications of this research are not limited to the sustainable development of Zibo City alone but extend to offer valuable insights for other small and medium-sized cities.

The notion of green development first emerged through the work of Boulding in 1966 [7]. This was subsequently amplified at the 2012 United Nations Conference on Sustainable Development (UNCSD), where green development was underscored as a conduit for fostering human equity, amplifying societal well-being, and mitigating environmental risks. A pivotal theme emphasized a reduction in capital consumption and the elevation of human capital as levers for stimulating economic growth, thereby spotlighting investments that prioritize environmental responsibility and resource efficiency [8]. Concurrently, ecologist Shijun Ma proposed a theory centered around socio-economic-natural complex ecosystems and spearheaded research into green development [9]. Moreover, the "green economy" concept, initially proposed by environmental economist David Pearce, has seen substantial development, thereby further advancing the discourse on this subject [10].

A cluster city is characterized by its composition of multiple clusters, each exhibiting relative autonomy and possessing an independent center with distinct functionalities [11]. The genesis of these cluster cities typically follows nature-oriented, resource-oriented, or policy-oriented mechanisms [12]. Resource-oriented cluster cities, in particular, confront issues of resource depletion and industrial transformation as they strive for sustainable development, as well as disparities in regional development. Consequently, examining the green development of resource-oriented cluster-type cities holds significant research value and representation.

Chinese scholarly discourse on urban green development levels has predominantly concentrated on macro-regions or city clusters, encompassing cities within the Yangtze River Economic Belt [13], city clusters situated in the middle reaches of the Yangtze River [6], eco-functional zones dominating Heilongjiang Province [14], cities located in Jiangxi Province [8], and development zones found in the Lanxi City Cluster [15]. However, the exploration of green development levels within individual regions of third- and fourth-tier cities remains significantly underdeveloped. Consequently, this study pivots its focus towards Zibo City, a locale distinguished by its characteristics of being both a cluster-type city and a regenerative city. This city confronts formidable challenges regarding its urban green transformation and pursuit of sustainable and efficient development.

2 Study Area and Research Methodology

2.1 Study Area

Zibo City, situated in East China and nestled in the middle of Shandong Province, straddles the Luzhong mountainous area and the North China Plain, displaying a topography that descends from the southern highlands to the northern lowlands. It comprises five districts—Zichuan, Zhangdian, Boshan, Linzi, and Zhoucun—and three counties—Huantai, Gaocheng, and Yiyuan—with the Zhangdian District serving as the governmental seat. As of 2021, Zibo's inhabitants represent 4.63% of the province's population, while its Gross Domestic Product (GDP) accounts for 5.06% of the provincial GDP. Additionally, its urbanization rate has reached 74.27%, and the city's GDP growth rate for 2021 stood second in the province, signifying it as a key player in Shandong Province's economic advancement. Being a regenerative city and an old industrial base in China, Zibo has the distinction of being the country's first city to be designated as a demonstration area for industrial transformation and upgrading. Hence, Zibo's level of urban green development is both representative and exemplary. This study, therefore, concentrates on the coupled and coordinated research of urban green development and urban land-use efficiency in Zibo City, with the aim of exploring sustainable urban development pathways and providing a scientific basis for urban development decision-making.

2.2 Urban Green Development Level Indices

This research, drawing upon relevant literature [12, 16] and aligned with the urban functional spaces of production, ecology, and lifestyle, adheres to the principles of scientific rigor, data accessibility, and accuracy. Consequently, the evaluation index system of the green development level has been constructed, focusing on three dimensions: green production, green ecology, and green life within the districts and counties of Zibo City. The specifics of this system are detailed in Table 1. Green development assesses the economic transformation level within the study area, incorporating indicators of economic development, pollution emission, and energy utilization. Meanwhile, green ecology evaluates the degree of regional environmental construction, and green life gauges the quality of the regional living environment.

2.3 Data Sources and Preprocessing

Following the guiding principles outlined in the 18th National Congress (2012), "to embark on a new path of urbanization with Chinese characteristics," and the 19th National Congress (2017), "to implement the concept of green development and promote the construction of ecological civilization," this study chooses the years 2014–2018 as the period of investigation. This selection enables an intuitive analysis of the serial effects of urban green development and land-use change. The data for evaluation indicators were sourced from the Zibo Statistical Yearbook, Zibo National Economic and Social Development Statistical Bulletin, and other such documents (2015–2022). Missing data were estimated using trend and interpolation methods, and the data were subsequently preprocessed through normalization.

Table 1. Evaluation indicator system for the green development level of districts and counties in Zibo City.

Target Layers	Standardized layer		Indicator layer
Evaluation of the level of urban green development in Zibo city	Green Manufacturing	Quality of economic growth	GDP per capita growth rate
			Percentage of secondary industry
			Percentage of tertiary industry
			Per capita disposable income
			General public expenditure
			Tax situation
		Pollution emission intensity	Industrial effluent discharge per unit GDP
			Industrial dust per unit GDP
			Industrial SO2 per unit GDP
			General industrial waste generation per unit GDP
		Resource utilization intensity	Total electricity consumption per unit GDP
			Total water consumption per unit GDP
			Built-up area per unit GDP
	Green Eco-Systems	Environmental construction	Area covered by greening
			Green space
			Number of parks
			Annual rainfall

(*continued*)

Table 1. (*continued*)

Target Layers	Standardized layer		Indicator layer
	Green Living	Green Behavior	Per capita water consumption
			Per capita electricity consumption
		Living environment	Population density
			Green space per capita
			Urban road space per capita

2.4 Entropy Approach-TOPSIS Modeling

TOPSIS (Technique for Order Preference by Similarity to Ideal Solution) is a method utilized for ranking data, gauging their proximity to the ideal solution based on the normalized values of the indicators. This approach assesses a system's level of development by calculating the Euclidean distance between the system's actual state and the ideal state [6]. Conventionally, the TOPSIS method primarily relies on expert judgments to assign weights, rendering the evaluation outcomes susceptible to human subjectivity. In contrast, the entropy weight method determines weights in line with the dispersion degree of different indicators, promoting objectivity in assignment [17]. By integrating insights from the relevant literature [6, 11–13], this study employs an entropy weight method-TOPSIS model, derived from the entropy weight method, to assess the level of urban green development in each district and county of Zibo City. The procedure is outlined as follows:

(1) Define indicator weights.
(2) Compute the weighted normalization matrix.
(3) Identify positive and negative ideal solutions.
(4) Evaluate the distance between the assessment subject and the superior and inferior solutions.
(5) Ascertain the relative closeness to depict the level of urban green development.

To facilitate a more comprehensive comparison and assessment of the level and spatio-temporal evolution of urban green development in Zibo City, this study organizes the calculated results of the green development levels of various districts and counties in ascending order on a year-by-year basis. Using the natural breakpoint method, the green development levels within Zibo City are classified into five grades. The foundations for these corresponding grades are presented in Table 2.

Table 2. Evaluation grade division of the urban green development level of districts and counties in Zibo city.

	Rank	1	2	3	4	5
Criteria	Score	(0,0.2381]	(0.2381,0.2851]	(0.2851,0.3291]	(0.3291,0.3883]	(0.3883,0.5808]
	value area	Low	Low	Medium	Medium	High

3 Empirical Results

3.1 Temporal Evolution Pattern of Green Development Levels of Districts and Counties in Zibo City

Utilizing the entropy weight method-TOPSIS model, this study evaluated the green development levels of each district and county in Zibo City from 2014 to 2021. Results indicate that the comprehensive green development index of each region within Zibo City demonstrated a general increasing trend from 2014 to 2021, though annual fluctuations were evident. From the perspective of the total green development comprehensive index, Zhangdian District, Linzi District, and Zichuan District presented high green development levels, while Boshan District, Gaocheng County, and Yiyuan County exhibited comparatively lower levels (see Fig. 1). Zhangdian District, as the urban center of Zibo City and a central transportation hub, possesses a robust economic base and city infrastructure. Over recent years, Zhangdian District has actively integrated new industries, continually promoting green development, resulting in its high green development level. Zichuan District and Linzi District, as old industrial bases of Zibo City, have made substantial progress in industrial transformation and ecological construction. By actively undertaking industrial transformation and ecological environment construction, these two districts have enhanced their green development levels. Conversely, Boshan District, located in Zibo City's southern mountainous region, has a relatively delicate ecological environment and outdated production capacities. The impacts of green development policies, such as retiring backward production capacities, are more pronounced in this district, leading to a lower green development level. Gaocheng and Yiyuan counties, mainly agricultural production areas with low industrial output, exhibit low urban green development levels due to their relatively weak industrial foundations.

The comprehensive green development index of Zibo City's districts and counties during the study period can be segmented into two phases (see Fig. 2). The first phase spans from 2014 to 2018, during which Zibo City's districts and counties actively enhanced investment attraction, augmented government fund investments, and fostered economic development. Concurrently, expenditures in ecological environment construction grew, notably increasing the urban green space, subsequently elevating the ecological environment construction score and creating a fluctuating upward trend in the green development index. Later in this phase, heavy industrial areas such as Zichuan District, Zhangdian District, and Linzi District witnessed increased industrial pollution emissions, population density, and electricity consumption, causing a decline in the green development index. Conversely, lighter industrial regions like Zhoucun District and Huantai

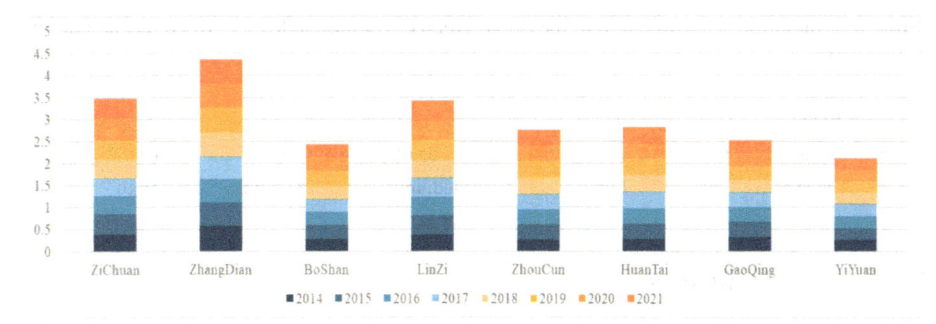

Fig. 1. Total level of urban green development in Zibo City by district and county.

County, endowed with superior ecological foundations and green development potential, saw steady progress in their green development levels. Overall, the enhancement of government funding and the strengthening of ecological environment construction under the new urbanization context positively influenced green development, with factors like industrial structure and population density also shaping the green development index trend across different districts and counties. After the 19th National Congress put forward the development directive of "implementing the concept of green development and promoting the construction of ecological civilization", Zibo City rapidly responded with a series of proactive measures, including the conversion of old and new kinetic energy and the "four increases and four reductions" three-year action plan. In the heavy industry sector, Zibo City curtailed crude steel and pig iron production, reduced coal consumption, and vigorously advanced the construction of green mines and geological restoration projects for closed mines. Besides, Zibo City continually encouraged the basic chemical industry to eliminate excess capacity. However, as Zibo City is an old industrial city, the transition from retiring excess capacity to a new type of industry significantly impacted its economy, especially as the chemical industry gradually became a pillar industry. This transition resulted in a decrease in the gross regional product of the districts and counties, affecting the quality of economic growth. Interestingly, in 2021, Zibo City's districts and counties completed the initial batch of new and old kinetic energy conversions, leading to economic recovery and quality enhancement. Simultaneously, in terms of environmental governance, Zibo City's districts and counties thoroughly implemented ten special activities for ecological and environmental protection, completed the task of air pollution control and scored higher in green ecology, further propelling the city's green development. Therefore, between 2019 and 2021, the overall fluctuating upward trend of Zibo City's districts and counties continued, with districts and counties like Linzi District and Huantai County reaching the peak value of the green development index.

Utilizing the entropy power method, an evaluation index system of urban green development was established for each region of Zibo City from 2014 to 2021. The findings revealed that green production within the urban production-ecology-life system had the most significant impact on green development, accounting for more than 50% annually.

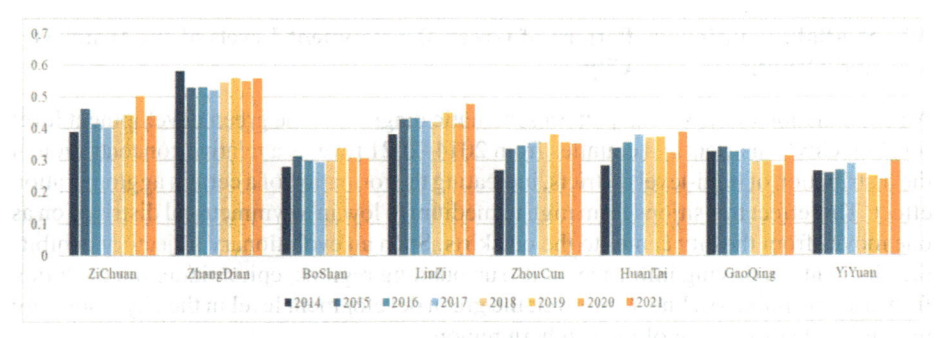

Fig. 2. Level of urban green development in Zibo City by district and county.

This demonstrates that transitioning urban production towards green production is pivotal for enhancing the level of urban green development. At the guideline layer, factors such as economic quality growth, pollution emission intensity, and environmental construction significantly influence the green development levels in the districts and counties of Zibo City. Furthermore, the weights of economic growth quality and environmental construction have been steadily increasing year by year. In contrast, the weights of pollution emission intensity and resource utilization intensity indicators have exhibited a negative correlation with the weights of economic growth quality and environmental construction. The weights of the remaining indicators have shown minor fluctuations. Conclusively, the level of urban green development in the districts and counties of Zibo City from 2014 to 2021 has been intimately tied to the quality of economic growth and the level of environmental construction (see Fig. 3). Improving high-quality economic growth and the level of environmental construction leads to enhanced resource utilization and a decrease in pollution emission intensity, thus fostering the city's green development.

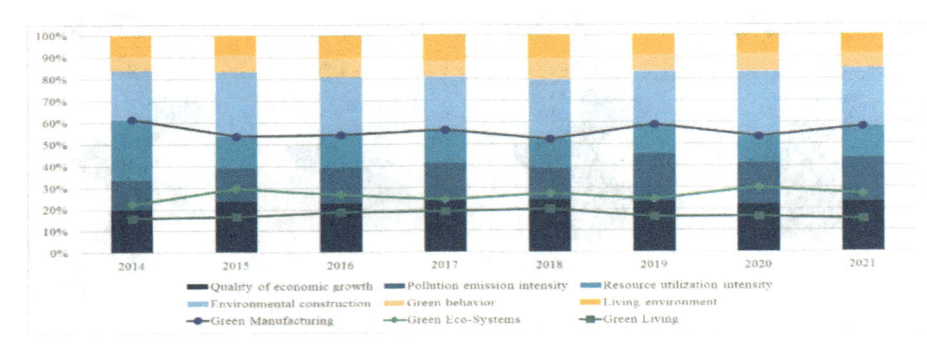

Fig. 3. Changes in the weighting of indicators in the green development level indicator system.

3.2 Spatial Evolutionary Pattern of Green Development Levels of the Districts and Counties in Zibo City

An examination of the spatial pattern schematic diagram of the green development level for Zibo City's districts and counties from 2014–2021 reveals a relative concentration in the distribution of high-level districts, indicating the formation of a certain agglomeration effect. This effect transitions from high to medium to low in a symmetrical distribution as one moves from the city center to the outskirts. Such an evolutionary trajectory exhibits the city center's driving influence on its surrounding regions, epitomizing the evolution from a single point to a line. Moreover, the green development level in the city's northern region is superior to that of the southern region.

As seen in Fig. 4, throughout the spatial-temporal shifts in green development from 2014 to 2021, an evident north-south disparity is observed in the level of green development among Zibo City's districts and counties. The number of high-level areas has expanded from two to three, primarily encompassing the city's economic hub and transportation nexus. Influenced by the city center, Huantai County and Zhoucun District have seen a steady augmentation in their green development levels, consolidating their status at the medium-high level. In contrast, Boshan District, Gaocheng County, and Yiyuan County oscillate between low levels of green development. Boshan District, an established industrial base, has achieved partial success in transitioning from excess capacity to newer industries. However, the fragile geographical environment and the diminishing radiation effect have resulted in significant fluctuations in its green development level.

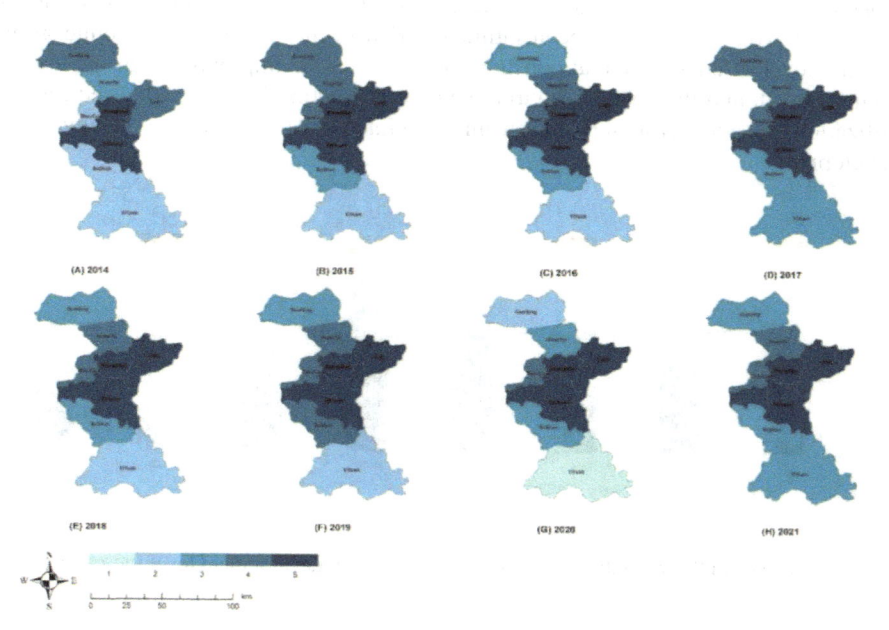

Fig. 4. Spatial pattern of the urban green development level of Zibo City by district and county.

Similarly, Gaocheng County, a leading agricultural producer with minimal industrial output, possesses a high ecological carrying capacity. Yet, due to ecological environment protection limitations, its green development level remains at a lower echelon.

The analysis of the disparate characteristics of Zibo City's green development levels indicates that these variances are influenced by a multiplicity of factors. The accelerated development of the central area catalyzes the enhancement of its peripheral regions. Conversely, districts and counties distant from the city center, which are impacted by restrictive factors, maintain a relatively low green development level. Collectively, a pronounced spatial imbalance in green development levels is apparent across Zibo City's districts and counties.

4 Conclusion

This study employs the Entropy Weight Method-TOPSIS model, comprehensively constructing an index system from the perspectives of green production, green ecology, and green life to measure the level of urban green development across districts and counties in Zibo City from 2014 to 2021. It quantifies the green development levels during this period and analyzes the spatial and temporal evolution patterns as well as trends of the primary indicators' weights, yielding the following key conclusions.

The yearly fluctuations in the level of green development among Zibo City's districts and counties from 2014 to 2021 are quite pronounced, demonstrating a generally oscillating upward trend. Within the study period, there was a decrease in low-level areas, an increase in medium-level areas, and a modest expansion in high-level areas. Zhangdian District consistently held the top rank for green development level among all districts and counties in Zibo City, with Zichuan District and Linzi District alternately securing the second and third positions. The level of green development in Huantai County has seen a gradual rise, consistently holding the fifth place across all districts and counties in Zibo City, whereas Boshan District, Gaocheng County, and Yiyuan County occupy the lower end of the ranking.

Between 2014 and 2021, there are notable regional disparities in the level of green development across the districts and counties of Zibo City. High-level areas are primarily located in the central region of the city, with the degree of regional green development decreasing from the city's center to its periphery. Simultaneously, the green development level among Zibo City's districts and counties reveals distinct spatial agglomeration characteristics. Zhangdian and Zichuan districts remain consistently within the high-level area throughout the study period, while Linzi District consistently holds a high-level status following its elevation to a high-level area in 2016. Huantai County and Zhoucun District progressively shifted from medium-level to medium-high level areas, while the remaining districts fluctuated between low and medium levels.

Based on the weights of the indicators computed via the entropy method, green production emerges as the pivotal factor influencing the green development level across districts and counties in Zibo City. This suggests that the transition towards green development in this old industrial city is primarily characterized by the guiding role of high-quality economic development, supplemented by environmental construction.

Going forward, there is a need to emphasize the directive role of high-quality economic growth, enhance resource utilization efficiency, and address pollution emissions, to facilitate efficient green development.

References

1. NBS China Statistical Yearbook (2020). http://www.stats.gov.cn/english/Statisticaldata/yearbook/
2. Fu, B.J., Zhang, L.W.: Land-use change and ecosystem services: concepts, methods and progress. Prog. Geogr. **4**(33), 441–446 (2014)
3. Fang, C.L., Yu, D.L.: Urban agglomeration: an evolving concept of an emerging phenomenon. Landsc. Urban Plan. **162**, 126–136 (2017)
4. Zhang, S.J., Liu, X.Y.: Spatial-temporal differences and influencing factors of urban land use efficiency in central plains urban agglomeration. Resour. Environ. Yangtze Basin **30**(10), 2417–2429 (2021)
5. Xie, X., Fang, B., Xu, H.Z.Y., He, S.S., Li, X.: Study on the coordinated relationship between Urban Land use efficiency and ecosystem health in China. Land Use Policy **102**, 105235 (2021)
6. Zou, L., Liu, H.: Regional difference and influencing factors of the green development level in the urban agglomeration in the middle reaches of the Yangtze River. Sci. China Earth Sci. **65**(8), 1449–1462 (2022)
7. Boulding, K.E., Jarrett, H.: Environmental Quality in Agrowing Economy: Essays from the Sixth RFF Forum. The Johns Hopkins Press, Baltimore (1966)
8. Xu, Y., Ouyang, W.H.: Dynamic measurement of the urban green development level and its influencing mechanism in Jiangxi Province. Resour. Environ. Yangtze Basin **31**(5), 1152–1168 (2022)
9. Ma, S.J., Wang, R.S.: The social-economic-natural complex ecosystem. Acta Ecol. Sin. **01**, 1–9 (1984)
10. Pearce, D.W., Anil, M., Edward, B.B.: Blueprint for a Green Economy. Earthscan, London (1989)
11. Zhang, R.J., Dong, H.Z.: Measurement of green development level of cities in the Yangtze river economic belt analyzing the spatial correlation structure. Stat. Decis. **38**(8), 118–123 (2022)
12. Zhang, Y.L., Wu, X.L.: Urban green development level and spatio-temporal difference of cities in the National Key Ecological Function Zones and adjacent non-ecological function zones. Acta Ecol. Sin. **42**(14), 5761–5777 (2022)
13. Wu, T.B., Sun, P.J.: Study on import trade potential and influencing factors of national woody forest products along "silk road economic belt." Areal Res. Dev. **40**(4), 32–38 (2021)
14. Zhao, Y.: Overall Urbanization Based Metropolis' Spatial Development: Dalian Case. Dalian University of Technology, Dalian (2014)
15. Xu, M.W.: Study on Gravity Model and Spatial Connection within Cluster Cities: Taking Zhongshan City, Guangdong Province, as an Example. South China University of Technology, Guangzhou (2022)
16. Li, G.D., Fang, C.L.: Quantitative function identification and analysis of urban ecological-production-living spaces. Acta Geogr. Sin. **71**(1), 49–65 (2016)
17. Wang, M.W., Chen, G.Y.: Entropy-based of set pair analysis model for optimization of land consolidation plans. Trans. Chin. Soc. Agric. Eng. **26**(6), 322–325 (2010)

Correlation Between Chinese Outbound Tourism Numbers and Chinese Outward Foreign Direct Investment Study
Development Insights in the Post-epidemic Era

Peili Yu(✉)

University of Pennsylvania, Philadelphia, PA 19104, USA
`peiliyu@sas.upenn.edu`

Abstract. Before the COVID-19 pandemic, the world's tourism industry maintained a steady growth trajectory, with an average annual growth rate of about 4%. Chinese tourists accounted for a larger share of world tourism market consumption. By 2013, China had become the world's largest outbound tourism market. According to data published by Statista, Chinese tourists accounted for 21% of the world's tourism spending 2016 (approximately US$261 billion), making them among the world's highest-spending international tourists. After entering the 21st century, the scale of China's outward foreign direct investment has increased and has been influenced by various factors. As the number of outbound trips increased following the improvement of the living standards of the Chinese people, the extent to which the tourism industry influenced China's outward investment also increased. This research investigates the relationship between the number of outbound Chinese travelers, a crucial indicator in the tourism domain, and its impact on Chinese outward foreign direct investment. Data from 26 countries across different continents were collected as the primary data source for this study. Through the research of mixed regression analysis and robustness test, it is found that the number of Chinese outbound tourists has a positive correlation with the impact of Chinese outward foreign direct investment. This outcome holds significant implications for informing China's Outward Investment policies and guiding global expansion strategies for enterprises in the post-pandemic era.

Keywords: Post-Epidemic Era · OFDI · Outbound Travelers · Spatial Patterns · Global Placement of Companies

1 Introduction

As a form of leisure and entertainment, tourism has an essential position in the development of society as a whole. Tourism can lead to the development of social benefits, and for nationals, they can expand their horizons and receive subtle education during their travels. For economic development, tourism drives the transformation and upgrading of consumer demand [1], promotes the development of new industries, boosts GDP to increase tax revenue, and promotes the transformation and upgrading of industrial structure. The government can continuously improve the improvement and modernization of the government service system according to the demand. With the increase in the number of Chinese outbound travelers, outbound tourism consumption has become a significant growth point of consumer demand, and this factor has a direct or indirect guiding effect on outward direct investment [2]. The COVID-19 epidemic lasted for several years and has impacted the world tourism industry and the pace of Chinese enterprises going abroad. In December 2022, China officially lifted control of the epidemic, Chinese people are gradually resuming outbound travel, and Chinese companies are gradually exploring and resuming outward investment. According to a report by the International Monetary Fund (IMF) in 2022, the epidemic significantly impacted the economies and employment opportunities of G20 member countries. The pace of China's outward foreign direct investment (OFDI) stagnated during the epidemic and has slowed in recent years due to a lack of overall strategy, among other reasons. The tourism-led growth hypothesis states that economic activity is affected by tourism in both the short and long term [3]. Therefore, exploring the impact of the number of Chinese outbound travelers before the epidemic on China's outward FDI will benefit the government in formulating policies to guide the development of the tourism industry and Chinese firms in exploring which countries to invest in.

The main research directions of the literature related to outward investment are the influencing factors of outbound direct investment [4], such as how the EU's FDI policy can correctly influence Chinese investment in the EU by changing the screening mechanism [5], as well as the current situation and problems of outward investment in the tourism industry, and the ways and choices of multinational operation of enterprises [6, 7].

On the one hand, existing articles focus on the outward direct investment of tourism [8]. Studies show that according to the spatial distribution analysis of data, the countries or regions of China's prominent foreign investment usually follow the order of the change of Chinese tourists' outbound travel destinations, and the funds change with the flow of people [9]. Moreover, foreign investment performance in foreign countries and regions, tourism is characterized by "trade first, then investment" [10]. There is also a bi-directional causal relationship between investment in tourism and international tourists, with increased investment driving tourism and vice versa [11]. According to Rasit's study on "10 ASEAN countries between 2004 and 2017", there is a positive correlation between foreign direct investment and tourism, and an increase in tourism will lead to an increase in foreign direct investment [3]. This theory helps assist the hypothesis of this paper.

On the other hand, in the study of tourism outbound investment choices. The "subject-motivator-process-effect" theory analyzes the tourism investment management of multinational corporations [12]. Li Xinjian and Cui Li mentioned in their 2013 article that the potential location of transnational (cross-border) operations is a prerequisite for promoting the rapid and healthy development of transnational (cross-border) operations of Chinese tourism enterprises [13]. When studying other countries, Jamaica, for example, was found to have a causal relationship between tourism expenditure and FDI inflows

[14]. Whereas, when studying the critical factors of inward FDI stock in the French hospitality sector, the results showed that bilateral FDI stock between France and investor countries is positively proportional to income and inversely proportional to the distance between them [15], a theory that will also be used as one of the references for the hypotheses of this paper.

These lines of research have mainly focused on the relationship between China's OFDI and other industries [16], with less attention paid to the relationship between China's tourism industry, especially the number of Chinese outbound travelers and China's OFDI. The existing literature focuses on the relationship between the two and the relationship between the tourism industry as represented by the hotel industry [17, 18], with more qualitative studies but fewer quantitative studies. Other tourism studies in the literature mainly focus on developed or tourism-oriented countries [19], and fewer studies link tourism to China's OFDI. This paper focuses on an essential variable in the tourism industry, the number of Chinese outbound travelers, and finds the relationship between China's OFDI and the number of outbound travelers as an influencing factor through the spatial and temporal distribution of the number of travelers and the quantitative distribution.

This paper will focus on the relationship between the major countries where the number of Chinese outbound travelers is located and the amount of Chinese outward direct investment these major countries received before the epidemic. By analyzing existing relevant studies and theoretical experiences, it will explore the definitions and influencing factors of the variables related to the number of Chinese outbound tourists, outbound countries, and Chinese outward foreign direct investment. The study will use preliminary data preliminaries that will constitute a short panel data analysis, followed by a mixed regression model constructed based on data and empirical tests, as well as a fixed effects test, to arrive at the results of the empirical analysis. The study's results will benefit the country in the context of the gradual recovery of China's outward foreign direct investment to strengthen the understanding of the associated influencing factors, from the macroeconomic and microeconomic aspects, for policymaking and policy adjustment to play a reference significance. At the same time, it will also be helpful to guide relevant enterprises to rationalize their global industrial investment layout in the post-epidemic era.

2 Model and Variable Setting

This paper focuses on the relationship between China's OFDI and the number of Chinese outbound tourists, and the potential influencing factors are processed and analyzed in the data, and a mixed regression model is selected for testing. The specific model is:

$$Y = \alpha + \beta_1 X + \beta_2 Z_1 + \beta_3 X * Z_1 + \beta_4 Z_2 + d \tag{1}$$

The dependent variable Y is China's direct outward investment flow, and the independent variable X is the number of Chinese outbound travelers in the country (region). The other variables Z_1 and Z_2 are the number of world heritage sites owned by the sample countries in different years and the continent where each country is located, respectively. In this model, according to the hypothetical situation, i.e., China's outward foreign direct investment is positively correlated with the number of outbound tourists. According to the existing data, it is hypothesized that the more Chinese outbound tourists in a country, the more direct investment of Chinese enterprises in that country will increase accordingly, so β1 in the hypothesis is positive. According to the attraction element in tourism, the number of local attractions will impact tourists' choices, so Z1 - the number of world heritage sites owned by the host country is explored as a variable. Usually, the more the number of world heritage sites, the more attractive it is for tourists, so β2 is assumed to be positive. Distance is an important consideration when tourists choose travel destinations, and this element is also applicable to Chinese tourists' outbound destination choices. Location will be more critical for outbound Chinese tourists when choosing travel destinations. The closer to China people will be relatively denser, showing the phenomenon of central agglomeration, so β4 is assumed to be positive (Table 1).

Table 1. Variable Name.

English Name	Chinese Name	Variable Explanation
Country	Country or area	Random area of countries selected as sample statistics
Year	Year	11 years of data from 2007–2017
Investment(Y)	China's outward investment	China's investment flows to specific countries or regions by year
Tourists(X)	China Outbound Tourism	Number of China's Outbound Tourism by country or region by year
No_heritage(Z1)	Number of World Heritage Sites	Number of World Heritage Sites by region to specific year
State(Z2)	Continents	Countries and regions are categorized differently according to the six continents
t*heritage(X*Z1)	Control Variables	Introduction of new control variables

Considering the addition of control variables to reduce the error, the X * Z1 variable is added to explore its relationship with Y. OLS regression, and fixed effects are used for short panel variable analysis. The empirical results are calculated by performing variable-by-variable control, and then the results are analyzed to conclude.

3 Empirical Testing

The empirical test is based on the existing data characterization and observable data to meet the requirement of non-repeating integers to determine that the test data constitute panel data. After the samples are individually numbered for each variable, the panel data structure is examined using Stata's xtdes, xtset commands. And the data examined in this paper constitute strongly balanced, which means balanced panel data. In this paper, $N = 26$, $T = 11$, N stands for 26 country data, T stands for 11 years of data, and $N > T$ constitutes a short panel data sample.

3.1 Mixed Regression

The selection criteria for modeling methods in Stata for panel data calculations usually depend on the type of dependent variable. In this paper, the variable pool is continuous variables in panel data. All individuals are considered to have the same regression formula, and there is no individual effect, which can be used to derive the measures using mixed OLS regression. Therefore, by constructing a mixed regression measurement model and substituting X, Z1, Z2, and X1 * Z1 as variables according to the formula to calculate their relationship with the dependent variable Y, respectively, the data are derived as shown in Table 2.

Table 2. Mixed regression results.

Variable	Investment-1	Investment-2	Investment-3	Investment-4
tourists	77.759*** (0.000)	75.769*** (0.000)	86.695*** (0.000)	86.695*** (0.000)
no_heritage		−1.52e+09** (0.014)	−1.33e+09*** (0.002)	−1.33e+09*** (0.002)
t*heritage			−84.04362*** (0.000)	−84.04362*** (0.000)
state				−1.90e+09** (0.042)
cons	1.47e+11 (0.5)	−1.04e+10 (0.964)	−5.83e+11*** (0.009)	−5.81e+11*** (0.009)
R2	0.9076	0.9088	0.9232	0.9232

Note: (1) *, **, and *** indicate significance at the 10%, 5%, and 1% levels, respectively (2) The test variables in the mixed regressions have less than 1% significance and are highly significant.

Analyzed explicitly from the perspective of the data of each variable, the situation is as follows

Tourists-China's Outbound Travelers: From the results in Table 2, the X variable of China's outbound travelers is significant at the 1% level with a p-value less than 1%. The coefficient of 86.695 is positive, indicating that the number of Chinese outbound tourists each year is closely and positively related to China's outward foreign direct investment. The number of Chinese outbound travelers positively and considerably impacts investment. The more outbound travelers, the more China's direct investment in the country. This is consistent with the actual situation, more Chinese outbound travelers, bringing more consumption and business opportunities, attracting Chinese enterprises to foreign direct investment.

no_heritage-Number of Natural World Heritage Owned by the Country: From the results (Table 2), the p-value of the variable Z1 for the number of world heritage owned by the destination country is less than 1%, i.e., significant at the 1% level. The coefficient is −1.33e+09, which indicates that the number of world heritage owned by the country is closely related to China's direct foreign investment. However, it is negatively correlated, i.e., the more world heritage owned by the country or region, the less China's direct foreign investment, which is inconsistent with the hypothesis. The reason is that the different thinking angles, according to the data, show that the more the country has world heritage, the less the Chinese investors can invest in the country's tourism attractions, so the direct investment is reduced, which is in line with the actual situation.

State-Tourism Destination Countries are Located in the Continent: According to the data assumptions, in addition to Antarctica, the remaining six continents are divided into 1–6 according to the distance from China (1 is the closest, 6 is the farthest, 1 for Asia, 2 for Europe, 3 for North America, 4 for Oceania, 5 for Africa, 6 for South America). From the results in Table 6-1, the p-value of the Z2 variable for the continent in which the destination country is located is less than 5%, i.e., significant at the 5% level. The coefficient is $-1.90e+09$, indicating a close but negative correlation between the continent where the country is located and China's direct outward investment. That is, the farther the country is from China, the smaller the amount of Chinese direct outward investment, which is consistent with reality. Cultural differences, policy differences, and international relations due to distance all impact Chinese OFDI [20, 21]. Generally speaking, the closer the distance, the closer the cooperation, the more able to enhance investors' investment confidence.

t*heritage-control Variables: From the results in Table 2, the p-value of the variable $Z1$, the number of Chinese outbound tourists arriving in the country X*the number of world heritage sites owned by the destination country, is less than 1% and significant at the 1% level. The coefficient is -84.04362, indicating that this control variable is closely related to the dependent Y.

3.2 Robustness Test

The underlying assumption of the mixed regression is that there are no individual effects, and to test this assumption, fixed effects are used to test with fixed effects for the Z2 continent when the data for the study of this paper has been calculated as a balanced panel. Repeated experiments are conducted by changing the parameters to explore whether the results remain relatively consistent and stable. From the data in this paper, the aim is to examine whether the test results remain significant after adjusting the classification criteria and whether the sign and significance change and if they do not, then they are robust.

The data were analyzed in comparison with the variables derived from the direct mixed regression to determine that the data needed to constitute a one-way fixed effect. This method allows for excluding time effects in constructing the fixed effects model. Excluding the time effect is mainly because the research in this paper does not consider the impact of time change on the study's results. Although the time trend in studying the economic development of countries and political relations is essential, this paper has been utilized to form a larger sample of data panel data to abate the impact of time. Therefore, only the continent Z2 is fixed, and the test results indicate that there is no significant change in the significance (see Table 3), which is manifested in the

Table 3. Fixed effects test results.

Variable	Investment-1	Investment-2	Investment-3
tourists	73.254***	76.233***	95.852***
	(0.000)	(0.000)	(0.000)
no_heritage		−1.51e+09	−6.38e+08
		(0.231)	(0.350)
t*heritage			−71.56233**
			(0.020)
cons	−1.29e+09**	1.51e+10	7.05e+09
	(0.025)	(0.257)	(0.353)
R^2	0.8161	0.4957	0.7368

Note: (1) *, **, and *** indicate significance at the 10%, 5%, and 1% levels, respectively (2) The independent variable x variable in fixed effects is significant at 1%, which is highly significant. (3) The introduced control variable t* heritage is significant at 5%, again with high significance.

fact that there is still a significant positive correlation between the number of outbound tourists from China in X variable and China's OFDI and the new variable formed by multiplying the number of outbound tourists arriving from China to the country X and the number of world heritage sites owned by that destination country in Z1 variable is still showing strong negative correlation significance. Slightly different from the mixed regression results is the measurement of the number of world heritage sites owned by the destination country Z1, which is insignificant. However, the negative coefficient is the same as that presented in Table 2 and has no significant impact on the overall robustness determination.

4 Conclusions and Policy Recommendations

4.1 Conclusion

From the data and empirical analysis in Tables 2 and Table 3, it can be seen that among all the variables, the X-variable, the number of Chinese outbound tourists, has the most significant impact on China's direct outward investment and presents positive coefficients and a significant p-value of 1% in both the OLS mixed regression and the fixed-effects test, which suggests that the number of Chinese outbound tourists has a significant positive and relevant linear relationship for China's OFDI. This paper draws on the theoretical constructs of previous literature, finds breakthroughs, and constructs relatively sound theoretical assumptions. At the same time, this paper utilizes data from 26 countries for 11 years from 2007–2017, constitutes panel data, and conducts an empirical test to analyze the impact of the number of Chinese outbound travelers on China's direct outward investment. After introducing time using the fixed-effects test and eliminating the time-series effects, the data results show a strong positive correlation between the number of Chinese outbound travelers and the two relevant variables of China's foreign direct outward investment. That is, the more the number of Chinese outbound travelers, the more China's outward foreign direct investment in the country.

The Chinese government vigorously pursued the "going out" strategy before Covid-19, especially encouraging Chinese enterprises to invest abroad. In the post-epidemic era, the number of Chinese direct foreign investments and Chinese outbound tourism has gradually increased and recovered. The study of the correlation between the two and their temporal and spatial factors provides a reference value for the formulation of China's macro policy and the micro-Chinese enterprises to go global better. At the same time, studying the distribution of continents and the correlation with the number of people can better help the Chinese government to formulate policies for investment risk assessment and market regulation and is also conducive to the adjustment and formulation of outbound development strategies by Chinese enterprises [22, 23].

4.2 Policy Recommendations

To effectively guide the outward investment of Chinese enterprises in the post-epidemic era and expect to realize the excellent effect of China's outward investment, this paper gives the following reference suggestions based on the results of empirical tests:

Encourage Tourists to Travel Out of China: Encourage Chinese tourists to travel out of China by formulating policies and publicity guidance. This will be helpful to encourage more Chinese investors to strengthen outward investment and enhance the confidence of Chinese enterprises to invest in the foreign market. At the same time, expanding the number of Chinese outbound travelers will help enhance the world's indirect understanding of China. This will indirectly attract more foreign tourists to travel to China, boosting China's domestic tourism market [24], forming a virtuous cycle of foreign investment within and outside the country and China's outward investment [25], and enhancing the ability to withstand economic risks in the post-pandemic era.

Rationally Guiding Investment Destinations: The Chinese government can formulate a list of investment destinations and incentive policies, improve outbound risk assessment and standardize investment criteria [26, 27]. This will help Chinese investors better understand the local cultural, legal, and political situation and learn more about the policies of countries or regions outside China regarding inward investment. Studies have shown that the difference between home and host country business environments is essential in enterprises' foreign outward direct investment (OFDI) location choice [28], and different political parties also influence investors' choices [29]. These reasonable ways of guiding investment destinations will help attenuate the decline of tourism attraction and investment attraction affected by distance, enhance Chinese enterprises' understanding of and confidence in the destination countries, and optimize the spatial structure of enterprises' global layouts.

References

1. Dai, B.: The internationalization of tourist enterprises and the research into their operations. Tour. Sci. 18–21 (2000)
2. Qin, Y.: Several implicit assumptions that outbound tourism drives the hotel industry's transnational operations. Tour. Tribune 8–9 (2011)

3. Rasit, N., Singkong, F., Aralas, S.: Tourism and foreign direct investment: an analysis for Asean countries. Malays. J. Bus. Econ. (MJBE) **6**, 283 (2020)
4. Götz, M., Jankowska, B.: On some aspects of state-owned enterprises' foreign direct investments (SOEs' FDI): the case of Polish SOEs' FDI (2017)
5. Rencz, F.: The determinants of Chinese foreign direct investment in the European Union. Asia Europe J. (2023)
6. Dikova, D., van Witteloostuijn, A.: Foreign direct investment mode choice: entry and establishment modes in transition economies. J. Int. Bus. Stud. **38**, 1013–1033 (2007)
7. Li, X.: New Theory on Transnational Management of China's Tourism Industry. China Economic Press, Beijing (2010)
8. Liu, M., Tang, J.: Research on "going out" path and mode of tourism enterprises in China. Econ. Geography 153–156 (2012)
9. Bao, F., Zhu, M.: An analysis of the characteristics and related factors of China's foreign direct investment in tourism industry. Commercial Res. 173–177 (2017)
10. Li, X., Yan, J., Chen, Y.: Characteristics and countermeasures of foreign investment of Chinese tourism industry. Resour. Dev. Market 225–227, 207 (2014)
11. Nonthapot, S.: Causality between capital investment in the tourism sector and tourist arrivals in ASEAN. J. Adv. Res. Law Econ. 2504–2511 (2017)
12. Song, C., Li, X.: A review and prospect of tourism transnational investment and operation. Tour. Tribune 134–144 (2018)
13. Li, X., Cui, L.: A study on potential locations of Chinese tourism company transnational/cross-border operation. Tour. Tribune 118–126 (2013)
14. Sarialioğlu Hayali, A., Küçükosman, A., Kpartor, K.: The relationship between foreign direct investment and tourism sector: the Jamaican case. Uluslararası İktisadi ve İdari İncelemeler Dergisi (2021)
15. Cró, S.R., Martins, A.: Foreign direct investment in the tourism sector: the case of France. Tour. Manag. Perspect. **33**, 100614 (2020)
16. Zheng, L., Liu, Z.: Spatial pattern of Chinese outward direct investment in the Belt and Road Initiative area. Progress Geography 563–570 (2015)
17. Ramón-Rodriguez, A.: Determining factors in entry choice for international expansion. The case of the Spanish hotel industry. Tour. Manag. **23**, 597–607 (2002)
18. Falk, M.: A gravity model of foreign direct investment in the hospitality industry. Tour. Manag. **55**, 225–237 (2016)
19. Chen, L., Tao, T.: Effects of inward investment on outward investment in international hotel industry. Bus. Manag. J. 131–144 (2014)
20. Huang, S., Cantwell, J.: FDI location choice: the role of locational ambidexterity. Multinatl. Bus. Rev. **25**, 28–51 (2017)
21. Song, C., Shi, S., Chen, J., Nijkamp, P., Li, X.: The influence of emigration on tourism outward foreign direct investment: evidence from China. J. Travel Res. **59**, 004728751984643 (2019)
22. Guo, T., Yi, R.: Thoughts on establishing the mechanism of prevention and control of overseas investment risk. Nat. Resour. Econ. China 29–31 (2013)
23. Song, T., Qian, X., Xue, J.: Risks and countermeasures of Chinese enterprises' overseas investment under the belt and road initiative. China Foreign Investment 38–40 (2022)
24. Li, T., Liu, J., Wang, L., Zhu, H., Yu, L.: Spatial differences in international investment in hotels and its driving factors in China. J. Geographical Sci. 1904–1919 (2017)
25. Fu, X., Buckley, P., Fu, X.: The growth impact of Chinese direct investment on host developing countries. Int. Bus. Rev. **29**, 101658 (2019)
26. Song, J.: Discussion on the current situation, problems and strategies of China's tourism foreign direct investment. Pract. Foreign Econ. Relat. Trade 80–84 (2019)
27. Wang, P.: The opportunities and challenges of china's foreign direct investment under the background of the belt and road initiative. Contemp. Econ. 11–13 (2017)

28. Qian, X., Liu, D., Huang, L., Li, H.: Distance of doing business and outward foreign direct investment: an empirical study of China. Rev. Dev. Econ. **26** (2022)
29. Lu, K., Biglaiser, G.: The politics of Chinese foreign direct investment in the USA. J. Asian Afr. Stud. **55**, 002190961987481 (2019)

Volatility Analysis Using High-Frequency Financial Data

Junchi Wang(✉)

Central University of Finance and Economics, Beijing, China
`2021310329@email.cufe.edu.cn`

Abstract. Stock market, whose total size exceeds 10 billion dollars, have boomed in the past few decades, becoming a crucial indicator of global economy. It is universally acknowledged that high-frequency data, stock price for instance, fluctuates dramatically during market crash as well as other financial events, creating numerous volatility clusters and jumps, which makes volatility analysis arduous and burdensome. Based on previous academic researches concerning Time Serie Momentum and Asset Pricing, I select several typical days with extreme financial events and conduct some empirical works such as analyzing RRV distribution of those days and calculating correlation coefficients, concluding four characteristics of the data including irrelevance, fat-tail and asymmetry, leverage effect and volatility clustering, and categorizing them to better unfold its overall distribution. My statistical works provide stock investors with an exhaustive and clear overall understanding concerning stock price volatility, helping them make better investment decisions and eventually receive better return during their stock investment.

Keywords: Stock price · volatility analysis · realized log return

1 Introduction

The total size of the world stock market has exceeded 10 billion dollars by the end of 2021, making it a non-negligible part in the world's financial system, significantly contributing to regions' social and economic developments. Thus, it's vital to study the factors of stock price fluctuation so as to stabilize the stock market as well as the global economy.

High-frequency data, as its name implies, is a set of data with a short interval of time, accurately reflecting the variation tendency. There are numerous buying and selling operations during trading time that only high frequency data provide us comprehensive and timely market information. Empirical analysis regarding stock market is mostly based on second-per-second stock price data.

2 Literature Review

Empirical asset pricing has long been concerned, analyzed by several methods including machine learning and deep learning. Besides, innumerable earlier essays focused on high frequency data modeling. Here's my literature review about stock market's theories, which can instruct my work.

Based on stocks' price, Moskowitz, T. and Yao, H. proposed Time Serie Momentum Theory, mentioning that each investment tool's excess return over the past 12 months provides investors with a positive indicator of its future returns, and the momentum of this time series partially reverses over longer periods of time. 'A heterogeneous portfolio of time series momentum ruses across all asset categories has provided numerous outlier returns, which is virtually unaffected by standard asset pricing factors, and performs best in extreme markets [1].' Besides, asset pricing included systematic risks, intriguing by four industry factors according to Pelger, M.: a market portfolio, an oil sector, an financial sector, and an power sector, both equally weighted. 'Stocks' exposure to these risk factors changes over time. These four consecutive factors bring intraday risk premiums, which could reverse overnight [2].' Additionally, similar to my empirical research, Pavel Savor and Mungo Wilson found that days with significant macroeconomic news often contain aberrant asset prices' behaviors. 'Additionally to an attractive increase in the average return on risky assets on announcement days, both the cross-sectional and time-varied return patterns are in accord with standard asset pricing theory. On days like these, stock market beta correlates closely with average returns [3].'

What's more, researchers using machine learning embodied special forecast on measuring assets' risks. 'We ascertain the optimum methods (trees and neural networks) and track their indicative tone-ups to allow for nonlinear divinable interactions ignored by other methods. All approaches approve on the same dominant set of indicative signals, including changes in momentum, volatility and liquidity [4].'

As for the researches regarding asset returns, Jeremiah Green summarized several characteristics during 1980–2014. 'We draw the conclusion that during 1980–2014, although 12 characteristics are independent determined factors in consecutive stocks as a whole, the accuracy of predictive return fell sharply in 2003, causing just two independent characteristics were seen as determinants from then on [5].' 'Looking empirically at the largest set of current 193 company characteristics, we conclude that our E-LASSO forecasts engender conspicuous cross-sectional out-of-sample R2 gains and consistently cause innumerable economic value [6].'

3 Empirical Analysis

3.1 Data Descriptions

The data I use in this scientific research is from Wharton Research Database, known as WRDS, regarding the second-by-second stock price data for each trading day between 2007 and 2014. I downloaded high-frequency prices of SPDR (ETF tracking the S&P 500 index) during these 8 years and then preprocess the data.

The S&P 500 Index is a broad market index released by S&P that reflects the overall market situation in the US stock market, which is one of the most vital indexes in US financial market, just as Dow Jones Industrial Average and Nasdaq Composite. Due to its wide selection of sample stocks, dispersed industries, good representativeness, and scientific and reasonable compilation methods, the S&P 500 is more favored by investors as a broader index than the other two, and is often used as a benchmark to measure investment performance.

The S&P 500 Index contains 400 industrial stocks, forty utility stocks, twenty transportation stocks, and forty financial stocks focused on significant exchanges in the United States. Based on 1942, the base period index is 10. At present, the index has risen above 2000 points.

My data includes 2014 trading days and each day contains 23401 trading seconds, corresponding to share price per second from 9:30 to 3 pm. To better substantiate my further conclusion, I preprocess the data by filling the gap using the last second's stock price and finally I get a stock price matrix with no vacancy value.

Bryan Kelly used IPCA method for the cross section of returns, enabling latent factors and time-varying loads to measure unobservable vigorous loads by introducing observable characteristics. 'Examining returns and features at the stock level, five IPCA factors has been found to elucidate the cross section of average returns more accurately than existing factor models and generate trivial and statistically insignificant abnormal intercepts associated with features [7].'

To better demonstrate the data concerning the returns of the stocks, I calculate log returns (LR) by taking the log on the prices and take the difference. Besides, I also get the realized volatility (RV) matrix, the squared log return, taking the difference every 100 s. Therefore, I can calculate relative realized volatility (RRV) matrix for following research. The equations are as follows.

$$LR_{T+1} = \log(price_{T+1}) - \log(price_T) \quad (1)$$

$$RV_{T+100} = \sum_{i=T+1}^{T+100} (LR_i)^2 \quad (2)$$

3.2 Visualizing the Log Returns and Realized Volatility in the Short Run

An Ordinary Day. On January 3rd, 2007, there was nothing happen during trading period, and log returns and RRVs of that day remained at relatively small figures. According to the graph below, log returns kept the values around 0 for the whole day and there was almost no abnormal point except at 10am. Moreover, most RRVs fluctuated around 1, demonstrating significant stability, making slight jumps during the beginning as well as the end of the day, which mostly controlled under 5 (Figs. 1 and 2).

One FOMC Announcement Day. On the FOMC announcement day, the committee will announce macroeconomic policies and the current socio-economic situation, which will affect the emotions of stock investors and finally reflects on stock price. On September 16th, 2008, the Federal Reserve acknowledged the increasing pressure on financial markets and hinted that it would consider lowering interest rates in the future. The FOMC considered that the credit squeeze, ongoing housing market contraction, and

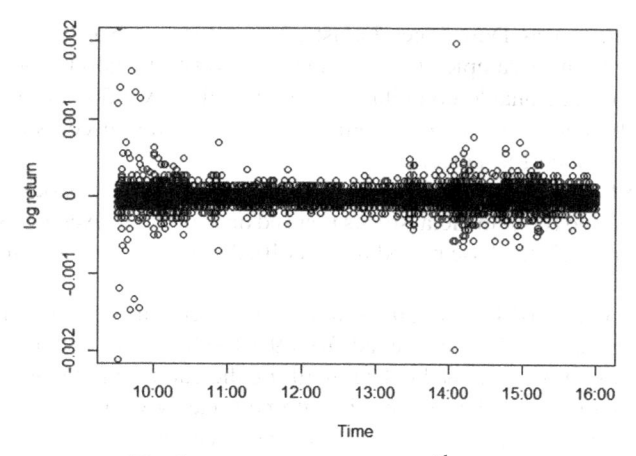

Fig. 1. Log return of January 3rd, 2007

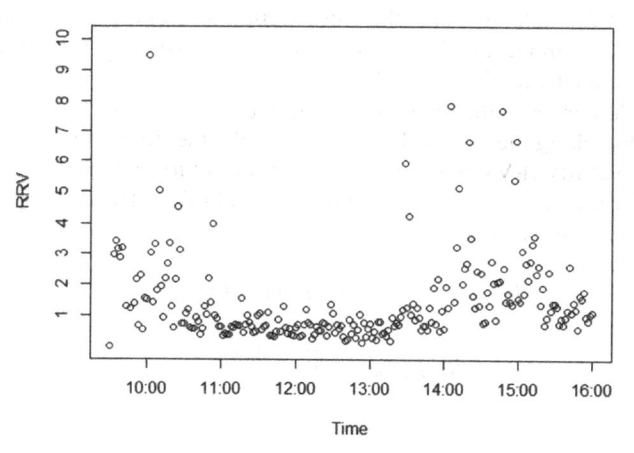

Fig. 2. RRVs of January 3rd, 2007

slowing export growth might drag down economic growth in the coming quarters. The announcement indeed intrigued negative market sentiment among shareholders. From these plots below, the log returns intensively distributed between plus and minus 0.001, often accompanied by jumps, which could reach to 0.005. RRVs were also quite unstable, mostly distributing from 1 to 3, while extreme values could approach 10, presenting more jumps and clustering than usual (Figs. 3 and 4).

The Flash Crash. On the flash crash day, one simple Thursday in 2010, the U.S. stock market experienced a sudden storm, and the Dow Jones industrial average, the beacon of global stock markets, plunged madly by nearly 1000 points, an unprecedented range. The flash crash began at nearly 3pm, leading to unstable stock prices (Fig. 5).

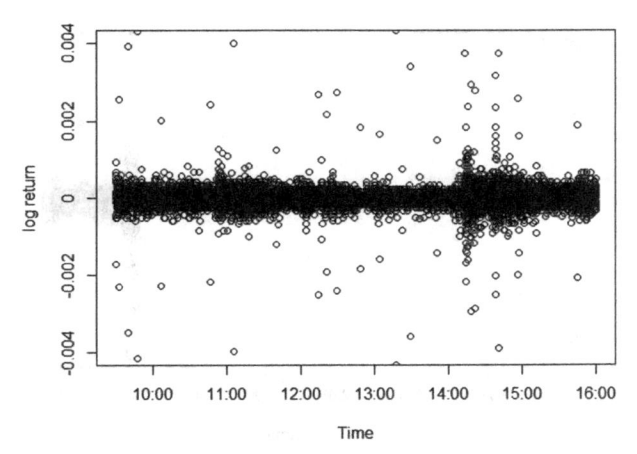

Fig. 3. Log return of September 16th, 2008

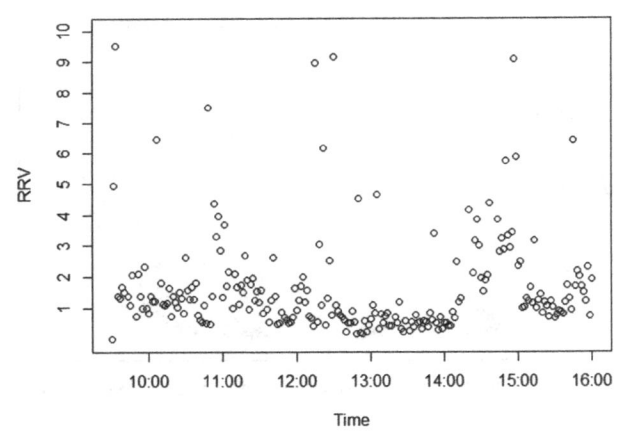

Fig. 4. RRVs of September 16th, 2008

According to the graphs, log returns exploded at 3pm and its maximum reached almost to 0.01. After that the log returns gradually stabilized, but still fluctuated from −0.002 to 0.002, embodying that the whole stock market was crashed dramatically. Meanwhile, the RRVs also presented this trend. RRVs remained under 2 before the flash crash happened at 3pm, and suddenly rose to nearly 16, keeping severe fluctuation until stock market closing (Fig. 6).

3.3 Summaries of High-Frequency Data Feature

The lag characteristics of mid to low frequency indicators are often quite obvious, which means that the frequency of mid to low frequency data is often at least monthly and usually only released in the middle of the second month. If used to analyze changes in economic and financial operations, it cannot reflect the latest situation. In contrast,

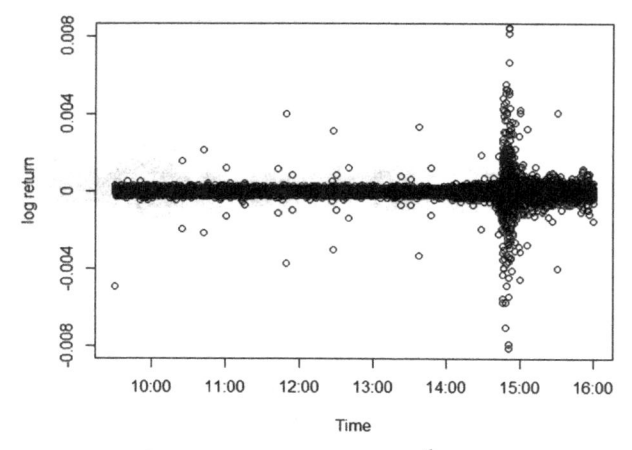

Fig. 5. Log return of May 16th, 2010

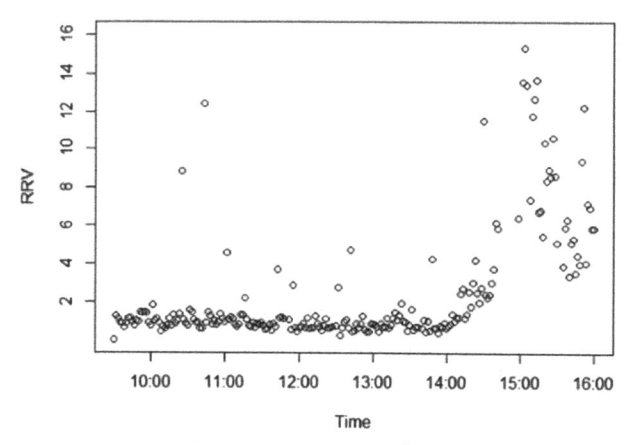

Fig. 6. RRVs of May 16th, 2010

high-frequency data are often used to observe or track short-term changes in economic operation, and based on this, in order to effectively reduce the dependence of researchers and decision-makers on mid to low frequency data and help to obtain more accurate conclusions.

To comprehensively understand these high-frequency data, I explore 5 features including irrelevance, fat-tail, asymmetry, volatility clustering/ jumping and leverage.

Irrelevance. For irrelevance, it's clearly to observe that the returns of asset prices at different time have very little correlation. Based on my second-per-second data, I decompose two time series per day. One time series get one day's log returns from second 1 to second 23400. The other series get the same day's log returns from second 2 to second 23401.

Then I calculate the correlation coefficient between these two series for this day. I repeat for all the dates to have a time series of correlation coefficients, and plot it for visualizing my work. In this scatter plot, each point represents one single day, and there are 2014 points in this plot. The horizontal axis of the scatter plot is the year, from 2007 to 2014, and the vertical axis is the covariance. The correlation of time series is definitely irrelevant as the points in the plot are evenly distributed between −0.5 and 0 without showing anywhere clustered (Fig. 7).

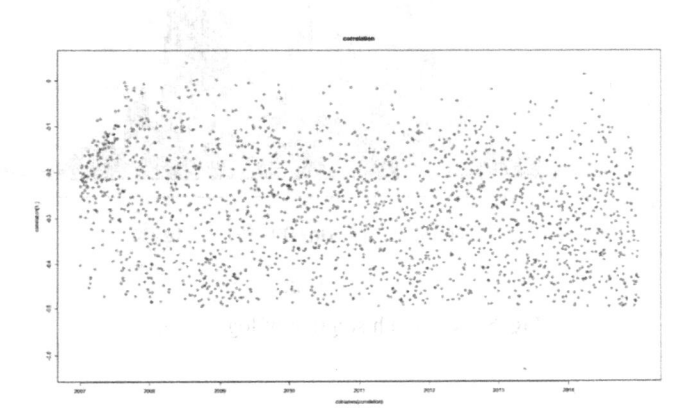

Fig. 7. Scatter plot of each day's correlation coefficient

Fat-Tail and Asymmetry. Fat-tail theory, also known as heavy-tail theory, indicating that empirical return distributions have thicker tails and more peaked centers than the standard normal distribution. Besides, observable returns are mostly asymmetric in favor of large deviations from the mean, showing a non-symmetric distribution of empirical return.

The following graph is the revised histogram of log returns between 2007 and 2014. The horizontal axis of the plot represents the year, and the vertical axis shows us the frequency of each group, which is separated by 0.01. The original log returns contain a large number of values near zero, resulting in the shape and scale of the histogram is not obvious, so I delete the absolute value less than $1e-04$ in the data to make the histogram more prominent. At the same time, I limit the value of the x-axis to between $-2e-04$ and $2e-04$ to make the fat-tail phenomenon significant. As for fat-tails, there are two obvious fat-tails, peaks in other words, distributing around $-7e-05$ and $7e-05$ in this graph. After eliminating those clustered data near zero, the fat-tails can be seen clearly and this histogram plot doesn't demonstrate the standard normal distribution (Fig. 8).

The graph below is also the histogram of log returns, and I process the data. In order to present the overall characteristics of log returns, this graph contains a much larger x-axis range than the previous graph. Meanwhile, I also delete values near 0 and exclude data with absolute values less than $4e-04$. It can be clearly seen from the graph that the histogram is not symmetric about 0, and there is a significant distribution difference between the left and right parts (Fig. 9).

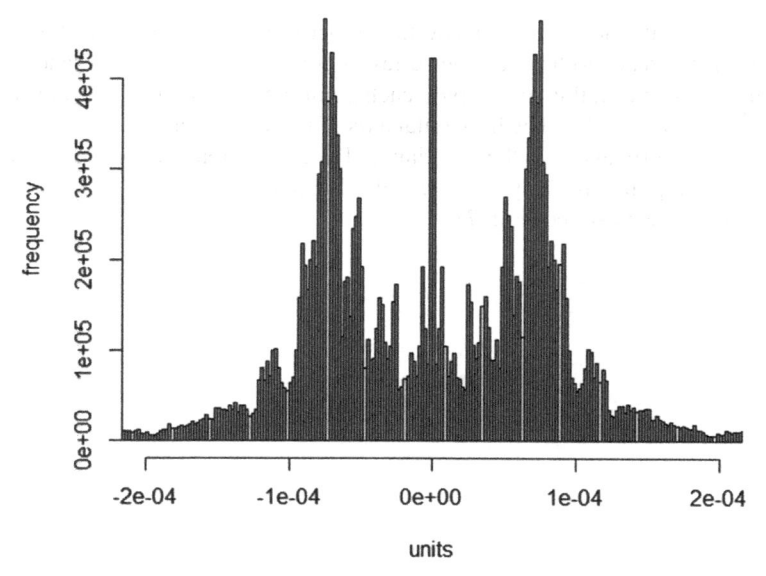

Fig. 8. Revised histogram of log returns

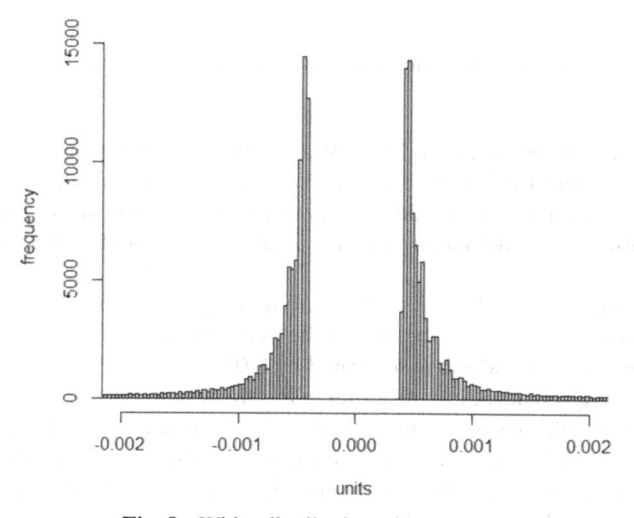

Fig. 9. Wider distribution of log returns

Leverage Effect. Leverage effect is a technique used by investors when purchasing stocks. Investors can use leverage to purchase more stocks and amplify their returns, while facing greater investment risks. The advantage of stock leverage effect is that investors can purchase a large number of stocks with less capital and obtain higher returns in a short period of time.

I have cumulative daily RVs and daily log returns by adding this data second-per-second, and I calculate the correlation between these two series over the whole 7 years. The result is -0.06062731, a negative number whose absolute value is close to zero, signifying the weak negative correlation between these series, which also proves that when future volatility is supposed to be high, return tends to be negative.

Volatility Clustering/Jumping. The changes in financial asset prices often follow large fluctuations, while small fluctuations follow small fluctuations, indicating that their fluctuations have a positive correlation. The analysis of the phenomenon of stock market volatility clustering in the academic field has deepened our understanding of the impact path and transmission mechanism of market volatility. Volatility clustering refers to the phenomenon where high and low volatility in the stock market often aggregate at a certain time period, and periods of high and low volatility aggregation alternate. In addition, the volatility of the stock market also exhibits asymmetric characteristics, that is, the impact of the positive and negative returns on future volatility is not symmetrical: generally speaking, when the return is negative, future volatility is more likely to change.

At present, academic research on stock volatility clustering mainly uses ARCH model and GARCH model to fit the volatility of stock prices. As for me, I've introduced a new metric called relative realized volatility, which is derived and calculated from realized volatility. It's obvious that RRV can measure the degree of change in asset investment return rate, and when RRV is large, volatility looks like jumped. The definition of RRV is as follows.

$$RRV_T = RV_T / (median\ of\ the\ RV\ over\ 5\ days) \qquad (3)$$

I do select some days and analyze the RRVs of those days. It's universally acknowledged that days whose RRVs clusters and jumps are extremely special. Thus, I select four days with significant financial events, market shocks, including Lehman Brothers bankruptcy, Chinese market crash, one FOMC announcement day and The Flash Crash, whose RRV plots have remarkable volatility clusters and jumps.

On the first day, the Lehman Brothers, with a history of 158 years, filed for bankruptcy, which triggered a chain reaction that led to chaos in the credit market. It can be seen from the figure that the RRVs remained stable around 0 for most of the trading day, with few jumping outliers. It is clearly that the points went up and down after 3pm, when the Lehman Brothers clarified their bankruptcy, representing big fluctuations in stock market. The volatility clustering was significant, as several large outliers were followed by a series of smaller RRVs' jumps (Fig. 10).

The second day happened a similar financial event: on February 27th, 2007, more than 900 stocks fell by the limit, and there were still more than 800 stocks on the limit at the close of 3 pm. Chinese stock market experienced a gigantic crush.

The figure below is that day's RRVs. It's obvious that at the beginning of the trading day, the RRVs fluctuated slightly between 0 and 1, but returned to calm around 10:15 and remained stable around 0. At 2 pm, the stock market crashed, and the RRVs in the picture soared up and down, with a maximum value far exceeding 10, and the volatility continued until the close of the market (Fig. 11).

On June 19th, 2013, one FOMC announcement day, 2pm was a breaking time that the Federal government declared to change the interest rate, leading a strong fluctuation

Fig. 10. RRVs of Lehman Brothers bankruptcy

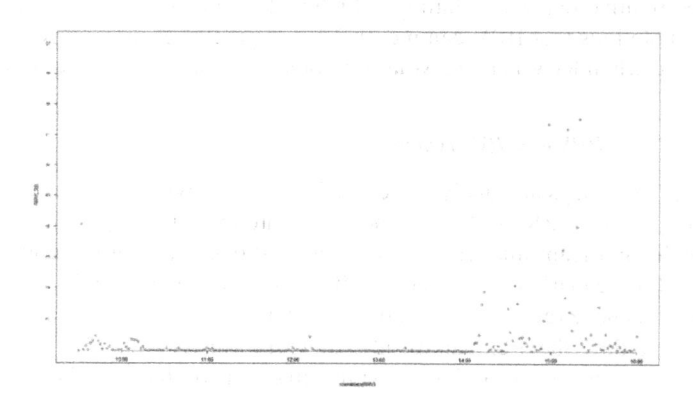

Fig. 11. RRVs of Chinese market crash

to the stock market, causing huge swings on that day's RRV plot. As usual, before the announcement was released, RRV performed very stably. After 2 pm, there was a significant fluctuation in the RRVs, and there was a significant clustering of fluctuations with the maximum around 1, showing a stepwise downward trend (Fig. 12).

Mentioned in part 3.2.3, on the flash crash day, the U.S. stock market experienced a sudden storm, which began at nearly 3pm. The graph below showed prominent volatility clustering, as big fluctuations followed with small jumps. It can be seen that RRVs reached at 4 at the beginning of the market crash. Then numerous smaller RRVs fluctuations followed and jumped between 0 and 0.5 (Fig. 13).

It is still a major question that whether RRV is a good candidate in exploring volatility clustering. Thus, it's crucial for us to look at RRV in a more macro perspective.

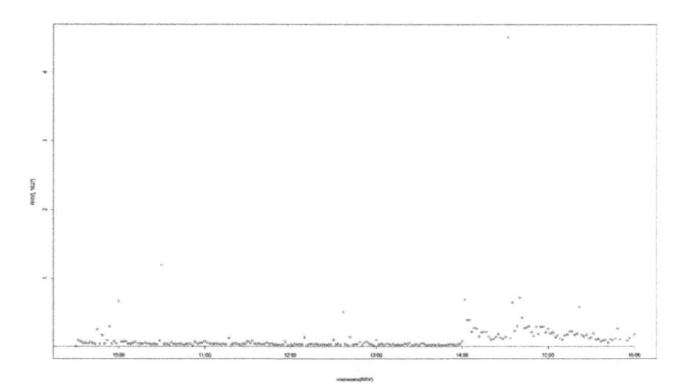

Fig. 12. RRVs of one FOMC announcement day

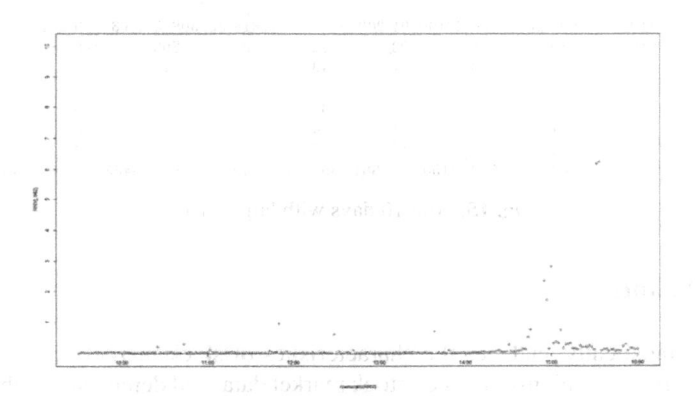

Fig. 13. RRVs of the flash crash

3.4 Overall Empirical Distribution of RRV

To better figure out the overall distribution of RRV, I gather all trading days between 2007 and 2014, containing 2014 days of price data. Like what I have done before, I calculate the RRV of these days, getting a matrix of 2014 days and 23401 s of each day. Then, I draw frequency histograms of all RRVs in the matrix. The distribution of RRV is skewed to the right, with the maximum value nearly 20000. There are 422 days whose maximum RRV is over 1000 and 130 days whose maximum RRV is over 2500 (Fig. 14).

Moreover, I select top 10 days where I have the largest RRVs in it, and I create a table with RRV intervals for better demonstration. As shown in the table, the maximum RRV on April 12, 2011 reached 20803.61, with a total of three days where the maximum RRV exceeded 10000. Observing the distribution of RRV over these days, it can be observed that the vast majority of RRVs are maintained at a very small level every day, ranging from 0 to 2.5. However, there are also a few abnormal values of large RRV, and the maximum RRV is accompanied by several smaller fluctuations in RRV. The distribution of RRV from 2.5 to 100 in the table reflects this well (Fig. 15).

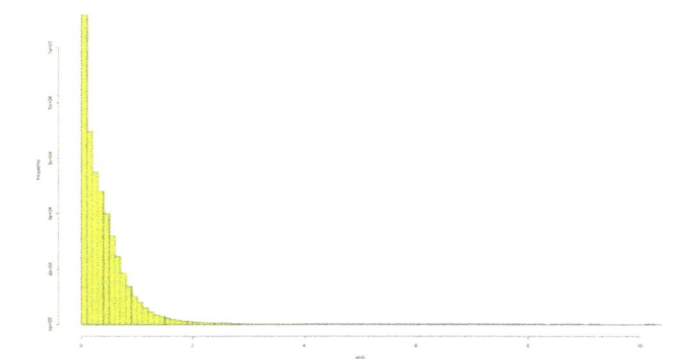

Fig. 14. Overall frequency histogram of RRV

Date	20110412	20090602	20121126	20100901	20080929	20110818	20130815	20081006	20140304	20111109
[0,2.5)	219	219	208	203	122	185	208	186	205	208
[2.5,5)	8	5	13	17	43	13	15	11	13	13
[5,10)	5	4	2	2	27	5	1	7	3	2
[10,100)	0	5	6	1	32	10	3	15	2	5
[100,1000)	1	1	4	1	4	10	2	2	0	0
Over 1000	2	1	2	11	7	12	6	14	12	7
Maximum	20803.61	20765.64	10553	9150.418	8814.355	8683.612	8658.672	8465.556	8031.402	7652.009

Fig. 15. Top 10 days with largest RRV

4 Conclusion

This paper statistically analyzes the characteristics of stock market prices, introduces four characteristics of high-frequency stock market data, and demonstrates the volatility clustering characteristics using the RRV research method. Finally, an overall analysis was conducted on the distribution of all RRVs from 2007 to 2014, providing a deeper understanding of the overall stock market, which can indeed help stock investors.

References

1. Moskowitz, T., Yao, H., Pederson, L.: Time Series Momentum. Chicago Booth: The Initiative on Global Markets, pp. 12–21 (2011)
2. Pelger, M.: Understanding Systematic Risk – A High-Frequency Approach (2020)
3. Savor, P., Wilson, M.: Asset pricing: a tale of two days. J. Financ. **113**, 171–201 (2014)
4. Gu, S., Kelly, B., Xiu, D.: Empirical asset pricing via machine learning. Rev. Financ. Stud. **33**, 2223–2273 (2020)
5. Green, J., Zhang, F., John, R.M.: The Characteristics that Provide Independent Information about Average U.S. Monthly Stock Returns (2016)
6. Han, Y., He, A., Rapach, D., Zhou, G.: Expected Stock Returns and Firm Characteristics: E-LASSO, Assessment, and Implications (2021)
7. Kelly, B., Pruitt, S., Su, Y.: Characteristics are Covariances: A Unified Model of Risk and Return (2018)

Can Environmental, Social and Governance Performance Alleviate Financial Dilemma?

Junyi Wang(✉)

School of Economics, Lanzhou University, Lanzhou, Gansu, China
wjydyxydyjz@163.com

Abstract. In the context of the increasing emphasis on sustainable development, enterprises, as integral components of society, play a crucial role in realizing sustainable objectives. ESG (Environmental, Social, and Governance) principles serve as a significant avenue for businesses to promote sustainable development. However, due to the external nature of ESG, many enterprises fail to prioritize its importance. This paper delves into the relationship between ESG and corporate financing constraints. Through an analysis of data from all A-share listed companies in China spanning from 2009 to 2020, the study concludes that ESG practices can significantly alleviate corporate financing constraints. This finding suggests that motivating companies to prioritize ESG fulfillment can yield positive effects on their financing capabilities. Additionally, this research contributes to a deeper understanding of ESG-related outcomes and sheds light on the influencing factors of financing constraints.

Keywords: ESG · Financing Constraints · Corporate Sustainability

1 Introduction

Since the Industrial Revolution, mankind's productivity and production technology have increased as never before, but this progress has also brought about an increasingly serious environmental, climate and resource crisis. Against this backdrop, people have begun to realize the need to cherish nature, and this increased awareness has received widespread attention from the international community [1]. Against this backdrop, corporate ESG (Environmental, Social and Governance) fulfillment has become one of the most important ways to achieve sustainable development. However, due to the externalities of ESG, many enterprises do not pay attention to it.

Currently, the ESG research literature covers a wide range of topics. There have been studies focusing on the impact of ESG on audit fees [2], on analysts' forecast accuracy [3], and on firms' financing costs through media monitoring [4], but there are fewer studies that directly investigate the impact of ESG on corporate finance costs. Therefore, this paper aims to fill this research gap. This paper utilizes the data of Chinese A-share listed companies from 2009 to 2020 to obtain that ESG can alleviate the financing constraints of enterprises.

The findings of this paper further enrich the relevant research on the consequences of ESG and provide a new perspective on the study of factors affecting corporate financing constraints. The findings suggest that a high level of ESG performance can alleviate corporate financing constraints and provide a low-cost source of capital for enterprises, and it is not just a moral obligation, but can bring real economic benefits to enterprises. Therefore, companies should realize the importance of ESG and incorporate it into their business decisions and strategic planning. This finding helps to promote the better application of ESG in practice and the realization of sustainable development.

This paper consists of 7 sections. The Sect. 2 is a summary of the relevant literature. The Sect. 3 explains this hypothesis in detail. The Sect. 4 mainly explains the samples, variable structure and data used in this paper. In the Sect. 5, we will discuss the conclusions and robustness verification of this paper, and conclude in the Sect. 6.

2 Literature Review

ESG refers to environment, society and governance. On the environmental front, companies need to focus on climate change, energy and resource use. On the social front, companies need to consider the interests of their stakeholders. In terms of governance, companies need to focus on the management structure, board of directors, and shareholder rights [5]. Therefore, ESG is not only a reflection of corporate social responsibility, but also have an important impact on the operation and financing constraints of a company.

The empirical results of Waddock and Graves show that CSR has a positive impact on the company's operating performance [6]. Li et al. showed that ESG information disclosure can effectively alleviate corporate financing constraints, and positive news reports can strengthen this [4]. Chen et al. found that ESG performance has a significant negative impact on the cost of equity financing and a positive impact on the cost of debt financing for firms [7]. Xiao et al. found that ESG assessment can effectively reduce the company's information and operational risks, thus reducing the auditor cost of the company [2]. At the same time, ESG can also reduce the financial pressure of enterprises [8] and improve the valuation of enterprises [9].

This review found that there is not enough empirical evidence in the existing literature to confirm the impact of ESG factor on corporate financing constraints. This is because the financing constraints is influenced by numerous factors. Therefore, further research is needed on the relationship between ESG and the financing constraints.

3 Hypothesis Development

Nowadays, more and more studies focus on the impact of ESG on corporate financing constraints, of which information risk and operational risk are two important research dimensions, because ESG is closely related to these two risks. The details are as follows.

ESG can reduce information risk and thus reduce the financing constraints. Eccles et al. found that introducing sustainability measures can reduce information risk by reducing agenda issues, improving corporate governance, and improving information quality [10]. Xu et al. found that the better the ESG responsibility performance, the stronger the sustainable competitive advantage, a competitive advantage that can help companies improve transparency not only in terms of surplus information, but also in terms of tone [11]. Xi and Wang found that ESG disclosure mitigates the risk of stock price collapse by reducing the degree of information asymmetry and reduces the risk of stock price collapse by reassuring investors [12]. The lower the information risk, the greater the trust investors have in the firm and the more willing they are to pay a higher price for the firm's stocks or bonds, thus reducing the firm's financing constraints.

ESG factors can also reduce operational risk, which in turn reduces the financing constraints. To avoid the negative consequences of low ESG ratings, such as share price volatility and higher costs, companies have an incentive to improve corporate governance and listen to the demands of various stakeholders, including employees, suppliers and customers, which leads to a reduction in operational risks and corporate irregularities [3]. Reduced operational risk for firms will make investors more willing to invest in the firm and will make it easier to obtain financing from financial institutions, thus reducing financing constraints.

Therefore, we draw a conclusion: ESG can affect financial constraints in two ways, namely, firm information risk and operational risk. The hypothesis, stated in alternative form, is as follows:

Hypothesis 1. *Ceteris paribus, ESG can reduce the financing constraints.*

4 Research Design

4.1 Sample Selection and Data Sources

In this paper, the data of A-share listed companies in China from 2009 to 2020 is selected as the preliminary sample, and exclude (1) financial enterprises and (2) ST*ST enterprises. The final sample consists of 33181 listed firms. The financial data involved in this article are all from Wind database and CSMAR database.

4.2 Empirical Model

The core objective of this study is to test whether ESG reduces the financing constraints of firms. To test the hypothesized mitigating effect of ESG on financing constraints, the following model is set.

$$FC_{i,t} = \beta_0 + \beta_1 ESG_{i,t} + \beta_i Controls_{i,t} + Industry + Year + \varepsilon_{i,t} \quad (1)$$

In the model, FC represents the degree of firms' financing constraints, ESG represents the level of firms' ESG ratings, Controls is a control variable, i and t represent different firms and years, Industry and Year are industry and year fixed effects, and ε is a randomized disturbance term.

4.3 Variable Definition

Dependent Variable. In the existing research, the financial restrictions of the company are measured as follows.

Single indicators, KZ index [13], WW index [14], SA index [15], Asset growth-cash flow sensitivity [16, 17], Cash-cash flow sensitivity [18].

This paper will use the SA index constructed by Hadlock and Pierce [15] to measure the company's financing constraints. Because the SA index contains two variables: IPO time and enterprise size, the SA index has strong externalities and can better avoid the endogenous factors and subjective factors among enterprises, and the conclusion is more robust; this theory adapts to the actual situation of China and is applicable to the national conditions of China [19, 20].

Independent Variable. Following Li et al. [4], we use the CSI ESG Rating as a proxy variable for ESG fulfillment.

CSI ESG Rating is a corporate ESG assessment system developed by CSI Data Institute. The rating system provides a comprehensive assessment of a company's ESG performance based on three dimensions: environmental, social and corporate governance. The rating criteria are divided into nine levels, and for the convenience of the study, the C-AAA levels are assigned 1–9 in this paper.

Control Variables. In order to eliminate confounding factors, improve internal validity, and enhance stability, so as to make more accurate interpretation and conclusion of the study, we add some control variables according to the existing literature. The specific control variables are defined and their values are shown in Table 1.

Table 1. Variable definition.

Variable Type	Variable Name	Variable Value Description
Explained Variables	Financing Constraints	Take the absolute value of SA $\left\| -0.737 \times \text{Size} + 0.043 \times \text{Size}^2 - 0.04 \times \text{Age} \right\|$
Explanatory Variables	ESG Rating Level	ESG rating of China Securities, assigned 1–9
Control Variables	Size	Natural logarithm of total assets at the end of the year
	PPE	Net fixed assets/Total Assets
	Lev	Total liabilities/Total Assets
	Indep	Number of independent directors/Total number of board of directors
	Board	Natural logarithm of the total number of board members

5 Empirical Results

5.1 Descriptive statistics Results

As can be seen from the descriptive data in Table 2, the level of financial constraints varies greatly. Meanwhile, the average score of ESG rating is 6.45, and the median is 6, that is, half of the enterprises' ESG ratings are lower than the average. The results indicate that the ESG levels of Chinese listed companies vary widely and there is still much room for improvement.

Table 2. Results of descriptive statistics.

Variable	N	Mean	SD	Min	p25	p50	p75	Max
SA	33181	−3.46	0.33	−4.15	−3.71	−3.44	−3.22	−2.43
ESG	33181	6.45	1.12	1.00	6.00	6.00	7.00	9.00
Size	33181	22.15	1.44	19.33	21.14	21.92	22.89	27.15
PPE	33181	0.21	0.17	0.00	0.08	0.18	0.30	0.71
Lev	33181	0.44	0.22	0.05	0.26	0.43	0.60	0.98
Indep	33181	0.38	0.07	0.25	0.33	0.36	0.43	0.60
Board	33181	2.29	0.26	1.61	2.20	2.30	2.49	2.94

5.2 Regression Results

Table 3 is an empirical analysis of ESG and corporate financing constraints. Column (1) is a regression with fixed effects of industry and year, and the result is −0.013, which is significantly negative at 1% level, which indicates that ESG can reduce the degree of financing constraints and validates hypothesis H1. In order to eliminate the influence of other factors on corporate financing constraints, column (2) is regressed again with the addition of control variables on the basis of column (1). The conclusion is −0.011, and significantly negative at 1% level, which shows that ESG can effectively reduce corporate financing constraints, further provides evidence for the hypothesis H1.

Table 3. ESG and financing constraints regression results.

	(1) SA	(2) SA
ESG	−0.013*** (−8.05)	−0.011*** (−6.84)
Size		−0.002 (−1.50)
PPE		−0.131*** (−11.15)
Lev		−0.272*** (−30.33)
Indep		0.361*** (15.36)
Board		−0.046*** (−6.72)
Constant	−3.381*** (−328.72)	−3.224*** (−97.51)
Industry	YES	YES
Year	YES	YES
N	33181	33181
r2_a	0.125	0.174

Note: *, * * and * * * indicate significance at the 10%, 5% and 1% level, respectively (two-tailed).

5.3 Robustness Test

In order to eliminate the effect of the epidemic on corporate financing restrictions, we exclude the data of 2019 and 2020, and take them as samples of empirical analysis, and get the following conclusions. In the column (1), the regression coefficient of ESG and financing constraints is −0.019, reaching a very significant negative value at 1% level. After adding the control variable in the column (2), the regression coefficient is −0.017, which reaches a very significant negative value at 1% level. This conclusion is consistent with the previous conclusion, which shows that the conclusion is correct (Table 4).

Table 4. Robustness test results.

	(1)	(2)
	SA	SA
ESG	−0.019***	−0.017***
	(−10.25)	(−8.85)
Size		−0.000
		(−0.03)
PPE		−0.130***
		(−10.23)
Lev		−0.295***
		(−30.12)
Indep		0.403***
		(15.45)
Board		−0.018**
		(−2.38)
_cons	−3.326***	−3.291***
	(−271.16)	(−90.33)
Industry	YES	YES
Year	YES	YES
N	25475	25475
r2_a	0.124	0.180

Note: The t-values are shown in parentheses. Here *, * * and * * * indicate significance at the 10%, 5% and 1% level, respectively (two-tailed).

6 Conclusion

Under the guidance of the idea of sustainable development, how to realize sustainable development is a very critical issue. Based on China's A-share listing data from 2009 to 2020, this paper empirically analyzes ESG on corporate financing constraints, and finds that ESG has a significant reduction effect on corporate financing constraints. Based on the conclusion of this study, companies should actively fulfill their environmental obligations, proactively release environmental information related to environmental protection, promote the development of the company in the direction of "green", and empower the company's high-quality development, so that the company can actively participate in environmental protection, climate governance, and charitable donations, so that it can obtain the support of external funds and resources and achieve the goal of sustainable development of the company.

References

1. Mei, X.Q.: Search up and down: the innovative spirit of environmental history. Soc. Sci. Front (03), 79–86 (2020)
2. Xiaofang, L.F., Wen, S., Hao, X., Huayu, S.: Do ESG ratings of listed companies affect audit fees? – a quasi-natural experiment based on ESG rating events. Audit Res. (03), 41–50 (2021)
3. Luo, K., Wu, S.: Corporate sustainability and analysts' earnings forecast accuracy: evidence from environmental, social and governance ratings. Corp. Soc. Responsib. Environ. Manag. **29**(5), 1465–1481 (2022)
4. Li, C.B., Shao, Y.M., Li, Z.Z., Li, M.S.: ESG disclosure, media monitoring and corporate financing constraints. Sci. Decis. **07**, 1–26 (2022)
5. Rau, P.R., Yu, T.: A survey on ESG: investors, institutions and firms. China Financ. Rev. Int. (2023)
6. Waddock, S.A., Graves, S.B.: The corporate social performance-financial performance link. Strateg. Manag. J. **18**(4), 303–319 (1997)
7. Chen, R., Zhao, X., Jin, H.: The impact of firms' ESG performance on their financing cost. Sci. Decis. Making **304**(11), 24-4 (2022)
8. Wang, L., Lian, Y., Dong, J.: A study on the mechanism of ESG performance on corporate value. Securities Market Herald (05), 23–34 (2022)
9. Wang, B., Yang, M.: A study on the mechanism of ESG performance on corporate value - empirical evidence from A-share listed companies in China. Soft Sci. (06), 78–84 (2022)
10. Eccles, R.G., Ioannou, I., Serafeim, G.: The impact of corporate sustainability on organizational processes and performance. Manag. Sci. **60**(11), 2835–2857 (2014)
11. Xu, X., Qiao, P., Huang, Q.: Can ESG responsibility performance convey more transparent information? Ind. Econ. Rev. **55**(02), 5–21 (2023)
12. Xi, L.S., Wang, Y.: Corporate ESG disclosure and stock price collapse risk. Econ. Issues (08), 57–64 (2022)
13. Lamont, O.C.P., Saa-Requejo, J.: Financial constraints and stock returns. Rev. Financ. Stud. **14**(2), 529–554 (2001)
14. Livdan, D., Horacio, S., Lu, Z.: Financially constrained stock returns. J. Financ. **64**(4), 1827–1862 (2009)
15. Hadlock, C., Pierce, J.: New evidence on measuring financial constraints: moving beyond the KZ index. Rev. Financ. Stud. **23**(5), 1909–1940 (2010)
16. Guariglia, A., Xu, L., Song, L.: Internal finance and growth: microeconometric evidence on Chinese firms. J. Dev. Econ. **96**(1), 79–94 (2011)
17. Zhang, J., Lu, Z., Zheng, W.-P., Chen, C.-Y.: Financing constraints, financing channels, and corporate R&D investment. World Econ. (10), 66–90 (2012)
18. Yu, W., Wang, M., Jin, X.: Political affiliation and financing constraints: information effects versus resource effects. Econ. Res. (09), 125–139 (2012)
19. Ju, X.S., Lu, D., Yu, Y.H.: Financing constraints, working capital management, and the persistence of firm innovation. Econ. Res. J. **1**, 4–16 (2013)
20. Jiang, F.X., Shi, B.B., Ma, Y.B.: Information releasers' financial experience and corporate financial constraints. Econ. Res. J. **6**, 83–97 (2016)

Reinforcement Learning for E-Commerce Dynamic Pricing

Hongxi Liu[✉]

Foothill College, Los Altos Hills, CA, USA
2932513173s@gmail.com

Abstract. With the quick development of artificial intelligence technology, it has been applied in many fields. Motivated by applications in financial services, we consider a seller who offers prices sequentially for online products, to maximize the long-term revenue, as well as increase costumers' satisfaction. This paper investigates how reinforcement learning methods can help optimize profits for e-commerce. We model the dynamic pricing problem as a Markov decision process and apply two reinforcement learning methods: Q-learning and Sarsa for pricing. Then, we give three predetermined demand models: linear-, quadratic- and exponential models with a variety of learning rates for numerical experiments. Results suggest that Q-learning has better performance than Sarsa as it achieves higher profits and lower volatility except the learning rate is 1.

Keywords: Dynamic Pricing · E-Commerce Platform · Reinforcement Learning · Pricing Strategy

1 Introduction

With the development of the Internet, online sales have become an integral part of our lives. E-commerce (short for electronic commerce) allows people to buy and sell goods or services on the Internet. Changes in the price of goods or services are an important issue which will also have an impact on consumers' shopping in the shortest time and directly affects companies' long-term profits. In the past, when retailers made pricing decisions and sales strategies based on the previous supply and demand of goods, as well as their experience. When they wanted to change prices, they had to write down the price on the tags. This takes a lot of time and effort. Retailers might not be able to adjust prices immediately, which may lead to profit loss. However, in recent decades, companies can collect online data and then analyze consumers' shopping habits and interests, and simultaneously adapt prices to meet consumers' needs. Consumers can obtain information about the items and easily compare prices of similar items on different e-commerce platforms. To maximize long-term profit, pricing correctly and quickly is crucial for retailers.

One popular method to solve this problem is dynamic pricing. It is the study of how demand responds to prices in a changing environment. It has been successfully applied in many industries such as hotel booking, airline ticketing, car rental and electricity. Nowadays, it has also been applied in emerging industries such as e-commerce (i.e., Amazon), and taxi services (i.e., Uber, Lyft). With the continuous development of artificial intelligence technology, increasingly more literature has investigated to use AI to solve dynamic pricing problems. Reinforcement learning (RL) is one of the most widely used technologies. It is a powerful tool in decision making, about learning the optimal behavior in an uncertain environment to obtain the maximum reward. In the RL framework, the agent (i.e., learner and decision maker) continually interacts with the environment (i.e., everything outside the agent). Thus, optimal behavior is learned through interactions with the environment and observations of how it responds. The decision-making problem is normally modeled as Markov decision processes (MDPs). Here, the agent selects actions based on the greedy policy.

In this paper, we investigate two commonly used approaches in RL: Sarsa and Q-learning. Sarsa is an on-policy value-based approach, that is, it is an updated based on the current policy. While Q-learning is an off-policy approach, and it is updated rule by the optimal policy. The policy we applied is ϵ-greedy policy, where ϵ is called the exploration rate. The greedy policy's principle tells the agent to take the action that can yield the highest expected rewards in the short-term and makes sure the next greedy policy is as good as or better than the current greedy policy. This action-selection rule is to choose the best action with probability $1 - \epsilon$ or choose a random action with the probability ϵ.

Our contributions can be summarized as follows. First, we set up an MDP model to solve the dynamic pricing problem on the e-commerce platform. Second, we consider three scenarios, assuming demand follows linear, exponential, and Poisson distribution models. Our results show the overall performance of Q-learning is better than Sarsa.

2 Literature Review

2.1 Revenue Management and Dynamic Pricing

Dynamic pricing applies the real-time dynamic adjustment to the price of an item to maximize revenue. This technique adapts itself from the studies of pricing and demands. Cournot introduces static price setting [1], then Evans proposes an alterable pricing strategy in his monopoly research. Simaan & Takayama then introduce variables in consideration of the relationship between price and supply [2, 3]. This development gives dynamic pricing an advantage to acquire greater speed in terms of pricing based on demand and consumption, which ensures the business remains competitive in the market. Den Boer for a comprehensive review including the historical origins, current development, and future directions of dynamic pricing [4].

Revenue management (RM) is an important pricing policy designed for perishable inventory, with staggering success in many industries that faces overbooking problems. Littlewood establishes the inventory control rule with two independent fares (as known as Littlewood's rule), and this rule indicates that discount fares are acceptable for booking if the revenue of the future full fare is exceeded, which marks the beginning of RM [5]. Then the success of RM broadens its influence, which finds concrete evidence in American Airline's annual report, as is shown by the approximately 1.4 billion dollars increase in the company's revenue during the last three years, and hence the expansion of business applications and research in this field. We refer to Belobaba for more account of the origin of RM, who also introduces a multi-period generalized version of Littlewood's equation [6]. The textbook by Talluri & van Ryzin provides further detailed explanations of the theories, applications, and overviews of RM [7].

Dynamic pricing is later introduced to revenue management to solve capacity control and optimization problems and has been successfully applied in conventional industries such as hotels, airlines, and electricity Talluri & van Ryzin [7]. The airline industry is a notable example of its real-life applications. McAfee & Te Velde illustrate the theoretical applications of dynamic pricing in the airline industry and compare their results based on the data of actual airline companies [8]. The hotel industry has adapted dynamic pricing due to its similarities to the airline industry, for minimizing their daily availability will generate optimal revenues. Abrate et al. study how dynamic pricing has impacted the European hotel market and how the method has contributed towards profitability based on a variety of variables [9]. Dong et al. find their research based on optimizing computationally efficiently the initial inventory decision, which is useful to both industries [10].

The wiring of the world economic establishment is fundamental to e-commerce and allows merchants to sell their products to consumers without ever encountering them. This advancement brings both opportunities and challenges to modern businesses because they are now facing more competition and more consumers. The method of Dynamic pricing now shows its significance in these unpredictable markets, and accurately setting the price can now determine the survival of online retailers. Chen et al. studied how the market share of products on Amazon, one of the largest e-commerce platforms, has been affected by dynamic pricing algorithms [11]. Garbarino & Lee, explains how dynamic pricing will affect Consumer Trust and how the consumer may feel unsatisfied when the pricing is unstable [12].

2.2 Reinforcement Learning

Reinforcement learning (RL) is a popular technique that has been researched extensively for decades. It includes different methods functioning within the same environment as Markov Decision Process describes. The work of Sutton & Barto provides a detailed introduction to RL, which elaborates on developed definitions and descriptions of the polities, algorithms, pioneering research, as well as its historical foundation [13]. RL has been researched and applied broadly in the field of traffic control. The work of Wiering et al. presents a set of multi-agent model RL systems for the traffic light, and this adaptable RL model has preformed the traditional non-adaptable system in the face of increasing traffic load [14].

Markov decision process (MDP) describes the environment of RL, and indicates that the agent environment enter-phase base of its policies. The agent adapts and improves based on the information returned from the value returned by the environment. Howard introduces MDP [15]. Now it has been used to solve the single-fare overbooking problems of the airline industry, see Rothstein for further information [16]. Ge Monacan also establishes several models and algorithms of MDP in his work. Song & Liu apply MDP to determine the potential rewards of electricity supply bidding [17]. B¨auerle &

Rieder explore how MDP can be applied to finances [18]. We focus on the method of temporal-difference (TD) learning, which includes Q-learning and Sarsa. Q-learning is an on-policy TD algorithm, in which the agent selects and learns from the action of other policies. Watkins provides an introduction and sophisticated description of Q- learning [19]. The work of Hester et al. demonstrates how deep Q-learning can be applied in simulated games and showed its advancement compared to traditional reinforcement learning [20]. Sarsa learning is an on- policy algorithm of TD learning, which learns from the value derived from the current policy. For a detailed overview of Sarsa, we refer readers to Rummery & Niranjan [21].

RL can effectively assist and improve dynamic pricing, as it is the self-adaptive policy that enhances the optimizations of revenues under complex conditions, and the success is notable both in academic research and real-life applications. Gosavii et al. use reinforcement learning to find solutions to problems in the airline industry and simulate such real-life issues as sudden cancellations and overbooking [22]. Lee et al. develop an algorithm that can find the most efficient chairing process of electric-powered vehicles and thus increases the reliability of the power grid while reducing the charging cost for customers [23]. Narahari et al. discuss a reinforcement learning approach for a single seller-owned electronic business, and how RL can improve dynamic pricing compared to other models they have developed [24]. The work of Raju et al. simulates how reinforcement learning with limited observable information can still improve current issues for dynamic pricing in a retail market [25].

3 Methodology

3.1 Markov Decision Process

Markov decision process (MDP) is a RL technique, which observes epochs in the duration of time and selects from the finite set of states, denoted by $s \in \mathcal{S}$. When the state is confirmed this process will take one action a from $\mathcal{A}$, which $\mathcal{A}$ represents the finite set of actions a available, denoted by $a \in \mathcal{A}$. This process is the agent environment interactions of MDP, where the choice selecting agent applies the mapping policy π and observes the outcome after applying the actions a to the environment. Then the agent will recognize s into the next state $s_{t+1} \in \mathcal{S}$ or s', and receive the new reward $r_{t+1} \in \mathbb{R}$ or r'.

In MDP, the agent continually interacts with the environment. The agent at each step t receives a representation of the environment's state, s_t and it selects an action $a_t \in \mathcal{A}(s)$. Then, as a consequence of its action the agent receives a reward, r_{t+1}. The key idea is learning through interaction, as shown in Fig. 1.

During this interaction, the agent must follow a principle to take an action which is the policy. The agent's action-selection behavior can be described by a *policy*, given by $\pi(s \mid a)$. We define the *optimal policy* by $\pi_\star$, which generates at least one policies that is equivalent to or greater than the current policy. The total *reward* function is defined by

$$G_t = \sum_{t=1}^{T} \gamma^{t-1} r_t \qquad (1)$$

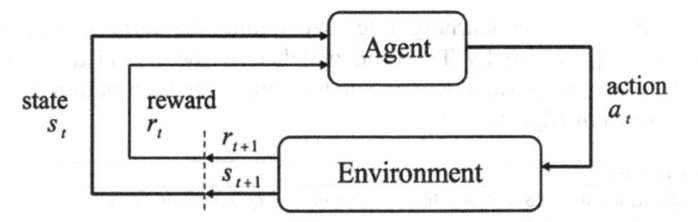

Fig. 1. The agent-environment interaction in an MDP.

It is the sum of discounted rewards at the time t, $\gamma \in (0, 1]$ is called the discount factor. If $\gamma = 0$, the agent only considers the immediate reward. If γ approaches 1, the agent's goal is to maximize the future reward.

The expected reward for state-action-next state is

$$r(s, a, s') = \mathbb{E}[G_t \mid s_{t-1} = s, a_{t-1} = a, s_t = s'] \quad (2)$$

where r is the total reward of $s \in \mathcal{S}$ and $a \in \mathcal{A}$, in which to agent takes the optimal possible a and applied to the s. $\mathbb{E}[\cdot]$ is the expected value for G_t, and G_t is the instantaneous reward after the agent environment interaction of s_{t-1} ors, into the next state s'.

The expected return of values $v_\pi(s)$ at the state s under the policy π is defined by

$$v_\pi(s) = \mathbb{E}_\pi[G_t \mid s_t = s] \quad (3)$$

where $\mathbb{E}_\pi[\cdot]$ is the expected value of total reward G_t under the policy π. If there is a terminal state, it is always zero. The expected return of values at the state s, denoted by $v_\star(s)$ given the optimal policy $\pi_\star$ is defined by

$$v_\star(s) = \max_\pi v_\pi(s) \quad (4)$$

This optimal policy will always generate a policy greater than or equal to the policy at this state s.

3.2 Temporal-Difference Learning (TD)

Temporal-Difference Learning (TD) is a reinforcement learning technique, including Q-learning and Sarsa, which are commonly used for evaluations and predictions. RL makes predictions based on previous experiences, where the agent environment interaction follows the generalized policy iteration using the TD methods.

In both methods, during each episode, from a current state s, we take an action a from s to another new state s', observing a reward r. The action a is taken following the current ϵ-greedy policy (given by the current Q-value function). Now we need to update $Q(s, a)$.

Sarsa, standing for State Action Reward State Action, is an on-policy value-based approach. It chooses next action a' following the same current policy above and using $r_t + \gamma Q(s', a')$ as target, given by

$$Q(s_t, a_t) \leftarrow Q(s_t, a_t) + \alpha[r_{t+1} + \gamma Q(s_{t+1}, a_{t+1}) - Q(s_t, a_t)] \quad (5)$$

where $\alpha \in (0, 1]$ is the learning rate. We define the term $Q(s_t, a_t) + \alpha[r_t + \gamma Q(s_{t+1}, a_{t+1}) - Q(s_t, a_t)]$ by TD-error, which uses the γ and α control the new value, plus the previous Q value will update the value of the estimation $Q(s_t, a_t)$. Sarsa algorithm is shown in Algorithm 1.

Algorithm 1: Sarsa

1　Initialize $Q(s, a)$ for all $s \in \mathcal{S}$, $a \in \mathcal{A}$ arbitrarily except that Q (*terminal*, ·)= 0
2　**foreach** *episode* ∈*episodes* **do**
3　　Initialize s
4　　Choose a from s using policy from derived from Q(e.g., ϵ-greedy)
5　　**while** s *is not terminal* **do**
6　　　Take action a, observe r, s'
7　　　Choose a' from s' using policy derived from Q(e.g., ϵ-greedy)
8　　　$Q(s, a) \leftarrow Q(s, a) + \alpha [R + \gamma Q(s', a') - Q(s, a)]$
9　　　$s \leftarrow s'$
10　　　$a \leftarrow a'$
11　　**end**
12　**end**

Q-learning is an off-policy approach, and it chooses the greedy action a, i.e. the action that maximize the Q-value function at the new state $Q(s', a)$, given by

$$Q(s_t, a_t) \leftarrow Q(s_t, a_t) + \alpha[r_{t+1} + \gamma \max_a Q(s_{t+1}, a) - Q(s_t, a_t)] \tag{6}$$

The new action is taken as greedy or optimal policy, not using the current policy. The next step $Q(s_{t+1}, a_{t+1})$ shows that the policy's propriety is to maximize the immediate rewards, which means that the potential effect of the next action a_{t+1} is not being considered by this method. Q-learning algorithm is shown in Algorithm 2.

Algorithm 2: Q-learning

1　Initialize $Q(s, a)$ for all $s \in \mathcal{S}$, $a \in \mathcal{A}$, arbitrarily except that $Q(terminal, \cdot) = 0$
2　**foreach** *episode* ∈ *episodes* **do**
3　　Initialize s
4　　**while** s *is not terminal* **do**
5　　　Choose a form s using policy derived form Q(e.g., ϵ-greedy)
6　　　Take action a, observe r, s'
7　　　$Q(s, a) \leftarrow Q(s, a) + \alpha \left[R + \gamma \max_a Q(s', a) - Q(s, a)\right]$
8　　　$s \leftarrow s'$
9　　**end**
10　**end**

3.3 Problem Formulation

In our case, we would like solve the revenue maximization problem through pricing. At time t, we set price to be p_t, and define the function of demand by $D(p_t)$. Then the expected revenue, denoted by r_t, at time t, is given by

$$r_t = \mathbb{E}[p_t D(p_t)] = p_t \mathbb{E}[D(p_t)] \tag{7}$$

Since the demand $D(p_t)$ is unknown, we will give three examples of the distribution of demand later. This function r_t is the instantaneous revenue. We here focus on the total revenue over selling horizon T, denoted by R_T, which is the sum of all instantaneous revenues, and given by

$$R_T = \sum_{t=0}^{T} \gamma^t r_t \qquad (8)$$

We normally choose γ close to 1.

We give an example of the three common functions of demand: linear, quadratic, and exponential models.

When the demand function is a linear model, we assume

$$\mathbb{E}[D(p_t)] = \alpha_0 - \alpha_1 p_t \qquad (9)$$

where $\mathbb{E}[D(p_t)]$ is the expected demand at price p_t. Parameters α_0, α_1 are constants, where α_0 is the initial value for demand and α_1 is the changing rate of demand with price. We also assume that $\alpha_1 \geq 0$ since the demand decreases when the price increases.

When the demand function is the quadratic model, that is

$$\mathbb{E}[D(p_t)] = \alpha_0 - \alpha_1 p_t - \alpha_2 p_t^2 \qquad (10)$$

Here we add another variable, $\alpha_2 p_t^2$, which considers the rate to the squared price and then exacerbates the changing rate of demand, and we assume that $\alpha_2 \geq 0$.

$$\mathbb{E}[D(p_t)] = \alpha_3 p_t^{-\alpha_4} \qquad (11)$$

with constants $\alpha_3, \alpha_4 > 0$.

4 Experimental Results

Sarsa for a variety of different step-sizes (i.e., learning rate) α, and choose prices based on the ϵ-greedy policy. Recall that Q-learning and Sarsa depend on the choice of discount factor γ, step-size α and exploration rate ϵ. Unless specified, we use default parameter settings of $\epsilon = 0.1$ and $\gamma = 0.9$. Here, α varies from $0.1, 0.3, 0.5, 0.7, 1.0$ Performance of Q-learning and Sarsa, measured by average reward, is considered as a function of the number of episodes T. Then we run for $T = 50,000$ episodes.

Figure 2 shows the results of Q-learning and Sarsa when demand follows a linear model. We can see that when T is large enough, both Q-learning and Sarsa algorithms converge to the optimal policy. However, Q-learning and Sarsa show different performances given different α. In specific, when $\alpha = 0.5, 1.0$, Sarsa outperforms Q-learning, giving Sarsa converges at 750,000 while Q-learning is at approximately 650,000.

When $\alpha = 0.3, 0.7$, Q-learning shows better performance than Sarsa, the average reward of Q-learning is around 750,000, and Sarsa is about 700,000.

Figure 3 shows the results of Q-learning and Sarsa when demand follows an exponential demand model. In this case, Q-learning and Sarsa have similar performance, that is, the average reward increases with the increase of α. Q-learning performed better than Sarsa when $\alpha = 0.1, 0.3, 0.5, 0.7$. However, when $\alpha = 0.3$, Q-learning has a sharp increase in its average rewards for episodes around 22,000. When $\alpha = 1.0$, Sarsa and

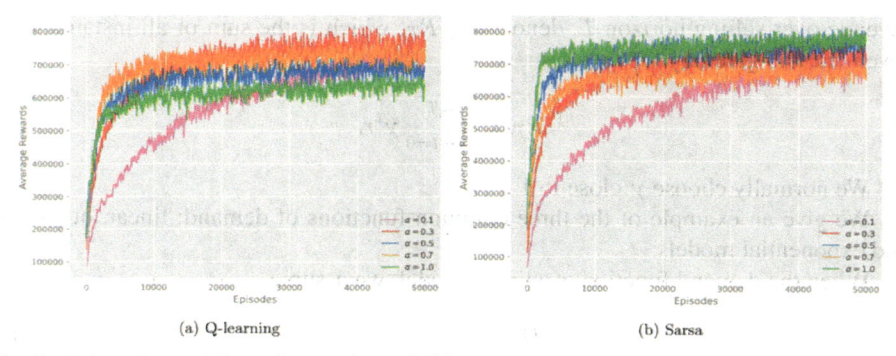

Fig. 2. Q-learning and Sarsa for a variety of different step-sizes $\alpha = 0.1, 0.3, 0.5, 0.7, 1.0$, when demand follows a linear model.

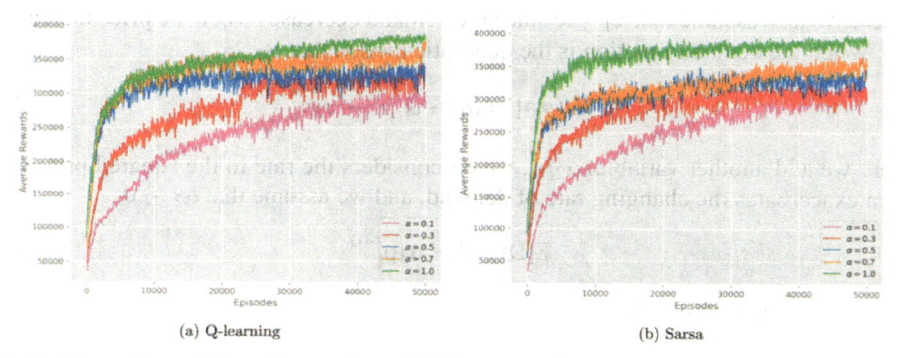

Fig. 3. Q-learning and Sarsa for a variety of different step-sizes $\alpha = 0.1, 0.3, 0.5, 0.7, 1.0$, when demand follows a exponential model.

Q-learning converge to similar average rewards, approximately 375,000, and both have the highest stability.

Figure 4 shows the results of Q-learning and Sarsa where demand follows a poisson distribution model. It can be seen that the overall performance of Q-learning is better than Sarsa in terms of the average rewards and stability, except for $\alpha = 1.0$, where Sarsa converges to 275,000 faster with less volatility.

(a) Q-learning (b) Sarsa

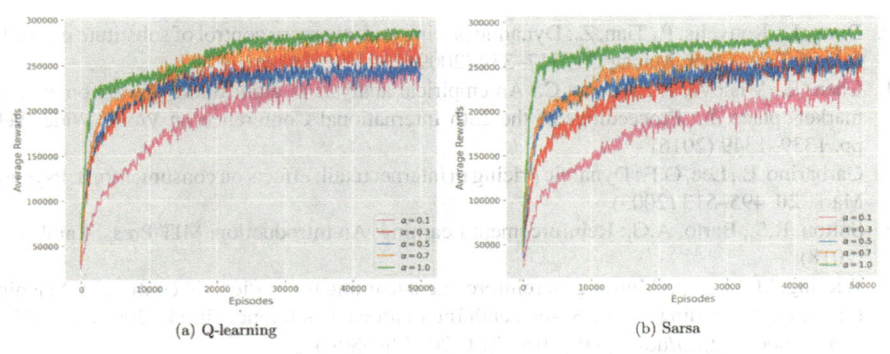

Fig. 4. Q-learning and Sarsa for a variety of different step-sizes $\alpha = 0.1, 0.3, 0.5, 0.7, 1.0$, when demand follows a Poisson model.

5 Conclusion

In this work, we investigated a reinforcement learning framework for dynamic pricing on the E-commerce platform. We modeled the dynamic pricing as a Markov Decision Process and then defined the state space, action space, and reward function. We consider three different demand models: linear, quadratic, and exponential functions, with different learning rates α. We showed that Q-learning pricing policy outperformed Sarsa pricing policy in most cases.

Reinforcement learning-based models for dynamic pricing are now an active area of research. An equally important issue concerns the computational efficiency of learning-based mechanisms. The development of powerful market simulators is another critical area. We considered a simulated case, which is too simple and not realistic. Thus, we would like to consider real market data, including buying behavior.

References

1. Cournot, A.A.: Researches into the Mathematical Principles of the Theory of Wealth. Macmillan Company, New York [c1897] (1927)
2. Evans, G.C.: The dynamics of monopoly. Am. Math. Mon. **31**, 77–83 (1924)
3. Simaan, M., Takayama, T.: Game theory applied to dynamic duopoly problems with production constraints. Automatica **14**, 161–166 (1978)
4. Den Boer, A.V.: Dynamic pricing and learning: historical origins, current research, and new directions. Surv. Oper. Res. Manag. Sci. **20**, 1–18 (2015)
5. Littlewood, K.: Forecasting and control of passenger bookings. Airline Group Int. Federation Oper. Res. Soc. **12**, 95–117 (1972)
6. Belobaba, P.: Air travel demand and airline seat inventory management. Ph.D. thesis Massachusetts Institute of Technology (1987)
7. Talluri, K., van Ryzin, G.: The Theory and Practice of Revenue Management. Springer, Boston (2005). https://doi.org/10.1007/b139000
8. McAfee, R.P., Te Velde, V.: Dynamic pricing in the airline industry. Handb. Econ. Inf. Syst. **1**, 527–567 (2006)
9. Abrate, G., Fraquelli, G., Viglia, G.: Dynamic pricing strategies: evidence from European hotels. Int. J. Hosp. Manag. **31**, 160–168 (2012)

10. Dong, L., Kouvelis, P., Tian, Z.: Dynamic pricing and inventory control of substitute products. Manuf. Serv. Oper. Manag. **11**, 317–339 (2009)
11. Chen, L., Mislove, A., Wilson, C.: An empirical analysis of algorithmic pricing on amazon market- place. In: Proceedings of the 25th International Conference on World Wide Web, pp. 1339–1349 (2016)
12. Garbarino, E., Lee, O.F.: Dynamic pricing in internet retail: effects on consumer trust. Psychol. Mark. **20**, 495–513 (2003)
13. Sutton, R.S., Barto, A.G.: Reinforcement Learning: An Introduction. MIT Press, Cambridge (2018)
14. Wiering, M.A., et al.: Multi-agent reinforcement learning for traffic light control. In: Machine Learning: Proceedings of the Seventeenth International Conference (ICML 2000), pp. 1151–1158 (2000). https://doi.org/10.1109/ITSC.2014.6958095
15. Howard, R.A.: Dynamic Programming and Markov Processes. Wiley, Cambridge (1960)
16. Rothstein, M.: An airline overbooking model. Transp. Sci. **5**, 180–192 (1971)
17. Song, H., Liu, C.-C.: A computational tool for trading in a competitive electricity market. In: 2000 IEEE Power Engineering Society Winter Meeting. Conference Proceedings (Cat. No. 00CH37077), vol. 1, pp. 26–27. IEEE (2000)
18. Bäuerle, N., Rieder, U.: Markov Decision Processes with Applications to Finance. Springer, Heidelberg (2011)
19. Watkins, C.J.C.H.: Learning from delayed rewards. Ph.D. thesis King's College Cambridge, UK (1989). http://www.cs.rhul.ac.uk/~chrisw/new_thesis.pdf
20. Hester, T., et al.: Deep q-learning from demonstrations. arXiv preprint arXiv:1704.03732 (2017)
21. Rummery, G.A., Niranjan, M.: On-Line Q-Learning Using Connectionist Systems. Technical Report TR 166 Cambridge University Engineering Department Cambridge, England (1994). http://mi.eng.cam.ac.uk/reports/svr-ftp/auto-pdf/rummery_tr166.pdf
22. Gosavii, A., Bandla, N., Das, T.K.: A reinforcement learning approach to a single leg airline revenue management problem with multiple fare classes and overbooking. IIE Trans. **34**, 729–742 (2002)
23. Lee, J., Lee, E., Kim, J.: Electric vehicle charging and discharging algorithm based on reinforcement learning with data-driven approach in dynamic pricing scheme. Energies **13**, 1950 (2020)
24. Narahari, Y., Raju, C., Ravikumar, K., Shah, S.: Dynamic pricing models for electronic business. Sadhana **30**, 231–256 (2005)
25. Raju, C., Narahari, Y., Ravikumar, K.: Learning dynamic prices in electronic retail markets with customer segmentation. Ann. Oper. Res. Oper. Res. **143**, 59–75 (2006). https://doi.org/10.1007/s10479-006-7372-3

Impact of ESG Performance on Firm Value and Its Transmission Mechanism: Research Based on Industry Heterogeneity

Xingzhuo Liu(✉)

School of Finance, Nankai University, No. 38, Road Tongyan, Haihe Education Town, Jinnan District, Tianjin, China
lxz_yy@163.com

Abstract. Since the basic framework of ESG disclosure was established by CSRC in The Governance Guidelines for Listed Companies in 2018, China's ESG system has been improved markedly. The disclosure of ESG helps to encourage market participants to pay attention to the impact of economic behavior on environment and society, and eventually promote the pluralistic development of society spontaneously. The findings suggest that overall ESG combined score has a significant and positive relationship with the listed companies in the four industries- energy industry, industrial industry, consumer discretionary industry and healthcare industry. Besides, the results show that for most industries (expect materials industry, consumer staple industry, and utilities industry), the long-term impact is slightly higher than that in the short term, indicating that firms can enhance their competitiveness and increase their value through ESG investment. From the perspective of ESG indexes, firms, investors and regulatory authorities, this paper concludes that all market participants should play a role in building ESG system; firms are supposed to emphasize ESG management in their daily business activities; investors can consider ESG performance more and deepen the concept of value investment; regulatory authorities are expected to create a proper environment for ESG construction and establish sounder ESG disclosure rules.

Keywords: ESG Performance · Firm Value · Industry Heterogeneity · Transmission Mechanism · Financing Constraints

1 Introduction

With the aim of promoting green development and ensuring the harmony between humanity and nature, the 20th CPC (the Communist Party of China) National Congress put forward the policy of accelerating the optimization of industrial structure and promoting the green transformation of enterprises by means of improving low-carbon economic system. Under the guidance of Five-sphere Integrated Plan, it is of vital importance to get the most out of the multi-agent pattern by motivating residents, companies and other entities to participate in social construction, to assume their own responsibilities, and to promote social progress spontaneously during the process of realizing new era's development objectives.

However, China's ESG transmission mechanism still needs time to be matured. For example, whether ESG disclosure has received enough attention from investors remains a question. Meanwhile, if related costs are considered, ESG investment may squeeze out other investment opportunities, resulting in reducing ESG investment. In order to find whether ESG performance has incentive effect on companies, I gain the impact of ESG performance on firm value in different industries, and further study the specific transmission mechanism about how ESG performance has an influence on firm value. This research helps to analyze the difference of the impact of ESG performance on firm value in different fields. Also, the results give theoretical basis and practical reference for formulating incentive policies for certain industry and promoting coordinated development among various fields.

This paper is organized as follows: Sect. 2 reviews the literature about prior research in ESG field. Section 3 discusses different theories and presents basic hypothesis. Section 4 outlines data sources, variables and empirical models. Section 5 shows the prime results.

2 Literature Review

Shareholder theory [1] believes that the maximization of shareholders' interests is what companies consider most, so it is predicted that ESG performance is negatively associated with firm value. Resource dependence theory [2] emphasizes that companies rely on their environment to succeed. Thus, it is expected that ESG performance has a positive relationship with enterprise value.

According to [3], among 2020 articles which discuss the relationship between ESG performance and firm value, 58% of these papers find a positive relationship; 8% find a negative relationship; 13% find no relationship; 21% have mixed results and fail to gain a clear conclusion. Using the data of Chinese listed power generation enterprises in 2016, [4] prove that high ESG performance will lead to better financial performance, and provide an important reference for the disclosure of information on social responsibility and the importance of supervision. Korean companies are selected as representatives of emerging markets, and ESG is used as the substitute for CSR (Corporate Social Responsibility). It shows that CSR has a significant positive impact on firm value [5]. Conversely, [6] employ the panel data of Italian companies from 2007 to 2015. Their findings show that ESG performance is negatively correlated with corporate financial performance. However, in multinational studies, it turns out that ESG performance has no relationship with firm financial performance [7]. There still exist more complex results. The study of Norwegian listed companies from 2010 to 2019 presents the conclusion that there is a positive correlation between ESG and Tobin Q, but a negative relationship between ESG and ROA [8].

In addition, some studies focus on the long or short term impact of ESG performance on firm value. CSR investment will increase the cost of enterprises in the short term and affect their strategic layout [9]. There is a significant and positive correlation between social responsibility of Chinese high-tech companies and their firm financial performance in the long term, while the correlation in the short term is not significant [10]. The difference between the long-term and short-term impact of ESG performance on firm value is worth exploring.

Above is about overall ESG score. When lacking ESG at the early stage, most of Chinese literature choose one direction (E, S or G) to do research. Taking unit sewage fee as the measurement of environmental performance, [11] finds that "E" performance has a positive relationship with financial performance. [12] construct two models of the relationship between firm value and social responsibility and the relationship between firm value and governance from the perspective of "S" and "G". Their findings show that social responsibility at time t is negatively correlated with firm value, but social responsibility at time t − 1 is positively correlated with firm value, which means that assuming social responsibility is conducive to the increase of long-term firm value. With the establishment of China's ESG system and the inclusion of Chinese corporate data in MSCI and other international databases, literature on empirical research on ESG is gradually enriched. Based on Huazheng ESG rating system, it is found that Chinese listed companies with high ESG performance have higher firm value [13].

Existing literature focuses on the characteristics of the company itself, such as ownership, scale, and pollution [14], but hasn't consider the difference among industries. [15] compare the long-term and short-term impact of ESG perfomance on firm value among several sectors. This paper enlightens me to study industry heterogeneity.

3 Theories, Variables and Methodology

3.1 Theories

ESG Performance and Firm Value. The relationship between ESG performance and firm value is controversial. According to shareholder theory, since shareholders are the owners of companies and they enjoy the remaining claim on benefits of business activities, the main purpose of a company must be to maximize shareholders' interests. However, assuming social responsibility cannot directly bring profits to shareholders and might increase financial risk of a company. Therefore, it is waste of time for companies to care about ESG performance [1].

On the other hand, in terms of stakeholder theory, companies should consider the interests of potential investors, creditors, government and other non-shareholders. If companies meet the demands of these related entities, they will gain adequate financial support and ensure long-term effective operation. In the absence of channels to show their external value, ESG can serve as an appropriate measurement of how much companies take the interests of stakeholders into account [6]. Similarly, resource dependence theory [2] emphasizes the significance of environment around companies. These two theories believe that ESG performance has a positive impact on firm value.

Financing Constraints and Firm Value. Financing constraints represent the difficulty for enterprises to obtain funds. When its own fund cannot satisfy investment needs, a firm have to supplement funds through external financing. However, financing constraints will reduce the accessibility of external financing, cut down the net income of investment, and ultimately decrease firm value.

ESG Performance and Financing Constraints. Stakeholder theory and resource dependence theory point out that enterprises can meet the demands of stakeholders so that they will overcome financing difficulties. The disclosure of ESG reflects their responsibilities, which will attract potential investors and increase financing channels [17]. In addition, the disclosure of ESG indicates that an enterprise has good credit and low risk. Thus, ESG is able to weaken the negative impact of financing constraints on firm value.

Long-Term and Short-Term Effect. In the long term, ESG reflects responsibility and sustainability of enterprises, which is conducive to improving corporate long-term performance. However, in the short term, ESG investment may not timely be transformed into advantages, and might reduce firm competitiveness due to the costs [9]. Therefore, although ESG is conducive to reducing financing constraints and increasing firm value in the long term, it may increase financial burden and reduce firm value in the short term.

3.2 Variables

Dependent Variables. Tobin Q is the proxy variable of firm value. Tobin Q is calculated as the quotient of a company's market value divided by its book value. Tobin Q allows for equity value, which reflects investors' expectations for the prospects of the company. At the same time, it considers long-term replacement costs, which have to do with the ability to make sustainable investment [18]. In the robustness tests, I replace Tobin Q with EPS. EPS is calculated as the quotient of a company's net profit divided by its equity.

Independent Variables. ESG score (ESG performance) is the weighted average of scores from all aspects of ESG.

Environmental performance takes environment management, energy and climate change, waste gas, raw materials and waste, waste water, water resources, biodiversity, and green construction and green finance account.

Social responsibility performance presents whether companies maintain a good relationship with its stakeholders and acquire loyalty and trust from employees, suppliers and consumers.

Governance performance mainly considers the issues related with directors and shareholders, the implementation of anti-monopoly, and the ability to deal with events.

Regulatory Effect. The regulatory effect happens if both ESG performance and financing constraints have a impact on firm value. High ESG performance helps to weaken financing constraints of enterprises and increases firm value. Based on this premise, I create the variable that represents financing constraints and the interaction term of ESG score and financing constraints.

I use SA index [19] as the proxy of financing constraints. Through the size and the duration of companies, SA index reflect the difficulty of financing faced by companies. The larger the value of SA index is, the stricter financing constraints are. The following formula calculates SA:

$$SA = -0.737 \times Ln(asset) + 0.043 \times [ln(asset)]2 - 0.04 \times duration$$

In this formula, the asset is the total assets from the annual report, and its unit is adjusted to 10 million RMB. The duration is the difference between the year that we use to do research and the year of its establishment.

Control Variables. Considering the impact of other firm characteristics on firm value, I use the logarithm of the total assets, the leverage to control the size and capital structure of the enterprise [14].

3.3 Methodology

Basic Model. In order to test the (short-term) impact of ESG performance on firm value and ensure the rationality and simplicity, I construct the model as follows:

$$TobinQ_{i,t} = \beta_0 + \beta_1 ESG\ Score_{i,t} + \beta_2 Ln\_Asset_{i,t} + \beta_3 Lev_{i,t} + \varepsilon_{i,t}$$

In this formula, i stands for the company, t represents the year, and β0 is the intercept term, εi,t is the random error term.

If β1 is significant and positive, the results support hypothesis 1a; if β1 is significant and negative, the results support hypothesis 1b; if β1 is non-significant, the results support hypothesis 1c.

Long-Term and Short-Term Effect Model. In order to compare the long and short term effect, I divide ESG performance at time t into two parts- ESG performance at time t − 1 and the difference of ESG performance at time t and ESG performance at time t − 1.

L.ESG represents ESG performance at time t − 1, and it will be employed to be measure the long-term impact of ESG performance on firm value; D.ESG represents the change of ESG performance, which reflects new increased or decreased ESG investment, and it will be employed to be measure the short-term impact of ESG performance on firm value.

$$ESG = L.ESG + D.ESG$$

$$L.ESG = ESG\ Score_{i,t-1}$$

$$D.ESG = \Delta ESG\ Score_{i,t} = ESG\ Score_{i,t} - ESG\ Score_{i,t-1}$$

The model is constructed as follows:

$$TobinQ_{i,t} = \beta_0 + \beta_1 L.ESG + \beta_2 D.ESG + \beta_3 Ln\_Asset_{i,t} + \beta_4 Lev_{i,t} + \varepsilon_{i,t}$$

If both β1 and β2 are significant, and the value of β1 is larger than that of β2, the results support hypothesis 2.

Regulatory Effect Model. To study the impact of financing constraints on firm value, I construct the following models:

$$TobinQ_{i,t} = \beta_0 + \beta_1 ESG\ Score_{i,t} + \beta_2 SA_{i,t} + \beta_3 Ln\_Asset_{i,t} + \beta_4 Lev_{i,t} + \varepsilon_{i,t}$$

If β2 is significant and negative, the results support hypothesis 3.

The coefficients of the interaction term of ESG performance and financing constraints reflect the regulatory effect of ESG performance on firm value through financing constraints. The model is constructed as follows:

$$TobinQ_{i,t} = \beta_0 + \beta_1 ESG\ Score_{i,t} + \beta_2 SA_{i,t} + \beta_3 SA_{i,t} \times ESG\ Score_{i,t} + \beta_4 Ln\_Asset_{i,t} + \beta_5 Lev_{i,t} + \varepsilon_{i,t}$$

Assuming that hypothesis 3 is true, if β3 is significant and positive, the results support hypothesis 4.

4 Results

4.1 Descriptive Statistics

Table 1 lists descriptive statistics of the whole sample, and descriptive statistics of certain industry are shown in the appendix.

Among all industries, the industries with high average value of ESG scores are healthcare (6.186) and IT (6.124). The mean of the whole sample is 5.898, the median approximates the mean, and the overall distribution is reasonable. This indicates that WIND ESG rating can reflect the comprehensive firm quality, and the follow-up study is reasonable.

When it comes to E,S,G scores, the industry with the highest average value of environment scores is healthcare (2.079), the industry with the the lowest scores is real estate (0.887), and other industries have similar scores; the industries with higher social responsibility scores are healthcare (4.431) and materials (4.328), the industries with lower social responsibility scores are consumer staple (2.891) and real estate (1.836), and the gaps of scores between industries are large, indicating that different attitudes towards social responsibility among industries are distinct, and that the subsequent industry research is of significance; the governance scores are similar.

Table 1. Descriptive statistics.

Variable	N	Mean	SD	Min	Median	Max
TobinQ	13108	1.787	2.050	0.0250	1.265	55.55
EPS	13108	0.359	1.016	−8.797	0.260	39.91
ESG Score	13108	5.898	0.816	2.650	5.840	9.380
Env	13108	1.522	1.956	0.000	0.850	10.00
Soc	13108	3.876	1.866	0.000	3.800	10.00
Gov	13108	6.289	1.001	1.200	6.320	9.650
SA	13108	−3.707	0.358	−5.722	−3.729	−1.293
Ln_Asset	13108	22.39	1.363	16.41	22.23	28.64
Lev	13108	0.460	1.592	0.008	0.433	178.3

4.2 Correlation Results

Table 2 lists the of correlation between the variables. Except the corporate governance score (significant at the 10% level), the correlations between other independent variables as well as control variables and Tobin Q are significant at the 1% level. The correlations between independent variables as well as control variables and EPS are significant at the 1% level.

The relationships between ESG score, environment score, social responsibility score, financing constraints, and leverage are all positively correlated with Tobin Q, and other variables are negatively correlated; except for financing constraints and leverage, the correlation between other variables and EPS are all positive.

Table 2. Pearson Correlation Matrix.

	TobinQ	EPS	ESG Score	Env	Soc	Gov	SA	Ln_Asset	Lev
TobinQ	1								
EPS	0.138***	1							
ESG Score	0.050***	0.157***	1						
Env	−0.061***	0.100***	0.580***	1					
Soc	0.063***	0.075***	0.809***	0.348***	1				
Gov	−0.017*	0.155***	0.539***	0.192***	0.197***	1			
SA	0.361***	−0.097***	−0.024***	−0.182***	0.074***	−0.109***	1		
Ln_Asset	−0.382***	0.221***	0.130***	0.272***	0.015*	0.202***	−0.682***	1	
Lev	0.196***	−0.055***	−0.046***	−0.00300	−0.024***	−0.036***	0.025***	0.00900	1

t-statistics in parentheses,*** $p < 0.01$, ** $p < 0.05$, * $p < 0.1$.

5 Conclusion

With the purpose of studying how to promote industry transformation. This research analyzes the impact of ESG performance on firm value from the perspective of various dimensions, and take industry heterogeneity into account. Also, this paper considers the long-term and short-term effect by dividing ESG score at time t into ESG score at time $t − 1$ and the difference of ESG score at time t and ESG score at time $t − 1$.

Based on the conclusions above, the suggestions are given as follows:

First, all market entities are expected to play a role in building ESG system. At present, China's ESG system still has a long way to go, with few rating agencies and immature rating methods. Government should increase publicity to encourage individuals and enterprises to participate in establishing ESG system.

Second, enterprises should spontaneously improve their own ESG performance. First, improve the overall ESG system and fully integrate ESG into the construction of firm culture and concept; second, to merge ESG into daily operation, such as product development, employee education, customer service and so on; third, strengthen ESG disclosure and reduce information asymmetry between firms and investors, and maintain a good reputation.

Third, investors need to consider ESG performance when making investment decisions. Expect macro environment and financial performance, the information about ecological protection, social responsibility, corporate governance and other non-financial information is also of great significance. Integrating ESG into strategic investment strategic helps to realize the value investment and pursue the long-term interests.

Fourth, government regulatory authorities are supposed to create a proper environment for ESG construction. In order to strengthen ESG disclosure, it is necessary to extend the scope of ESG disclosure, establish related laws and regulations, cultivate the culture of disclosing information completely and accurately, and improve ESG disclosure system.

After analyzing data of different industries, it can be found that the impact of ESG performance on firm value has industry heterogeneity, and the transmission mechanisms of different industries are not consistent. This research simply considers the transmission mechanism of financing constraints. The follow-up research can continue to study other transmission mechanisms. For example, it could be dug into from the perspective of innovation ability and investor attention.

References

1. Friedmann, F.M.: Capitalism and freedom, Article no. 111977 (1962)
2. Pfeffer, J., Salancik, G.R.: The External Control OG Organizations: A Resource Dependence Perspective. Stanford University Press, San Francisco (1978)
3. Whelan, T., Atz, U., Holt, T.V., Clark, C.: ESG and financial performance: uncovering the relationship by aggregating evidence from 1,000 plus studies published between 2015–2020, NYU Stern Center for Sustainable Business, Rockefeller Asset Management (2021)
4. Zhao, C., et al.: ESG and corporate financial performance: empirical evidence from China's listed power generation companies. Sustainability **10**(8), 1–18 (2018)
5. Yoon, B., Lee, J., Byun, R.: Does ESG performance enhance firm value? Evidence from Korea. Sustainability **10**(10), 3635 (2018)
6. Landi, G., Sciarelli, M.: Towards a more ethical market: the impact of ESG rating on corporate financial performance. Soc. Responsib. J. **15**(1), 11–27 (2019)
7. Lopez-de-Silanes, F., McCahery, J.A., Pudschedl, P.C.: ESG performance and disclosure: a cross-country analysis. Social Science Electronic Publishing (2020)
8. Giannopoulos, G., Fagernes, R.V.K., Elmarzouky, M., Hossain, K.A.B.M.A.: The ESG disclosure and the financial performance of Norwegian listed firms. J. Risk Financ. Manag. **15**, 237 (2022)
9. Vance, S.: Are socially responsible corporations good investment risks? Manag. Rev. **64**(1), 18–24 (1975)
10. Zhu, N., Zhu, L., Kong, Y., et al.: Research on the synergistic influence of technological innovation investment and social responsibility undertaking on financial performance. Account. Res. (2), 57–63, 95 (2014)
11. Hu, Q.: Research on the correlation between environment performance and financial performance of listed companies. China's Population Resour. Environ. **22**(06), 23–32 (2012)
12. Yu, X., Wu, W.: Research on governance, social responsibility and firm value. Contemp. Econ. Res. (05), 74–78 (2014)
13. Xu, M., Liu, C., Hu, Y., et al.: Empirical study on the impact of ESG performance of listed companies on firm value–take A-share listed companies as an example. China Asset Appraisal **256**(07), 27–37 (2021)

14. Zhang, L., Zhao, H.: Does environment, social responsibility, and governance (ESG) performance affect firm value?—empirical research based on A-share listed companies. Wuhan Financ. **238**(10), 36–43 (2019)
15. Rojo-Suárez, J., Alonso-Conde, A.B.: Short-run and long-run effects of ESG policies on value creation and the cost of equity of firms. Econ. Anal. Policy **77**, 599–616 (2023). ISSN 0313-5926
16. Edward Freeman, R.: Strategic Management: A Stakeholder Approach. Cambridge University Press, Cambridge (1984)
17. Martin, P.R., Moser, D.V.: Managers' green investment disclosures and investors' reaction. J. Account. Econ. **61**(1), 239–254 (2016)
18. Naeem, N., Cankaya, S., Bildik, R.: Does ESG performance affect the financial performance of environmentally sensitive industries? A comparison between emerging and developed markets. Borsa Istanbul Review (2022). ISSN 2214-8450
19. Hadlock, C.J., Pierce, J.R.: New evidence on measuring financial constraints: Moving beyond the KZ index. Rev. Financ. Stud. **23**(5), 1909–1940 (2010)

Author Index

A
Ahmad, Munir 1649
Ali, Asghar 1649

B
Bai, Yichuan 873
Bu, Zicheng 1295

C
Cai, Heyu 1315
Chen, BoYong 188
Chen, Jiaxuan 1949
Chen, Liang 1664
Chen, Mingfei 679
Chen, Rufeng 490
Chen, Shuying 1818
Chen, Xiangjun 1577
Chen, Xinyu 1987
Chen, Yajing 1437
Chen, Yu 273
Chen, Yuanyuan 2001
Chen, Yuxin 752
Chen, Ziqi 998
Cheng, Jia 1043
Cheng, XiangLin 1960
Chengye, Yang 1848
Chi, Guangqing 299

D
Dai, Liwen 119
Deng, Shifeng 1274
Ding, Manting 400
Dong, Liqi 690, 1274
Dong, Tingxuan 716
Du, Jianhang 1842
Du, Longzheng 1842
Duan, Yujiang 633

E
Edjah, Benjamin Kofi Tawiah 180

F
Fan, Shiqi 611
Fang, Xinru 1530
Feng, Yining 796
Fu, Bolin 669
Fu, Xinran 1361

G
Gan, Zhaoxuan 863
Gao, Qian 1274
Ge, Caixiaoyang 18
Ge, Fengfan 633
Gong, Qichao 1075
Gong, Ziqing 752
Guo, Ziqi 129

H
Hamid, Syed Ali Raza 1705
Han, Fang 400
Han, Le 1130
Han, Xiao 784
He, Bo 1426
He, Jintian 1882
Hong, Haozhe 1903
Hong, Jiayi 969
Hou, Qing 299
Hou, Yishan 1684
Hu, Jiahang 98
Hu, Yongheng 1842
Hu, Yuqing 1405
Huan, Chen 373
Huang, Fumian 235
Huang, Heqing 885
Huang, Lanjie 1371
Huang, Lvqin 291

Huang, Minrui 1156
Huang, Shengran 1025
Huang, Wensi 1606
Huang, Yiguo 1315
Huang, Yuting 1933

J
Jiamei, Liu 500
Jiang, Jiayue 1778
Jin, Yangjie 1455

K
Kong, Yile 925

L
Lang, Chenyu 1218
Lei, Feiyue 1242
Lei, Mengyan 382
Li, Aiqi 1548
Li, Chutian 1382
Li, David Tai 1156
Li, Jialin 1797
Li, Jiatong 566
Li, Junyuan 168
Li, Qijing 1083
Li, Xiangyu 598
Li, Yinwei 1
Li, Yiping 642
Li, Yufan 729
Li, Yunong 796
Li, Zeyao 986
Li, Zixuan 1720
Liang, JiaYou 391
Liu, Boyu 478
Liu, Hongxi 2051
Liu, Huimin 1094
Liu, Jiaqi 9
Liu, Lin 1914
Liu, Ming 1285
Liu, Minne 2010
Liu, Nanqi 652
Liu, Qing 828
Liu, Runbang 1327
Liu, Wenzheng 1445
Liu, Xiaochen 41
Liu, Xilin 1112
Liu, Xingzhuo 2061
Liu, Xinyi 1570
Liu, Yangmeng 1094

Liu, Yuqing 642
Lu, Yike 1064
Lyu, Shizhe 662

M
Ma, Jiajun 328
Ma, Kaixvan 1933
Ma, Miaoxuan 915
Ma, Tianqi 555
Ma, Zihao 168
Mehdi, Mirza Nasir Jahan 1705
Meng, Lu 1242
Mo, Tian 511

P
Pan, Shiqi 1873
Pang, Keyou 1694
Peng, Tianqi 1746

Q
Qi, Changyou 652
Qi, Xianya 849
Qi, Yijia 1231
Qian, Haonan 1112
Qin, Jingyu 796
Qiuge, Song 443
Qu, Shengyang 1265

R
Rao, Xiao 977

S
Shen, Bing 1522
Shi, Xinyu 626
Shi, Yiling 1606
Song, Chenwen 1720
Song, Xinyi 253
Su, Jianuo 1455
Su, Rixin 937
Su, Yiru 421
Sun, Ruixuan 642
Sun, Yuhan 1303
Sun, Yuyao 521
Sun, Zhenwu 998

T
Tang, Zihao 893
Tao, Yuankai 796

Tong, Xueyao 1018
Tong, Yuting 262

W

Wang, Chuhan 1252
Wang, Daoer 155
Wang, Hui 1008
Wang, Jiali 1971
Wang, Jiaxin 400
Wang, Junchi 2031
Wang, Junyi 2043
Wang, Keqing 669
Wang, Meixin 1778
Wang, Moran 247
Wang, Qing 199
Wang, Shikang 88
Wang, Sirui 1503
Wang, Siying 1630
Wang, Xiaodan 1675
Wang, Xiaoke 1831
Wang, Xiaoyu 998
Wang, Xueyan 1765
Wang, Yanshu 836
Wang, Yifan 1413
Wang, Yijing 1102
Wang, Yimeng 1924
Wang, Yingtong 1175
Wang, Yuping 314
Wang, Yuxi 1075
Wang, Yuyan 365
Wang, Zixuan 1455
Wei, Dan 1778
Wei, Zhuoer 1130
Wen, Haoyun 1112
Wen, Zhixing 633
Wu, Yinming 771

X

Xi, Ying 1559
Xi, Yirong 1143
Xiao, Gengqiang 321
Xiao, Mengzhen 1778
Xiao, Tianrui 1720
Xiao, Zhijia 1785
Xie, Qiaoyu 576
Xing, Ziyi 1035
Xinrui, Hu 350
Xinyu, Zhang 338
Xu, Beining 1252

Xu, Haosen 1197
Xu, Jiangjia 1120
Xu, Yifei 1684
Xu, Zehao 1185
Xu, Zihui 642

Y

Yan, Haocheng 280
Yang, Qijie 885
Yang, Yihan 1863
Yang, Yining 1809
Yang, Yunhao 63
Yang, Yuwei 1778
Yang, Ziyao 702
Yao, Zhuang 959
Yi, Sitian 588
Yi, Siyan 1094
Yin, Jiawen 566
Yin, Jiayun 1597
Yu, Jinhao 1893
Yu, Liu 27
Yu, Peili 2021
Yu, Yuting 466
Yuan, Mingze 129
Yuan, Siyun 1491
Yuan, Yuyang 1054

Z

Zang, Zhengjie 1616
Zhang, Aimiao 903
Zhang, Fengyi 307
Zhang, Huangzhiyi 431
Zhang, Huijia 1694
Zhang, Huiqi 414
Zhang, Jia 400
Zhang, Jiaheng 1513
Zhang, Jiaxi 214
Zhang, Jintian 1206
Zhang, Lei 224
Zhang, Qianwen 1252
Zhang, Qiaozhi 534
Zhang, Rui 566
Zhang, Shuyan 1130
Zhang, Xiyuan 168
Zhang, Yiwei 804
Zhang, Yizhen 1315
Zhang, Yuqing 738
Zhang, Zhuohao 188
Zhao, ShuaiJie 391

Zhao, Xinran 544
Zhao, Zhihan 146
Zheng, Chenhao 108
Zheng, Lixiang 456
Zhong, Yiming 98
Zhou, Shuai 299
Zhou, Shuye 1684
Zhou, Tianxin 669
Zhou, Wenjie 1606
Zhou, Xi 1641
Zhou, Yiqian 947
Zhu, HaoYuan 391
Zhu, Minxing 1474
Zhu, Siyuan 815
Zhu, Xitong 925
Zhu, Yuli 1075
Zhuge, Junjie 652
Zong, Zhuofan 137

9789819705221VOL03